The SAGE Handbook of

International Corporate and Public Affairs

This is the first Public Affairs book to cover all the major continents and give in-depth insights and guidance on business, government policy and international trade communication. It will make a substantial contribution to the development of dialogue between nations and businesses worldwide.

Xiaoying Zhang, Professor of International Journalism and Communication, Beijing Foreign Studies University

As our profession continues to evolve it is critical that lobbyists and public affairs professionals have all the information and tools at their disposal. This Handbook is one of those resources all professionals should have sitting on their desk – I know I do.

Paul A. Miller, President, National Institute for Lobbying & Ethics, Washington, DC

This Handbook provides essential reading and analysis for practitioners, potential clients and academics. It will help politicians, public officials and the media to better understand that corporate and public affairs are not black arts; but prudent tools of good governance for those determining or being affected by the decisions of government at every level.

Lord Tom McNally, Chair of the Youth Justice Board and former Deputy Leader of the House of Lords

An essential companion, offering a rich account of the development of the field as well as its applications. It will be welcomed by students of the subject for years to come.

C. Michael Hall, Professor of Marketing, University of Canterbury, New Zealand

In this increasingly important, but under-examined field, no other collection of material comes close to giving such a comprehensive view of the development of public affairs research, teaching and practice.

Geoff Allen, Founder of the Australasian Centre for Corporate Public Affairs

This is an incredibly timely book that explores the global phenomena of public affairs in a way that answers the naive superficiality of the anti-lobbying narrative.

Neil Collins, Emeritus Professor of Government, University College Cork, Ireland

Read this book and you will understand the forces that are impacting your organization and how to engage in the process in a thoughtful, results-oriented way.

Amy Showalter, The Showalter Group and Author of 'The Underdog Edge'

An edited volume of scope and substance, featuring a cadre of authors with impeccable credentials as thought leaders to inform the new realities of public affairs.

Louise Heslop, Professor Emeritus of Marketing, Carleton University, Canada

A pragmatic discipline must remain open-ended because there is no predicting what strategic adaptations may work best. This handbook is educational in the best sense.

John G Blair, Professor Emeritus of American Literature and Civilization, University of Geneva

A must-read publication for every globally-minded government relations and corporate affairs professional whether they're operating in London, Washington DC, Kenya or Korea.

Craig Hoy, Executive Director, PublicAffairsAsia

This is the book and guide on international Public Affairs that every businessman, politician and practitioner must have.

Henry Sun, International Director of Business Research Institute, University of Chester

The SAGE Handbook of

International Corporate
and Public Affairs

Edited by

Phil Harris and
Craig S. Fleisher

reference

Los Angeles I London I New Delhi I Singapore I Washington DC I Melbourne

Los Angeles | London | New Delhi
Singapore | Washington DC | Melbourne

SAGE Publications Ltd
1 Oliver's Yard
55 City Road
London EC1Y 1SP

SAGE Publications Inc.
2455 Teller Road
Thousand Oaks, California 91320

SAGE Publications India Pvt Ltd
B 1/I 1 Mohan Cooperative Industrial Area
Mathura Road
New Delhi 110 044

SAGE Publications Asia-Pacific Pte Ltd
3 Church Street
#10-04 Samsung Hub
Singapore 049483

Editor: Delia Martinez Alfonso
Editorial Assistant: Matthew Oldfield
Production Editor: Sushant Nailwal
Copyeditor: Sunrise Setting Ltd.
Proofreader: Derek Markham
Indexer: Avril Ehrlich
Marketing Manager: Alison Borg
Cover design: Wendy Scott
Typeset by Cenveo Publisher Services
Printed by
CPI Group (UK) Ltd, Croydon, CR0 4YY

At SAGE we take sustainability seriously.
Most of our products are printed in the UK
using FSC papers and boards. When we
print overseas we ensure sustainable
papers are used as measured by the
PREPS grading system. We undertake an
annual audit to monitor our sustainability.

Editorial arrangement and Introduction © Phil Harris and
Craig S. Fleisher, 2017

Part I © John Mahon, 2017
Chapter 1 © Craig S. Fleisher, 2017
Chapter 2 © Duane Windsor, 2017
Chapter 3 © Richard McGowan, 2017
Chapter 4 © Fruzsina M. Harsanyi and Geoff Allen, 2017
Chapter 5 © Shannon Blair Creighton and Martin Meznar, 2017
Part II © Phil Harris, 2017
Chapter 6 © Howard Viney, Paul Baines and Laura Stegen, 2017
Chapter 7 © Ian N. Richardson, 2017
Chapter 8 © Alberto Bitonti, 2017
Chapter 9 © Amy D. Meli and Edward A. Grefe, 2017
Chapter 10 © Simon Bryceson and Simon Levitt, 2017
Chapter 11 © Bruce I. Newman, Wojciech Cwalina and Andrzej Falkowski, 2017
Chapter 12 © Mordecai Lee, 2017
Part III © John M. Holcomb, 2017
Chapter 13 © Catie Snow Bailard, 2017
Chapter 14 © Michael Hadani, 2017
Chapter 15 © Laura Bernal-Bermudez and Tricia D. Olsen, 2017
Chapter 16 © Justin Greenwood, 2017
Chapter 17 © Shannon A. Bowen, 2017
Chapter 18 © Jeffrey A. Hart, 2017
Part IV © Carla Millar, 2017

Chapter 19 © Rinus van Schendelen, 2017
Chapter 20 © Alberto Bitonti and Phil Harris, 2017
Chapter 21 © John Mahon, 2017
Chapter 22 © Andréa Cristina Oliveira Gozetto and Clive S. Thomas, 2017
Chapter 23 © Ronel Rensburg and Olebogeng Selebi, 2017
Chapter 24 © Geoff Allen, 2017
Chapter 25 © Andrew Hughes, 2017
Part V © Craig S. Fleisher, 2017
Chapter 26 © William D. Oberman, 2017
Chapter 27 © Craig S. Fleisher, 2017
Chapter 28 © John M. Holcomb, 2017
Chapter 29 © John Mahon, 2017
Chapter 30 © Irina Lock and Peter Seele, 2017
Chapter 31 © Arco Timmermans, 2017
Part VI © Danny Moss, 2017
Chapter 32 © Clive S. Thomas and Kristina Klimovich, 2017
Chapter 33 © David Irwin and Kariuki Waweru, 2017
Chapter 34 © Conor McGrath, 2017
Chapter 35 © Koji Haraguchi and Ronald J. Hrebenar, 2017
Chapter 36 © Goodluck Charles, 2017
Chapter 37 © Gianluca Vinicio Aguggini, 2017

Library of Congress Control Number: 2016957757

British Library Cataloguing in Publication data

A catalogue record for this book is available from the British Library

ISBN 978-1-4462-7611-2

Contents

List of Figures

List of Tables

Notes on the Editors and Contributors

THE EDITORS

Phil Harris is Executive Director of the Business Research Institute at the University of Chester, Previously Dean of University of Chester Business School from 2009 to 2014 and holds the Westminster Chair of Marketing and Public Affairs at the University. Past Chairman of the Marketing Council (UK) PLC, Board member of the Chartered Institute of Marketing, Professor of Marketing at the University of Otago, New Zealand and Founding Director of the Centre for Corporate and Public Affairs at Manchester Metropolitan University.

Prior to becoming an academic he held positions in the international chemical, foods and radio industries with ICI, RHM and Radio Luxembourg and has chaired or been a board member of the American Marketing Association, Academy of Marketing, and the Australian and New Zealand Marketing Academy. He has been a candidate for the UK and EU Parliaments and is a past chairman of the Liberal Party and advisor to a number of business and governmental organisations.

Phil is regarded internationally as one of the founders of research and theory development in political marketing and strategic public affairs management (lobbying). He has just completed two books: The *International Handbook of Corporate and Public Affairs* with Craig S. Fleisher for SAGE (2017) and *Lobbying in Europe: Public Affairs and the Lobbying Industry in 28 EU Countries* with Alberto Bitonti for Palgrave (2017). His current activities focus on China, entrepreneurship, family business, business competitiveness and global public affairs and management education. He holds visiting professorships in Beijing, Jiangsu, Wuhan and Xiamen.

Craig S. Fleisher is the Chief Learning Officer and Director of Professional Development at Aurora WDC, a 20+ year old professional services firm headquartered in Madison, Wisconsin, USA. Craig holds academic roles as a long-serving graduate faculty member in the Executive Master of Science in Communication Management (EMScom) at the Università della Svizzera italiana (USI) in Lugano, Switzerland and Professor (adj.) in Business Information Management, Faculty of Business, Tampere University of Technology, Finland. He was previously President of the Canadian Council for Public Affairs Advancement and served as a board member of the Center for Public Affairs Management (Washington, DC), European Center for Public Affairs, Public Affairs Association of Canada, and George Washington University Graduate School of Political Management. He is the Regional Editor for the Americas of the *Journal of Public Affairs*.

A Fellow and Meritorious award winner in strategy and competitive intelligence, Craig is an award-winning instructor and top-cited author in business and strategic analysis, managing corporate and public affairs and social issues in management. He is an active keynote speaker, having addressed audiences in over 50 nations, and an advisor to senior executives in many class-leading organizations around the globe. He has written several acclaimed books, including *Assessing, Managing and Maximizing Public Affairs Performance* (1997), *Public Affairs Benchmarking: A Comprehensive Guide* (1995), *Strategic and Competitive Analysis* (2003), *Handbook of Public Affairs* (2005), *Business and Competitive Analysis* (2nd Ed, 2015) and has also published over 150 articles and chapters. He has previously served as dean, graduate program director, university research chair and/or professor at the Universities of Calgary, New Brunswick, Wilfrid Laurier, Windsor (Canada), Coastal Georgia (USA), and Sydney (Australia). He holds a PhD in Business Administration from the Katz Graduate School of Business, University of Pittsburgh.

THE CONTRIBUTORS

Gianluca Vinicio Aguggini was born on July 6, 1990 in Torino, Italy. He graduated in Foreign Languages applied to Business and Management at Catholic University of Sacred Heart in Milan, attaining his Bachelor degree in 2013. In order to enrich his marketing background and in line with his international vocation, he moved to London to pursue a Masters of Science in Marketing at Queen Mary University, where he was awarded First-Class Honours in 2015. After working in Milan as a Fashion Buyer Coordinator, he is now Business Development Associate at Condé Nast International in London. His long-term objective is to keep a strong connection between his career in the fashion industry and the editorial world, which he constantly looks at thanks to his passion for writing.

Geoff Allen has been a Civil Servant and Senior Advisor to the Australian Treasurer and Leader of the Opposition. He was co-founder, architect and foundation CEO of the Business Council of Australia. He has chaired a number of Australian Government advisory councils including its Trade Development Council, Trade Negotiations Advisory Group, and is currently Chairman of The Australian Statistics Advisory Council. He was a member of the Australian Government's Foreign Affairs Council and Prime Minister's Business-Community Partnership. He was National Chairman of the Committee for Economic Development of Australia and Director of a number of public companies. He was founder of Australia's largest independent public policy and economics consultancy and The Australian Centre for Corporate Public Affairs.

He pioneered the teaching of business government relations in Australia as Senior Research Fellow and subsequently as adjunct professor at the Melbourne Business School. He was Deputy Chairman of that School for ten years. He has been consultant to boards and senior managements of major companies and to governments, including personal assignments for the Australian Prime Minister. He was made Member of the Order of Australia for services to business government relations and public affairs.

Catie Snow Bailard earned her PhD in Political Science from UCLA and is an Associate Professor at George Washington University in the School of Media and Public Affairs. Catie's research agenda seeks to broaden the field of political communication by focusing on political outcomes beyond the American borders and media technologies beyond legacy broadcast media. In acknowledgment of her work, Catie received the 2012 Sanders-Kaid Award from the International Communication Association for the best paper published in political communication for her study, 'Testing the Internet's Effect on Democratic Satisfaction: A Multi-Methodological, Cross-National Approach'. She was also awarded the 2015 Best Book Award by the American Political Science Association in the field of Information Technology and Politics for her book, *Democracy's Double-Edged Sword: How Internet Use Changes Citizens' Views of their Government.*

Paul Baines is Professor of Political Marketing at Cranfield University. Paul was Managing Editor, Europe of the *Journal of Political Marketing* from 2010–13. He is author/co-author of more than a hundred published journal articles, book chapters and books on marketing issues. Over the last eighteen years, Paul's research has particularly focused on political marketing, public opinion and propaganda. Paul is (co-)editor and co-author of *Political Marketing* (Sage Publications, 2011), with Sir Robert Worcester, Roger Mortimore and Mark Gill, of *Explaining Cameron's Comeback* (Indie Books, 2015) and a four-volume set on *Propaganda* with Nicholas O'Shaughnessy (Sage Publications, 2012). Paul has worked on various communication research projects for the UK Foreign and Commonwealth Office, Home Office and Ministry of Defence. He is Director of Baines Associates Limited.

Laura Bernal-Bermudez is a DPhil candidate in the Department of Sociology of the University of Oxford, where she researches access to justice for victims of corporate human rights violations. She focuses on business and human rights in Colombia, but has participated in the creation of large-N databases of abuses occurring in Latin America. Her published work can be found in peer-reviewed journals in Colombia, including International Law Revista Internacional de Derecho Internacional and Vniversitas.

Alberto Bitonti is Professor of Politics at IES Abroad Rome and at the Umbra Institute of Perugia (Italy), as well as a Fellow at LUISS Guido Carli University of Rome (Italy) and at the School of Public Affairs of the American University in Washington DC (United States). He holds a PhD in Political Theory (University of Roma Tre, 2011). His research is grounded in Political Theory, Philosophy of Science and Political Science, and focuses on lobbying and public affairs, philosophy of power, political influence and communication. He is editor of Lobbying in Europe (Palgrave MacMillan, 2017, with Phil Harris), and author of Classe dirigente, a book on the Italian ruling class (Datanews, 2012), besides several book chapters. He is an activist for various organizations promoting open government, transparency and innovation in the political world.

Shannon A. Bowen is Professor of Public Relations at the University of South Carolina; she is the 2011 winner of the Jackson Jackson and Wagner Behavioral Science Research Prize. She has published scores of studies on many aspects of ethics in professional practice, and is co-editor of *Ethical Space, The International Journal of Communication Ethics*. Her professional experience includes working on Capitol Hill followed by her years as a research analyst and strategist for dozens of election campaigns as well as for corporate clients. Her doctorate is from the University of Maryland in the excellence theory tradition of James E. Grunig, as well as in business management, and was the ICA outstanding dissertation award winner. Her recent books include *An Overview of the Public Relations Function* and *Excellence in Internal Relations Management.*

Simon Bryceson is a Political Consultant, and has worked with over 300 corporations in Europe, North America, South America, Russia and Australasia. He is currently chairperson of

Harwood Levitt Consulting, a Public Affairs strategy consultancy based in Brussels. Simon was awarded the Order of the British Empire (MBE) for his services to politics in 1992. Previously, he held the position of General Secretary of the British Liberal Party between 1982–1987. For 7 years Simon was the Head of Public Affairs of Burson-Marsteller in London. He holds a degree in Politics from the University of York.

Goodluck Charles works with the University of Dar es Salaam Business School (UDBS) as a Senior Lecturer in the Department of Marketing. Over the last fifteen years he has taken a number of posts at the University including Deputy Director of the University of Dar es Salaam Entrepreneurship Centre (UDEC) and the School Coordinator of Research and Publications. He is currently the Coordinator of the Centre for Policy Research and Advocacy (CPRA), hosted by UDBS. He has researched and published on entrepreneurship and private-sector development, public–private dialogue and policy advocacy, family business, micro-financing and business environment.

Shannon Blair Creighton was recently named the MBA Director at Limestone College in Gaffney, South Carolina, after four years as a university Lecturer at Appalachian State University, North Carolina. Shannon is also currently finishing his DBA in International Business from Walden University with a research focus on reducing workplace discrimination. He has higher education experience in financial aid, student development, assessment, student club advising, strategic planning, diversity management, international travel experiences.

Wojciech Cwalina is Professor in the Department of Marketing Psychology at the SWPS University of Social Sciences and Humanities, Warsaw, Poland. His publications include numerous articles on political marketing, social psychology and media psychology, as well as chapters and books. The author of *Television Political Advertising* (TN KUL, Poland, 2000) and co-author of four books including *A Cross-Cultural Theory of Voter Behavior* (Haworth Press, 2007) and *Political Marketing: Theoretical and Strategic Foundations* (M.E. Sharpe, 2011). He is a member of the editorial board in *Psychologia Społeczna* (*Social Psychology*) and *Journal of Political Marketing*.

Andrzej Falkowski is Professor of Psychology and Marketing, and Head of the Department of Marketing Psychology at the SWPS University of Social Sciences and Humanities, Warsaw, Poland. He has been a Fulbright Scholar at the University of Michigan. His publications include numerous articles in consumer behavior, political marketing, and cognitive psychology journals, as well as chapters and books. He is co-author of *A Cross-Cultural Theory of Voter Behavior* (Haworth Press, 2007) and *Political Marketing: Theoretical and Strategic Foundations* (M.E. Sharpe, 2011). He is advisory editor of the *Handbook of Political Marketing*, and editorial board member of *Journal of Political Marketing*.

Justin Greenwood is Professor of European Public Policy at The Robert Gordon University (Aberdeen, UK) and a Visiting Professor at the College of Europe. He is the author of *Interest Representation in the EU* (Palgrave Macmillan), the subject of his career of long specialism, as well as *Inside the EU Business Associations* with the same publisher. He has also recently published articles on the European Transparency Register and the European Citizens' Initiative. He is currently the Principal Investigator on a UK Economic and Social Committee (ESRC) funded project examining information flows between the three EU legislative institutions and civil society organisations during the course of informal 'trilogue' negotiations, through which most EU legislation is agreed at first reading.

Edward A. Grefe has spent more than 40 years in Communications and Politics. He started his career with *The Washington Post* and continued his early journalism with *The Baltimore News American* for which he wrote a front page series on reading problems in that city in 1964. He worked for three Members of Congress in the late 1960s. Ed's many campaigns include candidates seeking to become US Senator, US Congressmen, Governor, and Mayor. In working with organizations seeking victory in legislative battles at the city and village level, in particular, he and his firm have been involved in over 350 grassroots campaigns. He has also worked on political campaigns and community advocacy efforts in several foreign countries – including Australia, Canada, Costa Rico, Ecuador, Mexico, and France. He has taught at the Graduate School of Political Management at George Washington University since 1995; and has taught as well at Duquesne University (Pittsburgh, PA), Leiden University (The Hague, The Netherlands), and Rosario University (Bogotá, Colombia).

Michael Hadani is the TransAmerica Corporation Professor of Business Policy at the School of Economics and Business Administration at Saint Mary's College of California. He received his PhD from the Martin J Whitman School of Management at Syracuse University. Apart from teaching strategy and global strategy to MBA and executive MBA students at the graduate school of business, Michael's research into corporate political activity has been published in the *Strategic Management Journal, Journal of Management, Journal of Business Research, Business & Society* and the *Journal of Organizational Behavior* and has appeared on several national media outlets. Michael also serves on the board of the *Journal of Management* and on the board of *Business & Society*.

Koji Haraguchi, a native of Japan, has his PhD in Political Science at the University of Utah and works at Yamanashi University's International College of Liberal Arts in Japan.

Fruzsina M. Harsanyi is a Consultant on Public Affairs, a Visiting Scholar at The American University, Washington, D.C., Director of the Global Government Relations Forum, and Senior Advisor to Interel, the global public affairs consultancy, headquartered in Brussels. Her consulting practice focuses on the strategic role of public affairs in business, on international public affairs and on public affairs as a leadership function. She has 30 years' experience managing the public-affairs function for several US and non-US multinational corporations, including Tyco International Ltd (Vice President, Global Public Affairs) and ABB Inc (Senior Vice President, Public Affairs and Corporate Communications). She has been on the faculty of the Corporate Public Affairs Institute in Melbourne, Australia for 20 years, where she delivered the annual oration in 2010. She has lectured on public affairs in the US and abroad, including at Georgetown University, Leeds University Business School in the UK and the Asia Public Affairs Institute in Hong Kong. She co-authored 'Creating a Public Affairs Function in Countries without a Public Affairs Culture', published in the *Journal of Public Affairs*, 2011.

Jeffrey A. Hart is Emeritus Professor of Political Science at Indiana University, Bloomington, where he taught international politics and international political economy from 1981 to 2012. His first teaching position was at Princeton University from 1973 to 1980. He was a professional staff member of the President's Commission for a National Agenda for the

Eighties from 1980 to 1981. Hart worked as an internal contractor at the Office of Technology Assessment of the US Congress 1985–6 and helped to write their report, *International Competition in Services* (1987). His books include *The New International Economic Order* (1983), *Interdependence in the Post-Multilateral Era* (1985), *Rival Capitalists* (1992), *Globalization and Governance* (1999), *Managing New Industry Creation* (2001), *Technology, Television, and Competition* (2004), *The Politics of International Economic Relations*, 7th edition (2009), and he has published scholarly articles in *World Politics, International Organization*, the *British Journal of Political Science, New Political Economy*, and the *Journal of Conflict Resolution*.

John M. Holcomb is a Professor of Business Ethics and Legal Studies and has over 35 years of teaching experience at the Universities of Denver, California (Berkeley), Maryland, Rutgers, and George Washington University. He has taught executive education programs in the US, Canada, and the United Kingdom, and has consulted to corporations, trade associations, and think tanks. He has written many articles and book chapters on the legal, political, and ethical aspects of business. His publications focus on corporate governance, corporate political activities, crisis management, and NGOs. He is former Chairman of the Colorado Commission on Judicial Discipline and has a JD degree from Georgetown University and MA in Political Science from Vanderbilt University.

Ronald J. Hrebenar is Emeritus Professor of Political Science at the University of Utah. He is author or editor of 17 books on Japanese and American politics in the subfields of interest groups, lobbying and political organization. He was a Fulbright Professor of Political Science at Tohoku University and Fulbright Distinguished Chair of Political Science at the University of Vienna.

Andrew Hughes is a Lecturer in Marketing in the Research School of Management, where he teaches marketing at both undergraduate and postgraduate levels. He is considered to be one of the leading researchers in political marketing in Australia and has given numerous interviews on politics and political marketing to international and national television, print and internet outlets. His past research has examined the role of stakeholders in political marketing, personal brands in political marketing, and the role of negative advertising. His thesis, 'The relationship between advertisement content and pacing on emotional responses and memory for televised political advertisements' was nominated for ANU's prestigious thesis prize, the J.G. Crawford Award.

His main areas of research include emotions in television advertising, emotional responses in marketing and strategy generally, communications, personal branding, and political and non-profit marketing.

David Irwin is a Social Entrepreneur and Consultant in enterprise and economic development working with clients such as DANIDA, Department for International Development, International Labour Organisation and the International Trade Centre. He advises on regulatory reform and the business-enabling environment and supports business associations to undertake projects to influence public policy. He works mainly in the UK and Sub-Saharan Africa. From early 2000 to 2002, he was Chief Executive of the Small Business Service, an executive agency of the Department of Trade and Industry, with responsibility for managing all of the UK Government's small business support programmes and a role as the 'strong voice for small business at the heart of Government'. Before joining SBS, he co-founded Project North East (PNE), one of the UK's leading enterprise and economic development agencies, and was its chief executive for

20 years. He was awarded the Queen's Award for Enterprise Promotion in 2009. David has a BSc in Engineering Science and Management from Durham University and an MBA from Newcastle University. He is a Fellow of the RSA. He has a particular interest in the factors that lead business associations to success in their influencing activities.

Kristina Klimovich has a Master's degree in International Affairs from the New School University in New York City and a Bachelor's degree in Social Sciences from the University of Alaska Southeast. She has extensive experience conducting interest-group research as a graduate research assistant. Kristina also has broad experience working for non-profit advocacy, research and aid organizations. She is currently promoting innovative sustainable financing strategies as a Fellow at PACE*Nation*.

Mordecai Lee is Professor at the University of Wisconsin-Milwaukee. He earned a PhD in public administration from Syracuse University (NY). Prior to joining the academy in 1997, he was a guest scholar at the Brookings Institution in Washington (DC), legislative assistant to a Member of Congress, elected to three terms in the Wisconsin State Legislature's State Assembly and two terms in the State Senate, and executive director of a faith-based NGO engaging in public policy advocacy. He has written extensively about public affairs in American government. His books include *The Philosopher-Lobbyist: John Dewey and the People's Lobby, 1928–1940* (2015), *Promoting the War Effort: Robert Horton and Federal Propaganda, 1938–1946* (2012), *Congress vs. the Bureaucracy: Muzzling Agency Public Relations* (2011) and *The First Presidential Communications Agency: FDR's Office of Government Reports* (2005). He co-edited *The Practice of Government Public Relations* (2012) and edited *Government Public Relations: A Reader* (2008). He has also authored several score articles in scholarly journals on public affairs in American government.

Simon Levitt is a Founder and Partner of Harwood Levitt Consulting, a Public Affairs strategy consultancy in Brussels. Simon has designed global and European Public Affairs strategies for the world's leading companies in the healthcare, FMCG, and food/drink sectors. He also works with foundations, and other civil society organisations on environment and development issues. Simon trains senior management on how to integrate Public Affairs effectively into their organisations, and his experience spans New York, London, and Brussels. He has lectured on Public Affairs and business strategy at Solvay Business School and United Business Institutes in Brussels since 2013 and has over 15 years of experience of the Brussels lobbying environment. Simon holds a degree in Classics from Oxford University.

Irina Lock is Assistant Professor of Corporate Communication at the University of Amsterdam, the Netherlands. She received her PhD from the Università della Svizzera italiana, Lugano, Switzerland.

John Mahon is the John M. Murphy Chair of International Business Policy and Strategy/ Professor of Management at the Maine Business School, University of Maine. He was the founding director of the School of Policy and International Affairs at UM. From 2004 to 2006, was Provost ad interim; from 2007–2010 he was Dean, College of Business Public Policy and Health. Prior to Maine, Mahon was a Professor of Strategy and Policy/Chair of the Strategy and Policy Department at the School of Management, Boston University. He received his DBA from Boston University, his MBA (with honors) from Bryant College, and his BS in Economics from the Wharton School at the University of Pennsylvania. He is the author or co-author of nearly 300 cases, papers and book chapters.

Richard McGowan is a Professor of the Carroll School of Management at Boston College. The focus of his research is on the interaction of the Business and Public Policy processes especially, as they relate to the gambling, tobacco, alcohol and marijuana industries.

Father McGowan has published seven books entitled: *State Lotteries and Legalized Gambling: Painless Revenue or Painful Mirage*, Quorum Books (October,1994); *Business, Politics and Cigarettes: Multiple Levels, Multiple Agendas*, Greenwood Press (September, 1995); *Industry as a Player in the Social and Political Arenas*, Quorum Press (June, 1996) and *The Search for Revenue and the Common Good: An Analysis of Government Regulation of the Alcohol Industry*, Praeger Books (May, 1997); *Government and the Transformation of the Gaming Industry*, Edward Elgar Publishing Inc. (July, 2001). In 2012, He published *The Gambling Debate*. His latest book, *Privatize this?* was published last year. He is finishing a book, entitled, *Lotteries: The Key to Understanding the Gambling Industry* and will begin a book entitled, *The Ethics of Disgust and the Sin Industries*. He has also published over a hundred referred articles in various academic journals and made over numerous academic and professional presentations.

Conor McGrath is Lecturer in Public Relations at Ulster University. He has worked for a Member of Parliament and as a lobbyist in the UK. Conor serves as Deputy Editor of the *Journal of Public Affairs* and as Practice Editor of *Interest Groups and Advocacy*. He is a former President of the Political Studies Association of Ireland, Chair of the Northern Ireland Government Affairs Group, Chair of the Education Sub-Council at the Public Relations Institute of Ireland, and Chair of the Research and Publications Committee at the European Centre for Public Affairs. His research interests include: lobbying regulation; the historical evolution and development of lobbying in the UK and US; professionalization of the lobbying industry; media coverage of Northern Irish politics; and fictional portrayals of lobbying and lobbyists.

Amy D. Meli serves as Senior Vice President for Grassroots Consulting at Aristotle. In this role, Amy helps her clients achieve their public affairs goals by building durable and effective grassroots programs. Over the past 14 years, Amy has managed grassroots programs for Fortune 500 companies, nonprofit groups, and other organizations; established and managed third party coalitions; and advised clients on the effective use of software in accomplishing their public affairs goals. Prior to her work at Aristotle, Amy worked on Capitol Hill for then-Congressman Richard Burr and the House Energy and Commerce Committee. Amy holds a BA from Virginia Tech in Political Science and Communication Studies, and a graduate degree in Political Management from The George Washington University Graduate School of Political Management, where she is currently an adjunct professor teaching Grassroots Politics.

Martin Meznar is a Professor and Associate Dean for International Programs and Assessment at the Walker College of Business at Appalachian State University (Boone, NC). He holds a PhD in International Business from the University of South Carolina. Much of his research centers on public affairs management in multinational corporations and on corporate social issues management. Prior to joining Appalachian State Dr Meznar taught at Arizona State University and before that at the University of Victoria, in British Columbia. His research has been published in a variety of academic journals, including the *Academy of Management*

Journal, Human Relations, Business & Society, Journal of International Management, Journal of Public Affairs and Latin American Business Review.

Carla Millar is a Fellow of Ashridge at Hult International Business School, Professor of International Marketing & Management at the University of Twente, and Professor of Public Affairs, University of Chester. As an executive in major MNCs she conceptualized and launched many international brands; as an academic she is a former Business School Dean and CEO; was CEO of City University Business School's Management Development Centre, a professor at RUG, Groningen, a visiting professor at ANU, Canberra & ESSEC, Paris, published over 100 academic papers, and guest edited a dozen Special Issues of peer reviewed Journals. For the *Journal of Public Affairs* she co-guest edited the much cited SIs on 'Public Affairs in Central and Eastern Europe' (2014) and on 'Multi Stakeholder Public Policy and Governance in China' (2014) after the special issue on 'The Sustainability Challenge – Influencing the change' (2012) and on 'Looking into the Abyss: Global Unethical Leadership' (2010), which offered international reflections on leadership in the face of corruption and manipulation. Currently she is guest editing the JPA SI on 'Value Creation in Knowledge Intensive Institutions: Priorities for Governance and Public Affairs' due in 2017.

Her current research focuses on leadership, ethics and innovation, transparency, multi-age driven organisational change, knowledge intensive industries, branding and reputation, comparative public affairs, and national governance bundles.

Danny Moss is Professor of Corporate and Public Affairs at the University of Chester Business School and co-director of the University's International Centre for Corporate & Public Affairs Research. Previously he worked at Manchester Metropolitan University, and the University of Stirling, specialising in the field of Public Relations and Corporate Communications, and co-founding the annual Global Public Relations Research Symposium held at Lake Bled, Slovenia. Danny Moss is the founding co-editor of the *Journal of Public Affairs* and has published work in a wide range of journals and has authored a number of books, most recently *Public relations: A managerial perspective* (2011).

Bruce I. Newman (PhD) is Professor of Marketing and Wicklander Fellow in Business Ethics in the Department of Marketing, Kellstadt Graduate School of Business at DePaul University, USA. He has held visiting scholar positions at several universities, including Stanford University, the University of California-Berkeley, and more recently at Meiji University in Tokyo, Japan. His publications have appeared in top academic journals, including the *Journal of Consumer Research, Journal of Business Research, Psychology & Marketing*, among others. Bruce has published 15 books, some of which have appeared in Chinese, Korean, Hungarian and Italian. His most recent book is *The Marketing Revolution in Politics: What Recent U.S. Presidential Campaigns Can Teach Us About Effective Marketing* (Rotman-UTP Press, 2016, Award-Winner in the Business: Marketing & Advertising category of the 2016 International Book Awards). He is the founding Editor-in-Chief of the *Journal of Political Marketing*, now in its fifteenth year. Dr Newman is a recipient of the Ehrenring (Ring of Honor) from the Austrian Advertising Research Association, and advised senior aides in the Clinton White House of 1995–1996 on communication strategy. Dr Newman has been invited to give Keynote Addresses in over 30 countries.

William D. Oberman is Associate Professor and Chair of the Department of Management, Marketing, and Entrepreneurship at the John L. Grove College of Business, Shippensburg

University. He completed his doctoral work in Business Environment & Public Policy and Strategic Planning & Policy at the Joseph M. Katz Graduate School of Business, University of Pittsburgh. In addition to Shippensburg, he has taught business & society, ethics, public affairs, leadership, and strategic management at the University of Pittsburgh, the University of New Mexico, and the Pennsylvania State University. His research interests include business involvement in the public policy process, corporate social responsibility, the roles and responsibilities of leaders and followers in large organizations, and social networks and organizational governance.

Andréa Cristina Oliveira Gozetto is a Political Scientist specializing in interest groups and political advocacy. She earned her PhD from the Universidade Estadual de Campinas (UNICAMP) in 2004 and her Master in Political Sociology from Unesp-Araraquara in 1998. She is also academic coordinator of the MBA in Economics and Management-Government Relations at the Fundação Getulio Vargas (FGV) MGM, visiting professor of the Public Management MBA at the Senac and advisor/researcher in the Local Public Administration MBA at Federal University of São Paulo (Unifesp). Andréa works as consultant for the National Industry Confederation (CNI). She has authored many articles on Brazilian lobbying. These include: *Interest Groups in Brazil: a new era and its challenges* (2014).

Tricia D. Olsen is the Marcus Faculty Fellow and an Assistant Professor at the University of Denver where she researches and teaches about business ethics, human rights, and sustainability in emerging economies. Dr Olsen's current research is on business and human rights, which involves the creation of a large-N database of historical trends of businesses' human rights practices in Latin America. She also writes about the development, and ethics, of microfinance across Brazil and Mexico. Her work has been published in the *Journal of Business Ethics, Human Rights Quarterly, Journal of Human Rights, and Journal of Peace Research*. Olsen has received support from Fulbright-Hays, the British Academy/Leverhulme, USAID, among others. She has consulted with the UN Working Group on Business and Human Rights and the Global Business Initiative.

Ronel Rensburg is Professor and Head of the Communication Management Division, as well as Director of the Center for Communication and Reputation Management at the University of Pretoria, South Africa. She holds a a PhD in Communication Science from the University of South Africa (Unisa). Much of her research centers on strategic communication management in the business environment and on reputation management. She is a Fellow of the Public Relations and Communication Management Institute of southern Africa (PRISA) and has published a variety of articles and books on these subject matters.

Ian N. Richardson is Director of Executive Education and Director of the MSc Strategic Public & Political Marketing at Stockholm University. In addition to advisory board responsibilities at Cranfield School of Management and Cracow University, he's also a member of the European Club Association (ECA) Scientific Advisory Panel. Prior to his doctorate at Cranfield, which explored consensus in transnational elite networks, Ian was a business leader in the magazine publishing and internet sectors. At the height of the dotcom era, he was Chief Operating Officer of the most well-funded internet start-up in Europe and has managed a number of pan-European digital information businesses. He has advised – and continues to advise – numerous organisations within the sector. As lead author of 'Bilderberg People: Elite Power and Consensus in World Affairs' (Routledge, 2011), and a political contributor to the

Huffington Post, Ian also provides advice and consulting on issues related to political strategy, public affairs and public diplomacy.

Rinus van Schendelen has been Full Professor in Political Science since 1980 and is Emeritus since 2005 at Erasmus University Rotterdam, the Netherlands (NL). His special interest has always been 'influencing decision-making', nowadays also called public affairs management. He published more than forty books and 200 articles in academic journals. His current leading title is 'The Art of Lobbying the EU: More Machiavelli in Brussels' (1st ed. 2002, 4th ed. 2013 and translated in German, Polish, Czech and Bulgarian. For over 35 years he advised all sorts of interest groups (governments, NGO's, companies etc.) for their EU-affairs. He is associate at PA Bureau Brussels in the EU capital. In NL he co-founded four PA 'King William' and other groupings of PA practitioners and at the EU level he co-founded and chaired for ten years the Research Committee of the then European Centre for Public Affairs.

Peter Seele is Associate Professor of Corporate Social Responsibility and Business Ethics at the Faculty of Communication Sciences at the Università della Svizzera italiana in Lugano, Switzerland.

Olebogeng Selebi is a Lecturer and PhD student from the University of Pretoria. Her research focus is primarily on public, intercultural and business communication. She currently holds an MCom degree in Communication Management. Ms Selebi teaches Business Communication Skills to approximately 2,000 first-year BCom students a year while also lecturing Strategic Corporate Communication Management as well as Reputation Management on Honours level. In addition to her teaching responsibilities, she provides two one-day communication workshops to actuaries who form part of the Actuarial Society of South Africa. In the past, she provided communication training for participants in the Albertina Sisulu Executive Leadership Programme in Health (ASELPH).

Laura Stegen was a Postgraduate student on the MSc in Management and Corporate Sustainability 2014–15 at Cranfield University.

Clive S. Thomas is a Senior Fellow at the Thomas S. Foley Institute for Public Policy and Public Service at Washington State University, in the State of Washington in the US, and a Visiting Professor at the University of São Paulo in Brazil. His publications include several books and articles on interest groups in US, European, Asian and Latin American politics, including *A Research Guide to US and International Interest Groups* (Praeger, 2004). His most recent publications are included in a Special Double Issue of the *Journal of Public Affairs*, published in Fall 2014, titled 'Interest Groups and Lobbying in Latin America: A New Era or More of the Same,' of which he was the guest editor. He also runs the political consulting firm PAS–Political Advocacy Strategies.

Arco Timmermans is Professor of Public Affairs at the Faculty of Governance and Global Affairs at Leiden University, the Netherlands. He obtained his PhD in the political and social sciences at the European University Institute in Florence, Italy. Former positions were at the Delft University of Technology, Twente University and the Montesquieu Institute in the Hague where he was research director. Arco's research and teaching is about comparative public policy and public affairs, focusing on the dynamics of issue attention, coalition building, grassroots lobbying, and the professionalization of public affairs in the Netherlands. He has published in journals such as the *European Journal of Political Research, Policy Studies Journal, Comparative Political Studies, Interest Groups & Advocacy*, the *Journal of Common Market Studies*, and he is a co-editor of the Palgrave book series *Comparative Studies of Political Agendas*. He is the co-founder of the Netherlands project in the international Comparative Agendas Project. The chair he holds is a unique collaboration between Leiden University and the Netherlands Association for Public Affairs, seeking to promote the dialogue between research and practice. Arco also wrote numerous newspaper columns and comments in various media on news issues relating to public affairs and politics.

Howard Viney is a Visiting Fellow at Open University Business School (OUBS), having previously been Senior Lecturer in Strategic Management there and at Cranfield University. He is also a Programme Director for the Centre for Management Development at London Business School. Prior to joining OUBS, Howard was a research fellow and lecturer at Middlesex University. His research interest is primarily focused upon stakeholder–management issues and nonmarket strategies and he is particularly interested in non-traditionally competitive industries, the marketized public sector and utility organizations. He has published over 20 academic papers, co-edited two books and presented his work at numerous international conferences.

Kariuki Waweru is an Advocacy Manager at the Business Advocacy Fund. He supports business associations in Kenya to identify, clarify and understand their economic-policy issues and then supports them as they advocate public-policy reform.

Duane Windsor obtained his PhD from Harvard University, is a Rice University alumnus (BA) and is now Lynette S. Autrey Professor of Management in the Jesse H. Jones Graduate School of Business there. He was editor (2007–14) of the journal *Business & Society*, founded in 1960 and sponsored by the International Association for Business and Society (IABS), from which he received the 2014 Distinguished Service Award. He served as elected programme chair and head of IABS and of the Social Issues in Management (SIM) Division of Academy of Management, from which he received the 2009 Sumner Marcus Award for Outstanding Service. He has published several books and monographs, his recent work focusing on corporate social responsibility and stakeholder theory. His articles have appeared in *Business & Society, Business Ethics Quarterly, Cornell International Law Journal, Journal of Business Ethics, Journal of Business Research, Journal of Corporate Citizenship, Journal of International Management, Journal of Management Studies, Journal of Public Affairs* and *Public Administration Review*.

Acknowledgments

In putting together the SAGE *Handbook of International Corporate and Public Affairs* there are many people we owe thanks to. It has been a long task and one which at times has seemed very daunting. 'Where do you start and when do you end?' we kept on saying. The discipline continues to evolve and remains dynamic. We hope we have done it credit in an international context. Thanks are due to many.

There are many unsung heroes such as our doctoral students and fellow researchers who typed and did background research for us or shared ideas, invariably at the last moment and at breakneck speed. These included Darby Best, Albert Carter, Wing Lam, Henry Sidsaph, Sarah Soriano, Sally Williamson, Sen Yang, Ying Zhao and the library and research staffs of our respective institutions. We also would particularly like to thank the support of our respective universities in Chester, UK and Lugano, Switzerland (The Università della Svizzera Italiana, Switzerland) and employers (Aurora WDC, Madison, Wisconsin) and research support given by the School of Journalism and International Communications at Beijing Foreign Studies University without whose support and investments of resources we would never have been able to produce what we believe is a groundbreaking global guide to effective international corporate and public affairs. Also to organizations across the world such as the Academy of Marketing Political Marketing Group, the Australian Centre for Corporate Public Affairs (ACCPA), Business Research Institute, University of Chester, Canadian Council for Public Affairs Advancement (CCPAA), European Centre for Public Affairs (ECPA), Foundation for Public Affairs (FPA), International Association of Business and Society (IABS), International Association of Business Communicators (IABC), International Public Relations Research Symposium, Public Affairs Association of Canada (PAAC), Public Relations Consultants Association (PRCA), International Centre for Corporate and Public Affairs Research, Chester, US Public Affairs Council and its Center for PA Management (Washington, DC) and the *Journal of Public Affairs* and its publishers, John Wiley & Sons. The latter, which has become the leading journal in the corporate and public affairs field and with the support of its distinguished editorial board helped in the development and underpinning of the work.

Most importantly we thank SAGE and our superbly creative and supportive editor, Delia Alfonso Martinez, who encouraged and supported us at every stage of the development of the *Handbook* regardless of the time and other pressures. Also to Matthew Oldfield of SAGE who has helped manage and coordinate contributions in a timely, professional and effective manner and also to our India based production group of Rudrani Mukherjee, Sushant Nailwal and team for their dedication in producing a first class manuscript. Finally, and perhaps most important to us, can we thank Irene Harris, Angela, Zachary, Austin, and KJ Fleisher for their patience, support, and good humour. As always, it was freely given and gratefully received and has provided the support and sustenance which we needed to put together what we feel is a primer and handbook for a great global business discipline that makes a strategic difference.

Phil and Craig

Introduction: The Continuing Development of International Corporate and Public Affairs

Phil Harris and Craig S. Fleisher

Irresolute princes, in order to avoid present dangers,
follow the neutral road most of the time,
and most of the time they are ruined

Niccolo Machiavelli, The Prince *(trans George Bull)*

The management and oversight of public affairs (PA) is a critical boardroom skill that resides with the Chief Executive and those engaged in multi-complex strategic political management work, particularly those working at and across the international business, government and politics interface. This has become of paramount importance to modern business in a very competitive and rapidly globalizing world where strong and focused leadership on corporate communication, issues management, governmental and regulatory issues and soft power (Nye, 2004) can often be pivotal to whether an organization fails or succeeds (Fleisher, 2012; Griffin, 2016, Sun and Harris, 2014; Titley, 2003). As one senior executive commented in a conversation with one of the authors, there are 1) those who are good at public affairs and

politics and their businesses succeed, and 2) those who do not understand the subject and they are either no more or in decline.

Public Affairs is often seen by many as a senior, strategic service of modern global management, combining transnational negotiation skills, networks and an understanding of governmental policy processes to operate in a regulated and complex world internationally (Moss et al., 2012). One plea that is worth emphasizing is that Public Affairs Management (PAM) is still an advanced and sometimes ultra-discrete industry and profession, thus it rarely gets taught at Business, Commerce, Communication, and Management Schools; this needs to change or otherwise we are not teaching the realities of politics, political institutions, stakeholder interests and public policy to future business and corporate executives (Fleisher, 2003b).

Most businesses, government agencies, state and private media, and NGOs have a stake, especially in democracies and emerging democracies, in cultivating a dialogue that is informed, fact driven, timely, responsive and progressive. Population growth, environmentalism and sustainability, the need for improved quality of life, military and cyber security, human rights, and sustainable economic and ecological practices are among the broad issues shaping the public agenda for nations across the globe. Constructive dialogue depends on accurate information, inclusive commitment to human interaction, and the willingness to think long- as well as short-term.

In the latter part of the last century (1990s onwards) a number of authors, practitioners and researchers began to regularly meet and share ideas in the field of corporate public affairs and as a result journals such as the *Journal of Public Affairs* (Wiley) and *Journal of Political Marketing* (Taylor and Francis) were launched to name just a few that specialized in this growing important area of practice and study. Both are now in their 16th volumes. Contextual developments also stimulated us to spend over two years in developing and putting together the first major handbook in the subject matter area entitled the *Handbook of Public Affairs* (2005) by Sage which had a relatively 'Who's Who' list of well recognized experts and contributors to outline the basic tenants and issues around the discipline internationally. After further reprinting and publishing of the Handbook and the passage of a decade, we agreed with authors, practitioners and researchers that it was time to develop a new replacement volume, The *SAGE Handbook of International Corporate and Public Affairs (IHCPA)*. This Handbook is totally new and includes original, previously unpublished work on such areas as Asia, South America, Africa and social media, amongst others. As such, it more fully reflects our modern internationalizing world and the increasing complexity, variability and diversity of advocacy, communicating, influence and policy making.

In this chapter, the authors discuss several key themes that appear throughout this current volume. They traduce the origins of the field, describe its definition and activity boundaries, elaborate on why the field has emerged and continues to evolve in response to various forces, identify a number of field-specific practices that have been identified in the research as being associated with effective public affairs, examine the research on assessing the performance of PA activity, and describe the research on PA at the individual level and what competencies practitioners should have to practice it successfully. They close the chapter by summarizing some of the enduring facts that have been developed about the field, offering a smattering of these in both descriptive and prescriptive forms.

DEFINING THE BOUNDARIES OF PUBLIC AFFAIRS

For well over fifty years, numerous studies have been conducted of the PA function in various nation-states, industry and temporal contexts (e.g., in the USA alone, see Boston University PARG, 1981; Denis & Holcomb, 1996; Dunn et al., 1979; Fleisher, 2005a; Gollner, 1984; Public Affairs Conference Report, 1966). All of these survey-related research efforts were aimed at documenting the expansion of the field. Despite efforts to use these to inductively draw the field's boundaries, none of them were able to establish a definite set of activities as to what activities were or should be included in the field, and what was/were not. The inability to achieve consensus as to its conceptual and/or practical boundaries has been one of a number of hindrances that some observers have noted in the accepted professionalization of the field (Fleisher, 1998). Having stated that, there are enough commonalities seen in these empirical studies to at least provide a Pareto optimal (the 80–20 rule) boundary of activities and organizations around the globe most frequently observed are, in alphabetical order, shown in the Table I.1:

Table I.1 The organizational activities that commonly constitute public affairs

Brand management/ Brand image	Corporate giving/ Philanthropic activity	Crisis management	Government relations/ Lobbying	Investor and financial relations	Public Relations	Stakeholder engagement/ Management
Change management/ Cultural change/ Organizational change	Corporate marketing	Employee communications	Industry association liaison	Issues management	Regulatory affairs	Web site/Intranet communication and management
Consumer affairs	Corporate (social) responsibility (CSR)	Environmental/ Ecological affairs	Interest group relations	Legal influence with respect to public policy matters	Social enterprise activities	
Corporate citizenship/ Engagement	Corporate sponsorships	External Communications	International public affairs	Media relations	Social media monitoring & interaction/Blog management	

The mix and importance of these functions covered will depend on which business sectors and areas of government the public affairs practitioner's organization is operating in. Also, this will be affected by whether they are based in a consultancy looking after a range of clients, or employed within a corporate or not-for-profit organization focused on a particular issue or business. There are also affects emanating from unique public policy factors that need to be accounted for such as the policy institutions targeted, and the history and cultures of the geographic areas for which the PAM practice is focused.

Public affairs is the term usually used to describe communication activities in relation to government, pressure groups and sometimes financial affairs at a corporate level, i.e., excluding customers/prospects and probably employees. Many people have the impression that 'Public Affairs' is another way of describing government affairs/relations or lobbying. Others perceive it as classic Public Relations or the second leg of political marketing after electoral campaigning (Sun, 2007; 2008). Lobbying still tends to have a negative image with many segments of the public, and although almost everyone is attempting to do it, few organizations explicitly claim that they either are or employ professional lobbyists.

Decades of research and scholarship have shown that lobbying is an international activity of major significance with key focal points of activity being centered on political capitals, like Brussels, Geneva, London and Washington and more recently Beijing, Berlin, Brasilia and Hong Kong (van Schendelen, 2010; Zetter, 2008). Lobbying has long been an integral part of Public Affairs Management, which is strategic international business communication focused on informing public policy, whether that is conducted by legislatures, officials, policy makers and/or those that influence regulatory frameworks. PAM can operate at local, regional, national or an international level (John, 2002; McGrath, 2006; McKittrick, 1990; Miller, 1991).

There are increasing amounts of published research in this field (Griffin, Fleisher, Brenner & Boddewyn, 2000). It is an area of professional practice that has seen substantial growth over the past decades (Harris & Moss, 2001). Public affairs and particularly government relations/lobbying, have evolved from an occasional tactic adopted by organizations to amend relevant legislation to become a managerial approach and strategy for achieving competitive advantage (Marx, 1990; Schuler, Rehbein & Cramer, 2002).

The lack of consensus around the term 'Public Affairs' makes it problematic to conceptualize research in the field, and thus to utilize existing work to suggest what 'best practices' might look like (Windsor, 2005). It has also made it difficult to identify and to document demonstrated practices, though practitioners constantly seek to better understand these (Fleisher, 1995; Fleisher & Hoewing, 1992). One attempt to summarize what appear to be two main themes running through the area, which seeks to define the scope of public affairs, is outlined in the following extract:

> The lingua franca of what appears to be the principal two arms of public affairs – government relations/lobbying and community relations/corporate responsibility – can be seen as 'dialogue at both a societal and government level'. By implication, those working in the public affairs field increasingly are required not only to be proficient communicators, but to have a sound appreciation of how the political parties work, develop policy, are influenced, run campaigns and are funded. Moreover, the type of issues and challenges that normally fall within the public affairs domain generally require far more complex and sophisticated solutions than those required when tackling market-related promotional campaigns. (Harris and Moss, 2001, p.108)

There is a lack of consensus about what public affairs is experienced by academics and professional practitioners alike (Fleisher, 2007). This is exacerbated by the discipline calling upon a range of skills such as diplomacy, law, international relations, government affairs, politics, marketing, communications, public relations, organizational behaviour, environmental science, trade relations and an awareness of stakeholders and policy issues (Shaw, 2005). Windsor (2005, p.401) notes that, 'There is no "grand" theory of public affairs – no integrative or overarching framework', but he does also go on to draw attention to the various theoretical debates which surround this area and which can inform academic thinking on public affairs, as do Getz (2002) and Griffin (2005). In Schuler's (2002) view, this lack of a single – central – theory makes it problematic for researchers to extend knowledge, while others suggest that a grand theory is unachievable, and even if it could be achieved, might be not desirable (Hillman, 2002).

Other boundaries might encompass public policy, issues management, crisis management, public relations and stakeholder relations (Harris & McGrath, 2012; Harris & Moss, 2001). While there may be some variation in the way functional boundaries are understood within different organizations and equally, within companies around the world, what does emerge clearly, is that issues management is a particularly significant component of the work of the public affairs function (for example, see Mahon's chapter 29 in this volume). As is in evidence in the USA, there is a reasonable amount of overlap among organizations who have membership in issue management's best established professional association, the Issue Management Council (established 1988) and the largest public affairs association, the Washington, DC-based Public Affairs Council (established in 1954). Moreover, it is in the context of issue management work, that senior management and other functional units (e.g., products, legal, financial, etc.) are most likely to see at first hand the value of public affairs. Indeed, it is worth noting that one recent article cited Unilever Plc as one of the 'leading adopters of issues management' (Wartick and Heugens, 2003), but highlighted the potential for even greater synergies between issues management and public affairs.

WHY PUBLIC AFFAIRS CONTINUES TO EVOLVE

The rapidly increasing strategic role of public affairs has been spurred on by the trend towards increased privatization, regulation and stakeholder activism. This together with the globalization of business operations and a surge in transnational government legislation and policy making, (i.e., Asian Pacific Economic Cooperation [APEC], European Union [EU], North American Free Trade Area [NAFTA], World Trade Organization [WTO] etc.) and banking Asia Infrastructure Investment Bank (AIIB) has forced organizations of all types to pay greater attention to their relationships with government nationally and internationally at every level. The formal approval of mergers, acquisitions, alliances, and takeovers is increasingly under government scrutiny as it attempts to regulate markets and trade. The regulation of auditing and the large accountancy groups like banking and financial services groups is now much on the world's public affairs agenda and exercising leading corporate, political and research minds as they attempt to produce good corporate governance. A closer look at the impact of regulation and regulatory behavior on corporations as well as how they respond to it is provided by Fleisher in Chapter 27 of Part 5 of this volume.

A good example of regulatory impact on the shape of international business is the attempts to shore-up global financial practice and procedure by intervention in the world money markets and regulation of the banking and finance business post the 2006 financial crash. The impact of over-regulation after an event was summed-up in 2011 to the authors by a colleague in the City of London, who commented, that they were 'being regulated into the stone-age'. Obviously the financial industry and its associated businesses have had to respond by being much more active to address what has at times been a crisis in confidence worldwide. This has led to greater scrutiny of banking practices and financial operations worldwide resulting in increased regulation and intervention by state governments, the recent revelations around HSBC and its operations in Switzerland are a good case in point (Swiss Info, 2015). The Greek Economy and its position in the Euro (aka what has been termed GREXIT) has dominated much of European political thought and policy making over the last two years. The Euro Zone instability crisis is a growing area of research looking at the study of political power and political risk. The marketing of policy making has had to be conducted via public affairs experts and government leaders to respective constituents, whilst the results of citizen concern and referendums have primarily had to be managed by European State Governments, the European Central Bank and the International Monetary Fund. The BREXIT campaign in the UK at a time of mass migration, human diaspora and instability in the Middle East and Northern Africa has stretched this significantly. Not too dissimilar situations have occurred in many business sectors before such as in the oil, chemical and nuclear industries to name just a few and the public affairs practitioner has been to the fore in each of these situations in trying to ensure stability and a long term strategic view is taken. The leave result (BREXIT) of the UK Referendum on Membership of the Union in the UK in June 2016 has brought a change of Prime Minister, Government and direction of the UK in its relations to the EU. Precisely what the changed relationship will be is unclear, but trade will be at the heart of it and Public Affairs Management will be critical to the success of developing new policies and relationships.

The increasing role of government as regulator as old corporatist linkages break down under globalization is a phenomenon that public affairs practitioners and corporations have to deal with on a daily and yet strategic basis. Among other things, the transfer of publicly owned businesses to the private sector such as energy, telecommunications, water utilities and increasingly government services and the potential entrance of the Chinese RMB currency as a formal world trading currency has directly stimulated the increasing importance of the public affairs area.

The growth of increasingly powerful and well-organized stakeholders in the form of activist citizen or interest groups has also influenced the growth of the field. Pressure groups, which are capable of mobilizing strong opposition to organizations whose policies they disagree with, has further stimulated public affairs work, stakeholder programs, political campaigning and lobbying activity (Lerbinger, 2006). Technological advances within the media now allow events in virtually any part of the world to be screened almost instantaneously, subjecting the behavior of organizations even in the most remote parts of the globe to worldwide media and public scrutiny. The growth of social media and cause and campaign activities using this medium has necessitated regular tracking and management of corporate and societal communication in this medium – a phenomenon called by one observer as being the move to 'Public Affairs 2.0' (Fleisher, 2012). The global dialogue on trade, commerce, and investment involves business executives, government officials, and representatives of non-governmental organizations (NGOs). Not surprisingly, this dialogue often includes environmental (ecological), social and community issues. Thus the entire business government-society relationship is frequently open to discussion, debate, and redefinition throughout the world, especially in democratic and emerging democratic political contexts.

Technological advances within various media now allow events in virtually any part of the world to be screened almost instantaneously, subjecting the behavior of organizations even in the most remote parts of the globe to world-wide media and public scrutiny (see Ch. 9 by Meli and Grefe in this volume for more on these phenomena). The global dialogue on trade, commerce,

and investment involves business executives, government officials, and representatives of non-governmental organizations (NGOs). Not surprisingly, this dialogue also often includes environmental (ecological), social and community issues. Thus the entire business-government-society relationship is open to near-constant discussion, debate, and redefinition throughout the world.

WHAT WE HAVE LEARNED AND STILL HOPE TO LEARN ABOUT SOME KEY PUBLIC AFFAIRS PRACTICES

Researchers at the University of Central Florida examined the central issue of what is best practice in any disciplinary field and how best practice can be researched (Myers, Smith and Martin, 2004). The paper reviewed a number of studies of best practice in a variety of contexts, including healthcare, public administration and public affairs, highlighting the lack of robustness in the way the term 'best practice' has been used in corporate and public sector body reports and emphasizing the lack of consensus in defining the term 'best practice'. The authors point to one of the more useful definitions of best practice in the public affairs context advanced by Overman and Boyd (1994, p.69) as, 'the selective observation of a set of exemplars across different contexts in order to derive more generalizable principles and theories'. This definition contains several key observations:

- Its emphasis on the use of exemplars – the 'best of the best' – highlights the need for careful judgement in determining which cases should be included in best practice research;
- It is important to draw evidence from multiple sources and contexts to increase the generalizability and utility of the findings; and
- Research into best practice should be done less for its own sake than as a means of deriving useful principles and theories.

Myers et al. go on to suggest a useful three-fold taxonomy of best practice based on what they see as a hierarchy of evidence – evidence based practices, best practices, and emerging/promising practices:

- Evidence Based Practices (EBPs) are those practices which are supported by a substantial body of outcome-based research;
- Best Practices (BPs) are practices which are supported by a substantial body of research findings generally acknowledged as superior or state of the art; and
- Emerging Practices (EPs) are believed by at least some knowledgeable professionals or professional groups to represent superior approaches.

The authors suggest that most of the best practice schemas in corporate and public affairs they have observed failed to meet the highest classification of EBPs, and hence they conclude that there is a need for greater rigour and objectivity in setting criteria and conducting research to determine best practice guidelines in fields such as public affairs.

Much generic advice on 'best practice' is available in the academic literature. One review asserts that identifying 'best practice' requires a comprehensive analysis of all comparable cases, which would suggest that establishing 'best practice' in absolute terms is inevitably a difficult and elusive goal, 'Any empirical attempt will fall short' (Bretschneider et al. 2005, p. 320). It does, however, go on to note that what organizations can seek to do is identify what constitutes 'good' practice and in so doing discover ways of improving organizational performance. It may be that the quest for 'best practice' is better directed toward developing consistently 'better' practice in all areas over time, benchmarked against peer companies. As one author puts it, 'Benchmarking encourages quantum rather than incremental learning…. Its principal utility is as a check against complacency built on past success' (John, 2002, p.32). Fleisher and Burton (1995) suggest a number of reasons why benchmarking can be useful in the public affairs field. These reasons are summarised in Figure 1 below.

While several of these rationales may appear to overlap, this listing helps make clear the range of benefits which can accrue from a serious and sustained effort to move towards determining best practice in public affairs.

What any 'best practice' audit should result in is a deeper awareness among practitioners

Figure I.1 Benefits of benchmarking in public affairs

Benchmarking Public Affairs can help the Organization to:

- Enhance internal communication and coordination between public affairs and both senior management and other functional units, as the audit process can in itself raise the unit's visibility within the organization;
- Demonstrate public affairs' willingness to improve its value by adopting more scientific or empirical methodologies for measuring performance, similar to those which are commonly used in other functional units such as marketing, production and manufacturing;
- Identify technologies used by other organizations in their successful execution of PA which can then be adopted;
- Produce longitudinal, systematic information on the basis of which management and resourcing decisions can be made;
- Highlight areas of relative efficiency and effectiveness – and uncover ones that have opportunities and room for improvement;
- Evaluate the performance of the public affairs unit – in its own right, compared against other organizations, and indeed individual staff performance within the unit;
- Serve as an 'early warning system' by flagging up areas in which change and challenges will emerge in the future;
- Assist in setting managerial priorities for future work, and in documenting how effective particular activities have been to date; and
- Aid the organization and improve its internal decision-making processes by enhancing the objective information available.

that even in the highest-performing organization, there will always be scope for further development and improvement. No company, or functional unit, is going to be the best in class across the whole range of its activities – to say nothing of the fact that it will not be undertaking all the possible activities which could be done. Ideally, it will serve to highlight not only areas where existing standards can be raised, but also areas in which new activity would be beneficial. Some form of benchmarking can therefore always be useful, particularly if it is systematic, designed as a learning process rather than as self-justification, based upon valid comparisons with peer organizations, acted upon, and repeated regularly. Benchmarking oneself against well-regarded peers allows the big picture of public affairs and the individual fields of activity within it to be subjected to detailed scrutiny annually or on a rolling basis, whereby components are looked at on a set schedule which allows a whole program of evaluation every 3–4 years.

Both the academic and professional literatures concentrate overwhelmingly on public affairs as it is practiced in advanced Western democracies. In order to arrive at any unified model of what best practice in corporate and public affairs might look like, it is essential that some element of cross-cultural awareness be built in (Fleisher, 2005a), and this will be especially important for its practice in emerging democracies and non-democratic contexts. Corporate and public affairs executives and staff increasingly need to be able to manage and implement campaigns across a number of nations (Dunn et al., 1979; Lodge, 1990; Mack, 1997; Zetter, 2008). Indeed, they may need to ensure both that a global campaign is sensitive to individual and diverse national cultures, and that activities in one country are integrated into and are harmonious with a global strategy. Organizations thus face a tremendous challenge in ensuring that their public affairs staffs have the necessary skills and knowledge to operate internationally. Fleisher (2003b; 2007) lists seven

subjects which effective international public affairs practitioners are required to have knowledge of and skills in:

- Intercultural competence;
- The ways in which society impacts upon public affairs;
- Local policy making processes;
- National understandings of what public affairs involves;
- Multi-lingual to working standards;
- International ethical standards; and
- The management of external consultants and partners.

The way in which public affairs is structured within an organization is clearly another critically important factor in its capacity to be effective. Although the literature on the structuring of public affairs is limited, the function's location within the organizational hierarchy and particularly in terms of access to top management is widely recognized as a key to public affairs achieving its full potential. While there is very limited empirical evidence, there is at least an anecdotal sense that all too often public affairs fails to adequately communicate its role and value to the rest of the organization. Here a range of factors could be at play. First, public affairs is a relatively specialized function, and as such tends to be quite small numerically and thus limited in what it can do. Second, public affairs may suffer in practical ways from the ambiguity surrounding its scope and from its general inability to date to establish itself as a recognized profession. Third, practitioners are perhaps more inclined to devote time and energy to promoting the organization externally and influencing its environment, rather than to feeding back the views of outside stakeholders to senior management and engaging in corporate discussions about external policies.

As Griffin and Dunn (2004, p. 215) acknowledge, 'there is no indication of a universal or "right" way to structure corporate PA departments'. What works for one company may be entirely contrary to another company's philosophy and organization.

Mack (1997) identifies three primary models by which a public affairs function may be organized:

- Centralized – here, one executive has responsibility for the entire public affairs programme and staff, and public affairs undertakes activities on behalf of the whole organization.
- Decentralized – a central public affairs team will co-ordinate activity, but most public affairs staff are based within the organization's business units which set their own priorities and programmes.
- Dispersed – an issues manager within each operating unit will handle that section's public affairs with little or no central co-ordination, but it is regarded very much as an issue-driven process rather than as a wider functional role.

Fleisher (1998, p.9) notes the irony that while public affairs 'relies upon effective communication to position the organization in its external marketplace', this expertise can be 'less evident in trying to position the function within the organization'. This view is supported by some empirical evidence. For example, respondents to a Dutch survey were asked to define what was meant by public affairs and to account for how much time they spent on particular activities, and in both cases respondents overwhelmingly noted external rather than internal priorities (de Lange, 2000). Fully 60% of the definitions of public affairs identified were clearly about communicating to and influencing the outside world, while the remainder were generic descriptors such as building networks and dealing with socio-political change; none explicitly suggested that public affairs was about influencing the organization on behalf of stakeholders. If public affairs is to significantly deepen internal understanding of its importance, staff must devote more time to internal communication and must become better equipped in what one scholar has termed 'functional multilingualism … the operational languages of finance, marketing, human resources, and so on' (Gollner, 1984, p.9) so that they are able to communicate with colleagues in other departments in ways which are meaningful to those colleagues.

Any company which wishes to review the effectiveness of its existing public affairs function arguably needs to focus on four interrelated areas:

- Enterprise level: how are the organization's values, behaviors and activities positioned vis-à-vis stakeholders in the societies within which it operates?
- Corporate level: how is corporate and public affairs structured and managed within the organization as a whole?
- Department level: what policies and processes are employed within the corporate and public affairs function itself?
- Individual level: what professional backgrounds/ skills and key personal competencies do corporate and public affairs staff need to bring to their role?

Clearly there is very little in the way of clear prescription within the literature about what processes might be put in place to ensure regular interaction between public affairs and senior management (Blumentritt, 2003). One area in which current corporate public affairs appears on the face of it to fall very short of what might be regarded as 'best practice' – but which nonetheless attracts more comment from activist groups than from academics – is that of internal processes intended to ensure senior oversight. Marx (1990) makes the point that a board-level public affairs committee should only focus on the relatively few issues which are most critical to the organization and on which the organization can have a positive influence. Examining examples of companies where such committees operate, Marx found that they dealt exclusively with no more than a handful of issues, which tended to be those issues that were identified as being of direct importance to the organization's business strategy, relatively short-term (so that their impact would be felt over the next 1–3 years), and on which the firm could potentially have a significant affect. A recent survey of 100 leading companies suggests that relatively few had a board-level committee which had responsibility for lobbying activities; among those which do are Chevron, ExxonMobil, Ford, Johnson & Johnson, Texas Instruments and BP (SustainAbility and WWF, 2005). Using Dow Chemical as an example, Lerbinger (2006, p.420) asserts that establishment of what he terms a 'public interest committee' that would act as the board-level focal point for oversight of public affairs would be a 'useful structural addition to corporate governance'.

A similar point was made by Langton (1982, p.112) who described a public policy committee as 'a powerful asset' for a firm in signalling to middle management that senior executives were focused on the 'socio-political aspect of corporate performance'. Mack (1997, p.61) emphasises managerial commitment over all else – 'The essential elements in any organization's government relations program are top management support, top management support, and top management support'. It should not be assumed that such high-level support is automatic – a recent survey conducted by McKinsey found that only one-third of CEOs mentioned engaging with host governments in their primary overseas markets as one of their personal top three priorities (Dua et al., 2010).

None of these models is likely to be appropriate in all places, at all times, for all companies (Dunn et al., 1979; Windsor, 2005). If best practice in public affairs is taken to mean the search for a single answer from which absolute effectiveness will then flow, then it is likely to prove a futile and fruitless quest. What research can uncover, however, is what factors are important contributors to the performance of a public affairs department. For example, whether there is any correlation between the size of a public affairs unit and success, or between the seniority of a public affairs head and the function's involvement in the corporate planning process. One survey of Canadian practitioners concluded that the

key elements in an effective government relations unit were:

- The head of the unit must have credibility and authority within the organization;
- Good contacts and relationships with government and policymakers;
- The unit plays a significant role in the business strategic planning process;
- Commitment and support for public affairs from the CEO; and
- The unit achieves visible successes so that it is seen to add value to the organization (Baetz, 1992).

However, to what extent such elements can be considered to constitute some of the key criteria for 'best' or demonstrated practice in public affairs remains open to debate – a debate which we will address again later in this chapter. Another element that has been researched, discussed and debated over the years is what qualities should individuals have who want to be successful PA practitioners? We will examine this matter at greater depth in the next section.

COMPETENCIES REQUIRED FOR EFFECTIVE MANAGEMENT AND PRACTICE OF PUBLIC AFFAIRS

What does appear to come through clearly is that as with all corporate units, success is heavily dependent upon personnel – recruitment of the 'right' people and providing them with the appropriate in-career training – is a fundamental precondition of effectiveness (Hawkins, 2004; Shaw, 2005). The question of competencies – those essential knowledge, skills, abilities and experiences (KSAEs) – that are needed to practice PA effectively has also been a central element of both practical and scholarly interest (Fleisher, 2003b; Shaw, 2005; van Schendelen, 2002). If organizations are going to have success in their PA endeavours, it behoves them to have the appropriate type, level and quantity of human capital needed to accomplish the organization's PA mission.

There have long been questions asked in PA professional events about whether there is a reasonable supply of entry-level positions available in the field, meaning those that might be suitable for a recent post-secondary, bachelor degree earning university graduate. Some observers have suggested that the complexity and criticality of the work may mean it is likely to be more suitable for experienced practitioners, with them having served at least a few years in the organizations and industry sectors to be able to adequately communicate positions in public policy contexts and among relevant stakeholder groups (Shaw, 2005). There is a view held by some that practitioners should hold knowledge of both sides of the organization's PA boundary – meaning that the practitioner understands the culture, history, offerings, and strategy of the organization, as well as the culture, institutions, practices and people who make the relevant public policy decisions impacting on the organization (Fleisher, 2003b).

Public affairs positions, especially at more senior levels, are arguably particularly difficult to fill, given the cross-boundary nature of their work (cutting across communication, management and politics, in addition to the product-specific knowledge required); consequently, there is a pressing need for these individuals to bring cross-disciplinary skills to the role (Fleisher, 2003b; van Schendelen, 2002). Paradoxically, however, little scholarly or professional research has focused on the question of the core personal qualities and professional competencies required by public affairs staff (Shaw, 2005; Titley, 2003; van Schendelen, 2002). According to one observer, 'The task of identifying, defining, describing the characteristics, and measuring competencies in nearly all PA [public affairs] activity areas ... is one ripe for academic research' (Fleisher, 2003b, p.80). As part of a survey of in-house lobbyists in the US higher education sector, Ferrin (2003) found a diverse spread of educational backgrounds and career profiles, which he

attributed to the prevalence of three dominant views when an institution is hiring a lobbyist:

- First, that there is no particular background required to produce the generic practitioner, rather personal qualities are a more significant predictor of effectiveness;
- Second, that it is essential to bring some particular political knowledge or experience to the role, perhaps through a primary degree or through having worked as an aide to a politician. The rationale here appears to be that a professional who comes equipped with an understanding of how the political process works can relatively easily acquire the sector or product specific knowledge which a given organization needs; and
- Third, that by contrast it is most important for the practitioner to have been fully immersed in the organization and its issues in order to be viewed by policymakers as credible, with political expertise picked up on the job. Clearly this view would imply that public affairs staff are recruited internally from other units of the organization, rather than externally from the political class.

Charles Mack (1997, p.98) suggests that the ideal lobbyist should possess skills akin to the ideal salesperson:

> Government relations is, in a sense, a specialized form of marketing. In that same sense, direct lobbying is often face-to-face selling. The same qualities required to be successful in sales are needed in a successful lobbyist: cordiality and charm, persistence, understanding of the product (i.e. the position the 'issue sales person' is advocating), and the persuasiveness needed to make the 'purchaser' (the public policy-maker) want to buy the 'product'.

One key factor mentioned by Mack is charm, or personality. And, certainly personality is important – but there is evidence that, over time, expertise becomes more significant. An article by Conor McGrath, 2006 presents the most systematic available survey of the personal characteristics, which appear to be most important to public affairs personnel: listening skills, courtesy, relationship skills, honesty, integrity and credibility.

ASSESSING THE PROCESSES OF AND RESULTS OF PUBLIC AFFAIRS ACTIVITY

If the public affairs function is not sufficiently well understood by senior executives, it runs the risk of being regarded rather like an insurance policy, as a cost rather than a strategic benefit. In other words, its purpose may be clearer at times of crisis than in periods of routine. The analogy, however, breaks down quickly in one crucial respect – if one has an insurance policy it will come into effect following a crisis and delivers what it is supposed to, while public affairs cannot effectively be turned off for long periods and then immediately triggered to solve a grave difficulty. It is important, therefore, that public affairs should find ways of demonstrating to the organization its proper role and value, to better explain what it does and why that is important. Providing that can be achieved, public affairs will then enjoy elevated credibility within the organization on an ongoing basis. One report, by an NGO working on sustainable development issues, advocates that organizations should consider six key factors as a means of gauging whether their lobbying efforts are appropriate; the areas are applicable to public affairs more generally. According to AccountAbility (2005), these six measures are:

1   Alignment – are the organization's activities consistent with its stated core values and business principles?
2   Materiality – are activities focused on those public policy issues of greatest potential significance to the organization?
3   Stakeholder Engagement – is the organization open to constructive dialogue with outside groups?
4   Reporting – is information about the organization's activities and positions transparent and accessible?
5   People – is the company clear about who represents it on public policy issues?
6   Processes – are suitable internal mechanisms in place to ensure that activities are both appropriate and effective?

One of us suggested almost a quarter of a century ago (Fleisher, 1993), that assessment of public affairs should not focus entirely on what it delivered but also on how it is delivered, and what consequences or impacts occur as a result. Also that corporate and public affairs units can and should undertake internal quality management programmes, in order to demonstrate their value to the organization. This would entail:

- Crafting a public affairs mission statement as an explicit statement of the reason for existence of the unit, the internal and external 'customers' the unit seeks to serve, its relationship with other functional units, and the customer-driven needs it aims to meet;
- Setting key, prioritised, objectives for the unit which define how it needs to operate in order to achieve its mission;
- Identifying the 'products' which the unit provides to each of its customers, so that the purpose of each activity can be made clear, and ultimately evaluated by surveying the customer groups. In addition, the production costs of each activity can be quantified;
- Assessing the efficiency of the internal processes through which products are delivered – for instance, the cost-effectiveness of the resources needed to implement an activity and the physical form of the product, reductions in redundancies and overlaps, elimination of activities which do not add value; and
- Measuring the effectiveness of each product, again by receiving feedback on its quality and levels of satisfaction derived from customers.

One of the key attributes of an effective public affairs department for Andrews (1996) is that it should make a positive contribution to the organization's financial performance. This, however, presents immediate difficulties as regards metrics and evaluation, highlighting the challenge of how one measures with any degree of accuracy the impact of public affairs. As a senior European practitioner puts it, 'Often, public affairs is seen as a function driven by activities which are triggered by external forces instead of being driven by what the company needs for which its public affairs managers are working' (Jonnaert, 2005, p.24). The very process of making explicit what strategic objectives are derived from business requirements and how those objectives are to be translated into activities, and then going on to connect the two by measuring progress achieved, can in itself demonstrate to other managers the role and value of public affairs for the organization as a whole (Laird, 1996).

Laird (1996) takes this idea one step further, when he proposes that public affairs can and should partly refocus its attention away from externally generated public policy issues and towards internally generated business issues. What he suggests is that if a public affairs unit was to proactively identify issues which have a direct impact on how the organization's business units are able to perform, that would in itself improve the perception by colleagues that public affairs adds value to the organization. The methodology here is termed 'Quantifying Impacts', and begins with public affairs asking operating staff what changes in their external environment would have the greatest impact on profitability (either by reducing costs or increasing profits). According to Laird (1996, p.254), business units operate on the basis of the restrictions and limitations they already face, as those personnel 'cannot fully appreciate or assess the potential for changing the external limitations'. Once those potential changes are identified, analysed and quantified, public affairs can then begin to work towards achieving the most significant, for instance, by seeking to amend legislative or regulatory requirements.

CONCLUSION

We see Corporate and Public Affairs as a growing, important, and relatively underappreciated field within some sectors, but most prominently – the academic one. Though we both have lengthy academic backgrounds, we will not hide our observation that there is not nearly enough interactions among post-secondary instructors and researchers and practitioners. Though managers/practitioners, researchers and scholars in the field continue to seek to better elaborate field-setting issues of, among other important topics, definition consensus (and whether it is even helpful to achieve this), activity boundaries and what does and does not constitute the management of PA practice, what quality and types of practices are and are not associated with desirable results, and what characteristics the ideal or optimal PA practitioner should exhibit.

Ongoing research which the authors and scholarly colleagues have embarked upon suggests that several characteristics of public affairs have long-term staying power. Several of the aspects we have greater confidence in as having achieved consensus about, with respect to public affairs, are that it:

- Is concerned with changing, driving or educating public opinion around socio-political issues which affect the organization's business performance, image and activities;
- Involves the organization's relationships with external or nonmarket stakeholders, and is most effective when adopted in a genuinely regular and on-going dialogical manner. It is always best to start early and regularly provide information rather than respond last minute when the decision has almost already been taken on previous dialogue and thinking. This also shows that the organization has not been watching policy formation and influencing it long term and strategically;
- Acts as a boundary-spanning activity which crosses a number of functional units and professional disciplines and involves the management of the business/political interface;
- Through advocacy, communication, and engagement, it seeks to protect and enhance the organization's reputation as a central purpose;
- Is based around the management of politics, public policy issues and their life cycle; The electoral or change cycle in a political or public policy institution, such as the appointment in November 2012 of the new Chinese Central Committee, the

formation of a majority Conservative Government in the UK in May 2015 or of direct relevance the election of SYRIZA as the governing party in Greece in 2015, or the US Presidential elections of 2016 indicates and signals to the knowledgeable PA practitioner when is best to exert influence and get things done or not;

- Managing CSR in all its global forms and iterations (Breitbarth and Harris, 2008 and Breitbarth, Harris and Aitken, 2009);
- Should be closely bound up with organizational strategic planning processes and personnel; and
- Has systems, activities and human capital that are all capable of demonstrating, through meaningful measures what their contribution is to the organization and a variety of its desired results.

In summary, corporate and public affairs is a field of practice with varying degrees of institutionalization around the globe that provides outstanding experiences and career paths for motivated individuals. It has demonstrated itself to be socially, financially and intellectually rewarding, and provides its practitioners with opportunities to affect genuine change in shaping how organizations and their stakeholders engage in issues, policy and politics.

REFERENCES

AccountAbility. 2005. Towards Responsible Lobbying: Leadership and Public Policy. AccountAbility: London.

Andrews L. 1996. The relationship of political marketing to political lobbying: An examination of the Devonport campaign for the Trident refitting contract. *European Journal of Marketing*, 30 (10/11): pp. 68–91.

Baetz MC. 1992. Rethinking the government relations unit. *Canadian Journal of Administrative Sciences*, 9(4): 310–324.

Blumentritt TP. 2003. Foreign subsidiaries' government affairs activities: the influence of managers and resources. Business & Society 42(2): 202–233.

Boston University Public Affairs Research Group (BU-PARG), 1981. *Public Affairs Officers and Their Functions: Summary of Survey Responses*,

monograph, Boston: Boston University School of Management; and the unpublished results of a 1986 survey by the same group.

Breitbarth T and Harris P. 2008. The role of corporate social responsibility in the football business: Towards the development of a conceptual model. *European Sports Management Quarterly*, 8, (2): 179–206.

Breitbarth T, Harris P and Aitken R. 2009. Corporate social responsibility in the European Union: a new trade barrier? *Journal of Public Affairs*, 9(4): 239–255.

Bretschneider S, Marc-Aurele FJ and Wu J. 2005. 'Best practices' research: a methodological guide for the perplexed. *Journal of Public Administration Research and Theory*, 15(2): 307–323.

de Lange R. 2000. Public affairs practitioners in the Netherlands: a profile study. *Public Relations Review*, 26(1): 15–29.

Dua A, Heil K and Wilins J. 2010. How business interacts with government. Survey published January 2010. http://www.mckinsey.com/industries/public-sector/our-insights/how-business-interacts-with-government-mckinsey-global-survey-results (accessed 24 March 2016).

Dennis L and Holcomb J. 1996. Historical Antecedents: Public Affairs in Full Flower – 1975–1985. In *Practical Public Affairs in an Era of Change*, (Ed.) L. Dennis. New York: PRSA & University Press of America.

Dunn SW, Cahill MF and Boddewyn JJ. 1979. *How Fifteen Transnational Corporations Manage Public Affairs*. Crain Books: Chicago.

Ferrin SE. 2003. Characteristics of in-house lobbyists in American colleges and universities. *Higher Education Policy*, 16(1): 87–108.

Fleisher CS. 2012. Anniversary retrospective, perspective and prospective of corporate public affairs: Moving from the 2000+ PA model to Public Affairs 2.0. *Journal of Public Affairs*, 12(1): 4–11.

Fleisher CS. 2007. Developing the public affairs body of knowledge. *Journal of Public Affairs*, 7(3): 281–290.

Fleisher CS. 2005a. The global development of public affairs. In *The Handbook of Public Affairs*, (eds) Harris P and Fleisher CS. Sage: London, pp. 5–30.

Fleisher CS. 2005b. The measurement and evaluation of public affairs process and performance. In *Handbook of Public Affairs*, (eds) Harris P and Fleisher CS. Sage: London, pp. 145–159.

Fleisher CS. 2003b. The development of competencies in international public affairs. *Journal of Public Affairs*, 3(1): 76–82.

Fleisher CS. 2002. The state of North American higher education in corporate public affairs. *Journal of Public Affairs*, 1(4) and 2(1): 436–440.

Fleisher CS. 1998. Are corporate public affairs practitioners professionals? A multi-region comparison with corporate public relations. Paper presented at the Fifth Annual Bled Symposium on International Public Relations Research.

Fleisher CS. 1997. Assessing, Managing, and Maximizing Public Affairs Performance: With Reports, Techniques, and Case Histories from Nearly Two Dozen Leading Organizations and Professionals Around the Globe (eds) Brian Hawkinson, and Natasha Blair. Public Affairs Council.

Fleisher CS. 1995. *Public Affairs Benchmarking*. Washington, DC: Public Affairs Council.

Fleisher CS. 1993. Quality management for corporate staff functions: the public affairs example. *Total Quality Management*, 4(2): 159–164.

Fleisher CS and Burton S. 1995. Taking stock of corporate benchmarking practices: panacea or Pandora's box? *Public Relations Review*, 21(1): 1–20.

Fleisher CS and Hoewing R. 1992. Strategically managing corporate external relations: New challenges and opportunities. *Strategic Change*, 1(5): 287–296.

Getz KA. 2002. Public affairs and political strategy: theoretical foundations. *Journal of Public Affairs*, 1(4) and 2(1): 305–329.

Gollner AB. 1984. Public relations/public affairs in the new managerial revolution. *Public Relations Review*, 10(4): 3–10.

Griffin JJ. 2016. *Managing Corporate Impacts: Co-Creating Value*. University of Cambridge Press, UK.

Griffin JJ. 2005. The empirical study of public affairs. In *The Handbook of Public Affairs*, (eds) Harris P and Fleisher CS. Sage: London, pp. 458–480.

Griffin JJ and Dunn P. 2004. Corporate public affairs: commitment, resources, and structure. *Business & Society*, 43(2): 196–220.

Griffin JJ, Fleisher CS, Brenner SN and Boddewyn JJ. 2000. Corporate public affairs research: Chronological reference list Part 2 (1958–84) *Journal of Public Affairs*, 1(2): 169–186.

Harris P and Moss D. 2001. Editorial: in search of public affairs: a function in search of an identity. *Journal of Public Affairs*, 1(2): 102–110.

Harris P and McGrath C. 2012. Cited on page one of Written Evidence submitted to the UK Parliament, Political Constitution and Reform Committee, London. http://www.publications.parliament.uk/pa/cm201213/cmselect/cmpolcon/153/153vw11.htm

Hawkins A. 2004. Developing the public affairs talent pool. Public Affairs Newsletter, September: 15.

Hillman AJ. 2002. Public affairs, issue management and political strategy: methodological issues that count – a different view. *Journal of Public Affairs*, 1(4) and 2(1): 356–361.

John S. 2002. *The Persuaders: When Lobbyists Matter*. Palgrave Macmillan: Basingstoke.

Jonnaert E. 2005. Public affairs and measurement: myth or reality? In *Everything Flows: Essays on Public Affairs and Change*, (Ed.) Spencer T. Landmarks: Brussels, pp. 23–28.

Laird NL. 1996. Public affairs: profit center? In *Practical Public Affairs in an Era of Change: A Communications Guide for Business, Government, and College*, (Ed.) Dennis LB. University Press of America: Lanham, MD, pp. 251–265.

Langton JF. 1982. Board policy committees. In *The Public Affairs Handbook*, (Ed.) Nagelschmidt JS. Amacom: New York, pp. 109–112.

Lerbinger O. 2006. *Corporate Public Affairs: Interacting with Interest Groups, Media, and Government*. Lawrence Erlbaum Associates: Mahwah, NJ.

Lodge GC. 1990. *Comparative Business-Government Relations*. Prentice Hall: Englewood Cliffs, NJ.

Machiavelli N (trans. George Bull). 1992. *The Prince*. Penguin, London.

Mack CS. 1997. *Business, Politics, and the Practice of Government Relations*. Quorum Books: Westport.

Marx TG. 1990. Strategic planning for public affairs. *Long Range Planning*, 23(1): 9–16.

McGrath C. 2006. The ideal lobbyist: personal characteristics of effective lobbyists. *Journal of Communication Management*, 10(1): 67–79.

McKittrick CE. 1990. Governmental programs at IBM. In *Comparative Business-Government Relations, Lodge GC*. Prentice Hall: Englewood Cliffs, NJ, pp. 219–225.

Miles MB, Huberman AM. 1994. *Qualitative Data Analysis: An Expanded Source Book*. Sage: Thousand Oaks.

Miller C. 1991. Lobbying: the need for regulation. In *The Commercial Lobbyists* (Ed.) Jordan G. Aberdeen University Press: Aberdeen, pp. 164–172.

Moss D, McGrath C, Tonge J and Harris P. 2012. Exploring the management of the corporate public affairs function in a dynamic global environment. *Journal of Public Affairs*, 12 (1): 47–60.

Myers S, Smith, HP and Martin, LL. 2004. Conducting best practices research in public affairs. Working Paper No. 3. Center for Community Partnerships, University of Central Florida: Orlando.

Nye JS. 2004. *Soft Power: The Means to Success in World Politics*. Public Affairs: New York.

Overman E and Boyd J. 1994. Best practice research and postbureaucratic reform. *Journal of Public Administration and Theory*, 4(1): 67–83.

Public Affairs Conference Report. 1966. Public affairs in national focus, Report number 5, New York: National Industrial Conference Board.

Schuler DA. 2002. Public affairs, issues management and political strategy: methodological approaches that count. *Journal of Public Affairs*, 1(4) & 2(1): 336–355.

Schuler DA, Rehbein K, and Cramer RD. 2002. Pursuing strategic advantage through political means: a multivariate approach. *Academy of Management Journal*, 45(4): 659–672.

Shaw P. 2005. The human resource dimensions of public affairs: staffing, training, career paths, competencies, and salaries. In *The Handbook of Public Affairs*, (eds) Harris P and Fleisher CS. Sage: London, pp. 123–144.

Sun H. 2007. International political marketing: a case study of its application in China. *Journal of Public Affairs*, 7: 331–340.

Sun, H. 2008. International political marketing: a case study of United States soft power and public diplomacy. *Journal of Public Affairs*, 8: 165–183.

Sun H and Harris P. 2014. Crises Management: Reflections from International Political Marketing and Public Affairs, The Harmony of Civilisation and Prosperity for all: China and the World, Tradition, Reality and Future. paper presented in the sub-theme session 'Conflict or Cooperation? Relations between the Rising China and Its Neighbors' 11th Beijng Forum, 7–9 November 2014, Peking University, China.

SustainAbility and WWF UK. 2005. Influencing Power: Reviewing the Conduct and Content of Corporate Lobbying. SustainAbility and WWF UK: London.

Swissinfo. 2015. Retrieved from http://www.swissinfo.ch/eng/in-depth/pressure-on-the-financial-sector (accessed 20 July 2015).

Titley S. 2003. How political and social change will transform the EU public affairs industry. *Journal of Public Affairs*, 3(1): 83–89.

van Schendelen R. 2010. *More Machiavelli in Brussels: The Art of Lobbying the EU*, third edition. Amsterdam University Press: Amsterdam.

van Schendelen R. 2002. The ideal profile of the PA expert at the EU level. *Journal of Public Affairs*, 2(2): 85–89.

Wartick SL and Heugens PPMAR. 2003. Future directions for issues management. *Corporate Reputation Review*, 6(1): 7–18.

Windsor D. 2005. "Theories" and theoretical roots of public affairs. In *The Handbook of Public Affairs*, (eds) Harris P and Fleisher CS. Sage: London, pp. 401–417.

Zetter L. 2008. *Lobbying: The Art of Political Persuasion*. Harriman House: Petersfield.

PART I

The Essential Foundation of Public Affairs

John Mahon

Corporations throughout the world have to deal with the new competitive realities of 24/7 competition, new products and services from unexpected sources that are released to the market unexpectedly, chaos engendered by terrorists and fear of terrorism – all of which demand constant corporate attention and require the investment of corporate resources quickly and efficiently. In this explosion of competitive and broad-sweeping environmental challenges what can easily be lost is the parallel growth in NGOs and their ability to pursue challenges in the non-market arena. This non-market arena (the legislature, the regulatory agency, the judiciary and the 'court of public opinion') is where the rules under which competition is conducted are determined, where the basic 'social license' to operate can be questioned and revoked and where organizations are often caught totally by surprise. It requires skills in assessing issues, their

development and emergence and in working with and building coalitions with stakeholders. The corporate function that deals with this non-market arena is public affairs and this part of the Handbook draws together the critical thinking of academics and practitioners who have broad, deep experience with corporate public affairs.

We begin with a revisiting of the development of corporate public affairs office by Craig S. Fleisher. Dr Fleisher has broad academic and professional public affairs experience and as such bridges the academic and practitioner worlds in his understanding of the field. Dr Fleisher builds on the earlier work that he did for the first edition of this handbook (Fleisher, 2005) and offers us a clear definition of public affairs noting that it includes 'those management processes that help an organization better relate to and effectively perform in its nonmarket environment'. Fleisher offers a thoughtful table reflecting what he terms the 'swinging pendulum' of the public's view of US government involvement in business over 50 years. He traces out in detail the evolutionary path of public affairs and how globalization has increased the complexity of the environment and the challenges facing public affairs in what he terms the 'macro' environment. He draws our attention in particular to the rise of social media and how social media allows geographically distant stakeholders to communicate with one another in real time, to develop strategies for action and to form coalitions on a global basis to pressure corporations and industries simultaneously on a global scale for action.

Having laid bare the challenges of the 'macro' environment, Fleisher turns his attention to the 'micro' environment of public affairs by examining the relational targets of public affairs activities and developing a typology that addresses these targets, the tactics that are used, the functions required for involvement and success and who is responsible for these actions within the organization (he calls this 'performers').

He then draws his analysis into a set of seven prescriptions that he has previously identified and argues that they are the 'new public affairs'. But in his work here he adds an additional set of three prescriptions that reflect the shift in the practice of public affairs.

Fleisher concludes his analysis with a concern that public affairs still does not meet some of the key criteria to rise to a broadly accepted professional status in most parts of the globe, and that the field and function still has broad untapped opportunities and promise going forward.

Dr Windsor builds on the foundation provided in the previous chapter in Chapter 2, entitled 'Theoretical Lenses and Conceptual Models for Understanding Public Affairs'. He draws careful distinctions between a theoretical lens and a conceptual model and sets a context for our understanding of public affairs. He weaves in various theoretical models but notes that the public affairs dimension,

although a vital organizational function, continues to search for an identity, theory and conceptualization, effective structure, best practices and social legitimacy – a significant indictment of the function, but which in some ways echoes Dr Fleisher's concerns with the failure of public affairs to achieve broadly accepted professional status.

Dr Windsor further refines his analysis, by looking closely at the discipline bases in which theoretical lenses and conceptual models are grounded, and provides us with a list of seven key disciplines that public affairs draws upon. The chapter draws together a very large literature base to deepen our understanding of public affairs and to allow for a rich discussion of the appropriate conceptual models.

To clarify his meaning of conceptual models he offers two examples, the Black–Scholes option pricing approach and the work of Allison and Zelikow (1999) in their analysis of the Cuban Missile Crisis of October 1962. Dr Windsor uses these two models to illustrate the use of assumptions in viewing and analyzing situations and to demonstrate that different conceptual models for interpreting situations adds richness to our understanding of the situation under analysis. He then develops a very general and abstract conceptual model of exercising political influence on a public policy process (and inserts considerations of illegal and immoral actions).

Dr Windsor then points out the importance of communications to stakeholders for the practice of public affairs and develops a second model for our consideration. He concludes his analysis by addressing the normative dimension of public affairs looking at both business ethics and corporate social performance perspectives.

Can we increase the rigor and power of our analysis with regards to public affairs research? This is essentially a question addressed by Dr McGowan in his chapter entitled 'Examining the Public Affairs Scholarship: What we've Learned (and still don't know) from the Empirical Studies of Public Affairs'.

We are shifting from the focus on theoretical lenses and conceptual models to assessing and using data with statistical methodologies to achieve results. McGowan uses articles published in the *International Journal of Public Affairs* as the source for his analysis. He justifies this selection and focuses on three different time periods to assess the state and use of empirical research in public affairs beyond simple descriptive analysis.

In the first period (2001–5) he notes that 33 percent of the published articles had empirical data (using the categories of descriptive statistics, hypothesis testing, and regression) and provides a description of the methodology used. This is, as he notes, not a particularly strong showing of statistically based empirical research. He highlights one article that did use a logistical regression. He concludes that this period was one of increasing interest in public affairs research that utilized statistical methodology.

The second period (2006–10) saw an increase in use of statistical analysis (from 33 to 40 percent) and more interestingly there was an increase in the use of hypothesis testing and regression and the variety of statistical methods increased dramatically, and the focus of these articles were on public affairs, issues management, and public policy. He identifies two articles as illustrative examples of the empirical statistical work being done during this period.

The use of statistical methodology during the third period (2011–15) shows that there was no appreciable (or to use a more rigorous term, no statistically significant) increase in the use of statistical methodologies – the number of articles rose from 40 to 42 percent – however, there is a move toward greater use of hypothesis testing and regression methodologies. He identifies one paper that used time-series analysis. He concludes that there has been a substantial increase in the use of statistical methodologies in public affairs research over the last 15 years and suggests that our understanding of the performance impact of public affairs can be significantly enhanced by use of data and more rigorous analysis.

McGowan then moves to suggestions for future public affairs empirical research and in particular the use of two methodologies – intervention analysis – of which there are two alternatives, ARIMA and Panel Regression, and provides examples of how they might be used to explore public affairs research.

Having addressed the history and development of public affairs, theoretical and conceptual lenses to use in considering public affairs and the growing use of more sophisticated statistical methodologies in public affairs research, we turn our attention to achieving the strategic potential of public affairs. This is addressed by two exceptionally experienced public affairs practitioners from Australia (Geoff Allen) and the United States (Fruzsina Harsanyi) in their work entitled 'Achieving the Strategic Potential of Public Affairs'. It is an appropriate compliment to Fleisher's earlier chapter where he raises concerns about the future of public affairs on a global stage and offers a practical 'lens' for looking at public affairs that compliments the work of Windsor in this part (Fleisher, 2005). The authors also address how the public affairs function looks at different levels of maturity and ties in nicely with Fleisher's time line and his prescriptions for action. They begin their analysis with a very clear warning: 'Where once the arc of history was moving toward greater integration, today separatist movements are gaining strength. Political chaos, violence and terrorism confront citizens, companies and governments on a daily basis'.

As this introduction is being written we have seen the growth of ISIS and its ability to bring chaos and death to almost any locale (e.g., the recent tragic bombings in Paris and Brussels). Allen and Harsanyi also note that business' social and political performance environment has become an increasing element in competition between firms and the creation of corporate value. This places even greater importance on the public affairs function in corporations, especially in large and/

or global organizations to deal with issues and challenges never before seen.

Allen and Harsanyi identify three levels of maturity with regards to the public affairs function – immature, consultant, and a mature function. In the immature state, public affairs are on the fringes of corporate decision making and activities and is often seen as expendable when economic conditions contract. The consultant state is where public affairs are seen as a specialized resource serving line management. In this state, public affairs responds to line manager needs and demands. The tragedy here is that line managers, with no expertise, determine what is important for public affairs to act on and they (line managers) decide what information is to be made available and shared with public affairs. This is akin to asking an opera singer to perform brain surgery. As might be expected, the consequences of action here can be disastrous as actions taken occur far too late to have significant impact. Harsanyi and Allen offer several examples of this situation based on their practical experience and involvements. The net result is that the organization often finds itself in a defensive posture, acting too late and unable to alter or change the situation to a more reasonable impact on the firm.

They then shift their focus to the 'mature' public affairs function and identify several characteristics of this state. These include a seat at the table with senior managers; specific contributions that are seen as performance enhancing and not simply as a cost; sub-functions that are closely integrated to achieve a holistic approach to issues (and they provide a visual for what they mean by this); engendering a sophisticated approach to company and functional planning; and an international geographical scope and business practice. This is the centerpiece of their argument and analysis. Harsanyi and Allen expand on all of the characteristics in detail and illuminate them with examples drawn from corporations around the world.

But this is not enough; they address what they term 'public affairs at level IV' where public affairs has a deep understanding of the business, where the function is highly valued and where public affairs are full partners in shaping organizational strategy. At this level, public affairs is defined in a uniquely different manner '… as the leadership function that manages risk and creates opportunities … shaping organizational strategy and influencing the socio-political environment to deliver beneficial outcomes …'.

The authors provide a very useful chart that addresses all of these public affairs' states on a variety of dimensions. The discussion and presentation here allows a thoughtful practitioner to position her or his public affairs function and clearly identify what 'state' their function is at this time – and more importantly how and where they might consider moving the public affairs function in the future. As always, Harsanyi and Allen's discussion is richly textured with corporate examples from a variety of industries. They argue, as Fleisher did in the opening chapter, that public affairs has made substantial progress over the last 50 or so years, but it is yet to achieve its full potential.

But if the demands on public affairs practitioners are increasing in complexity, where do public affairs professionals obtain their early introduction to this field. This topic is addressed in the chapter by Creighton and Meznar entitled 'The Status of Instruction in Public Affairs: Peace in the Eye of the Hurricane?'.

They perform an extensive analysis of the collegiate education available in public affairs, noting that its physical location in academe is essentially all over the map. Public affairs is addressed in public administration, in political science, in public relations, in communications in public policy, and in business program (see Table 5.1 for a listing of all the titles under which public affairs is taught at the collegiate level). Although they do not note it, the lack of a consistent intellectual home likely hurts the development of the field and unlike finance and marketing, for example, practitioner and professional support of education is difficult to obtain. Yet it is this diversity of educational 'homes' that does contribute to the vibrancy of public affairs.

It is likely that the more relevant education of public affairs practitioners occurs in executive programs where mid-level and higher management can be exposed to public affairs, and given their operating background and real world experience come to a greater recognition of the value of public affairs.

Creighton and Meznar provide us with a comparative ranking of the top 50 public affairs education programs in Table 5.5 and observe that over a ten-year period there has not been much change in these rankings. They raise a telling point in that they did not look at syllabi across these programs and over time so there is no easy method to assess whether the content of the programs have adjusted to the changed environment of public affairs. Their focus was clearly on academic instruction in public affairs and not on the professional training available to public affairs professionals (through such institutions as the Public Affairs Council, the Issues Management Council, public relations professional programs and the like). It is this author's opinion that the currency of public affairs is more likely to be found in professional programs and executive programs and not in academic programs. Academic programs may provide the basics of public affairs tools and techniques, but actual experience and professional training is more likely to hone and develop the emerging techniques and tools that will eventually find their way into academic instruction.

Creighton and Meznar do note that public affairs is still not widely recognized as an organizational function in undergraduate business education and as such the vast majority of business graduates are ill prepared to deal with the non-market environment, to understand how it impacts on corporate success, choices, and reputation. Unlike many fields (accounting, finance, etc.) there is no clearly recognized professional certification program for public affairs professionals and this is an area in which the profession needs to consider going forward into the future.

These chapters provide a challenge to the professional public affairs officer on a variety of levels – understanding the development of the field, where the opportunities and challenges lie for both professional and intellectual development. Public affairs is a critical organizational function constantly in search of recognition by line managers and whose skill set and boundary spanning activities offer the firm warning of dangers and opportunities for success, new products and services, enhanced reputation and serve as the foundation for the corporation's attempts to be citizen and maintain is social license to operate.

REFERENCES

Allison, G. and Zelikow, P. 1999. *Essence of Decision: Explaining the Cuban Missile Crisis.* 2nd edn New York: Longman.

Fleisher, C. S. 2005. 'The Global Development of the Public Affairs,' in P. Harris and C. S. Fleisher (eds.) *Handbook of Public Affairs*, London: Sage: 5–30.

Corporate Public Affairs: Revisiting the Development of the Field

Craig S. Fleisher

This chapter addresses the development of the field of corporate public affairs, from its origins to its current position. It builds upon an examination I wrote over ten years ago about how the field had developed (Fleisher, 2005), adding a contemporary analysis of how the field has and may likely continue to grow in the foreseeable future. Corporate public affairs is the function in business and commercial entities that has the primary managerial responsibility for addressing both issue (Heath and Palenchar, 2009) and stakeholder phenomena (Freeman, 1984), affecting the organization in its external or nonmarket environment. Though the field remains specialized in practice and unfamiliar to many in the general, global public, and even among some top executives, it has steadily grown from its roots to a position of respectability in some organizations, institutions, nation states, and occupations (Pinkham, 2013; 2005).

Since the early days of commerce and governance, business and government have always held an interdependent relationship. Businesses rely on governments to establish and enforce the 'rules of the game', scope the 'playing field', and act as an adjudicator or arbiter in solving business disputes. Among other things, governments rely on businesses and commercial enterprises to generate wealth, employ citizens, and to develop products and services that meet stakeholders' needs (Harris and Fleisher, 2005). When both business and government operate together at peak levels, national standards of living nearly always rise and the nation state tends to increase its attractiveness, gravitas, and international influence. When one, the other, or both operate sub-optimally, more adverse relative outcomes are produced.

Though the definitions of public affairs have been evolving and are often changing with the times that provide its contexts (Harris and Fleisher, 2005), for the purposes of this chapter (corporate) public affairs (PA) includes those management processes that help an organization better relate to and effectively perform in its nonmarket environment (Baron, 1999). The market environment, with which most students of business are familiar, includes the interactions between businesses and other parties that take place within markets or through private agreements such as contracts. The nonmarket (NM) environment, which is more familiar to students of government, political affairs or studies, includes legal, political, and social arrangements that structure the nature of interactions occurring outside, but in relationship to markets and private agreements (Baron, 1995). The NM context affects every industry and company differently and can do so at multiple levels including local, provincial/state, regional, national, or international – thus providing opportunities for competitive advantage to those organizations that can favorably guide and manage their entity's interactions with it (Keim, 2005). Nonmarket issues can be narrow to wide-ranging and include, among others, corporate responsibility, environmental protection, health and safety, international trade concerns, legislative policy and politics, regulatory matters, technology issues, and policy (Holcomb, 2005a).

The professionals who specialize in dealing with and helping organizations manage issues and their interactions with stakeholders in the NM environment are known as public affairs officers (i.e., analysts, specialists, managers, directors, VPs, etc.), otherwise known as PAOs. Public affairs work interrelates government relations, issue management, corporate and social responsibility, information dissemination, media communication, political education, and strategic communications advice. Public affairs practitioners seek to influence public policy institutions and processes, build and maintain a strong organizational reputation and find common ground with their organization's

stakeholders (Davidson, 2015). They also use a variety of concepts, frameworks, models, tools, and techniques that are somewhat unique for managing organizational, issue and stakeholder interactions (Showalter and Fleisher, 2005).

A FUNCTION ROOTED IN PUBLIC POLICY AND BUSINESS INTERACTION

The function has a long history, although the 'corporate' facet of public affairs was a latter twentieth century development. Corresponding to which parts of the globe one examines, PA developed at a different pace and in unique or path-dependent ways through the years (Allen, 2005; Holcomb, 2005b; Pedler, 2005).

Governments and public policy have grown in size, magnitude, and impact; correspondingly, the necessity of business to respond to it has also grown. For the purposes of this chapter, public policy are actions (or a plan of action) undertaken by government officials to achieve a broad purpose that likely affects a sizable portion of a nation's citizens (i.e., its publics). It follows that the public policy process is the means by which specific public policies are established, implemented, evaluated, and changed. This process is often conceived of in terms of three over-riding stages: public policy formation, public policy formulation, and public policy implementation (Buchholz, 1992). The ideological objective of the public policy process is designed to generate governmental decisions and actions that are reflective of the publics' best interests.

In attempting to best meet the publics' best interests, the process can often invite interested policy stakeholders to the consultative table. As such, business organizations and other interest groups have significant potential to influence public policy decision making. This basis forms the foundation by which the organization's public affairs professional receives his/her legitimacy and mandate. The public policy

Table 1.1   The swinging pendulum of how the public generally viewed US government involvement in business activity over 5 decades

Decade	Administration (during the decade)	Key social/business events, issues, and trends	Public's view
1970s	Nixon (1970–3) Ford (1973–6) Carter (1977–80)	Firestone radial tires Ford Pinto gas tanks Gender role flexibility Genetic engineering 'Green' revolution Middle East violence Oil and energy crises P&G Rely tampon recall Recessionary economies	The end of the Vietnam war, oil shocks, continuing regional conflict, need for continued scientific advancement (e.g., space exploration, nuclear power) and social unrest led to heavy involvement by the federal government in most sectors. US citizens looked to the government for solutions to these increasingly difficult social conditions and problems.
1980s	Reagan (1981–9)	Cold War ends Developing world debt crises Economic liberalization Exxon Valdez oil spill Global warming aware Internet, PC use grows J&J Tylenol tampering Major droughts War on drugs	The public had grown weary of the heavy federal government role in the economy and other sectors they experienced during the turbulent 1970s and under presidents Nixon, Ford, and Carter. Under Reagan, the government played less of a role – particularly with respect to the monitoring and regulation of business activity, some even seeing it as nearly invisible or inactive.
1990s	HW Bush (1990–3) Clinton (1993–9)	Alternative/new media Bre-X gold mining scam Dot-com bubble grows Dow Corning implants GATT updates/WTO Genetic engineered crops Greenspan's 'irrational exuberance' Kyoto Protocol/UNFCCC	The end years of the 'Reagan Revolution' of the 1980s left citizens wanting government to play a larger role again. Federal government spending grew quickly under Bush, and continued growing under Clinton. The Clinton government played a much more activist role in international and social affairs.
2000–10	Clinton (2000) GW Bush (2001–08) Obama (2009)	9/11 Bank failures Dot-com bubble burst Enron Government bailouts 'Great recession' Health-care reform Mobile phones take off Satellite broadcasting	US citizens grew tired of the heavy federal activity of the late 1990s. GW Bush was elected on a platform of a reduced role for the federal government, but the attacks on the World Trade Center changed this. Washington DC bailed out industries (airline transportation, auto manufacturing, etc.) and spent heavily on defense and homeland security.
2010–present	Obama (2010–16) TBD (2017–20)	Frothy capital markets Hacking accounts Mobile payments Possible national bankruptcies Slow global recovery Social media growth Sustainability thrusts Takada air bag recalls	President Obama has continued increasing government's role in most citizens' activity. Under his administration, major changes were made in education, health care, and social sectors. With an election in 2016, will Americans once again seek a decreased involvement of the federal government, or a continuation of it?

process provides the key venue in which the PA professional performs his/her craft.

Inputs to the public policy process, usually generated by interested and knowledgeable stakeholders like citizens, politicians, interest groups, legal experts, and concerned commercial interests among others, help mold a government's policy decisions and strategies to confront perceived and actual stakeholder problems. Stakeholder's objectives for public policy outcomes may either be wide and high-minded or narrow and mostly self-serving. Governments are also served by public policy by using tools involving combinations of incentives and penalties to prompt stakeholders under their auspices to act in ways that achieve policy goals.

Public policy effects are the outcomes that emanate out of government regulatory actions. Regulation includes those actions taken by government to establish rules which businesses or other groups must follow and which then shape their behavior. It is a primary way of accomplishing public policy. During the 1960s and 1970s, economic and social regulation, as well as the desire of citizens to be active in the shaping of responses, took on even more influence in many countries, and, as such, businesses needed to develop ways to interact with those agencies and governmental bodies and stakeholders who sought to alter or change their behavior (Holcomb, 2005b).

THE MACRO-CONTEXT UNDERLYING THE DEVELOPMENT OF CORPORATE PUBLIC AFFAIRS

The nature of government's involvement in business over the decades has created the key macro-environmental dynamic for which PA units must effectively function (Harris and Fleisher, 2005). The nature of this involvement, in terms of its depth, breadth, direction, pace, sequence, and scope, among other things, means that business and commercial interests must establish and nurture effective

working relationships with other stakeholders in the public policy and nonmarket contexts. In general, business decision makers prefer to have as much discretion as possible over the ground rules by which they operate; nevertheless, much public interest experience dictates that citizens go back and forth between the swings of pendulums asking for more and less government involvement in business activity. Table 1.1 provides a clearer sense of the swings in the US since the 1970s.

The political system and risks associated with it for business and commercial interests are ever-changing. Political risk includes the likelihood that a business's investments will be adversely impacted by governmental policy. In some countries, we have witnessed episodes of the nationalization of businesses by government (Wikipedia, 2015). Some countries are deemed to have corrupt governance systems (Transparency Index, 2014). In others, businesses may look to their federal governments to provide protection of their operations and/or the right to exist. Businesses have long sought to influence government in order to gain access to consumers or customers, and even to sell to the governments themselves (for example, aerospace, defense, infrastructure-building contracts, etc.). As such, risks can often cut both ways, and it becomes the realm of the PA officer to help manage the business response to managing these risks, among others.

By the 1970s corporations had evolved and become more complex, utilizing multiple departments to accomplish tasks, and had begun to interact with numerous, increasingly sophisticated, stakeholder groups on the organizational periphery (International Conference on Public Affairs, 1971). As such, corporate public affairs had developed into a boundary spanning function by the early 1970s. Boundary spanning departments are those units within an organization that reach across the organization's boundary line to interact with groups and people in society. Building positive and mutually beneficial relationships that span organizational boundaries became a growing part of managers' roles; more specifically to this chapter, it became the central factor underlying the work of the public affairs specialist. Corporate social responsibility (CSR), community and environmental affairs, issue and stakeholder management took on the central focus of PA officers, activities that remain core to PA practice to the current day (Holcomb, 2005b).

Despite there being a general trend toward less governmental involvement in business, the 1980s saw the continued growth of public affairs departments, particularly in areas like association relations, government relations, grassroots, lobbying, political action committees, and political education (Fleisher, 2005; Lusterman, 1985). Many of these developments were documented by large scale studies of the field and in dissertations (see, for example, Lusterman, 1985; Mahon, 1982; Post et al., 1982). Professional associations, like the US Public Affairs Council in Washington, DC, took on greater prominence and roles educating and informing the coming generation of PA officers.

The 1990s brought with it a new emphasis on managing public affairs and focused heavily on institutionalizing the function amongst other business functions. Among other things, PA officers renewed their focus on integrating PA activities with planning and strategy at different organizational levels, using technology to automate routine functions in the communication and event planning arenas, and measuring and evaluating their results and outcomes in terms understandable to other (non-PA) executives (Fleisher, 1997). The US Foundation for Public Affairs (1999) had found by the end of the decade that the function had achieved a higher degree of valued interaction with top executives and board-level governance functions, executives earned high levels of compensation mostly in line with similarly educated officers of other (i.e., non-PA) advisory functions, and the function was using many of the same kinds of tools and techniques that other managers had adopted, ranging from balanced scorecards, mission/vision development, continuous improvement, and better evaluation methods.

DRIVERS OF CORPORATE PUBLIC AFFAIRS ACTIVITY SINCE 2000

The turn of the century has produced changes confronting contemporary PA offices and officers. Business is confronted by a wide range of external forces, many of which can determine whether an enterprise or industry will be successful, or not. Issues in the forms of regularly changing policies, politics, and laws, events like elections and referenda, and trends such as those associated to demographic cohorts taking precedence in the workforce will continue to mean a prominent role for public affairs policy and practitioners. One immediate consequence for practitioners is the need to be able to take the 'pulse of stakeholders' on a continuing basis, as well as in quickly understanding the meaning of the metrics gathered amongst this fast flow of data.

In many parts of the globe, there has been a gradual erosion and loss of public trust in institutions. Recent outbreaks of diseases, political meltdowns of the economies of entire nation states, and continuing controversies surrounding which people should and should not be allowed to live and work in nation states remain unresolved in most iterations. Public affairs practitioners today have to help sustain not only their brand and corporate reputations, but also the integrity and public support of the institutions within which they ply their craft.

The globalization of world markets has added a layer of complexity to policy making and planning for most organizations. Whereas in past decades, these decisions and actions could be made and taken locally, today they cannot. Social media, efficient air transport, and digital information exchange have all combined to allow for freer travel and access between individual members as well as business stakeholders of different nation states. This means that PA practitioners must keep up with, or even lead the way, in terms of recognizing how to exploit distance-shrinking technologies, be both global and local (aka, glo-cal) in terms of their thinking and acting, and more globally and culturally astute than ever before (Fleisher, 2003; Harsanyi and Schmidt, 2012; Judd, 2008, 2009, 2010).

Communication in the public affairs realm has also taken on new meanings in recent decades (Davidson, 2015; EMRC, 2011). The rapid rise of the Internet, the continued growth of social media, and the automation, monitoring, and tracking of behaviors, discussions, and transactions all converge to powerfully shape the new public affairs context. Public affairs practitioners have to be masters of the new digital domains, and leverage communication skills that are evolving as quickly as the technologies that underlie their emergence (EMRC, 2011; Fleisher, 2012; Van Dijk, 2012).

Changing technologies have led to the ability to improve the quality, quantity, and pace of communication within organizations, as well as between organizations and their stakeholders. This can be a double-edged sword, making progress easier for those organizations that have always taken a strategic PA approach to their interactions and plans, but making progress far more difficult for those organizations that would prefer to ignore or brush away controversies underlying issues their stakeholders have with their corporate behaviors (Oliver and Holzinger, 2008). These technologies also allow for mass customization of message delivery, as can be done through social media-driven grassroots approaches that have long been a mainstay of the PA portfolio (Althaus, 2009).

Public affairs also should benefit from the growing focus on the interplay between the organization, its environment, and strategy (Men and Hung, 2012). Public communication takes on a re-emphasized and more strategic role in the new social-media age, thus providing organizations and their stakeholders

more opportunities than ever before to communicate with one another (Davidson, 2015). Public affairs practitioners should continue to take a prominent role in helping decision makers to craft strategies that recognize the need and relevancy of boundary spanning, buffering and/or bridging (Meznar and Nigh, 1995).

Last but not least, organizations of all types, as well as their key managers in PA and other functions, must become increasingly capable of dealing with significant change and greater complexity (Harsanyi, 2010; The Centre for Corporate Public Affairs, 2010). As such, they will have to keep abreast of emerging knowledge inside and monitor developments adjacent to their fields, constantly expand and stretch their experiential and social-media horizons – particularly as they pertain to reputational concerns (Albrecht, 2000; Mahon and Wartick, 2012). They should also learn new concepts, models, and frameworks in areas of analytics, intelligence, and networking to help them make better and faster sense of the perceived and actual complexity they and their organizations will encounter (Fleisher, 2012).

THE MICRO-CONTEXT UNDERLYING THE DEVELOPMENT OF THE 'NEW' CORPORATE PUBLIC AFFAIRS

Competent PA professionals enable their organizations to favorably participate in the public policy process. As such, it describes the array of activities that are utilized by PA professionals in facilitating the organization's participation within the public policy process. All of these activities enable the organization to relate to particular stakeholders in the public policy environment.

A reasonable way I have used for several decades to categorize PA activities is by the primary relational targets of PA activities:

1   government relations (GR)
2   public/stakeholder relations (P/SR)

3   community relations (CR)
4   organizational relations (OR)
5   political relations (PolR).

It must be acknowledged that not all PA departments perform all five of these activities, but nearly all perform at least two of them, and the more established and well-entrenched ones usually do three or more. Though there may be some overlap between the listed categories, but these five tend to be easily distinguishable in practice.

Table 1.2 breaks down this categorization into four smaller components. The first component is called 'targets', referring to the particular stakeholder group that the organization is trying to influence in the nonmarket or public policy environment. The second category is called 'tactic'. This refers to the generic role the organization assumes in relating to the targeted public policy stakeholders. The third category, called 'functions', refers to the ways these activities are organized within the organization itself. Finally, the fourth category, 'performers', identifies those individuals or groups who act in association with the PA professional on behalf of the business in relating to the organization's public policy environment targets.

So, just how have these PA activities been evolving since the turn of the century? In a 2001 article I noted how I had observed a shift in practice away from more classical and/or 'traditional' PA practices toward a 'new' model that I expected would be most prominent in that decade (i.e., 2001–10) (Fleisher, 2001). I suggested this shift had been catalyzed by half a dozen internal and external trends that had been driving practice, more specifically known as driving forces. As an effective strategic management response to these driving forces, at the time I offered seven prescriptions for practicing what I described as the 'new public affairs'. The prescriptions are summarized in the following sub-sections.

To Manage Public Affairs as an Ongoing, Year-Round Process Both Internally and Externally

Contemporary public affairs practice has continued to evolve in relative importance from the one I witnessed at the start of the new century (Moss et al., 2012; McGrath et al., 2010). Public policy institutions and processes have remained powerful influencers of the corporate playing pitch and often are the catalysts for so-called 'un-leveled' business playing fields (Mack, 1997; Oliver and Holzinger, 2008). In other words, the public policy arena remains an important arena in which competitive advantage may at least be episodically or temporarily achieved. Witness over the last decade any number of approved or disapproved mergers and acquisitions, unique content requirements, unusual safety standards, or tightened governance regulatory policies. Public policy institutions still matter to senior executives and their organizations' potential success, and the passage of time seems to only re-emphasize that point even further (Men and Hung, 2012).

Stakeholders have also repeatedly demonstrated that they will actively seek to protect or enhance their claims or stakes in the public policy arena (Carroll, 2005). The most effective stakeholders realize that they are most influential at moving their causes by being active throughout the year as opposed to just the periods around elections or voting. This is, at least in part, because most politicians or elected officials act year round in doing those things to both please their constituents and also to position themselves to get enough votes to win their next election. As such, more organizations than ever have ensconced public affairs processes within their strategic decision-making processes, and more public affairs practitioners have become trusted members, or at least advisors to, their top management teams (Griffin and Dunn, 2004; Oliver and Holzinger, 2008).

Table 1.2   The different relations that constitute public affairs practice

GOVERNMENT RELATIONS (GR)
1) Targets: governmental representatives at multiple levels
2) Tactic: political lobbying
3) Functions:
    a) International/transnational government relations
    b) Federal or national government relations
    c) Provincial/state/canton government relations
    d) Municipal or local government relations
    e) Regulatory affairs/compliance
4) Performers: corporate lobbyists, contracted lobbyists, association or coalitional lobbyists, designated organizational
    representatives such as senior executives, managers, or corporate legal counsel

PUBLIC/STAKEHOLDER RELATIONS (P/SR)
1) Targets: organizational 'publics' in society at large
2) Tactic: stakeholder communication
3) Functions:
    a) Customer relations/consumer affairs
    b) Employee relations and communication
    c) Events organization
    d) Investor and other financial relations support
    e) Issues/advocacy and/or image advertising
    f) Media/social-media relations
4) Performers: organizational communications experts, contracted
    PR professionals

COMMUNITY RELATIONS (CR)
1) Targets: the organization's communities
2) Tactic: climate building on a geo-locational basis
3) Functions:
    a) Charitable donations/corporate philanthropy
    b) Volunteerism
4) Performers: community relations professionals, organizational members, community interest group participants

ORGANIZATIONAL RELATIONS (OR)
1) Targets: organizational decision makers (line and staff)
2) Tactic: issues management
3) Functions:
    a) Crisis management
    b) Issues identification/monitoring
    c) Issues analysis
    d) Issues response
    e) Strategic business planning
4) Performers: the PA professional

POLITICAL RELATIONS (PolR)
1) Targets: organizational employees or associated employees
2) Tactic: political education, internal advocacy
3) Functions:
    a) Associations/organization partnerships
    b) Constituency building/grassroots activity
    c) Political action committees (PACs)
    d) Political education
    e) Political risk assessment/analysis
4) Performers: the PA professional, employees, community members, customers, owners

To Cultivate and Harvest the Capability to Build, Develop, and Maintain Enduring Stakeholder Relationships

Companies made major inroads during 2001–10 in managing their stakeholder relationships. That decade saw the publication of more stakeholder reports or their rough equivalents, more permanent structures dedicated to stakeholder dialogue ranging from continuing committees of the board of directors to permanent quasi-public/private groups dedicated to addressing shared issues, and many other new forms of stakeholder dialogue in between (Carroll, 2005; Freeman, 2000). Some companies have even appointed individuals with 'stakeholder' in their official titles, and even a small smattering of 'chief stakeholder officers' made their first appearances.

Despite the great deal of progress made in recognizing the importance of stakeholders over the past few decades, there are still several areas of stakeholder management that have room for improvement (Carroll, 2005). For example, stakeholders, especially non-financially-oriented ones, are still overlooked. Most organizations remain averse to appointing chief stakeholder officers or stakeholder management committees of their boards of directors. Many of the opportunities for P/SR improvement will need to be driven by educational institutions as opposed to those in the line of fire, or by associations who are well served to organize meetings, but are not as adept in developing the body of knowledge needed to better perform stakeholder management or corporate responsibility efforts (Griffin and Prakash, 2014). A myriad of cross-institutional opportunities remain for better P/SR knowledge building and practice sharing, if only we can get individuals within those institutions to better recognize their shared challenges and interests.

To Influence Stakeholders Using Refined Information (i.e., Intelligence)

In the last two decades, PA observers saw the rise of applications of Baron's concept of the four I's – the I's standing for interests, institutions, issues, and intelligence (Baron, 1995). Intelligence in this framework meant having actionable information about the relevant interests (i.e., stakeholders), issues and institutions that would allow an organization unique insight into the resolution of a non-market matter (Baron, 1999). Intelligence usually involves internal public affairs officers systematically doing both primary and secondary research at the intersection of the four I's (Fleisher, 2010/11). Social media research for public affairs, which I have often termed SMint (short for Social Media Intelligence) has also gained dramatically in prominence in recent years and is expected to continue to gain in prominence in the future.

Research activities of all sorts have continued to grow in strategic and tactical importance in most of the larger and more sophisticated multinational PA offices (Harsanyi, 2010). There is far greater use today of networks for research, both in the newer digital as well as more traditional personal domains like subject matter expert (aka, SME) networks. Research applications and processes themselves have become more sophisticated and real-time for many public affairs shops as the emphasis on developing intelligence has grown in prominence (Gupta, 2011).

To Recognize the Importance of Managing the Grassroots

The grassroots, or grassroots lobbying as it is otherwise known, are normally used to support and supplement traditional access-based lobbying; however, these efforts must be real, authentic grassroots, not automated, instant, or manufactured 'Astroturf' campaigns (Sourcewatch, 2015). Developing genuine support for an issue is significantly different from when 'front groups' intentionally manipulate uninformed persons to create the appearance of support. Approaches that rely upon misinformation, deception, intimidation, or bullying tactics of what public affairs guru Ed Grefe terms the 'family' or 'friend' stakeholder categories have been shown to be both ineffective and damaging in the long term to those organizations using them (Grefe and Linsky, 1996). Additionally, approaches that rely on groups using impersonal email, social-media-based lists, or electronic petitions, whereby most people who sign up are unaware and uninformed of what they are actually supporting, have also created net damage to both the political system and also to those associations, corporations, political interests, PR firms, and other politically active organizations who were found to have funded and originated these efforts (Sourcewatch, 2015).

I expect to see more use of the grassroots in the coming decades, as well as more unfortunate and ill-advised use of manufactured grassroots by some less-informed, passionate single-caused or fringe groups as well. These Astroturf grassroots efforts, in particular, will be fertilized by the ease of how these groups can be organized via social media. It is very convenient, and too tempting to some groups not to wander into public policy debates via Twitter, Facebook, corporate blogs, and like social media channels (Walker, 2014). Nevertheless, organizations and public policy makers alike – who effectively participate via these channels – will increasingly come to recognize that they will require an equal, if not even higher level of differentiated PA communications competence as the more traditional channels atrophy.

To Communicate in an Integrated Manner

Over the last three to four decades, formal research processes have been used more often in developing public affairs communication campaigns. However, there are still prominent examples where the research was used in a manipulative, one-directional manner to support the organization's original positions as opposed to modifying practices based on the research findings – the so-called 'damned lies and statistics' phenomenon described by Best (2001). The last ten years have seen the manipulative use of research reaching heights previously unseen. This occurred because so many individuals and groups were keen on using their own studies, communicating them out via digital channels and social media, and then reporting them as 'truisms'. Unfortunately, many readers of these items lacked the attention span, knowledge, and sophistication to determine the credibility, source bias, validity, or generalizability of this research. In Best's (2001) terms, there are still far more awestruck, cynical, and naive audience members than critical ones in these public policy debates.

I had expected at the start of the century that the integration of communication would someday seamlessly cut across functional groups such as corporate communications, government relations, marketing, public affairs, and public relations (Fleisher, 2001). Some powerful examples of this cross-functional integration actually occurred during this period, but they were more the extremes than the mean in my estimation. Unfortunately, this full integration across these external-facing communication functions still remains among the minority of (corporate) public affairs campaigns (Gupta, 2011). This state of affairs is even more likely to be true when the campaign is targeted on an issue that has a heavy electoral, lobbying, or regulatory element associated with its resolution (Kanol, 2015).

To Continuously Align Values and Strategy with the Public's Interests

I had considered the ability to be politically germane over time, whereby an organization is able to consistently align and adapt its policies and actions with the public's values (Freeman, 2000), to be a key indicator of whether the new PA model I had anticipated was actually in place. When and where this alignment was continuously managed, the organization's reputation improves (Roberts and Dowling, 2002), and creates the context for the most effective managerial utilization of the entire range of public affairs tools (Showalter and Fleisher, 2005). Ethics and ethical sensitivity was expected to be prominent since understanding the organization's stakeholder relationships is critical in achieving harmony between the organization and its stakeholders (Wiedmann, 2006). Executed properly by its PA function, stakeholders were expected to come to trust the organization, not necessarily agreeing or disagreeing with it but recognizing that it deserved to be a credible voice in the development of effective public policy (Davidson, 2015).

This was a continuous challenge for many organizations over several decades. The problem was not in organizations generally lacking the commitment or desire to create the alignment I referred to, but rather in effectively managing the constant tension between their own evolving global strategies and an oft-changing public interest. Because of the rapid growth and stakeholder uptake of expanding new media channels, public attitudes and opinions – the two key elements underlying the often imprecise aggregated set of values we call the 'public interest' – would shift more rapidly, and often more unexpectedly, than previously. This changed context often meant that organizations would have to take a far more proactive role in helping to shape the debate underlying the formation of public interest, a role that at least some prominent organizations had historically refrained from doing and remained more comfortable 'on the outside, looking in'. It also meant that the organizations would have to be able to take a better pulse and more effectively monitor the shifting foundations of the public interest and the environmental trends associated with that (Albrecht, 2000), a task that can require a level of research sophistication that some organizations still have not managed to achieve internally, despite major advances in doing this dynamically online with sophisticated analytical applications in recent years, or were unwilling to outsource to external experts like agencies or consultants.

To Improve External Relations Using the Accepted Facets of Contemporary Management Practice

My observations suggest we generally witnessed an improvement of the use of accepted facets of contemporary management in the practice of corporate public affairs (Foundation for Public Affairs, 2005, 1999). This occurred in the first place because more public affairs officers were exposed to business and management principles and scholarship. For example, more and more senior public affairs officers wielded management credentials like MBAs or attended specific executive development programs like the impressive residential institutes or similar high-level executive programs offered by The Centre for Corporate Public Affairs headquartered in Melbourne, Australia, US-based Public Affairs Council (Washington, DC), Boston College Center for Corporate Citizenship, and Issues Management Council (Leesburg, VA), among others. There have also been a plethora of training and informational webinars, short courses, social-media-based resource sites, blogs and other distance-friendly educational events offered that have expanded the reach of PA knowledge to individuals who previously lacked access to it. Having stated that, the scholarship on what works and doesn't in practice and theory across a range of PA management phenomena, including lobbying, grassroots, political contributions, political education, advocacy, and issue management, and performance measurement remains relatively underdeveloped and in need of a research infusion (Davidson, 2015; Kanol, 2015).

The typical MBA graduate would still be relatively naive about corporate public affairs, issue management, corporate communication, corporate citizenship, government relations, business and public policy, business–government relations, etc., relative to the well-established functional activities like accounting, finance, marketing, or operations (Fleisher, 2010/11). On the other hand, PA-related concepts like corporate social performance (Mahon and Wartick, 2012), corporate and community citizenship or stewardship, reputation management (Mahon and Wartick, 2012), sustainability (Millar et al., 2012), ethics, and governance have made inroads and frequently interact with corporate PA agendas. Much like the situation back in the 1970s and 1980s, very few institutions of higher education in North America offer undergraduate or graduate degree programs or even majors in the corporate PA field; even fewer have research chairs or institutes dedicated to the study of phenomenon within this subject matter area. Fortunately, the Journal of Public Affairs (Wiley) continues to publish and entered its second decade in 2011, thereby passing a major milestone for the development or professionalization of any field of study.

Despite some scattered and uneven progress having been made during 2001–10, strategic public affairs activity generally remains a peripheral element in the executive management of most companies as we began the second decade of the new millennium (Fleisher, 2010/11). Though they still tend to have greater internal influence in companies and industries that are more highly regulated (for example,

aerospace, bio/pharma, defense, energy, IT, etc.), senior public affairs executives are only occasionally noted in broad studies of organizational influence as being critical to the performance of their organizations – exemplified in an important manner by relatively few being quoted in annual reports or offering comment at annual shareholder meetings (Heath and Palenchar, 2009). The best ones usually only get a seat at the decision-making table, but rarely as central a one as the chief financial officer, marketing officer, or chief operating officer holds (Gupta, 2011). Last but not least, top PA officers continue to have to work hard at gaining and maintaining prominence in many businesses' strategic planning efforts, as they generally still do not have a 'guaranteed' spot at these strategic planning or decision-making tables, assuming they have the needed resources to be a significant force in the first place (Griffin and Dunn, 2004).

As I re-examined that piece ten years later, I realized several shifts had occurred in practice (Fleisher, 2012). As such, I had suggested three additional practices that had arisen and taken on significance. I labeled the new model that included all ten of these practices something called 'Public Affairs 2.0'. The three additional practices are outlined below.

To Build, Cultivate and Mobilize the Appropriate Alliances and Partnerships From Amongst all of Its Networks

Organizations who 'win' in public policy battles are those who are 'in' with those who align with the group's and the public interests, in other words, demonstrating keen levels of corporate responsibility (Griffin and Prakash, 2014). Developing personal networks has always been important in government relations and lobbying activities; consequently, knowing the right individuals like the influential staffers in a key elected official's office, could be the difference between moving policy in the desired direction or not (Mack, 1997). The networks that will be most valuable in the PA 2.0 environment though will encompass a greater variety of parties; the organization's grassroots membership, association members, popular media people, policy 'influentials', and both competitor (i.e., 'strange bed-fellows' – Grefe and Linsky, 1996) and supportive organizations within the organization's industry. Those organizations that can collaborate with their traditional public policy critics, such as interest groups generally on the 'other side of the fence', will have advantages when moving forward with positions to their public policy makers. Indeed, being able to gain the occasional willingness of critics to support important organizational public policy positions will be a key skill for PA 2.0 practitioners (Showalter, 2011; Van Dijk, 2012).

These networks have become one of the most critical assets of effective public affairs 2.0 teams. They will require resources (i.e., human, informational, temporal, technical, and financial) to build, intelligence to activate and lead the needed issue alliances, collaborations, and partnerships, and technology to optimize the delivery of targeted, multi-directional communications (i.e., calls to action, issue portals, public affairs-dedicated social media). This will also mean that organizations will face an ongoing challenge in attempting to communicate the value of investing still-scarce resources in (public affairs) assets that don't fit neatly in most CEO's financial lexicon of balance sheets, income statements, and quarterly or annual results. Astute PA 2.0 officers will liken these investments to financial vehicles like hedging, futures contracts, and risk management that these business executives more quickly discern.

To Understand the Responsibilities of Being a Global Citizen, and Apply Their Understanding Locally

Even though international public affairs practice has never really become a discipline in its own right, most companies today must operate in a globalized context. North American companies will succeed most when they can actually do business with the 95 percent of customers who live outside of the USA, many of whom are becoming viable consumers of discretionary products and services. Nevertheless, there are still many stakeholders who oppose the seeming onslaught of this force, and there will be continuing opposition to free trade and globalization itself. For example, maintaining so-called 'level playing fields', achieving 'fair' access to new national markets, agreeing upon fair levels of tariffs or fees, and ownership arrangements will continue to be prominent for business in the present decade. Sometimes, organizations will be challenged to set up their PA operation in countries where the national cultures would find this activity 'foreign' (Harsanyi, 2010). More locally, many communities will not want to do business unless an employer is a neighbor of choice (Burke, 1998). As such, the public policy challenges inherent in expanding trade, among other political matters, will remain vital to corporate interests, thereby providing public affairs officers ample opportunities to make a difference to their organizations (Getz, 2001).

Because of this force, public affairs competencies will increasingly be an area in which all business executives must be familiar (Harsanyi and Schmidt, 2012). Effective PA 2.0 officers over the period 2011–20 will display a set of competencies that would not have been necessarily needed a decade or two ago in many of their organizations (Fleisher, 2003; Moss et al., 2012). They will benefit from the increasing research like that published in the Journal of Public Affairs and by specialist think tanks. Additional help will come from professional development attention being devoted to practicing public affairs in different nation states and regions such as those being conducted under the auspices of, for example, the studies on managing public affairs in the EU, India, and China conducted by the Foundation for Public Affairs (see, for example, Judd, 2010, 2009, 2008), The Centre for Corporate Public Affairs (2010), and/or PublicAffairsAsia (In House, 2011). Another promising development has been the fast growth of public affairs consultancies and advisory services, as well as technical information applications or solutions that can automate formerly inefficient, manual tasks. Specialist PA agencies will provide not only gainful employment to individuals who want to practice public affairs but also expertise and resources that will extend the reach of in-house public affairs teams of organizations who are needing to employ these resources.

To Master the Evolving Communication Channels Provided by Digital and Social Media

Digital media has been increasing in its influence in shaping policy in most modern democracies (Van Dijk, 2012). It is used by interests on all sides of policy matters for tracking issues and tracking the pulse of the public interest or specific publics, sending messages out to stakeholders, encouraging financial donations, issuing 'calls to action', gathering intelligence, and for announcing events or meetings, among other things. As such, candidates, elected officials, politicians, policy makers, and their office staff members are recognizing its growing importance in carrying out their public responsibilities. Social media platforms like Facebook, Google+, Instagram, LinkedIn, Pinterest, SlideShare, Twitter, and YouTube are allowing political stakeholders to reach audiences that used to be beyond their reach using the traditional media. Additionally, blogs, online surveys, web pages, and wikis are allowing public officials to communicate with their constituencies in new ways, many of which are proving to be mutually beneficial. In many cases, social media are complementing the traditional means of communication, although in others, it is supplanting them (EMRC, 2011).

The Public Affairs 2.0 operation will be working to move today's present unidirectional communication (i.e., getting the message out to audiences) into multi-directional conversations and dialogs. These practitioners will also spend many hours monitoring, tracking, and managing social media as a daily task (Gupta, 2011). Although new media will continue to grow in prominence, traditional media remain important for moving trends in the long run and PA 2.0 practitioners will not lose sight of the need to stay on top of those channels as well (EMRC, 2011). Most importantly, the PA 2.0 practitioner will be able to move both strategically and tactically between the new social and traditional media channels in order to maximize the likelihood that their messages are being effectively and efficiently communicated and achieving the desired organizational objectives (DiStaso et al., 2011).

CONCLUSION

The field of corporate public affairs (PA) has made great strides over the last five decades, having come from humble origins primarily based in lobbying activity to being a fully fledged, valued strategic management function and competitive difference maker in some companies and industries. Although it still fails to meet some of the key criteria for it to rise to a broadly accepted professional status in most parts of the globe as I had first suggested nearly two decades ago (Fleisher, 1998), it has continued to make progress as a field since the turn of the millennium. The field and function remain essential in some companies, industries, and nation states, while still filled with untapped opportunity and promise in others.

This Handbook, the second one edited by my colleague Phil Harris and myself for SAGE, provides a useful yardstick to gauge its progress. The chapters and authors we selected look at PA from numerous perspectives, angles, and viewpoints. They show much of the progress and promise I have discussed in this chapter. Ten or twenty years from now, whether keen observers of the field will see continued progress or more unfulfilled opportunity will ultimately have to be judged by the test of time.

REFERENCES

Albrecht, K. 2000. *Corporate Radar: Tracking the Forces That Are Shaping Your Business.* AMACOM: New York.

Allen, G. 2005. An integrated model: the evolution of public affairs down under. In P Harris and CS Fleisher (eds), *Handbook of Public Affairs*, Sage: London, pp. 338–60.

Althaus, M. 2009. Discovering our (corporate) grassroots: European advocacy 2.0. In Johnson, DW (ed), *Routledge Handbook of Political Management*, New York: Routledge, pp. 477–94.

Baron, DP. 1995. *Business and its Environment*, 2nd edn, Prentice Hall: New York, pp. 177–90 and 199–217.

Baron, DP. 1999. Integrated market and non-market strategies in client and interest group politics. *Business and Politics*, 1(1): 7–34.

Best, J. 2001. *Damned Lies and Statistics: Untangling Numbers from the Media, Politicians, and Activists.* University of California Press: Berkeley, CA.

Buchholz, R. 1992. *Public Policy Issues for Management.* Prentice Hall: Englewood Cliffs, NJ.

Burke, E. 1998. *The Principle of the Neighbor of Choice.* Praeger Publishing: Westport, CT.

Carroll, A. 2005. Stakeholder management: background and advances. In P Harris and CS Fleisher (eds), *Handbook of Public Affairs*, Sage: London, pp. 501–16.

Carson, R. 1962. *Silent Spring.* Boston, Mass: Houghton Mifflin.

Davidson, S. 2015. Everywhere and nowhere: theorizing and researching public affairs and lobbying within public relations scholarship. *Public Relations Review*, 41(5): 615–627.

DiStaso, MW, McCorkindale, T, and Wright, DK. 2011. How public relations executives perceive and measure the impact of social media in their organizations. *Public Relations Review*, 37(3): 325–8.

EMRC. 2011. *Digital Media and Capitol Hill.* Emerging Media Research Council: Raleigh, NC.

Fleisher, CS. 1997. *Assessing, Managing, and Maximizing Public Affairs Performance: With Reports, Techniques, and Case Histories from Nearly Two Dozen Leading Organizations and Professionals Around the Globe.* Public Affairs Council: Washington, DC.

Fleisher, CS. 1998. 'Are corporate public affairs practitioners professionals? A multi-region comparison with corporate public relations', paper presented at the Fifth Annual Bled Symposium on International Public Relations Research, Bled.

Fleisher, CS. 2001. Emerging US public affairs practice: the 2000+ PA model. *Journal of Public Affairs*, 1(1): 44–52.

Fleisher, CS. 2003. The development of competencies in international public affairs. *Journal of Public Affairs*, 3(1): 76–82.

Fleisher, CS. 2005. The global development of public affairs. In P Harris and CS Fleisher (eds.), *Handbook of Public Affairs*, Sage: London, pp. 5–30.

Fleisher, CS. 2010/11. Five decades on the periphery: examining international public affairs through strategic lenses. *International Studies of Management and Organization*, Winter, 40(4): 82–94.

Fleisher, CS. 2012. Anniversary retrospective, perspective and prospective of corporate public affairs: moving from the 2000+ PA Model toward Public Affairs 2.0. *Journal of Public Affairs*, 12(1): 4–11.

Foundation for Public Affairs. 2005. *The State of Corporate Public Affairs.* Public Affairs Council: Washington, DC.

Foundation for Public Affairs. 1999. *1999–2000 State of Corporate Public Affairs.* Public Affairs Council: Washington, DC.

Freeman, RE. 1984. *Strategic Management: A Stakeholder Approach.* Pitman: Boston, MA.

Freeman, RE. 2000. The link between stakeholders and business ethics. *Corporate Public Affairs*, 10(1): 15–16.

Getz, K. 2001. Public affairs and political strategy: theoretical dimensions. *Journal of Public Affairs*, 1(4): 305–29.

Grefe, E and Linsky, M. 1996. *The New Corporate Activism*. McGraw Hill: New York.

Griffin, JJ and Dunn, P. 2004. Corporate public affairs: commitment, resources, and structure. *Business and Society*, 43(2): 196–220.

Griffin, JJ and Prakash, A. 2014. Corporate responsibility initiatives and mechanisms. *Business and Society*, 53(4): 465–82.

Gupta, S. 2011. Enhancing the role of corporate communications: a practice-based approach. *Corporate Reputation Review*, 14(2): 114–32.

Harris, P and Fleisher, CS. 2005. Introduction: the development of a sub-discipline and major area of research. In P Harris and CS Fleisher (eds), *Handbook of Public Affairs*, Sage: London, pp. xxxi–xxxvi.

Harsanyi, FM. 2010. Public affairs: a leadership competence for the twenty-first century. *Corporate Public Affairs*, 20(2): 10–14.

Harsanyi, FM and Schmidt, S. 2012. Creating a public affairs function in countries without a public affairs culture. *Journal of Public Affairs*, 12(1), pp. 86–97.

Heath, RL and Palenchar, M. 2009. *Strategic Issues Management: Organizations and Public Policy Challenges*, 2nd edn. Sage: Thousand Oaks, CA, pp. 20–2.

Holcomb, JM. 2005a. Public affairs, corporate scandals, and regulation: policy actors and actions. In P Harris and CS Fleisher (eds), *Handbook of Public Affairs*, Sage: London, pp. 537–60.

Holcomb, JM. 2005b. Public affairs in North America: US origins and development. In P Harris and CS Fleisher (eds), *Handbook of Public Affairs*, Sage: London, pp. 31–49.

International Conference on Public Affairs. 1971. *Public Affairs in the US and Europe*. Conference Board: New York.

Judd, E. 2008. *Good Guanxi: Managing Government Relations in China*. The Foundation for Public Affairs: Washington, DC.

Judd, E. 2009. *The Jugaad Principle: Managing Government Relations in India*. The Foundation for Public Affairs: Washington, DC.

Judd, E. 2010. *Opening Doors in Brussels: Managing Government Relations in the EU*. The Foundation for Public Affairs: Washington, DC.

Kanol, D. 2015. Comparative lobbying research: advances, shortcomings and recommendations, *Journal of Public Affairs*, 15(1): 110–15.

Keim, G. 2005. Managing business political advocacy in the United States: opportunities for improved effectiveness. In P Harris and CS Fleisher (eds), *Handbook of Public Affairs*, Sage: London, pp. 418–33.

Lusterman, S. 1985. *Managing International Public Affairs*. The Conference Board: New York.

Mack, C. 1997. *Business, Politics and the Practice of Government Relations*. Quorum Books: Westport, CT.

Mahon, JF. 1982. *The corporate public affairs office: structure, behavior, and impact* Doctoral dissertation. Boston University School of Management: Boston, MA.

Mahon, J and Wartick, SL. 2012. Corporate social performance profiling: using multiple stakeholder perceptions to assess a corporate reputation. *Journal of Public Affairs*, 12(1): 12–28.

McGrath C, Moss D, and Harris, P. November 2010. The evolving discipline of public affairs. *Journal of Public Affairs*, 10(4): 335–52.

Men, LR and Hung, CJF. 2012. Exploring the roles of organization–public relationships in the strategic management process: towards an integrated framework. *International Journal of Strategic Communication*, 6(2): 151–73.

Meznar, MB and Nigh, D. 1995. Buffer or bridge? Environmental and organizational determinants of public affairs activities in American firms. *Academy of Management Journal*, 38(4): 975–96.

Millar, C, Gitsham, M, and Mahon, J. 2012. The sustainability challenge: can public affairs influence the necessary change? *Journal of Public Affairs*, 12(3): 171–6.

Moss, D, McGrath, C, Tonge, J, and Harris, P. 2012. Exploring the management of the corporate public affairs function in a dynamic global environment. *Journal of Public Affairs*, 12(1): 47–60.

Oliver, C and Holzinger, I. 2008. The effectiveness of strategic political management: a dynamic capabilities framework. *Academy of Management Review*, 33(2): 496–520.

Pedler, R. 2005. The history and development of public affairs in the European Union and the United Kingdom. In P Harris and CS Fleisher (eds), *Handbook of Public Affairs*, Sage: London, pp. 50–5.

Pinkham, D. 1995. Foreword. In P Harris and CS Fleisher (eds), *Handbook of Public Affairs*, Sage: London, pp. xxiv–xxv.

Pinkham, D. 2013. 'Why Can't DHS Better Communicate with the American People?' Written Testimony of Douglas G. Pinkham, President, Public Affairs Council before the United States House of Representatives Committee on Homeland Security Subcommittee on Oversight and Management Efficiency Hearing. Available online at: http://docs.house.gov/meetings/HM/HM09/20130614/100875/HHRG-113-HM09-Wstate-PinkhamD-20130614.pdf [accessed May 21, 2016].

Post, JE, Dickie, RB, Murray Jr, EA, and Mahon, JF. 1982. The public affairs function in American corporations: development and relations with corporate planning. *Long Range Planning*, 15(2): 12–21.

The Research Pacific Group/PublicAffairsAsia. 2011. *The 2011 State of the Industry (In House) Report*. The Research Pacific Group/PublicAffairsAsia.

Roberts, PW and Dowling, GR. 2002. Corporate reputation and sustained superior financial performance. *Strategic Management Journal*, 23(12): 1077–93.

Showalter, A. 2011. *The Underdog Edge: How Ordinary People Change the Minds of the Powerful and Live to Tell About It*. New York: Morgan James Publishing.

Showalter, A and Fleisher, CS. 2005. The tools and techniques of public affairs. In P Harris and CS Fleisher (eds), *Handbook of Public Affairs*, Sage: London, pp. 109–22.

Sourcewatch. 2015. Astroturf, Available online at: http://www.sourcewatch.org/index.php?title=Astroturf [accessed June 30, 2015].

The Centre for Corporate Public Affairs. 2010. Surviving the storm: the state of Australian public affairs. *Corporate Public Affairs*, 20(2): 1–9.

Transparency Index. 2014. Available online at: https://www.transparency.org/cpi2014/results [accessed Jun 23, 2015].

Van Dijk, JAGM. 2012. Digital democracy: vision and reality. *Innovation and the Public Sector*, 19: 49–62.

Walker, ET. 2014. *Grassroots for hire: public affairs consultants in American democracy*. Cambridge University Press: Cambridge, UK.

Wiedmann, K-P. 2006. Corporate social responsibility, stakeholder alignment and corporate success: research questions, basic framework, and empirical evidence. Paper presented at the 10th Reputation Institute Conference on Reputation, Image, Identity, and Competitiveness, New York, NY, May 25–28.

Wikipedia. 2015. Nationalization. Available online at: https://en.wikipedia.org/wiki/Nationalization [accessed June 25, 2015].

Theoretical Lenses and Conceptual Models for Understanding Public Affairs

Duane Windsor

INTRODUCTION

This chapter identifies and explicates theoretical lenses and conceptual models for understanding public affairs as an organizational function and associated set of activities. Lenses and models assist with systematized thinking and research about the public affairs function. Public affairs essentially concern management communication with and mobilization of organizational stakeholders, with particular emphasis on influencing public policy affecting the organization and its stakeholders. The function lies at the interface of public relations and external political strategy of an organization.

A theoretical lens is a relatively broad perspective or viewpoint, typically grounded in one or possibly more disciplines, such as economics or communications, for interpreting empirical phenomena and suggesting policy recommendations for adoption and implementation. A conceptual model is an abstract and general explanation of something – whether an intellectual construct or a phenomenon – designed to assist with knowledge or understanding. A theoretical lens is broader and focuses one's attention on a phenomenon in a particular way. A conceptual model is narrower and expresses how one thinks something works or will work, drawing on one or more theoretical lenses. Both lenses and models embed some set of basic assumptions. A conceptual model typically comprises in addition a set of concepts (or ideas) which can be described by propositions, and a set of relationships among the concepts. A conceptual model is not a physical working model like a prototype or an executable software program but rather an intellectual formulation. These basic definitions will be developed in the section entitled 'Theoretical Lenses and Conceptual Models'.

The opportunity and need for the public affairs function exists in all organizations across business, governmental, and voluntary sectors. This expression is abstract and general; purpose, structure, and activity vary empirically and such variations should inform conceptual models. The emphasis in this chapter is on corporate public affairs in privately owned or publicly traded profit-seeking business organizations operating in markets, but the same function occurs in social enterprises whether operated as business or as nonprofit organizations (NPOs) (Young, 2000). Corporate public affairs constitute a subset of organizational public affairs. Much of the same information is applicable to governmental or NPO public affairs. Nongovernmental organizations (NGOs) seek to influence businesses as well as governments. Public affairs for governmental entities involve specialized issues, such that the public sector must be treated differently in various important respects.

The chapter is organized following this introduction into four major sections. The next section explains the theoretical and conceptual situation concerning public affairs. The third section addresses the rich theoretical roots of public affairs and associated literature. The fourth section identifies and discusses specific theoretical lenses and conceptual models. The final section considers the less developed normative dimension of public affairs and ends with a discussion of the future of public affairs theorizing and conceptualization. A necessary but not sufficient assumption for public affairs is that the activities involved are legal and honest – an assumption revisited in this final section.

THEORETICAL AND CONCEPTUAL SITUATION CONCERNING PUBLIC AFFAIRS

This section lays out basic assumptions and logical definitions for discussing public affairs theoretically and conceptually. Theories bearing on public affairs come from a number of disciplines. Two key conceptual

models, discussed in the fourth section, concern how public policy processes work and how effective organizational communications work.

According to stakeholder theory, an increasingly important theoretical lens in public affairs, one can divide an organization into internal stakeholders and external stakeholders. A stakeholder is an individual or set of individuals affected by or affecting the focal organization. Some stakeholders are primary, some stakeholders are secondary. Accordingly, there are internal relations and external relations. Internal relations – especially with employees – tend to fall under management directly rather than under public (meaning external) relations. But sometimes the channel for influencing external relations is through employees or other internal stakeholders. A political action committee (PAC) solicits funds from management.

While sometimes overlapping with internal relations, public affairs are principally a subset of external relations or external affairs (Boddewyn, 1974). External relations are sufficiently important to support a serious proposal that organizations consider appointing a chief external officer (Doh et al., 2014). Because public affairs are broader than just public relations while embedding aspects of the organization's political strategy (Windsor, 2002), authors today sometimes use the broad term public affairs and lobbying (Davidson, 2015; Somerville, 2012). Grunig (Grunig et al., 1992: 4) defines 'public relations as "the management of communication between an organization and its [internal and external] publics"' (citing Grunig and Hart, 1984: 6). An interesting issue then is whether public affairs is a topic within public relations (see Davidson, 2015) or particularly in combination with lobbying cuts across multiple disciplines.

Paraphrasing Windsor (2005), the public affairs function operates at the interface among community relations, corporate communications and public relations, corporate philanthropy, image and reputation management, issues management, legal affairs, media relations, political influence efforts and business–government relations, and stakeholder management activities. So regarded, the public affairs function is broad in scope (see den Hond et al., 2014). Following Harris and Moss (2001: 110), the definition of public affairs is the organizational function that manages relationships with organizational stakeholders, and especially those relationships that may have implications for public policy affecting the organization. Marketing communications and public relations tools are part of this relationship management (Harris and Moss, 2001: 110). A function is not necessarily a particular structure for managing such relationships. Accepting that modern public affairs historically grew out of community relations and political lobbying, the general tendency, in practice and scholarship, has been to regard public affairs activities as narrowly concerned with communities, issues, politics and external stakeholders (Harris and Moss, 2001). Corporate philanthropy, legal affairs, and media relations have tended to be independent concerns. This tendency, beginning to be reversed in global practice, ignores the integrative effects of these activities in combination (Harris and Moss, 2001) in strategically responding to and shaping the firm's nonmarket environment and the firm's and industry's social legitimacy (Zavattaro, 2014).

Public affairs is a broad function that, regardless of how it is organized within a specific business, encompasses how a business engages with its multiple and diverse stakeholders for purposes of explaining business policies and views on public policy issues. The role of public affairs is driven by the external environment of business, which will continue to become more global and at all levels of government more politicized and with more stakeholders more effectively mobilized. The scope of issues is thus steadily expanding in both market and nonmarket environments. Public affairs activity is most diverse for multinational enterprises

operating across multiple national jurisdictions. The purpose for a business is to establish a positive reputation and image among and positive relationships with stakeholders. The public affairs function encompasses corporate social responsibility (CSR), issue management, government relations including lobbying and campaign support, grassroots mobilization, media communications, and stakeholder communications. There is a wide array of relevant stakeholders such as business and trade associations, customers and clients, elected and appointed government officials, employees, local communities, media, nongovernmental organizations (NGOs), philanthropic (charitable) organizations, research organizations, shareholders, unions, and voters. This emphasis would tend to exclude business relationships such as competitors, distributors, franchisees, partners, and suppliers. Public diplomacy, defined as transmission of information and views to influence foreign policy of countries, is also an element. 'Social license to operate' is a rising public affairs concern (Ihlen and van Ruler, 2007), as is environmental sustainability. One can include governments (elected politicians and appointed civil servants) within the scope of external stakeholders, but governmental affairs is focused on lobbying and is thus quite different from communicating with nongovernmental external stakeholders.

Employees are internal stakeholders of an organization and for a business organization investors might be regarded similarly. Within an organization, governmental affairs, human resource management, investor relations, and labor relations may or may not be bundled with public affairs. Functionally, there may be overlaps of these functions with public affairs. For instance, a public affairs unit may undertake grassroots mobilization of employees for purposes of influencing public policy (Lord, 2003; Walker, 2014). In this instance, employee communication falls under the public affairs function, just as would grassroots mobilization of customers. Rolling out a new benefits program for employees falls under the human resource management function.

A working assumption of this chapter is that public affairs and governmental affairs functionally work in tandem to influence public policy – whatever management structure is adopted within an organization. One can think in terms of influencing governments and influencing nongovernmental stakeholders who in turn may influence governments. Public affairs and governmental affairs are important dimensions of organizational strategy (Windsor, 2002). One unifying dimension is successful strategic issue management (Mahon and Waddock, 1992), which can be more broadly about social issues and more narrowly about public policy issues, and its relationship to reputation management (Scott and Walsham, 2005). Another unifying dimension is successful stakeholder management. One empirical study concluded that primary stakeholder management has a positive effect on shareholder value, while social issue management has a negative effect on shareholder value (Hillman and Keim, 2001).

Davidson (2015), viewing public affairs as a subset of public relations, conducted a content analysis of a selected set of academic journals during the period 2000 to 2013 for the purpose of assessing how scholars have theorized and conducted research. The keywords for searching were 'public affairs' and 'lobbying'. The set of journals in the order reported by Davidson (2015: 620) comprised *Public Relations Review, Journal of Communication Management, Public Relations Inquiry, PRism, Public Relations Quarterly, Public Relations Journal, Journal of Public Relations Research*, and *Journal of Public Affairs*. The study located 104 articles, about 69 percent of which were in *Journal of Public Affairs* (Davidson, 2015: 620). Davidson is particularly interested in whether, and if so to what degree, concerns about support of corporate power and the resulting impact on legitimacy of democratic institutions have been addressed. Davidson finds that there is a low level of research into public affairs, with most of that published research coming from US and European institutions. The most widely reported perspectives are stakeholder theory and rhetorical (or discourse) theory. Davidson asserts that scholarship emphasizes functional objectives of organizations rather than civic concerns with corporate power and institutional legitimacy. Somerville (2012) points to the importance of interest group theory, discourse theory, and framing and storytelling theory. Framing and storytelling concern how something is presented to an audience.

THEORETICAL ROOTS OF PUBLIC AFFAIRS LENSES AND MODELS

Windsor (2005) in the first edition of this handbook addressed 'theories' and theoretical roots of public affairs. The emphasis was on the corporate public affairs function, whereas the present chapter expands the scope to organizational public affairs in nongovernmental sectors. The present chapter does not extensively repeat the 2005 references, which can be located in the earlier book and which are partly dated after more than a decade of scholarship and consulting. The present chapter draws on the theories and theoretical roots from the 2005 book. However, the general approach of the 2005 chapter remains broadly accurate in this author's judgment: public affairs constitute a broad and dynamically changing assignment at the interface between an organization and its external nonmarket environment. While a vital organizational function, the public affairs dimension remains in search of identity, theory and conceptualization, effective structure, best practices, and social legitimacy. The present chapter focuses on theory and conceptualization.

One can identify a relatively large number of theoretical lenses. Farmer (2010) makes the case for 'epistemic pluralism' using multiple lenses, and lists for public administration the following lenses: traditional, business, economic, political, critical, poststructural or postmodern, psychoanalytic, neuroscience, feminist, ethical, and data. One picks the lens or set of lenses judged most appropriate to the topic.

Theoretical lenses and conceptual models are typically grounded in one or more disciplines. There is no 'grand' theory of public affairs – no integrative or overarching framework. Theoretical roots lie in several disciplines, at the interface of which public affairs research lies. Key disciplines for public affairs include communications and public relations, economics, organizational sociology, political science, and strategic management. The normative dimension adds the disciplines of businesses in societies, business ethics and corporate social responsibility, and ecological (or sustainability) systems. In the absence of an overarching framework, limited theories and models deal, in relative isolation and drawing on different theoretical roots, with piecemeal aspects of public affairs.

A discipline is a body of scholarship with defined focus, scope, and boundary. Typically there are well established journals for publishing research. The seven key disciplines, listed here alphabetically, are businesses in society and business ethics, communications and public relations, ecological systems, economics, organizational sociology, political science, and strategic management. These seven disciplines are explained in greater detail in Windsor (2005), who drew on the pioneering taxonomic treatment by Getz (2002). One can argue over definition and boundary of a discipline, but the point is that theorizing and conceptualization of public affairs and lobbying will tend to draw on one or more of these bodies of scholarship. The following describes the relevance of economics, organizational sociology, political science, and strategic management in that sequence. Since communications and public relations are broad disciplines, partly grounded in psychology and marketing, the description is handled in the fourth

section through focus on a conceptual model of communications. The description of the businesses in society discipline, the business ethics discipline, and the ecological systems discipline is handled in the final section on normative considerations and the future of public affairs scholarship.

Economics is the science of rational (i.e., utility-maximizing) allocation of scarce (i.e., limited) resources (Lawniczak, 2009). The mainstream of economic research concerns market behavior: the demand and supply activities of buyers and sellers. The firm on the supply side of a market sells to some customer in order to maximize its economic wealth. While at the microeconomic level the science focuses on behavior of economic actors, at the macroeconomic level the science is concerned with aggregate outcomes including social welfare outcomes. Four economic approaches bear on public affairs and lobbying: collective action theory, public choice theory, transaction cost theory, and game theory.

Collective action theory concerns the costs to individuals of coming together for joint action, typically through pressure groups and coalitions of firms. Individuals, or firms, might lead, follow, or 'free ride' on the actions of others. 'Rational ignorance' is a condition in which an individual is sufficiently satisfied with outcomes to avoid paying to acquire costly information or to vote. Public choice theory applies a demand-and-supply or market perspective to group decisions. An organization may operate in at least three identifiable 'marketplaces' for market goods and services, public policies (including governmental goods and services), and public opinion (i.e., image, reputation, and perceived legitimacy). Transaction cost theory works from the insight that any transaction between two or more parties will involve some economic cost. These transaction costs influence governance arrangements, private party bargaining solutions, and public policy choices. Transaction cost in combination with information asymmetry underlies institutional economics (Hwang, 2015). Game theory is formal mathematical or informal logical modeling of interactions among interdependent actors, such as the competitors in an oligopolistic industry or the participants in a multistakeholder collaboration or dialogue. By definition, a 'game' comprises two or more players (who can compete and/or cooperate), stakes or outcomes, and a set of (disputable) rules for defining winner and loser. Friedrich's (1963) 'rule of anticipated reactions' for political strategy instructs players to consider likely countermoves. Game-theoretic reasoning can apply to interactions between an organization and a regulator, bargaining between a multinational enterprise and a host country government, or lobbying interactions with legislators.

The term organizational sociology is used to define what is often labeled macro-organizational theory, in distinction to micro-organizational behavior. Macro theory draws on sociology; micro theory draws on psychology. Macro theory is grounded in sociological analysis of groups and organizations. The public affairs function is an organizational buffer against, or bridge with, the external environment. Research suggests that buffering and bridging depend on a degree of environmental uncertainty in relationship to organizational power to resist or offset external pressures, such as environmental activism. Organizational sociology provides two abstract perspectives concerning relationship of organization and external environment: resource dependence theory and institutional theory.

Resource dependence theory views the organization as dependent on and extracting resources from an uncertain and changing environment. The firm seeks to reduce such external dependency. One approach is to reduce uncertainty through information gathering. Another approach is manipulation of the environment through influencing public opinion. Which approach is more beneficial and/or more costly may be contingent on situational conditions.

Institutional theory interprets the environment as a concrete system of formal or informal rules, requirements, and institutions for which the firm can develop internal political capital. Outsourcing political capital – to external consultants or lobbyists, for instance – increases external dependence, bringing institutional theory into an interface with resource dependence theory.

Political science is the study of governments and political behavior. The discipline thus includes both institutional and psychological behavioral perspectives. Two dimensions of political science are particularly pertinent to the study of public affairs. One dimension addresses the demand side of public policy in studying how pressure group politics influences governmental policy outputs directly through 'public politics' directed at government and indirectly through 'private politics' directed at businesses in particular (Baron, 2009; Hillman and Hitt, 1999). The other dimension addresses the supply side of public policy in studying how legislative, regulatory or administrative, and judicial institutions and processes function.

The dominant model of the demand side of US democratic politics remains an interest group theory in which organized, mobilized interests compete for public policy outputs. By definition, an interest group is a latent pressure group; a pressure group is mobilized and active. Pluralism and collective action theory in combination shape the demand side of public affairs literature. Mobilization of interests and intensity of commitment to action may (or may not) influence government policy outputs. The supply side of US democratic politics emphasizes an expected bias toward status quo policies of governmental institutions. This bias implies that status quo policy is costly to change. Legislators seek re-election; bureaucrats seek expansion of resources.

Cutting across economics, organizational sociology, and political science is what has been labeled political economy. This approach examines how variations in political institutions, structures and cultures affect public affairs activities and outcomes (Somerville, 2012).

Key aspects of strategic management theory relevant to public affairs are agency theory, the behavioral theory of the firm, integrated strategic management theory, and population ecology theory. Agency theory is a game-theoretic model of the contracting and monitoring relationships between a wealth-seeking principal and an agent possessing asymmetric information about effort and talent. The model can be applied to businesses (investor versus employee) or governments (citizen versus legislator or bureaucrat). Agency theory tends to predict empire building or underperformance depending on conditions. The behavioral theory of the firm addresses the internal dynamics of political coalitions within organizations. A key notion is slack (i.e., excess resources not fully deployed), permitting experimentation or buffering against external pressures. There remains considerable disagreement within strategic management scholarship concerning how to integrate external environment, internal capabilities or competencies, and internal resources into a fully integrated theory. Rehbein and Schuler (2015) apply a resource-based view (RBV) to the relationship between community programs and political strategy. Strategic management also has a now rich literature on integrating market and nonmarket dimensions of organizational strategy. At the interface between resource dependency theory and strategic management theory, population ecology theory views organizations as a natural population of entities competing for limited resources and space. A political ecology variant is relevant to public affairs.

THEORETICAL LENSES AND CONCEPTUAL MODELS

Generally, a theoretical lens is broader in scope and a conceptual model is narrower in scope. A theoretical lens functions more like an interpretive heuristic; a conceptual model functions more like a computational algorithm.

One illustration of combining theoretical lenses involves an approach to describing relationships among the environmental strategy, financial performance, and environmental performance of a business (Clemens and Bakstran, 2010). The authors take two theoretical lenses and two strategic purposes widely used in the strategy literature, and reasonably relevant to the problem. Relevance is both a matter of the authors' view and subject to being reasonably persuasive to readers. The two theoretical lenses are strategic choice and the resource-based view. The two strategic purposes are the stakeholder interest and the shareholder interest. These two purposes might be in conflict or might be complementary, depending on conditions, choices, and resources. The authors can construct different models of the relationship of environmental strategy to financial performance and environmental performance. A shareholder-oriented purpose may yield a different arrangement than a stakeholder-oriented purpose, and such arrangement will interact with the theoretical lens (strategic choice versus resource-based view).

Theoretical Lenses

A theoretical lens is a way of looking at an empirical phenomenon from the perspective or viewpoint of a theoretical framework. A theoretical framework invokes a set of basic assumptions about reality, typically drawing on a discipline in doing so. These assumptions guide scholarly inquiry and interpretation. The assumptions direct attention to specific information and provide ways for interpreting the information. There are no standardized criteria for selecting a theoretical framework to use, or virtually any topic can be looked at in a number of ways. For public affairs, economic, organizational, political, and strategic perspectives seem reasonably applicable. Multiple perspectives may be a partial safeguard against biased interpretation. Some research progress may be achieved by considering how to integrate two or more such perspectives (Okhuysen and Bonardi, 2011). For interpreting strategic change, Rajagopalan and Spreitzer (1997) generated an integrative framework building on the theoretical synergies of rational, learning, and cognitive lenses.

Conceptual Models

A conceptual model is a mental rather than physical model of something – whether an intellectual construct or a phenomenon – designed to assist with knowledge or understanding (Embley and Thalheim, 2014; Gentner and Stevens, 2014). Like a theoretical lens, a conceptual model invokes some set of basic assumptions about reality. Generally, a conceptual model is more specific and draws on one or more theoretical lenses. For instance, Mahon and Waddock (1992) used public policy, corporate strategy, process models, and multiple perspectives to understand the evolution of issues management. Two examples of conceptual models are the Black–Scholes option pricing approach and a three-model analysis of the Cuban Missile Crisis of October 1962.

The Black–Scholes option pricing model, or the option pricing formula or derivatives pricing theory, involves a number of basic assumptions about pricing scenarios. The model is a formula widely used on Wall Street and by option traders to determine a fair price (i.e., mutually agreeable to demand and supply sides) for a call or put option based on a limited number of factors such as stock volatility and days to expiration (Black and Scholes, 1973).

An analysis of the Cuban Missile Crisis of October 1962 comprises three conceptual models for interpreting events (Allison, 1969; Allison and Zelikow, 1999). The approach is not to assert an empirical conclusion, as such. Rather each conceptual

model takes a different theoretical perspective on the events, adding in sequence additional richness to understanding. In the first conceptual model, the analysis assumes that the government acts as a unitary rational actor in making decisions. Basically, either the president finalizes the decision or the decision-making group unanimously reaches the same decision. The theoretical perspective upon which the model draws is rational decision making in which the metaphor is a chess game played against an opponent. The president has advisors, but makes the moves (and there are limited rules, resources, and options). In the second conceptual model, the analysis assumes that the government is divided into sub-units which act in accordance with predetermined standard operating procedures (SOPs). Asked for options, the air force will recommend bombing (by the air force); the navy will recommend blockade (by the navy); and the army will recommend invasion (by the army, and no need for the marine corps). The theoretical perspective upon which the model draws is organization theory in which the metaphor is that the president is like a quarterback of a team that has predesigned plays as options. In the third conceptual model, the analysis assumes that the sub-units engage in political bargaining or negotiation, based upon preprogrammed and thus entirely predictable views: the state department prefers diplomacy; the military services prefer military action. The theoretical perspective upon which the model draws is intra-organizational politics.

As illustrated by the two examples, a conceptual model follows a process of abstracting general elements from a study of the real world, physical in the case of ecological or sustainability systems and social in the case of public affairs more generally. Conceptual modeling is intended to provide a meaningful understanding of something real (or imagined).

Two conceptual models are particularly important for public affairs and lobbying. One model is for prediction of outcomes of the public policy process (Sabatier, 2007). The other model is for effective communication with stakeholders. Public policy outcomes reflect some interaction among politics, interest group pressure, and public affairs activity (Somerville, 2012).

Figure 2.1 depicts a very general and abstract conceptual model of exercising political influence on a public policy process. The model differentiates among a demand side and a supply side, linked together by influence channels. The basic model is illustrative rather than detailed. A political influence – whether individual, group, or organization – attempts to obtain desired outputs (i.e., increased benefits or reduced costs) from the public policy process. Legal influence channels include legal campaign funding and advertising, provision of information to government, grassroots mobilization, and pressure in various forms for policy outputs. There are in reality also corrupt channels for illegal money and pressure – shown in italics for distinction. The field of public affairs necessarily and properly excludes illegal and immoral actions. Nevertheless, Figure 2.1 would be logically incomplete if not recognizing corruption.

Since the early 1960s, the American National Election Studies (ANES) has estimated general interest in politics by the proxy of asking respondents how often they follow public affairs (Robison, 2015). Robison reports a number of defects in this approach. There are also other surveys since the mid-1980s (Robison, 2015). The Internet may be altering the diversity of public affairs issues considered by individuals, based on an analysis of the 2004 and 2008 ANES data sets (Lee et al., 2014a). The increase in agenda diversity in 2008 relative to 2004 occurred even after controlling for socio-economic status, political interest, and traditional media use. However, campaign exposure played a mediating role such that the effects of Internet use disappeared.

Public affairs mean influencing stakeholders through performance activities and outcomes and through communications efforts of various types including propaganda. There is an enormous literature in communications and public relations that cannot be referenced here. There is a substantial overlap of public affairs and public relations in which communications strategies and tactics play a vital role. Public opinion toward business in general and toward a particular industry or firm is a latent reservoir of support or opposition.

An important conceptualization anchors on the four models of public relations developed by Grunig and Hunt (1984). The first model is that of press agent engaged in potentially cynical publicity which is favorable to the organization. The model features one-way communication from organization to target external public(s). This communication is pure propaganda, and the meaningless information used in the propaganda can be inaccurate in various dimensions. Propaganda works on the recipient's emotions. Propaganda typically involves little research beyond the selection of media to be used. The second model is that of public information. The model still features one-way communication from organization to target external public(s). However, the emphasis

Figure 2.1 A basic conceptual model of political influence on public policy process

Demand Side	Legal Influence Channels	Supply Side	
Political Influencer	Legal Campaign Funding and Advertising Information to Government Grassroots Mobilization Pressure for Policy Output *Illegal Money and Pressure* *(Corruption) Disallowed*	Public Policy Process	Public Policy Outputs

shifts to organizational image maintenance and enhancement through meaningful information. Even so, the information and media are selected in order to appeal to the recipient's emotions. Research expands slightly to address readership and readability, in particular. The third model is that of two-way asymmetric public relations. The model shifts to two-way communication with feedback from recipients. The goal is to maximize the impact of messages on recipients, to the benefit of the sending organization only. Another way of expressing this goal is to say that it operates to manage stakeholder expectations (Olkkonen and Luoma-aho, 2014). The model emphasizes scientific manipulation or persuasion of recipients. Research expands further to address refinement and strengthening of impact. The fourth model is that of two-way symmetric public relations. Two-way communication aims at reaching mutual understanding with the target external public(s). The purpose is to strengthen recipient support of the organization, but there is an increased emphasis on meaningful feedback from recipients. The authors argue that two-way communication is the best approach for social responsibility of the organization. The fourth model underlies the 'Excellence Theory' of public relations (Grunig et al., 1992, 2002; Tyma, 2008). This argument has been criticized as idealistic (see Jackowski, 2007). Crisis communication arguably should be viewed as involving special conditions (Fussell Sisco et al., 2010).

Figure 2.2 depicts a very general and abstract model of communication to stakeholders. This model is an adaptation of Grunig and Hunt (1984), who differentiate among four communication models: one-way propaganda, one-way information, two-way asymmetric feedback manipulated by the communicating organization and not the target, and two-way symmetric discourse between communicator and target. At the right side of the model, a target audience selects actions and provides feedback to the communicator. There may be two or multiple target audiences in a particular instance. In practice, this approach is highly situational with respect to defining and targeting publics (Grunig, 1997). A vital research problem concerns whether there is an integrated communications model and strategy for organizations (Niemann-Struweg, 2014), including social media (Kietzmann et al., 2012) and big data (Neuman et al., 2014), which are of growing importance.

The Grunig and Hunt models involve tacitly a distinction between one-way propaganda and two-way discourse (Weaver et al., 2006). There is a tacit assumption in stakeholder literature that effective dialogue is desirable for successful organization–stakeholder relationships (Lehtimaki and Kujala, forthcoming). A recent study (one of a number by Finnish scholars) of the Fray Bentos pulp mill investment in western Uruguay, by the Finnish company Botnia, illustrates that such effective dialogue does not always occur (Lehtimaki and Kujala, forthcoming). Opponents of the project, including Argentina, ultimately could not halt the startup and operation. Botnia's communications efforts did not build consensus support

Figure 2.2   A basic model of communication to stakeholders, based on Grunig and Hunt (1984)

Communicator	Communication Models	Target Audience(s)

Communicating Organization	One-Way Propaganda
	One-Way Information
	Two-Way Asymmetric
	  Feedback from Target
	Two-Way Symmetric
	  Discourse with Target
		Target Actions and Feedback to
		Communicator

or shared meanings among all stakehold-ers. The study separates the history of the struggle into three time frames: investment, conflict, and political. The struggle simply expanded into a multi-party international dis-pute when Uruguay decided to proceed and Finland decided not to intervene.

Selection of communications strategy is important. Skard and Thorbjørnsen (2014) report that whether publicity (i.e., third-party communication to reduce consumer skepti-cism) or direct advertising concerning CSR initiatives is better strategy depends on repu-tation of the social sponsor. Publicity is supe-rior to advertising when the social sponsor has a positive reputation. However, advertis-ing is superior to publicity when the social sponsor has a poor reputation. How well brand and cause fit together is also a consid-eration for consumers.

THE NORMATIVE DIMENSION AND FUTURE OF PUBLIC AFFAIRS THEORIZING AND CONCEPTUALIZATION

Ethics and corporate social responsibility (CSR) are receiving increasing attention in public affairs, lobbying, and public relations literatures (see Bartlett, 2011; Powell, 2012; Warren, 2012). Some of this attention focuses on particular issues such as health (Lee et al., 2014b) or fair trade (Moxham and Kauppi, 2014). Much of public relations research is subject to the comment that it is managerial, instrumental, or psychological-behavior in orientation (Ihlen and van Ruler, 2007). A corporatist perspective (Somerville, 2012) suggests that management communication is afforded privilege and instrumental status in much of public affairs scholarship. Privilege and instrumentality have been criticized from a postmodernist discourse perspective (Pal and Dutta, 2008).

The combined discipline of businesses in societies and business ethics (partly overlapping and interpenetrating) addresses the nonmarket environment, emphasizing business responsibilities and impacts. It is the natural (but not exclusive) home base of much public affairs scholarship. Businesses in soci-eties, a label capturing the global character of business scientifically examines descrip-tive empirical and instrumental dimensions. Business ethics philosophically addresses the normative dimension. Three central research streams are important: prescriptive business ethics, corporate social responsibility and global corporate citizenship constructs; the corporate social performance (CSP) frame-work embedding triple bottom line (TBL) performance; and stakeholder management theory.

The mainstream conceptual model of corporate social responsibility was devel-oped by Carroll (1991). He depicted CSR as a pyramid with economic responsibili-ties (broadly goods and services, jobs, and profits) at the foundation. Legal and ethi-cal responsibilities are the next two levels in that order. Philanthropic responsibilities form the apex of the pyramid. Economic and legal responsibilities are mandatory, ethical behavior expected and tax-deductible phi-lanthropy desirable. Carroll is explicit that all four dimensions are infused with moral duty. This pyramid can be cross-walked to stakeholder categories. Carroll has demon-strated that the CSR model can be aligned with the more recent construct of corporate citizenship (Council on Foundations, 1996). Empirical studies by Carroll and colleagues suggest managers often think in this order. Subsequent work by Carroll focused on the economic, legal, and ethical spheres with the discretionary or philanthropic sphere removed as a different kind of considera-tion. Adam Smith (*The Theory of Moral Sentiments*, 1790 [1759], VI.ii.2) defined citizenship as legal obedience and good citi-zenship as effort to advance the welfare of the whole commonwealth.

Wood (1991) reformulated the corporate social performance (CSP) perspective into an outcomes-oriented framework or model. The model combines CSR motives (or principles corresponding to determinants empirically), socially responsive organizational processes, and social outcomes of corporate activities. This approach reformulation is tripartite: the three dimensions just listed are each subdivided into three elements or subdimensions. The three motives are social legitimacy, internal or organizational dynamics for 'public' responsibility, and individual morality. The three elements of organizational processes are environmental assessment, issues management, and stakeholder management. The three outcomes are social policies, social programs, and social impacts. The CSP model can be used for empirical investigation and be cross-walked to Carroll's responsibilities model and to the firm's stakeholder groups. The notion of multiple performance outcomes suggests triple bottom line (TBL) performance such as financial, social, and ecological performance. Jensen (2001) argues that managers can handle only one decision criterion (i.e., wealth): everything else must be a constraint on that objective and not a competing target.

Stakeholder theory is increasingly viewed as a necessary perspective for public affairs research. One recent study links stakeholder and institutional theories (Doh and Guay, 2006); another recent study links stakeholder and communications theories (Paul, 2015). A stakeholder is any individual or group or category of individuals who can affect or be affected by the focal firm and thus could have interest in collaboration with management. Examples include ecology activists, communities, customers, employees, investors, media, governments, and suppliers. Nature and stakeholders might be excluded from this definition.

If not a stakeholder logically, nature must be regarded as a crucial, perhaps the overriding, aspect of corporate social performance. Nature is the fundamental requirement for human life or high material quality of life. Ecological systems thinking and evidence is vital to an appreciation of corporate and

stakeholder impacts on natural ecological systems. Increasingly, organized activist pressure groups advocate stronger environmental improvements. The triple bottom line approach includes ecological impact as a performance dimension.

A basic assumption for public affairs theorizing is that the activities are legal and honest, or as an alternative expression not irresponsible (Windsor, 2013). There is some empirical evidence in support of a thesis that in developing countries where corruption is rampant and law enforcement weak, firms tend to rely on illegal bribery; in advanced countries where there is less corruption and law enforcement is stronger, firms tend to switch to legal lobbying (Bennedsen et al., 2011; Campos and Giovannoni, 2007; Harstad and Svensson, 2011). Kaufmann and Vicente (2011) draw an important distinction between legal corruption and illegal corruption. The assignment of methods of influencing government to either category may reflect citizen pressure (or its absence) rather than a normatively based prescription. The distinction is pertinent with respect to public affairs and lobbying, which in theory could aim at moving methods from illegal to legal status. The most effective control against corruption is transparency (Veksler, 2016).

The external environment of all organizations – and especially businesses, NGOs, and governments – will continue to become more global, more politicized, and more actively mobilized (Johnson et al., 2015; Lee and Kim, forthcoming; Windsor, 2007). These changes are likely to be highly contextualized (Millar and Köppl, 2014; Titley, 2003). Public affairs scholarship remains multidisciplinary rather than interdisciplinary, focused on improving the art of practice, largely descriptive and barely predictive, and highly instrumental without being as yet sufficiently strategic (Steyn and Niemann, 2014).

An essential consideration in moral judgment concerns whether the individual manager or other employee of an organization has the quality of moral imagination or moral recognition (Godwin, 2015; Mencl and May, 2016). Jurkiewicz and Giacalone (2016) conceptualize (i.e., model) an ethical organization in terms of three components: law-abiding, exercising strong ethical leadership in daily operations and policies, and conducting ongoing monitoring processes to ensure compliance. The authors describe specific techniques for compliance.

Davidson (2015) makes recommendations concerning future directions for research in public affairs. Since one finding is that research in the global south (i.e., outside the US and Europe) is invisible, an implicit recommendation is for desirable globalization of scholarship. A second recommendation is an advocacy for emphasizing discourse (i.e., two-way symmetric communication as defined by Grunig and Hunt, 1984) into the definition of public affairs. A third recommendation is that academic public relations should assume responsibility for the field and in a way that equitably balances organizational versus societal concerns.

REFERENCES

Allison, G. (1969) 'Conceptual models and the Cuban Missile Crisis', *American Political Science Review*, 63(3): 689–718.

Allison, G. and Zelikow, Philip D. (1999) *Essence of Decision: Explaining the Cuban Missile Crisis*. 2nd edn. New York: Longman.

Baron, D. P. (2009) 'A positive theory of moral management, social pressure, and corporate social performance', *Journal of Economics & Management Strategy*, 18(1): 7–43.

Bartlett, Jennifer L. (2011) 'Public relations and corporate social responsibility', in Øyvind Ihlen, Jennifer L. Bartlett, and Steve May (eds), *The Handbook of Communication and Corporate Social Responsibility*. Oxford, UK: Wiley-Blackwell, pp. 67–86.

Bennedsen, M., Feldmann, S. E., and Lassen, D. D. (2011, June 28) 'Lobbying and bribes – A survey-based analysis of the demand for influence and corruption', CESifo Working Paper Series No. 3496. http://ssrn.com/abstract=1873891

Black, F. and Scholes, M. (1973) 'The pricing of options and corporate liabilities', *Journal of Political Economy*, 81(3): 637–54.

Boddewyn, J. J. (1974) 'External affairs: A corporate function in search of conceptualization and theory', *Organization and Administration Sciences*, 5(1): 67–111.

Campos, N. F. and Giovannoni, F. (2007) 'Lobbying, corruption and political influence', *Public Choice*, 131(1): 1–12.

Carroll, A. B. (1991) 'The pyramid of corporate social responsibility: Toward the moral management of organizational stakeholders', *Business Horizons*, 34(4): 39–48.

Clemens, B. and Bakstran, L. (2010) 'A framework of theoretical lenses and strategic purposes to describe relationships among firm environmental strategy, financial performance, and environmental performance', *Management Research Review*, 33(4): 393–405.

Council on Foundations (1996) *Measuring the Value of Corporate Citizenship*. Washington, DC: Council on Foundations.

Davidson, S. (2015) 'Everywhere and nowhere: Theorising and researching public affairs and lobbying within public relations scholarship', *Public Relations Review*, 41(5): 615–27.

den Hond, F., Rehbein, K. A., de Bakker, F. G. A., and Kooijmans-van Lankveld, H. (2014) 'Playing on two chessboards: Reputation effects between corporate social responsibility (CSR) and corporate political activity (CPA)', *Journal of Management Studies*, 51(5): 790–831.

Doh, J. P. and Guay, T. R. (2006) 'Corporate social responsibility, public policy, and NGO activism in Europe and the United States: An institutional-stakeholder perspective', *Journal of Management Studies*, 43(1): 47–73.

Doh, J. P., Lawton, T. C., Rajwani, T., and Paroutis, S. (2014) 'Why your company may need a chief external officer: Upgrading external affairs can help align strategy and improve competitive advantage', *Organizational Dynamics*, 43(2): 96–104.

Embley, David W. and Thalheim, Bernhard (eds) (2014) *Handbook of Conceptual Modeling: Theory, Practice, and Research Challenges*. Heidelberg and New York: Springer.

Farmer, David J. (2010) *Public Administration in Perspective: Theory and Practice through Multiple Lenses*. Armonk, NY: M.E. Sharpe.

Friedrich, Carl J. (1963) 'Influence and the rule of anticipated reactions', in Friedrich, C. J., *Man and His Government: An Empirical Theory of Politics*. New York: McGraw-Hill, pp. 199–215.

Fussell Sisco, H., Collins, E., and Zoch, L. (2010) 'Through the looking glass: A decade of Red Cross crisis response and situational crisis communication theory', *Public Relations Review*, 36(1): 21–7.

Gentner, Dedre and Stevens, Albert L. (eds) (2014) *Mental Models*. New York: Psychology Press (Hillsdale, NJ: Lawrence Erlbaum Associates, 1983).

Getz, K. A. (2002) 'Public affairs and political strategy: Theoretical foundations', *Journal of Public Affairs*, 1(4)–2(1): 305–29.

Godwin, L. N. (2015) 'Examining the impact of moral imagination on organizational decision making', *Business & Society*, 54(2): 254–78.

Grunig, J. E. (1997) 'A situational theory of publics: Conceptual history, recent challenges and new research', in Danny Moss, Toby MacManus, and Dejan Verčič (eds), *Public Relations Research: An International Perspective*. London and Boston: International Thomson Business Press, pp. 3–48.

Grunig, James E. et al. (eds) (1992) *Excellence in Public Relations and Communication Management*. Hillsdale, NJ: Lawrence Erlbaum Associates.

Grunig, James E. and Hunt, Todd T. (1984) *Managing Public Relations*. New York: Holt, Rinehart, and Winston.

Grunig, Larissa A., Grunig, James E., and Dozier, David M. (2002) *Excellent Public Relations and Effective Organizations: A Study of Communication Management in Three Countries*. Mahwah, NJ: Lawrence Erlbaum Associates.

Harris, P. and Moss, D. (2001) 'Editorial. In search of public affairs: A function in search of an identity', *Journal of Public Affairs*, 1(2): 102–10.

Harstad, B. and Svensson, J. (2011) 'Bribes, lobbying and development', *American Political Science Review*, 105(1): 46–63.

Hillman, A. J. and Hitt, M. A. (1999) 'Corporate political strategy formulation: A model of approach, participation, and strategy decisions', *Academy of Management Review*, 24(3): 825–42.

Hillman, A. J. and Keim, G. D. (2001) 'Shareholder value, stakeholder management, and social issues: What's the bottom line?', *Strategic Management Journal*, 22(2): 125–39.

Hwang, K. (2015) 'Contracting in local public organizations: the institutional economics perspective', *Journal of Public Affairs*, 15(3): 237–42.

Ihlen, Ø. and van Ruler, B. (2007) 'How public relations works: Theoretical roots and public relations perspectives', *Public Relations Review*, 33(3): 243–8.

Jackowski, M. (2007) 'Conceptualizing an improved public relations strategy: A case for stakeholder relationship marketing in Division I-A Intercollegiate Athletics', *Journal of Business and Public Affairs*, 1(1). http://www.scientificjournals.org/journals2007/articles/1016.htm

Jensen, M. C. (2001) 'Value maximization, stakeholder theory, and the corporate objective function', *Journal of Applied Corporate Finance*, 14(3): 8–21.

Johnson, J. H., Mirchandani, D. A., and Meznar, M. B. (2015) 'The impact of internationalization of US multinationals on public affairs strategy and performance: A comparison of 1993 and 2003', *Business & Society*, 54(1): 89–125.

Jurkiewicz, C. L. and Giacalone, R. A. (2016) 'How will we know it when we see it? Conceptualizing the ethical organization', *Public Organization Review*, 16(3): 409–20.

Kaufmann, D. and Vicente, P. C. (2011) 'Legal corruption', *Economics & Politics*, 23(2): 195–219.

Kietzmann, J. H., Silvestre, B. S., McCarthy, I. P., and Pitt, L. F. (2012) 'Unpacking the social media phenomenon: towards a research agenda', *Journal of Public Affairs*, 12(2): 109–19.

Lawniczak, R. (2009) Re-examining the economic roots of public relations. *Public Relations Review*, 35(4): 345–52.

Lee, S. and Kim, B. (forthcoming) 'A time-series analysis of international public relations expenditure and economic outcome', *Communication Research*. doi: 10.1177/0093650215581370 (online before print April 19, 2015).

Lee, J. K., Choi, J., and Kim, S. T. (2014a) 'All things considered? Investigating the diversity of public affairs issues that individuals think about in the Internet age', *Computers in Human Behavior*, 32(March): 112–22.

Lee, K., Conklin, M., Cranage, D. A., and Lee, S. (2014b) 'The role of perceived corporate social responsibility on providing healthful foods and nutrition information with health-consciousness as a moderator', *International Journal of Hospitality Management,* 37(February): 29–37.

Lehtimaki, H. and Kujala, J. (forthcoming) 'Framing dynamically changing firm–stakeholder relationships in an international dispute over a foreign investment: A discursive analysis approach', *Business & Society.* doi: 10.1177/0007650315570611 (online before print February 12, 2015)

Lord, M. D. (2003) 'Constituency building as the foundation for corporate political strategy', *Academy of Management Executive,* 17(1): 112–24.

Mahon, J. F. and Waddock, S. (1992) 'Strategic issues management: An integration of issue life cycle perspectives', *Business & Society*, 31(1): 19–32.

Mencl, J. and May, D. R. (2016) 'An exploratory study among HRM professionals of moral recognition in off-shoring decisions: The roles of perceived magnitude of consequences, time pressure, cognitive and affective empathy, and prior knowledge', *Business & Society*, 55(2): 246–70.

Millar, C. J. M. and Köppl, P. (2014) 'Perspectives, practices and prospects of public affairs in Central and Eastern Europe: a lobbying future anchored in an institutional context', *Journal of Public Affairs*, 14(1): 4–17.

Moxham, C. and Kauppi, K. (2014) 'Using organisational theories to further our understanding of socially sustainable supply chains: The case of fair trade', *Supply Chain Management: An International Journal*, 19(4): 413–20.

Neuman, W. R., Guggenheim, L., Jang, S. M., and Bae, S. Y. (2014) 'The dynamics of public attention: Agenda-setting theory meets big data', *Journal of Communication,* 64(2): 193–214.

Niemann-Struweg, I. (2014) 'An integrated communication implementation model for the post-2000 business environment', *Public Relations Review*, 40(2): 184–92.

Okhuysen, G. and Bonardi, J.-P. (2011) 'Editors' comments: The challenges of building theory by combining lenses', *Academy of Management Review*, 36(1): 6–11.

Olkkonen, L. and Luoma-aho, V. (2014) 'Public relations as expectation management?', *Journal of Communication Management*, 18(3): 222–39.

Pal, M. and Dutta, M. J. (2008) 'Public relations in a global context: The relevance of critical modernism as a theoretical lens', *Journal of Public Relations Research*, 20(2): 159–79.

Paul, K. (2015) 'Stakeholder theory, meet communications theory: media systems dependency and community infrastructure theory, with an application to California's cannabis/marijuana industry', *Journal of Business Ethics,* 129(3): 705–20.

Powell, Mel (2012) 'Ethics and the public relations management process', in Danny Moss and Barbara DeSanto (eds), *Public Relations: A Managerial Perspective*, London: Sage, pp. 422–39.

Rajagopalan, N. and Spreitzer, G. M. (1997) 'Toward a theory of strategic change: A multi-lens perspective and integrative framework', *Academy of Management Review*, 22(1): 48–79.

Rehbein, K. and Schuler, D. A. (2015) 'Linking corporate community programs and political strategies: A resource-based view', *Business & Society*, 54(6): 794–821.

Robison, J. (2015) 'Gaps in political interest: Following public affairs in surveys from Gallup, Pew, and the ANES', *International Journal of Public Opinion Research*, 27(3): 406–16.

Sabatier, Paul A. (2007) *Theories of the Policy Process*. Boulder, CO: Westview Press.

Scott, S. V. and Walsham, G. (2005) 'Reconceptualizing and managing reputation risk in the knowledge economy: Toward reputable action', *Organization Science*, 16(3): 308–22.

Smith, Adam (1790 [1759]) *The Theory of Moral Sentiments*. London: A. Millar, 6th edition.

Skard, S. and Thorbjørnsen, H. (2014) 'Is publicity always better than advertising? The role of brand reputation in communicating corporate social responsibility', *Journal of Business Ethics*, 124(1): 149–60.

Somerville, Ian (2012) 'Managing public affairs and lobbying: Persuasive communication in the policy sphere', in Danny Moss and Barbara DeSanto (eds), *Public Relations: A Managerial Perspective*, London: Sage, pp. 167–92.

Steyn, B. and Niemann, L. (2014) 'Strategic role of public relations in enterprise strategy, governance and sustainability: A normative framework', *Public Relations Review*, 40(2): 171–83.

Titley, S. (2003) 'How political and social change will transform the EU public affairs industry', *Journal of Public Affairs*, 3(1): 83–9.

Tyma, A. W. (2008) 'Public relations through a new lens: Critical praxis via the "Excellence Theory"', *International Journal of Communication*, 2: 193–205.

Veksler, A. (2016) 'Lobbying in the sunshine – hiding behind transparency?' *Journal of Public Affairs*, 16(1): 39–49.

Walker, Edward T. (2014) *Grassroots for Hire: Public Affairs Consultants in American Democracy*. New York: Cambridge University Press.

Warren, Richard (2012) 'Corporate social responsibility', in Danny Moss and Barbara DeSanto (eds), *Public Relations: A Managerial Perspective*, London: Sage, pp. 394–421.

Weaver, Kay, Motion, Judy, and Roper, Juliet (2006) 'From propaganda to discourse (and back again): Truth, power, the public interest, and public relations', in Jacquie L'Etang and Magda Pieczka (eds), *Public Relations: Critical Debates and Contemporary Practice*. Mahwah, NJ: Lawrence Erlbaum Associates, pp. 7–21.

Windsor, D. (2002) 'Public affairs, issues management, and political strategy: Opportunities, obstacles, and caveats', *Journal of Public Affairs*, 1(4)–2(1): 382–415.

Windsor, D. (2005) '"Theories" and theoretical roots of public affairs', in Phil Harris and Craig S. Fleisher (eds), *The Handbook of Public Affairs*. Thousand Oaks, CA: Sage Publications, pp. 401–17.

Windsor, D. (2007) 'Toward a global theory of cross-border and multilevel corporate political activity', *Business & Society,* 46(2): 253–78.

Windsor, D. (2013) 'Corporate social responsibility and irresponsibility: A positive theory approach', *Journal of Business Research*, 66(10): 1937–44.

Wood, D. J. (1991) 'Corporate social performance revisited', *Academy of Management Review* 16(4): 691–718.

Young, D. R. (2000) 'Alternative models of government-nonprofit sector relations: Theoretical and international perspectives', *Nonprofit and Voluntary Sector Quarterly*, 29(1): 149–72.

Zavattaro, S. M. (2014) 'Using legitimacy as an organizing lens for public administration', *Public Administration Review*, 74(4): 535–9.

Examining the Public Affairs Scholarship: What We've Learned (and still don't know) from the Empirical Studies of Public Affairs

Richard McGowan

INTRODUCTION

In reviewing the ten years of articles that involve the topic of public affairs, empirical methods are certainly not the preferred method of cataloguing the various aspects of public affairs that scholars analyze. There are many reasons for this but it is apparent when reading this literature that it is extremely difficult to determine what exactly is a 'successful' outcome for a public affairs' strategy. Most public affairs' questions lend themselves to substantial long term case studies that involve political, social and economic issues. Yet empirical methods might provide public affairs researchers with the ability to come to more focused results particularly in regards to economic and political aspects of public affairs issues.

This chapter will first review what has been accomplished in terms of empirical research in public affairs. This section will be divided into three parts. The first part will comment on the type of empirical research

that was attempted by public affair scholars from the period of 2001–5. The other two time periods will be 2006–10 and 2011–14. Hopefully, this division will allow the reader to experience both the breadth of empirical research as well as the progression that empirical research has taken during the past 15 years of public affairs research activity.

The second part of the chapter will make suggestions for future empirical questions that public affairs researchers might attempt to analyze using empirical research methods. Suggestions will also be made about what would be the appropriate methods to be employed.

A BRIEF REVIEW OF EMPIRICAL PUBLIC AFFAIRS RESEARCH

Each part of this section will comment on the amount, type, and variety of empirical public affairs scholarship during the period of time.

The definition of empirical research was 'liberal' in the sense that includes any article that has descriptive statistics, hypotheses testing or more advance techniques such as regression.

First Time Period: 2001–5

One can readily surmise from Table 3.1, that empirical public affairs research did not come easily to researchers in public affairs. Only 33 percent of articles published during the period between 2001 and 2005 had any sort of empirical material. The vast majority (80 percent) of what could be called empirical material contained descriptive statistics such as percentages, means, medians, etc. but little or no traditional statistical testing. However, 15 percent of the empirical analysis did contain traditional hypothesis testing utilizing such test statistics as the paired and unpaired 't' test where the researcher tested whether or not there was a statistically significant difference between groups or individuals and an article that employed analysis of variance to test whether there was a difference between three or more groups.

The most sophisticated piece of public affairs empirical research that was published during this period involved logistic regression. It was a piece written by Ge, Veeman and Adamowicz (2005) entitled, 'Consumers' search behaviour for GM food information'. In a logistic regression the dependent variable is a dummy variable and the parameters of the regression are estimated by a maximum likelihood estimation. In essence, the authors were trying to see if consumers were aware that a particular product had GM information and whether or not it made a difference in their purchasing habits. The results of the logistic regression were displayed in a typical fashion and the outcome was written in a clear and concise fashion. This article certainly demonstrated that scholars who were interested in public affairs/public policy were capable of employing advanced empirical methods. These results could easily be utilized as a basis for conducting an extensive case study of how the GM issue is being handled by public affairs managers of GM firms.

Second Time Period: 2006–10

While the percentage of public affairs articles using empirical material went up slightly (33 to 40 percent), what is striking about Table 3.2 is that the quality of the empirical analysis has risen sharply. Less than half of the empirical articles are merely descriptive statistics. The variety of statistical methods employed increased dramatically. Within the hypotheses testing component, the use of non-parametric tests acknowledges that data in public affairs is not 'normally distributed'. These tests allow the public affairs researcher to establish that there is a relationship between categories. That is important in itself. Clearly it does not

Table 3.1 2001–5 (33% of the public affairs articles had empirical data/analysis)

Methodology	% breakdown	Description of Methodology
Descriptive Statistics	80	Percentages and Financial Data
Hypothesis Testing	15	'p' values for Pair and Unpaired 't' Analysis of Variance
Regression	5	Simple and Logit regression

Table 3.2 2006–10 (40% of the public affairs articles had empirical data/analysis)

Methodology	% breakdown	Description of Methodology
Descriptive Statistics	46	Percentages and Financial Data
Hypothesis Testing	40	'p' values for Pair and Unpaired 't' Factor analysis, Correlation Non-parametric tests (Chi square)
Regression	14	Multiple and Multinomial logit, Hierarchical

indicate causality nor does it establish what exactly the relationship is.

One method that was employed during this period was factor analysis. The goal of factor analysis is to group variables. For example, assume there are ten independent variables that you think are related to the dependent variable. You might want to ask the question: Which variables are closer or similar to each other? A factor analysis classifies the ten variables into two or more groups of similar variables. An excellent example of the value of factor analysis for public affairs scholars is 'How to become your own worst adversary: examining the connection between managerial attribution and organizational relationship with public interest stakeholders', by Mattingly (2007). The paper does a first rate job in enumerating those characteristics of CEOs that led to difficulty in dealing with public interest groups.

Finally, in the area of regression analysis, there was much more an emphasis on multiple regression models, that is, including many more independent variables in determining the dependent variable. An interesting example of using a multiple regression methodology to explore a complex topic was Tian and Deng's (2007) article, 'The determinants of corporate political strategy in Chinese transition'. In this article, Tian and Deng utilized a hierarchial multiple regression model where higher powers of the independent variable account for a curved relationship between some of the independent and dependent variables. So Tian and Deng established that certain circumstances have a much more powerful influence on outcomes than others. In other words, the authors were able to show that various independent variables do not have to be linearly related to the dependent variable.

Overall, during this second time period (2006–10), the sophistication of the empirical methods that were employed went up significantly. While only 40 percent of public affairs articles employed empirical methods, the empirical results made a substantial contribution to our understanding of public affairs as well as issue management and public policy.

Third Time Period: 2011–15

For the period 2011–15, (please refer to Table 3.3) there was not a significant change in the use of empirical methods, although there does appear to be a shift is the use of traditional statistical analysis. One of the more innovative public affairs papers that published during this period was Chong, Halcoussis and Phillips (2011), 'Does market volatility impact presidential approval?'. It is one of the few articles over the past 20 years that utilized time series and the corresponding difficulties one encounters when time is a factor in achieving meaningful empirical results. It also utilized the Eta program which allowed the authors to aggregate 18 different economic factors that determine market volatility. This paper certainly paves the way for other public affairs scholars to utilize a combination of factor analysis along with a longitudinal data.

So over the past 15 years where are public affairs' scholars in relationship to empirical research? Clearly this section has shown that there has been a substantial increase in public affairs research that utilized empirical research. The other aspect is that the empirical (statistical) methodology has become much more complex and multifaceted. In the second section of this article, there will be suggestions on how to expand the use of empirical research as well as methodologies that might be employed.

Table 3.3   2011–14 (42% of the public affairs articles had empirical data/analysis)

Methodology	% breakdown	Description of Methodology
Descriptive Statistics	33	Percentages and Financial Data
Hypothesis Testing	50	'p' values for Pair and Unpaired 't' Analysis of Variance, Correlation Non-parametric tests
Regression	17	Simple and Multiple Regression Logit Eta (Time Series)

SUGGESTIONS FOR FUTURE PUBLIC AFFAIRS EMPIRICAL RESEARCH

One of the surprising elements missing in a great deal of the empirical research in public affairs is the time element. When an extensive case study of a public affairs issue is analyzed clearly there is an element of time that is involved. So the suggestions in this section are to supplement the richness that only a case study can provide. The empirical analysis that includes time will enable the researcher to make a commentary on how various measures influenced the outcomes of public affairs initiatives.

The element of time allows the researcher to conduct what is commonly known as intervention analysis. Two types of intervention models will be proposed that are commonly available in the majority of statistical packages (MINITAB, SPSS, STATA, and SAS are just a few packages that can be utilized).

ARIMA TIME SERIES INTERVENTIONS

An ARIMA (autoregressive integrated moving average) time series intervention ordinarily focuses on the null test hypothesis: Did an intervention have an impact on the time series. So for example a public affairs researcher might ask the question: How did increasing the legal age (from 18 to 21) to purchase cigarettes in California affect cigarette sales? The first step in this analysis is to estimate the appropriate ARIMA model for the time series. Clearly the researcher would need to develop an expertise for ARIMA modeling. But the beauty of ARIMA Intervention analysis is that the intervention itself can be modeled.

In general, the impact of the intervention has two characteristics: onset and duration.

So that the intervention can be modeled in four different ways using the cigarette example:

1 Abrupt and permanent: Sales went down immediately and stayed down permanently.

2 Gradual and permanent: Sales went down gradually and stayed down permanently.
3 Gradual and temporary: Sales went down gradually but returned to their previous level.
4 Abrupt and temporary: Sales went down immediately but eventually started to rise again to previous levels.

It has to be emphasized that in order to utilize this procedure two requirements are necessary. First, the social process under study has been operationalized as a time series; second, there is a discrete intervention that divides the time series into two components, one consisting of pre-intervention observations and the other consisting of all post-intervention observations.

This ARIMA Intervention analysis alone can't make a case for 'causality' alone. It is, however, a powerful tool especially in conjunction with a case study that has enumerated all of the factors that constitutes a complex public affairs situation.

There are numerous books on time series analysis and forecasting where this technique is examined. One example would be the 'little' green book series published by Sage entitled, *Interrupted Time Series Analysis* by McDowall, McCleary, Meidinger and Hay.

There is another way in which ARIMA analysis that would be of interest to public affairs scholars. One might be able to evaluate a policy to see if there is a gap in performance. For example, suppose that the soft drink industry started a campaign explaining its position on sugary drinks. One could use ARIMA to forecast sales given that there is no campaign and then compare what the actual sales were to see if there is a significant gap between the forecast and the actual. It would be a very intuitive and graphic way of explaining the results of an action by a firm, industry, or government.

PANEL REGRESSION

With ARIMA intervention analysis, the time series was the sole focus of analysis. A richer and fuller study would combine time series and cross-section data such as observations on thousands of individual firms, states, or industries simultaneously over a long period of time. Hence, a panel regression involves a regression where the researcher and the time effects are viewed as 'transitions' or discrete changes of state. Panel data often are produced by large, multi-year survey projects and provide a source of material for analysis.

However, while utilizing panel data, the researcher is confronted with two problems. First, there is often a problem with homoscedasticity (constant variance of the error term) that is associated with cross-sectional data. Second, time series data often has the problem that the data is serially correlated (data points are not statistically independent).

So while the data is very rich there can be numerous problems with this data. The most common method of dealing with these problems is called 'the random effects model'. This model is based on the assumption that the intercept for each cross-sectional unit is drawn from a distribution that is centered around a mean intercept. Again, there are many statistical packages (MINITAB, SPSS, STATA, SAS) that will allow the researcher to conduct a random effects model if that researcher has been able to assemble various variables (cross-section) over time. For example, in the previous cigarette sales data let us suppose that other states follow California's example of raising the age limit to purchase cigarettes, one might use as cross-sectional data the excise tax rate for each state, changes in GDP, the number of smoking prohibitions laws, and a dummy variable for the change in age requirement for monthly sales over a five-year period. Hopefully this rather 'richer' data set would allow the researcher to see if there is an interaction between these cross-section variables over time.

CONCLUSION

Over the past 15 years there has certainly been an increase in empirical studies in the public affairs area. By the end of past 15 years, nearly 50 percent of public affairs articles contain data and the majority of those articles utilize statistical analysis. Yet compared to other fields of study such as economics and management these figures are incredibly small. It is a rare article that is published in economics or management journals that would not almost be exclusively empirical or have mathematical proofs defining a new theory to test.

But one of the problems that public affairs scholars face is that research in this area combines social, political, and economic aspects. To conduct a study that combines these three aspects naturally leads to a rich descriptive case study. But the problem with this methodology is whether one can generalize any conclusions that are applicable and relevant to other situations.

Hence, it would seem that public affairs scholars will by necessity combine case studies with appropriate statistical analysis. In this article one fruitful avenue that blends well with case studies would be an emphasis on time series analysis. There are of course numerous other methodologies that could and should be explored. Overall, the state of empirical analysis for public affairs is healthy and appropriate. There should be no rush to employ statistical methodology for what some might perceive as 'rigor'. Hopefully public affairs scholarship will continue to attract researchers from various disciplines who can utilize their unique viewpoints and analytical approaches to further the analysis of complex public affairs.

REFERENCES

Chong, J., Halcoussis, D., and Phillips, M. (2011). Does market volatility impact presidential approval? *Journal of Public Affairs* (14723891), 11(4), 387–394. doi:10.1002/pa.410

Ge, G., Veeman, M., and Adamowicz, W. (2005). Consumers' search behaviour for

GM food information. *Journal of Public Affairs* (14723891), 5(3/4), 217–25. doi:10.1002/pa.23.

Mattingly, J. E. (2007). How to become your own worst adversary: Examining the connection between managerial attributions and organizational relationships with public interest stakeholders. *Journal of Public Affairs*, 7(1): 7–21.

Tian, Z. and Deng, X. (2007). The determinants of corporate political strategy in Chinese transition. *Journal of Public Affairs*, 7(4): 341–56.

FURTHER READING

Adelaja, A. O., Gibson, M. A., and Racevskis, L. A. (2010). Transaction costs and inter-jurisdictional cooperation: an application to land use collaboration. *Journal of Public Affairs* (14723891), 10(4), 265–79. doi:10.1002/pa.358.

Aitken-Turff, F. and Jackson, N. (2006). A mixed motive approach to lobbying: applying game theory to analyse the impact of co-operation and conflict on perceived lobbying success. *Journal of Public Affairs* (14723891), 6(2), 84–101. doi:10.1002/pa.216.

Albrecht, C., Campbell, C., Heinrich, D., and Lammel, M. (2013). Exploring why consumers engage in boycotts: toward a unified model. *Journal of Public Affairs* (14723891), 13(2), 180–9. doi:10.1002/pa.1473.

Babor, T. F., Ziming, X., and Damon, D. (2010). Changes in the self-regulation guidelines of the US Beer Code reduce the number of content violations reported in TV advertisements. *Journal of Public Affairs* (14723891), 10(1/2), 6–18. doi:10.1002/pa.347

Baines, P. and Worcester, R. M. (2005). When the British 'Tommy' went to war, public opinion followed. *Journal of Public Affairs* (14723891), 5(1), 4–19. doi:10.1002/pa.1.

Bhate, S. (2007). Health of the nation: An individual or a corporate social responsibility? A preliminary investigation into consumer perceptions. *Journal of Public Affairs* (14723891), 7(2), 164–80. doi:10.1002/pa.255.

Black, L. D. and Härtel, C. J. (2004). The five capabilities of socially responsible companies. *Journal of Public Affairs* (14723891), 4(2), 125–44.

Boddy, C. P., Ladyshewsky, R., and Galvin, P. (2010). Leaders without ethics in global business: Corporate psychopaths. *Journal of Public Affairs* (14723891), 10(3), 121–38. doi:10.1002/pa.352.

Boon, E., Wiid, R., and DesAutels, P. (2012). Teeth whitening, boot camp, and a brewery tour: a practical analysis of 'deal of the day'. *Journal of Public Affairs* (14723891), 12(2), 137–44. doi:10.1002/pa.1415.

Campbell, C., Piercy, N., and Heinrich, D. (2012). When companies get caught: The effect of consumers discovering undesirable firm engagement online. *Journal of Public Affairs* (14723891), 12(2), 120–6. doi:10.1002/pa.1413.

Castle, D., Finlay, K., and Clark, S. (2005). Proactive consumer consultation: The effect of information provision on response to transgenic animals. *Journal of Public Affairs* (14723891), 5(3/4), 200–16. doi:10.1002/pa.22.

Challen, C. (2001). Think global, talk local: Getting the part political message across in the age of the Internet. *Journal of Public Affairs* (14723891), 1(3), 254–65.

Constantelos, J. (2007). Interest group strategies in multi-level Europe. *Journal Of Public Affairs* (14723891), 7(1), 37–53. doi:10.1002/pa.243.

Deacon, D. and Monk, W. (2001). 'New managerialism' in the news: Media coverage of quangos in Britain. *Journal of Public Affairs* (14723891), 1(2), 153–66.

Deng, X. (2009). Patterns of internationalization of Chinese firms: Empirical study based on strategic approach. *Journal of Public Affairs* (14723891), 9(4), 301–12. doi:10.1002/pa.331.

Dolnicar, S. and Hurlimann, A. (2011). Water alternatives: Who and what influences public acceptance? *Journal of Public Affairs* (14723891), 11(1), 49–59. doi:10.1002/pa.378.

Evanson, R. K. (2008). Economic interest groups and the consolidation of democracy in the Czech Republic. *Journal of Public Affairs* (14723891), 8(1/2), 33–49. doi:10.1002/pa.283.

Gordon, R., Hastings, G., and Moodie, C. (2010). Alcohol marketing and young people's drinking: What the evidence base suggests for policy. *Journal of Public Affairs* (14723891), 10(1/2), 88–101. doi:10.1002/pa.338.

Grefe, E. (2003). E-campaigning: What it is and how to do it. *Journal of Public Affairs* (14723891), 3(1), 21–26.

Griffin, J. J. (2004). Corporate restructurings: Ripple effects on corporate philanthropy. *Journal of Public Affairs* (14723891), 4(1), 27–43.

Hall, D. V., Jones, S. C., and Hoek, J. (2011). Direct to consumer advertising versus disease awareness advertising: consumer perspectives from down under. *Journal of Public Affairs* (14723891), 11(1), 60–69. doi:10.1002/pa.379

Hemphill, T. A. (2003). Self-regulation, public issue management and marketing practices in the US entertainment industry. *Journal of Public Affairs* (14723891), 3(4), 338–57.

Henneberg, S. C. (2006). Strategic postures of political marketing: an exploratory operationalization. *Journal of Public Affairs* (14723891), 6(1), 15–30. doi:10.1002/pa.39.

Holtzhausen, L. and Fourie, L. (2011). Employees' perceptions of institutional values and employer-employee relationships at the North-West University. *Journal of Public Affairs* (14723891), 11(4), 243–54. doi:10.1002/pa.417.

Hrebenar, R. J., McBeth, C. H., and Morgan, B. B. (2008). Interests and lobbying in Lithuania: A spectrum of development. *Journal of Public Affairs* (14723891), 8(1/2), 51–65. doi:10.1002/pa.281.

Illia, L. (2003). Passage to cyberactivism: How dynamics of activism change. *Journal of Public Affairs* (14723891), 3(4), 326–37.

Jernigan, D. H. and Ross, C. (2010). Monitoring youth exposure to advertising on television: The devil is in the details. *Journal of Public Affairs* (14723891), 10(1/2), 36–49. doi:10.1002/pa.349.

Johnson Jr., J. H. and Meznar, M. B. (2005). Public affairs perceptions and practices: A ten-year (1993–2003) comparison. *Journal of Public Affairs* (14723891), 5(1), 55–65. doi:10.1002/pa.5.

Jones, S. C. and Eagleton, K. (2012). What do Australian consumers think about current advertising standards? *Journal of Public Affairs* (14723891), 12(4), 315–25. doi:10.1002/pa.424.

Jones, S. C. and Reid, A. (2010). The use of female sexuality in Australian alcohol advertising: Public policy implications of young adults' reactions to stereotypes. *Journal of Public Affairs* (14723891), 10(1/2), 19–35. doi:10.1002/pa.339.

Kemp, B., Randle, M., Hurlimann, A., and Dolnicar, S. (2012). Community acceptance of recycled water: can we inoculate the public against scare campaigns? *Journal of Public Affairs* (14723891), 12(4), 337–46. doi:10.1002/pa.1429.

Knight, J. G., Mather, D. W., and Holdsworth, D. K. (2005). Consumer benefits and acceptance of genetically modified food. *Journal of Public Affairs* (14723891), 5(3/4), 226–35. doi:10.1002/pa.24.

McDowall, D., McCleary, R., Meidinger, E. E., and Hay, R. A. (1990) *Interrupted Time Series*, 2nd Edition. CA: Sage.

Mahon, J., and Wartick, S. L. (2012). Corporate social performance profiling: using multiple stakeholder perceptions to assess a corporate reputation. *Journal of Public Affairs* (14723891), 12(1), 12–28. doi:10.1002/pa.433.

McGrath, C. (2003). 'Family Businesses Distributing America's Beverage': Managing government relations in the National Beer Wholesalers Association. *Journal of Public Affairs* (14723891), 3(3), 212–24.

McGrath, C. (2008). The development and regulation of lobbying in the new member states of the European Union. *Journal of Public Affairs* (14723891), 8(1/2), 15–32. doi:10.1002/pa.284.

Meznar, M. B., Johnson Jr., J. H., and Mizzi, P. J. (2006). No news is good news? Press coverage and corporate public affairs management. *Journal of Public Affairs* (14723891), 6(1), 58–68. doi:10.1002/pa.35.

Moll, R. (2003). Ford Motor Company and the Firestone tyre recall. *Journal of Public Affairs* (14723891), 3(3), 200–11.

Moloney, K. (2001). The rise and fall of spin: Changes of fashion in the presentation of UK policies. *Journal of Public Affairs* (14723891), 1(2), 124–35.

Moss, C. B., Schmitz, A., and Schmitz, T. G. (2006). First-generation genetically modified organisms in agriculture. *Journal of Public Affairs* (14723891), 6(1), 46–57. doi:10.1002/pa.41.

Nelson, J. P. (2010). Alcohol, unemployment rates and advertising bans: International panel evidence, 1975–2000. *Journal of Public Affairs* (14723891), 10(1/2), 74–87. doi:10.1002/pa.348.

O'Cass, A. (2001). The internal-external marketing orientation of a political party: Social implications of political party marketing orientation. *Journal of Public Affairs* (14723891), 1(2), 136–52.

Ormrod, R. P., Zaefarian, G., Henneberg, S. C., and Vries, P. (2015). Strategy, market orientation and performance: The political context. *Journal of Public Affairs* (14723891), 15(1), 37–52. doi:10.1002/pa.1494.

Patrón-Galindo, P. (2004). Symbolism and the construction of political products: Analysis of the political marketing strategies of Peruvian President Alejandro Toledo. *Journal of Public Affairs* (14723891), 4(2), 115–24.

Pedler, R. H. (2001). Envisaging the future: Scenarios and public affairs practice. *Journal of Public Affairs* (14723891), 1(2), 113–23.

Pinsky, I., El Jundi, S. J., Sanches, M., Zaleski, M. B., Laranjeira, R. R., and Caetano, R. (2010). Exposure of adolescents and young adults to alcohol advertising in Brazil. *Journal of Public Affairs* (14723891), 10(1/2), 50–8. doi:10.1002/pa.350.

Plangger, K. (2012). The power of popularity: how the size of a virtual community adds to firm value. *Journal of Public Affairs* (14723891), 12(2), 145–53. doi:10.1002/pa.1416.

Prasad, A. and Shivarajan, S. (2015). Understanding the role of technology in reducing corruption: A transaction cost approach. *Journal of Public Affairs* (14723891), 15(1), 19–36. doi:10.1002/pa.1484.

Ramasamy, B., Yeung, M. H., and Au, A. M. (2008). Can holidays boost consumption? The case of Hong Kong. *Journal of Public Affairs* (14723891), 8(4), 281–7.

Richards, D. C. (2003). Corporate public affairs: Necessary cost or value-added asset? *Journal of Public Affairs* (14723891), 3(1), 39–51.

Schilliger, L. K. and Seele, P. (2015). Company level localization and public affairs officers' educational background in Switzerland. *Journal of Public Affairs* (14723891), 15(1), 98–106. doi:10.1002/pa.1525.

Schuler, D. A. (2002). Public affairs, issues management and political strategy: Methodological approaches that count. *Journal of Public Affairs* (14723891), 1/2(4/1), 336–55.

Schwartz, J., Hoover, S., and Schwartz, A. (2008). The political advantage of a volatile market: the relationship between Presidential popularity and the 'investor fear gauge'. *Journal of Public Affairs* (14723891), 8(3), 195–207. doi:10.1002/pa.291.

Sibiano, P. and Agasisti, T. (2013). Efficiency and heterogeneity of public spending in education among Italian regions. *Journal of Public Affairs* (14723891), 13(1), 12–22. doi:10.1002/pa.1404.

Smith, G. (2011). Assessing the effectiveness of ethics legislation in influencing parliamentary attitudes toward corruption: a cross national comparison between the UK and Ireland. *Journal of Public Affairs* (14723891), 11(2), 100–10. doi:10.1002/pa.390.

Steiner, A. and Jarren, O. (2009). In the twilight of democracy: public affairs consultants in Switzerland. *Journal of Public Affairs* (14723891), 9(2), 95–109. doi:10.1002/pa.316.

Strömbäck, J. (2007). Antecedents of political market orientation in Britain and Sweden: analysis and future research propositions. *Journal of Public Affairs* (14723891), 7(1), 79–89. doi:10.1002/pa.241.

Strömbäck, J., Grandien, C., and Falasca, K. (2013). Do campaign strategies and tactics matter? Exploring party elite perceptions of what matters when explaining election outcomes. *Journal of Public Affairs* (14723891), 13(1), 41–52. doi:10.1002/pa.1441.

Szeto, R. F. (2010). Chinese folk wisdom: Implications for guarding against unethical practices by Chinese managers. *Journal of Public Affairs* (14723891), 10(3), 173–85. doi:10.1002/pa.355.

Tang, R., Tang, T., and Lee, Z. (2014). The efficiency of provincial governments in China from 2001 to 2010: Measurement and analysis. *Journal of Public Affairs* (14723891), 14(2), 142–53. doi:10.1002/pa.1518.

Turner, J. (2001). Trouble with Ken: New Labour's negative campaign in the selection and election process for London mayor. *Journal of Public Affairs* (14723891), 1(3), 239–53.

Wallis, D. (2001). Outfoxing Leviathan: Campaigning down Mexico way. *Journal of Public Affairs* (14723891), 1(3), 229–38.

Wang, P. (2014). Government intervention and the empowerment process: Citizen involvement in the 2010 Shanghai World Expo. *Journal of Public Affairs* (14723891), 14(2), 130–41. doi:10.1002/pa.1517.

Ward, S. and Lewandowska, A. (2006). Validation of a measure of societal marketing orientation. *Journal of Public Affairs* (14723891), 6(3/4), 241–55. doi:10.1002/pa.235.

Waters, R. D. and Williams, J. M. (2011). Squawking, tweeting, cooing, and hooting: Analyzing the communication patterns of government agencies on Twitter. *Journal of Public Affairs* (14723891), 11(4), 353–63. doi:10.1002/pa.385.

Wenjing, S. and Hooker, N. H. (2005). Improving recall crisis management: Should retailer information be disclosed? *Journal of Public Affairs* (14723891), 5(3/4), 329–41. doi:10.1002/pa.32.

West, G. E. and Larue, B. (2005). Determinants of anti-GM food activism. *Journal of Public Affairs* (14723891), 5(3/4), 236–50. doi:10.1002/pa.25.

Yang, A. (2013). Building global strategic alliances in the virtual space: a structural analysis of international nonprofit and nongovernmental organizations' transnational relationship networks. *Journal of Public Affairs* (14723891), 13(3), 239–50. doi:10.1002/pa.1463.

Zhilong, T. and Xinming, D. (2007). The determinants of corporate political strategy in Chinese transition. *Journal of Public Affairs* (14723891), 7(4), 341–56. doi:10.1002/pa.273.

Zyglidopoulos, S. C. (2004). The impact of downsizing on the corporate reputation for social performance. *Journal of Public Affairs* (14723891), 4(1), 11–25.

Achieving the Strategic Potential of Public Affairs

Fruzsina M. Harsanyi and Geoff Allen

INTRODUCTION

This chapter is written to reflect the practical experience of the two authors rather than making any attempt at theory building.

Their experience is more than a combined 80 years, and includes work in the civil services of two countries, political offices, public affairs in major global companies, advisory council roles to governments, management consulting, and business school research and teaching. They have provided public affairs advice to, and gained insights from, a great many major companies on six continents.

Beginning with a description of the function at different levels of maturity, the authors focus on what it should look like at the highest level. Strategic public affairs as a leadership function is the level at which, in the authors' judgment, public affairs will have achieved its full potential.

THE BUSINESS CONTEXT FOR PUBLIC AFFAIRS

The emergence of public affairs as a distinct field can be traced to changes in the socio-political environment of business in the 1960s and 1970s. Dramatic shifts in community sentiment led to a fundamental change in the expectations of the community about how corporations should behave, and a strong push for regulatory intervention. The business response was defensive, slow, and sporadic. Business was not able to protect its prerogatives from the great wave of social legislation, much of it driven by a new breed of issues advocates.

It was in this context UCLA academic Neil Jacoby (1974) postulated a new model of the firm in which it became a corporate activist. He proposed: ' ... a new theory of enterprise behavior, which I call the social environment model because its central tenet is that the enterprise reacts to the total social environment and not merely to markets' (Jacoby, 1974).

The most novel and important characteristic of the social environment model is the explicit recognition that corporate behavior responds to political forces, public opinion, and government pressures. Whereas both classical and managerial theory ignored the impact of political forces, the social environment theory analyzes corporate behavior as a response to both market and nonmarket forces because both affect the firm's costs, revenues, and profits (Jacoby, 1974, p. 235).

In 1982 the Conference Board reported on an international survey that illustrated the worldwide nature of the shift. In the United States 96 percent of the executives interviewed said outsiders are having an increasing influence on company decision-making. Among European executives, the figure was 98 percent. Since the 1970s and 1980s this pressure on companies and corporate performance has been unabated.

Government intervention has been the means by which corporate critics have attempted to achieve their goals and the pervasiveness of regulatory intervention on companies has continued to grow.

By 2011, in a study of 1,400 senior executives in major companies across the globe, McKinsey & Co. found that government and regulator stakeholders (at 53 percent of respondents) were seen as the second most likely stakeholders to affect the economic value of their companies after customers (72 percent) but before employees (49 percent) and investors (28 percent). North America (71 percent) and Europe (60 percent) were the most likely geographies where dependence on government is greatest. A significant number believed that the level of their involvement would increase (McKinsey & Co., 2011).

For most companies of scale, the business environments have continued to evolve rapidly into the twenty-first century. Major shifts in the centers of wealth and power have impacted the dynamics of business–government relationships. From an environment of

relative stability in the bipolar world of two great powers, we now have national governments, multilateral organizations, and international government agencies competing for power, and emerging economies flexing their muscles. Where once the arc of history was moving toward greater integration, today separatist movements are gaining strength. Political chaos, violence, and terrorism confront citizens, companies, and governments on a daily basis.

Business itself has been going through a great transformation with the rapid globalization of financing, design, production, and supply. The cultures and expectations of suppliers, staff, and religious and language groups can be very diverse. The boards and executive teams of major companies are increasingly drawn from a multiplicity of countries in a global executive market.

The power of social media and rising expectations of companies by the expanding middle class of both developed and developing countries are creating new external challenges for companies. Despite the vision of a stateless corporation projected in the 1960s, national governments are still the legal authority within borders; they share regulatory and other power with provincial and local governments as well as with international authorities. Companies may be stateless in their operations, but need governments to provide stability and security.

Companies have to reach far beyond their traditional markets, which used to be in developed countries, to emerging markets because their customers and competitors are there. Today, as the countries that were once labeled underdeveloped are becoming saturated, new candidates are identified for their growth potential. These present new risks and new opportunities. Even globalization as a phenomenon has changed and many companies are re-evaluating their global strategy in light of 'underwhelming' profits and 'unanticipated risks' (Rothfeder, 2015, pp. F1, F4).

It is apparent that we have reached a stage where business' social and political performance environment has become an important element in the competition between firms and the creation of corporate value. As Stanford academic David Baron suggests, 'Successful management requires frameworks for analyzing nonmarket issues, principles for reasoning about them, and approaches to formulate strategies to address them' (Baron, 1993, p. 5).

A SPECIALIST FUNCTION: THREE LEVELS OF DEVELOPMENT

While accountability for business performance in this complex global social and political environment is, and must remain, with the whole organization, corporate structures, and specialist competencies have evolved to manage activity and provide advice and leadership – the public affairs function.

The still evolving practice of public affairs can be seen as operating at different levels of maturity from reactive and defensive to proactive and offensive, from siloed and operational to integrated and strategic. These changes have taken place over time, but are far from universal, even in some otherwise sophisticated major firms.

Level I: An Immature Function

At the lowest level of maturity, practitioners can have acknowledged special skills while being seen as somewhat exotic and separate from the core of business management. On the communications side the role is largely a public relations orientation, a combination of portraying the organization in the most positive light through external messaging and fighting issue or reputation fires. Government relations is largely technical and reactive. The focus is on monitoring and when necessary on mounting evidence and argument with government to defend against regulatory pressures, often with heavy dependence

on peer group collaboration in industry associations.

Practitioners at this low level of functional maturity are likely to be given information about company thinking on a 'needs to know' basis. They tend to acquire only incidental knowledge of the early stages of corporate planning and at best they are fully briefed with what more senior executives determine is relevant information after decisions are made and directions set.

A natural consequence of this is that their skills and connections are deployed at a late stage in the cycle of issues, to fight on the agenda and framing propositions of issues adversaries, and with little opportunity to take advantage of opportunities that exist in the nonmarket environment. When practitioners are seen principally as defensive troubleshooters or image-makers, and are not seen to understand finance, technologies, or markets like a 'business person', there is no good reason for them to be in the corporate information loop.

During normal business periods, the importance of public affairs is not obvious and it may seem expendable. Activities such as building relationships, developing data for use in advocacy, educating internal stakeholders, and meeting with line managers to learn of their issues are often seen as nonessential by operations managers who do not understand the contribution public affairs can make. One manager asked his public affairs vice president what would happen if his budget were dramatically cut for six months! Would anybody know the difference?

Level II: Consultant to Line Management

A small step up in the evolution of the function towards its strategic potential is the concept of public affairs as consultant, or specialist resource, to serve line management.

Here the function brings expertise to needs that are identified by other managers qua clients. This is often complemented by the common practice of periodic negotiations, leading to effective contracts between business units and public affairs to establish what contribution to the business can be made by, and what the business' expectations are for, the function. Not infrequently this determines a business unit's contribution to the overall company public affairs budget. Seeing public affairs as internal consultant led to a phase where it was common to demand internal charging to make costs and perceived benefits transparent. In some cases the provision of this support has been made contestable with external providers, which reinforces the notion of public affairs as a cost center and it became common to place the function with other 'back of the house shared services'. This positioning and concept of the function seriously limits its capacity to strategic thinking and early identification and management of emerging issues affecting the business environment.

Even when some of the best-in-class public affairs operations have been established, they have been pushed into a defensive posture when a change in management brings in executives who do not understand or have little interest in the function. The role model presented by the CEO is a powerful influencer of the behavior of managers down the line. It is not uncommon for highly engaged and externally focused CEOs to be succeeded by those who have no appreciation of public affairs. This leads to diminishment of its potential contribution and in one extreme example in a major firm the function was abolished following a change of CEO.

In some companies public affairs practitioners become too closely aligned with the CEO. In these personality-driven cases, public affairs maintains its influence as long as the CEO is its protector. When that changes, practitioners are at risk or the function repositioned. This problem is often compounded when executives turn to general organization consultants or remuneration consultants hired to constrain costs or establish internal work value comparisons, who see the function at its immature level and undervalue the discipline.

As with the earlier level, an important limitation of the function as consultant is that other managers without relevant expertise determine what is important and what is relevant information to be made available. The history of business is replete with examples of serious failure and economic loss because operations managements did not see the implications of their decisions on external stakeholders and how they were likely to react.

Most practitioners will have numerous examples. They include the marketing department of a beverages company preparing to launch an alcoholic drink at young women as politicians debate advertising restrictions for alcohol; the company choosing to trial a new risky product roll-out in the marginal electorate of a hostile and influential politician; the US company that had its technical manual obviously translated into Mandarin for the Chinese market in Taiwan at a peak period of political tension; and the investor relations team promoting aggressive employment reduction in politically sensitive rural areas the day before the CEO was to meet relevant politicians and the press in the nation's capital.

An inadequate understanding of the potential contribution of the function means that there is no opportunity for practitioners, with their more finely attuned antennae to stakeholders and socio-political dynamics to alert the organization to potential issues emerging that can impact the business and suggest alternative approaches.

Level III: A Mature Function

The authors note that as far back as 1995 the CEO of the world's largest mining company endorsed the value of the function and suggested it had gone beyond the role of servicing line managers. He said:

> In essence, they (public affairs executives) are the acknowledged authority on the social and political

environments and their effects on our business. As such they are playing an increasingly strategic role in planning, issues management and the creative use of public policy to further company goals'. (Prescott, 1995)

This is a fair characterization of what we call the mature level of public affairs. It has a number of central elements. Those discussed are that the function has 1) a seat at the decision-making table; 2) its specific contributions are seen as business performance enhancing rather than a cost to an organization; 3) its sub-functions and those close to its functional boundary are closely integrated to achieve a holistic approach to issues; 4) it has a sophisticated approach to company and function planning; and 5) it is international in geographic scope and business process.

Seat at the Table

At the mature level, public affairs is at the strategy table and routinely participates in senior management meetings. Heads of function have ready access to the highest levels of decision-making and a presence with the board. It is able to determine the potential for risks and opportunities arising from the non-market environment and accordingly is fully informed at an early stage of planning and decision-making and has the power to intervene with advice on any relevant issue.

Apart from the opportunities that come from early identification and proactive management of issues, in a number of cases in the authors' experience this has led to an organization adopting a second or third best approach but the only one that was reasonably achievable.

To achieve this standing in an organization the public affairs team must have a sufficiently sophisticated understanding of the enterprise overall, its markets, financials, competitive environment, and the technical and other nature of its processes and products. Its executives need to speak the business language of the firm and be seen as peers of the senior management team.

A Business-Performance-Enhancing Function

Apart from engaging in decision-making at a senior level, public affairs supports the achievement of organization objectives in a number of ways. They include facilitating the support and maintenance of good relations and a strong reputation with nonmarket actors including governments and NGOs and using a variety of tools at its disposal.

There has been growth in recognition of the importance of reputation to business success. While there has always been a link seen between reputation and business performance, the work of Charles Fombrun and his successors have attempted with some success to quantify the financial impact of reputational capital. They have demonstrated that the value of a positive reputation is very substantial, and conversely, for example, reputational damage from behaviors that don't meet community expectations, or crises mismanaged, can have a dramatic impact on equity value (Fombrun, 1996).

One example of the recognition of this is of the CEO of one of the world's largest companies being 'let go' by its board at least in part because a report showed the company's relationships with key non-market stakeholders had been poorly managed and its reputation had deteriorated (AFR, 2015). In another case the board of a utility company concerned with the business impact of the CEO's reputation sought to add reputation metrics as a significant criterion for establishing his compensation.

The evolution from corporate philanthropy to corporate community investment as a competitive tool further illustrates the way in which one of these tools within the function has moved from the non-strategic mode to its mature level and in doing so provides more focused support for the achievement of corporate strategy.

In developed western economies at an early phase of functional maturity financial contributions were treated as philanthropic donations without a close connection to corporate strategy.

There was a long-standing cultural tradition of 'giving back to the community' and in the USA a legal framework that required giving to be 'disinterested' to achieve tax benefits. By the early 1990s companies were starting to realize the potential of their social contributions to support specific corporate objectives, and for example the US-based Public Affairs Council had identified the emergence and growth of 'strategic philanthropy'. By the late 1990s public-affairs-driven community investment initiatives were being used to engage with 'influencers', including government agencies, and build constructive alliances with often hostile NGOs.

Multinationals working in Asia started using their corporate contributions to form alliances with government and aligned with government priorities with the aim of building relations and facilitating market entry. Activity was addressed to government-preferred projects and partners in China and Vietnam for example, with sponsored schools and communist party welfare NGOs. Unilever strongly associated their imaginative health and nutrition activities in remote communities with brand awareness and facilitated micro-finance for underprivileged families to build their distribution chain. There are many such examples.

In a study for the Australian government in 2007, companies were asked whether corporate community investment was 'peripheral to business'. Only 10 percent of CEOs were seen to agree while 82 percent disagreed, or strongly disagreed. Ninety-three percent of CEOs said some return-on-investment (ROI) justification was sought and of these 24 percent demanded 'tangible' ROI justification (Centre for Corporate Public Affairs, 2007).

As a tool of the company's overarching commercial objectives, community investment will normally be connected to media strategy, community, and interest group relations, reputation, regulatory, and other public policy, and is important to the employment and motivation of employees. Enlightened self-interest and the use of community investment as a competitive tool had long been a minimum explicator of corporate social engagement, so the breathless reception of Porter and Kramer's 'strategic insight' called 'shared value' in 2006 was somewhat surprising (Porter and Kramer, 2006).

Integrated/highly Coordinated Function

While many companies still run government affairs and communications in separate silos with separate reporting lines through the organization (and this was the dominant model until the new millennium) the authors strongly believe that the best contribution can be made when these activities, together with employee communications and community investment, are managed holistically. While now accepted by most leading practitioners and their advisers, this is often neither understood nor adopted by line managers and organization designers.

The value of the integrated function (see Figure 4.1) is apparent when one considers that the external social, political, and regulatory environment is conditioned by a multitude of stakeholders interacting with and influencing each other as well as the company. Corporate and industry reputation in the community generally impacts business legitimacy with both commercial and political consequences. Media is both influenced by and has an influence on the articulation and development of issues with all stakeholders including staff and government. Local communities exert political influence and can veto, delay, or lead to costly conditions on development. Employees need to understand issues facing an organization and its approach to them, especially where they are controversial. Consequently successful management of significant issues normally requires a holistic approach to the external environment.

There are a number of business functions that are sometimes integrated in the public affairs team at a mature level but are more often managed separately. Where in some countries investor relations are managed in public affairs, in others the function may report through the CFO. Regulatory affairs can be managed from within or outside the function. This usually depends on the scale of the company or more importantly the technical nature of regulation in the industry. Marketing communications is often located here, but is more usually within marketing departments, again depending on the nature of an enterprise. In all these, as with legal departments, the closest possible working relationships are required across functional boundaries and this often leads to physical co-location.

One of the most important developments in the evolution of public affairs is the recognition that for public affairs to be effective, it must be connected to line management. As noted, public affairs at the mature level knows and understands the business and operations and other managers understand what to expect of public affairs.

Public Affairs and Planning
The public affairs mindset and toolbox is critical to optimal corporate strategic planning. Just as the development of strategy relies on public affairs' authoritative voice, so does planning, which is the implementation of strategy. Plans require an understanding of the future environment, and of the social and political environments in which an organization operates.

It is not uncommon now for public affairs to provide a chapter on the social and political context of the plan period to go alongside sections on the economic, financial, market, and competitor analysis in written corporate plans. One company adopted the practice of undertaking a regular 'future issues review' involving external stakeholders as part of the planning cycle. This was then used to sensitivity-test the draft overall strategic plan and specific proposals and investment bids of the business units.

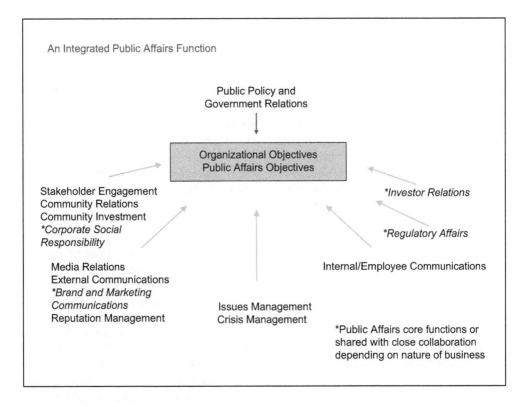

Figure 4.1   An integrated public affairs function

The focus on strategy for public affairs influences the way planning within and for the function itself is undertaken. At an early stage in the evolution of public affairs, sub-function plans were written around their separate activities. There was the separately developed media plan, the government relations plan, the community relations plan, and employee communications plan. These plans also tended to focus on process, products, and activities – often ends in themselves – rather than being firmly rooted on identified imperatives of business plans. Accordingly, the focus shifts from maintaining government contacts to pursuing government policy for business purposes; from communications activities to winning support by staff and external stakeholders for the achievement of organization objectives.

The contribution of public affairs to the strategic goals are best enabled, as noted, when the sub-functions are fully integrated and seen as tools for a holistic pursuit of these major business objectives. In many companies where public affairs is at the mature level, the function is not integrated, but is managed in a highly coordinated fashion.

The crisis Toyota faced in 2009–10 validates the importance of long-term investment in various sub-functions in order to have them ready in time of crisis. Toyota in the US spent years of careful strategic deployment of resources in developing relationships with elected officials, investing in communities, dealers, and customers. It created a presence for the company as a valued member of the community. When faced with a crisis that could have brought down the company, their dealers and customers did not desert Toyota. Both the governors of the states where they had factories and employees spoke up for the company. When asked whether all the investment in public affairs was worth it, the former head of function said, 'While it couldn't prevent a crisis, it ensured that the crisis was not deeper and longer' (Cooper, 2015).

International Public Affairs

International public affairs has been identified as an important focus for more than 30 years.

In the US, in a 1982 article, it was identified as having critical input into the strategic planning process, which itself was described as being in its infancy (Bergner, 1982). On the other side of the globe in Australia, the Centre for Corporate Public Affairs, founded in 1990 was breaking new ground in advancing the practice of public affairs. And yet managing internationally did not appear on the agenda of its popular professional development institute until a decade later. In parts of Europe, and in Asia, Latin America, and Africa, public affairs as a profession was practically non-existent. Managing public affairs as a global function was rare; international public affairs was little more than domestic public affairs, albeit in multiple locations, with a focus on issues arising from bilateral government relations or issues involving foreign subsidiaries.

The public affairs function expanded beyond its domestic scope when corporate organization itself changed to meet the requirements of the global economy. Stakeholders and issues crossed borders, as did non-governmental organizations, the latter developing increasingly sophisticated strategies to harass and hold companies accountable.

Positive reputations earned in one country could be destroyed by unattended crises in another country. Whatever public affairs managers did at their best domestically, like their domestic counterparts in general management, they now had to learn to do when managing across borders.

Companies over recent decades have been going through phases of centralization and decentralization affecting different lines of authority and accountability. With the internationalization of business these become even more complex with matrix structures and multiple reporting lines creating additional challenges. Despite attempts in some companies to present these as separate entities to different stakeholders, governments, NGOs, the social and traditional media, and investors see one company within and across geographies.

Accordingly, as the function matured, mechanisms and conventions were established within public affairs teams to help ensure consistency in reputational attributes, a cohesive approach to issues and stakeholder interaction, and clarity in the accountability for leadership on issues, regardless of formal structures.

A LEADERSHIP FUNCTION: PUBLIC AFFAIRS AT LEVEL IV

The function, however, achieves its highest potential when it goes beyond the mature stage, which is largely keeping the company informed of the external environment and managing risks emerging from it. This is the level where public affairs has a deep understanding of the business, where the function is valued by sophisticated operations managers, and where public affairs professionals are full partners to the business shaping organizational strategy. We see the function pushing on the boundary of this characterization to what we call public affairs as a leadership function (see Figure 4.2).

Although they may vary in budget, staff size, scope of responsibility, and reporting structure, public affairs is an established part of the overall organization in most large western companies. It operates at different stages of development from early to mature in the second decade of the twenty-first century. However, the authors believe the function still has to evolve further to achieve its potential to what we are calling public affairs as a leadership function.

At this level, we define **public affairs as the leadership function that manages risk and creates opportunities by shaping organizational strategy and influencing the socio-political environment to deliver beneficial outcomes for the organization and society**.

The essential characteristics of public affairs at this level include 1) re-defining what it means to be a strategic function; 2) being fully institutionalized and embedded as a core function and at an appropriate level and authority in the company; 3) global in its

---

Evolution of Public Affairs

Immature	Consultant	Mature	Leadership
PR orientation	Resource/ consultant	Part of management Integrated/ coordinated	Strategic partner Integrated
Need to know	Need to know	Seat at the table	Institutionalized
Reactive	Reactive/active	Active/proactive	Proactive
Trouble shooter Philanthropy	Authoritative specialist CSR	Manage risks Community investment International	Create opportunities Global Holistic business/ social focus

Figure 4.2　Evolution of public affairs

perspective and reach; 4) extended as a leadership competence for general management; 5) populated with quality professionals with leadership competencies who are regarded as business partners; and 6) having a holistic business and societal focus.

Re-Defining Strategic Function

'Strategy' and 'strategic' are vastly over-used words today. They are often used to describe what are merely plans and actions to achieve long-term objectives. Strategy is much more: '…the strategy-making process involves creativity, innovation, and change…' (Harrison, 2013, p. x). While strategy-making in the forward-looking, long-term planning sense exists at the mature level of public affairs, it has certain distinctive characteristics at the leadership level.

At this level, strategic public affairs goes beyond knowing the business to being a true business partner, taking action to anticipate problems, to smooth the way, protect operations and mitigate risks. As a leadership function its role is also to create opportunities including to proactively impact both the business model and or the socio-political environment in which it operates.

It is easier for operating managers to understand risk mitigation than opportunity creation, especially for those who define risk primarily in negative terms. Creating opportunity means seeing something that is not there, that may come into being if certain conditions are satisfied. It involves imagination and vision together with a deep understanding of the existing environment and a realistic assessment of the building blocks needed to bring the new environment into being. This is public affairs at the strategic, leadership level.

This can involve a dynamic, high risk, high stakes effort requiring the closest collaboration between line and staff functions. It exists already where organizations are under significant pressures including in industries that are highly regulated and where the nature of the market is rapidly changing. Under these

conditions, strategic public affairs can engage in or lead processes that will fundamentally change the model.

An example is an insurance company covering flood insurance in a community facing catastrophic damage season after season. With payout liabilities mounting for the company and premiums rising for the insured, the company decided to drop out of the market. But that wasn't the end. Corporate public affairs worked to push government and the community to put in flood levees, thereby providing flood protection and enabling the company to re-enter the market to the benefit of both the insured (lower premiums) and the company (lower payouts).

In the US health-care industry the commercial market is morphing into a different market; where product development, delivery mechanisms, incentives, hospital administration, patient care, and the regulators overseeing all this are changing. This is an environment in which we see not only risks, but a competitive advantage from changes in the environment. Here the role of public affairs is to identify new stakeholders, develop new relationships with them, and then fully understand their needs and aspirations. It begins with a re-assessment of the constituents as well as of the relationship. Where once doctors were the industry's key constituent, in the emerging model patients are. Where once it may have been a forced dependence, in the future it will be built on a new convergence of interest with stakeholders. The role of public affairs in this case is to help shape the business model while at the same time working with lawmakers and regulators to ensure alignment between public policy and private interests.

Another example of public affairs playing a major role in strategy-making comes from a distribution company facing major barriers to market entry from licensing authorities at the provincial and local levels. Despite the approach favored by the rest of the management team that wanted to fight politically and 'take on' the national regulator through legal and other means, or to capitulate to a less favorable business outcome, public affairs led an alternative stakeholder-focused strategy that ultimately, with modest business adjustments, overcame objections and facilitated propitious market entry.

Yet another example of public affairs leading strategic thinking in a company exists in the coal industry in Australia. Companies normally take regulatory constraints as givens and manage within them, and while opportunities can arise from government initiatives, government relations and public policy work is normally defensive. CRA (now part of Rio) and others in the New South Wales coal industry were operating in a hostile industrial environment that threatened the sustainability of the industry. The relevant unions had captured crucial management prerogatives in the operation of the mines including effective day-to-day control of the workforce and led extremely wasteful and productivity limiting restrictive work practices. These extreme industrial conditions were underpinned by coal industry-specific arbitration institutions established by legislation and regulation.

The public affairs leadership involved in strategy discussions took the view that what were widely perceived as 'industrial realities' could be overturned and that the public and governments would support radical change if the issues were exposed and reasonable alternatives recommended. They proposed a campaign to do this and seek public and policy-maker support for change. Despite the certainty of lost production and heavy short-term losses it was agreed and a range of public affairs tools were deployed with support at the highest levels of management. The unions led a global campaign to tarnish the reputation of the company, teaming with a variety of anti-business NGOs and targeting environmentalists, churches, and shareholders.

Commissioned research established international productivity benchmarks. The government was successfully lobbied to conduct its own study of comparative productivity and costs to the economy. In a comprehensive communications program monographs and research papers were published regularly and were accompanied by media briefings, releases, and letters to the editor that quoted the research results graphically. The major thrust, however, was dialogue with a strategically selected group of 'influencers' who were likely, in due course, to have an impact on community attitudes and the public policy environment.

Correspondence was initially established with around 200 recipients in the media, government, academia, and others, and this built to a list of 3,000 as the campaign rolled on. The coal industry's issues were successfully reframed to be ones of public interest rather than the normal perception of industrial standoff between capital and labor. The union had lost credibility in a series of industrial conflicts as the company and others in the industry won back legitimacy with key stakeholders. Normalization of conditions in industrial relations through legislative and regulatory change enabled the industry's ongoing viability.

Institutionalized and Embedded as a Core Function

Institutionalizing or embedding the function means making it impervious to changes in management or the personality preference of individual managers. Of course public affairs like other staff functions has to adjust to changes in style and priorities that come with new management. The level of resources and focus of activities will always depend on a range of factors. These include the size and profile of a business in a sector, and its vulnerability to, or opportunities in, the external environment. The mining industry in Australia put more resources into the function when environmental and indigenous issues were at their peak. Big 'pharma' has had its turn, and at time of writing the heat is on the fast food industry and banks.

As noted above the attitudes of company leadership, especially the CEO, are critical to the ability of the function to reach its potential and its use as a competitive tool. Practitioner and academic Robert Healy notes that, CEOs can be laggards who play catch-up on external issues, reluctant participants, or political entrepreneurs with social and political advantage as a priority. These characteristics broadly reflect the stages in the evolution of public affairs to providing leadership. Entrepreneurial first movers place ' … a positive value on political participation…[they]…believe as an article of faith that governments, politics, media and social media are rationally exploitable … [they]…have made investments in political resource capacity and have risk tolerance to exploit that capacity' (Healy, 2014, p. 64). He notes that firms like Apple, Starbucks, and Microsoft that did not appreciate their political vulnerability, suffered by not having an affirmative political culture, and had to make significant late adjustments to their political preparedness.

Crises can sometimes lead to a cultural shift and embedding public affairs within a company. The US-based Tyco is a good example. A successful global conglomerate, Tyco faced a perfect storm of crisis in 2002. In the wake of corporate scandal, its stock price crashed, its reputation was devastated. At this very same time, a tax issue, which labeled companies that had incorporated in tax haven countries 'financial traitors', became a focus of public attention in a presidential election year. Tyco, incorporated in Bermuda years earlier through a company it acquired, was denounced as an 'inverted company'. This was a time when having a sophisticated public affairs function would have been critical. Tyco had a public affairs function in name only. It had no one in the company confronting it with the consequences of a range of behaviors that offended critically important stakeholders. When trouble struck it had no relationships with lawmakers and regulators, no brand recognition, and no credibility to deliver a critical message.

New leadership understood the important role public affairs could play as an integral part of business in developing and executing the strategy to re-build Tyco (Figure 4.3). Tyco went on to split into three publicly traded companies, all with a robust public affairs function embedded in their senior teams.

Unfortunately, this longevity is not the experience in every company. When the crisis is over, the value of public affairs may recede in corporate memory unless the function is understood and fully embedded in the company's leadership. A pro-business

Figure 4.3   Public Affairs as an integral part of business operations

political environment can have a soporiphic effect on companies. At an association meeting in the US during the Bush administration, a group of corporate lobbyists expressed concern that their budgets might be cut because their executives did not feel threatened by government decisions. The scene quickly changed with the advent of the Obama administration with its increased focus on regulating industry. A short-term view would have gutted public affairs offices, a mistake often made by businesses who turn their 'swords into plowshares' as soon as a crisis is over.

Given the significance of the function to achieving corporate objectives as discussed earlier in this chapter, public affairs will only achieve its potential when it is seen as critical to organizational performance as other functions and embedded as fully as is the more traditional marketing, finance, human resource, and legal functions. It cannot be vulnerable to the vagaries of line management or external consultant ignorance or underestimation. It has to be seen as an integral activity by the leadership of a modern corporation.

Public Affairs as a Global Function

Public affairs as a global function goes beyond what we describe at the mature level as international public affairs, or bilateral government relations, just as global companies (Shell, Unilever, ABB) differ from traditional multinationals in terms of how they manage people, products and processes across borders.

Unlike the international model, operating globally is a game changer for public affairs in three respects. First, public affairs executives have to deploy state-of-the-art communications technology and sophisticated management tools to oversee a complex network of people, organizations, and programs. Building trust among teams from diverse cultures and working with country managers who may or may not have public affairs competencies, requires leadership skills at the highest level.

Second, stakeholders and issues increase dramatically on the global plane and have to be managed across borders. For example, an agriculture company that considers food security a key issue maps hundreds of stakeholders with thousands of influencers as the beginning of its process of managing the issues. Based on this an elaborate engagement strategy is devised and executed.

Third, public affairs executives have to be able to navigate diverse cultures. They have to deal with enormous challenges in understanding how to position their company; whether to be low or high profile; whether to rely on direct advocacy or work through associations; whether the phrase 'public affairs' even has meaning in a given culture. The scope of public affairs is also evolving. In the US it always includes government relations and may also include stakeholder engagement, issues management, community relations, corporate social responsibility, and communications.

In Europe, public affairs is mostly synonymous with a narrow definition of 'boots on the ground' government relations without the communications sub-functions. In Asia, it's a mix of government relations and marketing communications or business development driven by the experience of American, European, and Australian multinationals; the prevailing indigenous models exhibit the characteristics of an insiders environment, i.e., the decision-making process and the opportunities to access and influence outcomes by stakeholders is not transparent. In Latin America it's more personality-driven than programmatic. In emerging economies, it varies with how hospitable the political structure is to participation by outsiders. In Australia, an integrated model including all sub-functions is the norm.

In general, we can say that the principles of public affairs are global, although their application is local. These global principles go to the way companies understand and respond to business and social cultures and expectations, legal frameworks, power structures, modes of influence, and appropriate ways they should respond to these factors.

Companies considering entering new markets to source, invest or sell, or placing expatriate managers into a new geography, need to have a sophisticated awareness, not only of the financial, and market environment but also of the social and political context in which the business proceeds. This can simply mean trends and sensitivities in the regulatory environment, or customer and workforce culture. However, it also means understanding the political system and dynamics, the local power structures and shifting influences, the views and interests of relevant key players, and the role of domestic competitors in influencing the commercial or regulatory environment.

These factors can have a major effect on the viability of a new investment, positioning for a competitive bid for government contracts, assets or licenses and so on. There are many examples of failure due to an inadequate understanding of political dynamics, the embrace of connections with failing political standing, and successes from knowing what non-commercial buttons to press.

International companies seek comfort in market entry through joint ventures, local management international political risk consultants but have been slow to use the expertise that exists internally for analysis of the social and political environments and their implications for businesses.

There are examples to the contrary. One company known to the authors required public affairs to make an assessment and comment on the social and political context, including political risk of all significant proposals for new market or global product development proposals before decisions were made. This sort of analysis and engagement in decision-making within geographies has been common given the insights and skill sets of the public affairs team, and needs to leverage off the monitoring and active management of global issues – environment, human rights, health, and other issues when the profession is functioning optimally.

The Discipline as a Leadership Function for Operating Managers

The fourth condition for public affairs to achieve its true potential as a strategic function is for the discipline itself to become a leadership competence for operating managers.

This was said eloquently by a leading business statesman as far back as 1990.

> Management from the grass roots to the board room should be thinking about these [public affairs] issues intrinsically when business plans are being made as well as in the everyday process of managing. It is important that we value the capacity to deal with the social and political environment as an important part of the abilities that go into making a manager ... performance in this area must have increasing weight in the way in which our managers are recruited, trained, evaluated, and rewarded because of the critical nature of these issues to the successor lack of success of our enterprises ...

> We can do our sums, be great at production and marketing, fine tune our cashflows, manage people – we can do all of those things well, but fail badly if we haven't managed the social and political issues. (Parbo, 1990)

Twenty-first century leadership needs managers who are more than traditional, transaction-oriented business people. They are operating in an environment where transparency and trust are as important as traditional measures of quality and price. They have to understand the context in which they operate and know what is required to achieve business objectives in that context.

While function leaders need to think and act like other senior executives, the strategic potential of the function can only be achieved when the whole organization shares an understanding of public affairs imperatives. Any manager of a company can impact its reputation and standing with stakeholders and affect its license to operate.

Embedding a culture of awareness and sensitivity to the socio-political environment is not easy. As is the case in law or accountancy the appropriation of public affairs understanding and 'literacy' does not require general managers or others in staff functions to become specialists, however, the boundary spanning activities of the public affairs function becomes more demanding and crucial as executives move up the organizational hierarchy.

There are a number, but relatively few cases where public affairs practitioners have become the CEO or chairman of major companies. However, recognition that external relations such as high level stakeholder engagement, involvement in public policy, and understanding the implications of social and political pressures is critical for senior management. This has led some companies to require a rotation of duty in public affairs departments as a component in the development of 'high potential executives'.

A parallel can perhaps be drawn with information technology. It is a leadership competence that is a relative newcomer to the suite of executive functions that has gained acceptance because of changes in the environment of business. Because of the dramatic changes in technology, it has been necessary for businesses to adapt, to build capacity, and to have in-house expertise at the staff and leadership levels to manage it. Not every executive is an IT expert, but every executive knows how to exploit the value of the laptop and other devices that give him a window into the potential of information technology. Apart from using it for basic communications and for financial and process knowledge management they watch the news or consume it digitally; many are on Facebook and have Twitter accounts. Every executive has to be concerned about cyber-security.

There has been a slower embrace of public affairs as a core management function by line managers. Embedding a culture of awareness and sensitivity to the socio-political environment is not easy. Managers with technical and financial backgrounds often see the world through their own lenses of science and rationality, and expect stakeholders to think and act as they would. This expectation of 'rational' behavior of stakeholders has seen the loss of hundreds of millions of dollars in the authors' own experience.

In one not untypical case a CEO, concerned that his senior team were not significantly cognizant of the potential impact of external factors, commissioned a medium term external issues audit to confront them with potential challenges to their capacity to meet their business objectives. The need to manage within a social and political context is often ignored in corporate training, job specification, and recruitment.

An underlying cause of corporate failure or underperformance is the common mismatch in management incentives, for example for financial performance in a short time frame at the cost of longer-term objectives. The mantra of 'on time, on budget' has driven behavior at the cost of longer term and more valuable reputation or stakeholder support. However, an increasing number of companies have sought to more closely align management behavior with public affairs imperatives by specifying capacity to relate to stakeholders and sensitivity to external issues as a positive attribute in recruitment and, more importantly placing performance in this area as a material criterion for remuneration at risk.

Public Affairs as a Profession

The fifth condition for public affairs to achieve its potential is for public affairs practitioners themselves to take their profession to a higher level of professional development. At the leadership level, they must be fully competent in their profession as well as full business partners. This requires a sufficiently sophisticated understanding of the enterprise overall, its markets, financials, competitive environment, and the technical and other nature of its products. For their advice to be taken seriously and to be relevant practitioners need to speak the business language of the firm and appreciate the decision-making environment of the line manager. More junior practitioners may overstate the importance of an issue or of their role when they operate only from the perspective of their external stakeholders. In spanning the boundary between the company and its social and political environment the public affairs executive needs to share the corporate objectives and culture, while maintaining the objectivity and empathy with the outside world to keep the company attuned and develop effective strategies to engage.

As a broad generalization, at the early stage in its evolution the function in developed western countries when it was not appropriately valued or seen as strategic, departments were staffed by second career journalists (who could write) and mid-career government officials (who knew their way around government). The public relations industry was also a source of recruitment and there were a number of examples of semi-redundant line managers being parked in the function to await retirement.

As the strategic relevance of the function became more apparent and it was repositioned in organizational hierarchies, more senior people with serious business and political backgrounds were appointed. The growth of human capital in the function is illustrated by the educational qualifications of its staff. Data from Australia and the US illustrates a significant shift from graduate to post-graduate qualifications.

The question is asked about whether the function qualifies as 'a profession'. Unlike many professions, practitioners are not required to have formal endorsement by regulation or professional associations. They are not trained in any specific academic stream that is well aligned to the broad sweep of the function. Indeed relationships between practitioners and the academy are seriously deficient.

Received academic wisdom is that there is no integrating theory of public affairs but rather it is an eclectic mix of a number of other disciplines such as political science, sociology, economics, and communications. These theoretical silos are supposed to, but do not easily, come together to provide an integrated approach to public affairs. For this reason high level, specialist public affairs courses are lacking and the authors believe academic preparation for careers is best done in business schools where decision-making is taught holistically rather than in separate academic streams.

The function by now, however, has a valued professional identity, professional connectedness, and since the 1970s has developed its own systems and technology, framework of theory and knowledge. Its professional toolbox includes for example political advocacy, political risk analysis, issues management, stakeholder theory, business strategy, and risk communications.

However, as noted above, to achieve their strategic potential and required influence, we reiterate that leaders in the function need to have, and be seen to have, the language, understanding and mindset of the line managers with whom they are collaborating in decision-making. Accordingly, the authors are quick to advise aspiring young practitioners to pursue business education for their development. We are also asked whether or not peers from other disciplines or line management can make a transition to senior roles in public affairs. There have been a number of very successful such transitions, but they have only proved successful when the executive has very special skills, interests and a high level of emotional intelligence.

A Holistic Business–Society Focus

At the strategic leadership level, public affairs is clearly concerned with outcomes that benefit the business. But the authors hasten to add that the benefit to business in the long term is only possible if it also benefits society. There exists now a large body of research and practice that points to the importance of the business–society nexus. Whether defined narrowly as 'the business of business is business' or more broadly as the value-driven business, there is no question that companies must meet the challenge of the twenty-first century's premium on transparency and trust. They must do this by engaging with stakeholders and delivering business results that are achieved by means of a holistic focus on both business goals and social expectations.

LOOKING TO THE FUTURE

Public affairs has come a long way since the 1960s, but it has not yet achieved its full potential. It will always be about spanning the boundary between the corporation and the nonmarket environment. It will always be about managing the context in which the firm operates by engaging with stakeholders and working the issues. At the next level, it will be a business partner fully integrated at the highest levels of leadership proactively shaping strategy to create opportunities by influencing the environment in which business operates.

REFERENCES

The Australian Financial Review, May 30, 2015, p. 45.

Baron, David P. (1993). *Business and its Environment*, 3rd edn. Saddle River, New Jersey: Prentice Hall.

Bergner, Douglas (1982). 'International public affairs and strategic planning', *Perspectives*, January.

Centre for Corporate Public Affairs. (2007). 'Corporate Community Investment in Australia', *Report for the Prime Minister's Community Business Partnership, Australian Government Department of Prime Minister and Cabinet, Canberra.*

Cooper, Josephine S. (February 12, 2015). 'Presentation', Global Government Relations Forum, Washington, D.C.

Fombrun, Charles (1996). *Reputation: Realizing the Value from the Corporate Image*. Boston, MA: Harvard Business School Press.

Jacoby, N.H. (1974). 'The Corporation as Social Activist' in S.P. Sethi (ed.), *The Unstable Ground: Corporate Social Policy in a Dynamic Society*. Los Angeles, CA: Melville Publishing Company.

Harrison, Ross (2013). *Strategic Thinking in 3D*. Dulles, VA: Potomac Books.

Healy, Robert (2014). *Corporate Political Behavior: Why Corporations Do What They Do in Politics*. New York, Routledge.

McKinsey & Company, 'Managing government relations for the future,' *McKinsey Global Survey*, 2011.

Palmer, Anna (2005). 'Tyco's complete makeover,' *Influence* III, 2. 26–31.

Parbo, Arvi (1990). Speech at Official launch of the Centre for Corporate Public Affairs, Melbourne. November.

Porter, M.E. and Kramer, M.R. (2006). 'Strategy and society: the link between corporate competitive advantage and corporate social responsibility' *Harvard Business Review*, December, 1–14.

Prescott, John (1995). Managing Director of BHP Ltd, Oration, Centre for Corporate Public Affairs, Melbourne.

Rothfeder, Jeffrey (2015). 'The great unraveling of globalization,' *Wall Street Journal*, April 26, pp. F1, F4.

The Status of Instruction in Public Affairs: Peace in the Eye of the Hurricane?

Shannon Blair Creighton and Martin Meznar

As we set upon our task of reviewing the status of public affairs instruction, we were struck by how little appears to have changed since this volume was last published in 2005. The same schools seem to be offering the same programs – and the status quo seems little changed. Conversely, society and business practices have changed dramatically. Google went public in 2004 – and has been changing our information based society in dramatic ways. Facebook, Instagram, and Twitter have come of age. Gay marriage is legal in all 50 US states. One might argue that the job of the public affairs professional is much more challenging today. Yet we did not observe significant changes in public affairs education. Are we sitting calmly in the eye of a storm raging around our established university programs? It seems to be a possibility. Yet, trying to understand the current state of public affairs education is not an easy task, for at least two reasons:

1 The domain of the public affairs field is, almost by necessity, difficult to define. In a world of increasingly permeable boundaries between organizations and their environment, boundary-spanning functions such as public affairs are increasingly difficult to 'nail down'. Establishing the limits of this boundary spanning function is extremely difficult and probably ill-advised.

2 In part because of its lack of clear boundaries, public affairs education does not fit neatly into a specific program area or college across universities. Public affairs training can be found in business programs, political science programs, public administration programs, public policy programs, and so on. Thus it is difficult to put together a comprehensive picture of public affairs programs.

In our attempt to provide a somewhat cogent overview of the state of public affairs education, we have found it necessary to deal with these issues as follows:

First, we have followed Boddewyn's (2012) lead in viewing public affairs as focusing primarily, though not exclusively, on the non-market area of firm operations. Competitive strategies, marketing strategies, financial strategies, mergers and acquisitions (portfolio strategies), and so on are part of the market environment in which the firm competes. In the approach we take in this chapter, the public affairs function deals primarily with non-economic stakeholders such as political and social actors. Put differently, functional level strategies, business level strategies, and corporate level strategies deal primarily with the firm's market environment. Enterprise level strategies (Freeman, 1983; Meznar and Johnson, 2005), which deal with the legitimacy of a firm based on its role in society, would include the firm's non-market environment and thereby be the domain of public affairs.

Second, we have attempted to be inclusive – rather than exclusive – in identifying public affairs educational programs. Courses of study that consider non-market actors in their analysis of corporate activities and strategies fall within our understanding of the field. As such, public administration, social issues, business/government relations, and even corporate philanthropy would be included under the 'public affairs' banner. These topics are covered in a variety of disciplines from business to public administration and from lobbying to political science.

As we try to synthesize and organize our description of the current state of public affairs education, we are indebted to Craig Fleisher (2005) for giving us a framework and benchmark for this chapter. We have attempted to make our description consistent with his framework by following up data sources quoted in 2005 and updating that information. In this chapter, we rely on data provided by the National Association of Schools of Public Affairs and Administration (NASPAA) and the Council on Public Affairs to summarize public affairs programs in existence today. Our purpose is to provide a reasonably comprehensive list of programs that will serve as a resource to our readers. Where available, we have provided practical information on each program including program size, length, cost, and accreditation status. This information is summarized ahead, with the comprehensive list of 246 programs

included in the appendix. After this descriptive part of the chapter, we discuss the major changes which have occurred in the field over the last ten years. Finally, we discuss some of the biggest threats and opportunities, in our view, facing public affairs as discipline.

PUBLIC AFFAIRS PROGRAMS AVAILABLE TODAY

Public affairs education has been a growing field in institutions of higher education. NASPAA reports memberships at almost 300 institutions. There have been 185 programs that have achieved accreditation through NASPAA. Many of these programs offer undergraduate, graduate, online, and executive level programs. Table 5.1 lists the different program titles that were included in our research and how many programs utilized each title.

The majority of these programs are housed in a public affairs or public administration related department. Several other programs are located in political science or government-related departments. Other departments include business-related departments and colleges of arts and sciences.

The price tag varies widely across these programs, from less than $8,000 to over $100,000. Of the schools that offer state subsidized education, the average in-state tuition was approximately $21,500 and the average out of state tuition was $65,800. For private schools and online universities that do not differentiate tuition based on residency, the average cost was approximately $42,300. The NASPAA accredited programs have an average in state tuition of $21,160 and a non-resident average of $65,808. The average program costs for private and online programs that are accredited by NASPAA is $35,797. Twenty-six public affairs programs are offered entirely online. The average cost of these programs is $23,532. There are at least 13 more programs that offer online

Table 5.1   Program titles within the domain of Public Affairs

Program Name	Number of Programs
Executive Master of Public Administration	3
Executive Master of Public Management	1
In-Career Master of Arts in Public Policy and Management	1
Key Executive Master's Degree	1
Master of Engineering and Public Policy	1
Master of Health Administration	1
Master of International Affairs	1
Master of International Development	1
Master of Planning	1
Master of Public Administration	175
Master of Public Administration: Health Administration	1
Master of Public Affairs	14
Master of Public Management	2
Master of Public Policy	24
Master of Public Policy and Administration	7
Master of Public Service Management	1
Master of Science in Administration	1
Master of Science in Management	1
Master of Science in Public Administration	1
Master of Science in Public Affairs	1
Master of Science in Public Policy	1
Master of Science in Public Service	1
Master of Science in Urban Policy Analysis & Management	1
Masters of Public Administration	1
MBA for Business, Government and Not For Profit Management	1
Master of Professional Studies Public Administration	1
Master's in Public Policy & Management	1
Total	246

classes or certificate programs. Table 5.2 lists the 25 MPA programs with lowest tuition.

Of the programs that reported their current enrollments, the average enrollment was 118, which is skewed by some of the larger programs such as New York University (910), CUNY (802), and Baruch College (638). The median enrollment is 90. Table 5.3 represents some of the largest reported programs.

As with the other statistics mentioned earlier, the length of the programs varies widely. Most programs can be finished in two full academic years, requiring between 36 and 45 credit hours. Some programs are much longer, depending upon how the program is structured. See the Appendix for a comprehensive list of the number of credit hours required by each program. All executive and in-career programs are between 36 and 45 credit/semester hours. Table 5.4 lists the schools that have reported offering executive programs.

CHANGES IN PA EDUCATION OVER THE LAST DECADE

Despite dramatic changes in technology, social norms, and legislation, there have been few changes in the rankings for PA programs between US News and World Report's 2004 and 2012 findings. Table 5.5 lists the top 50 programs as ranked based on 2004 data and the rankings published in 2012. Upwards of 90 percent of the programs listed in the top 50 in 2004 remained in the top 50 in 2012. Table 5.5 lists the rankings for both years.

Further, there were approximately 250 programs in existence in 2004 (Koven, Goetze and Brennan, 2008) and we have identified 256 programs in our study ten years later. However, this apparent lack of change (as far as PA education) in the last decade begs the question of changes in the content of public affairs training. We did not compare the syllabi of PA core courses from ten years ago to what is currently being covered. Certainly, social media has transformed how grassroots campaigns are deployed, how social issues are managed, and how corporate reputations are built and demolished. The Public Affairs Council has sponsored recent seminars on topics such as 'Digital Media and Advocacy', 'Measuring and Communicating the Value of Social Media for Public Affairs', 'Messaging Matters: Tailoring Your Communications Strategy to Different Platforms', and 'Tweets

Table 5.2   Program costs

School Name	Program Name	Est. Program Cost
Georgia Regents University	Masters of Public Administration	$7,716.00
The University of North Carolina at Charlotte	Master of Public Administration	$8,256.00
The University of Texas at Brownsville	Master's in Public Policy & Management	$8,926.84
Savannah State University	Master of Public Administration	$9,666.00
University of Nebraska at Omaha	Master of Public Administration	$9,730.50
Georgia College & State University	Master of Public Administration	$10,368.00
University of Nevada, Las Vegas	Master of Public Administration	$10,491.00
University of Oklahoma	Master of Public Administration	$10,929.30
Southern Utah University	Master of Public Administration	$11,108.25
Southern University and A&M College	Master of Public Administration	$11,298.50
University of Arkansas at Little Rock	Master of Public Administration	$11,700.00
The University of Texas at Tyler	Master of Public Administration	$11,913.00
University of Central Florida	Master of Public Administration	$12,102.72
Wichita State University	Master of Public Administration	$12,119.25
University of West Georgia	Master of Public Administration	$12,260.00
Indiana University, Northwest	Master of Public Affairs	$12,531.84
New Mexico State University	Master of Public Administration	$12,556.00
Brigham Young University	Master of Public Administration	$12,620.00
Indiana University-Purdue University, Ft. Wayne	Master of Public Affairs	$12,739.35
Florida Atlantic University	Master of Public Administration	$12,755.82
University of Southern Indiana	Master of Public Administration	$12,774.24
University of New Orleans	Master of Public Administration	$12,872.00
Appalachian State University	Master of Public Administration	$12,965.75
Valdosta State University	Master of Public Administration	$12,980.00
Missouri State University	Master of Public Administration	$13,000.00

for Advocacy'. It is unclear, however, especially given the apparent stability of academic programs, how much the content of PA education is adjusting to the new tools available for public affairs professionals. Additional research is needed in this area to determine the extent to which programmatic content is staying abreast of technological and social change.

CHALLENGES TO PUBLIC AFFAIRS EDUCATION

Keeping Current in this Dynamic Field

Social media has changed the way and speed with which social issues arise.

Affinity groups of stakeholders can form around any issue almost instantly. Tweets can wreak havoc with a corporation's reputation in milliseconds. Campaign funding is under increasing scrutiny. New legal decisions on gay rights are transforming the social landscape across all 50 states. Platforms for advocacy advertising are continuously multiplying. The effectiveness of the public affairs officer is heavily dependent on mastery of these tools for shaping public opinion. Curricula in public affairs management programs must (1) equip students to master these tools, (2) refine the concept of stakeholder groups to deal with changing coalitions and narrower interests, and (3) prepare students to handle social issues life cycles that peak much more quickly than in the past.

Table 5.3   Largest programs based on enrollment

School Name	Program Name	Number of Reported Students
New York University	Master of Public Administration	910
John Jay College of Criminal Justice, CUNY	Master of Public Administration	802
Baruch College/ City University of New York	Master of Public Administration	638
Harvard University	Master of Public Policy	477
Indiana University, Bloomington	Master of Public Affairs	393
University of Washington	Master of Public Administration	389
University of Colorado, Denver	Master of Public Administration	381
George Mason University, School of Public Policy	Master of Public Policy	369
The Pennsylvania State University at Harrisburg	Master of Public Administration	300

Finding a Place in the Undergraduate Curricula Core

Despite the number of programs identified and detailed in this chapter, public affairs management is still not widely recognized as a specific function. While there are benefits to maintaining the wide breadth of the discipline, this breadth comes at a price. As business professors, it is the authors' opinion that a well designed business curriculum should expose students to the critical role non-market stakeholders play in corporate survival and success. New generations of students, with their interest in sustainability, social entrepreneurship, social enterprises, B corporations, and non-governmental organization management suggest now is the time to infuse more business curricular content on managing beyond the single bottom line. A required business course on managing non-market stakeholders would

go a long way toward defining the scope of public affairs management – at least in business school. If accrediting agencies such as AACSB, AMBA, and EQUIS would adopt such a recommendation, interest in public affairs as a discipline and career would increase significantly. Without such a slot in the business curriculum, it is hard to see how the field will coalesce and move forward.

More Continuing Education and Professional Certification

Given the multitude of career paths that can be subsumed under the public affairs umbrella – as well as the dynamism of the field alluded to earlier, public affairs professionals will need to be continuously honing their skills as technology, legislation, and social norms evolve. It will never be sufficient to offer graduate or undergraduate degrees in public affairs management. Our professionals should be the experts on social media applications. They should be the most up to date on changes in public opinion, legislation, and emerging issues. This is not possible without continual training opportunities. Organizations such as the Public Affairs Council in Washington, DC have a vital role to play in this area. Though important, it is not enough to keep discussing how to demonstrate to upper management the value of the public affairs function. Professional organizations must facilitate the sharing of the latest technology and expertise so that public affairs personnel embody knowledge that is vital to the success of the firm.

OPPORTUNITIES IN PUBLIC AFFAIRS EDUCATION

The opportunities we see in PA education are very closely related to threats mentioned above. As stakeholders become more diverse, more engaged in social media, and even quicker in

Table 5.4   Executive Programs

School Name	Program Name
American University	Key Executive Master's Degree
Baruch College/City University of New York	Master of Public Administration
Bridgewater State University	Master of Public Administration
Brigham Young University	Master of Public Administration
California State University, San Bernardino	Master of Public Administration
Carnegie Mellon University	Master of Public Management
Columbia University	Master of Public Administration
George Mason University, School of Public Policy	Master of Public Policy
Georgetown University	Master of Public Policy
Golden Gate University-San Francisco	Executive Master of Public Administration
Harvard University	Master of Public Policy
Indiana University, Bloomington	Master of Public Affairs
New York University	Master of Public Administration
Ohio University	Master of Public Administration
Ohio University	Executive Master of Public Administration
Pace University-New York	Master of Public Administration
Portland State University	Master of Public Administration
Portland State University	Executive Master of Public Administration
Princeton University	Master of Public Policy
Rutgers University, Camden	Master of Public Administration
Rutgers University, Newark	Master of Public Administration
Seattle University	Master of Public Administration
Southern University and A&M College	Master of Public Administration
Syracuse University	Master of Public Administration
The Ohio State University	In-Career Master of Arts in Public Policy and Management
The Ohio State University	Master of Public Administration
The University of Texas at Austin	Master of Public Affairs
The University of Utah	Master of Public Administration
The University of West Florida	Master of Science in Administration
University of Colorado, Denver	Master of Public Administration
University of Delaware	Master of Public Administration
University of Maryland, College Park	Master of Public Policy
University of Maryland, College Park	Executive Master of Public Management
University of Michigan-Ann Arbor	Master of Public Policy
University of Minnesota	Master of Public Affairs
University of Missouri-Columbia	Master of Public Affairs
University of Pennsylvania	Master of Public Administration
University of Pittsburgh	Master of International Development
University of South Florida	Master of Public Administration
University of Washington	Master of Public Administration
Upper Iowa University	Master of Public Administration

Table 5.5   Program rankings compared

2004 Ranking	School	2012 Ranking	School
1	Syracuse University	1	Syracuse University
2	Harvard University	2	Indiana University – Bloomington
3	Indiana University – Bloomington	3	Harvard University
4	University of Georgia	4	University of Georgia
5	Princeton University	5	Princeton University
6	University of California – Berkeley	6	New York University
7	University of Southern California	7	University of California – Berkeley
8	Carnegie Mellon University	8	University of Southern California
9	University of Michigan – Ann Arbor	9	Carnegie Mellon University
10	American University	10	University of Kansas
11	Duke University	11	University of Washington
12	George Washington University	12	American University
13	SUNY – Albany	13	George Washington University
14	University of Kansas – Lawrence	14	University of Michigan – Ann Arbor
15	U of North Carolina – Chapel Hill	15	University of Wisconsin – Madison
16	University of Texas – Austin	16	Arizona State University
17	Georgetown University	17	Duke University
18	New York University	18	Florida State University
19	University of Chicago	19	SUNY – Albany
20	University of Wisconsin – Madison	20	University of Kentucky
21	Columbia University	21	University of Minnesota (Twin Cities)
22	University of California – Los Angeles	22	U of Texas Austin
23	University of Maryland – College Park	23	Georgetown University
24	University of Minnesota – Twin Cities	24	Georgia State University
25	University of Pittsburgh	25	Rutgers – Newark
26	Arizona State University	26	University of Chicago
27	Florida State University	27	U of North Carolina – Chapel Hill
28	Georgia State University	28	Columbia University
29	Johns Hopkins University	29	Ohio State University
30	Rutgers University	30	University of Colorado – Denver
31	University of Nebraska – Omaha	31	University of Maryland – College Park
32	University of Washington	32	Texas A&M University
33	Virginia Polytech	33	University of Missouri
34	University of Kentucky	34	University of Nebraska – Omaha
35	Cornell University	35	University of Pittsburgh
36	Indiana University Purdue University	36	Cornell University
37	Northern Illinois University	37	University of Arizona
38	Texas A&M University	38	University of Delaware
39	University of Colorado – Denver	39	University of Illinois – Chicago
40	University of Delaware	40	Virginia Tech University
41	University of Missouri – Columbia	41	Cleveland State University
42	Cleveland State University	42	George Mason University
43	Naval Postgraduate School	43	Johns Hopkins University
44	Ohio State University	44	University of Pennsylvania

Table 5.5 Program rankings compared

2004 Ranking	School	2012 Ranking	School
45	University of Pennsylvania	45	City University of New York – Baruch
46	City University of New York – John Jay	46	Naval Postgraduate
47	George Mason University	47	Northern Illinois University
48	University of Arizona	48	Portland State University
49	University of Illinois – Chicago	49(tie)	Rutgers – New Brunswick
50	University of Utah	49(tie)	University of Connecticut
		49(tie)	University of Virginia

adopting new technology platforms, public affairs education needs to adapt accordingly.

Becoming More Diverse

To its credit, NASPAA has included a requirement for diversity related planning and programs into its accreditation standards for MPA and MPP programs. However, the lack of diversity in public affairs programs in higher education has been a concern since the 1960s and continues to be an issue (Ryan, 2012). The concept of diversity has been neglected in curricula and research in public affairs (Hewins-Maroney and Williams, 2007). In a recent study, Sabharwal and Geva-May (2013) found that a majority of public affairs programs in the United States had less than 34 percent of their student body from underrepresented populations and these programs with low enrollment numbers also have a lower percentage of faculty from diverse backgrounds. Less than half of the NASPAA accredited programs indicated that they addressed issues related to race in their curriculums. For public affairs education to be successful, it must be representative of the population that it is designed to serve, and up until this point it has failed to do so in terms of diversity (both race and gender). Until we train a more diverse group of students in public affairs management, organizations will struggle to manage relations with a very diverse set of stakeholders.

Dominating Social Media and Analytics

As Post, et al. (1982) so aptly put it, a public affairs unit serves a dual role, 'that of a window out of the corporation through which management can perceive, monitor, and understand external change, and simultaneously, a window in through which society can influence corporate policy and practice'. Thanks to social media and other developing technologies, the amount of information available both as the organization looks out the window and as society looks in has escalated dramatically. To be effective in this new environment, the public affairs officer must be an expert in broadcasting and retrieving information through social media and other emerging platforms (Price, 2013). The boundary-spanning role requires it. Given the huge volumes of information now available, interpretation of that data will require proficiency in 'big data' management and analytics. For public affairs managers to successfully accomplish their responsibilities, their training must include the latest information gathering and disseminating technologies as well as a strong foundation in data analysis tools such as analytics. By equipping students with such skills, PA programs will ensure the relevance of and reliance on public affairs officers in their corporate responsibilities.

More Mid-Level Career Training

Because of the new technologies, applications, and platforms that seem to appear each week, it would be impossible for boundary spanners to keep up with the tools necessary to do their jobs without continual training. We see a vital role for professional education in the future of the public affairs manager. The programs listed in Table 5.4 are certainly an important step in this direction. Without this training, we believe we are dooming public affairs workers to eventual failure. Given the static propensity of academic programs, we believe professional organizations (such as the Public Affairs Council, Business Roundtable, or The Centre for Public Affairs) must take leadership in this area. The training must be practical, current, and concrete. Universities may be able to contribute with well targeted executive education programs or graduate certifications – but the idea of continual training must be at the core of the public affairs professional's culture.

CONCLUSION

It is a great time to be part of the public affairs field. Students are increasingly interested in the interface between business and society. There are new tools to help businesses both understand their environment and help them interpret it properly. The competitive environment is making it increasingly clear to business that new consumers must be wooed on a variety of levels, not just offered the lowest price. The stakeholder model – including non-market stakeholders – is increasingly part of the evolving business paradigm. Organizational boundaries are more and more permeable and boundary spanning is increasingly complex. The need for public affairs education is greater than ever – as is the importance of the public affairs function to the organization. However, public affairs instruction must keep up with social and technological change. There is a storm of change going on out there. We must make sure that the tools we offer our students are the ones most suited to the challenges they face.

REFERENCES

Boddewyn, Jean J. (2012). Beyond 'The evolving discipline of public affairs', *Journal of Public Affairs*, 12(1), 98–104.

Fleisher, C. (2005). Educating present and future public affairs practitioners: Model programs. In P. Harris and C. Fleisher (eds) *The Handbook of Public Affairs,* London: Sage, pp. 517–536.

Freeman, E. (1984). *Strategic Management: A Stakeholder Approach.* Boston: Pitman.

Hewins-Maroney, B. and Williams, E. (2007). Teaching diversity in public administration: A missing component? *Journal of Public Affairs Education*, 13(1), 29–40.

Koven, S., Goetze, F., and Brennan, M. (2008). Profiling public affairs programs: The view from the top. *Administration and Society*, 40(7), 691–710.

Meznar, M. B. and Johnson, J. (2005). Business–government relations within a contingency theory framework: Strategy, structure, fit, and performance. *Business and Society*, 44(2), 119–43.

Post, J. E., Murray, E. A., Dickie, R. B. and Mahon, J. F. (1982). The public affairs function in American corporations: development and relations with corporate planning. *Long Range Planning*, 15 (April), 12–21.

Price, Tom. (2011). *Beyond Control: How Social Media and Mobile Communication Are Changing Public Affairs.* Public Affairs Council, Washington DC.

Ryan, S. E. (2012). Assessing diversity in public affairs curriculum. *Journal of Public Affairs Education*, 18(4), 757–74.

Sabharwal, M. and Geva-May, I. (2013). Advancing underrepresented populations in the public sector: approaches and practices in the instructional pipeline. *Journal of Public Affairs Education*, 657–79.

US News and World Report (2004, 2012) Best graduate schools (n.d.). Available at http://www.usnews.com/usnews/edu/grad/rankings/about/07pub_meth_brief.php

Appendix

School Name	Dept	Program Name	Numbers of Students (if known)	Cr. Hrs.	Est. price for program	Out of state cost	NASPAA Accredited	Online program?	UG	Executive
Albany State University	College of Arts & Humanities	Master of Public Administration	70	36	$18,775.00	$35,785.50	yes		y	
American University	Department of Public Administration and Policy	Key Executive Master's Degree	50	36	$65,808.00	$65,808.00	yes		y	y
American University	Department of Public Administration and Policy	Master of Public Administration	149	42	$64,092.00	$64,092.00	yes		y	
American University	Department of Public Administration and Policy	Master of Public Policy	132	39	$59,514.00	$59,514.00	yes		y	
American University in Cairo		Master of Public Administration	28	34	$37,044.00		no			
American University in Cairo		Master of Public Policy	12	33	$37,044.00		no			
Appalachian State University	Department of Government & Justice Studies	Master of Public Administration	60	42	$12,965.75	$34,914.25	yes			
Arizona State University	School of Public Affairs	Master of Public Administration	163	42	$52,649.00	$75,044.00	yes	Online courses	y	
Auburn University at Auburn	Department of Political Science	Master of Public Administration	47	42	$53,802.00	$93,870.00	yes		y	
Auburn University at Montgomery		Master of Public Administration	47	36	$13,556.00	$29,216.00	yes		y	
Ball State University		Master of Public Administration	41	36	$31,080.00	$72,786.00	no			
Baruch College/City University of New York	School of Public Affairs	Master of Public Administration	638	42	$21,080.00	$41,018.60	yes		y	y
Binghamton University	Department of Public Administration	Master of Public Administration	136	42	$19,022.50	$29,880.00	yes			
Boise State University	Department of Public Policy and Administration	Master of Public Administration		39	$13,269.75	$22,831.25	yes			

(Continued)

School Name	Dept	Program Name	Numbers of Students (if known)	Cr. Hrs.	Est. price for program	Out of state cost	NASPAA Accredited	Online program?	UG	Executive
Bowie State University	Dept. of Management, Marketing and Public Administration	Master of Public Administration		36	$17,904.63	$28,344.63	yes			
Brandeis University		Master of Public Policy	52	16	$90,852.00		no			
Bridgewater State University	Dept. of Political Science	Master of Public Administration	32	45	$16,852.50	$16,852.50	yes			y
Brigham Young University	George W. Romney Institute of Public Management	Master of Public Administration	109	40	$12,620.00	$25,240.00	yes			y
California State Polytechnic University, Pomona	Political Science Department	Master of Public Administration	60	52	$19,276.00	$32,172.00	yes			
California State University, Bakersfield	Department of Public Policy & Administration	Master of Public Administration	100	50	$14,037.50	$26,437.50	yes		y	
California State University, Chico	Department of Political Science	Master of Public Administration	53	42	$14,511.00	$30,135.00	yes		y	
California State University, Dominguez Hills	Department of Public Admin and Public Policy	Master of Public Administration	151	45	$14,810.00	$31,550.00	yes	MPA Degree	y	
California State University, Fresno	Department of Political Science	Master of Public Administration	32	36	$15,365.50	$28,546.00	yes		y	
California State University, Fullerton	Division of Politics, Administration, and Justice	Master of Public Administration	114	42	$13,266.19	$28,890.19	yes		y	
California State University, Long Beach	Graduate Center for Public Policy & Administration	Master of Public Administration		39	$13,476.00	$27,984.00	yes	MPA Degree		
California State University, Los Angeles	Department of Political Science	Master of Science in Public Administration	69	48	$15,218.00	$27,122.00	no			
California State University, San Bernardino	Department of Public Administration	Master of Public Administration	200	48	$14,802.08	$26,706.08	yes	MPA Degree	y	
California State University, Stanislaus	Department of Political Science and Public Administration	Master of Public Administration	100	42	$23,910.00		yes			y

Institution	School/Department	Degree							
California State University, Sacramento		Master of Public Policy and Administration	70	36	$13,224.25	$27,732.25	no		
Carnegie Mellon University	H. John Heinz III College, School of Public Policy and Management	Master of Public Management	109	14	$67,667.00		yes		y
Central Michigan University	Department of Political Science and Public Administration	Master of Public Administration	120	36	$18,972.00		yes	Online courses	
Clark Atlanta University	Department of Public Administration	Master of Public Administration		12	$27,635.00		yes		
Cleveland State University	Maxine Goodman Levin College of Urban Affairs	Master of Public Administration	154	42	$22,318.80	$41,953.80	yes		y
College of Charleston	Department of Political Science	Master of Public Administration	71	39	$36,430.00	$94,324.00	yes		
College of William and Mary		Master of Public Policy	48	50	$26,200.00	$58,800.00	no		y
Columbia University	School of International Policy and Affairs	Master of Public Administration		57	$108,018.00		yes		
Columbia University	School of International Policy and Affairs	Master of International Affairs		54	$108,018.00		yes		
Cornell University		Master of Public Administration	118	16	$64,000.00		no		
CUNY City College		Master of Public Service Management	14	45	$15,195.00	$35,100.00	no		
DePaul University	School of Public Service	Master of Science in Public Service	184	52	$34,060.00		yes		
DePaul University	School of Public Service	Master of Public Administration	183	52	$34,060.00		yes		
Duke University		Master of Public Policy	131	51	$83,022.00		no		
East Carolina University	Department of Political Science	Master of Public Administration	35	45	$13,654.00	$38,858.00	yes	Online courses	y
Eastern Kentucky University	Department of Government	Master of Public Administration	56	39	$17,745.00	$30,420.00	yes	MPA Degree	

(Continued)

School Name	Dept	Program Name	Numbers of Students (if known)	Cr. Hrs.	Est. price for program	Out of state cost	NASPAA Accredited	Online program?	UG	Executive
Eastern Michigan University	Department of Political Science	Master of Public Administration	144	40	$22,372.20	$39,816.20	yes			
Eastern Washington University		Master of Public Administration	164	60	$14,559.28	$33,846.12	no			
Florida Atlantic University	School of Public Administration	Master of Public Administration		42	$12,755.82	$38,955.42	yes		y	
Florida Gulf Coast University	Division of Public Affairs	Master of Public Administration	56	36	$13,441.68	$46,823.76	yes	MPA Degree		
Florida International University	School of International and Public Affairs	Master of Public Administration	196	42	$15,957.90	$37,800.00	yes		y	
Florida State University	Askew School of Public Administration & Policy	Master of Public Administration	122	42	$20,131.44	$46,650.24	yes			
Franklin University		Master of Public Administration		40	$18,560.00		no	Online only		
George Mason University	Department of Public & International Affairs	Master of Public Administration	293	36	$25,821.00	$47,997.00	yes		y	
George Mason University, School of Public Policy		Master of Public Policy	369	36	$25,821.00	$47,997.00	no		y	y
Georgetown University	McCourt School of Public Policy	Master of Public Policy	284	48	$95,508.00		no			y
Georgia College & State University	Department of Government and Sociology	Master of Public Administration	97	36	$10,368.00	$36,948.00	yes		y	
Georgia Institute of Technology		Master of Science in Public Policy		46	$29,472.00	$59,984.00	no			
Georgia Regents University	Department of Political Science	Masters of Public Administration	6	36	$7,716.00	$26,316.00	yes			
Georgia State University	Andrew Young School of Policy Studies	Master of Public Administration	138	39	$13,752.00	$44,733.00	yes		y	
Golden Gate University-San Francisco		Executive Master of Public Administration	95	36	$25,740.00		no		y	y

Institution	Department/College	Degree							
Governors State University	College of Business & Public Administration	Master of Public Administration	108	45	$13,815.00	$27,630.00	yes		y
Grambling State University	Department of Political Science and Public Administration	Master of Public Administration		45	$13,925.50	$32,363.50	yes		y
Grand Valley State University	School of Public, Nonprofit, and Health Administration	Master of Public Administration	178	42	$23,604.00		yes		y
Hamline University		Master of Public Administration	90	48	$23,760.00		no		
Harvard University		Master of Public Policy	477	18	$40,416.00		no		y
Idaho State University		Master of Public Administration	25	39	$15,468.00		no		
Indiana State University		Master of Public Administration		36	$17,100.00	$26,892.00	no	Online only	
Indiana University South Bend	Department of Political Science	Master of Public Affairs		39	$19,317.48	$32,852.82	yes	MPA Degree	y
Indiana University, Bloomington	School of Public & Environmental Affairs	Master of Public Affairs	393	48	$41,552.00		yes		y
Indiana University, Northwest	School of Public and Environmental Affairs	Master of Public Affairs		48	$12,531.84	$29,523.84	yes		y
Indiana University-Purdue University Indianapolis	School of Public & Environmental Affairs	Master of Public Affairs	164	48	$18,557.28		yes	Certificate programs	y
Indiana University-Purdue University, Ft. Wayne	Department of Public Policy	Master of Public Affairs		39	$12,739.35	$28,846.35	yes		y
Jackson State University	Department of Public Administration	Master of Public Policy and Administration	61	42	$13,732.00		yes		
Jacksonville State University	College of Arts and Sciences	Master of Public Administration		42	$14,658.00		yes		
James Madison University	School of Public Policy and Administration	Master of Public Administration	58	42	$18,228.00		yes		y
John Jay College of Criminal Justice, CUNY	Department of Public Management	Master of Public Administration	802	42	$20,260.00		yes	MPA Degree	y
Johns Hopkins University		Master of Public Policy	74	96	$97,920.00		no		

(Continued)

School Name	Dept	Program Name	Numbers of Students (if known)	Cr. Hrs.	Est. price for program	Out of state cost	NASPAA Accredited	Online program?	UG	Executive
Kansas State University	Department of Political Science	Master of Public Administration		40	$14,517.00	$31,149.40	yes			
Kean University	Dept. of Public Administration	Master of Public Administration	189	48	$37,200.00		yes		y	
Kennesaw State University	Department of Political Science and International Affairs	Master of Public Administration		36	$13,156.00		yes			
Kent State University	Department of Political Science	Master of Public Administration		36	$21,728.00		yes	MPA Degree		
Kentucky State University	School of Public Admin, Social Work, and Criminal Justice	Master of Public Administration		42	$16,716.00	$25,158.00	yes		y	
Long Island University	Department of Health Care & Public Administration	Master of Public Administration	153	42	$46,620.00		yes		y	
Long Island University, Brooklyn	School of Business, Public Administration and Info Sciences	Master of Public Administration		48	$53,280.00		yes			
Louisiana State University	Public Administration Institute	Master of Public Administration		45	$16,297.20		yes			
Marist College		Master of Public Administration		42	$31,500.00		No	Online only		
Midwestern State University	College of Health Sciences and Human Services	Master of Public Administration		36	$13,023.00		No	Online only		
Mills College		Master of Public Policy	32	36	$65,240.00		No			
Mississippi State University	Department of Political Science and Public Administration	Master of Public Policy and Administration	70	42	$14,784.00		yes			
Missouri State University	Political Science Department	Master of Public Administration	26	39	$13,000.00	$22,216.00	yes	Online		
Morehead State University	School of Public Affairs	Master of Public Administration	43	40	$16,214.00		yes	courses		

Institution	Department/School	Degree						
Naval Postgraduate School	Graduate School of Business and Public Policy	Master of Science in Management	40	48	$32,000.00		yes	
New Mexico State University	Department of Government	Master of Public Administration		42	$12,556.00	$33,572.00	yes	
New York University	Robert F. Wagner Graduate School of Public Service	Master of Public Administration	910	45	$81,188.00		yes	y
North Carolina State University	School of Public and International Affairs	Master of Public Administration	102	40	$15,704.00		yes	
Northeastern University	Department of Political Science	Master of Public Administration	141	42	$53,340.00		yes	MPA Degree
Northern Illinois University	Department of Public Administration	Master of Public Administration	75	44	$15,363.92		yes	
Northern Kentucky University	Dept. of Political Science and Criminal Justice	Master of Public Administration	90	39	$20,826.00		yes	
Oakland University	Department of Political Science	Master of Public Administration	77	40	$25,490.00		yes	y
Ohio University		Master of Public Administration	42	36	$32,752.00		no	y
Ohio University		Executive Master of Public Administration	29	36	$25,000.00		no	y
Old Dominion University	Department of Urban Studies and Public Administration	Master of Public Administration	117	39	$18,096.00		yes	
Oregon State University	School of Public Policy	Master of Public Policy	65	46	$16,200.00	$27,936.00	yes	
Pace University-New York		Master of Public Administration	160	39	$37,440.00		no	y
Park University		Master of Public Affairs	256	36	$17,280.00		no	
Pepperdine University		Master of Public Policy	118	64	$93,540.00		no	
Portland State University	Division of Public Administration	Master of Public Administration		60	$18,952.00		yes	y
Portland State University	Division of Public Administration	Executive Master of Public Administration	45	45	$36,000.00		yes	y
Portland State University	Division of Public Administration	Master of Public Administration: Health Administration	60	60	$18,952.00		yes	

(Continued)

School Name	Dept	Program Name	Numbers of Students (if known)	Cr. Hrs.	Est. price for program	Out of state cost	NASPAA Accredited	Online program?	UG	Executive
Princeton University		Master of Public Policy		1	$45,350.00		no		y	y
Princeton University		Master of Public Affairs	60–80 per year	2	$90,700.00		no		y	y
Regent University		Master of Public Administration	13	36	$23,400.00		no			
Rutgers University, Camden	Graduate Department of Public Policy & Administration	Master of Public Administration	165	42	$38,556.00		yes			y
Rutgers University, New Brunswick	Edward J. Bloustein School of Planning and Public Policy	Master of Public Policy	48	48	$31,776.00		yes			
Rutgers University, Newark	School of Public Affairs and Administration	Master of Public Administration	278	42	$32,736.00		yes		y	y
Saint Louis University	College of Education and Public Service	Master of Public Administration	10	36	$37,800.00		yes			
Sam Houston State University		Master of Public Administration	47	36	$14,055.00	$28,095.00	no			
San Diego State University	School of Public Affairs	Master of Public Administration		36	$16,845.00		yes			
San Francisco State University	Department of Public Administration	Master of Public Administration	180	42	$15,484.00		yes			
San Jose State University	Department of Political Science	Master of Public Administration	128	36	$13,476.00	$19,428.00	yes			
Savannah State University	Department of Political Science and Public Affairs	Master of Public Administration	22	36	$9,666.00	$28,764.00	yes			
Seattle University	Institute of Public Service	Master of Public Administration	166	54	$36,396.00		yes		y	y
Seton Hall University	Center for Public Service	Master of Public Administration		39	$56,667.00		yes	Certificate program		
Southern Illinois University at Edwardsville	Department of Public Administration & Policy Analysis	Master of Public Administration	138	39	$17,916.00	$39,028.00	yes			

Institution	Department/School	Degree							
Southern Illinois University, Carbondale	Department of Political Science	Master of Public Administration	65	40	$23,877.20	$64,933.20	yes		y
Southern University and A&M College	Department of Public Administration	Master of Public Administration	182	54	$11,298.50		yes		
Southern Utah University	Department of Political Science & Criminal Justice	Master of Public Administration	87	36	$11,108.25	$34,193.25	yes		
State University of New York, The College at Brockport	Department of Public Administration	Master of Public Administration	97	2	$14,805.00	$27,525.00	yes		
Suffolk University	Department of Public Management	Master of Public Administration		42	$56,941.00		yes		
Syracuse University	Maxwell School of Citizenship and Public Affairs	Master of Public Administration	136	40	$55,768.00		yes		y
Tennessee State University	Department of Public Administration	Master of Public Administration	80	42	$16,689.00	$38,337.00	yes		
Texas A&M International University	Department of Public Affairs and Social Research	Master of Public Administration	119	42	$17,275.00	$32,653.00	yes		y
Texas A&M University	Bush School of Government and Public Service	Master of Public Policy and Administration	90	48	$22,000.00	$22,000.00	yes	Certificate program	
Texas Southern University	Barbara Jordan-Mickey Leland School of Public Affairs	Master of Public Administration	136	48	$14,244.00	$24,644.00	yes		
Texas State University	Department of Public Administration	Master of Public Administration		36	$13,765.20	$27,805.20	yes		
Texas Tech University	Department of Political Science	Master of Public Administration		36	$18,093.00	$32,961.00	yes		
The Evergreen State College	Department of Public Administration	Master of Public Administration	90	60	$21,756.00	$46,484.00	no		
The George Washington University	Trachtenberg School of Public Policy and Public Admin	Master of Public Administration		40	$64,275.00	$64,275.00	yes		
The George Washington University	Trachtenberg School of Public Policy and Public Admin	Master of Public Policy		40	$64,275.00	$64,275.00	yes		
The Monterey Institute of International Studies	Department of Public Administration	Master of Public Administration	77	60	$82,432.00		no		y

(Continued)

School Name	Dept	Program Name	Numbers of Students (if known)	Cr. Hrs.	Est. price for program	Out of state cost	NASPAA Accredited	Online program?	UG	Executive
The New School	The Milano School of Int'l Affairs, Management, and Urban Policy	Master of Science in Urban Policy Analysis & Management		42	$62,712.00		yes			
The Ohio State University	John Glenn School of Public Affairs	In-Career Master of Arts in Public Policy and Management	128	38	$30,363.90	$74,405.90	yes			Y
The Ohio State University	John Glenn School of Public Affairs	Master of Public Administration	94	52			yes			Y
The Pennsylvania State University at Harrisburg	School of Public Affairs	Master of Public Administration	300	36	$37,632.00	$49,864.00	yes	MPA Degree	y	
The Pennsylvania State University at Harrisburg	School of Public Affairs	Master of Public Administration		36	$28,224.00	$37,404.00	yes		y	
The University of Alabama		Master of Public Administration	14	36	$14,739.00	$37,425.00	No			
The University of Alabama at Birmingham	Department of Government	Master of Public Administration		39	$15,075.00	$34,536.00	yes			
The University of Arizona	School of Government & Public Policy	Master of Public Administration	81	42	$25,400.00	$67,800.00	yes		y	
The University of Edinburgh		Master of Public Policy	25	1	$22,330.00		No			
The University of Georgia	School of Public and International Affairs	Master of Public Administration	142	41	$18,420.00	$48,139.00	yes			
The University of Illinois at Chicago	Department of Public Administration	Master of Public Administration	136	52	$22,508.00	$46,504.00	yes	Certificate programs		
The University of Kansas	School of Public Affairs and Administration	Master of Public Administration	125	38	$13,737.80	$32,279.10	yes			
The University of Memphis	Division of Public and Nonprofit Administration	Master of Public Administration		39	$22,338.00	$41,858.00	yes			
The University of New Mexico	School of Public Administration	Master of Public Administration	253	42	$15,167.36	$44,167.04	yes			
The University of North Carolina at Chapel Hill	School of Government	Master of Public Administration	186	45	$52,830.00		yes	MPA Degree		

Institution	Department	Degree							
The University of North Carolina at Charlotte	Department of Political Science	Master of Public Administration	75	39	$8,256.00	$33,598.00	yes		
The University of North Carolina at Greensboro	Department of Political Science	Master of Public Affairs	55	43	$13,581.00	$40,479.00	yes		
The University of South Dakota	Department of Political Science	Master of Public Administration	34	42	$29,950.20	$52,508.40	yes		
The University of Tennessee at Chattanooga	Dept of Political Science, Public Admin and Nonprofit Mgmt	Master of Public Administration	34	36	$19,340.00	$51,576.00	yes	Certificate programs	Y
The University of Tennessee, Knoxville		Master of Public Policy and Administration	31	39	$24,712.00	$61,548.00	no		
The University of Texas at Arlington	School of Urban and Public Affairs	Master of Public Administration	157	4	$17,420.00	$30,452.00	yes		
The University of Texas at Austin	LBJ School of Public Affairs	Master of Public Affairs	227	43	$35,626.00	$57,294.00	yes		
The University of Texas at Brownsville		Master's in Public Policy & Management	36	36	$8,926.84	$22,754.44	no		
The University of Texas at Dallas	School of Economic, Political and Policy Sciences	Master of Public Affairs	66	42	$26,932.00	$52,024.00	yes		y
The University of Texas at El Paso	Institute for Policy and Economic Development	Master of Public Administration	85	39	$13,866.00	$32,882.00	yes		
The University of Texas at San Antonio	Department of Public Administration	Master of Public Administration	179	39	$13,192.00	$39,888.00	yes		
The University of Texas at Tyler	Arts and Sciences	Master of Public Administration	13	36	$11,913.00	$26,041.20	no		
The University of Toledo	Department of Political Science & Public Administration	Master of Public Administration	23	36	$19,746.00	$35,250.00	yes	Online courses	
The University of Utah	Department of Political Science	Master of Public Administration		14	$18,647.76		yes		Y
The University of Vermont	Dept of Community Development & Applied Economics	Master of Public Administration	34	36	$21,996.00	$55,584.00	yes		

(Continued)

School Name	Dept	Program Name	Numbers of Students (if known)	Cr. Hrs.	Est. price for program	Out of state cost	NASPAA Accredited	Online program?	UG	Executive
The University of West Florida		Master of Science in Administration	150	36	$13,572.00		No			Y
Troy University	Department of Political Science	Master of Public Administration		36	$17,784.00		yes	MPA Degree & Certif. Programs		
University at Albany	Nelson A. Rockefeller College of Public Affairs & Policy	Master of Public Administration	147	44	$25,034.00	$47,714.00	yes		y	
University of Alaska Southeast	School of Management	Master of Public Administration		36	$14,940.00	$30,060.00	No	Online only		
University of Arkansas		Master of Public Administration	25	42	$16,797.48	$41,475.42	No		y	
University of Arkansas	Department of Political Science	Master of Public Administration		42	$16,797.48	$41,475.42	yes		y	
University of Arkansas at Little Rock	Institute of Government	Master of Public Administration	90	39	$11,700.00	$26,910.00	yes			
University of Baltimore	School of Public and International Affairs	Master of Public Administration		42	$29,778.00	$43,176.00	yes	MPA Degree		
University of California, Los Angeles		Master of Public Policy	109	80	$31,164.18	$55,654.18	no			
University of Central Florida	Department of Public Administration	Master of Public Administration	167	42	$12,102.72	$45,079.02	yes		y	
University of Chicago		Master of Public Policy	288	18	$88,176.00		no			
University of Colorado, Colorado Springs	School of Public Affairs	Master of Public Administration	133	39	$24,428.00	$42,788.00	yes			
University of Colorado, Denver	School of Public Affairs	Master of Public Administration	381	39	$17,964.00	$43,020.00	yes	MPA Degree		Y
University of Connecticut	Department of Public Policy	Master of Public Administration	82	45	$28,365.00	$67,309.00	yes			
University of Dayton	Department of Political Science	Master of Public Administration	15	39	$22,815.00	$22,815.00	yes			

Institution	School	Degree					
University of Delaware	School of Public Policy and Administration	Master of Public Administration	55	36	$65,000.00	$65,000.00	yes	Y
University of Hawaii at Manoa		Master of Public Administration	50	39	$14,760.00	$41,220.00	no	
University of Houston		Master of Public Administration	24	35	$13,642.00	$32,262.00	no	
University of Illinois at Springfield	College of Public Affairs and Administration	Master of Public Administration	208	40	$18,184.00	$30,884.00	yes	MPA Degree
University of Kentucky	Martin School of Public Policy & Administration	Master of Public Administration	66	42	$22,624.00	$49,328.00	yes	
University of La Verne	Department of Public and Health Administration	Master of Public Administration	79	39	$36,744.00		yes	y
University of Louisville	School of Urban & Public Affairs	Master of Public Administration	36	42	$26,252.00	$50,736.00	yes	
University of Maryland, Baltimore County	Department of Public Policy	Master of Public Policy	43	37	$18,424.00	$43,952.00	yes	
University of Maryland, College Park	School of Public Policy	Master of Public Policy	291	48	$46,728.00		yes	Y
University of Maryland, College Park		Executive Master of Public Management	64	30	$47,250.00		yes	Y
University of Maryland, College Park		Master of Professional Studies Public Administration	28	36	$26,460.00	$57,636.00	yes	
University of Maryland, College Park		Master of Public Management	24	36	$26,460.00	$57,636.00	yes	
University of Maryland, College Park		Master of Engineering and Public Policy		36	$26,460.00	$57,636.00	yes	
University of Massachusetts Amherst		Master of Public Policy and Administration	57	37	$22,131.00	$44,961.00	no	
University of Massachusetts Boston		Master of Science in Public Affairs	24	36	$22,527.00	$43,638.00	no	
University of Miami		Master of Public Administration	37	48	$85,920.00		no	

(Continued)

School Name	Dept	Program Name	Numbers of Students (if known)	Cr. Hrs.	Est. price for program	Out of state cost	NASPAA Accredited	Online program?	UG	Executive
University of Michigan-Ann Arbor		Master of Public Policy	199	45	$45,492.00	$82,768.00	no		y	Y
University of Minnesota		Master of Public Affairs	123	30	$38,916.00	$59,481.00	no	Online courses		Y
University of Minnesota	Humphrey School of Public Affairs	Master of Public Policy	214	30	$38,696.00	$54,324.00	yes	Online courses		
University of Missouri-Columbia	Harry S. Truman School of Public Affairs	Master of Public Affairs	184	45	$16,344.00	$42,183.00	yes	MPA Degree		Y
University of Missouri, Kansas City	Henry W. Bloch School of Management	Master of Public Administration	115	36	$14,430.36	$34,088.00	yes			
University of Missouri, St. Louis	Public Policy Administration Masters Program	Master of Public Policy and Administration	95	40	$13,420.00	$34,016.00	yes			
University of Nebraska at Omaha	College of Public Affairs & Community Service	Master of Public Administration	209	39	$9,730.50	$27,183.00	yes	MPA Degree		
University of Nevada, Las Vegas	Department of Public Administration	Master of Public Administration	99	39	$10,491.00	$38,311.00	yes			
University of New Hampshire	Department of Public Administration	Master of Public Administration	59	36	$13,500.00	$26,420.00	no			
University of New Orleans	Department of Political Science	Master of Public Administration	32	42	$12,872.00	$27,220.00	yes			
University of North Carolina, Wilmington	Department of Public and International Affairs	Master of Public Administration	79	42	$17,079.75	$47,307.10	yes		y	
University of North Dakota	College of Business and Public Administration	Master of Public Administration		36	$15,037.92		yes	MPA Degree and Certificate programs	y	
University of North Florida	Department of Political Science & Public Administration	Master of Public Administration	100	42	$20,722.38	$43,853.46	yes			
University of North Texas	Department of Public Administration	Master of Public Administration	90	42	$15,070.35	$30,280.35	yes		y	

Institution	Unit	Degree						
University of Oklahoma	Department of Political Science	Master of Public Administration		36	$10,929.30	$29,793.30	yes	
University of Oregon	Department of Planning, Public Policy & Management	Master of Public Administration	45	72	$21,384.00	$34,598.00	yes	
University of Pennsylvania		Master of Public Administration	111	36	$72,612.00		no	Y
University of Pittsburgh	Graduate School of Public and International Affairs	Master of International Development	76	48	$42,884.00	$69,320.00	yes	Y
University of Pittsburgh	Graduate School of Public and International Affairs	Master of Public Administration	75	48	$42,884.00	$69,320.00	yes	
University of Puerto Rico – Rio Piedras Campus	Roberto Sanchez Vilella School of Public Administration	Master of Public Administration	107	37			yes	
University of San Francisco	School of Management	Master of Public Administration	146	38	$42,180.00		yes	y
University of South Carolina	Department of Political Science	Master of Public Administration	45	48	$24,048.00	$51,540.00	yes	
University of South Florida	Dept of Government & International Affairs	Master of Public Administration	68	45	$20,856.00	$42,252.00	yes	Y
University of Southern California	Sol Price School of Public Policy	Master of Public Administration	289	41	$67,549.00		yes	MPA Degree y
University of Southern California		Master of Planning	142	48	$78,719.00		no	
University of Southern California		Master of Public Policy	127	48	$79,019.00		no	
University of Southern California		Master of Health Administration	109	48	$79,019.00		no	
University of Southern Indiana		Master of Public Administration	40	36	$12,774.24	$24,136.56	no	
University of Virginia – Frank Batten School of Leadership and Public Policy		Master of Public Policy	77	48	$51,400.00	$93,116.00	no	y

(Continued)

School Name	Dept	Program Name	Numbers of Students (if known)	Cr. Hrs.	Est. price for program	Out of state cost	NASPAA Accredited	Online program?	UG	Executive
University of Washington	Daniel J. Evans School of Public Affairs	Master of Public Administration	389	72	$38,478.00	$69,060.00	yes			Y
University of West Georgia	Department of Political Science and Planning	Master of Public Administration	27	36	$12,260.00	$33,356.00	yes			
University of Wisconsin-Madison	School of Public Affairs	Master of Public Affairs	54	42	$23,728.80	$50,382.56	no			
Upper Iowa University		Master of Public Administration		36	$17,964.00		no	Online only		Y
Valdosta State University	Department of Political Science	Master of Public Administration	107	36	$12,980.00	$35,732.00	yes	Online courses		
Villanova University	Department of Political Science	Master of Public Administration	70	36	$27,000.00	$32,400.00	yes	MPA Degree		
Virginia Commonwealth University	L. Douglas Wilder School of Govt. & Public Affairs	Master of Public Administration	91	36	$19,168.50	$36,940.50	yes	Online courses		
Virginia Polytechnic Institute & State University	Center for Public Administration & Policy	Master of Public Administration		36	$18,190.50	$36,582.00	yes			
Wayne State University	Department of Political Science	Master of Public Administration	62	42	$25,846.00	$53,854.50	yes		y	
West Chester University of Pennsylvania	Department of Public Policy & Administration	Master of Public Administration	147	36	$22,026.42	$31,347.42	yes			
West Virginia University	Division of Public Administration	Master of Public Administration	78	45	$19,485.00	$52,740.00	yes			
Western Carolina University	Department of Political Science & Public Affairs	Master of Public Affairs	57	36	$17,584.00	$38,398.00	yes			
Western Kentucky University	Department of Political Science	Master of Public Administration	57	39	$21,177.00	$29,757.00	yes			
Western Michigan University	School of Public Affairs & Administration	Master of Public Administration		39	$20,682.00	$43,806.00	yes			

Wichita State University	Hugo Wall School of Urban and Public Affairs	Master of Public Administration	75	39	$12,119.25	$27,120.60	yes	
Willamette University	Atkinson Graduate School of Management	MBA for Business, Government and Not For Profit Management	202	60	$75,200.00		yes	
Wright State University	Department of Urban Affairs & Geography	Master of Public Administration	54	36	$19,623.00	$33,336.00	yes	y

Expanding the Boundaries: Public Affairs and its Relationship to other Key Disciplines

Phil Harris

Marco Polo (1254–1324) was the son of Niccolo Polo, a Venetian merchant, and is famous for his book *Livres des merveilles du monde* (*Book of the Marvels of the World*, also known as *The Travels of Marco Polo*, *c*.1300), which was the first book to introduce Europeans to Central Asia and China. Polo's father and uncle had already made one visit to China in 1260 and Marco joined them for a second journey in 1271. They spent the next 20 years living in the Beijing area and travelling in the service of Kublai Khan throughout China, Asia, Middle East and Southern Russia. They knew at first hand the trade of the Silk Road and wrote in depth about business and manufacture around Guangzhou (Canton) and other major Chinese cities.

There is evidence that Marco travelled widely throughout the Mongol Empire both as trader and public servant, and in his work he gives extensive insights into the workings of the Chinese Mongol State, its communications, culture, public affairs, trade system and technology. He is the first writer to report the use of coal as an energy product in use in China and the development of transparency, fair dealing and financial security throughout the Mongol Empire. He also alludes to the corporate and public reputation of many rulers and states. He also records trips to India and Burma and assesses the growing trade between China and Europe. *The Travels* is seen as the first guide to China and Asia by a European and gives an insight into the changing nature of communication and the depth of global trade stretching from Europe to Asia, and insights into early consumer markets and political and public management. In many ways, it is a primer in global trade, power and communication and therefore, much like Machiavelli's works lends itself to being a guide book to the realities of the then known world (Jay, 1964, Skinner, 1981; Harris, Lock and Rees, 2000).

We have seen a resurgence of interest in the Silk Road Concept both culturally and economically, through such initiatives as 'One Belt, One Road' and regular explorations of culture, history and trade in academic and policy discourse and research (Millar and Mahon, 2014; McCormack and Blair, 2016). The 'One Belt, One Road' initiative – the Silk Road Economic Belt and the 21st Century Maritime Silk Road – is a key part of China's development strategy. The *Vision and Actions on Jointly Building the Silk Road Economic Belt and the 21st-Century Maritime Silk Road* (the 'Vision and Actions') issued by the National Development and Reform Commission on 28 March 2015 outlines the initiative's framework, co-operation priorities and co-operation mechanisms. (National Development and Reform Commission, 2015). Corporate Social Responsibility (CSR) and municipal government effectiveness are equally global and Chinese issues (Lam, 2014; Tang et al., 2014).

The world is becoming smaller as populations and trade grows, reflecting a modern renaissance in business and culture activity, connecting together Western and Eastern cultures, organisations and people. Business is changing as we see the impact of the internet on trade resulting in a reduction in physical shipments of goods world-wide in a conventional sense, but an overall increase in volume in total trade as more products are made available via digital online activities and the downloading of products or viewing and interaction online via mobile phone, tablet, PC or work stations. A good example is that Computer software and music is increasingly purchased online via digital downloads thus reducing physical shipments.

The internet is now the connective tissue of global trade. We can see this with the rise of Amazon, Alibaba global ecommerce businesses and the likes of Alipay, an online payment system which accounts for approximately half of all online payment

transactions within China (*The Economist*, 23 March 2013).

Corporate public affairs has grown dramatically in the last decade, reflecting a growth in world trade and regulation, and a boom in international intellectual property rights, pressure group activity and global social media advocacy. International trade has led to a boom in international relations work. Doha has become the prime annual world gathering and forum for those who need to know and want to have influence. The Young Presidents Organization sees itself as the world's premier network of chief executives and business leaders who can make a difference.

In this section of the *International Handbook of Corporate and Public Affairs*, we focus on those disciplines and subjects impacting upon the development of the discipline.

The first chapter is entitled, 'Public Affairs and Marketing' and is written by Howard Viney, Open University Business School, Milton Keynes, UK, Paul Baines and Laura Stegen of Cranfield University, UK. They outline how marketing can be utilised to underpin the effective performance of an organisation's public affairs strategy. They outline four marketing-public affairs case studies to underpin their analysis and reflection: 1) the UK fracking debate; 2) the UK food industry and the obesity debate; 3) attempts to liberalise and enter the US online gaming industry; and 4) UK airport capacity planning. The chapter highlights how public affairs and marketing are interlinked primarily through stakeholder evaluation and citizen and organisation engagement via the notion of stakeholder marketing. Interface activities include the use of market research/opinion surveys to understand the nature and dynamic of public opinion and to measure the effectiveness of the communications used by a campaign or organisation to change that opinion, environmental scanning exercises to understand the nature of impending issues/legislation and stakeholder mapping to identify engagement strategy options. The authors provide a word of caution in using marketing in public affairs campaigns: if used unethically, it risks damaging further the credibility of public affairs practitioners and the causes for which they are campaigning.

The next chapter, 'International Relations and Public Affairs' is by Ian N. Richardson of Stockholm Business School, Stockholm University, who was lead author of the insightful and pioneering text on international relations, *Bilderberg People: Elite Power and Consensus in World Affairs* (Richardson et al., 2011). He argues in this chapter that it is critical to have an understanding of theory development in international relations before assessing, from a strategic perspective, the complexities presented by a multi-layered and highly interdependent game in international politics. This leads, in turn, to a discussion of the nature of the relationship between preferences, interests and institutions within such a setting – and highlights the risks of too rationalistic and mechanistic an approach to international public affairs. Finally, using a descriptive account and a case study on Google's recent handling of the censorship issue with China, he outlines the dangers facing Multi-National Corporations (MNCs) that venture into the complex milieu of contemporary international relations which can be seen in the AT&T work by Brown (2016). The case raises a number of important questions related to the nature of business political engagement and, particularly, serves to highlight the risks associated with such activity.

'Public Affairs and Political Philosophy' is by Alberto Bitonti of the American University, Rome. He argues that we must deal with the fundamental question concerning the relationship between public affairs and the theoretical discussion around the concept of public interest, as this relationship lies at the very heart of any reflection on political philosophy and public affairs.

After an analysis of the concepts of *interest* and *public*, he describes five different ideal types of conceptions of public interest, where each of them provides a different theoretical

framework able to define public affairs and lobbying, as well as democracy itself. He argues that political philosophy and public interest have much to offer the underpinning of the emerging public affairs discipline and will allow practitioners to understand the complexities and policies around issues in more depth.

The next chapter is entitled, 'Public Affairs and Information Science/Systems' and is authored by Amy D. Meli who is Vice-President Grassroots Consulting at Aristotle Inc, Washington DC and one of the international leaders in grassroots campaigning Edward A. Grefe of George Washington University.

They focus on technology that supports mass mobilisation, which they see as the key use of information science systems to support public affairs. Second, they assess how it can be used to build real on-going dialogues with those who engage in public affairs campaigns. They discuss and review tracking stakeholders, their relationships and activities and use these methods to assess what people are saying about the organisation. Finally, they look to the future at potential developments, applications and trends in information science and systems and posit suggestions as to where they are going and how they will impact upon public affairs campaigning.

'Public Affairs and Ecology' is by Simon Bryceson and Simon Levitt who are internationally well-regarded corporate communications and public affairs practitioners with over 50 years of industry experience between them. They argue that it is crucial for businesses to be aware of managing the environment. In their chapter, they ask why actively managing controversial issues is on the increase for many corporations. The chapter utilises three case studies: Unilever, Greenpeace and the Common Fisheries Policy; BP and climate change; and Monsanto and GM foods from the environmental world to test their argument. They argue that ecological issues have become a management responsibility for large corporations because of political failure. As this failure becomes more severe, the public give up increasingly on politics and therefore, their last resort for change can only be found in campaigns and pressure group activity. They argue that the ecological and environmental movements since the mid 2000s are just the beginning and managing dialogue is critical.

'Political Marketing and Public Affairs' is by the leading international figure in the field of political marketing, Bruce I. Newman of De Paul, Chicago and his expert collaborating colleagues, Wojciech Cwalina and Andrzej Falkowski both of University of Social Sciences and Humanities (SWPS), Warsaw, Poland. They use the United States as a research base to explore the role of political parties and other bodies such as political action committees and interest groups to assess the influence of money to affect political outcomes at election time as well as to pass laws that benefit one group in society over another. They investigate the role of political funding that comes from lobbying efforts on the part of corporations and the impact it has on campaign budgets, tactics and the general ethical condition that exists in US politics today. The chapter ends with the introduction of an innovative Strategic Framework for Lobbyists that can be used as the basis for the development of marketing strategies.

The final chapter is by Mordecai Lee, Professor of Urban Planning, University of Wisconsin-Milwaukee, who is a former member of Wisconsin State Assembly and Wisconsin State Senate and is entitled, 'The Practice of Public Affairs in Public Administration'. He argues that the field of public affairs initially emerged with a focus primarily on its practice in the business sector, secondarily on the Non-Governmental Organisation (NGO) sector, and with only modest attention to its practice within the public sector. He makes the very strong case that, up to now, the public affairs literature has paid little attention to its practice in government, specifically in public administration, and secondarily that the context of civil

service work is so qualitatively different from the corporate and NGO sectors that it justifies separate treatment within the overall subject of public affairs. An understanding of public administration, he argues, allows one to better understand the development of policy and its implementation

These chapters substantially strengthen our knowledge of corporate public affairs and its operation and potential evolution. We hope they bring insights and inspiration to the practitioner, student and researcher.

'Everyone sees what you appear to be; few experience what you really are'.

(Niccolo Machiavelli, *The Prince*, trans. Bull, G. 1992).

REFERENCES

Brown, R. S. 2016. AT&T's establishment of a political capability. *Journal of Public Affairs*, 16(1): 57–65, February.

The Economist. 2013. Alibaba: the world's greatest bazaar. 23 March, London.

Harris, P., Lock, A. and Rees, P. (eds), 2000. *Machiavelli, Marketing and Management*, Routledge, London.

Jay, A. 1964. *Management and Machiavelli*, Pfeiffer Press, San Diego, CA.

Lam, M. L-L. 2014. Toward a 'harmonious society' through corporate social responsibility. *Special Issue: Public Policy and Governance in China, Journal of Public Affairs*, 14(2): 105–15, May.

Machiavelli, N. 1992. *The Prince*, trans. George Bull. Penguin, London.

McCormack, J. and Blair, J. G. 2016. *Thinking through China*, Rowman and Littlefield, Lanham.

Millar, C. C. J. M. and Mahon, J. F. 2014. Multi-stakeholder public policy and governance in China: an analysis. *Special Issue: Public Policy and Governance in China, Journal of Public Affairs*, 14(2): 85–92, May.

National Development and Reform Commission. 2015. *Vision and Actions on Jointly Building Silk Road Economic Belt and 21st-Century Maritime Silk Road*, Ministry of

Foreign Affairs and Ministry of Commerce, Beijing, China.

Polo, Marco. 1958. *The Travels of Marco Polo*, (trans. R. Latham), Penguin, London.

Richardson, I., Kakabadse, N. and Kakabadse, A. 2011. *Bilderberg People: Elite Power and Consensus in World Affairs*, Routledge, London.

Skinner, Q. 1981. *Machiavelli*, Oxford University Press, Oxford.

Tang, R., Tang, T. and Lee, Z. 2014. The efficiency of provincial governments in China from 2001 to 2010: measurement and analysis. *Special Issue: Public Policy and Governance in China, Journal of Public Affairs*, 14(2): 142–53, May.

Public Affairs and Marketing

Howard Viney, Paul Baines and Laura Stegen

INTRODUCTION

The chapter addresses the important question of how, if at all, marketing can support the effective performance of an organisation's non-market strategy/corporate political strategy. We present a range of arguments which suggest that marketing can enhance public affairs (also known as corporate political activity (CPA), business-government relations), but the extent to which a particular approach can be successful is context dependent and public affairs professionals need to develop expertise with a portfolio of marketing techniques. The chapter also explores the stakeholder marketing and lobbying interface. The aim is to explore the extent to which techniques that are familiar and well-practised in the area of marketing can be deployed to improve the performance of organisational lobbying. Through a series of cases, we explore how a range of techniques have been used to achieve different outcomes or address emerging public affairs issues.

The work extends existing work undertaken by the authors to identify and exemplify lobbying practices as levels of relationship engagement (LRE) (Baines and Viney, 2010; Viney and Baines, 2012). The focus here is upon how companies engage with the wider general public to reinforce more formal information, providing rhetorical or legal engagements. We therefore conduct this debate in the context of our five-stage framework, arguing that the practices we discuss – to mobilise grassroots support – can be deployed at any stage but are more likely to be of value at Stage 3 or Stage 2 LRE. This is where organisations are not able to benefit from close proximity to decision-makers or where efforts to exploit proximity have not been successful, but they have the opportunity to revise or challenge legislation/regulation and manage the implications of a legislative/regulatory change.

We begin the chapter by reviewing a number of related literatures to provide the grounding for our discussion, namely a brief introduction to key concepts in stakeholder theory, a discussion of the emergence of political marketing and a reflection on some of the practices of CPA.

MARKETING'S CONNECTION TO PUBLIC AFFAIRS: STAKEHOLDER THEORY

Freeman (1984: 25) defines a stakeholder as 'any group or individual who can affect or is affected by the achievement of the firm's objectives'. This work and this definition mark the emergence of stakeholder theory and the beginning of a contentious conversation, which continues to this day, as to who is, and who is not, a stakeholder and how an organisation should respond to stakeholder claims. Freeman's view was that stakeholder theory was very much a managerial theory, focused upon the instrumental question of how an organisation should manage its interactions with stakeholders in order to enable the firm to achieve its objectives more effectively. But other views have also emerged.

Instrumental Stakeholder Theory

In their seminal work on the emerging stakeholder theory, Donaldson and Preston (1995) identified three main types of use to which authors had put stakeholder theory to work. These include: 1) descriptive/empirical (i.e., as a tool to categorise observable behaviours), 2) instrumental (i.e., as a tool to enhance the organisational performance) and 3) normative (i.e., as a means of discussing the corporate social responsibility of business). As use of the theory has developed and evolved, a tension has emerged between the instrumental and normative perspectives, and

the theory has tended to become associated with scholars keen to identify what organisations ought to be doing to acknowledge the interests of a wider stakeholder community, suggesting the normative perspective has become more prevalent. However, as we have noted, this is in contrast to Freeman's (1984) more instrumental perspective that the role of stakeholder theory was to enable organisations to manage their stakeholders more effectively. In our examination of the application of marketing techniques to public affairs through the application of the Stakeholder Mapping Matrix, we adopt a more instrumental perspective and see the use of stakeholder theory more in terms of issue mitigation than observing the responsibility of business to be even handed with all constituencies.

An instrumental perspective on stakeholder theory therefore argues that while the main purpose of managers in a for-profit organisation remains to fulfil their fiduciary responsibility towards their owners, this task is rendered more complex by the emergence of a significant and varied group of alternative stakeholders whose interests may differ from those of shareholders, but which are also demanding of attention. Instrumental stakeholder theory argues that managers are not responsible for meeting all of these various stakeholder claims; rather that they are responsible for steering the organisation through these various and often divergent claims. This creates a challenge for the public affairs function to manage these interactions, particularly when there is a possible public interest aspect to the interaction, in such a way as to ensure that organisational performance is maximised while the effects of potential constraints are mitigated.

Stakeholder Identification and Salience Theory

Any discussion of instrumentalism in stakeholder theory requires a conversation about how organisations identify which stakeholders they should be paying attention to/seeking to manage effectively. One persuasive contribution to this literature has been work by Mitchell et al. (1997) on stakeholder salience, which sought to determine who and what truly counts to organisations as they address their stakeholder community. Their theory has very strong normative roots; the identification of the various attributes that comprise the model are based upon a normative assumption 'that these variables define the field of stakeholders: those entities to whom managers *should* pay attention' (Mitchell et al., 1997: 854, emphasis in original). However, the model itself permits description; organisations can use the model to identify which stakeholders can be aligned to which classes and so answer the question of which are truly important to managers in an organisation. In addition, it is an unstated potential outcome of the work that the model can also be used for instrumental purposes, suggesting ways in which an organisation can develop contingency approaches to managing their stakeholders based upon the insight provided by the application of this model.

Of particular interest in Mitchell et al.'s (1997) work is that they conclude by discussing the critical role of legitimacy and its centrality to the whole stakeholder question. They argue that much of the work of leading stakeholder theorists is focused upon understanding the bases of legitimacy (Mitchell et al., 1997: 882), whereas the reality of determining what really counts for organisations is much more complex than simply assuming that legitimate claims are upheld and illegitimate claims ignored. Their work, emphasising consideration of the relative power of a stakeholder and the urgency of their claim combined with an understanding of the bases of the legitimacy of that claim, offers an opportunity for a more realistic assessment of what truly counts.

The theory represents a powerful argument and has been widely accepted albeit with limited empirical assessment (Parent

and Deephouse, 2007). Agle et al.'s (1999) testing of the model has been used to justify a variety of conclusions drawn by researchers operating in the field. These include identifying a positive relationship between CEO values and corporate social performance (Goll and Rashid, 2004; Choi and Wang, 2007) and an organisation's ethical norms (Hemingway and MacLagen, 2004; Hemingway, 2005); and the positive impact of incentivisation as a catalyst for firm-level social responsibility (Husted and De Jesus Salazar, 2006), although this is alternatively interpreted as managers being instrumental in choosing to be socially responsible if it suits the interests of the firm (Godfrey and Hatch, 2007; Maitlis and Lawrence, 2007); as well as reaffirming the importance of resource dependency in stakeholder relations (Maitlis and Lawrence, 2007). The theory has also been used to support empirically formally intuitive assumptions about the existence of differences between stakeholder groups in terms of their relative importance to firms (Dentchev and Heene, 2004).

A significant point to emphasise, we suggest, is that the power and urgency of a claim is often ultimately intricately linked to the legitimacy of the claim, something that their own testing (Agle et al., 1999) helped to demonstrate. In this testing of the theory, the authors determined that power (based on some form of contractual relationship) tends to confer legitimacy upon a claim, which when allied to the perception of urgency (either from the stakeholder or from the manager anxious to please a powerful, legitimate stakeholder) leads to these claims being given priority. This finding has led critical observers to conclude that Agle et al.'s (1999) work has therefore provided evidence, for example, of managers being instrumental in choosing to be socially responsible if it suits the interests of the firm (Godfrey and Hatch, 2007; Maitlis and Lawrence, 2007) as well as reaffirming the importance of resource dependency in stakeholder relations (Maitlis and Lawrence, 2007). The theory, for all its descriptive power, has simply reaffirmed existing suspicions of the skewed normative biases of traditional competitive organisations. This is at odds with much writing on stakeholder theory from a normative tradition, which seeks to emphasise what organisations ought to do.

Stakeholder salience is a relevant concept for us given this chapter's focus upon public affairs which are aimed at mediating an organisation's relationship with broader public opinion. As we consider the various examples of engagement with public opinion, we reflect upon how stakeholder identification and salience theory can explain some of the choices made. We now turn to how stakeholder engagement has been addressed in the marketing literature.

STAKEHOLDER MARKETING AND MOBILISATION

Stakeholders, identified as entities who are affected by, or can affect, a given company, are ever more becoming the focus point of marketing management (Bhattacharya and Korschun, 2008; Gundlach and Wilkie, 2010). Gundlach and Wilkie (2010) argue that a firm can better observe the impact of marketing activities on society through its interdependent stakeholder relationships. The stakeholder marketing concept recognises that other entities are relevant target audiences for marketing activities, not just customers (Bhattacharya and Korschun, 2008).

The importance of stakeholders is also embedded in grassroots lobbying and political marketing through concepts of relationship management and network theory (Andrews, 1996; Freestone and McGoldrick, 2007; Henneberg and O'Shaughnessy, 2009; Walker, 2012). The profitable and mutually beneficial relationships that Harris and McGrath (2012) mention are fundamental to any business, hence the relationship to

stakeholders is of great importance. However, there is an evident lack of literature which combines the notions of grassroots lobbying with stakeholder engagement (Ihlen, 2007; Harris and McGrath, 2012; Walker, 2012). The objective of any grassroots campaign is to sell (Fraser, 1979), further, issues should be stated in terms of public or consumer impact, in order to generate a large following (Fraser, 1979; Andrews, 1996; Freestone and McGoldrick, 2007; Walker, 2012). This macro environmental approach (Fraser, 1979) correlates with the aim of this chapter, which is to explore how marketing techniques can be used to enhance the public affairs function. The assumption here is that stakeholders make up part of the macroeconomic environment of firms.

Dealing with stakeholders is a long-term relationship engagement (Frooman and Murrell, 2005; Shropshire and Hillman, 2007; Henneberg and O'Shaughnessy, 2009; Hughes and Dann, 2009; Harris and McGrath, 2012; Hillebrand et al., 2015). Thus, lobbying should be seen as an ongoing or continuous dialogue between two parties and not as a singular strategic campaign (Ihlen, 2007; Harris and McGrath, 2012). Walker (2012) describes the term as 'stakeholder-based lobbying', to proactively include stakeholders in a firm's political strategies and not merely respond to external demands. Stakeholder marketing also recognises the broader societal impact of marketing activities (Bhattacharya and Korschun, 2008).

Hillebrand et al. (2015) argue that stakeholder marketing is gaining more significance in the marketing field and that stakeholders are increasingly becoming interrelated, further affecting a firm's performance. In addition, they argue that by driving the focus away from the central stakeholder, the customer, to multiple stakeholders, firms will gain both tangible and intangible benefits, including knowledge and reputation (Bhattacharya and Korschun, 2008; Hillebrand et al., 2015). As our cases will demonstrate, marketing can play a decisive role in changing public perceptions of contentious strategic decisions.

GRASSROOTS LOBBYING AND MARKETING

One way to approach a campaign designed to influence public opinion would be to incorporate tools and techniques used in grassroots lobbying. However, most of the available literature on grassroots lobbying is set in the US, where lobbyists head to Washington to influence politicians whilst having a sound basis on which to agree 'back home' (Page, 2003). This is a typical approach which firms follow to influence public policies or regulations in their favor (Fraser, 1979; Cooper, 1993; Walker, 2009; Harris and McGrath, 2012). By clearly communicating and increasing public understanding of issues facing business as well as society, companies can either significantly fail or significantly gain from engaging in such activities (Sethi, 1979), such as annoying constituencies (Ihlen, 2007) or achieving a policy change in favor of the business (Cooper, 1993; Lock and Harris, 1996; Page, 2003; Walker, 2009; Harris and McGrath, 2012).

Sethi (1979) identified a dual role of corporations who engage in grassroots lobbying, first, to increase public awareness of issues facing business; and second, to increase the quality and quantity of information available to the public. This, in turn, will lead to improved public decision-making. This concept is also outlined in the UN Global Compact on responsible lobbying, where firms are encouraged to engage in any form of lobbying openly and truthfully (AccountAbility and The Global Compact, 2005). In the past, lobbying often occurred behind closed doors. However, Harris and McGrath (2012) stress the importance of firms having to show their value-for-money proposals to policy-makers with regards to public funding, for example.

This also encompasses a firm's responsibility to lobby for its society (Bauer, 2014).

Whereas lobbying has an indirect effect on the general public, grassroots lobbying uses the general public, often within particular constituencies, to influence policy-makers. Either way, these campaigns are mostly directed at influencing policy decision-makers, rather than the general public itself (Fraser, 1979; Baysinger et al., 1985; Walker, 2012). Therefore, it needs to be assessed as to what degree a grassroots lobbying campaign will be effective in changing public opinion on a particular strategic position. Most of the literature on grassroots lobbying focuses on persuading a very precise or narrow audience (Harris and McGrath, 2012), yet Walker (2012) links grassroots lobbying campaigning with stakeholder mobilisation. In addition, he advocates how stakeholders' views need to be proactively incorporated into the political strategy of a firm. In other words, to use stakeholders to support the grassroots campaign by activating them, as they have further reach than the firm on its own. Contrary to this, Cooper (1993) would suggest a 'grasstop' strategy where, for example, the local mayor or union president – a person representing grassroots public opinion – is approached instead of the general public itself.

There is a clear indication that grassroots lobbying involves the use of concepts from marketing (Fraser, 1979; Cooper, 1993; Walker, 2012) and more precisely from political marketing (Harris and McGrath, 2012). The lobbying element in grassroots lobbying emphasises the objective of a sales pitch (Fraser, 1979; Cooper, 1993; Andrews, 1996; Walker, 2009; Harris and McGrath, 2012; Walker, 2012); however, Sethi (1979) opposes this view. He presents it rather as idea or issue communications, thus keeping the objective distinct from messages of selling. Harris and McGrath (2012) on the other hand, emphasise the importance of persuasion, yet the concern is not to come across as a salesperson, as this can trigger negative reactions; rather it is to promote standpoints based on attitudes and beliefs to convince voters (Easton, 2009).

POLITICAL MARKETING AND PUBLIC AFFAIRS

The political marketing literature often makes liberal use of marketing concepts, such as the communications process (Andrews, 1996; Lock and Harris, 1996; Egan, 1999; Baines et al., 2002), as well as exchange theory, coinciding with concepts from lobbying (Andrews, 1996; Egan, 1999; Henneberg and O'Shaughnessy, 2009; Hughes and Dann, 2009). Andrews (1996) highlights the importance of political communication being viewed within the political context, as marketing communication is viewed within the marketing context. The emphasis is on how various actors try to achieve their objectives in the given context, such as competitors, employees, unions, government departments, local press or MPs. It is vital that research is conducted within this context to assess the current situation. Hence, it is crucial to be informed about the target audience, as a central concept of political marketing involves communicating messages along themes appealing to said audiences (Freestone and McGoldrick, 2007).

Nevertheless, situations occur in which the message sent out by political marketers and those received by the general public are interpreted differently by different audiences (Freestone and McGoldrick, 2007). Hence, the message being delivered needs to be simple (Fraser, 1979) and easy to understand by various audiences (Andrews, 1996), in order to limit the possibility of multiple interpretations. Baines et al. (2014) differentiate between 'intended positioning' and 'actual positioning' of the image of a party in a voter's mind. This concept can also be applied to lobbying, where the issue that the company frames to government may not be

received and considered in the exact same way it was framed by the company, not least because the government has other angles and concerns to consider. Hence, there is a difference between what companies try to convey to the public and what resonates in the public's mind or that of the government actor. Therefore, the question arises as to how to communicate different messages about the same issue to differing target audiences, in order to achieve the desired 'actual positioning' in a selected target audience member's mind. This, however, fully contradicts the notion of responsible lobbying of communicating the same message openly to all audiences (Bauer, 2014; AccountAbility and The Global Compact, 2005).

There is also a notion that influence in political marketing is shifting, as the focus is no longer on players who are directly involved, but rather activities are becoming more dependent on those indirectly involved (Henneberg and O'Shaughnessy, 2009). Cooperation and collaboration are also becoming increasingly important tactics in achieving the desired objectives (Cooper, 1993; Andrews, 1996; Egan, 1999; Henneberg and O'Shaughnessy, 2009; Walker, 2012), particularly for example between actors within the media and political entities. The mobilisation and influence of stakeholders has become more central to strategies within political marketing (Freestone and McGoldrick, 2007; Henneberg and O'Shaughnessy, 2009; Hughes and Dann, 2009; Harris and McGrath, 2012; Walker, 2012). Taking this argument further: 'Stakeholder engagement and stakeholder offerings of value are a central part of the political marketing definition'(Hughes and Dann, 2009, p. 249).

In summary, we can observe that organisations need to be aware of the claims of various stakeholders, and, if they view their relationships instrumentally, they should seek to manage those claims in the best interests of the firm, a process in which public affairs professionals will have a significant role to play. The marketing and public affairs literatures appear to offer a wide range of opinions on how to help public affairs professionals in this process, and, as we will discuss, these options are already being called into use.

MARKETING AND PUBLIC AFFAIRS IN PRACTICE

One important element of public affairs is scanning the political environment. This activity is often undertaken as part of the environmental scanning process. Typically, this is undertaken as part of a PESTLE, DEEPLIST or STEEPLE[1] exercise by senior (marketing) managers. Below, we discuss in more detail some key elements of political environmental scanning.

Political Environmental Scanning

When undertaking environmental scanning, the firm or organisation's political environment is analysed. Political environmental analysis considers the interaction between business, society and government before legislation is enacted, when it is still in preparation or in dispute. Political environmental analysis is critical in environmental scanning as companies can identify potential legal and regulatory changes in their industries and have a chance to impede, influence and alter that legislation. Political environmental scanning should therefore be an early warning system for impending high-impact legislation. Many authors of marketing strategy textbooks suggest that the political environment is outside the control of any one individual company. However, there are circumstances when an organisation or an industry coalition can affect legislation in its own favour. Typically, we would identify this as Stage 5 or Stage 4 LRE, influencing/co-creating and informing/revising legislation/regulation respectively. Public affairs, properly undertaken, can actually provide a company

with a competitive advantage over its rivals, when they develop a better public affairs capability as they respond faster to environmental changes. Organisations can therefore outperform other organisations over time if they can manage their relationships with government and regulatory bodies better than their competitors (Hillman et al., 2004; Lawton and Rajwani, 2011). For example, MasterCard and the US government actively intervened in Russia to halt the Russian government from creating its own credit company and extinguishing market opportunities for MasterCard (Harding and Parfitt, 2010).

Legislation is a technical area and thus few firms understand how to influence legislation without employing specialists. Special industry lobbyists might be hired to represent clients with government decision-makers and regulators and provide advisory services on how to design strategic communication campaigns. Generally, there are several ways in which marketers might conduct public affairs. It can be undertaken by employing specialist public affairs firms or engaging the lobbying branch of a larger public relations consultancy (e.g., Weber Shandwick or Bell Pottinger). Where it is legal, a politician might be engaged on the company's board. Politicians have also often been paid a fee to provide advice on a particular matter, but this often requires that they are not serving as a minister in the area on which they are providing advice. In Britain, over the years, payments to MPs have come under considerable scrutiny and the UK Parliament has set up a log for Members to outline their private interests, although it has stopped short of introducing a formal, legal professional code of conduct for public affairs practitioners. Quite often, however, firms develop their own inhouse public affairs capability, although this frequently constitutes no more than a small team. Where a company does not have the resources or the reach to have much impact with government, it might decide to promote its stance on an issue through a trade or professional body instead.

It is important to note that public affairs requires a different process in different countries, as the legislative and public communication systems differ, for example, considerably between the US and Europe, as well as in the Gulf countries of the Middle East or in China (Zetter, 2014).

Stakeholder Mapping

Identifying stakeholders is a particularly critical process in public affairs practice. Stakeholders include organisations or actors with whom the organisation has a relationship and which impact on the operations of the organisation, including shareholders (or trustees), regulatory bodies, charity or not-for-profit partners, supply chain partners, employees and customers.

Earlier, we introduced the concept of stakeholder identification and salience theory (Mitchell et al., 1997), which offers guidance on how companies can identify those stakeholders which are truly important to them. This is done by estimating their power as well as the legitimacy and urgency of their claims over the firm. However, this approach does not clarify the type of response that an

organisation might pursue to manage its relationships with any class of stakeholder. For this purpose, an organisation might choose to deploy the Stakeholder Mapping Matrix (see Figure 6.1). This framework identifies two attributes – Power (in common with Mitchell et al.'s (1997) work) and Interest (which may be seen as a hybrid attribute, synthesising the two other attributes used by Mitchell et al. – legitimacy and urgency). The key advantage of using this framework, therefore, is that it suggests which marketing options will be of benefit in managing the stakeholder interface when they possess a particular set of attributes.

The matrix identifies four types of stakeholder, based on high/low levels of interest in the organisational issue and high/low levels of power that they exert over it. Group A denotes those stakeholders with high levels of interest and power. These are key stakeholders who need to be engaged on the issues. Those with high interest but low levels of power, Group B, should be informed about the company's activities in order to maintain their interest. Group C are those organisations with high power but low interest. Despite their low interest, it is important to continually feed these organisations with information

	High	Power	Low
High	ENGAGE (A)		MAINTAIN (B)
Interest			
Low	*INFORM OR SATISFY (C)*		*REVIVE OR DISREGARD (D)*

Figure 6.1:   The Stakeholder Mapping Matrix
Source: Adapted from Scholes (2001)

concerning the organisation's activities either to increase their interest so that they can exert their power in the company's favour or alternatively to seek to keep them satisfied if it appears that they might exert their power against their interests. An organisation's relationships with those stakeholders who have low power and low interest should either be disregarded or revived (but in the latter case only where there is clear potential in the relationship for an increase in power or interest or both after some intervention).

Once key stakeholders have been identified, it is important to profile those stakeholders and their interests. Thomson and John (2007) suggest a number of key questions that can be asked in relation to stakeholders and public affairs, including:

- What are the stakeholders' motivations?
- What interests do the stakeholders have around your lobbying issue?
- What are stakeholders' current perceptions of your organisation?
- What are the stakeholders' perceptions around the current issue?
- Who or what influences those current perceptions?
- Who else do these stakeholders influence?
- What information do the stakeholders need from your organisation?
- What role do you want different stakeholders to play?
- What can be done to improve stakeholders' support?
- What can win around those stakeholders who are negative on your issue or if they cannot be won around, how can their opposition be mitigated?
- How important are the stakeholders to your argument?

Whilst some of these questions might be ascertained from discussions internally within the company, it is likely that much of the information required would need to be gleaned by commissioning public opinion surveys and/or from social media analysis. We now move on to consider how use of these types of approaches has helped organisations to develop marketing led/marketing-influenced public affairs campaigns and the reasons why a particular set of options has been chosen.

MARKETING AND PUBLIC AFFAIRS: SOME CASE EXAMPLES

This next section discusses some high-profile examples of public affairs campaigns which make use of marketing techniques in a range of industries. This section shows how marketing techniques can deliver greater performance for a company's public affairs function. Cases include the following examples:

(a) The current debate around fracking in the UK (e.g., Cuadrilla).
(b) The food industry and healthy eating practices (e.g., McDonalds' healthy eating programme and Mars, who have recently decided not to advertise directly to children).
(c) The online gaming industry and attempts to enter the US market or efforts by US gaming to change state legislation to liberalise gaming (e.g., in Pennsylvania and New York – changes which have badly affected the industry in Atlantic City).
(d) The UK airport industry and capacity planning – Heathrow versus Gatwick.

As we have noted, some stakeholder theorists (Freeman, 1984) argue that while the main purpose of managers in a for-profit organisation remains to fulfil their fiduciary responsibility towards their owners, this task is rendered more complex by the emergence of a significant and varied group of alternative stakeholder groups whose interests may differ from those of shareholders but which are also demanding attention. Stakeholder theory argues that managers are not responsible for meeting all of these various stakeholder claims; rather that they are responsible for steering the organisation through these various and often divergent claims. This creates a challenge for the public affairs function of managing these interactions in such a way as to ensure that organisational performance is maximised while the effect of potential constraints are mitigated.

We discuss some high-profile examples of the effects of this dilemma being faced in a range of industries, how some companies are rising to this challenge, and how some companies have had to change their initial choices to reflect the effect of dynamic public opinion.

A key question with respect to Case A is whether the public has sufficient power (and interest) to justify an 'engage' strategy (see Figure 6.1). Stakeholder Salience theory (Mitchell et al., 1997; Agle et al., 1999) identifies three key attributes – power, legitimacy and urgency – that stakeholders possess, which determines the responses organisations should make to stakeholder interests based upon the presence or lack of these categories. Their work acknowledges that coalitions

---

Case A: The current debate around fracking in the UK

Hydraulic fracturing, or as it is more commonly and widely described 'fracking', is a technique designed to recover gas and oil deposits from shale rock. It is an extremely controversial process in that while it creates the potential for positive social and economic benefits (namely, it provides access to cheap, domestic, energy supplies) it 'may' also be environmentally damaging. Fracking therefore presents a uniquely twenty-first-century dilemma – how to access cheap, reliable, domestic energy sources (which is a socially positive outcome), but in a way that does not cause concerns regarding the environmental impact of the process.

To date, fracking has received an extremely negative press in the UK, despite the positive aspects of the story. The extent to which this negativity is justified is difficult to establish; how it might be explained, less so. The majority of fracking activity is being undertaken by existing energy companies, many of whom have very poor reputations with interest groups representing the environment, and this is particularly the case with the big oil companies. This creates a febrile environment where advocacy or lobbying is likely to be extremely emotive, not least after the US Oscar-nominated documentary *Gasland*, which featured stories of the nightmare situations of what can happen when fracking goes wrong. Could marketing and public relations help? Apparently so. Cuadrilla and its agency, PPS Group, won a PR Week award in 2011 for 'best issues and crisis management' (Anon., 2011) for its stakeholder engagement programme, including obtaining fact-finding visits to fracking sites by major politicians.

More generally, the choice of marketing approach will depend upon how high the power possessed by the general public stakeholder is seen to be. If the public are a highly interested, but essentially disempowered constituency, then a strategy of 'maintain' (see Figure 6.1) to keep interest high in the sub-group which do not oppose fracking based upon an evidence base would be appropriate, and this has tended to represent the choices of fracking companies to date. Cuadrilla, the UK-based oil and gas exploration company, emphasises many positive benefits from its operations – in terms of jobs, energy security and tax revenues as well as community outreach projects – in its day to day marketing. However, it has also engaged in an evidence-based approach to attempt to dispel concerns about the implications of its actions for the local environment. It has stressed that it is complying with all appropriate industry regulations and has formed strong relationships with regulatory bodies to ensure its compliance. In competition, the opposing view that fracking is unnecessary (because other technologies are available) and harmful to the environment is represented by a number of anti-fracking groups, including Greenpeace and Friends of the Earth, and encapsulated in the 'Frack off' and Refracktion movements. Both the frackers (Cuadrilla) and the anti-frackers have engaged in advertising to support their issue positions, and both Cuadrilla (see Anon., 2013) and Greenpeace (see Casson, 2015) have had their ads banned for making misleading or exaggerated claims by the Advertising Standards Authority.

The key question is whether the industry would benefit from engaging more effectively with its stakeholder community? One aspect of this more aggressive engagement strategy by the frackers was to advocate for, and assist in the funding of, an independent body – the Task Force on Shale Gas – in September 2014 to develop an objective perspective on the pros and cons of fracking and to provide a platform for the evidence of the situation to be heard beyond the more emotive court of public opinion, where by August 2015, in a survey by the Department for Energy and Climate Change (DECC, 2015), more people in Britain opposed fracking (28 per cent) than supported it (21 per cent), although nearly half the public had not made up their minds (46 per cent). Eighteen months previously, the situation was reversed when 21 per cent opposed and 27 per cent supported. It seems that the anti-frackers may now be winning the PR battle.

of stakeholders can provide power where it might be missing if a stakeholder group operates alone. In the case of the 'fracking' debate, the challenge for the industry results from the coalition of public opinion organised by non-governmental organisations (NGOs, e.g., Frack Off, the British Anti-Fracking Action Network, Refracktion), as well as the UK Green Party and publicised by local and national broadcast media. This coalition of interests promotes those opposed to fracking from what Mitchell et al. (1997) call discretionary stakeholders (possessing only a legitimate interest in the organisation's activities) to a dominant stakeholder (possessing legitimacy and power) or even a definitive stakeholder (possessing legitimacy, power and an urgent desire to have their interests recognised).

The 'fracking' case suggests that when an issue becomes so emotive that public opinion is unlikely to be swayed by even the most persuasive evidence-based initiative, there is a need to enhance the approach to more fully engage with the interested stakeholder group, even if that group does not possess direct power. Case A therefore represents a competition (with NGOs) to influence public opinion. The potential benefits of an 'engage' strategy over and above an 'inform/satisfy' strategy can be witnessed with respect to our second case (see Figure 6.1), which looks at how prominent food and beverage companies have engaged with the public health lobby (see Case B).

In both examples quoted in Case B, the companies have modestly engaged with stakeholder groups by adjusting their product and service offerings in a way which intends to address stakeholder concerns and which will impact bottom line performance, rather than simply resorting to an information-based approach which, as the 'fracking case' illustrates, has a tendency to be drowned out by media messages. It might be possible to identify this approach as a 'satisfy' approach (see Figure 6.1) as both companies have made an attempt to meet their critics halfway,

but both instances have more in common with attempting to engage with their critics. In such a way, a compromise is found which satisfies public concerns but does not do too much damage to the bottom line. Case B represents an attempt to achieve a compromise with public opinion.

In both Cases A and B, the aim is to influence individual members of the public, who may or may not have an awareness of a collective identity. In Case C, the aim is to influence collective public opinion in a situation where the collective possesses real political power.

Our gambling case represents a different type of collaboration – government and casinos working together to attempt to win public support. For quite different reasons, state governments and casino operating companies have found common cause in attempting to convince the voting public to set aside any moral objections they may retain against legalised casino gambling to support public referenda to change local anti-gambling laws. These various campaigns, conducted in a number of US states, provide a clear example of an 'engage' strategy (see Figure 6.1) as the target of the campaign – voters – have the ultimate power to sanction a change in the law. Traditionally, an individual citizen would be identified as having limited power, but voters acting collectively do possess the power to approve or dismiss the law change making the effort by this unlikely coalition necessary and appropriate. An 'engage' strategy is therefore appropriate when the support of the target community is a necessity rather than something which is worthwhile but not critical.

A correlation appears to be forming. The greater the stakeholder group's power, the more likely an 'engage' strategy is required as predicted by Scholes (2001). But, as stakeholder identification and salience theory (Mitchell et al., 1997) has suggested, it is also likely that power is not the only determinant for the choice of engagement approach. Our final case emphasises the other attributes that stakeholders can possess – legitimacy and urgency.

Case B: The food industry and healthy eating practices

The linking of people's eating choices and their general health and well-being has become an increasing dilemma for a number of globally recognised food and beverage manufacturers. Some of these companies are retailing items which, if eaten in moderation are harmless indulgences, but when eaten to excess may contribute to damaged health. The dilemma they face is that a manager's fiduciary responsibility to maintain the bottom line involves addressing the challenge of encouraging greater consumption, but not to the extent that they may become villains in the eyes of non-ownership stakeholders (such as government or health care pressure groups). So, how have some companies addressed this challenge using marketing techniques?

Mars, the US-based confectionery company, has developed a radical marketing approach to counteract the threat offered by opponents suggesting it is damaging children's health – since 2007, it no longer directly markets to children under 12 (Derbyshire, 2007). Confectionery and toy manufacturers have long been accused of encouraging 'pester power' by advertising directly to children who have no discretionary spending ability in order that they appeal to their parents and hence make the case for a transaction. Mars took the lead in addressing this widely criticised approach and, in so doing, made it clear that a child's consumption of food was to be moderated by its parents and that it would not directly try to influence this conversation.

McDonald's, the US fast food company, has faced severe criticism for the calorific content of its menu, and it has responded by adjusting that menu to emphasise individual choice as it seeks to counter a variety of negative perceptions. Its marketing message has emphasised variety and the availability of alternative options thereby stressing that dining decisions are a product of individual choice, shifting responsibility back upon the consumer. The availability of calorific information, which was resisted by companies in the industry at the outset, is now embraced as part of the 'helping the consumer make informed choices' agenda within the industry.

Neither Mars nor McDonald's has fundamentally changed its offer, but it has recognised that changing the message – a child's food consumption is determined by adults, an individual is free to make their own consumption decisions and may make better decisions if better informed – may improve how they are perceived by other stakeholder groups. These approaches may harm the bottom line in the short term, but understanding the implications of stakeholder theory suggests that developing a longer-term perspective has greater value in the future. Such an approach is important as both companies are in the front line were the various governments around the world likely to introduce a 'sugar tax' – a tax on goods with high sugar content – in order to stem the epidemic of obesity in country populations and the associated public health costs involved. Only Denmark has introduced the law – and subsequently repealed it (Snowdon, 2015), but many other governments have considered it. In Britain, Public Health England recommended it, but the government seems loathe to adopt their advice (Meikle, 2015).

The airport expansion case acknowledges the potential benefits of mobilising public opinion in support of, or opposition to, a contentious public policy decision. The Heathrow and Gatwick campaigns both used marketing techniques extensively to create grassroots support for their campaigns in order to positively influence the Davies Commission. We would interpret this as an initial attempt to 'inform' interested stakeholder groups, which increased into an 'engage' strategy as the reality of competition became more evident (see Figure 6.1). Subsequently, now that a recommendation has been made and a decision is to be taken, it is clear that these techniques will be deployed against the successful campaign. However, a key difference may be that the pro-expansion campaigns were supported by significant financial resources making it possible to secure the services of a number of professional public relations agencies. The anti-Heathrow campaign does not enjoy this type of financial backing and must rely on more traditional public oppositional approaches at the grassroots level. But access to new tools such as social media, the government's online petition service, and the ease and low cost of creating and publicising an online presence provide the new anti-Heathrow expansion alliance with considerable advantages not enjoyed by their predecessors.

In both the Stage One (supporting the bids) and Stage Two (opposing the choice of Heathrow) cases, the target of the marketing campaigns holds little or no power but has urgent and, in the case of groups opposing

> ### Case C: Encouraging the building of casinos in the US
>
> In all of our cases so far, organisations have been seeking to make use of marketing techniques to influence public opinion to achieve organisational objectives. In this case, alongside organisational objectives, marketing is used to achieve public policy objectives. In the US, states possess considerable rights to determine laws and regulations which would be set by national governments in many other countries. One particular area where this is true is that of casino (as well as online) gambling and gaming. Traditionally, outside the well-known resorts of Las Vegas and Atlantic City, moral and ethical concerns have restricted the development of casino gambling in many states. However, there has been a recent increase in the number of states permitting casino development, with a similar trend emerging in the area of online gambling. In the early 1990s, only 6 states allowed casino gambling operations; over the following 25 years, that has increased to 20 (although if you include native American casino operations, the number rises to 30).
>
> The increase has been widely attributed to the potential casino operations' offer to increase both the tax base in a state as well as being an engine for economic development, creating service industry and tourism jobs in a country with a preference for low individual and corporate taxation. Put simply, some states have identified legalised gambling as a way to fund public sector spending requirements when citizens are both unwilling to pay taxation but expect service provision. The public affairs challenge is that the decision to change state legislation on gambling requires affirmation through state referendum, and marketing efforts are deployed to convince voters that permitting casino gambling will be beneficial.
>
> For example, in late 2014, a public ballot, which was intended to test the 2011 law permitting casino gambling in Massachusetts, was defeated. Defenders of the casino law developed a focused political marketing effort, funded by the casino companies, making the argument that the gambling industry would create jobs and opportunities in otherwise economically challenged communities. These positive economic messages also required assurances that regulation would be effective and support would be provided to gamblers who face addiction issues, in order to make a more convincing argument.

the runway expansion plan, legitimate cases. Case D shows how in an increasingly connected world, companies need to understand stakeholder relationships and be agile in developing appropriate responses from a full portfolio of marketing and public affairs techniques.

DISCUSSION

We have identified a number of different scenarios to illustrate how marketing techniques can be deployed in a range of different public affairs scenarios. In all instances, the aim of the actions was to positively influence public opinion – in favour of fracking, casino expansion, and the idea of airport expansion as well as to develop a positive attitude towards products which had been increasingly criticised on a number of counts, particularly their link to obesity and marketing to children. In most cases, public affairs have sought to 'inform'

the stakeholder community, but where the power of the stakeholder is immediately evident or has become evident (through the emergence of coalitions of stakeholders), the strategy has been to 'engage'. The exception to this conclusion has been in the case of the major food companies. This example is different as it does not deal with an immediate issue, but rather one which has existed for longer and is likely to continue to be persistent. In this case, the companies have taken competitive decisions which have acknowledged the interests of a certain group of stakeholders (i.e., a 'satisfy' approach) and are now seeking to use marketing techniques to demonstrate that they have chosen to satisfy these stakeholders and, having done so, to 'maintain' the new understanding which they hope has emerged (see Table 6.1 for a summary of which stakeholder engagement strategies the main companies used). The food example is therefore a more mature situation and the companies are seeking to manage opinion rather than direct it.

Case D: Airport planning

In July 2015, the Airports Commission, an independent body set up in 2012 to address the seemingly intractable problem of the limited capacity at UK airports, made a recommendation to the UK Parliament that a third runway at Heathrow should be approved. The report marked the culmination of three year's' work by the Commission but also the end of 'Stage One' of a substantial public relations campaign by the major London airports (Heathrow and Gatwick), which was estimated to have cost £3.3 million in advertising to London commuters alone. The owners of both Gatwick Airport (Gatwick Airport Limited, majority owned by Global Infrastructure Partners) and Heathrow Airport (BAA plc, owned by Ferrovial), have both taken out full page adverts in broadsheet newspapers as well as advertising extensively on the London public transport network. The 'Gatwick obviously' campaign aimed to build grassroots support for its lobbying campaign to build a second runway in order to meet Britain's airport expansion needs. Heathrow's 'Taking Britain further' campaign also sought to make the case for a third runway, mainly by arguing that it would have a stronger positive impact on the economy.

Both airports have therefore actively been engaged in seeking to mobilise grassroots support, and both developed extensive and sophisticated campaigns emphasising the potential benefits of a decision in favour of their respective airports for the local, regional and national economy, jobs and leisure transport. The intent of both campaigns (which deployed marketing, public relations and lobbying activities) appears to have been to mobilise grassroots support in order to influence the Davies Commission, a tactic which was criticised as 'subverting democracy' (Milmo, 2014). A key element in both campaigns was to emphasise how a positive choice for Heathrow or Gatwick would improve linkages between London, the North and Scotland with the Scottish government offering backing for the Gatwick bid and regional airports around the UK, including Aberdeen, Glasgow, Liverpool, Leeds Bradford and Newcastle, all offering their support to an expanded Heathrow (LJLA, n.d.).

The work of the Commission has been lauded as being open and eager to obtain the views of a wide range of interested stakeholders. However, the Davies Commission's recommendation of a third runway at Heathrow (see Airports Commission, 2015) is no guarantee that construction will begin as Parliament must ultimately support the recommendation. As Howard Davies, Chair of the Commission notes, this is not the first time expansion at Heathrow has been approved and past plans were 'subsequently set aside in the face of local opposition' (Airports Commission, 2015: 4). 'Stage Two' of the public relations campaign is therefore intended to influence Parliament when it comes to consider the recommendation. As Davies implied, a positive response to the recommendation is not a foregone conclusion, and there exists an inbuilt opposition to the recommendation including the former London Mayor, Boris Johnson, whose parliamentary constituency (Uxbridge) sits next door to Heathrow. The focus of the campaign is again to mobilise grassroots opposition and a number of groups, including The Campaign to Protect Rural England and Stop Heathrow Expansion, local groups such as HACAN and CHATR, and the current London mayor, Sadiq Khan, who supports a second runway at Gatwick over a third runway at Heathrow (Murphy, 2015). There is also no doubt that Gatwick will not be complacent (it continues its Gatwick Obviously campaign), or that Heathrow will become complacent: it is also continuing its public advertising on the issue. A July 2015 Ipsos MORI poll indicated that the general public were marginally in favour of expansion at Gatwick (Ipsos MORI, 2015) whilst a survey of MPs in September 2014 indicates a majority of MPs felt that Heathrow should be the airport that is expanded (Ipsos MORI, 2014). Given the next battle is likely to be at Parliament, we can expect a hotly contested political marketing battle for the hearts and minds of MPs next.

Table 6.1:   Stakeholder engagement strategies employed in different scenarios

Case	Stakeholder Engagement Strategy (after Scholes, 2001)
Fracking expansion	Companies began by seeking to INFORM, but increasingly have had to ENGAGE as coalitions of stakeholders were built that increased their power
Food and health	Companies made adjustments to their strategy which were intended to SATISFY and having reached an outcome which appears to work aim to MAINTAIN
Casino expansion	Companies and government have sought to ENGAGE to obtain support from a powerful stakeholder
Airport expansion	In Stage One of the process the companies sought to INFORM initially with the tendency to ENGAGE emerging as competition increased; in Stage Two the successful company is likely to seek to INFORM although if the coalition of interests ranged against them are successful then they may need to REENGAGE

The examples do provide evidence that a range of marketing approaches is available to public affairs professionals to assist in their activities. The fracking example indicates that it is possible to escalate as the situation demands as estimations of the relative power of interested stakeholders changes, as does the airport expansion example. The casino example indicates that these techniques can be used to proactively seek an outcome, while the food company example demonstrates how once a compromise situation has been reached, marketing techniques can be deployed to maintain this outcome to avoid it becoming damaging again or to require the deployment of more active forms of engagement.

Nevertheless, we would like to express a note of caution regarding how marketing in support of public affairs might be more widely perceived if used improperly. Public affairs is already viewed with suspicion, with the practice of 'lobbying' in particular variously described as a 'grabbing-hand' (Shleifer and Vishny, 2002), enforcing already unfair competition, reinforcing existing market failure (Henderson, 2001) and resulting in outcomes which are morally reprehensible (Gowthorpe and Amat, 2005) or an affront to fairness (Charki et al., 2011). Marketing, with its active connotation in support of public affairs, might be interpreted as an aggressive act on the part of an organisation which may not be welcome in the court of public opinion (as, to some extent, the examples in Cases A, C and D might suggest) and public affairs professionals are well advised to measure the benefits of such activity against the costs.

The discussion of how marketing might support public affairs is arguably complicated by its location between a variety of different literatures: the stakeholder, the public affairs, CPA, business-government relations and the marketing literatures. The argument that marketing may be of benefit in this field is likely to be strengthened by the development of a specific language, located in political marketing, which establishes and defines the concepts, ideas and approaches which might be of value to public affairs professionals in this important, highly valuable but potentially contentious area.

SUGGESTIONS FOR FURTHER RESEARCH

Public affairs research is constantly troubled by the lack of openness on the part of organisations to discussing their activities in this area. This chapter therefore makes a request that more attention be paid to the stakeholder-public affairs-marketing interface, despite the challenges this involves. It is clearly a critical concern as the importance of managing diverse stakeholder expectations increases. We also call for greater organisational engagement with research as the potential benefits can be identified in practice as well as from the theoretical dimension. In this chapter, we have scratched the surface in terms of considering how marketing is applied to public affairs campaigns from a small selection of case studies. Further research should consider the issue more systematically using a large array of cases, including from within specific jurisdictions, to tease out how marketing might support the public affairs function with differing effects in different countries/trade blocs.

A key theme within public affairs discussions concerns the alignment of market and non-market strategies (Lawton et al., 2014), for example, considering how the development of a public affairs capability might help generate sustainable competitive advantage, and there is clearly real potential to extend this to the area of marketing. Such an alignment might consider what benefits accrue to an organisation that aligns its market and non-market efforts formally. To some extent, some companies are already doing this, for example, Mars' challenging of Unilever's 'anti-competitive' dominance of the ice-cream market in the EU in the 1990s (see McDowell, 1996).

CONCLUSION

This chapter highlights how public affairs and marketing are linked together through the process of stakeholder evaluation and engagement. Whilst marketing has traditionally considered the supremacy of the customer, raising their concerns above all others, more recently, marketing, and particularly stakeholder marketing, suggests that marketing activities should be designed to maximise the benefits for all stakeholders, or help manage the stakeholder relationships when the interests of stakeholders are in conflict. This chapter therefore builds on Hult et al.'s (2011) work by exploring both the legal/regulatory stakeholder as well as the local community/general public stakeholder. From that perspective, marketing and public affairs are interlinked through marketing activities related to increasing grassroots support for issues and legislative-change initiatives. Such activities include the use of market research/opinion surveys both to understand the nature and dynamic of public opinion and to measure the effectiveness of the communications used by a campaign or organisation to change that opinion; environmental scanning exercises to understand the nature of impending issues/legislation; and stakeholder mapping to understand how to develop an engagement strategy with different stakeholders (i.e., whether or not to engage, maintain, inform/satisfy or revive/disregard). At the parliamentary consideration of a bill, marketing communications, particularly around issue advertising, might also be used to increase the salience of an organisation's stance on a particular issue, in much the same way that a political party attempts to raise its political capital with the electorate through political marketing techniques. Marketing communication

approaches, designed to engage target audiences, can also be utilised to frame matters and build arguments in situations where issues are contentious and potentially very damaging for an organisation if managed inexpertly. At this stage, other measures of effectiveness might also include: the number of opinions former meetings secured, the number of mentions in Parliament or questions asked about the issue, coverage in the media, reputation of the organisation touting a particular campaign stance before and after the campaign, the number of opportunities to input into government policy-making, and the number of actual inputs to government policy (Thomson and John, 2007).

Note

1 PESTLE stands for Political-Economic-Socio-cultural-Technological-Legal-Ecological. DEEPLIST stands for Demographic-Economic-Ecological/Environmental-Political-Legal-Informational-Social-Technological. STEEPLE stands for Social-Technological-Economical-Environmental-Political-Legal-Ethical. Of these approaches, PESTLE is probably the most commonly used method.

REFERENCES

AccountAbility and The Global Compact. (2005) Towards Responsible Lobbying. Leadership and Public Policy. Retrieved from: http://www.accountability.org/images/content/0/7/079/Responsible Lobbying Full Report(1).pdf [accessed on 26 August 2016].

Agle, B., Mitchell, R. and Sonnenfeld, J. (1999) 'Who matters to CEOs? An investigation of stakeholder attributes and salience, corporate performance and CEO values', *Academy of Management Journal*, 42(5): 507–25.

Airports Commission (2015) Airports Commission: Final Report. London: Airports Commission. 1 July. Retrieve from: https://www.gov.uk/government/publications/airports-commission-final-report [accessed 31 October 2015].

Andrews, L. (1996) 'The relationship of political marketing to political lobbying', *European Journal of Marketing*, 30(10/11): 76–99. doi:10.1108/03090569610149809.

Anon. (2011) 'PR Week awards 2011: Issues and crisis management', *PR Week*, 26 October. Retrieve from: http://www.prweek. com/article/1100817/prweek-awards-2011-issues-crisis-management [accessed 31 October 2015].

Anon. (2013) 'Fracking leaflet banned over "misleading" claims', *BBC News*, 24 April. Retrieve from: http://www.bbc.co.uk/news/uk-england-lancashire-22284340 [accessed 31 October 2015].

Baines, P. and Viney, H. (2010) 'The unloved relationship? Dynamic capabilities and political-market strategy: a research agenda', *Journal of Public Affairs*, 10(4): 258–64.

Baines, P., Harris, P. and Lewis, B.R. (2002) 'The political marketing planning process: Improving image and message in strategic target areas', *Marketing Intelligence and Planning* 20(1): 6–14.

Baines, P., Crawford, I., O'Shaughnessy, N., Worcester, R. and Mortimore, R. (2014) 'Positioning in political marketing: how semiotic analysis adds value to traditional survey approaches', *Journal of Marketing Management*, 30(1/2): 172–200.

Bauer, T. (2014) 'Responsible lobbying', *Journal of Corporate Citizenship*, 53 (March): 61–76.

Baysinger, B.D., Keim, G.D. and Zeithaml, C.P. (1985) 'An empirical evaluation of the potential for including shareholders in corporate constituency programs', *Academy of Management Journal*, 28(1): 180–200.

Bhattacharya, C.B. and Korschun, D. (2008) 'Stakeholder marketing: beyond the four Ps and the customer', *Journal of Public Policy and Marketing*, 27(1): 113–16.

Casson, R. (2015) Fracking bonkers? Decision to ban our ad shows twisted logic. *Greenpeace UK*, 6 May. Retrieve from: http://www.greenpeace.org.uk/blog/climate/asa-decision-ban-greenpeace-anti-fracking-ad-shows-twisted-logic-20150506 [accessed 31 October 2015].

Charki, M., Josserand, E. and Charki, N. (2011) 'Toward an ethical understanding of the controversial technology of online reverse auctions', *Journal of Business Ethics*, 98: 17–37.

Choi, J. and Wang, H. (2007) 'The promise of a managerial values approach to corporate philanthropy', *Journal of Business Ethics*, 73: 345–59.

Cooper, M. (1993) 'Winning in Washington: from grasstops to grassroots', *Public Relations Quarterly*, 38(4): 13–15.

DECC (2015) DECC Public Attitudes Tracker – Wave 14: Summary of Key Findings. London: Department for Energy and Climate Change, August. Retrieve from: https://www.gov.uk/government/uploads/system/uploads/attachment_data/file/450674/PAT_Summary_Wave_14.pdf [accessed 31 October 2015].

Dentchev, N. and Heene, A. (2004) 'Managing the reputation of restructuring corporations: send the right signal to the right stakeholder', *Journal of Public Affairs*, 4(1): 56–72.

Derbyshire, D. (2007) 'Mars to scrap advertising aimed at under 12s', *The Telegraph*, 6 February. Retrieve from: http://www.telegraph.co.uk/news/uknews/1541721/Mars-to-scrap-advertising-aimed-at-under-12s.html [accessed 2 November 2015].

Donaldson, T. and Preston, L. (1995) 'The stakeholder theory of the corporation: concepts, evidence, and implications', *Academy of Management Review*, 20(1): 65–91.

Easton, M. (2009) 'Emotion, rationality, and the European Union: a case study of the discursive framework of the 1994 Norwegian referendum on EU membership', *International Social Science Review*, 84: 44–65.

Egan, J. (1999) 'Political marketing: lessons from the mainstream', *Journal of Marketing Management*, 15(6): 495–503.

Fraser, E. (1979) 'Marketing public policy through grass roots action', *Public Relations Quarterly*, 24(2): 16–25.

Freeman, R.E. (1984) *Strategic Management: A Stakeholder Approach*. Boston, MA: HarperCollins.

Freestone, O.M. and McGoldrick, P.J. (2007) 'Ethical positioning and political marketing: the ethical awareness and concerns of UK voters', *Journal of Marketing Management*, 23(7/8): 651–73.

Frooman, J. and Murrell, A.J. (2005) 'Stakeholder influence strategies: the roles of structural and demographic determinants', *Business & Society*, 44(1): 3–31.

Godfrey, P. and Hatch, N. (2007) 'Researching corporate social responsibility: an agenda for the 21st century', *Journal of Business Ethics*, 70: 87–98.

Goll, I. and Rashid, A. (2004) 'The moderating effect of environmental munificence and dynamism on the relationship between discretionary social responsibility and firm performance', *Journal of Business Ethics*, 49: 41–54.

Gowthorpe, C. and Amat, O. (2005) 'Creative accounting: some ethical issues of macro- and micro-manipulation', *Journal of Business Ethics*, 57: 55–64.

Gundlach, G.T. and Wilkie, W.L. (2010) 'Stakeholder marketing: why "stakeholder" was omitted from the American Marketing Association's official 2007 Definition of Marketing and why the future is bright for stakeholder marketing', *Journal of Public Policy and Marketing*, 29(1): 89–92.

Harding, L. and Parfitt, T. (2010) 'Wikileaks cables: US "lobbied Russia on behalf of Visa and Mastercard"', *The Guardian*, 8 December. Retrieve from: http://www.theguardian.com/world/2010/dec/08/wikileaks-us-russia-visa-mastercard [accessed 31 October 2015].

Harris, P. and McGrath, C. (2012) 'Political marketing and lobbying: a neglected perspective and research agenda', *Journal of Political Marketing*, 11(1/2): 75–94.

Hemingway, C. (2005) 'Personal values as a catalyst for corporate social entrepreneurship', *Journal of Business Ethics*, 60: 233–49.

Hemingway, C. and MacLagan, P. (2004) 'Managers' personal values as drivers of corporate social responsibility', *Journal of Business Ethics*, 50: 33–44.

Henderson, D. (2001) *Misguided Virtue: False Notions of Corporate Social Responsibility*, London: Institute of Economic Affairs.

Henneberg, S.C. and O'Shaughnessy, N.J. (2009) 'Political relationship marketing: some macro/micro thoughts', *Journal of Marketing Management*, 25(1/2): 5–29.

Hillebrand, B., Driessen, P. and Koll, O. (2015) 'Stakeholder marketing: theoretical foundations and required capabilities', *Journal of*

the Academy of Marketing Science, 43(4): 411–28.

Hillman, A.J., Keim, G.D. and Schuler, D. (2004) Corporate political activity: a review and research agenda, *Journal of Management*, 30(6): 837–57.

Hughes, A. and Dann, S. (2009) 'Political marketing and stakeholder engagement', *Marketing Theory*, 9(2): 243–56.

Hult, G.T.M., Mena, J.A., Ferrell, O.C. and Ferrell, L. (2011) 'Stakeholder marketing: a definition and conceptual framework', *Academy of Marketing Science Review*, 1: 44–65.

Husted, B. and De Jesus Salazar, J. (2006) 'Taking Friedman seriously: maximizing profits and social performance', *Journal of Management Studies*, 43(1): 75–91.

Ihlen, O. (2007) 'When lobbying backfires: balancing lobby efforts with insights from stakeholder theory', *Journal of Communication Management*, 11(3): 235–46.

Ipsos MORI. (2014) MPs' attitudes to Heathrow airport expansion. *Ipsos MORI*, 7 September. Retrieve from: https://www.ipsos-mori.com/researchpublications/researcharchive/3442/MPs-attitudes-to-Heathrow-Airport-expansion.aspx [accessed 30 October 2015].

Ipsos MORI. (2015) Most Britons believe airport capacity should be increased. *Ipsos MORI*, 27 July. Retrieve from: https://www.ipsos-mori.com/researchpublications/researcharchive/3606/Most-Britons-believe-airport-capacity-should-be-increased.aspx [accessed 30th November 2015].

Lawton, T. and Rajwani, T. (2011) Designing lobbying capabilities: managerial choices in unpredictable environments, *European Business Review*, 23(2): 167–89.

Lawton, T., Doh, J. and Rajwani, T. (2014) *Aligning for Advantage: Competitive Strategies for the Political and Social Arenas*. Oxford, UK: Oxford University Press.

LJLA (n.d.) LJLA joins with other UK airports to back Heathrow expansion. *Liverpool John Lennon Airport*. Retrieve from: http://www.liverpoolairport.com/ljla-joins-uk-airports-heathrow-expansion/ [accessed 31 October 2015].

Lock, A. and Harris, P. (1996) 'Political marketing – vive la difference!', *European Journal of Marketing*, 30(10/11): 21–31.

Maitlis, S. and Lawrence, T. (2007) 'Triggers and enablers of sensegiving in organizations', *Academy of Management Journal*, 50(1): 57–84.

McDowell, M. (1996) 'An ice-cream war: bundling, tying and foreclosure', *European Journal of Law and Economics*, 3: 197–220.

Meikle, J. (2015) 'Public Health England obesity report: the key points', *The Guardian*, 22 October. Retrieve from: http://www.theguardian.com/society/2015/oct/22/public-health-england-obesity-report-key-points [accessed 31 October 2015].

Milmo, C. (2014) 'London airports' PR blitz is "subverting democracy"'. *The Independent*, 12 December. Retrieve from: http://www.independent.co.uk/travel/news-and-advice/london-airports-pr-blitz-is-subverting-democracy-9922081.html [accessed 31 October 2015].

Mitchell, R., Agle, B. and Wood, D. (1997) 'Toward a theory of stakeholder identification and salience: defending the principle of who and what really counts', *Academy of Management Review*, 22(4): 853–86.

Murphy, J. (2015) 'Labour mayor contender Sadiq Khan rejects third runway at Heathrow'. *Evening Standard*, 16 June. Retrieve from: http://www.standard.co.uk/news/mayor/labour-mayor-contender-sadiq-khan-rejects-building-third-runway-at-heathrow-10323138.html [accessed 28 August 2016].

Page, M. (2003) 'Grassroots lobbying takes hold in rural America', *Rural Telecommunications*, 22(6): 52–7.

Parent, M. and Deephouse, D. (2007) 'A case study of stakeholder identification and prioritization by managers', *Journal of Business Ethics*, 75(1): 1–23.

Scholes, K. (2001) 'Stakeholder mapping: a practical tool for public sector managers' in K. Scholes, G. Johnson *Exploring Public Sector Strategy*, JUpper Saddle River, NJ: Prentice Hall, pp. 165–84.

Sethi, S.P. (1979) 'Grassroots lobbying and the corporation', *Business and Society Review*, 29 (Spring): 8–14.

Shleifer, A. and Vishny, R.W. (2002) *The Grabbing Hand: Government Pathologies and Their Cures*, Cambridge, MA: Harvard University Press.

Shropshire, C. and Hillman, A.J. (2007) 'A longitudinal study of significant change in stakeholder management', *Business and Society*, 46(1): 63–87.

Snowdon, C. (2015) 'A tax on sugar won't work as the shipwreck of the Danish fat tax shows', *The Spectator*, 22 May. Retrieve from: http://health.spectator.co.uk/a-tax-on-sugar-wont-work-as-the-shipwreck-of-the-danish-fat-tax-shows/ [accessed 31 October 2015].

Thomson, S. and John, S. (2007) *Public Affairs in Practice*. London: Kogan Page/CIPR.

Viney, H. and Baines, P. (2012) 'Engaging government: why it's necessary and how businesses should do it', *The European Business Review*, Sept-Oct: 9–13.

Walker, E.T. (2009) 'Privatizing participation: civic change and the organizational dynamics of grassroots lobbying firms', *American Sociological Review*, 74(1): 83–105.

Walker, E.T. (2012) 'Putting a face on the issue: corporate stakeholder mobilization in professional grassroots lobbying campaigns', *Business and Society*, 51(4): 561–601.

Zetter, L. (2014) *Lobbying: The Art of Political Persuasion*. Petersfield, UK: Harriman House.

International Relations and Public Affairs

Ian N. Richardson

Consistent with theoretical developments elsewhere, the internationalization of firms, and the implications of rampant globalization processes in general, have been prominent themes in the public affairs literature in recent years (see, for example, Drogendijk, 2004; Fleisher, 2005; Burrell, 2012; Johnson Jr et al., 2015). As countless contributions have made clear, however, the firm-specific considerations that have accompanied such developments, while growing in significance, are nothing new. Instead, the strategic demands of firm internationalization, non-market as well as market, might best be seen as building on a considerable legacy of international trade – a legacy that has always had, at its heart, an essential political interrelatedness between private interests and the interests of states. Through consideration of theories of international relations (IR), this chapter seeks to contextualize the role of interests – specifically multinational business interests – and, in so doing, highlight the

instrumental value and, at times, precarious nature, of firm/state interrelatedness in contemporary international bargaining. The purpose is not to present a definitive statement of the role of interests in IR – such an objective is practically impossible – but, instead, to discuss important issues and specificities related to international public affairs practice that are highlighted by advances in IR theory.

The chapter presents an overview of theory development in the IR domain before considering, from a strategic perspective, the complexities presented by a multi-layered and highly interdependent game in international politics. This leads, in turn, to a discussion of the nature of the relationship between preferences, interests and institutions within such a setting – and highlights the risks of too rationalistic and mechanistic an approach to international public affairs. Lastly, a descriptive account of the dangers facing MNCs that venture into the complex milieu of contemporary IR is presented with the inclusion of a case study on Google's recent handling of the issue of censorship in China. The case raises a number of important questions related to the nature of business political engagement and, more specifically, serves to highlight the risks associated with such activity.

THEORIES OF INTERNATIONAL RELATIONS

In some ways, the fields of IR and public affairs share similar characteristics. Both are formed at the confluence of numerous, often unrelated, domains and continue to exhibit a theoretical pluralism; both have tended to be descriptive and intrinsically linked with real-world developments for theoretical advances; and both are characterized by ongoing debates related to the defining nature of their discipline. That being said, IR is clearly more interdisciplinary than the less evolved field of public affairs and, since the early 1990s, has found itself pulled in directions that have called into question the fundamental boundaries of the field – a theme that will be returned to shortly.

Most orthodox accounts of the IR field present theoretical advances as being, in a sense, historically chronological and related to material developments in international politics over the past 100 years. In addition to describing a stream of paradigms, often conflicting, the subject of the field's three (or four) 'great debates' is also invoked as a means of explaining the historically contested nature of the domain. Certain IR scholars have challenged this account of the field's development (see Schmidt, 2002) while, elsewhere, the continued use of such field-specific totems, as a means of providing coherence and identity within the domain, has been defended (see Waever, 2013). Notwithstanding these differences, one thing remains abundantly clear: the field of IR lacks precise definition and, moreover, appears some way from reconciling – if indeed reconciliation is desirable and

attainable – the diverse theories, concerns and methodologies of its various constituencies. As if to emphasize the extent of the field's theoretical plurality, a recently edited text on *Theories of International Relations* (see Schieder and Spindler, 2014) presents a collection of no fewer than 18 perspectives on the subject – and this is by no means intended to be a definitive statement.

To present an exhaustive account of theory development in IR is beyond the scope of this chapter but, suffice it to say, most advances speak – directly or indirectly – to the question of how we conceive of public affairs practice in the international political setting. For the purposes of contextualizing a discussion of interests, public affairs and IR, what follows is an extremely brief summary of some of the most significant contributions and debates in the IR field.

Idealism vs Realism

The theoretical distance between two dominant early theories, those of idealism and realism, constituted the first 'great debate' in IR in the first half of the twentieth century. The essential distinction is that, while idealism (see, among others, the work of Angell, 1910; Woolf, 1916 and Zimmern, 1936), which provided the impetus for IR thinking between the establishment of the League of Nations at the end of the Great War, and the outbreak of the Second World War, placed great faith in the ability of people and nations to overcome their differences in favour of greater international harmony, realism (see Carr, 2001[1939] and Moregenthau, 2005[1948]), which was very much influenced by events leading to, and during, the Second World War, viewed international politics as a struggle for power between nations. Peace, in so far as it is achievable, is not the product of enlightened and harmonious minds but, instead, the outcome of a balance of power between states driven by interests, greed, insecurity and power. Such an approach 'revolves around the notions of state sovereignty and its logical corollary, international anarchy. Sovereign states, recognizing no higher authority, are in an international state of nature; the resulting security dilemma forces them to live in a condition of mutual competition and conflict' (Lijphart, 1974: 43). At heart, realism is associated with certain key tenets that continue to resonate within the IR domain despite considerable challenges in the intervening period: namely, that the sovereign state is the most important actor; state behaviour is rational; states are unitary actors; there exists a clear delineation between national and international politics; and, ultimately, states pursue power (Schmidt, 2002).

Post-War Challenges to Realism

Meaningful intellectual challenges to the post-war creed of realism occurred with functionalist approaches (Mitrany, 1933, 1948; E. B. Haas, 1964, 2003[1958]), systems theory (Easton, 1953, 1957; Kaplan, 2005[1957]) and game theoretical accounts (see the seminal work of Von Neumann and Morgenstern, 2007[1944]) which, from somewhat differing perspectives, highlighted the capacity of a world system to influence the behaviour of individual nation states – directly or otherwise – in sharp contrast to the realist depiction of international politics as a dependent variable of state behaviour. The realist movement, and IR field more generally, was initially resistant to such developments, preferring instead to buffer the pre-existing identity of the emergent field, but the 'behavioural revolution' of the 1950s is widely credited with precipitating the second 'great debate' in IR: that related to the nature of scientific knowledge production that took place between descriptive traditionalists and empirical positivists.

It would be wrong to suggest that any one occurrence or theoretical contribution turned the tide against the traditional realist perspective, but clearly developments in the post-war

era, and what is widely regarded as a more complex and interdependent era of international politics, led to alternative theories – notably game theory – with an emphasis on problems of cooperation rather than conflict (Snidal, 1985a, 1985b). Significantly, with the work of Waltz (1979), realist – or, more specifically, neo-realist – accounts of IR incorporated arguments that accepted the structural effects of a world system in determining state preferences and behaviour. Remaining faithful to the realist conception of an egotistical, power seeking, state, neo-realism posits that states pursue their interests within the context of a world system based on a structurally uneven distribution of capabilities. In order to counter the threat of too great a polarity in IR, states will seek to rebalance power in their favour through the use of internal (economic and military) and external (alliance) strategies. Since an escalation of this kind is likely to impact the relative capabilities of other states, it's argued that escalation will be avoided, and mutual security enhanced, in favour of a 'balance of power'. This 'defensive' form of neo-realism is, however, accompanied by a more 'offensive' strand (see Mearsheimer, 2001) that, seeking to explain state aggression, views utility maximization through the development of hegemonic power as the ultimate end of states.

Interdependence and Complexity

In a slightly less pessimistic vein, and echoing liberal and neo-functionalist themes, Keohane and Nye (1977) introduced the idea of complex interdependency in sharp contrast to the neo-realist depiction of IR. Complex interdependence refers to a situation where multiple channels of contact connect societies and where relations of mutual dependency – specifically economic – create reciprocal effects between actors in different countries. This world politics paradigm has evolved over time and is now widely described as neoliberal institutionalism with its emphasis on non-state actors, including international institutions, on forms of power beyond military, on the role of interdependence between states in the international system, and on the importance of cooperation in international politics (Milner, 2009). Neoliberal institutionalism and its interdependence narrative has emerged as a dominant paradigm within the IR field and, for obvious reasons, is closely associated with various globalization and international trade themes. The normative and philosophical differences between neo-realist, neoliberal institutionalist and critical 'structural' contributions from fields such as global politics, world systems theory and international political economy, came to represent an inter-paradigm version of a third 'great debate' in the 1980s. Curiously, others in the field saw the epistemological divide between positivism and post-positivism in the domain as the defining third 'great debate', which, unsurprisingly, has led to confusion. It has been suggested in some quarters that this could have been avoided by accepting that the field had, in fact, entered a fourth 'great debate', precipitated by a deep questioning of the positivist agenda in IR between reflectivists and rationalists (see Waever, 1996).

Undoubtedly, the most significant reflectivist turn in IR over the past 25 years has been the profound influence of constructivist theory (see Wendt, 1992, 1999), which challenges underlying materialistic, rational actor, explanations of state behaviour. Constructivism is concerned with the socially constructed and embedded nature of norms and 'reality' in the international community. Rationality is, at the very least, contingent on a socially constructed and accepted appreciation of what constitutes rational behaviour at any given time. The role of shared understanding and underlying beliefs in constraining and shaping behaviour is seen, therefore, as critical to any understanding of how states make sense of the challenges they face. It also opens the door for consideration of how strategizing behaviour aimed at reframing underlying norms, beliefs

and ideas – for instance, on the part of transnational actors such as NGOs and MNCs – might be effective in achieving specific ends. The concept of norm entrepreneurship which, it has been suggested, might create 'norm bandwagons' and 'norm cascades' (Sunstein, 1995: 6–7), is of particular interest, with numerous examples of how issue saliency and public opinion in the international setting are being cultivated in this way (see, among others, Nadelman, 1990; Finnemore and Sikkink, 1998; Payne, 2001).

Globalization, Transnationalism and States

The adoption of alternative approaches – critical, constructivist and postmodern theories to name but a few (Schieder and Spindler, 2014) – has presented a challenge to longstanding conceptions of IR where, for some at least, 'the rigidity of the old discipline has been replaced by an "anything goes" attitude that, while undoubtedly entertaining, is perhaps a little too indiscriminate in its affection for the new' (Brown, 2004: 289). However distasteful these developments may be to some in the field, they are in some ways a reflection of significant changes that have taken place in world politics during this period. A period in which the structural determinants of the Cold War have given way to a much more fluid era of international cooperation than was previously the case. This pattern of behaviour has been accompanied and, to some extent, reinforced by the effects of globalization – effects that have necessitated considerable soul searching on the part of IR scholars related to the role and centricity of states in the international system.

The development of supranational bodies and global political discourses, coupled with the emergence of powerful, transnational, non-state actors, has challenged the idea that the nation state, and relations between nation states, should be the focus of attention when it comes to developments and politics in the international setting. Certainly non-state actors are a feature of international affairs today in ways that were not the case, to the same extent at least, in the past. But there is widespread acceptance of the view in IR that such influence is frequently overstated and highly context dependent. Moreover, there is 'little systematic evidence to sustain claims that the transnational "society world" has somehow overtaken the "state world"' (Risse, 2002: 251) in terms of explanatory value or meaningful governance.

At this time, the idea that states have somehow been, or are likely to be, displaced is largely discounted in IR in favour of an acknowledgement of the much more profound interrelationship that exists between states and non-state actors in every sphere of government. To this end, some contemporary perspectives – specifically constructivist accounts – of non-state actor influence in politics have tended to soften the idea of it as an exogenous intervention and emphasize, instead, collaboration and embeddedness through advocacy coalitions (Sabatier and Jenkins-Smith, 1993; Sabatier, 1988), epistemic communities (Adler, 1992; P. M. Haas, 1992), and regimes (Krasner, 1982; Stone, 1989; Wilson, 2000). None of this, however, should detract from what, to this day, remains the fundamental concern of IR scholars: namely, providing a satisfactory account of why states behave as they do. And, irrespective of the extent to which states, and state policy formation processes, are steered by interests, it's important to recognize that they remain the critical regulatory conduit in international bargaining.

INTERNATIONAL PUBLIC AFFAIRS PRACTICE AND THE MULTI-LEVEL GAME

Despite considerable reference to the subjects of internationalization and globalization in the public affairs domain, theory development

and research activity have for the most part been concerned with the idiosyncrasies of individual markets and the strategic firm-level challenges of running a public affairs function within an increasingly globalized context. The emergence of intergovernmental organizations (IGOs) such as the European Union is one obvious exception but, while there have been beautifully descriptive accounts of the history, purpose and challenges facing the bloc (see, in particular, the contributions of Spencer, 2005) the emphasis has tended towards an analysis of emergent institutional arrangements and, more pointedly, their significance for public affairs practice.

Consideration of the broader concerns of IR – and specifically the question of how state preference and behaviour are determined in the international setting – has been largely absent from scholarly accounts in the public affairs field. In its place, we see international public affairs presented as being in some way an extension of the firm's strategic public affairs function at a higher, or more transcendental, regulatory level. The importance of ensuring alignment of interests at all levels of government is seen as a strategic objective, but less consideration has been given to whether and how these levels are interconnected in the first instance. Instead, there exists a more rationalistic portrayal in which, states, regulatory authorities and, indeed, firms are presented as distinct unitary actors with reasonably identifiable interests, motivations and agendas. Within such a depiction, the role of the strategic public affairs function is simply that of ensuring the most optimal reconciliation possible – between external stakeholder demands and firm interests – at all levels of government for shareholders of the firm.

Coming to Terms with the Multi-Level Game

An acceptance of the 'levels of government' metaphor is extremely prevalent in the international public affairs literature and, in fact, has considerable heuristic support in the policy sciences field (the 'nested institutional setting' of Kiser and Ostrom, 1982 providing an obvious example). But the hierarchical institutional structure of the nation state, where political actors are identifiable by degrees of authority and functional specification, is situated within what is widely accepted in IR terms to be an anarchic system of international governance – that is to say, one lacking the order of subordination and a sovereign authority (Waltz, 1979).

The two 'levels', national and international, interact profoundly with each other, but the critical issue remains of how to make sense of the interactions (Knopf, 1993; Gourevitch, 2002). Putnam's (1988: 434) description of a two-level game provides a starting point for understanding – in game theoretical terms at least – some of the critical challenges:

> The politics of many international negotiations can usefully be conceived as a two-level game. At the national level, domestic groups pursue their interests by pressuring the government to adopt favorable policies, and politicians seek power by constructing coalitions among those groups. At the international level, national governments seek to maximize their own ability to satisfy domestic pressures, while minimizing the adverse consequences of foreign developments. Neither of the two games can be ignored by central decision-makers, so long as their countries remain interdependent, yet sovereign. Each national political leader appears at both game boards. Across the international table sit his foreign counterparts, and at his elbows sit diplomats and other international advisors. Around the domestic table behind him sit party and parliamentary figures, spokespersons for domestic agencies, representatives of key interest groups, and the leader's own political advisors. The unusual complexity of this two-level game is that moves that are rational for a player at one board (such as raising energy prices, conceding territory, or limiting auto imports) may be impolitic for that same player at the other board. Nevertheless, there are powerful incentives for consistency between the two games. Players [..] will tolerate some differences in rhetoric between the two games, but in the end either energy prices rise or they don't. The political complexities for the players in this two-level game are staggering. Any key player at the international table who is dissatisfied with the outcome may upset the game board, and conversely, any leader who fails to satisfy his fellow players at the domestic table risks being evicted from his seat. On occasion, however, clever players will spot a move on one board that will trigger realignments on other boards, enabling them to achieve otherwise unattainable objectives.

The unusual complexities of this two-level game fundamentally affect the bargaining capacity and approaches of actors at the international level. In stark contrast to the idea that state interests guide clear policy preferences, which in turn determine optimal and minimal bargaining positions, Putnam (1988) introduces the more fluid concept of 'win-sets' to describe a broader array of possible and acceptable outcomes. Understanding the win-sets of one's counterpart in international negotiations involves interpreting the many differing institutional and stakeholder demands placed on the negotiator at the domestic level. The narrower these demands, the less room for concession and the less flexible the negotiation stance. The broader the win-set, the greater the opportunity for finding mutually acceptable accords – assuming, of course, that concessions and gains result in acceptable win-sets on both sides. From a game theoretical perspective, it makes sense to signal a constrained win-set, thus strengthening one's negotiation stance, but this risks the possibility of failing to reach an agreement. In some ways, stable democracies, which are often seen as being less agile in international bargaining because of powerful domestic audiences (Fearon, 1994; Mansfield et al., 2002), have both advantages and disadvantages in this regard since their domestic situation and political constraints are more transparent to counterparts.

Interdependence and Interplay

There is, it should be stated, another important reason for exercising caution when viewing the levels of political discourse as in some way distinct. Today, more than ever, neither level conducts its business in a vacuum and significant underlying interdependencies can be seen to exist between nation state and the international political context. This renders any attempt to empirically understand the actions of one, while holding the other constant, a somewhat questionable exercise. As Gourevitch's (1978) 'second-image reversed' contribution suggests, there is a major problem with viewing foreign policy as a dependent variable of national political discourse and domestic interests when that discourse is itself influenced by exogenous factors, considerations and expectations. Indeed, the interdependence of actors and actions can quickly lead to a level of complexity that becomes unfathomable even where unitary actors and simple interactions are concerned (Allan and Dupont, 1999).

These complexities become even more pronounced when we acknowledge the mediating effects of IGOs, such as NATO and the EU, in international politics. Indeed, some have suggested that, in the case of the latter, regional governance should be seen as a critical stakeholder in a three-level game (Patterson, 1997; Larsen, 2007; Hwang and Kim, 2014; Reslow and Vink, 2015). Elsewhere, there have been calls to 'bring transnational actors back in' to our consideration of effects at all levels (Risse-Kappen, 1995) – after all, transnational actors can influence win-sets at the national level, influence interstate negotiations and create paths and dialogue between actors at all levels. In short, while institutional arrangements can mitigate the influence of transnational actors (TNAs) at the national level, and the strength of international institutions and compliance directly affects the ability of TNAs to influence national and international discourse 'from above', we should be under no illusions about the ability of TNAs to shape and constrain intra- and interstate narratives in ways that might directly impact policy outcomes (Risse-Kappen, 1995).

Available research on attempts by TNAs to impact international political discourse, points to three general influence strategies (Risse, 2002: 268–9):

- Through domestic lobbying of individual powerful states thereby exploiting the dynamics of the 'two-level game'. This might take the form of direct state lobbying efforts or, where national public opinion can be harnessed to increase pressure on domestic governments (which might not otherwise take a position on an issue likely to damage pre-existing relations with another state), TNAs can look to create a 'boomerang' pattern or effect (Keck and Sikkink, 1999).
- Through the development of coalitions with international organizations which, in turn, have the effect of pressuring individual states from both 'above' and 'below' – an approach that has been particularly favoured in the European Union.
- Through coalition building efforts with smaller states – in particular, through the provision of knowledge-based resources.

Leaving aside the age-old empirical question of whether these strategies result in adapted preferences and modified policy outcomes, it's worth noting a couple of important assumptions that underpin depictions of the relationship between interests and state/interstate preferences in accounts of this kind: the first is that the relationship is almost always seen as unidirectional (from interest to state) where the state is, at best, deriving a resource – often legitimacy – rather than seeking to proactively and instrumentally guide the preferences of external interests in line with those of its own; the second is that policy actors at various levels have reasonably identifiable interests, preferences or positions that need to be in some way caressed or modified. Unfortunately, such assumptions – however necessary from the perspective of a more instrumental strategic perspective – could, in many instances, prove to be erroneous.

Given the game theoretical implications of contemporary international bargaining, it is entirely conceivable that states might seek to utilize, even manipulate, special interests – whether domestic or transnational – for the purposes of achieving more preferable accommodations at the international table.

In other words, while MNCs might willingly take part in their own game when it comes to state and interstate discourse, they should be careful not to unwittingly become a participant in someone else's. It's for this reason, when considering state preferences, where there exists a general tendency in IR to model actors in a rationalistic and monolithic fashion (Bendor and Hammond, 1992), that we develop a far more nuanced – even political – understanding of state motivation, interests and preferences.

INTERESTS, PREFERENCES AND INSTITUTIONS

Notwithstanding the heavily contested nature of theory development in the IR domain, there is little disagreement between scholars over the critical role played by interests and preferences in international politics (Frieden, 1999). However, there are, it should be noted, significant problems highlighted by the IR literature when it comes to ascribing interests and preferences to actors which have considerable relevance for public affairs practice.

First, there is the question of how states define their preferences – a fundamental question in political science and, in IR, one that continues to evade satisfactory explanation (Frieden, 1999). A longstanding account, notably related to trade policy, is that, because of the differential impacts of international trade on various industrial sectors (based on factor or sector specific dynamics), and differing levels of competitiveness within those industry sectors, specific interests lobby government in support of their preferences (Frieden, 1999). Two important contributions, the first suggesting that concentrated interests take precedence over dispersed or fragmented forms (Schattschneider, 1935) and the second, building on the logic of collective action in stable societies (Olson, 1965), and highlighting how narrow, well organized, and entrenched interests might lead

to national economic decline (Olson, 1982), further call into question the idea of aggregated state preferences based upon pluralistic or 'encompassing' logics rather than 'distributive' ones (Olson, 1982). For his part, Olson (1982) was firmly of the belief that 'distributive' coalitions, those that sought disproportionate gains for the few, hold an increasingly dominant position in stable societies but there remain complex questions over the nature and extent of such influence. Indeed, most fundamentally, there remains no theory of how preferences are aggregated in government: the involvement of policy actors is largely ignored as is the impact of their preferences and ideas, and economic conditions that might constrain or shape the decisions of government are absent in such theories. Consequently, they stop short of a complete explanation of trade policy (Milner, 2013).

Second, if we take the question of how aggregated foreign policy preferences are defined, we see the state typically cast in pluralistic terms as an arbitrator of interests. Accepting that there may well be deep-seated cleavages in business support for international trade policies, and that such economic decisions have direct political consequences, it is important to recognize the mediating effects of government institutions on resulting policy preferences. Emphasizing the political dimensions of preference formation, which include consideration of whether, and at what cost, interests can be satisfied (Verdier, 1994), creates a causal discontinuity between the notion of underlying interests and resulting government preferences. Meaning, in turn, that we should exercise caution when attempting to deduce interests from preferences and, indeed, the strategies employed to achieve those preferences. For those concerned with anticipating or interpreting government preferences, the challenge is significant since 'it is never inherently obvious whether action is the result of preferences or strategies, underlying interests, or the environment in which they play themselves out' (Frieden, 1999: 46).

The implications of this difficulty in interpreting the meaning of, and underlying motivation for, state behaviour will not be lost, of course, on international public affairs practitioners. In the first instance, states and government agencies might not necessarily disclose their interests or preferences or, more problematical perhaps, might for a variety of reasons signal misleading interests or preferences. In the second instance, states and governments are not unitary actors; they are comprised of numerous departments and agencies with, at times, entirely different interests and motivations. The most clear-cut example of this exists in the area of trade which, for obvious reasons, is most concerned with building and maintaining harmonious relations with trading partners. Interests and preferences in this area may well be at odds with those in other agencies where such considerations run secondary to more immediate political concerns. Gourevitch (2002), for instance, describes how the US Commerce Department and its trade-related agencies constantly pressed Japan for trade concessions while its State and Defence Departments prefer to maintain a degree of goodwill with the country because of broader Asian security concerns. In the third instance, political preferences can change – sometimes quickly – which makes stationary assumptions related to actor preference in the international setting, however well-conceived, potentially vulnerable.

THE MULTINATIONAL CORPORATION AND POLITICAL ADVOCACY

What the chapter has so far sought to emphasize is the profound complexity of the international political system and, critically, the importance of complementing rationalistic assumptions with a greater understanding of the relationship between interests and preferences at and within all levels and spheres of governance. Within such a

depiction, the role of the policy entrepreneur will remain that of identifying 'windows of opportunity' for the advancement of particular agendas (Kingdon, 1984), but, in some instances, they may be called upon to take a less pragmatic, and more inflexible, advocacy position. At a time when Western consumer societies are demanding more in terms of ethical standards from their brands, the option of remaining passive on issues likely to create problems, especially across territories, becomes more difficult for the MNC. In rationalistic terms, this may mean balancing reputational costs against the short-, medium- and long-term commercial gains of remaining passive. If we accept that economic motivation might not be the only cause of preferences, however, it might also mean that we see more MNCs take pro-active advocacy positions, which, by implication, could bring them headlong into the murky waters of international politics.

One such example is that of Google in China. The case raises important questions about epistemic communities and regimes, the nature of the relationship between state and domestic MNC interests, rationalistic accounts of firm behaviour and the contingent nature of state preferences in IR. It also highlights the profound risks associated with engagement of this kind. It should be noted that the description is largely inferred by the sequence of reported events – an approach that, for reasons described earlier, has obvious shortcomings.

Google in China

Case Study reprinted with kind permission: Richardson, I. N., Kakabadse, A. P., & Kakabadse, N. K. (2011: 154–60). *Bilderberg People: Elite Power and Consensus in World Affairs*. Abingdon, UK: Routledge.

In January 2010, Google Inc. stoked political tensions between the US and China, and staggered the investment community by announcing that in light of cyber-attacks on its server infrastructure, which had originated in China – specifically attempts to access the Gmail accounts of Chinese human rights activists – it was no longer prepared to censor search functionality in the country.[1] Since establishing its Chinese search business in 2006, Google had consistently struggled to reconcile itself to the government's censorship demands.[2] And its founders and executives were clearly wounded by ongoing criticisms that it had compromised its integrity and its commitment to *Do No Evil* by entering into a written agreement with the Chinese government to filter out banned topics from its local service. Its provocative statement, therefore, was more than just corporate posturing – it reflected a deep-seated anxiety related to compromised principles and, specifically, the democratic principle of free speech. David Drummond, SVP, Corporate Development and Chief Legal Officer at Google, made it clear that it was prepared, if necessary, to abandon its Chinese business rather than continue to compromise over the issue:

We launched Google.cn in January 2006 in the belief that the benefits of increased access to information for people in China and a more open Internet outweighed our discomfort in agreeing to censor some results. At the time we made clear that 'we will carefully monitor conditions in China, including new laws and other restrictions on our services. If we determine that we are unable to achieve the objectives outlined we will not hesitate to reconsider our approach to China. These attacks and the surveillance they have uncovered – combined with the attempts over the past year to further limit free speech on the web – have led us to conclude that we should review the feasibility of our business operations in China. We have decided we are no longer willing to continue censoring our results on Google. cn, and so over the next few weeks we will be discussing with the Chinese government the basis on which we could operate an unfiltered search engine within the law, if at all. We recognize that this may well mean having to shut down Google.cn, and potentially our offices in China'[3].

Human rights activists and free speech advocates heaped praise on Google over a stance that had clearly embarrassed and angered the Chinese government. Investors were more luke-warm in their appreciation of the move,

simultaneously recognizing the lack of immediate damage to Google's international revenues but identifying the longer-term business implications of not being present in the world's most internet connected market. Elsewhere, Google's announcement, set against a backdrop of worsening political relations between the US and China – primarily related to currency and balance of trade issues – was a timely political gift for the US government who were quick to express support for the company. Speaking on the subject of internet freedom just days after the announcement, US Secretary of State Hillary Clinton proclaimed that:

New technologies do not take sides in the struggle for freedom and progress, but the United States does [...] We need to synchronize our technological progress with our principles [...] Increasingly, U.S. companies are making the issue of internet and information freedom a greater consideration in their business decisions. I hope that their competitors and foreign governments will pay close attention to this trend. The most recent situation involving Google has attracted a great deal of interest [...] The internet has already been a source of tremendous progress in China, and it is fabulous. There are so many people in China now online. But countries that restrict free access to information or violate the basic rights of internet users risk walling themselves off from the progress of the next century. Now, the United States and China have different views on this issue, and we intend to address those differences candidly and consistently in the context of our positive, cooperative, and comprehensive relationship [...] This issue isn't just about information freedom; it is about what kind of world we want and what kind of world we will inhabit. It's about whether we live on a planet with one internet, one global community, and a common body of knowledge that benefits and unites us all, or a fragmented planet in which access to information and opportunity is dependent on where you live and the whims of censors. Information freedom supports the peace and security that provides a foundation for global progress. Historically, asymmetrical access to information is one of the leading causes of interstate conflict [...] it's critical that people on both sides of the problem have access to the same set of facts and opinions.[4]

The Chinese government's position, however, was unequivocal. Google was reneging on a written promise and behaving in a way that it believed to be 'totally wrong'.[5] The state controlled Xinhua news agency, quoting an unnamed official within the State Council Information Office, relayed the view that 'Google has violated [the] written promise it made when entering the Chinese market by stopping filtering its searching service and blaming China in insinuation for alleged hacker attacks'.[6] It made clear that any move on the part of Google to offer an uncensored Chinese search service would not be tolerated – the company would 'pay the consequences'[7] for any transgressions. Furthermore, it attacked Google for its 'intricate ties' with the US government and took a sideswipe at the company's cooperation with US intelligence agencies.[8] As the stand-off intensified, it was clear that any attempt by Google to maintain an illegal uncensored service would, under the circumstances, be extremely inadvisable. In an attempt to circumvent the restrictions, Google took the decision in March 2010 to direct its Chinese search queries through its uncensored Hong Kong based servers – a decision that further angered Chinese officials. In another statement from Google, its spokesperson David Drummond explained the move:

> Figuring out how to make good on our promise to stop censoring search on Google.cn has been hard. We want as many people in the world as possible to have access to our services, including users in mainland China, yet the Chinese government has been crystal clear throughout our discussions that self-censorship is a non-negotiable legal requirement. We believe this new approach of providing uncensored search in simplified Chinese from Google.com.hk is a sensible solution to the challenges we've faced – it's entirely legal and will meaningfully increase access to information for people in China. We very much hope that the Chinese government respects our decision, though we are well aware that it could at any time block access to our services.[9]

Demonstrating, perhaps, the rather transitory and expedient nature of political indignation, the US administration was said to be dismayed at the inability of Google and the

Chinese authorities to come to an agreement[10] although it's unclear whether the dismay was aimed at Chinese insistence on censorship or Google's apparent escalation of the standoff. In a statement, National Security Council spokesperson, Mike Hammer, confirmed that the White House was informed of the company's decision concerning Hong Kong before the announcement was made.[11] Appearing to put some distance between the administration and Google, he stressed that bilateral ties between the countries were 'mature enough to sustain differences' and that Google's actions were motivated ultimately by its own interests.[12] Similarly, the Chinese authorities began to play down the significance of the dispute. In a press briefing, Qin Gang, a spokesman for the Chinese Foreign Ministry, argued that Google's move would be dealt with 'according to the law' and that it represented an isolated act by a commercial operation. It would not, he said, affect China-US ties 'unless politicized' by others.[13] At this point, it appeared that the Google situation had become, in effect, something of an irritation for both governments.

In the days and weeks before the expiration of Google's licence in China, tensions were allowed to diffuse sufficiently enough for renewal of the licence to be the least damaging outcome for all concerned. Sensitive searches made by mainland Chinese visitors to the Hong Kong based Google servers were effectively blocked by the government and, in the days before the licence renewal, Google appeased the authorities by ending the automatic redirection of Chinese traffic to its Hong Kong based website. Instead, its homepage featured a link, for those who wished to use it, to the Hong Kong servers.

Since the end of 2009, Google has seen its share of the Chinese search market fall from 35.6 per cent to 21.6 per cent (November 2010)[14] and it currently runs a distant second place to dominant local search business, Baidu. Despite this, and the possibility of punitive market conditions in the years ahead, Google executives continue[d] to publicly question the long-term viability of Chinese censorship. At a November 2010 meeting of the Council on Foreign Relations, a bastion of the US foreign policy establishment, Google's Chairman and CEO, Eric Schmidt, opined that China's attempt to control internet usage would ultimately fail as ever more Chinese people went online and found expression:

> Ultimately, the people will win over the government. The yearning is so strong. [...] China heavily invests in policing the web, using a large organization of regulators estimated between 30,000 to 50,000 people [...] The question is at what point will there be so many Chinese people online that such mechanisms break down in terms of censorship and so forth? [...] If you think about the scale, they've got a billion phones that are trying to express themselves. It will be difficult in my view to completely keep up with that.[15]

As the Google/China conflict played out during the course of 2010, it became increasingly difficult to understand, notwithstanding the US administration's claim that Google was acting in its own interests, what possible commercial motivation the company could have had for its stance. Cynics might suggest, of course, that the company looked to gain materially through the enhanced reputation of its brand, but the risks associated with the move make it difficult to see this as anything other than a happy consequence of what must have been, despite all suggestions to the contrary, a genuinely principled position. Google's executives were undoubtedly aware from the outset of the likely commercial repercussions of their actions. And, certainly, if we take the muted response of its competitors and other US corporations active in China, as an indicator of such things, there was, and is, a conspicuous absence of corporate criticism of the Chinese authorities. Google's actions were not driven by anything resembling an immediate business consideration; what they represented, in fact, was a remarkable blurring of the lines in contemporary world politics.

The political power of transnational corporations has always been understood in terms of economic self-interest. And, indeed, there are many examples of how this self-interest is shaping the world in which we live. Individual governments, for their part, have long championed their business interests overseas – to the extent that it's sometimes difficult to understand what other motivation there is for foreign policy. But Google's stand-off with the Chinese government represents something quite different. It's clear that the US administration was aware of, and supported, the initial action taken by the company. Aside from the benefit of forcing the Chinese into a defensive position over the breached security of US business interests, the administration was no doubt interested to see where Google's actions might lead. In particular, with US interests reporting a harshening of environmental conditions in China, it provided an opportunity to see how the authorities dealt with full frontal resistance from powerful transnational business interests. In the course of subsequent bilateral discussions with the Chinese, however, it seems the administration concluded that wider US interests were best served by encouraging an end to the stand-off. Google, having threatened to pull out of China over the dispute, in the event opted for a quieter resolution. Whether this decision was the product of second thoughts and consideration of their other Chinese businesses, the fact that they were left isolated over their actions, a concern for Chinese employees, pressure from shareholders or, more interestingly, administration influence, is impossible to know with any certainty, but it seems highly unlikely that it was a decision taken without consideration of interests beyond its own.

Google's stand against the Chinese government may, ultimately, prove to have been little more than an expression of the will of its founders, but it has forced us to re-think the strategic alignment of corporate and governmental agendas in international relations. It highlights the proximity and interdependence of corporate and political decision making and, crucially, the networked values and motivations that underpin it. And, while many will applaud the courage and conviction of Google for taking what it sees as its corporate responsibility and brand values seriously, others may see its moralizing, liberal internationalist, stance as representative of something quite new in international politics: the corporation as a proxy for the wider economic and political interests of its government.[16]

Prior to the events of this case, Google's search business in China had grown rapidly and, in 2009, was estimated to represent approximately one-third of the Chinese market. At the end of 2015, analysts estimate its market share at no more than 2–3 per cent and, furthermore, the company is reported to have experienced difficulties with a number of its other services in the country. While Google's advertising revenues from mainland China have continued to grow, its stand-off with the Chinese government has allowed Baidu, the Chinese search engine giant, to dominate in its home market and, potentially, pose a threat to Google's business outside of the country. Critically, without its core search business to drive Chinese revenues, Google remains, to all intents and purposes, a spectator on the sidelines of the largest internet market in the world – a market that represents its single most obvious source of growth. As principled as its stand in China may have been, it seems inconceivable that efforts are not being made, at all levels, to reach a reconciliation.

Google's decision to challenge the Chinese authorities has clearly had devastating consequences for its business operations in the country, but the effects of what is, in political terms, rather more than a regulatory difference of opinion have been felt well beyond Google. In what some might see as a retaliatory gesture on the part of US legislators, Chinese telecommunications firms HUAWEI and ZTE were effectively frozen

out of the US market in 2012 when a congressional report alleged, because of their relations with the Chinese government and a lack of cooperation with the committee, that they posed a threat to US national security. US government agencies were immediately 'off limits' for both companies and, when the chairman of the congressional committee responsible for the report appeared on television and encouraged viewers to 'find another vendor', US business and consumer confidence in both firms was further impacted. Faced with impossible conditions, and citing the politicized nature of developments, HUAWEI and ZTE pulled their operations out of the US.

Notwithstanding the fact that there may have been legitimate causes for concern, the timing of the report – coupled with a lack of substantive evidence – has led to accusations of protectionism and, more generally, the suspicion that both MNCs had become unwitting pawns in a much larger game.

CONCLUSION

The field of IR is vast. It's disciplinary and interdisciplinary interests go well beyond anything crudely highlighted in this chapter, but there are obvious theoretical areas that have the capacity to profoundly influence the way we conceive of public affairs practice in the international domain. The focus of this chapter has been to enrich, rather than discard, rationalistic accounts of firm and state behaviour in international public affairs. The inclusion of institutional factors, as critical mediating influences, will come as no surprise to practitioners of public affairs but, situated as they are within a complex, multi-levelled setting, their implications become even more pronounced.

The more immediate contribution of the chapter is the attempt to draw attention to an area of public affairs scholarship that, for pressing reasons, would benefit from further theoretical inquiry. In the area of international public affairs, we should look to develop a more interactive understanding of states, the international system, supranational authorities and TNAs, and try to avoid the temptation of unitary actor assumptions (Gourevitch, 2002). In short, while there's considerable heuristic value in simplifying the strategic challenges of public affairs practice in the international context, the fluid complexities of contemporary IR between states, and increasing numbers of non-state actors, require a more sophisticated appreciation of preferences and interests in, what remains, an anarchic world political system.

Notes

1   See BBC. (13 January 2010).
2   See Helft, M. and Barboza, D. (22 March 2010).
3   Drummond, D. (12 January 2010).
4   Rodham Clinton, H. (21 January 2010).
5   *Reuters*. (22 March 2010).
6   English.xinhuanet.com. (23 March 2010).
7   See Pomfret, J. (13 March 2010).
8   See BBC. (21 March 2010).
9   Drummond, D. (12 January 2010).
10 See BBC. (23 March 2010).
11 *AFP*. (22 March 2010).
12 *AFP*. (22 March 2010).
13 See Helft, M. and Barboza, D. (22 March 2010).
14 Kan, M. (2010).
15 Kan, M. (2010).
16 The Chinese government, for instance, argued that the US government was using the internet to 'subvert power' in China. See Pomfret, J. (13 March 2010).

REFERENCES

Adler, E. (1992). The emergence of cooperation: national epistemic communities and the international evolution of the idea of nuclear arms control. *International Organization*, 46(1), 101–45.

AFP. (22 March 2010). White House 'disappointed' no Google, China deal. Retrieved 13 November 2010 from http://www.google.com/hostednews/afp/article/ALeqM5gFISWXUaNq8MQN43wfERHAcLpP0Q

Allan, P. and Dupont, C. (1999). International relations theory and game theory: baroque modeling choices and empirical robustness. *International Political Science Review*, 20(1), 23–47.

Angell, N. (1910). *The Great Illusion: A Study of the Relation of Military Power in Nations to the Economic and Social Advantage*. New York and London: G. P. Putnam's Sons.

BBC. (13 January 2010). Google 'may pull out of China after Gmail cyber attack'. Retrieved 31 December 2010 from http://news.bbc.co.uk/2/hi/business/8455712.stm

BBC. (21 March 2010). China denounces Google 'US ties'. Retrieved 13 November 2010 from http://news.bbc.co.uk/2/hi/8578968.stm

BBC. (23 March 2010) Google stops censoring search results in China. Retrieved 12 November 2010 from http://news.bbc.co.uk/2/hi/business/8581393.stm

Bendor, J. and Hammond, T. (1992). Rethinking Allison's models. *American Political Science Review*, 86(2), 301–22.

Brown, C. (2004). Political theory and international relations. In G.F. Gaus and C. Kukathas (Eds.), *Handbook of Political Theory* (pp. 289–300). London: Sage.

Burrell, M. (2012). A decade of change and continuity in public affairs. *Journal of Public Affairs*, 12(1), 74–6.

Carr, E.H. (2001/1939). In M. Cox (Ed.), *The Twenty Years' Crisis: 1919–1939. An Introduction to the Study of International Relations*. Basingstoke, UK: Palgrave Macmillan.

Drogendijk, R. (2004). The public affairs of internationalisation: balancing pressures from multiple environments. *Journal of Public Affairs*, 4(1), 44–55.

Drummond, D. (12 January 2010). A new approach to China. Official Google blog. Retrieved 10 November 2010 from http://googleblog.blogspot.com/2010/01/new-approach-to-china.html

Easton, D. (1953). *The Political System: An Inquiry into the State of Political Science*. New York: Alfred A. Knopf.

Easton, D. (1957). An approach to the analysis of political systems. *World Politics*, 9(3), 383–400.

English.xinhuanet.com (23 March 2010). China says Google breaks promise; totally wrong to stop censoring. Retrieved 13 November 2010 from http://news.xinhuanet.com/english 2010/china/2010-03/23/c_13220853.htm

Fearon, J.D. (1994). Domestic political audiences and the escalation of international disputes. *American Political Science Review*, 88(3), 577–92.

Finnemore, M. and Sikkink, K. (1998). International norm dynamics and political change. *International Organization*, 52(4), 887–917.

Fleisher, C.S. (2005). The global development of public affairs. In P. Harris and C.S. Fleisher (Eds.), *The Handbook of Public Affairs* (pp. 5–30). London: Sage.

Frieden, J.A. (1999). Actors and preferences in international relations. In D.A. Lake and R. Powell (Eds.), *Strategic Choice and International Relations* (pp. 39–76). UK: Princeton University Press.

Gourevitch, P. (1978). The second image reversed: the international sources of domestic politics. *International Organization*, 32(4), 881–912.

Gourevitch, P. (2002). Domestic politics and international relations. In W. Carlsnaes, T. Risse and B.A. Simmons (Eds.), *Handbook of International Relations* (pp. 309–28). London: Sage.

Haas, E.B. (1964). *Beyond the Nation State: Functionalism and International Organization*. Stanford, CA: Stanford University Press.

Haas, E.B. (2003/1958). *The Uniting of Europe: Political, Social and Economic Forces, 1950–57*. Notre Dame, IN: University of Notre Dame Press.

Haas, P.M. (1992). Introduction: epistemic communities and international policy coordination. *International Organization*, 46(1), 1–35.

Helft, M. and Barboza, D. (22 March 2010). Google shuts China site in dispute over censorship. *New York Times*. Retrieved 14 November 2010 from http://www.nytimes.com/2010/03/23/technology/23google.html

Hwang, K.S. and Kim, H.J. (2014). Three-level game theory and the strategy of EU-Korea FTA negotiation. *Journal of East Asian Affairs*, 28(1), 85–130.

Johnson Jr, J.H., Mirchandani, D.A. and Meznar, M.B. (2015). The impact of internationalization of U.S. multinationals on public affairs strategy and performance: a comparison at 1993 and 2003. *Business and Society*, 54(1), 89–125.

Kan, M. (2010). China's internet censorship will fail in time. IDG News Service. Retrieved 12 November 2010 from http://www.macworld.com/article/155454/2010/11/google_china.html

Kaplan, M.A. (2005/1957). In A. Ware (Ed.), *System and Process in International Politics*. Colchester, UK: ECPR Press.

Keck, M.E. and Sikkink, K. (1999). Transnational advocacy networks in international and regional politics. *International Social Science Journal*, 51(159), 89–101.

Keohane, R.O. and Nye, J.S. (1977). *Power and Interdependence: World Politics in Transition*. Boston, MA: Little, Brown & Co.

Kingdon, J.W. (1984). *Agendas, Alternatives, and Public Policies*. Boston, MA: Little, Brown & Company.

Kiser, L.L. and Ostrom, E. (1982). The three worlds of action: a metatheoretical synthesis of institutional approaches. In E. Ostrom (Ed.), *Strategies of Political Inquiry* (pp. 179–222). Beverley Hills, CA: Sage.

Knopf, J.W. (1993). Beyond two-level games: domestic-international interaction in the intermediate-range nuclear forces negotiations. *International Organization*, 47(4), 599–628.

Krasner, S. (1982). Structural causes and regime consequences: regimes as intervening variables. *International Organization*, 36(2), 185–205.

Larsen, M.F. (2007). Trade negotiations between the EU and South Africa: a three-level game. *Journal of Common Market Studies*, 45(4), 857–81.

Lijphart, A. (1974). The structure of the theoretical revolution in international relations. *International Studies Quarterly*, 18(1), 41–74.

Mansfield, E.D., Milner, H.V. and Rosendorff, B.P. (2002). Why democracies cooperate more: electoral control and international trade agreements. *International Organization*, 56(3), 477–513.

Mearsheimer, J.J. (2001). *The Tragedy of Great Power Politics*. New York: W.W. Norton & Company.

Milner, H.V. (2009). Power, interdependence, and nonstate actors in world politics: research frontiers. In H.V. Milner and A. Moravcsik (Eds.), *Power, Interdependence, and Nonstate Actors in World Politics*. Princeton, NJ: Princeton University Press.

Milner, H.V. (2013). International trade. In W. Carlsnaes, T. Risse and B.A. Simmons (Eds.), *Handbook of International Relations* (pp. 720–45). London: Sage.

Mitrany, D. (1933). *Progress of International Government*. New York: Elliots Books.

Mitrany, D. (1948). The functional approach to world organization. *International Affairs*, 24(3), 350–63.

Moregenthau, H. (2005/1948). *Politics among Nations: The Struggle for Power and Peace* (7th ed.). London: McGraw-Hill Higher Education.

Nadelman, E.A. (1990). Global prohibition regimes: the evolution of norms in international society. *International Organization*, 44(4), 479–526.

Olson, M. (1965). *The Logic of Collective Action*. New York: Schocken.

Olson, M. (1982). *The Rise and Decline of Nations: Economic Growth, Stagflation, and Social Rigidities*. New Haven, CT: Yale University Press.

Patterson, L.A. (1997). Agricultural policy reform in the European Community: a three-level game analysis. *International Organization*, 51(1), 135–65.

Payne, R.A. (2001). Persuasion, frames and norm construction. *European Journal of International Relations*, 7(1), 37–61.

Pomfret, J. (13 March 2010). China holds firm against Google, says firm must obey its laws. Washington Post.com. Retrieved 12 November 2010 from http://www.washingtonpost.com/wp-dyn/content/article/2010/03/12/AR2010031203564.html

Putnam, R.D. (1988). Diplomacy and domestic politics: the logic of two-level games. *International Organization*, 42(3), 427–60.

Reslow, N. and Vink, M. (2015). Three-level games in EU external migration policy: negotiating mobility partnerships in West Africa. *Journal of Common Market Studies*, 53(4), 857–74.

Reuters (22 March 2010). Google 'totally wrong' on censorship move. Retrieved 13 November 2010 from http://www.reuters.com/article/idUSTOE62L05C20100322

Risse, T. (2002). Transnational actors and world politics. In W. Carlsnaes, T. Risse and B.A. Simmons (Eds.), *Handbook of International Relations* (pp. 255–74). London: Sage.

Risse-Kappen, T. (1995). *Bringing Transnational Relations Back In*. Cambridge, UK: Cambridge University Press.

Rodham Clinton, H. (21 January 2010). Remarks on internet freedom. State Department transcript. Retrieved 11 November 2010 from http://www.state.gov/secretary/rm/2010/01/135519.htm

Sabatier, P.A. (1988). An advocacy coalition framework of policy change and the role of policy-oriented learning therein. *Policy Sciences*, 21(2–3), 129–68.

Sabatier, P.A. and Jenkins-Smith, H.C. (1993). *Policy Change and Learning: An Advocacy Coalition Approach*. Boulder, CO: Westview Press.

Schattschneider, E.E. (1935). *Politics, Pressures and the Tariff*. New York: Prentice-Hall.

Schieder, S. and Spindler, M. (2014). *Theories of International Relations*. Abingdon, UK: Routledge.

Schmidt, B.C. (2002). On the history and historiography of international relations. In W. Carlsnaes, T. Risse and B.A. Simmons (Eds.), *Handbook of International Relations* (pp. 3–22). London: Sage.

Snidal, D. (1985a). The limits of hegemonic stability theory. *International Organization*, 39(4), 579–614.

Snidal, D. (1985b). Coordination versus prisoners' dilemma: implications for international cooperation and regimes. *American Political Science Review*, 79(4), 923–42.

Spencer, T. (2005). In P. Harris and C.S. Fleisher (Eds.), *The External Environment of Public Affairs in the European Union and the United Kingdom*. London: Sage.

Stone, C.N. (1989). *Regime Politics: Governing Atlanta, 1946–1988*. Lawrence, KA: University Press of Kansas.

Sunstein, C. R. (1995). Social norms and social rules. John M. Olin Law & Economics Working Paper no. 36 (2d Series). The Coase Lecture, Autumn. University of Chicago. Retrieved from http://www.law.uchicago.edu/files/files/36.Sunstein.Social.pdf (accessed 29 September 2016).

Verdier, D. (1994). *Democracy and International Trade: Britain, France and the United States, 1860–1990*. Princeton, NJ: Princeton University Press.

Von Neumann, J. and Morgenstern, O. (2007/1944). *Theory of Games and Economic Behavior*. Princeton, NJ: Princeton University Press.

Waever, O. (1996). The rise and fall of the inter-paradigm debate. In S. Smith, K. Booth and M. Zalewski (Eds.), *International Theory: Positivism and Beyond* (pp. 149–85). Cambridge, UK: Cambridge University Press.

Waever, O. (2013). Still a discipline after all these debates. In T. Dunne, M. Kurki and S. Smith (Eds.), *International Relations Theories: Discipline and Diversity* (pp. 306–27). Oxford, UK: Oxford University Press.

Waltz, K. (1979). *Theory of International Politics*. New York: McGraw-Hill.

Wendt, A. (1992). Anarchy is what the state makes of it: the social construction of power politics. *International Organization*, 46(2), 391–425.

Wendt, A. (1999). *Social Theory of International Politics*. Cambridge, UK: Cambridge University Press.

Wilson, C.A. (2000). Policy regimes and policy change. *Journal of Public Policy*, 20(3), 247–74.

Woolf, L.S. (1916). *International Government*. New York: Brentano's.

Zimmern, A. (1936). *The League of Nations and the Rule of Law, 1918–1935*. Edinburgh, UK: R & R Clark.

Public Affairs and Political Philosophy

Alberto Bitonti

INTRODUCTION

What does Political Philosophy have to do with Public Affairs? Well, we can say that without some premises of Political Philosophy, the whole Public Affairs field could not exist. Let us see why.

While in many respects Political Philosophy indicates the problems and the challenges concerning large institutional, governmental and societal processes (processes of primary interest to Public Affairs specialists), this discipline is also able to provide the Public Affairs industry itself with legitimacy overall, a legitimacy that many are continuously tempted to put into question (elected officials and citizens *in primis*). In fact, Political Philosophy provides the theoretical framework in which Public Affairs activities are deployed, even without a conscious awareness of the actors involved. That framework is represented by the debate on political authority, on the values shaping

public arenas in modern democracies, or on how to best pursue good government and good policies (Deutsch, 1971; Christman, 2002; Kymlicka, 2002; Dryzek et al., 2006).

When dealing with lobbying and Public Affairs, elected officials, civil servants, citizens, as well as scholars and practitioners might stumble into sentences such as 'this policy enhances the Public Interest', or 'our counterpart's proposal is a commitment to the special interests of the X lobby, clearly against the General Welfare'. Well, when we hear such expressions, involving the politics of interests, the General/Public Interest, the Common Good and the special/particular interests, where do we actually draw the line between the Public Interest and the particular or private interests? Is there only one Public Interest? And if that's the case, how would this Public Interest relate to all the particular interests? And consequently – once we perhaps realize that promoting our (or our clients') vision into the public arena through an intelligent activity of Public Affairs has exactly to do with the composition of our claims with the Public Interest – can we answer the questions concerning our intervention in the democratic process defending the legitimacy of it? Therefore, in general, what is the role and the legitimacy of pressure/interest groups and their PA actions in modern democracies?

These are some theoretical questions that those who study or work in the PA sector face sooner or later (even subconsciously), and that Political Philosophy helps to properly assess and discuss, without slipping into superficial, rhetorical or mistaken solutions.[1]

Throughout the history of ideas, philosophers, constitutionalists, political scientists and economists (among others) gave very different answers to the above-mentioned questions. In this chapter, I analyse some of these answers, trying to go beyond the boundaries of single disciplines, even if departing from a political theorist's point of view. The aim here is to provide some theoretical explanations concerning the idea of Public Interest (a rather slippery political concept!) and its relationship with private/particular interests, as this relationship lies at the very heart of the game for influence typical of Public Affairs arenas (where all interests somehow claim to be ultimately complying with the 'Public Interest').

In the first part of the chapter, then, I briefly describe the semantic ambiguity of the terms interest and public, among the main causes of confusion and misunderstandings in the political language.

In the second part of the chapter, I first explain the difference between concept and conception, demonstrating that in Political Philosophy different authors have supported various conceptions of the concept of Public Interest, and then I examine some of these conceptions, claiming that the legitimacy of private/particular interests in the public arena and the legitimacy of the Public Affairs industry depend on the conception we choose to adopt.

THE AMBIGUITY OF INTEREST

The word interest hides an ambiguous and multi-faceted concept, which is greatly responsible for much of the confusion surrounding the field of interest politics and the concept of Public Interest. In spite of a limited etymological significance (interest derives from the Latin *inter esse*, 'be between', which may refer to the difference between two sums of money in the practice of money lending, or to the belonging to a specific group, see Ornaghi and Cotellessa, 2000), it is a fact that the concept of interest has a great importance for Public Affairs. This is not only because an interest is what lies behind every interest group (Bentley, 1908; Truman, 1951) but also because the idea of interest is used very frequently in the political, economic or social fields, both on the analytical plan – in order to explain human behaviours (where interests seem to play the role of strong motives to action) – and on a more practical plan, where the interest is used to persuade someone of the rightness or the convenience of a position or a policy (a typical example is 'Do as I say because it is in your interest to do so'; a famous remark about it is by Frederik the Great of Prussia, who in a letter to Voltaire wrote: 'it's not enough to show the virtue to men, you need to use the spur of interest, without which very few would follow the right reason').

In other words, the concept of interest can be used to:

1 Define the perimeter of any interest group (analytical-theoretical function).
2 Explain individual or social actions (analytical-hermeneutic function).
3 Frame issues in a particularly compelling and effective way (practical-conative function).

The width of functions of the concept is a symptom of its semantic richness; nevertheless, a number of meaningful questions are hidden just behind such a large domain. Some of these questions are: do we conceive an interest as strictly economic and material or do we consider also non-material interests? Can interests refer only to single persons or to collective realities as well? Furthermore, is an interest conceived in subjective or objective terms? The answers to these questions can make a huge difference in terms of political analysis and action. For example, if an interest can be conceived objectively, this means that – in general – everyone could indicate what the interest of someone else is. This also means that people can be mistaken about their own interests (not recognizing their true objective interests), and so someone else may be justified in trying to promote that particular objectively-determined interest, even against someone else's will (a typical case of this kind is that of parents and children, where the latter would like to play all day, and the former would push their counterparts towards homework, whose importance would be sustained by an objective interest in an education). If, instead, we consider an interest as a synonym of want, or preference, we imply that the content of each interest can only be subjective, that nobody can be mistaken about their interests *ex definitione*, and that there cannot be a justification of coercive acts (or laws or policies) in terms of the interests of those who are coerced. Evidently, through a few simple theoretical arguments, these questions and the definition of what an interest is may lead us to reconsider the whole structure of political society, its procedures and assumptions, as well as the same conception of democracy and civil rights.

Notwithstanding such breadth in the range of meanings (or maybe just thanks to that), in the history of political ideas the term interest has always been very fortunate since its introduction in around the thirteenth century (Ornaghi and Cotellessa, 2000). Departing from its strictly economic meaning, in the Political Theory of the Renaissance (in authors such as Alonso de Castrillo, Niccolò Machiavelli or Francesco Guicciardini), the concept of interest develops further, becoming one of the factors which should guide the actions of princes and political leaders,

as a general synonym of advantage or utility (Bitonti, 2014). Moreover, between the sixteenth and the seventeenth centuries, the concept of interest also began to appear in the 'formulas' of interest (or reason) of State, national interest and, of course, Public Interest[2] (in authors like Giovanni Botero, Traiano Boccalini, Henri de Rohan or Fabio Albergati). In the following centuries, interest makes a theoretical 'step back' (in terms of collective entities), mainly referring to the different social classes and their irreconcilable motives, in authors like Joseph von Görres, Karl Marx, Friedrich Engels or Lorenz von Stein. It is at this time that interest appears once again, connoted by an economic aspect, as the strongest divisive element in modern societies.

Thanks to the contributions of Arthur Bentley and David Truman, in the twentieth century interest is generally put at the base of the group theory, where each group is exactly determined by a specific interest (Bentley, 1908). As evidenced by Cochran (1973), much of contemporary political science literature (especially American) is based on interest politics (Latham, 1952; Meynaud, 1965; Olson, 1965; Davies, 1985; Baggott, 1995; Herrnson et al., 1998; Panebianco, 2000; Michalowitz, 2004; Andres, 2009, to name but a few; consider also the analyses published in scholarly publications such as the *Journal of Public Affairs* or *Interest Groups & Advocacy*). As Lasswell puts it, 'we think of politics in terms of participants (with identifications, demands, expectations; with control over base values) interacting in arenas (situations in which decision outcomes are expected) employing strategies to maximize value indulgences over deprivations by influencing decision outcomes and hence effects' (Lasswell, 1958: 208).

The work of analysis of the political arena and the ability to map all the relevant groups and the interests at stake in any policy-making process is essentially the first phase in any Public Affairs strategy. That is one of the problematic fields where Political

Philosophy can help, clearly assessing the different aspects involved in the identification of an interest. A concept whose meanings and connotations may vary very widely, as we tried to explain.

THE MULTIDIMENSIONAL CONCEPT OF PUBLIC

If possible, the concept of public is even more complex than interest. When we refer to the Public Interest, what public are we concerned with? And when we say Public Affairs, whose or what kind of affairs are we discussing precisely?

As pointed out by Habermas, the 'usage of the words "public" and "public sphere" betrays a multiplicity of concurrent meanings' whose 'origins go back to various historical phases' (Habermas, 1989: 1). Political Philosophy is probably the main perspective through which one can delimit and properly understand the connotations of the concept of public, because essentially 'the public is a political state' (Dewey, 1927).

Theoretically, the concept of public can refer to three different denotations:

1   The institutional subject (the State), for instance in expressions such as 'the Public Sector' or 'public institutions' (the governmental players in a wide sense).
2   The social collective subject, for instance in expressions such as 'public opinion' or 'public problem', where the actual reference is to a vast group of people who are identified as some kind of collectivity (as social players in a wide sense).
3   The objective dimension of something denoted by a general and abstract character of publicity, for instance in expressions such as 'public meeting' (where, in abstract, everyone can participate) or 'public service' or 'publicity of Parliamentary proceedings' (that everyone is entitled to know without distinctions).[3]

Thus, the two former meanings have a subjective dimension (referring to: the State/ Government and the society/people), whereas the latter has an objective dimension (referring to the abstract character of publicity of something in general).

As mentioned above, the public is deeply shaped by political contours (in all the three denotations), having to do with the proper domain of intervention by the State, or with the identification of relevant communities or collective rights.

On the semantic-etymological plan, the word public comes from the Latin *publicus*, originally from *pop-licus* and *populus*, i.e., people; thus public defines what belongs to the people, concerns the people, what is done or known to everybody, as opposed to private. So we arrive at the fundamental question concerning how to distinguish the realms of public and private, and consequently Public Affairs from private affairs.

Habermas can help us understand the historical meaning of this distinction:

> The German word *privat*, which was borrowed from the Latin *privatus*, can be found only after the middle of the sixteenth century, having the same meaning as was assumed by the English 'private' and the French *privé*. It meant as much as 'not holding public office or official position', *ohne öffentliches Amt*, or *sans emplois, que l'engage dans les affaires publiques*. 'Private' designated the exclusion from the sphere of the state apparatus; for 'public' referred to the state that in the meantime had developed, under absolutism, into an entity having an objective existence over against the person of the ruler. The public (*das Publikum, le public*), was the 'public authority' (*öffentliche Gewalt*) in contrast to everything 'private' (*Privatwesen*). The servants of the state were *öffentliche Personen*, public persons, or *personnes publiques*; they were incumbent in some official position, their official business was 'public' (*öffentliches Amt, service public*), and government buildings and institutions were called 'public'. On the other hand, there were private individuals, private offices, private business, and private homes; Gotthelf speaks of the *Privatmann* (private person). The authorities were contrasted with the subjects excluded from them; the former served, so it was said, the public welfare, while the latter pursued their private interests. (Habermas, 1989: 12)

The idea of a private space separated by the public domain thus seems to develop distinctively in the Modern Age, following the affirmation of modern State, of the liberal idea of the rule of law and of individual rights, to be 'protected' and kept separated from the sphere of the public authority.

In his famous speech on the difference between the liberty of the Moderns and the liberty of the Ancients, Constant (1819) highlights how the citizens of ancient republics were free in the public space, as they participated in the discussion and in public political deliberations, but they were totally subjected to the same authority of which they were part. The liberty of modern republics, instead, is the liberty of civil rights, where individuals are free to use (and abuse) their freedom without any public interference. The same concept was explained by Berlin (1969) 150 years later in terms of positive liberty (that of political rights, where a citizen contributes to choose who governs) and negative liberty (that of civil rights, where a citizen enjoys a private space where the public authority is not entitled to enter). According to Berlin, both liberties coexist and are necessary in modern democracies (Berlin, 1969).

The idea of a private sphere slowly arises in a long historical process involving the Christian idea of person, the disruption of old empires, the advent of free cities and of national states, the development of modern capitalism (from the cities of Italy and the Netherlands in the Late Middle Ages), the Protestant Reformation and the invention of the printing press.

The new dimension of the private sphere – as opposed to the public sphere of political authority – lays the foundation for a fundamental dichotomy: that between the State and civil society, as the two major players of modern polity. Now, we do not intend civil society here as opposed to natural society (as it is in the political philosophy of Hobbes, Locke, Rousseau, Ferguson or Kant), but rather as the body of citizens pursuing their own interests in the private space, as described

by Althaus in his *Politica methodice digesta* (1603) and later by Hegel in his *Philosophy of Right* (1821). Hegel depicts a civil society marked by the autonomy from the State, by the aim of the satisfaction of private wants (through work and trade), guaranteed in its property rights by the administration of justice, and with a focus on the pursuit of particular interests (1821: par. 188).

Thus, a new version of the public emerges. The concept can keep referring to the governmental sphere of political authority (according to the first subjective denotation, mentioned before), but now it also refers to what concerns the citizens in their common interests, in their private sphere as civil society (recalling our second subjective denotation, but also the third objective one). Habermas analyses this new version of the concept in terms of bourgeois public sphere, typical of the era of the Enlightenment, based on the rational critical debate of Public Affairs (whereas the rational critical character will be lost in the mass society of modern Public Opinion).

In conclusion, we can finally state that Public Affairs are public in a variety of ways and that the semantic and theoretical ambiguity of the concept of public is reflected both in our comprehension of Public Affairs as a discipline and a profession, and in the philosophical attempt to understand the fundamental concept of Public Interest. Public Affairs are public because they may concern the relationship of an organization with the State and public institutions (public decision-makers in general); Public Affairs are public because they may concern the relationship of an organization with the general public, with civil society as depository of the Public Opinion (be that media, customers or stakeholders in general). Lastly, Public Affairs are public because they may concern general issues, to be discussed publicly and where in abstract everyone may have a stake.

If the philosophical contours of both the concept of interest and of public are so complex and ambiguous, the problematic character of the idea of Public Interest may now appear an obvious consequence. The second part of the chapter is dedicated to this idea.

CONCEPTIONS OF PUBLIC INTEREST

The plurality of denotations, dimensions and interpretations of both the concepts of interest and public results in several conceptions of the Public Interest itself. By conceptions, in Political Philosophy, we mean different visions, systems of thought, articulated philosophical constructions of one single concept (Rawls, 1993; Maffettone and Veca, 1997). Therefore, we observe one concept (the Public Interest) and several conceptions of it (the specific content given to the concept). In fact, despite using the same expression (Public Interest), in the history of ideas, political theorists, economists, jurists and politicians referred to very different things, institutional recipes, political programmes, economic policies, etc. Of course, this was possible because of the recalled vagueness (and ambiguity) of the expression (Sorauf, 1957; Schubert, 1960), which led some to even deny the utility of such a concept overall, if not for rhetorical purposes.

Before analysing these different conceptions, it is necessary to make some additional remarks on the concept. We use the expression Public Interest (singular form and capital letters) to refer to the general principle, design or basic political structure shaping a political society overall. We do not use the expression to refer to a collective interest (stemming from a particular group, as big as that may be) or to one interest (among many) which may claim to be 'public'. It is also something different from a national interest, as the latter may be defined the interest of a nation (or a State?) among many (Bitonti, 2014).

In order to define the concept of Public Interest, there would be good arguments to support all three denotations of the public mentioned before, referring to it as the basic institutional and political idea founding how

political society and its government work, or as a universalistic attempt to provide a general and abstract principle of good government. After all, the different conceptions of the Public Interest provide (different) answers to the basic question concerning how a political society is organized, and how it should be governed as a 'well-ordered society' (according to a common expression used by Contractualists).

Now, a number of studies and reflections have been developed on different conceptions of the Public Interest (Leys and Perry, 1959; Friedrich, 1962; Barry, 1965; Cochran, 1974; Mitnick, 1976; Lewin, 1991; Lewis, 2006; Box, 2007; Galston, 2007).

What follows is an attempt to draw a fundamental typology of conceptions of Public Interest, intending to deploy a useful and complete approach to illustrate them all under one single conceptual scheme.

The whole typology is composed of five different types; each type represents a particular conception of Public Interest. Of course, these are ideal-types (Weber, 1922), meaning that actual conceptions should broadly fall under the domain of one of them, as they represent idealized versions of real philosophical visions developed by various authors in the history of political theory.

The five types of conceptions of Public Interest are 1) the formal, 2) the substantive, 3) the realist, 4) the aggregative and 5) the procedural. Each of them has a distinctive vision concerning the role of government and of interest groups and lobbies in the governmental process, and hence of the legitimacy of the Public Affairs industry itself in the political sphere. Let us now analyse each of the five ideal-types, reserving some more general remarks on the relationship between each of them and Public Affairs in the following paragraph.

The formal conception

The formal conception of the Public Interest is a naïve conception, which claims that the

Public Interest is whatever the formal governmental authority says it is. Thus, the content of the Public Interest is tied to a subject (the authoritative body, be it a legislative assembly, the executive power, the administrative official, whatever embodies the formal authority in a given situation), and not an object: that is why it can be considered a naïve and tautological conception. It is formal because it focuses on the form of a decision and not on its actual content. In some extreme cases, the exclusive connection with the authority of power may even leave room for an arbitrary Public Interest (as contradictory as this may sound), because – according to this conception – it is the sheer will of the sovereign which represents the Public Interest *ex definitione*. Evidently, in absolute monarchies or other monocratic institutional assets, this could result in Public Interest being the will of just one person.[4] In a democratic environment, it is not different:

> In an elected democratic polity the public interest is whatever the majority in Congress or the president say it is. One version of this is principal-agent theory; another is agency-capture theory; and another is the administrative law argument that the constitution and the laws express the public interest and any significant deviation from them is a breach of the public interest. (H. George Frederickson, quoted in Lewis, 2006: 694)

This conception of the Public Interest is the one we find in many legislative acts and documents, where the adherence to the Public Interest is simply implied and presumed. Of course, public managers and administrative officials find themselves in a difficult position: their decisions are presumed to be the expression of the Public Interest (as they act on behalf of the State, the government, etc.), but they have to determine what the Public Interest is in each particular case. Scholars in the field of administrative studies in particular tackled the problem of an actual definition of the Public Interest for the first time (Freund, 1928; Leys, 1943). These authors claimed that the problem depended on the vagueness and ambiguity of several legislative provisions, which leads to a wide administrative discretion and to big problems of interpretation. The solution proposed would then be to push law-makers to solve any issue of interpretation by writing clearer laws and better defining the goals of the administrative action, letting public officials determine only the best ways (the means) to achieve those pre-established goals (the ends).

Now, a number of criticisms may be raised against this conception. As said, it is a naïve conception, because it is stuck in a circular tautology, not telling anything about the actual content of the Public Interest. It also leaves room for a regressive rationale, which goes around the problem of a definition of the Public Interest without solving it. In fact, if those who have to apply the Public Interest criterion in a given situation must always refer to somebody else's decision, administrative officials can refer to law-makers, who in their turn can refer to the basic values of a Constitution, but then the process has to stop somewhere (Kelsen, 1920). In the end, we will always find an arbitrary will, without any external foundational justification.

There is only one case where the formal conception of the Public Interest would not be naïve, tautological or regressive: that is the case when we believe that those who make the decisions are different from all other men because of a different epistemic condition. This means that they would be the best interpreters of the Public Interest not because of form, but because they would grasp the substance of it, knowing something that others do not. However, in this case, we would find ourselves in a different conception of the Public Interest, the substantive one.

The substantive conception

The substantive conception of the Public Interest is the one where there is a clear identification of the ultimate goal of society as a whole, and where someone is presumed to know it, understand the substance of it. That ultimate goal is considered an absolute Good, and that is why this conception can lead to absolutist political visions.

This conception can be found in 'strong' political doctrines of many political thinkers, who generally aim to build a completely new political (and social) order by looking at the ultimate Good of society. Two examples of this conception, famously recalled by Popper in his remarks against totalitarianism (1945), are Plato and Marx. Both of them identified the Public Interest in the greatest good (the Republic based on the knowledge of Good for Plato, the society without any classes for Marx), and gave someone the 'honour' of knowing this greatest good (because of a different epistemic condition: they know something others do not), and thus leading the historical process towards it. It is the philosophers for Plato (the only ones able to escape the cave of appearances and go beyond the deception of human perceptions), and the Communist vanguard of the proletariat for Marx (the only ones able to start the revolution and lead towards the ultimate goal of a society without classes, even through a phase of dictatorship). Plato and Marx are only two examples, but this conception is much more common than one might think, easily detectable in all absolutist doctrines.

Another characteristic of this conception is that it usually espouses an organicist and holistic vision of society, where the whole counts more than the single parts, and therefore where the interests or the rights of individuals may (or should) be sacrificed in favour of the greater good for society as a whole. That greater good is the substance of the Public Interest (hence, we call this conception substantive).

Two general features of that substance (in all the various forms that political thinkers gave to it) are Truth and Unity. Truth is deemed the foundation of each substantive vision (it can be a historical Truth, a theological one, an economic or political Truth),

and it is usually lived as a body of undisputed dogmas. Unity instead refers to the elimination of conflicts from society – because of the recognition of the Truth by everyone – as the realization of the ultimate goal of the greater Good, where everything gets its place as a part of the coherent picture of the whole.

If we go back to what we said about the different denotations of the interest, we may say that the substantive conception of the Public Interest reflects the objective denotation of interests, where the interests of everyone are conceived objectively. This means that people may be unaware of their 'true' interests and that someone may know them on their behalf. If you think about it, this entails a paternalist vision, or – in the most extreme cases – a totalitarian conception of politics, where the State or a public agent in general is entitled to make decisions even 'against' the citizens, for their own good.

However, several philosophical arguments can be brought against this conception, such as the fallibility of human knowledge (Popper, 1945), the heterogony of ends (Wundt, 1886) or all the anti-holistic theses, among many others.

If the substantive conception of the Public Interest has the highest degree of ethical claims (the Public Interest is equivalent to the greatest good of the whole society), the opposite vision is the one of those who believes that there is no such thing as the Public Interest.

The realist conception

According to the realist conception of the Public Interest, there is no Public Interest at all. In other words, there is no realistic approach possible to the concept, which remains confined to the field of ethical norms.

Those who espouse the realist conception adopt a 'scientific' mind-set, focusing on value-free descriptions of the reality

(Weber, 1922). This conception is typical of political scientists, who – from the time of Machiavelli onwards – began to analyse politics for what it actually was, in its 'effectual truth' (Machiavelli, 1532), and not for what it ought to be, on moral grounds. Therefore, when they analysed the concept of Public Interest, they realized that in history everyone saw different things in it and that it is not possible to use the concept in objective terms, with precise empirical specifications. That is why, instead of trying to determine what the Public Interest is, 'political scientists might better spend their time' (Schubert, 1962: 176). In fact, instead of pursuing a normative non-scientific concept, political scientists prefer to focus on the analysis of the governmental processes, on the fight between different interest groups to influence public policies, on the real networks of power in society.

Pragmatically, this conception claims that the Public Interest is just a label given to public policies (like in the formalist conception), or a rhetorical argument used to persuade others of one's positions, without any real rational foundation. Therefore, everyone claims to promote the Public Interest (even those supporting completely different programmes!), without considering that Public Interest always results in 'whatever happens to be the speaker's own view as to a desirable public policy' (Dahl and Lindblom, 1953: 501).

In general, the realist conception portrays individuals and groups as actors with different motives, beliefs, values and political positions, all fundamentally irreconcilable. 'The society itself is nothing other than the complex of the groups that compose it' (Bentley, 1908: 222), that is why we cannot even speak of one public, but of several different publics. In the end, 'we do not need to account for a totally inclusive interest, because one does not exist' (Truman, 1951: 51).

To sum up, political society and the same governmental process are a kind of arena where some win and some lose, according to a brutal criterion of relative force (where force and power derive from multiple factors, such as the size of groups, their resources, connections, techniques, ability to influence, etc.). That is the harsh reality of the realist conception, where the scientific consideration of actual reality is everything that counts and where the Public Interest is considered only a formal label, a rhetorical device or a philosophical normative concept to be left out of the field of value-free political science.

The aggregative conception

If according to the realist conception the Public Interest does not exist (or better, does not make sense under a scientific empirical perspective), in the aggregative conception we go back into the world of Political Philosophy and normative ethics.

In the aggregative conception, the Public Interest refers to that institutional or constitutional framework that allows a high number of groups and individuals with different visions, beliefs and preferences to live together as free and equal in a peaceful society.

Interests are not objectively conceived (as in the substantive conception), but are inherently subjective: everyone (every individual and every group) is the best judge of one's own interests, and no holistic reconciliation of visions is possible. Conflicts cannot be resolved by a single 'true' vision realizing an ultimate social unity.

Here, though, we find some basic values (fundamental liberties, equality of rights, peace) founding political society. The Public Interest then is exactly entrenched in those basic values, after which most modern democracies are shaped. Unlike the substantial conception, the aggregative one accepts (and preserves) different doctrines, beliefs and 'truths', because it recognizes a *de facto* polytheism of values in society; it upholds the fundamental right of individuals to live as freely as possible, only making it possible to do it in a compatible way with everyone else's freedom.

In this conception of the Public Interest, differently from the substantive conception, there is not one comprehensive Truth, or a fundamental Unity of everyone as parts of a whole. Society is conceived as composed of individuals, with different values, beliefs, comprehensive doctrines (Rawls, 1993); therefore, the basic structure of political society, the constitutional order or the institutional framework represent the Public Interest only as long as they respect and guarantee this basic assumption, made by free and equal individuals living together in peace. Liberal doctrines may be easily categorized under this conception, for example in the versions of open society (Popper, 1945) or of political liberalism (Rawls, 1993).

The essential idea founding the aggregative conception of the Public Interest is the *discordia concors* ('harmonic discord'), in which the agreement concerns the basic rules of social and political life, and the discord concerns the ends and the different moral visions, left to the private sphere of individuals.

The procedural conception

The fifth and last conception of the Public Interest to take into consideration is the procedural one. In the procedural conception, the Public Interest does not lie in a form, or in a substantive vision of absolute good or in some basic political values, but instead refers to a process, to a procedure. This conception does not point to a final goal, but focuses on the process through which it is possible to build a rational consensus of free and equal individuals in an ideal speech situation (Habermas, 1984; Apel, 1987). It aims to describe a policy-making process where fundamentally all the relevant stakeholders are involved, have an equal voice and are free to speak their opinion without any form of coercion or deception.

Following such process, and with public reason as a criterion for discussion (Kant, 1784; Rawls, 1993), the content of a deliberation will produce a decision in the Public Interest (being such not in itself, but as result of that particular process).

> The process view of the public interest regards individuals as participants in dialogue about what is in the public interest and what the public sector should do about it. Instead of packages of predetermined interests, individuals are perceived as people with interests who can learn from social interaction. In such interactions, they acquire new information about public issues and become aware of the perceptions and desires of others. They may find their interests changing or, even if their interests do not change, they may be willing to compromise for the good of the larger community. (Box, 2007: 588–9)

Under the procedural conception of the Public Interest, we can categorize all the theories concerning deliberative democracy and those reflections that weigh the due process of decision-making more than the same outcomes of the final decisions.

PUBLIC AFFAIRS IN THE DIFFERENT CONCEPTIONS OF THE PUBLIC INTEREST

Very ambitiously, we can say that most reflections on the Public Interest and on good government, developed by political philosophers over the centuries, may fall under one of the ideal-types of conceptions described above. But what do the different conceptions tell us about Public Affairs as an industry, where a great part of the job has exactly to do with the identification of particular or private interests, their relationship with the Public Interest and the influence of public decisions? Ultimately, how does Political Philosophy frame Public Affairs and lobbying overall?

As anticipated, the answer depends precisely on the conception of the Public Interest you adopt.

In the formal conception, the Public Interest is whatever the government decides. This conception finds potential applications in all types of political regimes (democratic and non-democratic), so that it says almost nothing on the actual content of the Public Interest in the end. However, we may probably define the approach of this conception towards Public Affairs as moderately negative: in fact, the basic idea is that any attempt to influence or change public policies represents an undue intervention towards decision-makers who already have the right answer in principle. Anyhow, the result will always be a decision in the Public Interest: that is why in the end we can only refer to a moderately negative vision of Public Affairs.

The approach of the substantive conception is much more definite instead. The idea of an absolute good shaping institutional designs and public policies is strongly incompatible with particular or private interests seen as inherently negative. In fact, particular points of view miss the whole picture, literally representing only a part, a partial vision, a biased stand: they are contrary to the Public Interest, as they represent only the expression or factions, lacking the full vision, characterized by ignorance, evilness or selfishness. The true Public Interest is only known to someone enjoying a different epistemic condition (those who know the Truth in its ultimate substance), and everyone else's position is just a dangerous deviation from the path of the 'true' Public Interest. Not an easy environment for Public Affairs then!

The realist conception does not take a normative stand (it is morally neutral); it just analyses politics and society for what they are: an arena where all fundamentally claim to have the Public Interest on their side, and where different interest groups compete with each other in order to gain power or to influence those with power. Public Affairs are the weapon of that competition: it is just the way politics works, and any moral consideration is out of place.

The procedural conception too has an ambiguous attitude towards Public Affairs, as in the ideal speech situation all stakeholders should only use reason in order to build a general consensus, and influencing others should only be a pure matter of content and critical reasoning.

The aggregative conception is evidently the most favourable to Public Affairs because of its liberal structure base, where all have the right to participate in the political process as free and equal, trying to promote their particular interest and maximizing their utility, competing with each other democratically. It is not just the way the world goes (as for the realists), but it is also morally good: the differences of opinions, of interests, of preferences, of points of view, is at the basis of liberal democracy. Therefore, Public Affairs are a natural and positive element of democracy itself, where an infinite number of interest groups participate in the governmental process, providing their expertise, their point of view, representing a (big or small) portion of society, exercising a fundamental political right, in a framework where the Public Interest is the democratic game itself.

CONCLUSION

In this chapter, we dealt with the fundamental question concerning the relationship between Public Affairs and the theoretical discussion around the concept of Public Interest, as this relationship lies at the very heart of any reflection of Political Philosophy on Public Affairs.

After an analysis of the concepts of interest and public, we described five different ideal-types of conceptions of Public Interest, where each of them provides a different theoretical framework able to frame Public Affairs and lobbying, as well as democracy itself. We think it will be a useful exercise for the reader to try to capture the nuances of one or other conception in the words of politicians and other players of the PA arena. There may be some surprising results.

In the first edition of this Handbook, in the chapter about the theoretical roots of Public Affairs, Duane Windsor concluded by writing that 'Corporate Public Affairs in the twenty-first century should focus on two central issues. One issue concerns definition of "the" Public Interest in a pluralistic democracy. The other issue concerns development of the competencies and resources needed to manage international Public Affairs in an expanding global arena' (Windsor, 2005: 413). We strongly hope that with this chapter we have made some progress towards at least addressing the former, highlighting the precious contributions that Political Philosophy can offer to Public Affairs.

or in their dealings with strangers for their own peculiar purposes are called private. So a theatre, or a place of amusement, is said to be public, not because it is actually visited by every member of the community, but because it is open to all indifferently; and any person may, if he desires, enter it. The same remark applies to public houses, public inns, public meetings, & c. The publication of a book is the exposing of it to sale in such a manner that it may be procured by any person who desires to purchase it: it would be equally published if not a single copy was sold. In the language of our law, public appear to be distinguished from private acts of parliament, on the ground that the one class directly affects the whole community, the other some definite person or persons' (1832: 233–4).

4   In fact, it is worth noting that this conception – as well as the other conceptions we are going to describe – can find applications in different historical times, and in a variety of political regimes.

Notes

1   Even if, after all, 'Political philosophy has no special access to fundamental truths, or reasonable ideas, about justice and the common good, or to other basic notions. Its merit, to the extent it has any, is that by study and reflection it may elaborate deeper and more instructive conceptions of basic political ideas that help us to clarify our judgments about the institutions and policies of a democratic regime' (Rawls, 2007: 1).

2   In truth, the application of the concept to the collective dimension of the political community (or polity, or State) was not new, as it can be found in classical texts such as some of Cicero's orations or Tacitus' *Annals*, recalled and commented – as in the best humanist tradition of the time – by authors like Giovanni Botero or Traiano Boccalini. In the ancient texts one can already find a reference to the concept in the notions of 'utilitate publica' (Tacitus, *Annals*, Liber XIV, 44) or 'rei publicae commodo' (Caesar, *De bello gallico*, Liber Sextus, XXXIII).

3   This third objective notion is very well defined by George Cornewall Lewis in his *Remarks on the Use and Abuse of some Political Terms*: 'Public, as opposed to private, is that which has no immediate relation to any specified person or persons, but may directly concern any member or members of the community, without distinction. Thus the acts of a magistrate, or a member of a legislative assembly, done by them in those capacities, are called public; the acts done by the same persons towards their family or friends,

REFERENCES

Althaus, Johannes 1603. *Politica methodice digesta, atque exemplis sacris et profanis illustrata*, Herborn, Germany: Corvinus.

Andres, Gary J. 2009. *Lobbying Reconsidered. Under the Influence*, New York: Pearson Education.

Apel, Karl-Otto 1987. The problem of philosophical foundations in light of a transcendental pragmatics of language. In Baynes, K., Bohman, J. and Mccarthy, T. (eds.) *After Philosophy. End or Transformation?* Cambridge, MA: MIT Press, pp. 250–290.

Baggott, Rob 1995. *Pressure Groups Today*, Manchester, UK: Manchester University Press.

Barry, Brian M. 1965. *Political Argument*, London, Routledge.

Bentley, Arthur F. 1908. *The Process of Government; A Study of Social Pressures*, Chicago, IL: The University of Chicago Press.

Berlin, Isaiah 1969. *Four Essays on Liberty*, Oxford, UK: Oxford University Press.

Bitonti, Alberto 2014. Un'analisi semantica e teoretica del concetto di interesse. In Campi, Alessandro and De Luca, Stefano (eds.) *Il realismo politico. Figure, concetti, prospettive di ricerca*, Soveria Mannelli, Italy: Rubbettino, pp. 669–96.

Box, Richard C. 2007. Redescribing the public interest. *The Social Science Journal*, 44(4): 585–98.

Christman, John 2002. *Social and Political Philosophy. A Contemporary Introduction*, London: Routledge.

Cochran, Clarke E. 1973. The Politics of Interest: Philosophy and the Limitations of the Science of Politics. *American Journal of Political Science*, 17(4): 745–66.

Cochran, Clarke E. 1974. Political science and 'the Public Interest'. *The Journal of Politics*, 36(2): 327–55.

Constant De Rebeque, Henri Benjamin 1819. *De la liberté des Anciens comparée à celle des Modernes* (speech at the Athénée Royal in Paris).

Dahl, Robert A. and Lindblom, Charles E. 1953. *Politics, Economics and Welfare: Planning and Politico-Economic Systems Resolved into Basic Social Processes*, New York: Harper.

Davies, Malcolm 1985. *Politics of Pressure. The Art of Lobbying*, London: BBC.

Deutsch, Karl W. 1971. On political theory and political action. *The American Political Science Review*, LXV: 11–27.

Dewey, John 1927. *The Public and Its Problems*, New York, Holt.

Dryzek, John S., Honnig, Bonnie and Philips, Anne (eds.) 2006. *The Oxford Handbook of Political Theory*, Oxford, UK: Oxford University Press.

Freund, Ernst 1928. *Administrative Powers over Persons and Property: A Comparative Survey*, Chicago, IL: University of Chicago Press.

Friedrich, Carl J. (ed.) 1962. *The Public Interest*, New York: Atherton Press.

Galston, William A. 2007. An old debate renewed: the politics of the public interest. *Daedalus*, 136(4): 10–19.

Habermas, Jürgen 1984. *Vorstudien und Ergänzungen zur Theorie des kommunikativen Handelns*, Frankfurt am Main, Germany: Suhrkamp.

Habermas, Jürgen 1989. *The Structural Transformation of the Public Sphere. An Inquiry into a Category of Bourgeois Society*, Cambridge, MA: MIT Press.

Hegel, Georg W.F. 1821. *Grundlinien der Philosophie des Rechts*, Berlin: Nicolaischen Buchhandlung.

Herrnson, Paul S., Shaiko, Ronald G. and Wilcox, Clyde (eds.) 1998. *The Interest Group Connection. Electioneering, Lobbying, and Policymaking in Washington*, Chatham, NJ: Chatham House Publishers.

Kant, Immanuel 1784. Beantwortung der Frage: Was ist Aufklärung? *Berlinische Monatsschrift*, Berlin: Haude und Spener.

Kelsen, Hans 1920. *Vom Wesen und Wert der Demokratie*, Tübingen, Germany: Mohr.

Kymlicka, Will 2002. *Contemporary Political Philosophy. An Introduction*, Oxford, UK: Oxford University Press.

Lasswell, Harold D. 1958. *Politics: Who Gets What, When, How. With Postscript*, Cleveland, OH: Meridian Books.

Latham, Earl 1952. *The Group Basis of Politics: A Study in Basing Point Legislation*, Ithaca, NY: Cornell University Press.

Lewin, Leif 1991. *Self-Interest and Public Interest in Western Politics*, Oxford, UK: Oxford University Press.

Lewis, Carol W. 2006. In pursuit of the public interest. *Public Administration Review*, 66(5): 694–701.

Lewis, George C. 1832. *Remarks on the Use and Abuse of some Political Terms*, London: B. Fellowes.

Leys, Wayne A.R. 1943. Ethics and administrative discretion. *Public Administration Review*, 3: 10–23.

Leys, Wayne A.R. and Perry, Charner M. 1959. *Philosophy and the Public Interest*, Chicago, IL: Committee to Advance Original Work in Philosophy.

Machiavelli, Niccolò 1532. *Il Principe*, Rome: Antonio Blado.

Maffettone, Sebastiano and Veca, Salvatore (eds.) 1997. *L'idea di giustizia da Platone a Rawls*, Rome: Editori Laterza.

Meynaud, Jean 1965. *Les groupes de pression*, Paris: Presses Universitaires de France.

Michalowitz, Irina 2004. *EU Lobbying. Principals, Agents and Targets: Strategic Interest Intermediation in EU Policy-Making*, Münster, Germany: LIT Verlag.

Mitnick, Barry M. 1976. A typology of conceptions of the public interest. *Administration & Society*, 8: 5–28.

Olson, Mancur 1965. *The Logic of Collective Action; Public Goods and the Theory of Groups*, Cambridge, MA: Harvard University Press.

Ornaghi, Lorenzo and Silvio Cotellessa 2000. *Interesse*, Bologna, Italy: Il Mulino.

Panebianco, Stefania 2000. *Il lobbying europeo*, Milan, Italy: Giuffrè.

Popper, Karl R. 1945. *The Open Society and its Enemies*, London: G. Routledge & Sons.

Rawls, John 1993. *Political Liberalism*, New York: Columbia University Press.

Rawls, John 2007. *Lectures on the History of Political Philosophy*, Cambridge, MA: Belknap Press of Harvard University Press (ed. by Samuel R. Freeman).

Schubert, Glendon A.J. 1960. *The Public Interest: A Critique of the Theory of a Political Concept*, Glencoe, IL: The Free Press.

Schubert, Glendon A.J. 1962. Is there a public interest theory? In Friedrich, C.J. (ed.) *The Public Interest*, New York: Atherton Press, pp. 162–176.

Sorauf, Frank J. 1957. The public interest reconsidered. *The Journal of Politics*, 19: 616–39.

Truman, David B. 1951. *The Governmental Process; Political Interests and Public Opinion*, New York: Knopf.

Weber, Max 1922. *Wirtschaft und Gesellschaft*, Tübingen, Germany: Mohr.

Windsor, Duane 2005. 'Theories' and theoretical roots of public affairs. In Harris, Phil and Fleisher, Craig S. *The Handbook of Public Affairs*. London: Sage, pp. 401–17.

Wundt, Wilhelm M. 1886. *Ethik: Eine Untersuchung der Thatsachen und Gesetze des sittlichen Lebens*, Stuttgart, Germany: Enke.

9

Public Affairs and Information Science/Systems

Amy D. Meli and Edward A. Grefe

INTRODUCTION

Our goal is two-fold. First, to focus on the technology that supports grassroots mobilization – the primary focus of information science/systems that today support public affairs. Our second goal is to discuss how to make the best use of technology on two levels: by making it the servant of the organization's vision; and, by building real, human relationships with those one would engage in public affairs campaigns.

As to the primary goal, the functional areas of public affairs we will cover include:

1 Tracking stakeholders: their relationships, their activities, media hits, what people are saying about the public affairs campaign of a corporation or trade association on social media, etc.
2 Identifying potential supporters: data mining in its many forms to build coalitions.
3 Communication tools used to enhance one's message and generate action: the web, social media, outreach to the media, constituent mobilization online and offline, etc.

This technology supports political campaigns, lobbying efforts, and community outreach programs. We will present case studies to illustrate how this technology is being used by public affairs professionals to support the goals of their organization. The future may be uncertain when it comes to technology, but two things can be said for sure. First, that updates to existing programs will have occurred between the time this paragraph is written and the time it is read. Second, new technologies will emerge before the book is published.

Our plan, therefore, is to focus initially on the existing technology and how it is being used. That information alone will make the reader a better tactician, a better manager.

We will also attempt to look ahead to see what technology may be in the offing. Crystal ball gazing is always a bit 'iffy'. But some tech trends may become reality.

As to our second goal, we will discuss two concepts underlying successful public affairs efforts supported by technology. These two concepts include:

1 The primacy of one's vision. Technology should remain servant to the vision of the organization. In other words, the tool should serve the vision instead of the tool shaping the vision.
2 Appreciating that technology works best when it supports real, existing, human relationships.

Understanding the importance of these two concepts, we believe, will enable the reader to be more than a tactician, to become a strategist. Strategist lead organizations as they are charged with helping the organization achieve its vision. They have tactician-managers reporting to them.

BRIDGING: THE VIEW TEN YEARS AGO

In 2005, in the chapter on information systems, Scott Castleman and Ed Grefe discussed Information and Communications Systems and Technologies (ICSTs). The term ICST suggests a unified communications approach that embraces audio-visual systems, telecommunications, and the software or apps necessary to access, store, transmit, evaluate, and manipulate information.[1]

Similarly, in 2005, the chapter discussed 'heterarchies'. Heterarchies[2] are an important term useful for academics' discussions on the concept of how groups divide and unite at various times. In academic circles, heterarchies are linked to 'adhocracy',[3] defined as a flexible, adaptable, and informal organization that is defined by its lack of formal structure.

ICST was an accepted term in the mid-2000s. Today, we prefer the more familiar IT, – or 'information technology'. IT covers all that ICST referred to a decade ago. When public affairs professionals discuss both the length of time for which a group is to

be organized and the degree of formality in organizing that group, the professionals tend to lump all such discussions under the general heading of 'advocacy'. Thus, for our purposes, the word 'advocacy' will cover all coalition building opportunities today both in general and in discussing the linkage of software and apps for mobilizing groups.

THE FUNCTIONAL AREAS OF PUBLIC AFFAIRS SUPPORTED BY TECHNOLOGY

Tracking Stakeholders

At its core, managing a grassroots organization involves building and managing relationships – both those between your organization and your stakeholders, and between stakeholders and decision-makers. In this section, we will look at the different ways that public affairs managers can track these relationships, and the pros and cons for each system.

Stakeholder databases and the danger of relying on tribal knowledge

The history of contact management systems can be traced back to the early 1990s. They replaced what we call tribal knowledge, or any unwritten information that is not commonly known by others in a company.

All grassroots campaigns have a system for managing relationships, whether formal or ad hoc. Some organizations use no technology at all to track relationships. Instead, public affairs managers rely upon 'tribal knowledge'[4] to identify and document relationships.

For example, the Washington office of one large corporation had no organized way of collecting the relationships that employees had with public officials. Each time the head of government affairs needed to find an employee that had a relationship with an elected official, the grassroots manager went through the time-consuming process of calling around to each of the company's branch managers to identify the right person. In this case, the information was stored in each branch manager's head, and the information was never centralized or documented.

Public affairs managers who spend more than a few years in the job can gradually begin to gather all of the information in their own head. But as new staff members assume the role of public affairs manager, the process begins all over again. Worst case? The original staff member leaves. The group has no legacy data to pass along.

The major drawback of the tribal knowledge system is that it requires the public affairs manager to be reactive in his or her approach. The amount of time required each time to collect information from each stakeholder and reach out to impacted individuals makes proactive outreach impractical. More importantly, the lack of a centralized database prevents public affairs managers from using relationship data to inform public affairs strategies.

Why Use a Stakeholder Database?

Stakeholder databases allow public affairs managers to use data when creating a public affairs strategy, run metrics for upstream reporting, and easily track people's interests based on behavior and interactions. Currently, public affairs managers tend to use one of three different approaches when acquiring a database: building a home-grown system, piggybacking on systems used by other departments, and obtaining one's own public affairs database. The positives and negatives of each approach are summarized in Table 9.1.

Home-grown systems

Some organizations have gathered information and use home-grown databases in order to track parts of those relationships. Many public affairs managers keep Excel spreadsheets of Access databases that list each person in a grassroots organization, their contact information, and information pertinent to the grassroots program. This system works well for organizations that don't have budget set aside for stakeholder tracking systems or that use the information infrequently.

Piggybacking on systems used by other departments

In corporate environments, organizations typically purchase Customer Relationship Management (CRM) systems, which are designed to track sales and customer relationships.[5] Popular CRM systems include Salesforce.com, SAP, Oracle, and Microsoft Dynamics CRM.[6] Features typically include the ability to track people and organizations, their contact information, interactions with customers, and information about the business relationships that the company has with each of its customers. Some systems also have the ability to manage communications, including blast emails and social media tracking.

While the primary use of these CRM systems is to track the company's relationship with its customers and prospective customers, in the past few years, some CRM providers have started to open their systems to track public affairs information. For example, Salesforce.com has opened its API so that software vendors can build public affairs functionality into the company's existing CRM, including zip-to-district matching and online advocacy tools.

For trade associations, this trend is less common. The primary purpose of most association software programs is to track the organization's relationship with its members and prospective members – for memberships and contributions. Public affairs managers for these groups – including NGOs – may be able to leverage existing association management systems to track some limited public affairs information as well.

Dedicated public affairs database

Finally, many public affairs managers opt to purchase software designed specifically to

Table 9.1   Pros and cons of stakeholder databases

Database type	Pros	Cons
Home-grown	Inexpensive. Easy to set up. No jumping through hoops with IT.	Often limited tracking capability. Only one person can access.
Piggybacking on existing CRM	Expense comes out of another department's budget. Integration between departments. Leverages information gathered by other parts of the organization.	Public affairs department does not own the system. Could require customization. Often limited public affairs functionality. Requires public affairs manager to share information with other departments.
Dedicated public affairs database	Custom made for public affairs. The number of products on the market provides a variety of different approaches to data management.	Cost. Takes time to set up. IT security review process can take time and resources.

manage and track public affairs activities. There are a number of companies offering such databases, but in the US in particular, each system tends to have the following in common:

- The ability to store individuals (employees, retirees, shareholders, volunteers, etc.) with contact information for each.
- The ability to view stakeholders by geographic region, including by state, zip code, and legislative district. Most systems integrate zip-to-district matching into their software packages so that any record in the system is appended with legislative district information.
- Up-to-date legislator data, including name, district information, biographical information, photo, and contact information. Most systems provide Federal and State legislator data.
- Searching and exporting functionality so that public affairs managers can prepare management reports. Most public affairs CRMs integrate activity management into the database so that public affairs managers can manage email messaging to grassroots supporters, communications between grassroots supporters and political decision-makers, and other public affairs activities. A more exhaustive review of activity management is discussed later in this chapter.
- Some CRM systems also provide legislative staff, local legislators, and/or federal agencies.
- Some systems incorporate other external or government affairs functions, including PAC contributions, charitable contributions, public relations, and lobbying activity.

The media: outreach and tracking

In addition to internal stakeholders and legislators, some public affairs managers may need to track their organization's presence in traditional and/or digital media. While this task is typically relegated to the media or public relations department of an organization, we will provide a brief overview of media tracking capabilities.

Back in the 1990s, several companies created databases designed to track media outreach and coverage for public relations organizations. Since that time, the market has matured and consolidated, leaving fewer players in the space. Since 2010, those players have purchased companies offering products that track social media outreach and coverage, and have integrated those features into their core products. This leaves media tracking databases that come in two flavors:

1. Public relations tracking databases: These systems will track *both* traditional *and* social media.
2. Social media tracking databases: These systems contain all of the social media tracking features contained in public relations databases, but lack traditional public relations tracking features.

In a public relations database, managers can track news from traditional media outlets in the following ways:

- By key word or company name.

- By publication type (most systems will identify 'top tier' media outlets versus other media outlets).
- By tone, so that managers can track positive, negative, or neutral coverage.

Public affairs managers can also generate reports on media coverage over time, find trends in positive/negative media coverage over a period of time, and track journalists' coverage of different topics by key word and beat.

Most public relations tracking systems also contain a database of journalists so that managers can identify and contact journalists based on the publication they work for, the beat they cover, and the articles they have written. Managers can also distribute press releases via a wire service using the software.

The trend of consolidation has extended into the social media tracking space. Since 2010, each of the large public relations software companies has purchased one or more social media tracking firms, allowing each of the PR software companies to integrate social media tracking into its suite of features. Whether through a PR database or a standalone social media tracking system, social media tracking features include:

- Identifying key words and hashtags that are trending on Twitter, Facebook, blogs, and other social media.
- Tracking mentions of your organization across multiple social media platforms.
- Generating trend reports of mentions and coverage over time.
- Managing an organization's social media posts across platforms.

Building a Database: Identifying Potential Supporters

When building grassroots programs and developing grassroots campaigns, it is often practical to combine the process of identifying potential supporters and getting them to take some action on your organization's behalf.

For example, one client needed to influence the outcome of a vote in the House of Representatives, and needed to generate a large volume of calls to key legislator offices to communicate support for the issue.

Since the client did not have a large number of grassroots supporters in a handful of key legislator districts, it was necessary to develop a phone outreach program that targeted voters who, research showed, would be receptive to the client's issue. Callers educated potential allies about the issue and determined whether they were supportive. Those who were supportive were patched through to their legislator's office during the same phone call.

While such programs may be the only option when an organization has no natural constituency in a specific political district, such programs are both expensive and usually for one-time use. For those organizations seeking a permanent and committed organization, we discuss later an education and activation process that assures greater longevity and loyalty.

Why Organizations Need to Identify Supporters

Some organizations are lucky enough to have a built-in nationwide network of members or customers in each legislative district and, as a result, don't need to identify outside supporters. For example, the AARP (The American Association of Retired Persons) has over 37 million members located in every State and Federal Congressional district in the nation. Many members are well-connected and politically savvy, so it is rare that the association needs to reach outside its membership for additional grassroots support.

However, most organizations do not have this depth and breadth of support, or need to demonstrate widespread support for an issue outside of its core membership. In these cases, an organization will often need to identify and recruit people from outside its core membership to take an action on behalf of the organization's political issues. There are a number of ways to accomplish this task, depending upon the organization's budget and goals. We discuss a few of these methods below.

When this book was last published, public affairs professionals had developed sophisticated ways to push information out to supporters and potential supporters. Public affairs managers could blast email lists of people with information about political issues. Organizations could robo-call individuals to remind them to vote in upcoming elections. In 2016, we are starting to see more emphasis on pulling individuals into grassroots networks. Three ways to 'pull in' supporters include online petitions, digital advertising, and coregistration.

Online Petitions

Many studies of the most effective ways to reach Members of Congress have concluded – based on surveys of both legislators and their staffs – that the best way to present one's ideas is in person. In descending order, the next best ways include by phone, by mail, and by email. Petitions are ranked at the bottom, on a par with or below automated postcards. Hence, to make the leap to supporting online petitions as somehow being effective is, to us, pure folly.

However, online petitions have grown in popularity because they are effective ways to identify members who support an organization's cause. Because online petitions are easy to sign and are seen by the public as effective ways to show support for an issue, U.S. citizens are increasingly more inclined to sign online petitions[7] for the issues they support.

This growth in popularity has been fueled by online petition sites, where individual citizens and organizations can create online petitions on almost any subject. People who sign petitions on these sites can create profiles for themselves so that they can return to the sites and sign petitions on other issues that they support.

The top two online petition sites, change. org and Care2, have over 100 million members combined – a target-rich environment for organizations seeking support from ordinary Americans. Organizations wishing to contact petition signers outside of the online petition platform must pay a fee to obtain the signer's contact information. Once the organization has added that individual to the organization's grassroots network, the organization can then contact these supporters to communicate with legislators in ways that are more likely to influence the legislative outcomes.

All this said, we offer a note of caution. Engagement via petitions is part of what is now being referred to as 'clicktivism'. We believe Malcolm Gladwell supports this position. His article in *The New Yorker*, entitled, 'Small change', notes that online petitions get a ton of people to sign for one simple reason: 'by not asking too much of them'.[8]

Digital Advertising

A large professional association supported a public health issue that had the support of a large majority of the U.S. population. But a small, vocal minority of the population was dominating social media with viral articles in opposition to the association's position. How could the association get its message to the people in support of their issue so that they could be recruited into the association's grassroots network? The organization recruited supporters using online ads.

Online advertising is currently in its 'wild wild west phase' – there are very few people in public affairs who truly understand how the process really works, and there are a wide variety of products and pricing structures. Over the next several years, we expect that this part of the industry will mature. In the meantime, we will provide a brief introduction to the different types of online advertisements, how they work, and how they can be used.

There are many ways to deliver ads online. A few of the most popular are discussed here.

Video ads

Video ads can come in many forms. On YouTube, advertisers place ads prior to the start of a video (the industry term for this is pre-roll) or at certain points in the middle of longer videos. Other online video sites like Hulu offer similar formats. Some websites allow video display ads (meaning that instead of an image and text incorporated on the top or side of the page, a video is available).

Search ads

All of the major search engines offer search ads, which can appear at the top or along the side of a search results page. Typically, ads are displayed when certain terms are used in the search, meaning that advertisers are able to target their ads to people who are interested in certain topics.[9]

Social media ads

Each social network handles advertisements differently, and the types of ads available are constantly evolving as the social network changes. In general terms, social networks like Facebook and Twitter allow organizations to promote their pages and posts, which would appear inside a user's regular feed, or to place advertisements in different parts of the user's screen. The real value of social media is being able to target individuals based on information tracked by each social network.

Display ads

Display ads encompass a wide variety of advertisements that are placed directly on websites. Some are simple images with text while others can contain animation or video. Display ads can be targeted in a variety of ways. One popular method is called 'retargeting', which allows an advertiser to identify and serve ads to people who have been to their site recently.

Mobile ads

Mobile ads are similar to display ads, but are formatted to be displayed on mobile devices.

While at first glance, digital advertising may seem like a slightly more modern take on traditional advertising, there are several features that distinguish it from traditional forms of advertising. These include:

1   **Measurability:** Unlike broadcast advertising, digital advertising allows an organization to measure exactly how many people are responding to an ad. For a pre-roll ad, how many people watched the ad all the way through without skipping it? For a display ad, how many clicked on the ad to learn more? For an ad with a call for action, how many people completed the action, and which URL were they coming from before they came to the organization's website? With online advertising, all of these questions have answers.

2   **Enhanced targeting capabilities:** Digital advertisers have the ability to target individuals with more precision and specificity than any other medium today. First, an explanation of how this works. Let's say an organization wants to start placing ads that recruit individuals to join in a nationwide campaign to ban texting and driving. That organization hires a digital advertising firm. That firm places a piece of code on the organization's website that will allow the website to track the exact individuals who visit the organization's site. The advertiser doesn't know the identity of each individual, but it does know a host of demographic information, including age, gender, geographic location, and political affiliation.

3   **Profile building:** Over time, the advertising firm is able to build a profile of the individuals who visit the organization's website. In this case, let's say the firm finds that supporters of the texting and driving ban are women aged 35–49 with teenagers in the household living in suburban areas. With this profile information in hand, the advertising firm can place ads to other suburban, middle-aged moms – digital 'lookalikes'.[10] Since the organization only pays for individuals who take an action (click on the ad, watch a video ad all the way through, etc.), this is also a cost-effective way to target.

4   **Prospect conversion:** The ability to convert prospects immediately: in the 1990s, we witnessed the advent of issue ads on TV – many may remember the Harry and Louise ads sponsored by the health insurance industry against President Clinton's health care proposal. These ads were

extremely effective in generating public support for the insurance industry's position and always contained a call for action at the end. In the case of Harry and Louise, viewers were asked to call a toll-free number to learn more about the issue.[11] This call for action was effective in generating support, but required the supporter to switch media – they had to go from watching a TV ad to picking up the phone and making a call. Digital advertising provides a way for people to go straight from watching an ad to taking an action without changing media. From a display ad, a user may click to go straight to an online petition, streamlining the process of taking action and leading to less drop-off between viewing the ad and taking an action.

5 **Ease of message testing:** Many savvy advertisers will incorporate digital advertising into their message testing strategy. For example, the same organization seeking legislation that would ban drivers from texting while driving produces two different ads with slightly different messages – one is more positive and the other is more negative. During the early days of the advertising campaign, that organization places a small number of each ad. The performance of each ad in the early period will determine which ad is used as the campaign progresses.

Coregistration

Coregistration is a term for something that you may have already experienced online. Have you ever booked a hotel room online and as a part of the process been asked if you're interested in receiving information about beach vacations through one of the hotel booking company's partners? If this has ever happened to you, then you've experienced coregistration.

Coregistration is a cost-effective way to obtain additional people for an online mailing list. Typically, an organization goes through a broker who works with a number of websites to place 'partnership' language immediately after an online transaction. Individuals who are presented with this language have an option of opting in to receive additional information. Organizations pay a small fee for each email address collected, and after the organization receives the individual's contact information, they are free to contact that individual as part of their opted-in email list. This process allows marketers to quickly build a list of individuals who have opted in for more information.

Microtargeting[12]

A corporation operating in a large and geographically diverse state needed to get statewide support for a bill in the state's legislature. The corporation had about 1,000 employees in the state who were all concentrated in a sparsely populated corner of the state.

The decision-makers on the bill in the state House and Senate all lived outside of the corporation's footprint, leaving it with no natural allies to support passage of the bill. Complicating matters, the bill's main opponent had long-standing relationships with key legislators and thousands of constituents in the exact districts that the corporation hoped to influence. How could it find enough supporters in key areas to gain statewide support of the bill?

The corporation in the above example decided to employ microtargeting to recruit supporters to their cause. Message testing indicated that Republican primary voters and business owners were the two groups most likely to support the issue. The corporation reached out to these individuals by phone and invited them to join an advocacy group that supported the issue. Over the course of a few weeks, the corporation was able to recruit enough statewide support for the bill to pass both houses of the legislature and reach the Governor's desk for signature. The bill was one of two in the state to be signed into law by the Governor that year.

This organization was able to accomplish its goal using microtargeting as part of its strategy. Microtargeting uses consumer data and demographics to identify the interests of specific individuals and influence their thoughts or actions. An important goal of microtargeting is to know the target audience so well that those messages get delivered through the target's preferred communication channel.[13]

Today, there are a growing number of data sources available to compile the information that can be used for microtargeting. Some of these sources include:

- **Voter data**: There are several vendors that compile the voter file from each state and/or local election authority. Most of these companies will sell the voter file to clients for a per-record fee. The voter file usually includes name, address, phone number, party affiliation (if collected by the state), date of birth, gender, and vote history. Other fields, described below, are often appended by vendors to provide a more in-depth description of each voter.
- **Legislative district data**: Any address can be matched to the appropriate federal, state, and sometimes local legislative district, allowing users to identify individuals in priority districts.
- **State and Federal contributor data**: Some vendors will append the voter file with the political contributions that voters have made to political candidates and other fundraising committees. This information can help to identify people who have strong relationships with legislators and other influential individuals, and also helps identify people who are the most involved in the political process.
- **Consumer data**: The credit rating agencies collect a vast amount of data about U.S. consumers, including their purchasing habits, household income, home ownership, interests and hobbies, and hundreds of other pieces of information. Consumer data is often appended to the voter file.
- **Social media information**: Recently, vendors have started offering the ability to identify a person's online profile, including their social networks and their online influencer score.
- **Political activity databases**: Some partisan data providers allow their clients to search for data based on voters' activity in other campaigns. For example, if Smith for Senate is looking for people who might support his campaign, his campaign might look for people that planted yard signs for his predecessor, or who volunteered for a House campaign during the last election cycle. This data, however, is typically available only to partisan political campaigns.
- **Behavioral data (for nonprofits)**: Some vendors provide the ability to microtarget based on other clients' behavioral data. For example, an environmental nonprofit is looking to obtain new advocates or donors. The vendor allows the group to communicate with people who are members or donors to other environmental nonprofits. The information would include the donations to specific organizations, the specific amounts and times.

If there is time, organizations will conduct research prior to a campaign to identify messages that resonate with different segments of the voting public or will identify different segments that are likely to support an issue prior to purchasing any data. Increasingly, microtargeting is combined with digital advertising to test both messages as well as conduct issue communications.

Data Mining

A nonprofit organization had a large membership, but a relatively small advocacy network. The client knew that some of the organization's members were already involved in the political process and were likely to support the organization's grassroots efforts if they knew more about how the organization was working to support its members' interests. But they lacked the ability to communicate with these individuals via email and didn't have the capacity to reach each of them by phone. How could the organization find the people who were already involved in politics to know which people to reach out to?

In this situation, the nonprofit organization used data mining to learn more about its own members before conducting outreach. The organization started with its own membership file, which contained names and addresses.

They then sent the file to a vendor who identified matching records in the voter file. When a match was found, the vendor appended voter, political contributor, and consumer data to the file, which provided a wealth of additional information about the nonprofit's members. From there, the nonprofit identified its most politically active members to recruit for involvement in the organization's advocacy program.

With data mining, the organization uses the same data as detailed in the Microtargeting section above. However, instead of selecting segments of the voter file based on an individual's characteristics, the organization adds microtargeting data to its own membership list. This information can be used in a variety of ways – voter registration drives, advocacy program recruitment, and message targeting are just a few examples.

Communicating With and Engaging Supporters

People communicate with each other differently now than they did since the last *Handbook of Public Affairs* was published. Email and SMS (sending text messages) were popular then and remain equally important as tools. Anecdotally, we have friends who tell us they often text their teenager from their living room while he is sitting upstairs in his bedroom. Newer ways of communicating are part of our continual technological evolution. In public affairs, they include:

Tele-town Halls
In the previous edition of this book, we discussed what, at the time, was an emerging concept: The electronic town hall.

> H. Ross Perot proposed, during his unsuccessful 1992 bid for president of the United States, the concept of the 'electronic town hall'. The electronic town hall [would be] a place in the virtual world, the World Wide Web, where citizens could be educated and voice their opinion on a myriad of issues great and small.[14]

That technology has been slow to develop, but in 2016, what we now call 'tele-town halls' is a popular and effective way to educate and engage advocates.

Phone advocacy has been around since the phone was invented, if only in the informal sense of one neighbor asking another to support a candidate or cause. Phone bank advocacy in political campaigns and in grassroots lobbying has been in use since the 1980s.

Recently, however, advocacy practitioners have started using tele-town halls in order to both educate and activate members.

In a tele-town hall, an organization reaches out by phone to a group of people (from as small as 25 people to over 10,000). These people are invited to join a tele-town hall on a particular topic. Those who are interested in the topic stay on the line and are able to listen to a presentation on the topic. During the course of the call, the presenter will ask if people are interested in taking an action on the issue. Those who are interested in taking an action are prompted to dial a number on their keypad. There is typically an opportunity for questions and answers towards the end of the call.

The organization hosting the tele-town hall receives a report with the contact information of those participating in the call. The host also receives information about those who asked questions or agreed to participate in a follow-up activity. In our experience, this is a cost-effective way to identify people who are supportive of an organization's issue and willing to take an action.

The value of the tele-town hall lies in the ability to communicate directly with potential supporters and engage in an in-depth conversation on an issue. Only those who are the most interested participate in the entire call, allowing the host to identify the people who are the most engaged on the issues.

Communication via social media
As previously mentioned, an important part of targeting is communicating with people by using their preferred communication channel. For examples:

- Americans spend an average of 42 minutes per day on Facebook alone.[15]
- Millions of viewers have learned algebra from the Khan Academy on YouTube.[16]
- Social networks like Twitter and Snapchat are gaining popularity.

These new technologies represent media networks important to advocates. We will address the three media that advocacy organizations have been able to most effectively use in support of their public affairs goals.

Facebook

Often, organizations will establish a Facebook profile, and then communicate with advocates using that medium. For example, during the recent Supreme Court case surrounding gay marriage, the Human Rights Campaign (HRC) encouraged its followers to update their profile picture to communicate their support for gay rights.[17] The most recent campaign in April 2015 received 109,000 shares, amplifying the HRC's message to not only supporters on social media, but to the networks of its supporters.

Twitter

Although Twitter's user base is smaller than that of Facebook, a growing number of journalists, celebrities, and other influentials are active on the platform. For this reason, advocates are often active on Twitter to promote their issues.

For example, during the 2012 Presidential campaign, Governor Mitt Romney made a comment about decreasing funding for public media like PBS (Public Broadcasting Service).

In response, Neil deGrasse Tyson, astrophysicist and former host of the PBS program *Nova ScienceNow*, tweeted his support for PBS funding. This tweet was available in the feeds of deGrasse Tyson's 3.7 million

followers, and was retweeted 59,000 times – amplifying the original message to the numerous other Twitter users (see Figure 9.1).

YouTube

Since YouTube is a video medium that allows anyone to upload content, advocacy organizations have an opportunity to educate and engage people in a very personal way. While relatively few organizations use this medium frequently, it can be effective when done consistently.

The National Hospice and Palliative Care Organization encourage its members to record video testimonials about the way that hospice care has touched their lives or the lives of their loved ones (see Figure 9.2). These touching stories help people – including public officials – with no direct exposure to hospices to understand the impact they can have.[18]

What we have explored so far is existing technology and its uses. We have also suggested how some see the future unfolding in terms of emerging technologies on the horizon. Knowing about technology and how to implement a communications plan based on it is important for any public affairs manager.

We believe moving beyond manager to lead the public affairs activities of an organization requires appreciating two contingent factors: the primacy of a vision that sees technology as servant, not shaper of action; and, the importance of real human relationships to insure that the use of one's technology helps to achieve one's goal.

Figure 9.1: Tweet from Neil deGrasse Tyson

Figure 9.2:   YouTube video of a hospice patient telling her story

THE PRIMACY OF VISION

The examples above provide an overview of the tactics and strategies available to a public affairs manager looking to engage his or her grassroots advocates. However, these strategies are useless unless paired with an organization's vision.

Our experience suggests that many people confuse strategy with vision. Strategy is an action, ideally the next appropriate action towards achieving an organization's vision; or, an appropriate action to defend achieving that vision when a threat looms. Strategy is what we do. Vision is why we do it.

To put it another way in a corporate setting:

> Vision is timeless. It's based on who/what *you* want to do. It's why you've got an organization in the first place. It must be specific enough that everyone can use it to decide if their work is moving the company forward. Progress towards the vision must be measurable.[19]

That measurement may consist on any number of barometers from PE [profits to earnings] ratio, to sales, or to gains in productivity.

Nonprofit organizations need a vision as well that clarifies why they exist. One suggested approach:

> Your vision is your dream. It's what your organization believes are the ideal conditions for your community; that is, how things would look if the issue important to you were completely, perfectly addressed. It might be a world without war, or a community in which all people are treated as equals, regardless of gender or racial background.[20]

A company or trade association may prefer using the word *mission* or *goal* rather than *vision*. But it is a statement that clarifies to the community why the existence of that organization is important to certain individuals. Within that broad context, the organization's vision, mission, or goal should be:

• Understood and shared by members of the community.

- Broad enough to include a diverse variety of local perspectives.
- Inspiring and uplifting to everyone involved in your effort.
- Easy to communicate – for example, short enough to fit on a T-shirt.[21]

Helen Keller, born deaf and blind in 1880, put it more parochially, when asked: 'What's worse, losing one's sight or one's hearing?'

Her response: 'The only thing worse than being blind is to have sight, but no vision'.[22]

The strategy is the *raison d'être* for the existence of an organization or for the pursuit of an outcome for an issue. Vision gives the strategy a rationale, why we are undertaking this strategy.

F. John Reh, management consultant and writer in the field, suggests the following hierarchy:

- Vision: what you want the organization to be; your dream.
- Strategy: what you are going to do to achieve your vision.
- Tactics: how you will achieve your strategy and when.[23]

We would add a fourth – *Programs* – before Tactics. Programs include advertising, research, fund raising, grassroots, coalition building, various eleemosynary programs, social media, and other online activities. Tactics are then the actions – running the advertisement, focusing the research on an organization or individual who may be an ally or an antagonist, operating a phone bank or an email blast, reaching out to potential allies, undertaking various online activities, including social media.

Beginning with a vision, we are able to develop a strategy when confronted with an opportunity or a threat, challenge our team whose jobs include running one or more programs, and develop tactics that are measurable in terms of achieving our strategy.

We view online activities, including social media, as being programs operated by the organization. Selecting the appropriate tactics – among them those noted above – should be guided by both the strategy and the vision of the organization.

LINKING HIGH-TECH ± HIGH-TOUCH

We believe the vision of the organization should place a premium on building on what we call high-touch over high-tech.

High-tech tools, including smart phones, tablets, social networks, and the like, are essential tools in today's world. That said, there are many challenges both to their use and to dealing with them when a crisis occurs. We have long believed, from our own experience and from a 'gut' perspective, that high-tech works best when coupled with high-touch, that is when married to personal relationships. Now, research – both formal and anecdotal – supports our 'gut' perspective.

> It is tempting to differentiate mobilizing and organizing strategies based on whether they are online or offline techniques. Online techniques lend themselves easily to mobilizing because they make targeting and list-building much easier and more efficient than before.
>
> Associations can build much larger and more targeted prospect pools of supporters with online technology than with traditional organizing strategies. The work of building relationships, fostering community, and creating interdependent work, in contrast, seems to depend largely on offline interactions.[24]
>
> ... In fact, a robust debate has emerged about whether or not online tools can be effective vehicles for collective action. Critics of the new forms of political activity have argued that their focus on quick and easy tasks amounts to nothing more than mere 'clicktivism', or worse yet, 'slacktivism', replacing meaningful political action with shallow tasks. Again, to quote Malcolm Gladwell's critique of online activism, 'the revolution will not be Tweeted'.[25]

In an article published in 2012, entitled 'The key to social media success within organizations',[26] two researchers at MIT, Quy Huy and Andrew Shipilov, reported a number of observations that support the need to link high-tech with high-touch – even the subtitle of their article, 'What determines whether an internal social media initiative brings business benefits? One essential – but often overlooked – factor is how employees feel about the organization'. Their study underscored the need for trust.

Based on the survey of 1,060 global executives in 2010, Huy and Shipilov discovered that 'to be successful, internal social media initiatives must focus first and foremost on the development of emotional capital, which we define as the aggregate feelings of goodwill toward a company and the way it operates'.

Their view is supported by another study published in 2013. In a chapter entitled 'Social media in internal communications: a view from senior management',[27] Tanja Sedja and Gorazd Justinek noted that if the internal media is out of touch with the true culture of the organization, the result may be that, while the organization's message 'dominate[s] the internal airwaves … sadly just a few people truly listen in'.

One example from our own experience is of an oil company that was spending millions on advertising and internal promotions to ballyhoo how good a company they were. Our focus groups with employees prior to launching a grassroots effort of employee-volunteers raised a counter thought. As one said, while others nodded, 'If we are such a good company, how come our lobbyist in Washington is being sent to jail?'

Huy and Shipilov's research emphasized: *Build community first*. It is a process based on developing emotional capital.

Emotional capital, report the MIT researchers, is built on a foundation of four pillars – authenticity, pride, attachment, and fun.

Authenticity is the most critical as it is the basis of trust. If the organization, in particular its leaders, are not trusted, social media will not correct the problem. In fact, as we know from whistle-blower articles appearing in the mainstream media, disgruntled employees in an organization in which people do not trust the organization, may well use social media clippings to embarrass the organization publicly.

If authenticity is real, and people trust the organization and its leaders, pride is engendered when people's accomplishments are recognized. As the research shows, financial rewards are important, but equally important is peer praise.

Of particular interest to we who work daily in the political environment is the finding on the importance of attachment. Too often we find clients insisting that we discuss only corporate issues and their importance to each person's employment. What Huy and Shipilov have now documented is how employees see their attachment to many things as providing a more substantial link than employment alone. To quote:

> Employees' attachment to the company is generated when employees feel that they belong to a community with shared values and interests. Some of these values are directly related to work, while others go beyond direct work-related interactions. Contrary to common belief in the pre-social media world, social media users often do not consider time spent on non-work-related discussions within social communities as wasted from a professional standpoint.

> When employees identify common non-work-related interests among each other and forge informal bonds, they will eventually start discussing work-related matters even outside of formal work hours, thickening the information exchange throughout the organization as well as increasing traffic in the company's social media communities.[28]

What this reinforces is our own beliefs, based, on our own practical experience, on the need to build relationships between all levels and among all employees on a much broader basis than simply the political issue *de jour*. Good programs encourage communications on subjects of many interests to employees. The topics for employee dialogue can range from engagement in Little League activities and stamp collecting to both the rationale for, and the practical challenges to, implementation of company policies. Doing so insures far more powerful social networks to call upon when political problems arise and employee response is needed.

Today we know that high-tech works best when it is married to high-touch. Online activities must work hand-in-hand with the offline programs, and work best when in support of offline activities rather than in control. The example that presents the best of this concept comes from the tactics used both MoveOn.Org and by the Obama campaigns.

We, along with other consultants, stress the need for fun as a requisite part of political participation. Again, Huy and Shipilov's research documents our long-held belief.

Huy and Shipilov recommend four steps for instituting a successful social media platform internally:

1 Identify leaders who are authentic and who[m] employees trust.
2 Help those people develop social media skills.
3 Ask them to build social media communities that emphasize authenticity, pride, attachment, and fun. In short, build emotional capital.
4 Deploy social media tools sequentially. Start with wikis and podcasts, and roll out social networking only after enough emotional capital has been built.[29]

A fifth step suggests the need to expect incremental benefits. Improved information exchange, motivation, morale, and reduced turnover will only occur 'after emotional capital has been developed'. Or to say the same from our perspective: social media – high-tech – cannot replace high-touch.

Anecdotally, a clear demonstration of combining high-touch with high-tech during the Obama campaign in 2012 was shared with us by a Dean at The George Washington University. It involved door-to-door efforts (high-touch), to re-engage a 2008 activist, the Dean's son (via high-tech).

The volunteer doorbell ringing that day was told that the Dean's son was not home. A week later, the volunteers returned. This time

the Dean was home and was able to tell them that his son was away at college.

'Why are you looking for him?' the Dean asked.

'Well, he was very active in 2008 and we note he has not yet gotten involved in this campaign. We are trying to reach him to get him involved', they replied.

'You're wasting your time', the Dean told the volunteers.

'Why is that?' they asked.

'He's disappointed by Obama's inability to do the things he said he would do, so he plans to just sit out this campaign'.

The volunteers then thanked the Dean for his time and left.

A week later, he received a call from his son.

'Dad, you're not going to believe this. I'm getting flooded with emails and Facebook postings from friends of mine from all over the country urging me to get involved in the Obama campaign. They are bothered that I have not joined the effort to re-elect Obama and deny Romney the Presidency, and are urging me to do so'.

'How'd they know I had dropped out of the campaign?'

What had happened is what we call the linkage of 'high-tech' with 'high-touch'. The visit to the home of the previous Obama supporter was the high-touch. Without that personal visit – the 'high-touch' – it is doubtful that the Obama team would have known of the disaffection of the Dean's son.

'High-tech' then kicked in as databases indicated people to whom the Dean's son was linked who were active in helping Obama get re-elected. In turn, the activists were contacted and asked to reach out to their friend, the Dean's son. The marriage of high-tech and high-touch is essential to achieve an outcome of positive engagement – one works well *only* if coupled with the other.

Han's study notes: 'The shift in the strategies employed by MoveOn and the Obama campaign, as well as other developments, demonstrated the power that civic associations can create by blending online and off-line mobilizing and organizing'.[30]

The Obama campaign recognized the distinction. They saw technology as a tool. Tools simply helped implement our plan. Tools should not dictate strategy nor control one's vision of an outcome for an issue. The caveat we will repeat is often two-fold: have a plan, one that involves real people in the planning process; then, determine what and how tools may be used to enhance one's communications needs.

We stress high-touch, as do those who have now done the empirical research. Even before such studies, 'gut' reactions such as ours were prevalent. For example, Han now documents 'Mobilizers ... do not seek to transform people's interests as they recruit them for action. They focus instead on building their base ... [They] allow people to self-select the level of activism they desire'.[31]

Her research underscores and affirms Saul Alinsky's dictum, 'Take people from where they are, not where you want them to be'.[32] Alinsky is, for many organizers, the 'godfather' of community organizing, a process, in our experience, far closer to mobilizing to deal with an issue or legislation than political campaigns.

Similarly, as Han reviews the role of training and notes the value of teaching members how to present their views to Members of Congress, her story supports what many practitioners have known for years.

Han chooses to keep anonymous the groups she studied. One she calls the National Association of Doctors (NAD). She cites a situation in which a Member of Congress voted the way the NAD wanted him to vote. The Member was asked by an NAD member whether the NAD member's contact had had a role in how the Member voted.

The Member replied: 'Absolutely because I felt like you had my back. I felt like I had a group of doctors out there who would say this is a good thing from a medical point of view'.[33]

Her study supports one of the notions from *Fighting to Win: Business Political Power*,

1981.[34] In a chapter entitled 'Building a fire', the author notes how politicians will tell a lobbyist to build a fire, by which s/he means, 'give me cover'. As a result, the politician may want to support the group's view. With appropriate cover from constituents, s/he can do so.

Given a choice, say between doing 'what is right, and what will get me re-elected', the politician will usually do what will get him/her re-elected. But, s/he can do both if s/he can demonstrate – based on the information given to the politician by the organization's network of volunteers – that there are people in his/her district who support the organization's position. The politician is echoing what Franklin Roosevelt would say to lobbyists: 'You have convinced me, now go out and force me'.

Beyond what has been advanced as the best way to build organizations, and now supported by empirical research, there is an equally important reason for building – through 'high-touch' – a group of people committed because they believe in the vision of the organization. That reason: to have the resources to defend oneself when under attack by social media.

We firmly support the use of technology as part of a public affairs mobilization plan. Social media has impact. In one sense, social media we would argue is today, the most important form of *broadcasting*. Its power to expand awareness of an issue is awesome.

There is a major caveat, however. To those who lobby or seek to build community support, *awareness* alone is rarely sufficient. Ultimately, in the political environment, *action* is needed and specific types of *action* that will cause those in power to change.

Thus, while vital and immensely complementary in building a communications effort, the challenge is to remember that technology is subordinate to the vision and the strategy. Just like other new technologies before it, social media is simply a tool that may or may not factor into an organization's strategy. Whether it is used will depend largely upon the audience the organization is targeting, the desired outcome, and the decision-makers' presence on different social media platforms.

There are some who question social media's place in advocacy campaigns at all. For example, crisis manager Eric Dezenhall's *Glass Jaw* characterizes social media, and Twitter specifically, as an attack-centric technology with little use for corporate public affairs managers who are looking to drive public policy outcomes.[35] While, in theory, he says, social media encourages, dialogue, in practice, 'promotes social warfare'.[36]

We believe that Hall goes too far, but his analysis does have merit. If used carelessly, social media has the potential to do more harm than good. Take the example of McDonald's failed hashtag campaign in 2012.

During that campaign, the company launched a hashtag, #McDStories, and encouraged customers to relay their fond memories of McDonald's on Twitter. Instead, individuals used the hashtag to tell some of the stories that the company had most wanted to downplay, including the health content of its food and fair pay for its employees. McDonald's media staff stopped promoting the hashtag within two hours of the campaign's launch.

We know that citizen groups can and have used social media to advance their causes. The first notable use happened back in 2010 with the Arab Spring, but more recently, activists have used hashtags like #blacklivesmatter and #takeitdown to draw attention to racial injustice. As this chapter goes to print, #takeitdown has played a significant role in pressuring the South Carolina legislature to remove the confederate flag from the South Carolina capitol.

Technology is a two-edged sword. What is *not* two-edged has now been demonstrated with empirical research. Namely, that an organization that builds social capital among its employees and within the communities in which it does business has less to fear from social media. Those who trust the organization will be among the first on the frontline as the organization's staunchest online defenders.

Best practices for social media use evolve just as quickly as the technologies themselves. Five years ago, public affairs officers may have used social media primarily to monitor conversations online. But social media managers are now using social media to more actively engage customers and other stakeholders. Han's study underscores both Dezenhall's observations and this thought:

This is not a simple story about the power of offline versus online organizing. Instead, it is a story about how associations can blend both online [transactional] and offline [transformational] strategies to build their activist base. Associations face a constant challenge between investing in membership and investing in members. Investing in membership helps build breadth, but investing in members helps build depth.[37] Han goes on:

> People often confuse mobilizing with organizing but ... they are quite different. When mobilizing associations do not try to cultivate the civic skills, motivations or capacities of the people they are mobilizing. Instead, they focus on maximizing the numbers by activating people who already have some latent interest. Organizers, by contrast, try to transform the capacity of their members to be activists and leaders.[38]

Her study supports our contention: 'that the best way to get people involved and keep them involved is engage not only in transactional mobilizing but also in transformational organizing'.[39]

We believe that those organizations that have a vision which includes building human capital, and strategies that match that vision, will be in a position to reach out to communities and grow and reach their goals. Solid research now confirms what we have learned from our own on-the-ground experience.

People matter. Including them in the process in a meaningful way is essential. That means following a process that will instill trust. Invite them to participate. Listen and respond to concerns they raise. Involve them in decision-making. Overcome fears by training all on how to be effective. Acknowledge their participation. And do all of this person-to-person.

Then, use the tools we have described to communicate with one's troops, expand their participation, and amplify their effectiveness. The tools exist. We have focused on those to use. We guarantee that if one uses them in support of a program based on high-touch engagement, the tools will be effective, the public affairs program a success.

Notes

1 http://en.wikipedia.org/wiki/Information_and_communications_technology
2 http://en.wikipedia.org/wiki/Heterarchy
3 http://en.wikipedia.org/wiki/Adhocracy
4 http://www.isixsigma.com/dictionary/tribal-knowledge/
5 Zeng, Yun E., Wen, Joseph H. and Yen, David C. (2003).
6 http://www.forbes.com/sites/louiscolumbus/2013/04/26/2013-crm-market-share-update-40-of-crm-systems-sold-are-saas-based/, original citation is Gartner report: *Market Share Analysis: Customer Relationship Software*, Worldwide, 2012.
7 http://www.congressfoundation.org/storage/documents/CMF_Pubs/cwc_citizenengagement.pdf, p. 21.
8 http://www.newyorker.com/magazine/2010/10/04/small-change-malcolm-gladwell
9 https://www.thinkwithgoogle.com/products/search-ads.html
10 http://adage.com/article/dataworks/alike-models/239590/
11 C-SPAN 2009, https://www.youtube.com/watch?v=Dt31nhleeCg
12 One definition of microtargeting to which we subscribe: 'Micro-targeting is (also called micro-targeting or micro-niche targeting) is a marketing strategy that uses consumer data and demographics to identify the interests of specific individuals or very small groups of like-minded individuals and influence their thoughts or actions. An important goal of a micro-targeting initiative is to know the target audience so well that messages get delivered through the target's preferred communication channel'. http://searchcio.techtarget.com/definition/microtargeting
13 http://searchcio.techtarget.com/definition/micro-targeting
14 Harris, Phil and Fleisher, Craig (2005).
15 http://www.adweek.com/socialtimes/social-media-minutes-day/503160
16 https://www.youtube.com/user/khanacademy/videos?flow=grid&sort=p&view=0
17 http://www.hrc.org/red
18 Hospice Action Network (25 August 2011), https://www.youtube.com/watch?v=g1CYud8Ik8
19 http://www.steverrobbins.com/articles/vision-strategy-tactics. Steve L. Robbins, PhD has assisted many organizations in developing the necessary skills and environment that fully utilize the diverse human resources that abound in our world, including Microsoft, Toyota, PepsiCo, Nordstrom, NASA, NSA, General Mills, Pfizer, Benjamin Moore Paints, Bristol-Myers Squibb, Herman Miller, Gerber Foods, the Federal Reserve Bank, National Cancer Institute, Trinity Health system, and a host of others.
20 http://ctb.edu/en/table-of-contents/structure/strategic-planning/vision-mission-statements/main. The Community Tool Box is a service of the Work Group for Community Health and Development at the University of Kansas. © 2014 Community Tool Box. All Rights Reserved.
21 http://ctb.edu/en/table-of-contents/structure/strategic-planning/vision-mission-statements/main. The Community Tool Box is a service of the Work Group for Community Health and Development at the University of Kansas. © 2014 Community Tool Box. All Rights Reserved.
22 http://www.brainyquote.com/quotes/quotes/h/helenkelle383771.html
23 http://management.about.com/cs/admin-accounting/a/vst.htm. F. John Reh (2014), Management and Leadership Expert.
24 Hahrie Han (2014), p. 17.
25 Hahrie Han (2014), p. 18. While the criticism is valid, there are multiple recent examples of organizations that have been able to convert 'slacktivists' into real advocates. The common thread in all of those examples – the organization was able to successfully convert individuals from taking an inconsequential action online to participating in something more meaningful, often offline. Nonprofits often call this process the 'ladder of engagement', whereby an individual begins by participating in some nominal activity and gradually 'moves up' to more meaningful activities.
26 Quy Huy and Andrew Shipilov (Fall 2012).
27 Sedej, Tanja and Justinek, Gorazd (2013), pp. 86–8.
28 Quy Huy and Andrew Shipilov (Fall 2012).
29 Quy Huy and Andrew Shipilov (Fall 2012).
30 Hahrie Han (2014), p. 21.
31 Hahrie Han (2014), p. 15.
32 Saul D. Alinsky (1971), p. xix.

33 Hahrie Han (2014), p. 38.
34 Edward A. Grefe (1981).
35 Eric Dezenhall (2014), p. 103. Dezenhall worked in the Reagan White House as an aide to Michael K. Deaver. He now heads a firm he co-founded, Dezenhall Resources. He teaches a course on crisis management and marketplace defense to MBA students at Georgetown University's McDonough School of Business.
36 Eric Dezenhall (2014), p. 102.
37 Hahrie Han (2014), p. 4.
38 Hahrie Han (2014), p. 8.
39 Hahrie Han (2014), p. 88.

REFERENCES

Alinsky, Saul D. (1971). *Rules for Radicals*, Vintage Books.

C-SPAN (2009). *'Harry and Louise* health care advertisements', online video clip, https://www.youtube.com/watch?v=CwOX2P4s-lw (accessed 15 April 2015)

Dezenhall, Eric (2014). *Glass Jaw*, New York: Hatchette Book Group, p. 103.

Gartner (2012). 'Market share analysis: Customer relationship software, worldwide, 2012', https://www.gartner.com/doc/2441815/market-share-analysis-consulting-services (accessed 16 April 2015)

Gladwell, Malcolm (4 October 2010). 'Small change: Why the revolution will not be tweeted', *The New Yorker*, http://www.newyorker.com/magazine/2010/10/04/small-change-malcolm-gladwell (accessed 13 April 2015)

Goldschmidt, Kathy and Ochreiter, Leslie (2008). *Communicating with Congress. How the Internet Has Changed Citizen Engagement.* Washington, DC: Congressional Management Foundation. p. 21.

Grefe, Edward A. (1981). *Fighting to Win: Business Political Power*, New York: Harcourt Brace Jovanovich.

Han, Hahrie (2014). *How Organizations Develop Activists*, Oxford, UK: Oxford University Press.

Harris, Phil and Fleisher, Craig (2005). *The Handbook of Public Affairs*, London: Sage, pp. 162–3.

Human Rights Campaign (June 2013). 'Picture Equality', http://www.hrc.org/red

Huy, Quy and Shipilov, Andrew (Fall 2012). 'The key to social media success within organizations', *MIT Sloan Management Review*, http://sloanreview.mit.edu/article/the-key-to-social-media-success-within-organizations (accessed 15 April 2015)

Khan Academy (29 August 2014). 'You can learn anything', online video clip, https://www.youtube.com/watch?v=JC82Il2cjqA (accessed 16 April 2015)

Nagy, Jenette, and Fawcett, Stephen. 'An overview of strategic planning or VMOSA, *Community Toolbox*', University of Kansas, http://ctb.ku.edu/en/table-of-contents/structure/strategic-planning/vmosa/main (accessed 12 April 2015)

Reh, F. John (18 December 2014). 'Vision, strategy, and tactics', http://management.about.com/cs/adminaccounting/a/vst.htm (accessed 12 April 2015)

Robbins, Stever. 'Setting strategic direction: vision, strategy, and tactics', http://www.steverrobbins.com/articles/vision-strategy-tactics (accessed 12 March 2015)

Sedej, Tanja and Justinek, Gorazd (2013). 'Social media in internal communications: A view from senior management', in Tanya Bondarouk and Miguel R. Olivas-Lujan, *Social Media in Human Resources Management.* UK: Emerald Group Publishing Ltd, pp. 86–8.

Zeng, Yun E., Wen, Joseph H. and Yen, David C. (2003). 'Customer relationship management (CRM) in business-to-business (B2B) e-commerce', *Information Management & Computer Security*, 11(1): 39–44.

10

PA and Ecology

Simon Bryceson and Simon Levitt

INTRODUCTION

Attitudes to the natural world vary, yet resources lie at the heart of political arrangements everywhere. The question of 'what to do' with these resources is almost always mired in heated political and philosophical dispute; as such, understanding the ecology landscape has become a core part of the work of the public affairs professional, and looking to the future, its importance is likely to rise.

Over the last decades, corporations have increasingly found themselves having to deal with controversial issues within the ecology landscape. The traditional view, that politicians are powerful rational actors, is still held in c-suites around the world. In reality, large sections of the political system are profoundly dysfunctional, meaning the c-suite's expectation of political 'power' and 'rationale' seldom plays out in a way they anticipate or want. This is especially true in the realm

of ecology due to the wide-scale nature of the challenges faced.

European Commission President Jean-Claude Juncker explains the political issue well, 'we all know what to do, we just don't know how to get re-elected after we've done it'. Peter Mair and Richard Katz (2009) expand on this, likening the political sphere to a cartel. Political parties, now highly professional, collude and set the scope debate. In such a system, 'the goals of politics become self-referential' (p. 755). This results not only in several issues being intentionally overlooked, but also in a diminished capacity for problem-solving in public life. Despite this new political modus operandi, corporations' senior management has failed to recognise that their 'traditional' model of political operation is obsolete.

In this chapter, we will ask why actively managing controversial issues is on the rise for many corporations. We will walk through three case studies from the environmental world to test our hypothesis. Throughout this chapter, we will see that ecological issues have become a management responsibility for large corporations because of political failure. As this failure becomes more acute, and the public give up increasingly on politics, their last resource for change can only be found in campaigns. As we will see in the course of this chapter, the movements since the mid 2000s are just the beginning.

To unpack the case studies, we must first understand the three major drivers that have fuelled a shift in public opinion concerning the fundamental nature of corporate social responsibility:

1 The resolution of the argument about companies' use of natural resources and their responsibility towards said resources.
2 The emergence of pressure groups as drivers of public opinion on controversial issues.
3 The fragmentation of media as a limitation on political action in the environmental arena.

THE MARKET, COMPANIES AND THE USE OF NATURAL RESOURCES

A 20-year battle of philosophical concepts played out in the 1970s and 1980s. This battle resulted in many ideological scars and, in part, explains the current attitudes of senior managers in the Board Room to the natural world – a view that often seems out of touch with the world at large.

The fundamental question fought over was, 'to whom does the natural world belong?'

At one end of the spectrum is a body of opinion represented by the phrase 'wise use' (Botkin, 2000). This body of opinion, influential with management thinking in the United States in the 1970s and 1980s, would today be known and represented by organisations such as the *Heartland Institute* or the *Cato Institute*.

'Wise use' rests very much in the tradition of what Macpherson (2010) calls 'possessive individualism' (a branch of liberal individualism), taking the view that society is a contractual arrangement in which the notion of ownership is critical to liberty and thus to personal development. This view is not inimical to the conservation of the natural environment, but stands in direct opposition to the other powerful historical force in this debate. At the other end of the spectrum, we have what we will call the 'concern for the commons'.

The 'concern for the commons' view holds that the notion of ownership is inconsistent with the primacy of sustaining an environment suitable for mankind and other life. Central to this is the idea of externalities – a cost or benefit that affects a party who did not choose to incur said cost or benefit. This view argues that the costs of production, like pollution, should be borne by the corporation, not the public. The incorporation of externalities into operating costs is a shared goal of most liberal politicians. Over time, this view has become a multifaceted movement that we will call here the 'concern for the commons'.

Underlying both the 'wise use' and 'concern for the commons' positions is a further question: is the marketplace consistent with environmental sustainability?

Milton Friedman (1975), on behalf of the 'wise use' camp, argued vigorously and persuasively that it was the legal duty of a joint-stock company to pursue the interests of its shareholders; and these interests are predominantly financial. Other concerns of the shareholders, be they social, political or spiritual, would or should be pursued through more suitable human institutions. Many saw this as a reasonable division of labour, responsibility and action.

In the 1970s and 1980s, one can see why justifying a strong concept of individual ownership was attractive to those wary of government power. Friedman gathered a large and loyal following in the business community, arming them with logical and philosophical stances that justified the extraction, use and disposal of natural resources – such activity allowed us to have and run cars across the world after all. The reason this history is important is because many of these followers now occupy the highest levels of the corporate triangle.

From the 1980s onward, the 'concern for the commons' camp steadily gained the upper hand. In 1987, the Montreal Protocol became arguably the most important (and successful) international agreement yet, placing strong limits on the 'wise use' of the commons. Catalysed by the movement surrounding climate change, most people today would attribute some responsibility to corporations for their resource use. Examples of this are numerous and have even caused large financial trusts to take radical action. Syracuse University repurposed $1.18 billion from extractive into clean energy. The Rockefeller Brothers Fund divested from fossil fuels in 2015. Such is the attention, regulators and politicians are even debating laws around 'extended producer responsibility', essentially arguing that corporations should have to pick up litter if it has their brand on it.

The relevance of this to public affairs and ecology is that, regardless of your personal position, a working knowledge of the main arguments in this debate has become a prerequisite for creating a consensus for action amongst senior management. Couching recommendations inside a 'possessive individualistic' or 'common good' envelope can make the difference between action or not. Moreover, the scars from battles in the 1970s and 1980s have sown the seeds of some of the more curious actions of corporations over the years.

In each of the three case studies used to illuminate this chapter, the senior managers of the companies had to engage in an internal debate that centred on these fundamental issues of ownership and control. In truth, this debate might have remained largely theoretical were it not for a second factor: the emergence of highly professional pressure groups.

THE EMERGENCE OF ENVIRONMENTAL PRESSURE GROUPS

Environmental pressure groups such as Friends of the Earth, World Wide Fund for Nature (WWF) or Greenpeace, are phenomena that emerged in the 1960s in Europe and North America. Of course, previously there had been organisations that were concerned with environmental issues, from the preservation of birdlife to the establishment of national parks; however, the aggression was new as was the target – corporate reputation and the brand.

In the United Kingdom, the iconic moment was the Friends of the Earth campaign against Cadbury-Schweppes (see Figure 10.1) concerning the non-returnable bottles they started to manufacture (Doherty and Doyle, 2013). It was to be the first of many such campaigns, the weapon of choice – brand damage. It was to become a standard tactic of the environment movement and a major driver of corporate management concern about the environment and public opinion.

As we all know, corporations spend a great deal of time and money creating 'brand character', which in turn becomes 'brand equity'. The new and aggressive tactics threatened that equity by publicly challenging the integrity of individual brands. Professional organisations challenged the brand character of major corporations, connecting the actions of the corporation with the public's perception of the brand.

Nike, Kimberley Clark, BP, Shell, Exon, Lego, Monsanto, Unilever; some of the biggest brands or brand holders in the world have become the subject of such campaigns. Although each company responded to these campaigns in a manner consistent with their own culture, there are undoubtedly a number of common themes.

These pressure groups caused a constant internal tension. Some saw the commercial imperative as the defence of the brand. By complying with the regulatory legal frameworks, companies fulfilled any 'ethical' obligation. Consumer-facing departments saw

Figure 10.1 Friends of the Earth campaigners place empty bottles outside the London HQ of Cadbury Schweppes in 1971, to promote re-use

https://www.foe.co.uk/living/40th_anniversary_gallery_31282

strong commercial reasons to reject 'wise use' because of the potential impact of brand damage. This tension, between a desire to interpret one's own role in legal and commercial terms, whilst being constantly faced with demands to accept ethical criteria separate from, and superseding, legal responsibilities, played out in the boardroom and the executive management committee of many targeted companies. Executives were asking themselves, 'Why am I dealing with this controversial issue rather than the politicians?' Many still are today.

Matters of legislation and regulation are normally perceived by senior managers as the appropriate sphere of action of politicians – 'they set the rules and we operate within them'. There is sometimes a degree of confusion and resentment when it is realised that politicians themselves may not wish to take a position on a controversial subject. The frustration of the managerial class is particularly acute when the politician will not defend a decision that has been arrived at by scientific and regulatory bodies for which they are responsible.

The reason that politicians would not defend these positions publicly was simply because the pressure groups had mobilised sufficient opinion in the opposite direction;

why would a politician take the risk? When politicians make decisions on genetically modified (GM) food, they are generally not thinking about any of the research and data showing GM food not to be harmful to human health (Vox, 2015). The power mobilised by environment movements against GM foods is such that image-conscious, risk-averse politicians now prefer to avoid making decisions.

A theme across all these case studies is that government checked itself out of every one of these debates.

THE FRAGMENTATION OF THE MEDIA AS A LIMITATION ON POLITICAL ACTION

Coincident with the rise of the pressure group, and possibly causally related to it, is the diminishing capacity of the politician to act as advocate on controversial issues. Changes in the modern media environment are the source of much commentary. Two elements of those changes, however, are directly relevant to corporate senior management's perception of the diminishing role of the politician. The first of these is simply the diminishing time which the politician has to present any kind of complex case to the general public. Adatto (1990) and Hallin (1992) ran the numbers and – worryingly for the politicians – demonstrated that their 'sound-bite' TV airtime had reduced from over 40 seconds in the 1960s to just 7 seconds by the 1980s. No one can make a complex argument in 7 seconds. (For a recent update of Hallin's study, see Bucy and Grabe 2007.)

The second major driver of change is the explosion in the number of media outlets. The development of social media, Twitter, Facebook and the endless stream of new arrivals, combined with an ever greater multiplicity of television channels, the majority of which contain little or no contemporary political commentary, again leads to a diminished capacity to articulate a complex case.

Many of the most controversial debates around corporate behaviour and environmental issues involve a complex mix of judgement and scientific data. This does not make them susceptible to easy characterisation, particularly when that characterisation is aimed at simplification for a mass audience. A frequently heard complaint from members of the executive committee of large corporations is that their opponents are able to mobilise 'emotion' in a way in which the corporate world cannot or should not. From this perspective, the media coverage of these complex issues is inherently biased against the complexity of the corporate position and in favour of the professional emotionalism of the pressure groups (Ornstein and Mann, 2000). Pressure groups do not accept the notion of 'value free' science; for them the decisions on what research to fund are frequently driven by commerce. This raises a question for them: 'to what extent does commercially driven science distort "real science"'. As a consequence, they regularly call for scientists doing regulatory work to be without ties to commercial organisations; moreover they rely more on emotional communication than a scientific style.

If the drivers of corporate management concern about social and environmental responsibility are ideological ('wise use' versus brand protection) and pragmatic (a reaction to the emergence of highly professionalised pressure group campaigns), then they are also surely political. Their concern is driven by an attempt to fill the perceived vacuum of the politician, unable or unwilling to defend complex legislative or regulatory outcomes.

PA AND ECOLOGY IN PRACTICE

Let us see these three factors in practice. In the following three case studies, in addition to highlighting some of the professional issues for public affairs operatives, we will try to highlight the interaction between these three crucial factors: ideological, reactive to pressure group activity and the adoption of a more overtly political role by the corporation.

UNILEVER, GREENPEACE AND THE COMMON FISHERIES POLICY

Fisheries in Europe are regulated by the Common Fisheries Policy. The policy has two objectives: first, to allocate fairly which country can catch which fish; second, to set a limit on the total number of fish that can be caught in European waters.

The second objective has proved hard to achieve. This is because of the relatively simple political law of concentrated versus diffuse interest, as conceptualised by Mancur Olson (1965). It is in the interests of fishermen to catch as many fish as possible, this year. As consumers, it is in the interests of all of us that a large number of fish are not caught this year in order to ensure the longer-term sustainability of fish. However, our interest is more diffuse than that of the fishermen. Consumers face a huge hurdle to effective organisation on this issue as a result. Conversely, when the fisheries ministers of European countries sit down to debate the year's fishing quotas, they know that fishermen are a powerful lobby that can cause them trouble. Because of the geographic concentration of fishermen, in any country with an election system based on geographic constituencies, the minister's party could lose a meaningful number of seats at the next election.

This is a classic 'problem of the commons', where conflicts between our 'wise use' camp and conservation become prominent. The seas have been open to the public as a common resource since time immemorial. What has brought that into question is the exhaustion, or alleged exhaustion, of certain species of fish. As a consequence, the pressure for a

greater degree of regulation had risen. Yet the political system seemed to fail to respond to that pressure. The problem was a real one; certain fish stocks were indeed running out. There was a solution, at least in the long term: fishing regulation based on sustainability of fish stocks. However, this solution was confounded, at least in the view of many of those involved at the time, because of a breakdown in the political process.

The result is that every year in Europe, too many fish are caught. In the 1990s, this problem was becoming acute in respect of cod in the North Sea. Greenpeace decided that this required a major campaign. Greenpeace realised that it was difficult to attack the regulators (even though this was their responsibility), because the regulators were more frightened of fishermen than any other constituency. In such situations, it is also difficult to attack individual national governments, because they in turn blame other governments and 'Brussels'. It is difficult, in turn, to attack 'Brussels', because there is such a tenuous link between 'Brussels' and media that changes public opinion.

Greenpeace needed another target and looked towards brands. At the time, the largest single buyer of fish in the world was Unilever. Unilever owned the major frozen fish businesses of Birdseye Walls, Langlese Iglo and Gorton's in the US. Additionally, Unilever was a major purchaser of fish oil sourced from smaller fish for the production of its margarines.

In early 1996, Greenpeace started planning a campaign against Unilever in Europe, in order to highlight the unsustainable nature of European fisheries. When Unilever became aware of the impending campaign, the company faced a strategic option. It could prepare to defend itself in communications terms on the basis of the status quo, by arguing (correctly) that it was not responsible for the problem being highlighted. This would have been the corporate reaction in 99 per cent of cases. Alternatively, it could choose to engage on the issue, which it did.

Unilever recognised two important points. One, that although the problem was not the company's fault, it would be possible for opponents to connect the problem to the company's brand over an extended period of time. Two, the aforementioned politics of the Common Fisheries Policy meant that any problem with European fisheries would at least get far worse before the correct regulatory action was taken, and that this could become a major issue for media criticism.

The required behavioural change could be achieved in two ways. The first is regulation, which in this case was not working. The second is a market-based mechanism. Unilever engaged in a dialogue with the Worldwide Fund for Nature (WWF), which had successfully established a market-based mechanism in the forestry sector previously: the Forest Stewardship Council (FSC). What Unilever and WWF now planned was a Marine Stewardship Council – the MSC. The MSC was to be set up as an independent organisation whose role was to certify sustainable fisheries. Any fishery around the world could apply to be examined by the MSC, and if it were successfully certified as sustainable, any fish sold from that fishery could be labelled as MSC-certified.

The MSC was launched and is today certifying fisheries from around the world. The on-pack logo of 'MSC-certified' is slowly gaining market awareness, which will encourage the supply chain to move towards wider certification. Today, driven by Unilever, there is now a fully fledged market-based mechanism in place in Europe to encourage the fishing supply chain to maintain sustainable fisheries.

What did all this mean for Unilever? Greenpeace did not campaign against the company, so a threat was avoided. Rather, Unilever was applauded for its action in playing a meaningful role in sustainability. Unilever's market position and brand, which had briefly threatened to be its weakness on the issue, were instead used by the company to good effect: within weeks of its announcement, most of its competitors and most of the retailers in the UK had signified they would only source MSC-certified fish in the future (most of the largest retailers globally have now made this pledge). So, over time, MSC labels would become a marketing requirement; in the meantime an MSC label could be seen as part of a premium brand promise (and price). Perhaps most importantly, Unilever helped its business in a more fundamental way – Unilever's future fish business depended on there being a sustainable supply of fish.

For Unilever, it had become increasingly difficult to argue anything like a 'wise use' case. The obvious problem was, no matter how wise the use by Unilever may be of the natural resource, it was part of a broader industrial process that was alleged to be threatening the existence of that resource. This is the very essence of this kind of brand vulnerability on ecological questions and at the heart of the public affairs professional's work in this area. The pressure groups have moved astutely to hold the commercial brand responsible for the political failure. The management at Unilever radically diminished the threat to the brand through its response to the issue.

The other thing of note was the way in which a commercial organisation and a pressure group were able to set up an organisation like the MSC. Since this was largely brought about by public concern on the issue of fish stock conservation: why were the politicians not reacting to that pressure?

There seems to be a gap between what was politically possible and what the science showed was necessary. Which brings us to BP and climate change.

BP AND CLIMATE CHANGE

Climate change has emerged as a major issue for us all. In the mid 1990s, this was represented by substantial amounts of media coverage of the emerging science. That coverage often focused on potential 'villains' and the large oil companies were obviously brand vulnerable on the issue.

Initially, the industry's collective response to climate change, and the brand vulnerability it brought, was to dispute the scientific evidence (Van Den Hove et al., 2002). The major companies formed the Global Climate Coalition, in part to fund science questioning the emerging orthodoxy on climate change. Climate change was not happening; it was not happening as quickly as some stated; its potential consequences were being overstated; or the contribution of man-made carbon emissions was overstated.

In early 1997, BP pulled out of the Global Climate Coalition. Its recently installed CEO, John (now Lord) Browne, announced BP's change in position, which the company widely communicated to the media, politicians and pressure groups (Browne, 1997). This was a very carefully thought through action on the part of the corporation. In looking at it as an example of the way in which a company has responded to an ecological question, it is important to note the significance of individual commitment (see Lowe and Harris, 1998; Rowlands, 2000).

Browne and other senior figures in BP believed strongly in what they were saying: the balance of accumulating evidence on climate change had reached a point which they believed required precautionary action, particularly where that action was intrinsically desirable in any case.

For the oil industry to continue with a position of denial of the principle would be pointless, but also damaging to future commercial interests, both with regard to loss of reputation along with a diminished ability to affect the precise set of outcomes, i.e., the future legal framework of the business.

By publicly communicating its position when it did, BP became a participant in the debate rather than a victim of it. There was much still to fight for: the future contribution of hydrocarbons versus other energy sources;

the timescale for action; the role of hydrocarbons in the 'hydrogen economy'; the mechanisms for carbon capping ('cap and trade' permits versus taxation); and the allocation of permits (grandfathering versus auctioning). By moving from denial to acceptance of the principle, BP was able to participate in the debate and offer a view on the specifics. Its point of view was listened to because its position was sufficiently surprising and progressive for the time.

As with any business move, the first mover reaps the greatest advantage. Where companies and industries in similar situations have gone on to be attacked again and again, BP and Browne were praised. President Clinton publicly praised the company and invited Browne to join his 'group of wise men' on climate change (Lowe and Harris, 1998). The company was congratulated by Prime Minister Blair on the floor of the House of Commons. BP's move was widely and positively discussed in the media around the world, and the company was publicly congratulated by Greenpeace.

Then there was the financial community. One often underrated element of issues management is the reputation of the company's management. If a company can demonstrate creative thinking ahead of its competitors on an issue of public interest, this implicitly implies an ability to think ahead of its competitors on operational issues. It can only have been helpful that Browne was voted the second most admired global businessperson by the Financial Times (2007).

Most 'oil' companies are in fact hydrocarbon companies, in that they also extract and sell gas, and in some cases coal. Coal's chemical composition has a low ratio of hydrogen to carbon atoms. Oil has a higher hydrogen to carbon ratio, meaning, in percentage terms you release less carbon when you burn it. Gas has an even higher ratio of hydrogen to carbon. If a tax were introduced based on the percentage of carbon released, it would have different consequences for each state of matter. Therefore, all other conditions being equal, in a carbon-restricted market, the price of oil goes up a little relative to coal and the price of gas goes up by a great deal.

Just before BP's communications on climate change, effectively accepting a carbon-restricted future, it had acquired Arco, a company with one of the highest gas-to-oil ratios in the industry. Additionally, BP was already planning a merger with Amoco. Amoco had the highest gas-to-oil ratio in the industry, i.e., ahead of time, BP was investing in a carbon-restricted future.

There can be few greater challenges than the explanation of the oil industry's case in a time of public concern about climate change. What BP was doing was repositioning itself on the whole issue in a way consistent with its commercial operations and, where possible, enhancing those operations in a way which was to serve it well into the future.

The issue of how humanity collectively uses natural resources again emerges as a concern which is focused on commercial organisations, the brand, by a variety of pressure groups and media coverage. Further, there again seems to be an element of the commercial organisations being held responsible for issues that would more normally be thought to be the realm of the politician.

MONSANTO AND GM FOODS

From the mid 1990s onwards, the emergence of GM food and ethical boundaries for biotechnology became an issue of increasing public debate. As the leading producer of GM foods, Monsanto became one of the most controversial companies in the world. Unlike Unilever and BP, Monsanto represents the consequences of failing to inform the general public about the activities and science behind a company's operations. Would a different strategy have produced a different result?

Monsanto enraged the ecology and environment movement, culminating in 2013 with the million-strong worldwide 'March against Monsanto'. Other multinational corporations produce GM foods and have a worse environmental track record than Monsanto, yet the company is still seen as one of the world's most unethical companies. What is it about Monsanto that has created so much hostility?

Monsanto began developing their biotechnology industry in the 1980s after closing its chemical industry arm. In 1996, Monsanto launched their first GM food product, Roundup Ready soy, a genetically engineered soybean seed, and Roundup Ready corn and cotton seeds followed in 1997.

Through genetic engineering, seeds under the Roundup Ready brand are designed to prevent threats to crops such as rootworm and thereby lead to a reduction of pesticide use amongst farmers.

From 1995 to 2000, the CEO of Monsanto, Robert B. Shapiro, initiated a series of mergers and acquisitions to develop and expand Monsanto in the agricultural bio-technology sector. Instead of rolling out Monsanto's Roundup Ready brand gradually, the senior management of the company decided to push its products fast to attain market share. As the company quickly outgrew its competitors, the initial success backfired: although US regulators approved Monsanto's crops, the company did not prioritise explaining the science behinds its GM food technology to the public.

Indeed, Monsanto was the subject of much criticism within the industry for its determination to move with speed. Several attempts were made to form a united industry position that would have left Monsanto less isolated. These frequently foundered on cost. Was there any public education campaign about the first products into the market place or around the technology itself?

The development of bio-technology applied to agriculture had been controversial from the start. When launching their Roundup

Ready brand and GM seeds, Monsanto framed the issue of Roundup Ready products that can deliver higher crop output, which is necessary to feed an ever-increasing global population. Instead of building consensus amongst environmental groups and engage with the public early about the science behind its products, Monsanto largely left the science and GM food safety debate to the regulating authorities. A classic case of not understanding that approval is not the same as persuasion; that the approval process does not automatically confer legitimacy in the eyes of the public.

The issue of GM food safety and labelling of products has become a polarising issue for the public all over the world. Through the increased use of new types of media such as social networks, blogs and other online platforms, criticism of Monsanto's activities has become commonplace. Perhaps most striking about such networks is that the safety of GM food products is constantly questioned despite the fact that Monsanto's products are perhaps some of the most tested for 'food safety' reasons in human history. The general scientific consensus states that GM foods are safe, yet pressure groups framed the debate of GM foods in these scientific terms. With the debate framed along the threat towards human health, ethical – as opposed to scientific – issues were overlooked. The importance of property rights, farmers' rights, supply chain sustainability and distribution of resources in the developing world were completely excluded from the public debate on GM foods. According to PEW Research Center (2015), 57 per cent of Americans still think that GM foods are unsafe to eat. Almost 20 years since Monsanto started its GM food operations, there is still a huge public resistance to bio-technology, with which Monsanto and the industry still struggle.

Perhaps one of the most infuriating aspects of Monsanto's behaviour to the ecology movement has been the challenge of GM foods around nature, ownership and the 'wise use' concept. Monsanto held patents on crop seeds which the environmental movement saw as a new development, as the company was now able to exert control over the food supply chain. This in turn drew in the development movement and other elements of the social justice campaigning world. This hostile public perception also precipitated various legal disputes between farmers and Monsanto over seed planting rights. Being the strongest party, Monsanto would largely emerge victorious from such court cases, but the constant legal involvement turned into negative PR as the company gained a reputation for being aggressive and litigious even over minor violations. The assertion of legal right independent of political, and thus commercial, consequence is another recurring theme in public affairs and ecology; it overlooks the 'outrage factor' and political reaction to it.

Some parts of the environmental movement also considered GM foods to be 'artificial', (i.e., manipulated by modern technology) as opposed to 'natural' food, which is free from any human intervention. The view that manipulating food with modern technology is morally irresponsible has been advocated by groups such as Greenpeace. The argument becomes both philosophical (what is natural?) and practical; to what extent are GM foods likely to be responsible for lost biodiversity? These views correlate with the increased popularity of organic food, whose market has grown enormously, partly as a reaction to the perceived 'industrialisation' of food production. The failure of Monsanto to engage with the more pragmatic pressure groups that held such views caused the debate about agricultural bio-technology to be dominated by the most ideological of the groups. When an industry fails to engage with public concern, then that concern will be articulated by the most media attractive of opponents, which in many cases are the most one-sided. Failure to address the more pragmatic groups means they have no interest in differing from the more ideological ones.

It is common in public affairs work in the field of ecology and the environment for senior management to characterise all critics as ideologically driven and unscientific. The problem with this position is that it tends to become self-fulfilling. By adopting an adversarial stance to all critics, the most pragmatic or data oriented critics find themselves aligned with the most entrenched and data indifferent ones. Whereas BP and Unilever sought out critics of the status quo with whom they could work, Monsanto became increasingly isolated, even within the industry.

Rather interestingly in Monsanto's approach, the corporation focused almost exclusively on persuading farmers about the 'wise use' validity of its practices with GM foods, assuming that there would be little public interest (or that the public did not have a right to have an interest in their commercial transaction with Monsanto). This enabled the ecology movement to frame the public debate entirely on its own terms and left Monsanto facing an uphill battle to win any favourable opinions.

After becoming a target for constant campaigning, legislators, who would have a natural authority in trying to shape public opinion, even though their power to do so is much diminished, have become reluctant to be identified with Monsanto. The call for labelling of GM food products by campaigners has caused lawmakers all over the world to stay away from trying to lead on any debate on GM products. This has damaged the brand value of Monsanto as regulators in Europe and elsewhere have introduced mandatory GM food labelling or resisted the introduction of GM crops, thereby leaving Monsanto to fight recurring PR and regulatory battles over its products. In fact, in September 2015, France sought an opt-out from the EU's GMO Directive, which approved and foresaw the cultivation of certain EU-approved GM crops. Scotland and Latvia are expected to follow suit. With public campaigns also resisting the implementation of the GMO Directive, the challenge to win public support seems to have become a losing battle.

CONCLUDING REMARKS

Clearly, public concern about different environmental issues rises and falls. It is therefore part of the public affairs professional's role to continually assess which of these issues is becoming more salient. This is a complex matter since it involves estimating public opinion at a point in the future and is subject to almost limitless variables. Second, it is difficult to know in advance how an issue, which is being addressed in the regulatory or legislative environment, might or might not impact on the company and shareholder value. This is because both the precise nature of any regulatory outcome is difficult to predict until the last moment and because it is difficult to estimate the extent to which political controversy will leave the company isolated.

The first two examples which we have used in this chapter are of companies which took fundamental ecological questions, humanities relationship to the oceans and to the life within them, and the emerging threat of climate change, and tried to gain some kind of 'first mover advantage'. There is also the reverse need: that of a company to avoid becoming isolated.

The third example relates to the misunderstanding, or perhaps miscalculation of public reaction to the operation of a company, namely the introduction of GM organisms in food. In this case, it is worth remembering that there is much debate over both the science of GM food and whether, if public affairs professionals had handled the introduction of the product more effectively, public opinion would have been more receptive. The example also demonstrates the potentially damaging impact an inadequate public affairs handling and what failure to explain the commercial operations behind a company might cause.

Conversely, a pressure group campaigning against a brand is usually intending to isolate that brand. It may also be intended to use it as an example of wider industry bad practice, but more sophisticated campaigners are looking to divide the relevant industry on the question at hand.

Most countries in the liberal democratic world have seen pressure group campaigns that are focused on a particular company or brand, rather than the ecological, developmental or social problem that is said to be 'the issue'. A public affairs professional therefore needs to have a constantly updated analysis of the company's operations to ensure that any procedure or product that might have the 'outrage factor' is identified and monitored. However, identifying in advance what a combination of pressure group activity, media narrative and political context that may arise as the public opinion weather is a difficult task.

The case studies in this chapter show that ecological issues have become a management responsibility for large corporations because of political failure. However, they are examples of a much wider phenomenon that goes beyond environmental concern. The origins of this political failure are made clear by Peter Mair (2013) in *Ruling the Void: The Hollowing out of Western Democracy*. In the future, as this issue becomes more acute and the public give up increasingly on politics, their last resource for change will only be found in campaigns. The movements of recent decades are just the beginning.

REFERENCES

Adatto, K. (1990), *Sound Bite Democracy: Network Evening News Presidential Campaign Coverage, 1968 and 1988*. Cambridge, MA: Harvard University, Joan Shorentstein Barone Center.

Botkin, D.B. (2000), *No Man's Garden: Thoreau and a New Vision For Civilization and Nature*. Washington, DC: Island Press.

Browne, J. (1997), 'Addressing global climate change', speech at Stanford University, California. Retrieved 21 August 2015, from: http://www.bp.com/content/dam/bp/pdf/speeches/1997/Addressing_Global_Climate_Change.pdf

Bucy, E. and Grabe, E. (2007), Taking television seriously: a sound and image bite analysis of presidential campaign coverage, 1992–2004. *Journal of Communication*, 57, 652–75.

Doherty, B. and Doyle, T. (2013), *Environmentalism, Resistance and Solidarity: The Politics of Friends of the Earth*. Basingstoke, UK: Palgrave Macmillan.

Financial Times (2007), 'Sun King of the oil industry'. Retrieved 16 September 2015, from http://www.ft.com/intl/cms/s/0/2a42aa08-a261-11db-a187-0000779e2340.html#axz z3k0WncDt5

Friedman, M. (1975), *There's No Such Thing As a Free Lunch*. London: Open Court Pub Co.

Hallin, D.C. (1992), Sound bite news: Television coverage of elections, 1968–1988. *Journal of Communication*, 42(2), 5–24.

Lowe, E.A. and Harris, R.J. (1998), Taking climate change seriously: British Petroleum's business strategy. *Corporate Environmental Strategy*, 5(2), 22–31.

Macpherson, C.B. (2010), *The Political Theory of Possessive Individualism, Hobbes to Locke*. OUP Canada: Oxford University Press.

Mair, P. (2013), *Ruling the Void: The Hollowing of Western Democracy*. London: Verso.

Mair, P. and Katz, R. (2009), The cartel party thesis: a restatement. *Perspectives on Politics*, 7(4), 753–66.

Olson, M. (1965), *The Logic of Collective Action: Public Goods and the Theory of Groups*. Cambridge, MA: Harvard University Press.

Ornstein, N. and Mann, T. (2000), *The Permanent Campaign and its Future*. Washington, DC: American Enterprise Institute Press.

PEW Research Center (2015), 'Public and scientists' views on science and society'. Retrieved 16 September 2015, from http://www.pewinternet.org/2015/01/29/public-and-scientists-views-on-science-and-society/#_Chapter_3:_Attitudes

Rowlands, I.J. (2000), Beauty and the beast? BP's and Exxon's positions on global climate change. *Environment and Planning C*, 18(3), 339–54.

Van Den Hove, S., Le Menestel, M. and De Bettignies, H. (2002), The oil industry and climate change: strategies and ethical dilemmas. *Climate Policy*, 2(1), 3–18.

Vox (2015), 'Poll: Scientists overwhelmingly think GMOs are safe to eat. The public doesn't'. Retrieved 16 September 2015, from   http://www.vox.com/2015/1/29/7947695/gmos-safety-poll

11

Political Marketing and Public Affairs

Bruce I. Newman, Wojciech Cwalina
and Andrzej Falkowski

This chapter will explore the link between political marketing and public affairs. In the United States, where the emphasis will be placed in this chapter, there have been efforts on the part of political parties and other political action committees and interest groups to use the influence of money to affect political outcomes at election time as well as to pass laws that benefit one group in society over another. We will investigate the role of money that comes from lobbying efforts on the part of corporations and the impact it has on campaign budgets, tactics, and the general ethical condition that exists in politics today. The chapter ends with the introduction of an innovative 'strategic framework for lobbyists' that can be used as the basis for the development of marketing strategies.

THE ROLE OF LOBBYING IN THE UNITED STATES

In general, the role of lobbyists in the United States can be broken down into three main

areas: business, union, and special interest (Baumgartner and Leech, 2001; Scholzman et al., 2012). Business lobbyists usually hire firms such as public affairs companies to conduct their business for them. These public affairs companies are beginning to understand and use the tactics and strategies that have been well documented in the political marketing literature to date. Unions seem to be more active at the grassroots level and tend to concentrate more on influencing their own members. Special interest groups are more active with respect to issue advocacy advertising, and less sophisticated with respect to their use of political marketing methods (Gerrity, 2010). Although the link between political marketing and lobbying has been touched on in the literature in political marketing (Andrews, 1996; Davies and Newman, 2006; Harris, 2001; Newman, 1999a, 1999b, 2002b; Williams and Newman, 2013), this chapter will be the first serious analysis of how the two can be merged into a very powerful knowledge base to be used by lobbyists to impact the decision making of

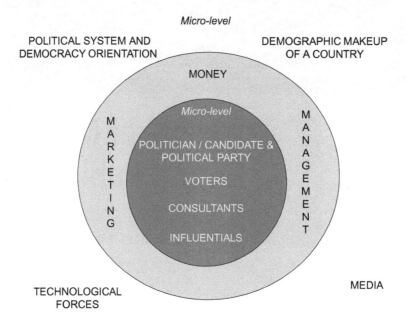

Figure 11.1:   The macro and micro view of political marketing (Cwalina et al., 2012: 267)

political parties and politicians in their role as governing officials.

This relationship between political marketing and lobbying should be located in a broad perspective linking the so-called macro and micro factors affecting the political behavior (Cwalina et al., 2016). These factors constitute a network of mutual causal influences both within a particular level and also between them. Figure 11.1 illustrates the view of political marketing integrating factors at different levels of analysis.

The detailed analysis of these factors, and cause-and-effect relations between them at the various stages of a political campaign, has been presented by Cwalina et al. (2012). Note the following elements that are important in building relationships between public affairs as a specialized form of lobbying and political marketing:

1   *Money, marketing, and management.* It is obvious that political marketing is closely related to management. In the macro perspective, the management is first of all the result of financial regulations defining the directions of

marketing campaigns' development and the level of investment (costs) in 'creating' information and political events. The costs of sending this information to voters is also included in those calculations. Furthermore, with the use of sophisticated marketing techniques comes the high cost of consultants to carry out marketing functions. From this perspective, the absolute foundation for any marketing action is managing the finances – getting financial resources (focus on the donators) and spending them in the most efficient way to achieve campaign goals (Herrnson and Campbell, 2009). Managing the finances directly determines the importance of such elements of political marketing at the micro level as political consultants and candidates and the political parties.

2   *The voter.* Controlling the voters' behavior is an essential task of political marketing. Indeed, candidates, to be successful, have to understand the voters and their basic needs and aspirations and the constituencies they represent or seek to represent. Marketing orientation in politics means that in order for the political campaign to be successful, one needs to understand the voter because the voter is the key figure in all democracies. Understanding the voters requires finding their accurate position in social

structure, to know their needs and goals, and psychological features. On the other hand, in the light of integration of the fields of political marketing and public affairs, of particular importance is that 'understanding' the voter is also related to how he or she receives, processes, and interprets political information; how he or she evaluates politicians and their proposals and then takes decisions and implements them. The public affairs companies are involved in controlling the process of collecting and interpreting political information by voters, as, for example, business organizations, civil right groups, or labor unions.

3   *The politician/candidate and the political party.* In the political marketing process, candidate image and issue positions are used jointly for positioning politicians and their platforms, which is based on a combination of cognition and affect (Baines, 1999; Ben-Ur and Newman, 2010; Cwalina et al., 2011; Cwalina and Falkowski, 2015; Smith, 2005). The established politician message (platform) is then disseminated on the voter market in a direct or indirect way. It should be stressed that although a politician's positive image may be related to his or her real traits, it is more often that the general public may decide who a charismatic leader is. Thus, the most important issue in creating any image is selecting those features that will lay the foundations for further actions. Business lobbyists make the selection of such features and use the newspapers editors and media personalities for their presentation to voters.

4   *The political consultants.* This is 'the product managers of the political world'. (O'Shaughnessy, 1990: 7). The consultants are in a position to help a politician craft a winning image that resonates well with citizens. They do it in both ways, either focusing their campaign strategy on the national party organization and on the mobilizing force of strong party organizations, or concentrating on available financial resources and on the strategic positioning of their candidates and developing messages that appeal to the expectations of specific target groups. Naturally, sources of information enabling the effectiveness of the consultants are the results of the activity of lobbyists on the political market.

5   *Influentials.* These include lobbyist businesses, which are of particular importance in the integration of political marketing and public affairs.

They refer to, for example, the formal organization and its leader (e.g., labor unions, civil rights groups, business organizations, environmental movements); the religious groups and churches; and the public figures such as newspaper editors, experts, or media personalities whose influence is exerted indirectly via organized media or authority structures. For example, the establishment of the Equal Rights Amendment movement, the National Organization of Women, and the active role of the League of Women Voters in United States have significantly influenced changes in legislation as well as including gender rights issues in party platforms and getting women involved in politics – both as voters and candidates. Likewise, the American Association of Retired Persons, as a lobby group for older people, with a membership of 34 million, is a real power on the political market. Thus, the influentials function as gatekeepers, which limit information by selective editing, increase the amount of information by expansive editing, or reorganize the information through reinterpretation. Influentials set the agenda by making some issues and politicians' personal characteristics more salient to the public, and, in consequence, more important.

The integration of the fields of political marketing and public affairs as a hybrid model for lobbyists constitutes an important step for governments around the world that are increasingly forced to find ways of identifying business opportunities for corporations in their respective countries. It is in the interest of corporations to use political activity to secure greater sales and avoid regulation costs that make it more difficult for them to compete for business around the world. So, it should not be surprising to know the literature finds that the most consistent explanatory factors of political activity have been firms' size, degree of government regulation, and the amount of firm or industry sales to the government (Grier et al., 1994). Among the top 500 corporations in the United States, close to 60 percent have political action committees, and the mean contribution to candidates running for public office was $80,349 (Mitchell et al., 1997).

WHAT IS A PAC?

A PAC is an acronym that stands for the term political action committee, which is set up to raise and spend funds to support candidates for public office. Special interests (like the American Heart Association and trade associations like the National Roofing Contractors Association) use their PACs to make known and further their positions on issues and policies that affect their industry. PAC money is used to support politicians who have helped these organizations in their fight on Capitol Hill. In other words, by contributing to political campaigns, PACs hope to influence both who is elected and what they do when they are in office.

So which organizations have given the most amount of money since the mid 2000's in the United States? According to Opensecrets.org, a website devoted to the dissemination of information on lobbying, the following list of donors covers the top 10 from 1989 to 2015:

1   Service Employees International Union: $222,434,657.
2   ActBlue: $160,637,963.
3   American Federation of State, County and Municipal Employees: $93,830,657.
4   National Education Association: $92,972,656.
5   Fahr LLC: $75,289,659.
6   American Federation of Teachers: $69,757,113.
7   Las Vegas Sands: $69,440,942.
8   National Association of Realtors: $68,683,359.
9   Carpenters and Joiners Union: $67,778,534.
10 International Brotherhood of Electrical Workers: $63,572,836.

If we look at the figures at recent single elections, such as in the 2013–14 cycle, it becomes clear that the list of the top 10 contains almost all of the same organizations listed above, with only three exceptions – Bloomberg L.P., NextGen Climate Action, and Elliott Management Corporation. When we compare this list with the top 10 from the 2011–12 cycle, we find on both the same four organizations: Las Vegas Sands, ActBlue, Service Employees International Union, and National Education Association.

There is clearly a consistency in influence coming from the same lobbyists. This makes it more clear for the candidates running for election, as well as the politicians sitting in office, to know where to turn for money to finance their re-election bids as well as pet projects in Congress. In his analysis of four consecutive elections in the 1980s, Snyder (1992) found a remarkable degree of persistence in PAC contributions for both the investor and ideological PACs. It is understandable, because contributors must develop a relationship of mutual trust and respect with politicians (especially officeholders) in order to receive tangible rewards for their investments.

If we look overseas to identify the PACs that are spending the most on foreign elections, the following companies rise to the top five in the 2013–14 cycle:

1   GlaxoSmithKline: $744,999.
2   HSBC North America: $566,920.
3   UBS Americas: $468,100.
4   DaimlerChrysler: $440,100.
5   Credit Suisse First Boston: $379,250.

If we go back to the last congressional cycle and track the source of money from PACs and soft and individual donations, the amount of money coming from business, labor, and ideological organizations breaks down in the following way in 2014 (as of March 2015):

1   Business: $1,675,242,051 (41 percent to Democrats and 59 percent to Republicans).
2   Labor: $140,729,752 (89 percent to Democrats and 11 percent to Republicans).
3   Ideological: $255,667,633 (51 percent to Democrats and 49 percent to Republicans).

IMPACT OF SPENDING ON ELECTION OUTCOMES

Perhaps most important and germane to this discussion is not necessarily the amount of money spent on election campaigns, but the impact (or correlation) of the money spent on individual campaigns and the outcomes of that spending. According to Smith (1995: 93), the 'purpose of campaign contributions is to buy access, not votes'. Then, donations may influence whom politicians talk to, the amount of energy they devote to particular issues, and what they do in informal settings. In an authoritative edited book on the financing of the 2000 congressional election, Magleby (2002: 127) concluded that most of the candidates who raised and spent the most money won, and most of those candidates also happened to be incumbents. This of course stands to reason, as those members in Congress who have the most influence in the legislative process will be in the best position to influence laws that impact on corporations and other interested parties. A very interesting statistic is the breakdown of contributions for House of Representatives candidates (Table 11.1).

Only in the case of incumbents did the largest percentage of money come from PACs. The PAC's main job is to get the maximum return on their donations, seeking to win influence and goodwill with as many lawmakers as possible in Washington. There will not be a return on their investment if the recipients of their donations don't win office. Because of this, PACs are very careful where they invest their money, thereby not taking the risk on non-incumbents with whom they are not sufficiently familiar to trust to carry out the favors they seek. Furthermore, as demonstrated by Snyder's analysis (1992), representatives running for House seats in

small states receive significantly higher investor contributions than representatives running for House seats in large states. This is because contributors who are interested in developing and maintaining long-term relationships with candidates will consider a candidate's political future as well as her or his current office when making their contribution decisions. 'Given two similar candidates running for two offices that are similar in all respects except that only one office is a natural "stepping-stone" to a higher office, a contributor who treats his contributions as long-term investments should contribute more to the candidate running for the "stepping-stone" office' (Snyder, 1992: 20). Then, House representatives from small states (in terms of population) are more likely to move to the Senate than representatives from populous states.

The way in which PACs get around the limitations of the law in their support of candidates and parties is to spend their money and influence on 'issue ads'. Issues costing more money, involving a greater departure from the status quo, and affecting more people will attract more attention (Baumgartner and Leech, 2001). Issue or 'third-party' advertisements which raise specific concerns or even attack or support a candidate are considered to be non-political as long as they do not call for the open support or defeat of a particular candidate in an ad (Bergan and Risner, 2012; Cwalina et al., 2011; Reyes, 2006). This is where the influence of political marketing becomes very significant. This was part of the Supreme Court ruling in its landmark 1976 *Buckley v. Valeo* decision that set the

Table 11.1 Contributions for House candidates in 2000 election (%)

Contributor	Incumbents	Challengers
Individual over $200	15	18
Individual $200–$1000	36	39
Political action committee	41	17
Parties	1	3
Candidates	1	18
Miscellaneous	6	4

Source: Magleby (2002: 126)

Table 11.2   Top spending on the top 10 issues

Industry	Total spending – $
1. Miscellaneous	41,294,326
2. Human rights	14,286,766
3. Environment	6,797,000
4. Gun rights	6,680,759
5. Republican/Conservative	6,024,761
6. Pro-Israel	1,500,000
7. Abortion policy/Pro-choice	799,168
8. Abortion policy/Pro-life	715,000
9. Gun control	420,000
10. Women's issues	340,000

Source: Opensecrets.org

rules for the current set of election laws. The use of issue ads became very popular during the course of elections that took place in the 1990s when religious rights groups began to make targets of selected politicians. Since then, several PACs followed suit to express their rights as citizens of the United States by paying for such issue ads that clearly favored one candidate over another. The political parties themselves in fact have relied on issue ads to support their own cadre of candidates in recent elections.

According to year 2000 data, the most amount of money spent on the top 10 issues based on ideological/single-issue ads broke down into the categories in Table 11.2.

As one looks at money spent by lobbyists in recent elections in the United States, the following conclusions can be drawn:

1   Contributions from PACs to congressional candidates continue on an upward spiral.
2   Growth in soft money spending, particularly by the Democratic Party, has been essential to the party's success in recent key congressional races.
3   Parties and PACs will continue to see redistricting changes happening in upcoming elections, which will make their job even more difficult.
4   PACs are spending millions of dollars on issue advocacy in more targeted congressional races.
5   PACs are increasing their independent expenditures because they are able to directly urge voters to vote for or against a particular candidate, However, all independent expenditures must be reported to the FEC.

6   PACs that gave the most in recent elections were corporate PACs in direct contributions to candidates, followed by trade associations, labor PACs, ideologically oriented PACs, with cooperatives giving the least amount of monetary support.
7   Groups like the NRA, the Christian Coalition, and the AFL-CIO are semi-permanent, full-service, independent electoral organizations that work just like political parties.
8   A large proportion of PAC activity is shielded from public view, as more groups learn to take advantage of opportunities to influence electoral policies through such devices as soft money contributions to the political parties and issue advocacy advertising.

Some say the United States is in an era characterized by the 'permanent campaign' where political fund raising is continual and there is a blurring of election and policy-making activity. While many have made the argument that the increase in the number and influence of political action committees implies the decline of political parties and the emergence of the influence of special interests, it is clear that the PAC system owes much of its structure to the party system. PACs are formed by groups that are sensitive to electoral shifts and partisan conflict. This sensitivity to the ebb and flow of the party system also implies that most PACs are likely to favor one party or the other.

THE IMPACT OF LAWS ON LOBBYISTS

Under amended FECA 1979, parties can spend money on pins, bumper stickers, voter registration, get-out-the-vote drives, and the spending does not count against the party contribution or coordinated expenditure limits for any candidate. The law also permits parties to set up a separate account for fund raising called 'non-federal' or 'soft' money for party activities not expressly connected to candidates.

In *Buckley v. Valeo* (1976), the Supreme Court majority ruled that there should be mandatory limits on campaign spending. Candidates spending their own money, as well as independent expenditures, are violations of a constitutional right to free speech and unconstitutional. This case applies to state and local elections as well. *Buckley v. Valeo* allows interest groups to skirt the full disclosure intention of FECA because of the right to free speech. Supreme Court footnotes to the case state that limits on spending or contributions apply only to express advocacy (i.e., 'vote for', 'elect', 'defeat', 'for Congress'). Without these words, the advocacy spending is beyond the scope of FECA and the source of the funding or the amount need not be disclosed. PACs may engage in unlimited express advocacy for or against a candidate via 'independent expenditures'. Unlimited express advocacy represents internal communications with their own members, and unlimited and undisclosed issue advocacy often supports or opposes a candidate. PACs may raise unlimited money for electoral purposes, but face spending constraints on direct contributions.

There have been some very significant changes put into law in the United States that will have an impact on the effectiveness of lobbyists. On 10 December 2003, the Supreme Court ruled that Congress was justified in seeking to purge national politics of the big money campaign contributions with laws that will limit large donations from corporations, unions, and individuals. Opponents of the laws objected to the limitation of free speech (provided for by the First Amendment of the Constitution of the United States) that some argued was inherent in the passing of the laws ruled justified by the Supreme Court. According to the new laws, soft money contributions (namely those contributions to political parties for use other than advocating a candidate's election or defeat) that until now gave local and state parties unlimited transfers of monies to be used for issue/ideological advertisements, will now effectively be eliminated.

Hard money contributions (contributions to individual candidates to support or defeat them) will now be limited to $2,000 per election, $25,000 per year to national parties and $5,000 per year to a single PAC. There will be a complete ban on issue ads, which are broadcast ads from independent groups, including unions and corporations, that do not advocate the election or defeat of candidates, yet refer directly to them, within 60 days of an election or 30 days of a primary. This law is the first major campaign finance legislation in 30 years, and is often referred to as McCain-Feingold (also known technically in Congress as legislation S.1593) after its main sponsors, Senators John McCain and Russell Feingold. The law took effect from the 2004 elections. This law will have a very big impact on funds that allowed soft money contributions to political parties to be used to get out the vote and build party strength, and not to support a particular candidate. However, many critics argued that campaigns turned to soft money donations to circumvent campaign finance rules. The national political parties have raised hundreds of millions of dollars, which have in fact been used to help support specific campaigns. The central provision of McCain-Feingold prohibits parties from soliciting, receiving, or spending soft money.

STRATEGY DEVELOPMENT BY LOBBYISTS

Firms cannot legally contribute corporate funds to PACs, but firms can grant permission for trade associations or professional PACs to solicit their employees for contributions. Many decisions on legislation are often made in a last-minute frenzy as legislators prepare to adjourn for the legislation session, so lobbyists need to know when to act and how to act, as legislation comes up fast. It is crucial that each member of the subcommittee working on a Bill a PAC is interested in is contacted by the committee about the Bill and gets constituents who support the Bill to contact committee members. Next, contact should be made by all members of the full committee to get their support. The Bill may be in committee for years, so there is ample time for a PAC to get constituents to contact committee members. PACs can influence a Bill at any point in the process from committee to joint committee to either House to conference committee to the executive.

The key step in moving a PAC's Bill to a successful vote in committee (which is the most critical step) is choosing the most influential person in the committee to join the cause of the PAC. To get the PAC Bill through committee, a PAC will also want to approach the strongest committee member from the minority side. PACs should help committees set up hearings on the Bill and be present at mark-up sessions (because the legislator or staff person may need to contact someone from the PAC at a moment's notice, and because last-minute words with an undecided committee member are important, and because it sends the message to the legislators that the PAC is concerned about a particular Bill).

PACs should try to make connections with legislators' staff members who have a lot of 'behind the scenes' power and get updates on their Bill. PACs should recognize those staff members who have helped them. (This involves spending of some kind.) Most PACs use ideological, access-oriented, or mixed strategies when contributing to candidates. PACs that use ideological strategies are similar to the two major political parties (democrats and republicans) with respect to the fact that they seek to influence the political process through the election.

Ideological PACs give money to candidates in highly competitive races to encourage the career of up-and-coming young politicians. Ideological PACs rarely make contributions for the purpose of gaining access to legislators, because these committees seek to push specific issues that are linked to fundamental policies and issues that politicians will rarely compromise on. Access-oriented committees make contributions mainly to gain a foothold with members of Congress who are in a position to affect regulations and appropriations on those laws that affect the specific industry in which the organization operates and that is represented by the PAC. Access-oriented committees consider campaign contributions a tool for strengthening their relationship with important government officials. They see that contributions create goodwill to make it easier for their lobbyists to influence the legislative process. Access-oriented PACs give more money to incumbents, and it does not have to be a competitive election for them to give money.

Mixed strategy PACs, which include primarily trade associations and labor unions, give some money to candidates that share their views and some money to incumbents they want to keep accessible to them. It is not unusual to see committees recruiting and training candidates to run for public office, as well as serving as advisors to their campaigns in the primary and general elections. So the question that arises now is: how can a lobbyist use the knowledge base in political marketing to carry out their functions?

THE ROLE OF POLITICAL MARKETING IN POLITICS

Politicians have relied on basic marketing skills to get elected, going back to the earliest campaigns in US history. Candidates have relied on campaign buttons, posters, political rallies, and campaign speeches to inform voters about what they stand for, who they are, and how they will help them achieve their dreams. Once in office, these same candidates turn into politicians who have to work hard to put into legislation those laws that will allow them to go back to the same voters at the next election cycle with promises fulfilled. Getting those promises fulfilled takes much more than simply relying on marketing to win office, but must depend on a whole new set of marketing methods to govern with. This is where the intersection of public affairs and marketing finds its most interesting connection, and that is the use of marketing by lobbyists to impact on the choice of laws that a politician attempts to enact (Harris et al., 1999; Harris and McGrath, 2012; McGrath, 2006; Newman, 1994). The same principles that operate in the commercial marketplace hold true in the political marketplace: successful organizations have a market focus and are constantly engaged in doing research to better understand their customers' wants and needs. In other words, marketers must be able to anticipate their customers' wants and needs, and then develop innovative products and services on a regular basis to keep their customers brand loyal and devoted to their companies. Politicians have a similar orientation and are carrying out research on a regular basis to determine how best to represent their constituency and attempt to increase the quality of life of citizens by using the most efficient means available to them as a steward of the government (Cwalina et al., 2011; Kotler and Kotler, 1999; Newman, 2002a; Newman and Sheth, 1985b).

Political marketing can be defined as:

[t]he processes of exchanges and establishing, maintaining, and enhancing relationships among objects in the political market (politicians, political parties, voters, interests groups, institutions), whose goal is to identify and satisfy their needs and develop political leadership. (Cwalina et al., 2009: 70)

This definition can be broadened to include the use of these same methods by lobbyists who seek to influence public opinion in an attempt to influence politicians to pass laws that benefit the companies they represent.

It has literally become impossible not to incorporate a marketing orientation when running for office, or for that matter when running the country. Politics today has become more than just a campaign to get elected and re-elected, but is increasingly becoming a fully fledged marketing campaign that relies on all the same processes as a corporation would use to succeed in the marketplace. The same advanced technological methods used by corporate America to market products are being used by politicians to market themselves and their ideas. The modern-day politician at all levels of office must rely on marketing not only to win the election but also to be successful as a leader after entering the White House (Butler and Collins, 1999; Cwalina et al., 2011; Gouliamos et al., 2013; Newman and Perloff, 2004; Perloff, 1999; Wring, 1999). Advances in the telecommunications industry, especially interactive technology, have opened up the possibilities for corporations that are in the business of lobbying government (Johnson, 1999; Newman, 2016). To better understand the role of political marketing for lobbyists, it is critical to first understand how government is changing. Only by understanding the needs of government officials and politicians will it be possible for lobbyists to impact their decision-making process over legislation.

MAKING THE LEAP TO LOBBYING

The use of political marketing by lobbyists presents several different leaps in logic. Because lobbyists have to deal with many different government officials, particularly those in Congress, the job is very difficult. If lobbyists are going to successfully sell themselves to government officials, and at the same time help politicians to sell their ideas to the people and Congress, then a framework must be used that translates the value proposition that exists between government and lobbyists. A theory of political choice behavior developed by Newman (1981) and tested on several elections (Cwalina et al., 2008; Newman, 1999b, 1999a; Newman and Sheth, 1985a, 1987) proposes a number of cognitive beliefs that may come from a wide range of sources, including the voter, word-of-mouth communication, and the mass media. In addition, the theory incorporates the influence of an individual's affiliation with groups of people in his/her social environment (Lazarsfeld et al., 1944) and the influence of party affiliation and past voting behavior (Campbell et al., 1960). The usefulness of this theory can be found in the comprehensiveness of the range of voter beliefs that are covered in so few cognitive constructs. As such, it has the potential to be used by Congress as a very powerful communication tool to develop appeals that highlight the distinctiveness of what Congress can offer interested parties over the internet.

The fundamental axiom of the theory is that a voter/citizen is a consumer of a service offered by a politician, and, similar to consumers in the commercial marketplace, voters choose candidates based on the perceived value they offer them. The same logic can be applied to citizens seeking services from Congress. The theory proposes that there are five distinct and separate cognitive domains that drive the voter's behavior. A key proposition of the theory is that voter behavior can be driven by a combination of one or more of the domains in a given election. The generic nature of the theory makes it useful for anyone interested in understanding the relative importance of various issues, policies, and other service offerings to citizens from government. The theory includes the following components:

1   *Political issues.* This dimension represents the policies a candidate advocates and promises to enact if elected to office. It captures the rational considerations of a voter that normally would revolve around issues that people feel in their pocketbooks. This construct captures the same kind of appeals that are used by companies who appeal to consumers with products that promise high quality, lower prices, and other benefits that have a rational appeal.

2   *Social imagery.* This represents the stereotyping of the candidate to appeal to voters by making associations between the candidate and selected segments in society (e.g., the support that opinion leaders give to a politician). The use of imagery can be very powerful here as the candidate or political party manufactures an image in the minds of voters on the basis of his/her associations, with the possibility of that image being either positive or negative in the mind of the voter, depending on which group it is that the candidate is trying to associate him or herself with. The adaptation of this component in the commercial marketplace manifests itself through the use of prominent and well-known spokespersons for companies who are used in advertisements and commercials. Similar to the same process that is used in politics, companies create an image for their product through the sheer association of the product or company with the personality who is used.

3   *Candidate personality.* Imagery in politics is perhaps the most important avenue that can be used to sell a candidate or political party. Whereas the use of imagery was described through the use of the Social Imagery component in the model, it is also represented through the personality of the candidate in a slightly different way. Here, the candidate (or political party) is emphasizing personality traits to help reinforce and manufacture an image in the voter's mind. When we compare this to the consumer in the marketplace, marketers do play on emotions by using the right setting, appeals, and background to create a mood which affects the consumer's decision to purchase a particular brand.

4   *Situational contingency.* This dimension represents that aspect of a voter's thinking which could be swayed by 'hypothetical events' described by competing parties or candidates during the course of a campaign. Winning elections is often based on getting a small percentage of voters to switch their allegiance to another candidate or party. Marketers also rely on this dimension as the basis for appealing to consumers and getting them to switch from one brand or company to another. Common practices used to implement this value proposition come in the form of sales promotions, giveaways, and advertisements, all unexpected events from the consumer's point of view that are aimed at altering his or her behavior. In the government, this may be shaped by news and media reports that affect voters' and citizens' perceptions of government.

5 *Epistemic value.* This dimension appeals to a voter's sense of curiosity or novelty in choosing a candidate. Marketers rely on this tactic when appealing to consumers' desires to acquire the latest and newest products in the marketplace. Whereas the theory as it exists can be applied by lobbyists in their effort to affect the decision making of government officials, it may be more useful to make some conceptual changes in the model so that it has a more direct application to the role of the lobbyist in government.

LINKING PUBLIC AFFAIRS, LOBBYING, AND POLITICAL MARKETING

The specific link between public affairs and lobbying is a much debated issue. However, this linkage was well put in an article in the *Journal of Public Affairs*, a leading source on the role of public affairs and lobbying in the world today:

> [f]rom a pragmatic point of view, the industry is engaged, one way or another, in the application of pressure and influence to produce political outcomes that are beneficial to its clients. To succeed in this enterprise requires knowledge and understanding of the prevailing political culture and dynamics of decision-making. This culture is undergoing fundamental change and the industry is falling behind in its grasp of what is happening. In any event, we are likely to see a radical transformation in the practice of public affairs in Europe, to the extent that the public affairs industry will be un-recognizable in ten years' time. (Titley, 2003: 85)

The elections in the United States, especially the 2004 campaign of Howard Dean, support a similar theme that is spelled out in the Titley (2003) article, which is that the change that will dominate politics in the future does not rest necessarily with the elites in the formal political institutions, but with the power of public opinion. Specifically, in the case of the 2004 US presidential election, the candidacy of Howard Dean documented the fund-raising ability of a virtual unknown, and without the

consent of the political elites in the Democratic Party. Through innovative use of the internet, Dean was able to raise money from millions of small donors who allowed him to lead all other competitors going into the start of the primary season. However, after losing the Iowa caucus, it became clear that even extraordinary fund-raising ability was not enough to make him successful, and he subsequently lost the nomination to John Kerry. This is in stark contrast to the large sums of money that President Bush was able to raise in his bid to get re-elected in 2004. The President relied on the funds from lobbyists who represented corporations that the Bush administration supported during his tenure with favorable legislation. The case for less reliance on political party ideology (Newman, 2001a, 2001b) is well made and sheds light on the need for models of citizen/voter choice behavior that can be used to understand and respond to the needs and wants of citizens in an effort to affect public opinion. As Titley (2003) makes the case for the movement from rational-based campaigns designed around few political actors to value-based arguments targeted to many political actors, it is necessary to begin to develop and adapt models that have been historically used by political marketers for use in the public affairs industry.

As we have witnessed in the United States, the Howard Dean candidacy proved that it is possible for any interested party that represents a particular ideology to have an impact on public opinion. This same technology will enable corporations to work with both the elite political actors and the citizenry to impact the development of legislation, and not be put in a position to respond to the impact of these same methods being used against corporations by single-issue interest groups. This is where public affairs, lobbying, and political marketing intersect. Instead of relying on public affairs and lobbying as tools for corporations to further their own business and political interests, political marketing will take this discussion a step further by shedding light on how political actors are using political marketing techniques to drive their policy-making and electioneering decisions. Once the decision-making process of politicians and political parties is made more clear in light of the political marketing paradigm shift that has taken place over the past few decades, only then will lobbyists be in a position to understand how to best partner with government to affect their own business and political interests (O'Shaughnessy, 1999).

The ability of public affairs officials to rely on both rational and emotional appeals will mean a better understanding of the political marketing model. As such, it is in the interests of public affairs officials to scrutinize carefully how political marketing has shaped campaigns in recent decades around the world as they compete for more scarce resources from government. An integrated framework of public affairs and political marketing will be necessary to bridge this knowledge gap. Such a framework will fill the vacuum that exists in the public affairs industry today. This will facilitate the interplay between public affairs executives and other stakeholders in the corporation who have a direct impact on public opinion (e.g., product and brand managers, marketing research directors, marketing strategists, and other corporate players who are involved in the marketing process within a corporation).

Since we do live in an era of manufactured images (Newman, 1999c), it will become imperative that public affairs executives and lobbyists understand the tools by which organizations and individuals can shape and manufacture images in the commercial and political marketplaces.

A STRATEGIC FRAMEWORK FOR LOBBYISTS

The basic premise behind the strategic framework for lobbyists stems from the political marketing literature that emphasizes the importance of first understanding the needs and wants of the voters before establishing a campaign platform as a candidate or sitting politician (Cwalina et al., 2011; Newman, 1994, 1999a, 1999b, 1999c; Newman and Verčič, 2003). To the lobbyist, it is imperative that there be a very clear understanding of both the politician and his/her constituency. With this in mind, the following framework puts forward four different components that allow the lobbyists the ability to draw a political profile for the party or politician before embarking on strategy development.

If we take the strategic framework for lobbyists presented in Figure 11.2, several similarities to the 'theory of political choice behavior' emerge.

Ideological Posture

This component reflects the issues and policies that a political party or politician supports on a philosophical level. The lobbyist will be interested in measuring the specific issues and policies that reflect the ideological orientation of the party/politician. This component is measured by a number of statements about the issues and policies that either are of interest to the party/politician or will have a direct impact on the success of that person or party in an upcoming election:

Please indicate whether you agree or disagree that each of the following issues is important to you:

I believe my party/candidacy requires me to:

1 Increase health care benefits.
2 Reduce taxes for corporations.
3 Etc.

The list of 'hypothetical' issues is determined with qualitative research that is pertinent to the party/politician at the point in time when the lobbyist is seeking to get their support.

Emotional Commitment

This component reflects the personal commitment that a party or politician has towards

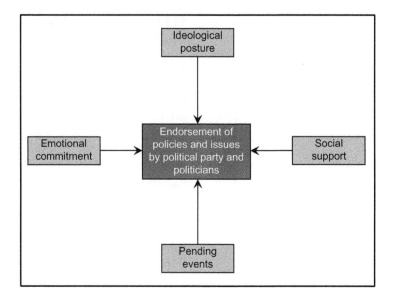

Figure 11.2:   Strategic framework for lobbyists

a particular segment of voters or supporters, as well as his/her own personal emotional attachment to specific issues or policies that can ostensibly help an interested organization (both profit and non-profit). This component is measured by identifying a list of feelings that reflect the party/politician's commitment to the group or issue:

> Parties and politicians support certain groups in society as well as specific issues for many personal and political reasons. Please indicate whether you experience any of the feelings I have listed below in your support of the following groups of people and issues:
>
> *I support the following issue because:*
>
> 1   I am fulfilling my promise to ...
> 2   Standing up for the rights of ... is important to me.
> 3   Etc.

The lobbyist will fill in the issue that is important to the organization that he/she is representing. The list of 'voter/interest groups' is determined with qualitative research that is pertinent to the party/politician at the point in time when the lobbyist is seeking to get their support.

Social Support

This component reflects the support that a party/politician receives from a segment of voters, an interest group, a political action committee, or any other significant group of people who could influence the decision of a party or individual politician. This component takes into consideration the importance that a group of people has on the development of the image of the party/politician. However, this goes beyond the simple stereotyping of the party/politician to address the support that the group gives to a party/politician in the form of money or a volunteer network at election time. A political party or individual politician may choose to seek the support of various groups of people to manufacture an image in the minds of voters on the basis of the association of these groups to the party/politician. This component is measured by identifying a list of groups of voters/interest groups/PACs and determining how likely it is that each group supports the party/politician in some capacity.

> In this section, I have listed a number of groups of people who are likely to be supportive of party X/ politician Y. For *each* group of people, I'd like to know which you think is most or least likely to support the party/politician with money or volunteer help:
>
> 1 National Rifle Association.
> 2 Democrats.
> 3 Republicans.
> 4 Elderly citizens.
> 5 Etc.

The lobbyist will fill in the groups that are important to the organization that he/she is representing. The list of 'voter/interest groups' is determined with qualitative research that is pertinent to the party/ politician at the point in time when the lobbyist is seeking to get their support.

Pending Events

This component represents the impact of events in the world and in the specific country of the party/politician that will have a temporary impact on the voting record of the party/politician. This component is measured by listing a number of 'hypothetical events' that might influence the party/ politician to support a specific issue or group of people:

> Certain conditions motivate parties/politicians to behave differently than their voting record might indicate. Do you believe that the following situations would influence you to switch your support for issue X/group Y?
>
> *I would switch my support for issue X if I knew:*
>
> 1 I would lose an upcoming election.
> 2 I could attract more voters.
> 3 My party leadership would stop supporting my causes.

STRATEGIC IMPLICATIONS OF THE FRAMEWORK

The strategic framework for lobbyists can be used to identify the specific appeals that are laid out for the politician to use in an effort to get legislation passed in Congress (in the United States), in Parliament (in the United Kingdom), or in any other political body that decides on which laws are passed in a country. This often means that a politician will have to rely on standard marketing research methods to identify the needs and wants of citizens as well as the thinking of the politician to better position the ideas of the politician.

In politics, market segmentation has been traditionally used by political parties and politicians to target specific messages to different segments of people (Baines, 1999; Cwalina et al., 2009, 2011). For example, during the 2004 US presidential race, on the Democratic side, Howard Dean realized early on that Democrat voters were very angry about President Bush's decision to invade Iraq. With that knowledge, Dean set out to separate himself from the rest of the candidates running for the Democratic nomination by making his feelings on the war the centerpiece of his campaign. That market segmentation strategy worked quite well until the voters in the early primaries decided that they wanted not only a candidate who cared about that issue but someone who was electable. Ultimately, the segment of voters who supported Howard Dean began to slip away because of his loss in the Iowa caucus and the increasing importance of electability in the campaign.

There were of course other voter segments casting ballots in the Democratic primaries. There were the voters who might have voted for Bush and supported his initial efforts in Iraq, but became more disillusioned over time as the media began to run stories on the absence of intelligence to support the idea that Iraq had weapons of mass destruction. These voters may have participated in the open primaries where states allow voters from either one of the two major parties to vote. Another segment could have consisted of voters who had lost their jobs since President Bush entered the White House, and were looking for a candidate who looked like he/she was able to restore the lost jobs in the country. We could of course list other segments, but the key point is that each of these segments represents a different group of voters who are looking for something different in a President.

Once the multiple voter segments have been identified, the candidate has to position him/herself in the marketplace. Positioning is a multi-stage process that begins with a politician making a determination of his/her own strengths and weaknesses as well as his/her opponents' strengths and weaknesses. The key elements here include: (1) creating an image of the candidate that emphasizes the individual's particular personality traits, and (2) developing and presenting a clear position on the country's economic and social issues. These elements may be used jointly for positioning politicians via policies on issues or via image and emotions. The goal of message development is to set and establish the campaign platform. It evolves over the course of the permanent political campaign (during both the election period and the governing period). The campaign platform is defined in terms of candidate leadership, image, and the issues and policies the candidate advocates. It is influenced by several factors, including the candidate, the lobbyist, and, most important, the voters. The manufacturing of an image is carried out in the media by emphasizing certain personality traits of the candidate, as well as stressing various issues (Newman, 1999c). For example, during the 2000 US presidential campaign, George W. Bush realized that as a perceived outsider to Washington, he was in a good position to criticize the system which the incumbent (Bill Clinton) had governed for the previous eight years. Similarly, Howard Dean's appeal initially centered around the same message, namely that he

was an outsider to Washington, DC, and was not contaminated by the influential people and organizations who affect the governing process.

Interest groups also engage in agenda setting (i.e., in making the issue salient and important) and framing campaigns in order to influence the way the public and decision makers prioritize and conceptualize policy issues (e.g., Baumgartner, 2009; Cwalina et al., 2015; Lakoff, 2009). Framing, as defined by Entman (2007: 164), is the 'process of culling a few elements of perceived reality and assembling a narrative that highlights connections among them to promote a particular interpretation'. Therefore, framing refers to subtle alterations in the statement or presentation of judgments or choice problems, and framing effects refer to changes in decision outcomes resulting from these alterations. Interest groups tailor their frames in order to realize numerous goals: they consider how their frames will resonate with the public, members of the media, and politicians (Gerrity, 2010). According to McGrath (2007: 278), 'what lobbyists seek to do when they frame issues is to find a form of words which expresses the policy problem as they see it and suggests the policy solution which they desire'.

The segmentation and positioning of politicians continues after a politician gets into office as the individual and party that he or she represents attempts to appeal to various segments of the population by passing legislation that is favorable to one group over another.

The key issue arises as to the use of the strategic lobbying framework to enable a political party or politician to more effectively segment and position the image and platform of the person or party. The framework presented in this chapter puts the party/ politician in a position to make a determination with respect to the marketing strategy that should be used to influence public opinion. The lobbyist can use the strategic framework to collect information on the thinking of the politicians and voters to determine how best to position the message a politician/party sends to the multiple segments that need to be addressed. These multiple segments include: the Congress (or Parliament if it is the United Kingdom); selected segments of citizens; leaders of influential interest groups; other political leaders who will be influential in passing legislation; the media who will report on the efforts of the lobbyist and the organization he or she represents; governments in other countries who have a vested interest in the passing of legislation; and of course the sitting government which stands to either benefit or be hurt by the legislation.

REFERENCES

Andrews, L. (1996). The relationship of political marketing to political lobbying: An examination of the Devonport campaign for the Trident refitting contract. *European Journal of Marketing*, 30(10/11), 68–91.

Baines, P.R. (1999). Voter segmentation and candidate positioning. In B.I. Newman (Ed.), *Handbook of Political Marketing* (pp. 403–20). Thousand Oaks, CA: Sage.

Baumgartner, F.R. (2009). Interest groups and agendas. In L.S. Maisel and J.M. Berry (Eds.), *Oxford Handbook of American Political Parties and Interest Groups* (pp. 519–33). New York: Oxford University Press.

Baumgartner, F.R. and Leech, B.L. (2001). Interest niches and policy bandwagons: Patterns of interest group involvement in national politics. *Journal of Politics*, 63(4), 1191–213.

Ben-Ur, J. and Newman, B.I. (2010). A marketing poll: An innovative approach to prediction, explanation and strategy. *European Journal of Marketing*, 44(3/4), 515–38.

Bergan, D. and Risner, G. (2012). The power of citizen-group public-policy advertising: Messages don't need third-party validation to increase salience among pockets of voters. *Journal of Advertising Research*, 52(4), 405–20.

Butler, P. and Collins, N. (1999). A conceptual framework for political marketing. In B.I.

Newman (Ed.), *Handbook of Political Marketing* (pp. 55–72). Thousand Oaks, CA: Sage.

Campbell, A., Converse, P.E., Miller, W.E. and Stokes, D.E. (1960). *The American Voter*. New York: John Wiley & Sons.

Cwalina, W. and Falkowski, A. (2015). Political branding: Political candidates positioning based on inter-object associative affinity index. *Journal of Political Marketing*, 14(1–2), 152–74.

Cwalina, W., Falkowski, A. and Newman, B.I. (2008). *A Cross-Cultural Theory of Voter Behavior*. New York: Haworth Press/Taylor & Francis Group.

Cwalina, W., Falkowski, A. and Newman, B.I. (2009). Political management and marketing. In D.W. Johnson (Ed.), *Routledge Handbook of Political Management* (pp. 67–80). New York: Routledge.

Cwalina, W., Falkowski, A. and Newman, B.I. (2011). *Political Marketing: Theoretical and Strategic Foundations*. Armonk, NY: M.E. Sharpe.

Cwalina, W., Falkowski, A. and Newman, B.I. (2012). The macro and micro views of political marketing: The underpinnings of a theory of political marketing. *Journal of Public Affairs*, 12(4), 254–69.

Cwalina, W., Falkowski, A. and Newman, B.I. (2015). Persuasion in the political context: Opportunities and threats. In D.W. Stewart (Ed.), *Handbook of Persuasion and Social Marketing, Volume 1*, (pp. 61–128). Santa Barbara, CA: Praeger.

Cwalina, W., Falkowski, A. and Newman, B.I. (2016). Political marketing: The multidisciplinary approach. In W.L. Benoit (Ed.), *Praeger handbook of political campaigning in the United States, Volume 1: Foundations and campaign media* (pp. 101–119). Santa Barbara, CA: Praeger.

Davies, P.J. and Newman, B.I. (Eds.) (2006). *Winning Elections with Political Marketing*. New York: The Haworth Press.

Entman, R.M. (2007). Framing bias: Media in the distribution of power. *Journal of Communication*, 57(1), 163–73.

Gerrity, J.C. (2010). Building a framing campaign: Interest groups and the debate on partial-birth abortion. In B.F. Schaffner and P.J. Sellers (Eds.), *Winning with Words: The*

Origins and Impact of Political Framing (pp. 60–77). New York: Routledge.

Gouliamos, K., Theocharous, A. and Newman, B.I. (Eds.) (2013). *Political Marketing: Strategic Campaign Culture*. New York: Routledge.

Grier, K.E., Munger, M.C. and Roberts, B.E. (1994). The determinants of industry political activity, 1978–1986. *American Political Science Review*, 88(4), 911–26.

Harris, P. (2001). Machiavelli, political marketing and reinventing government. *European Journal of Marketing*, 35(9/10), 1136–1154.

Harris, P., Lock, A. and Roberts, N. (1999). Limitations of political marketing? A content analysis of press coverage of political issues during the 1997 U.K. general election campaign. In B.I. Newman (Ed.), *Handbook of Political Marketing* (pp. 539–58). Thousand Oaks, CA: Sage.

Harris, P. and McGrath, C. (2012). Political marketing and lobbying: A neglected perspective and research agenda. *Journal of Political Marketing*, 11(1–2), 75–94.

Herrnson, P.S. and Campbell, C.C. (2009). Modern political campaigns in the United States. In D.W. Johnson (Ed.), *Routledge Handbook of Political Management*, (pp. 11–23). New York: Routledge.

Johnson, D.W. (1999). The cyberspace election of the future. In B.I. Newman (Ed.), *Handbook of Political Marketing* (pp. 705–24). Thousand Oaks, CA: Sage.

Kotler, P. and Kotler, N. (1999). Political marketing. Generating effective candidates, campaigns, and causes. In B.I. Newman (Ed.), *Handbook of Political Marketing* (pp. 3–18). Thousand Oaks, CA: Sage.

Lakoff, G. (2009). *The Political Mind: A Cognitive Scientist's Guide to Your Brain and its Politics*. New York: Penguin Books.

Lazarsfeld, P., Berelson, B. and Gaudet, H. (1944). *The Peoples Choice: How the Voter Makes up His Mind in a Presidential Campaign*. New York: Columbia University Press.

Magleby, D.B. (Ed.) (2002). *Financing the 2001 Election*. Washington, DC: Brookings Institution Press.

McGrath, C. (2006). Grass roots lobbying: Marketing politics and policy "beyond the beltway". In P.J. Davies and B.I. Newman (Eds.), *Winning Elections with Political Marketing* (pp. 105–130). New York: The Haworth Press.

McGrath, C. (2007). Framing lobbying messages: Defining and communicating political issues persuasively. *Journal of Public Affairs*, 7(3), 269–80.

Mitchell, N.J., Hansen, W.L. and Jepsen, E.M. (1997). The determinants of domestic and foreign corporate political activity. *Journal of Politics*, 59(4), 1096–113.

Newman, B.I. (1981). The Prediction and Explanation of Actual Voting Behavior in a Presidential Primary Election. Unpublished doctoral dissertation, University of Illinois at Urbana-Champaign.

Newman, B.I. (1994). *The Marketing of the President: Political Marketing as Campaign Strategy*. Thousand Oaks, CA: Sage.

Newman, B.I. (1999a). A predictive model of voter behavior: The repositioning of Bill Clinton. In B.I. Newman (Ed.), *Handbook of Political Marketing* (pp. 259–82). Thousand Oaks, CA: Sage.

Newman, B.I. (Ed.) (1999b). *Handbook of Political Marketing*. Thousand Oaks, CA: Sage.

Newman, B.I. (1999c). *The Mass Marketing of Politics: Democracy in an Age of Manufactured Images*. Thousand Oaks, CA: Sage.

Newman, B.I. (2001a). An assessment of the 2000 US Presidential election: A set of political marketing guidelines. *Journal of Public Affairs*, I(3), 210–16.

Newman, B.I. (2001b). Image manufacturing in the United States: Recent US Presidential Elections and beyond. *European Journal of Marketing*, 35(9–10), 966–70.

Newman, B.I. (2002a). The role of marketing in politics. *Journal of Political Marketing*, I(I), 1–5.

Newman, B.I. (2002b). Broadening the boundaries of marketing: Political marketing in New Millennium. *Psychology and Marketing*, 19(12), 983–6.

Newman, B.I. (2016). *The Marketing Revolution in Politics: What Recent U.S. Presidential Campaigns Can Teach Us about Effective Marketing*. Toronto, Canada: Rotman-University of Toronto Press.

Newman, B.I. and Perloff, R. (2004). Political marketing: Theory, research, and applications. In L.L. Kaid (Ed.), *Handbook of Political*

Communication Research (pp. 17–43). Thousand Oaks, CA: Sage.

Newman, B.I. and Sheth, J.N. (1985a). A model of primary voter behavior. *Journal of Consumer Research*, 12(2), 178–87.

Newman, B.I. and Sheth, J.N. (1985b). *Political Marketing: Readings and Annotated Bibliography*. Chicago, IL: American Marketing Association.

Newman, B.I. and Sheth, J.N. (1987). *A Theory of Political Choice Behavior*. New York: Praeger.

Newman, B.I. and Verčič, D. (Eds) (2003). *Communication of Politics: Cross-Cultural Theory Building in the Practice of Public Relations and Political Marketing*. New York: Haworth Press.

O'Shaughnessy, N. (1990). High priesthood, low priestcraft: The role of political consultants. *European Journal of Marketing*, 24(2), 7–23.

O'Shaughnessy, N.T. (1999). Political marketing and political propaganda. In B.I. Newman (Ed.), *Handbook of Political Marketing* (pp. 725–40). Thousand Oaks, CA: Sage.

Perloff, R.M. (1999). Elite, popular, and merchandised politics: Historical origins of presidential campaign marketing. In B.I. Newman (Ed.), *Handbook of Political Marketing* (pp. 19–40). Thousand Oaks, CA: Sage.

Reyes, G.M. (2006). The Swift Boat Veterans for Truth, the politics of realism, and the manipulation of Vietnam remembrance in the 2004 presidential election. *Rhetoric and Public Affairs*, 9(4), 571–600.

Scholzman, K.L., Verba, S. and Brady, H.E. (2012). *The Unheavenly Chorus: Unequal Political Voice and the Broken Promise of American Democracy*. Princeton, NJ: Princeton University Press.

Smith, G. (2005). Positioning political parties: The 2005 UK general election. *Journal of Marketing Management*, 21(9), 1135–49.

Smith, R.A. (1995). Interest group influence in the U.S. Congress. *Legislative Studies Quarterly*, 20(1), 89–139.

Snyder, J.M. (1992). Long-term investing in politicians; or, give early, give often. *Journal of Law & Economics*, 35(1), 15–43.

Titley, S. (2003). How political and social change will transform the EU public affairs industry. *Journal of Public Affairs*, 53(l), 85–9.

Williams, C.B. and Newman, B.I. (Eds.) (2013). *Political Marketing in Retrospective and Prospective*. New York: Routledge.

Wring, D. (1999). The marketing colonization of political campaigning. In B.I. Newman (Ed.), *Handbook of Political Marketing* (pp. 41–54). Thousand Oaks, CA: Sage.

The Practice of Public Affairs in Public Administration

Mordecai Lee

DOES PUBLIC AFFAIRS INCLUDE ITS PRACTICE BY GOVERNMENT?

The field of public affairs initially emerged with a focus primarily on its practice in the business sector, secondarily in the non-governmental organization (NGO) sector, and with only modest attention to its practice within the public sector. For example, the 2010 survey of the field by McGrath et al. (2010) focused largely on the literature's application to for-profit organizations. Similarly, a large proportion of articles in the *Journal of Public Affairs* (*JPA*) were about businesses. The contents of the first edition of this *Handbook* focused mostly on the corporate world and, to a lesser extent, NGOs (Harris and Fleisher, 2005). Given that a key focus of public affairs is government relations, then by definition does that mean government doesn't conduct relations with itself and therefore the public sector should be excluded from the field of public affairs?

On the other hand, *JPA* has routinely published articles relating to public affairs in the public sector. This conveyed that the generic scope of public affairs as a field of inquiry could be viewed as extending to governmental agencies as well (for example, Heinze et al., 2013; Laursen and Valentini, 2013; Alaimo, 2016), even if not primarily or at the same level of interest as the business sector. Hence, the important signal by the editors of this new edition of the *Handbook* to include an initial exploration of public affairs as it applies to the public sector. It is hoped that this recognition will contribute gradually to a common perception that public affairs is a pan-sectoral enterprise, not ghettoized to the business sector (and, somewhat less, to NGOs).

Still, government is different. Different from what? From the corporate sector and NGOs. The differences and similarities need to be identified in order to clarify if public affairs is applicable to the public sector and, if applicable, how practiced. One approach, embodied in the discipline of organization theory, tends to view all large modern organizations as more similar than different, such as in management, structure, performance measurement, strategic planning, IT, reporting, accountability, operational vs. functional activities (earlier called line vs. staff), and headquarters vs. field. Accepting this premise, then public affairs would be universal to all sectors and largely similar wherever practiced. In that sense, the sectoral affiliation of the organization engaging in public affairs would be a minor distinction.

From the opposite perspective, Sayre quipped that 'business and public administration are alike only in all unimportant respects' (1958: 245). This gets to the heart of the *qualitative* difference between business and government. A for-profit business has owners who hold stock in it. These owners receive payments as their prorated share of the company's profits and they vote in elections of members to the board of directors. Corporations generally operate in a competitive or regulated marketplace. Profits and long-term survival are measures of success. (NGOs usually have no owners and are self-perpetuating. No financial benefits inure to, for example, its members (unless it's a cooperative). If a nonprofit is ever liquidated, its assets do not accrue to any individuals.) In contrast, a government agency is owned by the public-at-large, is accountable to elected officials, generally has a social purpose, and has a basic duty to serve the public interest. Government agencies usually have a monopoly on the service they provide and, hence, do not have a competitive marketplace they need to survive in. Deaths of government agencies are relatively rare. Finally, governments can force citizens to do or not do something. There are penalties for noncompliance, including incarceration and fines. Corporations and NGOs have no such power.

Bannister identified at least 19 generic characteristics which were mandatory values in public administration compared

to business (2010: 42). For example, for the American national government, Congress has enacted about 75 general management laws, which circumscribe and control in great detail the operations of all federal agencies (Wamsley, 2004: 226–8). These constraints and limitations are as inherent to public administration as they are abhorrent to business administration.

Flowing from the distinctions between the corporate world and government are some obvious implications for the practice of public affairs. For example, by definition, government agencies would not have a mission of *corporate* social responsibility (CSR), if only because they are not corporations. More substantively, social responsibility is indivisible from the *raison d'être* of public administration to serve the public interest. Similarly, the duty of transparency is obligatory in public administration (with some understandable exceptions) and wholly nonexistent as a legal obligation or conventional practice in the corporate world. At most, NGOs are expected to be somewhat translucent, but this is usually not a duty imposed by law. Another example of the implications of differences between business and public administration is the role of public reporting (Lee, 2002). Government agencies have a proactive obligation to report on their activities to the citizenry, while the legal obligation of corporations to report externally tends to be limited to its shareholders and regulators.

After surveying communication professionals in the public and private sectors, Liu et al. (2010: 211) documented that the fields of practice were distinctly different. They concluded that given the significant variations they found in sector-based practices, 'it is time for communication scholars to catch up' with further research premised on those intersectoral differences.

Given these differences in business and government management, and their impact on public affairs, how – if at all – does a researcher identify this more specific enterprise of public affairs in the public sector?

PUBLIC AFFAIRS AS AN ELEMENT OF PUBLIC ADMINISTRATION

For public affairs in the public sector, what's in and what's out? Before examining the practice of public affairs in government, there is an important distinction to make about boundaries. Politics and elections, of course, are in the public sector. While they are fascinating and have perennial appeal to the media, that is not the entirety of the public sector. Rather, the *bulk* of the public sector – whether measured in staffing, spending, or other standard metrics of modern organizations – is outside politics. It is in the other major segment of the public sector: public administration. This is the world of civil servants, permanent employees of the government, whose salaries are funded by taxpayers (and other coerced payments such as fees), and who hold office permanently, *regardless of election results*. Based on the early template set by the British tradition of civil service, these employees are – at least theoretically – recruited, selected, hired, promoted, compensated, and fired based on merit. Therefore, it follows that the bulk of public affairs activities in the public sector are in public administration, not in politics.

Modern Western democracies are dominated by large government agencies implementing the programs and public policies formally and legally enacted by elected officials, usually those comprising the legislative institution. In parliamentary systems, the government in power (usually called prime minister and cabinet) is rooted in parliament itself, reflecting a majority membership of the parliament (sometimes one party, sometimes a coalition of parties). The American template wholly separates the legislative branch from the leadership of the executive branch, with the President and his/her administration not being members of Congress. The French model is something of a mix of both, given the role of a separately elected President vis-à-vis the traditional parliamentary system, including a prime minister. There are, of course, other variations.

Regardless of the precise structure of the legislative body in modern Western democracy, the commonality is that authoritatively enacted policies, once adopted, are usually handed off to the bureaucracy to implement. Yes, the heads of these agencies are often political appointees who are part of the governing coalition, but their power over the permanent civil servants of their agency is sometimes tenuous to modest. Ministers come and go, the bureaucracy is there forever.

Sometimes these agencies are the direct deliverers of public services, sometimes the contractors for other organizations to do so. Regardless, these bureaucracies are an important, but often overlooked and overshadowed component of the public sector compared to the excitement of politics. While bureaucracies can be, and are, dominant in nondemocratic countries (such as China and Russia) as well, the focus here is on the practice of public affairs in democratically based public administration. Why? Because a central function of public affairs is responsiveness and sensitivity to the public in general and to autonomous elected lawmakers in particular. Stating it a bit baldly, in an authoritarian political system, public administration does not need to engage in sophisticated public affairs. It needs only to be responsive to the dictator. That is an in-house activity. On the other hand, public affairs is inherently an out-of-house oriented activity due to the nature of democracy and, especially, elected legislatures.

Hence, the premise of this chapter is twofold: that public affairs exists in the public sector as well as in the corporate and NGO sectors and that the bulk of public sector public affairs takes place within public administration, rather than in the relatively separate realm of politics and elections.

A limitation to providing a literature review of public sector public affairs is that much of the research literature on this general subject is geo-centric and country specific. This is understandable due to variations in governmental structures by nation and by a tendency of some writers to be more interested in their own country than in international generalizations. As a mild antidote to that tendency, while the next two sections focus on American practice, they are followed by a section on the (English language) literature regarding public relations (PR) as a component of public affairs from scholars based in Western Europe and elsewhere.

AMERICAN NOMENCLATURE AND PRACTICE

The contemporary academic subject of public affairs is generally treated in the literature as encompassing external communication aimed at publics and at governmental decision-makers, such as lawmakers. However, as used in the US, public affairs tend to have two other common meanings, which are quite different from the nomenclature used in the literature.

First, public affairs is often used as a synonym for public administration and other aspects of government. Many universities have schools of public affairs, which offer degrees in public affairs, public policy, and public administration. The credentialing association for these schools and training programs is the Network of Schools of Public Policy, Affairs, and Administration. It sponsors an academic peer-review journal called *Journal of Public Affairs Education*. Hence, the subject of this chapter could lightheartedly be described as the practice of public affairs in public affairs.

A second American usage of public affairs is as a synonym for PR and other external communications programs by government agencies. For example, it is common in the federal government for each cabinet department to have a subcabinet level assistant secretary for public affairs. Similarly, most of the larger executive branch agencies outside the cabinet (usually called independent agencies) have an Office of Public Affairs or some

variation on that term. This usage emerged as a way to lower the visibility of the practice of PR in the American public sector because politicians tended to be hostile to the concept of PR in public administration (Lee, 2011a). Such a negative view of government PR is not limited to the US and is relatively common, such as in Australia (Glenny, 2008). Therefore, another breezy title of the subject of this chapter could be the practice of public affairs as a component of public affairs.

(*Note to readers*: To avoid confusion between this American usage and the general academic and professional subject matter of this *Handbook*, hereafter all discussions of the latter will be referred to as generic public affairs. Absent that qualifier, the meaning will be based on American usage, namely PR in public administration.)

The political hostility to PR in public administration is oddly counter-balanced by legislators' enthusiasm for a robust legislative relations apparatus by the same department. Based on the literature, one could almost say (without one's tongue too firmly in cheek) that the US Congress never met a budget for a federal agency's PR which was too low nor a budget for legislative liaison which was too high (Lee, 2009).

Given such confusing usages and political perspectives, the subject matter of this chapter could be called public sector public affairs, governmental public affairs, or public affairs in public administration.

THE US CONGRESS DEFINES AND DEBATES GOVERNMENTAL PUBLIC AFFAIRS, 2011–2012

Assistant Secretaries for Legislative Relations and PR in the President's Subcabinet

By the beginning of the twenty-first century, nearly all cabinet departments had an assistant secretary for public affairs and, separately, an assistant secretary for legislative relations (Lee, 2008a, 2011b). These officials were members of the President's subcabinet and therefore, part of the administration. Even though subcabinet positions are, by definition, of lesser importance and power than cabinet positions, all presidential appointments to the cabinet and subcabinet required the same process for confirmation by the US Senate. Officials nominated by the President could not take office before and until approved by a vote of the Senate.

Hence, presidential appointments to these two assistant secretaryships involved in generic public affairs required approval by the US Senate. As all other subcabinet officers, this process entailed extensive paperwork (including an FBI background and security check), a public hearing by a standing committee to examine the appointee and hear other testimony pro and con, then a committee vote, then a vote on the floor of the Senate.

In 2011–12, the US Congress considered *de novo* the long-standing approach requiring all presidential appointments to be reviewed in depth by the Senate and subject to a confirmation vote. Were all nominations equal in importance and thus requiring such a detailed confirmation process? In that context, where did generic public affairs rank? Were assistant secretaries for PR and Congressional liaison as important as other assistant secretaries? If not, *how* much less? Furthermore, were the two assistant secretaryships equal in importance to each other?

During the Clinton and Bush presidencies, there had been increased partisanship toward their nominations for major offices, including the cabinet, subcabinet, and senior positions in independent agencies. When the majority in the Senate was held by the party other than the President's, appointments took increasingly long periods of time before a confirmation vote. This was viewed by the opposition party as a way of undermining the effectiveness of a president's administration. Such tactics were exacerbated during President

Obama's first term, when the minority Republicans in the Senate used parliamentary procedure and dilatory tactics, including the need for 60 votes (of 100, called cloture), to prevent or delay floor votes on presidential nominations.

Finally, a group of moderate Senators from both parties concluded that the appointment process had indeed become dysfunctional. Given their partisan perspectives on what the problem was, there were only a few proposed reforms they could agree on. One was that there were too many executive officers requiring Senate confirmation. This clogged up the system and prevented in-depth consideration of major appointments, which all could agree were truly important. The question was which offices were not as important as, say, Secretary of Defense or Under Secretary of the Treasury, the second highest official in that department?

For this aspect of the problem, attention quickly focused on the C-suite found in nearly every federal department or independent agency, such as chief information officer, chief financial officer, inspector general, and chief human capital officer. These offices were usually at the assistant secretarial level. To become an assistant secretary, each office required nomination by the President and confirmation by the Senate, the identical process as major appointments.

Proposed Bill

After several false starts in earlier Congresses, in 2011, Senators from both parties introduced a Bill (called S. 679, meaning the 679th Bill introduced in the Senate during that two-year session of Congress) to cut significantly the number of nominations requiring Senate confirmation. Their list of offices no longer requiring *any* Senate confirmation included all assistant secretaryships relating to legislative affairs and public affairs. Instead, the President would appoint people to be assistant secretaries of public affairs and

Congressional relations directly. No Senate consideration or confirmation would be required. Nominees would take office immediately upon the President's appointment.

Explaining the rationale of the Bill, one of its senior sponsors said 'many of these positions have little or no policy role, such as the Assistant Secretary for Legislative Affairs at the Department of Commerce ... or assistant secretaries for public affairs' (*Congressional Record* [henceforth *CR*], 30 March 2011, S1990). Here was a significant political perspective deeming the federal practice of generic public affairs (comprising both legislative relations and PR) as relatively minor in the universe of federal power. The Bill was referred to the Committee on Homeland Security and Governmental Affairs. It recommended the Bill for passage, stating that the Bill would only eliminate the requirement of Senate confirmation for 'non-policymaking or lower level positions' including all 'legislative and public affairs positions' (US Senate, 2011: 6–7).

Senate Floor Debate

The debate on the floor of the Senate over the merits of the Bill presents an unusual opportunity for analysis. Typically, American legislation is vertical, in the sense that it usually deals with one department or agency (or a small handful) at a time. Hence, the annual appropriations Bills for small passels of agencies is a way for Congress to impose its will on a retail basis, agency by agency. This proposed legislation in 2011 was unusual in that it was horizontal, affecting all cabinet departments equally. This meant the debate would be wholesale, about the generic nature and importance of all similar positions throughout the executive branch. Therefore, the debate provides a real world political perspective on how federal legislators viewed the practice of generic public affairs, whether by assistant secretaries for legislative relations or assistant secretaries for public affairs.

The Bill came up for debate on the floor of the Senate in June 2011. Explaining and summarizing the version of the Bill approved by the Committee, its major co-sponsors were at pains to justify exempting assistant secretaryships in public affairs and legislation relations from any Senate confirmation. One said that most of the offices to be removed from Senate confirmation were merely 'in the areas of legislative and public affairs, [and] internal management positions' (*CR*, 22 June 2011, S3996). In other words, they viewed the practice of generic public affairs in the federal government as a relatively ministerial activity, little more than messengers of information, whether aimed at the public-at-large or at the legislative branch. These were errand boys and girls. It was a striking declaration of the relative importance of generic public affairs in government. Most importantly, the assertion was that these assistant secretaries did not make policy or even participate in the policymaking process.

Not everyone agreed. The conservative Heritage Foundation quickly issued a report criticizing this viewpoint (along with several other features of the Bill). Assistant secretaries for Congressional relations were important positions because 'both the executive branch and the Congress rely [on them] to ensure clear and accurate communications and smooth interaction between the executive branch and Congress'. Similarly, Congress relies on assistant secretaries for public affairs 'to ensure truthful explanations to the public of what goes on in executive departments' (Addington, 2011: 2, note 5). These arguments resonated with some conservative Senators. James DeMint (R-SC) quickly submitted an amendment to the Bill to retain the requirement of Senate confirmation to both assistant secretaryships (Amendment 511, *CR*, 22 June 2011, S4008).

Fellow conservative Orrin Hatch (R-UT) concurred with DeMint. In particular, Hatch's view was propelled by the fierce feudalism of the Senate's entrenched committee system, especially their respective jurisdictions.

Hatch was the ranking minority member of the Finance Committee. The Committee's empire included aspects of the Department of Health and Human Services (HHS) and the Treasury Department. Eliminating the requirement of Senate confirmation for assistant secretaries for legislative relations and public affairs would diminish the power of the Committee, which Hatch hoped someday to be chair of (if, as a result of a national election, his party became the majority party in the Senate). Hatch injected a particularly partisan tone to his position, linking it to the controversial Affordable Care Act (aka Obamacare), which had been enacted in the preceding session of Congress. Criticizing the implementation of the Act and calling for its repeal was a major plank of the Republican agenda at the time. Hatch pointed out the role that the two assistant HHS secretaries were playing in the rollout of the new law. 'In light of the controversial passage, and now implementation, of Obamacare, does it really make sense to relinquish direct oversight over the Assistant Secretary of Legislation?' Similarly, he noted that 'some Members of this body have been concerned with how HHS has publicly discussed health care reform and have taken issue with the accuracy of information provided to the public' (*CR*, 22 June 2011, S4015). Therefore, he argued, it was equally important to retain Senate confirmation of the HHS assistant secretary for public affairs, too.

Hatch's jurisdictional parochialism crossed party lines. Committee chair Max Baucus (D-MT) and Hatch sent a jointly signed letter of protest to the Committee which had recommended the Bill. The Committee on Homeland Security and Governmental Affairs, they wrote, should not be tinkering with the power of another committee. Using a bipartisan, but committee-centric, tone, they pointed out the importance of assistant secretaries for legislative relations. They

> advise the Secretaries of these agencies on Congressional input to help formulate policy for

their respective agencies. These assistant secretaries serve as Congress' conduit to the Treasury Department and HHS. And they are the primary point of contact for Congressional members and staff, collect Congressional inquiries, and coordinate agency responses. As such, Congress has a direct interest in ensuring that the nominees who fulfill these roles remain accountable to not only the Secretaries of Treasury and HHS, but also to Congress. (*CR*, 22 June 2011, S4016).

Here was an important political and operational description of the role of legislative liaison in the federal government. These were not unimportant positions.

Their joint letter also described the value of assistant PR secretaries. They

> are responsible for communicating to the media and the public information about the myriad policies and programs implemented by these agencies. It is imperative that these assistant secretaries carry out this role in an objective and transparent manner that adequately provides essential information to the public. Given the importance of the media in communicating policy options and shaping public opinion, it is appropriate for the Senate to continue to provide its advice and consent on this position. (S4016)

This position description of the role of PR in government similarly provides a clear statement of the importance of PR in public administration and that these officers were in the policymaking loop, not just automatons transmitting information to the citizenry. While not explicitly mentioned in their letter, accounts of the role of the Assistant Secretary of the Treasury for Public Affairs, Michele Davis, during the Wall Street meltdown in 2008 documented her role as an insider and contributor to policymaking throughout those tense months (Sorkin, 2011: 50, 67, 285–8, 514).

Compromise Proposal

The sponsors of the original Bill felt they had to compromise and address some of these concerns. Generally, good-government and reform legislation has little political sex appeal and is of little interest to the media and voters. Along with the inherent aspect of legislatures which tilt the process in favor of stopping action from happening, this Bill had little momentum and would not be able to overcome all such criticisms. Therefore, they decided to offer what's called a managers' amendment to yield partially to the bipartisan opposition. The amendment treated the two assistant secretaries differently. Assistant secretaries for legislation would continue to require confirmation while assistant secretaries for public affairs would, as originally proposed, no longer require any Senate consideration.

Charles Schumer (D-NY), one of the floor managers of the Bill (from the majority party), explained the rationale for the compromise: 'The Senate should have some say in determining who is going to give information the Senate and others need, but we don't think the public affairs positions should have to go through Senate confirmation. All these spokespeople report to Senate-confirmed individuals, where we have oversight' (*CR*, 29 June 2011, S4175).

DeMint was not placated by half a loaf. He insisted on pursuing his amendment so that the PR assistant secretaries would continue to require Senate confirmation. He argued that those assistant secretaries were in 'public affairs positions that interface on behalf of the public with the administration ... These folks need to be accountable to us and we need to make sure they respond to the American people'. In rebuttal, Susan Collins (R-ME) claimed that 'heaven help us if these public affairs people are making policy. They are not. They are just the messengers' (S4176). DeMint refused to back down and insisted on a roll call vote on his proposed amendment. His amendment was rejected by a vote of 25 to 74. The 25 votes in favor of his amendment were all cast by Republican Senators, while the 75 votes came from Democrats and Republicans. Hatch sided with DeMint while Baucus went along with the majority. The Bill, as amended by the managers' amendment, then passed 79–20 (S4178).

Appearances notwithstanding, the managers had not really accepted the principle that

assistant secretaries for legislative affairs needed a full-blown Senate confirmation process like a cabinet secretary. Their retreat was tactical, even misleading. Later that day, they proposed revising the Senate's internal rules for the new process of presidential nominations (assuming that the Bill would eventually become law). In the new rule, the Senate created a two-tier categorization of appointments requiring confirmation. There would continue to be the traditional confirmation process for major appointees. But for lesser positions, including assistant secretaries for legislative affairs, there would be a truncated procedure to speed up consideration. Such nominations would be referred directly to the Senate floor for a vote instead of to a committee. Unless any Senator objected and insisted on having that nomination go to a committee for full review, the nomination would automatically and quickly come up for a vote on the floor of the Senate. The Senate approved this revision to its rules 89 to 8 (S4208).

By this procedural maneuver, the Senate had created three tiers of presidential appointments. Generic public affairs was not in the top class and not considered very important. But, politically, there was now a distinction between the relative importance of legislative liaison and PR. From now on, assistant secretaries for Congressional relations would receive expedited Senate consideration and, barring an objection by a Senator to a specific nominee, would quickly come up for a floor vote as relatively non-controversial and relatively unimportant. Assistant secretaries for PR were deemed less important than that. They no longer required any Senate consideration and they took office immediately upon the President's appointment.

House of Representatives Floor Debate

There was one last twist to the story of S. 679. Even though the Bill had passed the Senate in June 2011, the House of Representatives did not take it up for more than a year. The Republican-majority House was less interested than the Senate in smoothing out the work of President Obama's administration. Even though the House has no role in the process of confirming presidential nominations, a bill changing the law on nominations did require House assent. (The resolution on revising Senate procedures did not.) Finally, on 31 July 2012, the House took up the Bill (without any routine referral to committee for initial consideration). It is plausible to infer of the delay that House Republicans wanted the new law in place in case their party's presidential nominee, Mitt Romney, would defeat President Obama in the November 2012 election. While it may have not been good for the goose, it would definitely be good for the gander.

The floor manager of the Bill, Jason Chaffetz (R-UT), described the changes to the status quo proposed in the Senate-approved version. Focusing on the principle of in-depth review of important nominations, he said, 'what's most important probably doesn't require Senate confirmation for the Assistant Secretary for Public Affairs'. Nonetheless, Louie Gohmert (R-TX) opposed the Bill. He argued that if any position was no longer important enough for detailed Senate consideration, then 'maybe they're irrelevant and immaterial enough that we can just do away with the positions' (*CR*, 31 July 2012, H5409). The Bill passed the House 261–116. Of the 242 GOP members, about half voted against it (H5448–9).

President Obama signed the Bill on 10 August 2012 (PL 112–166, 126 *Stat.* 1283–95).

In summary, the fight over revising the Senate confirmation process provided an insiders' glimpse into the perspective of national lawmakers on the practice of generic public affairs in federal administration. Neither the senior PR official nor the senior legislative relations official were of the highest importance. These were both lesser-tier roles. The new law demoted both the assistant

secretaries for legislative relations and the assistant secretaries for PR, but the former by one grade, the latter by two. Reflecting a certain degree of self-interest and parochialism, the federal legislative branch deemed Congressional liaison as important enough to continue to require a Senate confirmation vote (albeit through an expedited process), while PR was viewed as a non-policymaking role and therefore required no Senate confirmation at all. The clear political pronouncement was that legislative relations was a second-class position while PR was a third-class office. Here was as explicit a declaration as could be of how lawmakers viewed the relative importance of generic public affairs in government.

PR BY GOVERNMENT AGENCIES: EUROPEAN AND OTHER WESTERN LITERATURE

A common component of generic public affairs in the public sector is the practice of PR. To counterbalance the US-centric focus of the preceding section, there is a rich literature from European-based and other non-US researchers on PR and external communication in government.

As with the earlier discussions of the nomenclature used for generic public affairs in government, similar clarifications are important for this subtopic. First, a reminder that the focus here is on PR in public administration, in other words external communications emanating from permanent government agencies, which are largely staffed by career civil servants. Therefore, the highly interesting subject of political PR, such as elections and campaigns, is a wholly separate subject falling outside the scope of this chapter (Kiousis and Strömbäck, 2014).

Second, the term government communication would logically be assumed to be a synonym for PR in the public sector. Yet some authors have arbitrarily deemed that government communication does not include public administration. Canel and Sanders (2012) oddly, even bizarrely, defined government communication as *excluding* most of public administration. Understandably, they focused on the executive branch of government, viewing external communication activities by legislative and judicial institutions as a qualitatively different activity. Fair enough. However, they also eliminated entities which 'execute politically defined public policies but their primary end is the *provision* or *delivery* of public goods such as health and education'. They limited the focus of government communication to 'prime ministerial or presidential communication as well as mayoral or local and regional government communication' (Canel and Sanders, 2012: 86, emphasis in original). This was no mistake or typo. A year later, they repeated this definition in their international casebook (Sanders and Canel, 2013: 4). This is absurd. Government is not the same as politics. Neither is government synonymous with only elected executive officials and their direct appointees. By their arbitrary delineation, Canel and Sanders excluded the vast bulk of public affairs in the public sector, namely its practice in public administration. Their definition of government communication was tantamount to a subgenus of *political* communication, because they limited it to politicians in office (as opposed to candidates in elections). In a mild exculpation, one chapter of their casebook explicitly included public administration as a locus of government communication (Liu and Levenshus, 2013).

Notwithstanding Canel and Sanders, most academic researchers based in the disciplines variously called PR, mass communication, or communication have commonly used the nomenclature of government communication (or governmen*tal* communication) as including public administration, such as scholars based in the Netherlands and Australia (Vos, 2006; Young, 2007). A policy paper prepared by Ihlen and adopted by the government of Norway used a variation on that, referring to

government information (Ministry of Labor, 2001).

Regrettably, there is no uniform or widely used typology by international researchers for the subdivisions of government PR. Sometimes this is due to the disciplinary home of the writer, trends in terminology, or local usage. These sub-literatures cover a multiplicity of topics, some mutually exclusive, some overlapping.

Media relations is commonly associated with public administration PR. Laursen and Valentini (2013) examined the work of press officers at the EU Council. Using the CSR framework, researchers examined the pressures by the news media on local governments in Spain to release sustainability information (Cuadrado-Ballesteros et al., 2014). Another researcher examined the professionalism of the staff at the Information Division of the UK's Ministry of Defence (Elmer, 2000). From a practitioner perspective, Édes (2000) recounted in his experiences as an EU information professional working with counterparts in new democracies in eastern and central Europe. More recently, three European researchers have proposed a theoretical framework and analytical platform for the increasing importance of media relations in public administration. They called it the mediatization of public bureaucracies (Thorbjørnsrud et al., 2014).

Other non-US researchers have subdivided government PR into slightly different perspectives and subtopics. These include paid government advertising as a public sector counterpart to CSR (Kerr et al., 2008), policy communications (Gelders and Ihlen, 2010), customer orientation (Schedler and Summermatter, 2007), e-government (Van Der Meer et al., 2014) and transparency (Christensen and Lægreid, 2002).

Finally, for historians interested in UK practices, Williams-Thompson's (1951) oft-overlooked memoir recounted his experiences as chief information officer at the Ministry of Supply in 1946–49. Also, two reports on government information activities now serve as helpful historical markers of structures, missions, and proposed reforms in the 1960s and 1970s (Ogilvy-Webb, 1965; Clark, 1970).

The practice of media relations reflects the duty of government agencies to be openly accountable to the public as a means of enhancing democratic governance. These activities often reflect disseminating information for its own sake. In other words, they don't help accomplish the substantive policy mission of an agency. Instead, they contribute to an informed citizenry, the *sine qua non* of democracy. However, separately, public communication can also be motivated by utilitarian purposes that help accomplish a programmatic goal, including responsiveness to clients, increasing the utilization of available services, public education and advertising campaigns (sometimes called social marketing), promoting voluntary compliance with new laws and rules, and eliciting citizen cooperation as the eyes and ears of the agency (sometimes called co-production) (Lee, 2015).

When engaging in these kinds of activities, PR often overlaps with marketing and branding. Several recent volumes from Western European academics have focused on the importance of marketing and brand management in the public sector (Eshuis and Klijn, 2012; Pasquier and Villeneuve, 2012). More distinct foci on government external communication have included Wæraas and Maor's (2015) examination of organizational reputation and an exploration by two Israeli academics of municipal and national place marketing in times of crisis and controversy (Avraham and Ketter, 2008). US-based Zavattaro (2014) has also written on governmental marketing, especially by municipalities.

OTHER ELEMENTS OF GOVERNMENTAL PUBLIC AFFAIRS

Generic public affairs in government consists of more than media relations and PR. Some other discrete components identified in the literature include reporting, legislative liaison, crisis communications, and increased specialization.

Direct Reporting to the Public

The preceding section's focus on media relations in public sector PR is premised on the existence of an intermediary institution between government and the citizenry. This is counter-balanced by the practice of direct reporting of public sector agencies to the public-at-large (Lee, 2002). The tradition of these activities emerged in the UK and US during the nineteenth century in the form of annual reports (Frankel, 2006: 35–6, 179–80). More recently, there has been a focus emanating from the accounting profession called popular reporting, namely the reformatting of excessively detailed financial reports into a format which would be understandable and meaningful to the lay citizen. Mack and Ryan (2007) documented that stakeholders outside government were increasingly using the annual reports from Australian public agencies as sources of information of specialized interest to them. Some direct reporting entails online access to agency performance results. Meijer (2007: 182) studied the practices of Dutch public sector entities and concluded that the benefits of such accountability were also associated with each agency trying to avoid 'debating what these scores mean about the actual quality of their service'. A study of annual reports from Swedish municipalities found a great variance in social and environmental issues (Tagesson et al., 2013). Schatteman (2010) evaluated the reporting by Canadian municipalities in Ontario. In general, online communication and social media have led to the transformation of public reporting into e-reporting (Lee, 2005; Greitens and Joaquin, 2015). The benefits of providing inexpensive and accessible information will likely become more evident as the technology improves.

Legislative Liaison

As presented in the earlier section on Congressional debate over the importance of legislative relations, another element of generic public affairs in the public sector is legislative liaison by the bureaucracy. Generally, the American literature on external communication in public administration treats PR and legislative relations as wholly separate topics, instead of the more logical and common approach used in the public affairs literature regarding the for-profit and NGO sectors.

The distinct silos in the US public administration literature separating governmental PR from legislative liaison are also reflected in practice. Focusing on the national government, of 42 departments and major non-cabinet agencies, 39 maintained separate units responsible for PR and Congressional relations. Only three had an official who held joint responsibility for both. The National Science Foundation had a Director of the Office of Legislative and Public Affairs, the Agency for International Development (US AID) had an Assistant Administrator for Legislative and Public Affairs, and the Federal Housing Finance Agency had a Senior Associate Director for the Office of Congressional Affairs and Communications (US Congress, 2013; US Office of the Federal Register, 2013). These were clearly exceptions to the rule, namely the assumption in practice as well as in the academic literature distinguishing between PR and legislative relations as separate enterprises within generic public affairs in government.

In-depth and high quality academic literature on legislative relations in the public sector has been slow to emerge. Khademian and Sharif (2015: 157) sought to integrate the extant literature into a broader public administration perspective on agency liaison with elected legislative bodies. They concluded that there were four major obstacles to effective legislative relations: 'minimizing disruption, building goodwill, balancing accountability, and navigating the grey zone'. Cummings (2012) has written about federal agencies' Congressional relations and Scroggs (2000) related his experiences as an Army liaison officer on Capitol Hill. Abney (1988) researched state agency liaison with a state legislature (Georgia), but little has been written since, perhaps due to the differences among the 50 states and the difficulty of generalizations.

Crisis Communication

Crisis communication is a standard category within generic public affairs. However, in one of the few intersectoral studies on the subject, the authors documented distinct differences between corporate and governmental crisis communication. According to Kim and Liu (2012: 80–1), public sector agencies 'were more likely to emphasize providing instructing information (i.e. information that indicates what actions publics should take to protect themselves) … whereas organizations representing corporate interests tended to focus more on reputation management'. This differentiation is an example of the theme of this chapter, namely that generic public affairs in public administration is a distinctly different enterprise from corporate public affairs.

Recent literature on crisis communication in public administration focuses on the multiple functions which are embedded in such situations, including disseminating helpful information directly to the public-at-large, up-to-the minute briefings for the news media, notifying NGOs and intergovernmental partners of relevant developments, and disseminating information to far-flung staff within the agency (Lee, 2008b). The central premise of governmental PR in an emergency should be to convey competence and trust (Mastracci et al., 2012: 54–72). Assessing the communication failures of the US national government during Hurricane Katrina in 2005, Garnett and Kouzmin (2009) identified the significant expansion of privatization and outsourcing of key public administration functions as underlying those failures. From the more specialized perspective of public health, Ratzan and Meltzer (2005: 343–7) provided maxims and best practices for crisis communication.

Rapid technological developments, especially of social media, have led to a friendly debate in the literature. Crowe (2013) argued that social media have so revolutionized communication to the point that the traditional news media was quickly atrophying, and therefore crisis communication should focus almost entirely on social media. Others have argued that the news media continues to play a vestigial role in mass communication. Based on the principle of redundancy in crisis communication, they recommended continuing to include legacy media with other communication platforms in planning and operations of emergency public affairs (Duncan, 2014; Dunlap, 2014).

Professionalization and Specialization

There has been a noticeable trend toward bureaucratization of generic public affairs in the public sector to the point of creating distinct subfields of expertise and specialization. In the 1950s, Parkinson (1980 [1957]: 13–36) had light-heartedly but memorably identified a 'law' of government bureaucracy which he called the Rising Pyramid. By this he meant that public officials inherently want to increase their importance by increasing the number of civil servants who work for them without necessarily actually doing more work. After studying the American national government, Light (1995) more seriously termed the same phenomenon as thickening. These secular observations about civil service in general are valid and applicable to generic public affairs in the public sector.

One example of this trend has been the gradual increase in the number of cabinet departments with assistant secretaries in Congressional liaison and in public affairs (Lee, 2008a, 2011b). In turn, going down the hierarchy, these assistant secretaries have spawned deputy assistant secretaries, general deputy assistant secretaries, and associate deputy assistant secretaries. At least one department has upgraded the importance of PR by creating an undersecretary who oversees the assistant secretary for PR. This is at the State Department, which also has an Under Secretary for Public Diplomacy and Public Affairs.

Official titles used in the PR area suggest both a broad scope of functions and increasing specialization and professionalization. For example, in the US national government, under the rubric of public affairs, there are distinct professional functions including (in alphabetical order): brand review, broadcast media and technology, communication development, communication integration and strategy, communications planning and technology, constituent affairs, consumer communications, creative development, digital strategy, implementation of the Freedom of Information Act and personal privacy laws, media relations, national engagement, multimedia, public inquiries, public outreach, publications management, speechwriting, spokesperson, and web presence. The military have some unique units, including afloat media systems (Navy) and field bands (Army).

Similarly, the practice of legislative relations in US departments and agencies has spawned specialization, including (in alphabetical order): benefits legislative affairs, budget and appropriations, constituent services, corporate enterprise legislative affairs, information, investigations, legislative counsel, legislative development, legislative research analysis, operations, plans, policy, and programs. Several of the military services also maintain units for Congressional travel, commonly known as junkets (US Congress, 2013; US Office of the Federal Register, 2013).

The bureaucratization of PR work has also been reflected in the civil service system. In the federal government, the Office of Personnel Management (OPM, formerly the US Civil Service Commission) established a detailed position classification in public affairs. Its HR experts identified nine factors involved in public affairs work including required knowledge, complexity, scope and effect, personal contacts, and purpose of contacts. Using those criteria, they defined 12 levels of positions for public affairs specialists, from entry level to senior management (US OPM, 1981). OPM also created a separate career path for government information specialists (US OPM, 2012).

CONCLUSION

This chapter has made a two-fold argument. First, that up to now, the public affairs literature has paid little attention to its practice in government, specifically in public administration. Second, that the context of civil service work is so qualitatively different from the corporate and NGO sectors that it justifies separate treatment within generic public affairs.

These arguments are relatively preliminary in the context of the empirical research literature. While there has been a creditable amount of peer-review publications about government PR and, to a lesser extent, legislative relations, those writings tend to be stand-alone in terms of a perspective limited to the public sector and a perspective limited to one country or cluster of relatively similar countries (such as the EU).

Therefore, future research efforts are encouraged to address these limitations. There is a need for international and comparative research to build a reputable literature permitting generalizations about generic public affairs in public administration throughout the world or, at least, in larger clusters of countries. This would contribute to theory building for generic public affairs in the public sector. Simultaneously, there is a need for intersectoral comparative literature. In-depth research is needed to confirm or undermine the contention that governmental public affairs is significantly different from business and/or NGOs. This, in turn, would greatly contribute to further theory building in generic public affairs.

REFERENCES

Abney, Glenn. 1988. Lobbying by the insiders: Parallels of state agencies and interest groups. *Public Administration Review* 48: 911–17.

Addington, David S. 2011. *Speed up Nominations and Confirmations, But Do Not Enact S. 679*, WebMemo No. 3211, April 1. Washington, DC: Heritage Foundation.

Alaimo, Kara. 2016. Which government officials leak unauthorized information to the press in Washington? *Journal of Public Affairs* 16(1): 7–15.

Avraham, Eli and Ketter, Eran. 2008. *Media Strategies for Marketing Places in Crisis: Improving the Image of Cities, Countries, and Tourist Destinations*. Amsterdam, The Netherlands: Butterworth Heinemann.

Bannister, Frank. 2010. Deep e-government: Beneath the carapace. In Hans J. Scholl, ed., *E-Government: Information, Technology, and Transformation*, pp. 33–51. Armonk, NY: M. E. Sharpe.

Canel, María José and Sanders, Karen. 2012. Government communication: An emerging field in political communication research. In Holli A. Semetko and Margaret Scammell, eds., *The SAGE Handbook of Political Communication*, pp. 85–96. Los Angeles, CA: Sage.

Christensen, Tom and Lægreid, Per. 2002. New public management: Puzzles of democracy and the influence of citizens. *Journal of Political Philosophy* 10: 267–95.

Clark, Fife. 1970. *The Central Office of Information*. London: George Allen & Unwin.

Crowe, Adam S. 2013. *Leadership in the Open: A New Paradigm in Emergency Management*. Boca Raton, FL: CRC Press.

Cuadrado-Ballesteros, Beatriz, Frías-Aceituno, José and Martinez-Ferrero, Jennifer. 2014. The role of media pressure on the disclosure of sustainability information by local governments. *Online Information Review* 38: 114–35.

Cummings, Grace. 2012. Working with Congress: Building relationships across the constitutional divide. In Terry Newell, Grant Reeher and Peter Ronayne, eds., *The Trusted Leader: Building the Relationships That Make Government Work*, 2nd ed., pp. 293–317. Los Angeles, CA: Sage/CQ Press.

Duncan, Randall C. 2014. Emergency management and the media. In Michael J. Fagel, ed., *Crisis Management and Emergency Planning: Preparing for Today's Challenges*, pp. 157–76. Boca Raton, FL: CRC Press.

Dunlap, Jeremiah W. 2014. Communications and mass casualty events. In Michael J. Fagel, ed., *Crisis Management and Emergency Planning: Preparing for Today's Challenges*, pp. 141–55. Boca Raton, FL: CRC Press.

Édes, Bart W. 2000. The role of government information officers. *Journal of Government Information* 27: 455–69.

Elmer, Paul. 2000. Beyond professionalism: A government public relations model. *Corporate Communications* 5: 190–6.

Eshuis, Jasper and Klijn, Erik-Hans. 2012. *Branding in Governance and Public Management*. London: Routledge.

Frankel, Oz. 2006. *States of Inquiry: Social Investigations and Print Culture in Nineteenth-Century Britain and the United States*. Baltimore, MD: Johns Hopkins University Press.

Garnett, James and Kouzmin, Alexander. 2009. Crisis communication post Katrina: What are we learning? *Public Organization Review* 9: 385–98.

Gelders, Dave and Ihlen, Øyvind. 2010. Minding the gap: Applying a service marketing model into government policy communications. *Government Information Quarterly* 27: 34–40.

Glenny, Leanne. 2008. Perspectives of communication in the Australian public sector. *Journal of Communication Management* 12: 152–68.

Greitens, Thomas J. and Joaquin, M. Ernita. 2015. Improving the effectiveness of e-reporting in government with the concept of multiple accountability. In Aroon Manoharan, ed., *E-Government and Websites: A Public Solutions Handbook*, pp. 47–65. New York: Routledge.

Harris, Phil and Fleisher, Craig S. eds. 2005. *The Handbook of Public Affairs*. London: Sage.

Heinze, Jana, Schneider, Helmut and Ferié, Frederik. 2013. Mapping the consumption of government communication: A qualitative study in Germany. *Journal of Public Affairs* 13: 370–83.

Kerr, Gayle, Johnston, Kim and Beatson, Amanda. 2008. A framework of corporate social responsibility for advertising accountability: The case of Australian government advertising campaign. *Journal of Marketing Communications* 14: 155–69.

Khademian, Anne M. and Sparger Sharif, Fatima. 2015. Developing effective relations with legislatures. In James L. Perry and Robert K. Christensen, eds., *Handbook of Public Administration*, 3rd ed., pp. 157–79. San Francisco, CA: Jossey-Bass/Wiley.

Kim, Sora and Fisher Liu, Brooke. 2012. Are all crises opportunities? A comparison of how corporate and government organizations responded to the 2009 flu pandemic. *Journal of Public Relations Research* 24: 69–85.

Kiousis, Spiro and Strömbäck, Jesper. 2014. Political public relations. In Carsten Reinemann, ed., *Political Communication*, pp. 249–66. Berlin: De Gruyter Mouton.

Laursen, Bo and Valentini, Chiara. 2013. Media relations in the Council of the European Union: Insights into the Council press officers' professional practices. *Journal of Public Affairs* 13: 230–8.

Lee, Mordecai. 2002. Intersectoral differences in public affairs: The duty of public reporting in public administration. *Journal of Public Affairs* 2(2): 33–43.

Lee, Mordecai. 2005. E-reporting: Using managing-for-results data to strengthen democratic accountability. In John M. Kamensky and Albert Morales, eds., *Managing for Results 2005*, pp. 141–95. Lanham, MD: Rowman & Littlefield.

Lee, Mordecai. 2008a. Public affairs enters the US President's subcabinet: Creating the first assistant secretary for public affairs

(1944–1953) and subsequent developments. *Journal of Public Affairs* 8: 185–94.

Lee, Mordecai. 2008b. Media relations and external communications during a disaster. In Jack Pinkowski, ed., *Disaster Management Handbook*, pp. 387–99. Boca Raton, FL: CRC Press.

Lee, Mordecai. 2009. Too much bureaucracy or too little? Congressional treatment of Defense Department legislative liaison, 1950s–1990s. *Public Administration & Management* (online journal: http://www.spaef.com/pam.php) 14(2): 323–61.

Lee, Mordecai. 2011a. *Congress vs. the Bureaucracy: Muzzling Agency Public Relations*. Norman, OK: University of Oklahoma Press.

Lee, Mordecai. 2011b. Creating the first assistant secretary for Congressional relations (1941–1949) and subsequent developments: A case study of thickening in the federal bureaucracy. *Public Voices* 12(1): 27–45.

Lee, Mordecai. 2015. E-government and public relations: It's the message, not the medium. In Aroon Manoharan, ed., *E-Government and Websites: A Public Solutions Handbook*, pp. 3–21. New York: Routledge.

Light, Paul C. 1995. *Thickening Government: Federal Hierarchy and the Diffusion of Accountability*. Washington, DC: Brookings Institution Press.

Liu, Brooke Fisher and Blake Levenshus, Abbey. 2013. Opportunities, challenges and trends in US federal government communication. In Karen Sanders and María José Canel, eds., *Government Communication: Cases and Challenges*, pp. 59–78. London: Bloomsbury.

Liu, Brooke Fisher, Horsley, J. Suzanne and Blake Levenshus, Abbey. 2010. Government and corporate communication practices: Do the differences matter? *Journal of Applied Communication Research* 38: 189–213.

Mack, Janet and Ryan, Christine. 2007. Is there an audience for public sector annual reports: Australian experience. *International Journal of Public Sector Management* 20: 134–46.

Mastracci, Sharon H., Guy, Mary E. and Newman, Meredith A. 2012. *Emotional Labor and Crisis Response: Working on the Razor's Edge*. Armonk, NY: M. E. Sharpe.

McGrath, Conor, Moss, Danny and Harris, Phil. 2010. The evolving discipline of public affairs. *Journal of Public Affairs* 10: 335–52.

Meijer, Albert Jacob. 2007. Publishing public performance results on the Internet: Do stakeholders use the Internet to hold Dutch public service organizations to account? *Government Information Quarterly* 24: 165–85.

Ministry of Labor and Government Administration, Norway. 2001. *Central Government Information Policy: Goals, Principles and Consequences*, rev. ed. Oslo, Norway: Ministry of Labor and Government Administration.

Ogilvy-Webb, Marjorie. 1965. *The Government Explains: A Study of the Information Services*. London: George Allen and Unwin.

Parkinson, C. Northcote. 1980 [1957]. *Parkinson: The Law*. Boston, MA: Houghton Mifflin.

Pasquier, Martial, and Villeneuve, Jean-Patrick. 2012. *Marketing Management and Communications in the Public Sector*. London: Routledge.

Ratzan, Scott C. and Meltzer, Wendy. 2005. State of the art in crisis communication: Past lessons and principles of practice. In Muhiuddin Haider, ed., *Global Health Communication: Challenges, Perspectives, and Strategies*, pp. 321–47. Sudbury, MA: Jones and Bartlett.

Sanders, Karen and Canel, María José, eds. 2013. *Government Communication: Cases and Challenges*. London: Bloomsbury.

Sayre, Wallace S. 1958. The unhappy bureaucrats: Views ironic, hopeful, indignant (book review). *Public Administration Review* 18: 239–45.

Schatteman, Alicia. 2010. The state of Ontario's municipal performance reports: A critical analysis. *Canadian Public Administration* 53: 531–50.

Schedler, Kuno, and Summermatter, Lukas. 2007. Customer orientation in electronic government: Motives and effects. *Government Information Quarterly* 24: 291–311.

Scroggs, Stephen K. 2000. *Army Relations with Congress: Thick Armor, Dull Sword, Slow Horse*. Westport, CT: Praeger/Greenwood.

Sorkin, Andrew Ross. 2011. *Too Big to Fail: The Inside Story of How Wall Street and Washington Fought to Save the Financial System – and Themselves*, rev. ed. New York: Penguin.

Tagesson, Torbjörn, Klugman, Michelle and Lindvall Ekström, Maria. 2013. What explains the extent and content of social disclosures in Swedish municipalities' annual reports. *Journal of Management & Governance* 17: 217–35.

Thorbjørnsrud, Kjersti, Ustad Figenschou, Tine and Ihlen, Øyvnid. 2014. Mediatization of public bureaucracies. In Knut Lundby, ed., *Mediatization of Communication*, pp. 405–22. Berlin: De Gruyter Mouton.

US Congress, Joint Committee on Printing. 2013. *2013–2014 Official Congressional Directory, 113th Congress*. Washington, DC: Government Printing Office.

US Office of Personnel Management. 1981. *Position Classification Standard for Public Affairs Series, GS-1035* (https://www.opm.gov/policy-data-oversight/classification-qualifications/classifying-general-schedule-positions/standards/1000/gs1035.pdf)

US Office of Personnel Management. 2012. *Position Classification Flysheet for Government Information Series, 0306* (https://www.opm.gov/policy-data-oversight/classification-qualifications/classifying-general-schedule-positions/standards/0300/gs0306.pdf)

US Office of the Federal Register, National Archives and Records Administration. 2013. *United States Government Manual, 2013*. Washington, DC: Office of the Federal Register, National Archives and Records Administration.

US Senate, Committee on Homeland Security and Governmental Affairs. 2011. *Presidential Appointment Efficiency and Streamlining Act of 2011*. 112th Cong., 1st sess., Senate Report 112–24.

Van Der Meer, Toni G.L.A., Gelders, Dave and Rotthier, Sabine. 2014. e-Democracy: Exploring the current stage of e-government. *Journal of Information Policy* 4: 489–506.

Vos, Marita. 2006. Setting the research agenda for governmental communication. *Journal of Communication Management* 10: 250–58.

Wæraas, Arild and Maor, Moshe, eds. 2015. *Organizational Reputation in the Public Sector*. London: Routledge.

Wamsley, Barbara S. 2004. Technocracies: Can they bell the cat? In Thomas H. Stanton and Benjamin Ginsberg, eds., *Making Government Manageable: Executive Organization and Management in the Twenty-First Century*, pp. 204–28. Baltimore, MD: Johns Hopkins University Press.

Williams-Thompson, Richard. 1951. *Was I Really Necessary?* London: World's Press News Publishing.

Young, Sally, ed. 2007. *Government Communication in Australia*. Melbourne: Cambridge University Press.

Zavattaro, Staci M. 2014. *Place Branding through Phases of the Image: Balancing Image and Substance*. New York: Palgrave Macmillan.

PART III

Key Issues in the Development of Public Affairs

John M. Holcomb

This section on 'Key Issues in the Development of Public Affairs' includes six key issues that are having major impacts on the field of public affairs: digital media, corporate political activity, human rights and sustainable development, regulation of lobbying, ethics and professionalism, and globalization and multinational corporations.

Catie Snow Bailard, in her chapter on 'Public Affairs, Digital Media, and Tech Trends' examines digital media in the field of information and communications technology and their impact on public affairs. The chapter focuses on the type and range of information now available through digital media that are relevant to public affairs, and on the impact of digital media on various dimensions of public affairs. Those dimensions include the diffusion of political knowledge and evaluation of government and political leaders, their effects on governance and transparency,

and their effects on collective action efforts by citizens and interest groups.

Her chapter argues that use of information and communications technology (ICT) is essential for participation in a globalized political economy, and that it poses challenges to governments that attempt to limit and monitor the consumption of information by their citizens. The chapter also discusses the continuing problem of the digital divide, both within and between countries, on social, geographic, and political bases. The archival capacity of the internet is enormous, facilitating access to information on an immediate basis, and strengthening accountability of public officials to their constituents. The diversity of information sources is also growing, as individual citizens can post remarks or videos of events as they occur.

Communication costs also decline, in turn leading to greater efficiencies for political participation and more opportunities for consumer and citizen protest. Government and corporations often become more accountable and transparent as a result, and trust, political satisfaction, and democratic practices are often better realized. At the same time, diversity of sources and instant communication can lead to fragmentation in society and political polarization, as users seek out unreliable and sensational information. Digital media, accessed either through computers or mobile phones, can also be used for nefarious purposes that do not strengthen democracy but can be exploited for violence, terrorism, and cyber-attacks. Therefore, government and private actors must monitor digital media for such threats, which in turn leads to the ongoing debate between privacy and security.

The chapter on 'Corporate Political Activity and Public Policy Outcomes: New Realities and Increasing Challenges', by Michael Hadani, examines various forms of political activity, including lobbying, trade association activity, and most importantly political contributions. The chapter examines the legal, normative, and strategic challenges facing the politically active firm. The author offers a useful and sophisticated analysis of corporate political activity (CPA), from the perspectives of various disciplines. From a sociological perspective, the chapter examines how CPA serves the interests of individual companies, the business system, and of top managers. It does so by applying the elements of class-wide rationality, institutional theory, and ideology. It points out that firm-level political activity is often the most efficient, and that firms also participate politically to advance their institutional legitimacy, especially when they are in regulated industries. The chapter also cites recent studies attesting to the importance of the motivations and interests of top management in pursuing CPA.

In examining the political science literature, the chapter demonstrates that the vast writings on interest groups raise questions about the impact and efficacy of CPA. It sometimes does not represent the most efficient allocation of corporate resources and may lead to financial under-performance. It can also contribute to rent-seeking behavior and seeking special benefits from government, which can slow economic growth. Based on exchange and public choice theories, often cited by court decisions on CPA, corporations supply money to satisfy the demand of public policy actors, leading to the possibility of corruption. Studies are mixed or negative on the causal connection between CPA and corruption, though leading judicial decisions since 1976 have been based on the premise of exchange theory, and the possibility or likelihood that CPA above certain levels will lead to corruption. The chapter also examines CPA from the perspective of strategic management theory and applies resource dependency theory to explain the value of CPA.

Finally, the chapter provides a brief history of lobbying law and campaign finance law, and then explains the landmark Supreme Court decisions ranging from *Buckley* v. *Valeo* in 1976 to the most current cases, including the controversial *Citizens United* v. *Federal Election Commission* case in 2010 and *McCutcheon* v. *Federal Election Commission* in 2012.

In their chapter on 'Business, Human Rights, and Sustainable Development', Tricia Olsen and Laura Bernal-Bermudez explain how the agenda of business and human rights has developed, how companies typically respond, and how the issue has elevated expectations for corporate public affairs. The authors demonstrate that corporations must transform their approaches to human rights and adopt more collaborative strategies.

The chapter begins by examining the weaknesses of human rights standards adopted by nation states, in their attempts to apply global human rights norms. Covenants and treaties contain many such norms, and they also form the basis of various standards of the UN, such as the UN Commission on Transnational Corporations, the UN Global Compact, and of the Organization for

Economic Cooperation and Development. The first section in the chapter also discusses multi-stakeholder initiatives, such as Kimberley Certification Scheme, to reduce the flow of conflict diamonds, and the Extractive Industry Transparency Initiative, to reduce corruption in extractive projects. Most important are the more recent UN Guiding Principles on Business and Human Rights, following an approach of 'principled pragmatism'. Some nation states have also upgraded by adopting mandatory standards of corporate social responsibility, by requiring social performance reports by corporations, and by signing on to multi-stakeholder initiatives.

The chapter's second section discusses corporate collaborative efforts, including cooperation with the multi-stakeholder initiatives, e.g., by creating the World Diamond Council, adopting independent anti-bribery policies, supporting the Fair Labor Association and upholding the Workplace Code of Conduct. Union Carbide and the electronics industry also adopted self-regulatory measures in response to various safety and pollution hazards. This section of the chapter also includes a discussion of an important new database, allowing corporations to respond to allegations of human rights abuses. While some corporations may defend themselves against charges, others adopt proactive policies to prevent human rights abuses.

The final section of the chapter addresses new responsibilities for corporate public affairs, including due diligence to ensure compliance with human rights standards and to avoid human rights abuses. Secondly, it is important for public affairs to seek and ensure access to appropriate remedies, whether judicial or non-judicial, and to pursue voluntary remedies to human rights abuses. The chapter provides numerous examples of each. Overall, it is an impressive survey of ways to close the governance gap and the gap between policy and practice.

Justin Greenwood, in his chapter on 'The Regulation of Lobbying Activity', provides an informative global survey of lobbying regulation. Lobbying regulation seeks to foster transparency, accountability, and addresses issues of unequal access. Self-regulation occurs to an extent, but the more prevalent regulatory schemes are based on prohibition of certain forms of lobbying or based on disclosure. The chapter usefully distinguishes between group representation in corporatist and pluralist regimes. While the pluralist tradition encourages outside group participation in public policy formation through conventional lobbying, the corporatist tradition incorporates interest groups into the formal institutional setting, while discouraging external and commercial lobbying. In corporatist states, business associations and trade unions participate in public policy-making through institutionalized arrangements. Hence, corporatist regimes have resisted lobbying regulation, with less need for it, along with their resistance of the American model.

The difference between theoretical and actual regulation of lobbying and influence puts a premium on the monitoring of compliance with regulations of corruption. Here, intergovernmental organizations such as the World Bank and non-governmental organizations (NGOs) such as Transparency International can be important resources. Based on the effectiveness of monitoring and enforcement, compliance can range from evasion, to token gestures, to full adaptation to the regulations. Enforcement can include judicial enforcement, actions by an ombudsman, and consultation through online reporting.

Various regimes regulate lobbying either by focusing on the target of lobbying – the public policymaker – or on the lobbyist. Regulations of the targets include laws to prevent corruption, especially in the previously discussed area of campaign finance, and to control conflicts of interest by policymakers. Included in this good governance approach are rules preventing undue influence through acceptance of gifts, rules requiring the reporting of meetings with lobbyists, and rules limiting or requiring the reporting of outside income. Avoiding conflicts of interest is often accomplished through regulations of the revolving door between government jobs and later lobbying roles, by post-employment restrictions imposed on legislators and their staffs. Some countries have also imposed disclosure regulations or other restrictions on contacts with expert advisory groups, including NGOs.

The regulations that focus on lobbyists, rather than their targets, emphasize lobbying registration and disclosure. Incentivized registration includes provisions that lobbying organizations have a code of conduct, including the accuracy of information they transmit, as well as registration, as pre-requisites to participate in legislative hearings and bilateral meetings. Mandatory registration and disclosure are applied especially to commercial lobbyists, but may apply to NGOs as well. Journalists and watchdog organizations assist in ensuring compliance with the regulations.

In responding to all the foregoing trends in public affairs, it is important that practitioners are driven by an ethical sensibility. Shannon A. Bowen carefully examines its most important elements in her chapter on 'Values, Ethics, and Professionalism in Public Affairs'. She first examines values at the personal, organizational, and societal levels. Societal values in Western society include independence, liberty, and freedom, while Eastern society puts greater emphasis on collectivism. To know one's personal values is important in determining whether there is a fit with core organizational values, to resolve any conflict with an organization's culture, and to exercise leadership. Organizational values, whether codified or otherwise embedded in the organization's culture, often include integrity, ethics, and corporate citizenship.

In examining the importance of moral philosophy and ethics, the chapter focuses on the importance of being able to make trade-offs between conflicting rights (not just between what is right and what is wrong), and on the importance of rationality and consistency.

The chapter also explains the importance of utilitarianism, based on consequences and the greatest good for the greatest number. This normative framework assumes the ability to anticipate consequences and to account for unintended consequences, both difficult assignments.

Deontology is a competing and more highly principled ethical framework, with elements of its categorical imperative including duty, dignity and respect, and intention of a morally good will, irrespective of the consequences of one's actions. The rational calculation involved in applying deontology also requires that one universalize the principle applied to a particular situation to all similar situations. Applying both utilitarianism and deontology to public affairs requires an appreciation of organizational culture and the possible negative impact of a failure to apply ethical reasoning, resulting in crises and organizational failures.

The section on professionalism in public affairs examines the important roles of public affairs officers in advising top management on ethical dilemmas, to protect the credibility of the organization, and to advance the leadership role of the CEO. Ethical analysis is also crucial to issues management, both in anticipating emerging issues and in establishing priorities among those issues. Finally, professionalism is necessary to avoid corruption and to possess the moral courage to battle it.

The chapter by Jeffrey A. Hart, on 'Globalization and Multinational Corporations', begins by addressing the cultural aspects of globalization, whereby American multinational corporations (MNCs) contribute to the 'soft power' of the US. As creators of foreign direct investment (FDI), MNCs are the predominant owners of technology and account for half of global research and development spending. By using the global economy to lower their costs, MNCs are both the agents and beneficiaries of globalization.

The chapter demonstrates the expansion of MNC activity, both in terms of outflows from developing countries and inflows and out-flows from the developed world. Underlying causes of globalization include the role of international institutions such as the World Trade Organization and Organization for Economic Cooperation and Development (OECD), as well as advances in transportation and communications technologies. The chapter also discusses 'gravity models', which establish that countries in greater proximity on the bases of geography, language, religion, and a common set of democratic institutions trade and invest with each other more often than with more distant regimes. Opponents of globalization include orthodox Muslims, economic nationalists, and trade unions. Divisions within countries on globalization also exist, as unions oppose globalization while managers favor it. The chapter also discusses horizontal FDI, which occurs in order to have greater access to new customers, and vertical FDI, which exists to lower the costs of production through cheaper labor and materials.

The chapter further points out that regional integration is actually more prominent than globalization, which is often too costly and risky, and points to various important regional economic arrangements. While some maintain that the power of MNCs outstrips that of nation states, the chapter persuasively argues that is not the case, and that governments of nation states use tax policy, subsidies, and investment and trade policies to exercise leverage over MNCs. The chapter also chronicles the economic and social advantages, as well as the disadvantages, of MNCs.

Finally, the chapter provides short discussions of current issues associated with globalization and MNCs, including: government incentives to inward FDI and the possible consequence of a 'race to the bottom'; transfer pricing, tax havens and inversions; technology transfer; MNCs from emerging economies; intellectual property protection and piracy; dispute settlement; extraterritorial reach of national laws; and corporate social responsibility.

Public Affairs, Digital Media, and Tech Trends

Catie Snow Bailard

In recent years, popular movements ranging from Hong Kong, to the Middle East and North Africa, to Europe and North America have called global attention to digital technologies' capacity to facilitate political organization by citizens. Posting pictures and videos from the field, as well as sharing public statements and personal reflections online, have effectively enabled these movements to rally support from both domestic and international sources, report developments from the ground in near real-time, communicate their grievances to government leaders and other elites (who have sometimes responded in kind, online), and document police or military abuses. Each of these serves as a compelling illustration of the degree to which new information and communication technologies (i.e., ICTs) alter the various communication costs that are integral components of the processes of public affairs.

Before proceeding, it is worthwhile to note that there remains marked ambiguity and disagreement within the study and practice of public affairs as to how exactly to define public affairs. In a recent review of the field's literature, the editors of the *Journal of Public Affairs* conclude that, 'despite a period of marked growth and maturing of the discipline over the past decade, there is little evidence of a consensual definition and understanding of public affairs emerging amongst academics or practitioners' (McGrath et al., 2010: 346). As these editors cogently summarize (2010: 339), while some scholars define public affairs as the cushion that protects organizations from external threats and buffers relations with key stakeholder groups (Meznar and Nigh, 1995), other scholars see short-term political lobbying efforts and longer-term relationship-building with the government as the defining features of public affairs (Hillman and Hitt, 1999), while still others focus on public affairs as the facilitation and construction of relationships and interactions between members of the social and political spheres in order to bring corporate prefer-ences and public policy into alignment (van Schendelen and Van Schendelen, 2010).

While it is clear that disagreement regarding the exact definition and jurisdiction of public affairs remains, a common thread across these competing views is the importance of commu-nication – whether it be between stakehold-ers and representatives, for the sake of issue management, the shaping of media relations, or fostering community relations (McGrath et al., 2010: 340). Many of the most integral processes and relationships that fall under the umbrella of public affairs require the pack-aging and exchange of information between relevant actors and parties. Thus, to a large degree, the strategies and success of public-affairs efforts hinge on communication costs. And it is these communication costs that have been transformed by the changes brought to our information landscapes by new ICTs.

To explore the relevance and effects of ICT in the domain of public affairs, this chapter addresses three specific questions. The first section seeks to answer the ques-tions of what exactly are ICTs, and how do these technologies interact and build on one another to construct our contemporary infor-mation landscapes? The second explores how exactly these ICTs are changing the type and range of information available for public con-sumption in ways that are relevant to public affairs. The third and final discussion consid-ers the specific dimensions of public affairs where we are most likely to see the effects of ICT – specifically, how these ICTs affect citizens' political knowledge and relevant evaluations of their government and leaders, their effects on governance and transparency, and their effects on collective action efforts by citizens and interest groups.

WHAT ARE ICTS?

Exactly what the term 'information and com-munication technology' (most commonly abbreviated as ICT) actually denotes is nearly as contested as the debate surrounding the definition of public affairs. Historically, the use of this term is visible in scholarly work as early as the 1980s (Melody et al., 1986), but it was popularized in 1997 after its use by the UK's Independent ICT in Schools Commission, in their report on the state of technology in their education system. 'On a point of definition we talk in this report of ICT, adding "communications" to the more familiar "information technology". This seems to us accurately to reflect the increas-ing role of both information and communica-tion technologies in all aspects of society' (1997: 12).

In the following years, this term has evolved and become even more popular, but some portion of confusion over what exactly ICT denotes lingers. This is largely due to the continually changing set of relevant technol-ogies, which requires frequent updating and (often) expansion of the term. For the purpose of this chapter, however, it makes sense to adopt the broadest and most inclusive sense of the term. 'Thus, the term ICT is best seen as an umbrella term for a range of technologi-cal applications such as computer hardware and software, digital broadcast technologies, telecommunications technologies such as mobile phones, as well as electronic informa-tion resources such as the world wide web and CDRoms' (Selwyn, 2004: 346–7).

Arguably, the most common feature con-necting the newer technologies that fall under the ICT umbrella is their capacity to digitize information, as opposed to the mechanical, analog, and electronic systems that largely characterized earlier technologies. To digi-tize information means to convert assorted content (e.g., image, audio, video) into a single binary code (i.e., sequences of 0's and 1's). The technical capacity to digitize infor-mation was developed just before the turn of the 20th century; however, it was not until the 1950s that this technology was regularly utilized, albeit still in a limited capacity. Its use expanded further with television systems switching to digital technology and the introduction of home computers in the 1980s. It was not until the beginning of the 21st century, however, that digital technology became ubiquitous with the growth of the Internet and mobile technologies that dominate our present-day information landscapes (Digital Preservation Management, 2015). The primary significance of digital technology for contemporary information landscapes is the comparatively massive amount of information that can now be quickly and efficiently packaged for communication.

An important component of conceptualizing how these digital ICTs are reshaping our contemporary information landscapes is the increasing convergence of these technologies. 'In the spread of new ICTs there are overall tendencies of convergence: similar devices are used everywhere, with converging functions ... similar contents are available and access to them is facilitated through various devices' (Heller, 2008: 29). For example, whereas previously we thought of the Internet as primarily computer-based, individuals are increasingly accessing it through other devices, such as tablets and mobile phones. In fact, there are a growing number of individuals who access the Internet primarily or even exclusively through their phones (Kovach, 2015).

So, where is the line that demarcates computer-based from telephony-based information and communication activities? For example, how does one differentiate information attained online by individuals via their computers, which is then communicated by those individuals via mobile phones to their social media networks? Or, what if an individual takes a picture with his mobile phone of a protest event and posts it to a social media website, which is then picked up by a mainstream media outlet and posted on their own website as part of a developing story? Thankfully, there is no need to differentiate. Mobile phones and computers are not mutually exclusive components of contemporary information environments but instead are moving toward greater and greater convergence – meaning that the need and ability to differentiate between different technologies and their uses will continue to diminish. For example,

> The set of technologies known throughout most of the 1990s as 'the Internet' is steadily merging with other technologies ... As these technologies continue to evolve, what is actually 'the Internet' will become less clear and less important. The fundamental modes of communication that various technologies enable will become more crucial than the machinery involved. (Bimber, 2003: 8)

In addition to considering how these newer technologies converge with one another, it is also important to embed our understanding of these newer ICTs within the broader information landscape, in which these newer technologies also interact with older, traditional media technologies. This process is referred to as the hybridization of contemporary media systems. A leading book on how this process is unfolding is Andrew Chadwick's *The Hybrid Media System: Politics and Power* (2013). Chadwick offers a nuanced picture of how 'newer' and 'older' media interact, compete, cooperate, and co-opt each other and, in doing so, create the interdependent, negotiated, hybridizing media systems that characterize Britain and the United States today. As part of this consideration, Chadwick details how the Internet interacts with and influences the broadcast and newspaper industries, and vice versa, beginning with the structure of the Internet itself, and how it borrows from and builds on features of traditional media. Next, he discusses how actors in each media borrow from each other – such as how bloggers and journalists exchange tips and information, how norms are diffusing both ways in this relationship, and the specific practices that actors in both older and newer media utilize to blend the online with the offline and, in doing so, contribute to their growing interdependence with one another.

Before leaving this discussion, it is also imperative to recall that Chadwick's discussion of media hybridization is specific to the

UK and USA, which means it is primarily relevant to developed democracies. This is an important point, because media hybridization is also unfolding in developing democracies and non-democracies, but this process looks markedly different in these countries. In one example, consider the phenomenon of leapfrogging:

> ICTs are unique in a number of ways compared with the leading industries of the past that were responsible for industrial growth and development, such as steel, chemicals, and machinery. In many applications, and in some types of production, the conditions of entry for using and, in some cases, for producing ICTs do not require massive investment in fixed plant capacity or infrastructure or in the accumulation of experience ... All these features suggest that ICTs have the potential to support the development strategy of 'leapfrogging', i.e. bypassing some of the processes of accumulation of human capabilities and fixed investment in order to narrow the gaps in productivity and output that separate industrialized and developing countries. (Steinmueller, 2001: 193–4)

Next, consider the peculiar and complex dance between an authoritarian government's need to embrace ICTs in order to participate in the global market and their desire to maintain tight control over information flows in their nation – commonly referred to as the dictator's dilemma (Kedzie, 1997). ICT is becoming an increasingly inescapable prerequisite for participation in the global economy, impelling governments across the globe to promote Internet and mobile technology usage among their citizenry if they hope to become or remain economically competitive. While ICT expansion gels nicely with the political and social norms intrinsic to developed democracies, governments that have traditionally sought to monitor and limit the information consumed by their citizenry are increasingly confronted with the thorny task of balancing competing economic and political interests.

This does not imply that these authoritarian leaders have no choice but to passively welcome ICT technology into their countries. Rather, there may always be governments who refuse to tacitly accept such a trade-off – those who stand confidently at their shores with sieve in hand, hoping to greet the ICT tidal wave by funneling it through officially sanctioned channels. Indeed, at present it appears that a number of governments have implemented Internet regulations and content controls with reasonable success. China and Russia stand out as examples of relatively successful governmental Internet regulation (MacKinnon, 2008; Morozov, 2011a; 2011b). Nevertheless, as will be discussed at greater length in the following sections, no matter how sophisticated the regulatory and censorship systems, there is no disputing that these technologies have changed the informational relationship between these governments and their citizens in ways that are meaningful for public affairs.

Finally, how the process of media hybridization looks different in less developed countries also highlights the lingering problems associated with the digital divide. The term 'digital divide' was coined in the mid 1990s, at which time it referred to the divide separating those with and without computer access. The term then expanded as technology evolved to include access to the Internet and, more recently, access to broadband technology. While the actual technologies straddling the digital divide have transformed over the past decades, the essential meaning and significance of the term remains unchanged. It denotes the stark disparity in access to information, tools of political participation, and education and employment opportunities that differentiate those with and without access to digital technology.

A groundbreaking book regarding the Internet's digital divide is Pippa Norris's (2001) *Digital Divide: Civic Engagement, Information Poverty, and the Internet Worldwide*. Norris delineates and discusses three types of significant divide: 1) the social divide within countries between those with and without access, 2) the global divide between countries with more and less access, and 3) the political divide between those who use the Internet toward political ends and those who do not. As we will discuss in more detail in the following section, a large global divide still exists. A significant social divide also lingers, particularly within countries with lower Internet penetration rates – where young men with more education and higher socioeconomic status tend to be the most likely to be online (Christensen and Levinson, 2003; International Telecommunications Union, 2013). In addition to the monetary costs associated with using the Internet, the digital divide within many nations is further exacerbated by differences in education, literacy, and technical skills that facilitate Internet use (Mossberger et al., 2008).

Fortunately, there are some factors that offset the limitations engendered by the digital divide in these countries, at least to some extent. First, consider the positive externalities that Internet use bestows upon communities, which are understood as the 'social benefits beyond those reaped by the individuals who use the technology' (Mossberger et al., 2008: 3). In example, Mossberger, Tolbert, and McNeal argue that 'information available online helps citizens to be more informed about politics and more inclined to participate, then society as a whole profits from broader and possibly more deliberative participation in democratic processes' (2008: 3).

This also means that the benefits of access to a greater volume of more diverse information online extend beyond those who physically access that information – after all, information acquired online is not fated to only exist online. Instead, information acquired online is easily and often communicated to a broader audience through offline channels, updating the classic theory of the two-step flow of information. First articulated by Katz and Lazarsfeld in 1955 in reference to traditional media, the two-step flow theory of information posits that information attained from the mass media tends to move in two stages. In the first stage, opinion leaders are exposed to political information

directly from the media. Next, these opinion leaders pass this information along to those they interact with directly in their various social networks, often accompanied by their own interpretation. Thus, even in countries with limited Internet exposure, it is likely that some degree of the information attained online is diffused by Internet users to non-users in their social networks.

In conclusion, thanks to forces such as digitization, convergence, and hybridization, ICTs are profoundly reshaping contemporary information landscapes across the globe. Without doubt, how these processes are unfolding varies across different regions, suggesting that there will also be distinct implications for how these technologies impact public affairs across these countries. However, there are also some important commonalities across these countries in terms of how new ICTs are changing the nature of information to which citizens have access. This leads to the next question guiding this chapter: what effects do ICTs have on the type of information and communication capacity available to individuals across the globe?

HOW ARE ICTS CHANGING CONTEMPORARY INFORMATION LANDSCAPES?

Digital information and communication technologies are rapidly, profoundly, and simultaneously changing three structural properties of contemporary communication systems. How we encode information (i.e., how a technology packages information for transmission), the means for transmitting this encoded information (i.e., the technology that determines where we can send encoded information, how quickly, and at what cost), as well as the networks that determine who can send and receive that information (i.e., who are the receivers and who are the senders of encoded information within the network structures intrinsic to technologies) have changed dramatically with the advent of the Internet and mobile technology (Bailard, 2014). The resultant transformation to contemporary information landscapes is so profound that the term 'information revolution' is perhaps more appropriate now than ever before. As Clay Shirky (2008) reflects in *Here Comes Everybody*, 'We are living in the middle of the largest increase in expressive capability in the history of the human race. More people can communicate more things to more people than has ever been possible in the past, and the size and speed of this increase, from under one million participants to over one billion in a generation, makes the change unprecedented' (105–6).

This dramatic reshaping of contemporary information landscapes has direct and clear consequences for the quantity and range of information available to citizens across the globe, as well as the communication costs that are integral to organization. The following paragraphs explore the effect of newer ICTs on the volume and diversity of information available in ways that are meaningful for public affairs, as well as the significance of these technologies for the communicative processes that characterize collective action.

Volume of Information

The Internet's capacity to relay a seemingly limitless quantity of information stems from the virtual absence of space and time constraints online, which increases the volume of available information as well as making it more efficient for individuals to access that information (Bimber, 2001; Earl and Kimport, 2011; Mossberger and Tolbert, 2010; Scheufele and Nisbet, 2002). A 2015 report by Cisco estimates that, 'Annual global IP traffic will pass the zettabyte (1,000 exabytes) threshold by the end of 2016, and will reach 2 zettabytes per year by 2019. By 2016, global IP traffic will reach 1.1 zetta-bytes per year, or 88.4 exabytes (nearly one

billion gigabytes) per month, and by 2019, global IP traffic will reach 2.0 zettabytes per year, or 168 exabytes per month'. As an anchor point, the entire amount of printed information housed by all of the US Library of Congress was estimated to be 15 terabytes in 2012 (*Sydney Morning Herald*, 2012), which amounts to roughly 0.000015 (or 1/667,000th) of the amount of information predicted to pass through the Internet during a typical month in 2016.

A central component of the Internet's seemingly limitless space constraints is the archival function that it serves. Historically, the development of the written word and then the printing press had a profound effect on the availability of information, in a large part because these developments meant that information could now be archived. This made messages more permanent, thus increasing the quantity of information available for consumption by enabling the information packaged in a recorded message to abide well beyond the initial act of communication.

In comparative terms, the archival capacity provided by the Internet is staggering. In one estimate, on a typical day in 2012, 250 million photos were uploaded, 2 million blog posts were written, and 864,000 hours of video were uploaded to YouTube (Silverman, 2012). This has dramatically increased the amount of information that individuals can now access, on their own schedules and at their own inclination. No longer do individuals have to worry about missing the evening newscast, tracking down print editions of news stories that interest them, or visit libraries and shuffle through card catalogues to learn more about a topic of interest. There is a permanency, centralization, and ease of access provided by the Internet's archival function that is monumental in terms of the volume of information that is now accessible to individuals.

On the topic of time, it is also useful to briefly consider the immediacy provided by new technologies and how this also changes the volume of information to which individuals now have access. As Chadwick (2013) articulates, the Internet has changed the nature of the relationship shared by time and information. Social media specifically have played a large role in this development – reports and photos about developing events can be documented and reported from the field in nearly real-time and then distributed through social media feeds by elites, members of the news industry, or even ordinary citizens. Through Twitter, candidates and government officials are expected to be engaged in continuous, real-time engagement with the public. On the other hand, they are also able to immediately garner feedback from their constituents on a speech or event by analyzing the content of Twitter traffic. Thus, the immediacy and 'real-timeness' provided by the Internet also exerts a powerful influence on the volume of information available for the communicative processes integral to public affairs.

Finally, we cannot leave the subject of accessibility to information without returning to the limitations imposed by the digital divide, in terms of who actually has access to the vast stores of information provided by these technologies. Despite mushrooming growth of these technologies across the globe, there remain stark differences in access across regions and nations in terms of accessibility. By most measures, despite exponential growth over the past decade, sub-Saharan Africa continues to lag behind other regions. Latin America and regions of Asia tend to occupy a middle ground in terms of ICT access, with developed nations and parts of Asia occupying the highest levels of these measures (International Telecommunications Union, 2013). Looking to the future, however, some of these disparities are expected to diminish. For example, mobile service providers are shifting their concentration to developing nations, having reached saturation points in many developed countries. 'Existing business models and strategies show that lower revenues are compensated by masses of new subscribers. Also, studies

have shown low-income groups are prepared to spend proportionally more of their income on telecommunications' (International Telecommunications Union, 2008: 6). In recent years, these providers have produced increasingly affordable mobile devices and sold airtime in cheaper and cheaper packets, with many subscribers in these nations opting for pre-paid plans that offer such features as per-second billing.

Diversity of Information

In addition to providing a greater volume of information, the content of the information communicated via newer ICT is distinct from and supports a more diverse range of perspectives relative to traditional media. This is most directly attributable to the Internet's multipoint-to-multipoint configuration (Chadwick, 2006; Mossberger et al., 2008), which provides a convenient and accessible platform for the masses to contribute content – in the form of information, perspectives and opinions, anecdotes and personal experiences, memes, various creative works, and pictures and videos – to informational landscapes.

Contrast this with traditional broadcast media, such as the television and radio, which are configured as single-point-to-multipoint media, in which information emanates from a single source out to the masses. This meant that, during the broadcast era, the gatekeepers who determined which information made it past their posts exercised greater control over determining the content of information available for public consumption. And since these gatekeepers often faced institutional and commercial constraints, specific stories from specific perspectives were either more or less likely to make it past their posts (Graber, 1997), thus limiting the range of information and perspectives constituting traditional media landscapes.

The effect of the multipoint-to-multipoint configuration of the Internet on the changed role of traditional media gatekeepers, and the resulting increase in the diversity of information available for public consumption, are aptly summarized by Yochai Benkler (2006):

> The emergence of a networked public sphere is attenuating, or even solving, the most basic failings of the mass-mediated public sphere … It provides an avenue for substantially more diverse and politically mobilized communication than was feasible in a commercial mass media with a small number of speakers and a vast number of passive recipients. The views of many more individuals and communities can be heard. (465)

Of course, it is important to acknowledge that online news consumption in developed democracies tends to overwhelmingly frequent the websites associated with traditional news media outlets (Hindman, 2009). However, this does not mean they are exposed to the same *content* that they would be in a world without the Internet. This is evidenced by studies that compared the content of the print and online versions of major news organizations, which revealed that online news sites belonging to traditional media outfits provide individuals with different content and news stories than their own print versions (Althaus and Tewksbury, 2002; Maier, 2010).

Also consider that newsrooms do not have sufficient resources to position journalists and cameras in all places at all times where newsworthy events might happen. This means that the decisions regarding where and when to station these resources largely determines which stories a newsroom can report. Compare this to the Internet age, in which average citizens can contribute eyewitness accounts, information, and pictures and video footage to the public stage, expanding the range of perspectives and information available for public consumption. This capacity for user-generated content to shift the public dialogue is highlighted by the many instances in which stories that first broke on the Internet gathered enough steam that they eventually compelled the traditional media to also cover them – stories that may have never been told

in a pre-Internet era. Moreover, a number (albeit limited) of these stories have managed to attract enough widespread and sustained attention to influence the course of policy-making and related public affairs processes.

The Internet's capacity to increase the range of information available for public consumption is also evident even in countries with the most successful Internet censorship policies. Citing a number of earlier studies, Earl and Kimport (2011) highlight the Internet's capacity to spread messages that circumvent mainstream media even in 'hostile climates' and in ways that are 'more difficult for governments to block' (25). Accordingly, examples abound of users evading sophisticated Internet regulatory systems to disseminate political information that would otherwise remain suppressed.

In support of this, Larry Diamond writes, 'With recent technological revolutions, the ability to generate information and opinion has been radically decentralized' (2008: 99). This is because, as aptly summarized by Philip N. Howard (2010), whereas it was relatively efficient for states to control traditional media and costly for citizens to have their voices heard through those systems, the Internet has flipped this equation on its head. Instead it has become relatively cheap and efficient for citizens to disseminate information, and rather costly for governments to control that expression.

This has profound consequences for the diversity of information now available for public consumption relative to the broadcast era. As Andrew Chadwick (2006) explains, 'regulating television is actually pretty straightforward in comparison with the Internet' (7), which he attributes to the fundamental differences that distinguish the Internet from traditional broadcast media. These include the Internet being a multi-point-to-multipoint medium as opposed to television's single-point-to-multipoint configuration, the Internet being primarily globally oriented whereas television is more nationally oriented, the substantially lower entry costs of content production on the Internet versus television, and the existence of well-known technical fixes to state censorship available to Internet users, which include 'proxy servers, encryption, and other anonymity tools to route around controls' (7).

This is the case even in China, the nation with perhaps the most sophisticated regulatory system. This system combines the Great Firewall that actively blocks content deemed 'sensitive' from entering the nation, a more subtle approach of purposefully manipulating search engine results, with a large human force that monitors and then shames and punishes Internet users who do not conform to established guidelines. Despite all of these efforts at censorship, however, it is clear that 'the Internet in China often disseminates forbidden information and opinions through e-mail, instant messaging, blogs, and bulletin board forums or through political expressions disguised as non-political comments' (Lum, 2006: 2).

The potential for the Internet's multipoint-to-multipoint configuration to broaden the range of voices and perspectives available in countries with sophisticated censorship systems is particularly well illustrated by China's microblog website, Sina Weibo. This website is the nation's alternative to Twitter, which is officially blocked in China. Since its launch in 2009, Sina Weibo's popularity has mushroomed, with nearly 400 million users by the end of 2012 (Rigg, 2012). Not surprisingly, Weibo is actively censored by the government (Sullivan, 2012), which entails employing thousands of individuals who actively monitor the website for content deemed controversial or in violation of censorship regulations, which is then deleted. Nevertheless, Weibo still provides a platform to citizens to discuss controversial issues and criticize the Chinese government. Recent studies have revealed that, although there is clear evidence of censorship via deleted posts that referred to controversial topics (e.g., Falun Gong, specific political activists, pornography), the deletion of this content

is inconsistent and incomplete (Bamman et al., 2012). For example, an analysis of millions of social media posts to 1,400 distinct Chinese social media websites revealed that government censors are actually relatively permissive toward critical and even vitriolic discussion of the government by citizens, opting instead to concentrate their censorship activities on online content that seems to advocate some sort of offline activity or political organization (King et al., 2013).

Finally, the Internet and mobile technology also empower users to more successfully transcend intranational boundaries to share information that would otherwise likely remain muffled. For example, female Internet users constitute a sizeable percentage of the Saudi Arabian blogosphere: 'Young women make up half the bloggers in the kingdom ... lured by the possible anonymity of the medium, Saudi women have produced a string of blogs filled with feminist poetry, steamy romantic episodes and rants against their restricted lives and patriarchal society' (Ambah, 2006).

In conclusion, it is clear that more political information from more perspectives is now available for consumption than would be available in a world without the digital ICTs that have reshaped global information landscapes. This has important implications for the diversity of information available to various audiences that is integral to the practice of public affairs.

Improved Communication Between Group Members

Thus far, much of this section has focused on the multi-point to multi-point information-sharing largely enabled by the Internet and social media platforms. However, newer ICTs – particularly mobile technology – also facilitate one-to-one exchanges of information that are integral to collective action processes germane to public affairs. In Mancur Olson's foundational work, *The Logic of*

Collective Action (1965), a group's likelihood of organizing toward collective ends (e.g., forming an interest group, petitioning a government for action, policy advocacy on behalf of a group's interests, campaign activities, protest movements) hinges on a number of factors that determine the costs and benefits that group members expect as a result of participation in that collective action. One central determinant of these factors is how easily and cost-effectively a group can communicate and exchange information between its members.

The most visible of these communication costs are associated with coordination: how effectively can groups inform their members of the logistics of participation, typically referred to as organizational costs (i.e., the who, what, where, and when's)? Another prominent type of communication cost that groups incur are those associated with identifying, locating, and punishing free-riders who opt out of collective action, but who still seek to enjoy the public goods associated with that group's efforts. Additionally, lower communication costs also facilitate secondary processes that are often integral to collective action (i.e., the 'why's' of participation). For example, the likelihood of organization increases when group members (or group factions) can better bargain with one another in order to arrive at mutually satisfactory goals and a mutually beneficial course of action to achieve those goals. Collective action is also more likely to occur when group members better identify with one another and believe that they, in fact, do have common interests at stake, which justify the costs of working together to achieve their collective goals.

New information and communication technologies have drastically reduced the costs of communication, fundamentally reshaping contemporary information environments. This drastic reduction in communication costs has had profound consequences for collective action more generally. By 'lowering the costs of coordinating group action' (Shirky, 2008: 31), the expected goods of collective action will exceed the expected costs of that organization more often than in the past, which Shirky predicts will result in a surge in group activity toward a broader range of ends. In slightly more detail, Bimber, Flanigan, and Stohl articulate three specific ways in which reduced information costs provided by new technology will facilitate collective action: 'The need to accumulate resources in order to bear the costs of acquiring information about interests, the costs of distributing messages, and the labor and material costs of coordination are diminished substantially under certain circumstances by the availability of new technology' (Bimber et al., 2005: 374).

Thus, it is not surprising that scholars are revisiting the classic Olsonian logic of collective action in light of new technology (Lupia and Sin, 2003). As a result, a large portion of the recent scholarly work on new technology and collective action explores the potential for digital technologies to increase political participation and civic engagement (Earl and Kimport, 2011; Kenski and Stroud, 2006; Mossberger et al., 2008; Xenos and Moy, 2007). The processes of political participation and civic engagement are two key components of the public affairs processes where we are likely to see the effects of ICTs. Thus, the following and final section of this chapter considers the potential effects of ICTs on the processes germane to public affairs.

WHAT ARE THE RELEVANT EFFECTS OF ICT FOR PUBLIC AFFAIRS?

Thus far, this chapter has explored what ICTs are, how they are reconstructing information landscapes, and what effect these technologies have had on the volume and diversity of information as well as the communicative processes available to publics. The next logical step in this discussion is a consideration of where we are likely to see the relevant effects of these changes. Although there are a number of domains where ICT effects are relevant for public affairs – including the effects of these technologies on the structure and operation of traditional 'bricks and mortar' NGOs and interest groups, as well as in the corporate sphere – the following section considers the effects of ICTs within the realm of the citizen-government nexus. Specifically, this section examines the effect of ICTs on citizens' political knowledge and related political evaluations, political organization and protest, and government accountability and transparency.

Effects on Political Knowledge and Evaluations

A growing body of research shows that Internet exposure increases users' levels of political knowledge (Davis, 1999; Johnson and Kaye, 2003; Kenski and Stroud, 2006; Mossberger et al., 2008). In one example, a study of 14- to 22-year-old users substantiated the positive effect of Internet use on political awareness, also finding that the Internet's influence exceeded that of any other mass medium, including newspapers (Pasek et al., 2006). However, there are also some notable exceptions to these findings; studies that yield no empirical support for the Internet's capacity to increase political knowledge (Scheufele and Nisbet, 2002; Tewksbury and Althaus, 2000).

Somewhat straddling this divide is the work that explores the potentially deleterious effects of 'too much choice' of content in the contemporary media environment, which posits that the effect of the Internet on political knowledge is contingent on the individual and how he or she uses the Internet. Markus Prior, for example, argues that, 'Greater choice allows politically interested people to access more information and increase their political knowledge. Yet those who prefer nonpolitical content can more easily escape the news and therefore pick up less political information than they used to' (2005: 577). In his analysis, Prior finds

that, among individuals who express an interest in news, the use of cable television and Internet increases political knowledge; however, among those who report a strong preference for entertainment content, these media decrease their political knowledge over time. This suggests that the Internet's effect on political knowledge is likely contextual and variable across individuals and types of uses.

Skeptics have worried that the vast quantity of information on the Internet may actually inhibit information acquisition by overwhelming Internet users. However, research shows that individuals can develop appropriate organization and screening practices to minimize the risk of data glut (Hiltz and Turoff, 1985; Nielson, 1995). In support of this, Benkler notes the rise of 'nonmarket, peer-produced alternative sources of filtration and accreditation', which serve as mechanisms to filter, focus attention around, and then validate claims and their sources through informal peer-review (2006: 12).

Finally, while information acquisition is often the result of deliberate, purposive effort, users can also acquire information as a byproduct of using the Internet for other purposes. In Mossberger and Tolbert's (2010) words, '*online news may accidentally mobilize individuals* who are online for other reasons' (emphasis in original: 205). A report by the Project for Excellence in Journalism (Horrigan et al., 2004) found that 73 percent of Internet users 'bumped into news' after going online for another purpose. Underscoring the import of this sort of incidental exposure, Tewksbury, Weaver, and Maddex (2001) found that incidental exposure to news increased individuals' awareness of current affairs.

Taken as a whole, research suggests a net positive effect of Internet use on exposure to and acquisition of political information – however, these effects may be marginal at times and contingent on the context of use. Nevertheless, this effect on political knowledge means that ICTs alter the set of information that individuals draw upon to formulate political evaluations and attitudes that are integral to processes of public affairs, particularly campaign efforts on behalf of politicians or policies, participation drives, and public service efforts seeking to influence political behaviors. Specifically, research has substantiated ICT effects on evaluations of specific government officials (Hong, 2013), as well as broader measures of political trust, political satisfaction, support for democratic principles, and the strength of democratic practices available in one's nation (Bailard, 2012, 2014; Nisbet et al., 2012; Tolbert and Mossberger, 2006).

Effect on Collective Action Processes Integral to Grassroots Political Organization and Activity

Not surprisingly, how new ICTs affect political organization and activity in advanced democracies is a dominant theme among technocrats, politicians, and pundits. In an interview with the *Washington Post*, Al Gore proclaims that, 'what we're witnessing … is the rebirth of our participatory democracy' (Vargas, 2009). According to Japanese technocrat and entrepreneur, Joichi Ito, 'blogging will fundamentally change the (way) people interact with media and politics and provide us with an opportunity to overhaul our outdated democracies' (Kageyama, 2004).

Academics, on the other hand, have been relatively more circumspect in their proclamations. Two prominent scholars, Bruce Bimber and Clay Shirky, see the majority of change happening at the institutional and organizational levels. Bimber argues that 'technological change in the contemporary period should contribute toward information abundance, which in turn contributes toward postbureaucratic forms of politics', in which private political organizations, such as interest groups and civic associations, will take over many of the functions that were previously the domain of formal and traditional political institutions (2003: 21). Shirky

focuses on the Internet's capacity to facilitate grassroots political organization, 'by making it easier for groups to self-assemble and for individuals to contribute to group effort without requiring formal management … these tools have radically altered the old limits on the size, sophistication, and scope in unsupervised effort' (2008: 21).

Other scholars focus on the Internet's potential to facilitate democratic behavior at the individual level. The dominant theoretical framework motivating these studies derives from rational choice theory, which views the Internet as encouraging political behavior as a result of its capacity to make civic action – such as voting, volunteering, and donating – more efficient. By reducing the costs of civic activities, individuals become more likely to engage in this behavior as a result of the lowered threshold point at which the expected costs of the behavior begin to outweigh the expected benefits.

While one body of research substantiates the Internet's capacity to encourage political behaviors by individuals (Best and Wade, 2009; Johnson and Kaye, 2003; Jennings and Zeitner, 2003; Tolbert and McNeal, 2003; Xenos and Moy, 2007), another set of prominent studies reveal a null or negligible effect of Internet use on the political behavior of individuals (Bimber, 1998, 2001, 2003; Quintelier and Vissers, 2008; Xenos and Moy, 2007). Taking a broader view, a meta-analysis reviewed 38 Internet studies and concluded that the Internet did have a positive effect on political engagement – but this effect was substantively small and likely dependent on using the Internet specifically to gather news (Boulianne, 2009).

Another component of the consideration of ICTs' effect on political organization and activity is how these technologies are changing what contemporary political participation looks like. Earl and Kimport (2011) identify two avenues through which ICTs affect collective action. The first is through scaling up effects, increasing the 'size, speed, and reach of activism', without having a 'definitive effect on the process underlying activism' (2011: 14). They term these 'supersize' effects. The second avenue through which ICTs affect political organization occurs when activists leverage these technologies to encourage and engage in novel processes of organization or participation. They term this 'theory 2.0' of the effects of ICTs on collective action, which include the rise of short-term activism online, the decreasing requirement of conventional organizations to coordinate group members and actions, and the increasing number of diverse causes and issues around which people organize.

In sum, although it may prove impossible to empirically demonstrate that the use of ICTs has been a necessary or sufficient component of recent high-profile popular movements, taken as a whole academic research suggests these technologies do exert at least a moderate positive effect on political participation and organization. Moreover, these recent grassroots movements demonstrate that, regardless of whether they were necessary or sufficient, ICTs play a highly visible and central role in these activities (Castells, 2015).

Before leaving this section, however, it is essential to acknowledge that the effects of ICTs on political activity and organization may not always be constructive for the processes of public affairs. In example, motivated by the theory of selective exposure (Zillmann and Bryant, 1985), which contends that individuals prefer to expose themselves to information that reinforces rather than challenges their pre-existing attitudes and opinions, some argue that the proliferation of media options (particularly cable television and the Internet) may be further polarizing audiences (Stroud, 2008; Sunstein, 2001). Others argue that this multiplication of media choices is increasingly leading to the fragmentation of audiences, such that it will be difficult to focus and sustain public attention around a specific set of issues (Tewksbury, 2005; Tewksbury and Rittenberg, 2009). Thus, both the multiplication of media choices and the

fragmentation of audiences may serve as impediments to successful political organization to affect productive political change or influence policy.

However, these fears have received only mixed empirical support, with some studies showing marginal or nonexistent fragmentation and polarization resulting from online news consumption (Coleman and McCombs, 2007; Webster and Ksiazek, 2012). One such study compared face-to-face interactions, traditional media consumption, and Internet use and found no support for the argument that Internet users are highly ideologically polarized and segregated in the websites they visit (Gentzkow and Shapiro, 2011). They also found that the majority of Internet users tend to visit more centrist and moderate websites and also tend to visit multiple websites when gathering news. Moreover, they found that exposure to content online was markedly less ideologically segregated than the respondents' face-to-face interactions.

Finally, it is also true that terrorist and insurgent groups, authoritarian regimes, and militaries employ ICTs to achieve their own objectives. There are a multitude of examples of ICTs being used by authoritarian governments to successfully intimidate, dissuade, and even locate and punish would-be political organizers, either overtly or through cyber warfare efforts (Kalathil and Boas, 2001, 2003; Morozov, 2011a, 2011b). These tools have also been used by non-elite mobilizers, including (but not exclusively) terrorist organizations, to recruit followers and raise funds (Theohary, 2011; Weimann, 2006) as well as to organize toward destructive or violent collective action (Bailard, 2015; Pierskalla and Hollenbach, 2013; Warren, 2015).

The use of ICTs by non-state actors to organize for violence, particularly in the case of terrorist attacks against civilian populations, has exposed governments to fierce criticism by frustrated and fearful citizens, who fault their government for not effectively monitoring the social media and other digital communications that laid the groundwork for these plans of attack. One impediment these governments face in effectively detecting and monitoring these types of communications is the sheer amount of data that officials must filter through. A second impediment is the encryption of this data by these groups. A third impediment is the ability of government officials to quickly gain access to suspicious users' data from service providers, some of whom are reticent to violate the privacy of their users, while others simply do not have the capacity to decipher encrypted data. This is all further complicated by the continually morphing and inconsistent laws surrounding privacy matters and the parameters that determine governments' rights to access this data, both within and across national boundaries.

E-Government and Effects on Transparency and Accountability

Proponents of new ICTs cite the Internet's provision of a larger quantity of political information, as well as more efficient and direct channels of communication between citizens and their officials, as enhancing the accountability and transparency of governments. As these ICTs continue to disseminate, governments – democratic, democratizing, and non-democratic alike – increasingly confront evidence that they have lost some degree of control over information flows compared to what they enjoyed in the era of traditional broadcast media systems. In theory, this increases citizens' potential oversight of the government and its officials, by providing a broader and more accessible array of information about officials' activities, both past and present – a proposition well-supported by a number of recent scandals revealed online. Thus, officials today are aware that there is greater potential for their decisions and actions to be broadcast onto the national and even international stage, in a venue and context over which they have diminished control.

This by no means suggests, however, that governments are now entirely beholden to public opinion in the course of decision-making in the Internet age, nor are they likely to see themselves as such. But these governments are aware that they must, nevertheless, weigh the potential activation of latent public opinion in ways that might affect public-affairs efforts and outcomes at some point in the future. V.O. Key (1961) first introduced the concept of latent public opinion, which John Zaller later summarized as 'opinion that might exist at some point in the future in response to the decision-makers' actions and may therefore result in political damage or even the defeat at the polls' (2002: 2).

Turning to more proactive measures, many governments have constructed e-government websites to facilitate citizens' access to information about their government and provide a convenient conduit for citizens to contact their government officials. This effort has not gone unappreciated: 82 percent of American Internet users reported accessing e-government content in 2010 (Smith, 2010). The significance of accessing e-government websites is that this type of online activity can exert a positive impact on individuals' trust in their government in advanced democracies, as well as their perceptions of their government's responsiveness and effectiveness (Tolbert and Mossberger, 2006).

Moving away from the context of advanced democracies, new ICTs also have implications for the accountability and transparency of governments in developing democracies and authoritarian nations. Larry Diamond (2010) offers the term 'liberation technology' for these ICTs, which he argues also serve as 'accountability technology'. He argues that these tools have the potential to provide efficient and powerful tools for transparency and monitoring, even within non-democratic nations. In illustration of this, Diamond offers a multitude of examples from across the globe in which these technologies were utilized to expose government malfeasance and advocate for accountability, including the use of ICT to protest police brutality and change detention policies in China, expose corruption and human rights abuses in Malaysia and inform citizens of anti-corruption and human rights issues in Senegal.

In summary, new ICTs provide opportunities for accountability and transparency that were simply not possible under previous communication systems due to the high costs and barriers to entry that these previous information landscapes faced. By drastically lowering information and communication costs, ICTs have meaningfully changed the range and type of political opportunities that exist across all national contexts. Thus, the diminished communication costs yielded by ICTs have altered the toolset of citizenship and governance in potentially profound ways – with clear implications for accountability and transparency efforts.

However, it is important to remember that these altered toolsets will not automatically nor uniformly precipitate constructive political and social outcomes. It is true that they provide opportunities and tools toward political organization and governmental accountability that older technologies simply could not provide. However, there is no guarantee that these opportunities will always be successfully realized. And, when they are, there is no guarantee it will always be toward ends that are productive for public affairs. Nevertheless, the effects of ICTs are evident throughout the various spheres that constitute public affairs, providing new opportunities as well as new risks that change what the processes of public affairs look like today.

CONCLUSION

This chapter explored three specific considerations. The first section answered the question of what exactly are ICTs, and how do these technologies interact and build on one another to construct our contemporary information landscapes. The second section considered how exactly ICTs have changed the type and range of information available for public consumption in ways that are relevant to public affairs. The third section explored the dimensions of public affairs within the citizen-government nexus where the effects of ICT have been most prominent. Specifically, this section considered how these ICTs affect citizens' political knowledge and relevant evaluations of their government and leaders, their effects on collective action efforts by citizens and grassroots groups, and their effects on governance in terms of accountability and transparency.

Of course, this is just the tip of the iceberg. Other important spheres relevant to public affairs where new technologies are changing business as usual include how they affect the processes and structure of traditional, 'bricks and mortar' organizations such as NGOs, lobbying organizations, and interest groups. These technologies are also significantly altering the calculus and practice of public affairs for corporations – particularly in regard to image- and reputation-building efforts. For example, corporations are increasingly aware of the need to not only monitor but also endeavor to influence the content of social media discussion about their products and corporate image generally (Mangold and Faulds, 2009). On the flip side, there is also the growing use of ICTs by consumers and advocacy groups to mobilize boycotts of products or brands, further altering the relationship shared by corporations and consumers in the domain of public affairs. Whelan and colleagues (2013) provide a succinct summary of the degree to which ICTs have changed citizen-corporation relations and communication,

individual citizens, and the general publics they combine to form, are relatively and potentially empowered by the emergence of social media; so too is the power of corporations, and their (functional/formally organized) stakeholders, relatively and potentially tempered. Accordingly, our argument is not that social media make citizens, individually and/or collectively, more powerful than corporations and their stakeholders. Rather, it is that citizens are potentially enabled relative to corporations and their (functional/formally organized) stakeholders. (786)

In closing, the reduced communication costs afforded by new ICTs have meaningful implications for several processes germane to public affairs. Whether it be communication between stakeholders and their representatives, or campaigns deployed on behalf of issue management, shaping media relations, or fostering community relations – many of the most integral processes and exchanges that constitute public affairs require the packaging and exchange of information between relevant actors and parties. This portends large changes in what the practice and strategies of successful public affairs will look like into the foreseeable future as these technologies and their uses continue to evolve and reshape contemporary information landscapes

REFERENCES

Althaus, S. L. and Tewksbury, D. (2002). Agenda setting and the 'new' news: Patterns of issue importance among readers of the paper and online versions of the New York Times. *Communications Research*, *29*, 180–207.

Ambah, F. S. (2006). New clicks in the Arab world: Bloggers challenge longtime cultural, political restrictions. *The Washington Post*, November 12, A13.

Bailard, C. S. (2012). Testing the internet's effect on democratic satisfaction: A multimethodological, cross-national approach. *Journal of Information Technology & Politics*, 9(2), 185–204.

Bailard, C. S. (2014). *Democracy's doubleedged sword: How internet use changes citizens' views of their government*. Baltimore, MD: Johns Hopkins University Press.

Bailard, C. S. (2015). Ethnic conflict goes mobile: Mobile technology's effect on the opportunities and motivations for violent collective action. *Journal of Peace Research*, 0022343314556334.

Bamman, D., O'Connor, B., and Smith, N. A. (2012). Censorship and deletion practices in Chinese social media. *First Monday*, *17*(3), March 5. Retrieved from http://firstmonday.org/htbin/cgiwrap/bin/ojs/index.php/fm/article/view/3943/3169 (accessed 26 August, 2016).

Benkler, Y. (2006). *The wealth of networks: How social production transforms markets and freedom*. New Haven, CT.: Yale University Press.

Best, M. L. and Wade, K. W. (2009). The internet and democracy: Global catalyst or democratic dud? *Bulletin of Science, Technology & Society*, *29*, 255–71. doi: 10.1177/0270467609336304.

Bimber, B., Flanagin, A. J., and Stohl, C. (2005). Reconceptualizing collective action in the contemporary media environment. *Communication Theory*, *15*(4), 365.

Bimber, B. (2003). *Information and American democracy: Technology in the evolution of political power*. Cambridge, U.K.: Cambridge University Press.

Bimber, B. (2001). Information and political engagement in America: The search for effects of information technology at the individual level. *Political Research Quarterly*, *54*, 53–67.

Boulianne, S. (2009). Does internet use effect engagement? A meta-analysis of research. *Political Communication*, 26(2), 193–211.

Castells, M. (2015). *Networks of outrage and hope: Social movements in the internet age*. Cambridge, U.K.: Polity Press.

Chadwick, A. (2013). *The hybrid media system: Politics and power*. Oxford, U.K.: Oxford University Press.

Chadwick, A. (2006). *Internet politics: States, citizens, and new communication technologies*. New York: Oxford University Press.

Cisco (2015). The zettabyte era: Trends and analysis. *Cisco White Paper*. Retrieved from: http://www.cisco.com/c/en/us/solutions/collateral/service-provider/visual-networking-index-vni/VNI_Hyperconnectivity_WP.html (accessed 26 August, 2016).

Coleman, R. and McCombs, M. (2007). The young and agenda-less? Exploring age-related differences in agenda setting on the youngest generation, baby boomers, and the civic generation. *Journalism & Mass Communication Quarterly, 84*(3), 495–508.

Davis, R. (1999). *The web of politics: The internet's impact on the American political system.* New York: Oxford University Press.

Diamond, L. (2010). Liberation technology. *Journal of Democracy, 21*(3), 69–83.

Diamond, L. (2008). *The spirit of democracy: The struggle to build free societies throughout the world.* New York: Holt Paperbacks.

Digital Preservation Management. Timeline: Digital Technology and Preservation. Retrieved from: http://www.dpworkshop. org/dpm-eng/timeline/viewall.html (accessed 2015).

Earl, J. and Kimport, K. (2011). *Digitally Enabled Social Change.* Cambridge, MA: MIT Press.

Gentzkow, M. and Shapiro, J. M. (2011). Ideological segregation online and offline. *The Quarterly Journal of Economics, 126*(4), 1799–1839.

Graber, D. A. (1997). *Mass Media and American Politics. 5th ed.* Washington, DC: Congressional Quarterly Press.

Heller, Maria. (2008). "Global and European information society." In P. Ludes (ed.), *Convergence and fragmentation: Media technology and the information society (Vol. 5),* 29–36. Bristol: U.K.: Intellect Books.

Hillman, A. J. and Hitt, M. A. (1999). Corporate political strategy formulation: A model of approach, participation, and strategy decisions. *Academy of Management Review, 24*(4), 825–42.

Hiltz, S. R. and Turoff, M. (1985). Structuring computer mediated communication systems to avoid information overload. *Communication of the ACM, 28,* 680–9.

Hindman, M. S. (2009). *The myth of digital democracy.* Princeton, NJ: Princeton University Press.

Hong, H. (2013). Government websites and social media's influence on government-public relationships. *Public Relations Review, 39*(4), 346–56.

Horrigan, J. B., Garrett, K., and Resnick, P. (2004). The internet and the democratic debate. *Pew Internet & American Life Project,* October 27. Retrieved from: http://www.

pewinternet.org/2004/10/27/the-internet-and-democratic-debate/ (accessed 26 August, 2016).

Howard, P. N. (2010). *The digital origins of dictatorship and democracy.* New York: Oxford University Press.

Independent ICT in Schools Commission (chair: Dennis Stevenson). (1997). Information and communications technology in UK schools: an independent inquiry. London.

International Telecommunications Union. (2013). The world in 2013: ICT facts and figures. Retrieved from: http://www.itu.int/ en/ITUD/Statistics/Documents/facts/ ICTFactsFigures2013-e.pdf (accessed 19 August, 2016).

International Telecommunications Union. (2008). *African telecommunication/ICT indicators 2008: At a crossroads.* Geneva: International Telecommunications Union.

Jennings, M. K. and Zeitner, V. (2003). Internet use and civic engagement: A longitudinal analysis. *Public Opinion Quarterly, 67,* 311–34. doi: 10.1086/376947.

Johnson, T. J. and Kaye, B. (2003). A boost or bust for democracy? How the web influenced political attitudes and behaviors in the 1996 and 2000 presidential elections. *Press/Politics, 8,* 9–34. doi: 10.1177/1081180X03008003002.

Kageyama, Y. (2004). Japanese Internet star spreads blogging gospel. *USA Today.* Retrieved from: http://usatoday30.usatoday. com/tech/world/2004-05-30-japan-blogger_x.htm (accessed 19 August, 2016).

Kalathil, S. and Boas, T. C. (2003). Open networks, closed regimes. Washington, DC: *Carnegie Endowment for International Peace.* Retrieved from: http://www.asu.edu/ courses/pos445/Open%20Networks%20 Closed%20Regimes.pdf (accessed 19 August, 2016).

Kalathil, S. and Boas, T. C. (2001). The internet and state control in authoritarian regimes: China, Cuba, and the counter-revolution. *Carnegie Endowment for International Peace.* Retrieved from: http://www. carnegieendowment.org/publications/index. cfm?fa=view&id=728 (accessed 19 August, 2016).

Katz, E. and Lazarsfeld, P. F. (1955). *Personal influence: The part played by people in the flow of mass communications*. New York: Free Press.

Kedzie, C. (1997). *Communication and democracy: Coincident revolutions and the emergent dictators*. Arlington, VA.: RAND Corporation.

Kenski, K. and Stroud, N. J. (2006). Connections between internet use and political efficacy, knowledge, and participation. *Journal of Broadcasting and Electronic Media, 5*(2), 173–92.

Key, V. O. (1961). *Public opinion and American democracy*. New York: Alfred A. Knopf.

King, G., Pan, J., and Roberts, M. E. (2013). How censorship in China allows government criticism but silences collective expression. *American Political Science Review, 107*(02), 326–43.

Kovach, S. (2015). More people are using just their phones to access the internet than desktops. *Business Insider,* April 30. Retrieved from: http://www.businessinsider.com/mobile-internet-users-pass-desktop-users-2015-4 (accessed 19 August, 2016).

Levinson, D. and Christensen, K. (2003). *Encyclopedia of community: From the village to the virtual world (Vol. 3)*. Thousand Oaks: Sage, pp. 791–794. users-2015-4#ixzz3dQuKQXAL.

Lum, T. (2006). Internet development and information control in the People's Republic of China. (CRS Report RL33167). *Congress Research Service*. Washington DC: Library of Congress.

Lupia, A. and Sin, G. (2003). Which public goods are endangered? How evolving communication technologies affect the logic of collective action. *Public Choice, 117*(3–4), 315–31.

MacKinnon, R. (2008). Flatter world and thicker walls? Blogs, censorship and civic discourse in China. *Public Choice, 134*(1–2), 31–46.

Maier, S. (2010). All the news fit to post? Comparing news content on the web to newspapers, television, and radio. *Journalism Mass Communication Quarterly, 87*(3–4), 548–62.

Mangold, W. G. and Faulds, D. J. (2009). Social media: The new hybrid element of the promotion mix. *Business Horizons, 52*(4), 357–65.

McGrath, C., Moss, D., and Harris, P. (2010). The evolving discipline of public affairs. *Journal of Public Affairs, 10*(4), 335–52.

Meier, P. Retrieved from: http://blog.ushahidi.com/2012/01/12/haiti-and-the-power-of-crowdsourcing/ (accessed 19 August, 2016).

Melody, W. H., Mansell, R. E., and Richards, B. J. (1986). *Information and communication technologies: Social science research and training (Vol. 2)*. Swindon: U.K.: Economic and Social Research Council.

Meznar, M. B. and Nigh, D. (1995). Buffer or bridge? Environmental and organizational determinants of public affairs activities in American firms. *Academy of Management Journal, 38*(4), 975–96.

Morozov, E. (2011a). *The net delusion: The dark side of internet freedom*. New York: Public Affairs.

Morozov, E. (2011b). How the Kremlin harnesses the internet. *New York Times.* Retrieved from: http://www.nytimes.com/2011/01/05/opinion/05iht-edmorozov04.html?_r=0 (accessed 19 August, 2016).

Mossberger, K., Kaplan, D., and Gilbert, M. (2008). Going online without easy access: A tale of three cities. *Journal of Urban Affairs: 30*(5): 469–88.

Mossberger, K., Tolbert, C. J., and McNeal, R. S. (2008). *Digital citizenship. The internet, society, and participation*. Cambridge, MA: MIT Press.

Mossberger, K. and Tolbert, C. J. (2010). Digital democracy: How politics online is changing electoral participation. In J. E. Leighley (ed.), *The Oxford Handbook of American Elections and Political Behavior*. Oxford: Oxford University Press, pp. 200–18.

Nielson, J. (2005). *Multimedia and hypertext: The internet and beyond*. San Diego, CA: Academic Press.

Nisbet, E. C., Stoycheff, E., and Pearce, K. E. (2012). Internet use and democratic demands: A multinational, multilevel model of Internet use and citizen attitudes about democracy. *Journal of Communication, 62*(2), 249–65.

Norris, P. (2001). *A digital divide: Civic engagement, information poverty, and the internet worldwide*. New York: Cambridge University Press.

Olson, M. (2009). *The logic of collective action (Vol. 124)*. Cambridge, MA.: Harvard University Press.

Pasek, J., Kenski, K., Romer, D., and Jamieson, K. H. (2006). America's youth and community engagement: How use of the mass media is related to civic activity and political awareness in 14- to 22-year-olds. *Communication Research*, *33*(3), 115–35.

Pierskalla, J. H. and Hollenbach, F. M. (2013). Technology and collective action: The effect of cell phone coverage on political violence in Africa. *American Political Science Review*, *107*(02), 207–24.

Prior, M. (2005). News vs. entertainment: How increasing media choice widens gaps in political knowledge and turnout. *American Journal of Political Science*, *49*(3), 577–92.

Quintelier, E. and Vissers, S. (2008). The effect of internet use on political participation. *Social Science Computer Review*, *26*(4), 411–27. doi: 10.1177/0894439307312631.

Rigg, J. (2012). Sina Weibo exceeds 400 million users, sees increasing mobile traffic. *Engadget*, November 16. Retrieved from http://www.engadget.com/2012/11/16/sina-weibo-400-million-users/ (accessed 19 August, 2016).

Scheufele, D. A. and Nisbet, M. C. (2002). Being a citizen online: New opportunities and dead ends. *Press/Politics*, *7*(3), 55–75.

Selwyn, N. (2004). Reconsidering political and popular understandings of the digital divide. *New Media & Society*, *6*(3), 341–62.

Shirky, C. (2008). *Here comes everybody: The power of organizing without organizations*. New York: The Penguin Group.

Silverman, Matt. (2012). A day in the life of the internet. *Mashable*, March 6. Retrieved from: http://mashable.com/2012/03/06/one-day-internet-data-traffic (accessed 19 August, 2016).

Smith, A. (2010). Government online. *Pew Research Center.* Retrieved from: http://www.pewinternet.org/2010/04/27/government-online/ (accessed 19 August, 2016).

Steinmueller, W. E. (2001). ICTs and the possibilities for leapfrogging by developing countries. *International Labour Review*, *140*(2), 193–210.

Stroud, N. J. (2008). Media use and political predispositions: Revisiting the concept of selective exposure. *Political Behavior*, *30*(3), 341–66.

Sullivan, J. (2012). A tale of two microblogs in China. *Media, Culture & Society*, 34, 773–83. doi: 10.1177/0163443712448951.

Sunstein, C. R. (2001). *Republic.com*. Princeton, NJ: Princeton University Press.

Sydney Morning Herald. (2012). Optimism shines through experts' view of the future, March 24. Retrieved from: http://www.smh.com.au/national/optimism-shines-through-experts-view-of-the-future-20120323-1vpas.html (accessed 19 August, 2016).

Tewksbury, D. (2005). The seeds of audience fragmentation: Specialization in the use of online news sites. *Journal of Broadcasting & Electronic Media*, *49*(3), 332–48.

Tewksbury, D. and Althaus, S. L. (2000). Differences in knowledge acquisition among readers of the paper and online versions of a national newspaper. *Journalism & Mass Communication Quarterly*, *77*, 457–79.

Tewksbury, D. and Rittenberg, J. (2009). Online news creation and consumption: Implications for modern democracies. In A. Chadwick and Howard. P. N. (eds) *Routledge handbook of internet politics*, 186–200. Abingdon: Routledge.

Tewksbury, D., Weaver, A. J., and Maddex, B. D. (2001). Accidentally informed: News exposure on the world wide web. *Journalism and Mass Communication Quarterly*, *78*(3), 533–54.

Theohary, C. A. (2011). *Terrorist use of the internet: Information operations in cyberspace*. Collingdale, PA.: DIANE Publishing.

Tolbert, C. J. and McNeal, R. S. (2003). Unraveling the effect of the internet on political participation. *Political Research Quarterly*, *56*, 175–85. doi: 10.1177/106591290305600206.

Tolbert, C. J. and Mossberger, K. (2006). The effects of e-government on trust and confidence in government. *Public Administration Review*, *66*(3), 354–69. doi: 10.1111/j.1540-6210.2006.00594.x.

van Schendelen, M. P. and Van Schendelen, R. (2010). *More Machiavelli in Brussels: The art of lobbying the EU*. Amsterdam, Netherlands: Amsterdam University Press.

Vargas, J. A. (2009). The old ways of practicing democracy have come to an end: The internet lets everyone participate. *Washington Post*, January 1. Retrieved from: http://blog.cleveland.com/pdopinion/2009/01/politics_is_no_longer_local_it.html (accessed 26 August, 2016).

Warren, T. C. (2015). Explosive connections? Mass media, social media, and the geography of collective violence in African states. *Journal of Peace Research*, doi: 0022343314558102.

Webster, J. G. and Ksiazek, T. B. (2012). The dynamics of audience fragmentation: Public attention in an age of digital media. *Journal of Communication*, *62*(1), 39–56.

Weimann, G. (2006). Virtual disputes: The use of the Internet for terrorist debates. *Studies in Conflict & Terrorism*, *29*(7), 623–39.

Whelan, G., Moon, J., and Grant, B. (2013). Corporations and citizenship arenas in the age of social media. *Journal of Business Ethics*, *118*(4), 777–90.

Xenos, M. and Moy, P. (2007). Direct and differential effects of the internet on political and civic engagement. *Journal of Communication*, *57*(4), 704–18. doi: 10.1111/j.1460-2466.2007.00364.x.

Zaller, J. (2003). Coming to grips with VO Key's concept of latent opinion. *Electoral Democracy*, 311–36. Retrieved from: https://www.researchgate.net/profile/John_Zaller/publication/245700090_Coming_to_Grips_with_V.O._Key's_Concept_of_Latent_Opinion/links/55299e030cf29b22c9bf5108.pdf) (accessed 19 August, 2016).

Zillmann, D. and Bryant, J. (1985). Affect, mood, and emotion as determinants of selective exposure. In Zillmann D. and Bryant J. (eds) *Selective Exposure to Communication*, 157–90. Mahwah, NJ: Lawrence Erlbaum Associates.

Corporate Political Activity and Public Policy Outcomes: New Realities and Increasing Challenges

Michael Hadani

INTRODUCTION

Corporate political strategies, corporate political investments or corporate political activity (CPA) represent a growing non-market[1] strategic approach (Baron, 1995; Hillman and Hitt, 1999) common for firms today and growing in popularity. CPA involves various tactics, such as making political action committee (PAC) contributions to politicians' election and reelection campaigns, hiring lobbyists, hiring former members of Congress or staffers to work for firms, engaging in grassroots lobbying, and participating in trade organizations, among others, all aimed at generating political access (Austen-Smith, 1995; Truman, 1951). CPA in many cases tries to achieve outright political influence (Hasen, 2012; Hansen, 1991; Stratmann, 2002); it holds the potential of delivering significant returns on (political) investments for firms pursuing

such influence. Indeed, the *Boston Globe* recently reported that:

> By investing just $1.8 million over two years in payments for Washington lobbyists, Whirlpool secured the renewal of lucrative energy tax credits for making high-efficiency appliances that it estimates will be worth a combined $120 million for 2012 and 2013. Such breaks have helped the company keep its total tax expenses below zero in recent years.

Moreover, the article notes that, in 2013, corporations received a staggering 154 billion dollars in tax breaks, contained in 135 individual provisions of the tax code and a new tax appropriation bill. Whirlpool argued the tax breaks help retain jobs but has closed two plants in the US (during the same time period) and let go of over 800 employees (http://www.bostonglobe.com/news/politics/2013/03/16/corporations-record-huge-returns-from-tax-lobbying-gridlock-congress-stalls-reform/omgZvDPa37DNlSqi0G95YK/story.html [accessed 15 June 2015]).

As this story indicates, when firms are politically successful the benefits are not only staggering but can come at the expense of both the employees and the public at large without conclusively impacting the firm in the long term. One could still argue that companies such as Whirlpool use money gained via CPA to invest in building resources or research and development. However, Lux, Crook and Woehr's (2011) argue, in their recent meta-analysis that firms either tend to pursue market-based opportunities (such as investments in research and development) or political opportunities but not both. They note (p. 237): 'The results also indicate that economic opportunities are not significantly related to CPA.' The two, CPA and marker oriented activities, may act as substitutes, rather than complement one another, a notion long established (Olson, 1965; Stigler, 1971). Others have shown that, as firms shift resources to political avenues, they invest less in their competitive resources and collectively may lose market returns (Coates and Wilson, 2007; Olson, 1982); the value and outcomes of CPA are open to debate.

Yet research on CPA itself makes it harder rather than easier to arrive at substantive conclusions as to its value both to firms and to society at large, as different theoretical approaches to CPA make different assumptions as to the process and the value of CPA. At the same time there is a growing concern over the political power and sway firms hold today, given recent changes in US law and the normative notion that CPA may be akin to corruption (Teachout, 2014). Surprisingly, research on CPA in business, economics and political science has not fully integrated legal and related normative views on CPA, but rather focused on its instrumental and descriptive dynamics. Thus, the purpose of this book chapter is to provide an integrative review and analysis of the different theoretical views on CPA, taking into account the growing concerns over legal and normative

issues such as corruption, free speech, and value to society.

The structure of this book chapter is as follows: I first review major theoretical views on CPA originating from various theoretical disciplines, from sociology to strategy. I then introduce legal (and related normative) views on CPA and conclude with some open questions and ongoing debates regarding the dynamics and implications of CPA for managers today.

SOCIOLOGICAL VIEWS: CLASS-WIDE RATIONALITY, INSTITUTIONAL THEORY, AND IDEOLOGY

Sociology has made three important contributions to the study of CPA. The first is the view that businesses engage the government in order to push a market-oriented rationality rather than alternative ideologies, such as a social one (Getz, 2002); this approach has been termed 'class-wide rationality' (Clawson et al., 1998; Mizruchi, 1992). Useem's (1982) work argues that within corporate elites, specific values and ideologies are prevalent, reflecting collective beliefs that in the political arena may translate into the pursuit of common or cohesive business-wide ends. Thus, this approach focuses on a common or shared interest and on similar ideological fault lines that can predict interest group political action, and has also been used to explain the political activity of firms (Getz, 2002; Heinz et al., 1993). Although one can explain some of the political activity of firms from an ideological viewpoint, this approach was criticized as failing to account for the largely independent nature of firms' CPA (Getz, 2002; Gray and Lowery, 1997) and the understanding that, while CPA might be affected by shared interests, it is strongly affected by firm-level considerations (Rehbein and Schuler, 1999) as firms compete against each other in the political marketplace. For example, Wilson (1990) found that, while firms do participate in industry-wide trade organizations, as part of their political approach, these are perceived as less efficient than firm-level CPA tactics. However, new research has shown that the unit of analysis matters in this debate. Instead of looking at the firm as the unit of analysis and its CPA as the outcome, we may need to look at who initiates CPA and the political leanings of the firm. For instance, the top managers of the firm may be a more appropriate unit of analysis than the firm itself (Hadani et al., in press); this will be elaborated below.

A second, related approach is derived from institutional theory, which focuses on the forces that collectively shape institutional fields and corporate behavior. Firms, among other actors, seek to increase their legitimacy, since increasing legitimacy helps them survive, in particular under conditions of uncertainty (DiMaggio and Powell, 1983). In order to achieve this legitimacy, firms (among others) often engage in isomorphic behaviors, to increase institutional conformity, which will lead to higher legitimacy (Scott, 1995). For example, Staw and Epstein (2000) show how firms adopt managerial practices not because they are efficient (though they may be) but due to mimetic forces and their perceived legitimizing effects. Thus, firms might adopt CPA because they operate in regulated industries, have federal contracts (as shown in several studies) or are otherwise impacted by government action (Darves and Dreiling, 2002). Firms operating in more politically active industries might perceive a legitimizing need to do so themselves as a way to manage their image vis-à-vis the government. However, they may also engage in mimetic CPA since other firms engage in CPA (Mizruchi, 1989). From this viewpoint CPA may not be about pure profit maximizing but more about signaling legitimacy and 'keeping up with the Joneses'. It is important to note that the legitimacy that may drive CPA or its dynamics is not societal but is driven by the firm's political legitimacy needs (Hillman and Hitt, 1999).

Third, if we focus on the CEO as a major initiator of firm CPA, which many studies argue is the case (Blumentritt, 2003; Burris, 2001), then his or her political ideology may matter to the way the firm engages in CPA and specifically the political leanings of a firm's CPA. Recent scholarship has highlighted the need to focus not just on the role CEOs play in imitating and impacting CPA (Hadani et al., in press; Ozer, 2010), but also on how this person's own ideology matters. Extending upper echelon theory, Christensen, Dhaliwal, Boivie and Graffin (2015) argue that the different parties in the US exhibit different ideological belief systems and economic assumptions with regard to how wealth is obtained, the distribution and redistribution of wealth, and the role of government in general. Further, CEOs are likely to have personal ideological beliefs that reflect either a Republican or a Democratic leaning and these ideologies, as part of their belief systems, can paint their behavior as CEOs. Chin, Hambrick and Trevino (2013) find that CEOs' political orientation impacts firms' CSR. Specifically, they find that (1) liberal-leaning CEOs emphasize CSR more than conservative-leaning CEOs; (2) the association between a CEO's political ideology and CSR is moderated by a CEO's relative power; and (3) liberal CEOs emphasize CSR even when recent financial performance is low, unlike conservative CEOs who pursue CSR initiatives only if recent performance allows them to do so. These recent findings indicate that a CEO political belief system impacts corporate strategy and thus is also likely to impact the CPA of a firm, in particular the relative Democratic versus Republican tilt of a firm's CPA. This novel idea, if proven accurate, has important implications. It raises the possibility that CPA is truly not just about maximizing profits but is influenced by personal preferences and biases, as suggested by Hadani and Schuler (2013), who extend March and Simon's (1958) work on bounded rationality. In the context of CPA, managers are not only boundedly rational but may be bounded by their political viewpoints as well.

POLITICAL SCIENCE VIEWS ON CPA: INTEREST GROUP AND PUBLIC CHOICE THEORIES

Interest Group Approaches

First, interest group theory has been used to explain both the motivation for and the outcomes of CPA. Interest group theory views the structure of public policy making and some of its outcomes as reflecting a competition among various interest groups (trade associations, citizens' organizations, umbrella organizations, NGOs, and other collective parties) who have specific public policy demands at the state or the federal level (Hrebenar, 1992; Scholzman and Tierney, 1986; Thomas and Hrebenar, 1990). Traditionally, political science scholarship viewed the demands raised by interest groups and their lobbying as impacting government policy (Truman, 1971). Lowi (1969) argued that government policy is strongly impacted by actions of interest groups and Olson (1982) argued that such political activity can shift resources from productive to less productive means and harm the economy. In his original thesis published in 1965, Olson argues that the appearance of a politically active interest group is self-selective; groups that are able to organize and resolve collective action and coordination issues will appear and engage in political action. Consequently, they will become more dominant over other interested parties that did not resolve these issues; their agendas will become more dominant at the expense of other groups or the public since the political establishment is more susceptible to their pressure (Kollman, 1998).

However, interest groups are rational objective maximizers who wish to exert control in the advancement of their goals. As such, their success may be a double-edged sword, especially if their goals are economic or profit maximizing in nature, due to 'institutional sclerosis', a term coined by Olson (1982). Olson argued that political activity on behalf of interest groups, if effective in achieving political means, will shift resources from productive uses to rent-seeking ones and away from efficient allocation of resources such as the adoption of new technologies. In other words, he argued that if more interest groups are politically active economic drag or slowdown will occur. Coates and Wilson (2007) argue not only that interest groups are 'entrenched' in the public policy arena and as such are powerful actors, but that few macro-level empirical studies of the sclerosis hypothesis have been conducted. In a study of 55 countries they looked at the number of trade associations (that lobby governments) and the value and volatility of the stock market over 30 years of data. They find a negative association between the number of trade associations and the overall value of the stock market and its volatility, across different analytical approaches. They note (p. 345):

> In particular, a one percent increase in the number of interest groups in a country is associated with a direct reduction in average annual stock market returns of roughly 2–5%, and a reduction in the volatility of annual stock returns of roughly 6–14%. The findings clearly suggest that greater attention should be paid to the impact of interest groups on economic activity, by economists, policy makers, and financial practitioners alike.

The study's implications, though applying to macro-level analyses, are interesting at the micro level of the firm as they raise the question: does CPA lead to resource misallocation? This is a strong possibility given older studies that examine how CPA can impact barriers to entry (Dean et al., 1998; Esty and Caves, 1983) and newer ones that focus on the limits of CPA to achieve financial results (Hadani and Schuler, 2013; Sobel and Graefe-Anderson, 2014).

EXCHANGE THEORIES, THE POLITICAL MARKETPLACE VIEW, PUBLIC CHOICE AND CPA

Related to interest groups and elaborating their dynamics are political exchange theories, somewhat based on social exchange approaches (i.e., Blau, 1964), which assume that a quasi-economic exchange occurs between interest groups or firms and public policy officials. As noted by Hall and Deardorff (2006), these exchange models assume that implicit (or at times even explicit) exchanges occur between those providing money or information and those providing policy, such as votes. Thus, there is a form of non-market trade occurring between the two parties to this political transaction (Austen-Smith, 1995). The question here is, given the covert nature of this exchange and the illegality of outright bribes, how can the firm on the one hand and the legislator on the other enforce any exchange? One partial solution is to create repeated interactions between a firm or an interest group and a legislator to build relational capital and to reduce information asymmetry (Snyder, 1992). Stratmann (1991, 1998) argued that firms may make contributions both before and after votes on bills to make sure they reward expected outcomes and can discipline their counterparts from reneging on implicit promises. However, other studies have failed to find conclusive support for a simple exchange model based solely on a quid pro quo type of exchange, which has led other scholars to argue that donations to politicians (a common currency in exchange models) are all about buying time and not direct influence (Hall and Wayman, 1990). Still, as noted by Hall and Deardorff (2006), many questions remain as to the viability of simple exchange models. Regardless, an extension of such models, the political marketplace view of CPA, has become one of the most dominant in political science but especially in management and strategy scholarship.

The political marketplace theory has its roots in the work of Buchanan (1987) and others (Truman, 1951). At its core are two assumptions. First is the basic view of competition among interest groups seeking access and influence in the public policy arena. Second is the notion that public policy outcomes, whatever they may be, are a result of economic-like exchanges between constituents and other interested parties, such as firms and decision makers in the public policy sphere. As noted by Hillman and Keim (1995), public policy seekers wish to maximize their own limited set of interests. Relatedly, those seeking public policy outcomes are public policy demanders and those providing public policy outcomes are public policy suppliers. Market-like exchanges allow firms to offer votes, money, and information to legislators and their staff in return for access or at times outright influence (Hillman and Hitt, 1999). Though originating from political science, its elaboration and expansion have been primarily within the arena of strategic management described later on.

Somewhat similar to the above are public choice theories (Buchanan and Tullock, 1962), which acknowledge the self-interested nature of legislators. These theories depict the political process in general, and firms' CPA specifically, as an exchange process between policy makers and private actors, such as individuals, firms and other interested parties (Downs, 1957). In this context public policy makers provide or supply policy and private actors are public policy demanders, perceived as purchasers of beneficial policy (Getz, 2002). Public choice theory assumes that actors are rational and self-interested parties, and as such this theory tries to assess their incentives for political activity and can help us understand why firms employ specific tactics. There are different interpretations of the implications of this theory. First is a view reflective of exchange theories in which legislators respond to the needs and views of private actors, who provide money and information in return for specific policy outcomes; hence this theory helps explain why firms are politically active (Getz, 2002). Holcomb (1995) notes that public choice theory helps explain how the government works, and Keim and Zeithaml (1986) highlight the incentives and the behavioral constraints facing public policy officials; legislators focus on listening to and being responsive to their politically active constituencies because their support is crucial to winning reelection (Keim and Zeithaml, 1986). These politically active constituents may be the public or private interests, but by definition they represent those who are likely to stay actively informed about, and involved in, the public policy process and the political arena (Lord, 2000). As noted by Lord (2000), legislators have a strong self-interest to remain in office because their position provides them with continuous benefits such as pay, prestige, and power. This in turn raises the importance of constituency building.

ECONOMIC VIEWS ON CPA

The economics literature has contributed several theories to firms' CPA, collective action theory, and transaction cost theory. Collective action theory focuses on the collective benefits that accrue from firms' CPA (Olson, 1965). Since CPA is costly, and since it would benefit larger firms more than small ones, as they have more to gain from it, smaller firms would free ride on the CPA of larger firms (Olson, 1971). Empirically this approach, which focuses on the impact of industry concentration on firms' CPA, has received only mixed support (Esty and Caves, 1983; Hansen et al., 2005). Some suggest that, although collective action dynamics might affect CPA, it is not a central issue, as CPA represents more of a competitive action strategy (Grier et al., 1994; see also Baron, 1997). Further, collective action theory ignores the existence of information asymmetries between parties involved in political activities; they assume firms know the political actions of other firms and use a rational calculus of cost and benefits of the decision to be politically active. However, such assumptions are open to debate, as firms do not have full access to or understanding of the political activity of their competition, nor a full understanding of the political marketplace (Hillman and Hitt,

1999; Schuler et al., 2002). Neither are they fully economically rational in understanding and evaluating the costs and benefits associated with CPA (i.e., March and Simon, 1958). Thus, although the collective action model is a beneficial starting point, most researchers have moved to other theoretical frameworks to explain CPA (Getz, 2002).

Transaction cost theory, another economics-driven viewpoint, is concerned about which organizational arrangements are the most efficient from an economic cost perspective, examining ways in which firms internalize or externalize transactions, or shift firm boundaries for maximum economic efficiency (Williamson, 1985). Internalizing a transaction implies a firm is more committed to it as it needs to create permanent internal functions for it; contracting out may result in creating an agency problem and the firm would need to deal with the related risk associated with such a problem (opportunism, moral hazard issues, etc.). While transaction cost economics does not help explain firms' motivation for CPA, it can help explore the conditions under which firms will act independently or in unison to achieve political gains, or when firms will attempt to internalize or externalize their own political strategies, such as in the use of external or internal lobbying. Another example relates to firms joining trade or collective business associations, in which the ability to achieve the same economies of political scale is less likely if firms internalize the same type of political activity.

MANAGEMENT AND STRATEGIC MANAGEMENT VIEWS ON CPA

Work in management in general, and strategic management specifically, has focused on several related approaches to understanding CPA, among which resource dependence theory (RDT) and the aforementioned political marketplace theory are popular (Hadani and Schuler, 2013). Originally used to describe how organizations depend on their external environment and how this dependency should be managed to maintain autonomy and control over resources, RDT (Pfeffer and Salancik, 1978) describes a context under which an entity such as an organization relies on another entity for necessary resources and this reliance not only creates power differentials between the parties to the exchange, but also potentially constrains one party's action. Government actions and firms' dependency on such actions, such as under regulation, have always been viewed as constraining the ability of firms to exercise strategic freedom (Hillman and Hitt, 1999; Hillman, 2003; 2005). RDT has been used to explain both when and why firms become politically active and how they can manage this dependency (Hillman et al., 1999; Mezanr and Nigh, 1995). The main assumption here is that not only is it rational to try to manage government dependencies (Hillman et al., 2004), but that doing so can be an effective way to reduce socio-political uncertainty (Lord, 2000). Indeed, Oliver and Holzinger (2008) argue that effective political strategies can result in higher efficiency and legitimacy for firms, and that firms that are able to anticipate and implement governmental policies are likely to develop good relationships with key stakeholders such as the government, media, and public interest groups.

A second popular theoretical framework is the political marketplace approach, which originates from political science but has been expanded significantly by management scholars. The work of Bonardi, Hillman and Keim (2005) has explored when political markets are more or less attractive. Specifically, these scholars have explored the importance of political issue salience (election versus non-election issues), new issues versus existing ones, demand-side competition for political access, supply-side competition, and interaction between demand- and supply-side dynamics. Bonardi and Keim (2005) have

added a focus on the importance of widely versus narrowly defined political issues.

Based on the above, I provide a synthesis of major theoretical views in Table 14.1 below.

EMPIRICAL TRENDS

Empirical scholarship on CPA is complex, as empirical work on CPA relies on different theoretical views and may focus on one or more of two general CPA dynamics – the antecedents of CPA and the outcomes of CPA. With regard to the latter, research can be further subdivided into the impact of CPA on access to politicians, or impact on votes or election outcomes, or the direct impact of CPA on firm-level outcomes.

In terms of antecedents for CPA, Lux et al. (2011) conducted a meta-analysis focusing on the antecedents of CPA. They report that political incumbency, ideology, political competition, government regulation, and sales and industry concentration, among other factors, explain variance in the decision to engage in CPA. In terms of direct outcomes, Hillman et al. (1999) find a positive short-term market response to the appointment of politically tied directors, and Hillman (2005) later found that, for regulated firms, having former politicians on the board is positively associated with market value but not with accounting-based performance outcomes. Cooper, Gulen and Ovtchinnikov (2010) report that PAC contributions are positively associated with future stock returns, but mostly for firms that give to more politicians, firms that give to politicians holding office in the same state the firm is headquartered, and firms that give to Democrats rather than Republicans. It is important to note that Cooper et al. (2010) only examined firms that were politically active. Lux et al.'s (2011) meta-analysis reports a modest effect of CPA on firm performance measured as accounting returns. This latter finding is open to debate,

Table 14.1 Comparison of different disciplinary views on CPA

Theoretical discipline/ stream	Assumptions	Actors	CPA Foci	Scholarship examples
Political science				
Interest group theory	Public policy outcomes are a function of competition Actors are rational objective maximizers	Any interested party able to organize and overcome collective action problem Typically some collective interest groups	Competition impacts policy outcomes Policy outcomes reflect successful constituents' access Interest group has narrow objectives, which may not maximize social welfare or public good	Lowi (1969) Olson (1982)
Public choice theory	Public policy outcomes are impacted by the needs of the politically active and vocal groups and firms Actors are rational and sensitive to cost benefit analysis but the median voter cannot effectively monitor public policy outcomes and is likely to be indifferent, in and in many cases ineffectual, in setting public policy agendas or public policy outcomes	Interested parties are selfish utility maximizers (the public interest is sometimes ignored)	Public policy is an outcome of exchanges among participants A political marketplace exists with clear winners and losers Politics is a 'game' with no clearly defined 'common good' Policy suppliers are not necessarily beholden to normative expectations of right or wrong	Buchanan and Tollison (1984)
Sociology				
Institutional theory	Legitimacy is as important to survival as other rationales, such as economic efficiency	Any member of a specific institutional field seeks to maximize legitimacy by responding to different coercive and mimetic forces Isomorphic pressures increase strategic similarity Coercive isomorphism can originate from the government	Firms and interest groups seek to maximize political legitimacy and acceptance by following the political behavior of others or behaving in a similar manner Firms compete for political legitimacy	DiMaggio and Powell (1983) Mizruchi (1989, 1992)
Class-wide rationality	Firms that are more connected to each other through inter-firm networks and will exhibit strong cohesive class-wide ideology, which is focused on free market forces and reduced government intervention	Firms and their elites (top executives) CPA somewhat reflects similar ideological leanings	Class-wide rationality explains some variance in firms' CPA; more central firms reflect similar pro-business interests; peripheral firms may deviate from a class-wide rationality	Useem (1982) Burris (2001)

Economic views

Collective action theories	The benefits from collective action accrue to both politically active and non-politically active firms; smaller interest groups or actors have an incentive to free ride on those that bear the costs of organizing and becoming politically active	Firms and other interest groups CPA reflects a cost-benefit calculation	The antecedents of CPA of large versus smaller firms or large organized interests versus smaller ones	Olson (1965)

Management/Strategy

Resource dependence theory	Organizations are dependent on powerful institutions in their environment for critical resources (political, financial, normative)	Organizations and the government or society	Resource dependency constrains managerial (strategic) freedom and motivates CPA. CPA is used to reduce dependency and uncertainty and to increase the monitoring ability of the political environment	Pfeffer and Salancik (1978) Hillman et al. (1999) Hillman (2005)
Political marketplace (extension of public choice and interest group theory)	Similar to public choice theory; public policy outcomes are a result of market-like exchanges between public policy demanders and suppliers. The 'goods' exchanged are information, money or the promise of votes in return for votes, contracts or other beneficial public policy outcomes	Any interested party that can offer votes, money or valuable information may obtain political access but firms may gain a premium for access given their ability to solve collective action problems and due to firms' significant financial resources	The political marketplace is the critical arena in which CPA occurs. Both supply-side and demand-side competition affect political access and influence; issue saliency and visibility are important mediating factors	Bonardi et al. (2005) Bonardi and Keim (2005)

as their study involved regulated firms (such as utilities or universities) alongside non-regulated firms, and ignored recent large-scale studies (with larger samples) that report the exact opposite with regard to the impact of CPA on firm outcomes, which appears to be negative rather than positive (Aggarwal et al., 2012; Hadani and Schuler, 2013; Sobel and Graefe-Anderson, 2014). Hadani, Bonardi and Dahan's (in press) new meta analysis finds only weak effects of CPA on public policy outcomes and a statistically marginal effect regarding the direct impact of CPA on firm performance. Moreover, Igan, Mishra and Tressel (2009), as well as Kostovetsky (2009), report that CPA can increase risk taking and endanger the firm. Sobel and Graefe-Anderson (2014) found that not only is CPA not associated with firm- or industry-level outcomes, but it also contributes to higher executive compensation with no improvements to firm performance; CPA appears to insulate the firm from market discipline. In a similar vein others have argued that CPA may raise agency costs; institutional investors may oppose CPA (Coates, 2010; 2012; Hadani, 2012; Sobel and Graefe-Anderson, 2014).

In terms of indirect outcomes, such as votes, Ansolabehere, Snyder and Ueda (2004) reviewed almost 40 studies that examined whether PAC contributions impact voting outcomes, as well as conducting their own longitudinal analysis of the issue. They report that in 75 percent of cases donations to politicians do not impact their voting behavior and their own complex analysis reveals much of the same, if not worse; PAC contributions seem to be a very weak instrument for influencing voting outcomes. Studies on election outcomes are equivocal as well, and raise the importance of political issue context. While PAC money is intended to impact election outcomes (Stratmann, 1998), some studies do not find an effect on election outcomes (Abramowitz, 1988). The impact on election outcomes is also open to debate as the effect

of PAC money may be dependent on whether the politician is a challenger or an incumbent (Magee, 2002). Dharmapala and Palda (2002) find that, for a politician running for office, a narrow base of financial PAC support (one that could be expected from a candidate whose base of support is from firms) results in worse election campaigns for challengers, while having a negligible impact on incumbents. Their dataset was unique as it covered 13 years of data and over 650,000 donations. This analysis does not focus on the fact that in order to win elections those seeking office need to raise substantial amounts of money and that the ability of such candidates to raise funds strongly impacts their chance of winning (Ackerman and Ayres, 2002).

In terms of lobbying, the outcomes appear to be less equivocal in their impact on public policy or performance. Some find support that lobbying can impact public policy agenda setting and decisions such as the content of legislation itself rather than voting outcomes, especially for policy issues impacting a narrow constituency (Baik and Lee, 2012; Nelson and Yackee, 2012; see also Gawande et al., 2012), with at least partial support for a direct effect of lobbying on firm outcomes (Kim, 2008). However, others (Hadani and Schuler, 2013) report a negative association between lobbying and firm market value. Others note lobbying's ability to leverage the public policy arena. For example, Blau, Brough and Thomas (2013) report that, before and during the financial crisis, financial institutions that lobbied were more likely to receive TARP money and, when they received TARP money, they received more of it. Hill, Kelly, Lockhart and Van Ness (2013) find that firms that lobby have better excess returns than those that do not, but only when they engage less in PAC contributions. Kang (2015) finds that, for energy-sector firms, lobbying increases financial outcomes, echoing the work of Bonardi and colleagues (2006) regarding the ability of politically active utilities to increase their rate of return, above and beyond other relevant factors.

However, utilities face little competition for political access, which may make their CPA easier to leverage.

To summarize, while research on the antecedents of CPA is clear in its conclusions, research on CPA outcomes is more equivocal. CPA's ability to impact public policy outcomes has not been strongly supported in political science literature, especially for PAC contributions, while the ability of PAC contributions to impact election outcomes is open to debate. Lobbying efforts may fare better in impacting the content of legislation, though their impact on election outcomes naturally has not been explored. In terms of outright financial returns it is difficult to argue that CPA is effective or ineffective given the mixed results associated with studies that have examined direct linkages between CPA and different measures of firm financial performance.

A general look at both the theory and the empirical evidence supplied above reveals some common themes. First, most of the theorizing and indeed the empirical research on CPA is about the utility and self-interest needs of those participating in CPA, be these interest groups in general or firms specifically. This is a common thread across public choice and exchange theories as well as the resource dependence views on CPA. Second, almost all theoretical approaches used to describe the antecedents or outcomes of CPA skirt social issues (economic approaches have long acknowledged social costs and resource diversion as a result of CPA, often termed deadweight loss or allocation inefficiencies). Indeed, according to some theoretical views we cannot realistically expect legislators not to follow the needs of interest groups when these groups are politically active; since such groups or firms focus on their narrow needs, public policy outcomes may come to reflect narrow needs. The legal or normative considerations are of secondary import in most theorizing on CPA, to date, especially in management- or strategy-based research. While studies in political science,

economics, sociology and management/strategy often borrow or integrate insights from each other, in particular research in management (for example, Getz, 2002; Hillman et al., 2004; Lux et al., 2011), the legal view on CPA has rarely been integrated into mainstream management research on CPA.

LEGAL VIEWS ON CPA: HISTORY AND THEMES

As noted above, legal and normative analyses of CPA are almost absent from CPA scholarship and debate, with few exceptions (Alzola, 2013), and with the exception of legal scholarship published in law journals. This is exacerbated by the silo-like nature of research on CPA. Its perspectives on corruption, free speech and the public good, though meaningful and important, are mostly absent from some of the most oft cited CPA articles, and this creates a critical void that needs to be addressed as it provides important insights into understanding how CPA is viewed today. The history of how the law viewed the role of outside interests in the public policy process, below, provides these important insights.

Fear of outside influence on the public policy process in the US is as old as the republic itself. Indeed, since the inception of the US, the interaction between moneyed, for-profit parties and legislators, either at the state or the federal level, was viewed negatively and as reflecting dangerous corruption. Some of the speakers at the constitutional convention held in 1787 spoke against it; George Mason argued that government corruption (bowing to private interests) would 'end government'. As reviewed in Zephyr Teachout's 2014 book *Corruption in America*, early American conceptions of corruption originated from two related sources. The first was Aristotelian and republican and the second was Christian and puritanical. In both schools of thought, corruption occurs in the political arena where incentives exist for self-serving behaviors that come at the expense of the public (Teachout, 2014: 39–40). In this context a private intention to sway public policy for private ends was viewed as corrupt – the notion of a quid pro quo exchange, which some have come to set as a litmus test for corruption vis-à-vis CPA, combined with the purpose or intent of distorting public policy outcomes. Thus, legislative or political bribery was defined broadly, reflecting more than a quid pro quo type of exchange; officials were guilty of bribery if they treated one side more favorably than the other. In some states, giving something of value to a legislature was viewed as an intent to influence public policy and thus as corrupt. Individual states in particular were very concerned about the potential influence of private interests on state legislators; by the 1820s, most state constitutions outlawed any material exchanges between legislators and private individuals, since such exchanges were seen either as vote buying or attempting to achieve private gains from legislative outcomes (Teachout, 2014: 109).

In the 1850s, bribery statutes became broader, making it illegal to give money or valued goods to a legislator to receive a favor, assistance, or any legislative benefits in return. Federal statutory law also expanded with the passing of the first anti-bribery law in 1853. It prescribed punishment for anyone who promised something of value to officers or legislators of the government with the intent of impacting voting outcomes or laws, and punishment for those who accepted such benefits (Teachout, 2014: 116–117). After the civil war, anti-corruption statutes expanded to more states and further broadened the definition of corruption to cover attempts at influencing the behavior of publicly elected officials. This view dominated thinking at both the state and the national level. In 1907 the Tillman Act passed by Congress prohibited corporations from making both direct money contributions with regard to presidential or congressional elections and from making indirect 'independent expenditures' on their behalf;

violators (corporate officers) would be fined significantly and/or face prison terms of up to a year. The act, however, did not create an enforcement mechanism (Sitkoff, 2002). In 1910 the Federal Corrupt Practices Act was passed and among its provisions were campaign spending limits on political parties in (House of Representatives) general elections. In 1911 it was amended to include Senate and primary elections. Its original content and 1911 amendments required public disclosure of financial spending by political parties and candidates and set limits on the amount of money candidates were allowed to spend on their election campaigns. Thus for most of the 19th and at least part of the 20th century the legislature, reflecting public concerns, sought to curb outside and corporate influence on public policy outcomes in the US, realizing its potential for corruption.

However, gradually the agenda changed. Early Supreme Court decisions did not challenge the normative aspect of interest group impact or the corrupt impact of CPA, but rather focused on the procedural aspects of regulating how money was used in election campaigns or in politics in general. For example, in 1925 the Supreme Court removed candidates' spending limits on the grounds that the US Constitution did not grant Congress the authority to regulate primary elections or political party nomination procedures. The Taft-Hartley Act of 1947, though not primarily aimed at regulating political donations, prohibited independent donations from unions and corporations in support of or against candidates running for Federal elections. The Federal Elections Campaign Act (FECA) passed in 1971 (and its subsequent modifications and amendments in 1972, 1974, 1976, 1977 and 1979) solidified regulation over the exchanges among moneyed parties and those running for election or reelection campaigns at the federal level. Specifically, the law and its amendments set contributions limits from individuals to candidates and parties, set disclosure guidelines for legislators and parties receiving donations, and encouraged grassroots political activity as well as creating a system for public funding of elections (http://www.fec.gov/pdf/legislative_hist/legislative_history_1979.pdf [accessed 20 May 2015]). The legislative passage of FECA and its amendments not only recognized the ubiquitous nature of the exchanges between moneyed interest groups and politicians but also the need for government oversight. It is important to note that the campaign finance laws and regulation were amended and modified from 1971 through 2007 (http://www.fec.gov/law/feca/feca.pdf [accessed 20 May 2015]), indicating the increasing power of interest groups, the growing influence of business in politics, and public and political concern over the impact of money on the public policy sphere.

One of the most difficult issues for the law is lobbying. On the one hand, lobbying may reflect a legitimate exchange of information from concerned constituents to politicians (Hall and Deardorff, 2006; Hansen, 1991; Smith, 2000) and possibly a form of political participation or consumption (Ansolabehere et al., 2003) and, on the other, an attempt to tilt public policy in favor of the few, such as corporations, at the expense of many (Coates, 2010; Hasen, 2012). Historically, though, common law viewed lobbying as a proxy for bribery (and as creating a distorted incentive for legislators) and thus corrupt and, until the early 20th century, most state laws outlawed lobbying altogether (Teachout, 2014: 43, 167). The consensus view then was that lobbying contracts were a precursor to corruption, a view echoed by Supreme Court decisions of that time. At the state level, courts found that private lobbying or persuasion outside of public purview increased the risk of bribes and corruption (for example, in California, Kentucky, Oregon, Nebraska, Wisconsin, and Vermont, among other state courts) (Teachout, 2014: 159). Only in the mid 20th century, with the ascendance of the contractual view of lobbying as a professional contract between two individuals, did

lobbying gradually become accepted, and in 1946 Congress passed the Federal Regulation of Lobbying Act. The Lobbying Disclosure Act of 1995 and its 2007 amendments require that a person acting as a lobbyist register with the Clerk of the House of Representatives and the Secretary of the Senate. As stated by the law:

> The term 'lobbyist' means any individual who is employed or retained by a client for financial or other compensation for services that include more than one lobbying contact, other than an individual whose lobbying activities constitute less than 20 percent of the time engaged in the services provided by such individual to that client over a six month period.

> The term 'client' means any person or entity that employs or retains another person for financial or other compensation to conduct lobbying activities on behalf of that person or entity. A person or entity whose employees act as lobbyists on its own behalf is both a client and an employer of such employees. In the case of a coalition or association that employs or retains other persons to conduct lobbying activities, the client is the coalition or association and not its individual members' (http://lobbyingdisclosure.house.gov/lda.html [accessed 20 May 2015]).

The law requires lobbyists to report their activities as stated:

> No later than 45 days after the end of the semiannual period beginning on the first day of each January and the first day of July of each year in which a registrant is registered under section 4, each registrant shall file a report with the Secretary of the Senate and the Clerk of the House of Representatives on its lobbying activities during such semiannual period. A separate report shall be filed for each client of the registrant' (http://lobbyingdisclosure.house.gov/lda.html [accessed 20 May 2015]).

The 2007 amendments also require organizations that spend over $12,500 quarterly to register as lobbyists (http://lobbyingdisclosure.house.gov/amended_lda_guide.html [accessed 20 May 2015]).

Thus, gradually CPA became legitimate as long as its activities were disclosed, since such disclosure was viewed as a remedy for corruption, at least partially. One major issue remains, though, which is the issue of free speech.

MAJOR CHALLENGES AND EMERGING THEMES: LANDMARK LEGAL CASES

Historically CPA was not viewed through the lens of free speech until several state level court decisions, and in particular one landmark Supreme Court decision, shifted the legal discourse. Specifically, in 1975, FECA, and its 1974 amendments, were challenged in *Buckley* v. *Valeo*, in which Senator James A. Buckley and others sued Francis R. Valeo, who was an ex officio member of the FEC. The lawsuit argued that FECA violated the First and Fifth amendments (free speech and due process rights). In 1976 the Supreme Court's decision upheld most of the original content of the law but struck down candidate spending limits, following an interpretation and application of the First Amendment to political spending. The court also upheld the disclosure regime, contribution limits and the system for publicly funding elections. Legal scholars widely interpreted the case as reflecting four themes: 1) Money expenditure on elections is protected under the First Amendment; 2) Combating corruption and its appearance are legitimate reasons to limit free speech; 3) Campaign contribution limits are valid; 4) Campaign expenditure limits are not valid (Teachout, 2014: 208). It is worth noting though that, even after *Buckley* v. *Valeo*, limits on corporate contributions to candidates, prohibited by the earlier Tillman Act, were still legal.

However, from 1970 and beyond, as more and more corporations increased their CPA (Smith, 2012), legal scrutiny focused less on lobbying and more on campaign spending and contributions. In 1990 the Supreme Court decided *Austin* v. *Michigan Chamber*

of Commerce, ruling that limits on corporations using their own treasury money to make independent contributions are legal and are allowed under the First and Fourteenth Amendments. The court noted:

> The corrosive and distorting effects of immense aggregations of wealth that are accumulated with the help of the corporate form and that have little or no correlation to the public's support for the corporation's political ideas ... (and that) Corporate wealth can unfairly influence elections when it is deployed in the form of independent expenditures, just as it can when it assumes the guise of political contributions. We therefore hold that the State has articulated a sufficiently compelling rationale to support its restriction on independent expenditures by corporations(http://caselaw.lp.findlaw.com/scripts/getcase.pl?court=US&vol=494&invol=652 [accessed 15 April 2015]).

The Court clearly made a connection between corporate political actions and corruption in terms of 'unfair influence'. In 2002, Congress passed the Bipartisan Campaign Reform Act of 2002 (BCRA), referred to also as the McCain–Feingold Act. This law amended the FECA and banned unrestricted (soft) money donations made directly to political parties as well as limited the ability of corporations, unions and non-profits to publish issue advocacy ads within 30 days of a primary or caucus or 60 days of a general election, and prohibited any such ad paid for by a corporation (including a non-profit issue organization) or by unions and their general treasury funds. The law also limited the ability of political parties to use their funds for issue ads on behalf of candidates running for election or reelection campaigns. In 2003 the BCRA's constitutionality was challenged in the Supreme Court in *McConnell* v. *FEC*. The Court ruled that corruption was a concern when the legal system examines the regulation of money in politics and that a ban on soft money donations and limits on issue ads were legitimate and warranted (http://www.fec.gov/pdf/record/2004/jan04.pdf [accessed 12 August 2016]). This law and those that preceded it, back to the 1907 Tillman Act, reflect the understanding that, while bribery is a criminal offence and narrowly defined, the grey area of CPA is different yet warrants concern. The so-called political marketplace exchanges, often occurring behind closed doors, can still constitute questionable activity if they aim to change or to move existing legislative preferences (Stark, 1997). However, in 2010 the debate regarding CPA changed.

On January 21, 2010, the Supreme Court delivered its decision in *Citizens United* v. *FEC*. The case involved Citizens United, a conservative advocacy group that wanted to air a movie critical of Hillary Clinton within 30 days of the then-upcoming Democratic primaries and thus violating the BCRA Act of 2002. The district court of the District of Columbia prohibited the group from airing the movie, and the group appealed. The Supreme Court, in a 5 to 4 decision, ruled that corporations, unions and non-profits can make independent contributions for 'electioneering communications' or issue ads for or against candidates running for office. Direct contributions from corporate treasuries to candidates were still banned and regulation, oversight and disclosure on corporate spending was also viewed as legal (https://www.supremecourt.gov/opinions/09pdf/08-205.pdf [accessed 12 August 2016]). The law overturned *Austin* v. *Chamber of Commerce* as well as parts of the BCRA 2002 Act and is widely viewed as a doctrinal or seismic shift in legal thinking over the last 100 years, as it equated political speech with free speech without recognizing the possibility of corrupting the legislature (which some Supreme Court judges narrowly defined as explicit quid pro quo exchanges) – a notion in stark contrast to older Supreme Court decisions as well as to the widely held views of lower courts (*New York Times*, 21 January, 2010; http://www.nytimes.com/2010/01/22/us/politics/22scotus.html?_r=0; Teachout, 2014).

In 2014 the Supreme Court decided *McCutcheon* v. *Federal Election Commission*, in which the plaintiff claimed that existing aggregate limits on political expenditures in elections are unconstitutional under the First Amendment. On April 2, 2014, the Court ruled that aggregate spending limits are unconstitutional and that:

> Moreover, the only type of corruption that Congress may target is quid pro quo corruption. Spending large sums of money in connection with elections, but not in connection with an effort to control the exercise of an officeholder's official duties, does not give rise to quid pro quo corruption. Nor does the possibility that an individual who spends large sums may garner 'influence over or access to' elected officials or political parties. (http://www.fec.gov/law/litigation/mccutcheon_sc_opinion.pdf [accessed 1 May 2015]).

COMMON THEMES AND ONGOING DEBATES

As the historical review above depicts, over the last two centuries debates about the influence of moneyed interests on political decision making have been at the forefront of legal debate. Teachout's (2014) book, as well as media reporting from the 18th through the 21st centuries, also focuses on the influence of money on politics. While for over 150 years political contributions to politicians and lobbying of politicians were viewed with grave suspicion as leading to corruption, shifts in the legal arena based on recent Supreme Court decisions (beginning in 1976) have framed CPA as protected by free speech. While in the past CPA was defined broadly as intent to influence, as leveraging gifts and money-giving for private gain, and viewed as undue influence and thus as corrupt, since 2010 corruption has been defined narrowly as a quid pro quo exchange (Teachout, 2014; for a different view see Holcomb, 2016). In other words, while in the past CPA was legally viewed through the broad lens of harmful intention to influence public policy for private gain (which followed a broad definition of corruption), it has been replaced with a narrow definition of corruption and a basic First Amendment right built on the

Fourteenth Amendment and its application to corporate personhood. Recent legal scholarship is experiencing a lively debate regarding the consequences of the recent Supreme Court decisions, reflecting several related issues, as follows:

1   *Whose speech is it anyway?* Many legal scholars have noted that, given recent Supreme Court decisions – endorsing CPA as protected free speech – the risk of firms, and in particular of CEOs, engaging in political speech that does not correspond with those of firm shareholders is real. This has been noted even before 2010 (see Sitkoff, 2002) and more so after Citizens United by Bebchuk and Jackson (2012) and Coates (2012). The issue here is that shareholders cannot vote on firms' CPA as it is considered an issue relating to 'ordinary business' and as such under the purview of top management (Ciara Torres-Spilecy, 2010). Moreover, engaging in proxy activism against CPA can be at best advisory, as shareholder resolutions are non-binding in nature (Goranova and Ryan, 2014). Consequently, CPA can easily be defined as reflecting agency costs and not a strategy favored by institutional shareholders (Aggarwal et al., 2012; Bebchuk and Neemna, 2010; Coates, 2012; Hadani, 2012; Sitkoff, 2002; Sobel and Graefe-Anderson, 2014). Thus, free speech rights can reflect a conflict between the firm and its stakeholders. Earlier I noted the possibility of CPA being motivated by personal ideological preferences. If CEOs use CPA as a personal vehicle for expressing their own personal values and beliefs, which is what CEOs' political orientation is all about (Chin et al., 2013), then the so-called CPA reflects personal speech and as such may be problematic to firm shareholders and stakeholders, and raises a potential conflict between them and the firms.

2   *Disclosure matters.* Some scholars note that, to make sure politically active firms do not act against the will of shareholders, effective disclosure of CPA activities is necessary (Sitkoff, 2002: 1110–1111, 1116). Those concerned about the legal and normative implications of CPA (Stark, 1997; Teachout, 2014) have promoted disclosure as necessary. Some CPA disclosure is already mandated (PAC donations and lobbying expenditures' disclosures are required by law); however, so-called Super PACs face fewer disclosure rules and much of CPA is opaque as it occurs behind closed doors (Hadani, 2011). Bebchuk and Jackson (2013: 958) note:

> It will not be possible for researchers, and more importantly investors, to determine whether corporate spending on politics is beneficial for investors until there is adequate disclosure of such spending. At present, because much corporate political spending occurs under the radar screen, it is not possible to evaluate the extent to which such spending is consistent with investor interests. They also note the need to regulate disclosure, not just regarding direct spending but also regarding indirect political expenditures, such as making contributions to trade or umbrella organizations.

3   *Public policy can be a valid counter argument curbing the free speech view of CPA.* While on major issues or salient issues lobbying may not be effective, on narrow issues, which are most of the issues discussed in Congress (Hasen, 2012), lobbying is likely to be much more effective as competition for access is limited (Bonardi et al., 2005). Here the issue is the classical 'rent seeking' ability of CPA. Rent seeking is a form of so-called wealth transfers or wealth redistribution resulting from interest or corporate political action (Tollison, 1997, in Hasen, 2012), since not only does it move resources away from productive means to political ones (for the firm), it can also redistribute existing resources of the government and take them away from the public (Stearns and Zywicki, 2010). Moreover, Olson (1965) argued that political rent seeking can harm societies because it can shift the nature of legislation itself and result in economic inefficiencies. As noted earlier, there is strong empirical support for the notion that at least some forms of CPA distort economic allocation and cause economic damage at a national level (Coates and Wilson, 2007).

4   *Is corruption limited to quid pro quo exchanges?* As noted by Teachout's (2014) book, for most of the legislative history of the US, corruption with regard to the role of money in politics was defined broadly, as reflecting an intent to achieve private goals at the expense of the public. The issue here is not only that firms pursue their narrow agendas (which may not even enhance their long-term financial outcomes), but that in doing so they provide the opportunity and the means for legislators to focus on the needs of the rich and powerful at the expense of the public at large (Sitkoff, 2002), or just focus on private

political needs. Moreover, as noted by Stark (1997), if an exchange of information or money with a legislature occurred even without any explicit promise of return, quid pro quo corruption could still exist (Gordon, 1991). In management research, the definition of corruption is closely linked to the older legal views of CPA and to the actual process of engaging in CPA. For example, Ashforth, Gioia, Robinson and Trevino (2008) note that corruption 'is defined as the illicit use of one's position or power for perceived personal or collective gain' and 'Corruption implies a willful perversion of order, ideals, and, perhaps most important, trust – a "moral deterioration" in the words of the Concise Oxford English Dictionary'. They go on to raise the question of 'How would it look if your organizational practices showed up in a New York Times headline?' Given the covert nature of CPA, would most politically active firms be willing to openly report their behind-the-scenes interactions with public policy makers? While prior to 2010 firms used money indirectly, today they can directly spend corporate money for or against candidates running for office, and corporations' cumulative spending today is in the billions, based on data collected by the Center for Responsive Politics. Given that CPA is often directed by the top executives of the firm (Burris, 2001; Hadani et al., in press) and given the magnitude of current CPA expenditures, will CPA not translate into direct influence over legislative agendas and as such raise the legal risk for firms that are politically active?

To summarize, this chapter reviewed extant theorizing and empirical analysis of CPA. It has shown that existing theoretical approaches to the study of CPA and its dynamics, while of importance, are often limited in exposing the legal and normative limitations and risks associated with CPA and raise the need to further integrate law and a normative lens into the discourse of and research on CPA. I have shown that, both financially and strategically, CPA's viability is open to debate. Adding the legal lens to this debate further increases the scrutiny we should bring to the study of CPA. Pursuing CPA based on recent legal changes may cause a conflict with firm stakeholders and result in other negative normative risks. When the composition of the

Supreme Court changes in the future, the possibility looms of both the *Citizens United* and *McCutcheon* cases being overturned. That would in turn possibly lead to changes in CPA strategy, as corporations will need to adapt to a new legal environment.

Note

1 Unlike dealing with financial intermediaries and the product market, CPA occurs in the political arena and is termed non-market.

REFERENCES

Ackerman, B. and Ayres, I. 2002. *Voting with dollars*. New Haven, CT: Yale University Press.

Abramowitz, A. 1988. Explaining Senate election outcomes. *American Political Science Review*, 82(2): 385–403.

Aggarwal, R. K., Meschke, F., and Wang, T. Y. 2012. Corporate political contributions: Investment or agency? *Business and Politics*, 14(1): 1469–1508.

Alzola, M. 2013. Corporate dystopia: The ethics of corporate political spending. *Business & Society*, 52: 388–426.

Ansolabehere, S., De Figueiredo, J. M., and Snyder, J. M. 2003. Why is there so little money in US politics? *Journal of Economic Perspectives*, 17: 105–130.

Ansolabehere, S., Snyder, J. M., & Ueda, M. 2004. Did firms profit from soft money? *MIT Economics Working Paper No. 04–11*.

Ashforth, B. E., Gioia, D. A., Robinson, S. L., and Trevino, L. K. 2008. Re-viewing organizational corruption – Introduction. *Academy of Management Review*, 33(3): 670–684.

Austen-Smith, D. 1995. Campaign contributions and access. *American Political Science Review*, 89(3): 566–582.

Baik, K. H. and Lee, D. 2012. Do rent seeking groups announce their sharing rules? *Economic Inquiry*, 50(2): 348–363.

Baron, D. P. 1995. Integrated strategy: Market and nonmarket components. *California Management Review*, 37(2): 47–65.

Baron, D. P. 1996. *Business and its environment*. Englewood Cliffs, NJ: Prentice-Hall.

Baron, D. P. 1997. Integrated strategy and international trade disputes. *Journal of Economics and Management Strategy* 6(2): 291–346.

Bebchuk, L. and Jackson, R. 2013. Shining a Light on Corporate Political Spending, *Georgetown Law Journal*, 101: 923–967.

Bebchuk, L. and Jackson, R. 2012. Corporate political speech: Who decides? *Harvard Law Review*, 124: 83–117.

Bebchuk, L. A., and Jackson, R. J. Jr. 2010. Corporate political speech: Who decides? *Harvard Law Review*, 124: 83–117.

Bebchuk, L. and Neema, Z. 2010. Investor protection and interest group politics. *Review of Financial Studies*, 23: 1089–1119.

Blau, P. M. 1964. *Exchange and power in social life*. New York: John Wiley.

Blau, B. M., Brough, T. J., and Thomas, D. W. 2013. Corporate lobbying, political connections, and the bailout of banks. *Journal of Banking & Finance*, 37: 3007–3017.

Blumentritt, T. 2003. Government affairs activities at MNE foreign subsidiaries. *Business and Society*, 42(2): 202–263.

Bonardi, J.-P., Holburn, G., and Vanden Bergh, R. 2006. Nonmarket performance: Evidence from US electric utilities. *Academy of Management Journal*, 49(6): 1209–1228.

Bonardi, J.-P., Hillman, A., and Keim, G. 2005. The attractiveness of political markets: Implication for firm strategies. *Academy of Management Review*, 30(2): 397–413.

Bonardi, J.-P. and Keim, G. 2005. Corporate political strategies for widely salient issues. *Academy of Management Review*, 30(3): 555–576.

Buchanan, J. M. 1987. The constitution of economic policy. *American Economic Review, American Economic Association*, 77(3): 243–50.

Buchanan, J. M. and Tollison, R. D. 1984. *The Theory of Public Choice—II*. University of Michigan Press: Ann Arbor.

Buchanan, J. M. and Tullock, G. 1962. *The calculus of consent, logical foundations of constitutional-democracy*. Ann Arbor, University of Michigan Press.

Burris, V. 2001. Two faces of capital: Corporations and individual capitalists as political actors. *American Sociological Review*, 66: 361–381.

Chin, M. K., Hambrick, D. C., and Trevino, L. K. 2013. Political ideologies of CEOs: Illustrative evidence of the influence of executive values on corporate social responsibility. *Administrative Science Quarterly* 58: 197–232.

Christensen, C., Dhaliwal, D, Boivie, S., and Graffin, S. 2015. Top management conservatism and corporate risk strategies: Evidence from managers' personal political orientation and corporate tax avoidance. *Strategic Management Journal*, 36: 1918–1938.

Ciara Torres-Spelliscy, *Corporate Campaign Spending: Giving Shareholders A Voice* (Brennan Center 2010).

Clawson, D. Neustadtl, A., and Weller, M. 1998. *Dollars and votes: How business campaign contributions subvert democracy*. Philadelphia: Temple University Press.

Coates, J. C. 2012. Corporate politics, governance, and value before and after Citizens United. *Journal of Empirical Legal Studies*, 9(4): 657–696.

Coates, D. and Wilson, B. 2007. Interest group activity and long-run stock market performance. *Public Choice*, 133: 343–358.

Cooper, M. J., Gulen, H. and Ovtchinnikov, A. V. 2010. Corporate political contributions and stock returns. *Journal of Finance*, 65: 687–724.

Darves, D. and Dreiling, M. 2002. Corporate political networks and trade policy formation. *Humanity and Society,* 26(1): 5–27.

Dean, T. J., Vryza, M., and Fryxell, G. E. 1998. Do corporate PACs restrict competition? An empirical examination of industry PAC contributions and entry. *Business and Society*, 37(2): 135–156.

Dharmapala, D. and Palda, F. 2002. Are campaign contributions a form of speech? Evidence from recent US House elections. *Public Choice*, 112: 81–114.

DiMaggio, P. and Powell, W. 1983. The Iron Cage revisited: Institutional isomorphism and collective rationality in organizational fields. *American Sociological Review*, 48: 147–160.

Downs, A. 1957. *An economic theory of democracy*. New York: Harper.

Esty, D. C. and Caves, R. E. 1983. Market structure and political influence: New data on political expenditures, activity, and success. *Economic Inquiry*, 21: 24–38.

Gawande, K., Krishna, P., and Olarreagai, M. 2012. Lobbying competition over trade policy. *International Economic Review*, 53(1): 115–132.

Getz, K. A. 2002. Public affairs and political strategy: Theoretical foundations. *Journal of Public Affairs*, 1/2: 305–329.

Goranova, M. and Ryan, L. V. 2014. Shareholder activism: A multidisciplinary review. *Journal of Management*, 40: 1230–1268.

Gordon J.D. III, 1991. Consideration and the commerical-gift dichotomy. *Vanderbilt Law Review*, 44: 283–310.

Gray, V. and Lowery, D. 1997. Reconceptualizing PAC formation: It's not a collective action problem, and it may be an arms race. *American Politics Quarterly*, 25: 319–346.

Grier, K. B., Munger, M. C., and Roberts, B. E. 1994. The determinants of industry political activity: 1980–1986. *The American Political Science Review*, 88: 911–926.

Hadani, M. 2012. Institutional ownership monitoring and corporate political activity: governance implications. *Journal of Business Research*, 65(7): 944–950.

Hadani, M., Bonardi, J.P., and Dahan, N. (in press). Corporate political activity, public policy uncertainty, and firm outcomes: A meta-analysis. *Strategic Organization*, doi:10.1177/1476127016651001.

Hadani, M. and Schuler, D. A. 2013. In search of El Dorado: The elusive financial returns on corporate political investments. *Strategic Management Journal*, 34(2): 165–181.

Hadani, M., Dahan, N., and Doh, J. (in press) The CEO as chief political officer: Managerial discretion and corporate political activity. *Journal of Business Research*, DOI: 10.1016/j.jbusres.2015.03.046.

Hall, R. and Wayman, F. 1990. Buying time: Moneyed interests and the mobilization of bias in Congressional committees. *American Political Science Review*, 84(3): 797–782.

Hall, R. L. and Deardorff, A. V. 2006. Lobbying as legislative subsidy. *American Political Science Review*, 100: 69–84.

Hansen, J.M. 1991. *Gaining access: Congress and the Farm Lobby, 1919–1981*. Chicago: University Of Chicago Press.

Hansen, W. L., Mitchell, N. J., and Drope, J. M. 2005. The logic of private and collective action. *American Journal of Political Science*, 49: 150–167.

Hasen, R.L. 2012. Lobbying, rent seeking and the constitution. *Stanford Law Review*, 64: 191–254.

Heinz, J., Laumann, E., Nelson, R., and Salisbury, R. 1993. *The hollow core: private interests in national policy making*. Cambridge, MA: Harvard University Press.

Hill, M. G., Kelly, G., Lockhart, D. and Van Ness, R. 2013. Determinants and Effects of Corporate Lobbying. *Financial Management*, 42(4): 931–957.

Hillman, A. J. 2005. Politicians on the board of directors: Do connections affect the bottom line? *Journal of Management*, 31(3): 464–481.

Hillman, A. J. and Keim, G. 1995. International variation in the business-government interface. *Academy of Management Review*, 20(1): 193–214.

Hillman, A. J., Hitt, M. A. 1999. Corporate political strategy formulation: a model of approach, participation, and strategy decisions. *Academy of Management Review*, 24: 825–842.

Hillman, A. J., Zardkoohi, A., and Bierman, L. 1999. Corporate political strategies and firm performance: indications of firm-specific benefits from personal service in the US government. *Strategic Management Journal*, 20(1): 67–81.

Hillman, A. J., Keim, G. D., and Schuler, D. 2004. Corporate political activity: a review and research agenda. *Journal of Management*, 30: 837–855.

Hillman, A. J., Keim, G. D., and Schuler, D. 2004. Corporate political activity: A review and research agenda. *Journal of Management*, 30: 837–857.

Holcomb, J. (forthcoming) Corporate Governance: Ethics and Legal Compliance, Risk Management, and Political Activities. In Richard Leblanc (Ed.) *The Handbook of Board Governance: A Comprehensive Guide for Public, Private, and Not for Profit Board Members.*, San Francisco: Jossey Bass Wiley.

Holcomb, J. 1995. Citizen interest groups, public policy, and corporate responses. In Lloyd Dennis (Ed.) *Practical public affairs in an era of change*. (pp. 201–234). Lanham, MD: University Press.

Hrebenar, R. J. 1992. Change, transition, and growth in southern interest group politics.

In *Interest group politics in the southern state*, 321–52. Ronald J. Hebrenar and Clive S. Thomas (Eds.). Tuscaloosa: University of Alabama Press.

Igan, D., Mishra, P., and Tressel, T. A fistful of dollars: Lobbying and the financial crisis. IMF Working Paper, 2009. Available at www.imf.org/external/pubs/ft/wp/2009/wp09287.pdf (accessed 29 August 2016).

Kang, K. 2015. Policy influence and private returns from lobbying in the energy sector. *Review of Economic Studies,* 1: 1–43.

Keim, G. D. and Zeithaml, C. P. 1986. Corporate political strategy and legislative decisionmaking – a review and contingency approach. *Academy of Management Review,* 11(4): 828–843.

Kim, J. H. 2008. Corporate lobbying revisited. *Business and Politics,* 10: 1–23.

Kollman, K. 1998. *Outside lobbying: Public opinion and interest group strategies*. Princeton, NJ: Princeton University Press.

Kostovetsky, L. 2009. Political capital and moral hazard. Simon School Working Paper No. FR 10-05. Available at http://papers.ssrn.com/sol3/papers.cfm?abstract_id=1507227 (accessed 29 August 2016).

Liptak, A. Justices, 5-4, reject corporate spending limit. New York Times, January 21, 2010.

Lord, M. D. 2000. Constituency based lobbying as corporate political strategy: testing an agency theory perspective. *Business & Politics,* 2: 289–308.

Lowi, T. J. 1969. *The end of liberalism: Ideology, policy, and the crisis of public authority*. New York: Norton.

Lux, S., Crook, T., and Woehr, D. 2011. Mixing business with politics: A meta-analysis of the antecedents and outcomes of corporate political activity. *Journal of Management,* 37(1): 223–247.

Magee, C. 2002. Do political action committees give money to candidates for electoral or influence motives? *Public Choice,* 112: 373–399.

March, J. and Simon, H. A. 1958. *Organizations*. New York: Wiley Press.

Meznar, M. B, Nigh, D., and Kwok, C. C. 1998. Announcements of withdrawal from South Africa revisited: Making sense of contradictory event study findings. *Academy of Management Journal,* 41(6): 715–730.

Mizruchi, M. S. 1989. Similarity of political behavior among large American corporations. *American Journal of Sociology,* 95: 401–424.

Mizruchi, M. S. 1992. *The structure of corporate political action: Interfirm relations and their consequences*. Cambridge, MA: Harvard University Press.

Nelson, D. and Yackee, S. W. 2012. Lobbying coalitions and government policy change. *Journal of Politics,* 74: 339–353.

Oliver, C. and Holzinger, I. 2008. The effectiveness of strategic political management: A dynamic capabilities framework. *Academy of Management Review,* 33(2): 496–520.

Olson, M. 1965. *The logic of collective action; public goods and the theory of groups*. Cambridge, MA: Harvard University Press.

Olson, M. 1982. *The Rise and Decline of Nations*. New Haven, CT: Yale University Press.

Ozer, M. 2010. Top management teams and corporate political activity: Do top management teams have influence on corporate political activity? *Journal of Business Research,* 63(11): 1196–1201.

Pfeffer, J. and Salancik, G. R. 1978. *The External Control of Organizations: A Resource Dependence Perspective*. New York: Harper & Row.

Rehbein, K. A. and Schuler, D. A. 1999. Testing the firm as a filter of corporate political action. *Business and Society,* 38: 144–167.

Schuler, D. A., Rehbein, K., and Cramer, R. D. 2002. Pursuing strategic advantages through political means: A multivariate approach. *Academy of Management Journal,* 45: 659–672.

Schlozman, K. L. and Tierney, J. T. (1986). *Organized interests and American democracy*. New York: Harper & Row.

Scott, W. R. 1995. *Institutions and Organizations*. Thousand Oaks, CA: Sage.

Sitkoff, R. H. 2002. Corporate political speech, political extortion, and the competition for corporate charters. *University of Chicago Law Review,* 69: 1103–1165.

Smith, H. 2012. *Who stole the American dream?* New York, NY: Random House.

Smith, M. A. 2000. *American business and political power*. Chicago, IL: The University of Chicago Press.

Snyder, J. M. 1992. Long term investing in politicians, or, give early give often. *Journal of Law and Economics*, 35: 15–43.

Sobel, R. S. and Graefe-Anderson, R. L. 2014. The relationship between political connections and the financial performance of industries and firms. *Working Paper 14–18, Mercatus Center, George Mason University.*

Stark, A. 1997. Don't change the subject: Interrupting public discourse over quid pro quo. *Business Ethics Quarterly*, 7: 93–116.

Staw, B. M. and Epstein, L. D. 2000. What bandwagons bring: Effects of popular management techniques on corporate performance, reputation, and CEO pay. *Administrative Science Quarterly*, 45: 523–556.

Stearns, M. and Zywicki, T. 2010. Antitrust and public choice. At: http://masonlec.org/site/rte_uploads/files/Antitrust_FINAL.pdf (accessed 1 May, 2015).

Stigler, G. J. 1971. The theory of economic regulation. *Bell Journal of Economics and Management Science*, 2(1): 3–21.

Stratmann, T. 1991. What do campaign contributions buy? Deciphering causal effects of money and votes. *Southern Economic Journal*, 57: 606–620.

Stratmann, T. 1998. The market for Congressional votes: Is timing of contributions everything? *Journal of Law and Economics*, 41(1): 83–113.

Stratmann, T. 2002. Can special interests buy congressional votes? Evidence from financial services legislation. *Journal of Law and Economics*, 45: 345–373.

Thomas, C. S. and Hrebenar, R. J. 1990. Interest groups in the States. In Gray, V., Jacob, H., and Albritton, R. (Eds.) *Politics in the American States*. 5th ed. Glenview, IL: Scott Foresman.

Teachout, Z. 2014. *Corruption in America: From Benjamin Franklin's snuff box to Citizens United*. Cambridge, MA: Harvard University Press.

Truman, D. B. 1951/1971. *The governmental process. Political interests and public opinion*. New York: Alfred A. Knopf, Inc., 2nd edition.

Useem, M. 1982. Classwide rationality in the politics of managers and directors of large corporations in the United States and Great Britain. *Administrative Science Quarterly*, 27: 199–227.

Williamson, O. E. 1985. *The economic institutions of capitalism*. New York: Free Press.

Wilson, J. 1990. Corporate political strategies. *British Journal of Political Science*, 20: 281–288.

Business, Human Rights, and Sustainable Development

Laura Bernal-Bermudez and Tricia D. Olsen

Corporate public affairs have transformed over the past two decades. This is no more apparent than around the issue of business and human rights. Companies today, especially trans- or multi-national corporations, are faced with the challenge of addressing a variety of stakeholder concerns and must adopt new, innovative, and at times collaborative public affairs strategies to prepare for the external, non-market environment. This chapter explores how the agenda of business and human rights has developed, how companies typically respond, and concludes by outlining how this issue has changed corporate public affairs.

Why human rights? The human rights agenda has traditionally focused on states. Non-democratic states were the primary perpetrators of gross human rights violations. After the so-called 'third wave' of democracy (Huntington, 1991), beginning in the 1970s, in which democratic transitions spread across Latin America, Asia and the former Soviet Union, states and international regimes embraced new norms to ensure such widespread human rights abuses would not occur again.

Business, however, is often implicated in human rights violations, too. In Guatemala, in 2005, Monterrico Metals allowed public and private security forces to use their facilities to torture local community members protesting company operations (Business and Human Rights Resource Centre, Monterrico Metals Lawsuit, 2015). In Argentina, over 20,000 businesses have polluted the basin of the Matanza Riachuelo river over many years. According to Greenpeace, it is one of the most polluted basins in the world and, as such, has severely impacted the health of those living in the area (Greenpeace, Riachuelo [accessed online]; La Nación, 2013). In addition, companies have also committed abuses with non-democratic leaders or those involved in armed conflicts (e.g. Ledesma's facilities in Argentina were used as a detention center during the dictatorship (Dandan, 2012); Urapalma SA was involved in forced displacement of communities by paramilitary forces in Colombia (Ballvé, 2009).

More broadly, cases such as these bring into question the value of economic growth as distinct from sustainable development. Citizens, policymakers, and corporate leaders are paying more attention to the type – or quality – of economic opportunities that are available around the globe. Daly and Townsend (1993) capture this idea pithily: 'When something grows it gets bigger. When something develops, it gets different' (p. 267). A strong corporate public affairs strategy, today, requires that companies recognize that development can manifest itself in unexpected ways when economic growth is pursued in isolation from a basic respect for human rights. While this chapter focuses specifically on human rights, the discussion is also closely linked to the promulgation of sustainable development.

What are human rights? Human rights, as outlined in the Universal Declaration of Human Rights (UDHR), signed in 1948 and born out of the atrocities during World War II, are inalienable entitlements of all human beings.[1] The existence of rights necessarily entails duties to respect, protect and guarantee. Although the International Bill of Human Rights (i.e. the UDHR, the International Covenant on Civil and Political Rights (ICCPR) and the International Covenant on Economic, Social and Cultural Rights (ICESCR)) points to states as principal duty-bearers, the UDHR declares that 'every individual and every organ of society' shall strive to seek respect of these rights. Although companies are not yet bound by human rights treaties, this language is widely seen as opening the door for other duty-bearers to come on to the scene, including non-state actors such as corporations (Alston, 2005; Clapham, 2006).

States, however, are the signatories of the covenants and, thus, have a duty to protect human rights and ensure that third parties respect them (including business). Although not all states have ratified the ICCPR and the ICESCR (the United States, for example, is not a signatory of the International Covenant on Economic, Social and Cultural Rights), the UDHR is a powerful tool in applying legal and normative pressure to those states found in violation.

Given that states have a duty to protect human rights (and even to ensure non-state actors respect human rights), a discussion about business and human rights thus requires some overview of the state (see the section 'A New Agenda: Business and Human Rights' below). The next section, 'Corporate Responses to the Business and Human Rights Agenda', delves into existing empirical data on recent shifts in public policy to engage corporate actors in the effort to reduce human rights abuses. The chapter then discusses corporate responses to those initiatives both in terms of corporate policy and corporate practice. The final section, 'New Responsibilities for Public Affairs', contains a broader discussion as to what human rights policy and governance discussions mean for corporate public affairs, more generally. We also suggest a few considerations for firms, and the public affairs function specifically, to more effectively address human rights concerns.

A NEW AGENDA: BUSINESS AND HUMAN RIGHTS

The increased focus on business and human rights has been driven by multiple factors. First, multinational enterprises have more power and influence today than ever before. Some companies' assets are larger than the GDP of the countries in which they work. The largest 44 companies in the world, for example, generate over 11 percent of global GDP. General Motors (GM) produces more revenue ($135.59 billion) than the GDP of Hungary ($129 billion) where GM opened a plant in 1991.

Second, this trend is exacerbated by the fact that states, in turn, are thought to have weakened in the face of increased corporate power. Numerous scholars have lamented the fact that governments, in an increasingly globalized market economy, are weaker and are less capable (or willing) to regulate business (Aaronson, 2003; Abouharb and Cingranelli, 2009; Fourcade-Gourinchas and Babb, 2002; Kindermann, 2009). While some countries are unwilling to challenge foreign companies upon which their economies depend, jurisdictional issues also become quickly overwhelming (Clapham, 2006). It is sometimes unclear how to regulate companies that are domiciled in one country, have operations in a number of others, and may hold their financial assets in yet another country (Clapham, 2006). This challenge relates directly to the issue of human rights and is often referred to as the 'governance gap' (Deitelhoff and Wolf, 2013; Deva, 2014; Ruggie, 2013).[2]

Together, we suggest that these trends have opened up a space in which global norms – in this case, human rights norms – might be applied to business. As global human rights norms have been adopted by state actors in a majority of countries (albeit, to varying degrees), business is expected to do the same. As the examples in the introduction illustrate, when firms engage directly or indirectly in human rights violations they put their own future at risk. The costs of not doing so may involve reputational or operational risks, costs associated with legal liability, and possibly loss of consumer or investor confidence.

Scholars recognize these changes and that, in its place, we see the emergence of global governance. '[W]ith the intensified engagement of private actors, social movements, and the growing activities of international institutions, a new form of transnational regulation is emerging: global governance, the definition and implementation of standards of behavior with global reach' (Scherer and Palazzo, 2011: 909). Today, an increasing number of global institutions seek to promote global norms to shape the behavior of non-state actors (Avant et al., 2010).

Yet, global governance around human rights presents interesting challenges to traditional corporate public affairs. The human rights agenda, as an international norm promoted by international institutions, may be at times perceived as quite nebulous to the traditional public affairs office. What is expected of business? How should one assess human rights risks and prepare to mitigate allegations of human rights abuse? What does the business and human rights agenda mean for public affairs, in general? This section begins to answer these questions by providing some background to the global and domestic policy changes around business and human rights.

The Formation of a Global Human Rights Agenda

Since the early 1970s, worldwide initiatives have attempted to curb corporate human rights abuses. In 1974, the United Nations established the Commission on Transnational Corporations (UNCTC). The UNCTC created a code of conduct that, while not explicitly about human rights, sought to outline best practices with regards to international trade, treatment of foreign enterprises, dispute settlement, and jurisdiction, among other issues. The UNCTC only produced a series of drafts and was discontinued in 1992.

Other efforts during the 1970s were primarily voluntary in nature. In 1976, the Organization for Economic Cooperation and Development (OECD) issued Guidelines for Multinational Enterprises. A year later, in 1977, the International Labor Organization (ILO) published the Tripartite Declaration of Principles Concerning Multinational Enterprises. The Sullivan Principles on Apartheid and the US Foreign Corrupt Practices Act – both adopted in 1977 – were also part of this effort in the 1970s to change the norms and standards for global business. These initiatives, in general, were viewed as unsuccessful for failing to create long-standing and widely agreed-upon sets of standards (Sagafi-Nejad, 2008). Even so, they paved the way for additional efforts in the following decades. In the late 1990s and early 2000s a dual process of increased soft law (voluntary efforts) and the formation of hard law (international regulatory frameworks) was underway.

With regards to additional soft law mechanisms, the UN Secretary General Kofi Annan launched the Global Compact in 2000. It was created as a voluntary mechanism to facilitate discussions and best practices around corporate behavior and human rights. It urged companies to support and respect the protection of internationally recognized human rights and to ensure they were not complicit in the abuse of those rights. The Global Compact promotes 'shared values and principles' for states and non-state actors alike and represents one of the first efforts to encourage non-state actors to explicitly commit to respecting human rights. To date, the Global Compact has 15,900 corporate members (of which 7,000 are considered active). Approximately 5,000 non-business members have also joined the organization.[3] The same year, the Voluntary Principles on Security and Human Rights (VPs) were published, which provided guidelines to assess risk associated with employing or dealing with private and public security forces. The VPs were signed by prominent governments (the United States and the United Kingdom), key international NGOs, and more than 15 large multinationals working primarily in the extractive industry.

In 2003, two notable industry-specific voluntary initiatives were formed. The Kimberley Certification Scheme (KCS) is a multi-stakeholder initiative between states, NGOs and companies to reduce the flow of conflict diamonds that were fueling conflicts in Sierra Leone, Angola, and the Democratic Republic of the Congo, among other countries. The Extractive Industry Transparency Initiative (EITI) brought together another group of states, NGOs,

investors, and companies to bring greater transparency to state revenue associated with large-scale extractive projects and to reduce corruption and bribery. States and companies agreed to publicly disclose payments associated with large-scale extraction projects; increased transparency meant that citizens could hold states accountable for following through on commitments by spending rents from the extractive industry wisely. Both of these initiatives are discussed in greater depth below.

With regards to hard law, in the 1990s the UN gathered a group of five independent experts to draft a code of conduct for transnational corporations, or what is now known as the 'Norms on the Responsibilities of Transnational Corporations and Other Business Enterprises with Regard to Human Rights' (hereafter the 'Draft Norms'). The Draft Norms set out human rights standards for companies and drew heavily from existing international law in areas such as civil, political, economic, social, and cultural rights that addressed issues from labor concerns, to environmental issues, to consumer protection.

The breadth of the Draft Norms was met with some trepidation. The main point of controversy was that they placed direct, legal responsibility on corporations as 'organs of society', a term that is employed in the UDHR, as referenced in the introduction. The Draft Norms also included implementation mechanisms (monitoring, reporting and verification) and stipulated obligations of financial redress.

Businesses largely opposed the Draft Norms, as they wanted to avoid binding international law. States also fought this hard law initiative. Many developing countries questioned their ability (and willingness) to enforce a regulatory framework that was perceived as threatening by business upon which their economies depend. Developed states were hesitant to sign on to hard law mechanisms that would challenge state sovereignty through extraterritoriality.

In April 2004, amidst this political backlash, the UN Commission on Human Rights set them aside, declaring the Norms 'had not been requested by the commission and thus, would not be considered' (Mantilla, 2009).

When the Draft Norms were discarded due to the lack of support from key state and corporate actors, many within the United Nations were concerned that the business and human rights agenda might be abandoned completely. Kofi Annan appointed Harvard's Professor John Ruggie as the Secretary General's Special Representative for Business and Human Rights to revive the discussion. The Global Compact, spearheaded by Ruggie, was thus the precursor for today's leading initiative – the United Nations Guiding Principles on Business and Human Rights (UNGPs). Most notably, the UN Human Rights Council unanimously endorsed the Guiding Principles on Business and Human Rights in June 2011.

The UNGPs – the principal document for today's business and human rights agenda – outline principles that describe the role and responsibilities of business, the state, and civil society in aiming to reduce violations of human rights by corporate actors and to improve access to remedy for victims of such abuse. The three pillars of the UNGPs are: 1) the state duty to protect human rights; 2) the corporate responsibility to respect human rights; and 3) improving access to remedy for victims of corporate abuse.

The UNGPs embody a compromise in international standards around business and human rights. Ruggie adopted an approach of 'principled pragmatism', which is a combined effort of voluntary compliance and the promotion of global norms (Ruggie, 2013). While one pillar is explicitly about business conduct, compliance is voluntary. In the section below, we discuss some of the ways in which state behavior has changed as a result of the UNGPs. In subsequent sections, we focus specifically on corporate actors and implications for public affairs.

Domestic Implications of Global Business and Human Rights Norms

While the UNGPs have only been in effect for five years at the time of publication, we can already observe some ways in which this work has changed the domestic policy landscape.

A recent paper highlights that National Contact Points (NCPs), part of a complaint mechanism created in 1976 to monitor company compliance with the OECD Guidelines for Multinational Enterprises, have been revived and are utilized to submit human rights grievances. In the 1990s they fell into disuse, but in 2000 the OECD Guidelines were revised to expand their scope to be applicable to companies' operations in non-OECD countries. Under these guidelines, 'firms were advised to respect the human rights of those affected by their activities consistent with the host government's obligations and commitments – that is, consistent with whatever international human rights treaties a host government may, or may not, have ratified' (Ruggie and Nelson, 2015: 2). In 2011 the OECD adapted its Guidelines to include the companies' responsibility to respect human rights, and the due diligence requirement as outlined by the UNGPs (*ibid.*).

Ruggie and Nelson (2015: 13) assess the claims submitted to the NCPs and find that the 2011 reforms have had the following five points of impact:

> more human rights cases than other types of complaints; a greater diversity of human rights cases than in the past; a diversification of industries against which complaints are brought; the growing role of the Guidelines' due diligence provisions; and a higher admissibility rate for human rights cases than for others.

Yet, not all claims were acted upon. Between 2000 and 2011, NGOs and labor unions presented a number of complaints, out of which 40 percent were declared inadmissible primarily because it was not possible to verify the investment nexus (i.e. the firm did not have direct equity in the business accused of the violation) (Ruggie and Nelson, 2015). Most of the companies involved in these complaints are based in advanced and high-income economies.

In addition to the use of NCPs, we also observe that, contrary to the claim that states have weakened, some states are adapting to a more globalized context by regulating corporate behavior around corporate social responsibility (CSR) activities. Many countries have passed regulations for firms domiciled in the home country with regards to their CSR activities abroad. These regulations may relate to managing global supply chains, imposing CSR demands through public procurement, or regulating specific CSR standards for company policies (Knudsen et al., 2015). Denmark, for example, established a Council for CSR in 2008, which is charged with aiding, supporting, and informing the Danish government on matters related to Danish companies' social responsibility. The Council contributes to, and supports, the advancement of sustainability in the Danish private and public sector and consists of members from the government, trade organizations, NGOs, civil society, local municipalities and trade unions (Danish Council for Corporate Responsibility, 2016).

Sometimes countries have offered tacit support for multi-stakeholder initiatives (MSIs). The Extractive Industry Transparency Initiative (EITI), for example, was supported by the United States inclusion of Section 1502 in the Dodd-Frank Act. This regulation is the first of its kind requiring companies that file reports with the SEC to provide disclosure regarding the use of 'conflict minerals' in the manufacture of products or in products they contract to manufacture. This effort supports existing regional and international efforts to prevent the exploitation of particular minerals that finance armed groups in conflict zones, specifically the Democratic Republic of the Congo. States can also be more explicit in their approach and have played a leading role in the creation of MSIs, as was the case of the United Kingdom in creating the EITI and the Ethical Trading Initiative.

Furthermore, governments of emerging and developed economies have also adopted new forms of CSR regulation. The 2013 Companies Act in India requires that companies set up a CSR board committee that must ensure that the company spends 'at least two percent of the average net profits of the company made during the three immediately preceding financial years' on 'CSR' activities (Parliament India Companies Act, 2013: par. 135).[4] In Argentina, Law 2594 of the City of Buenos Aires requires companies with over 300 employees to report on their social and environmental performance (Legislatura de la Ciudad Autónoma de Buenos Aires, 2007). As of 2001, Australia required corporations listed in the Australian stock exchange and other investment firms to complete an annual CSR report. Since 1996, Belgian transnational corporations (TNCs) and Belgian subsidiaries of foreign companies have been required to report on their social performance in their annual accounts. And, also as of 2001, nationally listed French companies are required to submit a corporate sustainability report, which should include information on 'how they will ensure that subcontractors and subsidiaries comply with ILO's core conventions' (Abrahams, 2004: 35).

The UN Working Group on Business and Human Rights (UNWG) encouraged states to create a national action plan (NAP) as part of their responsibility to implement the Guiding Principles. A NAP is an evolving policy strategy developed by the state, in which it articulates priorities and actions it will adopt to support the implementation of business and human rights norms (UN Working Group on Business and Human Rights, 2014; International Corporate Accountability Roundtable and The Danish Institute for Human Rights, 2014).

By 2015, according to the UNWG, 10 countries had produced a NAP (most of them developed countries,[5] e.g. UK, the Netherlands, Italy, except for Colombia, which produced a NAP in December 2015), and 18 countries were either in the process of developing a NAP or had committed to developing one, including the United States, Germany and Brazil (UN Working Group on Business and Human Rights, 2014). To date, there is momentum around NAPs, particularly in Europe and the Americas, where the European Union and the Organization of American States have been actively encouraging states to engage with business and human rights (Business and Human Rights Resource Centre, 2015; International Corporate Accountability Roundtable and The Danish Institute for Human Rights, 2014). NAPs will, of course, have implications for the domestic norms in home and host states with which businesses will need to comply.

CORPORATE RESPONSES TO THE BUSINESS AND HUMAN RIGHTS AGENDA

Corporate responses to a shift in the international and, increasingly, national policies around business and human rights have been varied. Since the business and human rights agenda is relatively new, there is not a large body of empirical work on this topic to review.

In this section, we consider available empirical data of businesses' responses to the human rights agenda in two ways. First, we assess the corporate initiatives that aim to address issue-specific or industry-specific challenges. Second, we provide data on how corporations respond to allegations of human rights abuse. This section highlights the existence of a substantial disconnect between the proliferation of corporate participation in collaborative efforts with key stakeholders, as compared to their ability to respond effectively when allegations actually occur.

Engagement in Collaborative Initiatives

Corporations have a long track record of engaging with other stakeholders to address industry-specific issues (Abrahams, 2004; Baumann-Pauly et al., 2015). This may require cooperation with other firms in the industry in an effort to self-regulate. Or, it can also take shape through multi-stakeholder initiatives (MSIs), some of which were mentioned in the previous section. MSIs generally involve states and representatives from civil society, in addition to corporate leaders. Here we provide a few examples that are related to, or have been informed by, the business and human rights agenda.

Multi-Stakeholder Initiatives

The Kimberley Certification Scheme (KCS) is an MSI endorsed by the UN General Assembly. The KCS is the result of consultations between diamond-producing states, the international diamond industry and civil society organizations to certify that only 'conflict-free' diamonds enter the legitimate trade (Haufler, 2009). The KCS came into force in 2003 and its members include 81 states that represent 99.8 percent of the world diamond producers, the World Diamond Council (which represents the world diamond industry), and civil society organizations.[6] This effort has been criticized by Global Witness, one of the civil society organizations that initially supported the initiative (Global Witness, 2013). Global Witness withdrew its support in 2011, because KCS and its members failed to take into consideration a broader range of human rights concerns. Global Witness claims that lax standards have led to the certification of diamonds that are, in their view, tainted by human rights abuses (Global Witness, 2013). In addition, there is some question whether the KCS can be upheld as a model, given that weak national governments are meant to control borders that are rife with corruption, conflict and crisis (Haufler, 2009).

Despite its limitations, this initiative has produced changes in company policies. The World Diamond Council (WDC) is actively involved in the initiative, and created a Kimberley Process Task Force. Together, they have produced and promoted The Essential Guide to Implementing The Kimberley Process, which is a set of steps that all the WDC members and suppliers have to follow to effectively implement the system designed to eliminate conflict diamonds. De Beers, for example, had previously been criticized for not controlling the source of their diamonds. They have used the KSC to improve their performance on human rights compliance. De Beers requires every supplier to comply with the KCS, requiring a certificate to accompany every diamond.[7] Also, in 2014 the company established a new corporate governance structure that includes a sustainability committee, a social investment committee, a safety and sustainable development council and a human rights working group.[8] According to the company's 2013 report, it has been 100 percent compliant with the KCS since 2011.[9]

EITI is another well-known MSI that was launched in 2003 to improve the transparency of payments in the extractive industry. The EITI seeks to promote good tax governance, accountability, transparency and the prevention of corruption through the verification and full publication of company payments and government revenues. It recognizes the importance that these revenues have in transforming economies, reducing poverty, and improving the living conditions of the populations of resource-rich countries. Although EITI does not explicitly refer to human rights, corruption affects the state capacity to guarantee human rights when communities find themselves, for example, without access to healthcare or education.

The EITI has had broad support from companies and states, alike. Over 90 of the world's largest oil, gas and mining companies support the EITI. Although it is a state-led initiative, the EITI brings companies and civil society together with state actors to implement standards collaboratively. Companies recognize that their involvement in public policy and broader stakeholder engagement is necessary to maintain their social license to operate

(Hutton and Olsen, 2015). Most of the member companies support the implementation of EITI in the countries where they operate. They participate by submitting data to state authorities and providing support to prepare the reports and to implement the standards (e.g. BP in Azerbaijan and Indonesia; Barrick Gold in Peru and Zambia). For companies, this initiative helps improve the business environment and reduces political risk in countries where they operate.[10]

Company policies have changed as a result of their involvement in the EITI initiative. They have established internal mechanisms to facilitate external reporting about company payments to the state and to submit a report to EITI. Some firms, such as ExxonMobil, have been actively involved in helping to establish transparency agreements to regulate the disclosure of government information about revenues. Afren plc became a supporting company in 2014, after which it reviewed its Code of Conduct and Anti-bribery and Corruption policies (Afren plc, 2014).[11] Also, in 2009 Anglo American updated its Business Principles to reflect its commitment to EITI (EITI; Anglo American).[12] EITI, however, is not without its critics. It has been criticized for its lack of public participation (Aaronson, 2011; Global Witness, 2009). In addition, some have argued that EITI has little effect on level of democracy, political stability and corruption (Corrigan, 2014).

Our final example of a multi-stakeholder initiative is one of the oldest – the Fair Labor Association (FLA), which was founded in 1999. The FLA is a collaborative effort between companies, colleges and universities, and civil society organizations to address exploitative labor practices. They offer tools and resources to companies, and provide training to management, as well as conduct due diligence and advocacy campaigns to bring transparency to global supply chains. Many of the world's leading brands,[13] some of which have been involved in media exposés for having sweatshops in their supply chains, are now part of this initiative and use the FLA tools to improve performance. In 2012, for example, Nike, Adidas and Liz Claiborne were accredited for complying with FLA standards.

Like the other MSI initiatives, participating in them requires internal organizational changes as well. Companies not only have to change their internal policies (e.g. companies that join the FLA agree to uphold the Workplace Code of Conduct, and have to adjust their policies accordingly[14]), but must also be equipped to improve their partnership with suppliers in developing countries. After an FLA assessment in 2009, for example, Adidas and Nike employees worked closely with a Vietnamese apparel supplier to prevent forced labor, improve their respect for freedom of association, and protect the health and safety of the factory's workers. Previously, workers at this plant lacked the required work permits, they were forced to leave the union, and in some departments they were not given proper protective equipment (Fair Labor Association, 2009). The FLA worked with companies up the supply chain to remedy these issues.

Self-Regulatory Initiatives

In addition to MSIs, corporations have also worked together to address stakeholder concerns associated with corporate conduct. Self-regulatory initiatives often begin after a crisis to avoid harsh regulations. Responsible Care, for example, is a voluntary initiative created by companies in the chemical industry in 1985. Union Carbide spearheaded this effort after the Bhopal crisis, which still inflicts residents of the Bhopal region in India with long-term health concerns. This initiative has evolved, and in 2006 it launched the Responsible Care Global Charter at the UN-led International Conference on Chemicals Management (recently reviewed in 2014). Business associations in 60 countries, whose combined chemical industries account for more than 70 percent of global chemicals production, have joined the initiative.[15]

The Electronic Industry Citizenship Coalition (EICC) was founded in 2004 by a group of companies in the electronic industry (originally called the Electronic Industry Code of Conduct). In early 2004 CAFOD (Catholic Agency for Overseas Development) published the report 'Clean Up Your Computer: Working conditions in the electronics sector' (CAFOD, 2014), showing appallingly poor working conditions at computers and electronics manufacturers. CAFOD called on the big brands (i.e. Hewlett Packard, Dell and IBM) to implement a code of conduct (Lindsay, 2006). The EICC sought to create an industry-wide standard on social, environmental and ethical issues in the supply chain.[16] It began with only eight members. By 2015, it grew to include more than 100 electronics companies with combined annual revenue of approximately $3 trillion that directly employ over 5.5 million people. In addition to EICC members, thousands of companies that are next-tier suppliers to member companies are required to implement the EICC Code of Conduct.[17] In addition, the EICC has a number of initiatives on specific topics (e.g. conflict minerals and environmental sustainability, trafficked and forced labor) on which companies collaborate to create tools, guidance documents and mechanisms to jointly address these issues.

Responses to Allegations

Next, we seek to explore reactive strategies, or how companies respond to allegations of corporate human rights abuse. To do so, we draw from a unique dataset, the Corporations and Human Rights Database (CHRD), which captures allegations of corporate human rights abuse in Latin America between 2000–2014. The CHRD is the most systematic and comprehensive collection of data on corporate human rights allegations and draws from the Business and Human Rights Resource Center (BHRRC), a non-profit organization that has created an online archive of information about business and human rights since 2000.[18]

Of the 1,306 allegations in the CHRD, only 467 (36 percent) include a corporate response.[19] Of those that provided some type of response, over three in four companies denied the allegation (362 of 467), while nearly one in four acknowledged the allegation (112 of 467). Nearly one in ten (48 of 467) companies provided justification for the allegation, while nearly one in five (90 of 467) offered a plan for change. Only three percent of the companies (16 of 467) in the CHRD that provided a response offered an apology.[20]

When responding to an allegation from an external stakeholder, companies deny the allegation in a number of ways. At times, they suggest the claim does not take into account all the facts. Particularly, they may state that those presenting the claim do not take into consideration the validation of the company's operation by other bodies, including local, national and international communities or regulatory agencies. Muriel Mining Corporation, for example, faced allegations of not conducting prior consultations with affected communities in Colombia. They argued, instead, that they had letters of agreement from indigenous authorities allowing them to start the exploration phase (Muriel Mining Corporation, 2009). Alternatively, companies may refer to state approval of their operations through environmental impact permits, or other administrative permits. For example, GoldCorp ensured that the company's operation of the Marlin Mine in Guatemala had the support of the Ministry of Energy and Mines, which verified that there was no negative impact to the environment or the health of local populations (GoldCorp, 2011). Finally, companies may simply deny being involved in the abuse, and rather profess their commitment to business ethics by referring to their participation in global initiatives (such as the Global Compact) or their rating in international standards schemes. For example, AngloGold Ashanti, in response to

accusations of threats against indigenous communities opposing the company's operations in their lands located in the Department of Chocó in Colombia, denied being involved in the abuse. The company emphasized that it was signatory to the Voluntary Principles and dedicated to human rights and compliance with national and international standards (AngloGold Ashanti, 2011).

Companies may also question the validity of the claim. Some companies in the CHRD, for example, deny that their operations have negative human rights or environmental impacts. Barrick Gold, which operates the Pascua Lama gold mining project in Argentina, has been the target of resistance by local communities and environmental activists, who claim that the project has contributed to water pollution, diminishing glaciers and uses harmful chemicals (Regroupement pour la Responsabilité Social et L'Equité, 2008). The company has simply denied such claims: 'The Company denies that its operation of these projects is in violation of the OECD Guidelines' (Barrick Gold, 2011).

When the allegation involves a subsidiary, companies often resort to distancing their work from that of their suppliers. This was the case, for example, with Coca-Cola regarding the violence met by union members working in its subsidiary in Guatemala. The company argued that it had a minority share in INCASA, the local company (Hurtado, 2010). Also in Guatemala, the subsidiary of a Canadian company, Hudbay Minerals, was accused of employing a security company, whose personnel used violent tactics against local community members opposing the mine. Hudbay responded by denying all responsibility for the actions of security personnel hired by its subsidiary (Canadian Press, 2011).

Lastly, some companies seek to react proactively, especially when they see their competitors involved in accountability lawsuits and multimillion-dollar compensation schemes. Such firms take preventative measures to avoid being in the same situation in the future, therefore improving the standards of the sector. This was the case, for example, with Exxon Mobil, Royal Dutch Shell, Chevron and ConocoPhillips, who pooled US$1 million to form a joint venture to develop a response and containment system after the 2004 BP Gulf oil spill (McNulty, 2010; McNulty, 2011).

NEW RESPONSIBILITIES FOR PUBLIC AFFAIRS

Implications from corporate public affairs, as they relate to the business and human rights agenda, are most prominent in the second and third pillars of the UNGPs. Pillar two outlines the corporate responsibility to protect human rights and indicates that companies must adopt a due diligence process to avoid rights abuses and to address negative impacts with which they are involved. Pillar two also ties into pillar three, which promotes access to remedy through judicial and non-judicial mechanisms. While pillar two urges companies to both 'know and show' they are meeting their responsibilities, pillar three encourages companies – in collaboration with states and civil society – to provide redress. We take each component – due diligence and remedy provision – in turn to explore what, in practice, the business and human rights agenda means for public affairs.

Due Diligence

The corporate responsibility to respect human rights indicates that businesses must act with due diligence to avoid infringing on the rights of others and to address negative impacts with which they are involved. The second pillar offers a process for companies to both 'know and show' that they are meeting this responsibility, by which they become aware of, prevent, and address their adverse human rights impacts. The UNGPs hold that companies have the power to affect virtually all of the internationally recognized rights. Therefore, there is a responsibility of both the state and the private sector to acknowledge their role in upholding and protecting human rights. Due diligence consists of both a 'hard system', which includes policies and procedures that ensure the UNGPs are an integral part of business operation, and a 'soft system', which is about cultural shifts within an organization and engaging with external stakeholders (ECLT Foundation, 2015).

Certainly a cultural shift is underway as the business and human rights agenda is increasingly on the radar of industry leaders. A 2014 Economist Intelligence Unit Survey found that 85 percent of C-level business leaders believed human rights were a concern for business. The UNGPs and subsequent work by UN member states have likely played a role in this perception. A 2013 survey by the Global Business Initiative, for example, found that over 75 percent of corporate respondents were familiar with the UNGPs, over half of whom had heard about their development in 2010 or earlier. Just over 20 percent of respondents had heard of the UNGPs for the first time in 2012 or 2013. These trends – and the increased awareness of corporate engagement with the UNGPs – also play out in patterns around corporate policies and processes.

We see evidence of the so-called 'hard system' through the adoption of internal policies to avoid human rights abuses. Figures 15.1 and 15.2 display data drawn from Asset4's ESG (environmental, social and governance) dataset of publicly traded companies; the data in the figures are from a sample that includes the Russell 1000. Asset4 compiles its data using news and company reports, published in English. While Asset4 does not collect data specific to the UNGPs, the existing questions provide an interesting insight into the increased attention companies are paying to respecting human rights in general.

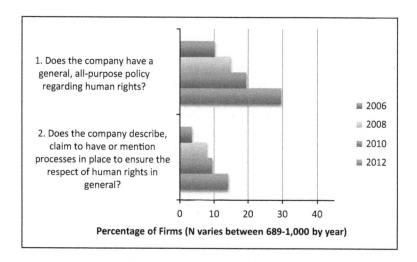

Figure 15.1   Data on company policy and practice around human rights, in general

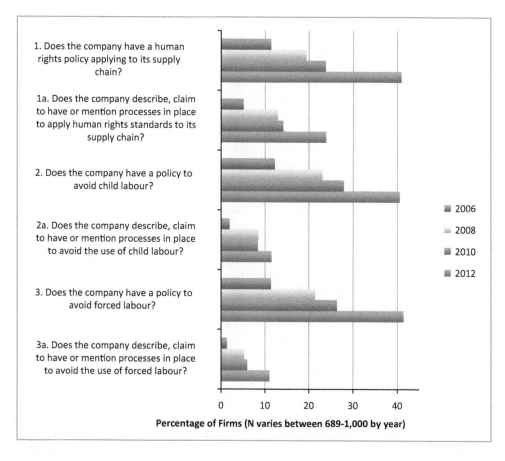

Figure 15.2   Data on company policy and practice specific to supply chain, child labor, and forced labor

There are a few interesting trends to high-light from Figures 15.1 and 15.2. We can observe a marked increase in policy and practice, both in general and with regards to specific human rights issue areas between 2006 and 2012. In Figure 15.1, we notice an increase (from 10 percent in 2006 to just under 30 percent in 2012) in companies that report having an all-purpose policy on human rights. Those numbers drop substantially, however, when asked about specific processes to ensure respect for human rights.

In Figure 15.2, we observe that policies on specific issue areas have more widespread adoption than generic human rights policies. Over 40 percent of the firms in this sample have a specific policy on supply chains, child labor and forced labor. As with Figure 15.2, there is a substantial disconnect between policy and practice. In Figure 15.2, for example, many more companies have policies (questions 1, 2 and 3) on an issue area than companies that report having processes in place to avoid such abuses (questions 1a, 2a and 3a). These data reflect the findings from the CHRD, discussed above in the section 'Responses to Allegations'. While companies are adopting policies around human rights, those policies are not adequately transforming into practice.

Access to Remedy

Access to remedy is the third pillar of the UNGPs, which notes that, while states should provide remedy through judicial or legislative means, companies also have a responsibility to redress any abuses to which they directly or indirectly contributed. The UNGPs, however, recognize that judicial remedy may only be appropriate in some circumstances and also promote the use of state-based or independent non-judicial remedy mechanisms, provided they are legitimate, equitable and transparent.

The CHRD also includes data on remedy and offers some insight as to the frequency

with which judicial or non-judicial remedy is employed. Of the allegations in the database, 38 percent had some type of judicial action. This can include civil, administrative, constitutional or criminal proceedings. Not all judicial activity, of course, results in a trial. Of the 498 allegations that had some type of judicial action in the CHRD, over half (57 percent) went to trial.

The prevalence of judicial mechanisms suggests that companies are willing to endure long legal battles to defend their operations or seek remedy themselves from the claims presented by communities and human rights defenders. A well-known example is the Chevron case in Ecuador, where the company defended its role in the clean up of the Oriente region in courts in Ecuador and in the US. This case began in 1993 with the last ruling occurring 20 years later in 2013.

The CHRD also points to an interesting subset of cases in which companies file libel lawsuits against those who have presented claims against them. Activists have called these actions Strategic Lawsuits Against Public Participation (SLAPP) and view them as retaliation and attempts to silence victims. Newmont Mining Company in Peru launched a suit in relation to the Minera Yanacocha, in which it sued a family for squatting on company land. In 2012 a local court convicted the family and ordered them to pay a fine in favor of the company. Similarly, in Argentina, Refineria del Norte SA resorted to constitutional procedures to request that the courts order indigenous communities to stop impeding the company's operations. The court ruled in favor of the company. And in Haiti, Cintas Corp filed a lawsuit for defamation against a human rights defender who accused the company of keeping employees in poor working conditions.

When conflicts persist, a number of cases in the CHRD illustrate that companies seek to reach out-of-court settlements with claimants. These settlements have resulted in compensation for victims, but generally do not include any recognition of liability by the company. BP, for example, was alleged to have contributed to environmental degradation in Colombia, particularly to the erosion of land caused by the construction of the Ocensa oil pipeline. Colombian peasants filed a lawsuit against the company in the United Kingdom. There was no admission of liability by the company, but BP did agree to create a compensation fund and organize workshops to help farmers cope with their changing environment. Although the amount of the settlement was not disclosed, it is believed that it was far from the £15 million that the farmers were asking the UK court (Verkaik, 2006). In the now infamous Niger Delta, Royal Dutch Shell ultimately sidestepped a lawsuit filed in the UK in 2012 and settled out of court with the Bodo Community for the pollution caused by two oil spills in Rivers State, Nigeria. The company accepted liability for the oil spills and in January 2015 agreed to a £55 million settlement with the community, a sum below the £300 million requested by the community as compensation (Shell Global, 2015).

The CHRD also illustrates that non-judicial remedy mechanisms are less common, despite their broad categorization – ranging from roundtable talks to grievance mechanisms. Only 24 percent of allegations in the CHRD involve some type of non-judicial remedy. Yet, corporate public affairs should consider non-judicial remedy seriously (Rees and Vermijs, 2008). A non-judicial remedy mechanism, if conducted in a transparent and fair manner, could reduce long and inefficient legal battles that may damage a company's reputation. We offer a few additional examples here that provide insight as to how companies can strategically utilize non-judicial remedy to address human rights abuses.

Some companies engage a respected, independent third party to validate and suggest remedy of specific claims. Such third party verification can bring clarity to whether an abuse occurred and, if so, an assessment of causes and remedy mechanisms to prevent future violations. This was the case with Pemex, after the collapse of the Usumacinta platform, located in the Bay of Campeche, in October 2007. As a result, 23 workers died and 65 were injured. The political party, Convergencia, and the union, Frente Unido de Marinos Mercantes, attributed the deaths and injuries to Pemex and its subcontractors, or the private companies in charge of the operation of the platform. They alleged that the subcontractors did not comply with minimum security standards (América Multimedios Agencia de Noticias, 2009).

Pemex requested the internal investigation to be conducted by Battelle Memorial Institute (BMI), the world's largest non-profit research and development organization. On October 31, 2008, BMI released the report, entitled 'Root Cause Analysis of the Usumacinta-KAB-101 Incident'. The report concluded that one of the primary causes was the lack of security training given to the workers. In response, Pemex changed its policies around security training and sought to tighten its monitoring of subcontractors' compliance with security measures (Battelle Memorial Institute, 2008; Pemex, 2008).

At times, companies have also sought to negotiate the remedy through multi-stakeholder roundtables. In the Peruvian case of Minera Yanacocha, mentioned earlier, Newmont was accused of polluting the environment and affecting local communities' health. Because the International Finance Corporation in part financed this project, the Compliance Advisor Ombudsman (CAO) of the World Bank Group oversaw a multi-stakeholder roundtable. This roundtable, created in September 2001, has served as an open forum for discussion and conflict resolution between more than 50 public and private stakeholders and the company. This roundtable also oversaw an independent participatory water impact study and led a participatory water-monitoring program (Oficina del Asesor en Cumplimiento/Ombudsman, 2007).

CONCLUSION

The business and human rights agenda has created a new challenge for corporate public affairs. Yet, this chapter highlights that there is an oft-forgotten temporal component to this approach. Companies focus on initial interactions with relevant stakeholders, but do not consider a long-term strategy for public affairs. Many business and human rights issues are long-term challenges, such as environmental degradation or labor relations. Moreover, stakeholder preferences may change over time, especially as norms change through domestic or international institutions. Unforeseen events may also require firms to respond effectively with little warning.

At a minimum, companies must have a strategic response for the varied stakeholders with whom they engage. In addition to domestic standards, multinational companies must also be aware of international norms and how these norms have shaped expectations around business conduct. From an organizational perspective, this requires distinct internal (policies and processes) and external (multi-stakeholder engagement, third party auditing) strategies to adequately prepare for potential human rights risks and address them, if abuses do occur.

Internally, in light of the proliferation of global and domestic norms and expectations, and the high risks for companies involved in human rights violations, firms need to have a) human rights policies and b) processes in place for grievance mechanisms. Such policies should be in adherence to the existing international norms on business and human rights. Complying with domestic laws and norms, in other words, may not be enough; public affairs offers must consider global governing institutions and the new norms they are creating.

Externally, corporate public affairs officers should be engaging with MSIs, which allow firms to make sense of their responsibilities in terms of business and human rights. MSIs facilitate sharing best practices and allow companies to keep in line with the other companies operating in the same industry, many of which are likely facing some of the same challenges regarding human rights in their operations. Firms should also engage with state actors in the creation of National Action Plans to identify particularly risky areas and ensure that regulatory practices are aligned with industry practice. When violations do occur, firms need to have processes in place to guarantee transparency of grievance mechanisms (i.e. non-judicial mechanisms) to ensure the legitimacy of the outcome. Companies can promote transparency through independent reviews and publication of third-party reports.

New demands and growing societal complexity have not only challenged the role of the state, they have also raised the bar for corporate public affairs. Firms must develop dynamic, yet enduring strategies to address the business and human rights agenda. Scholars and practitioners of corporate public affairs must acknowledge the importance of a long-term, yet adaptive perspective toward business and human rights.

Notes

1   While the term 'human rights' has initially been associated with physical integrity rights (i.e. murder, disappearance, kidnapping and illegal detention, torture), it is much wider than this and includes other sets of rights as well. The International Covenant on Civil and Political Rights (ICCPR), for example, delineates rights that a state may not take away from its citizens, including the freedom of speech or freedom of movement. The International Covenant on Economic, Social, and Cultural Rights (ICESCR) suggests the state has a duty to protect against violations of economic, cultural, and social rights (e.g. rights to education, physical and mental health, formation of trade unions).

2   We should also note that existing research challenges the notion that states have lost their agency and simply follow the dictates of globalization. Instead, scholars suggest that states

have been able to maintain domestic autonomy, even in the context of increased global governance. Olsen and Sinha (2013), for example, put forth a theory of 'relative divergence' to illustrate that states in emerging economies are employing new, innovative strategies that give shape to domestic industries, even with strong pressure to comply with international agreements. Similarly, Garrett (1998) argues that market integration co-exists with interventionist governments and greater policy divergence.

3 These numbers for corporate members include: Companies, Small or Medium-sized Enterprises and Micro Enterprise: See https://www.unglobal-compact.org/participants/search

4 http://www.bsr.org/en/our-insights/blog-view/india-companies-act-2013-five-key-points-about-indias-csr-mandate

5 http://www.ohchr.org/EN/Issues/Business/Pages/NationalActionPlans.aspx

6 http://www.kimberleyprocess.com/en/about

7 See De Beers Peace of Mind page: http://www.debeers.com/the-de-beers-difference/peace-of-mind/

8 See De Beers Governance page: http://www.debeersgroup.com/en/building-forever/our-approach/governance.html

9 See De Beers 2013 Report: http://www.debeers-group.com/content/dam/de-beers/corporate/documents/Sustainability/Sustainability%20Reports/Report%20to%20Society%202013.PDF

10 See the EITI company members page: https://eiti.org/supporters/companies

11 See Afren Management Systems page: http://www.afren.com/corporate_responsibility/business_conduct/management_systems/

12 See Anglo American Business Principles: http://www.angloamerican.com/~/media/Files/A/Anglo-American-PLC-V2/documents/approach-and-policies/social/businessintegritypolicy-may2014-english.pdf

13 See FLA members page: http://www.fairlabor.org/es/affiliates/participating-companies

14 See FLA Code of Conduct page: http://www.fair-labor.org/our-work/labor-standards

15 See http://www.icca-chem.org/en/Home/Responsible-care/

16 See EICC history page: http://www.eiccoalition.org/about/history/

17 Se EICC members page: http://www.eiccoalition.org/about/members/

18 Business and Human Rights Resource Centre: http://business-humanrights.org/

19 A response, as coded in the CHRD, is a statement – as published in a newspaper article, press release, company report, or other document – made by the corporation. Some of these responses were the result of the BHRRC's request for a response to a particular company on a particular violation, but not all violations recorded by the BHRRC were followed by a request for a company response. In this sense, the coders had to look for company responses using a Google search.

20 Note that company responses could fall in multiple categories. Thus, the percentages do not add up to 100.

REFERENCES

Aaronson, S. A. (2003). Courting international business. *The International Economy*. Washington, DC: EBSCO Publishing.

Aaronson, S. A. (2011). Limited partnership: Business, government, civil society, and the public in the Extractive Industries Transparency Initiative (EITI). *Public Administration and Development*, 31(1), 50–63.

Abrahams, D. (2004). *Regulating Corporations: A Resource Guide*. Geneva: United Nations Research Institute for Social Development.

Abouharb, M. R. and Cingranelli, D. L. (2009). IMF programs and human rights, 1981–2003. *Review of International Organizations*, 4, 47–72. doi:10.1007/s11558-008-9050-5.

Afren plc. (2014). Corporate Responsibility: Targets. Accessed July 2, 2015. Retrieved from http://www.afren.com/corporate_responsibility/targets/

Alston, P. (2005). *The 'not-a-cat' Syndrome: Can the international human rights regime accommodate non-state actors?* Oxford: Oxford University Press.

América Multimedios Agencia de Noticias. (2009). Presentaron diputados de Convergencia queja contra PEMEX ante CIDH. Accessed July 2, 2015. Retrieved from https://business-humanrights.org/es/presentarán-diputados-de-convergencia-queja-contra-pemex-ante-la-cidh-méxico

AngloGold Ashanti. (2011). Respuesta de AngloGold Ashanti a Reportes a Alegaciones de Comunidades Étnicas del Chocó Colombia. Retrieved from http://www.business-humanrights.org/Links/Repository/1010286/jump (accessed 2 July, 2015).

Avant, D. D., Finnemore, M., and Sell, S. K. (Eds.). (2010). *Who governs the globe?* NY: Cambridge University Press.

Ballve, T. (2009). El lado oscuro del Plan Colombia. *Verdadabierta.com*. Bogotá. Retrieved from http://www.verdadabierta.com/negocios-ilegales/captura-de-rentas-publicas/1969-el-lado-oscuro-del-plan-colombia (accessed 30 June, 2015).

Barrick Gold. (2011). Re: Barrick Gold Corporation statement on June 8, 2011, request by the organization FOCO-INPADE for review of alleged OECD Guidelines' violations in Argentina. Accessed July 2, 2015. Retrieved from http://business-humanrights.org/media/documents/barrick-gold-response-re-oecd-complaint-in-argentina-28-jun-2011.pdf

Battelle Memorial Institute. (2008). Root cause analysis of the Usumacinta-KAB-10 1 Incident October 23, 2007. Accessed July 2, 2015. Retrieved from https://www.academia.edu/1981028/Usumacinta_Accident_Report

Baumann-Pauly, D., Nolan, J., van Herdeen, A., and Samway, M. (2015). Industry-specific multi-stakeholder initiatives that govern corporate human rights standards – legitimacy assessments of the Fair Labor Association and the Global Network Initiative, SSRN Working Paper. Accessed June 30, 2015. Retrieved from http://papers.ssrn.com/sol3/papers.cfm?abstract_id=2576217

Business and Human Rights Resource Centre. Monterrico Metals Lawsuit (re Peru). Accessed July 1, 2015. Retrieved from http://business-humanrights.org/en/monterrico-metals-lawsuit-re-peru-0

CAFOD. (2014). Clean up your computer: Working conditions in the electronics sector. Accessed July 2, 2015. Retrieved from http://www.eldis.org/go/home&id=14913&type=Document#.V6uCYmViCb8 (accessed 29 August, 2016).

Canadian Press. (2011). HudBay defends against allegations in gang rape lawsuit. Accessed July 2, 2015. Retrieved from http://www.ctvnews.ca/hudbay-defends-against-allegations-in-gang-rape-lawsuit-1.624851

Clapham, A. (2006). *Human rights obligations of non-state actors*. Oxford: Oxford University Press.

Corrigan, C. C. (2014). Breaking the resource curse: Transparency in the natural resource sector and the extractive industries transparency initiative. *Resources Policy*, 40, 17–30. doi: 10.1016/j.resourpol.2013.10.003.

Daly, H. E. and Townsend, K. N. (1993). *Valuing the Earth: Economics, ecology, ethics*. Cambridge, MA: MIT Press.

Dandan, A. (2012). El poder económico detrás del poder military, Página 12. Accessed May 30, 2014. Retrieved from http://www.pagina12.com.ar/diario/elpais/1-190074-2012-03-21.html

Danish Council for Corporate Responsibility (2016). "Purpose and tasks," Accessed August 19, 2016. Retrieved from http://csr-council.dk/purpose_and_tasks

Deitelhoff, N. and Wolf, K. D. (2013). Business and human rights: how corporate norms violations become norm entrepreneurs. In Risse, T., Ropp, S. C., and Sikkink, K. *The persistent power of human rights from compliance to commitment*. Cambridge: Cambridge University Press.

Deva, S. (2014). *Regulating Corporate Human Rights Violations: Humanizing business*. Great Britain: Routledge.

ECLT Foundation. (2015). Implementing the corporate responsibility to respect of the UNGPs: Lessons and tools from the third UN forum on business and human rights. Accessed July 7, 2015. Retrieved from http://www.eclt.org/news-item/implementing-corporate-responsibility-respect-ungps-lessons-tools-3rd-un-forum-business-human-rights/

EITI. Anglo American. Accessed July 2, 2015. Retrieved from https://eiti.org/supporters/companies/anglo-american

Fair Labor Association. (2009). Enforcing freedom of association and protecting foreign workers in Vietnam. Accessed July 1, 2015. Retrieved from http://www.fairlabor.org/impact/case-studies/study/enforcing-freedom-association-and-protecting-foreign-workers-vietnam

Fourcade-Gourinchas, M. and Babb, S. L. (2002). The rebirth of the liberal creed: Paths to neoliberalism in four countries. *American Journal of Sociology*, 108(3), 533–579. doi:10.1086/367922.

Garrett, Geoffrey. (1998). *Partisan Politics in the Global Economy*. Cambridge, MA: Cambridge University Press.

Global Witness. (2009). Five challenges for the EITI to deliver. Accessed January 26, 2016. Retrieved from https://www.globalwitness.org/en/archive/five-challenges-eiti-deliver/

Global Witness. (2013). The Kimberly Process. Accessed July 1, 2015. Retrieved from https://www.globalwitness.org/campaigns/conflict-diamonds/kimberley-process/

GoldCorp. (2011). Response from GoldCorp to report raising concerns about the economic benefits and environmental risks of the Marlin Mine in Guatemala. Accessed July 2, 2015. Retrieved from http://www.business-humanrights.org/Links/Repository/1009013/jump

Greenpeace. Riachuelo. Accessed July 1, 2015. Retrieved from http://www.greenpeace.org/argentina/es/campanas/contaminacion/riachuelo/

Haufler, V. (2009). The Kimberley process certification scheme: An innovation in global governance and conflict prevention. *Journal of Business Ethics*, 89(4), 403–416.

Huntington, Samuel P. (1991). *The Third Wave: Democratization in the Late Twentieth Century*. Norman: University of Oklahoma Press.

Hurtado, P. (2010). Coca-Cola sued in US by Guatemalans over anti-union violence, Bloomberg. Accessed August 19, 201. Retrieved from http://www.insidecostarica.com/daily-news/2010/february/27/centam-10022703.htm

Hutton, Bruce and Tricia D. Olsen. 2015. Sustainability in the Developing World: An Exploration of Corporate Responsibility and Efficacy in Promoting Social Justice. In *Corporations as Stewards: Getting Beyond the Starting Blocks*, edited by James O'Toole, Ed Lawler and Susan Morhman, Greenleaf Publishing, pp. 205–225.

International Corporate Accountability Roundtable and The Danish Institute for Human Rights. (2014). National action plans on business and human rights: A toolkit for the development, implementation and review of state commitments to business and human rights frameworks. Accessed July 7, 2015. Retrieved from http://icar.ngo/wp-content/uploads/2014/06/DIHR-ICAR-National-Action-Plans-NAPs-Report3.pdf

Kindermann, D. (2009). Why do some countries get CSR sooner, and in greater quantity, than others? The political economy of corporate responsibility and the rise of market liberalism across the OECD: 1977–2007. Social Science Research Center Berlin (WZB). Retrieved from http://econpapers.repec.org/paper/zbwwzbkpw/spiii2009301.htm (accessed 15 July, 2016).

Knudsen, J.S., Moon, J. and Slager, R., 2015. Government policies for corporate social responsibility in Europe: a comparative analysis of institutionalisation. *Policy & Politics*, 43(1), pp.81–99.

La Nación. (2013). La cuenca Matanza-Riachuelo, entre los 10 lugares más contaminados del mundo. Accessed July 1, 2015. Retrieved from http://www.lanacion.com.ar/1635635-la-cuenca-matanza-riachuelo-entre-los-10-lugares-mas-contaminados-del-mundo

Legislatura de la Ciudad Autónoma de Buenos Aires. (2007). Ley 2594. Accessed July 1, 2015. Retrieved http://www.codigor.com.ar/brsa.htm

Lindsay, A. (2006). Electronics industry labour standards. ECCR Bulletin no. 60. Accessed January 26, 2016. Retrieved from http://www.eccr.org.uk/dcs/ElectronicsIndustryLabourStandards.pdf

Mantilla, G. (2009). Emerging International Human Rights Norms for Transnational Corporations. *Global Governance*, 15(2), 279–298. Retrieved from http://www.jstor.org/stable/27800755

McNulty, S. (2010). Oil groups form $1bn spill response unit. Financial Times. Accessed July 2, 2015. Retrieved from http://www.ft.com/cms/s/0/73c055f0-94f6-11df-af3b-00144feab49a.html

McNulty, S. (2011). Oil spill response system launched. Financial Times. Accessed July 2, 2015. Retrieved from http://www.ft.com/cms/s/0/30ed4a12-3aaf-11e0-9c65-00144feabdc0.html#axzz2XDJcJs3x

Muriel Mining Corporation. (2009). Response re Colombia solidarity campaign report. Accessed July 2, 2015. Retrieved from http://www.reports-and-materials.org/Muriel-Mining-response-re-Colombia-Solidarity-Campaign-report-16-May-2009.doc

Oficina del Asesor en Cumplimiento/Ombudsman. (2007). Construyendo Consenso: Historia y Lecciones Aprendidas de la Mesa de Diálogo y Consenso CAO-Cajamarca, Perú. Accessed July 2, 2015. Retrieved from http://www.cao-ombudsman.org/publications/documents/CAO_Monograph_IndWaterStudy_SpanishPart2.pdf

Olsen, Tricia D. and Aseema Sinha. 2013. Linkage Politics and the Persistence of National Policy Autonomy in Emerging Powers: Patents, Profits, and Patients in the context of TRIPS Compliance. *Business & Politics* 15(3), 323–356.

Parliament India. (2013) Companies Act. Accessed July 2, 2015. Retrieved from http://www.mca.gov.in/Ministry/pdf/Companies-Act2013.pdf

Pemex. (2008). PEMEX da a conocer los resultados de la investigación interna sobre el accidente en la plataforma Usumacinta, en el Golfo de México. Accessed July 2, 2015. https://sites.google.com/site/0902carlosr/accidente-en-la-plataforma-usumacinta

Rees, C. and Vermijs, D. (2008). Mapping grievance mechanisms in the business and human rights arena. Corporate social responsibility initiative John F. Kennedy School of Government Harvard University. Accessed July 7, 2015. Retrieved from http://accessfacility.org/sites/default/files/Rees%20%26%20Vermijs%20-%20Mapping%20Grievance%20Mechanisms%20in%20the%20Business%20and%20Human%20Rights%20Arena.pdf

Regroupement pour la Responsabilite Sociale et l'Equité. (2008). Recommendation to shareholders concerning Barrick Gold's Pascua-Lama project. Accessed July 1, 2015. Retrieved from http://www.business-human-rights.org/Links/Repository/114653/jump

Ruggie, J. G. (2013). *Just Business: Multinational corporations and human rights*. New York: W.W. Norton & Co.

Ruggie, J. G. and Nelson, T. (2015). Human rights and the OECD guidelines for multinational enterprises: Normative innovations and implementation challenges. Corporate Social Responsibility Initiative Working Paper No. 66. Cambridge, MA: John F. Kennedy School of Government, Harvard University. Accessed June 30, 2015. Retrieved from http://ecgi.ssrn.com/delivery.php?ID=6931021151220941230080001121020101240250
033010045057018088111124064104123106065116014024027057111007030003085068083005003114016011048088035048125121014026114125111041015071017071028080079067107122117002118002098097028090097100005005085030114029098&EXT=pdf&TYPE=2
Sagafi-Nejad, Tagi, and John H. Dunning. 2008. *The UN and Transnational Corporations: From Code of Conduct to Global Compact*. Bloomington, IN: Indiana University Press.

Scherer, A. G. and Palazzo, G. 2011. The new political role of business in a globalized world: A review of a new perspective on CSR and its implications for the firm, governance, and democracy. *Journal of Management Studies*, 48(4), pp. 899–931.

Shell Global. (2015). Shell's Nigerian subsidiary agrees £55 million settlement with the Bodo community. Accessed July 2, 2015. Retrieved from http://www.shell.com/global/about-shell/investor/news-and-library/2015/shells-nigerian-subsidiary-settlement-with-bodo-community.html

United Kingdom HM Government. (2013). Good business: Implementing the UN guiding principles of business and human rights. Accessed July 7, 2015. Retrieved from https://www.gov.uk/government/uploads/system/uploads/attachment_data/file/236901/BHR_Action_Plan_-_final_online_version_1_.pdf

UN Working Group on Business and Human Rights. (2014). Guidance on national action plans on business and human rights. Accessed July 7, 2015. Retrieved from http://www.ohchr.org/Documents/Issues/Business/UNWG_%20NAPGuidance.pdf

Verkaik, R. (2006). BP pays out millions to Colombian farmers. The Independent. Accessed July 1, 2015. Retrieved from http://www.independent.co.uk/news/world/americas/bp-pays-out-millions-to-colombian-farmers-408816.html

APPENDIX - LIST OF ACRONYMS

BMI	Battelle Memorial Institute
BP	British Petroleum
BHRRC	Business and Human Rights Resource Center
CAFOD	Catholic Agency for Overseas Development
CAO	Compliance Advisor Ombudsman of the World Bank Group
CHRD	Corporations and Human Rights Database
CSR	Corporate social responsibility
ECLT	Eliminating Child Labour in Tobacco Growing Foundation
EICC	Electronic Industry Citizenship Coalition
EITI	Extractive Industry Transparency Initiative
FLA	Fair Labor Association
GDP	Gross domestic product
GM	General Motors
ILO	International Labor Organization
ICCPR	International Covenant on Civil and Political Rights
ICESCR	International Covenant on Economic, Social, and Cultural Rights
KCS	Kimberley Certification Scheme
MSI	Multi-stakeholder initiatives
NAP	National action plan
NCP	National Contact Points
NGO	Non-Governmental Organization
Draft Norms	Norms on the Responsibilities of Transnational Corporations and Other Business Enterprises with Regard to Human Rights
OECD	Organization for Economic Cooperation and Development
Pemex	Petróleos Mexicanos
SEC	US Securities and Exchange Commission
SLAPP	Strategic Lawsuits Against Public Participation
TNC	Transnational Corporations
UDHR	Universal Declaration of Human Rights
UNCTC	United Nations Commission on Transnational Corporations
UNGPs	United Nations Guiding Principles on Business and Human Rights
UNWG	UN Working Group on Business and Human Rights
VP	Voluntary Principles on Security and Human Rights
WDC	World Diamond Council

The Regulation of Lobbying Activity

Justin Greenwood[1]

Whereas 'illiberal democracies' (Mair, 2014) have used 'lobby regulation' to justify measures of political control over dissenting organisations, regulation in liberal democracies involves a balancing act between preservation of civil and participatory rights (including those involving relationships between citizens and elected representatives) while seeking to address unwanted effects of 'lobbying'. Whilst 'lobby regulation' proposals continue to be popular among legislators, often responding to localised scandals, schemes have frequently failed to reach legislation through disagreements over how to operationalise them. Recent years, however, have seen a number of proposals coming downstream into law, reflecting a variety of factors linked to globalisation, associated policy learning and transfer (the Canadian Commissioner for Lobbying reports six countries consulting her expertise during the course of 2013–14; Office of the Commissioner of Lobbying in Canada,

2014), linkage across jurisdictions and improved mechanisms of horizontal and vertical accountability involving political institutions. A broad direction of travel involves adaptation of pluralistic traditions, embedding lobby regulation in a package of 'good governance' measures related to accountability and transparency, and seeking to address varying degrees of inequalities of access to political decision making.

A legacy of self-regulatory practice remains alongside statutory schemes, with innovation driven by attempts to ensure the continued survival of host organisations, and statutory codes of practice often working from instruments devised during self-regulation. Enforcement of schemes remains an enduring challenge, with a mixture of sanctions ranging from reputational consequence to criminal sanctions. Enforcement is backed by comparative best practice resources offered by intergovernmental fora, and vigilance from professionalised watchdog organisations linked across borders, offering web-based databases for active monitoring.

Measures to regulate lobbying can be distinguished by those aimed at the lobbied (targets of lobbyists) and at lobbyists. Those for the lobbied emerge first because of the greater ease of identifying, and controlling, the target constituencies involved in different branches of government, whereas defining and controlling a 'lobbyist' invokes a more complex set of issues involving civil and political rights. Disclosure regulations seeking compliance by lobbyists range from schemes in which a lobbyist is explicitly defined, to those relying on incentives for lobbyists to identify themselves. Incentivised self-identification schemes tend to be broad in scope, whereas statutory schemes offering definitions of lobbying and lobbyists tend to be less encompassing, sometimes based around a single category such as commercial lobbyists.

The chapter starts with an assessment of the context of lobby regulation, and in particular with a comparison of pluralist and corporatist traditions, as well as the impact that globalisation has made in shifting the balance towards pluralist traditions of lobbying. The chapter continues by identifying the components of a pluralist regulatory system, assessing measures regulating the behaviour of those who are lobbied, followed by an analysis of measures regulating the behaviour of lobbyists.

THE CONTEXT OF LOBBY REGULATION

Lobby regulation comes in a variety of guises. It is frequently understood as a challenge for rational-legal systems of government to limit 'distortion of public policy decisions on account of purchase of influence by private interests' (Andersson and Hayward, 2009, p. 749). Yet beneath this veneer lies a set of issues with widely diverging frames of reference, extending into the concept of 'good governance'. Sometimes the frame of reference extends into much wider terms of economic, social and political inequalities, occasionally underpinned by mechanistic assumptions that wealth easily translates into political influence. The means of seeking influence by a wide range of advocacy organisations ('NGOs'), too, have increasingly come under scrutiny (Economist, 2000; Independent, 2014). Lobby regulation schemes have frequently appeared as proposals in legislatures during the course of the last century, but (with the notable exception of the USA) often failed to progress beyond proposals. Executive branches of government in many other jurisdictions have shown increasing responsiveness to these proposals in more recent years, linked to pressures of globalisation described later in this chapter. Commercial practitioners have traditionally responded to these pressures by leading the introduction of self-regulatory schemes, but which have had limited durability in resisting pressures for statutory regulation. Self-regulatory instruments have extended to other groups of practitioners, including NGOs. Statutory schemes differ widely in intention and operationalisation.

Liberal democracies working in pluralist traditions seem to have the longest established traditions of schemes to regulate lobbying (e.g. North America), but if the frame is widened to consider corporatist traditions in parts of Europe and Latin America, then dialogue between organised civil society and political institutions can be placed in a similarly well-established tradition of regulation. Liberal democracies with a corporatist tradition have a highly regulated environment in which organised segments of society, mainly based around business associations and trade unions, participate in institutionalised arrangements to mediate their interests. They involve formal mechanisms incorporating 'representative' associations into government, the establishment of elevated rights inside political institutions, or through delegated policy responsibilities. These are legitimised as mechanisms of interest inter-mediation between key (mainly producer) societal interests, whereas 'lobbying' is per-ceived in more hostile ways in corporatist and statist traditions as a market mechanism car-rying the potential for political influence to follow wealth. In countries with Napoleonic traditions, political institutions and competi-tion between parties have been viewed as the only legitimate way to reconcile different interests in society, discouraging the devel-opment of commercial lobbying practice (Council of Europe, 2013). Commercial lob-bying services were therefore much slower to take hold in countries with corporatist tra-ditions, and regulatory instruments in such countries tended to emerge at a much later stage than in North America (Pross, 2007; Dos Santos and Teixera da Costa, 2014).

Yet it is difficult to sustain generalisa-tions throughout the 'corporatist'/'pluralist' dimensions. Even the United Kingdom, with long-established traditions of commer-cial lobbying (and a claim to the origins of the word 'lobbying', from the entrance hall to the Parliament where Members might be engaged before their entry into the voting chamber), only passed a statutory regulatory scheme in 2014, much later than those estab-lished in countries with corporatist traditions elsewhere in Europe and in Latin America. The need for political systems to operate on the basis of consent requires mechanisms to structure dialogue with political institu-tions, and these are as commonplace in plu-ralist systems as in corporatist traditions. Mechanisms designed for transparency, con-sultations, and degrees of accountability are highly developed throughout liberal democ-racies and are not uncommon in countries with established authoritarian regimes, albeit with varying degrees of effectiveness. And some countries with corporatist traditions, such as Sweden and Norway, have the great-est depth of transparency regimes to be found anywhere in the world, yet have resisted lobby regulation measures, based on a resist-ance to the 'Americanisation' of politics.

The breadth and depth of issues involved in lobby regulation can be further consid-ered through an examination of the approach of authoritarian regimes to civil society organisations. A guru of Russia's recent re-definition, Sergey Karaganov, recently pro-claimed 'no more liberal democracy' for the country, in a narrative asserting the estab-lishment of an 'authoritarian democracy' over a temporary period of flirtation with 'liberal democracy' in the post-Soviet era (BBC, 2015; see also Paraszczuk, 2013). In this 'authoritarian democracy', tolerance for critical voices is constrained by a 2015 Act of the Russian Duma (Parliament) banning 'undesirable' international organisations per-ceived as a threat to 'public order' (Guardian, 2015). In 2012, President Putin signed a law in which NGOs in Russia in receipt of for-eign funding, and thus organisations from countries with longer-established traditions of civil rights, would be registered as foreign agents (Guardian, 2012), since enforced by a vigorous regime of punitive inspection vis-its applied to critical organisations (Human Rights Watch, 2015). Civil rights are a fea-ture of liberal democracies with constitutions (e.g. the First Amendment to the American constitution), but the incorporation of free-dom of speech and assembly into the 1936 constitution of the USSR shows how partici-patory rights need to be embedded in longer-established traditions to operationalise them. The conflict between theoretical and actual respect for civil rights and participation has also arisen in other post-Soviet countries dominated by a single political party, most recently in Hungary (Economist, 2014). Yet even in countries where civil rights pre-date the establishment of political rights, over-tones of political control can accompany lobby regulation schemes. In the United Kingdom, 'lobby regulation' was a frame used for targeting the balance of regula-tion in the form of the 2014 *Transparency of Lobbying, Non-party Campaigning and Trade Union Administration Act of 2014'*. The Act was framed as a way to tackle lobbying scandals. It aimed at the registration of public affairs consultancies, political activities of trade unions and at political campaigning by a wide range of advocacy and charitable organisations.

Globalisation has brought with it a variety of pressures which have helped to transform a number of lobby regulation proposals into legislation. Global firms are in concept disruptive to established national corporatist arrangements, and their practices as political actors have travelled across borders. Commercial public affairs companies which serve their needs have followed them into markets previously unfamiliar with 'lobbying', raising a series of issues relating to regulation. Corporatist practices have receded in favour of pluralist mechanisms involving transparency of dialogue between wider civil society and political institutions. And globalisation has facilitated the mobilisation of critical voices by the simple means of finding like-minded others through the internet, bringing dialogue into public arenas. Mechanisms of policy learning and transfer are thereby enabled (OECD, 2014).

Where politics has itself become a form of market place for ideas and contestation, so regulatory forms have emerged that facilitate open contestation in ways that seek to provide legitimacy. And intergovernmental executive institutions that help to sustain the prevailing framework of international regulated markets offer key monitoring resources. Foremost among these are the *Worldwide Governance Indicators* sponsored by the World Bank, offering six dimensions of governance, including regulatory quality, voice and accountability, and control of corruption, discussed further below. International cooperation fora, such as the Organisation for Economic Cooperation and Development (OECD) and the Council of Europe's *Commission for Democracy through Law* (the 'Venice Commission') gather and disseminate comparative best practices, with a particular focus on lobby regulation. These chart the establishment in recent years of lobby regulation regimes in member countries, including those with corporatist traditions as well as those where only political institutions have been vested with the 'general interest'. Thus, within the past five years statutory lobby regulation schemes – named as such – have reached the status of legislation in Austria, Chile, France, Hungary (with an interruption), Ireland, Mexico, the Netherlands, Slovenia, and are on the point of doing so in Brazil. There are longer-established instruments in Georgia, Israel, Lithuania, Peru, Poland, Australia (with an interruption) and other pluralist-based systems, most notably Canada, the European Union and the United States, discussed further below, as well as the recent scheme in the United Kingdom.

What does a Pluralist Regulatory System Look Like?

Archetypal pluralist systems, as above, are based on elaborated systems of checks and balances seeking to diffuse power, supported by administrative systems with varying legal status. Transparency International places elements of a comprehensive lobby regulation system into three categories involving transparency, integrity and equality of access (Mulcahy, 2015). Consistent with an emphasis on 'participatory democracy', participation in formalised arrangements of consultation with governing institutions is an activity sometimes excluded from the scope of contacts disclosure within lobby regulations. Written communications are sometimes excluded from schemes where there are freedom of information arrangements that provide for their disclosure. Given the central place of legislatures in representative democracy, regulatory components directed at legislatures tend to be lighter than provisions involving executives, but in both cases the balance of regulation lies more upon the lobbied than upon lobbyists (primarily involving transparency). Whereas the balance of measures for the lobbied involve both prohibition and transparency, the emphasis of measures for lobbyists from civil society are more centred on disclosure.

Transparency underpins exchanges between civil society and political institutions. Whilst this rests on a popular assumption that 'sunshine is the best disinfectant', there is some evidence that the results of transparency mechanisms produce no better effect than widespread resignation in highly corrupt countries (Bauer and Grimes, 2014). And, as noted, some of the countries with the strongest traditions of transparency do not have lobby regulation schemes. The impact of transparency depends on the effectiveness of accountability arrangements. Accountability to the public (vertical accountability), accompanied by arrangements of oversight between political institutions (horizontal accountability), reinforce each other. Freedom of information (FoI) measures provide a means to address asymmetries of information and enrich public debate, and are made operational by elites (legislatures, journalists, NGOs, researchers).

The depth of these measures in design and practice influences the extent of public deliberation, a key property for improvement of the quality of, and acceptance of, public policies. The response that organisations make to external measures or regulations can take a variety of forms, ranging from evasion (where strong ideologies prevail), cosmetic discourse of responsiveness while internal practices remain essentially the same, re-interpretation (adapting external demands to fit its external practice) and full adaptation (Moodie, 2015). This framework seems to capture the responsiveness of public administrations to lobby regulation proposals, with proposals in some countries (e.g. Italy, Norway, Ireland) making seemingly little headway over long periods of time. Nonetheless, Ireland's Regulation of Lobbying Act of 2015 illustrates the way in which pressures to regulate can be cumulative over time.

A frequent pattern in lobby regulation involves acts of entrepreneurship by legislators seeking to develop a political profile, marketing a regulatory solution by linking their proposal to a recent scandal event, much in the manner predicted by Kingdon's model of agenda setting in which solutions search for problems (Kingdon, 1984; see also Greenwood, 2011, for an account of the establishment of the EU's Register of Interest Representatives in 2008). Schemes in smaller countries have sometimes emerged from the localised force of a single 'scandal' event (e.g. Austria, Slovenia), whereas in others a scandal has remained insufficiently salient to establish a lobby regulation. But where a number of salient scandal events recur over the course of a period of time, the cumulative effect is sufficient for the establishment of a scheme. The United Kingdom and Ireland are among examples of this latter pattern, whereas in Norway five attempts to introduce lobby regulation since 1995 have failed, partly because of the loss of institutional memory, and partly because the specific incidents they related to were more 'issues' than high saliency 'scandals'.

Mechanisms of enforcement include judicial oversight systems, or an Ombudsman through which public complaints can be channelled more informally. The success of an Ombudsman depends upon its ability to assert itself, determined by the level of powers invested in the office and the support of a legislature in pursuing enquiries directed against the Executive branch of government. The opening of an 'own enquiry' by an Ombudsman frequently stems from complaints lodged by watchdog advocacy groups. Built-in periods of review, and other reflection devices, produced by political institutions are also important opportunities for development of regulatory schemes, to be used by professionalised advocacy groups.

Central to pluralist systems are systems of public consultation, facilitated by online devices, in which contributions are published (as in the case of two-thirds of OECD member states – OECD, 2014) and/or summarised, and expert advice is subject to partial or full transparency arrangements. Information obtained from consultation and expert input is used to help regulatory impact assessments, with cost-benefit assessments of different policy options under consideration made public, often accompanied (in design, if not always in practice) by public justification of policy choices within the frame of published consultation responses. Around one-half of OECD countries use the concept of a 'legislative footprint' in the form of a document identifying consultees and further details of the consultative process (OECD, 2014).

Enforcement of consultation mechanisms in pluralist systems depends upon the extent to which they have legal status, although some corporatist style 'compact' agreements between governments and organised civil society provide a quasi-legal alternative, and apparently effective, means to establish and enforce standards (Will and Kendall, 2009).

Thus, experience over time provides a means for development of these components of 'structured dialogue'. Whilst components can be found in many territorial settings, the effectiveness of arrangements for them can vary significantly, sometimes involving cultural influences (see, for instance, the case study of Ghana by Yeboah-Assiamah and Alesu-Dordzi (2015)). The United States has a long experience of pluralist-based administrative law traditions, founded on a strong public frame of transparency discourse, underpinning its long established experience with lobby regulation. In the USA, lobby regulation schemes date back to 1935 at the federal level and the vast majority of states with their own provisions to the early 1950s (Chari, Hogan and Murphy, 2010). Public transparency forms the core of these, with registers of lobbyists based on public disclosure and conformity with a code of conduct, and measures to regulate the lobbied.

The limitation of these measures is illustrated by the Jack Abramoff case in the United States, elevated to the status of feature film as *Casino Jack*, involving systemic and high-level corruption between lobbyists, public officials and legislators, along with jail term sentences

served from 2006. The case, centred on conning tribal Indian Casino owners that looming regulation was ahead but avoidable through political contributions, is notable because it originated in the most highly regulated lobbying system in the world at the time, in which long-established traditions of administrative law cover both lobbyists and the lobbied. The case was quickly cited as direct justification for a lobby regulation scheme by a European Commission Vice-President (Kallas), now known as the EU's Transparency Register, in turn characterised as the vanguard of a 'new wave' of lobby regulation in Europe (Holman and Luneburg, 2012, p. 91).

The EU has had its 'lobbygate' scandals too, most notably in 2011 when three Members of the European Parliament (MEPs) agreed to submit amendments to legislative proposals in return for payment from a fake lobbying firm established in a journalistic 'sting' investigation. One of the MEPs involved is now serving out his jail term in Austria with a day release programme that allows him to work for a consultancy (The Local, 2015). The effectiveness of lobby regulation instruments is considered in the following sections, examining arrangements that regulate the lobbied and lobbyists. The prospect of 'regulatory capture' provides a strong narrative for lobby regulation advocates and journalists, and a result for political institutions to avoid.

OPERATIONALISING LOBBY REGULATION: REGULATING THE LOBBIED

Regulatory measures for the lobb*ied*, such as government employees and members of legislatures, emerge before those for lobbyists because of the greater ease of identifying, and controlling, the target constituencies involved, as distinguished from the civil society groups engaged in political decision making. Prohibition of outright corruption is a key element, but the scope of the definition of corruption can vary substantially, as discussed below, with some even making provision for criminal prosecution. Sanctions for defined elements involve a mixture of criminal, civil and organisational disciplinary provisions, supported by codes of ethics and conduct, and arrangements for providing information about transgressions. Conflict of interest disclosure arrangements for activities that may give rise to suspicion of bias and partiality play centre-stage. Codes to which officials are required to comply can embrace a wide range of provisions, such as stipulations in Slovenia not to participate on a subsidised basis in invited conferences and training courses (OECD, 2014).

Corruption, 'Good Governance' and Disclosure

Transparency International (TI) brands itself as 'the global coalition against corruption', with its flagship *Corruption Perception Index* (CPI) offering an established resource that monitors perceptions of corruption in countries throughout the world. CPI is a benchmark much used as a point of reference, carrying substantial economic and political consequences involving decisions of investment, aid and inclusivity (Andersson and Hayward, 2009). Yet its basis as a perception index indicates the difficulties of establishing a fixed definition of corruption and the means used to address it. Counter-accusations of corruption have been used by regimes as a means to frame and deter critics (see, for instance, Ajai, 2013 in a case study of Nigeria).

There is no universal definition of corruption, but instead interpretations that have acquired currency through iterative use, or those which are too broad for application (Andersson and Hayward, 2009). Nonetheless, tackling the problem lies in wider arrangements for 'good governance', which

> is seen as being participatory, accountable, transparent, responsive, consensus orientated, effective and efficient, equitable and inclusive, as well as following the rule of law. In general, the good governance

approach has implied a straightforward – if very broad – approach to tackling corruption, focusing on improving political accountability, strengthening civil society, promoting competition via markets and the private sector, imposing institutional restraints on power and reforming public sector management. (Andersson and Hayward, 2009, p.751)

These authors note how much of the focus has been upon reducing opportunities for corruption and increasing the risk of detection and related punishments. At its most severe, the consequences of criminalising officials is intended as a deterrent to lobbyists or clients in seeking to exert undue influence. Estonia's anti-corruption Act makes a criminal offence from decisions that bring about 'unequal or unjustified advantages' with a key paragraph offering definition that

> there is corrupt use of an official position if the public official
>
> (acting in his or her official capacity) makes a decision or performs an act that violates his or her official duties in his or her own interest or in that of any third person, if this brings about unequal or unjustified advantages for the official or the third person from the point of view of public interest. (OECD, 2014, p.64)

The approach of placing requirements upon officials, backed by disciplinary sanction, is also intended to increase the efficacy of compliance mechanisms involving disclosure. Disclosure components vary, but are loosely based on the concept of avoiding anything that may give rise to the perception of, or possibilities for, 'undue influence'. Thresholds are often provided for refusal and acceptance of gifts and hospitality, accompanied by public registers where gifts fall in the 'acceptable' zone, with exceptions for minutiae (such as cheap consumables). Around half of OECD countries make guidelines available online (OECD, 2014).

Administrations can seek to achieve disclosure of meetings between public officials and lobbyists by placing the reporting responsibility on officials (La Pira and Thomas, 2014). The extent of this is illustrated by a provision of Slovenia's Integrity and Prevention of Corruption Act of 2010, which

> requires that, at every contact with a lobbyist, a lobbied official should record: the name of the lobbyist; whether the lobbyist has identified him- or herself in accordance with the provisions of the Integrity and Prevention of Corruption Act; the area of lobbying; the name of the interest group or any other organisation for which the lobbyist is lobbying; any enclosure; and the date and place of the lobbyist's visit. The lobbied official should sign his or her record of the meeting with the lobbyist and forward a copy of the record to his superior and the Commission for the Prevention of Corruption within three days. The Commission keeps records for five years. (OECD, 2014, p.69)

The counter-argument lies in whether the expense of disclosure should be borne by public funds, but in highly regulated systems there are arrangements for disclosure by lobbied and lobbyists to the extent that information from the two sets of disclosures can be cross-checked and used for compliance purposes. Professional transparency watchdogs have played a key role in bringing disclosure features to wider audiences through tailored websites that provide information about potential conflict of interest issues and interactions between officials, legislators and advocacy organisations. TI Europe's *EU Integrity Watch*, launched in mid-2015, takes the concept of offering pointed information for public consumption well downstream, in bringing together information from a number of different disclosure databases of EU institutions into a single, easy to use, portal. There, the public is presented with information as to which members of the legislature have significant outside income, and which senior members of the European Commission held meetings with which lobby organisations, following the introduction of mandatory disclosure measures for the latter in 2014. The portal offers summary data on headcounts of lobbyists, as well as the most active organisations and categories of advocacy organisations. These portals are useful for journalists in regular need of stories with potentially high impact, thus offering a

means to enforce disclosure and make political institutions responsive to systemic regulatory improvements.

A further type of component covering the 'lobbied' involves supportive measures aimed at learning and best practice, including dissemination of rules and guidelines to those taking up office, training, and helpline desks where questions arise over implementation. Research among officials in the European Commission suggests that officials tend to make similar judgements as to the boundaries of acceptable behaviour (Nastase, 2014).

Nonetheless, results from the OECD survey on Lobbying Rules and Guidelines of 2013 indicate there is limited use of supportive measures among a core group of their members ('OECD10') with lobby regulation schemes in place. Thus, only Canada, Germany, Slovenia and the USA provide officials in both executive and legislative branches of government, and Poland only in the legislative branch, with information about requirements, while Austria, France, Hungary, Italy (regional-level schemes) and Mexico reported none at all. Similarly, only Germany, Slovenia and the USA reported providing training, with case studies, to both branches of government, and only Austria, Canada, Germany, Slovenia and the USA offer advisory helplines (OECD, 2014). The annual report of the Canadian Commissioner of Lobbying in Canada for 2013–14 documents an active role played in providing training for public officials as well as others (Commissioner of Lobbying in Canada, 2014).

'Revolving Doors'

Arrangements that prevent serving members of legislatures from simultaneously undertaking advocacy for third parties have become common, though not universal, governance features, replacing simple disclosure mechanisms. Measures to regulate 'revolving doors' between the public and private sectors have also become integrated features of lobby regulation schemes, with 'cooling-off' provisions involving post-employment restrictions in around half of OECD countries, and screening arrangements to avoid potential conflicts of interest from pre-public employment in around one-third (OECD, 2014).

With their working knowledge of political institutions, specific legislative topics and range of established networks, former members of legislative and executive branches of government are attractive recruits for lobby-related organisations. High-profile examples involve former presidents and ministerial posts taking up subsequent advisory positions with organisations related to corporate lobbying, bringing extended pressures for regulation (Mulcahy, 2015). Regulatory measures vary across countries between those that are addressed to the executive and legislative branches of government, the level of seniority of posts covered by the arrangements, and the length of period involved (Canada, at five years, is the longest). A variation involves imposing shorter periods of post-employment restriction but applied retroactively to cover a longer period, and by placing a restriction on lobbying involving any topic on which the official had worked during a period preceding the end of employment. Senior officials of the European Commission are forbidden from lobbying on topics on which they worked for three years before leaving post, applied for one year after leaving office. Six countries have arrangements covering both branches of government and most public officials (Canada, Germany, Korea, Mexico, Portugal and the USA) (OECD, 2014). Determining which posts are lobby-related inevitably involves degrees of judgement that require interpretation, in which ethics committees exercise scrutiny of cases referred to them.

Because post-employment measures involve placing restrictions on future employment prospects, their introduction requires negotiations with civil service staff unions over compensatory elements that vary according to existing contracts. Restrictions on members of legislatures are generally lighter, in recognition of the fixed-term nature of legislatures as compared with the permanent contracts of public officials, and the limited types of employment to which former members might be suited to perform. Thus, a Member of the European Parliament will only lose access to former Members' facilities (building entry, a parking space, etc.) if they undertake lobbying activities after their time as an MEP, compared to an outright ban on members of the executive, enforced by the prospect of loss of some pension entitlements. Former members' familiarity with cities where legislatures are based also contributes to making a route to the 'other side' of political institutions a well-trodden pathway, with almost half of retiring members of the US Congress now taking up lobbying-related positions (OECD, 2014).

In a striking study of former 'staffers' of US Senate offices who became lobbyists, Blanes, Vidal, Draca and Fons-Rosen (2010) found their income as lobbyists declined by a quarter once the Senator left Congress.

Regulatory arrangements covering office staff of a member of a legislature vary, but (as in the European Parliament) can parallel staff regulations applicable to executive branches of government. Thus, staff would not be allowed to lobby the legislature for a designated period of time (five years in the case of the EP) after leaving their jobs in the legislature. LaPira and Thomas find inadequate arrangements in the US to regulate the post-employment condition of 'staffers', who mainly gravitate towards commercial lobbying positions (LaPira and Thomas, 2014).

Expert Advisory Groups

Sources of policy advice are subject to a high degree of contestation, and the prospect for substantive politics to lurk behind technical advice. Standard devices for the use of expertise in political systems involve arrangements for transparency, centred on public registers, disclosure arrangements and those aimed at the avoidance of conflict of interests, and plurality of sources. Regulatory policy making requires a high degree of technical expertise, and the degree of politicisation is high in regulatory-based regimes such as the European Union, where the European Parliament has been successful in making the European Commission responsive to demands for procedural changes through its control over budget lines (Moodie, 2015). The Commission depends upon input from over 1,200 expert groups, with experts from national administrations accounting for 70% of members (Moodie, 2015), followed by scientists, and in some groups nominees from organisations throughout civil society (Gornitzka and Sverdrup, 2011). Gornitzka and Sverdrup's study is the only assessment to date covering the entire range of EU expert groups, finding no support for claims of regulatory capture, but rather one of heterogeneity where societal interests are involved with expert groups. Claims that business groups outnumber NGOs miss the diversity within each of these constituencies, and business groups often divide and take competing political positions. Rather than being excluded, a seemingly greater problem for NGOs involves their ability to service a large number of groups, with one citing membership of 40 expert groups (Panichi and Ariès, 2015). Nonetheless, advocacy groups have politicised the role of expert groups, resulting in the European Parliament temporarily withholding funding for them. Additionally, the European Ombudsman made a recommendation that calls for applications to take part in expert groups to be made public.

OPERATIONALISING LOBBY REGULATION: REGULATING LOBBYISTS

Most lobbying regulations focus on the activities of lobbyists, based around registration and disclosure. One objection to registration is that

it may create the perception of a 'two-tier' system of access which deters the exercise of participatory rights, an objection most powerfully voiced by representatives of NGO sectors, most recently voiced in the UK just before the turn of this century (Committee on Standards in Public Life, 2000). It is a mark of the shift in civil society in approaches to lobby regulation that such an objection is now rarely heard from NGOs, whose campaigns have now shifted more towards the achievement of a 'level playing field' for participation in political decision making with business-related organisations. This has involved an acceptance by NGOs that their activities also have to fall within the scope of regulation, including reluctant acquiescence in wearing the mantra 'lobbyist'. Producer organisations, too, have come to adapt to regulation as a means of accepting the designation as an 'accredited lobbyist'.

The first parts of this section cover the scope of regulation by comparing incentivised schemes with those that are mandatory in law, together with the disclosure elements involved, followed by analysis of arrangements for monitoring and compliance. A final section examines the continued presence of self-regulatory schemes alongside those run by political institutions.

BREADTH OF SCOPE: THE EUROPEAN UNION'S LOBBY REGULATION SCHEME

The European Union's Transparency Register

> covers **all** activities designed to influence – **directly** or **indirectly** – policymaking, policy implementation and decision-making in the EU institutions, no matter where they are carried out or which channel or method of communication is used. (Joint Transparency Register Secretariat (JTRS) 2015: original emphasis)

Whilst the emphasis in the revision of the scheme in 2015 is thus upon actions rather than agents in its definition, the predecessor maintained the stress upon *activities carried out with the objective of directly or indirectly influencing policy and decision making,* in which all organisations engaged in such activities were 'expected to register', with accompanying guidance identifying, *inter alia*, informal networks, and conferences aimed at exerting influence, within its scope. As such, the scheme has the widest embrace of organisational coverage to be found anywhere, with currently in excess of 9,000 organisations around the globe, including public authorities and universities who have chosen to publish their own entry on a register. The scheme is designed to attract a large number of organisations to fall within the scope of regulation, starting with a change of name in 2011 from the 'Register of Interest Representatives' (ROIR) to the 'Transparency Register' (the ROIR nomenclature had deterred some, notably think tanks and churches, from making an entry). The ability of organisations to publish their own entry directly to a public web interface for free means that the Transparency Register has been plagued by publicity seekers with little or no connection to EU lobbying (Greenwood and Dreger, 2013).

The act of registration requires public disclosure of a limited set of information about organisations, including income, spending and staffing levels, and some degree of identification of individuals. Registration also requires agreement to abide by a code of conduct, the provisions for which are unremarkable other than explicit provision for organisations to take responsibility for the accuracy of information conveyed during lobbying. The scheme has until now been voluntary, although the incoming 2014 European Commission has announced the intention to conclude an agreement with other EU institutions in 2015 to upgrade its status to mandatory. The basis of the scheme, incentivising registrations but with policing and sanction arrangements centred primarily on reputational mechanisms, has led lobby regulation

activists to question what mandatory regulation might mean in practice.

Incentives to join the Transparency Register are related to access to, although not accreditation by, political institutions, of which the most important is a pass to facilitate access to the European Parliament. Registration is a pre-requisite for inclusion in hearings, expert and advisory groups, and for bilateral meetings (but not including chance encounters) at senior levels, and pressure applied at lower levels, in the European Commission. These factors, strengthened during the course of 2014 and 2015, have made registration *de facto* mandatory, resulting in a rash of additional registrations, as well as an improvement in the quality of data entered by registering organisations (*Financial Times*, 2015). Some law firms have used the cover of client confidentiality as a reason not to register and make the associated public disclosures (Greenwood and Dreger, 2013). The strengthening of incentives introduced by the incoming (Juncker) Commission in 2014 has squeezed their scope to operate without registration to the point that a number have broken rank and joined the Register.

Mandatory Schemes

Schemes that are mandatory in law are much less embracing in scope than incentivised schemes because of the need to specifically identify their targets. Lobbyist Registration schemes that are mandatory in law exist in Australia, Austria, Canada, Ireland, Lithuania, Mexico, Poland, Slovenia, the United Kingdom and the United States. Schemes in Australia, Poland and the United Kingdom are narrowly drawn around commercial lobbyists only, while schemes in Canada and Hungary take in extensive categories of others, including law firms, in-house lobbyists from profit and non-profit (including charitable) sectors, think tanks, media organisations and churches, with schemes in other countries lying in between these poles (JTRS,

2013; OECD, 2014). Nonetheless, regulatory provisions for commercial lobbyists are more extensive than those covering other lobbyists in all jurisdictions, including the EU, because of the greater need to identify information about those interests seeking to influence decision making.

The basic components of schemes aimed at commercial lobbyists involve registration and disclosure, with the most extensive requirements for disclosure in schemes in Austria, Canada, Ireland, Slovenia and the USA. Because the schemes in Europe were based around design elements of schemes in Canada and the USA, and have very few registrations following a recent launch (2015, in the cases of Austria and Ireland), the focus in this section is primarily on the design and operationalisation of schemes in Canada and the USA. More detailed description of regulatory measures in Canada and the USA can be found in Holman and Luneburg (2012).

Lobbyist registration schemes in North America exclude from the scope of regulation any lobbyists (in Canada, other than commercial lobbyists) who spend less than 20% of their time (self-defined, thus introducing scope for non-compliance) on lobbying activities within a quarterly reporting period (and in the USA, spending below $3,001). Otherwise, communication with either the legislative or executive branches of government triggers registration, although in the USA fewer members of the executive branch are covered compared to blanket provisions applicable to communication with all those working in the legislative branch (Holman and Luneburg, 2012). In addition to registration of lobbyists, separate activity reports cover information about the lobbying organisations and individuals on a quarterly basis (political contributions are the subject of disclosure in the USA on a half-yearly basis), and activity reports, required on a monthly basis in Canada about oral communications. Subjects of disclosure include the names of lobbyists (and any positions previously held in government) as well as employing organisations, targets of lobbying (extending to named department/officials), beneficiaries of lobbying (extending down to the identification of subsidiaries), subjects of lobbying and lobbying coalition members and (in Canada) the methods of lobbying.

Oversight

Monitoring of regulatory arrangements involves a mixture of oversight from observers, and from government itself. The source of stories potentially available from lobby registers and databases makes for a high degree of journalistic coverage, with *Politico* (in Brussels and Washington) offering specialised weekly e-news with a regular feature listing new registrations each week, as well as feature stories. Outside of the political circuit and trade magazines, the *Financial Times* has a regular stream of coverage using lobby data sources. Professionalised watchdog organisations, often drawing on substantial levels of funding from governmental organisations and trust sources, provide scrutiny and analysis, and use their websites to highlight systemic weakness, with some aggressively featuring individual cases and actively using complaint procedures.

Official oversight arrangements vary across jurisdictions between units attached to either the executive or legislative branches of government, or in some cases a jointly established unit. These units may be dedicated to lobbying or integrity oversight, or perform a range of duties related to administrative measures that structure dialogue with civil society. These offices undertake sample checks on data provided, as well as administer the schemes they oversee. The Office of the Commissioner of Lobbying in Canada has 28 full-time employees dedicated to the work of the office, with specialised directorates devoted to registration, and investigative, activities. The latter includes taking a 5% sample of the monthly communication reports and the power to open comprehensive Administrative Reviews, with ongoing powers to refer outcomes to a more formal investigation and to the judicial authorities. By way of contrast, the European Commission/Parliament Joint Transparency Register Secretariat (JTRS) has the equivalent of four full-time staff attached to the work of the register.

Sanctions work on the basis of reputational consequences, which follow from reporting of transgressions, and forms of penalties vary from exclusion from incentivised registers, to civil and criminal penalties. Four countries (Austria, Canada, Germany and the USA) have provision for jail terms. Canada and the USA provide for fines of up to $200,000, and in the USA up to five years' imprisonment for corrupt violation of the Lobbying Disclosure Act (OECD, 2014). Nonetheless, resort to judicial proceedings is rare, with the first case arising in Canada in 2013.

Self-Regulation

Self-regulatory schemes can begin as a response to public criticism, with an intention to head off the prospect of avoiding statutory regulation, over which the subjects have little control. An alternative perspective is that professions generally seek regulation as a means of consolidating and developing a status, and of distinguishing themselves from others. Often, they involve an entrepreneurial act by an individual or small network, in which the prospect of establishing a platform for an organisation to showcase a profile, or even hold out the prospect of future employment, may be an incentive. The establishment and survival of an organisation depends upon its ability to differentiate itself from others operating in the field (Gray and Lowery, 1996; Lowery and Gray, 1997). As jurisdictions have developed statutory regulation, organisations with self-regulatory codes have to find a way to sustain themselves by finding a niche of added value, or risk being marginalised. One form of adaptation is to extend membership, and thus the

scope of self-regulation, beyond the categories of practitioners covered by statutory schemes. This option is available in countries where statutory regulation is narrowly drawn around commercial practitioners, and where there is no government-defined code of conduct for lobbyists, such as the United Kingdom.

International NGOs (INGOs) (e.g. Amnesty International, Greenpeace and Transparency International) have also developed self-regulatory codes, including the International NGO Accountability Charter (established 2005, revised 2014), which includes the requirement to submit an annual review to an independent review board. The code has attracted criticism for lacking many of the provisions that its members advocate for statutory regulatory instruments (Vibert, 2007), and in particular for its lack of sanctions.

CONCLUSION

Lobby regulation schemes comprise measures aimed at the lobbied and lobbyists. Measures for the lobbied are established first because of the greater ease of identifying, and controlling, the target constituencies involved, and their ease of demarcation from the participation of civil society in political decision making. Both elements involve a mixture of prohibition and disclosure, with civil society organisations increasingly providing attractive web-based resources seeking to facilitate the matching of disclosure reports from public officials and lobbyists. One perspective involves placing the balance of responsibilities upon public officials for reporting, with sanctions for contravention of such strength that they act as a deterrent to lobbyists. 'Cooling-off' provisions involving post-employment restrictions exist in around half of OECD countries.

Lobbyist registration schemes that are mandatory in law exist in over ten countries, with a notable recent trend being the establishment of schemes in countries with corporatist or statist traditions. In small countries, a localised scandal of high saliency has been sufficient to establish a scheme, while in others the cumulative effect of events has contributed to their establishment. A first starting point involves registration schemes narrowly drawn around commercial lobbyists, whereas incentivised voluntary registration schemes, in which reputational elements provide the main sanction, are more widely embraced.

Globalisation has been a key feature in the development of components of lobby regulation, involving three contributory factors. One involves the growth of trade across borders involving multi-national firms and the regulatory challenges involved, followed by commercial public affairs firms seeking to service their needs. A second involves the linkage of protest across borders, facilitated by the internet. A third involves linkage of regulatory schemes, with those in the north American continent increasingly providing a reference point for the development of schemes elsewhere. These have helped to place lobby regulation components firmly within measures for 'good governance', in which equality of access to decision making has become an established feature, based around pluralist regimes of checks and balances, founded on mechanisms of transparency and accountability.

Note

1 Professor of European Public Policy, Robert Gordon University, Aberdeen, United Kingdom; Visiting Professor, College of Europe.

REFERENCES

Ajai, O. (2013) *Corruption can Bite: Nuhu Ribadu's EFCC and Anti-Corruption Drive in Nigeria*, available as Case 213–040-1 from The Case Centre, http://www.thecasecentre. org/educators/ accessed on 2 July 2015.

Andersson, S. and Heywood, P. M. (2009) 'The Politics of Perception: Use and Abuse of Transparency International's Approach to Measuring Corruption'. *Political Studies*, 57: 746–767.

Bauer, M. and Grimes, M. (2014) 'Indignation or Resignation: The implications of transparency for social accountability', *Governance*, 27, 2: 291–330.

BBC Radio 4 'Today' programme 2 June 2015, http://www.bbc.co.uk/radio/player/ b05wxzxs accessed on 25 June 2015.

Blanes, I., Vidal, J., Draca, M. and Fons-Rosen, C. (2010) 'Revolving Door Lobbyists', Centre for Economic Performance Discussion Paper No. 993, London School of Economics, http://personal.lse.ac.uk/blanesiv/revolving. pdf accessed on 23 June 2015.

Chari, R., Hogan, J. and Murphy, G. (2010) *Regulating Lobbying: a Global Comparison*. Manchester: Manchester University Press.

Committee on Standards in Public Life (2000) Reinforcing Standards: review of the First Report of the Committee on Standards in Public Life, Volume 1 (the Neill Committee). London: HMSO.

Council of Europe (2013) Report on the Role of Extra-Institutional Actors in the Democratic System (Lobbying), European Commission for Democracy through Law (Venice Commission), Study 590/2010, CDL-AD(2013) 011, http://www.venice.coe.int/webforms/ documents/default.aspx?pdffile=CDL-AD(2013)011-e accessed on 23 June 2015.

Dos Santos, L. A. and Teixera da Costa, P. M. (2014) Brazil: lobby regulation, transparency and democratic governance, in OECD (2014), *Lobbyists, Governments and Public Trust, Volume 3: Implementing the OECD Principles for Transparency and Integrity in Lobbying*, OECD Publishing, http://www.oecd.org/governance/lobbyists-governments-and-public-trust-volume-3-9789264214224-en.htm doi: 10.1787/9789264214224-en accessed on 23 June 2015: 109–124.

Economist (2000) Angry and Effective, http:// www.economist.com/node/374657 accessed on 3 July 2015.

Economist (2014) Donors: Keep Out, http:// www.economist.com/news/

international/21616969-more-and-more-autocrats-are-stifling-criticism-barring-non-governmental-organisations accessed on 25 June 2015.

Gray, V. and Lowery, D. (1996) 'A Niche Theory of Interest Representation', *The Journal of Politics*, 58, 1: 91–111.

Financial Times (2015) Goldman forced to reveal 14-fold rise in spending on EU lobbying as rules bite, *Financial Times*, 29 April 2015, p. 11.

Gornitzka, A. and Sverdrup, U. (2011) 'Access of Experts: Information and EU Decision-making', *West European Politics*, 34, 1: 48–70.

Greenwood, J. (2011) 'The lobby regulation element of the European Transparency Initiative: between liberal and deliberative models of democracy', *Comparative European Politics*, 9, 3: 317–343.

Greenwood, J. and Dreger, J. (2013) The Transparency Register: A European vanguard of strong lobby regulation? *Interest Groups & Advocacy*, 2, 2: 139–162.

Guardian (2012) Russia plans to register 'foreign agent' NGOs, *Guardian*, 2 July 2012, http://www.theguardian.com/world/2012/jul/02/russia-register-foreign-agent-ngos accessed on 25 June 2015.

Guardian (2015) Russia bans 'undesirable' international organisations ahead of 2016 elections, *Guardian*, http://www.theguardian.com/world/2015/may/19/russia-bans-undesirable-international-organisations-2016-elections accessed on 25 June 2015.

Holman, C. and Luneburg, W. (2012) 'Lobbying and Transparency: a comparative analysis of regulatory reform', *Interest Groups and Advocacy*, 1, 1: 75–104.

Human Rights Watch (2015) World Report 2014: Russia, http://www.hrw.org/world-report/2014/country-chapters/russia?page=1 accessed on 25 June 2015.

Independent (2014) Former Greenpeace leading light condemns them for opposing GM 'golden rice' crop that could save two million children from starvation per year, http://www.independent.co.uk/news/science/former-greenpeace-leading-light-condemns-them-for-opposing-gm-golden-rice-crop-that-could-save-two-million-children-from-starvation-per-year-9097170.html, accessed on 3 July 2014.

Joint Transparency Register Secretariat of the European Commission and European Parliament (2015) Who is expected to register, http://ec.europa.eu/transparencyregister/public/staticPage/displayStaticPage.do?locale=en&reference=WHOS_IS_EXPECTED_TO_REGISTER accessed on 4 August 2016.

Kingdon, J. (1984) *Agendas, Alternative and Public Policies*. New York: Addison Wesley.

LaPira, T. and Thomas, H. (2014) 'Revolving Door Lobbyists and Interest Representation', *Interest Groups and Advocacy*, 3, 1: 4–29.

Lowery, D. and Gray, V. (1997) 'How some Rules just don't matter: the Regulation of Lobbyists', *Public Choice*, 91: 139–147.

Mair, P. (2014) 'Democracies'; in D Caramani (2014, 3rd edn) *Comparative Politics*. Oxford: Oxford University Press, 79–95.

Moodie, J. R. (2015) Resistant to Change? The European Commission and Expert Group Reform, *West European Politics*, http://dx.doi.org/10.1080/01402382.2015.1041824 accessed on 23 June 2015.

Mulcahy, S. (2015) Lobbying in Europe – hidden influence, privileged access. Brussels: Transparency International Europe, http://www.transparency.org/whatwedo/publication/lobbying_in_europe accessed on 1 July 2015.

Nastase, A. (2014) 'Catering to Organizational Needs in Ethics Management: the Case of the European Commission', *International Journal of Public Administration*, 37, 2: 93–105.

OECD (2014) *Lobbyists, Governments and Public Trust, Volume 3: Implementing the OECD Principles for Transparency and Integrity in Lobbying*, OECD Publishing, http://www.oecd.org/governance/lobbyists-governments-and-public-trust-volume-3-9789264214224-en.htm doi: 10.1787/9789264214224-en accessed on 4 August 2016.

Office of the Commissioner of Lobbying of Canada (2014) Annual Report 13|14, https://ocl-cal.gc.ca/eic/site/012.nsf/eng/h_00918.html accessed on 5 July 2015.

Panichi, J. and Ariès, Q. (2015) 'Nerds, techies and lobbyists: The Commission is planning to overhaul the extensive system of expert groups', *Politico* http://www.politico.eu/

article/expert-groups-transparency-lobbying/ accessed on 4 July 2015.

Paraszczuk, J. (2013) Russia Spotlight: Former Putin Adviser Karaganov Calls For 'New National Identity', EA World View 14 November, http://eaworldview.com/2013/11/russia-spotlight-former-yeltsin-adviser-karaganov-calls-new-national-identity/ accessed on 26 June 2015.

Pross, A. P. (2007) Lobbying: Models for Regulation, Organisation for Economic Cooperation and Development, Organisation for Economic Cooperation and Development (OECD), http://www.oecd.org/gov/fighting-corruptioninthepublicsector/expertgroupon-confictofinterestwithaspecialsessiononlob-byingenhancingtransparencyandaccounta-bilityparis07-08june2007.htm accessed on 17 January 2013.

The Local (2015) Jailed ex-interior Minister granted day release, 12 January 2015, Kronen Zeitung, http://www.thelocal.at/20150112/ former-minister-granted-prison-day-release accessed on 4 July 2015.

Vibert, F. (2007) NGO Codes of Conduct: monitored self-regulation, London: European Policy Forum http://www.epfltd.org/ accessed on 14 July 2008.

Will, C. and Kendall, J. (2009) 'A New Settlement for Europe: Towards "Open, Transparent and Regular Dialogue with Representative Associations and Civil Society"? in Jeremy Kendall (ed.) *Handbook on Third Sector Policy in Europe:* Multi-level Processes and Organized Civil Society. Cheltenham: Edward Elgar, 293–316.

Yeboah-Assiamah, E. and Alesu-Dordzi, S. (2015) 'The calculus of corruption: a paradox of "strong" corruption amidst "strong" systems and institutions in developing administrative systems', *Journal of Public Affairs*, doi: 10.1002/pa.1576, http://onlinelibrary. wiley.com/doi/10.1002/pa.1576/abstract accessed on 1 July 2015.

Values, Ethics, and Professionalism in Public Affairs

Shannon A. Bowen

FACING ETHICAL CHALLENGES

Readers who study or work in public affairs will have already realized that the ethical challenges faced by our field are myriad, often convoluted, and always complex. Defining issues, conducting research, communicating internally and with governments, various publics, and non-governmental organizations (NGOs) requires a delicate balancing of the right and the good with competing duties and obligations to numerous parties. This chapter is organized into three main sections of values, ethics, and professionalism, to offer a useful framework for moral decisions for academics and professionals alike. It will not attempt to catalog the plethora of ethical challenges that could arise in everyday public affairs because to do so would prove sheer folly. Instead, this chapter seeks to provide readers with an understanding of moral responsibilities, methods of analyses, and articulated rationale to approach and resolve moral dilemmas in public affairs.

Arguably, ethical challenges in public affairs are more complex than those found in any other arena (Bowen, 2011). Due to the magnitude of our work, hundreds or thousands of people can be impacted by the consequences of one decision and the moral principles involved are significant. Economies can change, power can shift, values can evolve, and societies can transform due to the work done in public affairs. Business-sector activities intertwining with government and public policy create weighty decision ramifications and the responsibility to engage in ethical analyses is, therefore, a pressing issue for the development of public affairs. That development can help the field itself because public affairs must continue to advance in both ethical sophistication and functional responsibility. A 2012 study by the Foundation for Public Affairs found that only 41% of organizations have a public affairs and communication function integrated into management and, 'More surprisingly, only 23% have an integrated structure for government affairs and CSR' (Judd, 2015, p. 6). Providing analyses of shared values, ethics, responsibilities, and core principles is one way that public affairs can increase not only its own credibility and professional standing but also enhance the ethical rectitude of organizations within society.

VALUES: PERSONAL, ORGANIZATIONAL, SOCIETAL

Values are the core tenets of beliefs supporting moral judgements. Values are personal or individual and learned through many forms of socialization and study (Rokeach, 1973). Values are also held by organizations as part of an organizational culture, evidenced in mission, vision, goals, and reward or punishment systems. Values can also be seen at a societal level. DeGeorge (2010) expounded, 'The morality of a society is related to its mores, or the customs that a society or group accept as being right and wrong, as well as those laws of a society to add legal prohibitions and sanctions to many activities considered to be immoral' (p. 12). Common values in Western society include independence, liberty, voice, and freedom, or in Eastern society more collectivism and face-saving measures, for example.

For public administrators, ethical awareness begins with the ability to identify personal values, organizational values, and broader social values that may impact decisions. The first step in becoming ethically engaged is to take a thorough inventory of one's personal values. What are the principles of primary importance that you believe should be upheld? What are the values that you believe are worth fighting for and potentially would sacrifice to uphold? If you had to rank those values on a list in priority order, which values would hold the top several spots? Other questions related to decision-making preference may also be helpful, such as: Are you the type of person who would rather be just and fair to all involved or would rather consider the consequences to all involved?

Knowing those core values before they are challenged or involved in a dispute of conflicting loyalties can be invaluable when attempting to resolve an ethical dilemma. Further, they allow the decision-maker to know when a good fit of common values may be achieved with an organization, or when a conflict with an organization's culture may arise (Smircich and Callas, 1987). In a similar manner, you can then identify spoken or unspoken organizational values, societal values, and cross-national values that may be in opposition or complementary. Reflecting on these values for a few brief moments may prove invaluable later on when engaged in issues management.

Organizational values have much to do with leadership and mission, and are communicated via internal relations, reward systems, and training programs, as well as components of organizational culture both clear and nebulous. Ethical leader behaviors illustrate organizational values and also serve to influence perceptions of leader credibility and trustworthiness, power-sharing, and symmetrical communication, engaging employees within an organization (Men, 2015).

Organizations may have a codified list of values that they strive to enact, or the values may be more organic, arising of their own devices from the organization's culture (Sims, 1994). However, even when they are not codified or formally discussed, members of an organization can almost always articulate its values (Goodpaster, 2007). Participants in Bowen's (2015) study, in which some organizations had values statements and other organizations did not, had no trouble identifying the values of their own organization, such as integrity, ethics, citizenship, CSR, innovation, safety, social responsibility, and quality. In that study, and in organizations without codified values, participants would often talk about the pervasive nature of values by describing it as 'in our DNA' (Bowen, 2015, p. 11).

Seeger (1997) offered these general characteristics of values: 1. Values have hierarchical priorities; 2. Values are dynamic and change over time; and 3. Individual and social identity both depend upon values. Using that understanding to help determine priorities, a changing environment, and core identity can enrich ethical organizational decision-making. Five additional values for organizations were offered by Rieke and Sillars (1993): competition, production, future thinking, cost-benefit analyses, and success. Though originally geared toward for-profit corporations, those values can also be applied in a not-for-profit environment when examining how to maximize the achievement of organizational goals. All organizations must operate under some type of logistical constraints for time and resources, even NGOs. Therefore, a commonality of goal attainment may be a shared value across organizations, ultimately sharing these values as well. Public affairs can develop and strengthen the responsibilities it holds by incorporating these values into the ethical considerations of issues, and contested matters of fact, values, and policy.

Other common values can also be identified across different types of organizations and even societies, and are a useful starting ground for the discussion of ideas and resolution of conflict. Using common values to begin such discussions may be illustrative of integrative or collaborative solutions to common problems. Common values may also provide a fertile ground for inventing options for mutual gain (Lewicki, Litterer, Saunders, and Minton, 1993). Common values that cross cultural and societal boundaries do exist (Sriramesh, 2009), and include basics such as the values of being communicated with honestly and dealt with fairly, not being murdered, property ownership, and not being enslaved (DeGeorge, 2010). More refined common values can also be

identified across numerous cultural boundaries with further examination (Bowen and Erzikova, 2013), such as the right to debate, hold an opinion, or to participate in decisions that affect one's life. Examining the core values that guide interests of multiple parties may help public affairs to begin to identify common ground across divergent boundaries (Bowen, 2011).

Values provide a common basis for understanding moral dilemmas. Moral philosophy offers a way to rigorously study moral dilemmas, and ethics seeks analytical and rational frameworks with which to consistently guide decision-making (Bowen, 2008a). In essence, ethics allows us to analytically and rigorously analyze the values, priorities, and principles, which guide or should guide our decisions. Ethics is a way to put values into action. A brief overview of the moral philosophy supporting ethical analyses is needed before one can understand how to apply the analytical frameworks of ethics in public affairs.

MORAL PHILOSOPHY AND ETHICS

The study of moral philosophy is far more complex than simple judgments of right or wrong, because ethics allows for rigorous analyses of contested values, dual loyalties, multiple claims of right, and competing responsibilities. A common adage is that you do not need ethics to know right from wrong; you need ethics to determine right from most right. The complex initiatives often involved in public affairs necessitate assigning priorities to organizational values, understanding national and multinational values, and resolving competing claims of publics and stakeholders. DeGeorge (2010) wrote that ethics in the general sense seeks a systematic way to determine 'the rules that ought to govern human conduct, the values worth pursuing, and the character traits deserving development' (p. 13).

Ethicists seek rationality and consistency as a way to guard against capriciousness, bias, prejudice, selfishness, and any of the other prudential factors that would destroy the rigor of a moral analysis. In that manner, objective judgment or independence is essential; Sullivan (1989) noted that morality was 'living autonomously' (p. 44).

Moral philosophers divide ethics into three categories: meta-ethical approaches that seek to understand the larger questions of how we draw moral conclusions; normative ethics that seeks to derive a consistent, coherent, and analytical system of ethical judgements or principles; and descriptive ethics that describes moral practices (DeGeorge, 2010). Normative ethics that helps to guide decision-making is the focus of this work.

Before moving to the analytical frameworks of normative ethics, it is important to note that materialism, a descriptive type of ethics, often describes the motives of the ethically unaware. Materialism holds that the decision-maker should seek to satisfy his or her own needs first in a competitive arena. Materialism is based on self-interest and results in bias; thus it has found little resonance within ethics. Despite the ethical flaws in materialism, self-interested decisions commonly occur in business and public affairs. Materialism often describes what happens when ethics is lacking rather than offering a normative ideal to which public affairs should aspire. Normative ethics holds that self-interest alone does not make a decision ethical but brutal and egoistic, and a more powerful standard of analysis must be used to determine right.

Normative ethical approaches are more rigorous, time-consuming, and difficult to implement than using materialism, intuition, or instinct. Yet the rigor and strength of a normative ethical analysis offer a new level of insight and defensibility to public affairs decisions. Although normative ethics is an enormous field, it can be simplified by looking at the two converse approaches to ethical analyses: utilitarianism and deontology.

Utilitarianism

Utilitarianism uses consequences, or predicted, potential consequences of a decision in order to determine the ethical course of action. The *utility* of a decision – what the decision does – determines whether it is ethical, using outcomes as a basis rather than moral principle. In general, the best decision will maximize good outcomes and minimize bad outcomes, known also as the maxi-mins test or the utilitarian calculus. Utilitarianism was developed by Jeremey Bentham, but refined and popularized by his student, John Stuart Mill (MacIntyre, 1966). Overall, utilitarianism seeks to maximize the greatest amount of good for the greatest number of people while minimizing potential harm. Although there are two different forms of utilitarianism, act and rule, both forms determine ethics based on potential outcomes of different options (Mill, 1861/1957).

Act utilitarianism uses the ethics of one unique situation to arrive at a prediction of that which produces the greatest happiness or good for the greatest number of people. In that approach, the decision that maximizes good and minimizes bad is the ethical course of action, predicted in all the specificity of the unique situation. The maxi-mins principle is used to determine the maximum good outcomes and the minimum harms as the ethical course of action.

Rule utilitarianism does not confine the analysis to the specifics of one situation, but seeks wisdom from prior cases or similar situations, still seeking to maximize the outcomes that are considered intrinsically valuable, for the greatest number of people, while minimizing negative outcomes (Elliott, 2007). Those outcomes to be maximized could be happiness, knowledge, honor, kindness, honesty, friendship, and other principles or concepts that would be good when maximized (MacIntyre, 1966). Defining the good is a challenge in any form of ethics, but in the utilitarian framework normally relies upon happiness or 'the greater good for the greatest number of people' standard (MacIntyre, 1966). In rule utilitarianism, the maxi-mins rule uses wisdom from prior cases, along with weighing outcomes, to help determine the maximum intrinsic good and the minimum harms. Act utilitarianism has the benefit of giving guidance in a very specific and unique case, pondering all of its complexities. Rule utilitarianism has the benefit of learning from the past and deciding what the moral principle to be maximized should be. Each type of utilitarian analysis can be helpful, especially when considering an issue with potentially large public impact.

The utilitarian idea gets to the heart of the public interest or the greater good as a reason for conducting public affairs ethically. By looking at the consequences alone rather than moral principle, utilitarianism does not ensure a truly ethical outcome. However, its use does focus on the public interest rather than selfish materialism, so it is thought to produce more positives than negatives. It is an intuitive and fast form of analysis that allows consistent implementation. The decisions that arrive via utilitarianism are normally understandable and defensible. Utilitarianism is useful in public affairs because the outcomes of the decisions made using a utilitarian framework should benefit the public interest, as in the greatest good for the greatest number, without bias or capriciousness. Rule utilitarianism is generally thought to provide a more analytical framework than act utilitarianism (DeGeorge, 2010). Yet, act utilitarianism provides a quick analysis of a very specific situation and helps to thoroughly understand potential outcomes. Utilitarianism must be implemented with the utmost objectivity because the theory has a significant number of pitfalls.

Pitfalls of Utilitarianism

Utilitarianism provides a rather simple yet consistent means through which public administrators can analyze decisions and predict potential consequences. The idea of conducting ethical activities in the interest of the greatest good for the greatest number of people is a morally worthy one. Yet the very simplicity that is the strength of act utilitarianism and even rule utilitarianism can also be the cause of the following pitfalls, which must be guarded against.

Future consequences, including actions and reactions of stakeholders and publics, must be predicted with accuracy. Unpredictable outcomes cannot be accounted for by utilitarianism. Much research is required in order to thoroughly understand all of the options and potential outcomes of each possible decision before a conclusion is reached, and is often a costly and error-prone process. The values of publics must be known and understood in order to accurately predict how they would respond to each potential action. Unintended consequences must be successfully anticipated and planned for in order to minimize negative outcomes or harms. Serving the greatest good for the greatest number of people can lead to a tyranny of the majority. The decision-maker must guard against ignoring the valid concerns of a minority. Utilitarianism does not allow drastic sacrifice or true harms to a small public in order to benefit the majority; the amount of harm allowed is minimal. And finally, most troubling to ethicists, utilitarianism equates ethics and moral principle with numbers of people rather than looking at the greater arguments behind the issue. For example, if 50 people are on each side of an argument, no ethical decision is possible; worse, if one person changes sides, that person, by creating a majority, has determined the ethics of the entire issue.

Accurately forecasting future repercussions of organizational actions among multiple publics is difficult at best. Research, both informal and formal, helps to thoroughly understand the issue and the desires, interests, values, and priorities of different stakeholders and publics. In seeking to weigh the number of positive outcomes for the greatest number of people, rule utilitarianism has an advantage in that its research also includes historical or similar cases to help guide the decision. Conducting research should also help the public administrator to be familiar with potential options to resolve an issue. Research can be used to create a number of alternatives, and then these alternatives could be examined in detail for their potential consequences before any decision is made using an act utilitarian approach.

Utilitarianism serves as a powerful means of protecting the public interest and is the basis of much of Western society and judicial systems (Elliott, 2007). For instance, in creating the greatest good for the greatest number of people, the United States government mandated vaccinations, despite the harm that vaccinations cause to a few. The greater good for the greatest number of people was seen as the propagation of disease resistance; thus vaccination is deemed ethical. The main strength of utilitarian theory is that it acts with the public interest in mind, as defined by the greatest number of people aided by a decision. Using a utilitarian analysis requires information and research, an analysis that is based on careful prediction and forecasting, and vigilance against the pitfalls of the framework. It is often most suited to less complex ethical dilemmas, or those with a significant component of public interest (Jiang and Bowen, 2011). The second overall approach to ethics is a more rigorous deontological approach that can be combined with a utilitarian analysis, or used in place of it as a standalone framework for ethics.

Deontology: Kantian Theory

The 18th-century Prussian philosopher Immanuel Kant (1724–1804) used ancient conceptions of ethics to inform his thinking, but arrived at a complex, rigorous, theoretically sophisticated, and practically unassailable – yet practical – test of ethics known as deontology (Scruton, 1982). Deontology is based on the study of duty or moral principle rather than consequences. Consequences are only one factor among many in this form of decision-making and are not used alone to determine the ethical nature of the decision (Kant, 1793/1974). Still, the important consideration in this ethical framework is underlying moral principle.

Deontology is entirely based on rational decision-making and objective moral autonomy. Rationality is necessary so that any logical decision-maker would arrive at the same decision no matter where they are in time, space, culture, and so on. The Law of Autonomy is necessary to keep bias and capriciousness out of decisions, basing them entirely on equality and that which is universalizable, or could be applied equally to everyone (Sullivan, 1989). This analytical framework requires rigorous rational analysis of all decision options available from each perspective of various stakeholders and publics. Moral autonomy is essential because ethical decisions cannot be compromised by bias, selfishness, fear of retribution, or similar (Bowen, 2006). Moral autonomy asks if you have the independence that is necessary to engage in an objective, rational analysis (Scruton, 1982). Autonomy is a moral construct that differs from authority, as official decision-making responsibility. Rationality and autonomy rely upon one another in that one must be able to engage in the moral analysis without being compelled in any particular direction to result in a rational conclusion, and autonomy indicates that one must have the freedom to do so (Kant, 1793/1974). If one is rational and morally autonomous, an analysis can be conducted using Kant's categorical imperative.

Implementing Deontology: The Categorical Imperative

Kant's categorical imperative consists of three tests that can be applied universally, meaning that any rational person, anywhere, and at any time, would arrive at the same conclusion. Rationality frees the decision-maker of cultural biases as well as selfish preferences and allows him or her to weigh the merits of the action based on logic alone (Sullivan, 1989). Kant's categorical imperative is so named because all people have a responsibility and moral obligation to follow it that is derived from their rationality.

Using an issues management framework (discussed in more detail in Chapter 29 of this volume) to solve potential problems means that potential decision options – possible solutions to the issue at hand – be identified and vetted. In a deontological approach, the potential decision options to solve an issue should be investigated with all three tests of the categorical imperative. The tests of Kant's (1785/1993) categorical imperative include duty, dignity and respect, and intention or a morally good will. A potential option should be judged ethical when it passes all three tests of the categorical imperative, not simply one or two.

In the categorical imperative's first test, Kant asked us to consider the universal nature of the action and whether we could obligate all others, as a universal law, to do the same thing that we are about to do (Paton, 1967). If the action upholds a duty to universal moral principles, then all other people would also agree that the action is ethical despite their particular perspective. The universal test of duty asks the decision-maker to make a reversible decision, meaning that he or she uses empathy to place him or herself in the position of the other involved publics, rationally distancing his or her own interests and organizational interests to be just one factor among many. If you still see the logic, rationality, and moral principle driving the decision from these vantage points of other publics or stakeholders then the decision is ethical. Kant did not state that everyone must agree with the decision, simply that it must be logically understandable from all viewpoints (Baron, 1995).

The universal moral norms that Kant used as this standard hold that any person, public, or constituency, from their own vantage points, could logically evaluate the option as ethical. Kant offered the test of universality to help ascertain an underlying moral principle that most people could logically evaluate as ethical. Universal moral principles generally include concepts that we can argue are good prima facie: honesty, industriousness, liberty, knowledge, and so forth (Sullivan, 1989). A universal norm does not obligate everyone to agree with the decision, only to arrive at a logical conclusion valuing the moral principle involved. If the test of universality is met, meaning that all rational decision-makers could enact the universal law requiring the option, then it is ethical and one moves on to the second form of the categorical imperative.

The second formula of the categorical imperative involves the dignity and respect of persons (Paton, 1967). According to Sullivan (1994), Kant is the premier philosopher of equality because his theory mandates that all people are equal by virtue of their rationality, and respect for that equality is morally obligated. To apply the second test of the categorical imperative, a public affairs manager should ask, 'Does this potential option offer dignity and respect for all publics involved in the issue?' The moral principle underlying this test is that dignity and respect are based on an innate moral good, and disregarding others or preference in one's own interest strips equality from the situation. If an action violates human dignity or respect, it is deemed unethical. Again, stakeholders and publics do not have to agree with or like the decision. Reasonable parties often disagree; however, the key is doing so while maintaining dignity and respect for other views. For instance, some publics may disagree with the type of protests used by those against the International Monetary Fund (IMF); however, they should respect the right of the protesters to employ a moral evaluation ending in protest. To disrespect another erodes the moral autonomy necessary to create one's own independent judgments that are an essential component of deontology. If the option maintains dignity and respect of stakeholders and publics, one can move on to the third test of Kantian analysis.

The third test of the categorical imperative is Kant's most stringent test of morality (Sullivan, 1989). Kant held that good will or good intention is the only morally incorruptible motive to guide action (Scruton, 1982). Kant (1930/1963) argued, 'If our conduct as free agents is to have moral goodness, it must proceed solely from a good will' (p. 18). Deontological theory holds that *only* decisions made from a basis of goodwill or pure moral intention are ethical, even if it is ultimately the same decision that is enacted from a nefarious motive. For instance, designating funds to build a new interstate highway in a Congressman's district in exchange for his vote on a particular issue is unethical. Funding the new interstate highway because it is needed to relieve traffic congestion is the ethical decision. The result is the same – the new highway is funded – yet the first situation is based on unethical selfishness, while the latter situation meets this test because it is based on good intention.

In the public affairs arena, intentions should be examined routinely, especially when financially or politically motivated issues drive a decision. This final test of the categorical imperative shows that the intention to do the right thing, the morally good will, is the only ethical motive for action (Sullivan, 1989). If an analysis reveals that an option is simply glossed-over self-interest, it is unethical regardless of the outcome. But if an option is based on an intent to do the right thing, it meets the test of goodwill. Deontology holds that an option is ethical when it passes all three tests of categorical imperative.

When considering various options to resolve an issue, the three tests of the categorical imperative can be applied to each option. Doing so results in a rigorous moral analysis and a multisided understanding of the issue from various perspectives, both inside the organization and of external publics and stakeholders. The core tenets of a deontological framework – rationality, autonomy,

dignity and respect, and good intention – are argued by philosophers (Paton, 1967; Scruton, 1982; Sullivan, 1989; Baron, 1995) to result in the most stringent ethical analysis offered by moral philosophy. Considering an action thoroughly through the lens of deontology normally means that the organization is acting from moral principle and if the action is challenged it is morally defensible.

Several studies have found that issues managers often use a deontological approach to ethical reasoning in their decision-making. In applying deontology, a public affairs professional can explain decisions to management, stakeholders, constituencies, legislators, governmental/regulatory bodies, the media, competitors, NGOs and international interests.

Applying Utilitarianism and Deontology in Public Affairs

To apply moral philosophy in public affairs, it is first necessary to recognize what type of issue needs ethical analysis. Recognizing an ethical issue is often trickier than it seems. One study (Bowen, 2002) found that issues managers and one global pharmaceutical firm rarely labeled any problem an ethical issue because of the belief system that hiring good people would summarily result in ethical decisions. That same study compared an exemplary organization, a leader in ethics, and found that issues were commonly and frequently discussed in terms of ethics (Bowen, 2002) and therefore concluded that candid and frequent discussions of ethics resulted in a more ethical organization overall.

Other studies have found that an organizational culture is more important to ethical decision-making than codes of ethics or 'assumed' ethics once onboarding is complete (Sims, 1994; Sims and Brinkman, 2003; Goodpaster, 2007). In actively discussing an organization's ethics, the internal culture related to ethical decision-making is strengthened and organizational values are both examined and reinforced (Bowen, 2015). There are many cases that offer examples of an inattention to ethics destroying an organization, such as the dishonesty surrounding the bankruptcy of A.H. Robins in the Dalkon Shield case (Gini, 2004) or the defective DC-10 being sold to airlines as a safe plane (Gini, 2004). Landmark cases such as these are common, yet one need only look to each day's news to see evidence of ethical inattention, laxity, ignorance, or even a disdain for ethics, in public and government affairs. Unfortunately, these acts of ignorance can bankrupt companies, damage economies, cost taxpayers, and destroy the public trust that citizens place in both business and in their government or elected officials. The cost of inattention to ethics is high.

Despite mounting evidence that ethics creates longer-term and more stable, lasting relationships between organizations and publics (Grunig, 1992, 2014; Goodpaster, 2007; Bowen and Hung-Baesecke, 2013), some people may still perceive ethics as too complicated or onerous to consider. Further, several studies have found that, although top communicators advise management on ethics, many say that they lack the formal training or knowledge to do so (L'Etang, 2003; Bowen, 2008b; Fawkes, 2012). This chapter seeks to simplify ethics to a practical level in which it can be applied on a daily basis to all types of public affairs issues, large and small, as part of the growing professionalization and higher-level responsibility of public affairs.

PROFESSIONALISM IN PUBLIC AFFAIRS

Increasing the ethical rectitude and understanding of those in the public affairs arena would, no doubt, serve to advance the field, increasing its credibility, professionalism, and resulting in higher levels of strategic

decision-making responsibility. It would also help to create more ethically responsible organizations, be they private, government, or NGO entities. In so doing, an ethically responsible organization fulfills a positive social role for communicators (Rawlins, 2007, 2009; Stoker and Rawlins, 2010), helps to create civil discourse (Taylor, 2010), facilitates a better understanding between governments and the organizations within them (Bowen, 2010), and helps to create organizations with more ethical rectitude (Baker and Martinson, 2002; Bowen and Gallicano, 2013), strategy that is ethically aligned with that of publics (Botan, 1997), and reflective communication (Van Ruler and Verčič, 2005).

Professional communicators are often called upon not only to make ethical decisions but also to advise on ethics. Issues managers and public relations practitioners report that they are required to counsel the leaders of their organizations on ethical dilemmas (L'Etang, 2003; Bowen, 2002). About 65% of public relations practitioners in a recent worldwide study reported directly to the highest-ranking person in their organizations or said that they had regular access to counseling that person (Bowen et al., 2006). They reported that there were many reasons for being called to counsel a CEO, including a crisis, an ethical dilemma, an issue high on the media agenda, their credibility within the organization, or having a leadership role or influence in the organization (Bowen, 2009).

In studying ethics and professional public relations, Wright (1982, 1985) found that the age, gender, and experience of professional communicators were related to their ethical expertise. In general, females may be more sensitive to ethical problems yet males receive more ethics training (Bowen et al., 2006). With age and experience, professional communicators become more deontological or duty-based in their decision-making (Wright, 1985). Pratt, Im, and Montague (1994) also found that public relations practitioners are more likely to use deontology in their decision-making, likely due to the powerful and rigorous framework that approach offers, as did Bowen (2004a) when studying the ethics of issues management. Berger and Reber (2006) added that the role of resistance, or actively working on behalf of more rigorous understanding of issues within an organization, may be required of professional communicators engaged in high-level issues management. These findings argue for a high level of moral understanding, principled behavior, analytical power, and moral courage.

In applying these studies to public affairs, it is clear that public affairs officers will be called upon to counsel on ethics, the values of interest groups, and defining issues, even more so if media attention or conflict is present. Those kinds of issues commonly arise with elected officials, in government agencies, nonprofits, lobbying firms, heavily regulated industries, interest groups, private businesses, and the many support services that also play a role in public affairs, such as public diplomacy initiatives. The ethical theories and forms of analyses put forward in this chapter can be used by professionals in government public affairs, NGOs and interest groups, or in corporate public affairs. All sides of the communication function in public affairs must manage public policy issues, or the way in which their organizations interact with publics, government bodies, and stakeholders (Heath and Palenchar, 2009). Heath (1997) explained: 'Public policy issues are those with the potential of maturing into governmental legislation or regulation (international, federal, state, or local)' (p. 45). Whenever legislation and regulation are involved, the stakes are high and the publics are many, with conflicting interests. In short, competing interests and values of different groups within society lend themselves to ethical dilemmas. Conflicts of values are common in the public affairs arena and the best time to prepare for ethical challenges is before you are in the middle of the complex moral dilemma.

PREPARING PUBLIC AFFAIRS PROFESSIONALS FOR CONDUCTING ETHICAL ANALYSES

Ethics and public affairs intersect in the function called issues management. Public policy issues faced by governments, legislators, regulatory agencies, lobbyists, interest groups, and businesses must be monitored and managed on a continual basis. Public opinion and the interests of stakeholder groups can change rapidly and dramatically, creating a dynamic and often turbulent communication environment that requires issues management (Lerbinger, 2006).

Perhaps the most critical phase of issues management in an ethical sense is the first step: identifying a new or emerging issue or problem. Issues are researched, defined, and articulated early in the issue identification stage, including understanding the potential ethical components of an issue. Those ethical components may require later analysis and resolution. A potential issue problem or conflict escalates in importance when it can affect the future of the organization (Buchholz, Evans, and Wagley, 1994). Predicting the potential impact of an issue should help prioritize it in importance for research, analyses, and issue monitoring. Numerous sources should be monitored to track emerging and known issues.

When an issue of potential importance emerges, conducting formal and informal research to understand the issue is essential. In this issue monitoring phase, understanding the problem and problem recognition (Grunig, 1992) and importance that stakeholders and publics assign to an issue helps to prioritize it for resolution (Buchholz, Evans, and Wagley, 1994).

Undoubtedly the most ethically vital step is to conduct a rigorous analysis of an issue using all known sources of information to fully understand the situation. That analysis can be conducted in utilitarian terms if the issue is one involving public interest, or deontological terms for the more complex issues involving competing interests. Ignoring the ethical components of an emerging or monitored issue is exceptionally dangerous to an organization. Media attention to a potential ethical problem can drastically alter the organization's ability to solve the problem while maintaining good relationships with stakeholders and publics. Additionally, if a potential ethical dilemma enters the public policy arena of potential legislation and regulation, an organization loses the ability to define the issue, and will often emerge with less autonomy over its own operations, as well as the increased expense of compliance with the regulation and monitoring.

In determining how to resolve an issue, various decision alternatives, or issue action options, are explored. With the gathering of research and the understanding of various competing values, an ethical analysis can be conducted and discussed. A number of ethical decision-making models for use in issues management, government relations, and public relations exist (Bowen, 2004b, 2005, 2010, 2011; Bowen and Gallicano, 2013, Tilley, 2005). Although those models are useful and applicable, it helps for practicality to simplify their constructs and apply them

directly to public affairs related to the constructs discussed in this chapter. Please refer to Figure 17.1.

Using the Ethical Consideration Triangle offered in Figure 17.1, many varied publics and stakeholders can be considered, as well as each of the other groups inside the triangle as compared with each point of the triangle. In beginning to use the Ethical Consideration Triangle, a few screening questions are offered as general consideration to help the public affairs officer maintain the rational moral autonomy (independence or lack of bias) required by a deontological analysis. This tool can be employed by groups of decision-makers and used as a discussion springboard, or it can be used by an individual decision-maker.

Each point of the Ethical Consideration Triangle corresponds to one form of Kant's categorical imperative, discussed in more detail earlier in this chapter. Fleshing out the many publics and stakeholder groups related to an issue and then considering each according to the moral principle offered in each of the three points of the triangle allows for a rigorous analysis. In deontology, all three points of the Ethical Consideration Triangle

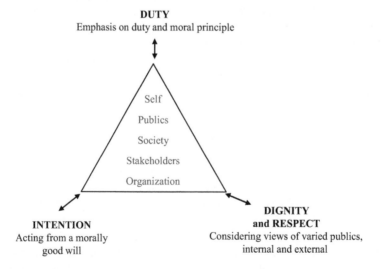

Figure 17.1   Ethical Consideration Triangle

must be cleared affirmatively in order for the decision to be ethical.

The experienced issues manager will pose such questions as: What decision alternative maintains rational duty to moral principle? Am I analyzing the situation autonomously, that is, independently, and without bias? Which option creates a morally principled decision? Am I maintaining dignity and respect for the differing and divergent views of all of the publics and stakeholders on this issue? Are there integrative options that incorporate the interests of other stakeholders and publics as well as that of the organization? Is this decision option really made from good intention alone or is there some type of bias involved? Which option holds good intention when resolving the issue?

Although a deontological analysis is a formidable undertaking, it provides a defensible solution and contested territory, especially for issues of high potential media interest or conflict. Although various stakeholders and publics may not agree with the organization's solution, when it is explained in the rational terms of deontology, they can understand the decision. Such decisions also offer explanatory power for media relations. Although the solutions offered may not be perfect, they should be more long lasting and less objectionable than less rigorously analyzed choices.

Issues managers, along with public relations professionals and frequently lobbyists, enact the strategy that was chosen to resolve the issue, often called an issue action plan or issue action strategy. Various modes of communication may be undertaken to inform, persuade, or change public opinion. Evaluation research will then be conducted to determine how much change related to the public policy issue has been effected and whether or not the campaign needs to continue. Organizations normally manage multiple issues at any given time, and reassign changing issue priorities. The perpetual cycle of issues management allows public affairs officers to identify, analyze and ethically consider the conflicting values involving an issue before it reaches a more difficult level of problem resolution or crisis management. However, some problems cannot be averted.

THE PROBLEM OF CORRUPTION

Corruption in government, lobbying, public affairs, and business, appears to be at an epidemic level. Every person who works in public affairs must confront corruption at some point. According to the Edelman (2014) *Trust Barometer*, public trust in government is even lower than trust in business, though both are at record lows. Public demands for accountability have increased in recent years, meaning that government, business, and NGOs cannot exist as amoral organizations. Without an ethical value system and the professionalism to guide moral behavior, government, business, and NGOs often end up in scandal, crisis, the subject of new government regulations and/or fines, and with decreasing support from former supporters. Despite these obvious negative outcomes, many people in positions of power use their influence for personal benefit, engaging in corrupt practices such as selling votes for campaign donations. Kant (1785/1993) argued that selfishness is the very core of corrupt human behavior and must be guarded against rigorously and analytically at every turn. Even when it is unintentional, selfishness can taint communication and corruption can creep in on the unaware. Lovari (2015) found that politicians using social media often did so with 'a dark side ... in a self-interested way' (p. 17).

There are a few points to understand about corruption that can help to identify and confront it. As Kant (1785/1993, 1930/1963) pointed out, corruption is often based on prudential self-interest, and the actions that would further one's self-interest, not only for financial gain but for many other desirable outcomes. Further, it is often based on power and authority, because it implies the ability to enact initiatives and also the authority to silence subordinates or those who may question the decision. Corruption often assumes a norm of reciprocity which allows a quid pro quo agreement to be enacted, granting a favor for a later benefit. If that norm of reciprocity is broken, the corrupt often become vengeful, retributive, or even criminal, feeling entitled to do so because of the level of personal risk they have undertaken. Finally, corruption generally requires secrecy in order to operate. Secrecy is generally a warning that a potential ethical violation is afoot because honesty does not require whispers, couched nods, and quiet handshakes.

These hallmarks of corruption can help the public affairs manager avoid the potential ethical traps involved when dealing with the corrupt. If a potentially corrupt situation, person, office, or organization is encountered, returning to the Ethical Consideration Triangle can help to distance oneself from the situation and analyze it rationally. Some difficult choices lie ahead if corruption is encountered. The first response in the face of corruption should be one of honesty. Honesty is a general protection because it is always assumed and it has moral value in and of itself. Trying to correct the situation with honesty may be enough to end the corrupt behavior. For example, 'No, we are not offering a campaign donation, we want to win your vote on the merit of our issue' may end donation-seeking in return for favorable voting. It may also alienate the legislator, but it does maintain ethical rectitude, protection, and credibility for the lobbyist in this example.

Professional standards are a good start (Grunig, 2000) but often more is required in terms of moral analyses in the face of a complex dilemma. Going further in the face of corruption may require more morally courageous behavior. Moral courage means acting upon ethical principle and conviction alone or in the face of disapproval, retribution, or even threat. If manipulation is occurring in a situation, for example, the public affairs manager may have to confront executives in order

to argue for a more direct interpretation. In that case he or she may need to prepare to leave the position, be dismissed, or seek other employment.

Whistleblowing, or making a hidden corruption public to media or regulatory agencies, is often the last resort when facing entrenched corruption. The communication manager may have to blow the whistle or go public with an issue when his or her ethical analysis reveals a greater moral duty to the principle of honesty than a duty to the corrupt organization. Those who blow the whistle on corruption must be sure of their analysis, and use judgment that is not clouded by a personal connection to the situation. Kant calls upon the public administrator to distance him or herself from a situation, making the decision as a pure observer rather than immersed participant in order to heighten impartiality (Zingale, 2013). If that analysis reveals corruption that cannot be corrected, changed or reversed, the person's greater moral duty is to honesty as a universal principle that underlies both communication and society.

Whistleblowing requires moral courage in that immediate reactions can be harsh (DeGeorge, 2010). Some whistleblowers use the utilitarian standard of acting in the public interest as their ethical *raison d'être*, while others report duty to act according to their moral values. Going public with corruption is a difficult choice but often whistleblowers become cultural heroes due to their moral courage and selfless behavior.

WHY BE ETHICAL?

In public affairs, reputation and ethical behavior are inextricably and forever linked because the public policy arena is just that, public. Competing values, differing definitions of importance, cultural norms, beliefs, and ideologies will always come into conflict when dealing with divergent publics and stakeholders. Ethics can help resolve these complex dilemmas and do so while further-ing organizational relationships. Sometimes, organizations need to be reminded of how important ethical considerations are to their credibility and long-term reputation, and that job will fall to the public affairs manager. Ethics may fall by the wayside in the rush to conduct business or legislation expediently. However, not considering ethics in public affairs is a shortsighted mistake. Additionally, incorporating ethical theories into the opera-tions of the field serves to heighten its profes-sionalism and social responsibility (Grunig, 2014).

Ethically responsible issues management can help an organization build long-term, trusting relationships with publics and stake-holders, creating an enhanced reputation and the credibility that comes with ethical aware-ness. Often issues management can deal with problems internally, responding and changing organizational actions and policy in a manner that averts crises and conflict. Using the Ethical Consideration Triangle for managing issues should offer public affairs professionals the opportunity to foster more ethical accountability and responsiveness in their organizations and build a better reputa-tion in the public affairs arena.

REFERENCES

Baker, S. and Martinson, D. L. (2002). Out of the red-light district: Five principles for ethi-cally provocative public relations. *Public Rela-tions Quarterly*, 47(3), 15–19.

Baron, M. W. (1995). *Kantian ethics almost without apology.* Ithaca, NY: Cornell Univer-sity Press.

Berger, B. K. and Reber, B. H. (2006). *Gaining influence in public relations: The role of resistance in practice.* Mahwah, NJ: Law-rence Erlbaum.

Botan, C. (1997). Ethics in strategic communi-cation campaigns: The case for a new approach to public relations. *Journal of Busi-ness Communication*, 34(2), 188–202.

Bowen, S. A. (2002). Elite executives in issues management: The role of ethical paradigms in decision making. *Journal of Public Affairs*, 2(4), 270–283.

Bowen, S. A. (2004a). Organizational factors encouraging ethical decision making: An exploration into the case of an exemplar. *Journal of Business Ethics*, 52(4), 311–324.

Bowen, S. A. (2004b). Expansion of ethics as the tenth generic principle of public relations excellence: A Kantian theory and model for managing ethical issues. *Journal of Public Relations Research*, 16(1), 65–92.

Bowen, S. A. (2005). A practical model for ethi-cal decision making in issues management and public relations. *Journal of Public Rela-tions Research*, 17(3), 191–216.

Bowen, S. A. (2006). Autonomy in communica-tion: Inclusion in strategic management and ethical decision-making, a comparative case analysis. *Journal of Communication Man-agement*, 10(4), 330–352.

Bowen, S. A. (2008a). Foundations in moral philosophy for public relations ethics. In T. Hansen-Horn and B. D. Neff, *Public relations: From theory to practice* (pp. 160–180). Boston: Pearson Allyn & Bacon.

Bowen, S. A. (2008b). A state of neglect: Public relations as corporate conscience or ethics counsel. *Journal of Public Relations Research*, 20(3), 271–296.

Bowen, S. A. (2009). What communication professionals tell us regarding dominant coa-lition access and gaining membership. *Jour-nal of Applied Communication Research*, 37(4), 427–452.

Bowen, S. A. (2010). The nature of good in public relations: What should be its norma-tive ethic? In R. L. Heath (Ed.), *Handbook of public relations* (pp. 569–583). Thousand Oaks, CA: Sage.

Bowen, S. A. (2011). Ethics in government public relations. In K. Stewart, M. Lee, and G. Neeley (Eds.), *The practice of government public relations* (pp. 155–177). London: Taylor & Francis.

Bowen, S. A. (2015). Exploring the role of the dominant coalition in creating an ethical culture for internal stakeholders. *Public Rela-tions Journal*, 9, 1–23. Available: http://www.prsa.org/Intelligence/PRJournal#.VYxDil7bLIU (accessed 5/4/2016).

Bowen, S. A., Heath, R. L., Lee, J., Painter, G., Agraz, F. J., McKie, D., and Toledano, M. (2006). *The business of truth: A guide to ethical communication*. San Francisco, CA: International Association of Business Communicators.

Bowen, S. A. and Erzikova, E. V. (2013). The international divide in public relations ethics education: Advocacy versus autonomy. *Public Relations Journal*, 7(1), np. http://www.prsa.org/Intelligence/PRJournal/Documents/2013BowenErzikova.pdf. Accessed 5/14/2016.

Bowen, S. A. and Gallicano, T. D. (2013). A philosophy of reflective ethical symmetry: Comprehensive historical and future moral approaches in the excellence theory. In K. Sriramesh, A. Zerfass, and J. N. Kim (Eds.), *Public relations and communication management* (pp. 193–209). London: Taylor & Francis.

Bowen, S. A. and Hung-Baesecke, C. J. (2013, May). *Is ethics a precursor to authentic organization-public relationships?* Paper presented at the 11th Annual International Conference on Communication and Mass Media (Atiner), Athens, Greece.

Buchholz, R. A., Evans, W. D., and Wagley, R. A. (1994). *Management responses to public issues: Concepts and cases in strategy formulation (3rd ed.)*. Upper Saddle River, NJ: Prentice Hall.

DeGeorge, R. T. (2010). *Business ethics* (7th ed.). Boston, MA: Pearson.

Edelman (2014). *Edelman trust barometer*. New York, NY: Edelman.

Elliott, D. (2007). Getting Mill right. *Journal of Mass Media Ethics*, 22(2, 3), 100–112.

Fawkes, J. (2012). Saints and sinners: competing identities in public relations ethics. *Public Relations Review*, 38(5), 865–872.

Goodpaster, K. E. (2007). *Conscience and corporate culture*. Hoboken, NJ: Blackwell.

Gini, A. (2004). *Case studies in business ethics* (5th ed.). Upper Saddle River, NJ: Prentice Hall.

Grunig, J. E. (Ed.). (1992). *Excellence in public relations and communication management*. Hillsdale, NJ: Lawrence Erlbaum Associates.

Grunig, J. E. (2000). Collectivism, collaboration, and societal corporatism as core professional values in public relations. *Journal of Public Relations Research*, 12(1), 23–48.

Grunig, J. E. (2014). Introduction: Ethics problems and theories in public relations. *Revue Internationale Communication sociale et publique*, 11, 15–28.

Heath, R. L. (1997). *Strategic issues management: Organizations and public policy challenges*. Thousand Oaks, CA: Sage.

Heath, R. L. and Palenchar, M. J. (2009). *Strategic issues management: Organizations and public policy challenges*. Thousand Oaks, CA: Sage.

Jiang, H. and Bowen, S. A. (2011). Ethical decision making in issues management within activist groups. *Public Relations Journal*, 5(1), np. http://www.prsa.org/SearchResults/download/6D-050101/0/Ethical_Decision_Making_in_Issues_Management_in_Ac. Accessed 5/4/2016.

Judd, E. (2015). *A shared vision for corporate good: How smart companies are creating value through CSR and public affairs*. Washington, DC: Foundation for Public Affairs. Available: http://pac.org/files/csr_report.pdf. Accessed 5/16/2016.

Kant, I. (1785/1993). Metaphysical foundations of morals. In C. J. Friedrich (Ed.), *The philosophy of Kant: Immanuel Kant's moral and political writings* (pp. 154–229). New York: The Modern Library.

Kant, I. (1793/1974). *On the old saw: That may be right in theory but it won't work in practice*. Translated by E. B. Ashton. Philadelphia: University of Pennsylvania Press.

Kant, I. (1930/1963). *Lectures on ethics* (L. Infield, Trans.). Indianapolis, IN: Hackett Publishing.

L'Etang, J. (2003). The myth of the 'ethical guardian': An examination of its origins, potency, and illusions. *Journal of Communication Management*, 8(1), 53–67.

Lerbinger, O. (2006). *Corporate public affairs: Interacting with interest groups, media, and government*. Mahwah, NJ: Lawrence Erlbaum Associates.

Lewicki, R. J., Litterer, J. A., Saunders, D. M., and Minton, J. W. (1993). *Negotiation: Readings, exercises, and cases* (2nd ed.). Boston, MA: Irwin.

Lovari, A. (2015, May). *Investigating the role of social media managers in the public sector, between new competencies and dark sides: An empirical Italian study*. Paper presented at the annual conference of the International Communication Association, San Juan, Puerto Rico.

MacIntyre, A. (1966). *A Short History of Ethics*. New York: MacMillan.

Men, L. R. (2015). The role of ethical leadership in internal communication: Influences on communication symmetry, leader credibility, and employee engagement. *Public Relations Journal*, 9, 1–22. Available: http://www.prsa. org/Intelligence/PRJournal#.VYxDil7bLIU (accessed 17 May, 2016).

Mill, J. S. (1861/1957). *Utilitarianism*. New York: The Liberal Arts Press.

Paton, H. J. (1967). *The categorical imperative: A study in Kant's moral philosophy*. New York: Harper & Row.

Pratt, C. B., Im, S. H., and Montague, S. N. (1994). Investigating the application of deontology among US public relations practitioners. *Journal of Public Relations Research*, 6(4), 241–266.

Rawlins, B. (2007). Trust and PR practice [Electronic Version]. *Institute for Public Relations*. Retrieved from http://www.instituteforpr. org/wp-content/uploads/Rawlins-Trust-formatted-for-IPR-12-10.pdf (accessed 22 August, 2016).

Rawlins, B. (2009). Give the emperor a mirror: toward developing a stakeholder measurement of organizational transparency. *Journal of Public Relations Research*, 21(1), 71–99.

Rieke, R. D. and Sillars, M. O. (1993). *Argumentation: Critical decision making* (3rd ed.) New York: Harper Collins.

Rokeach, M. (1973). *The nature of human values*. New York: The Free Press.

Scruton, R. (1982). *Kant*. Oxford: Oxford University Press.

Seeger, M. W. (1997). *Ethics and organizational communication*. Cresskill, NJ: Hampton.

Sims, R. R. (1994). *Ethics and organizational decision making: A call for renewal*. Westport, CT: Quorum.

Sims, R. R. and Brinkman, J. (2003). Enron ethics (or, culture matters more than codes). *Journal of Business Ethics*, 45(3), 243–256.

Smircich, L. and Calas, M. B. (1987). Organizational culture: A critical assessment. In F. M. Jablin, L. L. Putnam, K. H. Roberts, and L. W. Porter (Eds.), *Handbook of organizational communication: An interdisciplinary perspective* (pp. 228–263). Newbury Park, CA: Sage.

Sriramesh, K. (2009). The relationship between culture and public relations. In K. Sriramesh and D. Verčič (Eds.), *The global public relations handbook: Revised and expanded edition, theory research and practice* (pp. 47–61). New York: Routledge.

Stoker, K. and Rawlins, B. (2010). Taking the BS out of PR: Creating genuine messages by emphasizing character and authenticity. *Ethical Space: The International Journal of Communication Ethics*, 7(2–3), 61–69.

Sullivan, R. J. (1989). *Immanuel Kant's moral theory*. Cambridge: Cambridge University Press.

Sullivan, R. J. (1994). *An introduction to Kant's ethics*. New York: Cambridge University Press.

Taylor, M. (2010). Public relations in the enactment of civil society. In R. L. Heath (Ed.), *The Sage Handbook of Public Relations* (pp. 5–15). Thousand Oaks, CA: Sage.

Tilly, E. (2005). The ethics pyramid: Making ethics unavoidable in the public relations process. *The Journal of Mass Media Ethics*, 24(4), 305–320.

Wright, D. K. (1982). The philosophy of ethical development in public relations. *IPRA Review*, April 22, np.

Wright, D. K. (1985). Can age predict the moral values of public relations practitioners? *Public Relations Review*, 11(1), 51–60.

Van Ruler, B. and Verčič, D. (2005). Reflective communication management, future ways for public relations research. *Communication Yearbook*, 29, 239–273.

Zingale, N. C. (2013). The phenomenology of sharing: Social media networking, sharing, and telling. *Journal of Public Affairs*, 13(3), 288–297.

18

Globalization and Multinational Corporations

Jeffrey A. Hart

INTRODUCTION

The term 'globalization' began to appear frequently in scholarly works on international political economy (IPE) in the 1990s. One way to define globalization is in terms of an increase in international interconnectedness, or interdependence, but its distinctiveness from interdependence derives primarily from the increased role of multinational corporations (MNCs)[1] in the contemporary world economy. Some authors stress the cultural side of globalization, arguing that globalization results in a homogenization of global culture (see, for example, Appadurai, 1996; Hopper, 2007). They observe that all urban centers feature the same boutiques selling products with the same logos, everyone watches the same movies and the same TV programs, and everyone eats at the same restaurants and drinks the same beverages. In this sense, the logos and branding efforts of MNCs are symbols of

globalization. Opponents of this viewpoint stress the continuing cultural differences within and across nations. Some even argue that globalization enhances both convergence and divergence of cultures. Joseph Nye (2004) has highlighted the possibility that cultural globalization, to the extent that it is dominated by US firms, is a form of 'soft power'. But most of the politics of globalization focuses not on culture but on its economic aspects and the role of MNCs in globalization.

A multinational corporation is 'an enterprise that engages in foreign direct investment (FDI) and that owns or controls value-added activities in more than one country' (Dunning, 1992, p. 3). The MNCs of the post-WW2 period are different from those of earlier periods in being more focused on manufacturing and services than on extraction of raw materials and commodities (Dicken, 2015) and more likely to be financed by a combination of foreign direct investment (FDI) and local capital rather than international portfolio investments (Gilpin, 1972). In addition, contemporary MNCs are the predominant owners of proprietary technology. MNCs account for at least 50% of R&D spending worldwide (Keller, 2009; Zeile, 2014). In the United States and elsewhere, most patents are awarded to MNCs (Florida, 2005; OECD, 2008). In the last two decades of the twentieth century, competing MNCs from a growing number of economies have created geographically dispersed 'value chains' to take advantage of lower R&D, production, and distribution costs made possible by lower barriers to trade and investment flows (Borrus and Zysman, 1997; Ernst and Kim, 2002; Gereffi, 1996; Gereffi et al., 2005; Sturgeon, 2002; Sturgeon, 2007; Sturgeon and Gereffi, 2009).

I will concentrate here on research about the relationship between economic globalization and multinational corporations. Economic globalization is the increasing integration of input, factor, and final product markets coupled with the increasing salience of MNCs in the world economy and their creation of cross-national value-chain networks (Hart and Prakash, 1999). MNCs are both beneficiaries and agents of globalization. MNC globalizing strategies would not be possible without a certain amount of globalization; globalization increases as MNCs

exercise their options to pursue these strategies. The process of globalization is not complete and probably never will be, so much of the scholarship on globalization deals with whether there is more or less of it in a given period and what the constraints are on increases in globalization.

THE EXPANSION OF MNC ACTIVITY

In 2014, the global stock of inward and outward FDI was around $26 trillion, up from about $2.2 trillion in 1990. Global flows of inward and outward FDI were around $1.5 trillion in 2014, up from around $400 billion in 1995 (UNCTAD, 2015).[2] There has been substantial fluctuation in flows over the past few decades but the general trend is up. While most outflows originate in the industrialized nations, recently outflows from developing countries have grown more rapidly, especially from China. The United States is still the largest source of outflows and it has the largest stock of both outflows and inflows. Inflows are going increasingly to the developing world: 55% in 2014 (see Figure 18.1 below). A small number of developing countries are responsible for a large proportion of the developing world's inflows and outflows: China is currently the largest recipient of

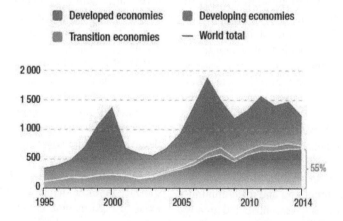

Figure 18.1   FDI inflows, global and by group of economies, 1995–2014 (Billions of dollars)

Source: UNCTAD, FDI/MNE database (www.unctad.org/fdistatistics).

inflows, followed by Hong Kong, Singapore, Brazil, India, Chile, Mexico, and Indonesia (UNCTAD, 2015, p. 5).

UNDERLYING CAUSES OF GLOBALIZATION

As to the underlying causes of globalization, some scholars emphasize the role of international institutions, such as the World Trade Organization or the Organization for Economic Cooperation and Development, in setting the rules for the world economy (Simmons et al., 2008). Others focus on the role of changes in transportation and communications technologies that make it less costly to manage far-flung economic activities (Friedman, 2007; Keohane and Milner, 1996). Still others argue that the preferences of key national actors, particularly the United States, are central to explaining the recent trend toward globalization (Spero and Hart, 2009). It is quite likely that all three of these factors have played a role in recent decades. As the process of globalization continues, however, the growing international presence of MNCs from countries other than the United States means that explanations based solely on the preferences of the US government are becoming less and less useful.

Also, it has been difficult until recently to establish a specific international regime for investment. The international trade regime bears some of the burden of establishing rules for investment and there are a variety of forums for the resolution of disputes over investment. There has been rapid growth in bilateral investment treaties (BITs) (Elkins et al., 2006). Nevertheless, international investment remains more dependent on national legal systems and self-enforcement than on international regimes.

Advances in computing and telecommunications technologies have contributed greatly to the ability of MNCs to manage themselves and to take advantage of having operations in different countries and in different time zones. An example of this is the widespread use of call centers in India by firms based in the rest of the world. Thomas Friedman (2007) provides a number of other examples in his various books on globalization.

GRAVITY MODELS AND CONSTRAINTS ON GLOBALIZATION

The main obstacle to globalization is distance. Generally, the costs of managing far-flung economic activities go up as distance increases. Distance is measured not just in terms of geography, but also in terms of culture (language, ethnicity, religion, etc.). 'Gravity models' are used to measure the impact of these various forms of distance (Feenstra, 2004; Fratianni et al., 2011). They start from the assumption that bilateral trade and investment flows depend primarily on the size of the markets of the two countries involved and the distance between them. Geographic distance is a major factor in those analyses, but so are linguistic and other cultural differences. For example, pairs of countries in which a majority of the population speaks the same language are considerably more likely to engage in trade and foreign direct investment. US firms are more likely to invest in Britain or Ireland than in France or Germany; Chinese firms are more likely to invest in countries with Chinese-speaking populations (Oh et al., 2013; Selmier and Oh, 2013). Shared religion plays an important role in enhancing trade and investment flows among countries (Hergueux, 2011).

Domestic politics constitute another form of constraint. In general, countries with democratic regimes are more likely to trade with and invest in other countries with democratic regimes. This is partly a function of the fact that democracies are more likely to exist in high-income countries than in low-income countries. But it is also a function of a common set of institutions that are shared by democratic systems, such as the rule of law and an independent judiciary (Bénassy-Quéré et al., 2005).

Certain countries seem disinclined to encourage FDI of any sort. The Soviet Union was generally hostile to FDI. Contemporary Japan is often singled out as a country that is hostile toward inward FDI but not outward FDI. After the 1978 reforms and until fairly recently, China was considered to be hostile to outward FDI but relatively accepting of inward FDI. Until recently, India did not encourage inward FDI. Countries with authoritarian regimes tended to trade with and invest in other countries with similar regimes. This was especially true during the Cold War, but that pattern has continued after the breakup of the Soviet Union.

Since the end of the Cold War, a major split has developed between the Islamic countries and the West over a variety of conflicts, which has a major cultural dimension. Orthodox Muslims are particularly concerned about the erosion of morality that accompanies the growing presence of MNCs. They see the culture of the West as represented in MNC merchandising to be contrary to the moral and religious principles that they would like to see preserved in the Muslim world. They also see MNCs as agents of Western imperialism. As a result, they are much more willing than other groups to forego the benefits of FDI inflows (Friedman, 1999).

Economic nationalists within all countries tend to oppose both outflows and inflows of FDI. Public opinion survey research has focused on how attitudes toward trade and investment contrast by variables at the individual or group levels. One of the key determinants is how an individual is connected to the national and global economies: in particular, whether or not the individual depends on goods and services that are traded internationally. Individuals in 'non-traded' goods and services industries tend to be accepting or indifferent to increases in international trade and investment flows. Individuals in traded sectors are accepting only if their

sector is internationally competitive. If they perceive trade or investment to be threatening to domestic employment they will oppose it (Scheve and Slaughter, 1998).

In addition, support for globalization on the part of members of trade unions in the industrialized countries tends to be declining globally because of downward pressure on wages caused by a combination of the introduction of new production technologies and the difficulty of competing with low-wage labor in the developing countries (Pew Research Center, 2014). The managers of MNCs, in contrast, tend to favor further liberalization of world trade and investment flows. Although they have some stake in preserving the advantages that accrue to them from having learned about and adapted to the laws and practices of a wide variety of countries, still they tend to favor liberalization because it makes it easier for them to enter new markets.

These differences in attitudes within countries play an important role in international negotiations over trade and investment regimes. The current debate in the United States over the Trans-Pacific Partnership (TPP) is a good example of this. US trade unions are strongly opposed to the TPP because they see it as a threat to employment. Legislators who represent districts or states where unions are politically powerful tend to oppose the TPP. Senator Harry Reid, for example, is a strong opponent of TPP (O'Keefe, 2015). When President Obama wanted recently to visit a place where support for the TPP was strong, he picked the world headquarters of Nike Corporation in Beaverton, Oregon.

TWO TYPES OF FDI: HORIZONTAL AND VERTICAL

A central puzzle economists pose is why multinational firms choose to establish an overseas presence rather than simply export goods and services. The two main answers are (1) to gain access to potentially large markets that would

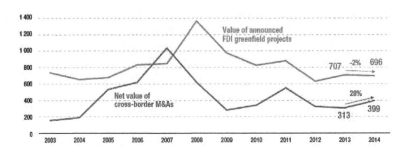

Figure 18.2 Value of cross-border M&As and announced greenfield projects, 2003–2014 (Billions of dollars)

Source: UNCTAD, cross-border M&A database for M&As (www.unctad.org/fdistatistics); Financial Times Ltd, fDi Markets (www.fDimarkets.com) for greenfield projects.

otherwise be closed – called horizontal foreign direct investment (HFDI) – and (2) to gain access to low-cost local inputs as part of a strategy of global competitiveness – called vertical foreign direct investment (VFDI) (see also Cuervo-Cazurra et al., 2015 for other possible motives). In general, HFDI typifies relationships between pairs of developed economies and VFDI typifies relationships between pairs of countries where one is developed and the other is developing (Navaretti and Venables, 2006).

MNCs sometimes set up 'greenfield' operations abroad rather than simply merging with or acquiring a local firm. Mergers and acquisitions used to account for the dominant share of FDI flows, especially to high-income countries. But greenfield investments are growing in importance because of the shift toward investing in developing countries. Most host countries prefer greenfield investments over mergers and acquisitions (see Figure 18.2).

With regard to VFDI, the central question is how a firm will divide its production processes across different locations with different factor prices in the presence of 'trade costs' and 'disintegration costs'. VFDI flows between two countries will not occur unless factor endowments are sufficiently different. However, factor price equalization will occur over time, partly as a result of VFDI flows, and so VFDI may eventually be replaced by HFDI.

Why are the international operations of firms sometimes organized internally, in wholly owned subsidiaries, and sometimes externally, under arms-length contracts with independent local producers? The main reason given for internalization is market failure connected with arms-length contracts. According to Navaretti and Venables (2006), there are three types of market failures: the hold-up problem, the dissipation of intangible assets, and principal-agent relationships between multinationals and local firms. The hold-up problem occurs when a local firm has to make investments that are specific to the contracting relationship. The potential losses caused by an altered relationship result in underinvestment. The dissipation of intangible assets occurs when a foreign firm cannot avoid losing control over valued assets because it has a contractual relationship with a local firm. The principal-agent problem occurs because of hidden actions or hidden information about local market conditions. The local firm may have an interest in concealing local market information from the foreign firm.

The more recent literature on global value chains argues that many MNCs have opted for replacing or supplementing the establishment of overseas subsidiaries with contractual relationships with local or regional firms. These MNCs have adopted modularization strategies as part of a broader global competitiveness effort where components manufacturing and assembly may be done in low-wage or low-cost locations. This necessarily involves a major effort to implement global standards for technology and interfaces. Because of lower coordination and transportation costs, the final products can be marketed anywhere in the world with sufficient guarantees of quality to make them globally competitive (Sturgeon and Gereffi, 2009). So, for example, Korean flat panel display firms contract with Japanese and US glass firms to supply them with specialized glass for displays (Murtha et al., 2001), and Taiwanese assembly firms such as Foxconn help Apple to assemble iPods in Taiwan (Linden et al., 2009) and iPhones in China.

THE OLI MODEL (ALSO CALLED THE ECLECTIC MODEL)

Many scholars employ an eclectic model pioneered by John Dunning and his collaborators to explain the behavior of MNCs: the so-called OLI model. OLI stands for ownership, location, and internalization. According to this model, an MNC must have market power that derives from ownership of some specialized knowledge. It must consider the particular foreign location advantageous for new investments relative to alternative locations including the home market. Finally, it must prefer to operate overseas facilities that it controls rather than simply contracting with local firms. Again the focus is on the importance of market imperfections and transaction costs in creating incentives for overseas activities of MNCs (Dunning, 1992).

The OLI model has its defenders and detractors. A volume edited by Cantwell and Narula, (2004) emphasizes the need to simplify and operationalize key variables.

Globalization vs. Regionalization

Some scholars argue that what we have witnessed so far is not globalization per se, but rather regionalization of the world economy.

Alan Rugman and his collaborators have argued this forcefully in a number of empirical studies (Rugman, 2001a; Rugman, 2001b; Rugman and Girod, 2003; Rugman and Oh, 2008). Rugman believes that the difficulties of coordinating activities across large distances combined with the generally long-term nature of FDI means that fully global strategies are too costly and too risky for most multinational corporations. Most MNCs choose to focus on regional strategies instead.

One of the reasons that the analysis of trade and FDI data seems to bear out Rugman's argument is the efforts of certain regions, most notably the European Union but also North America and Latin America, to integrate their economies through free trade areas and common markets. Inter-regional trade and investment flows are considerably higher as a result than extra-regional trade and investment flows (Akhter and Beno, 2003).

Also, some regions have fewer constraints to integration. There may have been substantial efforts to improve regional transportation and communication infrastructures and to take advantage of regional culture commonalities to encourage trade and investment flows. An additional impetus has been to promote regional integration as a way of lessening dependence on extra-regional economies. In the case of Western Europe, the challenge of competing with the United States played an important role in convincing the citizenry to support regional integration efforts. In Eastern Europe, affiliation with the European Union serves as a signal to foreign investors that FDI is welcome in an affiliated country (Akhter and Beno, 2011; Bevan and Estrin, 2004).

With the recent rise of the Chinese economy and the earlier growth in Japan and Southeast Asia, there have been significant changes in Asia-based regional integration efforts. All the factors that have influenced regionalization in North America, Western Europe, and Latin America are starting to influence regionalization in Asia. Besides the Asian Development Bank (ADB), the Association of South East Asian Nations

(ASEAN), and the somewhat weaker South Asian Association for Regional Cooperation (SAARC), China has recently led the way to forming an Asian Infrastructure Investment Bank (AIIB) (Rimmer, 2014, Chapter 9).

THE CONTINUING ROLE OF THE GOVERNMENTS OF NATION-STATES

Some students of globalization argue that the governments of nation-states have become increasingly irrelevant as globalization proceeds (Strange, 1996). The main decision-making power about the allocation of economic resources, they argue, is increasingly in the hands of MNCs who have many locational options and are not necessarily loyal to any particular country, including the 'home country'. In the absence of credible global intergovernmental governance, MNCs become the main governors of the world economy.

Others argue that the governments of nation-states still ultimately control the direction of globalization: what has been globalized can be reversed in their view, especially during times of conflict (Doremus et al., 1998; Pauly and Reich, 1997). They cite examples of historical periods in which this has occurred, but also more recent examples of reversals of trade and investment flows. The great reduction of investment flows during and after World War I is the main historical example (Wolf, 2004, Chapter 8), while the major shifts in bilateral economic relationships between, for example, the United States and Venezuela or between Russia and the Ukraine are more recent examples. War and other forms of militarized conflict are strongly and negatively related to FDI flows (Bussman, 2010).

Even in the absence of conflict, however, national governments still possess many policy instruments that can affect the level and quality of MNC activity. The most obvious is the power to assess and collect taxes, but there are many other sources of leverage. For example, some countries favor domestic firms by granting them subsidies and other forms of preferential treatment. Some nurture 'national champion' firms in high-technology industries (Hart, 2001). Some countries offer technical and scientific assistance to domestic firms that is not available to foreign firms. Some governments attempt to control MNCs by limiting access to their domestic markets through licensing requirements or other entry barriers. They may require that firms establish joint ventures instead of wholly owned subsidiaries. Still others impose export requirements.

Finally, governments of nation-states continue to play a dominant role in international intergovernmental institutions such as the World Bank, the International Monetary Fund, the Organization of Economic Cooperation and Development, and the international economic summits of the Group of 8 (G8) and the Group of 20 (G20). While MNCs increasingly have a seat at the table in what used to be exclusively intergovernmental forums (see Levy and Prakash, 2003), they still cannot match the capabilities of the governments of large and powerful nation-states in global governance.

THE CONSEQUENCES OF MNC-LED GLOBALIZATION

Who benefits and who loses when globalization increases, especially through the global spread of MNC activities? There are clearly many benefits from globalization (see, for example, Bhagwati, 2007). Consumers have access to many products and services at lower prices than they would otherwise have. Producers and consumers may have better access to capital, technology, marketing experience, and managerial expertise. The managers and employees of internationally competitive MNCs benefit, as do their shareholders and other investors. The dispersion of economic activity globally creates job opportunities for many citizens of those host countries that have received inflows of FDI and are successful in producing products that can be sold globally. Ideally, the presence of MNCs should increase the level of competition in local markets (unless MNCs have used mergers or acquisitions merely to reduce competition).

Critics of MNCs argue that they often engage in anti-competitive practices, that they do not employ or transfer the latest technologies, that they do not adequately train local workers and managers, that they tend to import crucial components instead of sourcing them locally (thus increasing trade deficits), that they fail to recognize the rights of workers and exclude union members from their facilities, that they engage in environmentally unsustainable practices, etc. (see, for example, Rodrik, 2011). The most common criticism of MNCs deals with the loss of control. Even though subsidiaries of MNCs are subject to local laws and regulations, the critics argue that local authorities are unable to counter MNC lobbying for special treatment and that MNCs, unlike local firms, can credibly threaten to move to a new location if they do not get what they want. When MNCs finance their overseas operations entirely on local capital markets and fail to use any FDI funds to invest in a new facility, critics argue that they are not contributing to the overall level of investment but are merely displacing local firms and crowding them out of local capital markets. It is a matter of empirical research as to whether the defenders or the critics of MNCs are right or wrong.

ISSUES ASSOCIATED WITH GLOBALIZATION AND MNCS

Specific policy issues associated with globalization and MNCs include but are not limited to the following categories:

INCENTIVES FOR INWARD FDI

Government officials charged with promoting economic development are interested in attracting new investment flows, both domestic and foreign. Many of the same policies that are attractive to domestic investors are also attractive to MNCs: access to resources and infrastructure, pools of appropriately skilled labor, business-friendly regulations, acceptable tax rates, etc. Occasionally, officials have to go the extra mile to attract foreign firms, especially when the firms have no experience of investing in that particular location. Besides going on trade missions to the home country of the MNC, officials might offer tax holidays and other inducements not available to other firms. Such inducements are not always popular with the locals, however, especially if the cost of inducements is outsized relative to the number of resulting jobs. In addition, the temptation to relax regulations or reduce taxes in one location can produce 'races to the bottom', which end up cancelling any local advantage (Dadush, 2013).

TRANSFER PRICING, TAX HAVENS, AND INVERSION

One of the more controversial aspects of MNC activity is the use of creative accounting to ensure that profits are located in countries with the lowest rates of taxation. One of the ways to do this is with transfer pricing (Rugman and Eden, 1985). A particularly graphic example recently was the very low taxes paid globally by Apple Corporation because of a deal negotiated in 1991 with the government of Ireland. Apple apparently shifted taxable revenue from its global operations to its Irish subsidiary in order to avoid taxes. While the usual corporate tax rate for MNCs in Ireland is around 12.5%, Apple negotiated a tax rate of 2%. Both the US government and the European Union criticized this deal widely, and Ireland was asked to end that particular tax loophole (Duhigg and Kocieniewski, 2012).

The research on transfer prices indicates that MNCs engage in the practice in a limited manner, enough to show that some taxes are shifted to low-tax locations (Grubert and Mutti, 1991; Grubert, 2012). Some firms advise MNCs on how to do this without being too obvious. There have been significant efforts within the OECD to promulgate guidelines on transfer pricing (OECD, 2010).

More recently, public officials have expressed concerns about the attempt of some MNCs to change their headquarters to low-tax locations. This is generally done by merging with a firm in a low-tax location. A recent example is the attempt by the US pharmaceutical firm Pfizer to become a British corporation by merging with AstraZeneca. According to the Department of the Treasury, effective US corporate tax rates declined from 29% in 2000 to 17% in 2013 as a result of inversions and transfer pricing. President Obama called these practices 'unpatriotic' in a speech delivered in July 2014 and Secretary of the Treasury, Jack Lew, issued new regulations meant to reduce the tax savings achieved by inversions.

So far there is no strong international regime regulating transfer pricing, tax havens, and inversions. The OECD has adopted guidelines but they are voluntary. The global evasion of taxes by MNCs is likely to remain an issue for a long time to come (Palan et al., 2009).

TECHNOLOGY TRANSFER

Since MNCs are generally better able to generate new technologies than non-MNCs and to own intellectual property rights associated with those technologies, a key issue is whether or not locals can gain access to MNC technology at a reasonable price. More importantly, locals will want to participate in the creation of new technologies themselves, if possible. These sorts of questions are lumped into a category called 'technology transfer'. Technology transfer does not require that MNCs share intellectual property directly but simply that locals have sufficient access to the underlying technology to develop their own solutions to problems. When this occurs, the positive spinoffs from MNC-related technology transfer can be significant and long lasting.

One of the ways this can occur is if the MNC establishes a local research and development facility. There is a growing body of literature on the factors that influence the decision to do this (Dunning, 1994; Narula, 2014; Teece, 1977). One important factor is strong enforcement of intellectual property laws (Zeile, 2014). Another is investment in the education and training of skilled workers (including scientists and engineers). In some industries, a key factor is investment in physical infrastructures necessary for research and development, such as computer networks and advanced telecommunications facilities (Donaubauer et al., 2014).

MNCS FROM EMERGING ECONOMIES

The dominance of US-based MNCs was greatly reduced from the 1970s onward when first MNCs based in Western Europe and Japan and later MNCs based in Southeast Asia (particularly Korea and Taiwan) began to establish a strong presence outside their regions. The latest set of big players in global FDI flows includes Brazil, Russia, India, and China (the BRICs) and the formerly communist countries of Eastern Europe. That group of countries is often referred to as the 'emerging markets', (see Figure 18.3).

One key question addressed by scholars is whether these new MNCs behave differently from older MNCs and whether a new set of theories is necessary to explain their behavior. Several scholars argue that the answer to these questions is that existing theories are sufficient (Alon et al., 2011; Ernst and Kim, 2002; Narula, 2012).

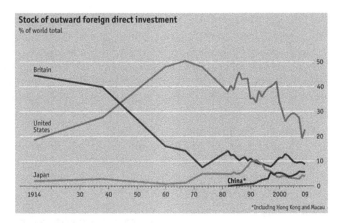

Figure 18.3   Percentage of Global FDI Outflows by Country, 1914–2019

Source: UNCTAD; 'Multinational Enterprises and the Global Economy' by J.H.Dunning

Recently scholars have been paying particular attention to Chinese FDI because of the rapid growth of the Chinese economy and a recent policy shift toward encouraging outward FDI (Shambaugh, 2012). The record of inward FDI in China is also a subject of a number of studies. Most FDI inflow into China is directed toward gaining access to the large and rapidly growing domestic market. Outflow, in contrast, started primarily as a means to improve access to foreign deposits of energy and raw materials. More recently, however, Chinese outflows are directed toward industrialized nations as a means to gain access to advanced technology and markets for high-value-added goods and services. Chinese outward FDI is controlled disproportionately by state enterprises and not by private firms.

depend heavily on patents and licensing fees complain frequently and loudly about the fact that their intellectual property is insufficiently protected in some markets. For example, the US-based film and recording industries want China to clamp down on what they call the 'piracy' of their intellectual property via the illegal copying of CDs and DVDs.

Several efforts have been made to create new international regimes for the protection of intellectual property. Within the WTO, the agreement on Trade Related Intellectual Property (TRIPS) deals with this question, but remains a thorn in the side of the governments of developing nations. A section of the still secret draft of the Trans-Pacific Partnership deals with this issue (for an overview see Flinn et al., 2012).

INTELLECTUAL PROPERTY

Because MNCs create and own intellectual property in a variety of important technologies, the governments of nation-states are often concerned about guaranteeing access to those technologies at reasonable cost. Each country has its own laws governing intellectual property. Some are stricter and more strictly enforced than others. MNCs that

DISPUTE SETTLEMENT

MNCs have a strong incentive to create new institutions for the settlement of investment disputes. Although there are some legal protections available to them to prevent appropriation of their property without adequate compensation, there is still a long way to go. From the MNC perspective, a key issue is how to resolve disputes between themselves and other MNCs and both home and host governments. MNCs rely increasingly on bilateral investment treaties and national courts to handle these disputes, but there are a number of alternative forums that have evolved over time.

In 1995, the OECD began negotiations on new rules for international investment called the Multilateral Agreement on Investment (MAI). In February 1997, a draft of the agreement was leaked to a public advocacy organization in the United States (Public Citizen), provoking a series of anti-globalization rallies and demonstrations that ended with a suspension of the negotiations (Graham, 2000). Since then, there have been a variety of proposals for new investment dispute resolution regimes.

The International Center for the Settlement of Investment Disputes (ICSID) was set up within the World Bank Group in 1966 to provide facilities for conciliation and arbitration of investment disputes. Disputes may be referred to ICSID under the provisions agreed to in BITs and free trade agreements (FTAs) if the parties agree to do so. The figure below (Figure 18.4), shows the growth in the number of cases referred to ICSID between 1972 and 2014. Over a third of the disputes are settled or dismissed before a final ruling is made (ICSID, 2015).

The most recent proposal is for an Investment Framework Agreement (IFA) within the World Trade Organization. According to proponents, the IFA would not replace existing BITs or investment chapters in FTAs and would be open to a much broader set of countries (Hufbauer and Stephenson, 2014). So the effort to create a multilateral agreement continues alongside the bilateral and minilateral efforts.

EXTRATERRITORIALITY

When MNCs operate across national boundaries in ways that national governments consider to be prejudicial to their interests, it becomes tempting to pass legislation or enforce laws that are 'extraterritorial': that is, they apply to the operations of firms outside the territorial jurisdiction of national legal regimes. A good example of this is the anti-bribery laws that have been applied to the foreign behavior of US-based MNCs. Those laws apply not only to activities that occur in foreign countries, but also to the action of foreign firms that have US subsidiaries. The main reason MNCs oppose extraterritoriality

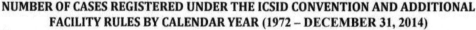
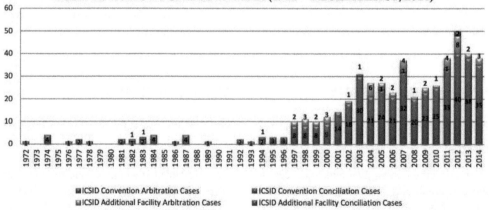

Figure 18.4   Annual number of investment disputes registered by ICSID, 1972–2014

is that it forces them to do what they consider to be impossible: to comply with potentially contradictory laws and regulations in more than one jurisdiction.

Issues of extraterritoriality come up whenever trade or investment sanctions are applied by governments seeking to change the behavior of others. In 1997, the Canadian subsidiary of Wal-Mart was required to comply with US laws regarding the trade embargo with Cuba (Clark, 2004). In 2012, the US government imposed restrictions on the activities of US subsidiaries of foreign MNCs as part of the larger effort to get Iran to stop developing nuclear weapons. Two foreign banks were prohibited from having access to US banks while they were doing business with Iranian firms. Organizations such as the International Chamber of Commerce are opposed to the application of extraterritorial laws because, in their view, the result is unnecessary barriers to trade and investment flows. Also opposed, for obvious reasons, are the governments of countries negatively affected by such laws.

CORPORATE SOCIAL RESPONSIBILITY

Because of the great variety of public image problems that have been generated by MNC activities, many firms have adopted strategies for highlighting their potentially positive contributions by advertising widely their goals for 'corporate social responsibility' (CSR). CSR is 'a self-regulatory mechanism whereby a business monitors and ensures its active compliance with the spirit of the law, ethical standards, and international norms' (McWilliams and Siegel, 2001).

Almost every major MNC has a website in which a number of pages are devoted to enumeration and illustration of its CSR activities. These pages usually include information about what the firm is doing to preserve the environment, to collect and distribute charitable contributions from its employees, to

encourage its employees to engage in public service of various kinds, and to conduct business in an ethical manner. Skeptics claim that such activities are 'window dressing' and not terribly meaningful, but others argue that CSR can lead to a shift in corporate behavior toward good global citizenship, particularly in the area of supporting human rights (Ruggie, 2013).

CONCLUSION

Existing research on MNCs and globalization indicates a variety of potential directions for future research and for tasks to be undertaken by public affairs managers of both governments and MNCs interested in changing (for the better, hopefully) the rather poor image that MNC-led globalization has among the general population worldwide. Ironically, it is likely that these efforts are more necessary in the industrialized world than in the developing regions because, so far at least, globalization has a good reputation for reducing global inequality (especially in big countries such as China and India) in the developing world but not in developed regions (Pew Research Center, 2014). In the industrialized world, MNCs and MNC-led globalization are blamed for environmental degradation, exploitation of Third World workers, undermining democracy, tax evasion, and the hollowing out of the middle classes. In the developing world, the problem is usually one of a lack of transparency and accountability (Stiglitz, 2008). Not all of these negative images are justified, of course, but they are increasingly common and deeply held. In short, MNC-led globalization has a legitimation problem.

It is not clear what efforts on the part of MNCs themselves can reduce this negativity. It is more likely that strengthened international economic governance institutions with direct representation not just of governments and MNCs but also of other stakeholders are

needed in a broader effort to legitimize globalization (de Burca et al., 2014; Higgott et
al., 2000; Levy and Prakash, 2003; Scherer
et al., 2006).

Notes

1 Multinational corporations are also referred to as
   multinational enterprises (MNEs), transnational
   corporations (TNCs), and transnational enterprises (TNEs).
2 Stocks are a measure of cumulative flows over
   time. They represent the value of the MNCs'
   share of fixed investment. Whereas flows can
   fluctuate dramatically, stocks are somewhat more
   stable because they reflect the underlying value
   of accumulated investments.

REFERENCES

Akhter, Syed and Colleen Beno (2011) 'An
   Empirical Note on Regionalization and Globalization', *Multinational Business Review*,
   19(1): 26–35.
Alon, Ilan, John Child, Shaomin Li, and John R.
   McIntyre (2011) 'Globalization of Chinese
   Firms: Theoretical Universalism or Particular-
   ism', *Management and Organization Review*,
   7(2): 191–200.
Andreas Georg Scherer, Guido Palazzo, and
   Dorothèe Baumann, (2006) 'Global Rules
   and Private Actors – Towards a New Role of
   the Transnational Corporation in Global
   Governance', *Business Ethics Quarterly*, 16:
   505–532.
Appadurai, Arjun (1996) *Modernity at Large:
   Cultural Dimensions of Globalization.*
   Minneapolis: University of Minnesota
   Press.
Bénassy-Quéré, Agnès, Maylis Coupet, and
   Thierry Mayer, (2005) 'Institutional Determi-
   nants of Foreign Direct Investment', Centre
   d'Etudes Prospectives et d'Informations
   Internationales, CEPII Working Paper No.
   2005–05.
Bevan, Alan A. and Sol Estrin (2004) 'The
   Determinants of Foreign Investment into
   European Transition Economies', *Journal of
   Comparative Economics*, 32: 775–787.

Bhagwati, Jagdish (2007) *In Defense of Globalization.* New York: Oxford University Press.
Borrus, Michael and John Zysman (1997) 'Globalization with Borders: The Rise of Win-
   telism as the Future of Global Competition',
   Industry and Innovation, 42(2): 141–166.
Bussman, Margit (2010) 'Foreign Direct Investment and Militarized International Conflict',
   Journal of Peace Research, 47(2): 143–153.
Cantwell, John and Rajneesh Narula, eds.
   (2004) *International Business and the Eclectic Paradigm: Developing the OLI Framework.* New York: Routledge.
Clark, Harry L. (2004) 'Dealing with US Extraterritorial Sanctions and Foreign Counter-
   measures', *Journal of International Law*,
   25(1): 455–489.
Cuervo-Cazurra, Alvaro, Rajneesh Narula, and
   C. Annique Un (2015) 'Internationalization
   Motives: Sell More, Buy Better, Upgrade, and
   Escape', *The Multinational Business Review*,
   23(1): 25–35.
Dadush, Uri (2013) 'Incentives to Attract FDI',
   in Global Agenda Council on Global Trade
   and FDI, *Foreign Direct Investment as a Key
   Driver for Trade, Growth, and Prosperity: The
   Case for a Multilateral Agreement on Invest-
   ment.* Geneva: World Economic Forum.
De Burca, Grainne, Robert O. Keohane, and
   Charles Sabel (2014) 'Global Experimentalist
   Governance', *British Journal of Political Sci-
   ence*, 44(3): 477–486.
Dicken, Peter (2015) *Global Shift: Mapping the
   Changing Contours of the World Economy,
   7th edition.* New York: The Guildford Press.
Donaubauer, Julian, Birgit Meyer, and Peter
   Nunnenkamp (2014) 'The Crucial Role of
   Infrastructure in Attracting FDI', *Columbia
   FDI Perspectives*, 133.
Doremus, Paul M., William W. Keller, Louis W.
   Pauly, and Simon Reich (1998) *The Myth of
   the Global Corporation.* Princeton, NJ:
   Princeton University Press.
Duhigg, Charles and David Kocieniewski (2012)
   'How Apple Sidesteps Billions in Taxes', New
   York Times, April 28, retrieved from http://
   www.nytimes.com/2012/04/29/business/
   apples-tax-strategy-aims-at-low-tax-states-and-
   nations.html?_r=0 (accessed 20 August, 2016).
Dunning, John H. (1992) *Multinational Enter-
   prises and the Global Economy.* Reading,
   Mass.: Addison-Wesley.

Dunning, John (1994) 'Multinational Enterprises and the Globalization of Innovatory Capacity', *Research Policy*, 23(1): 67–88.

Elkins, Zachary, Andrew T. Guzman, and Beth A. Simmons (2006) 'Competing for Capital: The Diffusion of Bilateral Investment Treaties', *International Organization*, 60: 811–846.

Ernst, Dieter and L. Kim (2002) 'Global Production Networks, Knowledge Diffusion, and Local Capability Formation', *Research Policy*, 31(8): 1417–1429.

Feenstra, Robert C. (2004) *Advanced International Trade: Theory and Evidence*. Princeton, NJ: Princeton University Press.

Flinn, Sean M., Brook Baker, Margot Kaminski, and Jimmy Koo (2012) 'The US Proposal for an Intellectual Property Chapter in the Trans-Pacific Partnership Agreement', *American University International Law Review*, 28(1): 105–205.

Florida, Richard (2005) 'The World is Spiky', *The Atlantic*, 296(3): 48–51.

Fratianni, Michele, Marchionne, F., and Chang Hoon Oh (2011) 'A Commentary on the Gravity Equation in International Business Research', *Multinational Business Review*, 19(1): 36–46.

Friedman, Thomas L. (1999) *The Lexus and the Olive Tree: Understanding Globalization*. New York: Anchor Books.

Friedman, Thomas L. (2007) *The World is Flat, 3.0*. New York: Picador.

Gereffi, Gary (1996) 'Commodity Chains and Regional Divisions of Labor in East Asia', *Journal of Asian Business*, 12: 75–112.

Gereffi, Gary, J. Humphrey, and Timothy J. Sturgeon (2005) 'The Governance of Global Value Chains', *Review of International Political Economy*, 12(1): 78–104.

Gilpin, Robert (1975) *US Power and the Multinational Corporation: The Political Economy of Foreign Direct Investment*. New York: Basic Books.

Graham, Edward M. (2000) *Fighting the Wrong Enemy: Antiglobal Activists and Multinational Enterprises*. Washington, DC: Institute for International Economics.

Grubert, Harry (2012) 'Foreign Taxes and the Growing Share of US Multinational Income Abroad: Profits, Not Sales, Are Being Globalized', *National Tax Journal*, 65(2): 247–282.

Grubert, Harry and John Mutti (1991) 'Taxes, Tariffs, and Transfer Pricing in Multinational Corporate Decision Making', *The Review of Economics and Statistics*, 73(2): 285–293.

Hart, Jeffrey A. (2001) 'National Champions', in R. J. Barry Jones, ed., *Encyclopedia of International Political Economy*. London: Routledge.

Hart, Jeffrey A. and Aseem Prakash (1999) 'Introduction', in Jeffrey A. Hart and Aseem Prakash, eds. *Globalization and Governance*. London: Routledge.

Hergueux, Jerome (2011) 'How does religion bias the allocation of Foreign Direct Investment? The role of institutions', *International Economics*, 128(4): 53–76.

Higgott, Richard A., Geoffrey R.D. Underhill, and Andreas Bieler, eds. (2000) *Non-State Actors and Authority in the Global System*. London and New York: Routledge.

Hopper, Paul (2007) *Understanding Cultural Globalization*. Boston: Polity.

Hufbauer, Gary and Sherry Stephenson (2014) 'The Case for a Framework Agreement on Investment', *Columbia FDI Perspectives*, 116.

ICSID (2015) Background Information on the International Centre for Settlement of Investment Disputes. Retrieved from https://icsid. worldbank.org/apps/ICSIDWEB/about/ Documents/ICSID%20Fact%20Sheet%20-% 20ENGLISH.pdf (accessed 20August, 2016).

Keller, Wolfgang (2009) 'International Trade, Foreign Direct Investment, and Technology Spillovers', NBER Working Paper 15442, retrieved from http://www.nber.org/papers/ w15442 (accessed 20 August, 2016).

Keohane, Robert O. and Helen V. Milner (1996) *Internationalization and Domestic Politics*. New York: Cambridge University Press.

Levy, David L. and Aseem Prakash (2003) 'Bargains Old and New: Multinational Corporations in Global Governance', *Business and Politics*, 5 (2003): 131–150.

Linden, Greg, Kenneth L. Kraemer, and Jason Diedrick (2009) 'Who Captures Value in a Global Innovation Network? The Case of Apple's iPod', *Communications of the ACM*, 52(3): 140–144.

McWilliams, Abagail and Donald Siegel (2001) 'Corporate Social Responsibility: A Theory of the Firm Perspective', *Academy of Management Review*, 26: 117–127.

Murtha, Thomas P., Stefanie Ann Lenway, and Jeffrey A. Hart (2001) *Managing*

New Industry Creation: Global Knowledge Formation and Entrepreneurship in High Technology. Stanford, Calif.: Stanford University Press.

Narula, Rajneesh (2012) 'Do We Need Different Frameworks to Explain Infant MNEs from Developing Countries?', *Global Strategy Journal*, 2: 188–204.

Narula, Rajneesh (2014) *Globalization and Technology: Interdependence, Innovation Systems, and Industrial Policy*. New York: Wiley.

Navaretti, Giorgio Barba and Anthony J. Venables (2006) *Multinational Firms in the World Economy*. Princeton, NJ: Princeton University Press.

Nye, Joseph (2004) *Soft Power: The Means to Success in World Politics*. New York: Public Affairs.

Oh, Chang Hoon, W. Travis Selmier, and D. Lien (2013) 'International Trade, Foreign Direct Investment, and Transaction Costs of Languages', *Journal of Socio-Economics*, 40: 732–735.

O'Keefe, Ed (2015) 'The Trans Pacific Partnership Is in Trouble on Capitol Hill. Here's Why'. *Washington Post*, February 9, Retrieved from http://www.washingtonpost.com/blogs/the-fix/wp/2014/02/19/why-the-trans-pacific-partnership-is-in-trouble-on-capitol-hill/ (accessed 20 August, 2016).

OECD (2008) *Compendium of Patent Statistics*. Paris: Organization for Economic Cooperation and Development.

OECD (2010) *Transfer Pricing Guidelines for Multinational Enterprises and Tax Administrations*. Paris: Organization for Economic Cooperation and Development.

Palan, Ronen, Richard Murphy, and Christian Chavagneux (2009) *Tax Havens: How Globalization Really Works*. Ithaca, NY: Cornell University Press.

Pauly, Louis W. and Simon Reich (1997) 'National Structures and Multinational Corporate Behavior: Enduring Differences in the Age of Globalization', *International Organization*, 51(1): 1–30.

Pew Research Center (2014) *Faith and Skepticism about Trade, Foreign Investment*. Washington, DC: Pew Research Center.

Rimmer, Peter J. (2014) *Asia-Pacific Rim Logistics: Global Context and Local Politics*. Cheltenham, England: Edward Elgar.

Rodrik, Dani (2011) *The Globalization Paradox: Democracy and the Future of the World Economy*. New York: Norton.

Ruggie, John G. (2013) *Just Business: Multinational Corporations and Human Rights*. New York: Norton.

Rugman, Alan M. (2001a) *The End of Globalization: What it Means for Business*. New York: Random House Business Books.

Rugman, Alan M. (2001b) 'The Myth of Global Strategy', *International Marketing Review*, 18(6): 583–58.

Rugman, Alan M. and Lorraine Eden, eds. (1985) *Multinationals and Transfer Pricing*. New York: St. Martin's Press.

Rugman, Alan M. and Stephane Girod (2003) 'Retail Multinationals and Globalization: The Evidence is Regional', *European Management Journal*, 21(1): 24–37.

Rugman, Alan M. and C. H. Oh (2008) 'Friedman's Follies: Insights on the Globalization/Regionalization Debate', *Business and Politics*, 10(2): 1–14.

Scheve, Kenneth and Matthew Slaughter (1998) 'What Determines Individual Trade Policy Preferences?', *NBER Working Paper Series*, 6531.

Selmier, W. Travis and Chang Hoon Oh (2013) 'The Power of Major Trade Languages in Trade and Foreign Direct Investment', *Review of International Political Economy*, 20(3): 386–514.

Shambaugh, David (2012) 'Are China's Multinational Corporations Really Multinational?', *East Asia Quarterly*, 4(2), retrieved from http://www.eastasiaforum.org/2012/06/21/are-chinas-multinational-corporations-really-multinational/ (accessed 20 August, 2016).

Simmons, Beth A., Frank Dobbin, and Geoffrey Garrett (2008) 'Introduction: The Diffusion of Liberalization', in Beth A. Simmons, Frank Dobbin, and Geoffrey Garrett, eds., *The Global Diffusion of Markets and Democracy*. New York: Cambridge University Press.

Spero, Joan Edelman and Jeffrey A. Hart (2009) *The Politics of International Economic Relations, 7th edition*. Boston: Cengage.

Stiglitz, Joseph E. (2008) 'Regulating Multinational Corporations: Toward Principles of Cross-Border Legal Frameworks in a Globalizing World Balancing Rights with Responsibilities', *American University International Law Review*, 23(3): 451–558.

Strange, Susan (1996) *The Retreat of the State: The Diffusion of Power in the World Economy*. New York: Cambridge University Press.

Sturgeon, Timothy J. (2002) 'Modular Production Networks: A New American Model of Industrial Organization', *Industrial and Corporate Change*, 11(3): 451–496.

Sturgeon, Timothy J. (2007) 'How Globalization Drives Institutional Diversity: The Japanese Electronics Industry's Response to Value Chain Modularity', *Journal of East Asian Studies*, 7(1): 1–34.

Sturgeon, Timothy J. and Gary Gereffi (2009) 'Measuring Success in the Global Economy: International Trade, Industrial Upgrading, and Business Function Outsourcing in Global Value Chains', *Transnational Corporations*, 18(2): 1–35.

Teece, David (1977) 'Technology Transfer by Multinational Firms: The Resource Cost of Transferring Technological Know-How', *The Economic Journal*, 87: 241–262.

UNCTAD – United Nations Conference on Trade and Development (2015) *World Investment Report*. New York and Geneva: United Nations.

Wolf, Martin (2004) *Why Globalization Works*. New Haven, Conn.: Yale University Press.

Zeile, William J. (2014) 'Research Spotlight: Multinational Enterprises and International Technology Transfer', *Survey of Current Business*, 94(9): 1–9.

PART IV

Regional Development and Localised Approaches to Public Affairs

Carla Millar

This section presents general patterns, specificities and idiosyncrasies of public affairs (PA) from a regional perspective, covering six continents, plus a special chapter on the 'Brussels Bubble' – public affairs in the EU context with its focus on institutions such as the European Commission and the European Parliament.

The diversity of the situations described is striking. It calls into question whether there is a single 'correct' approach – represented by 'advanced' practice – or whether, as I believe:

1 There is no one leading public affairs model that works best globally and is aimed for and converged towards in all countries and environments.
2 Public affairs is culture bound, anchored in history, institutions and the prevailing business system.

This leads me to identify and find evidence in the contributions for a number of key factors

which could help bring public affairs on to a higher plane worldwide:

(a) Understanding culture and institutions
(b) Professionalisation and understanding of best practice on a regional, and sometimes national, basis
(c) Integrity and, to a certain extent, transparency.

TOWARDS ONE IDEAL PUBLIC AFFAIRS MODEL?

One of the questions that can be raised concerns to what extent public affairs can have one academic subject matter, or one ideal model or code of practice, and to what extent there is a trend towards convergence, a hierarchy amongst countries, a route towards such an ideal public affairs model. For this to be true one would expect to be able to track levels of development and match them to the development stages of countries and their economic/institutional structures.

The World Bank classifies countries and changes classifications when necessary. Then there are definitions of groups of emerging markets, such as BRIC, Next 11, etc. (see Table P IV.1). None of these classifications seems to provide the type of hierarchy and route towards a particular ideal model or standard for public affairs and research has not yet produced any evidence for other variables that might correlate with a putative development track for public affairs.

Possibly an analogy exists with corporate governance, where similar questions have been raised about convergence towards one model (Millar, 2014). Here there were major differences, despite superficial steps to modify governance regimes to accommodate globalising companies. Some patterns did, however, emerge when considering the complex or 'bundle' of formal and informal governance arrangements. Millar et al. (2005) found that these roughly matched differences amongst three types of business system ('the way we do business here') corresponding to differences in how people approached questions of business interaction, especially exchange.

Next to the 'market-driven', 'capitalist', 'Anglo-American' business system, there exists a 'communitarian', 'community-driven', 'continental European' business system, and emerging markets operate according to yet another type of business system, often emphasising societal and trust-building priorities.

Corporate governance includes a formal component – governance rules and regulations with legal or quasi-legal force – and because of this can easily be viewed in terms of nations setting those rules. The practical effects, however, depend also on informal institutions, particularly the prevailing commercial practice and attitude to exchange, which may lead to different outcomes, and may motivate companies (or even the authorities) to diverge from the idealised model. And within countries there are likely to be different groups which diverge from the assumed 'standard' behaviour and even the most carefully crafted sets of regulations may impact organisations from such groups in unintended ways.

PUBLIC AFFAIRS IS CULTURE BOUND

A recent special issue of the *Journal of Public Affairs* on 'The State of Public Affairs in Central and Eastern Europe', which I co-guest edited, argues that 'Public affairs is embedded in the democratic and political landscape, linked to the institutions, values and way of life in a particular country. This landscape is influenced by history, wars and political regimes, from centuries back to the more recent history' (Millar and Köppl, 2014: 4); similarly, Chapter 21 in this volume on North America states: 'The roots of public affairs are shown to lie in urban and community affairs, corporate philanthropy and public relations.'

Public affairs is an activity that is not only culture bound, but history, environment and business-systems bound. Thus research in

Table P IV.1   The World Bank classifies countries

By Region	By Income	By Lending
• East Asia and Pacific	• Low-income economies	• IDA
• Europe and Central Asia	• Lower-middle-income economies	• Blend
• Latin America & the Caribbean	• Upper-middle-income economies	• IBRD
• Middle East and North Africa	• High-income economies	
• South Asia	• High-income OECD members	
• Sub-Saharan Africa		

public affairs has to be contextualised and linked to formal and informal institutions. In such international research an institution-based view of strategy and organisation theory may be developed (Kostova and Hult, 2016).

Looking at public affairs as the bridge in communication and influencing between business, government/public administration and society, it can be observed that throughout the world government institutions seem paralysed by the lack of long-term political vision. As a result, government is easily subject to external influences. Public affairs actually is in a very early, embryonic stage of development in terms of long-term vision and interests. The profession of the public affairs consultant will progressively find its natural place, acting as a catalyst for the development of business–government–society linkages.

For public affairs, as for corporate governance, the environment is dominated by the two contrasting major legal systems: that practised in Anglo-Saxon countries such as the United States and United Kingdom, and that practised in continental Europe as well as Asian countries such as Japan, Korea or Taiwan. These lay the foundations for informal and formal aspects of business systems (North, 1990; Choi et al., 1999). The business relationships include such issues as the role of trust and the intangible aspects of exchange transactions.

Co-evolution theory (Flier et al., 2003; Millar et al., 2009) offers one approach to understanding the link between such legal and relationship differences and the institutions and practices that exist within societies, and may provide a framework for charting the public affairs universe as well as for addressing the related ethical questions.

There are two major dimensions which can influence the evolution of a national business system. First is the strength of the ties between organisations and institutions. A system could have very strong linkages between institutions and organisations, as in many collective societies in Asia and in continental Europe (Choi, 1992). The second dimension is the relative proportion, and thus importance, of formal versus informal institutions that determines the performance of legal systems, and the separation between institutions and organisations (Millar et al., 2009).

A visualisation of the comparison of the formal and informal business systems can be found in Figure P IV.1 which shows that in formal systems there is a larger share of the centre circle for formal institutions than for informal institutions, whereas in informal systems the share of informal institutions

Informal business system   **Formal business system**

Figure P IV.1   Informal versus formal business systems

Source: Adapted from North (1990) and Choi, et al. (1999)

versus formal institutions gives the informal institutions a larger position. Here the
strength of ties is shown by the links between
the four forms of organisation being mutual
and direct in the informal system, whereas in
the formal business systems the lines are dot-
ted ones only, depicting very weak links.

The role of informal institutions in underpinning social norms and values is a source of
differences between the systems. In informal
systems, the linkages between the four major
forms of organisation in society – economic,
political, educational and social organisations – are close and intertwined. This is
similar to the close interaction between banking, corporations, government and financial
markets (Whitley, 1994; Choi et al., 1999),
and is prevalent in countries like Germany
and France in continental Europe, and
Japan, Korea, Taiwan and Singapore in Asia.
The legal system in these countries mainly
provides a framework for (ethical) behaviour
and trust; it can be seen as providing basic
prohibitions and parameters beyond which
it is not permissible to go, but enforceable
rights only as a recourse of last resort if other
ties are insufficient. In formal systems, on
the other hand, the linkages between the four
major types of organisation in this model –
economic, political, educational and social –
are, relatively speaking, weaker. This is typical
of common law countries such as the USA
and the UK which countries also tend to rely
much more on formal, legal contracts in economic and business transactions.

One of the distinctive features of informal
systems is the significance of non-anonymous
peer reviews and monitoring based on trust.
Here lies a clear link with norms and values apparent in such society and how and
where communication between organisation
and institution takes place. For public affairs
the lesson may be that considerable sensitivity will be required to find the borderline
between using close ties and links as would
be expected as part of the normal conduct of
business and using them in ways that are prohibited as corrupt.

FACTORS TO BRING PUBLIC AFFAIRS ON TO A HIGHER PLANE

Understanding Culture and Institutions

Differences in the cultural and business environment as discussed above will have their
effects on the institutions and organisations
operating in these business systems, including public affairs, as predicted by co-
evolution theory (Millar et al., 2009). Chapter
20 on Europe congruently argues, 'Studying
and understanding how public affairs vary in
the different corners of Europe can help PA
professionals master this complex and multi-
faceted landscape effectively.'

Professionalisation and Understanding of Best Practice in the Region

There is a great need to counter the risk that
public affairs will be viewed on the basis of
the behaviour of amateur or inexperienced
claimants to the title; while professionalisation may call for different emphases in different contexts, it will be a valuable move to
improve the reputation as well as the effectiveness of the industry.

Integrity and, to a Certain Extent, Transparency

Critical issues such as increased regulation of
lobbyists and greater transparency about the
decision-making processes are argued to promote opportunities to assess the weight given
to different interests. Media can play an
important role by providing the public with
information and allow them to take a stand
and engage with lobbyists. Integrity within
the public affairs industry, however, will
always prevail over any form of forced
behaviour and practice.

THE CHAPTERS IN THIS HANDBOOK

The chapters that follow each have their own structure reflecting the preferences and priorities of the authors and the salient characteristics of the region; however, reflecting what I have discussed above, you will find that attention is paid to history and evolution, including terminology development and current use of terms; the development of PA, interest groups, government relations, the local environment and/or market – that is, the diversity in, and distinctness of, the region; the economic, political, social and cultural context and regulation, including a critique of activities; some words on the PA profession as it is – its development, standing, education and training, with the names of relevant and important players, and an indication of the strength of consultants versus corporates; and last but not least, the current state of public affairs, views on a best practice model and gaps to be bridged, with indications of future directions and challenges.

Chapter 21 on North America underlines that the public affairs function is a dynamic, evolving component of any large corporation, and especially of those corporations engaged in international business. Public affairs is not without challenge, however, and the interplay of public affairs, non-governmental organisations (NGOs) and the external environment will continue to compel corporate action and engagement in the marketplace of ideas. Fundamental to corporate defence (and offence) here is a well-organised public affairs department.

Whilst in Latin America 'government relations' is still a young practice, the consolidation of democratic systems throughout the region is enabling those agents more inclined to interact with governments on a permanent and open basis, such as business organisations, to develop professionally.

Europe is probably the most diverse continent with more than forty nation-states and some of the oldest democratic traditions. Important decisions concerning financial, trading, environmental and social policies affecting markets worldwide are taken in Europe every day, with centres such as Brussels, Berlin, Geneva, London and Paris as hubs of a complex web of power. Public affairs engages in multiple ways with that power.

In the uncommon EU system, managing PA requires much preparatory homework and understanding of the European institutions, the formal and informal decision-taking routes, and the pressures from member states – traditional lobbying being only one tool to achieve objectives – whose importance is justified by the EU's power to dictate the legislative context in twenty-eight member states.

In Africa, lobbying gives citizen groups, associations, labour unions and the private sector the opportunity to converse with government, and with lawmakers increasingly relying on lobbyists for information, PA plays an important role 'that usually accompanies proposed legislation'. This emphasises the importance of communication for successful lobbying. Lobbying in South Africa is highly regulated; regardless of this, it plays an important role in relation to the tender process and the corruption and fraud that plague it. Investment in PA professionalisation offers the opportunity to improve communication.

Asia on the whole has yet to embrace a consistent model in the area of PA and there seems to be much scope for development, with Japan and Korea leading.

In Australia the practice of public affairs varies from early learning to a mature stage owing to the variation in business environments. Easy proximity of business and government in New Zealand allows communication skill to be dominant in the understanding and practice of public affairs. In the Pacific islands a limited number of practitioners in a large but sparsely populated region leads to an ecology in which PA efforts are largely supported by staff in offshore corporate or regional offices.

I trust you will enjoy the exciting journey this section of the Handbook offers and wish you a great read.

REFERENCES

Choi, C.J. 1992. Asian Capitalism versus Western Civilization. Oxford University, Queen's College and Templeton College working paper.

Choi, C. J., S. H. Lee and J. B. Kim. 1999. Countertrade: Contractual Uncertainty and Transaction Governance in Emerging Economies. *Journal of International Business Studies* 30: 189–202.

Flier, B., F. A. J. van den Bosch and H. W. Volberda. 2003. Co-Evolution in Strategic Renewal Behaviour of British, Dutch and French Financial Incumbents: Interaction of Environmental Selection, Institutional Effects and Managerial Intentionality. *Journal of Management Studies* 40: 2163–87.

Kostova, Tatiana and Thomas M. Hult. 2016. Mayer and Peng's 2005 Articles as a Foundation for an Expanded and Refined International Business Research Agenda: Context, Organisational and Theories. *Journal of International Business Studies* 7 (1): 23–33.

Millar, Carla C. J. M. 2014. To Be or Not To Be: The Existential Issue for National Governance Bundles. *Corporate Governance, an International Journal* 22 (3): 194–8.

Millar, Carla and Peter Köppl. 2014. Perspectives, Practices and Prospects of Public Affairs in Central and Eastern Europe: A Lobbying Future Anchored in an Institutional Context. *Journal of Public Affairs*, special issue on 'The State of Public Affairs in Central and Eastern Europe', 14 (1): 4–17.

Millar, C. C. J. M., T. Eldomiaty, B. J. Hilton and C. J. Chong. 2005. Corporate Governance and Institutional Strategic Transparency in Emerging Markets. *Journal of Business Ethics* 59 (1–2): 163–74.

Millar, Carla C. J. M., Chong-Ju Choi and Philip Y. K. Cheng. 2009. Co-evolution: Law and Institutions in International Ethics Research. *Journal of Business Ethics* 87 (4): 455–61.

North, D. 1990. *Institutions, Institutional Change and Economic Performance.* Cambridge: Cambridge University Press.

Whitley, R. 1994. Dominant forms of economic organization on market economies. *Organization Studies*, 15: 153–82.

19

Public Affairs in the Uncommon European Union

Rinus van Schendelen

What is special about managing one's public affairs (PA) in the European Union (EU)? The answer here comes from three specific questions. Why is the EU an uncommon political playing-field? What characterizes interest groups at the EU level? What may be an interest group's SWOT (strengths, weaknesses, opportunities and threats) vis-à-vis this EU?

WHY IS THE EU AN UNCOMMON POLITICAL PLAYING-FIELD?

The EU of now twenty-eight European (27, if UK really leaves) states may look to be just another multi-state system like the US, China or India. By three features it is not.

1   *An artificial and gradually natural construct.* The sixty years' young EU is based on a treaty, concluded in 1958 by six state-governments, often

renewed since and now signed by twenty-eight different states that, in the past, have often hindered or even warred with each other. The treaty is a contract between distrusting partners that assign parts of their 'sovereign powers' to the EU, often in different ways, as many states have stayed outside the 'Schengen area' (which allows free movement of people) and the euro and/ or have their opt-ins and opt-outs. The treaty's essence is its mechanism of common legislation that, by binding the member-states, overrules conflicting domestic laws and rules. Those wars are over so far, but not the inter-state issues that are now forwarded by interest groups from governments and civil societies in the member-states, which thus might better be called member-countries. The EU is more a union of common laws than of values shared by many citizens across borders. Rising EU-scepticism (voiced by up to 30 per cent of voters in 2014) shows their growing involvement, which makes the EU gradually a more 'natural' system (Leconte, 2010).

2   *Skeleton versus flesh-and-blood.* The treaties define the formal framework of institutions, structures, procedures, authorities, competences,

budget and more, in short a skeleton that tells the body how it must function. Its daily 'flesh-and-blood' functioning is not so much in contradiction but different, as everything not forbidden by treaty can be done by consent. The treaty text suggests that the Council of Ministers, in which all member-states have one seat but unequal voting power, is the main institution. Sometimes this is true, for example when a treaty change is being prepared (member-states must reach unanimity) and on defence policy (hardly EU powers). Usually the Commission (COM), being by treaty the executive institution that holds the (almost) 'exclusive privilege of drafting legislative proposals', sits in the driver's seat. Inside all institutions, it is not the top level but the middle level that usually handles the decision process vis-à-vis a policy theme that always stands at issue among many stakeholders, all together called an 'arena', as is described hereafter. In order to obtain influence, defined as 'making a difference in the desired direction', the most experienced interest groups step in at these lower levels and particularly in the earliest COM-phase, where 'the games are still fairly open'.

3   *Not an ordinary system.* The EU has the exceptional scale of twenty-eight member-states and twice the US population, but is neither a multi-state government like the USA nor a platform like the United Nations (UN). By treaty it must leave vital political processes, such as communication, participation or law maintenance (Almond and Powell, 1966), largely to the member-states, although it can influence these via soft policy means, like subsidies and benchmarks. It is basically a mechanism that aggregates issues among the countries and settles these for a while by making laws and rules that overrule the domestic ones, a capacity that the UN does not have. It is a sort of 'non-state statehood' (Neyer and Wiener, 2011). In some policy domains (competition, agriculture) it is powerful, in others (social affairs, energy) less so, and in yet others (security, health) it is weak. However, in these last areas it can wield influence by using strong powers like one on competition, as it does in, for example, the domains of social affairs and health. Compared with 'ordinary systems', the EU is under-resourced. Its annual budget (€160 billion in 2015, of which above 90 per cent spent on subsidies) is about 80 per cent of that of the central government of the small country

of Austria, and its total staff (45,000 persons, including 10 per cent who are linguists) is about 40 per cent of that of the central government of the Netherlands, a small country with only one language.

The Flesh-and-Blood of the Main EU Institutions

Pragmatic PA experts don't complain about the peculiarities of a playing-field, but take the facts as they are and search for optimal ways to win and not to lose (in itself a fine win) on their targets. They see the institutional flesh-and-blood processes, which start at the COM, as very useful knowledge. Various handbooks describe these processes in detail (Buonanno and Nugent, 2013; Richardson, 2012; Wallace et al., 2014). The main characteristics of the treaty-based institutions are as follows:

1   *The European Commission* of twenty-eight Commissioners (the College) exerts, with the help of its approximately forty Directorates-General/Services (DGs), its 'exclusive privilege' to draft proposals along two routes. One is by legislative process that needs approval either by the Council alone (the 'special legislative procedure', SLP) or by both the Council and the European Parliament (EP) (the 'ordinary legislative procedure', OLP). The other route is largely managed by the COM itself, but now in its executive role of making the detailed rules (called 'delegated or implementing acts'), for which it is empowered either by treaty (like in the field of competition) or by laws. The total annual production of laws and rules is about 2,500 on average (Van Schendelen, 2013, 80 for figures), of which about 15 per cent are laws and 85 per cent rules. In cross-national perspective, the COM is an extremely small bureaucracy, having only 14,000 policy staff (other staff total 24,000 people), recruited from all twenty-eight (and more) countries. A policy unit has on average seventeen staff and thus is keen to obtain relevant policy information and support. Inevitably, the COM manages its work differently from national bureaucracies. It 'insources' about 100,000 experts from all sorts

of national and European interest groups into its 2,000 expert committees, each of which is run by a *dossierchef* (mid-level civil servant) and has experts from very different stakeholders around the table. Through their diverse input of information and support and their discussions, the experts help (willy-nilly and almost for free) the dossierchef to define the issues at stake (in a green paper) and identify the solution to the problem (a white paper) in feasible ways. The dossierchef turns the white paper into a draft legal text, to be approved by the EP and/or the Council as laws (the 15 per cent) or by the COM as rules (the 85 per cent); in order to implement the acts, the COM must go through about 350 special committees ('comitology') composed of mainly national government experts. In all mentioned committees, in return for their useful information and support, experts from interest groups obtain positions that offer the chance to influence the COM texts. This smart 'Commission Method' can be seen as a superb PA performance and opportunity (Van Schendelen, 2013, 92–8), to which we return at the end of this chapter.

2 *Three representative institutions.* Most powerful is the EP, as it usually shares the strong power of the OLP. Its 751 directly elected members (MEPs) from the twenty-eight EU member-states (EU-28) represent more than 200 national political parties that, in order to obtain EP facilities and influence, have to join one of about ten so-called 'political groups', for example the conservative EPP or the socialist S&D. The micro-ideologies of these 200 or so parties inevitably disappear in the EP, where the cross-national political groups function like occasional platforms, bound together more by common interests than by common ideology. The dominant definition of 'politics', which is 'party politics' at domestic levels, is 'interest politics' inside and among the EP groups. The driving interests regarding any dossier (policy idea or proposal) are usually negotiated between a 'rapporteur' of the relevant EP commission, one or more 'co-rapporteurs' from other commissions, and, as they all have a party-political profile, 'shadow rapporteurs' from other groups – in total, a varying team of about fifteen MEPs for any dossier. The leaders of the commissions and the groups negotiate about the remaining issues, in order to create aggregated influence at the plenary voting. Additionally, the EP has about forty 'intergroups', namely cross-party

groups of MEPs that act as an interest group for special themes like rural areas, disability or youth. Two other representative institutions are the Committee of the Regions and the Economic and Social Committee, the one representing regional and local governments and the other socio-economic interest groups. Both are composed of members who are indirectly elected or nominated by some body at home and hold only advisory powers (SLP). In the 'flesh-and-blood' of the EU decision-making they can still have influence. All three institutions are very open to being influenced in Brussels, and their members in their home countries too. Through them an interest group can cast its shadow on the COM when preparing a proposal and/or influence a proposal once this is on their agenda.

3 *The Council of Ministers* is the place of the EU-28 governments. It works via eight specialized Councils, such as those for Justice and Transport, which all fall under the General Council and are chaired by a twice-a-year rotating member-state. Under the OLP the various Councils decide by a weighted majority, and under the SLP usually by consensus (a slowly made wide agreement without voting) and seldom by unanimity (which would make one veto deadly). Their decisions are prepared by Coreper, the body of all twenty-eight Permanent Representations (PRs, 'EU Embassies'), and negotiated in advance in almost 300 working groups of national civil servants. Special are the Foreign Affairs Council (FA ministers) and the European Council (heads of state), chaired by an appointed person and usually deciding by consensus. Since the mid-2000s, the Council members, in theory most powerful as treaty-makers, have in practice displayed increasing difficulty in coming to a common position under OLP or SLP. One cause is the enlargement from EU-15 (until 2004) to EU-28, and another the less stable composition of the Council. With twenty-eight governments there are about six regular domestic elections annually, alongside some forced ones, together close to one-third of the Council. Any new government alters some policy positions of its predecessor. In its negotiations with the EP and the COM, which have stable five-year terms, the Council is increasingly the loser. Interest groups find it difficult to influence the Council being 'the mum oyster of Brussels' directly, but through the PRs they can collect information, and through domestic

politics they may influence the Council indirectly, which requires co-ordinated actions from interest groups.

4   *More institutions and agencies.* There are eight (more specialized) institutions more. One is the EU Court of Justice (Luxembourg). Its treaty-based jurisprudence overrules (parts of) EU laws and rules that it sees as conflicting with the treaties, so forcing the COM to draft adjustments. Another example is the European Central Bank (ECB, Frankfurt), which is responsible for the stability of the euro. As the outcome of European Council agreements in 2011 on new mechanisms to improve control of the fall-out of the post-2007 financial crises, it is co-responsible with the COM (and partially the IMF) for the financial stability of state governments and private banks (Snyder, 2012). Next to these institutions, there are about forty agencies and/or authorities, such as Europol (on policing) and the EFSA (on food safety). They are not treaty-based, but more-or-less decentralized parts of the COM, often in a joint-venture with the governments and located in a member-state. Most function like the 'Commission Method' (expert committees) mentioned above, but have their own directorate. They advise the COM on taking measures by legislative proposals or delegated acts regarding the substance and/or management of their policy field. A few agencies, such as the ERC (on research) and the EASME (on small and medium-sized enterprises) have regulatory powers that they apply through comitology (implementing acts). Interest groups can influence an agency particularly via experts who come to its meetings from external interest groups.

Typifying the EU as an Uncommon Playing-Field that Requires Adjusted PA

The essence of the uncommon EU can be summarized as follows:

1   *Top-down machinery.* The binding priority of EU laws and rules over the national codebooks is the most centralist EU characteristic. EU decisions that are sent as guidelines or recommendations to the member-states are not formally binding but can influence them as 'soft laws or rules'.

In particular EU subsidies seduce many interest groups to do what the EU wants them to do, even if there is no formal obligation.

2   *Bottom-up machinery.* The ways these laws and rules get into the EU codebook ('Official Journal') show that the EU functions strongly from the bottom up. Its 'centre' is a configuration of highly separated or fragmented powers. It collects many strong inputs from its decentralized layers and, thanks to the unparalleled openness and accessibility of the COM and EP, from countless interest groups. In the languages of continental Europe, the EU is like a federal (bottom-up) system; only in the UK is this F-word viewed as the centralist opposite (thus, can better not be used).

3   *Complex and dynamic polyarchy.* A better and value-free catchword for the EU is that of 'polyarchy': an open system that for its output effectiveness depends on negotiations among its interdependent parts. No part really rules ('archy'), but many together ('poly') can, which is seen as 'the best feasible democracy' (Dahl, 1971). The EU system looks extraordinarily complex and dynamic, like 'a labyrinth built on a trampoline'. True enough, every political system has its complexities and dynamics, but the EU has them at all systemic levels together: citizens, officials and politicians, institutions, regime principles and constitutional framework (Norris, 2011).

Effectively influencing a system is never a free choice, but always system-dependent too. What works in one city, state or case often fails in another. The uncommon scale and nature of the EU requires from interest groups very different PA expertise that is adjusted to the EU system. The overarching catchword for this is *anticipatory homework*: any influence effort must be anticipated and managed as a campaign through rather different territory, full of challenging actors and factors from both inside and outside the EU at different levels that all together determine any outcome. The six specifics of EU-bound PA are as follows [Van Schendelen, 2013, ch. V]:

1   *Home front.* As each interest group has its discord of tasks, agendas, emotions and more, it must permanently bring this 'home front' to cohesive action. PA must be the responsibility of the board (or the principal of a consultant) and

be assisted by a PA unit (and maybe a Brussels' front-officer). By mutual briefing and debriefing, this PA unit is interconnected with other staff units (such as 'legal' and 'sales') and with line experts on the substance; the latter are also useful for, for example, COM expert committees. The PA unit's first job is to collect sound information (symbol I), not by (fixed) antenna but by (moving) radar, about current and arising EU issues, arenas and dossiers. The outcome is a long-list full of opportunities and threats (daydreams and nightmares) that all look relevant.

2   *Strategy.* The long-list has to be critically analysed, that is all information has to be turned into intelligence (symbol I^2). Are the assumed facts of a daydream really true and is the dream really desired, and, similarly, what about a nightmare? The good answer comes from mid-term strategic thinking. The radar goes on to collect information, now about the many other stakeholders and officials on a dossier, particularly the possible opponent or ambivalent ones, and, also, the interests they have. This enables each dossier to be assessed for how feasible the group's desires are. Should it expect a tailwind, headwind or an unpredictable one? The I^2 often results in re-assessments and/or a shortened long-list. For each confirmed dossier sharp and measurable targets for the EU's decision-outcome are set.

3   *Critical mass.* A single interest group can influence the EU only if it is sufficiently supported by other groups: sectoral ones (in its interest domain), preferably also cross-sectoral (from other domains, e.g. business plus NGO) and, in the EU, always cross-national ('one passport cannot score'). The collected support from interest groups with similar interests on a dossier it organizes as a common platform. Its long-list is converted to a 'shared-list' of dossiers to be managed on as many platforms. The basic form of an EU platform is the sectoral European federation or association (EuroFed) (Greenwood, 2011). An interest group needs this 'critical mass' (symbol M) in order to achieve greater effectiveness (symbol E1) and efficiency (symbol E2) of its own influence efforts. By influencing not solo ('solo-list') but together, the reward can be multiplied influence at divided costs. In short, PA at the EU level requires the management of $2E= MI^2$. A lot of work, but without alternative.

4   *Action planning.* The basic level of PA management is, from now on, a platform. Thanks to its earlier I^2, many an interest group can take a rather free ride and limit itself to remote control of the common PA. For every platform a common strategy with common targets must be negotiated. On what is not common, every partner is free to act alone or otherwise. On the common targets of a platform, a common action plan must be based. The best PA method here is 'to think backwards' from the inner circle of the EU final decision-makers and then to 'act forwards' to them. The collection of I for I^2 goes on always, now also including the opponent platforms, the maps of procedures and deadlines, and the observer-only stakeholders such as mass media that may intervene. This review of the arena is the 'PA war map' that enables definition of the main tactical approaches and technical methods. Like a military action scenario, it is regularly reviewed.

5   *Implementation.* The 'proof of the pudding' of all anticipatory homework (thanks to the platform at largely divided costs) must come from the rewards of multiplied influence. For the operational activities, easy dos and don'ts can't be applied, as what is better to do or to leave always depends on the arena situation to be read from the PA war map. In this phase one has to be conscious of and act prudently regarding the limits of PA on the Sender's side, in the Communication channels, inside the Arena, on the Receiver's side (for example, officials, MEPs) and in the watching Environment, together making up the SCARE limits of PA (Van Schendelen, 2013, ch. VII). In PA, 'details' don't exist, as they may contain the devil (or the saint). Many losses and gains are a result of seemingly small details.

6   *Evaluation.* At regular intervals, the leading question is 'where can it be (or could it have been) done better?' Often, the possible improvements need better anticipated homework rather than more resources, as excellence depends more on quality as on quantity of people or 'more on grams of brains as on kilos fte's'. Good or bad luck and the limits of PA always play some role. The question then is: were they really unpredictable or rather foreseeable? An evaluation can benefit from critical mass again, such as from staff and line on the home front, partners on the platform, receivers (for example, dossierchefs, rapporteurs) and, once the arena is over, opponents and informed journalists.

This EU-adjusted PA is, like any campaign through challenging territory, seldom 100 per cent excellently performed. The ultimate criterion is that one's performance has been better than that of the opponents and has brought the edge over them. Later in the chapter we'll apply the six specifics of EU-adjusted PA as *proxy measures* of strengths (and their opposites as weaknesses) as part of a broader SWOT.

WHAT CHARACTERIZES INTEREST GROUPS AT THE EU LEVEL?

Major questions now are: Is there a regulatory framework vis-à-vis interest groups that try to influence the EU? What are the quantities of diverse interests and interest groups? What is the quality of the influence performance of interests groups? What are new trends in influencing the EU? Is PA at the EU level a profession?

The Regulatory Framework for Influencing the EU

So far we have avoided the word *lobbying* and only used the general idea of influencing and the modern idea of methodical PA management that largely equals the formula $2E= MI^2$ and starts at home. The etymological meaning of lobbying, coming from late medieval Italy, is 'entering the *lobia*' (the porch) of the local ruler's *palazzo*, in order to collect information on how to elicit a favour from him or her. It is corridor-behaviour, going around. If power is concentrated in one or a few persons, it may still work. If power is dispersed among many, as is the case of the EU, influencing by only lobbying is a utopia, as it would require countless visits to numerous people in every phase of any dossier. Neither the sending interest group nor the receiving official, politician or stakeholder can afford this inefficiency. In the internet

era, the I for MI^2 can much better (2E) be collected by desk research than by lobbying. In the 'premier league of Brussels PA', desk research is often 85 per cent of all work, filled up with about 15 per cent of lobbying in order to secure missing information or support from somebody (Spencer and McGrath, 2008). Social media are the least used cyber-tools, as they are seen as risky in terms of security and privacy and as useless for fine-tuned negotiations (BM, 2013; EurActiv, 2009). A different meaning of lobbying is prominent at country level, where it is often taken not as means of preparation but as 'dirty practices' like bribery, roguery or corruption. As nothing is good or bad by itself and only by its valuation, dirty practices can happen by lobbying, PA and any influencing too. A useful concept must have, however, not a biased but a neutral meaning.

In their European Transparency Initiative (ETI, 2014; Greenwood and Dreger, 2013), which renewed the rules of conduct and registration for interest groups, the COM and EP (the Council abstained), ignoring the notion of PA management, defined lobbying in a third way as 'all activities carried out with the objective of directly or indirectly influencing the formulation or implementation of policy and the decision-making processes of the EU institutions, irrespective of where they are undertaken and of the channel or medium of communication used'. The substantive word is 'influencing', indeed the valid one. Calling this 'lobbying', the COM and EP pass over the notions of 'corridor-behaviour' and 'dirty practices' and use the word as a neutral term that only covers what they, as 'receivers of lobby efforts', experience and take it as 'pars pro toto' for the substantive whole that can yield either clean or dirty practices. Lobbying they explicitly praise for its positive contributions to better EU decision-making. The code of conduct is basically about transparency of interests and accountability of doings. COM officials and MEPs have their own 'codes of good behaviour'. In 2014 the COM ordered its Commissioners and highest officials to register their contacts with interest groups in a public register. Under Council pressure, lobby groups from national governments and political parties are explicitly exempted from all registers and codes.

The real control on the conduct of lobby groups comes, however, not from the ETI, but from the *social control* ('mother of all control', the E of SCARE) that is exerted by watchdog NGOs, such as TI, Alter-EU, CEO and Finance Watch, often with support from the COM and EP. According to (what they see as) the spirit rather than the letters of the ETI, they watch the conduct of lobby groups and publicly name and shame any group that has its appearances against it. Such a group is soon penalized by isolation in its EuroFed and closed doors at the COM and EP, in short out of PA business for a while. Other groups seeing this take the lesson, become more prudent and internalize this limit of PA better. At country level, the German parliament has the oldest (1972) register (2,100 registrants in 2014) and code. In 2015 ten of the twenty-eight national parliaments (not the governments) have a register and code too (Holman and Luneburg, 2012), but hardly any have NGOs that promote the enforcement of the texts by social control, such as at EU level. The most notorious EU scandal since 2010 has been 'Dalligate', in which the Health Commissioner John Dalli was accused of being involved in a bribery attempt to lift the EU ban on selling snus, as revealed by Swedish Tobacco company, the alleged partner in bribery; Dalli resigned but the case remains unclear as a result of lack of hard evidence. The number of scandals at the EU level is indeed much lower than at the domestic level (TI, 2015).

What are the Quantities of Diverse Interests and Interests Groups in the EU?

To probe new themes for legislation, the COM often launches an Online Consultation (OC). It publishes the results on the internet and in a report ('blue paper') that often shows tens of thousands of responding interest groups (Quitkat, 2011). It is a gold mine for discovering the wide diversity of interests in Europe on a new theme and for efficiently identifying the stakeholders that responded and their interests at stake (the needed I for one's I^2). This diversity of interests is clearly caused by the diversity of the EU countries, as shown by the EU's socio-economic indicators (COM/DG Eurostat). A prominent interest in the one country, such as energy, health or a rural area, may be different or absent in another one. Influencing the EU thus is an excellent way to discover the realities of Europe and to grasp why the EU is so uncommon and still under (re)construction. The OC respondents are only a sample of all interests on a theme, as many other interests may lack group structure or, if they have one, may be in disorder or temporarily inactive, but may sooner or later enter the arena. An intelligent interest group wants to search, beyond the boundaries of an arena, for such unorganized interests or silent interest groups that may be useful for its own 2E. The COM annually spends about €1billion on temporarily supporting newly arising interests and interest groups in order to include them in its 'Commission Method'.

In early 2016, the ETI had about 10,000 registered interest groups and lobbyists, the latter acting in-house (as employees of an interest group) or as consultants. They have the following backgrounds: 48 per cent from trade, occupational and business entities, 33 per cent from NGOs, think-tanks and civil institutions like universities and churches, 13 per cent from consultancies and 5 per cent from regional and local authorities and other similar agencies. Is this the full picture? Certainly not. The registrants are largely Brussels-based, 15 per cent each from Germany, France and the UK and for 40 per cent from the twenty-five other countries (Wonka et al., 2010). For influencing the EU, most interest groups rely, usually through their national umbrella, on their EuroFed and only occasionally send somebody to Brussels. The many commuting lobbyists usually make an appointment that is registered at the counter. The *c.* 100,000 experts of the expert committees, the many people from national governments and some other groups don't have to register. Nowhere is there a tally of all people inside any organization who are involved in influencing efforts in the EU. In short, the real numbers are much bigger than shown by this ETI tip of the iceberg. The tip represents the hard core of Brussels lobbying: the groups and people who are there permanently or frequently. Their hubs are the thousand or so standing EuroFeds (Greenwood, 2011). Some examples are Business Europe (employers' organizations), ETUC (trade unions), UEAPME (SMEs), CEMR (regional and local governments), EBU ('for the blind'), EPA (parents' groups) and FIEP (national police). They have a high membership from the EU-28, are often open for groups from outside the EU, and work as machineries that must bring the very different interests of their sectoral members more on one line, in short for creating the sectoral mass (M) needed for influence.

What is the Quality of the PA Performance at the EU Level?

In theory, the ideal measure of PA quality is that one's influence efforts produce the desired difference at the greatest possible effectiveness and the lowest possible costs (2E). Such a causality cannot, however, be measured perfectly, as the outcome is always the product of many actors and factors and as real life never offers a control situation (Hume, 1748). The results of one's influence efforts can only be stated in terms of plausibility that should be subject to critical debate and refutation, as they may contain much nonsense. For example, the popular belief that influences success mainly depends on resources like budget, networks or positions,

lacks good evidence (Beyers and Kerremans, 2007). They may be helpful, sometimes necessary, but never sufficient, and show many exceptions, for example, 'rich tobacco' that loses from 'poor health NGOs'. The best possible *proxy measures* of PA performance are the six specifics of anticipatory homework, mentioned above. The question is: is there a strong factor that explains why EU interest groups perform differently on the continuum of poor versus excellent PA?

1   *By nationality.* In the first decades of the EU most interest groups reflected in their influence efforts the ways and styles they were used to in their own country. In those times most interest groups relied on their domestic ministry's connection to the then mighty Council (only SLP, no OLP). The directly inviting infrastructure of EuroFeds was still small by quantity and fragile by quality. PA was still largely unknown, as it came from the USA to the EU in the 1980s. All this has become history. The groups from the pre-2004 member-countries are now mainly driven by their own interests instead of their passport, shop only occasionally in their national capital, make easily cross-national coalitions in a EuroFed or ad hoc platform, and hear about PA in the EU there. Most interest groups from the post-2004 EU-13 (mainly ex-USSR) initially took the national route, as they had to get their group better adapted to the EU and familiarized with the EU infrastructure, which is becoming reality now (Millar and Köppl, 2014). The differences between interest groups from old and new countries are rapidly diminishing. 'The French' don't exist and neither do the twenty-seven others.

2   *By background.* PA was brought from the US to the UK by transatlantic multinational firms and from the UK to the continent by Anglo-Dutch ones, like Unilever and Shell. The better-structured interest groups still belong to the family of multinationally organized (MNO-like) groups, but not anymore only from business but also NGOs (such as Greenpeace), EuroFeds (like above) and networks of agencies (like E-Reg on car registration). They have internalized the European diversity of interests. As applies to every generalization, one cannot reversely conclude that each MNO-like group is well-organized, as every board can be nonchalant (and many are). The

next best group, by some distance, includes groups from the extremely diverse world of SMEs, such as farmers with their EuroFed COPA, research institutes (EARTO) and the water suppliers (EUREAU) that often get their many small members to a common position, but most SMEs, again, have not yet achieved that. Third best are some semi-autonomous regions (like in Germany and Spain) and metropolitan areas (like Paris-banlieue), in contrast to the majority of regions and cities that are still weakly organized and are happy with a fine EU profile and some subsidies rather than influencing crucial EU decisions. Most national ministries, once often strong players, are at the continuum's lower end. Usually lacking PA experts, they approach the EU via their policy experts, focus on the Council (the end-phase of the 15 per cent laws, mainly OLP now), mistake their treaty powers for real influence and suffer from domestic political instability. At the lowest end stand the national parliaments and political parties, in recent research described as the 'losers or victims of EU integration' (Mattila and Raunio, 2012; Ladrech, 2010). Background is no factor at the continuum's lower end and a weak one at the upper end.

3   *By reputation.* One's reputation may contribute to one's final performance. A nice guy is more readily invited and taken on board than a bad guy, even if both are important. Two recent surveys offer information about the reputation of interest groups. One, held among 600 politicians and officials from eighteen state governments and EU institutions (BM, 2013), found that half (50 per cent) of all respondents had at some point refused access to a lobbyist. The most negative aspect of lobbying was seen by 26 per cent to be 'lack of transparency': 55–65 per cent considered trade associations, sectoral groups, companies, trade unions and NGOs as transparent and only 16–27 per cent viewed PA agencies, think-tanks, law firms and mass media in the same way. The effectiveness of lobbying they attribute to the interest groups runs almost parallel to the assessed transparency. On both assessments the EU respondents are more positive than the national ones. The second survey is the COM's Anti-Corruption Report (Commission, 2014). It defines corruption as 'any abuse of power for private gain' and presents on a range of variants (for example, bribery, nepotism and cartels) perceptions of both citizens and businessmen in twenty-seven countries. Every country is perceived as more-or-less corrupt, but the north-western countries less than the others. Corruption is said to happen most in the triangle of political parties, officials and companies. Fresh reputation data portray the Commission as having more transparency, integrity and accessibility than any national government and the EP as medium (TI, 2015). This may be explained by favourable EU factors, such as the strong interest competition, the social control by NGOs, the living sense of prudence, the insignificance of party politics and the wider use of PA. In short, a good reputation is necessary: some categories of groups have it for some time (but many single members of them not) and it is certainly not sufficient for a strong PA performance.

4   *By experience.* Newcomers from new member-states or foreign countries often start ill-prepared. They mistake the EU as being more-or-less like their own political system and PA as similar to lobbying, advocacy or public relations. They may depart soon or learn rapidly by trial and error or thanks to their socializing EuroFed. Among the most experienced groups one can find the better organized and operating ones, such as some MNOs, SMEs, regions and big cities, ministries and even some party family. They influence not alone but via a cross-national and cross-sectoral platform and learn how to become better prepared for the EU. On a specific dossier, for example, a Ministry of Industry then follows its leading industrial group that is part of a crucial EuroFed and, for example, 'green' political parties follow Greenpeace. Long-term EU experience seems to be a factor of PA quality, as it helps to internalize the uncommon EU mechanism, improve the anticipatory homework and pay heed to the limits of PA. Many interest groups that have long acted in Brussels, however, have hardly learnt, forget their lessons and/or rely on routine and easy dos and don'ts. Even experience is not such a strong factor that it explains excellence.

Are There New Trends of Influencing the EU?

Five years ago we mentioned three new trends: more interest groups start as self-reliant players, go through an appropriate EuroFed that delivers supportive M and obtain greater interest in the game of 'Triple P' (by which loyal Persons are put on strong Positions in friendly made Procedures, so building their own uphill citadel in order to beat the downhill opponents before a match starts) (Van Schendelen, 2011). The first two trends have become regular practice. The third one looks to be already in the past. It may be that interest groups that tried to gain more control over the EU's increased complexity since the mid-2000s (for example, the thirteen new member-states, treaty change, serious crises) by re-inventing the old Triple P game, have felt that, owing simply to that greater complexity, the game has become utopia. Citadels may still exist, but more by coincidence than by engineering, only for a short time and in a distant policy domain. Strong new trends are the following:

1   *Multiple routing.* Part of PA homework has become, for every dossier, the figuring out of smart routes to the decision actors and factors in the fragmented EU system. The 'national route' has gained a new meaning. Instead of the regular or selective route to the national capital, it is now to 'the rest of one's own country'. Already here an interest group can find sectoral and cross-sectoral stakeholders with similar interests on its dossier(s). Many of these stakeholders are connected to platforms across EU countries and to EuroFeds, and some even to countries like the USA and Japan or institutions like the World Health Organization (WHO) and World Trade Organization (WTO) that influence the EU too. Thus, a group can start to collect broader 'critical mass' (M) at home and, once this snowballs, see multiple (international, transnational and global) routes to the many EU decision points. By 'backwards thinking' from these to where it stands, it can select the routes that can optimally contribute to its final 2E.

2   *Flexible platforms.* The thousand or so EuroFeds are still the hubs for influencing the EU. Since the 2004 expansion to EU-28, many have got difficulty aggregating the more diverse interests to a common position. Many of their leading members now prefer an ad hoc platform in a light construction with hotel meetings during the life of a dossier. They use their EuroFed as 'shopping centre' for creating a fine-tuned ad hoc platform, of which the total number is estimated to have increased above those thousand EuroFeds. Here they are also free from the national associations that still run many EuroFeds. The COM and EP too have a preference for platforms with cross-sectoral rather than only sectoral M (as EuroFeds have).

3   *Circular PA.* Until recently most interest groups had a special unit for PA in the EU, the so-called upstream. For managing the downstream effects of EU decisions in their countries, they had their old unit for domestic PA. Since in many areas the EU policy process is circular to and from the countries, the PA must become circular too. Many a PA challenge at home now comes from the EU downstream. Thanks to the priority of EU laws over national ones, domestic challenges can often be better solved by PA in the EU than by domestic PA. For example, the case of the 30 per cent of domestic electors being sceptical about the EU and paralysing their government via parties is so far hardly a concern of domestic PA, but is a serious one for the EU unit. Such a problem is solved by integrating the two units as one team that manages a challenge wherever it arises. Side-effects of this trend appear to be that the better developed PA expertise at the EU level obtains dissemination at home and the same for the two other trends of multiple routing and flexible platforms. Domestic PA becomes slightly Europeanized.

Is PA in the EU a Profession?

Influencing others is an activity as old and widespread as humankind. Only a few are paid for it as employees or consultants and have it as their occupation. For it to be a profession, as, for example, for an engineer or lawyer, much more is needed, such as at least appropriate education, independent examination, publicly certified diploma and further training (McGrath, 2015; 2005). The education must cover both its substantial contents and the methodical discipline that creates and refutes knowledge and insights.

Usually, the government or, on its behalf, an institute sets the minimal requirements and often much more, for example regular inspections and jurisdiction. For the universal activity and/or the occupation of 'influencing others', such minimal requirements exist nowhere in the western world. The aforementioned registers and codes are no substitute, as they ask from lobbyists specific information and conduct at the entrance of official doors, but leave their competences and skills as they are. Lobbying and PA thus are a free activity, sometimes an occupation and *not a profession*, as also applies to the job of a politician. The often young practitioners come from very different trainings and previous jobs, learn mainly by doing, and have employers or principals with different expectations of their skills, as surveys show (Althaus, 2015; Timmermans, 2015).

It is thus up to the practitioners to develop by *self-regulation* occupational and, in future, maybe professional standards. Their associations should do this. The first one arose in the USA (1954), followed by the UK in the mid-1990s and by continental Europe in the 2000s (see listed websites). The initiative came usually from consultants who, not shielded by an employer, felt the cold wind of the citizens' distrust in lobbying directly and wanted self-regulation that could suggest public recognition (even if only shared by colleagues). Most associations took as their name not 'lobbying' but 'public affairs' (whatever it may mean) and established self-regulation that is mainly a code of conduct towards people outside, like politicians, principals and journalists. Nowhere did they define the basics of what they think they have in common, let alone an educational curriculum and all the other characteristics of a profession. In a few European countries, some practitioners and/ or scholars have develop(ed) a PA masters programme as an academic discipline, such as political science, communication science or business management (McGrath, 2015; Van Schendelen, 2013, ch. VI). They have invented their own definitions, basic courses,

skills and so on, without taking PA as a discipline that needs methodical thinking too. At the EU level there are two associations, SEAP for in-house people and EPACA for consultants, which leave the substance of PA as it is. Some universities and consultancies sell 'dos and don'ts' training on 'how to influence the EU'.

In Europe, the transition from occupation to profession has a long way to go. It is hardly clear what the practitioners are doing in practice, but most look like 'medieval' lobbyists, without preparing the work of $2E = MI^2$, and anyhow can't be qualified by professional standards. Therefore, we distinguish here only between 'excellent' (well-prepared) and 'poor' efforts to influence others, based on the proxy measures detailed above. This is not a personal approach, but grounded on a great deal of serious literature, research, surveys and participatory observations (Van Schendelen, 2013) and not unique (McGrath, 2015; 2006). The more excellent practitioners, to be found mainly at the EU level, might initiate better self-regulation and bring their occupation to a profession. Otherwise, the citizens' distrust in domestic lobbying may politicize the occupation and finally lead to public regulation by or on behalf of the government.

WHAT MAY BE AN INTEREST GROUP'S SWOT VIS-À-VIS THIS EU?

With regard to its EU environment, every interest group has *internally* its Strengths and Weaknesses and *externally* its Opportunities and Threats, in short its SWOT. A well-organized interest group identifies its SWOT as standard practice with as input the collected I^2 and as output the updated strategic proposals to the board. This way it can perform better in the near future. Because no two interest groups are the same in every respect vis-à-vis the EU, we can raise here only SWOT challenges that are frequently relevant to many groups. As no group has ever been identified as fully 100 per cent strong or weak or fully in the winning or the losing mood, the following appetizer can be useful to all.

Internal Strengths Vis-à-Vis the EU?

1   *Is the PA excellent?* On the proxy quality measures, an interest group may show particular strengths, such as (almost) always operating not alone, but on platforms with varied stakeholders selected in an early phase. The group can then consider increasing its PA ambitions for the EU, for example getting a line expert inside a COM/DG, making an EP intergroup or getting a seat in comitology.

2   *Following the new trends?* Given the notified strengths, it can also decide to spend energy on better following the fresh PA trends of multiple routing, flexible ad hoc alliances and particularly the circular PA. All three make the two sides of the 2E coin even shinier.

3   *Is the group well-respected?* A respected position in its market or policy domain and ultimately in public opinion makes the interest group vis-à-vis other stakeholders and officials a 'nice guy', who can more easily collect important stakeholders for joint influence actions, so improving its 2E further.

4   *Good negotiation skills?* The EU and the routes into it require good negotiation skills. One makes friends by one's supply side and deals by one's demand side, and the two must be fine-tuned at the right time. In case of just 'bad luck' (no fault) a feasible 'loss compensation scenario' must be within reach.

5   *Lesson learning?* One learns less from one's own strengths, and more from the factors leading to a success. Was it maybe 'good luck'? Were the opponents really weak or did they have an even better compensation prize? If such questions are regularly posed and systematically answered, they help maintain excellence.

Internal Weaknesses Vis-à-Vis the EU?

1   *Weak internal organization?* In most interest groups this is the daily situation. For example:

PA is not a Board's responsibility, intelligence is absent, strategy is hardly criticized and PA is done in hope alone. Such a group is seldom invited on to a platform, must act alone, and obtains poor 2E and maybe worsening returns, boomerangs.

2   *Unfamiliar with the EU?* A group holding the value-judgement that 'the EU is really a labyrinth on a trampoline' demonstrates that it is unfamiliar with this 'foreign' EU. Instead of targeting the dossierchef or rapporteur, it goes for help to compatriots inside the EU that are seldom relevant on the matter. Once it gets lost, its board or the principal sees PA at the EU level as a waste of resources, and so it becomes.

3   *Reliance on domestic politics?* Some groups still rely on the old national route and hope to get a free ride from a ministry into the EU. Usually they get a polite ear and go home with false hope in the ministry's EU influence at home and in the EU. Instead of dreaming about the rewards from influencing the EU, they can better pay the costs of adaptation to what others decide.

4   *Circular PA?* This logical new PA trend is still absent in most groups with PA units at home and in the EU. Then, the one unit may not know or may even hinder what the other does. Often, the home unit, having the older position inside the group, opposes the circular integration. By intervention the board can improve its 2E both at home and in the EU.

5   *Learning for improvement?* In theory a weak group can make the greatest jump forwards, but in practice it often has big problems making the correct take-off and jump. To improve its PA in the EU, its board must direct its group first of all to study its failed cases and its stronger competitors, to internalize the PA homework (see above) and to act particularly prudently on the current dossiers.

External Opportunities Vis-à-Vis the EU?

1   *Honey and money?* The finest honey of the EU is the laws and rules that favour one's specific interest and replace twenty-eight codebooks with one. They offer big rewards. Smaller attractions are EU subsidies (the 90+ per cent of annual EU budget) that need a legal basis too and, once this is decided, bring a great deal of

red tape. By influencing the proposals for laws and rules, a group can get both better honey and less paperwork.

2   *Going via member-countries?* The construction of a fine-tuned M (platform) for better 2E can best start at home in one's sector, roll out to cross-sectoral partners there, move through all of them to other countries, and be filled up by shopping groups in some EuroFeds. The platform can offer a strong position vis-à-vis the institutions. Only integrated PA at home and in the EU can deliver such a platform efficiently.

3   *Enjoying EU polyarchy?* A polyarchical system may be rather unpredictable, but it also holds better moments and more open doors that one only has to identify. By negotiating skillfully, an interest platform can influence the timing of decisions, support from the inside and the final compromise made. Good PA management allows the fruits of polyarchy to be plucked.

4   *Having insourced experts?* The COM expert committees and the EP intergroups can be most helpful for influencing the substance of laws and delegated rules. The experts are recruited for their expertise but have an interest group's background. Each committee and intergroup is a small polyarchy and a form of insourced democracy. Any board should try to befriend people inside.

5   *Getting uphill position?* Although harder to realize than in the past, an uphill position in an arena remains a dream, because it implies better 2E and a tailwind for one's interests. Its build-up requires from PA management early planning (before an arena starts), silent upframing (reframing up to high social values) of its core interest (more 'general interest'), precise timing (ready at EU decision moments) and low public attention ('technical').

External Threats Vis-à-Vis the EU?

1   *Slope of social playing-field?* EU decisions can make an interest group's position in its market or policy domain more or less level. Each can be seen as a problem or a blessing. A more level one can threaten one's home privileges and a less level one its interests in cross-border expansion. Mid-term strategic thinking must give the answer to the question of which it is better to strive for. The EU trend is towards more level.

2   *Costs of (not) influencing?* Influencing the EU costs a lot of work, time, people and so on. Doing nothing brings the costs of complying with what others have decided. Both options have their balance sheet of costs and rewards that can be estimated and compared in advance and help the PA management to take the better decision. This is one standard method for stabilizing the long-list.

3   *New issues and scandals?* New arena-bound issues may arise during the influence process and partners on one's platform may be scandalized. Such events may threaten one's own position. Most new issues can be foreseen through anticipatory homework. Scandals can be minimized by respecting the SCARE-limits of PA, by selecting the partners prudently and by having a scandal management scenario within reach.

4   *Getting downhill position?* Many factors may make an arena's wind less friendly or even cold and bring one's platform downhill. They may come from, for example, politics in member-states (elections), at EU level (new COM), foreign countries (such as Ukraine) and/or global level (financial crises). As PA homework shows, no group is ever the sole loser. The many others suffering the same fate can strengthen one's M.

5   *Decline of domestic support?* At home, each interest group needs legitimacy and support amongst citizens. The rising EU-scepticism voiced by political parties and mass media may threaten its licence to operate in the EU. The interest groups operating in both the EU and often near the citizens at home can counter the decline by telling the citizens why the EU ('heaven nor hell') is at least relevant.

CONCLUSION

More than at the domestic level, in the uncommon EU system PA management must do a great deal of anticipatory homework, here laid down in six critical proxy measures. Traditional lobbying through corridors is only supplementary. The PA management at the EU level is, in short, the management of $2E= MI^2$. The work intensity is justified by the high relevance of the EU, which by its laws and rules can overrule the twenty-eight member-countries. Most interest groups are still in some phase of discovering and learning the EU basics, such as the system itself, the diversity of interests, the countless interest groups, the new trends and thus the basics of PA in the EU too. The SWOT above shows that each group has room to perform better in the EU and to gain more from it.

REFERENCES

Almond, G. and G. Powell (1966), *Comparative Politics*, Boston: Little Brown.

Althaus, M. (2015), 'Recruiting the competent lobbyist in Germany', in McGrath (2015), 76–100.

Beyers, J. and B. Kerremans (2007), 'Critical resource dependency and the Europeanization of domestic interest groups', in D. Coen, ed., *EU Lobbying: Empirical and Theoretical Studies*, Oxford: Oxford University Press.

BM (2013), *Guide to Effective Lobbying in Europe*, Brussels: Burson-Marsteller.

Buonanno, L. and N. Nugent (2013), *Policies and Policy Processes of the EU*, Basingstoke: Palgrave.

Commission (2014), *Anti-Corruption Report* (COM 2014/38), Brussels: European Commission.

Dahl, R. (1971), *Polyarchy*, New Haven: Yale University Press.

ETI (2014), *The European Transparency Initiative*, Brussels: European Commission and Parliament, available at http://europa.eu/eu-law/have-your-say/index_en.htm (accessed 28 June 2016).

EurActiv (2009), *Corporate PA Survey 2009*, Brussels, www.euractiv.com.

Greenwood, J. (2011), *Interest Representation in the EU*, Basingstoke: Palgrave.

Greenwood, J. and J. Dreger (2013), 'The transparency register: a European vanguard of strong lobby regulation?', *Interest Groups and Advocacy*, 2 (2), 139–62.

Holman, C. and W. Luneburg (2012), 'Lobbying and transparency: a comparative analysis of regulatory reform', *Interest Groups and Advocacy*, 1 (1), 75–104.

Hume, D. (1748), *An Enquiry Concerning Human Understanding*, London: Cadell.

Ladrech, R. (2010), *Europeanization and National Politics*, Basingstoke: Palgrave.

Leconte, C. (2010), *Understanding Euroscepticism*, Basingstoke: Palgrave.

McGrath, C. (2005), 'Towards a lobbying profession', *Journal of Public Affairs*, 5 (2), 124–35.

McGrath, C. (2006), 'The ideal lobbyist', *Journal of Communication Management*, 10 (1), 67–79.

McGrath, C., ed. (2015), 'Learning to lobby', special issue of *Interest Groups and Advocacy*, 4 (1), 1–100.

Mattila, M. and T. Raunio (2012), 'Drifting further apart on EU: national parties and their electorates', *Western European Politics*, 35 (3), 589–606.

Millar, C. and P. Köppl, eds (2014), 'Public affairs in central and eastern Europe', special issue of the *Journal of Public Affairs*, 14 (1), 1–83.

Neyer, J. and A. Wiener, eds (2011), *Political Theory of the EU*, Oxford: Oxford University Press.

Norris, P. (2011), *Democratic Deficit*, New York: Cambridge University Press.

Quitkat, C. (2011), 'The Commission's online consultations', *Journal of Common Market Studies*, 49 (3), 653–74.

Richardson, J., ed. (2012), *Constructing a Policy-making State?* Oxford: Oxford University Press.

Snyder, F., ed. (2012), 'Financial market regulation and economic governance', special issue of *European Law Review*, 18 (1), 1–161.

Spencer, T. and C. McGrath, eds (2008), *The Future of Public Trust*, London: Dods.

TI (2015), *Lobbying in Europe: Hidden Influence, Privileged Access*, Berlin: Transparency International.

Timmermans, A. (2015), 'The moving stages of PA in the Netherlands', in McGrath (2015), 25–39.

Van Schendelen, R. (2011), 'New trends of PA management at the EU level', *Journal of Public Affairs*, 12 (1), 39–46.

Van Schendelen, R. (2013), *The Art of Lobbying the EU: More Machiavelli in Brussels*, Amsterdam: Amsterdam University Press.

Wallace, H., M. A. Pollack and A. R. Young, eds (2014), *Policy-making in the European Union*, Oxford: Oxford University Press (7th edn).

Wonka, A., F. R. Baumgartner, C. Mahoney and J. Berkhout (2010), 'Measuring the size and scope of the EU interest group population', *European Union Politics*, 11 (3), 463–676.

WEBSITES

On the European Union

www.europa.eu   The most important EU site.

www.ecprd.org, www.ipex.eu and www.cosac.eu   EU parliaments' sites.

www.votewatch.eu   Independent site on EP Vote Statistics.

www.theparliament.com   News bulletin on the EP.

www.epthinktank.eu   The EP Research Services site.

www.amicuria.eu and www.curia.europa.eu Sites on the Court and its cases.

www.euractiv.com and www.euobserver.com Information sites.

www.agenceeurope.com   Daily news bulletin.

www.publications.eu   Site on EU publications.

www.europeanvoice.com and www.neurope.eu   Weeklies on EU.

www.eureporter.co.uk   Weekly newspaper on European countries.

www.eufeeds.eu and www.presseurop.eu Dailies on EU.

www.europeanbusinessreview.eu   Business review on EU.

www.europeanagenda.eu   Daily EU news on people and events.

www.thebrusselsconnection.be   Site   on Brussels'EU quarter.

On 'Public Affairs' Management Facilities and Circles

www.dods.eu   The leading directory of interest groups.

www.eurobrussels.com   The European Affairs Jobs site.

www.seap.be and www.epaca.org   Brussels-based PA networks.

www.theecpa.eu and www.appc.org.uk   UK sites on PA.

www.degepol.de and www.bdp-net.de   Two German PA-related sites.

www.afcl.net   The site of French PA consultancies.

www.alpac.at and www.oepav.at   Two Austrian sites.

www.bvpa.nl and www.apaa.cz   Dutch and Czech PA sites.

www.public-affairs.ch Swiss PA site.

www.aescop.com and www.ilchiostro.org Spanish and Italian sites.

www.pac.org, www.theaapc.org and www.alldc.org   US PA sites.

www.paceurope.eu   Pan-European network.

www.publicaffairsworld.com   PA services site.

On Academic Studies

www.sgeu-ecpr.org   The Political Science Research Group on the EU.

www.uaces.org   UK-based site on contemporary studies on Europe.

www.elprg.eu   The European Legislative Politics Research Group.

www.parties-and-elections.eu   The site about all elections in Europe.

www.ceeol.com   Central and Eastern European Online Library.

www.eustudies.org   US-based association of scholars on the EU.

www.councilforeuropeanstudies.org   US site on European studies.

www.ccsenet.org   Canadian scholars, also studying the EU.

20

Public Affairs in Europe

Alberto Bitonti and Phil Harris

To found a great empire for the sole purpose of raising up a people of customers, may at first sight appear a project fit only for a nation of shopkeepers.

It is, however, a project altogether unfit for a nation of shopkeepers; but extremely fit for a nation whose government is influenced by shopkeepers. (Adam Smith, *The Wealth of Nations*)

INTRODUCTION

Adam Smith's comments apply as much to the world and Europe now as they did in the eighteenth century to the UK, as we have seen the development of the world trading market, the internet and global regulatory influence and power. The world is increasingly run by shopkeepers and very full of customers.

Public affairs are at the heart of Europe, reflecting that it is the largest developed consumer market in the world, comprising more than forty national states and most of the key international businesses. Financial systems, organisations and regulatory bodies are based there.

The headquarters of the European Union in Brussels, which represents the 28 member states of the EU, has around it probably the largest concentration of the public affairs industry in the world,[1] reflecting the fact that the EU's economy is approximately 25 per cent of the world's GDP and it has a geographically concentrated population of more than 500 million at the centre of the modern world trade routes.[2]

In addition to this, the Eurasian Economic Union (EEU), headquartered in Moscow and representing the key former USSR states, including Russia, Belarus and Kazakhstan (totalling approximately 176 million citizens), is also there, right on the eastern side of the European continent. Other states not in these economic zones include Iceland, Norway, Ukraine, a number of smaller states and of course Switzerland. Switzerland, partially as a result of its historic neutrality and centrality in Europe, has become the home of one of the main headquarters of the United Nations, of several UN agencies (such as the World Health Organisation, the International Labour Organisation, the International Telecommunications Union and the World Intellectual Property Organisation) and of a number of other international bodies, such as the World Trade Organisation, the International Committee of the Red Cross and the International Organisation for Standardisation. The annual meeting of the World Economic Forum is also held in Switzerland (in Davos), bringing the top business and political figures together to discuss critical economic, environmental, health and societal issues impacting on the globe.

If we widen the perspective to the 47 member states of the Council of Europe, covering the whole European continent with their total population of around 800 million people and broad GDP close to 40 per cent of the world's output, we can obtain a clear picture of the influence of the area and understand why public affairs has grown to be the substantive industry it is in the continent. Europe is the home in currency terms and finances to the Euro, UK Pound, Swiss Franc and the Russian Rouble amongst others. It exerts a leadership role in setting the standards in environmental, financial and market regulations, with centres such as Brussels, Geneva, Berlin, London, Moscow and Paris all playing pivotal roles in fields relevant to worldwide markets.

Considering all of this, it is evident how Europe as a continent appears an extremely interesting area to study for those dealing with public affairs in complex scenarios.

In order to gain a picture of public affairs in Europe, we have decided to look at four major countries belonging to the EU, one from the west (the UK), one from the south (Italy), one from the east (Bulgaria) and one from the north (Sweden). The result in the UK of the European Referendum on Membership of the EU in June 2016, with a Narrow BREXIT vote to leave shows both the

tensions and differences within Europe. It will inevitably take time to work out the best way forward for the EU and UK and lead to a significant growth of the public affairs industry in London and Brussels to deal with ongoing relations and trade deals. The chronic shortage of trade deal experience and negotiators in the UK has delayed and highlighted the complexity of the area. In contrast to the chapter on PA at EU institutional level, we chose to take into consideration these four case studies as they differ not only as to geographical collocation, but also for cultural, institutional and political reasons, thus representing a wide variety of public affairs environments (a more complete and detailed analysis is developed in Bitonti and Harris, 2017). In the next paragraphs we'll give an overview of the public affairs industry in each of these four countries, trying to gain some general insights about the character of public affairs in Europe in our conclusion.

THE UK

In 1994 the phrase 'Machiavellian marketing' (Harris, 1994) was coined in Manchester to sum up exerting pressure and influencing government for strategic gain. This conceptualisation of political lobbying as part of marketing was born against a backdrop of a dramatic rise in lobbying in the UK and a major growth over the previous two decades in the public affairs industry. Interestingly the term *lobby* is often more associated with Westminster than Washington, as it refers to a number of halls where Members of Parliament can meet constituents or visitors to discuss interests. Thus dialogue to influence policy and decision making in the lobbies of the oldest large-scale parliament in Europe gave the name to a whole professional activity: *lobbying*, indeed.

If we look at the UK parliament it appears very much like a medieval maze, which is a distinct feature of older European parliaments and to some extent equivalent legislatures

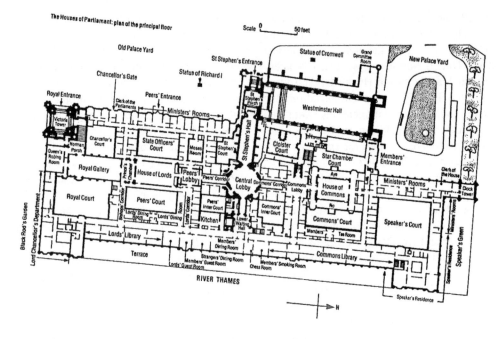

Figure 20.1   Plan of the prime floor of Westminster Parliament

around the world. The map in Figure 20.1 is that of Westminster, where the UK parliament meets and Machiavelli would have been very much at home, watching intrigues and power being used to influence policy. From the map you can see it has endless lobbies, corridors and courts, an ideal place for intrigue and for the light and the dark of policy making, where public affairs professionals come into play.

Professional large-scale lobbying and the development of the public affairs industry received a major boost in the UK in the 1980s, when the Conservative Government's monetarist policy and privatisation of state-owned industries led to much reshaping and change of ownership of the business land-scape. Lobby or lose out seemed to be the order of the day. Thus occasional lobbying became a thing of the past, moving to a much more sophisticated public affairs manage-ment approach, where communications spe-cialists, corporate lawyers, strategic business management figures and regulators moved into the arena to set strategy for corporate gain and advantage. In the 1990s a number of

companies and organisations focused on pub-lic affairs had emerged, and it had become a distinct boardroom function.

This process has further evolved over time throughout the UK via local and regional government influences, for instance on the evolution of retail development and green belt policy. More recently the announced divestment of Royal Bank of Scotland shares and sale of the Post Office are good exam-ples of the ongoing process of transferring ownership to the private sector. Public affairs influence around these issues is inevitable and has played a major part in financial, tele-communications and infrastructure invest-ments. One of the current largest public affairs campaigns is around the development of Heathrow Airport, to ensure it is the world's largest airport hub. This is an ongoing public affairs campaign involving government, busi-ness interests, counter pressure groups and local residents, much like the development there of Terminal Four was a decade ago.

It has been suggested that the subject of this area is very much part of political marketing and has a number of common characteristics that are associated with what has come to be called 'relationship marketing' and particularly business-to-business marketing.

Research suggests that many of the theoretical constructs developed and used by those associated with the Industrial Marketing and Purchasing (IMP) group of marketing internationalist and network-orientated researchers offer appropriate tools and models to understand this complex area. Work in the area (Harris et al., 1999; Griffin et al., 2001; Moss et al., 2012) confirms the substantial growth of political lobbying and public affairs work, which has been particularly stimulated by globalisation and the rise of national and international regulatory activity. Politicians and government officials have confirmed the increasing importance of this activity and the need to provide quality information, to understand the international political system and to have good personal ethical values to maintain integrity and trust and gain regular entry into the decision-making process.

The key functions which a number of practising public affairs figures have identified as being essential to fulfilling their role include the following:

- Understanding own organisation's communication and decision-making process
- Knowing the policy formulation and policy-making process
- Network of contacts in area of operation
- Dealing with the civil service
- Dealing with parliament
- Dealing with politicians
- Dealing with ministers
- Dealing with the media
- Dealing with regulators
- Dealing with local and regional government
- Dealing with trade bodies
- Dealing with transnational government and associated bodies
- Contacts with party organisations
- Managing relationships with policy think tanks, etc.
- Coalition building with others around mutual policy interests
- Managing relationships with community stakeholders

- Gaining access to regular sources of policy information.

These functions form the core area of political lobbying and associated marketing activity in the UK but also more widely the developing lobbying functions in Europe. They predominantly cover external relationships and avenues for exerting policy influence. Yet, the attention paid thus far by business and management and political science research and teaching has tended to downplay or ignore many of these key lobbying functions.

In the UK, lobbying has its origins as an organised process just prior to the Second World War. Early forms of it were evidenced alongside the Port Wine Trade and associated tax levels and exemption as early as the 1950s (Sousa, 1999). However, until the 1990s many politicians in the UK denied the existence of lobbying, with the Labour Party suggesting in 1996 that it was going to ban lobbying if elected in 1997, which of course it did not. In October 1994, the Standards in Public Life Committee under Lord Nolan was established. The committee was established by Prime Minister John Major in response to concerns that conduct by some politicians was unethical, arising from exposures of some parliamentarians' activities in the press. The committee's original terms of reference were:

> To examine current concerns about standards of conduct of all holders of public office, including arrangements relating to financial and commercial activities, and make recommendations as to any changes in present arrangements which might be required to ensure the highest standards of propriety in public life. (Nolan, 1995)

The term *public office* includes ministers, civil servants and advisers, Members of Parliament and UK Members of the European Parliament, members and senior officers of all non-departmental public bodies and of national health service bodies, non-ministerial office holders, members and other senior officers of other bodies discharging publicly funded functions, and elected members and senior officers of local authorities.

Nolan made a number of recommendations, but the core proposals were set out in the Seven Principles of Public Life, which are now seen as the core principles for ministers and officials to follow (see Box 20.1). The Nolan Principles have been adopted widely in the UK and internationally.

The focus of lobbying and much public affairs work has tended to be on government departments and parliament, and influencing regulatory legislation and government policy. In the late 1990s there was a steady increase in lobbying to influence local government around developing retail outlets and associated infrastructure improvements.

The prime reasons for the growth of political lobbying and strategic public affairs work in the UK can be seen longitudinally in Table 20.1.

Table 20.1 uses a stages model adapted from the conceptualisation, constructs and framework of Rostow's (1960) work 'The Stages of Economic Growth', which outlines the key political policy issues and economic and social background to the rise of lobbying in the UK and its growing strategic importance for management.

The steady evolution of change within the British business economy and government policy making is outlined in Table 20.1. Public affairs activity began to increase in response to government selling public assets and monopoly licences to the private sector and the steady rise in government activity. The rise of globalisation and the emergence of trade blocs that adopt a strong harmonisation and regulatory approach in economic and social policies were all significant factors in the growth in levels of activity and the strategic importance of the management of political lobbying and public affairs work.

Throughout the period to the late 1970s, the relationships between business and government were orderly in the sense that both parties knew what the likely intentions of the other party were. Contact was regularised via trade organisations, trade unions and formalised structures between government and business interests (Winch, 1969; Middlemas, 1986; Kavanagh and Morris, 1989; Cook and Stevenson, 1996). This regularised network broke down in the late 1970s in the UK and alternative mechanisms became necessary to influence government (Lawson, 1992; Hutton, 1995; Marr, 1995; Andrews 1996; Harris and Lock, 1996). In addition,

---

Box 20.1   The seven principles of public life

- **Selflessness** – Holders of public office should act solely in terms of the public interest. They should not do so in order to gain financial or other benefits for themselves, their family or their friends.
- **Integrity** – Holders of public office should not place themselves under any financial or other obligation to outside individuals or organisations that might seek to influence them in the performance of their official duties.
- **Objectivity** – In carrying out public business, including making public appointments, awarding contracts, or recommending individuals for rewards and benefits, holders of public office should make choices on merit.
- **Accountability** – Holders of public office are accountable for their decisions and actions to the public and must submit themselves to whatever scrutiny is appropriate to their office.
- **Openness** – Holders of public office should be as open as possible about all the decisions and actions they take. They should give reasons for their decisions and restrict information only when the wider public interest clearly demands.
- **Honesty** – Holders of public office have a duty to declare any private interests relating to their public duties and to take steps to resolve any conflicts arising in a way that protects the public interest.
- **Leadership** – Holders of public office should promote and support these principles by leadership and example.

Table 20.1   Evolution of modern public affairs and lobbying in UK

Period/Government Policy Making	Main Economic & Societal Trends for Business
1940s	
Impact of Second World War	Command Economy
Full Employment Policy	
Nationalisation: Bank of England, Coal,	Creation of Welfare State
Cable & Wireless, Civil Aviation,	
Electricity, Gas, Transport and	State Control
Iron and Steel Industries	
Creation of National Health Service	
House Building Act promotes Council Houses	
1950s	
Denationalisation of Iron and Steel,	State Control in a Mixed Economy End of Empire
Formation of European Community	
UK does not join	

600 pages of legislation on average year pass through Parliament per annum (Hansard Society, 1992)

1960s	
Incomes Policy introduced	Government Intervention
Re-nationalisation of key industrial sectors. Creation of	
Dept of Health and Social Security	
Entry to EC rejected in 1963 and 1967	Mixed Economy
1970s	
Rolls Royce taken into public ownership	State Control & Intervention
Three-Day Week/Miners Strike	
1973 joins EC, confirmed by referendum 1975	
British Leyland formed	
National Enterprise Board	Mixed Economy
In 1976 Government intervention in economy	
reaches 49 per cent of GDP	
IMF Loan	
Aircraft and Shipbuilding Act, establishes	
British Aerospace and British Shipbuilders	
1979, Privatisation of BP and council house sale policy	Start of Privatisation Policy
1980s	
Privatisation: Aerospace, Cable & Wireless,	Anti-Corporatism Move to De-Regulation and
Amersham International, National Freight,	Privatisation Growth of UK Government
Britoil, British Ports, Enterprise Oil, Jaguar,	Regulatory Policies
British Telecom, Gas, British Airways,	
Royal Ordinance, Rolls Royce, Airports	
Authority, Rover Group, British Steel and	
Water	
DHSS divided into Health and	
Social Security Departments.	
Increasing EU intervention	Rising EU Regulation
1986 Single European Act	

(Continued)

Table 20.1   Evolution of modern public affairs and lobbying in UK (*Continued*)

Period/Government Policy Making	*Main Economic & Societal Trends for Business*
2000 pages of legislation go through parliament in an average year (Hansard Report, 1992)	
1990s	
Privatisation: Electricity and Rail track	Emergence of the Regulatory State in UK, EU,
Maastricht Treaty in EU (formerly EC)	Trade blocs
Allows extension of community policy	
Involvement into Economic and Monetary	
Union, Environment and Defence. Treaty of	
European Union 1991. Leave ERM.	
Labour Electoral Landslide 1997	
Do not join first wave of EURO	BSE Crisis at height 1998
Scottish and Welsh Parliaments formed	
2000s	
Public Private Partnerships	Major capital projects initiated, hospitals
9/11 Impact	schools etc.
2001 and 2005 Labour Electoral wins	
Iraq War 2003	
Remain outside Euro Zone	
EU enlargement goes Eastwards	
Blair is replaced by Brown as PM	
Financial Crash 2008	Regulation of Financial system and banks.
2010s	
Coalition Conservative/Liberal Democrat	Austerity budgets
Government formed 2010	Cuts in Public Sector budgets
Scottish Independence Referendum	Public Sector freeze in expenditure
Treaty of Lisbon	
Conservative Government formed May 2015	
Estimate that 10,000 pages of legislation now goes through parliament (authors Source), (Based on author's research and adaptation of Rostow [1960] historic stages model)	

government increasingly adopted the role of regulator of a number of key public and private sector business areas from which it had been forced for fiscal reasons to withdraw (Foster and Plowden, 1996).

The increasing regulatory role of government in the economy and society can be seen in a comparison of the amount of legislation generated in the key time periods (which is indicated in Table 20.1), which shows a trebling in legislation between the 1960s and 1990s. This has doubled again in the past decade. There is clearly an emerging correlation between the increasing amount of legislation by government to regulate markets and increases in political lobbying activity to amend or stop regulation.

The volume of legislation from the UK, Welsh, Northern Irish and Scottish assemblies and parliaments suggests that only proactive organisations will be able to take a strategic approach and use political lobbying for competitive advantage, as these actors will be monitoring potential developments rather than just responding to emerging legislation. This, because of scale, gives advantage to larger organisations that can maintain many of the tracking and intelligence-gathering systems and processes suggested by issues management approaches (Heath, 1990; 1997). Alternatively, to exert pressure and influence, one has to be part of a confederation of interests, such as the Confederation of British Industry (CBI), Chambers of Commerce, Federation of Small Businesses or Institute of Directors in the business sector.

The Rise of Regulation

Lobbying and public affairs management has grown as a result of business and non-governmental organisations wishing to influence government regulatory policy. As government has sold its ownership of control of various sectors of the economy – utilities, broadcasting, etc. – it has tried to shape the direction of these now private companies or organisations and their interests through regulation. In fact, the last part of the twentieth century and early part of the twenty-first century has seen government at every level develop regulation. To influence that regulation leads to strategic gain for the organisation. If you can shape the market to your advantage then you win, and lobbying is about shaping that regulation so that it suits you and your interests.

There has been a growth in public affairs work and particularly lobbying because as government has withdrawn from its role of being owner in the economy it has attempted to regulate and set the business environment for companies to operate in. However, the more competitive companies and NGOs influence that regulation to their own competitive advantage. Regulation of the industry has been erratic until recently, with a focus most recently on a register of lobbying companies rather than on in-house public affairs work. Only 7 of 19 European countries have measures in place to regulate lobbying, according to a comprehensive report by Transparency International (TI). These countries are the UK, Austria, France, Ireland, Lithuania, Poland and Slovenia.

In their recent study, TI scored each country plus the European Commission, the European Parliament and the Council of the EU on transparency, integrity and equality of access. Overall marks indicated the strength of a country's or organisation's lobbying regulations and efforts to promote ethical lobbying. The UK scored 44 per cent overall, exceeding the 31 per cent average score. TI applauded the level of self-regulation among UK professional bodies, citing the CIPR and APPC codes of conduct as well as a vigorous complaint mechanism. Areas for improvement included the oversight of the lobbying register and greater transparency in the public sector, such as the way in which politicians declare their interests. The UK's lobbying register was launched on 25 March 2015, a year after the Lobbying Act was introduced, and had 53 listed agencies at the time of going to press (Sulit, 2015).

Slovenia ranked first with an overall score of 55 per cent, thanks to a 'fairly robust' lobbying register and an anti-corruption agency that regularly sends out reports of public sector and lobbying contacts. It is also the only country with mandatory 'cooling-off' periods before former MPs assume lobbying positions that potentially create conflicts of interest.

Hungary and Cyprus received the lowest marks in the TI study, the former due to ill-designed regulations coupled with 'a culture of impunity' surrounding political influencing and the latter for its non-existent lobbying laws.

Lobbying is part of modern political communication. As politicians become increasingly isolated and short of quality information, effective lobbying fills up that vacuum and allows good decision making (and of course sometimes bad decision making). Globalisation means that to gain competitive edge transnationally, public affairs campaigns are used to influence transnational bodies such as the EU, WTO, NATO, etc.

Another trend is of course accountability. Lobbying has to be seen to be accountable like government and to be of a high ethical standard. As society has higher demands, so it will want its voices heard; society will become more consumer driven and government will have to become more responsive to consumer needs. Consumers need to lobby for quality of life and for resources to be spent on priority areas. All that we can say is that we can be sure of one thing: as government increasingly develops a regulatory society, so lobbying and public affairs will grow. As regards training this is still very much focused on the job and expertise is bought in or headhunted. There are some specific PA courses, notably at Brunel, Chester and Cranfield universities but these are limited and there needs to be a major development of strategic work in this area to support this booming industry.

SWEDEN

The Swedish case is quite interesting, and can be used as a good example of the situation in Nordic countries.

The Swedish constitution in its current form dates from 1975, and rests on the key principles evolved in many European states in the eighteenth and nineteenth centuries as part of the transformation to a modern democratic and transparent society. Sweden has been at the forefront of democracy, being for instance the first country to introduce freedom of the press in 1776. The need for transparency and quality reportage is indeed very evident throughout all of Swedish society,[3] as this long tradition of openness and transparency reflects a strong respect of the rule of law and very low levels of perceived and experienced corruption (De Fouloy, 2015).

The political and administrative system is divided into three levels: national, regional and local/municipal. The political parties operating on regional and local levels are broadly the same as those that operate at the national level. General elections are held every four years, with national,

regional, and local elections always held on the same day. There are 349 members of the national parliament (Riksdag). Parties must receive at least 4 per cent of national votes or 12 per cent in a single constituency, to be represented in the Riksdag, which limits the number of parties involved in political decision-making processes at the national level. There are currently eight parties represented in the Riksdag. The Prime Minister is formally elected by the parliament but is proposed by the Speaker of Parliament (for a more detailed analysis, see Hedlund, 2017).

Sweden is divided into 290 local municipalities and 20 regions. Based on the concept of thematic autonomy, each of these wields great decision-making power within their geographical area. Municipalities and regions have the authority to decide on many issues; they have the right to raise taxation and local rates or service delivery fees, but also receive significant subsidies from the government.

The political culture in Sweden has a number of distinct features, all of which have consequences for public affairs. The political culture is characterised by cooperation and consensus. Similar to the UK, there is a significant trend to pluralism and a fast-moving multi-dimensional state where social media and transparency are to the fore. This allows for greater lobbying opportunities in a very well-defined, transparent public affairs environment.

Politics today, however, are characterised by a general trend of political pluralism marked by increased complexity and speed. This enables more extensive lobbying as the lobbyists often serve as sources of information for politicians. According to De Fouloy (2015), 'Sweden's population of lobbyists has gone from around 100 some 20 years ago, to somewhere between 700 and 800 today. As many as 37 percent of former lawmakers, top aides and appointed senior public servants have gone on to work as lobbyists after the end of their political tenure'.

Public affairs – and lobbying specifically – is something that Sweden is very much in denial about. There's plenty of it going on, of course, but many choose to believe that Sweden's self-proclaimed transparency makes public affairs practice essentially one of glorified information provision. This is far from the truth, but it does mean that there would be a reluctance to engage directly with a tabooed subject such as lobbying rather than, say, strategic communication or external relations.

The pre-eminent Swedish institution in this area is Berghs School of Communication and it runs a one-year programme called Strategic Communication (http://www.berghs.se/kurser-utbildningar/strategisk-kommunikation-heltid). One of the courses on this programme is called Samhällskontakter which is 'public affairs' in Swedish. It's taught over three to four weeks and has been led by the Director of Corporate Affairs at British American Tobacco in Sweden. There are, of course, other Swedish universities and training companies offering courses in PR and communication, but apart from the course at Berghs and the MSc in Strategic Public and Political Marketing at Stockholm University there are no other institutions offering a course in public affairs.

During the past decade, though, the parliamentary situation has become more complex following the break-up of what was effectively a Swedish social democratically dominated state. Since 2010, eight different parties are represented in the parliament and, as a result, growing difficulties to form political majorities can be observed, also stimulating a growth in public affairs around various key economic and social issues. Even without specific lobbying regulations, the Swedish case appears a good example of how political and civic cultural elements directly affect the way public affairs and lobbying are perceived and experienced in a given environment.

ITALY

Italy is very different from the environment of UK or Scandinavia; in fact, public affairs in the countries on the southern shores of Europe presents quite distinctive features. A very typical case for this area is represented by Italy (with some analogies to be found in Spain, Portugal and Greece), through which we will try to shed some light on the most important elements of the public affairs industry of this area of Europe.

In Italy the concepts of public affairs and especially the term *lobbying* are considered with suspicion, owing to philosophical, historical, legal and communicational reasons.

The philosophical reason is in the prevailing conception of the public interest, deemed by the common feeling as a substantial normative standard to be 'preserved' by public decision-makers. According to this conception, public decision-makers ought to keep their point of view as pure as possible in order not to be influenced by private or particular interests, thus considering lobbying a potential dangerous distortion from public interest itself (this vision is better explained in Chapter 8 of this volume and in Bitonti and Harris, 2017).

The historical reason lies in the role of political parties (and additionally of trade unions and the industrialists' confederation) in the public decision-making process. At least until the last decade of twentieth century, political parties were considered the only strongly legitimate actors of political participation, so public affairs and lobbying activities could not find room outside this framework, in a kind of 'closed competition' for political representation easily won by political parties.

The legal reason is represented by the absence of any specific regulation of lobbying in the country. This contributes to covering a whole area of activities with shade and opacity, thus putting legitimate public affairs activities and illegitimate actions of influence-peddling on the same plan.

This brings us to the last reason, which we may define as 'communicational': much of the public discourse about public affairs and lobbying is biased by this very substantial

confusion about the differences between lobbying and influence-peddling, apparently not
sufficiently clear to most journalists working
in Italian media.

It is not a surprise, then, that most lobbyists and PA professionals in the country (both
consultants and in-house) often choose more
'neutral' labels such as 'institutional affairs' or
'government relations' to describe their jobs.

Significant changes, though, have affected
the Italian political system in recent decades,
producing a more fertile ground for public
affairs in the country, despite the aforementioned strong prejudices. In fact, the conditions and the degree of development of the
PA industry may be seen as dependent on
a number of factors in the Italian political
system that have changed significantly over
time.

Among the most important factors, we
must consider the institutional structure of
the government and the party system.

After the fascist era and the Second World
War, Italy took the form of a parliamentary
republic, according to the newly written constitution approved in 1947. This means that
most power lay in the hands of the legislative
branch (made of two democratically elected
chambers – the Chamber of Deputies and
the Senate), whereas the executive branch
(appointed by the President of the Republic,
who in his turn is elected by the Members of
the Parliament) has to receive the 'confidence'
of the parliament itself. However, in order to
better understand the real functioning of the
governmental process, this institutional set-
up needs to be analysed in combination with
the party system, which has contributed to
'bending' the system in different directions at
different historical times. A first period (usually known in Italy as 'the First Republic')
is identified from 1948 to 1992–3. During
these 45 years, which overlap with a looming
Cold War, Italy witnessed a polarised pluralist party system (Sartori, 1976), where the
Christian Democrats (considered the defenders of Italy's permanence in the Western
bloc) always held the majority of votes, in

opposition to a very strong Communist Party
(counting on around one third of the electorate), to the Socialist Party and other minor
parties[4] (Colarizi, 1996). In that scenario,
political participation was very high and it
found expression mainly through political
parties (this is evident from indicators such as
electoral turnouts[5] and political party memberships[6]), also thanks to a proportional electoral law. An additional element to consider
in the picture is the strong intervention of the
state in the economic field, with major state-
owned enterprises in all the strategic sectors
(public utilities, energy, transportation, telecommunications, defence, etc.).

As a result, political parties were the main
actors of both the institutional and social
environment, able to make the most relevant
decisions even in the economic sphere, leaving little or no room for a professional and
autonomous public affairs industry.

Many of these factors saw substantial
changes after 1992–3, changes which determined the beginning of the so-called 'Second
Republic'.[7] The fall of the Soviet Union, the
end of the Cold War, the explosion of huge
scandals of corruption and bribery which
struck the parties running the country for
decades, the adoption of a new electoral
law (mostly majoritarian, in contrast to the
old proportional system) and the creation of
brand new political parties caused a sudden
change of the whole Italian political system
(Guarnieri, 2006). In the following decades –
at least until 2013 – the political system saw
the emergence of a two-pole party system
(centre-right and centre-left), which governed alternatively for twenty years,[8] pushing
Italy towards a majoritarian set-up (Lijphart,
1999). The new situation was also favoured
by the increasing personalisation of the
political sphere (with a new role of political marketing and political communication,
especially on TV) and by a growing concentration of substantial power in the executive
branch (through a bigger use of decree laws
in comparison with the past). We must also
combine this with a vast process of economic

reforms, which privatised many of the previously state-owned enterprises in a wide liberalisation effort.

These changes created much more favourable conditions for the growth of a public affairs industry, which actually began to rise in those years.

In the new era of the Second Republic, political parties, labour (trade unions) and industrialists' organisations kept playing a predominant role, but evidently the need for political representation could not be fulfilled only by these actors any more. In fact, several new subjects appeared on the public scene – small and medium-sized enterprises, NGOs, the old state-owned enterprises now having to compete in an open market, as well as many new associations of citizens, eager to influence the government, even without and outside political parties[9] (Antonucci, 2014). This is how a true public affairs industry could be born and slowly begin to thrive, in the form of both in-house lobbyists and external consultants for hire.

Unfortunately, the public perception of the professionals working in the PA sector has not changed much since then: in the public discourse, as well as in most news reports, lobbyists are still viewed with suspicion as something obscure or having to do with corruption (Transparency International Italia, 2014).[10] Much of this negative fame derives – among the other factors mentioned above – from the absence of a specific regulation of lobbying.

Even if several legislative attempts at lobbying regulation have been made since 1976, none of these bills became a law, presumably because of the cultural diffidence mentioned above, which brings most politicians to deny the role of interest politics at least in the public discourse (contributing to keeping the whole field of interests' representation in the shade). Of course this does not mean that lobbying activities do not take place in most decision-making processes.

Even beyond the constitutional covering of lobbying (which is guaranteed by various

provisions in the Italian Constitution, such as articles 2, 3, 18, 49, 50), some indirect regulation actually exists: for instance, in the rules regulating the functioning of the Chamber of Deputies and the Senate, some specific rules are dedicated to the process of formation of a bill and to the preliminary assessment of the effects of any proposed piece of legislation, also through the consultation of stakeholders in hearings (article 79 of the Rules of the Chamber of Deputies; article 43 of the Rules of the Senate). A similar provision affects the Executive Branch and the preliminary analysis of decisions to be taken by the Council of Ministers (Law No. 50 of 1999 and Law No. 246 of 2005; see Petrillo, 2011), even if no provisions regulate the consultation processes in detail or describe standard procedures.

Considering the absence of a specific lobbying regulation (a few experiments have only recently been launched by the Chamber of Deputies and by some Ministries), it is hard to estimate the number of people working in the PA industry in Italy. The only available data concern the number of associates in a few professional associations dedicated to PA, namely Il Chiostro (specifically dedicated to lobbyists, having around 100 members) and FERPI (dedicated to the wider world of public relations, having around 850 members). Alongside various initiatives to promote the culture of transparency in PA and other training opportunities, Il Chiostro elaborated an Ethical Code to be subscribed to by all the members of the association, providing guidelines of ethical conduct and sanctions for the transgressors.

In addition to the education and training activities provided by professional associations, a number of university courses and Masters programmes have been created in the 2000s, symptoms of the growing interest in the world of public affairs, the standing of which is still far from being socially recognised (mainly because of the reasons aforementioned), but which offers an increasing number of job opportunities both as in-house PA professionals in organisations (still the predominant form of employment) and as consultants in agencies.

To conclude, the Italian industry of PA is definitely growing, at least since the advent of the 'Second Republic' in 1992–3, with major problems deriving from the lack of specific regulation and from the strong prejudices which still survive in the public opinion against the word *lobbying*. The abolition of state-funding for political parties (abolished in 2014, completely coming into effect in 2017), the constant growth of political think tanks as well as a thriving private sector (both for-profit and not-for-profit), will definitely continue to favour the growth of the PA industry, especially in a country such as Italy where important initiatives against corruption[11] have been recently implemented (often under the impulse of EU institutions), and where the political game maintains a crucial role in shaping important sectors of the economy and society.

BULGARIA

Our last case, Bulgaria, is quite useful in order to illustrate some of the characteristics of the PA industry in Eastern Europe, specifically as a country that belonged to the former Soviet bloc and witnessed a quick transition to democracy in the 1990s (even if with specific features within the Central and Eastern European general picture; see Mihova, 2014).

In fact, even if lobbying activities exist in both democratic and non-democratic regimes (with very different channels and modalities of course; see Pirgova, 2002), for the purposes of this chapter we can say that public affairs in Bulgaria came into existence only after 1990, with the democratic transition.

Now, considering the lack of a pre-existing democratic environment with its social and political features (such as a lively civil society, a mature political arena, trust towards institutions), it is not surprising that most of the lobbying activities in the new democratic

set-up saw foreign actors take a prominent role (Lewis and Benson, 2014). In fact, especially in the first phase of democratic transition, the same institution-building process of Bulgarian political society was strongly affected by the intervention of foreign subjects (governments as well as private organisations), aiming to remove the traces of the previous regime and to promote their respective strategic interests (Mavrov, 2011; Dineva, 2017), with think tanks emerging as leading actors of the new democratic policy-making process (Lavergne, 2008).

The fragmented Bulgarian society, experiencing in those years unknown levels of social differentiation and disintegration (Tsakova, 2005), appeared more a battle-ground for the entities aiming to design the new political equilibria than the actor playing its natural role as main character of the new phase.

In fact, especially in the first years of the post-Communist transition, many civil society organisations appeared strongly politicised, backed by the main national political parties, or dependent on foreign funding for their survival. The absence of an autonomous social activism led some even to deny that lobbying in the positive sense was possible in Bulgaria, even years after.[12]

It is worth mentioning how the very perception of lobbying and public affairs in Bulgaria is strictly dependent on whether a national or international framework is considered, and that there is a wide dissonance between what experts and the public refer to as *lobbying*. If experts conceive lobbying activities according to the Western or American meaning (Duvanova, 2009), in general the word has 'become a term used to explain any practice or phenomenon that remains non-transparent, non-public, "behind the scenes" in the political-institutional process' (Transparency International Bulgaria, 2014).

No differently from other countries of Europe, philosophical, historical, cultural and legal reasons can be pointed out as responsible for the diffident approach towards this field of activities (Millar and Köppl, 2014).

The conception of the relationship between the state and private interests and the cultural and political heritage deriving from 50 years of Communism – are two predominant factors determining the vision of lobbying in Bulgaria. Be that as it may, the legal framework of interests' representation has an immediate impact on the public perception as well.

As is the case in Italy, there is no specific regulation of lobbying activities in Bulgaria, in spite of a clear constitutional cover (the right of every citizen to petition and make proposals to the public authorities, stated in article 45 of the Bulgarian Constitution). However, relevant pieces of legislation can be found elsewhere, such as in the law on conflicts of interests (adopted in 2008) and the law on political parties (adopted in 2005), in addition to other normative provisions concerning some special laws (the Trade Act, the Public Procurement Law, the Concessions Law, the Municipal Ownership Law, the State Property Law, the Law on Commodity Exchanges and Wholesale Markets, the Law for the Civil Servant and the Law for the Administration), aiming to regulate the disclosure of information, the prevention of potential conflict between private and public interests or the objective, impartial and lawful exercise of power and obligations of service (Mavrov, 2011).

In particular, it is worth mentioning the Law on Political Parties, regulating the overall activity of political parties, their funding opportunities, participation in commercial companies and reporting obligations. Specifically, political parties are not allowed to receive funds from legal entities, from religious institutions, from foreign governments, companies or NGOs or to receive anonymous donations, and both political parties and election candidates are not allowed to receive donations from physical persons beyond the limit of 10,000 leva (around €5,000) per year. In addition, political parties have to keep a public register (which needs to be available on their websites) including information about all the donations received, the properties, the annual financial statement and election campaigns' financial statements.

According to Mavrov, the 'main flaw associated with the transparency of financing of the election campaigns is that in this sphere there are almost no existing regulations and the ones that do exist are not harmonized and coordinated', thus creating a possibility for corruption practices and other abuses (Mavrov, 2011; Transparency International Bulgaria, 2014).

So, while corruption continues to be perceived as a major problem by the majority of the population, as far as the PA industry is concerned the lack of a coherent and systematic regulation of the representation of interests determines a picture where the equality of access to decision-makers is quite low and where a transparent and open governmental process is still a long way from being achieved.

In addition to that, a weak civil society continues to play a crucial part in the story. Even in recent years, the picture of Bulgarian NGOs appears to have deteriorated, with many organisations barely striving to survive and many quitting their activities, and with little or no monetary help provided for them in public budgets (Dineva, 2017).

Considering this scenario, it is not surprising that lobbying and public affairs still lack an autonomous professional standing, with no training courses or professional Masters programmes dedicated to this activity, and with no professional associations representing the category, except for the wider-range association representing PR agencies, the BAPRA (Bulgarian Association of Public Relations Agencies).

Without an autonomous professional standing and a proper (moral but also juridical) legitimacy to exist, lobbying activities in Bulgaria will continue to be inappropriately associated with the bad public image mentioned above, as something obscure and dull, having more to do with influence-peddling, corruption and clientelism than with democracy. Rise in public attention towards this field is visible anyway, testified by a number of bills on lobbying presented in the Bulgarian National Assembly in the past 15 years and by a growing number of publications on this topic.

The entry of Bulgaria into the European Union in 2007 has certainly represented a spark for greater attention towards the whole Bulgarian PA industry, considering the European Union's constant concerns about corruption both at governance level and as regards EU funds (Mihova, 2014). Analysts and politicians express different views on how to deal with lobbying in the country (Mavrov, 2011; Transparency International Bulgaria, 2014; Dineva, 2017), but it is evident that the model of consultation and interests' representation expressed by the EU Commission appears to be very influential for Bulgarian experts, whose main concern, however, is the adoption of a model consistent with Bulgarian social and political characteristics, and not adapted mechanically from a foreign environment that is different to the Bulgarian context. This is a concern that can certainly be shared by many Eastern European countries.

CONCLUSION

Europe is one of the most diverse continents in the world, with more than 40 nation states within its borders and some of the oldest and most established democratic traditions and parliaments. As a matter of fact, important decisions concerning financial, trading, environmental and social policies affecting markets worldwide are taken in Europe every day, with centres such as Brussels, Berlin, Geneva, London and Paris fulfilling the role of hubs of a huge and complex web of power. Public affairs live on that power, and are nurtured by the relationships between these centres of power and decision making and the various subjects in society: corporations, NGOs, etc. That is why studying and

understanding how public affairs vary in the different corners of Europe can help PA professionals to deal with this complex and multi-faceted landscape, made of different historical backgrounds, institutional systems, political traditions and cultural attitudes.

In order to shed some light on this complex reality, we chose to give an overview of the public affairs industries in four different European countries. In the UK a long democratic tradition has produced a thriving public affairs industry; in Sweden a strong culture of participation seems to shape the natural contours of lobbying and political influence. In Italy the predominant role of political parties is a heavy legacy of the twentieth century, but new opportunities were created within a renovated political system; in Bulgaria an ongoing process of civil society development seems to be the beacon for totally overcoming the non-democratic past, changing the way businesses and NGOs deal with the government and public decision-makers.

In all the countries analysed, critical issues seem to be an increased regulation of lobbyists and a greater transparency of the decision-making process, so that everyone can assess the weight of the different interests in play, also stimulated by the growth of cyberadvocacy. The increasing scale and quality of the industry and its increasing professionalism appear to be general trends in Europe, with what was once an amateur's industry being driven by professionals who are now operating across continents and often have transnational backgrounds themselves.

The presence of great international organisations (in particular the European Union) and the economic and political relevance of the various actors on the European scene contribute to make this continent a fundamentally critical landscape in order to assess what we have called a huge and multi-faceted web of power: a web that every public affairs professional needs to unravel, if one aims to be influential in modern politics and business, where global and local dimensions become increasingly intertwined.

Notes

1 In fact the area close to the EU buildings in Belgium has come to be known as Brusslington, reflecting the pivotal role the EU plays in allowing businesses and organisations to influence and shape legislation and regulation of trade and the environment worldwide.

2 The population of the EU (more than 508 million people in 2015) is not homogenous and shows widely varying trends and different demographics, with a declining population in the east and some signs of growth in the west. The UK has the fastest population growth rate, followed by France and Germany amongst major countries, thus explaining some aspects of migration across the continent.

3 This Nordic style is very evident across Scandinavia and can be seen very clearly in such popular TV shows as *Borgen* and popularist writing across the whole Scandinavian area.

4 Even if there was a clear political opposition between Christian Democrats and the Communists, it would be more appropriate to frame the political balance of the time as a consensual (consociation) one (Lijphart, 1999).

5 The electoral turnout in the national political elections went from 92.23 per cent in 1948 to 90.62 per cent in 1979. Then it slowly began to decrease in the following decades; in 2013 it was 75.20 per cent (data from the Archive of the Elections of the Italian Ministry of Interior).

6 In 1948 the sum of the party members of the main parties (Communist Party, the Christian Democrats and the Socialist Party) was 3,741,622, in a population of 29,117,554 electors, meaning that 12.85 per cent of the electors were members of a party; the same ratio slightly decreased to 9.58 per cent in 1979 (data from Istituto Cattaneo of Bologna). These are very high percentages in comparison with other Western democratic countries.

7 Even if this definition does not reflect any change in the Italian constitutional charter (as usually is required by similar definitions, such as the French case). The constitution was not touched, but the changes in the political system were so relevant that a substantial transition to a completely new phase was apparent to political analysts, justifying this definition of 'Second Republic'.

8 In the political elections of 2013, this bi-polar trend was broken by the very good results of a third 'pole' alternative to both centre-right and centre-left, the Five Star Movement party (see Diamanti et al., 2013). It is still too early, though, to assess whether the tri-polar dynamic will be a lasting feature of the new Italian political system or not.

9 Political parties which saw their role as social and economic actors diminishing because of the new context. The same political participation (traditionally exerted through party membership and electoral turnout) began to change and to become more variegated. Sign of this can coherently be found in a decreasing electoral turnout (82.88 per cent in 1996, 80.51 per cent in 2008, 75.20 per cent in 2013) and in much smaller party memberships.

10 In slightly better views (unfortunately but meaningfully shared even by some practitioners), the lobbying profession has to do with the number of politicians you know, more than with the ability to conduct a professional campaign of interests' representation.

11 On the connection between lobbying and corruption see Campos and Giovannoni (2007).

12 Such is the thinking of Vladimir Kisiov, former Chairman of the Local Parliament of Sofia, quoted by Mavrov (2011).

REFERENCES

Andrews, L. (1996). The Relationship of Political Marketing to Political Lobbying: An Examination of the Devonport Campaign for the Trident Refitting Contract, *European Journal of Marketing*, 30 (10/11), 76–99.

Antonucci, M. C. (2014). *Lobbying e Terzo Settore. Un binomio possibile?*, Rome: Edizioni Nuova Cultura.

Bitonti, A. and Harris, P. (eds.) (2017). *Lobbying in Europe. Public Affairs and the Lobbying Industry in 28 EU countries*, London: Palgrave Macmillan.

Campos, N. F. and Giovannoni, F. (2007). Lobbying, Corruption and Political Influence, *Public Choice*, 131, 1–21.

Colarizi, S. (1996). *Biografia della Prima Repubblica*, Rome and Bari: Laterza.

Cook, C. and Stevenson, J. (1996). *Britain since 1945*. London: Longman.

De Fouloy, C. D. (2015). Lobbying Landscape in Sweden [Online]. Brussels: Association of Accredited Public Policy Advocates to the European Union. Available: http://www.aalep.eu/lobbying-landscape-sweden [accessed 5 August 2015].

Diamanti, I., Bordignon, F. and Ceccarini, L. (eds.) (2013). Un salto nel voto. Ritratto politico dell'Italia di oggi, Rome and Bari: Laterza.

Dineva, D. (2017). Lobbying in Bulgaria, in Bitonti, A. and Harris, P. (eds.), *Lobbying in Europe, Public Affairs and the Lobbying Industry in 28 EU countries*, London: Palgrave Macmillan.

Duvanova, D. S. (2009). Business Representation in Eastern Europe: The Failure of Corporatism?, in McGrath, C. (ed.) *Interest Groups and Lobbying in Europe: Essays on Trade, Environment, Legislation, and Economic Development*, New York: Edwin Mellen Press.

Foster, C. D. and Plowden, F. J. (1996). *The State under Stress: Can the Hollow State be Good Government?* Buckingham: Open University Press.

Griffin, J. J., Fleisher, C. S., Brenner, S. N. and Boddewyn, J. J. (2001). Corporate Public Affairs Research: Chronological Reference List, *Journal of Public Affairs*, 1 (1), 9–32.

Guarnieri, C. (2006). *Il sistema politico italiano*, Bologna: Il Mulino.

Hansard Society (1992). *Making the Law: Report of the Hansard Society*, London: Hansard Society.

Harris, P. (1994). *Political Lobbying or Machiavellian Marketing in Britain. Proceedings of the British Academy of Management Conference, University of Lancaster, 12–14 September*. Published paper in proceedings of the British Academy of Management Conference, University of Lancaster, 12–14 September.

Harris, P. and Lock, A. (1996). Machiavellian Marketing: The Development of Corporate Lobbying in the UK, *Journal of Marketing Management*, 12 (4), 313–28.

Harris, P., Moss, D. and Vetter, N. (1999). Machiavelli's Legacy to Public Affairs: A Modern Tale of Servants and Princes in UK Organisations, *Journal of Communication Management*, 3 (3), 201–17.

Heath, R. L. (1990). Corporate Issues Management: Theoretical Underpinnings and Research Foundation, *Public Relations Research Annual*, 2, 29–65.

Heath, R. L. (1997). *Strategic Issues Management: Organizations and Public Policy Challenges*, Thousand Oaks, California: Sage.

Hedlund, A.-K. (2017). Lobbying in Sweden, in Bitonti, A. and Harris, P. (eds.) *Lobbying in Europe. Public Affairs and the Lobbying Industry in 28 EU countries*, London: Palgrave Macmillan.

Hutton, W. (1995). *The State We're In*, London: Jonathan Cape.

Kavanagh, D. and Morris, P. (1989). *Consensus politics from Attlee to Thatcher*. Oxford, UK: Blackwell.

Lavergne, D. A. (2008). *La 'main invisible' de la transition: think tanks et transition démocratique en Bulgarie après 1989*, Paris: École des hautes études en sciences sociales.

Lewis, G. and Benson, P. (2014). The evolution and current state of public affairs in Hungary, *Journal of Public Affairs*, 14 (1), 67–75.

Lijphart, A. (1999). *Patterns of Democracy. Government Forms and Performance in Thirty-six Countries*, New Haven: Yale University Press.

Lawson, N. (1992). *The View from No.11: Memoirs of a Tory Radical*, London: Bantam.

Marr, A. (1995). *Ruling Britannia*, London: Michael Joseph.

Mavrov, B. (ed.) (2011). *Transparency in Lobbying in Bulgaria*, Sofia: European Institute.

Middlemas, K. (1986). *Power, Competition and the State*, 2 vols., London: Macmillan.

Mihova, M. (2014). The State of Public Affairs in Bulgaria, *Journal of Public Affairs*, 14 (1), 76–83.

Millar, C. C. J. M. and Köppl, P. (2014). Perspectives, Practices and Prospects of Public Affairs in Central and Eastern Europe: A Lobbying Future Anchored in an Institutional Context, *Journal of Public Affairs*, 14 (1), 4–17.

Moss, D., McGrath, C., Tonge, J. and Harris, P. (2012). Exploring the Management of Corporate Public Affairs Function in a Dynamic Global Environment, *Journal of Public Affairs*, 12 (1), 47–60.

Nolan, M. (1995). *First Report of the Committee on Standards in Public Life*, London: HMSO.

Petrillo, P. L. (2011). *Democrazie sotto pressione. Parlamenti e lobby nel diritto pubblico comparato*, Milan: Giuffrè.

Pirgova, M. (2002). *Balgarskiiat parlamentarizam v usloviiata na globalen prehod*, Sofia: Paradigma.

Sartori, G. (1976). *Parties and Party Systems: A Framework for Analysis*, Cambridge: Cambridge University Press.

Sousa, C. (1999). *So You Want to be a Political Lobbyist? Guide to the World of Political Lobbying*, London, Politicos.

Sulit, M. (2015). UK among Seven out of 19 EU Nations to Regulate Lobbying, says Anticorruption Watchdog, *PR Week*, 16 April.

Transparency International (2015) Report on Lobbying in Europe, Hidden Influence: Privileged Access, Transparency International Secretariat, Berlin.

Transparency International Bulgaria (2014). *Lobbying in Bulgaria: Interests, Influence, Politics*, Sofia: Transparency International Bulgaria.

Transparency International Italia (2014). *Lobbying e democrazia. La rappresentanza degli interessi in Italia*, Milan: Transparency International Italia.

Tsakova, I. (2005). *Lobizam i demokratsiia*, Sofia: Avangard Prima.

Winch, D. (1969). *Economics and Policy: A Historical Survey*, London: Hodder and Stoughton.

21

Public Affairs in North America

John Mahon

CORPORATE PUBLIC AFFAIRS

Corporate public affairs is that arm of the organization that deals with interactions between the organization and the marketplace of ideas. This marketplace of ideas includes such areas as the legislative, judicial, and regulatory functions of government as well as dealings with non-government organizations, the media and the general public. This marketplace of ideas is crucial as it is in these locales that the rules of competition are created and enforced. That is, such actions as the banning of tobacco commercials on radio and television, taxation and trade policies all occur in this marketplace and can have profound impacts on competition and the marketplace for goods and services.

This external non-market environment is becoming increasingly intrusive and active in its attempts to influence and shape organizational actions and decisions on a global, regional and national scale (Coen, 1997;

Dill, 1958; Eelis, 1958–9; Hegarty et al., 1978; Weidenbaum, 1980). Public affairs is the center of the organization's actions to anticipate, plan and respond in a thoughtful and articulate manner to issues, problems and situations. These problems/issues/situations can arise as a result of corporate actions (for example, the recent emissions problems with Volkswagen automobiles worldwide). They can arise from legislative and regulatory proposals, media and special interest group actions and so on. This can involve the individual firm and the industry as a whole (as well as multiple industries in concert) dealing with issues and problems at all levels.

Both for-profit and not-for-profit organizations have public affairs departments. The existence of these departments recognizes the critical role played by the marketplace of ideas in, as noted, setting the rules of competition and the significant additional costs that actions in this arena can impose on organizations. Finally, organizations of all types are recognizing that their legitimacy as a societal actor is related to how they are perceived by government and the broader society at large.

THE HISTORICAL DEVELOPMENT OF PUBLIC AFFAIRS IN NORTH AMERICA

The historical development of public affairs in North America is best seen through its emergence in the United States. What we now address as public affairs activities and organization can trace its roots back to three streams of development starting in the 1920s. These three areas – corporate philanthropy, urban and community affairs, and public relations – were major contributors to the modern public affairs function and office (for an in-depth treatment of the emergence and development of public affairs in the United States; see Mahon, 1982).

At the turn of the century business leaders had a negative attitude regarding the public and its role in business affairs. J. P. Morgan, a famous financier, once observed that 'I owe the public nothing' and his counterpart, William Vanderbilt, at the time agreed, offering his view that 'The public be damned.' This relationship can be captured broadly in Figure 21.1 which reflects the view that business saw itself as the dominant force in relationship to government and society (see Galambos [1975], Garraty [1966], Josephson

[1962] and Morison [1965] for a lively reporting of these relationships over time).

This relationship, with business dominating government and societal affairs, existed for some time, but as with most relationships, it changed gradually over time. As public tolerance of business actions waned, government stepped in to control some of the worst situations. Chandler (1980) argued that the growth of government involvement in business and the switch to an adversarial relationship was a direct result of business taking self-serving advantage during non-regulated times. In halting steps, government began to insert itself in the affairs of business both at the industry level (banking, insurance, airlines) and at issue-specific level (health, safety, employment). The government saw itself as the best representative of the public interest with regards to uncontrolled and unconstrained business activities. As such, the relationship noted in Figure 21.1 altered to that shown in Figure 21.2 below.

Over time, a third set of actors became involved – non-governmental organizations or public interest groups that also want to influence business and government and argue that they, too, represent the broader interests of society, leading to the dynamic environment that business faces today as shown in Figure 21.3.

This broad historical background reflecting changes in the relationship between business, government and society sets the stage for considering how philanthropy, urban and

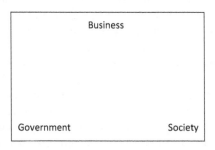

Figure 21.1   Early business-government-society relationships

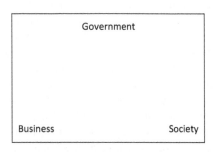

Figure 21.2   Evolving business-society relationships

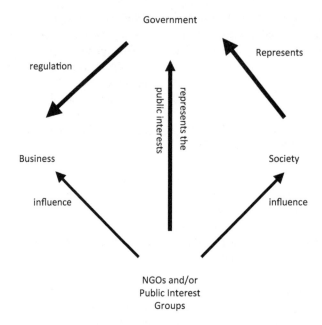

Figure 21.3   The current chaotic state of business-government-NGOs-society relationships

community affairs, and public relations con-tributed to the development and growth of public affairs. Corporate philanthropy and urban and community affairs developed in the 1970s (*California Management Review*, 1969a, 1969b), whereas public relations is much older, beginning at the turn of the century in the early 1900s.

Urban and Community Affairs

Cohn (1971) analyzed the growth in urban and community affairs following riots in major American cities (Watts, Newark and Detroit). The initial experiences of busi-nesses in these endeavors was not very posi-tive. Cohn notes that the firms moved too fast and too far and that executives realized that running a business was not the same as man-aging urban and community affairs. Even though efforts continue in this area, business activity is viewed with cynicism as many see it as the firm's attempt to achieve favorable impacts on their reputation.

Corporate Philanthropy

Heald (1970) and Koch (1979) have analyzed the growth in corporate philanthropy in the twentieth century. Heald documents the stormy relationships between business, soci-ety and government over corporate giving and community involvement. It is clear from his analysis that businesses more often than not were dragged into philanthropic activities by intense outside pressures (the public inter-est groups and non-governmental organiza-tions noted earlier). Koch, taking a different view, attempted to address how firms can use philanthropic activities in a more meaningful and organizationally relevant manner. He noted that firms could reap substantial tax advantages and provide more benefits to soci-ety at large by developing clear strategies for corporate philanthropy – an earlier precursor of what is today known as strategic corporate philanthropy. Strategic corporate philan-thropy is embroiled in controversy today. Shareholders are not always supportive of their 'monies' being used in this manner, and external groups see these activities as a skeptical and cynical approach by firms to curry favor with external actors to the firm.

Public Relations

Tedlow (1979) looks at the 'corporate image makers' and chronicles the origins and activities of public relations from 1900 to 1950. He clearly sees the development of public relations as the response of firms to growing governmental and societal interference. The original focus of public relations was on government, regulatory agencies, politicians and leaders of organized labor. Over time, however, the focus of public relations migrated and in general, public relations became the conduit of information about noteworthy activities from the firm to the general public using the mass media. The firm became more interested in controlling the coverage of the firm by the mass media, and as a consequence, relationships with government were left to the government relations function in the organization. Tedlow puts it best when he observes that:

> The development of public relations should be seen within this context. Businessmen knew well the power of public opinion. They respected its impact on the conduct of strikes, on legislation, on sales and on their own morale. As firms grew larger, they came to realize the importance of controlling the news which they could not avoid generating. (1979: 18)

Public relations became the responders to attacks on the corporation and in dealings with the media. As a consequence, many firms had several different entities dealing with the external environment and lacked a clear co-ordinating function to bring them together.

THE DEVELOPMENT OF THE MODERN PUBLIC AFFAIRS FUNCTION

The 1970s saw a dramatic rise in interest in the public affairs function in large American corporations (see, for example, but by no means limited to, Brown, 1971; Epstein, 1969; Post, 1979). Griffin et al. (2001a, 2001b) provide an extraordinarily detailed chronological reference list to corporate public affairs research for two distinct periods – 1958–84 and 1985–2000 – which reflects the growing interest of academia in public affairs (see also Gruber and Hoewing, 1980; McGrath, 1976, 1977; Morris, 1980). But the media also recognized the growing importance of public affairs. *Business Week* observed that:

> Call it 'PR' or 'Public Affairs', Pfizer and most other major corporations are making a carefully planned effort to communicate with multiple audiences, influence opinion, and create an environment more favorable to what they perceive to be in their direct interest. They are taking PR far beyond traditional functions of image building and getting the company's name in the paper – or keeping it out. (January 22, 1979: 49)

In 1980, the Boston University Public Affairs Research Group (PARG, 1981) published what was the first extensive comprehensive survey of public affairs departments in the United States – 1,000 of the largest firms were solicited, and more than 400 responded to a detailed survey. This provided the first look into what public affairs departments were doing, their staffing and budget levels. The survey also addressed government relations, corporate planning, and managing of emerging issues. The survey asked what activities or functions are considered within public affairs and the top four responses were: community relations (85 percent of firms considered this part of public affairs); government relations (85 percent); corporate contributions (72 percent); and media relations (70 percent). Specialized relationships, such as dealing with shareholders and consumers, seem to be handled elsewhere in the corporation. Fifty-nine percent of respondents developed their public affairs function in 1970 or later.

At the federal and state level the two primary activities are regular correspondence with politicians and lobbying. At the federal level the third most performed activity was using political action committees. It is clear from these results that public affairs was focused on government relationships and activities and on community relations, corporate contributions and media relationships. In follow-up work (Foundation for Public Affairs, 2005; Griffin, 1997; Post and Mahon, 1981; Post et al., 1981, 1982) it became clear that one way to view public affairs was as a 'window out' for the corporation to view and act on the external environment and a 'window in' for government, NGOs and society to impact corporate decisions and activities. Specifically, according to Post et al.:

> The public affairs function in American companies appears to be converging around a basic set of responsibilities and activities. At the risk of some over-simplification, the essential role of public affairs units appears to be that of *window out* of the corporation through which management can perceive, monitor, and understand external change and simultaneously a *window in* through which society can influence corporate policy and practice. This boundary spanning role primarily involves the flow of information to and from the organization. In many firms it also involves the flow of financial resources in the form of political contributions to elected and would be elected officials and charitable contributions to various stakeholder groups in society. (1982: 13)

As we will see, there have been follow-up surveys regarding public affairs, but this 'window-in window-out' distinction seems to hold up until this very day.

Although there have been many attempts to draw sharp distinctions between public affairs and public relations, the lines still remain blurred in corporate America. To many, the role of public relations is more reactionary, putting the best face on corporate actions after the fact, whereas public affairs is more proactive, attempting to position the corporation to deal with issues and situations *before* they become problems.

In 1996, Post and Griffin, in cooperation with the Foundation for Public Affairs, conducted a follow-up survey to ascertain what changes have occurred with regards to public affairs (Post and Griffin, 1996; more information can be found in Griffin, 1997). This survey was sent to 1,100 firms and more than 260 corporations responded. They show that corporations have greatly increased their activity in grassroots programs, international public affairs and community relations. For the first time there were differences in manufacturing versus non-manufacturing firms. Manufacturing firms tend to spend more time with international public affairs while non-manufacturing firms spend more time with grassroots programs. Political involvement continues to be complex in America. Eighty percent of the respondents now have political action committees, and trade associations and business associations are used by nearly every company now. Issues management has become more prominent as well and involves both public affairs professionals and operating managers.

In 2005, the Foundation for Public Affairs did another survey of public affairs sent to 510 firms with more than 150 corporations responding. As might be reasonably expected, public affairs continues to evolve. Their data suggests that most firms have a reasonably well-developed issues management capability and more companies than in the past have a presence in Washington, DC. The top six activities that public affairs engage in are now: federal government relations (95 percent respondents engage in this); state government relations (85 percent); political action committees (83 percent); issues management (82 percent); local government relations (79 percent); and three activities at the 75 percent level – business/trade association oversight/assessment, direct corporate political contributions and grassroots programs. The Public Affairs Council (PAC) had conducted an annual state of the public affairs function since 1992 and the reports are available from them. For those interested in a year-to-year snapshot of public affairs development these reports serve as a rich and substantive data bank.

It is clear that public affairs has been, and will continue, refining and refocusing its efforts: for example, corporations more recently have segmented government relations into federal, state and local relations and pursued more capability in international public affairs and issues management. This division of public affairs activities is not the case at the moment in Europe – but with more and more political and regulatory power moving to Brussels, European firms will have to develop public affairs capabilities that deal with local issues, national issues and European Union issues for the first time (see McGuire et al., 2012).

Let us turn our attention to three of the more interesting developments in public affairs that reflect the local environment and political and legal context in the USA – the growth in political action committees and corporate philanthropy, issues and stakeholder management, and international public affairs.

Political Action Committees and Corporate Philanthropy

As noted earlier, it is in the marketplace of ideas that changes to the rules under which corporations engage with one another, with government and with society are determined. In addition to the more traditional approach, lobbying – support of political candidates in running for election and re-election – can afford access and on occasion support for corporate positions. However, corporations are not alone in attempting to influence political leaders – individuals, non-government organizations and other groups also attempt to gain advantage and exercise their will. Lobbying and political action committees are activities that can be used to blunt other actors' attempts at influencing and changing the rules and/or to impact and change the rules that support corporate positions.

The political campaign funding laws in the United States are unique and often cause confusion for those outside the United States. The original focus of these laws was to prevent undue influence on political elections by wealthy individuals and corporations and unions. There were strict dollar limits on how much an individual could give, and corporations and unions were banned from making contributions to political action committees (independent organizations that raise money for support of a candidate or overall party, for example, Republican or Democratic candidates). These laws have changed dramatically in the past few years. The aforementioned limits were mostly eliminated in two sweeping Supreme Court decisions.

The first decision, in January 2010, has had the most impact on campaigns and on corporate contributions. In the 'Citizens United' case, the ban on corporate and union independent expenditures and financing electioneering communications was removed. This means that corporations and unions can spend unlimited sums of money on ads and other political tools calling for the election or defeat of a political candidate. This has led to an explosion in independent advertising and communications for and against political candidates. It has led to the rise of what is termed 'Super PACS' who receive enormous sums of money from corporations, unions and individuals. Individuals are able to contribute large sums because of the second decision, also by the Supreme Court (April 1, 2014), that struck down limits on contributions by wealthy individuals to candidates and political action committees. These two decisions have engendered a great deal of debate that may result in further modifications at a later date in campaign financing laws.

Corporate Contributions

While political action committees and lobbying are more direct measures to engage political actors and participate in the marketplace of ideas, corporate philanthropy affords another, more indirect path of influence. In general, corporate philanthropy consists of charitable donations to not-for-profit organizations and communities. The form of the donation can be in cash, in resources or in employee volunteer time. These donations are often handled via a company-sponsored foundation (but it is not required by law). The idea, beyond just good works, is that the organization will receive favorable reputational enhancement from these activities that could be mobilized to support action in the marketplace of ideas.

As the economy waxes and wanes, the funds available to the firm also expand and contract. In addition, the requests for such philanthropy often exceed what the individual firm can do. One response is that firms have adapted by allowing employees to volunteer their time to charitable and community organizations. This provides several advantages to the firm and public affairs as employee volunteers can be a source of emerging issues and concerns in the community that may require corporate action, and also a reputational asset for the firm in the community.

As a consequence of limited financial resources, corporate 'strategic' philanthropy has grown significantly in recent years. Corporate strategic philanthropy comprises the processes by which a corporation targets all of its charitable activities and involvements around specifically chosen issues or causes that support its own business objectives and goals. In essence, a corporation is trying to simultaneously achieve a direct benefit for its own narrow interests and provide benefit(s) to those who are the recipients of these charitable actions. One of the more popular approaches is to devote a portion of the profits of a good to a specific charity. For example, Avon Products ran a program where the purchase of its products that featured a 'pink ribbon' resulted in some of the profits being given to organizations supporting breast cancer research (Avon Corporation, 1999). Note that the corporation increases its sales (and profits) and enhances its reputation, and that the recipient organizations receive an influx of funding.

Porter and Kramer offer a more sophisticated view and approach to philanthropy, noting that:

> A handful of companies have begun to use context-focused philanthropy to achieve both social and economic gains. Cisco Systems, to take one example, has invested in an ambitious educational program – the Cisco Networking Academy – to train computer network administrators, thus alleviating a potential constraint on its growth while providing attractive job opportunities to high school graduates. By focusing on social needs that affect its corporate context and utilizing its unique attributes as a corporation to address them, Cisco has begun to demonstrate the unrealized potential of corporate philanthropy. (2002: 59)

To be clear, Porter and Kramer are putting a twist on corporate strategic philanthropy away from charitable donations to involvements and donations that directly impact on the competitive positioning of the firm (what they term the corporate context). They offer another example, that of American Express, which:

> has funded Travel and Tourism Academies in secondary schools, training students not for the credit card business, its core business, but for careers in other travel agencies as well as airlines, hotels, and restaurants ... (the program) operates in ten countries and more than 3,000 schools with more than 120,000 students enrolled. It provides the major social benefits of improved educational and job opportunities for local citizens ... The economic gains are also substantial, as local travel clusters become more competitive and better able to grow. That translates into important benefits for American Express. (2002: 62)

Issues and Stakeholder Management

Organizations looking toward the future attempt to assess which issues (differences that exist in facts, values or policies) are going to gain visibility and traction in the marketplace of ideas, that impact on the firm and therefore require organizational planning and action.

It can be reasonably argued that Howard Chase developed the term issues management in the mid-1970s. He launched the Issues Management Association – now known as the Issues Management Council (see: http://issuemanagement.org) – and wrote some of the earliest articles on this topic (1977, 1984). Johnson has defined issues management as 'the process by which the corporation can identify, evaluate and respond to those social and political issues which may impact significantly upon it' (1983: 22). For example, changes in federal taxation policies are an issue of concern to corporations. Concerns about nuclear power, cloning of animals, food safety, drug pricing and availability are all examples of issues that could engender corporate interest and responses. Chase offered a further refinement of 'strategic issues management' (see also Ansoff, 1980) as:

> the capacity to understand, mobilize, coordinate, and direct all strategic and policy planning functions, and all public affairs/public relations skills, toward the achievement of one objective: meaningful participation in creation of public policy that affects personal and institutional destiny. (Chase, 1982: 1–2)

Issues management has evolved to be the long-term assessment arm of corporations (and of public interest groups) of potential issues that will gain attention and demand action – especially action in the marketplace of ideas. Issues management is discussed in further detail in this Handbook. There is notion of an issues lifecycle – that is, that issues evolve and emerge over time. In the initial stages of an issue the firm has very different choices for action than when an issue emerges full blown. An initial issue, just emerging, offers the firm the opportunity to contain the issue and to keep organizational resource commitment to a minimum. As an issue unfolds, more stakeholders enter into the fray, requiring greater expenditures of resources and moving the organization from containment strategies to coping strategies.

When an issue reaches a resolution stage (which can be temporary) the firm has no further option but compliance with the terms of the resolution.

The key lesson here is that corporations engaged in the marketplace of ideas attempt to predict which issues among an enormous set of potential issues are likely to demand corporate action and commitment of resources and/or changed behavior. Wartick and Mahon (1994) provide an extensive, thorough review of issues management as a concept and develop a clear definition of what constitutes a corporate issue.

Stakeholder Management

Issues management can aid us in the identification of topics that might arise for resolution. But 'issues' do not move toward analysis, discussion and debate without the involvement of stakeholders – both those for, against and neutral with regards to a specific issue. As such, when an issue moves from a potential stage to where it is actually being advanced and discussed, those who have an interest in the resolution of the issue (stakeholders) become engaged. These stakeholders will attempt to move the issue to an arena where they have an advantage over other stakeholders (for example, move away from a legislative solution to a regulatory solution or to a judicial resolution). In addition, stakeholders will attempt to define the issue an such a manner as to support their position and to build adherents and additional stakeholder involvement. Freeman is credited with the most useful definition of a stakeholder – 'any group or individual who can affect or is affected by the achievement of the organization's objectives' (1984: 46). Both corporations and NGOs attempt to manage these stakeholders, develop coalitions of support, and deny access, where possible, to stakeholders who do not support their position and preferred solution. Schattschneider (1960) has argued that in a contest between actors, one should focus not on the actors, but on the audience. Whichever actor (stakeholder) can

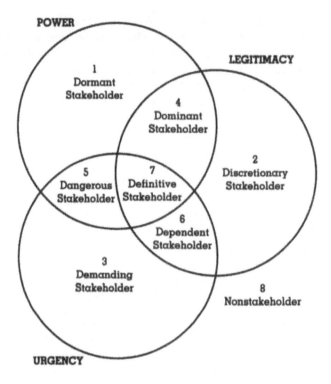

Figure 21.4 Criteria for evaluation of stakeholder influence

Source: Mitchell et al., 1997: 874.

bring the audience on their side will likely win the contest. To put it another way, stakeholder management is important in developing what appears to be widespread support for a specific position with regards to an issue.

At first read, Freeman's definition may appear so broad as to be unhelpful. We need to understand that stakeholders are always identified and defined in relationship to the specific issue and context under discussion. For example, the stakeholders around environmental issues are quite different than those stakeholders who have an interest in civil liberties or pharmaceutical issues.

Because of the difficulties found in operationalizing Freeman's view of stakeholders, many managers and public affairs professionals find it difficult to use in practice. Mitchell et al. (1997) have worked to make stakeholder management more relevant to the organization. They have offered

a classification scheme for stakeholders that provides a conceptual (and practical) tool to help organizations better understand stakeholders, utilizing characterizations of power, legitimacy and urgency (see Figure 21.4).

Power is a relatively easy concept to understand and apply. It simply asks what power the stakeholder has over the corporation and how it is exercised (for example, through the use of force – physical force or use of material or financial resources). Legitimacy, they argue, is distinct from power (and when linked, they create authority) and is a desirable social good. We recognize stakeholders as

'legitimate' based on the context of the issue or problem, the stakeholder's past history of involvement and their overall reputation. Finally, urgency represents the time sensitivity of the issue AND the importance of the issue or situation to a stakeholder – or as they observe urgency is 'the degree to which stakeholder claims call for immediate attention'. (1997: 867)

A careful look at Figure 21.4 demonstrates that stakeholders can have one, two or three of the characteristics of power, legitimacy and urgency in any combination. They argue that stakeholders who possess only one of these characteristics will be seen as unimportant by the organization (noted as 1, 2 or 3 in Figure 21.4) and they identify them as 'latent' stakeholders. Mitchell et al. (1997) offer detailed descriptions of each of these nine stakeholder categorizations that are beyond the scope of this chapter. They are 'latent' to the extent that they are not mobilized to action but could obtain the other characteristic at any time – the easiest path is to obtain one of the other two characteristics they are lacking.

Stakeholders that have at least two of these characteristics are what they term 'expectant' stakeholders (noted as 4, 5 or 6 in Figure 21.4). In essence, these types of stakeholders 'expect' something from the corporation and are willing to act on that expectation. As such, their importance to the corporation increases because these stakeholders can attempt to exercise their choices on corporate action and decision-making.

Definitive stakeholders possess all three characteristics – power, legitimacy and urgency (noted as 7, 8 and 9 in Figure 21.4). Any expectant stakeholder can become a definitive stakeholder by acquiring the one missing characteristic. From a corporate and public affairs view, these are the most dangerous stakeholders that the firm faces and they have the ability to significantly impact the unfolding of an issue and alter corporate decision-making and actions. As a consequence, public affairs managers are wise to attend to stakeholders in their order of impact on the firm – definitive, expectant, latent.

International Public Affairs

The growth of the internet and social media along with the internationalization of many NGOs and other public interest groups have forced public affairs departments to become more internationalized. The potential for an issue to arise virtually anywhere and to be championed in that country has never been higher. The challenge is that sophisticated NGOs and other groups can launch an issue in a country where 'winning' would be comparatively easy – and then leverage that win as they move into other countries.

The potential pressure points are so numerous that public affairs has to rely on country managers – often without much public affairs training and expertise – to keep corporations informed about these emerging issues that may be impactful on those corporations. Fleisher has offered a comprehensive list of why public affairs in international contexts is important and likely to become more important in the future. His list included such arguments as the growing distrust of multinational corporations and increasingly powerful convergence of information communications and technology. International public affairs skills and expertise is only going to increase in the future, and corporations, especially those that operate globally, will be disadvantaged without strong international public affairs skills. But what skills are needed to be a public affairs professional and how is the profession developing?

THE PUBLIC AFFAIRS PROFESSION

Creighton and Meznar in Chapter 5 of this Handbook explore in depth the educational aspects of the public affairs profession in colleges and universities. They identify the major institutions that engage in this education. They faced two challenges in this work: the first is the broad reach of education in public affairs – programs exist in public policy, business administration, public administration and public policy programs. This makes the development of the field challenging as each of these programs brings a different 'twist' or approach to what constitutes public affairs education and training. The second problem is that public affairs is clearly a boundary-spanning function, and with the constantly changing boundary between the firm and the environment, what exactly constitutes public affairs is a challenge.

They used, as a starting point, the National Association of Schools of Public Affairs and Administration (NASPAA) to identify programs in public affairs in more than 300 institutions – curiously, few of these programs include in their title 'public affairs'.

They note that public affairs education, in the formal sense, has remained static over the past ten years, despite changes in technology and the external environment. They do not, however, address the professional training available in public affairs outside the formal educational arena – and it is this level of education and training that is more dynamic and contemporary than that found on college and university campuses. Three of the largest, ongoing, visible professional groups in public affairs are the Public Affairs Council, the Centre for Corporate Public Affairs and the Issues Management Council. The European Centre for Public Affairs (ECPA) is a Brussels-based think tank that is, according to its web site (http://theecpa.eu), 'focused on best practice, training, and skills development in public affairs'. In addition, it provides the opportunity for networking, formal training and skill development programs and an opportunity for best practice and dialogue sessions. The activities and level of involvement of the ECPA has been uneven over the past several years and it is notably younger than the organizations we will discuss here.

Public Affairs Council (PAC)

The Public Affairs Council, located in Washington, DC (with an additional office in Brussels, Belgium), is the oldest professional, non-political, non-partisan association for public affairs professionals worldwide (see http://pac.org). Founded in 1954, it is arguably the broadest in its activities of all the professional public affairs associations.

At the time of writing this chapter it offers two professional certification programs, one in Political Action Committees and Grassroots Management and another in Public Affairs Management. The Certification in Political Action Committees and Grassroots Management requires the individual to choose a focus in either grassroots management or political action committees. It is a unique blend of formal programs offered by the PAC and community credits (for example, serving as a mentor for individuals involved with either a political action committee or a grassroots program). Individuals entering in the Public Affairs Management certification program must have a minimum of seven years' experience in broad areas of management and it takes from two to three years to complete. As with the previous certification program, this also requires formal and community-based activities.

In addition to these certification programs, the PAC runs a number of training programs (21 alone in October 2015) on such topics as: Creating an Election Year PAC Plan, Measuring and Communicating the Value of CSR, Advocacy for Regulatory Success, Strategic Planning for Public Affairs and other topics of immediate interest to the public affairs professional. These programs are offered both in physical form and via webinars.

The PAC also has an aggressive publications program. It publishes the *Impact* newsletter (published monthly in print); the *Catalyst* newsletter (electronically published with latest public affairs news from contemporary journals and resources); and *Pin Points* (Political Involvement Network Newsletter). Years ago the PAC also published a journal, *Public Affairs Review* (no longer published).

In addition to all of this, the PAC has a very active research foundation that works on reports and emerging trends and issues in public affairs. The Foundation for Public Affairs was established in 1976. It pioneered the analysis of large and influential interest groups via a biannual publication entitled *Public Interest Profiles*. In the 1980s this survey was taken over by the Congressional Quarterly Press.

The most recent reports provided by the Foundation include such topics as: *Corporate and Association PAC Benchmarking*; *The State of Corporate Public Affairs 2014–2015*; *Measuring and Communicating the Value of Public Affairs*; *Russian Renaissance? Managing Public Affairs in Today's Russia*; and *Beyond Control: and How Social Media and Mobile Communications are Changing Public Affairs*. Finally, the PAC had become increasingly involved in international public affairs, producing such reports as: *Building and Managing a Global Public Affairs Function*; *Managing Stakeholder Engagement on a Global Scale*; *O Memento Magico: Managing Public Affairs in Brazil*; and *Opening Doors in Brussels: Managing Government Relations in the EU*.

The Centre for Corporate Public Affairs

The Centre for Corporate Public Affairs (https://accpa.com.au), located in Sydney, Australia, was established in 1990. It has close affiliations with the Public Affairs Council and with the European Centre for Public Affairs and is heavily involved in professional education and leadership in public affairs in the Australia–Asia region.

Like the PAC, it offers professional development programs and activities on a broad scale, and regular telesymposiums and webinars, workshops, residential institutes and heads of function and senior practitioner roundtables, and special dialogues (for example, trade policy, reputation indexes).

The Centre publishes a Public Affairs Newsletter and has an extensive 'Knowledge Centre' on its web site that includes a wealth of resources for the practitioner (including such things as research reports, text of public orations, web-based resources, case studies and video interviews). It is equal in renown and involvement to the PAC in the USA.

The Issue Management Council

The Issue Management Council is the newest of the professional associations, with a narrow focus on issues management (which makes it unique). It is located just outside Washington, DC and offers training and consultations on issues management. Its leadership consists of practicing issues managers in some of the largest corporations in the world. It also publishes a newsletter and offers resources via its web site (http://issuemanagement.org). The Council is working on carving out a distinctive niche in public affairs education and training that complements the PAC, AACPA and ECPA.

All of the aforementioned organizations offer executive education programs and consultation services to the profession of public affairs. Public affairs tends to use consultants in lobbying and regulatory affairs as specialized knowledge is required for success in these arenas. In addition, broad national trade associations such as the National Federation of Independent Businessmen and the National Chamber of Commerce provide services to all industries whereas organizations such as the Pharmaceutical Manufacturing Association and the Chemical Manufacturers Association provide similar services to their related industries and membership.

In general, broad issues and situations at the specific industry level (for example, drug testing) and broad issues that cut across industries (taxation policies) are often handled by external consultants. Issues that strike at the heart of an individual corporation are the absolute domain of public affairs.

THE CURRENT STATE OF PA

Clearly, public affairs is a corporate function that has grown in both importance and influence within the corporation. There still exists some 'fuzziness' between public relations and public affairs in terms of which function is responsible for what specific activities. Public relations started out dealing with government, regulatory agencies, politicians – much of which is now the province of public affairs. There continues to be manoeuvring within large corporations between public affairs and public relations.

The falling of trade barriers, the formation of transnational trading partners (for example, the European Union, the Latin American Free Trade Association) and growing numbers of large multinational corporations (MNCs) has demanded a growing capability in international public affairs. It is a serious mistake to assume that the political and regulatory context in one nation is exactly the same as that in another nation. In addition, MNCs, because of their size and visibility, are becoming lightning rods of contention increasing stakeholder and NGO interest and activism.

All of these trends and others not mentioned serve to underscore the increasing importance of public affairs.

FUTURE DIRECTIONS AND CHALLENGES

There are a number of challenges that face the public affairs function going forward:

1 *Measurement.* How do we measure the success and performance of public affairs activities? This has been a significant problem for public affairs because of the broad nature of its activities. For example, many firms use simple rubrics in assessment – for example, if a firm loses in its attempts to influence legislation, that is considered 'bad' or a loss. However, the firm may have made significant gains in access, in its position in terms of being heard and in relationships with other stakeholders that are not captured by simple 'win/loss' characterizations. This author has argued that public affairs departments can be seen as cost-containment functions, or as profit-preservation functions or as preserving market access and/or opening up new markets.

Measurement will remain a constant problem for public affairs for the foreseeable future.

2 *Social media.* The explosive growth in social media (Facebook, Instagram, Twitter, etc.) has enabled the transmission of issues and concerns across borders in near-instant time and has reduced the time in which corporations can develop positions and respond to these media. It has also greatly increased the ability of NGOs to organize cross-border campaigns and launch multiple attacks in multiple arenas in multiple countries simultaneously. Some data on the impact of social media: 97 percent of generation Y use social media; social media have overtaken pornography as the #1 activity on the web; there are more than 50 million tweets a day; and if Facebook were a country, its membership would make it the third largest country in the world. There are more than 200 million blogs a day, and 34 percent of them offer opinions on products and brands – data suggests that 78 percent of consumers rely on and trust peer recommendations. President Obama in his first campaign used social media to an extraordinary extent – more so than ever in history. During his campaign 13 million people on his email list received 7,000 variations of more than 1 billion emails. Most large corporations have not determined how to use, monitor and respond to events in the social media world.

3 *Stakeholders' growing sophistication.* NGOs and other public interest groups are becoming more adept at organizing and sharing resources to challenge corporations. Some NGOs use their lobbying clout, while others use their fundraising abilities to tackle issues of importance to their membership – this means that corporations are facing constellations of stakeholders as opposed to the individual stakeholders of the past.

4 *Corporate social responsibility, corporate citizenship and sustainability demands.* As governments move away from social programs the expectations are growing that corporations need to pick up the 'slack'. This means that the legitimacy of the firm, its 'license to operate', is increasingly being challenged by NGOs and community groups demanding firms engage in more socially responsible actions and become better corporate 'citizens' (recall the Occupy movement of a few years ago). The United Nations, in response to these concerns, has created the Global Compact (https://www.unglobalcompact.org) – 'A call to

Table 21.1   UN Principles for Global Corporations

Human rights
Principle 1: Businesses should support and respect the protection of internationally proclaimed human rights; and
Principle 2: make sure that they are not complicit in human rights abuses.

Labor
Principle 3: Businesses should uphold the freedom of association and the effective recognition of the right to collective
    bargaining;
Principle 4: the elimination of all forms of forced and compulsory labor;
Principle 5: the effective abolition of child labor; and
Principle 6: the elimination of discrimination in respect of employment and occupation.

Environment
Principle 7: Businesses should support a precautionary approach to environmental challenges;
Principle 8: undertake initiatives to promote greater environmental responsibility; and
Principle 9: encourage the development and diffusion of environmentally friendly technologies.

Anti-corruption
Principle 10: Businesses should work against corruption in all its forms, including extortion and bribery.

Source: https://www.unglobalcompact.org/what-is-gc/mission/principles

companies to align strategies and operations with universal principles on human rights, labour, environment and anti-corruption, and take actions that advance societal goals.' The UN has developed a set of ten principles that those who join the compact must agree to (see Table 21.1).

The UN argues that:

Corporate sustainability starts with a company's value system and a principled approach to doing business. This means operating in ways that, at a minimum, meet fundamental responsibilities in the areas of human rights, labour, environment and anti-corruption. Responsible businesses enact the same values and principles wherever they have a presence, and know that good practices in one area do not offset harm in another. By incorporating the Global Compact principles into strategies, policies and procedures, and establishing a culture of integrity, companies are not only upholding their basic responsibilities to people and planet, but also setting the stage for long-term success. (https://www.unglobalcompact.org/what-is-gc/mission/principles)

As can be seen, the program is quite ambitious and impacts on corporate discretion, action and commitment of financial and other resources. The impact of this program is still being debated – it is new, and the reporting requirements for corporations seem to allow for a great deal of vagueness.

1   Performance assessments and demands across national borders of corporate performance and behavior. Two of the challenges in assessment of corporate behavior and action are (1) who is doing the assessment and (2) what criteria are they using in making this assessment? One could also address the time frame of corporate actions and how that aligns with any assessments being made. Mahon and Wartick offer a challenging example of this problem:

Suppose, for example, that MWC Corporation makes a multi-million dollar gift to Vrije Universiteit. MWC was able to provide this gift because it had been very profitable using low-wage, nonunion workers to brew beer. The river running next to MWC's major production facility in Cedar Falls, Iowa, is so polluted that the state environmental agency has issued a 'do not swim' and a 'do not fish' order for this waterway. MWC has had absolutely no role in the pollution of the river, and it is provable with data over time. MWC has been criticized by social activists in the Cedar Falls area for not providing job security since workers are laid off and rehired as demand for and production of the MWC beer ebbs and flows, but the Cedar Falls community in general appreciates MWC's near 100 percent involvement and leadership in important local activities and campaigns. All levels of government look favorably upon MWC because their profitability leads to substantial tax dollars even though within the past year the Federal Trade Commission had to order that MWC run a series of remedial ads designed to correct a false claim that disparaged competitors. Suppliers to MWC frequently compliment and cooperate with MWC because it always pays its bills on time and lives up to its agreement, but competitors believe that the use of low-wage, nonunion workers is anti-competitive given the high levels of unionization that exist elsewhere in the industry. Question: Is MWC socially responsible? Is it an example of 'good' corporate social performance? What are the key tradeoffs in the Corporate Social Performance (CSP) of MWC and can MWC's performance somehow be aggregated to come up with some 'bottom line' assessment of its *total* CSP? (Mahon and Wartick, 2005, pp. 140–1)

2   Soft law versus hard law decisions.

Holcomb (2006) provides the clearest analysis of this challenge for public affairs when he notes:

With the spread of globalization and the rise of codes passed by international organizations, there has been a growing tendency for courts to rely on such codes as 'soft law' in their decisions. As the distance between the 'hard law' of statutes and court precedence and the 'soft law' of codes narrows, so does the distance between legal obligations and voluntary self-regulation. How then do corporations define the range of various corporate responsibilities? (2006: 44)

CONCLUSION

It should be clear that the public affairs function is a dynamic, evolving component of any large corporation, and especially for those corporations engaged in international business. Public affairs is not without challenge, however, and the interplay of public affairs, NGOs and the external environment will continue to compel corporate action and engagement in the marketplace of ideas. The corporate defense (and offense) here is a well-organized public affairs department.

REFERENCES

Aguilar, F. J., 1967. *Scanning the Business Environment*. New York: Macmillan.

Ansoff, H. I., 1980. Strategic issue management. *Strategic Management Journal, 1*: 131–48.

Armstrong, R., and Jones, M., 1980. Education for public affairs. *Public Affairs Review, 1*: 39–49.

Avon Corporation, 1999. Avon's breast cancer awareness crusade, Retrieved from http://www.avoncrusade.com/ (accessed June 30, 2016).

Brown, J. K., 1971. *This Business of Issues: Coping with the Company's Environment*. New York: The Conference Board.

California Management Review, 1969a. Business and the Urban Scene. *California Management Review, 11* (Summer): Special Issue.

California Management Review, 1969b. The Social Environment – A New Corporate Response. *California Management Review, 12* (Fall): Special Issue.

Chandler, A., 1980. Government versus business: An American phenomenon, in John Dunlop (ed.), *Business and Public Policy*. Cambridge, MA: Harvard University Press.

Chase, H. W., 1977. Public issues management: The new science, *Public Relations Journal, 33* (5): 25–6.

Chase, H. W., 1982. Issue management conference – A special report. *Corporate Public Issues and Their Management, 7*: 1–2.

Chase, H. W., 1984. *Issues Management: Origins of the Future*. Stamford, CT: Issues Action Publication.

Coen, D., 1997. The evolution of the large firm as a political actor in the European Union. *Journal of Management, 30* (6): 837–57.

Cohn, J., 1971. *The Conscience of the Corporation: Business and Urban Affairs, 1967–1970*. Baltimore, MD: The Johns Hopkins University Press.

Dill, W. R., 1958. Environment as an influence in managerial autonomy. *Administrative Science Quarterly, 2*: 409–43.

Eelis, R., 1958–9. The corporate image in public relations. *California Management Review, 1* (4): 15–23.

Epstein, E. M., 1969. *The Corporation in American Politics*. Englewood Cliffs: Prentice-Hall.

Fleisher, C. S., 2005. The global development of public affairs, in P. Harris and C. S. Fleisher (eds.), *Handbook of Public Affairs*. London: Sage: 5–30.

Foundation for Public Affairs, 2005. *The State of Corporate Public Affairs*. Washington, DC: Foundation for Public Affairs.

Freeman, R. E., 1984. *Strategic Management: A Stakeholder Approach*. Boston, MA: Pitman.

Galambos, L., 1975. *The Public Image of Big Business in America, 1880–1940*. London: The Johns Hopkins University Press.

Garraty, J., 1966. *The American Nation*. New York: Harper and Row.

Griffin, J. J., 1997. Corporate Public Affairs in the 1990s: Structure, Resources, and Processes. Unpublished Doctoral Dissertation, Boston University School of Management, Boston, MA.

Griffin, J. J., Fleisher, C. S., Brenner, S., and Boddewyn, J., 2001a. Corporate public affairs research: Chronological reference list: Part 1: 1958–1984. *International Journal of Public Affairs*, *1* (2): 169–86.

Griffin, J. J., Fleisher, C. S., Brenner, S., and Boddewyn, J., 2001b. Corporate public affairs research: Chronological reference list: Part 2: 1985–2000. *International Journal of Public Affairs*, *2* (1): 9–32.

Gruber, W., and Hoewing, R., 1980. The new management in corporate public affairs. *Public Affairs Review*, *1*: 13–23.

Heald, M., 1970. *The Social Responsibility of Business: Company and Community, 1900–1960*. Cleveland: Case Western Reserve Press.

Hegarty, W. H., Aplin, J. C., and Cosier, R. H., 1978. Achieving corporate success in external affairs. *Business Horizons*, *21*: 65–74.

Holcomb, J. M., 2006. Public affairs in North America: US origins and development, in P. Harris and C. S. Fleisher (eds.), *Handbook of Public Affairs*. London: Sage: 31–49.

Johnson, J., 1983. Issues management: What are the issues? *Business Quarterly*, *48* (3): 22–31.

Josephson, M., 1962. *The Robber Barons*. New York: Harvest Books.

Koch, F., 1979. A strategy for corporate giving and community involvement, *The New Corporate Philanthropy*. Springer Books: 12–22.

McGrath, P., 1976. *Managing Corporate External Relations*. New York: The Conference Board.

McGrath, P., 1977. *Action Plan for Public Affairs*. New York: The Conference Board.

McGuire, S., Lindeque, J., and Suder, G., 2012. Learning and lobbying: Emerging market firms and corporate political activity in Europe. *European Journal of International Management*, *6* (3): 342–62.

Mahon, J. F., 1982. The Corporate Public Affairs Office: Structure, Behavior and Impact. Unpublished Doctoral Dissertation, Boston University School of Management, Boston, MA.

Mahon, J. F., and Wartick, S. L., 2005. Assessing corporate social performance: Linking strategy and stakeholders of the firm. *Global Business and Economics Review*, *7* (2/3) (October): 133–54.

Mitchell, R. K., Agle, B. R., and Wood, D. J. 1997. Toward a theory of stakeholder identification and salience: Defining the principle of who and what really counts. *Academy of Management Review*, *22* (4): 853–86.

Morison, S. E., 1965. *The Oxford History of the American People*. New York: Oxford University Press.

Morris, S., 1980. Managing corporate external affairs. *Management Review*, *69*: 48–53.

Porter, M. E., and Kramer, M. R., 2002. The competitive advantage of corporate philanthropy. *Harvard Business Review*, *80* (12): 56–69.

Post, J. E., 1979. 'The internal management of social responsiveness: The role of the public affairs department,' paper presented at a Seminar on the Corporation in Society: Planning and Management of Corporate Responsibility at the University of Santa Clara, CA, October.

Post, J. E., and Griffin, J. J., 1996. *The State of Corporate Public Affairs: Final Report*. Washington, DC: Foundation for Public Affairs and Boston University School of Management.

Post, J. E., and Mahon, J. F., 1981. 'Strategic management of external relations: How companies manage public affairs,' paper presented at the International Conference on Global Strategic Management, London, October.

Post, J. E., Murray, E. A., Dickie, R., and Mahon, J. F., 1981. Public affairs offices and their functions: Highlights of a national survey. *Public Affairs Review, 2*: 88–99.

Post, J. E., Murray, E. A., Dickie, R., and Mahon, J. F., 1982. The public affairs function in American corporations: Development and relations with corporate planning. *Long Range Planning, 15* (2): 12–21.

Public Affairs Research Group (PARG), School of Management, Boston University, 1981. *Public Affairs Offices and Their Functions: Summary of Survey Responses.*

Schattschneider, E. E., 1960. *The Semi-Sovereign People.* New York: Holt.

Tedlow, R., 1979. *Keeping the Corporate Image: Public Relations and Business.* Greenwich, CT: JAI Press.

Wartick, S. L., and Mahon, J. F., 1994. Toward a substantive definition of the corporate issue construct: A review and synthesis of the literature. *Business & Society, 33* (3): 293–311.

Weidenbaum, M., 1980. Public policy: No longer a spectator sport for business. *Journal of Business Strategy, 1*: 46–53.

22

Public Affairs in Latin America: The Gradual and Uneven Formalization of a Long-Time Informal Activity

Andréa Cristina Oliveira Gozetto and
Clive S. Thomas

INTRODUCTION

Joan Navarro, Vice Chairman of Public Affairs at Llorent & Cuenca, an international public affairs consultancy with offices throughout Latin America, summed up the present status and development of public affair in the region in this way:

> While it's gaining importance, government relations in Latin America is still a young practice, particularly if defined by US or European standards. Fortunately, the consolidation of democratic systems throughout the region is enabling the professional development of those agents more inclined to interact with governments on a permanent and open basis, such as business organizations. (Navarro, 2015)

In a region as vast as Latin America, four times the size of Europe, while there is no common pattern across the region regarding the development and current status of public affairs (or government affairs, as Latin Americans usually call the core activity of public affairs), Navarro's encapsulation is a good starting point.

Given specific differences in colonial experiences and particular paths of political development, there is no single Latin American identity. Lumping together the region's countries as *Latin America* is an oversimplification of these differences. Nevertheless, this is the way the region is often viewed by many scholars, the media and even governments. That said, we can identify some general characteristics of the socio-economic and particularly the political development of the region.

Some form of government relations has always existed in Latin America, but is in the process of moving from an informal to a formal activity. The development (or lack thereof) of public affairs has been shaped by the social, economic and particularly the political culture of the region. But because of varying levels of development, public affairs varies from country to country and even within countries.

Table 22.1   The countries of Latin America

Alphabetical Listing	Mexico and Central America	South America
Argentina	Costa Rica	Argentina
Bolivia	El Salvador	Bolivia
Brazil	Guatemala	Brazil
Chile	Honduras	Chile
Colombia	Mexico	Colombia
Central America		
Costa Rica	Nicaragua	Ecuador
Cuba	Panama	Paraguay
Dominican Republic	The Caribbean	Peru
Ecuador		Uruguay
El Salvador	Cuba	Venezuela
Guatemala		
Haiti	Dominican Republic	
Honduras	Haiti	
Mexico		
Nicaragua		
Panama		
Paraguay		
Peru		
Uruguay		
Venezuela		

From a socio-cultural and historical perspective, Latin America includes those countries with a Spanish, Portuguese and in one case (Haiti), a French colonial heritage. So the region excludes those countries and possessions of English and Dutch colonial origin, and some of French origin, as well as US possessions in the Caribbean. By this definition there are twenty Latin American countries (as listed in Table 22.1). Nineteen of these now have some form of democratic government. The exception is Cuba and so it is not included in this chapter.

While no direct research and writing has been conducted on public affairs as such in Latin America, there is a small body of literature on interest groups and lobbying in several countries, on individual interests, and some comparative studies. We draw on many of these throughout the chapter. Our major sources of information, however, are the findings from a survey developed specifically for this chapter. The survey was distributed to

public affairs practitioners in several countries across the region. The chapter also draws on previous original research by the authors.[1]

THE MEANING OF PUBLIC AFFAIRS ACROSS LATIN AMERICA AND THE USE OF TERMS IN THIS CHAPTER

We can take as the benchmark of the practice of public affairs the way it is viewed in Britain, many British Commonwealth countries and in parts of Europe: the promotion of the interests of a private business or corporation in its dealings with the public sector. This includes: promoting the business's image through public relations; issues of social responsibility, regarding business ethics and dealing with issues such as the environment; and interaction with government on public policy issues and actions that affect a business – commonly known as lobbying. However, because of the negative image of lobbying, many companies avoid the term and use euphemisms such as government relations, governmental affairs, corporate affairs or corporate relations.

The definitional boundaries of public affairs and lobbying are very porous and have grown increasingly so since the 1980s. This reflects that today many scholars and commentators use the term public affairs to include all entities that lobby from business to unions to environmentalists to social issue groups, such as gay rights and pro- and anti-abortion to community groups. Many scholars also include the role of government as a lobbyist as well as government as a target of lobbying. This broad view of the interests, groups and organizations involved in public affairs was reflected in many of the survey responses we received for this chapter.

While all the activities covered by the original meaning of public affairs as it applied to business are now part of what most businesses and a range of other groups, organizations and interests engage in across Latin America, it is rarely referred to as public affairs as such. In fact, there is no agreed upon term across Latin America to refer to all the activities embraced by the traditional meaning of public affairs. This also came through clearly in our survey research. One reason may be the newness of this activity in the region, as we will see later. What is traditionally referred to as public affairs is variously called public relations, public sector relations and corporate affairs, among other designations.

Private sector–government relations in working to affect public policy is embraced, as in other parts of the world, within the terms government affairs, governmental relations, corporate relations or corporate affairs. It is the government affairs activity in terms of the political advocacy role of business and other groups, organizations and interests that works to affect public policy in Latin America. That is the subject of this chapter.

Even though the term public affairs is not used in Latin America for the lobbying activities of business and other organizations, we use the term public affairs in this chapter to keep our terminology consistent with other chapters in this Handbook.

THE ECONOMIC, POLITICAL, SOCIAL AND CULTURAL CONTEXT

Since the conquistadores colonized what is now Latin America in the sixteenth century, and particularly since the region's push for independence two centuries ago and until very recently, Latin American politics has been known for various forms of eight related characteristics.

Latin America's Political Tradition

First has been a strong statist and monist view of government, often manifesting itself in state corporatist-type arrangements, resulting in a weak civil society. Second is the

persistence of personalism in politics, where personalities dominate and where institutionalism has been slow to take root. Third is elitism, mainly whites and often the military. Elitism had gone hand-in-hand with the fourth characteristic – the exclusion of several groups from political power, particularly many racial and ethnic minorities, indigenous peoples and women.

These first four elements have shaped the other four characteristics. Fifth has been a feeling of political alienation, in some cases a fear of government, among many citizens, coupled with and often reinforced by the sixth characteristic. This is a slow and often retrogressive movement towards broad political participation as countries alternated between dictatorships and various limited forms of democracy. Seventh is a very mixed, often deplorable record of civil liberties and human rights. Finally, there is political corruption, often very overt. Corruption has been endemic to political life, stemming from the dominance of personalism and informal political institutions in the political culture producing clientelism and other forms of particularist as opposed to formal political institutional relationships.

The Consequences for Government Affairs

Of the many consequences of these characteristics for government affairs and political advocacy, five are most enlightening.

First, it has led to very restricted access to the policy process. With the exception of some countries like Uruguay, Costa Rica and for a while Chile and Brazil, the process has been dominated by a small elite with little access by other groups. Second, until the 1980s and the return to or first experiences of democracy of most of the region's countries, government affairs activity was very personalized and dominated by the small elite. This, of course, is a very informal and loose definition of public affairs. These first two factors undermined the development of institutional structures and channels for government affairs, leading to the third factor, namely that it allows corruption to flourish. Although perhaps less than in the past, corruption flourishes to this day even in the more advanced democracies of the region. This was demonstrated by events in 2014 and 2015 in Chile, involving President Michelle Bachelet's son, and in a corruption scandal involving Brazil's national oil company, Petrobrás.

Fourth, and as a result of the first three factors, Latin American government affairs and political advocacy were dominated for centuries by power groups. These are politically influential individuals or cliques that often controlled the policy process. As we explain in the next three sections, these groups are part of all group systems, democratic and otherwise, but far more prominent in authoritarian systems like those in Latin America. And fifth, the exclusionary and authoritarian political systems that existed across the region for most of its history were not conducive to the development of a feeling of political efficacy (a feeling of the ability to influence government actions) by the mass of Latin American citizens. In fact, the tradition has been quite the contrary, tending to discourage political participation, in some cases making it impossible given the restricted franchise, not to mention that political activity, particularly actions opposing the regime, was very unwise during dictatorships.

What all this adds up to is a political tradition and political environment across most of Latin America that, for generations, led to a public affairs system that was highly informal and highly restricted in regard to those participating for it remains so in many countries today.

THE POLITICAL-CULTURAL CONTEXT OF GOVERNMENT RELATIONS

What has had a major influence on this development and the current status of public affairs is the socio-economic and particularly the political culture of the region.

Political culture is fundamental to the structure, operation and the policies of all political systems. Political culture is one part of the broader culture of a society. As such, it consists of the beliefs (the evaluation of the truth or falsity of ideas or purported facts) and attitudes (the outward expression of a belief or emotion about an idea, fact or person) regarding three elements: (1) The range of acceptable behavior by those involved in the political process; (2) the extent of government operations and power and the limits on them, if any; and (3) how individuals view their relationship to the political and governmental system, including their level of political efficacy.

Political culture is acquired through a process of political socialization. This process begins in early childhood and continues throughout life. Political-cultural values are transmitted by parents and families, peer groups, schools and colleges, the media, churches, government officials, and candidates for political office, among other socialization agents. Of the many aspects of Latin American political culture, six are particularly relevant for understanding the development and current status of government affairs in the region.

Family

Throughout Latin America the family is the dominant institution socially, psychologically and economically. Certainly, family is important in advanced democracies too – but not to the same all-pervasive extent. These relationships in Latin America persist to this day, rather akin to the political cultural traits of southern Europe and many developing countries.

In the long-standing democracies, there is a more or less clear line between the private sphere of the family and the public sphere; the line has been much less clear in Latin America. In many ways this is still true today.

The effects of this include directing public money to family members such as awarding contracts to relatives, nepotism, and pressuring interest group leaders and others to provide benefits to family members (Freyre, 1973; Holanda, 1996; Judd, 2011, 18–19; Rohter, 2012, Chap. 2).

Elitism

Elitism is part of and reinforced by the major socio-economic and political disparities in Latin America. From colonial times there was a small elite that was well educated, had large landholdings and later ran business enterprises and were involved in government through personal contacts and often as an elected or appointed official of a government. Besides large landowners and business people, this also included senior military officers and the clergy from the prominent institution of the Catholic Church. This elite was perhaps one or two percent of the population. Until well into the twentieth century in most countries, the mass of the population was poor, illiterate, very deferential, exploited by this elite economically and excluded from political participation of all types.

With their lock on political access and influence, the elites in most countries had no incentive to encourage increased political participation by the mass of society – in fact, quite the reverse. This stunted the growth of political institutions and perpetuated personalism based on informal and behind-the-scenes political dealings. There were exceptions, however, particularly in Chile, Uruguay and to some extent Brazil, where mass union movements and other interests developed to challenge the elite.

Political Corruption

Transparency International (TI), the international anti-corruption NGO, defines political corruption as 'the illegal use of private funds for personal gain' (Transparency International, 2014). The dominance of the family and the lack of political checks on elites were and remain major reasons for endemic and widespread corruption in Latin American politics. As indicated earlier, the practice is so entrenched that it even affects the more advanced democratic systems in the region.

What constitutes corruption, however, is largely determined by local cultural practices, and therefore, many actions would not be considered corruption in Latin America that would be considered so in Europe or the United States. Nevertheless, laws to fight corruption in several of the region's countries do use standards common in advanced democracies.

A Deep Public Skepticism of Interest Groups

The dominance of policy making by the elite and the all-pervasiveness of corruption have contributed to a deep skepticism of interest groups and those who work for and represent them. This skepticism goes much deeper than in the United States or Europe, partly owing to historical circumstances and the role of the media. Not only have civil elites been seen as corrupt over the years and in many cases today, but many members of the military are also viewed in this way. It was, in fact, during military rule between the 1960s and 1980s that the media, largely surreptitiously through underground activity, linked interest groups, interests and lobbying with corruption.

This interest group–corruption link has stuck in the public mind. It is reinforced by the lack of transparency of interest group and lobbying connections with government across much of the region. The default assumption is that if things happen behind closed door with no public scrutiny, something nefarious is happening.

Low Levels of Political Efficacy

Exclusion from the policy process for generation after generation, the serious risks of participating in politics during authoritarian regimes, and mass poverty and lack of education, are not conducive to a deep feeling of political efficacy among the mass of Latin Americans. Added to this is a strong strain of deference on the part of many. Again, to use the situation in Brazil, one legacy of this hierarchical element is a 'top-down' psychology in society where, for many Brazilians, government and politicians are seen as very remote (Santos, 2013).

In contrast, the elites have a high level of political efficacy and have had for generations. Through fair means or foul, they know that if they have the right contacts and the resources, they stand a very good chance of affecting public policy in their favor.

Minimal Knowledge of the Basics of Civic Engagement

A low standard of education for many Latin Americans combined with a low level of political efficacy, plus poverty and other factors, means that the majority of Latin Americans have very little knowledge of how their political system works. Furthermore, many citizens, and even some organizations, do not realize that they can go to government to present their cause (Judd, 2011, 16).

As political activism was a very risky business under authoritarian regimes, this meant that between the mid-1960s and the mid-1980s the generation that came of age in these years avoided political participation. Thus they never learned the ways of approaching and trying to influence government. Moreover, several interests involved in the protests of the latter years of military regimes have not moved beyond this indirect form of lobbying, often because they are not schooled in the techniques of sophisticated lobbying (Santos, 2013).

The Implications for Government Affairs

Clearly, the nature of this political culture in Latin America contrasts sharply with those of Western Europe, the United States and other long-standing and advanced democracies. Because political culture has a major influence on the conduct of public affairs, this means that there are some major differences in the conduct of political advocacy in Latin America. These include government affairs being in a nascent stage for most of the region; where government affairs operates, it is largely the province of a small elite, though less so since the return to democracy, a system that is less institutionalized and more personalized; government affairs being viewed very negatively by the mass of the population, in part due to the persistence of political corruption; and political advocacy still operates largely behind closed doors.

The rest of this chapter expands on these characteristics of Latin American government affairs as, in large part, shaped by the region's political culture.

THE DEVELOPMENT AND CONTEMPORARY STATUS OF INTEREST GROUP SYSTEMS IN LATIN AMERICA

Like the development of interest groups in all political systems, a broad way to view this development is as a transition from a system based predominantly on the operation of a few influential power groups to one more formalized – an institutionalization of the group system and the techniques used to influence government policy. Across the region there were several common power groups from before independence well into the twentieth century. These included the Catholic Church, certain elements of the military, landowners, family and patronage groups, and foreign influential forces including the British, French and Spanish and later the US government and various businesses from these countries. The influence of various foreign interests and interest groups has always been a major aspect of Latin American political systems. However, past and present there were and remain variations in the extent and influence of these various domestic and foreign power groups across Latin America.

Also, as in most political systems, it was economic interests that were the first to organize and to transition to more formalized interest groups. In some countries, such as Argentina, Chile and Costa Rica, this transition began in the latter half of the nineteenth century. For instance, the Uruguay National Chamber of Commerce dates back to 1867 (Piacenza and Benavente, 2009) and in Costa Rica the development of civil society in the late nineteenth century included the establishment of *colegios*, which are professional organizations including lawyers, doctors, engineers, journalists, architects, pharmacists and others (Booth, 1998, 95–8). In others, such as Paraguay, Bolivia, Haiti and some Central American countries, this group institutionalization process did not occur in a major way until the mid-twentieth century, and then, only to varying degrees. In still other countries, like Brazil, Peru and Colombia, the timeline of this transition fell somewhere in between.

In the first half of the twentieth century, in the relatively developed countries, an increasing number of formalized interests arrived on the political scene, mainly industrial, agri-business and labor groups. With some exceptions, like Uruguay and Costa Rica, these were usually co-opted by government in some form of state corporatist arrangements. Also, beginning in the 1920s, university students became a force in demonstrating for various causes, usually against dictators. Student groups remain very active today. Workers' protests also increased, though in most countries they were still excluded from the halls of power.

Even into the 1960s, civil society was weak in most countries and access to the policy-making process was more often than not still very restricted (again, with some exceptions down to the early 1970s in Uruguay and Chile, and Brazil until 1964). Throughout much of the region during the dictatorships of the 1960s to the mid-1980s, most groups were banned, particularly labor groups, and major controls placed on the media. As a result, with the exception of the three countries that remained more or less democracies during these years, Costa Rica, Colombia and Venezuela, the development of the interest group system was stymied and levels of political efficacy remained low. Corruption continued to be rife in all systems, including the military regimes as mentioned earlier. And as we will see in the next section, this had a major influence on the lack of development of a formalized process of public affairs.

Latin America's Contemporary Interest Group Systems

Since the return of democracy or the first move to democracy in several countries in the region during the 1980s (Cuba excepted and now Venezuela too), the policy process has become more open. In addition, range and number of interests and interest groups has expanded and, in most cases, the use of political advocacy strategies and tactics has broadened. As in the past, however, across the region a wide variation exists between the levels of development of group systems. In this regard Klimovich and Thomas (2014, 184–5) offer a useful way to categorize the range of systems on a spectrum from unified to bifurcated group systems.

Integrated systems are those where there is a high level of institutionalization of the system, widespread sophistication of advocacy group organization, general access of civil society groups to the policy-making process, widespread knowledge in society of lobbying strategies and tactics, and a high degree of competition between a wide range of formalized and informal interests.

Uruguay, Brazil, Costa Rica and Chile are examples of integrated systems. They are seen as approaching the level of sophistication in their advocacy systems of those in advanced democracies, like the United States and those of Western Europe.

In contrast, a bifurcated interest group system is one that has a low level of institutionalization, only a small minority of advocacy groups have sophisticated organizations, there is limited access of groups to the policy-making process, minimal knowledge in society of lobbying strategies and tactics, and a less competitive group system. Bifurcated systems are underdeveloped, predominantly elitist and usually characterized by social and protest movements among those not part of the elitist system. Therefore, the duality or bifurcation of the advocacy system is a result of the reality of two advocacy communities existing in a country: a small insider elite and the mass of society as outsiders.

Paraguay, Haiti and Guatemala are examples of bifurcated political advocacy systems. Even though the knowledge of the operation of advanced interest group systems in the established democracies is likely well-known among the small elite in bifurcated countries, the systems are not approaching the level of development of these advanced systems. Bifurcated systems are more akin to those in Eastern Europe immediately after the fall of communism and of many African countries today that have had mixed experience with democracy, such as Kenya, Zimbabwe and even South Africa.

This difference between integrated and bifurcated systems should not be seen as a clear division. It is, in fact, one of degree and is best represented by a continuum along a scale from the most integrated (which, in effect, means the most developed) to the most bifurcated (the least developed). Other Latin American countries, like Bolivia, Colombia and Panama, fall at various points along the continuum. Furthermore, neither are we

claiming that the two segments of bifurcated advocacy systems – the elite and outsider segments – are totally separate. Clearly they are not, as the outsider interests are working to influence the insiders and policy-makers. There is often much overlap between, and in some cases, as in Bolivia, increasing convergence of, the two parts of the system.

PUBLIC AFFAIRS–GOVERNMENT RELATIONS IN LATIN AMERICA: AN OVERVIEW

Overall, public affairs is in its infancy in Latin America as Joan Navarro indicates in the opening quote of this chapter. This nascent state of development was confirmed by the research conducted for this project. Generally, the activity is in a state of transition towards a more open and professional status. Reflecting the levels of political development, the position and influence of government affairs in Latin America varies greatly and it is hard to encompass the entire region in one short overview. There are different levels of maturity and sophistication in this area throughout the region.

Variations Across the Region

Public affairs across Latin America ranges from the highly developed, sophisticated and professional, on a par with the advocacy business in the United States or Europe, to no more than the old style of personal contacts and dealings far from public view that may involve corruption. Regarding individual countries, a sample of the returns from our survey revealed the following.

Brazil, Chile, Costa Rica, Uruguay and to a large extent, Argentina and Mexico have elements of their systems that, as largely integrated systems, are highly developed. Chile even has lobby regulation, which, as we will see later, is not common in the region. Besides corporate interests, in these countries, unions and major trade associations and other organizations also lobby, most notably government and various NGOs. At the other end of the scale are many citizens who have low levels of political efficacy and do not understand government affairs or how they can access government (Macário, 2013). Some of these engage in protests (often called manifestations in parts of Latin America) but generally lack knowledge of how to follow up such actions with direct lobbying of public officials.

Countries such as Ecuador, Colombia, Panama, the Dominican Republic and Bolivia fall in the middle range of the integrated–bifurcated scale. A lower level of government affairs professionalism exists in these countries, and an even larger segment of the population is ignorant of how to engage in political advocacy. Then there are the bifurcated systems in countries like Haiti, Paraguay and Honduras, where government affairs have a small elite with the mass of the population being left out in the political cold. Protests are the major way that the mass of the population engages in government affairs, but their successes are mixed and often meet with strong resistance from the government, sometimes even violence from the police or the military.

In general, the activity of government affairs at the professional level has developed considerably since the return to democracy. Major changes, for example, have taken place in Brazil since 2000 according to Luiz Santos, former Deputy Chief of Staff in the Office of the President of Brazil (Santos, 2013). One important influence on this development has been foreign businesses and multinational corporations from outside the region like Google, Mastercard, IBM, and automakers from Germany and Japan. These are important customers for public affairs professionals. Government relations professionals are crucial in countries that are protectionist in foreign trade like Brazil. Foreign companies count on these professionals in order to deal with these countries' numerous regulations and bureaucracy.

Organization of Public Affairs Activity

The organization of government affairs, more or less, falls into four categories: individuals and firms in the private sector; those working for corporations; those working for various associations, NGOs and other non-profits; and those in government.

All countries in the region have a community of private public affairs professionals. As the most populous country and one of the most developed, Brazil has the largest private public affairs community. This consists of individual operations such as Antonio Marcos Umbelino Lobo who runs the firm Umbelino Lobo (Lobo, 2013). There are also some international companies that engage in the broad area of public affairs. Two of the best-known are Burson-Marsteller, established in Switzerland with offices around the world and operations in twelve Latin American countries; and Llorent & Cuenca, a Spanish company with operations in Spain, Portugal and ten countries in Latin America.[2]

Besides hiring consulting and advocacy firms to aid in lobbying, businesses are increasingly hiring their own government relations staff. This is particularly the case with foreign companies. Google's operation in Brazil for example, has a division focusing on government relations with federal and state governments. Their major representative is Mariana Macário (Macário, 2013). Latin American domestic businesses from Mexico to Argentina also have government relations department, particularly the region's multinationals, like Teléfonos de México (TelMex).

Like their counterparts across the developed world, many professional associations, unions and other organizations have in-house lobbyists. In terms of political advocates, Uruguay provides three typical examples. One is Gustavo Pérez, a former president of the Central Council of the Uruguayan Bank Employees Association (AEBU), who remains a political advocate for his organization (Pérez, 2009). Another is

Claudio Piacenza, assistant manager for the Uruguayan National Chamber of Commerce, who deals with both legislative and executive branches of government (Piacenza and Benavente, 2009). The third example is that of Ignacion Munyo and Carlos Díaz, senior specialists for CERES, a conservative think tank focusing on macro-economic policy. They deal with the Uruguayan government to secure grants and also to advocate for their policy positions (Munyo and Díaz, 2009).

While not referred to as either lobbyists or political advocates, the fourth category of government affairs professionals is the representatives of government agencies and government corporations. These represent their agencies to the legislative and executive branches of government to provide information, advocate for the programs and budgets and also to protect their organizations' interests. Two examples from Brazil are Paulo Maurício Costa, who is a former legislative director for the federal Ministry of Justice, and Cintia Cury (2013), Director of Parliamentary Affairs for EMBRAPA (the Brazilian Enterprise for Agricultural Research).

The Extent of Professional Education

The respondents to our survey regarding formal education in public affairs reported no or only a few offerings. There are, however, an increasing number of courses and even some university degrees offered. Plus, there are some workshops held by private organizations and businesses, some by private consultants and some offered through professional conferences. The information we received tends to indicate that such professional training takes place more in the larger countries and integrated group systems, such as Argentina, Brazil, Costa Rica and Uruguay. The need for formal education in these countries is a reflection of the increasing complexity of strategies and tactics and the desire for the new breed of advocates to secure a more professional image, among other reasons.

As its formal professional training is the most developed, we can use Brazil to provide a range of examples. In 2015, Fundação Getulio Vargas (FGV), a prestigious private university in São Paulo, launched a Master of Business Administration (MBA) in Government Relations. Then there is the Brazilian Corporate Communication Association (ABERJE), the major goal of which is to promote professionalism. ABERJE holds conferences to enhance knowledge and skills of its members and also publishes books on government affairs. In terms of individual public affairs practitioners aiding in the education of political advocacy, one of the services that Antonio Marcos provides in his consulting practice is educating his clients on the dos and don'ts of political advocacy (Lobo, 2013). And as the in-house government affairs person for Google Brazil, Mariana Macário works to get others at the firm knowledgeable in government affairs and how it aids the company. Foreign businesses are particularly interested in improving professional training in public affairs.

STRATEGIES AND TACTICS

The extent of the types of strategies and tactics employed varies not only across the region but within countries. The variety of strategies and tactics range from the old ways based upon personal contacts alone sometimes involving corruption, to demonstrations and protests, to sophisticated operations using all the modern techniques of both direct and indirect methods by government affairs professionals. Here we briefly outline this range of lobbying approaches, beginning with what remains the major form of government affairs activity – personal contacts.

The Importance of Personal Contacts – Past and Present

Using personal contact is not only the most widely used lobbying technique but also the most necessary. Unless a lobbyist can communicate to the policy-maker the specifics of their issue or needs, they are not likely to be successful.

Certainly, personal contacts are fundamental in political advocacy in all political systems. But for historical and cultural reasons, and the underdeveloped nature of many political systems in Latin America, personal contact with policy-makers is by far the most used lobbying tactic, and in some cases the only one used by many groups, organizations and individual government affairs practitioners. The methods of what we can call old-style lobbyists were based on contacts through family, friends, business relationships, other personal connections and often involved corruption, even among the military. Mariana Macário, the Google government affairs person, tells of a member of Congress requesting money to aid her lobbying effort; she categorically declined.

The old-style lobbyist still thrives today in all Latin American countries alongside the government affairs professional. While these professionals work in more aboveboard ways, all our surveys and previous interviews of government affairs personnel clearly show that personal contact is also their major modus operandi in working to influence policy-makers. For example, in Uruguay, with less than 4 million people, a sort of friends and neighbors politics operates even for formalized groups of business and unions (Butler, 2009; Pérez, 2009; Piacenza and Benavente, 2009). Also, personal contacts are the major form of lobbying in countries with large populations such as Brazil (Santos, 2013: Lobo, 2013).

Personal contacts are also important because of the Latin American style of doing business in public affairs and the conditions of bureaucracy that pervade the region. Most policy-makers do not like the hard sell by lobbyists as in the United States and they do not generally like to deal with contract lobbyists, but prefer the members of an organization or group to lobby them. And while technical information is important, personal relationships take precedence over these (Cordoso, 1973). Alejandro Butler, who runs the government affairs consulting firm Improfit Casa de Comunicación in Montevideo, calls this the 'cousin syndrome' (2009). Introductions to policy-makers by friends or family give a lobbyist more credibility than their ability to provide technical information, though technical information is becoming increasingly important.

An important part of personal contact relates to 'fixing things', which is necessary because of the inherent bureaucracy stemming from the Iberian tradition. So getting around or over this stumbling block is essential. In Brazil this is called *jeitinho*, with the need to do so often arising because of the fabled Brazilian *papelada* (red tape), a longstanding legacy in Brazil and throughout the region (Lobo, 2013).

The Sophisticated Operations

For a long time it was thought that the work of government affairs just involved having an address book and organizing meetings. Today, at least at the professional level, public affairs is seen as a service that can assist a company, interest groups, NGO or other organization to use a range of strategies and techniques to benefit their cause. In so doing it can be of benefit to both the group and policy-makers. Also, businesses, unions and professional associations as well as NGOs are increasingly setting up government affairs divisions and employing sophisticated techniques beyond just personal contacts. In addition, there are the international consultancies. These tend to provide a range of services for their clients of which government affairs is often only one.

The international consulting firm LLorent & Cuenca is an example of a sophisticated operation. Its purpose is to provide clients with strategic counsel, research, program development and execution to further their business strategies and manage their reputation and their policy engagement. The activities are very diverse and public affairs is only part (but an important part) of what LLorent & Cuenca offers. In regard to public affairs, the company provides clients with three major services:

- Political intelligence: the anticipation of regulatory risks and scenarios.
- Institutional positioning: the improvement of the level of relations between the enterprises and the government and other public authorities.
- Lobbying: actions aimed at influencing the decision-making processes. These often include workshops and other training in political advocacy for clients.

In some countries, such as Uruguay and Chile where political parties are strong and have major influence over policy making, some groups and interests align with them. This includes business with conservative parties and unions with left-wing parties. This can be a major benefit when their party is in power in getting their issues on the policy agenda, but a disadvantage when their party is out of power.

Use of Social Media

Our survey question on the use of social media showed mixed results in its use. Some consultancies are beginning to use social media to promote the image of their clients and also to be more effective in getting messages over to policy-makers. At the other end of the scale, many businesses and the smaller – one or two person – consultancies said they do not use social media. Most of the respondents, however, saw its use as on the increase across the region.

Interestingly, throughout Latin America social media has probably been used more

by protest groups and others involved in demonstrations, such as students, indigenous groups and more traditional organizations like unions both blue and white collar. These have often used social media to coordinate their demonstrations and protests.

CONCERNS ABOUT INTEREST GROUPS IN LATIN AMERICA: THE ISSUES OF REGULATION

Few Latin American countries have any form of regulation regarding interest group and advocacy activity. Where the extent of transparency of government activities is more extensive, enforcement is often lax. According to many professionals in the government affairs profession across the region, it is, in large part, this lack of regulation and transparency that is at the root of the low esteem in which government affairs and its practitioners are viewed. Thus, regulation and transparency is seen as the single most important development to make the government affairs business more acceptable and as an essential part of a democratic society.

An important point to bear in mind when considering concerns about interest groups in Latin America and elsewhere in democratic systems is that successful regulation does not depend on lobby laws alone as Santos and Costa (2014) point out. Lobby laws need to be part of an open governance package that includes provisions for transparency of government actions, ethics laws, campaign finance regulations and conflict of interest provisions. However, space does not permit consideration of these other provisions in this article.

The Extent of Lobby Regulation Across the Region

Although many countries have considered enacting lobby laws, only three countries have such laws and they are very recent. Peru was the first to enact a lobby law in 2003, followed by Chile in 2010, and Mexico in 2011. The Mexican law, however, covers only the legislature (Ortega González, 2014). But in all three countries the laws tend to be very bureaucratic and are too restrictive and, therefore, have had the opposite effect than intended: instead of promoting transparency and professionalism, they have motivated circumvention of the regulations. While Brazil and Argentina do not have lobby laws, they do have laws providing for extensive transparency with respect to the executive branch.

The Pressures to Enact Lobby Regulations

Pressure to enact lobby laws and reform those in the three countries that have existing laws comes from several sources: the public, the media, foreign corporations (and many domestic ones), government affairs professionals, left-wing parties and interest groups, social movements, and international organizations, particularly the OECD (the Organization for Cooperation and Development).

Public pressure is, of course, the most amorphous of these pressures. But there is a general feeling among the middle class and other educated segments of society that regulation can end corruption or at least reduce it substantially. The public is egged on by the media which has done much to perpetuate the direct connection between lobbying and corruption.

Foreign corporations feel that enacting lobby laws and more extensive provisions for transparency will increase their ability to compete for contracts. They feel disadvantaged because of the extensive corruption and backroom deals that are done between domestic businesses and public officials. In addition, most foreign corporations need to engage in political advocacy and they would like fair competition in that activity

too. Lobby laws and transparency will also enhance their public image so that all can see that their lobbying activities are legitimate and professional. It is the desire to change the image of government affairs as being corrupt or at least shady and to demonstrate its legitimacy that most professional government affairs practitioners support regulation and increased transparency. Left-wing political parties and social movements favor regulation also to level the lobbying playing field.

Promoting transparency in lobbying as part of advancing pluralist democracy is also the major reason that the OECD has conducted several studies on lobbying in developing democracies, including countries in Latin America. The OECD has done so, in part, to assess the extent of corruption and make recommendations on how to deal with it (OECD, 2008, 2014a, 2014b). Much of the acceptance of the countries of Latin America in international organizations as legitimate democracies depends, in part, on the extent of public disclosure of activities involved in public policy making and citizen access to the actions of government.

Prospects for the Future

As Santos (2013) commented about Brazil, the political system is more open and accountable than it was even ten years ago. Furthermore, lobby regulation will come eventually. This is likely for most countries in the region, though more so in the integrated systems and those approaching that status. This, however, will likely be a slow and incremental process for five major reasons.

First, of course, there are political-cultural reasons and strong pressures from many political practitioners, both elected and appointed, and many of those working to influence government, who want to maintain the status quo. Second, and a related point, while they pay lip-service to reform, most politicians do not want reform. After all, the existing system was the one that got them where they are and change holds the fear of the unknown (Thomas, 2006). Third, the three countries presently with lobby laws have had mixed experiences with them, involving much bureaucracy and over-regulation. This not only encourages circumvention of the laws but does not provide a good example to other countries considering enacting such laws, and plays into the hands of those who oppose regulation. So, fourth, several countries, like Brazil, have been very tentative about adopting regulation because they fear it may not work if they have too little or too much regulation. Fifth, and a related point, there are many ways to regulate lobbying and finding the right balance is, indeed, a challenge even in long-established democracies like the United States (Thomas, 2006).

THE FUTURE OF GOVERNMENT AFFAIRS: ISSUES OF ADVANCING DEMOCRACY, INCREASED PROFESSIONALISM AND PUBLIC ATTITUDES AND AWARENESS

Given that government affairs is in the formative stage across Latin America, what will it take to advance it to approach the level of the activity in the USA and Western Europe? The first factor is the advancement of democracy, particularly in bifurcated systems. The second is increased professionalism of government affairs practitioners. Third is the need for a change in public attitudes towards government affairs.

The most democratic systems in Latin America, such as Uruguay, Costa Rica, Chile and Brazil, have the most developed, the most institutionalized, government affairs activity. In contrast, those countries with the least democratic systems, run by elites and with very low levels of political efficacy,

have bifurcated group systems, and a very underdeveloped government affairs system that is still largely informal and often corrupt.

If government affairs is to become more formalized and professionalized in Latin America, clearly the less-developed democracies have to transition into more pluralistic and participatory systems. What are the prospects that these developments in democracy will occur? The prospects for democracy to advance in the bifurcated group systems do not look promising. They face major hurdles, such as extreme poverty for most of the society, virtually no knowledge of the political system and an almost non-existent level of political efficacy. Haiti is probably the most extreme example of this but others, particularly Paraguay, are close. Perhaps more significant in terms of influences working against major advances in pluralist democracy is their long histories of authoritarianism and elite rule. The elites have no pressure on them to change their ways of influencing government, other than that from international organizations like Transparency International and the OECD, which they largely ignore. So, as in most of the history of these countries, a form of government affairs – based on the time-honored tradition of personal relationships – will continue; but the movement toward an institutionalized and professional form of political advocacy is likely a long way off. Again, from the surveys returned for this chapter, five points come across clearly on how the government affairs business can become more professional. In order of significance these are: increasing transparency and enactment of lobby laws; tackling corruption; dealing with the old-style lobbyist–policy-maker relationships; and changing public attitudes to political advocacy. We have dealt with four of these in the chapter so far, so here we make some brief comments about changing public attitudes.

As we have seen, one barrier to acceptance of government affairs specialists as legitimate professionals is the general negative attitude of the public towards politicians and all those involved in politics. This attitude has deep roots in the political culture of all countries, including those where government affairs is relatively advanced. Changing these attitudes very much depends on the same developments as advancing professionalism in government affairs, particularly tackling corruption and institute some form of meaningful transparency of the activity of political advocacy.

As to developing public awareness of the activity of public affairs and its potential benefits to the mass of society, this will take several developments. One is the continued advancement of democracy and its consolidation. This is necessary not only because of its increased pluralism and the increase in group activity, but also to allay the fears of joining groups and being engaged in political advocacy.

Certainly, a larger segment of the population will come to accept the activity of government affairs and some will participate in it. In general, however, all the familiar barriers to advancing political efficacy will take some time to overcome, probably several generations.

The Upshot

What this all means for the future of public affairs in Latin America is that an essentially bifurcated system will remain in three forms. One is that there will be a very small segment of the population, both professional government affairs people and old-style fixers, on one side and the mass of society on the other. Second, there will be the division within countries between the professionals and the old-style fixers. And third, there will likely continue to be a difference between the more advanced systems with the developed democracies and integrated government affairs systems and those of the less democratically advanced with bifurcated and essentially informal government affairs systems.

CONCLUSION: PUBLIC AFFAIRS/ GOVERNMENT RELATIONS IN A HIGHLY DIVERSE REGION

From what we have said in this chapter, five characteristics of the contemporary system of public affairs in Latin America stand out.

First, and probably the major characteristic, is its youth, its nascent condition even in the integrated group systems. Those who returned our surveys often commented that the public affairs business was far less developed than in the United States or Europe. This is not surprising given that many of these countries have only recently returned to the status of democracies where government affairs can be openly conducted.

Second, a wide range of levels of sophistication of government affairs across the region is apparent. There is a wide gap not just between the practices of political advocacy in integrated and bifurcated systems, but also within individual countries, including the most developed. These developed systems run the gamut from highly professional government affairs firms and professionals in private practice and in government, to the time-honored practices of the activities of power groups.

The activities of power groups are part of the third contemporary characteristic of government affairs in Latin America, namely the persistence of informal lobbying activity. This is largely the product of a deeply ingrained political culture that emphasizes family, friends and personal contacts and downplays the public interest. This results in much government affairs business being conducted behind closed doors and the continued widespread existence of corruption. These methods of doing political business are hard to change and they dominate how government affairs are conducted in the least-developed countries. But they also persist in integrated group systems.

Fourth, despite the persistence of the old style of lobbying, among professionals there is an increasing use of a range of techniques of lobbying, from personal contacts to grass-roots lobbying, to the use of the courts, to helping politicians get elected, to public relations campaigns and the purposeful use of protests and demonstrations. The trend across the region is, in fact, to use more sophisticated techniques in public affairs. In this regard, some of the most professional lobbyists and corporate communications/lobbying firms have a level of sophistication in their approach to political advocacy that rivals any Washington, DC or Brussels lobbying firms and their practitioners.

Fifth, even taking into consideration the increased activity in Latin America of public affairs by many trade associations, non-profits, environmentalists and NGOs, among others, the activity is still confined to a very small segment of the population. It will take major developments in the region before the mass of the population both understand and utilize the potential of public affairs.

So we can encapsulate the present status of public affairs in Latin America as follows: while the profession and the activity of political advocacy have advanced considerably since the return to democracy of most of the region's countries, government affairs has a long way to go to reach the highly sophisticated levels of the activity in the advanced democracies.

Notes

1   Regarding the surveys distributed for this chapter, a total of 50 were sent to government affairs consultant companies and individuals. We received 30 responses from the following countries: Argentina, Brazil, Chile, Colombia, the Dominican Republic, Ecuador, Mexico, Peru and Uruguay. As most were received from Brazil, by far the region's largest economy and with 35 percent of the region's population, most of the work in this chapter is based on surveys from Brazil. Other research comes from interviews by the authors in Brazil, Chile and Uruguay during the past ten years.

2   See the websites of these two companies at: www.llorenteycuenca.com for Llorent & Cuenca; and http://www.burson-marsteller.com/ for Burson-Marsteller.

REFERENCES

Booth, J. A. 1998. *Costa Rica; Quest for Democracy*. Westview Press: Boulder, CO.

Butler, Alejandro. 2009. Director, Improfit Casa de Comunicación [political consulting firm]. Personal interview by Clive Thomas, June 11.

Cardoso, F. H. 1973. 'Associated-Dependent Development: Theoretical and Practical Implications.' Chapter 6 in Alfred Stepan, ed., *Authoritarian Brazil: Origins, Policy and Future*. Yale University Press: New Haven, CT, pp. 142–78.

Cury, C. 2013. Director of Parliamentary Affairs, EMBRAPA (Brazilian Enterprise for Agricultural Research). Personal interview by the authors, Brasília, June 12, 2013.

Freyre, G. 1973. *Casa-grande & senzala*. José Olympio: Rio de Janeiro.

Gozetto, A.C.O. and C.S. Thomas. 2014. 'Interest Groups in Brazil: A New Era and its Challenges,' in Journal of Public Affairs, 14(3–4), 212–239.

Holanda, S. B. 1996. *Raízes do Brasil*. Companhia das Letras: São Paulo.

Judd, E. 2011. *O Momento Mágico: Managing Public Affairs in Brazil*. Foundation for Public Affairs, The Public Affairs Council: Washington, DC.

Klimovich, Kristina and Clive S. Thomas. 2014. 'Power Groups, Interests and Interest Groups in Consolidated and Transitional Democracies: Comparing Uruguay and Costa Rica with Paraguay and Haiti,' in Thomas (2014).

Lobo, Antonio Marcos Umbelino. (2013). Owner of the consulting firm Umbelindo Lobo. Interview by the lead author, Brasília, June 12.

Macário, M. 2013. Government Affairs Manager, Google Brazil. Personal interview by the lead author, São Paulo, July 16, 2013.

Munyo, Ignacion [senior economist], Carlos Díaz, [researcher/economist]. 2009. Center for the Study of Economic and Social Reality–CERES [Think tank dealing with macro-economic information]. Personal interview by Clive Thomas, June 11.

Navarro, Joan. 2015. Survey submitted to the authors.

OECD (Organization for Economic Co-operation and Development). 2008. *Lobbyists, Governments and Public Trust: Building a Legislative Framework for Enhancing Transparency and Accountability in Lobbying.* Organization for Economic Co-operation and Development: Paris.

OECD. 2014a. *Lobbyists, Governments and Public Trust: Building a Legislative Framework for Enhancing Transparency and Accountability in Lobbying.* Organization for Economic Co-operation and Development: Paris.

OECD. 2014b. *Lobbyists, Governments and Public Trust: Implementing the OECD Principles for Transparency and Integrity in Lobbying*, Volume 3. Organization for Economic Co-operation and Development: Paris.

Ortega González, Jorge. 2014. *Lobbying in Mexico.* Secretaría de Gobernacion: Paris.

Piacenza, Claudio [assistant manager], María Dolores Benavente [international affairs manager]. 2009. Uruguayan National Chamber of Commerce and Services. Personal interview by Clive Thomas, June 11.

Pérez, Gustavo. 2009. President of the Central Council, Uruguayan Bank Employees Association (AEBU). Personal interview by Clive Thomas, June 11.

Rohter, Larry. 2012. *Brazil on the Rise: The Story of a Country Transformed.* Palgrave/Macmillan: Basingstoke, England.

Santos, L. A. dos. 2013. Deputy Chief of Staff, Executive Office of the President of Brazil. Personal interview by the authors, Brasília, June 13.

Santos, L. A. dos, and Paulo M. T. da Costa. 2014. 'The Contribution of Lobby Regulation Initiatives in Addressing Political Corruption across Latin America,' in Thomas (2014).

Thomas, C. S. 2006. 'Transparency in Public Affairs: Lessons from the Mixed Experience of the United States,' in T. Spencer and C. McGrath, eds., *Challenge and Response: Essays on Public Affairs and Transparency.* Landmarks Press: Brussels, 41–8.

Thomas, Clive S. ed. 2014. 'Interest Groups and Lobbying in Latin America – A New Era or More of the Same?' *Journal of Public Affairs.* Special issue, 14 (3–4) (September–November).

Transparency International. 2014. *Corruption Perceptions Index 2013.* Available at: http://www.transparency.org/cpi2013/results (accessed June 30, 2016).

23

Public Affairs in South Africa

Ronel Rensburg and Olebogeng Selebi

FOUNDATIONS OF PUBLIC AFFAIRS

The study of public affairs is often confused with public relations but there are distinctions between the two which are even more pronounced in southern Africa. Public relations may often be utilised to implement public affairs tactics but cannot replace effective public affairs management. The Public Relations Society of America (PRSA) defines public relations in the following ways (Skinner, Mersham and Benecke, 2013:4): 'Public relations helps an organisation and its publics adapt mutually to each other' and 'Public relations is an organisation's efforts to win the co-operation of groups of people'.

Based on these definitions, one of the main purposes of public relations is to manage the cooperation of people and organisations through communication for the achievement of national and organisational goals. Public relations can therefore be used to administer and communicate government policy and

hence advance the success of these policies. Governments create a variety of policies, laws, rules and regulations for the betterment of the public environment. These policies often do not have the support of local communities, non-governmental organisations (NGOs) and private sector organisations that are required to fund some of the initiatives developed from these policies. Although these issues occur all over the world, they are a particular area of embattlement for the public sector environment in southern Africa. The effectiveness of these policies is impaired without effective communication and public relations efforts in the management and implementation of public policy.

According to Skinner et al. (2013: 5–6), public relations has the following characteristics:

- *Public relations is dynamic*: Public relations is not static. It changes constantly and can be adapted to the situation and circumstance in which it is required. In relation to public affairs it can be adapted to communicate a specific policy.

- *Public relations is analytical*: Proper public relations cannot be done without an analysis of the environment. The environment and situation that the public relations activity will take place in should be carefully analysed and completely understood. Therefore, with regards to public affairs and public policy, governments should fully understand the environment and stakeholders (publics) for which they create policies. This will assist in communicating these policies and receiving support from the public.
- *Public relations is planned*: Effective public relations does not happen haphazardly. Governments that do not have a specific, structured message to convey to the public should refrain from communicating. Effective communication should be planned and purposeful. It should also be goal-oriented and result from a situational or problem analysis.
- *Public relations implies action*: When governments create policies and communicate them, these policies should be executed. Governments that create policies and make unfulfilled promises to the general public develop a level of mistrust with their followers. Post-apartheid South Africa is currently not seeing clear results from the promises made in 1994, when the new democratic government took power. This reputation created as a result of unfulfilled promises can be difficult to transform and can lead to a disregard of future policies. In essence, effective public relations is proactive and not reactive and identifies the needs of the public, addresses them and communicates with the public before the societal issues are exacerbated by other factors. The authors of this chapter are of the opinion that effective public relations should also be *interactive* – prompting and maintaining engagement with the public and involving them in policies that might affect them from the outset.
- *Public relations efforts should be evaluated*: There should be ways of measuring the effectiveness of engagements with the public. This will assist in determining the right and wrong ways of communicating with the identified audience. Without measuring the success of communication strategies, governments run the risk of replicating the same mistakes of past communicative and policy efforts, and may fail to capitalise on their positive communicative habits.

- *Public relations emphasises adjustment*: Public relations efforts cannot be rigid. Therefore, as stakeholder habits (communicative and otherwise) change governments should adapt to this and communicate accordingly. If certain communicative efforts have failed in the past, the state should be adaptive enough in its efforts to communicate with the public and adjust to the needs of the audience. South Africa is a developmental state and as such it will be pivotal for public affairs in such a state to be *transculturally sensitive* with a continuous eye on *transformation*.

The above statements indicate that public affairs is managed through public relations, making public relations the overarching principle for managing public affairs. This is also the case in southern Africa.

According to Cutlip et al. (in Skinner et al., 2013:284), 'the purpose of public affairs itself closely resembles that of democracy. Abundant and accurate information is used by effective democratic governments to maintain responsive relationships with constituents, based on mutual understanding and continuing two-way communication.' This comparison between public affairs and democracy indicates that, like democracy, public affairs should take the feelings and opinions of stakeholders into consideration. Stakeholders should feel included in decision-making. Also, effective public affairs management demands that democratic governments respond to and address the concerns of the public while using the two-way communication model to ensure that all stakeholders participate in some way in the development of policy.

The main goal of public affairs is two-fold (Skinner et al., 2013:285):

- *Democratic governments should inform the populace of their actions and decisions*: In order for public affairs to be successfully exercised, governments should play an active role in informing the population of their plans and actions, and should respond to the concerns of the citizens.
- *Effective government administration needs the active involvement and backing of the popula-*

tion: Citizens play an important role in ensuring that state-owned facilities are administered correctly. Citizens should be willing to share information on the goings-on of their communities in order to assist government in providing for the needs of their unique societies.

PUBLIC AFFAIRS AND ITS RELATIONSHIP TO OTHER KEY DISCIPLINES

Public affairs focuses on building and maintaining the relationships between government and its main stakeholders. In order to do this, it should be integrated with other disciplines. Government's stakeholders include not only its citizens but also the private sector and other interest groups (such as trade unions, the media and non-governmental organisations (NGOs)).

Government and the Media

The relationship between the state and the media will have an impact on the public's attitude towards any government policy. The media are influential in terms of information on political and social events. Therefore, they would be an important conduit for the flow of information on government policy and for enhancing the relationship between government and its stakeholders. The media can be gatekeepers of the information the public receive on government policy. Although social media has reduced the impact of traditional media outlets to act as gatekeepers, they are still responsible for starting the conversation on government policies and making the public aware of state decisions.

In terms of influencing a nation's policy, communication can be viewed in two ways. Schneider and Janning (in Kamps, 2013:2) state that it can be viewed as an essential component in the development of national policy. On the other hand, it can be argued that government policy has an informal element that should be managed through effective communication (Benz; Sarcinelli and Tenscher in Kamps, 2013:2–3). This informality deals with the involvement of non-state bodies in the development of national policy.

Therefore, political parties have to do more than campaign for votes. Once they have succeeded in garnering sufficient votes they have the added responsibility of involving the public in the policies they develop. This indicates that in order for government policy to be effectively implemented it has to receive the support of all major stakeholders. This includes the media, business, trade unions and the general public, amongst many others. In this sense it creates a challenge and an opportunity for governments to use strategic communication as a way of going beyond using only political campaigning as a way of interacting with the public. Hence, public affairs could be considered a form of perpetual political campaigning and a way of using communication to maintain a positive image and continuously engage the public (Baugut and Reinemann; Jentges et al. in Kamps, 2013:3).

As stated previously, effective engagement with the public requires governments to be slightly informal in the way that they engage their stakeholders. In legal terms, 'informality' assists in separating the fixed rules stated in legislation from the more non-fixed rules that are an important part of implementing and practising the rules stated in the law (Görlitz and Burth in Kamps, 2013:3). The law is largely rigid and generalised. This indicates that a certain degree of informality would be needed to simplify (Mayntz in Kamps, 2013:3) and adapt these rules to different situations and scenarios in order to ensure that the most benefit is received from the practical implementation of these rules and laws.

According to Mayntz and Grunden (in Kamps, 2013:4) there are various ways to categorise and determine the formality or informality with which to enforce rules and laws:

1 relationships and networks
2 action and behaviour.

The implementation of national policy requires a degree of informality because of the different stakeholders that it affects and the needs and expectations they have. Yet, informality in government is often criticised and shunned (Kamps, 2013:6). The main argument is that informality gives a large degree of power to stakeholders which may lead to undesirable factors like corruption (Stüwe; Mayntz in Kamps, 2013:6), that negatively affect many southern African economies. Therefore, the implementation of the national policies, which require a degree of informality and adaptability, may be seen as counter-productive. To address this, national policies should be communicated well enough to stakeholders that their fears and concerns regarding the intentions of a nation's leaders are allayed. The main function of communication in doing this is to rally the backing of stakeholders and allow all parties involved (including the state) to communicate their desires and intentions (Steiner and Jarren; Vowe in Kamps, 2013:6).

As the possibility of corruption in government is a constant concern in the southern African environment, the media – traditional and social – have very pronounced roles to play. They are there to support but also criticise governments and government policies and the implementation (or non-implementation) of these. This often leads to a difficult state–media relationship in southern Africa. South Africa has one of the freest media on the continent of Africa, and the South African government is very often brutally under fire for its actions.

The Relationship Between Government and Trade Unions

South Africa has been infamous for having a complex political environment. The state of a nation's political affairs has an impact on the socioeconomic issues that it encounters. An example of this would be the effect that apartheid had on South African society and its economy. Owing to the political instability experienced before 1994, several countries developed sanctions against South Africa, making it difficult for trade to take place with other countries. Therefore, the political context in which national policy is introduced is an essential component to its effective implementation. Another important variable in the implementation and communication of national policy is the trade unions that represent a nation's workforce. Trade unions became powerful entities in their alliances with other political movements (like the Communist Party) in South Africa. Trade unions have an effective communication structure, a vast level of reach and influence, and the ideal should therefore be that they are in good standing with the government and be an important contributor to law and policy. For this to be effectively done, good communication structures should be developed between government and trade unions.

The South African political environment consists not only of political parties that are shaped by their own agendas, but also of trade unions that protect the interests of employees and are currently strong opponents to some of the interests of the ruling party – the African National Congress (ANC). The Congress of South African Trade Unions (COSATU) is the largest and most influential trade union in the country. COSATU was created in the mid-1980s during the apartheid era (Schiavone, 2007:378). The main aim of this party was to oppose that government and its policies (Schiavone, 2007:378). However, with the abolition of apartheid, the role of the COSATU evolved. The rise of national democracy caused trade unions also to become more democratic in the way that they led their followers. Therefore, the input of trade union members became an important part of decision-making.

Corporate Social Responsibility (CSR) as a way of Sustaining the Relationship Between Government and the Private Sector

One of the most important disciplines in public affairs is corporate social responsibility (CSR) because of its community outreach role in the private sector – assisting the state with providing public services. In this case, public affairs regulates the relationship between government, the private sector and the general public (citizens) in meeting state needs.

According to a report assembled for the World Bank (Fox, Ward and Howard in Kloppers, 2013:123–4), government has various responsibilities it has to fulfil in order to create an environment that enables and allows organisations to participate in activities that improve society and deal with societal ills. These roles and responsibilities of government are as follows (Fox et al. in Kloppers, 2013:124–30):

- *Legislative mandating*. In this role, government is required to deliver a particular level of legal standards that organisations have to adhere to. Government has the power to make laws and set legal standards. In order for these laws to be successfully implemented, they should be correctly communicated to the people and organisations the laws apply to. Clear legislation can be a good tool for the implementation of national policy. This legislation would provide organisations with stipulations on the best ways of going about fulfilling the implementation of national policy. The government also has power to create legislation that, if not adhered to, would lead to negative legal and monetary repercussions.
- *Facilitating*. Governments can use the authority they have to inspire organisations and the public to participate in societal projects. This is done by creating laws and setting up structures that ensure that national policies are effectively implemented. In this role, governments are facilitators that assist in the implementation of CSR projects that are in line with the policies of the nation. In this role the state would produce the environment necessary for organisations to participate in the implementation of national policy.

Government would also have to invest in communication that would raise private sector consciousness of the societal needs that this sector could become involved in as well as the benefits of their involvement. The support structures that have been put in place to assist participating organisations should also be emphasised.

- *Partnering*. The South African government has a variety of responsibilities. Attending to the many needs of its citizens without the assistance of the private sector is an impossible task. Therefore, if the state hopes to address the many socioeconomic issues the country has, interaction between the government and the private sector is imperative. Government policies should promote and enable this interaction. Also, these two sectors (private and public) cannot interact effectively without the existence of strong communication. Government largely depends on fiscal policy to determine the funds available to conduct its day-to-day activities but these funds are highly regulated. In order to effectively address the needs of the public it would need the participation of the private sector.
- *Endorsing*. Another role that government has to play is to endorse social projects that private organisations and business operate. In this instance, the state would have to openly show its support for these programmes. One way of doing this would be by offering rewards to participating organisations for being part of initiatives that are designed to help government reach its economic and social targets. Supporting CSR and community projects would assist government in taking a proactive role towards integrating public, private sector and social resources for the greater good. Another way that government could do this is by providing training to industry partners on conducting CSR initiatives correctly. National policies could be used as a strategic training tool that will provide a framework for the best ways that organisations can fit their CSR programmes into the larger national vision.
- *Enforcing*. This role is similar to the role that governments play when creating mandates for what is expected by the private sector. Enforcement supplements the government's mandating role. As stated in the section on government's legislative mandating role, creating legislation without having ways in which to enforce it would reduce the effectiveness of national policy. Therefore, the government should have structures to com-

municate and enforce the laws it creates. In this instance, mandating supplies a structure for regulating and implementing the legal blueprint for the implementation of national policy. Government can do this by creating regulatory bodies that have the main task of ensuring that organisations comply with the stipulations set by the state.

- *Legitimising*: As stated previously, government cannot attend to all societal issues on its own. The implementation of national policy requires a great deal of private sector investment and involvement. Therefore, legitimising CSR and proving the importance of it to the private sector is an important part of ensuring their involvement and participation in the implementation of policy. Legitimising the importance of CSR is not only for the private sector but for the public sector as well.
- *Standardising*: As the world has evolved, the way that governments execute their strategies should evolve and be in line with modern standards. Organisations and their practices have changed as a result of changing consumer needs, changing technology, and legislation that has transformed over the years. Therefore, the national policy has to prove its ability to align with modernity.
- *Leveraging*: The principle of leveraging is based on the fact that CSR in general and as a principle is more influential than the collective CSR projects that are run by an organisation or even in the nation as a whole. Leveraging resources can be a robust tool that government and the private sector can use to address societal issues.
- *Modelling/demonstration*: This indicates that government should not only stipulate what organisations have to do to be better members of society but also practically demonstrate their own roles and responsibilities in the policies they develop. Policies cannot be one-sided but should include the rights and responsibilities of all parties involved. These rights and responsibilities should be effectively communicated to all members of society.

At the onset of the King Report on Corporate Governance in South Africa, the activities of government and business were linked in more substantial ways. With the King III Report (2009), it became necessary for all private organisations that are listed on the Johannesburg Stock Exchange (JSE) – from 2011 – to make use of integrated reporting, where annual financial reporting would include organisations also reporting on their corporate social responsibility and sustainability programmes. This brought a stronger liaison between the private sector, their community engagement programmes and the government's public affairs activities.

In summary, each of the above role-players and individual disciplines is important, and interplays with public affairs, and therefore they require communication tailored to their needs and communicative habits.

EMERGING TRENDS IN PUBLIC AFFAIRS

Technology has changed the way stakeholders communicate and live their lives. This has affected all disciplines and disciplines that fail to adapt to this wireless world often will not be able to cater to a modern population.

Public Affairs and Social Media Communication

Social media is changing the way that people communicate with each other. It provides many benefits and increases the effectiveness of communication. Social media can be an effective tool not only for individuals and businesses, but also for governments to communicate with the general public.

Social media can be placed in the categories of either *consumer-generated media* or *user-generated media*. According to Hart (2011:114), social media is a term often used to describe the gathering of software that enables individuals, as well as communities, to collect and share information on a variety of topics. Regardless of the demographic segments that separate people, social media plays a significant role in uniting people from different demographics (Hart, 2011:114). In South Africa it can also unite people from various cultures.

Facebook has grown to have a database of millions of people. Therefore, considering the fact that a large number of the individuals that organisations are trying to attract are on Facebook, many organisations are using Facebook as a medium for reaching their target audiences. Governments cannot ignore social media as a way of communicating with the public. According to Carlston (2011:12), governments and organisations in general need not fear Facebook but should treat it as any other medium with which they can communicate with stakeholders. However, the immediacy of social media messages on Facebook and Twitter can also bring reputation damage to individuals, organisations and governments. Therefore, governments must ensure that the messages that are conveyed on social media platforms are in line with the overall image that the state is hoping to convey and should refrain from having multiple messages that divert from this image. Social media can therefore be an important tool not only for disseminating information to the public, but also for governments to engage the public on issues that concern them.

Social media may be an effective tool for improving the reputation of the state. The general public's and the private sector's perceptions of the government and its leaders impact on their opinion of national policy. Therefore, addressing the concerns of stakeholder groups on public social media platforms may improve reputations and emphasise the point that the state is conscious of the apprehensions and concerns of the public and is indeed addressing them. According to Barnett, Jermier and Lafferty (in Iwu-Egwuonwu, 2011:199), reputation is a valuable asset in public affairs based on, *inter alia*, three factors, namely, awareness, assessment and consolidation. Therefore, in order for reputation to be built and sustained in the long term, the general public would have to be aware of the presence of the government on online platforms. Once this has been well established, two-way communication between all parties involved can begin

and the alignment between assessment and consolidation can commence. Social media can become the nexus in awareness, assessment and consolidation.

THE REGIONAL DEVELOPMENT AND APPLICATION OF PUBLIC AFFAIRS

According to Strong (in Thornhill, 2012:129),

the state is something more than a mere collection of families, or an agglomeration of occupational organisations, or a referee holding the ring between the conflicting interests of the voluntary associations which it permits to exist. In a properly organised political community the state exists for society and not society for the state.

This notion that the government exists for the good of society seems often forgotten by those in power. The lack of government communication and consultation with stakeholders emphasises this point. Due to the fact that the main responsibility of government is to take care of the needs of its stakeholders, adequate knowledge of the stakeholder groups is a factor of importance. This cannot be established without communication between the state and all its stakeholders. Public affairs is the mechanism that can assist in establishing the stakeholder needs and how these needs can be met. This discipline can be applied in a variety of contexts with all of the state's stakeholders.

Technology and the vast level of scholarship on the subject of public affairs are both highly beneficial to modern governments. Leaders now have access to research and information on the history of past governments and their communicative habits that can be beneficial to modern states in their desire to build better relationships with their constituents and stakeholders at large. In the South African context, building these relationships between government and stakeholders can be complex because of the different stakeholder groups. An example of this is the number of government departments currently in South Africa. The departments are as follows (Anon, nd b):

- Agriculture, Forestry and Fisheries
- Arts and Culture
- Communications
- Cooperative Governance
- Correctional Services
- Defence
- Education
- Energy
- Environmental Affairs
- Government Communications and Information System (GCIS)
- Health
- Home Affairs
- Human Settlements
- Independent Complaints Directorate
- International Relations and Cooperation (Foreign Affairs)
- Justice and Constitutional Development
- Labour
- Mineral Resources
- National Intelligence Agency
- National Treasury
- Police
- Public Administration Leadership and Management Academy
- Public Enterprises
- Public Service and Administration
- Public Service Commission
- Public Works
- Rural Development and Land Reform
- Science and Technology
- Social Development
- South African Police Service
- South African Revenue Service
- South African Secret Service
- Sport and Recreation South Africa
- Statistics South Africa
- The Presidency
- Tourism
- Trade and Industry
- Traditional Affairs
- Transport
- Water Affairs
- Women, Children and People with Disabilities

Each of these departments has its own unique set of needs and demands. Figure 23.1 is an example of the structure of South African

governments and how they work (Hendrickse 2012:123). Although this example focuses primarily on the Ministry of Women, Children and People with Disabilities, the basic structure applies to most government departments. This highlights the vast number of issues that government has to communicate on as well as the stakeholders that should be conversed with.

South Africa's government is divided into three domains: national, provincial and local (Thornhill, 2012:128). Local governments were further divided into municipalities in 1998 (Thornhill, 2012:128). This extended the number of stakeholders that should be considered by government communicators. One of the unique features of South African government is that provincial and local governments are not necessarily used to implement the decisions of national government at the grassroots level. Each of the domains of government is considered autonomous and should collaborate with national government in the decision-making process. Therefore, provincial and local government leaders are important role-players in the way they function. Managing these domains can be difficult and requires strong administrative skills, leadership (Thornhill, 2012:128) and effective stakeholder communication.

To communicate with these varying stakeholders the South African government created the Government Communication and Information System (GCIS) which is a department with the sole purpose of communicating with government's internal and external stakeholders. According to its website, the GCIS has the following responsibilities (GCIS, nd a):

- to deliver expert services;
- to establish and observe criteria that promote effective government communication;
- to ensure that all government's communication can be clearly understood by its stakeholders; and
- to pre-emptively communicate all government's plans, decisions, policies, programmes and achievements to the public.

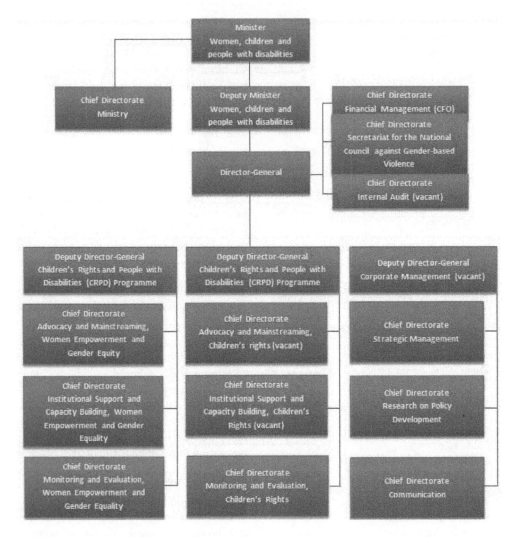

Figure 23.1   Example of South African government department structures

Source: Hendrickse (2012:123)

South Africa is a developing country with a variety of socioeconomic issues that should be addressed by the state. Unfortunately the levels of inequality, joblessness and poverty (indicated by the Gini-coefficient) have increased since the introduction of democracy in 1994 (Madumo, 2012:40). To deal with this issue, the government adopted the concept of being a developmental state, the purpose of which is to address the needs of those living in impoverished communities (Madumo, 2012:40). Furthermore, individual municipalities would be expected to play a more prominent role in eradicating poverty and social ills (Madumo, 2012:40). This would mean that the responsibility of dealing with socioeconomic issues would fall on municipal leaders. This increases the need for adequate communication. The government would need to communicate about not only its broader goals and objectives, but also its plans and strategies at a grassroots level. Stakeholders should be informed about both.

The national government also has a number of policies in place to deal with these socio-economic issues, but the burden of doing so cannot be totally handled by the government. As stated previously, this is the reason for interaction between the government and private sector. The partnership between the private and public sector can aid in development. Regardless of this, democracy should not be sacrificed for the sake of economic development (Thornhill, 2012:133). Real democracy cannot be achieved without adequate communication. Therefore, a developing nation like South Africa should ensure that the interaction of the private and public sector is regulated by policies that advocate for democracy in decision-making (Thornhill, 2012:133). Chapter 10 (section 195(1)) of the Constitution of the Republic of South Africa 1996, makes provisions for this in stating that (Thornhill, 2012:133):

- A substantial level of specialised ethics should be adhered to.
- Competent and cost-effective use of public funds should be encouraged.
- All public administration initiatives should be focused on development (both social and economic).
- The needs of society should be identified and met and all stakeholders should be involved in developing policy.
- All activities of public administration should be accounted for.

None of the above can be adhered to without effective communication with internal and external stakeholders.

CASE STUDIES OF PUBLIC AFFAIRS IN ACTION

According to Skinner et al. (2013:284), the objectives of government public affairs in South Africa are as follows:

- Informing citizens and stakeholders of government activities
- Promoting active cooperation in state initiatives

- Promoting citizen support for state initiatives
- Playing the role of an activist and defender of a nation's citizens
- Handling information internally
- Simplifying and aiding in the process of media relations
- Developing communities and the nation in general (both in terms of national identity and socio-economic development).

The above gives an indication of the goal of public affairs and the stakeholders that governments aim to reach through the public relations and communication efforts that form part of effective public affairs management. There are several examples of scenarios in which government could have or should have used better public affairs and public relations strategies for communicating with its interest groups. The controversial introduction of e-tolling in South Africa is an example of this.

E-Toll Programme

The e-toll programme implemented in South Africa comprises the electronic collection of tolls that road-users are required to pay for using the roads. The e-toll programme was created to pay for the approximately R20 billion highway upgrade initiative that took place between 2007 and 2011. Although the highway upgrade programme and the development of a better road network was welcomed by citizens, the financial implications were communicated ineffectively to the public. The government introduced the e-tolling programme as a mechanism for supplementing the funds that were used for improving the roads. Although this may be an effective way of replacing the funds used for road improvements, the lack of consultation with important stakeholders (such as citizens in general, the private sector and trade unions) on the cost they would incur in future for this was minimal. This led to severe opposition with the majority of road-users refusing to succumb. Citizens were requested to purchase an e-tag, which is a device used to monitor the number of times a person uses the highway. Owners fitted with the e-tag would be required to pay every time they used the road network. Most citizens did not purchase e-tags or register for e-tolling, and others are currently refusing to pay for e-tolling.

This civil disobedience led to the creation of organisations disapproving government's decision to introduce tolls. One of these organisations is the Opposition to Urban Tolling Alliance (Outa). Public opposition to the e-tolling structures led to government's decision to publish a gazette requesting the public to comment on proposed changes to the e-toll regulations by 26 September 2015 (Fin24, 2015). 'This gazette seeks to introduce a number of changes to the e-toll regulations, some of which are sincerely concerning,' said an Outa spokesperson (Fin24, 2015). According to du Preez (2015), Outa urged the public to comment on e-toll regulation changes.

This effort was a neutral to positive one on the part of the state in terms of public affairs management and communicating with the public. Although the process would have worked better had it been implemented sooner, the initiative that government took to consult with the public after the fact was – theoretically seen – a communication improvement. Outa said it has set up a page on its website 'which makes it easy for the public to submit comments' on the main issues in response to the notice in the gazette and states that 'it is important to know that the more the public participates in making such submissions, the stronger the people's case is to be heard' (Fin24, 2015).

Although the government has taken actions to remedy the effects of limited communication with the public, the lack of consultation during the introduction of the e-toll programme has created a scenario where the public feel that they are at war with the state. The outcome of this issue is still outstanding.

The South African government's response to the public's comments on e-tolling was to reduce the e-toll fees by half, while putting mechanisms in place to freeze licence discs for non-payers. Therefore, this would in essence force citizens to comply with the regulations. Drivers who do not comply would not be allowed to use their vehicles legally. The current reprieve is turning into government force – forcing the promotion and implementation of and selling something that South Africans did not ask for, have not been consulted on, did not agree to and do not want.

Cosatu (Congress of South African Trade Unions) was greatly opposed to the implementation of urban tolling in South Africa. Cosatu is the nation's largest trade union group, with twenty-one associated trade unions and almost two million members (workers). Therefore, Cosatu's influence is widespread, and its support of government policy would aid in the implementation of e-tolling.

In protest at e-tolling, Cosatu arranged a drive-slow on South Africa's main highways. 'The "drive-slow" was successful and raised awareness of the fight,' said the union federation's provincial secretary, Dumisani Dakile (Times Live, 2012). He further stated that 'this fight is not a fight for Cosatu only, it is a fight for South Africa' (Times Live, 2012). These statements create the impression that the state is at war with its main stakeholders with regards to the implementation of this particular policy. The main reason for this is the lack of adequate communication with stakeholders – from the very beginning. It also points to the lack of consultation in constructing policy.

Transport department spokesperson Tiyani Rikhotso said the government noted the protest action and respected the right of individuals and organisations to protest. He said the department consulted with the public when the process of e-tolling started in 2007 (see Figure 23.2). According to Rikhotso 'All matters of concern were adequately addressed with concerned parties in all these sessions. Assertions that this project is being forced on South Africans are therefore devoid of truth' (Times Live, 2012). This indicates that the state and the public's opinion of sufficient consultation regarding matters affecting the nation may differ as according to public opinion sufficient consultation on the matter was not done. This insinuates that the effectiveness of public affairs management and communication with the public is largely based on the opinion of the citizens. Government communication, in this case, should therefore be viewed as ineffective in the eyes of the public. If this is not achieved, government communication and consultation will always be deemed ineffective.

Figure 23.2   Trade union members protesting against e-toll system

Source: Times Live: http://www.timeslive.co.za/local/2012/12/07/e-toll-protest-a-success-says-Cosatu

Eskom Electricity Crisis

Another example of the importance of public affairs in handling national issues is the electricity crisis that took place in South Africa in recent years.

Owing to a lack of adequate state planning, South Africa found itself with an energy shortage. South Africa's energy producer, Eskom, was unable to produce enough energy for the nation's population growth and increased industrialisation. Eskom introduced the concept of 'load-shedding' which deals with the reduction of energy use through rationing and interrupting the energy supply at certain times and in varying regions around the country. This negatively affected the public, businesses and the economy in general.

Eskom CEO Tshediso Matona stated that the energy crisis was caused by both Eskom and the government (My Broadband, 2015). Matona further stated that 'the government co-owns the problem because some of the factors that led us into the situation have to do with policy' (My Broadband, 2015), namely the energy prices decided on by the National Energy Regulator of South Africa (Nersa). This indicates that the state, which is the main role-player in the creation of energy policy, has the responsibility of communicating and consulting with other important stakeholders before creating policy. Therefore, the responsibility lies with the state to communicate effectively with all stakeholders – in both the creation of policy and the way it should be implemented.

According to Hunter, Letsoalo and Mataboge (2015), the government disapproved of the way that Eskom communicated regarding the electricity crisis at its onset. Government communicators were of the opinion that Eskom's public openness with regards to the extent of the electricity crisis was detrimental to the reputation of the government. This led to an interruption in the communication between Eskom and the government leaders.

In order to remedy this, the government's National Executive Committee (NEC) and Cabinet made the decision to take control of several of Eskom's communicative duties in an effort to monitor and control the information that is supplied to the public (Hunter et al., 2015). This would also help them reach consensus on the information that should be kept from the public.

A Cabinet source said the government was worried about how Eskom's communications were affecting the government negatively. According to a government source, Eskom was 'saying things and they are not realising how it is affecting us politically' (Hunter et al., 2015). It was further stated that government was 'concerned. We can't have a state entity that is communicating a different message to what we are communicating' and that it was having trouble 'align[ing] Eskom's message to our political message' (Hunter et al., 2015).

Government questioned the reliability and validity of Eskom's communication therefore, and state officials had to prioritise meeting with Eskom's leaders to decide on the best ways to communicate with the public.

The main source of government's concerns came from a press release issued by Eskom's acting director general of the communications department, Donald Liphoko, which rebuffed a hoax insinuating that Eskom's main power grid could crash and lead to a nationwide absence of electricity for more than two weeks (Hunter et al., 2015). Liphoko guaranteed the public that the energy crisis was a 'priority at the highest level' (Hunter et al., 2015). The Cabinet source stated that this statement by Eskom was what prompted the government's appropriation of Eskom's communication.

Another government source stated that the goal of the state was not to take away Eskom's ability to communicate with the public but to 'implement certain levels of predictability and certainty in their communication' (Hunter et al., 2015). Therefore, the power utility was required to collaborate with government in its communication to the public. For this to be achieved, a clear line of communication would have to be established between the leaders of Eskom and the national government. As stated previously, government's aim in this regard was not to completely stop Eskom's communication but to ensure that both Eskom and the state in general had one central message to communicate. According to Liphoko, 'there is no decision that government is going to communicate on behalf of Eskom. Our position is to support the communication efforts of Eskom', but government 'reserves the right to speak on national matters. It's not only to give direction to the entities, but also to the nation' (Hunter et al., 2015).

TACTICAL APPROACHES TO EXECUTING PUBLIC AFFAIRS

There are various ways of implementing public affairs strategies with stakeholders. As stated in the previous section social media is one of the tactics that can be used to manage and execute strategies for government to communicate with its citizens and most important stakeholders.

According to Bertot, Jaeger, Munson, and Glaisyer (in Graham and Johnson Avery, 2013:1), 'social media tools can improve interactivity between a government and the public, and they reach populations that do not consume traditional media as frequently as others'.

Social media has various benefits to government in that it allows government to communicate with stakeholders on the platforms they use most. It also gives citizens (as government's main stakeholder) the ability to discuss national events and issues of national importance. It, in essence, gives them more of a voice and more influence. An example of this is the 'Fees Must Fall' student protests that took place in the last quarter of 2015. This campaign resulted from students' concerns regarding the cost of education at South African universities. Students and other stakeholders gathered at universities around the country to protest against the annual increase of university fees. With the creation of the hashtag '#FeesMustFall' students were able to influence stakeholders that they otherwise may not have been able to effectively reach. This hashtag and the use of social media enabled thousands of students from all over the country to mobilise themselves and grab the attention of the South African government, university leaders and even the world. This demonstrates the importance of social media as a tool for government's interaction with its main stakeholders. Therefore, understanding this platform can 'make or break' government's communicative strategies.

Social media can improve the state's capabilities to communicate with the population on important issues and manage their expectations and remain transparent (Graham and Johnson Avery, 2013:1). Without this, citizens may have different opinions or expectations of the state than was intended.

According to Skinner et al. (2013:286) there are a variety of factors that can act as obstructions to the communicative actions of the state and the state's ability to form and sustain a bond with the public, including:

- Credibility
- Public apathy
- Legislative hostility.

All of the above affect and are affected by the reputation of the government. The importance of reputation has increased in recent years and the development of various scales of measurement of reputation such as 'The Reputation Quotient' and the 'America's Most Admired Companies' article published by *Fortune* magazine on the reputations of America's most admired corporations (Bromley, 2002:35). According to Bromley (2002:36), reputation is a socially shared impression and is therefore based on collectives and not on heterogeneous collections of people. A collective is a 'relatively homogeneous group of people with a degree of common interest in a reputational entity, such as a company or a product or a person' (Bromley, 2002:36). Therefore, in order for governments to analyse and understand the way the public interprets reputation, they would have to understand how reputation is interpreted based on the common interests and social interactions that people have. These interactions determine stakeholder beliefs, attitudes and actions.

One important measure for assessing reputation is the Reputation Institute's RepTrak model. 'RepTrak Research is the world's largest and highest quality normative reputation benchmark database' (Fombrun and van Reel, 2015:2). According to the Reputation Institute's most recent findings, South Africa's reputation displayed the following (Fombrun and van Reel, 2015:12–27):

- Out of 175 countries, South Africa ranked the 67th with regards to the perceived level of corruption.
- The global reputation mean which evaluated 55 countries stands at 56.3, with South Africa ranking as the 40th country and scoring 49.7. In contrast to this, Canada has the best reputation, scoring 78.1, and Iraq scored worst with its reputation amounting to a score of 22.5.
- South Africa's reputation has reduced by 3.2 per cent in the past year.
- The internal reputation mean which evaluated 22 countries stands at 68.3, with South Africa ranking last and scoring 38.7. In contrast to this, Australian citizens have the best opinion of their country, scoring 90.1.

The above figures show the negative opinion that South African citizens have of the state. This opinion cannot be changed without effective communication on the part of the state. Aside from the use of social media, the reputation of a government can also be enhanced by its lobbying efforts and its ability to interact with a variety of stakeholders on important issues.

Lobbying gives citizen groups, associations, labour unions and the private sector the opportunity to converse with government on important issues regarding legislation, policies and other issues taking place in politics (Tusinski Berg, 2009:1). Lobbyists simplify complex problems and exhibit only the most important information to legislators, staff members or committees. Tusinski Berg (2009:1) states that 'this adds to the extensive research and evidence that usually accompanies proposed legislation. Increasingly, lawmakers rely on lobbyists for information.' This emphasises the importance of communication for successful lobbying. Lobbying in South Africa is highly regulated (Skinner et al., 2013:287). Regardless of this, it plays an important role in managing the regulation of activities and legislation surrounding the government's tender process and the corruption and fraud that plagues it (Skinner et al., 2013:287). The media plays an important role in this regard by providing the public with information on corruption and fraud and allows them to take a stand and engage lobbyists on remedying these issues.

In order to improve its communication, government should invest in continuous education that will assist it in communicating with its stakeholders. As stated previously, the state developed the Government Communication and Information System (GCIS) to assist government in its communication. The University of Pretoria's Centre for Communication and Reputation Management (CCRM), headed by Professor Ronel Rensburg, provides continuous education and training for communicators from the GCIS as well as government communicators

in general. Avenues such as this can aid in the improvement of government communication and the overall management of public affairs.

REFERENCES

Anon. nd a. *Government communication and information system.* [Online] Available from: http://www.gcis.gov.za/content/about-us [Accessed: 2015-11-23].

Anon. nd b. *South African government departments.* [Online] Available from: http://www.southafrica-newyork.net/consulate/government_departments.html [Accessed: 2015-11-23].

Bromley, D. 2002. Comparing corporate reputations: league tables, quotients, benchmarks, or case studies? *Corporate Reputation Review*, 5:35–50. [Online] Available from: www.reputationinstitute.com/crr/V05/Bromley.pdf [Downloaded: 2012-05-20].

Carlston, J. 2011. The 10 commandments of Facebook. *Franchising World*, 43(7):12–14. [Online] Available from: EBSCOHost: Business Source Premier: http://search.ebscohost.comlogin.aspx?direct=true&db=buh&AN=63009611&site=ehost-live&scope=site [Downloaded: 2012-04-09].

du Preez, E. 2015. Public urged to speak up on e-tolls regulations. [Online] Available from: http://www.fin24.com/Economy/Public-urged-to-speak-up-on-e-tolls-regulations-20150918 [Accessed: 2015-11-23].

Fin24. 2015. SA cuts Gauteng e-toll fees by 50% – as it happened. [Online] Available from: http://www.fin24.com/Economy/LIVE-Ramaphosa-lifts-veil-on-e-tolls-20150520 [Accessed: 2015-11-23].

Fombrun, C. and van Riel, C. 2015. 2015. Country RepTrak® the world's most reputable countries. [Online] Available from: https://www.reputationinstitute.com/CMSPages/GetAzureFile.aspx?path=~%5Cmedia%5Cmedia%5Cdocuments%5Ccountry-reptrak-webinar-2015-forweb_1.pdf&hash=07cf404f41364b36d38c8282897ec0e64c91ea20694cc77a075691f452e82d41 [Downloaded: 2015-11-23].

Graham, M. and Johnson Avery, E. 2013. Government public relations and social media: an analysis of the perceptions and trends of social media use at the local government level. *Public Relations Society of America*, 7(4):1–21.

Hart, L. 2011. Social media. In: Doorley, F. and Garcia, H. F. (eds.) *The key to successful public relations and corporate communication*. 2nd ed. New York: Taylor and Francis.

Hendrickse, R. 2012. Reshaping power: South Africa's gender machinery reviewed. *Administratio Publica,* 20(3):110–27.

Hunter, Q., Letsoalo, M. and Mataboge, M. 2015. Eskom's honesty irks ANC. [Online] Available from: http://mg.co.za/article/2015-02-12-eskoms-honesty-irks-anc [Accessed: 2015–11-23].

Iwu-Egwuonwu, R. C. 2011. Corporate reputation and firm performance: empirical literature evidence. *International Journal of Business and Management*, 6:197–206. [Online] Available from: www.ccsenet.org/journal/index.php/ijbm/article/download/7199.pdf [Downloaded: 2012-05-20].

Kamps, K. 2013. Informality matters: perspectives for studies on political communication. *Public Relations Society of America*, 9(1):1–22.

King, M. 2009. Corporate governance and King III. [Online] Available from: https://www.kpmg.com/ZA/en/IssuesAndInsightsArticlesPublications/Tax-and-Legal-Publications/Documents/Corporate%20Governance%20and%20King%203.pdf [Downloaded: 2015-11-23].

Kloppers, H. 2013. Creating a CSR-enabling environment: the role of government. [Online] Available from: http://reference.sabinet.co.za/webx/access/electronic_journals/sapr1/sapr1_v28_n1_a8.pdf [Downloaded: 2015-11-23].

Madumo, O. S. 2012. The promotion of developmental local government to facilitate a developmental state. *Administratio Publica*, 20(3):40–54.

My Broadband. 2015. *ANC government contributed to power crisis: Eskom CEO.* [Online] Available from: http://mybroadband.co.za/news/energy/116962-anc-government-contributed-to-power-crisis-eskom-ceo.htm [Accessed: 2015-11-23].

Schiavone, M. 2007. Social movement unions and political parties (in South Africa and the Philippines): a win-win situation? *African and Asian Studies*, 6:373–93.

Skinner, C., Mersham, G. and Benecke, R. 2013. *Handbook of public relations*. Cape Town: Oxford University Press.

Thornhill, C. 2012. Improving local government transformation in South Africa. *Administratio Publica*, 20(3): 128–43.

Times Live. 2012. E-toll protest a success, says Cosatu. [Online] Available from: http://www.timeslive.co.za/local/2012/12/07/e-toll-protest-a-success-says-Cosatu [Accessed: 2015-11-23].

Tusinski Berg, K. 2009. Finding connections between lobbying, public relations and advocacy. *Public Relations Journal*, 3(3):1–19.

Public Affairs in Australia and Oceania

Geoff Allen

This chapter is based on around forty years' practical experience in business–government relations and consultancy to boards and senior management of major companies on public affairs organisation and process.

Oceania is a highly diverse region. It includes a medium-sized developed country, Australia, and a small one, New Zealand. Depending on the definition of the region there are also up to fourteen developing countries in the area, most of which are remote island microstates with tiny populations scattered across the Pacific Ocean.

This chapter demonstrates the wide divergence in public affairs practice across the region due to scale, economic and social structures and business–government cultures.

Australia has a population of around 24 million, more than twice that of the rest of the region combined, including Papua New Guinea and New Zealand, and its economy is more than five times as large.

Australia's economy is ranked twelfth in the world by GDP. A number of the world's largest mining companies are Australian, as are four of the world's ten largest banks. It hosts substantial and long-standing operations of multinational companies across most sectors and it has been common for multinational companies to make Sydney or Melbourne the headquarters of their Asia–Pacific regional operations.

At one-fifth the size, New Zealand has a population of around 4.5 million and is ranked fifty-fourth in global GDP. It has only a small number of indigenous companies of significant scale, for example in the financial and utilities sectors; however, its largest company commands 30 per cent of the world's dairy exports. Many of its major companies are subsidiaries of Australian and other international companies, managed in tandem with overseas-based offices.

Papua New Guinea (PNG) is by far the largest developing country in Oceania with a population of just over 7 million, around 80 per cent of whom make a living from subsistence agriculture, mostly in isolated, rural, customary communities. It is one of the world's most culturally diverse countries with eight hundred living languages being spoken.

PNG is nevertheless resource rich and growing quickly because of a number of nation-building mining and energy projects led by large multinationals. This has led to a growth in its GDP ranking to 114th in 2014.

PNG has only a few indigenous companies of scale – one with substantial oil and gas holdings, a bank with branches elsewhere in the Pacific, an airline and a regional hotel chain. Its sovereign wealth funds, provincial governments and local communities have equity positions in a number of these domestic companies and multinational projects, designed to benefit locals from resource projects.

Fiji is a remote archipelago of more than three hundred islands, with a population of less than 900,000 (of whom almost 40 per cent are of Indian descent). Its economy stalled after a military coup and subsequent boycotts in 2009, but growth resumed with boycotts lifted following a democratic election in 2014 (which confirmed the coup leader as Prime Minister).

Fiji has a mix of industries including sugar, apparel, tourism, fishing and minerals. There are a few significant indigenous companies whose leadership is closely associated with the political and bureaucratic elite. Its interventionist and autocratic government has a stake in a number of listed and private enterprises.

The recently independent Timor-Leste, with a population of about 1.2 million, is one of the poorest countries in the world, notwithstanding increasing (but as yet poorly distributed) wealth from fledgling offshore oil and gas resources.

Many of these Pacific island countries became independent in the 1970s, but French Polynesia and New Caledonia remain French territories. Equally distributed, their combined population is less than 600,000, and includes a higher percentage of Europeans than the other Pacific microstates. They both also have a significantly higher GDP per capita.

The rest of the region is made up of countries with populations as low as that of the Marshall Islands with 56,000 and Tuvalu with 12,000.

Obviously there is a great variety in the way companies structure and manage public affairs in the various countries in Oceania, and it is rare outside Australia, New Zealand and a handful of expatriate companies in PNG, to find anything approximating an embedded public affairs function.

AUSTRALIA CONDITIONS PRECEDENT

Australia is a robust democracy with a broad base of industries. Nation-building agriculture has given way to minerals as its major export. There is a small but sophisticated manufacturing industry but services comprise the largest sector of the economy.

Since the 1980s there has been an expansion of Australian company operations into Asia, the USA and Europe. Throughout its history, however, Australia has depended on foreign capital; many multinational companies have contributed to its economy and the development of its business culture.

Australian business and public affairs practice has the major role in these areas in the region and accordingly its public affairs practice will be most fully explored in this chapter.

In order to understand the practice of public affairs in Australia, it is important to understand how it has evolved since the 1980s.

Divisions emerged as commodity exporters took their prices in international markets while their cost structures were impacted by protectionist policies and inefficient labour markets at home. The rapid escalation of social and political challenges to business in the 1960s and 1970s, particularly in the United States, took place with a lag in Australia but became manifest through the 1980s. As a result forest resources were being locked up, foreign ownership was under attack, and a strong push was being mounted to impose new constraints on banks. Resource companies complained that problems such as red tape, green tape and indigenous politics in developing new projects were driving exploration and resource development offshore. It became apparent that multiple stakeholders in the broader social and political environment were influencing corporate reputation, public policy and the overall achievement of corporate objectives. Business frustration was colourfully exhibited in a quote used in 1990 by the most senior business statesman of the time, Sir Arvi Parbo, to a group of senior public affairs practitioners.

> The external business environment is a little like the croquet game in Alice in Wonderland. The mallet Alice uses is a flamingo that lifts its head and faces the other direction just as Alice tries to hit the ball. The ball is a hedgehog. Instead of lying there waiting for Alice to hit it, the hedgehog unrolls, gets up, moves to another part of the court and sits down again. The wickets are card soldiers, ordered around by the Queen of Hearts, who changes the game at whim by barking out an order to the wickets to reposition themselves around the court.

> Substitute rules and regulations for the mallet, media and pressure groups for the hedgehog and Governments for the Queen of Hearts and you have a good description of the sort of environment we have to work in. (Parbo, 1990)

While there was great frustration about this business environment, companies were poorly equipped to deal with it. Much of the responsibility for the regulatory framework had been left to industry associations. However, they were not adequately focused on, or equipped to address, the emerging challenges.

Since the colonial period, before the separate colonies federated to form a national

government in 1900, there was a strong network of local industry associations, including chambers of commerce and chambers of manufacturers, largely focused on industrial relations and the trade protection of local industries. These state-based associations protected their membership and financial base and consequently power of the purse when they established dependent national peak affiliations after the federation. They did this by preventing direct company membership at that national level and by insisting company membership participate through the state organisations. Consequently, while senior executives of the larger national companies were involved in sector-specific organisations such as minerals and banking, large company leadership was largely absent from these formal peak councils of business. However, outside this formal representative structure strong informal systems operated and much of the business–government interaction was conducted in 'old boy networks behind closed doors', involving political and public service leaders and a small disconnected number of well-placed corporate chiefs.

In the mid-1980s, in reaction to the growing challenges to business, and without confidence in existing representative structures, a new organisation of the CEOs of the top one hundred companies, the Business Council of Australia (BCA), modelled in part on the US Business Roundtable, was formed to influence the direction of public policy. It immediately became a major business voice at the national level.

The BCA took a fresh approach to public policy. It engaged academics and policy leaders from within government and attempted to set an economic reform agenda by undertaking an unprecedented level of private sector economic and policy research. It used this research to stimulate debate and pursued public advocacy on the key issues of microeconomic reform and an open economy. This coincided with a receptive and activist political leadership built on a more assertive economic rationalist bureaucracy, and was received by a more sophisticated media commentariat with an appetite for serious debate.

This shift to more fulsome argument and evidence in public advocacy to influence government represented a shift to what has been called an 'outsider system', in contrast to the more opaque and clubby approach of network influence, styled an 'insider system'.

Within a few years a new breed of young, economically literate executives were appointed to lead the old guard of networked former bureaucrats appointed to other associations. They included one who became Australia's longest-serving foreign minister, one a highly successful trade minister and two who became CEOs and Chairs of major Australian companies.

The Business Council's recognition of how community opinion and community interest groups were instrumental in driving public policy led it to establish a Community Relations Committee of CEOs to reflect on business reputation and outreach. Its aim was for business to engage with, meet criticism from and win support from, the community.

This was an innovative approach for an organisation mainly concerned with policy issues such as taxation, economics and corporate law. Sir Arvi Parbo, quoted above, who was first chairman of the BCA, showed his support for this by opting to lead and be spokesman for that community-facing committee.

This reflected, and at the same time contributed to, a growing recognition in the major companies themselves that they needed to establish their own more rigorous, evidence-based advocacy at the corporate level to convince government of their positions, as well as win social and political legitimacy at the corporate level.

A quite dramatic shift in the focus of Australian companies to offshore investment in the 1980s also had the effect of broadening the interest of senior business leaders beyond the policy and regulatory activities of Canberra. Having been Canberra-centric they now had to focus on multiple political and regulatory environments and required alternative resources and points of contact with government within their companies.

Emergence of the Function

These factors – the new demand for evidence in policy advocacy, recognition that policy makers are influenced by community attitudes, and the need for additional government relations capability as companies expanded – underpin the development of the modern integrated public affairs practice in Australia. Until the late 1980s the separate external relations activities in major Australian companies were branded 'public relations' or 'communications' on the one hand and 'government affairs' on the other.

The public relations or communications function had been small even in the larger companies and was led most often by middle-aged journalists who had first careers in newspapers. Their activities were overwhelmingly to defend and promote corporate interests and image in the media, develop publications such as annual reports and promotional materials, and produce corporate feel-good employee newsletters. While there was usually ready access to corporate leadership the function was transactional rather than strategic, had limited influence, and was placed at best in middle management.

The government affairs function varied according to the needs of different industries. Former public servants, especially from industry departments, supported companies' regulatory tasks, for example by defending tariffs and import quotas, campaigning against dumping actions and working to protect sales tax arrangements. Former officials also worked in the larger resource companies to help them win exploration or development licences and limit government-imposed operational constraints.

As with public relations staff these government-facing specialists were mainly trouble-shooting and transactional and placed at modest levels in company hierarchies. Typically they were sole practitioners working closely with corporate economists and taxation specialists who outranked them in status and influence.

By the early 1990s an increasing appreciation of the importance of community opinion and third-party organisations in influencing policy and regulatory outcomes led to a closer integration of government and communications-focused efforts within companies. This influenced the forging of these two separate functions into a single external relations department that was to become known as 'public affairs' or 'corporate affairs'. The limited scale of most Australian corporations was also a factor in bringing the functions together; given the small number of staff in these functions, management synergies were captured by their structural integration.

In 1989, while these developments were unfolding, a retreat was held in the outskirts of Melbourne. Government relations and communications practitioners from major companies mostly from the BCA membership list (by now, some with 'public affairs' or 'corporate affairs' in their titles) were invited to sit down to discuss business–government issues with invited government leaders.

Several things became apparent at this meeting and in discussion with participants that followed.

First, while peers within industry-specific sectors were reasonably well connected, there had been virtually no contact between practitioners across sectors or across the five major Australian cities. They valued the opportunity to discuss issues of common concern and were keen to build an ongoing network.

Second, they felt at this point they lacked a professional identity and a conceptual framework for the changing and increasingly important roles they were performing. They also claimed to lack opportunities for continuous learning and the professional development of their staff.

The government affairs function in companies had not been clearly defined as a management discipline. While a number with communications backgrounds were members of the Public Relations Institute of Australia (PRIA), corporate practitioners from the larger companies no longer felt the organisation, or the way 'public relations' was perceived, reflected the broader nature of their emerging corporate task.

The facilitators of this conference suggested participants form a professional body to maintain contact, and provide research and professional development opportunities. They preferred, however, to avoid the complexities of establishing and running an incorporated professional association and asked the conference facilitators to provide this as a continuing service.

Subsequently, in 1990 the Centre for Corporate Public Affairs (the Centre) was established and quickly built to a relatively stable ongoing membership of the public affairs departments of around one hundred large companies and government enterprises in Australia, in due course some in New Zealand and a number affiliated in Asia.

While the model is different in a number of important ways and considerably smaller in scale, the Centre was inspired in part by the US-based Public Affairs Council, with which it has maintained a filial association.

Since 1990 the Centre has filled the gap in professional affiliation and development and is acknowledged to have helped shape the nature and standing of public affairs in Australia.

The major objectives of the Centre have been to instil a sense of a public affairs professional identity on the function and its various sub-functions, to provide a more strategic business orientation in public affairs, to develop staff, and to understand and share domestic and international best practice.

Since its establishment the Centre has led more than fifty senior practitioners on international 'best practice' study tours involving leading companies and academics in the

USA and UK. More than 1,300 Australian and New Zealand practitioners have participated in its intensive one-week residential 'Institute' at the Melbourne Business School. This broad-based programme, whose faculty has included leading international practitioners and academics, has assisted in the development of many of the current heads of the function in major firms who return to share their experiences. Its seminars and workshops have explored public affairs concerns at an early stage of their development, led by international leaders in their relevant fields. These have included Professors Post (function development), Fleischer (function measurement), Chess and Sandman (risk communication), Mahon (issues management), Fombrun (reputation), Freeman (stakeholder management), Griffin (CSR) and Grayson (community investment).

THE AUSTRALIAN MODEL

From the early 1990s scale was one factor in establishing Australia's integrated model. However, a more conscious rationale for this management approach to the social and political environment emerged to become firmly entrenched and characterise public affairs in Australia.

Since about 2000 this integrated model has been fully established with 75–80 per cent (varying over time) of major Australian companies incorporating communications, community relations and government relations functions in the same department.[1]

The integrated function in Australia now typically involves activities such as traditional and social media, other external relations and event management, government relations and public policy, issues management, employee communications, interest group relations, association liaison, community relations, community investment, corporate sponsorship and crisis management. This is based on a broad acceptance that major

issues will have government, media, community and staff dimensions, are impacted by reputation which in turn is impacted by corporate social responsibility (in its broadest definition), all needing to be managed strategically and holistically. Accordingly it is now common for plans for these sub-functions to be written and activities pursued, not as separate instruments aimed narrowly at discrete stakeholder groups, but as integrated professional tools focused on the achievement of key identified strategic business imperatives.

One example of this is the way corporate community investment (CCI) is used in the mining sector to deal with environmental clearance and access to indigenous land. A major study for the Australian government in 2007 found that 93 per cent of companies surveyed said they required a business case for CCI decisions, including 24 per cent that required a tangible ROI justification (Centre for Corporate Public Affairs, 2007).

A number of functions on the boundary of public affairs are sometimes included in, and sometimes managed outside, the portfolio of sub-functions. The requirements of particular industries normally predict their location.

Regulatory affairs is often co-managed by government relations staff within public affairs departments, but where the regulatory task is technical, such as in pharmaceutical industries or in the price regulation of utilities, this is often led by legal or other technical departments.

Consumer affairs can also be placed within public affairs, but, for example, with fast-moving consumer goods it is placed in marketing or in a separate structure where again the consumer issues are very technical.

The primary role in investor relations in listed companies shifted from public affairs in the early 2000s as a new investor relations specialisation sprang up with its reporting line to the Chief Financial Officer. While public affairs no longer has responsibility for analyst briefings and investor liaison, it still plays an important role in general communications and media issues, and in some companies the close working relationship between teams is deliberately underpinned by co-location on office floors.

Marketing communications is undertaken either within public affairs or marketing departments; brand management, while shared, can be led from either.

Employee communications has shifted around. Initially when publishing newsletters was the main game, the journalist skillset made public affairs the most relevant location. A surge of culture change activity shifted it towards human resources for a period, but it has since returned in most companies to public affairs departments given the boundary-blurring role of social media, and an important focus on engaging employees on the major issues facing companies.

The standing of the function is marked by its place in corporate hierarchies. Since around the year 2000, from more humble positioning in middle management, many of the heads of the function have moved through corporate hierarchies to report directly to the company chief executive. In the first two decades of the twenty-first century this has been the case in between 60 and 70 per cent of major companies. In most of the remainder they report through one level below the CEO, usually to an executive with a suite of staff functions, or to strategic development and planning. Around two-thirds are members of their senior management committees of corporate teams. It is also normal for the lead practitioners in decentralised business units to be members of their management teams.

Between 70 and 80 per cent of the senior practitioners in recent surveys claim they participate in the development of the company's strategic plans.

This picture is of course not uniform. Not all major companies are on board with the integrated model, or relative seniority of function leaders, and even where this has been achieved, fortunes of departments and their staff numbers fluctuate with frequent re-organisation.

Notwithstanding the rise of the function in corporate hierarchies and decision-making, the standing of public affairs is often not acknowledged by external observers such as journalists who refer to practitioners pejoratively as 'corporate flacks' or some operations managers who still call the function 'PR'. One factor is no doubt the relative newness of public affairs as a strategic management function.

From the consulting experience of the author it is apparent that operations managers are significantly less likely to value the strategic nature of the function than CEOs who themselves have to deal directly with external relations concerns. Where the standing and positioning of the function in organisational hierarchies has fluctuated, this has often been because of a change of CEO from a different company or business culture. In relation to formal reporting lines this has been the result of a trend towards reducing the number of executives within the CEO's formal span of control. The expectations of practitioners has become so high that in a number of major companies the head of public affairs has resigned because of this loss of direct formal reporting to the CEO.

Another issue emerging from change in CEO, or organisational philosophy, has been a lack of appreciation of the rationale for the integrated model. Practitioners universally support the model, but it is sometimes denied them by executives with overseas backgrounds, and frequently threatened by generalist organisational consultants with a limited appreciation of the potential role of the function and the need to understand and respond holistically to the non-market environment.

The fluctuation in organisational models between centralisation and decentralisation of the function between corporate headquarters and business units has been another issue for public affairs practice in Australia. As Australian companies went offshore to establish overseas subsidiaries in the last decades of the twentieth century, this issue became more complex and is resolved differently between companies and within companies over time.

Different views prevail on how much autonomy should be vested in business-unit or country-level public affairs compared with the need for control or cohesion from the centre. This again varies with CEO and organisational philosophies of companies at different times. Significant consequences for public affairs performance and outcomes for companies have followed both excessive centralisation and decentralisation. The most common resolution in Australia as elsewhere has been for dual reporting lines that of course create their own challenges.

In many decentralised business entities, limited scale and business circumstances require only one public affairs executive or a very small team to provide support across the variety of sub-functions.

In this situation some leading companies with adequate scale are pursuing what is known locally as the 'centre of excellence' model. Here the emphasis is on the provision of specialist support, professional development and coaching. Where scale permits, the leadership of each major sub-function in a company (for example, media, community relations, internal communications, or government relations and public policy) is resourced as a specialist source of expertise, best practice and innovation for each sub-function across the organisation as well as providing direct support when special needs arise.

While centres of excellence are normally located at the corporate centre, they can be distributed elsewhere to where expertise resides. In one company example, a business unit generalist practitioner who has most experience in crisis management leads the coaching and crisis management support when needed, across the company.

CAREER PREPARATION

Apart from the Centre for Corporate Public Affairs that has as its members exclusively the public affairs departments of companies, industry associations and government business enterprises, two other professional bodies exist in Australia. They are the PRIA and the International Association of Business Communicators. Both of these are individual member associations with networking and professional development activities. In both cases they are focused on the communications side at a relatively basic level, and the mass of their membership is outside the mainstream corporate sector.

Many universities have programmes in communications, public relations, media or journalism. Sub-streams of some include organisational communications where communications aspects of issues and crisis management and stakeholder relations in companies are explored. These courses are a major source of base-level entry into company teams, public relations agencies and communications roles in not-for-profit organisations. However, career preparation at tertiary level largely reflects old or limited thinking about the function; there are no tertiary offerings with the full scope of socio-political analysis, communications and government in the context of business management or business strategy. This is in contrast with programmes that prepare professionals in other functional specialisations such as accounting, marketing and logistics. This may be in part because of the relatively new status of the profession, and also a lack of developed academics in the field.

Equally disappointing is the fact that business schools in MBA, executive and other general management programmes have largely ignored the non-market context of modern management. The business school at Sydney University launched a Masters of Public Affairs programme in the 1990s. However, this was soon absorbed into the political science faculty and civil servants dominated enrolments before it was discontinued. For a number of years since the 1970s the Melbourne Business School ran a valued course covering business government relations and the social and political environment of business as an element of business strategy. However, this too has been discontinued, and business school teaching in the area tends to be limited to boundary subjects such as units on regulatory economics, business ethics, CSR, sustainability and marketing communications. Nowhere are the highly relevant programmes that are run in top-flight US business schools such as 'managing in the non-market system' (for example, at Stanford, Yale, MIT, UCLA) or 'business government and society' (Harvard).

As the function has climbed the corporate ladder towards its strategic business role, executives from a variety of disciplines including law, science and general management have joined the ranks of senior practitioners. Those who have come from the traditional communications, or narrow political or government backgrounds, are being encouraged to pursue more business-oriented professional development opportunities to equip them for their business roles.

LOBBYING AND PARTY FUNDING

Australia does not have the tradition of professional lobbying that exists, for example, in the USA. Given the modest scale of Australian business and government there is relatively easy access for large companies and national interest groups to politicians, regulators and bureaucrats. It is considered appropriate by both business and government for companies to undertake their own communications with government leaders and advisers. Indeed, politicians and bureaucrats frequently voice their strong preference for dealing with companies directly.

While time is a major constraint all round, it is considered best practice by both business and government for there to be full and frequent information flows between the sectors, and it is common for government relations practitioners to enjoy a trusted place at the centre of this process. Leaders of business associations are also constant and welcome intermediaries.

A few former politicians and party apparatchiks seek to play a more US-style lobbying role. They can occasionally gain access and a voice for smaller companies or where corporate government relations executives have been less than effective. But where professional advisers are used, the main game is with a small number of competent Canberra-based political consulting firms with connections across the political spectrum that are used most effectively for political intelligence and advice on strategy.

With the rising public demand for policy justification and increasingly sophisticated government and interest group sectors, the 1980s saw the birth and subsequent growth of economic and public policy consultancies. They are seen to be politically neutral, staffed mainly by economists with public policy backgrounds, and assist companies and associations to review issues and present their case. They are also used by governments to review programmes and assist in the development of policy.

Until the second decade of the twenty-first century, policy think tanks played a very limited role in policy thinking but have become a more important part of the 'outsider system' debates in the current decade. Some of these have party political connections but most are keen to assert their policy independence.

While not involving mainstream companies, several scandals around the turn of the century involving the lobbying activities of former politicians, particularly at the state government level, led to the development by both the national and state governments of lobbying registers and codes of conduct. These rules, however, are restricted to third-party representatives and do not include company executives. They are modest documents limited mainly to transparency provisions, such as the provision of client lists.

Party or candidate funding plays a lesser role in the Australian political system than in a number of other countries. There is some public funding for registered parties based on the number of votes they won in the previous election. The Labor Party is the beneficiary of political levies paid to it by affiliated trade unions as well as some corporate funding. The conservative parties rely heavily on fundraising activities of supporters and attract a greater level of corporate support. However, public companies are increasingly deciding not to fund political activities, limiting participation in small-scale fundraising activities such as paying for dinner with politicians or registering with inflated prices at party conferences.

As with the rules concerning lobbying, transparency of funding through the required publication of contributions is the designated control. The threshold for reporting of donations is around the modest $US 10,000 for any company or other organisation. Games are played to subvert the rules, such as the establishment of supporting coteries, but these are modest by international standards.

While these modest contributions might facilitate a meeting with a politician for those who would otherwise not have access, there is little evidence to suggest public funding influences policy or regulatory outcomes in any significant way.

Compulsory voting in Australia does not require strategies to get out the vote and there is very little party political activity within companies or with their staff, although individual executives may be active in parties outside their corporate roles. Generally, while voting proclivities of business leaders might be assumed, there is a strong emphasis on voting confidentiality and corporate bipartisanship, a factor that sometimes annoys conservative politicians who expect overt political support from the corporate sector.

The practice of public affairs in Australia has evolved from its PR and government affairs antecedents from the early 1990s to around 2005 and has largely stabilised at that point in concept, function and level of resources. Through this period and beyond, the quality and mainstream business orientation of its

leading executives has grown and its organisational model has been spread in Australian business cultures.

Following the professional development of public affairs, and building on experience gained by Australia's recent outward business expansion, a number of Australian practitioners now occupy important roles in non-Australian companies in the UK, USA and particularly in Asia.

NEW ZEALAND

As in Australia, the development of the public affairs function has been heavily conditioned, and can best be explained, by the history of the relationship between business and the political economy.

The Business Environment

New Zealand is a small country with a progressive one-state democracy based on a centralised unicameral legislative system. While there is a range of industries including manufacturing and minerals processing and an expanding tourism industry, agricultural and pastoral products are by far the largest export earners. Like most developed economies, the services sector is the dominant employer.

There are fewer than twenty indigenous companies of sufficient scale to warrant the establishment of a public affairs department of the kind we are discussing here. Four of the top ten are in the energy sector. Foreign companies, however, play a major role in the domestic economy, for example Australian companies dominate the local banking and finance sectors and make up almost half of the foreign affiliates operating in New Zealand. This, with the extensive trade and free movement of labour across the Tasman Sea, demonstrates the interconnectedness of these two economies.

A dramatic shift took place in the 1980s as the then highly protected and closed, centrally controlled economy was deregulated to become one of the most open in the OECD. State-owned enterprises were subjected to competition or privatised, agricultural subsidies were abolished, the exchange rate was floated, and other micro-economic reforms, such as in labour markets and taxation, were implemented.

Business-friendly regulatory frameworks and a strong international trading culture since the opening of the economy have made New Zealand a confident and outward-looking business environment.

The heavy government intervention and dirigisme of the pre-reform era had been marked by close relationships between business and government elites pursuing the protected status quo of 'New Zealand Inc.' in what was described above for pre-reform Australia as an 'insider system'. As in Australia, also, with a shift towards economic rationalism came more open public debate and contestability on policy. With increased scrutiny and the need to justify policy positions in recent years, companies deepened their research and evidence-based arguments. This work is now reflected in government submissions and public advocacy.

Accordingly, aspects of this 'outsider' or public advocacy and policy contestability approach arose with the advent of the country's dramatic spurt of micro-economic reform agenda and has led to this being an entrenched element in the relationship between business and its government and non-government interlocutors.

Notwithstanding this, the smallness of the business and government community and their close proximity in the two major cities (the political capital, Wellington, and business capital, Auckland) has meant that there is constant, full and informal communications between the sectors at various levels.

Politicians and government officials, by virtue of their continuous interaction with business leaders, are knowledgeable about the interests and wishes of major companies, and business executives have ready informal access to political and regulatory power. This clubbish dynamic is symbolised by what is called the 'Kuru Club'. (Kuru is the Maori name for the curled-up fern that graces the tail of Air New Zealand planes.) The Kuru Club is the jocular term for business and government frequent flyers – particularly between Auckland and Wellington – who are constantly meeting and interacting in Air New Zealand lounges.

Despite New Zealand consistently being ranked amongst the cleanest countries in Transparency International's Corruption Index, an attempt was made through a Green Party private member's bill in 2013 to establish by legislation a register of lobbyists and a lobbyist code of conduct. The proposed bill was based on Australian and Canadian models although it went beyond them to require the registration and disclosure of trade union, NGO and corporate lobbying.

In reality, given the frequency and informality of the networks, such legislation would have been impractical. The proposal was dismissed as being too broad and likely to discourage valued constituency engagement with politicians. The Chair of the Parliamentary Committee that recommended against the proposal tellingly said, 'New Zealand is a village. We know who the lobbyists are and what they are going to talk to us about' (Dyson, 2013).

Implications for Public Affairs

The nature of this easy interaction between senior levels of business and government has conditioned the shape of the public affairs function in New Zealand. It has meant that there is less need for the sort of specialised government relations and public policy resources that exist, for example, in Australia and many other developed countries. This, together with the modest scale of public affairs departments in the relatively small indigenous companies, has meant that dealing with government at a professional level is seen in most of them as an aspect of the communications task to be undertaken by an overall external relations function leader or staff member who is by name and self-identity a communications or stakeholder relations generalist.

Recognising the significance of government there has been an increasing intake to public affairs positions of executives from the bureaucracy or ministers' offices, although many of these had journalist or other communications backgrounds rather than policy roles. Mid-career entry to the profession has been from journalism, some from government, and from the few but active public relations or political advisory agencies. Indeed in this small market for professionals, career interaction between companies and these agencies is frequent.

Where a company has an Australian parent the language used to describe the overall function is likely to be 'public affairs' or 'corporate affairs' as it is in Australia, but for indigenous New Zealand companies 'communications' and to a lesser extent 'public relations' is the common term. As indicated this reflects the skewing of the function towards communications, relationship building, reputation management, 'sustainability' and community relations.

There is no received organisational orthodoxy. The function more normally sits lower than its Australian counterpart in organisation hierarchies and reporting can be through a greater variety of other functions, depending on how it is perceived in any company and the nature of the business. While some are direct reports to company chiefs or corporate services generalists, common reporting lines include through legal, marketing or human resources executives, or the CFO.

As in Australia it is not considered appropriate for major companies to undertake their direct communications with government through third parties; however, there is a small but active public relations and

political advisory network in New Zealand and one that is in relative terms greater than that in Australia. A greater propensity than in Australia to outsource these public affairs activities and others beyond government relations may well be explained by the scale of companies that limits the scale of staff and other resources in-house.

There has been little attention to the non-market environment in tertiary management education management training but there are undergraduate public relations, media or communications courses in most tertiary institutions, and graduates of these courses make up the large majority of base-level recruits to corporate communications departments.

Given the size of the professional community and the geographic proximity of the major business and government centres, there is a high degree of professional interaction; practitioners know each other well and often follow each other as they move from organisation to organisation.

PRINZ and the International Association of Business Communicators are active, the latter in the political capital, Wellington. These organisations are heavily public relations and communications focused, with consultants, fundraisers and others predominating as members. Their professional development activities are basic; however, a number of the senior practitioners in the field participate in a 'senior practitioners forum' hosted by PRINZ. As one public affairs practitioner said, 'We don't tend to meet in workshops or conferences to exchange ideas and best practice and so on because we are all very familiar with what each other is doing' (Allen, 2015a).

It is worthy of note that the communications function in government agencies – sometimes called public affairs – is strong and sophisticated in New Zealand, even more developed than in some leading companies, and arguably more advanced than their Australian counterparts.

In both countries government initiatives seem to lack legitimacy, certainly in the eyes of policy opponents, if there has not been stakeholder consultation, and increasingly this consultation is mandated in legislation. It is interesting to note that in both New Zealand and Australia government practitioners have led the way in innovative stakeholder engagement. Structured processes for community engagement, sophisticated social marketing and innovative uses of social media have all been the hallmarks of this leadership by the public sector.

PACIFIC ISLAND PUBLIC AFFAIRS

New Guinea

While it will remain a subsistence world for the large majority of the 7 million inhabitants of Papua New Guinea scattered in small tribal groupings across the country, the economy of PNG is undergoing major change due mainly to a number of large-scale, remote, oil and gas and mining projects.

The social and political environment of business is very complex. The Melanesian obligation of the powerful and wealthy to win and share resources with their families and tribal 'wantoks' (speakers of the same language) has complicated political and bureaucratic activity. Tribal obligations at senior levels of government have been one of a number of contributors to perceptions of corruption and political patronage that see Transparency International ranking PNG consistently around 150th in its Corruption Index. Questions of corruption and nepotism are also compounded by the structure of politics around individuals, regional jealousies and factions, which have led also to periods of instability and, for outsiders, difficulties in mapping complex motivations and points of decision.

Shifts in power through the first decades of the twenty-first century have seen a loss of influence of the bureaucracy and an accumulation of power in the hands of the executive, particularly the office of the Prime Minister. The parliamentary democracy left by well-meaning Australians following independence in the 1970s includes a proliferation of under-scale but active provincial governments with their own set of regulatory interventions, 'roads and bridges' focus, and overlapping responsibilities with the national government.

Notwithstanding this challenging environment there has been enough time since independence for a small, educated middle class to emerge and take its place in business and government. With this small and deeply connected emerging urban elite, relationships between business and government are personal and close, albeit sometimes tense. While power structures are dynamic and unpredictable, the smallness of the business and government elite makes access to decision makers informal and frequent.

There are several indigenous companies of scale, for example an airline, bank, hotel chain and an oil exploration company. The government has been building equity in many of these enterprises as well as taking minority positions in a number of the significant resource projects of multinational companies.

A small number of major multinationals in the resources sector, particularly from Australia, the USA and more recently China, are at the forefront of the country's development, and this is where we find the main action for the public affairs function.

The economic activity in this resources sector is in remote areas away from the urban centres. Companies seeking access to land for these projects must deal with shrewd villagers and small tribal groupings, seeking to leverage development for local benefit. Apart from significant contributions, for instance to local infrastructure and community services, local communities can be vested with 10 per cent of the equity in these local projects. Particularly challenging is the level of expectations of local groups and the complexity of the competing demands and power relationships of multiple tribal or village entities. The negotiation of local community agreements with local landholders can take a long time because of the extravagance of some expectations and dynamics within and between quarrelsome counterparties. This has led to considerable expatriate and local public affairs resources being deployed in community relations and negotiations.

The experience of one major resource project is not untypical. As one operations manager said,

> Frankly the company was having the crap beaten out of it publicly for the first six months. The project is crucial for the country but the company was making no progress. The landowner environment was particularly tough including a number of violent incidents. We significantly increased resources including expatriate expertise and turned it around big time. Public affairs was the key to our success. (Allen 2015b)

Because of the nature of the task the major structural divide in the function of public affairs in most of these resource companies is not government relations and communications, as is the case in many countries, but between these aspects of public affairs being managed together in the major centres on the one hand, and the highly resourced intensive community relations activity surrounding projects on the other.

Traditional media is not strong, has limited reach beyond PNG's few city centres and is not particularly influential. However, as in a number of developing countries, and with remote locations, social media is emerging strongly and is already playing a major role in how issues are seen and managed.

Expatriate companies, as in other developing countries, have embarked on serious localisation of employment policies, and have been taking advantage of the second generation of tertiary-educated leaders to play increasingly senior roles in companies. One downside has been that, as major companies arrived, many of the best-educated class of executives have abandoned government careers for more lucrative roles in companies, including a handful in public affairs. Mainly because of their capability as well as their forensic knowledge of local culture and political drivers, some of the most capable have assumed the role of country manager for these expatriate businesses.

Given the significance of government and the political authorising environment, much of the task of country manager here and elsewhere is stakeholder relations, especially with government, and engagement with other key stakeholders – the province of public affairs.

In part because of the complexities of local politics and the importance of personal relationships, expatriate companies also commonly avail themselves of a small group of well-placed consultants or retired advisers external to the firm. Most of these have political or public service backgrounds and are well regarded and connected to officials with influence, but the pool of talent, and experience and required gravitas is small with supply exceeding demand.

Notwithstanding this the local managements of multinationals working in Papua New Guinea frequently call on the relevant corporate public affairs expertise, for example in government relations or community relations, from their corporate or regional centres. Accordingly, they fly in to advise or assist directly on particular issues or to train local staff.

Several Australian and American companies have taken PNG nationals to their businesses overseas for public affairs training and experience, so it is reasonable to expect a small indigenous function to emerge, heavily influenced by the approach of the overseas companies training these functional pioneers. The scale of operations suggests they will develop as generalist practitioners with remits covering the interconnected areas of communications and government and community relations.

The Pacific Island Microstates

It is necessary for this chapter to generalise about public affairs in the remainder of Oceania. The region is made up of a number of island microstates with significant social and political differences. Most populations are between a quarter and half a million, but some are considerably less. Most achieved independence in the 1970s, although New Caledonia and French Polynesia remain French territories, albeit with considerable self-government. Indigenous populations are mostly Melanesian or Polynesian. Fiji has a large ethnic Indian population and there are significant European minorities in the French territories. Australia and New Zealand are big aid donors to the rest of the region and the destination for the majority of its exports. Five of these small economies have New Zealand dollars as their currency. A large percentage of these Pacific island populations live in traditional villages with national incomes in the range of US$2,000–6,000 per annum.

While political dynamics across the countries vary considerably, parliamentary democracies predominate. At the same time in a number of countries there remains a parallel traditional tribal authority structure in villages and clans and in central bodies such as Fiji's Great Council of Chiefs, New Caledonia's Customary Senate and Vanuatu's Council of Chiefs. They exercise considerable influence at various levels over local culture and national politics, but their influence over governments fluctuates over time.

As in Papua New Guinea, tribal loyalties and personality-based factions have led to political instability, occasional violence and complexities in government and relationships with the private sector. Many of these countries sit in the bottom quartile of political risk and corruption indices. Australia and New Zealand have had to provide troops and police in several countries to assist in peacekeeping and stabilisation programmes.

Although not always stable, and despite democratic constitutions, a number of the countries are run with autocratic political control, and with legal systems subject to heavy political influence. In Fiji, for example, a successful military coup was undertaken in the name of eliminating corruption and nepotism, but resulted in an erosion of the rule of law, discrimination in government support of businesses, and heavy censorship of the media to protect the political leadership.

The economies vary but products from the region include fishing, forestry, sugar, other agricultural products, and in some countries, tourism. Fiji has some minerals, New Caledonia has 25 per cent of the world's nickel and Timor-Leste is building a large sovereign wealth fund from its substantial offshore oil resources. While diminishing in significance, Vanuatu is capitalising on its tax haven status, and from its provision of shipping 'flags of convenience'.

In developing countries like the Pacific island states the external relations function is rare for indigenous companies. There are few of these of scale, and most of the larger company operations in these countries are by subsidiaries of international companies. Whether they are Australian or New Zealand companies or from other parts of the world, these expatriate businesses are likely to be part of regional structures, and have reporting relationships through Australia, New Zealand or Singapore. Chinese investment in the region is growing quickly, albeit from a low base.

The role of external 'representative' of these companies is most often carried by the most senior executive – usually expatriate – who is designated 'country manager' and it is added to his or her operational responsibilities. Where the business warrants it these managers focus on an individual country, but more often a line executive will have coverage of a number of the small states in which they do business. However, as the representative of these companies across the region, these country managers or equivalent have to perform many of the functions that in larger environments would fall to public affairs specialists.

What is not always appreciated is that when operational executives are called upon to fill these positions they may be unskilled and unprepared. They commonly have little experience in relations with complex stakeholders including political leaders and activists. Yet as major players in small local economies they are asked to assume particularly sensitive positions of community leadership, and risk being dragged into complex local politics, factional alignments, community investments in controversial areas and other areas of potential controversy.

While political and ethnic unrest was high and even violent in the Pacific in the early 2000s, one company with a significant presence in the downstream petroleum industry decided to change its business leadership in several small Pacific countries simultaneously. Only weeks before the transfer of executives with refinery, depot and distribution management, but little other experience, the company realised the complexity of the political and social environment facing these executives. As a result the company had to scramble to put together a crash course on Pacific island politics and public affairs generally as well as issues in each local country before they took up their appointments.

It is most common to support these country managers in their external relations activities and strategies remotely by public affairs teams in head offices. Some of the larger companies do employ indigenous and expatriate communications and community relations and occasionally public affairs generalists in the region. For example, several Australian banks have staff on the ground in Fiji, but with responsibilities for the function in the various island countries in which they operate. At their various levels, Pacific island staff are normally well connected to head office teams and, as with country managers, have the capacity to call on advice, and from time to time other resources to fly in from other parts of the company to assist with complex situations.

While there are a number of other tertiary institutions, twelve Pacific island countries co-own the University of the South Pacific with campuses spread across participating countries. The range of courses available includes journalism, politics and management, but these have made little impact to date on preparation for public affairs roles.

CONCLUSION

The practice of public affairs varies as greatly as the economies and business environments. As a generalisation, the public affairs function varies in major Australian companies but most are close to what is described as the 'mature phase' by Harsanyi and Allen in this volume. In smaller Australian companies and those with low vulnerability to regulatory or political pressures, the function is more likely to be at the early stage of development as described in that chapter.

Easy proximity to each other of business and government in New Zealand has meant that communications has the dominant weighting in the understanding and practice of public affairs. The limited scale of operations in their mainstream companies has meant government relations tends to be seen as just another communications activity.

The need for specialist community relations in PNG is a special case, but generally in the Pacific islands a limited number of practitioners are supported by staff in offshore corporate or regional offices. As in other small developing economies, external relations tasks are most commonly performed by country managers with operational responsibilities.

Note

1 This generalisation and those in following paragraphs made on the state of Australian public

affairs practice are based on the surveys of practitioners, Centre of Corporate Public Affairs, 'The State of Australian Public Affairs', 2009, 2012 and 2015.

REFERENCES

Allen, Geoff (2015a) Interview with senior New Zealand communications practitioner, June.

Allen, Geoff (2015b) Interview with US resource company executive, June.

Centre for Corporate Public Affairs (2007) 'Corporate Community Investment in Australia', Project for the Prime Minister's Community Business Partnership, p. 34.

Dyson, Ruth (2013) Labor MP, quoted in *New Zealand Herald*, 23 August.

Parbo, Sir Arvi (1990) Launch of the Australian Centre for Corporate Public Affairs, Melbourne, November, 1990.

Public Affairs in East and South-East Asia

Andrew Hughes

If you want one year of prosperity, grow grain. If you want ten years of prosperity, grow trees. If you want one hundred years of prosperity, grow people. (Unknown)

INTRODUCTION

In the second decade of the twenty-first century it is becoming clear just how important public affairs will be in the entire region. Whilst Asia itself geographically is a region that stretches from Turkey in the west all the way through to Japan and Russia in the east, this chapter will examine only East and South-East Asia, with special mention made of the subcontinent region that includes India and Pakistan.

This chapter will start by examining the importance of relationships in Asian public affairs. It will examine briefly the economic background of Asia, with a focus on the current high growth but with an eye on a future that will be more about maximising opportunities in maturing markets than capitalising on growth. Following this, Asian public affairs will be defined, based on a conceptual model centred on the Asian context of reciprocity in relationships. Next, the development of Asian public affairs during this century will be briefly discussed. A more in-depth analysis of the region's super powers – China, India, Japan and South Korea – will follow, along with a brief examination of some of Asia's future powers and rising nations. The chapter will conclude with some final points on the future development of public affairs in Asia.

CHALLENGES AND OPPORTUNITIES IN THE ASIAN CENTURY

Economic Growth and Public Affairs: Creating New Opportunities and Relationships

As the region enters the second half of the second decade of the 'Asian century', there is increasing concern over the likelihood of a more sustained Asian slowdown hitting the region. But this needs to be put into perspective. Slowdown for the Asian economies means a breather from the near double digit growth rates that were seen in the region in the early part of the Asian century. For example, in the case of the region's economic powerhouse, China, this means a target of growing at 6.5 per cent a year up until 2021, down on the 2015 figure of 6.9 per cent, but still nearly double the same figures set by Australia and many other advanced economies in the region (Sweeney and Shao 2016). Then there is the increase in the proportion of world GDP that the Asian region comprises (Figure 25.1), well into the 40 per cent range and remaining the fastest growing region into the foreseeable future (Austrade 2016).

However, this is why some see the next stage of economic development in Asia as being important in the development of the region as a whole – many countries are

coming out of a time of full capacity and growth in their economies and societies. This economic growth and reform contributed to a (largely) sustained period of political stability, which allowed the entry of many foreign multinationals into local markets along with other market-based reforms that led to growth (Bajpaee 2016). Whilst this naturally saw a growth in public affairs in the region, the latter was also helped by the existing predilection towards the importance of relationships and reciprocity of favours, or as the Chinese say *guanxi* (Ambler 1994; Wang 2007; Yeung and Tung 1996). The importance of relationships, especially in business, meant that multinational companies were able to achieve stronger relationships with Asian governments more rapidly and effectively than with the governments of the countries where they were based. This further aided public affairs development in the region as governments used large multinational

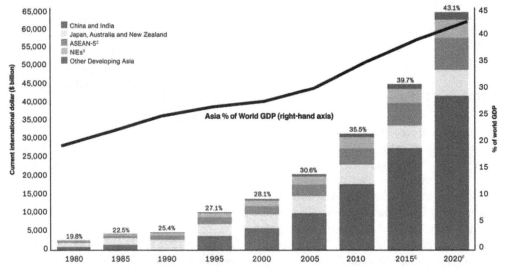

Note: The number on the bar represents the Asian economy as a percentage share of world GDP (PPP).

E = Estimate **F** = Forecast

1. An international dollar would buy in the cited country a comparable amount of goods and services a US dollar would buy in the United States. Local currency values are converted into international dollars using PPP exchange rates
2. Composed of 5 countries: Indonesia, Malaysia, Philippines, Thailand and Vietnam
3. Newly Industrialised Economies: Singapore, Hong Kong, South Korea and Taiwan

Figure 25.1   The rapid rise of Asia as an economic power: Asia % of World GDP from 1980–2020

Source: Austrade (2016), Why Australia? Benchmark Report 2016, p. 7.

corporations to develop, maintain and assist diplomacy and relations even when the governments themselves may have been in rivalry with each other.

This should not just be seen as a one-way relationship where the Western brands were gaining all the benefit, as the reciprocity of favours in the relationships also allowed Asian brands to enter foreign markets and establish relationships with foreign consumers. This allowed both Asian and Western brands to establish social capital, which public affairs functions in Asia see as a priority to develop and maintain (Putnam 1994). Whilst initially country of origin effects limited their development, over time these brands have been able to develop resonance with consumers across many categories from cars to appliances to food, which in turn has allowed the countries they come from to be perceived far more favourably than would have been the case if a model of Western liberal democratic metrics were used.

With the growth in technology, especially in mobile devices and online commerce in the form of apps, the world is seeing a second wave of Asian brands hit the market. Online brands and e-tailers such as Alibaba, Weibo, Rakuten, Amazon, Tmall, Jingdon and Suning to name just a few are experiencing growth which is the envy of their US and European counterparts. Forrester is predicting that the five key online markets in the region, namely China, Japan, South Korea, India and Australia, will have revenue of US$1.4 trillion by 2020, with China already being the largest e-commerce market in the world and already nine times the size of Japan and seventeen times that of South Korea (Yu 2016).

This online growth is introducing the next wave of consumers to the next wave of Asian brands, establishing new relationships and exchanges between Asia and the rest of the world in a digital space that shows no signs of slowing down. This space has created new opportunities for public affairs in the region as old values become

accepted as part of relationships of the next generation.

Globalisation and Public Affairs in an Asian Context

Asia has always seen itself and been seen by others as one of the most influential parts of the world in a political, financial and social sense. As Harris (2016) noted, Marco Polo and his observations on the Silk Road may have made the opportunities and potential of the Asian market more widely known in the West, and perhaps even been the start of the influence of public affairs in developing relationships between the two, but since then countries in the Asian region have sought to become global powers in their own right.

In a military context Asia has nearly always taken centre-stage in global affairs, especially since the end of the Second World War and the development of nuclear weapon capability by several nations in the region such as China, India, Pakistan and North Korea, not to mention of course that already held and shared by Russia and the United States and their allies. Whilst some of the world's largest armies are in Asia, military power in the modern era is more about cyber warfare and streamlined rapid reaction forces and no longer just about who has a nuclear arsenal. This has meant that the protection of strategic and national interests extends to the protection of corporate brands, which is where public affairs has assisted governments and defence organisations in developing messages that support the development of cyber defences and resources that may come at the price of civil liberties (ASPI 2015).

Public affairs' role in developing a narrative for governments where there exist political and military struggles in the region is also an important one. An example of this is the South China Sea where each nation with a current military presence or role is under domestic pressures to be seen to be protecting and preserving national interests, even though behind the scenes the strength of business and trading relationships between these nations is keeping channels open and trade flourishing (Goh 2008; Medeiros 2005). More than anywhere else on earth, Asia is the one place where every significant military force and power wishes to have not just a presence but also a sphere of influence, which can create tension when perhaps there needs to be more restraint.

Whilst military muscle still counts for many in Asia, it really acts more like the bouncer on the door than a true reflection of a nation's power as globalisation has turned economic power into the bargaining tool of choice (Rajan 2003). Economically there is no doubt that the five biggest economies in the region – China, India, Japan, South Korea and Russia – count themselves as world economic powers, reflected in their roles in global economic forums such as the G20, APEC and for some the G8 (Beeson 2014). But even rising powers just outside this select group, such as Indonesia, Turkey, Thailand, Malaysia, Singapore, Pakistan and the Philippines, can have a global reach owing to the size and growth of their economies and brands (Beeson 2014).

The Asian economic super powers are also distinguished by their large foreign exchange reserves, mainly in US dollars, which they can use to secure influences in nations and companies that they want either to build closer ties with or take a strategic interest in. This in itself can be a cause of tension, particularly in Western nations where the sale and ownership of national assets or companies raises domestic political pressures on political parties and candidates to protect national security and trade interests at the expense of free trade and lower trade barriers (Omestad 1989). In recent times in some Western nations sales of some assets and companies have even been blocked or restricted as a result of national security concerns over who may ultimately control an asset, such as the proposed 2015 sale of Australia's largest cattle producer to foreign owners. With mergers and acquisitions occurring on a constant basis in global markets, this issue may be one that continues well into the future (Serdar Dinc and Erel 2013), despite the best efforts of lobbyists and public affairs experts to allay xenophobic fears of foreign ownership.

With the globalisation of public affairs, methods once used only in Western markets are now finding a home in the business environment of the East, together with global firms representing clients and governments across a wide range of issues in many nations. Public affairs organisations have been able to capitalise on this: being able to build relationships and contacts with individuals within political and business organisations that, to those on the outside, may be secretive or may be opaque in terms of who exactly within the organisation holds power, has undoubtedly helped many clients of these firms.

The Asian Century: Politics with Asian Characteristics but Western Methods

The Asian century has highlighted the differences and similarities between the East and the West when it comes to politics. Whilst Western-style democracies struggle in Asia for the very good reason that they were designed for entrenched Western cultures and values, which can be at times totally opposite to the cultures and values in the East, modern Western-style methods have been widely accepted into Asian politics and business (Mahbubani 2008).

This means that the methods used to manage public affairs in Europe, the United States or other parts of the West such as Australia or New Zealand, are equally found in use and application in the East. Stakeholder management and engagement, events, government and business relations, social media strategies, reputational research, political lobbying and market research are all widely practised and used in the Asian region (Holtbrügge and Berg 2004); in fact it could be argued that the political, business and social culture and values of the East encourage these methods more than do that of the West.

There are those in the West who will argue that democracy is everything, but there are equally those in the East who will say that if your cultures and values encourage and reward positive and constructive partnerships and relationships between stakeholders then the outcome may very well be the same. This is the dilemma that many organisations coming from the West face: when does a close relationship cross the line between being one of influence and being one of corruption or abuse of power? Governments in the East have recognised that this is a serious issue and have started to become more aware and active in monitoring stakeholder relationships between companies and government officials and corporations, especially those from the West (Lovett, Simmons and Kali 1999).

This issue is one that Western brands need to be careful about as in their home markets any abuse of relationships in the East may be perceived as negatively as in the East. For example, claims of selling foreign products not fit for consumption in their home markets into foreign markets do not play out well for building brand value and equity regardless of the where, who, how, when and why of the situation, something that New Zealand dairy companies have recently found out (Stojkov, Noy and Sağlam 2016).

With more and more nations in the Asian region such as Bangladesh, Burma, Vietnam, Malaysia and Indonesia developing and modernising their political systems, public affairs will only see continued growth in the region as these systems adopt and implement Western methods for political governance, campaigns and management that fit their cultures and values. An example of this in social media is Indonesia – now the fourth biggest nation in the world for use of Twitter, and quickly climbing the ladder on use of other social media platforms such as Instagram, Facebook and Pinterest, now all part and parcel of modern political management and campaigns (De Zuniga, Puig-i-Abril and Rojas 2009).

The 3 Rs of Asian Public Affairs: Relationship, Relationship and Relationship

Asian public affairs at its core is founded on the Asian concept of relationship. Whilst many regions in the world see relationship as being important (Grönroos 1984; Gummesson 1994), in Asia the concept of a relationship is not just a business or public philosophy, it is a way of life which goes back thousands of years (Arias 1998). Some of the earliest relationship-building exercises in Asia, such as trade visits by Marco Polo, would now be seen as a form of public affairs (Harris 2016). Trade and commerce relationships are not just about transactions, but take a more individual, long-term perspective. Whilst called *guanxi* in China, this concept is found at the centre of business, political, social and wider networks all through the region (Arias 1998; Wang 2007). This common understanding of how relationships work in an Asian context has helped organisations and individuals quickly adapt more modern relationship marketing methods and concepts into Asian culture, or as Ambler (1994) states, make *guanxi* the third paradigm in marketing.

Often in Asia it is the relationship between individuals in organisations and the wider industry network, who may have attended schools or universities together, that is of most importance in a public affairs relationship context (Davies et al. 1995). When an individual leaves one organisation to go and work for another, their networks and relationships transfer with them, which is causing issues in Asian public affairs as this can negatively impact the development of an organisation (Arias 1998). This may also be a factor in the at times haphazard development of

Asian public affairs as individuals don't share knowledge in a public affairs organisation in the same manner as expected in the West. This means that unless a firm can replace one individual with one of similar knowledge, status and networks, then it can find itself having to seek a replacement with similar skills but requiring a substantial investment of time and resources to move that person to the same level as the previous one.

For organisations and individuals outside the region this highlights the need to have a local alliance or relationship in place before entering the market. Even then, the highly regionalised nature of many political and governance systems in Asia means that an organisation needs to still develop relationships in these markets before they can hope for any long-term success (Ambler 1994; Arias 1998). In Asian public affairs a very long-term timeframe and mindset is therefore required, or as an old Confucius saying states, 'The earth may be slow, but the ox is patient', so eventually any investment should pay off.

Asian Public Affairs Defined

This should start to build a picture of what Asian public affairs can be defined as being. A definition of Asian public affairs can assist those not familiar with the area in identifying activities that may indicate that public affairs is being carried out. A definition should not be seen as a method for establishing best practice, and as Harris and Fleisher (2005:97) state, a definition should be more about 'how the functions operate and the prime reasons for its existence'.

As noted by McGrath, Moss and Harris (2010) public affairs can be a particularly difficult area to define as it can change meaning in different cultures and contexts. They also note the fluidity of any definition in the minds of practitioners, who will tend to define it by function, method and objective, sometimes even specific to the practitioner

and firm itself. There is more consensus on the duality of public affairs as a function in the modern era – that is, objectives and functions can be external, such as government relations, lobbying, events, shareholder management, external stakeholders such as community interest groups, policy and public relations, communications and even marketing activities, and internally focused such as employee relations, corporate strategy and tactical advice to executives and other levels of the firm. Objectives themselves have also evolved into being broadly focused on relationships and engagement with all internal and external stakeholders, with specifics being concerned with the duality noted above through using relevant functions listed above. As McGrath et al. (2010) mention, in a way it is a bridge that allows two-way traffic between the external and the internal.

McGrath et al. (2010) state that a definition of public affairs needs to encompass the prime reason for the existence of public affairs in that particular construct. In the case of Asian public affairs this would mean relationships with stakeholders, or in particular, carrying out activities that lead to their creation, development and maintenance. Luo (2001) and Gao (2006) maintain that public affairs objectives in China can be either transactional or relational, that is with key outcomes being focused on a certain transaction, or on strengthening or creating a relationship, but regardless of objective, at their core they are still about *guanxi*. This emphasis on the importance of relationships in Asian public affairs is critical in any definition that relates to the region as it helps explain the dual emphasis that might be seen in any exchange that takes place between stakeholders: that is, the transactional exchange that occurs can't be more important than the value of the relationship that already exists between the stakeholders in the exchange.

But a field and region as broad as this, where there is a convergence of methods from marketing, communications, policy, public relations and management, also means that any definition needs to be flexible and fluid enough to recognise that the primary use of any of these methods is the achievement of a successful public affairs strategy (Moss et al. 2012).

Therefore, for the purpose of this chapter, the following definition will be used:

Asian public affairs is the use, development and application of a broad range of activities designed and implemented to create, develop and maintain relationships of value with the organisation's stakeholders.

The Rise of Stakeholders in Public Affairs in Asia

The relationship between stakeholders, public affairs and politics is well established (Hughes and Dann 2009). Stakeholder groups have increasingly turned to public affairs to achieve their objectives, and for some public affairs firms they may represent different stakeholders on the one issue or even act as a facilitator on an issue to achieve key objectives for all sides. As Getz (2002) noted, there is a need for further research into the relationship between stakeholder objectives, firm objectives and public affairs. As the second decade of the Asian century starts to

enter its twilight, it can be seen that in some relationships, when stakeholder objectives, firm objectives and political objectives of a government are in alignment, then the influence of public affairs activities is probably close to its zenith.

While it could be argued that the rise of stakeholders in Asia could also be attributed to a lack of democratic political systems, this can be countered by the fact that public affairs in all parts of the world, if anything more in democracies, has benefited from stakeholders who value the speed and direct action that representation by a public affairs firm or individual affords.

The Five-Attribute Model for Asian Public Affairs

Stakeholders in public affairs in Asia can be classified using a modified five-attribute model based on the work of Mitchell, Agle and Wood (1997). These five attributes are power, legitimacy, urgency, relationship and value (see Table 25.1). These attributes take into consideration the importance of relationships in Asian business, political and social contexts, and also the importance of the value that stakeholders seek to exchange in an actor-to-actor model (see Figure 25.2).

Table 25.1   Stakeholder exchange based attribute model definitions

Attribute	Definition	Based On
Power	'A relationship among social actors in which one social actor, A, can get another social actor, B, to do something that B would not'	Dahl (1957), Pfeffer (1981), Weber (1947), Hester, Bradley & Adams (2012)
Legitimacy	'A generalized perception or assumption that the actions of an entity are desirable, proper, or appropriate within some socially constructed system of norms, values, beliefs, definitions' (Mitchell et al. 1997, p. 869)	Weber (1947)
Urgency	'The degree to which stakeholder claims for immediate attention' (Mitchell et al. 1997, p. 869)	Mitchell et al. (1997)
Relationship	The level and intensity to which the actors have a connection, either past or present, and the length of time that such a connection has existed for	Grönroos 1984, Gummesson 1994
Value	Value is co-created in the exchange between actors, always determined by the beneficiary, and may be experiential, contextual and meaning-laden	Vargo & Lusch (2004, 2008)

These attributes can be used to build a conceptual framework with which to assess the influence of individual stakeholders in public affairs in either a broad or specific context not just in Asia but also around the world (Figure 25.2). Understanding the contextual nature of stakeholders in public affairs allows a picture to be constructed of how a certain stakeholder, or group of stakeholders, may behave in one country as compared with another, allowing for a comparison across political, business and social systems and to understand what value is being sought by stakeholders in different countries (McGrath et al. 2010). For example, a mining company may be active in certain countries at a certain time in South-East Asia but not others as the value it derives may be higher, relationships stronger and more powerful, but also there could be a greater sense of urgency due to changing power arrangements in government and society in that nation.

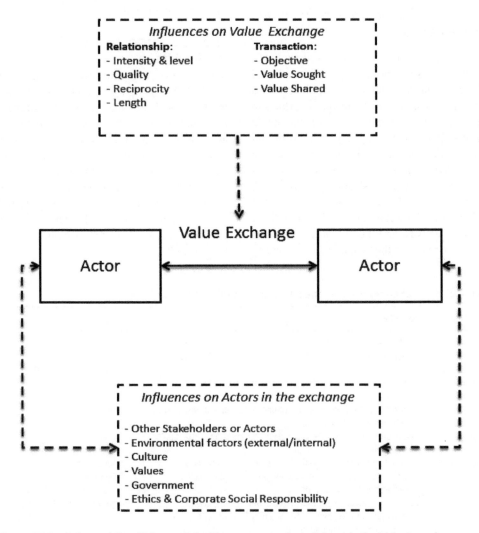

Figure 25.2   Asian public affairs stakeholder conceptual model – relationship & exchange

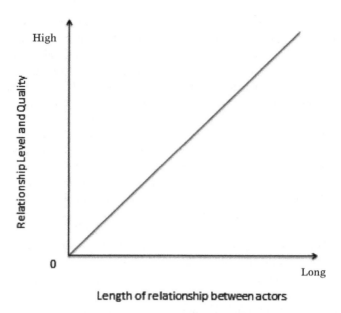

High

Relationship Level and Quality

0

Long

Length of relationship between actors

Figure 25.3   The relationship between relationship quality/level and length of time in Asian Public Affairs

Current State of Asian Public Affairs: Engagement with Stakeholders

It's not the technology that changes the world. It's the dreams behind the technology (Jack Ma, Chairman of Alibaba).

Asian public affairs is emerging from a period when the main objectives were focused on crisis management, events such as trade expos or shareholder meetings, and government relations and lobbying (Public Affairs Asia 2016). In more recent times non-government organisations (NGOs) have started to emerge as important influencers in the region, growing in size, resources and networks (Shen 2016). This is partly being driven by the growth in global business trends and interest in ethics and corporate social responsibility which have pushed some issues, such as supply chain ethics, gender balance on corporate boards, sustainability and good corporate citizenship, to the fore (Shen 2016). Yet whilst the more developed markets in the region such as Japan have developed strategies and methods to deal with NGOs, only in recent times have organisations and governments in India and China been creating strategies to deal with the types of issues non-government organisations constantly raise.

With the rapid rise of consumerism, technology, social media and the market-based reforms of many Asian economies, regional brands such as Tata, Tencent, Alibaba, ICBC, Huawei, Asian Paints, Hero, Sony, Samsung, Toyota and Kia, to name just a few, have been able to increase their value and customer bases to become global giants. These brands, and ones like them, that are now moving up fast on regional brand rankings, also suggest the importance of brand democracy to consumers in the region as a way of expressing themselves in a more Western way. Brand democracy can be defined as the perception that a consumer holds that they are free to choose from as many brands as possible in as open a market as possible with their rights protected as consumers by the government. But the growth in brands, especially that in value of brands that are designed specifically for local markets in Asia, also highlights the importance of relationships and brand resonance with consumers. The convergence of these marketing concepts into a form of democratic expression in a consumerist context should make researchers such as Grönroos (1984), Gummesson (1994) and Keller (1993) very satisfied indeed as their work is unified and used by practitioners to develop stronger brands and relationships across an entire region of the world.

An emphasis on relationships in marketing also makes issues such as sustainability, ethics and corporate social responsibility and consumer rights important ones in the region, especially because of the importance of relationships. Concerns over these issues are now important to many in and out of the region (Shen 2016; Zhu, Saarkis and Lai 2007), reflected in an increase in policy development, regulations and legislation around these areas, and with consumers being able to have more choice in Asian markets than ever before, Asian public affairs has started to work on initiatives and methods that create stronger relationships between brands and consumers on these issues (see Figure 25.3).

With digital transformation also comes the expectation that change and reform will occur at digital speeds, especially in the minds of the younger generations (Trendwatch 2016). In Asian public affairs this has meant that issues around the speed and level of reforms in industry, markets and government have become important. An example of this recently was in Japan where Prime Minister Shinzo Abe's efforts to modernise government and business practices to open markets more to foreigners and increase the proportion of women on corporate boards by the 2020 Tokyo Olympics have hit trouble (Pesek 2016).

Yet even in times of political and military conflict, public affairs is the bridge that allows relationships to be maintained and communications to be kept open (McGrath et al. 2010). In fact many would argue that public affairs has existed since the beginning of the first trading relationships. In a region as diverse in all facets as Asia is, it has been the ability of public affairs to bring everyone together in a commonality of interest – be that business, or even the famous ASEAN karaoke sessions – that has allowed for more contentious issues to be assuaged long before they can escalate and require the intervention of the super powers to resolve the matter. There is no doubt that the future for public affairs in Asia is as bright as that for the entire region, but as the nation analysis will highlight, there are still challenges that need to be overcome to ensure that this bright future becomes reality.

THE NATIONS

The Super Powers

China

At a new divergence: the relationship between public affairs, politics and business Of all the countries in the Asian region there is one that is only a small number of years away from being a true global super power in a political, military, business and social sense: China (Subramanian 2011). In fact it already has achieved super power status in business, politics and social levels, signalled by recent concerns over the magnitude of the effect on the world economy of any slowdown in China (Ogilvy Public Relations 2016; Wolf 2016). And in a military sense, with recent announcements on reforms and modernisation programmes across all levels and functions of the armed forces, such as the continued construction of carrier fleets, it is only a matter of time before China has a global reach and presence to start to rival that of the United States.

At the same time this has caused some frayed nerves inside and outside the region among those nations that can't compete with the growth, might and power of the Chinese business and military complex. However, whilst there have been some recent flare-ups and disputes in the region, and there has been a history of disputes between China and some of its neighbours, the difference between then and now in governance and politics make this of less of a concern going forward.

With an emphasis on *guanxi*, public affairs in China is growing rapidly, but it is also undergoing a time of development of the function from a low/medium-skilled sector to one that is medium/high skilled. Hampered by a previous reluctance to invest in the function and train skilled talent in the sector, the extent of public affairs knowledge and skills in China is the greatest threat to its immediate growth. However, medium- and long-term prospects are positive, helped by a need to fill the policy, engagement and stakeholder relationship vacuum left by the rapid development and modernisation of the economy and society.

Guanxi and Public Affairs

Guanxi has an important role in public affairs in China. The reciprocal nature of *guanxi*-based relationships influences the range of methods used in Chinese public affairs. As Guo (2006) and Luo (2001) noted, there is a duality to this in a public affairs sense – transactional value based on achieving specific short-term objectives, but then also the overarching relationship value which takes a much longer-term view of methods and functions used.

An example of this is the relationship China has with the United States. Whilst there may be political and military differences, usually short-term based on a specific issue, this has not translated into business and trading restrictions. If anything it is this aspect of the relationship, based around *guanxi*, which keeps the political and military side of it in check. This extends to many other relationships China has in the region where it has made very large investments and

established substantial trading links, but then have in some cases and for different reasons, such as with Japan, fluctuating political relations (King 2012).

This makes it essential for any business wishing to enter the Chinese market to engage with local communities, and to build alliances and relationships with key local stakeholders that will allow a firm to establish firm footholds in each of the key regions in China. For businesses that do enter the Chinese market, they need to plan for a certain level of risk as the economy and governance are still undergoing a significant modernising process started by President Xi Jinping and Premier Li Keqiang in the current five-year plan and committed to continue until at least the end of the next five-year plan in 2020 (Ogilvy PR 2016). Whilst this transition phase does pose certain risks, it will also allow for far more opportunities, for firms both in and external to China.

Back to the Future: Developing Public Affairs Methods with Chinese Characteristics

One key way foreign investors are developing public affairs capabilities that have Chinese characteristics is by supporting or setting up local think tanks, needed to assist with the development of public policy and innovations in China's transformation from old to new (Huang 2015). In a nation that has a large number of universities rapidly rising on the global ranking scales, and with a large number of keen local and foreign supporters and investors led by President Xi Jinping, China is also now home to some of the most innovative and leading think tanks and forums in the world, such as the Beijing Forum and, amongst others, the Chinese Academy of Social Sciences, China Institute of International Studies and the China Institutes of Contemporary International Relations (Xufeng 2009). With more than two thousand policy research institutions in China, the role of think tanks in developing and maintaining *guanxi* with stakeholders in

China can't be emphasised enough (Hornby 2015).

Traditional methods such as sponsoring major events like the Olympics or the rapidly developing Chinese Soccer League, hosting gatherings of business and political leaders, or supporting a local university through sponsored chairs, are also being adapted and used in China. Public affairs in China is about an integrated approach (Public Affairs Asia 2016), and not just about lobbying and advocacy, but about using methods from the West that can be adapted and used in the East that allow for the strengthening and development of *guanxi*. This may explain why modern methods that can be quickly and effectively adapted to local regions, such as social media, have become an important part of any integrated strategy in the region (Public Affairs Asia 2016).

Whilst Western social media brands such as Facebook, Twitter and Instagram are still to find a presence, Chinese social media brands Qzone, Weibo, Tudour and Youku are more than worthy replacements, and with more than 280 million micro bloggers the importance of a corporate blog can't be emphasised enough. In fact whilst some may see the blocking of foreign social media sites as nefarious, the development of locally owned, operated and created social media sites and industry would leave even the biggest Silicon Valley fan envious, especially with the average Chinese netizen spending on average 2.7 hours online every day (Nielsen 2012; Trendwatching.com 2015). Further, around the world there is an emerging trend among consumers to embrace local web content over international (Nielsen 2012), so the development of social media in China does need to be seen through an Asian lens and not a Western one.

Public affairs has a period of substantial growth ahead of it in China. Global firms are already active in the local market in nearly every large city and province in China. Reforms will open up new pathways and opportunities for business and trading

relationships between China and the rest of the world, but it will always be important to maintain both a strong sense and respect of *guanxi* and a strong product and brand that can be accepted and respected by the Chinese market. Doing these two things will ensure that an organisation's public affairs are always seen in a positive light in one of the most important economic markets in the world.

India

Rising Power Rising to Challenges?

India, the world's largest Western model democracy, may not be like China in terms of the economic power it wields, and indeed it faces more challenges than that of its largest regional neighbour, but it does offer to the astute firm a wide range of opportunities in a developing market. India is also entering a period when the need for reform of governance, the economy, political institutions and state-owned corporations is becoming more pressing than ever if the country is to become a global economic super power like its northern neighbour, China. With the Bharatiya Janata Party in charge of New Delhi, and with a Prime Minister in Narendra Modi who embraces the digital age if his use of Twitter and Facebook is anything to go by, a reformist agenda is slowly being implemented.

However, the speed of reform may very well be the biggest challenge to India in years ahead, even with its economic growth showing no signs of slowing or entering a recession. Economically India is performing well, with GDP growth double that of many Western economies at 7.5 per cent, inflation showing signs of also slowing down and a market-based economy (Wolf 2016). Of concern though is a falling balance of trade, falling gross investment levels against GDP and slowing credit growth, mainly connected to what seems to outsiders as a glacial-like speed in the reform process (Wolf 2016).

The difficulty the Indian government faces with the reform process is complicated by the lack of federal control over some states, an entrenched bureaucracy and state-owned corporations with near monopolistic powers that are unwilling to allow for free market reforms and increased private sector investment (Wolf 2016). Changing just one of these would likely be a lengthy and costly political battle for any party. There are also increasing concerns over the effects of development on the environment, linked by some to major industrial incidents such as Bhopal (Berg and Holtbrügge 2001), with attention on the need to modernise the economy not just about market reforms but also about protecting the environment and restoring the beauty of India where it has been altered in some places. Despite this, India has transformed its economy from one centred on an agrarian base, to one of services and high-tech manufacturing, led by brands such as Hero, Tata and Reliance amongst others (Wolf 2016).

Socially, India is also undergoing a period of transformation, with wider acceptance of the role of women in society, and attempts to break down caste barriers. Politically, it is also coming to a more settled relationship with former foe and regional power Pakistan, and forging closer ties to neighbour China. Narendra Modi's more inclusive style of governing has also impressed many around the world and has placed India in the top echelon of world powers and forums, and with an influential and keen expat community around the globe eager to assist with the creation of a modern nation, it is now up to India whether it wants to accept the challenge of becoming a global power or staying a regional one.

Public Affairs in India

Public affairs is a very necessary business function in modern-day India, where regulation and government relations can mean the difference between a foreign brand sinking and swimming in one of the most diverse markets on earth. Stakeholder management and engagement is as important in India as it is in all countries, but again the Asian region places perhaps a more multi-layered contextual

importance on relationships than might be expected in other regions of the world (Public Affairs Forum of India 2015). The lessons of neglecting relationships at a local level in India can be gleaned from errors in public affairs management involving foreign organisations, such as that arising after the Bhopal disaster in 1984 (Berg and Holtbrügge 2001).

However, one of the bigger challenges for a public affairs firm in modern India is that, in a nation of 29 states spread across thousands of kilometres and nearly as many cultures and languages, maintaining a presence in public affairs in each one can be costly and time consuming. Therefore it is important for a firm to allocate resources according to where they want and need to have the most influence, engagement and strongest relationships with stakeholders, more than a brand awareness across the nation. One way for an organisation to have an influence in India through public affairs is through the creation or support of a think tank (Public Affairs Forum of India 2015). In India, as in many other nations in Asia, the development and creation of think tanks to influence public policy and legislation is becoming an important tool in public affairs. Like China, India has a large and well-developed higher education sector that can provide staff and resources to support the creation of a think tank, along with the support of the most powerful leader in the nation, Prime Minister Narendra Modi.

Apart from providing an independent source of ideas and opinions on existing policy and legislation at both a local, state and federal level, these think tanks allow for a place where key stakeholders of an issue or area can meet each other informally and further strengthen their relationships with one another. In recent times brands such as Reliance, which supports the Observer Research Foundation, have started to align with key think tanks, and with the entry of Brookings and the Carnegie Endowment Institutions into India this will only continue (Jha 2015).

Social media is becoming an important tool in the public affairs toolbox in India. It is not hard to see why when the Prime Minister himself has more than 18 million followers on Twitter and 32 million likes on Facebook. Social media will only increase in use and influence as network speeds and coverage increase, and smart devices such as phones and tablets start to achieve wider penetration rates, making this means a more effective way to reach all of the states in India than using one of the more traditional forms of media such as print or television. This is of course not to mention the power of the high-tech and start-up industry, led by the hub of Bangalore which is worth tens of billions of US dollars in exports every year and provides a highly educated, English-speaking workforce that rivals the output of any other tech hub in the world but at a fraction of the wage costs (Kannan 2013).

There is still a role for the traditional methods of public affairs in India of lobbying, campaign management, advocacy, public and government relations, events, and issues management (Public Affairs Forum of India 2015). However, as with China, engagement with stakeholders is one of the keys to succeeding in India: many can learn a lesson from the way in which Tata Industries engages and involves local communities with its brand which has been important in overcoming any local concerns over industrial developments. Integrating public affairs methods with stakeholder management, and providing value for all in the relationship, provides a guide on how an organisation should approach public affairs in India.

Japan

Going for Growth?

Japan is one of the region's most influential and perhaps its most developed nation. Politically, economically, militarily and socially it stands as one of the most advanced in the world, although like many in the region it needs to decide whether to turn its challenges into opportunities for reform and modernisation or lose influence and power to one of the region's other developing powers. Economically Japan needs to reform and modernise its economy to stimulate growth, which politically may be a difficult path to go down considering the shaky nature of the Japanese political landscape (Kihara 2016).

However, as a highly developed economy that has slipped dangerously close to stagnation levels and resorted to massive government-backed asset-buyback schemes, time is running out on the policy options available to the government to increase domestic demand to protect the economy from the possibility of a long-term global slowdown and losing exports to regional neighbours such as China and India (Kihara 2016).

Similar to other countries in Asia, the concept and depth of relationships are important in understanding how and why public affairs activities are carried out in Japan (Cooper-Chen and Tanaka 2007). The importance of understanding the need for respect, hierarchy and harmony in a relationship, based on Confucianism, Shinto, Zen and Buddhist beliefs, can make stakeholder engagement and interaction much easier in Japan, but they can take a long time to develop (Cooper-Chen and Tanaka 2007). An example of this in practice is how many Japanese corporations have had close relations with one another that have been established over centuries and are valued through a long-term perspective that nearly all Japanese companies have when doing business.

This is perhaps why some Japanese brands have failed to adapt to the fast pace of some modern global markets where fortune favours the brave and relationships can be developed very quickly across cultures and nations; that is, they have not seen that some take a shorter-term view to creating value with other stakeholders and place more emphasis on actions in the short and medium term than the long term.

Public Affairs in Japan

Public affairs in Japan is primarily focused on the functions of media and government relations, crisis management, promotion and integration of brand strategies, internal activities and events, corporate social responsibility, issues management, stakeholder relations and foreign market public affairs activities (Yamamura and Shimizu 2009). This is based on a broader cultural and societial view on power needing to be exercised in a soft way, with consensus and acceptance, and not a harder more direct way (Kelly, Masumoto and Gibson 2002).

These functions are integrated with the importance of long-term relationship values of reciprocity, harmony, respect and hierarchy to guide the implementation of these functions and in what situations they are used (Cooper-Chen and Tanaka 2007; Yamamura and Shimizu 2009). For example, a heavy emphasis is placed upon how shareholder meetings are conducted, and internal activities with employees, who are usually guaranteed a job and generous living, health and education benefits for life, are nearly as important as external activities conducted in the market place.

Since the events of the 2011 Japanese tsunami and earthquake where some brands were seen to be disrespectful and disloyal to customers and employees (Batyko 2012), there has been a change in approach in methods used to manage crises and media relations. Message management and channels became important to organisations as customers and citizens alike began to trust less in the media produced by the organisations and trust more in what they saw in the media, especially social media networks such as Facebook, Twitter and local apps Line and GREE.

This has seen many large brands embrace social media as a message-management tool, not unique of course around the world, but also as a crisis management method, which was unique in the Japanese market. Japanese brands are also now more aware of how the local media can influence brand perceptions both domestically and in foreign markets (Mullcr and Simonsson 2015), again perhaps revealing that some of the old business and relationship beliefs are undergoing the first signs of change.

Whilst the Japanese market is currently mature in an economic sense, in a public affairs sense it is still growing as Western methods are adapted and implemented in Japanese business customs and norms.

South Korea

South Korea is one of the most developed nations in Asia. With an economy ranked 11th in the world on nominal GDP and 13th by purchasing power parity, low inflation, membership of the G20 and a highly advanced education, manufacturing and technology sector, led by global powerhouse and leader of the South Korean *Chaebol*, Samsung, South Korea can count itself as a regional economic power (Mu-hyun 2015). Add to this the unresolved conflict with North Korea that sees coalition partner and close ally the United States base nearly 30,000 military personnel at several locations through the Eighth Army and the Seventh Air Force, not to mention the huge military industrial complex that South Korea has established in its own right, and South Korea is also a regional power militarily and politically.

However, unresolved issues from the end of the Second World War and the Korean War mean that relationships have been uneasy with fellow regional powers, China and Japan, although business and trade relations and networks are starting to see closer ties slowly develop (Suk-hee 2012). Despite the tense relationship with North Korea that has ebbed and flowed since the 1953 armistice was signed to cease the 625 Upheaval, as it is usually referred to in South Korea, or the Fatherland Liberation War as it is called in the North, South Korea has managed to transform into one of the most modern and developed nations in the world.

The formation of the South Korean *Chaebol*, the largest and wealthiest of the South Korean brands and conglomerates that grew from an extraordinary period of growth when the economy grew at an average of 8 per cent per annum for nearly thirty years from the early 1960s to the early 1990s, has seen South Korean brands such as Samsung, Hyundai, LG, Kia and POSCO become known around the world (Mu-hyum 2015). In recent times free trade agreements with other economic powers such as China, the United States, the EU, Australia and Canada have set the scene for the decades to come as new markets are opened up in those nations.

Domestically, South Korea is similar to most other major liberal democracies in having two major political parties dominate the political landscape, in this case the conservative Saenuri Party and the liberal Together Democratic Party. Currently the President of South Korea, the highest office in the land, is held by the Saenuri Party's Park Geun-hye, the first female President in the history of the nation. Traditionally, especially under former President Lee Myung-bak, the Saenuri Party has taken a harder line to issues with regional neighbours such as North Korea and Japan, whereas the Together Democratic Party has taken a more open and conciliatory line to the North and to China.

Public Affairs in South Korea

Public affairs functions in South Korea have developed in line with the economy and in similar ways to those of other close neighbours, that is, with South Korean characteristics and context focused on maintaining strong relationships with stakeholders, but integrating Western methods. With close government support and aid helping many of the *Chaebol* develop, it was only natural that there were close links between the two (Mu-hyum 2015), especially through events such as the openings of manufacturing plants and regions, trade, markets and finance policy, and even foreign policy through opening manufacturing plants in countries where political and military relations are tense such as the Kaesong industrial zone on the border of North Korea. Influencing the *Chaebol*

therefore can mean influencing government policy, highlighting the development of advocacy and lobbying in South Korea as a public affairs method.

In more recent times an emphasis has been placed on developing crisis management within both corporations and the government itself. The close relationship between corporations and government meant that there was an assumption that one would protect the other; however, some recent events have proved this to be incorrect and highlighted the need for development of this function. Firstly, the Asian and global financial crisis revealed that some very large South Korean firms had borrowed large amounts of money which they had no ability to repay without government assistance. The largest of these firms, Daewoo, indeed was not able to repay its $US80 billion debt and collapsed, becoming the biggest financial collapse in the world (Mu-hyum 2015). Apart from the collapse itself the government was not prepared for any event of this magnitude and scrambled to try and repair the damage to its governance and business reputation domestically and internationally. More recent events such as the responses to Asiana Airlines Flight 214 crash in San Francisco (Gale 2013), and the Korean Airlines 'Nutgate' incident, revealed that crisis management still needs much work and attention in the public affairs arena.

Future Powers

Whilst public affairs is at its most developed and diverse in the regional powers, there are many nations in Asia that see themselves as being future powers in one critical metric or another in the decades to come and are developing public affairs in their own right that are worthy of mention.

Indonesia, Pakistan, Turkey, Thailand, Malaysia, Singapore and the Philippines are all nations that are seen as rising powers either politically, militarily, economically or socially. Indonesia, for example, has a rapidly expanding public affairs sector, again focused on government and corporate relations, but also with the development of think tanks and firms that specialise in the area that are both local and branches of the larger public affairs firms. Indonesia itself is undergoing a transition period from being an economy based on mainly agricultural and resource commodities to one focused on services and technology driven by a rapidly developing society that is becoming more and more consumption-based every day. With a robust democracy, close ties with most of the regional powers and global powers in China and the United States, and one of the most active and diverse media markets in the world, Indonesia presents a lot of opportunity for public affairs.

Pakistan is also worthy of mention. Apart from being a nuclear armed state, and undergoing a period of political change where foreign influences are minimised and the relationship with India settled, economically Pakistan is on the verge of a period of extensive growth and development. Although not as developed in a public affairs sense as other regional powers, it has a developing sector that still uses many of the methods of the past, such as media and campaign management, to great effect.

The development and use of public affairs in Turkey is also growing as quickly as the economy in the region. Although social media use has been restricted at times, this has not proved to be much of an impediment to public affairs. With close relationships between the government and corporations in Turkey, and in some cases even ownership, public affairs is centred around providing services to the government and corporations on relations, stakeholder management and engagement, and media management. In recent times, with the refugee crisis stemming from unrest in Syria, Iraq, parts of Africa and Afghanistan, crisis management has become important for the government and some corporations. This is especially so as Turkey edges closer to EU entry with assistance from some in Brussels such as the German delegation.

Singapore is a notable centre for public affairs in the region, favoured by many international firms as a hub for operations thanks to its central location in the Asia Pacific region, its highly advanced infrastructure and economy, political stability, access to a highly skilled, educated and bilingual labour market, and of course a very Westernised and high standard of living that makes it the envy of many in the region. It is no wonder Singapore's symbol is that of a very proud lion. Many international brands also have their regional headquarters in Singapore, and in development, use and methods of modern public affairs functions it is on a par with the regional super powers such as Japan, China and South Korea. For these reasons Singapore is often used as a benchmark by many developing nations as it is a nation nearly entirely dependent now on the high level of services it provides to other nations in the region and has moved away from manufacturing industries that placed its economy at risk from lower waged nations.

Whilst the future powers are on the whole still developing economically, politically, socially and militarily, public affairs is most definitely on the way up in these regions in use and functions, even if there is still a dearth of resources in some. They represent a crossroads in the use of traditional public affairs functions and methods, and the ways of the new methods centred around digital technology. But they also highlight the convergence of roles and functions in marketing, communications, public affairs and management that is being seen all around the region.

Nations on the Turn

In Asia there are a number of nations on the turn and rapidly developing. These nations, such as Bangladesh, Vietnam, Burma and Brunei to name a few, are also still developing their public affairs. These nations' public affairs expertise is typified by a reliance upon foreign firm expertise or expats who have returned with Western skills and knowledge. Development of public affairs is also hampered by a lack of technology and digital resources and infrastructure in many parts of government and business operations, especially away from the larger cities.

However, with markets in many of these nations developing rapidly thanks to investment, market reforms, increased political stability, cheap labour, and access to global markets, it can be expected that more firms will turn to the use of public affairs to strengthen relationships and engagement with stakeholders and drive positive messages about their brands.

There is also a generational change occurring where some of the old methods of public affairs that were adapted to the Asian culture and values system, such as maintaining close and lengthy stakeholder relationships and events based around major corporate announcements, have been retained whilst allowing younger generations to use digital and social media methods to drive new relationships with the West that have exposed local brands to global trade winds, with mixed results. But with the larger nations experiencing soft landings in the years ahead, these nations only have high growth times ahead of them if they can keep to their planned economic, market and governance reforms which will keep investment flowing in and lead to an increase in public affairs activities.

What is becoming more observable in these nations is how the public affairs specialist is the same person as the marketing specialist, the digital specialist, the comms specialist, the events and campaign specialist, and the media specialist, that is, one and the same person working in a modern-day mash-up position. As noted earlier in this chapter, there is a convergence of ideas and functions being seen in public affairs in Asia that perhaps makes it unique compared with other regions in the world owing to the scale and the diverse range of cultures and countries where this is happening.

CONCLUSION

Public affairs in Asia has a huge amount of potential, even after a decade of extraordinary growth that marked the start of the Asian century. With Asian brands only on the up in the global market, and with regional free trade agreements and market and economic reforms modernising many Asian nations, public affairs will only grow with these changes.

Public affairs in Asia is also helped by the existing set of norms, values and customs that place relationships and engagement with stakeholders of the firm at the centre of the Asian business model, even in the modern era of social and digital technologies. This has led to a more Asian style of public affairs, with Western characteristics and methods, where the value and length of a relationship internal and external to the firm can dictate what methods are used by a public affairs practitioner. For many exponents this means that they will feel that they are on a see-saw of being a strategic and tactical thinker one day, and then the very next, organising and running a small corporate event in a local region.

There are challenges, though, for public affairs in Asia. There is the convergence of ideas and methods between the old and the new as in some nations traditional forms of media still dominate owing to infrastructure and resource limitations on the use of newer forms of media. In China, for example, a public affairs practitioner needs to be familiar with use of technology both in and outside the firewall, and be able to operate and think across both Western and Chinese cultures and languages seamlessly for clients.

There is also a noticeable shortage of talented staff who can 'act local but think global' thanks to the rapid development of public affairs in the region. Loss of talent still stands as a major challenge for many firms that struggle to find and retain key staff who establish relationships with key stakeholders but then leave to pursue other opportunities in the region. Localisation is also a challenge for some practitioners who may be used to using modern public affairs methods in Western markets, but then struggle to go back to using older methods in regions where digital resources are minimal. Local firms also have to battle their global parents who can sometimes fail to understand just how much of a different region Asia is despite its acceptance of some aspects of Western lifestyles and consumerism, not to mention the diverse range of cultures and values that a public affairs team may have when they operate in this region.

The adaptation of corporate social responsibility and ethics in Asian firms and governments is also placing increased levels of expectations on companies that many are finding difficult to adapt to within the sector. This is perhaps caused by an over-reliance upon training to respond to crises, and not on being pro-active on this new corporate mindset.

However, in Asia the opportunities far outweigh these challenges. Firms continue to grow, staff continue to learn new skills that the Asian market wants and needs, and governments and stakeholders still want to engage and keep their relationships strong all across the region, even when there may be times of political and military conflict. The Asian public affairs century after all has only just begun.

REFERENCES

Ambler, T. (1994). Marketing's third paradigm: Guanxi. *Business Strategy Review*, 5(4), 69–80.

Arias, J. Tomás Gómez. (1998). A relationship marketing approach to guanxi. *European Journal of Marketing*, 32(1/2), 145–56.

Austrade, 2016, Benchmark Report 2016 – Austrade, file:///C:/Users/u4055366/Dropbox/2016%20Research/Harris%20-%20International%20Public%20Affairs/Australia-Benchmark-Report.pdf, accessed August 30, 2016.

Australian Strategic Policy Institute (ASPI). (2015). Asia Pacific cyber Insights, International Cyber Policy Centre, https://www.aspi.org.au/publications/asia-pacific-cyber-insights/ASPI-Asia-Pacific-Cyber-Insights.pdf, viewed 29 March 2016.

Bajpaee, C. (2016). Japan and China: The geo-economic dimension. *The Diplomat*, March 28, http://thediplomat.com/2016/03/japan-and-china-the-geo-economic-dimension/, viewed 28 March 2016.

Batyko, R. J. (2012). The impact of corporate culture on public relations in Japan: A case study examining Tokyo Electric Power and Toyota. *Public Relations Journal*, 6(3), 1–19.

Beeson, M. (2014). *Regionalism and globalization in East Asia: Politics, security and economic development*. Basingstoke: Palgrave Macmillan.

Berg, N. and Holtbrügge, D. (2001). Public affairs management activities of German multinational corporations in India. *Journal of Business Ethics*, 30(1), 105–19.

Cooper-Chen, A. and Tanaka, M. (2007). Public relations in Japan: The cultural roots of Kouhou. *Journal of Public Relations Research*, 20(1), 94–114.

Davies, H., Leung, T. K., Luk, S. T., and Wong, Y. H. (1995). The benefits of 'Guanxi': The value of relationships in developing the Chinese market. *Industrial Marketing Management*, 24(3), 207–14.

De Zúñiga, H. G., Puig-i-Abril, E., and Rojas, H. (2009). Weblogs, traditional sources online and political participation: An assessment of how the internet is changing the political environment. *New Media and Society*, 11(4), 553–74.

Gale, A. (2013). Why Asiana has a PR problem. *Wall Street Journal*, 10 July, http://blogs.wsj.com/korearealtime/2013/07/10/why-asiana-has-a-pr-problem/, viewed 20 March 2016.

Gao Y. (2006). Corporate political action in China and America: A comparative perspective. *Journal of Public Affairs*, 6(2), 111–21.

Getz, K. A. (2002). Public affairs and political strategy: Theoretical foundations. *Journal of Public Affairs*, 1(4), 305–29.

Goh, E. (2008). Great powers and hierarchical order in Southeast Asia: Analyzing regional security strategies. *International Security*, 32(3), 113–57.

Grönroos, C. (1984). A service quality model and its marketing implications. *European Journal of Marketing*, 18(4), 36–44.

Gummesson, E. (1994). Making relationship marketing operational. *International Journal of Service Industry Management*, 5(5), 5–20.

Harris, P. (2016). Monkey business, Marco Polo, and managing global public affairs and trade. *Journal of Public Affairs*, 16(1), 3–6.

Harris, P. and Fleisher, C. S. (Eds.). (2005). *Handbook of Public Affairs*. London: Sage.

Holtbrügge, D. and Berg, N. (2004). How multinational corporations deal with their sociopolitical stakeholders: An empirical study in Asia, Europe, and the US. *Asian Business and Management*, 3(3), 299–313.

Hornby, L. (2015). China to let 100 think-tanks bloom, *Financial Times*, http://www.ft.com/cms/s/0/115be32a-f234-11e4-b914-00144feab7de.html#axzz4Inf5Z6pB, accessed 30 August, 2016.

Huang, Y. (2015). The change in China's economy, *East Asia Forum*, http://www.eastasia-forum.org/2015/02/15/the-change-in-chinas-economy/, accessed 30 August, 2016.

Hughes, A. and Dann, S. (2009). Political marketing and stakeholder engagement. *Marketing Theory*, 9(2), 243–56.

Jha, P. (2015). India's most influential think-tanks. *Hindustan Times*, 16 August, http://www.hindustantimes.com/india/india-s-most-influential-think-tanks/story-emb0d-b2lmqltL8pKeYuZiL.html, accessed 17 March 2016.

Kannan, S. (2013). Bangalore: India's IT hub readies for digital future, BBC News, http://www.bbc.com/news/technology23931499, viewed 18 March 2016.

Keller, K. L. (1993). Conceptualizing, measuring, and managing customer-based brand equity. *Journal of Marketing*, 57(10), 1–22.

Kelly, W., Masumoto, T., and Gibson, D. (2002). Kisha kurabu and koho: Japanese media relations and public relations. *Public Relations Review*, 28(3), 265–81.

Kihara, L. (2016). BOJ keeps policy steady, offers gloomier view on economy, inflation, *Reuters*, http://www.reuters.com/article/us-japan-economy-boj-idUSKCN0WG2FF, viewed 18 March 2016.

King, A. (2012). *Japan and China: warm trade ties temper political tensions*, East Asia Forum, http://www.eastasiaforum.org/2012/10/22/japan-and-china-warm-trade-ties-temper-political-tensions/, accessed 30 August 2016.

Lovett, S., Simmons, L. C., and Kali, R. (1999). Guanxi versus the market: Ethics and efficiency. *Journal of International Business Studies*, 30(2), 231–47.

Luo, Y. (2001). Toward a cooperative view of MNC host government relations: Building blocks and performance implications. *Journal of International Business Studies*, 32(3), 401–20.

McGrath, C., Moss, D., and Harris, P. (2010). The evolving discipline of public affairs. *Journal of Public Affairs*, 10(4), 335–52.

Mahbubani, K. (2008). *The new Asian hemisphere: The irresistible shift of global power to the East* (Vol. 1). New York: Public Affairs.

Medeiros, E. S. (2005). Strategic hedging and the future of Asia-Pacific stability. *The Washington Quarterly*, 29(1), 145–67.

Mitchell, R. K., Agle, B. R., and Wood, D. J. (1997). Toward a theory of stakeholder identification and salience: Defining the principle of who and what really counts. *Academy of Management Review*, 22(4), 853–86.

Moss, D., McGrath, C., Tonge, J., and Harris, P. (2012). Exploring the management of the corporate public affairs function in a dynamic global environment. *Journal of Public Affairs*, 12(1), 47–60.

Mu-hyun, C. (2015). The chaebols: The rise of South Korea's mighty conglomerates, CNET, 7 April 7, http://www.cnet.com/au/news/the-chaebols-the-rise-of-south-koreas-mighty-conglomerates/, accessed 20 March 2016.

Muller, S. and Simonsson, E. (2015). Working with social media in Japan: In the case of H&M, IKEA and Volvo Corporation, Masters Project, University of Gothenburg, https://gupea.ub.gu.se/bitstream/2077/39854/1/gupea_2077_39854_1.pdf, accessed 29 March 2016.

Nielsen (2012). The Asian Media Landscape is Turning Digital, Nielsen, http://www.nielsen.com/content/dam/corporate/au/en/reports/2012/changing-asian-media-landscape-feb2012.pdf, accessed 23 March 2016.

Ogilvy & Mather, New report from O&M identifies 12 velocity markets that will reshape global growth, http://www.ogilvy.com/News/Press-Releases/June-2016-New-report-from-OM-identifies-12-velocity-markets-reshaping-global-growth.aspx, accessed 30 August 2016.

Omestad, T. (1989). Selling off America. *Foreign Policy* (76), 119–40.

Pesek, W. (2016). How Sharp is denting the Japan brand, *Barron's Asia*, 29 March, http://www.barrons.com/articles/how-sharp-is-denting-the-japan-brand-1459215209, accessed 29 March 2016.

Public Affairs Asia (2016). State of the Industry Report, Publicaffairsasia.com, http://publicaffairsasia.com/download_soi_pdf/, accessed 12 March 2016.

Public Affairs Forum of India (2015). Public affairs in India: The emerging landscape, www.pafi.in/pdf/Public-Affairs-in-India-The-Emerging-Landscape.pdf, viewed 18 March 2016.

Putnam, R. D. (1994). Social capital and public affairs. *Bulletin of the American Academy of Arts and Sciences*, 47(8), 5–19.

Rajan, R. (2003). Emergence of China as an economic power: What does it imply for South-East Asia? *Economic and Political Weekly*, 2639–43.

Serdar Dinc, I. and Erel, I. (2013). Economic nationalism in mergers and acquisitions. *Journal of Finance*, 68(6), 2471–514.

Shen, C. (2016). The 'new normal' for government relations practitioners in China, Publicaffairsasia.com, 9 March, http://publicaffairsasia.com/the-new-normal-for-government-relations-practitioners-in-china/, accessed 20 March 2016.

Stojkov, K., Noy, I. and Sağlam, Y. (2016). *The trade impacts of a food scare: The Fonterra contamination incident* (No. 4969). Victoria University of Wellington, School of Economics and Finance.

Subramanian, A. (2011). Inevitable Superpower: Why China's Dominance is a Sure Thing, *Foreign Affairs*, 90(5), 66–78.

Suk-hee, H. (2012). South Korea seeks to balance relations with China and the United States, Council on Foreign Relations, http://www.cfr.org/south-korea/south-korea-seeks-balance-relations-china-united-states/p29447, accessed 20 March 2016.

Sweeny, P and Shao, X. (2016) China says economy will 'absolutely not' experience hard landing, http://in.reuters.com/article/us-china-parliament-economy-idINKCN0W801D, accessed March 10 2016.

Trendwatching.com (2015). Future of digital consumerism in Asia, http://trendwatching.com/x/wp-content/uploads/2015/08/2015–08-PDC-DIGITAL-CONSUMERISM-IN-ASIA.pdf, accessed 22 March 2016.

Trendwatching, 5 Consumer Trends for 2016, http://trendwatching.com/trends/5-trends-for-2016/, accessed 30 August 2016.

Wang, C. L. (2007). Guanxi vs. relationship marketing: Exploring underlying differences. *Industrial Marketing Management*, 36(1), 81–6.

Wolf, M. (2016). India is a light in a gloomy world economy, *Financial Times*, 26 March, http://www.ft.com/cms/s/0/1dc01f08-e90c-11e5-bb79-2303682345c8.html#axzz44olUu5Gl, viewed 28 March 2016.

Xufeng, Z. (2009). The Influence of Think Tanks in the Chinese Policy Process: Different Ways and Mechanisms. *Asian Survey*, 49(2), 333–57.

Yamamura, K. and Shimizu, M. (2009). Public relations in Japan: Expert opinion on its Future. Research that Matters to the Practice, Institute for Public Relations, United States of America.

Yeung, I. Y. and Tung, R. L. (1996). Achieving business success in Confucian societies: The importance of guanxi (connections). *Organizational Dynamics*, 25(2), 54–65.

Yu, E. (2016). China e-commerce market to hit $1.1T by 2020, India $75B, http://www.zdnet.com/article/china-e-commerce-market-to-hit-1-1t-by-2020-india-75b/, accessed 30 August 2016.

Zhu, Q., Sarkis, J., and Lai, K. H. (2007). Initiatives and outcomes of green supply chain management implementation by Chinese manufacturers. *Journal of Environmental Management*, 85(1), 179–89.

PART V

Tactical Approaches to Executing Public Affairs

Craig S. Fleisher

The tactical execution of public affairs (PA) is an area of inquiry that likely sits closest to the corporate and PA practitioners studied by many of the scholars contributing in this SAGE Handbook. Although the PA field has been somewhat inhibited in its scholarly treatment of practice (McGrath, Moss and Harris, 2010), there are a better number of popular press treatments (e.g., often in the form of book length treatments or short social media-based videos) of how PA work is actually conducted, what works and does not, and how practitioners actually carry out the concepts, frameworks, ideas, models and theories that scholars like the ones writing in this volume aim to develop and understand. Building enhanced scholarly understanding upon these examinations of corporate and PA practice, this section expands upon Part 2 (Tools, Techniques and Organizing for Public Affairs) and Part 3 (Case Studies in Public

Affairs) of our earlier *The Handbook of Public Affairs* (Harris and Fleisher, 2005) and includes six, original treatments of selected PA practice, including coverage of the following:

- Ch. 26: Lobbying by William Oberman
- Ch. 27: Regulatory Affairs by Craig S. Fleisher
- Ch. 28: Judicial and Legal Influence Techniques by John Holcomb
- Ch. 29: Issue Management by John Mahon
- Ch. 30: Corporate Social Responsibility (CSR) and Involvement by Peter Seele and Irina Lock
- Ch. 31: Coalition and Network Building by Arco Timmermans

Lobbying is one of many public affairs tools (Showalter and Fleisher, 2005; Thomas, 2005), and arguably the most frequent one, that organizations deploy in pursuing advantages in the nonmarket, public policy or socio-political environments. Chapter 26 author William Oberman, who contributed a chapter on public policy processes and institutions in our prior handbook (Oberman, 2005), uses a resource-based view of the firm to argue that organizations employ two key resources in performing public affairs and lobbying, those being access (to public sector decision makers) and legitimacy (referring to the organization's participation and positioning in public policy processes). Oberman tackles a number of vexing dilemmas that have surrounded the use of lobbying, including ones about the actual value of information lobbyists provide to public policy officials, the relative value of political and policy-based information in determining outcomes, how much influence financial resources contribute toward the lobbying effort, whether connections or expertise generate greater influence, and on what bases politicians respond to the lobbying organization – whether that is predominantly political or personal. He notes that there is a growing volume of scholarly research which begins to provide explanations, and although there are a reasonable number of commonalities underlying the answers to these questions, valid explanations are often dependent on the specific contexts being examined.

In the second half of his chapter, Oberman expands upon the nuts and bolts of actual lobbying work and sheds new light about the lobbyists themselves. He shares scholarship which shows that effective lobbying nearly always is associated with the organization and its lobbying advocates having a deep understanding of governments and their policy-making processes. Among other factors, he notes the importance of doing thorough planning about strategic design, the use of collective support, forms and framing of messages, as well as choosing the most appropriate and receptive venues and targets of the lobbying effort. Last but not least, he does both scholars and practitioners a favor by noting how global forces, different levels and interdependencies constantly change the nonmarket environment, and reminds all

lobbying stakeholders of the importance of staying on top of these changes, adapting and remaining vigilant about these vital public affairs phenomena.

Unlike lobbying, which is used by nearly all public affairs executives in the execution of their tasks, Fleisher picks up an often under-appreciated and less utilized tool found in the arsenals of some PA practitioners in Chapter 27. He offers an argument for why managing regulatory affairs can be helpful in supporting an organization's efforts to find synergies across the market and nonmarket environments. Building on Oberman's Ch. 26 contribution in this section, Fleisher views regulatory processes and officials as being appropriate if less acknowledged venues and targets of PA influence. He offers a mini case study of the online transportation network company Uber to illustrate how important managing regulatory affairs can be to the success of a company, particularly when that company is offering new concepts, models, products or services that challenge the existing boundaries of the law and legal understanding of business/government interfaces. Uber is a disruptive technology-driven solution that solves a number of the public's transportation problems, and correspondingly, how this same technology puts the company into direct conflict with established interests, primarily in the form of the established and highly regulated taxi companies and drivers it is viewed to displace.

Fleisher offers an intelligence-driven model for managing responses in an organization's regulatory environment he calls 'Regulatory Affairs Competitive Intelligence', otherwise known as RACI. Like most other PA tools that are heavily dependent on the communication and transmission of often complex, specialized and timely information, RACI works best when it uses both primary and secondary sources of information. RACI practitioners can use a variety of existing conceptual models and taxonomies to sort, filter and analyze emerging and existing data. Done successfully, they can make asymmetric sense of potential regulatory developments in ways that can allow a forward-focused organization to work more complementarily with regulators than other stakeholders in the development or further refinement of the 'rules of the game' and therefore be a potential source of competitive advantage.

Holcomb addresses judicial influence techniques, another long-standing and established set of tools within the corporate and PA tool kit (Showalter and Fleisher, 2005). In Chapter 28, he notes that influencing US and increasingly, the international legal, judicial, rights and/or regulatory processes can mean high stakes. Civil and criminal settlements, government regulation and the 'setting of the rules of the commercial game' can all be 'life or death' decisions for businesses. Holcomb shares several areas where public affairs activity can particularly be a key influence: influencing the selection or elections of federal or state judges, educating judges, financially supporting legal foundations or more controversially – judicial candidates, filing friend-of-the-court (aka, Amicus Curiae) briefs, establishing litigation centers, selecting elite law firms to represent business interests, and affecting the 'gatekeeper role' played by courts in who does and does not get invited to participate in major cases impacting the business and economic system.

Holcomb produces a plethora of examples and evidence that shows that business can have significant impact on the judiciary. The necessity for business interests to employ these techniques should go without question, especially in nation-states whereby the judiciary has significant influence on law and public policy-making processes, as it does in most western democracies, for example. Nevertheless, Holcomb also identifies any number of possible ethical issues that can arise from the exercise of this tactic, and astutely reminds readers that the sword can be sharp on both sides – those groups who try and live by these tactics can also die by it. It is also a good reminder to

PA officers that ethics leads the law – in other words, doing the 'right' things before 'right' is actually enshrined in public policy or the law, and how it is prudent and worthwhile to stay out front of and above reproach when it comes to business-stakeholder interactions.

As Harris and I argue in the opening chapter of this book, issue management (IM), along with stakeholder engagement, remains a core and defining managerial role for most every veteran corporate and PA officer. In Chapter 29, Mahon describes IM tactics that are useful to any type of organization, equally appropriate to public-interest-groups and to international political and social action by corporations and other groups. Mahon refers to research and his own experience in recognizing that many line managers lack the needed competencies in this arena. He makes a strong case that what is needed is expanded, earlier recognition of political and social processes to resolve misunderstandings and difficulties before they enter the formal political, legal, and regulatory arenas. As such, taking what I have previously called preemptive strategy and action, whereby issues are defused while still embryonic in their life cycle, can be a critical advantage in both the market and nonmarket places. It can save the organization from expending valuable resources focused on issue resolution – which in its worst manifestation means managing an organization's responses to a full-borne crisis- and instead allow it to devote its resources to better meeting both existing and emerging business and societal needs and wants.

Issues get resolved through political contestation. Mahon notes there are two alternatives available to organizations in any political contest – deal with the issue and/or deal with those who are pressing the issue for resolution. Organizations need to be vigilant about what is emerging and how it evolves over its life cycle, be authentic in their stakeholder communication and engagement, and willing to change their behavior or positions if it can potentially result in a win-win, net beneficial outcome.

He observes that organizations usually do best by keeping seemingly adverse issues off of the public policy agenda and out of rule-making institutions. This way they can exercise maximum corporate discretion to deal with the issue, with lesser public and media involvement. If that tactic fails, the next best strategy is seizing the initiative and taking control of the issue and its definition, thus aiming to place it on an agenda more to the liking of the organization's choosing. Sometimes, this means the organization must change its own actions so that the contesting stakeholders no longer hold adverse opinions or views about how the organization is behaving. It is in the making of these changes – or not – that IM plays its hand most prominently at the market and nonmarket interface.

Lock and Seele note in Chapter 30 how another PA approach, that being corporate social responsibility (CSR), has increasingly become a compliance exercise in a number of countries. Given the bottom line effects that CSR practiced as a compliance exercise may have, they share how the political and corporate spheres will grow ever-closer. This creates a dilemma. On the one hand, corporations have become ever more active in the political arena through public affairs (PA) activities because legislation often determines success, failure, or even the 'license to operate' for corporations. On the other hand, researchers have observed a 'new political role of corporations' contributing to solving global public issues and improving community outcomes as part of their CSR, a recently developed theoretical stream known as 'political CSR'.

The authors offer a penetrating examination of this interaction in the case of Coca-Cola as a sponsor of the Olympic Games in London and how it interacted with the UK debate about sugar and obesity. The authors note throughout the case how stakeholders such as doctors' associations and communities got involved, as well as the London Assembly, a community board controlling the mayor of the City of London. What makes this case examination intriguing was how Coca-Cola's CSR strategy was in opposition to what the company planned as sponsor and how it was perceived by the public regarding public health. They end their chapter by proposing a form of strategic alignment between CSR and public affairs, particularly to safeguard the authentic and credible role of communities in the process of deliberation.

Coalitions and network building are two of the more prominent and potentially significant corporate approaches to influencing policy through PA activity. Author Arco Timmermans' arguments in Chapter 31 characterize how the context in which interest organizations and stakeholder groups move around issues establishes the underpinnings for forming lobbying coalitions. He notes how both network ties and positions matter, along with pre-established positive or negative reputations, for allies of a PA cause. Exchanging resources, a high level of tolerance for compositional diversity, and a good deal of compromising, among other things, are required in managing coalitions and securing desirable outcomes.

Timmermans notes that coalition leadership may not solely determine outcomes, but that it can be vital for catalyzing coalition formation, for enlarging a coalition, and for pushing members over sticking points in order to deliver for collective action. Steering coalitions gets more difficult as they grow. He notes that we still have much to learn about bandwagons and their effects in public affairs. He suggests that they are becoming more frequent, and can be a powerful veto mechanism, but they do not always provide a 'definitive push' for policy change.

CONCLUSION

The tactics used in corporate and PA work are evolving all the time, both as a response to changes in the nonmarket or public policy environment, as well as through purposeful and opportunistic innovation by PA practitioners themselves who aim to stay 'ahead of the curve'. Among these innovations, which can be found to some degree in all of the six topical subjects examined in this chapter are increasing use of social media for ongoing corporate and PA work, IT-driven reconnaissance to gather new and more expansive forms of data about the sociopolitical environment, the application of more powerful analytics and more sophisticated analysis methods and processes, and significant increases in the ability to generate feedback and feedforward. All of these driving forces allow an organization to communicate and learn, both more quickly and deeply, from its forays into nonmarket issues and stakeholder engagement. It also demonstrates one quality that has never gone away from this field, that being the desire of practitioners to constantly improve and strive toward greater professionalism, which come along with the associated public and organizational recognition of the importance and value of their unique efforts.

REFERENCES

Harris, P. and Fleisher, C. 2005. [Eds.] *The Handbook of Public Affairs*. London, UK: Sage.

McGrath, C. Moss, D. and Harris, P. November 2010. The evolving discipline of public affairs. *Journal of Public Affairs*, 10(4): 335–52.

Oberman, W. 2005. The external environment of public affairs in North America: Public policy process and institutions, pp. 56–70 in Harris, P. and Fleisher, C. [Eds.], *The Handbook of Public Affairs*. London, UK: Sage.

Showalter, A. and Fleisher, C. 2005. The tools and techniques of public affairs, pp. 109–122 in Harris, P. and Fleisher, C. [Eds.], *The Handbook of Public Affairs*. London, UK: Sage.

Thomas, C. 2005. Lobbying in the United States: An overview for students, scholars, and practitioners, pp. 281–303 in Harris, P. and Fleisher, C. [Eds.], *The Handbook of Public Affairs*. London, UK: Sage.

26

Lobbying Resources and Strategies

William D. Oberman

My chapter in the 2005 edition of the *Handbook of Public Affairs* reviewed key concepts underpinning academic understanding of the processes and institutions comprising the public policy system in the United States (US). Topics included the roles of and interaction among branches and levels of government, policy sub-systems, interest groups, and agendas. This chapter will provide a background on recent research into how groups with a stake in policy outcomes navigate in such systems, on the tools and resources they employ to gain access, and on how they translate that access to influence – in other words, on how groups lobby. Lobbying is a term with many definitions, but in the US context it historically refers to direct attempts to communicate with and influence public policy decision-makers. However, it can involve a broader range of public policy influence activities, such as electoral and campaign finance involvement, grassroots organizing, and advocacy advertising. If we think of public affairs in its broadest sense, as representing 'an organization's efforts to monitor and manage its business environment' (Public Affairs Council, n.d.), lobbying's role is clear and integral to this function. To the extent that government and public policy are part of organization's environment – and it is hard to think of situations in which that would not be the case – lobbying is another term for an organization's efforts to manage the government sector of its environment.

From a more conceptual or academic perspective, lobbying can be counted among the tools deployed by firms in their pursuit of strategic advantage. One theoretical approach to understanding the strategic management of business organizations is the resource-based view of the firm (Wernerfelt, 1984; Barney, 1991). This approach has been extended beyond traditional market-oriented strategy to include the non-market as well (Hillman and Hitt, 1999; Shaffer and Hillman, 2000; Rehbien et al., 2005; Oberman, 2008;

Bonardi, 2011). From the resource-based view perspective, public affairs for business organizations is about leveraging organizational resources into operational political influence as part of an overall strategy to use non-market resources to gain or maintain a competitive advantage in the market or, perhaps, as part of a coalition to increase or defend broader returns to an industry or economic sector. More specifically, an organization's public affairs capability can be seen as a catalytic resource available for use to 'capture', 'co-opt', or 'domesticate' latent political resources such as public sentiments, unorganized constituencies, and district-based representation, converting them into the operational resources of political access, legitimacy, influence, and, ultimately, favorable public policy that could be exploited by the organization (Oberman, 2008). In this chapter, we will focus on the leveraging and conversion process, the specific techniques used to develop the critical resources of access and legitimacy, and, from that base, to advocate for policy positions. This conversion process is called lobbying.

In the first section of this chapter, we will address what have been identified as the two fundamental resources of political strategy and lobbying: access and legitimacy. We will then take a look at current perspectives on the more 'nuts and bolts' aspects of lobbying. Most research on interest groups and lobbying has been conducted in the US context, although there is a large emerging literature on lobbying in the European Union (EU). We will attempt to incorporate a comparative perspective, noting differences between the US, EU, and other political contexts.

ACCESS AND LEGITIMACY

Access to public decision-makers and the *legitimacy* of an organization's participation and position in the political process can be seen as the two 'meta-categories' of political resources, pivotal in the establishment of political influence. To mix construction metaphors, they are both the pillars of the gateway between latent and realized influence and the foundation for effective communication between an organization and a political decision-maker. In the practical world of lobbying, access and legitimacy are closely intertwined and function on multiple levels. Access to a public official can be based on the connections of professional lobbyists, shared ideology, support for the organization in a legislative district, or long-standing membership in a particular policy sub-system. There is a robust interactive relationship with legitimacy.

Oberman (2008) noted that, for business in market-based systems, self-interest seeking is generally seen as legitimate in the economic sphere, but is questioned in the political sphere. Thus, a function of public affairs is to build legitimacy by aligning the self-interested socio-political claims of the organization with a view of the public interest held by at least some influential segments of society. This can involve altering the socio-political claims (more a function of general management than public affairs) or changing public perceptions of the company by aligning the company's claims with an existing view of the public interest or even changing a view of the public interest itself. The link between access and legitimacy in the political process may be extended to include a procedural element as well. Does the access to public decision-makers, and hence participation in the process, by an organization or interest lead to better public policy outcomes? Perhaps, a group's position may not be in alignment with widely shared views of the public interest, but if its access to decision-makers can provide information or logic that improves the policy process and outcomes, then this is legitimizing in itself. Thus, the ability to provide valuable information can bring with it access and procedural, if not full, legitimacy.

The value of information is indeed a strong thread running through the literature on lobbying.

Information can be valuable to politicians for both public and personal reasons. There is information directly related to policy and there is information that is political in nature. Policy information includes data and analyses pertaining to the problem that the policy is intended to address, realized and potential costs and benefits, technology, etc. (Hansen, 1991; Wright, 1996). To the extent that this information improves upon what is available elsewhere, it arguably has value for improving decision-making in the public interest. Political information pertains to the electoral consequences of policy decisions – how a policy will affect members of a politician's constituency and how they may react (McQuide, 2007) – which is absolutely an area of personal concern for any politician concerned with re-election. However, in a representative democracy, communicating the current and expected reactions of a politician's constituents to a policy is certainly a legitimate function, even if the politician is anticipated to respond out of personal rather than public interest.

Although most research on lobbying has until recently focused on the US context, a similar 'logic of access' (Bouwen, 2002) applies in other contexts as well. Bouwen, who noted that access is a pre-condition for influence, identified three information-based 'access goods' necessary for access to European-level institutions. The institutional structure of EU institutions and their position as supranational actors distinguishes them from US counterparts in form and detail, but not in the basic role played by information in the lobbying process. Bouwen proposes that the European Commission, the European Parliament, and the Council of Ministers will each demand different types of information from business interests in exchange for access. The Commission will have the greatest need for expert knowledge and will give the greatest lobbying access to large individual firms that possess cutting-edge technical information. The Parliament will have the greatest need for information about

European-level interests and give the greatest access to Europe-wide associations and less to national associations and individual firms. Finally, the Council of Ministers will have the greatest need for information about national interests and give the greatest access to national business associations and others representing national-level interests.

In developing countries or countries with less well-established democratic traditions, access is just as important, although its acquisition may have to be approached differently. For example, Yadev (2008) emphasizes the importance of working through party leaders rather than individual legislators in a country such as India with a highly centralized party power structure. The party, through the speaker, controls the flow of legislation in the Parliament, as well as the votes of individual members. Information remains a valuable 'access good', but it must be information useful to national party leaders, not to representatives of individual districts.

There is an ongoing discussion in the political science literature concerning the bases of access. Do political decision-makers grant access to a lobbyist because the lobbyist can provide valuable information about policy issues or, in the case of elected politicians, information that can aid their re-election? Is access granted on the basis of financial considerations, such as campaign contributions? Is access granted based on established 'connections'? Is it granted on the basis of shared beliefs or constituency representation?

One route of access is 'social', rather than ideological, financial, or constituency based. Often access is sought by hiring lobbyists with connections to important governmental decision-makers. One question that is raised regarding professional lobbyists is: Are they more valued for their expertise (information) in a given area of policy or for their inside connections? This question is mirrored in the discussion below about information and campaign contributions and illustrates a tension in the relationship between access and legitimacy. If professional lobbyists serve the public interest by providing a reservoir of expertise in a given policy domain, it would support the legitimacy of their access and participation (and their clients') in the public policy process. Conversely, if the value lobbyists provide clients who are able to afford their services is access through a social network tie, their contribution to the public interest is open to question. Recent research by Bertrand et al. (2011) suggests that expertise plays a relatively small role and that it is the personal ties maintained by lobbyists that provide value for their clients. Bolstering this view is work on 'revolving door lobbyists', which indicates that lobbying revenues of ex-Senate staffers-turned-lobbyists drop by 24% when the Senator for whom they previously worked leaves the Senate (Blanes i Vidal et al., 2012). The authors of this research describe the lobbying industry as a 'market for political connections' (2012: 3733).

For elected politicians, campaign contributions are often characterized as a means of buying access. Given the paucity of evidence that contributions actually buy votes, it has become the conventional wisdom that contributions are aimed at gaining access. Langbein (1986) provided empirical support for this thesis 30 years ago, concluding that one hour of access to a hypothetical average-workload member of Congress cost US$72,300. The access argument is supported by a stream of research conducted in the 1980s and 1990s demonstrating that political action committees (PACs) give more money to incumbents, congressional leaders, and members of committees relevant to interests, and that they follow-up contributions with contacts (Hojnacki and Kimball, 2001). Ansolabehere et al. (2002) found a strong link between lobbying and campaign contributions, concluding that the pattern of corporate PAC contributions is most consistent with an access strategy. Ideological and union PACs, on the other hand, tend to give in a manner that suggests their primary aim is electoral influence.

The direct access-for-money view has been challenged. Austen-Smith (1995) argued

that a purely contributions-for-access model would predict a pattern of contributions in which legislators with identical policy preferences to an organization would receive US$0 contributions. If the legislator knows the organization has policy preferences identical to his or her own and would be producing information valuable for his or her position, it would be in the legislator's interest to grant access to an organization even if it makes no monetary contribution. On the other hand, for the organization to gain access to legislators with increasingly dissimilar preferences, it would be necessary to make increasingly larger contributions. The less perceived value the organization's information would have for the legislator (as determined by a perceived mutuality of interest), the more he/she would 'charge' for time. (Contributions would drop to zero when a legislator was reached whose preferences were so dissimilar that neither side would realize any value in the exchange.) Yet, such a negative relationship between policy preference similarity and PAC contributions is the opposite of what is actually seen. PACs tend to give support to politicians with policy positions similar to their own. Austen-Smith concludes that in the absence of perfect information about an organization's preferences, a purpose of PAC contributions can be signaling the value of the information the organization can provide to the legislator. This explanation is consistent with the idea that PAC contributions are aimed at securing access, but it is the information lobbyists can provide that is most valuable to politicians, not the contributions themselves. Contributions are mere indicators that a group believes its policy preferences on a particular issue are aligned with those of the legislator and is willing to put money behind that belief. This signals to the legislator that the group may possess information he/she can use. Hall and Deardorff (2006) argue that lobbying is a form of 'legislative subsidy' (in the form of in-depth policy analysis and political intelligence) given by lobbyists to politicians who share their policy preferences. In effect, lobbyists subsidize politicians with valuable information in order to increase the effectiveness and level of the politicians' activities on issues of mutual interest. The role of campaign contributions in their view is that they indirectly affect legislative effort in a given area by facilitating the subsidization process. To the extent contributions buy access, the access is seen as being used by lobbyists not to request favors, but to offer assistance to the politician who is looking to advance policies reflecting their common interests.

In research at odds with the idea that campaign contributions secure access, Hojnacki and Kimball (2001) found that, controlling for other factors, such as an organization having a presence in a legislator's home district, PAC contributions were not a significant predictor of an organization's contact with a legislator. Their research indicated that the type of organization that is likely to have an affiliated PAC – those representing the material interests of well-defined groups – are also likely to have a presence in more districts than organizations without a PAC. It is the broader constituency representation that gives them access to a greater number of politicians, not the PAC contributions. They found that the strongest factors predicting an organization's contact with a legislator were support for the organization's position in the legislator's district and issues of importance for the organization before the legislator's committee.

What is interesting about the signaling explanation of PAC contributions is that it illustrates the intimate connection between access, legitimacy, and information. Rather than directly buying access, PAC contributions in this view are aimed at buying legitimacy, or at least procedural legitimacy, with the coin of legitimacy in this sense being the possession of valuable and relevant information that can increase the quality of public policy (at least from one point of view). Information is valuable in itself and should be sought by government decision-makers for the public good, as well as for their own interests. However, politicians need help identifying the sources of information. Contributions are a signal of the availability of valuable information, not a crass purchase of time. Whether or not this view captures the full reality of the role played by campaign contributions, it does demonstrate that this reality is complex. Further, it underlines the interconnectedness of all aspects of lobbying and public affairs in general. Lobbying cannot be approached in a piecemeal fashion. It must be managed strategically, with the tactics being employed as part of an integrated package of building access and legitimacy, information provision, and clear policy objectives.

THE NUTS AND BOLTS OF LOBBYING

Some aspects of lobbying seem to be common to most national contexts. Thomas and Hrebenar (2009) describe lobbying in terms of 'universal activities' common to all liberal democracies: (1) monitoring the activities of government and other interest groups; (2) making contacts in the government and with other groups; (3) building trust and credibility; (4) creating relationships with public officials that create need or obligation on the part of the official; (5) keeping harmony within the groups and with allies; and (6) continually refining strategies and tactics. We can identify the goals associated with these six activities as information accumulation, relationship building, and strategic design.

Information Accumulation

Information is the lifeblood of lobbying. Expertise in one's area of policy interest is critical. Every political issue tends to be surrounded by 'a community of professionals who spend careers immersed in the details of a given issue … who know what ever there is to know about their issues' (Baumgartner et al., 2009: 55–6). This includes detailed knowledge of not only the current players and their positions and arguments, but a mastery of the history and evolution of rationales, personalities, policies, and programs in the area, as well as an understanding of related international and state-level policies. Effective lobbyists will be aware of forces impacting the policy agenda and on top of all relevant developments. They will know the positions and predilections of politicians and bureaucrats who operate within their policy community. They will be fluent in the scientific and technical arguments advanced by all sides in the policy debate.

Support from a comprehensive corporate public affairs program can add to the lobbyist's knowledge base. Sophisticated environmental monitoring can provide strategic intelligence on developing social, economic, political, and technological trends that may impact the industry or organization. It can also lead to an appreciation of the interests, values, and organizational potential of the stakeholders associated with one's organization that may prove politically valuable.

Perhaps more important than technical support in developing a lobbyist's knowledge base is social support. Effective lobbyists must embed themselves in the relevant 'issue networks' (Helco, 1978). They must be 'plugged in' to the information streams that flow through the community of participants in policy-making in their areas of interest. Chalmers (2013) looked at what he called the 'social logic' of informational lobbying in the EU and determined that not all network ties are equal in the informational advantages they provide to lobbying groups. In a seminal piece of research, Grannovetter (1973) demonstrated that 'weak', or casual, network ties play a powerful role in the dissemination of information. For example, in finding a job, the best leads tend to come from casual acquaintances, rather than close friends. However, Chalmers found that in the EU lobbying context that 'strong', or close, ties are more valuable. While it is true that one is more likely to learn new information from casual acquaintances than from close friends (who by definition travel in the same circles and know the same things as you do), in lobbying the information problem is not quantity but quality. In fact, there is information overload. The greatest problem is sorting the wheat from the chaff. In this regard, information from close and trusted sources is generally more reliable and valuable than novel material from unfamiliar sources.

Relationship Building

Relationship building is directly related to access. We have discussed how access may be related to campaign contributions, delivery of valuable information, previous contact-providing employment, and other factors. However, there is a 'soft', social skill component to effective lobbying as well. Encyclopedic policy knowledge, a large bank account, and a list of acquaintances can only take you so far if you do not have the personality to bring those resources to bear. Based on 60 interviews with lobbyists in Europe and the US, McGrath (2006) identified key personal characteristics that the respondents felt necessary for success in the profession. These included an ability to listen and observe. Although lobbying is largely about providing information, it is not one-way communication. Effective interpersonal persuasion requires sensitivity to verbal and visual feedback. One lobbyist interviewed went as far as to suggest that women and gay men may have an advantage in this regard, although research by Nownes and Freeman (1998) has indicated little difference between male and female lobbyists in the tactics employed. General relationship skills are required, as well as a reputation for honesty and integrity. Credibility was seen as critical, as it should be in an activity so dependent on the transmission of reliable information. Overall, it seems the social skills and personality traits required for success in lobbying are very similar to those required for relationship marketing and sales.

Strategic Design

The strategic choices that go into the design of a lobbying strategy have been set out as the degree of inclusiveness, form of argument, venue, target, and delivery mode (Vining et al., 2005). We will use this schema to organize this section of the chapter. Inclusiveness refers to the orientation toward collective action or coalition formation, from going it alone through to expanding circles of coalition partners. Form of argument refers to the choice of the broad categories of how the issues would be framed. Venue refers to the level or levels of government at which influence is sought. Target refers to the intended audience – legislative, bureaucratic, executive, judicial, media, etc. Finally, delivery mode is the decision whether to 'outsource' lobby activities or maintain them 'in-house'.

Collective Lobbying

How is the choice of whether to lobby collectively or individually made and how is the collective to be structured? Organization for collective action in the public policy arena has been recognized as being problematic since Olson (1965) outlined the incentives for free-riding 50 years ago. Prior to that, pluralists had assumed that those with common interests would organize so as to pursue those interests in governmental policy venues. Olson presented a strong argument as to why most rational actors would choose not to commit resources to political struggles in the belief that they could simply sit back and enjoy the benefits of others' investments. A great deal of theorizing in political science since Olson has been aimed at explaining how interests organize in the presence of

incentives for free-riding. However, as pointed out by Hula (1999), the incentives faced by organizations or groups already committed to lobbying are different from those faced by groups who are deciding whether or not to get involved at all. Coalitions lend legitimacy to a position by demonstrating the number of groups supporting it. From a practical standpoint, working in a coalition spreads out the workload and allows a broader range of government officials to be reached. From the self-interested perspective of the individual lobbyist, being involved with coalitions sends a message to the employer or client organization that the lobbyist is 'doing something' and can increase individual visibility with the profession and policy community.

In increasingly complex policy domains, coalition organization requires interest groups that find themselves on the same general side of an issue, work out their differences and construct a consensus compromise position among themselves before going public. Presenting a more uniform policy position provides a clear signal to government officials on the strength of support for a policy (Nelson and Yackee, 2012). It may be better to compromise with people with whom one has minor differences and be part of the conversation on the consensus position than to follow a lone-wolf, interest maximization strategy and find oneself isolated between enemies and 'distant' friends.

Joining a coalition of groups with similar policy aims has some costs, in resources and in potential compromise, but a large majority of lobbyists believe it is an effective and efficient means of increasing influence with government decision-makers (Hula, 1999). Surprisingly, major academic studies have found little relationship between coalition lobbying and political success. Nelson and Yackee (2012) believe these negative findings are the result of researchers looking at the wrong things, such as policy *change*, and present evidence that coalitions that increase the uniformity of their message and are large, with a membership strategically constructed to pull in organizations with special knowledge or expertise who would not otherwise be involved, are quite influential in the policy process.

Making the decision to engage in a coalition strategy depends on the context of policy-making in a particular area. Taking a behavioral ecology perspective, Gray and Lowery (1998) liken variation in alliance activity to foraging behavior in animal populations. The answer to whether coalition lobbying is more effective than solo lobbying is that 'it depends'. Forming coalitions may be effective in the face of intense competition from policy opponents and in policy domains in which there is a large number of participants competing for access to policymakers. Situations requiring the signaling of wide-spread support, such as when major or controversial policy changes are sought, may require participation in a coalition, as would policies which have broad-based effects. In other cases, solo lobbying may be preferable.

Mahoney (2007a) found that lobbying groups in the US were far more likely to form ad hoc coalitions than those in the EU, attributing this to the desire of issues advocates in the US to signal the breadth of support for their position. According to Mahoney, when coalitions are formed in the EU context, the basis is usually resource sharing rather than the signaling of public support – although Coen (1998) saw alliance building in the EU as providing an opportunity for large firms to establish political credibility. Mahoney concluded that the greater prevalence of ad hoc coalitions in the US was driven by institutional differences, particularly the direct electoral accountability in the US that requires more sensitivity on the part of officials to public opinion.

Forms and Frames

Vining et al. (2005) discussed the 'form of argument' choice in terms of publicly presenting as issue as a matter of fact or science, in terms of efficiency, or as a social equity concern. Each of these approaches has its pros and cons, but they are all related to the idea of issue definition or framing. Any argument for a policy position must have a politically legitimate underpinning. The proposed policy must address an issue of public concern and be in general alignment with societal values. Issues are complex and multidimensional. By focusing on or drawing attention to particular aspects of an issue and providing value-based interpretations of those aspects, political actors can frame or define an issue in a way that creates a sense of need for the policy they are proposing.

The importance of the framing of problems or issues has long been understood in psychology (Kahneman and Tversky, 1984) and political science (Schattschneider, 1960; Cobb and Elder, 1973; Riker, 1986). From a lobbying perspective, getting people to accept your definition of an issue, to focus on the aspect of an inherently multidimensional reality that is most favorable to your side's position, is a crucial step in the influence process when issues are highly visible. Political actors attempt to manipulate definitions of political issues to expand or contract attention, concern, and participation in ways that advantage them. Colloquially, this is known as spin control. McGrath (2007) relates the process to advertising and product positioning. Conceptually, it is a major part of the effort to create the fundamental political resource of legitimacy.

A current example in the US is the controversy over the display of the Confederate battle flag. Supporters of the flag defend its public display by presenting it as a historical symbol of Southern heritage and as a memorial to the hundreds of thousands of soldiers who fought and died for a cause in which they believed. Detractors define it as a symbol of a defeated and wicked slave-based society and a continuing legacy of racism. Until recently, these competing definitions were held in sufficient balance that a number of Southern states continued to fly the flag over public buildings and incorporate it in official state symbols. A middle ground of people who may have been sympathetic to the detractor's definition tolerated the flag, perhaps out of respect for the sincerity and depth of feeling of the supporters or simply because it was a low-priority issue for them. However, a racially motivated mass murder triggered a sea change. The supporter's definition of the flag is rapidly losing acceptance and the legitimacy of their position is disintegrating.

In general, however, frames are relatively stable. As in the flag case, a shift in a dominant frame may be driven more by external factors than by the efforts of advocates. Baumgartner et al. (2009) argue that, despite frequently cited anecdotal examples, successful reframing is rare. Lobbyists or activists cannot simply choose what appears to be a favorable frame or spin for their issue at a given point in time and sell it to an accepting public. Such attempts will likely encounter both an active opposition and a skeptical media. Also, when a reframing opportunity appears, it can be difficult to suddenly change a line of argument and the view of reality in which one has been invested, especially if one is working with coalition partners who are likewise invested. At the individual level, lobbyists may have personal convictions associated with particular frames, as well as concerns about damage to their reputation and credibility from being seen as superficial 'spinners'.

In addition to attempting to frame an issue in a general sense, lobbyists or others may attempt targeted framing – framing an argument differently depending upon the target audience. Baumgartner and Mahoney (2008) reported that one-third of lobbyists interviewed in a EU survey said they focused on different dimensions of an issue when communicating with different audiences. However, two-thirds of respondents did not. This was explained by the majority group's concerns for transparency and not wanting to be seen as manipulative, as well as the desire

to maintain a consistent message. The bottom line is that reframing is not easy and not necessarily desirable in all circumstances. However, any group without an argument for its position tied to a definition of an issue that most people, or at least an influential set of people, would consider to be legitimately in line with societal values and the public interest is not likely to get far in influencing public policy.

Venues and Targets

Venue refers to the level (local, state, national, supranational), branch (legislative, executive, judicial), and specific unit (committee, agency, etc.) of government in which public policy is formulated or acted upon. Groups that want to influence policy sometimes have a choice of venue in which to focus their efforts. The idea of 'venue shopping' (Baumgartner and Jones, 1993) is well known – actors will strategically choose the most advantageous venue to pursue their policy objectives. This choice is said to be at the heart of political strategy (Pralle, 2003). If government bureaucrats are more sympathetic to a group's position than legislators, it makes sense to lobby the bureaucrats, provided they have sufficient room to maneuver in implementing legislative policy (Holyoke et al., 2012). If changing a law appears more likely to occur through the establishment of a new legal precedent than through the passage of legislation, it makes sense to pursue a litigation strategy rather than a traditional lobbying approach (Rubin et al., 2001).

Horizontal strategies involve choosing among venues at the same level of government. An example would be choosing whether to focus lobbying efforts on the committee in the US Congress that has oversight of a given regulatory policy, the federal agency charged with implementing the regulation, or both. In terms of horizontal strategy, one fact that is fairly well established is that there is a high correlation between lobbying the legislative branch and the executive branch (McKay, 2011). That is, groups tend to be active in both venues. At the US federal level, McKay found that most lobbyists work with the Congress or both Congress and agencies; few work with just agencies. A higher level of conflict on an issue seems to lead to lobbying across both venues.

Another research finding is that groups will be active where their opponents and coalition allies are active (Holyoke, 2003). Activity or presence does not imply intense effort. Sometimes a token effort at lobbying will be made in a venue in which opposition groups are dominant in order to signal to both supporters and opponents that the fight is still on. The real effort will be made in venues where officials are perceived to be ideologically aligned with or electorally dependent on the lobbying group (Holyoke et al., 2012). This finding is in line with the long-standing notion that lobbying effort tends to be concentrated on friends.

Vertical, or multi-level, strategies involve a choice among levels of government. In systems in which power is highly centralized, this choice may not exist, but it does in federal systems. In the US federal system this means a choice among local, state, and federal venues. In Europe, the choice is usually characterized as between national and EU levels, but can include sub-national levels as well. Constantelos (2007) noted that the choice between a 'national route' and 'Brussels strategy' depends on resources, domestic and international politics, and the scope of the membership and interests of political interest groups or associations. It has been argued that groups from countries with a more decentralized power structure will have more experience with domestic multi-level venues and be more comfortable expanding to the EU level (Schmidt, 2006), although Beyers and Kerremans (2012) did not find support for this. They also found little support for the hypothesis that groups with less access to domestic policy networks would seek to compensate by focusing their efforts

at the EU level. On the contrary, the groups most likely to be active at the EU level were those who were most active at the national level. EU-level participation seems more to be a case of the well connected getting better connected, than outsiders finding a venue that offsets disadvantages at the national level. At the sub-national level, domestic institutional structure does play the role one would expect. Constantelos found that regional interest groups in highly centralized France focused lobbying effort on the national government, while those in less centralized Italy focused on regional governments. In both countries, groups lobbied at multiple levels. For example, even when regional groups had national affiliates, the regional groups still chose to lobby at the national level themselves.

Vertical strategies are sometimes impacted by the fact that lower level government bodies are often mandated to implement policies created by higher level bodies. For example, in the US, state and local governments are mandated to implement federal policies under pain of losing dollars from the federal treasury. It is not uncommon that officials at the state level are opposed to the federal policy on ideological or practical grounds. An interest group having already lost at the federal level may choose to lobby the lower body to resist the federal level policy. Whether this approach makes sense depends on the amount of control the higher level body has over the lower (Holyoke et al., 2012).

Targeting involves the choice of which particular governmental decision-makers to focus lobbying activities on. We have already mentioned the tendency to focus on those who are friendly or like-minded. Targeting can also involve the choice of whether and what proportion of resources to devote to attempts at influencing the media and general public. Generally known as 'grassroots' or 'outside lobbying', Kollman (1998) notes that this approach plays two roles in the political process, signaling and conflict expansion. Groups choose the outside route to mobilize public opinion in support of their positions, with the aim of convincing members of the public to communicate their support to government officials. This signals to policy-makers something about the salience of an issue in the public mind. It also can expand a policy conflict (Schattschneider, 1960) to formerly quiescent groups, bringing them in on the side of the group with a successful outside approach. Outside advocacy tactics include press contacts, advocacy advertising, editorial writing, and public-relation campaigns; more focused grassroots tactics attempt to mobilize mass membership organizations and/or the general public (Baumgartner et al., 2009).

'Inside lobbying', direct contact with government officials, is the more common approach, used by almost all but the most alienated participants in the political process. Outside tactics are less ubiquitous, but still quite common and can be powerful. Outside tactics may have once been thought of as an available avenue of power to those who lacked traditional access, but they are employed by groups across the spectrum of political privilege. When privileged groups use these tactics, however, they sometimes come under suspicion. The term 'astroturf', usually attributed to the late US Senator Lloyd Bentsen, has been used to describe artificial grassroots campaigns in which well-funded, shadowy interests employ a variety of techniques to create an illusion of popular support for a position. A number of examples of these campaigns are well known (Lyon and Maxwell, 2004). Any advantage gained by these techniques is likely to be temporary and damaging when revealed.

Kollman (1998) proposes that the appropriateness of outside tactics depends on an issue's popularity and salience (importance for those who agree with the group's goals). He argues that attempts to use outside tactics on low popularity and low salience issues are rare and, when seen, can be considered astroturf. When popularity is high and salience is low, outside tactics can be used to expand the conflict. When popularity is low and salience

is high, targeted outside tactics can be used to allow the signaling of the importance of the issue for a particular group, while avoiding arousal of potentially hostile groups. If an issue is both popular and salient, groups should do all they can to make the popular support for them well known.

In an international comparison, Ishio (1999) looked at how groups in the US and Japan use inside and outside tactics. While groups in the US often employ both approaches, Ishio found that the structure of government in Japan, with party-selected candidates and a strong executive branch, combined with a cultural preference for consensual decision-making, gives Japanese interest groups less incentive than those in the US to employ outside lobbying tactics. Interestingly, however, on high conflict issues this tendency breaks down. Japanese groups are as likely as American groups to use outside tactics.

Make or Buy?

Most firms do not engage in lobbying. Hill et al. (2013) looked at 6,076 companies in the *Compustat* database (a compilation of financial and market information provided by Standard & Poor's), from 1999 to 2006 (23,974 firm-years) and found 3,042 firm-years of lobbying. That is, about 13% of companies reported expenditures lobbying the US federal government in any given year. This number falls in the typically reported range. It is known that the degree to which companies get involved in lobbying at the national level in the US is related to size, amount of government regulation affecting their industry, and sales to the government (Hansen and Mitchell, 2000; Brasher and Lowery, 2005). When companies do decide to lobby, they can choose to employ in-house lobbyists, lobbyists working directly for the company, or they can choose to contract with an independent lobbyist to represent their interests. Many firms follow a mixed strategy, using both in-house and contract lobbyists, perhaps depending upon the issue area. For example, Microsoft reported spending US$10,490,000 lobbying the US government in 2013. US$4,054,500 was paid to 23 independent lobbying firms and the rest spent directly (Opensecrets.org, 2015).

Various theories have been advanced to explain the choice between keeping lobbying in-house or contracting it out. One explanation is based on transaction costs or, in this case, the cost associated with the risk that sensitive information may be compromised through dealings with external lobbyists (De Figueiredo and Kim, 2004). When firms are concerned with leakage of sensitive information, they would be expected to use their own employees to represent their interests to government. In other situations, lobbying may be outsourced.

Another explanation involves the structure of policy-making networks. LaPira et al. (2014) used sophisticated social network analysis to divide the network made up of thousands of Washington lobbyists into core and periphery issue domains. The core issue domains, such as taxation, budget, health, trade, and defense, were dense with network connections. Other domains, such as travel and tourism, were more peripheral or 'niche' areas. It was found that in-house lobbyists were more likely to be active in core domains and contracted lobbyists in peripheral domains. The explanation for this was that organizations will invest in an in-house lobbying capability only in areas of continuing governmental interest. Areas which may only occasionally attract government attention can be left to contracted specialists.

Institutional Factors

At the beginning of this section, we noted the universal activities associated with lobbying listed by Thomas and Hrebenar (2009). However, these authors also pointed out that cultural and institutional factors create the 'rules of the game' for lobbying, especially in political contexts. These rules are likely to differ substantially among economically developed, long-standing democracies, emerging economies, and traditionally authoritarian states. However, differences in success factors and style have been noted between the most developed of polities. Institutional factors are said to drive US lobbyists toward more confrontational tactics, while those in the EU are pushed toward consensus-building.

Mahoney (2007b) looked at lobbying success in the US and EU. She found that while the US (with directly elected representatives) was more democratic on the surface than the EU (with appointed officials and parliament members accountable to national parties rather than directly to the public), policy outcomes in the US were more biased toward wealthy business interests. This was seen as largely due to institutional arrangements. In the US, it is possible to kill proposals at many stages in the process. In the EU, once the policy process starts, some policy change is inevitable. This forces EU policy advocates to work toward a balanced outcome. The game in the US tends to be winner-take-all; and the system of privately funded elections in the US has tended to advantage the side with the most money. Mahoney found that corporations in the US experienced at least partial success in their lobbying efforts 89% of the time, while citizen groups had no success 60% of the time. In the EU, results are more balanced. Despite these effects, Mahoney concluded that the context of the issue itself was more important in determining outcomes than institutional differences. The broader, more salient, and more conflictual the issue, the less likely lobbyists are to attain their goals in both the US and the EU.

Commentators have often contrasted the 'brash' style of American lobbyists with the 'soft-spoken' style characteristic of European lobbyists (Woll, 2012). Although, this has been attributed to political culture, Woll sees it as more a function of the institutional structure of the political systems. In the US, the system of private campaign finance means money plays a role that it does not in the EU. Likewise, the prevalence of lawyers and legal strategies in US public policy-making contributes to an adversarial environment. Lobbying has a shorter history in the EU, with economic interests traditionally suspect and represented through intermediary associations at the national level. This has been changing in recent years with the growth of individual company lobbying at the EU level. Although the day-to-day activities of lobbyists are similar on both sides of the Atlantic, Woll sees EU lobbyists as more interested in building consensus and long-term, trust-based relationships and less interested in pressure and confrontation than their US counterparts. The key factor, according to Woll, is that the EU is not a nation-state and must rely on cooperation among the member states. This creates a demand for consensus and compromise that acts as a strong constraint on the type of aggressive behavior seen in the US.

DISCUSSION

The core political resources possessed by any organization actively competing in the political arena are access and legitimacy. The process through which these resources are developed and converted into public policies that create or secure an advantage in the market place can be labeled lobbying. In this chapter, we have reviewed recent research perspectives on the goals, strategies, and activities associated with lobbying. There are certain commonalities in most democratic systems. Effective lobbying requires an in-depth knowledge and continuous monitoring of both the technical and political aspects of one's issue domain. This knowledge is valuable as an input into the development of public influence strategies, but also as an exchange good when

dealing with government officials. Effective lobbying requires the creation and maintenance of trust-based relationships with potential and existing coalition partners, politicians, bureaucrats, and other important actors in a policy community. Effective lobbying requires an understanding of government and the policy-making process. It requires an appreciation of all the routes through which one's objectives may be attained and the capabilities possessed by one's organization, potential allies, and the sympathetic publics for traversing these routes. Effective lobbying requires understanding how to communicate a message to government decision-makers, as well as how to frame it for the public. Finally, effective lobbying in the twenty-first century requires understanding the global, multi-level, and interdependent nature of the emerging political environment.

REFERENCES

Ansolabehere, S., Snyder, J.M., and Tripathi, M. (2002) Are PAC contributions and lobbying linked? New evidence from the 1995 Lobby Disclosure Act. *Business and Politics*, 4(2): 131–155.

Austen-Smith, D. (1995) Campaign contributions and access. *American Political Science Review*, 89(3): 566–581.

Barney, J.B. (1991) Firm resources and sustained competitive advantage. *Journal of Management*, 17(1): 99–120.

Baumgartner, F.R., Berry, J.M., Hojnacki, M., Kimball, D.C., and Leech, B.L. (2009) *Lobbying and Policy Change: Who Wins, Who Loses, and Why.* Chicago, IL: University of Chicago Press.

Baumgartner, F.R. and Jones, B.D. (1993) *Agendas and Instability in American Politics.* Chicago, IL: University of Chicago Press.

Baumgartner, F.R. and Mahoney, C. (2008). Forum section: The two faces of framing individual-level framing and collective issue definition in the European Union. *European Union Politics*, 9(3): 435–449.

Bertrand, M., Bombardini, M., and Trebbi, F. (2011) Is it whom you know or what you know? An empirical assessment of the lobbying process. NBER Working Paper Series, 16765 (http://www.nber.org/papers/w16765).

Beyers, J. and Kerremans, B. (2012) Domestic embeddedness and the dynamics of multi-level venue shopping in four EU member states. *Governance: An International Journal of Policy, Administration, and Institutions*, 25(2): 263–290.

Blanes i Vidal, J., Draca, M., and Fons-Rosen, C. (2012) Revolving door lobbyists. *American Economic Review*, 102(7): 3731–3748.

Bornardi, J.P. (2011) Corporate political resources and the resourced-based view of firm. *Strategic Organization*, 9(3): 247–255.

Bouwen, P. (2002) Corporate lobbying in the European Union: The logic of access. *Journal of European Public Policy*, 9(3): 365–390.

Brasher, H. and Lowery, D. (2006) The corporate context of lobbying activity. *Business and Politics*, 8(1): 1–23.

Chalmers, A.W. (2013) With a lot of help from their friends: Explaining the social logic of informational lobbying in the European Union. *European Union Politics*, 14(4): 475–496.

Cobb, R.W. and Elder, C.D. (1973) *Participation in American Politics: The Dynamics of Agenda Building*. Baltimore, MA: Johns Hopkins Press.

Coen, D. (1998) The European business interest and the nation-state: Large firm lobbying in the European Union and member states. *Journal of Public Policy*, 18(10): 75–100.

Constantelos, J. (2007) Interest group strategies in multi-level Europe. *Journal of Public Affairs*, 7: 39–53.

De Figueiredo, J.M. and Kim, J.J. (2004) When do firms hire lobbyists? The organization of lobbying at the Federal Communications Commission. *Industrial and Corporate Change*, 13(6): 883–900.

Grannovetter, M.S. (1973) The strength of weak ties. *American Journal of Sociology*, 78(6): 1360–1380.

Gray, V. and Lowery, D. (1998) To lobby alone or in a flock: Foraging behavior among interest groups. *American Politics Quarterly*, 26(1): 5–34.

Hall, R.L. and Deardorff, A.V. (2006) Lobbying as legislative subsidy. *American Political Science Review*, 100(1): 69–84.

Hansen, J.M. (1991) *Gaining Access: Congress and the Farm Lobby, 1919–1981* Chicago, IL: University of Chicago Press.

Hansen, W.L. and Mitchell, N.J. (2000) Disaggregating and explaining corporate political activity: Domestic and foreign corporations in national politics. *American Political Science Review*, 94(4): 891–903.

Helco, H. (1978) Issue networks and the executive establishment: Government growth in the age of improvement. In King, A. (ed.) *The New American Political System*. Washington, DC: American Enterprise Institute.

Hill, M.D., Kelly, G.W., Lockhart, G.B., and Ness, R.A. (2013) Determinants and effects of corporate lobbying. *Financial Management*, 42(4): 931–957.

Hillman, A.J. and Hitt, M.A. (1999) Corporate political strategy formulation: A model of approach, participation, and strategy decisions. *Academy of Management Journal*, 24: 825–842.

Hojnacki, M. and Kimball, D.C. (2001) PAC contributions and lobbying contacts in Congressional committees. *Political Research Quarterly*, 54(1): 161–180.

Holyoke, T.T. (2003) Choosing battlegrounds: Interest group lobbying across multiple venues. *Political Research Quarterly*, 56: 325–336.

Holyoke, T.T., Brown, H., and Henig, J.R. (2012) Shopping in the political arena: strategic State and local venue selection by advocates. *State and Local Government Review*, 44(1): 9–20.

Hula, K.W. (1999) *Lobbying Together: Interest Group Coalitions in Legislative Politics*. Washington, DC: Georgetown University Press.

Ishio, Y. (1999) Interest groups' lobbying tactics in Japan and the U.S.: The influence of political structures on and conflict on tactical choices. *Southeastern Political Review*, 27(2): 243–264.

Kahneman, D. and Tversky, A. (1984) Choices, values, and frames. *American Psychologist*, 39: 341–350.

Kollman, K. (1998) *Outside Lobbying: Public Opinion and Interest Group Strategies*. Princeton, NJ: Princeton University Press.

Langbein, L.I. (1986) Money and access: Some empirical evidence. *Journal of Politics*, 48(4): 1052–1062.

LaPira, T.M., Thomas, H.F., and Baumgartner, F.R. (2014) The two worlds of lobbying: Washington lobbyists in the core and on the periphery. *Interest Groups & Advocacy*, 3(3): 219–245.

Lyon, T.P. and Maxwell, J.W. (2004) Astroturf: Interest group lobbying and corporate strategy. *Journal of Economics and Management Strategy*, 13(4): 561–597.

Mahoney, C. (2007a) Networking vs. allying: the decision of interest groups to join coalitions in the US and the EU. *Journal of European Public Policy*, 14(3): 366–383.

Mahoney, C. (2007b) Lobbying success in the United States and the European Union. *Journal of Public Policy*, 27(1): 35–56.

McGrath, C. (2006) The ideal lobbyist: Personal characteristics of effective lobbyists. *Journal of Communication Management*, 10(1): 67–79.

McGrath, C. (2007) Framing lobbying messages: Defining and communicating political issues persuasively. *Journal of Public Affairs*, 7: 69–80.

McKay, A.M. (2011) The decision to lobby bureaucrats. *Public Choice*, 147: 123–138.

McQuide, B. (2007) Interest group informational lobbying: Policy vs. political information. In *Midwest Political Science Association 2007 Annual Meeting Paper*.

Nelson, D. and Yackee, S.B. (2012) Lobbying coalitions and government policy change: An analysis of federal agency rulemaking. *Journal of Politics*, 74(2): 339–353.

Nownes, A.J. and Freeman, P.K. (1998) Female lobbyists: Women in the world of 'Good Old Boys'. *Journal of Politics*, 60(4): 1181–1201.

Oberman, W.D. (2008) A conceptual look at the strategic resource dynamics of public affairs. *Journal of Public Affairs*, 8: 249–260.

Olson, M. (1965) *The Logic of Collective Action: Public Goods and the Theory of Groups*. Cambridge, MA: Harvard University Press.

Opensecrets.org (2015) Retrieved from: https://www.opensecrets.org/lobby/clientsum.php?id=D000000115&year=2013.

Pralle, S.B. (2003) Venue shopping, political strategy, and policy change: The internationalization of Canadian forest advocacy. *Journal of Public Policy*, 23(3): 233–260.

Public Affairs Council (n.d.) Retrieved from: http://pac.org/faq#WhatPA.

Rehbein, K.A., Schuler, D.A., and Doh, J.P. (2005) Firm political capital: A social network perspective. In *Academy of Management Annual Meeting, Honolulu, Hawaii, August*. Based on manuscript dated July (Vol. 12, p. 2005).

Riker, W. (1986) *The Art of Political Manipulation*. New Haven, CT: Yale University Press.

Rubin, P.H., Curran, C., and Curran, J.F. (2001) Litigation versus legislation: Forum shopping by rent seekers. *Public Choice*, 107: 295–310.

Schattschneider, E.E. (1960) *The Semisovereign People: A Realist's Guide to Democracy in America*. New York: Holt.

Schmidt, V.A. (2006) *Democracy in Europe: The EU and National Politics*. Oxford: Oxford University Press.

Shaffer, B.A. and Hillman, A.J. (2000) The development of business government strategies by diversified firms. *Strategic Management Journal*, 18: 509–533.

Thomas, C.S. and Hrebenar, R.J. (2009) Comparing lobbying across liberal democracies: Problems approaches, and initial findings. *Journal of Comparative Politics*, 2(1): 131–142.

Vining, A.R., Shapiro, D.M., and Borges, B. (2005) Building the firm's political (lobbying) strategy). *Journal of Public Affairs*, 5: 150–175.

Wernerfelt, B. (1984) A resource-based view of the firm. *Strategic Management Journal*, 5(2): 171–180.

Woll, C. (2012) The brash and the soft-spoken: Lobbying styles in transatlantic comparison. *Interest Groups & Advocacy*, 1(2): 193–214.

Wright, J.R. (1996) *Interest Groups and Congress: Lobbying, Contributions, and Influence*. Boston: Allyon & Bacon Publishers.

Yadev, V. (2008) Business lobbies and policymaking in developing countries: The contrasting cases of India and China. *Journal of Public Affairs*, 8: 67–82.

27

Managing Regulatory Affairs and Intelligence: The Often Hidden Domain of Public Affairs Practice

Craig S. Fleisher

UBER: A CASE STUDY IN THE NEED FOR EFFECTIVE MANAGEMENT OF REGULATORY AFFAIRS

'In 128 of our cities, we've got regulatory issues in about 128 of our cities,' Justin Kintz, Policy Director (for the Americas), Uber. (Hu, 2014)

Although it is generally viewed to be a force for progress, technological innovation can be a disruptive influence on many markets and impact society in a myriad of ways that few government officials might have anticipated. To understand how and why this happens, one only needs to look as far as a typical downtown street corner, where hailing a cab used to be commonplace. It has become less common in the larger cities where Uber operates. Part of the so-called new 'sharing economy' created by the rapid adoption and use of mobile devices, Uber is a fast-growing, capital-attracting company operating on all the major continents. It offers a service that lets passengers request a ride by simply tapping a freely available, user-friendly, mobile phone application; nevertheless, it is a technological innovation that represents a disruption to the established order of the markets it seeks to serve. As such, its entrance has caused its market rivals and, most importantly for the purposes of this chapter, stakeholders, in the form of policy-makers and regulators, any number of concerns and growing pains worldwide.

One stakeholder group that has taken particular notice of Uber's emergence is taxi cab companies and drivers. They are threatened by the rapid emergence of this newcomer 'on their turf'. At a minimum, Uber has caused many of these entities to lose revenues and ridership; at a maximum, it has put them out of business or work. In some large cities in North America and Europe, such as London, Paris, and San Francisco for example, where Uber has been established the longest, it has been publicly vilified by complaints among other things for forcing taxi companies to fold, causing taxi drivers to seek other gainful employment, encouraging passengers to ride in dangerous vehicles or with unsafe and untrained drivers, causing accidents or traffic snarl-ups, and/or for displacing the licensing regimes that had been established to protect these entities.

Social media such as Facebook and Twitter are full of individual commentators who liken the company to Star Wars' mega-villain Darth Vader, view it as a plague upon their cities, and want it eliminated. These Uber-averse stakeholders have usually called upon local officials to put a halt to Uber's presence and license to operate in these cities. They have achieved a few regulatory successes and garnered public attention, even sympathy, in selected locales; nevertheless, the company, the numbers of its drivers, and its ridership has continued to expand. Uber fights regulatory and stakeholder-related battles on a city-by-city basis, continuing to grow as more and more consumers clamor for the service and an increasing number of policy officials become convinced of the net benefits derived from allowing the company to operate in their jurisdictions.

The US state of Virginia provided a microcosm of the battle around this issue. Uber had been operating there despite the regulator's initial calls for it to cease and desist. The state's transportation secretary Aubrey Layne commented that,

> I think that the laws can be changed to accommodate them, but until they are, they are in violation. [...] I'd be the first to admit that technology is moving quicker than many of our laws. On the other hand, there is the safety of the public, and there is the due process of law that needs to be dealt with. (Hu, 2014)

Another regulatory combat zone for Uber is found in Boston, MA. Donna Blythe-Shaw, who represents the Boston Taxi Cab Drivers Association, says, '[Uber's drivers] are not properly vetted. Their prices are to lure you in, and so once they take over, then of course they can price and do whatever they want'

(Hu, 2014). On the other side, Uber's Hintz flatly states, 'We're pro competition, we're pro-consumer choice, and I think the market's going to decide a lot of these factors' (Hu, 2014). And in the middle of this contentious issue are the regulators, whose responsibilities are to uphold the laws and to protect the various publics affected by Uber's emergence.

The large US state of New York proved to be a major theatre of battle for the company with its regulators. New York City, in particular, was the front line in the fight between Uber and its policy rivals. The battle led to one of Uber's former policy managers, Bradley Tusk, to claim victory (Fiegerman, 2015). Tusk stated, 'Some of the public disputes companies like Uber and AirBnB have had to make the reality of regulation and politics far more apparent to founders and startups, which creates both a need on their end and (hopefully) an opportunity on ours'. In the early days, Tusk worked with Uber's Chief Executive Officer (CEO) and its general managers in its new markets to learn about and help the company leap over its regulatory hurdles. As time went on, he helped build up a team of Uber staffers and consultants to deal with government and media relationships. Because of his successful Uber experience, Tusk, who is someone who sees the need for technology startups like Uber to understand and manage their interactions with regulators even on a locality-by-locality basis, launched Tusk Ventures, a political consultancy firm that helps other disruptive, startup companies successfully navigate around their own regulatory hurdles.

In issues and policy marketplaces, where lawmakers and regulatory officials can set the terms and decide upon the license to operate for companies such as Uber, who and/or which stakeholders are going to succeed – Uber or those stakeholders opposed to it? Will the laws and regulations catch up with the innovation? How should policy-makers address disruptions like the one represented by Uber, which clearly represents the technological march of progress, but which also concurrently threatens the established market, regulatory and social order?

Make no mistake about it – Uber's emergence has created any number of legitimate regulatory issues (Baker, 2015). There is even an updating list dedicated to where Uber (and its market peer/rival Lyft) are facing regulatory issues (see http://www.buzzfeed.com/johanabhuiyan/here-is-where-uber-and-lyft-are-facing-regulation-battles-in#.gny0MW7aE). These regulatory affairs (RA) issues are a mixture of understanding, perceptions, and values intersecting with concerns and questions about ethics, governance, issues, stakeholders, and society, all of which sit squarely in the middle of the public affairs (PA) aegis.

WHAT IS REGULATION AND WHY DOES IT MATTER TO BUSINESSES?

Like many phenomena with which PA practitioners interact, regulation is present in much public life and may change with each new calendar year. And when it comes to business-related matters, seemingly insignificant or small regulatory shifts can send a business on a slippery slope and/or have magnified domino effects. Martin Mucci, the president and CEO of human resources outsourcing services company Paychex, said, 'Staying up to date with the ever-changing regulatory environment can be the difference between your business maintaining compliance and potentially facing steep IRS penalties' (Brooks, 2015). Any missteps in this environment can trigger corporate and personal, financial and/or criminal penalties, wasted resources, lost time, or new risks; on the other side of the continuum, they can result in missed, overlooked, or unleveraged opportunities to succeed.

It can be inherently difficult to define and generally entails a complex interplay of values, interests, and resources (Levi-Faur, 2011). Common characterizations of the term identify regulation as any ruling endorsed by a government or one of its authorized agencies where there is an expectation of stakeholder compliance in line with some public good. It includes legislation, regulations, quasi-regulations, and any other aspect of regulator behavior that can influence or compel specific behavior about what is and is not permissible by business and its interactions with the stakeholder community. On the opposite but related side of the regulatory continuum, deregulation would be the acts or processes for reducing or removing existing regulations. Other forms along the continuum of regulatory reform would include re-regulation or liberalization.

Regulations are usually used by governments to address stakeholder concerns that are not being adequately, properly, or timely addressed by business entities – to the satisfaction of those stakeholders. Commonly suggested motives for governments to regulate can include the desire to protect consumers, to achieve greater economic efficiency, to better protect the natural environment, to facilitate social justice, or to ensure security of supply of a particularly important product, resource, or service, among others (Levi-Faur, 2011). More recently, the push for 'transparency in government' has added significantly more need for regulatory filings and requirements (Besley, 2015). There is a common view that these increased filings will add greater transparency, which is particularly relevant to industries that are self-regulated. This will continue to gain in prevalence as governments at all levels struggle to demonstrate that they are taking action on 'bad apples' in self-regulating industries.

Regulations come in a variety of types. Two of the largest ones impacting businesses are (1) economic, which deals with aspects of a market, and (2) social, which addresses social outcomes or results (for example, benefits or externalities) of market behavior. Regulatory policies can affect whether or how much it costs a business to enter a market (entry regulation), what products or services will cost, what can and cannot be part of a product or service (content), and how and by what means a product or service is to be delivered (standards). The Uber case that began this chapter actually demonstrates all of these factors in a contemporary, global context.

The primary conceptual aim of most regulations is to address failures of markets to deliver desirable goods and services – whether economic, social, or environmental. When failures and associated harms are perceived by officials, regulation is executed by governments along a continuum of models. The following regulatory types, each of which has its own unique sets of advantages and disadvantages, are commonly used for resolving the aims of global regulators:

1 Command and control regulation: It imposes rules and standards about appropriate business behavior and is backed up or sanctioned by (criminal) penalties for business entities that break those rules.
2 Market-based regulation: These models channel market forces to influence competitive behavior through the means of laws, disclosure, tradeable permits, etc.
3 Incentive-based regulation: It uses grants, subsidies, or taxes as a way of encouraging compliance with the rules.
4 Self-regulation: This occurs where businesses or their designated association sets, monitors, and enforces rules by which members are supposed to adhere.

The state can also use other forms of regulatory models, such as direct action, establishing new rights or responsibilities, creating liabilities laws, or directing/requiring stakeholder compensation.

The regulatory process, institutions, and context are critical for business managers and professionals to understand because they are the filter between companies and their environment, as both business and society influence one another through public policy

(Federal Register, 2011). Regulatory decisions made by government agencies can be a source of the largest costs of doing business; consequently, corporations and business associations must bring to bear uncommon competences in managing this particular business–government relationship (National Association of Manufacturing, 2014).

Baron (1995) notes that, for managers, the challenge of understanding public policy environment (PPE) forces, such as government, interest groups, activists, and the public, is often more difficult than understanding the market environment. The PPE includes the interactions occurring within what is commonly referred to by business strategists as the STEEP sectors of the macro-environment: *s*ocial, *t*echnological, *e*conomic, *e*cological, and *p*olitical. Preston and Post (1975) in their seminal work on principles of public responsibility suggest that firms must monitor everything between the literal text of established laws and regulations, and the broad patterns of public action that may eventually impact the former.

WHY RA CAN BE AN IMPORTANT FOCUS WITHIN THE PA MANAGEMENT DOMAIN

PA professionals in enterprises are often responsible for a range of non-market and public-policy related duties (Fleisher, 2005). One of the more interesting, yet infrequently researched and written about in PA scholarship or taught in university classrooms, is managing relationships with regulatory actors/interests, institutions (that is, agencies) and processes (Griffin et al., 2001a, 2001b). The remainder of this chapter aims to explore the RA role from a PA perspective, to explain the regulatory context within which PA managers operate, to illuminate how RA can be strategically managed – focusing particularly on the development of strategic or competitive intelligence – and provide examples of actual practices derived from PA case studies and research, where RA roles have become institutionalized and professionalized.

Business decision-makers and leaders around the globe often complain about government regulations and how they limit or restrict commercial entities from freely achieving desired commercial or profit-making goals (Sparrow, 2011). Consumer, environmentally friendly, or financial oversight/compliance regulations, among others, are often viewed by executives as a waste of a business' time, money, or effort, and are often offered as a reason why profits are lower than they otherwise would have been (Bogardus, 2015). There are many other historical examples where government statutory requirements have been criticized, avoided, and/or violated by businesses. Additionally, the politics from both the left and the right that surround regulatory behavior can be confounding, with both sides battling back and forth, behind and in the public eye, about the kind of regulatory policy that will better the social condition (Levi-Faur, 2011).

North American business communities, for one, have generally been averse to any government law, regulation, compliance obligation, or tax levy that they see as undermining profitability or impeding their business operations (Davis, 2011). This same opinion is often shared in jurisdictions outside of North America as well. Since the enactment of anti-trust laws in the early twentieth century, followed by periodic increases in corporate tax rates and increasingly complex and restrictive regulatory laws governing the conduct of business, US business owners have seen a growth and bewildering array of complex regulations that have been sought after by stakeholders ranging from consumers, to employees, special interest groups, suppliers, all the way to political officials (Bogardus, 2015). National chamber of commerce groups who advocate for business interests are regularly speaking out against what they see as ever-burgeoning and expanding government

regulation of business activity, some calling it more complex than ever before (Yarbrough, 2013).

On the other hand, regulation has just as often been sought, requested, or advocated for by businesses and their stakeholders; in contrast to the anti-regulatory stance shared in the above paragraph, some enlightened executives realize that it can also simultaneously serve both an organization's commercial and societal goals (Dollinger, 2015; Drum, 2011). Indeed, in many countries, government agencies are established to support indigenous businesses by providing assistance, funding, information, or networking access to new markets. Examples of these would be agencies established to support small or emerging businesses, such as the US Small Business Administration, or Innovation, Science and Economic Development Canada's Small Business Financing Program. Other business leaders have recognized that managing regulatory processes strategically can, under certain conditions and contexts, allow an organization, sector, or industry to achieve a competitive advantage, exploit an opportunity for advantage based on the ensuing regulatory policy, or to strategically mitigate risks (Holburn, 2012). Some companies and industries have even come to recognize that managing regulatory and related non-market affairs can become a key capability in their decision-making and execution arsenals that should be managed just as carefully and professionally as other capabilities that potentially provide asymmetric advantages (Lawton et al., 2013, 2014).

WHAT ACTIVITIES DO RA PROFESSIONALS PERFORM?

Strategically managing RA by any sized business has grown more difficult through the years, often in proportion to the increased complexity of regulatory processes that must be navigated. Companies in some industries, such as the pharmaceuticals/life sciences, energy, utilities, defense and aerospace, health care, and medical products, among others, must operate RA units and regularly interact with regulators and various regulatory agencies. This interaction covers a gamut of functional business activity, ranging from compliance, to legal matters, to advertising and marketing, and beyond. Small and medium-sized businesses must manage RA typically without the benefit of PA units or internal RA specialists.

In a strategic context, management of the PPE requires an organization to manage four primary items, information, institutions, issues, and stakeholders, or as Baron (1995) calls them, *interests*. *Regulatory issues* are the currency of public policy debates and are defined here as gaps between an organization's actions and the expectations of those regulators (that is, stakeholders) who can impact its goals. *Information* is what stakeholders know about the relationship between

actions and consequences, and about the capabilities, desires, and resources of the issue players. *Stakeholders* are parties that either have or seek a stake in a particular regulatory issue. *Institutions* are those formally established establishments where regulatory policy is debated and established.

To manage these 4I's – as Baron's concept is now known – companies have increasingly realized the need to hire and manage qualified RA executives. Due to the policy and governance nature of RA tasks, many of these will come from, or work directly with, their PA counter-parts. The RA job is constantly changing, in line with the changing directives, processes, environment, and aims of the regulatory agencies within which an organization must interact. The 'typical' RA job requires more education, knowledge, and experience than ever before. Figure 27.1 shows a genericized job description for a RA director in the pharmaceutical industry.

Figure 27.1   Genericized job description for a senior regulatory affairs director*

Global Pharmaceuticals Company (GPC) – based in the US

Job Description

As the Senior Director of Global Regulatory Affairs (GRA) Intelligence, you will be in a leadership role managing a diverse range of activities combined with a technical role inspiring and leading cutting edge projects on a global basis. This role will influence and shape the image of the GPC global regulatory affairs organization.

You will be responsible for providing strategic direction, applying a full understanding of global issues liaising with the Regulatory Policy Groups (RPGs) and creating synergies and active collaboration with other intelligence, planning, and strategy roles within the GPC organization (e.g. competitive intelligence, research and development, business development). As the lead global regulatory affairs interface, you are accountable for the group's delivery of the external environment sections of the therapeutic area and product regulatory strategy documents (RSDs), as well as oversight for the group's delivery of responses to regulatory queries from product teams and GRA leadership to facilitate informed decision making.

This role has an impact on an entire function, therapy area or project. Because of this, we are looking for highly developed levels of conceptual thought, leadership without line management responsibility, and strategic vision to manage the highest level of risk and capitalize on competitive opportunities emanating from the regulatory environment.

High-level Expectations

- Provide a broad strategic view of global regulatory affairs issues.
- Work in a team capacity with Associate Directors to lead the horizon scanning process, and proactively monitor and interpret the external regulatory environment.
- Build a solid interface between the global regulatory affairs groups, the regional regulatory policy groups, and the global drug development organizations.
- Continually improve the alignment of intelligence efforts with other key GPC RA and related groups complementing the work of their organizations and avoiding duplication of effort.

Continued

- Oversee the analysis regarding whether GPC would benefit from participating in specific public commenting opportunities and identify critical aspects to address.
- Oversee the Call for Comments process and/or work collaboratively with the appointed Call for Comments Lead(s) to determine if the GPC position was accepted and the impact of GPC's externalization efforts.

Monitor, Analyze and Interpret the Environment

- Strategically monitor/search the external environment in line with therapeutic areas and regional identified priorities and bring emerging issues forward for higher/highest level consideration.
- Analyze and apply relevant intelligence findings in the context of current GPC business and project activities.
- Communicate insightful impact to facilitate awareness of business critical issues and informed decision-making by teams.
- Identify issues that impact the business now and in the near future with a view to predicting trends.
- Manage horizon scanning process and escalate items for consideration on global RA risk register.
- Work collaboratively and align with other policy/intelligence groups to optimize horizon scanning.
- Identify global RA priority external engagement and monitoring topics. Effectively communicate the output to the wider organization.
- Actively engage senior management and Regulatory Therapy Area Leads to solicit input and buy-in for key RA intelligence areas of interest.
- Work closely with other global RA and GPC representatives focus and prioritize intelligence areas of interest.

Manage Queries and RSDs

- Work collaboratively to effectively ensure the Global Regulatory Intelligence group responds to queries in support of robust RSD creation.
- Leads/oversee delivery of regulatory environment components of RSDs:
  - using knowledge of broad regulatory issues with emphasis on cross-cutting matters
  - leveraging institutional memory, and disease area specific investigations.
- Review and summarize assessment reports published by key regulatory authorities (e.g., European Medicines Agency (EMA) European Public Assessment Reports (EPARs); United States (US) Food and Drug Administration (FDA) Summary Basis of Approvals (SBAs); etc.) and output from relevant meetings (e.g. US FDA Advisory Committees), and ensure RSDs and environment documents reflect this intelligence.

Metrics

- Endorse/ implement change based on metrics.
- Coordinate collection and use of internal and externally gathered metrics.
- Communicate results of analysis to broader business, and use to shape external environment.

Account Management

- Manage relationships with external vendors such as CIRS, CMR, Tufts, etc. as well as professional services firms.
- Drive development of business case in order to acquire further services from suppliers which require additional budget.
- Within established budget parameters, optimize delivery of services from vendors and identify if further services are required.

Internal Engagement Management

- Create and lead overall internal engagement strategy.
- Build internal networks on complex regulatory topics.
- Manage relationship with senior management, e.g., legal, therapy area VPs, etc.
- Establish and leverage relationship with specific accounts (other GPC functions, policy and RA groups, etc.) as assigned.
- Identify gaps, analyze business requirements and implement improvements.
- Represents GPC on internal issue based teams.

Managing External Engagement

- Represent and advocate on behalf of GPC on broader regulatory and drug development intelligence topics.
- Represent the company on external networks for multiple and cross-functional topics and/brief senior management in advance of key meetings.
- Endorse, prioritize external engagement and monitoring topics.
- Provide a broad strategic view for regulatory intelligence issues that form the basis of the company's external engagement activities.
- Chair multiple topic external networks/committees, as appropriate.
- Develop networks with external senior RA staff.
- Provide timely, constructive feedback and coaching to direct reports and GPC colleagues.

*This was gathered from reviewing key competencies and requirements from job descriptions at sites such as GlassDoor, Indeed.com, and Salary.com, synthesized with an analysis of the profiles of the top 20 RA executives on Linkedin (see https://www.linkedin.com/title/regulatory-affairs-executive). Unsurprisingly, the pharmaceuticals industry is disproportionately represented in these advertisements and listings. Compared with other industries in which RA executives practice, it has the highest number of post-secondary degree programs, professional associations, and certification/credentialing programs, among other things.

RA competitive intelligence (RACI – pronounced 'racey') becomes most important from a strategic perspective in these industries because it allows organizations to gain a comprehensive understanding of the present, and even future, regulatory environment. For example, regulatory agencies often require companies to document their activities, and leave these available for certain time periods to public comment. This can provide an early warning to associated opportunities and threats. Moreover, these PPE-based opportunities and threats come in about half a dozen primary forms as the examples in Figure 27.3 suggest:

INDUSTRIES WHERE RA MANAGERS ARE PREVALENT AND REGULATORY INTENSITY IS HIGH

Almost any industry that is heavily regulated by governmental entities will employ RA practitioners. This will especially be true when organizations are required by law to regularly file documentation, comply with guidelines, and interact with their regulators. A month-long (June) 2015 search of companies seeking RA specialists shows that most common among these would be the 18 industries listed in Figure 27.2.

INTELLIGENCE ON THE REGULATORY ENVIRONMENT IS IMPORTANT

Companies must constantly monitor social and political factors, inside and outside their regulatory environment. Ignoring these areas has cost some companies a good deal of money, to say nothing of goodwill, because they have been forced to respond to public pressure or more burdensome government regulation (Oberman, 2005). Baron (1995) suggests that, beyond typical market considerations, success can depend on how effectively organizations deal with governments,

Figure 27.2   Main industries in which RA officials are regularly employed (circa 2015)

• Aerospace and defense	• Beauty products/cosmetics	• Business services
• Chemicals	• Construction (engineering)	• Education (higher, secondary, elementary)
• Energy and utilities	• Government and non-profit	• Financial services (banking, insurance, investments, etc.)
• Healthcare and life sciences (hospitals, medical devices/products, nutritionals, pharmaceuticals, veterinary)	• Hospitality, leisure, and travel	• Media (broadcast internet, social)
• Manufacturing (durables, nondurables)	• Retail and wholesale	• Software and networking
• Technology (New Product Development (NPD), discovery)	• Telecom	• Transportation (airline transport, shipping)

Figure 27.3 Overview of opportunities and threats for businesses in the public policy environment

	Opportunity	Threat
Consultation	Influence resultant policies or regulations	Co-optation
Expenditure	Acquire subsidies, grants, access to new customers	Temporary competitive disadvantage
Privatization	'Leveling' of the playing field or markets	Increased competition and rivalry
Regulation	'Control' competition and rivalry	Increased costs and expenditure of additional resources
Takeover	Customers with deep pockets	Potentially unfair, unpredictable, and formidable competitor
Taxation	Gain temporary competitive advantage	Reduce return on investment

interest groups, activists, and the public – non-market factors that include regulatory institutions and actors. In other words, external impacts, public issues, and stakeholders are important to management (Keim, 2005). In addition to Uber which has already been presented, consider the following examples. Should or how should government officials respond to and/or regulate:

- Google, which uses people's private information gathered while they surf the web using its market-dominant search engine or e-mail applications, thus profiting from the user's data collected in its commercial business operations? Is this acceptable? Should users be able to opt-out or protect certain forms of information, or be given some types of privacy rights?
- The rapid emergence of autonomous or self-driving cars on their roads, self-navigating boats on their waterways, or planes in their airspace? For example, one issue that arises is who will be responsible for damage or deaths ostensibly caused by one of these computer-operated conveyances? What if the conveyance was hacked by an entity bent on doing harm?
- Amazon and other package delivery services who want to use drones to efficiently and conveniently deliver their customers' packages? Among the issues that must be considered are how many can operate in what (private and public) spaces, at what times, and under what conditions?
- The price of a newly discovered drug that can eradicate long-standing diseases, but which cost the companies who discovered it billions of Euros in their gamble to try and bring it to the market?

- The desire of foreign operators to enter new international markets, where their presence might benefit consumers, bring new capital investment, and grow employment, but may also put some domestic entities out of business?

Businesses have existential responsibilities and are licensed to serve public interests, should comply with existing regulations, and work with regulators in their product spaces to deliver better, less costly/harmful, new, or alternative solutions (Preston and Post, 1975). Regulatory and other PPE officials seek stakeholder feedback and need to hear from affected parties, including the businesses that might be compelling the need for regulation and regulatory policy (Federal Register, 2011). Indeed, most veteran RA officials recognize that many regulatory agencies have 'windows of opportunity' whereby the agency is far more amenable to receiving stakeholder input and making suggested changes. All of these matters form the typical environment within which regulators and public policy-makers must make decisions, and business executives must do likewise.

The global regulatory climate tends to increase in complexity more often than it actually simplifies matters. This makes it more difficult for enterprises of any size to keep up with the regulations, to discern what they mean to their business, and/or to execute compliance processes. Furthermore, regulators often require companies to communicate their data and positions. It is often not just a matter of reacting to rules and compliance, but rather strategically managing regulatory matters, policy, and its environment. Strategic management requires enhanced sense-making, intelligence, and understanding of the future (Fleisher, 2016).

Some observers have noted that the nature of what companies compete for has changed. Companies compete with a multitude of other organized interests seeking attention, government support, funding, membership, and credibility in the community (Keim, 2005). Few senior executives dispute that fierce competition exists within governments for funding, in the media for space and time, in policy arenas for better outcomes, and among the general public for attention. Just as companies compete for customers and market share in the market place, companies also compete for stakeholders and share of mind or attention in the regulatory environment.

In what forms does some of this competition take place? Companies, such as those in the health care and life sciences space, compete to demonstrate the benefits or efficacy of their products and services, often doing this through the regulatory submission and review process. Advantages arise by gaining regulatory approval to show that a product more effectively treats a key, underlying condition than rivals' alternatives. Some companies send their executives to meet frequently with regulators, both on a compliance (that is, reactive, responsive) and advisory (that is, proactive, advance) basis. Others battle it out in the news media in attempts to win the 'battle of public opinion' that is thought to have indirect influence on the thinking of regulators and other policy officials. Companies also often spend considerable sums to convince local communities on the merits of a development project in order to get the community's officials backing to make some change. For example, US retailing giant Wal-Mart fought community by community during its rapid growth stage of the late twentieth century. It sought to gain zoning approvals to develop large-sized stores in rural neighborhoods, some of which were not pleased on initial glance because they thought that their existing, long-standing mom-and-pop retailing businesses might be put out of business shortly after Wal-Mart's arrival there.

Competing more effectively in the regulatory environment requires companies to develop regulatory intelligence. Intelligence is systematically gathered, and data and information processed about regulatory concerns that allow the organization's executives to make better decisions about forthcoming actions their company might take to most beneficially resolve the concern (Fleisher and Bensoussan, 2015). Intelligence is also a foundation of strategy development, and helps company's position themselves over time in their market, public policy, and regulatory spaces in which competition between rivals for policy exists.

Regulatory intelligence serves several key purposes for regulated or prospectively regulated organizations, including but not limited to the following strategic benefits:

1 To anticipate changes in the relevant (global) regulatory space: This is also known as developing distant or early warning in terms of what policy-makers and regulators might be considering.
2 To address forthcoming or proposed actions of market rivals: Being able to trump or raise costs of entry, foreclose or forestall actions can often allow a company to obtain or extend early-mover product/service market advantages.
3 To learn from another company's regulatory failures and successes: By benchmarking another company's submissions and experiences, learning can be applied to one's own processes in search of generating improved regulatory outcomes and results.
4 To more quickly identify and understand new products/services, regulation, and/or technologies and position one's own to be better aligned with converging trends.
5 To examine one's own regulatory strategies and tactics through and with a more objective lens: Through gathering and analyzing intelligence on their own and rival organizations, many companies have uncovered new ideas that allow them

to work more advantageously and effectively with their regulators and regulatory institutions, so as to become trusted by regulatory actors to have the public's best interests in mind.

6   To more effectively and efficiently implement the latest regulatory concepts, policies, practices, tools, and techniques.

DEVELOPING RA STRATEGY

Non-market competition requires management decision-makers to develop PPE strategies (Lawton et al., 2014). Because most managers are involved in PPE issues on an episodic as opposed to continual basis, they should have a parsimonious framework for formulating good strategies; unfortunately, few frameworks exist for this task (Baron, 1995). This chapter's author has developed one that has been benchmarked from a

number of leading organizations over the last decade on several continents. The framework suggests that the process of developing non-market/PPE strategy is an ongoing and sequenced compilation of issues and stakeholder management practices (see Figure 27.4).

Each step is important in the process. Each one needs to be satisfactorily done or the entire process can lose efficacy. Items listed under each step are in no particular order and every item listed may not be relevant or essential to every individual project. This process requires the active support of relevant human, information, and technological resources in order to improve both the quality and quantity of inputs for intelligence processes. It can also be applied in doing a one-time assessment of an organization's PPE, recognizing that the assessor will sacrifice a degree of comprehensiveness in taking a snapshot instead of viewing the motion picture.

Figure 27.4   Generic process for developing regulatory strategy

Preparatory step - Regulatory scanning and monitoring

a. Scan and monitor regulatory information sources – objective is to identify potential, emerging, or existing issues that could result in public policy or regulatory action affecting the firm.
    •   Internal stakeholder data – all relevant employees, shareholders, retirees
    •   External stakeholder data
        — Government at all levels, especially regulatory institutions, actors, and interests
        — Interest groups, shadow constituencies, activists
        — Media – both news and social media outlets
        — Public and other business stakeholders (including industry peers/rivals).

b. Forecast PPE trends and events.
    •   Trends – descriptions of social, technological, environmental, economic, or political/legal/regulatory (STEEP) movements over time
    •   Events – developments that change the future when they occur.

c. Define issues as controversies or disputes between the organization and stakeholders. The definition may only be an approximation (especially if issue is in an early stage of its life cycle) and redefinition may be necessary as the character of an issue evolves.

d. Perform preliminary assessment.
    •   Review current set of PPE and market-related objectives
    •   Objective: determine which few of the many issues are or are likely to be relevant
    •   The set of potentially important issues are eventually subjected to further tracking
    •   This assessment is subject to be altered as more information is gathered and the issues shift; over time, it is usually necessary to change the set of issues being tracked.

e. Identify the set of most significant issues that require further analysis.

f. Categorize and prioritize issues (use matrices).
    •   Combination of previous criteria + weighting system.

Step 1 – Issue definition and categorization

Write issue briefs for those issues prioritized as most significant – this includes a two page or less sized document summarizing the issue for management consideration. A useful issue brief will include a statement of the focus of the issue, a discussion of its background, a description of the trends, driving forces, and stakeholders associated with the issue, and a short note on the interaction of the issue with other issues on an organization's issue agenda. Place issue briefs in storage and retrieval system.

Step 2 – Issue attribute assessments

It is helpful to use multiple attribute classificatory techniques on each significant issue being considered.

a. Assess scope of issue
  - Institutional arena(s)
    - — Regulatory commissions/administrative agencies
    - — Courts (at multiple levels)
    - — Legislatures
    - — Executive departments/branch
  - Evolutionary scope (uses issue life cycle concepts)
    - — Formative stage/changing expectations
    - — Political stage
    - — Legislative/regulatory stage
    - — Judicial/litigation stage
  - Geographic scope
    - — Global, international, multinational, federal, provincial, regional, municipal, local, etc.

b. Assess issue urgency [high <-- medium --> low]
  - Responsibility [yes <-- possibly --> no] – does the organization have a responsibility to participate in issue resolution?
  - Manageability [high <-- medium --> low] – can the organization influence the issue's evolution and/or resolution? (Universal – Advocacy – Selective – Technical)
  - Visibility [high <-- medium --> low] – is the issue and/or the organization's response highly visible?

c. Re-assess criticality of issue [high <-- medium --> low]
  - Current/estimated breadth of operations affected
  - Estimated financial implications
  - Estimated non-financial (safety, health, social, temporal, etc.) implications.

Step 3 – Stakeholder identification and prioritization (per issue)

a. List the stakeholders and describe critical assumptions
  - Nature of interests (benefits/costs – moral and distributive – of issue to them)
  - Nature of power (resources, abilities, geographic distribution, etc.)

b. Assess stakeholder attributes
  - Direction of source
  - Opinion
  - Degree of power/strength
  - Immediacy of effect
  - Scope of effect
  - Probability of resolution.

c. Prioritize stakeholders
  - Develop and agree upon criteria
  - Employ weighting system.

Step 4 – Issue alternative plan generation

a. Review data

b. Develop programmatic alternatives
  - Assess programs
    - — Consider alternative stakeholder postures, organizational credibility

Continued

— Determine likely stakeholder reactions
— Calculate resources and costs required for program implementation.

c. Evaluate potential performance impacts of alternative selected.

d. Establish/formulate strategy
- Specify position being taken
- Specify programmatic objectives
- Contingency objectives.

Step 5 – Implementation considerations

a. Timing
- Proactive <-- interactive – reactive --> inactive
- Immediate <-- short term – medium term --> long term.

b. Techniques
- Communication: advocacy advertising, annual report, press releases, media presentation, and video news releases
- Participation: lobbying/government relations, involvement in business/industry associations, constituency building, grassroots, political contributions, coalition building, electoral support, and testimony
- Compliance: change plans, negotiation, legal resistance, litigation, and other judicial strategies.

c. Vehicles
- Company lobbyist, contracted lobbyist, senior officer, grassroots
- Peak association, trade association, industry association, professional association, ad hoc coalition.

d. Style
- Confront <-- neutral --> conciliate
- Resist <-- bargain – capitulate – terminate --> cessate.

e. Contingency possibilities.

BASIC INTELLIGENCE ACTIVITIES IN RA

A particular type of competitive intelligence, RACI, refers to the processes used for the development of actionable information through legal and ethical means about the regulatory environment that could affect a company's competitive position. RACI emphasizes the development of intelligence on regulatory institutions, processes, stakeholders, and issues that affect an organization's competitiveness. It also refers to the scanning and monitoring of the regulatory environment for opportunities to mold and shape future regulation, guidance, and policy. Actionable information means explicit recommendations communicated to decision-makers as to how an organization should respond to analyses, observations, and conclusions generated about regulatory opportunities and threats. RA professionals are

responsible for providing this intelligence to executives, but it is the executives that must make the judgements as to the RA's value.

There are a variety of activities conducted by RA practitioners in developing intelligence. These include but are not limited to the following 10 essential RACI tasks:

1 To analyze relevant intelligence findings in the context of current project activities and communicate the impact to facilitate awareness of business critical issues.
2 To catalyze and manage human intelligence, as well as RA subject matter expert (SME) networks.
3 To collect expert opinions and advice from RA officials, planning, policy, and strategy colleagues and disseminate it to key stakeholders.
4 To conduct intelligence processes and communicate product specific information to regulatory (product) teams where requested.
5 To develop effective and systematic approaches to RA data and information, and report activities.
6 To organize, facilitate collection, and submit comments on regulatory agency guidance.

7   To produce intelligence reports and product/project status reports for distribution capturing internal and external regulatory information.
8   To provide support to regulatory policy activities through research, data, and information assimilation.
9   To scan, monitor, and track key developments from regulatory authorities, special interest groups, trade associations, and other external stakeholders relevant to regulatory activities.
10 To support internal groups and/or functions through collaboration or collection and distribution of specific RA information.

As in most staff areas, organizations usually need much more (regulatory) information than can be obtained with available intelligence resources. RA activities can generally be organized using the traditional intelligence process 'wheel' involving planning, data collection, analysis, and evaluation/control. This section will particularly focus on the wheel's use in developing RACI.

Planning

The RA planning effort generally begins with an effort to identify regulatory intelligence topics, establishing objectives, defining actions, and identifying and deploying resources to address regulatory and top executives' (that is, user's) critical intelligence needs. Among the most critical tasks for those organizing a regulatory strategy effort is to define the *business issues* and *opportunities* the RACI team will address. This definition is usually constructed by surveying senior decision-makers as to their priorities and by carefully reviewing the organization's strategic plan and strategy. Questions to be asked here include the following: What kind of intelligence is expected and for whom? How will these individuals utilize the RACI? When do they need it? In what form can they best use it?

Setting objectives is also an integral activity performed during the planning stage. Robert Galvin (1992), head of Motorola, addresses the use of RACI in shaping Motorola's market environment as 'writing the rules of the game'. He stated:

> The first step in any defined strategy is writing the rules of the game honorably and fairly in a manner that gives everyone a chance with predictable rules. Our company has started industries. We have helped write standards. We have helped write trade rules. We have helped influence policies. We have helped write national laws of countries where we have engaged, always in a respectful way. We have never taken for granted that the rules of the game would just evolve in a fashion that would make for the greatest opportunity. With the right rules of the game, one's opportunity for success is enhanced.

The first and arguably most critical question that should be asked of any RACI effort is what is it that the organization hopes to achieve vis-à-vis the regulatory and larger PPE? Several objectives form the basic justification for RACI activities in business, including:

- *To identify new product and market opportunities* that may be available in the regulatory environment.
- *To provide early warning* of regulatory developments or stakeholder activities that represent potential business threats or opportunities.
- *To evaluate issue prospects* created within regulatory institutions in time to permit appropriate, enlightened, and realistic organizational responses.
- *To anticipate and understand policy-related shifts or trends* as the preparation for organizational planning and strategy development.

Others in use by organizations that could readily be added include: to successfully impact the outcome of issues that have the greatest impact on customer satisfaction, employee motivation and satisfaction, market share, and returns at all governmental levels; to make use of all available government assistance; to be perceived as a 'good corporate citizen'; and to give the highest corporate priority to environmental and public concerns.

As always, there are a number of key implementation issues that need to be considered during the planning or design stage. Some key RACI success factors to consider are: nurturing relevant internal executive clients by ensuring their support and understanding their RA needs; integrating the program with other organizational units to leverage the existing infrastructure; staying visible and bootstrapping resources; keeping the program lean and focused; ensuring that the program is self-funded if possible; delivering actionable products that provide value to clients; keeping the recipients in the feedback–feedforward loop; making ongoing enhancements to the effort's capabilities; and maintaining credibility.

Data Collection

At this stage, the RACI manager needs to determine answers to the following questions: (1) 'What are the available methods of data collection?' and (2) 'How do I choose the methods given the assignment?' Data collection involves legal and ethical activities to gather, screen, and organize raw data and processed information relevant to the regulatory needs being addressed or to overall organizational interests. The ethical component of RACI is critically important because its continuance in most advanced countries is predicated on the protection and maintenance of democratic principles; therefore, the regulatory area is one that receives particularly thorough decision-making scrutiny and regulation. Data collection tends to take on one of two primary formats: (1) ongoing, as is often the case with regulatory monitoring programs; or (2) it is targeted to acquire specific data.

RA collection mechanisms typically involve technical and human methods. Technology collection involves the use of digitized database applications and systems for scanning and monitoring such as those provided through online search and specialized RA solutions (Karami, 2012). Social media has gained in importance in recent years, and many countries have added easier access to their regulatory institutions and agencies to promote efficient communication. There are also specific on-line sources used specifically for RACI such as those provided by the agencies themselves and topically specialized publishers.

Human sources and methods (aka, HUMINT), those involving face-to-face communication, are a primary currency of RACI, public, and government affairs staff members. They involve networking with stakeholders and organizational colleagues, attending committee meetings and hearings, and interviewing issue and regulatory experts among other related activities. Most frequently, data collection will occur through the connections established between the organization's (either business or association) regulatory, public, or government affairs staff members, lobbyists, and the individuals comprising their personal networks. This can be especially helpful as many organizational members come from recent political or governmental positions and know the key players and pathways involved in navigating policy through the public decision-making and regulatory institutions.

Data gathering methods must always be documentable and reproducible for them to serve RACI effectively. Regulatory information is obtained through reliable sources and extracted fact-based primary information. Regulatory information types include: ad-hoc health authority queries (such as those filed in the US through Freedom of Information Act requests), advisory meetings, approvals, authority alerts and websites, laws, regulations, guidance, (public) regulatory databases, and regulatory news.

For accuracy and analytic integrity purposes, published data must always have official citation and reference sources cited. This becomes even more important as RA practitioners move into the next stage of RACI processing.

Analysis

Analysis, where the analyst attempts to draw conclusions or insights from the collected data, is generally viewed to be the most difficult and potentially the highest value-adding RACI process stage. It is accomplished by applying known methods and concepts to the data and sorting through what was collected for relevance. The area of public policy and regulatory environment analysis for managerial purposes is one that is generally deficient in terms of tool availability (Showalter and Fleisher, 2005). Some of the tools that are used in this stage are used specifically in RACI while others used are borrowed and adapted from several of the more traditional business or competitive analytic tool sets (Fleisher and Bensoussan, 2015).

An attempt has been made to classify the techniques according to the issues, stakeholder, and institutional approaches previously described. The approaches are classified by whether they are primarily focused on stakeholder data, issue data, institutional data, or a combination of two and three of these items. Each of these 40 plus approaches utilizes the data collected and attempts to deliver information and intelligence as an output. A reasonably comprehensive list of tools used in RACI is provided in Figure 27.5. It should be noted that not all companies in every industry will use all of these tools, but all of them can be and/or have been used at one time or another in the development of RACI or RA strategy.

Communicating RACI results and findings closes the loop between those who collect and analyze competitive information and those who use it to make decisions. Analyzed information must be disseminated via the appropriate means to the appropriate parties that can use it in decision-making and then act upon these decisions. This is the point at which information begins to take the form of intelligence since it provides direction to the organization to help it compete more effectively. Successful RACI is applied to critical, strategic management decisions because it provides senior executives with implications and strategic alternatives that can be effectively integrated into the strategic management process.

Figure 27.5   Range of analytical tools[a] commonly used in RACI activities

Issue-focus	Institutional-focus	Stakeholder-focus	Multiple-focus
• Crisis assessment and simulation	• Compliance analysis	• Assumption surfacing and testing	• Benchmarking
• Critical success factors	• Disruption analysis	• Audience analysis	• Communications mix assessment
• Issue mapping and analysis	• Early warnings	• Coalition/alliance mapping and analysis	• Comprehensive impact assessment
• Political and social risk analysis	• Industry evolution analysis	• Ethical analysis	• Cost/benefit analysis (issue, regulatory, social, stakeholder)
• Policy analysis	• Industry structure analysis	• Focus groups	• Futures
• Risk analysis	• Innovation analysis	• Hierarchy of effects modeling	• Geo-locational risk assessment
• Sensitivity analysis	• Institutional evolution analysis	• Interest group capability and resources analysis	• Life-cycle analysis (policy agenda, product/PLM)
• Simulations	• Institutional structure analysis	• Public opinion research	• Macro-environment (STEEP) analysis
	• Market analysis	• Reputational and social performance analysis	• Media (+social) content analysis
	• Mergers and acquisitions analysis	• Shadowing	• Regulatory impact analysis
	• Portfolio/pipeline analysis	• Social network and contacts analysis	• Scenario analysis
	• Regulatory rules analysis	• Stakeholder analysis or profiling	• Situation analysis
		• Value analysis	

[a] Some degree of overlap exists among a number/some of the tools listed above. Where the overlap among categories is heaviest or most frequent, the tools have been listed in the last column called combination focus. Otherwise, the tools are primarily focused on either one of issues, institution, or stakeholder-based data.

Evaluation/control

Last but not least, the entire program or effort must be assessed. There are three broad approaches to evaluating RACI: (1) the audit approach; (2) the analytic approach; and (3) the utility approach. The audit approach focuses on a systematic review of the outcomes of each RACI process stage and is conducted using (a) key indicator/indices, (b) service-oriented user reaction measures, or (c) a comprehensive Malcolm Baldrige National Quality Award-like instrument. The analytic approach attempts to apply the scientific method to RACI assessment either through experimental design, whereby the examiner assesses the effects of RACI 'treatments', or through recommendations on organizational outcomes. The objective of these approaches is to determine whether or not the introduction of RACI has the desired effects on relevant organizational outcomes. The last approach attempts to evaluate the dollar value of outcomes against the cost of producing them. A variant of this approach, the dollar criterion method, tries to estimate the financial impact of factors such as improved reputation, decreased stakeholder pressure, and legislative victories.

Implementing a RACI approach takes considerable effort and time, especially for organizations that lack institutional memory in RA. Nevertheless, there are several key steps that are almost always associated with implementing successful programs, including: establishing context, ensuring senior executive support, selecting a team and champion, conducting needs assessment, establishing a structure, involving key users, educating and involving employees, establishing a storage and retrieval system, and evaluating the process.

RACI AND ITS LINK TO KEY ORGANIZATIONAL PROCESSES

One of the most difficult connections to make is that between RACI and organizational outcomes. It can also be difficult to establish a clear association between most public policy-oriented activities and the bottom line (Fleisher, 1997). These two factors suggest that making the connection between RACI and organizational outcomes may be difficult; however, there are a number of reasonably tight connections that can be drawn through carefully planned and implemented research of the effect RACI may have on critical organizational processes. For example, it is reasonable to suggest that the effective performance of RACI should impact the following organizational processes:

- Change agentry: through effective RACI, organizational and environmental change can be eased, smooth transitions promoted, and affected stakeholders reassured.
- Crisis avoidance: Through study or issues and stakeholder positions, RACI can protect a favorable organizational position, minimize the erosion of a favorable position, retain allied stakeholders, and maintain normalized operations in difficult times.
- Decision-makers' awareness: Through RACI, senior decision-makers are counseled, using research and analyses, about what's happening in the regulatory environment, allowing them to make better informed decisions
- Issue anticipation: Through research and stakeholder liaison, RACI can provide distant early warning of social and political change and trends.
- Opportunity and threat detection: Through regular stakeholder interaction in generating RACI, new markets, products, allies, and positive issues can be uncovered and sociopolitical barriers removed.
- Social performance: Through research into stakeholder positions vis-à-vis issues, RACI can help to 'create reputation', and enhance economic success through earning the trust of key regulatory stakeholders that can influence the market.
- Stakeholder and institutional awareness: Through stakeholder and institutional targeting, RACI can pave the way for sales, fundraising, stock offerings, etc.

CONCLUSION

The central purpose of this chapter has been to provide PA professionals with a means to recognize their ability to provide value to executives and their organizations through their efforts as applied to the regulatory environment. A secondary purpose has been to give individuals already working on regulatory issues a sense of how their efforts can fit within the organization's intelligence and broader strategy processes. It is the author's view that this intersection remains mostly unexploited by companies and that the successful application and institutionalization of RACI can help companies achieve new, and often asymmetric, marketplace and sociopolitical advantages.

ACKNOWLEDGMENTS

The author wishes to thank his colleague Jim Miller of jamesfmiller.com, a long-time Canadian participant in and observer of public policy processes, for several helpful comments of this chapter.

REFERENCES

Baker, D. 2015. Uber's problems are real, and the regulatory solutions are simple. *The Conversation*, February 24, accessed June 20, 2015 from: http://www.cato-unbound.org/2015/02/24/dean-baker/ubers-problems-are-real-regulatory-solutions-are-simple.

Baron, D.P. 1995. The nonmarket strategy system. *MIT Sloan Management Review*, Fall accessed June 20, 2015 from: http://sloanreview.mit.edu/article/the-nonmarket-strategy-system/.

Besley, T. 2015. Law, regulation, and the business climate: The nature and influence of the World Bank Doing Business Project. *The Journal of Economic Perspectives*, vol. 29(3), Summer, pp. 99–120.

Bogardus, K. 2015. Effort to cut 'red tape' triggers lobbying battle in Senate. *E&E Daily*, May 22, accessed June 20, 2016 from: http://www.eenews.net/stories/1060019013.

Brooks, C. 2015. 10 regulatory changes that could affect your business this year. *Business News Daily*, January 15, accessed March 16, 2015 from: http://www.businesnewsdaily.com/7671-regulatory-isues-changes.html.

Davis, M. 2011. Government regulations: Do they help business? Accessed June 16, 2015 from: http://www.investopedia.com/articles/economics/11/government-regulations.asp.

Dollinger, M.J. 2015. An interview with Kerry Tassopoulos, Vice President–Public Affairs, Risk Management and Compliance at Mary Kay Inc. *Business Horizons*, vol. 58(5), September, pp. 581–588.

Drum, K. 2011. Corporations hate regulation, until they love it. *Mother Jones,* November 11, accessed July 1, 2016 from: http://www.motherjones.com/kevin-drum/2011/11/why-businesses-love-regulatory-complexity.

Federal Register. 2011. A guide to the rulemaking process. Accessed June 25, 2015 from: https://www.federalregister.gov/uploads/2011/01/the_rulemaking_process.pdf.

Fiegerman, S. 2015. The man who saved Uber in New York is looking for new start ups. Accessed August 5, 2015 from: http://mashable.com/2015/08/04/uber-regulatory-consulting/.

Fleisher, C.S. 1997. *Assessing, Measuring and Managing Public Affairs Performance*. Washington, DC: Public Affairs Council.

Fleisher, C.S. 2005. The global development of public affairs, pp. 5–30 in Harris, P. and Fleisher, C.S. (eds), *The Handbook of Public Affairs*. London, UK: Sage Publications.

Fleisher, C.S. 2016. Seeing the future – as clear as the cross-eyed javelin thrower? January 4, accessed June 15, 2016 from: https://www.linkedin.com/pulse/seeing-future-clear-cross-eyed-javelin-thrower-craig-s-fleisher.

Fleisher, C.S. and Bensoussan, B. 2015. *Business and Competitive Analysis: Effective Application of New and Classic Methods*. 2 ed. Upper Saddle River, NJ: Pearson.

Galvin, R. 1992. International business and the changing nature of global competition. Public speech given in October at Miami University, Oxford, OH.

Griffin, J., Fleisher, C., Brenner, S. and J. Boddewyn, 2001a. Corporate public affairs research: A chronological reference list: Part 1

1985–2000. *Journal of Public Affairs*, vol. 1(1), pp. 9–32.

Griffin, J., Fleisher, C., Brenner, S. and J. Boddewyn, 2001b. Corporate public affairs research: A chronological reference list: Part 2 1958–1984. *Journal of Public Affairs*, vol. 1(2), pp. 167–186.

Holburn, G.L. 2012. Assessing and managing regulatory risk in renewable energy: Contrasts between Canada and the United States. *Energy Policy*, vol. 45, pp. 654–665.

Hu, E. 2014. Uber's rapid growth pits innovation against existing laws. Article written on June 12 for National Public Radio, accessed June 18, 2015 from: http://www.npr.org/sections/alltechconsidered/2014/06/12/321008384/ubers-rapid-growth-pits-innovation-against-existing-laws.

Karami, A. 2012. An investigation on environmental scanning and growth strategy in high tech small and medium sized enterprises. *New Technology-Based Firms in the New Millennium*, vol. 9, pp. 99–108 in Groen, A., Oakey, R., Van Der Sijde, P., and Cook, G. (eds). Bingley, UK: Emerald Group Publishing.

Keim, G. 2005. Managing business political advocacy in the United States: Opportunities for improved effectiveness, pp. 418–433 in Harris, P. and Fleisher, C.S. (eds), *The Handbook of Public Affairs*. London, UK: Sage Publications.

Lawton, T., Doh, J. and Rajwani, T. 2014. *Aligning for Advantage*. Oxford, UK: Oxford University Press.

Lawton, T., Rajwani, T. and Doh, J. 2013. The antecedents of political capabilities: A study of ownership, cross-border activity and organization at legacy airlines in a deregulatory context. *International Business Review*, vol. 22(1), pp. 228–242.

Levi-Faur, D. 2011. Regulation and regulatory governance, ch. 1 in Levi-Faur, D. (ed.), *Handbook on the Politics of Regulation*. Cheltenham, UK: Edward Elgar Publishing.

National Association of Manufacturing. 2014. Executive Summary: The cost of federal regulation to the US economy, manufacturing and small business. Accessed June 25, 2015 from: http://www.nam.org/Data-and-Reports/Cost-of-Federal-Regulations/Federal-Regulation-Executive-Summary.pdf.

Oberman, W. 2005. The external environment of public affairs in North America: Public policy process and institutions, pp. 56–70 in Harris, P. and Fleisher, C.S. (eds), *The Handbook of Public Affairs*. London, UK: Sage Publications.

Preston, L.E. and Post, J.E. 1975. *Private Management and Public Policy*. Upper Saddle River, NJ: Prentice-Hall.

Showalter, A. and Fleisher, C.S. 2005. The tools and techniques of public affairs, pp. 109–122 in Harris, P. and Fleisher, C.S. (eds), *The Handbook of Public Affairs*. London, UK: Sage Publications.

Sparrow, M.K. 2011. *The Regulatory Craft: Controlling Risks, Solving Problems, and Managing Compliance*. Washington, DC: Brookings Institution Press.

Yarbrough, C. 2013. Why regulatory intelligence is more important than ever. Accessed June 23, 2015 from: http://www.pharmaceuticalonline.com/doc/why-regulatory-intelligence-is-more-important-than-ever-0001.

Influencing the Legal and Judicial Process

John M. Holcomb

INTRODUCTION

The stake of business in judicial decisions is greater than ever. Civil and criminal settlements involving corporations are reaching new heights, and government regulation continues to grow, with controversial and recent laws like the Dodd–Frank Act having been passed. Further, Congress seems often to be paralyzed in partisan logjams, and access to the executive branch is limited. Hence, more policy is determined by court cases, and business accomplishes little of real substance through its traditional lobbying of the other two branches of government.

In examining the growing necessity and opportunities to influence the US legal and judicial process, this chapter will focus particularly on the following avenues of influence: selection and election of judges, educating judges through support of think tanks, supporting the efforts of legal foundations, filing amicus curiae briefs, cooperating with the efforts of the US Chamber Litigation Center and elite appellate law firms, and focusing on big cases with major impacts on business and the economic system.

INFLUENCING JUDICIAL SELECTION

Influencing the selection of judges is an extremely important aspect of influencing the entire legal and judicial process. At the federal level in the US, the president appoints members of the federal judiciary, with the advice and consent of the Senate. At the state level, at least in 39 states, judges are elected. The tactics used to influence judicial selection depend on the selection system used. At the federal level, interest groups and corporations lobby the executive and legislative branches on judicial appointments and rate the appointees from their various perspectives. They can also make philanthropic contributions to organizations like the Federalist Society, which cultivate future candidates for the bench. At the state level, where elections are used, interest groups and corporations can make financial contributions in judicial elections.

Were judges appointed based only on objective criteria of merit, interest groups would have less incentive to try to influence the composition of the federal and state judicial branches. The effort to influence judicial appointments is based on the theory of legal realism, which holds that judicial decisions are based not just on the facts and the law as objectively viewed, but also based on the values and ideologies of the various judges.[1] That view conflicts with the assumption of the 'cult of the robe', that judges strip themselves of their biases when cloaked in the black robes, but the extensive literature on legal realism and judicial decision-making belies that assumption (Rowland and Carp, 1996; Segal and Spaeth, 1993, 2002). As corroborating evidence, studies of appellate court decisions demonstrate that judges and justices often vote together in blocks based on their common views and ideologies. For instance, scholars and court-watchers refer to the liberal and conservative wings of the US Supreme Court, and studies of voting patterns after each term of the Court examine how the two wings of the court often align against each other on critical decisions (Ciocchetti, 2013; Greenhouse, 2015; Liptak, 2015; Nyhan, 2015; Parlapiano et al., 2015).

Based on the premise of legal realism and the fact that judicial values do matter, business and other interest groups closely scrutinize the values of federal court nominees and take positions on their nomination. Those values are also easier to ascertain now than they have been in the past. While historically Supreme Court justices came from a variety of backgrounds, including elected political offices, current members of the Court all have experience as appellate court judges, with known voting records (Howard, 2015). While the Senate Judiciary

Committee cannot ask appointees how they would vote on any particular case or issue, committee members can probe their opinions on previous lower court cases. Likewise, business and other interest groups can infer the predisposition of Court appointees from their previous opinions, in deciding whether to support or oppose a nominee. Moreover, the president can appoint judges based on the same revealing information. Among all the variables affecting how a judge will vote on major issues, studies demonstrate that whether a Republican or Democratic president appointed a judge is the most important factor (Rowland and Carp, 1996).

A study of every member of the Supreme Court since 1946 is revealing:

> Justices appointed by Republican Presidents are on average considerably more likely to favor business than Democratic appointees. ... Republican Presidents appointed 13 of the 15 Justices most favorable to business, ... and Democratic Presidents appointed 13 of the 15 least business-friendly Justices, Brennan and Warren being the two Justices in this group who were appointed by a Republican President. On the current Court, no Justice appointed by a Republican President is less favorable to business than any Justice appointed by a Democratic President. (Epstein et al., 2013)

While Republican nominees to the highest Court have not always behaved as predicted, with Justices Harry Blackmon and David Souter being leading examples, most Justices appointed by George W. Bush and Barack Obama have behaved as each president would have hoped.

That same study found that the Roberts Court has been more friendly to business than either the preceding Burger or Rehnquist Courts, and far more friendly than the liberal Warren Court, even though the Court did turn right during the era of the Rehnquist Court (Savage, 1992) and then more so during the Roberts Court (Coyle, 2013). In fact, five of the 10 Justices most friendly to business since 1946 are currently serving on the Court, and that includes the two most pro-business Justices over that era

(Epstein et al., 2013). Another study, focusing on the 2011–12 term of the Court found the Justices taking a pro-business stance in key decisions (Ciocchetti, 2013). The major findings of the study are:

1 The Court's opinions came out strongly on the side of business with business interests receiving sixty-one out of seventy potential votes. This resulted in an eighty-seven percent success rate for business interests over the course of the Term. This high percentage is different from the previous Term at the Roberts Court where the Justices unanimously voted against business interests in a handful of cases.

2 These pro-business decisions did not occur in ordinary, run of the mill cases. Instead, the impact of these decisions is magnified because they each involved topics critical to America's economic recovery.

3 Perhaps surprisingly, the Court's liberal-leaning Justices voted with the Court's conservatives twenty-three out of a possible thirty-one opportunities – or seventy-four percent of the time – in the significant business impact cases. They did so in disputes that presented compelling arguments from both a conservative and liberal perspective and where such facts allowed for a strong four-Justice dissent. Such a split, however, occurred only once in the cases considered in the tally.

4 The Court was willing to both narrow and expand constitutional provisions/amendments and state/federal statutes to reach its desired result. There appeared to be no concerted effort to adhere to a minimalist or living Constitutionalist philosophy – at least in these significant business impact cases. (Ciocchetti, 2013)

The 2014–15 term of the Court, however, turned in a leftward direction (Parlapiano et al., 2015). That may turn out to be an aberration from long-term trends, however, and based on the nature of cases decided during that term.

Interest groups, including business, have been much more diligent in probing the records of Supreme Court nominees, and supporting or opposing them, since 1987, when President Reagan appointed Robert Bork to the Court, and the Senate denied him confirmation by a vote of 58–42 (Holyoke, 2014; Savelieff, 2012). There were 145 groups that lobbied on the Bork nomination, most of them opposing his confirmation (DeGregorio and Rossotti, 1995), including the National Education Association (NEA), American Civil Liberties Union (ACLU), Alliance for Justice, and People for the American Way, as well as feminist organizations (Banks and O'Brien, 2016; Holyoke, 2014; Howard, 2015). 'To Bork' a nominee, meaning to successfully disparage a nominee, has now entered the political lexicon as a verb, and Supreme Court nominations became more contentious ideological battles after Bork was denied confirmation. Since the battle over Bork, interest groups have closely scrutinized the records of nominees, with 81 groups having lobbied on the appointment of Clarence Thomas to the Court (Caldeira et al., 2000). The Alliance for Justice on the left, and the US Chamber Litigation Center on the right, each pour through the records, testimony, and voting patterns of judicial nominees to determine whether they should support or oppose those appointments (Danelski, 1990; Watson and Stookey, 1988).

ELECTION OF STATE JUDGES

Interest groups have even more directly influenced the election of state judges by making political contributions to their election campaigns. While 39 states have elected judges, the system is fraught with ethical and legal concerns (Gaylord, 2012; Geyh, 2012). Since judicial independence is the hallmark of the system, with it being more important for judges than for legislators and executive officials to exercise independent judgment, gaining influence with judges through political contributions could easily jeopardize independence and bias a judge toward a party in a case. While a system of elected judges therefore has many critics, its proponents claim that elections actually foster more independence, especially from the partisan influence of governors who might otherwise appoint them (Bonneau and Hall, 2009; Shugerman, 2012; Tarr, 2012). In order to mitigate that type of influence, most states with appointed systems have adopted the Missouri Plan, which creates a commission of experts to recommend a slate of candidates, from which the governor must then make the ultimate appointment. On a general level, business has supported the Missouri Plan, as opposed to judicial elections.

While proponents of judicial elections have to deal with criticisms related to sacrificing judicial independence, they maintain that elections do better serve the value of accountability. Whether judges should be accountable to the electorate, however, is another question. Based again on the premise of legal realism and on the view that courts do indeed make public policy, election advocates argue that courts should therefore be directly accountable to the electorate (Carrington, 1998). Meanwhile, others argue that courts serve as a check and balance on the elected branches of government and exist partially to protect minority rights against the 'tyranny of the majority'. Hence, accountability is far less important for the judicial branch, with judicial independence being of far higher value (Dinan, 2013; Gaylord, 2012; Geyh, 2012). One's view of the nature of the judicial process will determine where one stands on the trade-off between independence and accountability.

Whatever the merits or weaknesses of a system based on judicial elections, it is the system in place in 39 states, which returns us to the ethical and legal problems confronting contributors and other players. In states with judicial elections, the US Supreme Court has ruled in *Republican Party of Minnesota v. White*, 536 US 765 (2002) that judicial candidates are free to announce their positions on political and social issues, but also ruled in *Williams-Yulee v. Florida Bar*, 575 US 135 S.Ct. 1656 (2015) that a state prohibition against personal solicitation of campaign contributions by judicial candidates is constitutional. In the latter case, the compelling government interest in protecting the independence of the judiciary overrides any First Amendment interest of the judicial candidates.

The most important case related to the interests and freedom of corporate contributors is *Caperton v. A.T. Massey Coal Co.*, 556 US 868 (2009). With a US$50 million jury verdict being appealed to the West Virginia Supreme Court, Massey Chief Executive Officer (CEO) Donald Blankenship contributed US$3 million to the electoral campaign of his favored judicial candidate, Justice Benjamin, who won the election. Once on the court, Benjamin then voted to overturn the jury verdict in a 3–2 decision, thereby casting a deciding vote in the case. In the *Caperton* case, the Supreme Court overturned that decision and ruled that Justice Benjamin's participation in the case violated due process and that his recusal from voting would have been mandatory (Gibson and Caldeira, 2012; Howell, 2012). Based on this case, corporations or corporate officials should exercise restraint in the amount contributed to judicial elections, even when they are allowed by state law to contribute, so as not to provoke due process challenges. Further, aggressive political action, especially when connected to a case involving serious criminal charges, can create substantial reputational damage, as in the *Caperton* case.

Other examples also speak loudly. In Illinois in 2004, a judicial candidate won a US$9.3 million campaign for a spot on the state supreme court with US$350,000 in contributions from those affiliated with State Farm Insurance Company, and the judge went on to vote with State Farm in a US$1 billion national class action case (Chemerinsky et al., 2012). There was also an immediate payoff for Philip Morris, as the court overturned a US$10 billion punitive damages award against the company (Katz, 2015). A meta-analysis of several studies, and other references to those studies, have found a high correlation between judges who have received large contributions from businesses and law firms and then voted with those interests in subsequent litigation (Abramovsky, 2012; Goodman, 2012). Other political groups like the ACLU, National Association for the Advancement of Colored People (NAACP), and the National Rifle Association also attempt to influence judicial elections, but without the level of contributions that business can make (Gibson and Caldeira, 2013). Some critics believe such activity threatens the legitimacy of the courts (Brandenburg and Schotland, 2008; Gibson et al., 2011).

The most prominent business organization involved in funding state judicial elections is the Institute for Legal Reform, founded in 1998 as an operation of the US Chamber of Commerce. In 2004, the Institute won 12 of the 13 state judicial elections it had funded, and by then had spent more than US$144 million on such races, with a success rate of 80 percent (Katz, 2015). Original corporate sponsors of the Institute included Home Depot, State Farm, and AIG from the insurance industry; GM, Toyota, and Ford from the auto industry; Walmart and other retailers; and FedEx and Johnson & Johnson (Katz, 2015). In the year 2000 elections, the Institute targeted races in Ohio, Alabama, Indiana, Michigan, and Mississippi and won 12 of the 15 elections in which it had endorsed a judicial candidate or candidate for attorney general. State Farm's CEO and AIG's CEO Maurice Greenberg sat on the board of the Institute, which worked in tandem with the Law Enforcement Alliance of America in 'realigning the courts' (Katz, 2015).

Participation in a questionable and controversial system, such as judicial elections, also raises further questions for business organizations to consider. Corporations may be propping up a system that they otherwise oppose in concept. They might argue that they are just playing by the rules of the game, even if they believe the rules are wrong, but that may not be a satisfactory answer to corporate critics and to critics of the system of elected judges. One judicial ethicist even makes a case for the unconstitutionality of state judicial elections

(Freedman, 2013). While the Zecklin Center for Political Accountability at the Wharton School of Finance ranks corporations based on their disclosure of political activities, singling out expenditures on congressional races, it has not yet focused on expenditures on judicial races (CPA, 2014). That may be a next logical step for some rating organization to take, in which case companies like Massey Energy would not fare well.

Almost as problematic as contributions to state judicial elections are contributions to races for state attorney general positions, since the latter are also key actors in the administration of justice and should act with a high level of independence and integrity, avoiding any political cronyism. Scandals have touched the conduct of several attorneys general, based on their decisions in favor of well-connected contributors (Edmonds, 2014). An investigative report by *The New York Times*, based on 6,000 emails, found that lobbyists and lawyers used campaign contributions to push state attorney generals to 'drop investigations, change policies, negotiate favorable settlements, or pressure federal regulators'. The influence is more pernicious as the authority of state attorneys general has expanded to include multistate investigations of securities fraud and internet crimes (Lipton, 2014). There is even an organization called SAGE (Society of Attorneys General Emeritus), most of whose members lobby current attorneys general on behalf of corporate clients. Those clients include Devon Energy, Southern Company of Georgia, TransCanada, Bank of America, T-Mobile, Comcast, and Pfizer (Lipton, 2014a). Meanwhile, other former attorneys general now functioning as trial lawyers are coaxing their former peers to sue corporations for various abuses, with the trial lawyers doing the legal work and reaping substantial contingency fees while the states also collect handsome damages (Lipton, 2014b). The Chamber's Institute for Legal Reform has also been heavily involved in defeating candidates for attorney general viewed as unfavorable to business interests (Katz, 2015).

EDUCATING JUDGES

Corporations indirectly influence the legal and judicial process through support for programs that educate present or future judges. That training may not strive for objectivity but shares a perspective that may hopefully encourage judges to decide cases in a way that is helpful to business. The Law and Economics Center (LEC), founded by Henry Manne at the University of Miami, created the first educational program, for federal and state judges. The Center has since moved its operations, first to Emory University and now to George Mason University. The Mason Judicial Education Program sponsors an Economics Institute for Judges. Its approach is based on the Chicago school of economics, which emphasizes efficiency, and its programs provide training in basic and applied economics for federal and state judges. As one authority on law and economics states:

> Law and Economics gave conservative lawyers and, especially, legal academics a solid ideological and analytical foundation. Its reputation has risen, partly through the remarkable efforts of Judge Richard A. Posner, from eccentric to still controversial but unquestionably respectable. (Lowenstein, 2008)

The LEC's efforts are based on the likely valid assumption that many judges need a more solid foundation in microeconomics for their decisions. Undoubtedly, many business organizations would agree and therefore applaud and support the center's efforts. For that reason, several major corporations give financial support to the Center. For 2014–15, over 30 corporations made donations, including Altria, AT&T, Dow Chemical, ExxonMobil, General Electric, Ford Motor Company, Google, Johnson & Johnson, Merck, Qualcomm, Valero Energy, State Farm, and Visa. All of the foregoing would be considered corporations with sophisticated and highly visible public affairs operations.

Liberal critics, however, fear that education grounded in the Chicago school of economics will lead judges to render decisions friendly to business and more hostile to government regulation. The Center, however, states: 'For 38 years, the LEC has offered intellectually rigorous, balanced, and timely educational programs to the nation's judges and justices in the belief that the fundamental principles of a free and just society depend on a knowledgeable and well-educated judiciary' (http://www.masonlec.org, accessed on October 15, 2015).

Indeed, the Judicial Education Program has featured economists of various stripes in its programs over the years. Meanwhile, the Center still:

> recognizes that the US civil justice system imposes tremendous burdens on American businesses through high discovery costs, regulation through litigation, class action abuses, and litigation or the threat of litigation. Providing an unprecedented opportunity to improve the nation's judiciary, the JEP offers intense programs designed to build understanding of critical economic disciplines so that judges may apply this knowledge when assessing complex issues surrounding legal disputes. (http://www.masonlec.org, accessed on November 15, 2015)

That language would be music to the ears of business supporters and provides them the rationale to support the Center.

In earlier days, liberal groups raised questions about the tax-exempt status of the Center, and the tax deductibility of corporate donations to the Center, on the basis that such donations were not for a 'scientific, educational, or charitable' purpose, but to win more favorable treatment by the courts. That challenge was seen as specious, and business groups have never since had any legal concerns about donations to the Law and Economics Center (Houck, 1984).

Beyond support for the Law and Economics Center and its Economics Institute for Judges, corporations have also indirectly aided the cultivation of future legal and judicial talent by supporting the Federalist Society. As the

Society describes its role, 'the Society has created a conservative and libertarian intellectual network that extends to all levels of the legal community'. It notes that 'law schools and the legal profession are strongly dominated by a form of orthodox liberal ideology', and that 'it is founded on the principles that the state exists to preserve freedom, that the separation of governmental powers is central to our Constitution, and that it is emphatically the province and duty of the judiciary to say what the law is, not what it should be'. The Society has chapters at law schools throughout the country and lists the following business organizations among its donors: Koch Industries, Microsoft, Verizon, Lilly Endowment, Adolph Coors Foundation, BP America, Pfizer, ChevronTexaco, Chamber of Commerce, CME Group Foundation, Google, Aflac, Delta Airlines, ExxonMobil, Glaxo Smith Kline, Pepsi, Facebook, Devon Energy, and Hyundai America.

While the Law and Economics Center and the Federalist Society are appropriate vehicles for corporations to create a more favorable climate for business in the legal system, there are other think tanks that serve the same end and also defend the role and interests of business in the legal system (Pierson, 2015). Most prominent among them is the American Enterprise Institute for Public Policy Research (AEI), founded in 1938 as a small community of scholars, with a staff of 200. It enjoys the support of many corporate donors, and Daniel A. D'Aniello, one of the founders of the Carlyle Group, launched its Capital Campaign for Free Enterprise and American Progress with a US$20 million gift. The founders of Eagle Capital Management have endowed the Beth and Ravenel Curry Chair of Free Enterprise with a US$3 million grant, and State Farm Mutual Automobile Insurance Company has endowed the James Q. Wilson Chair in American Politics and Culture with another US$3 million grant. Peter Wallison, a prominent AEI fellow, was a leading dissenting member of the Financial Crisis Inquiry Commission and identified the policies of

Fannie Mae and Freddie Mac, not the policies of banks, as leading causes of the housing collapse. He has also been a major critic of the Dodd–Frank Law and has argued for its repeal (Wallison, 2015).

Libertarian policy think tanks such as the Cato Institute and the Competitive Enterprise Institute also actively promote free market positions in Congress and in the courts. They engage in a wide range of public policy research and litigation. The Cato Institute's priorities have included anti-tax and anti-regulatory positions, as well as support for privatizing public services, school choice, privatizing social security, legalizing gay marriage, and legalizing marijuana, along with opposition to campaign finance reform, donor disclosure, and the Dodd–Frank Act. Cato also submitted an amicus brief in favor of corporate free speech and against the campaign finance limits in the *Citizens United* case.

Cato was established with seed money from Koch Industries and the Koch family, though its financial base is now much more diverse (Stefancic and Delgado, 1996). According to http://www.sourcewatch.org/index.php/Cato_Institute, the following corporations have donated to Cato in the past, in spite of the think tank's pure libertarian position and opposition to corporate welfare: Altria, American Petroleum Institute, Amgen, Comcast, Consumer Electronic Association, Ebay, ExxomMobil, FedEx, General Motors, Honda North America, Microsoft, Pepco Holdings, R.J. Reynolds Tobacco Company, TimeWarner, Toyota, Verisign, Verizon, Visa, Volkswagen, and Wal-Mart.

The Competitive Enterprise Institute (CEI), founded in 1984, operates as both a think tank and advocacy group in favor of free market solutions to social and economic problems. It has lobbied and litigated against many environmental and consumer regulations and has been critical of fuel economy and climate change regulations. Similar to Cato, CEI is essentially a libertarian think tank. Though difficult to attract corporate support for some of its positions, it has enjoyed support from the Amoco Foundation, Coca-Cola, CSX Corporation, FMC, Ford Motor Company, General Motors, Philip Morris, Pfizer, ExxonMobil, and Texaco (http://www.sourcewatch.org/index.php/ Competitive_Enterprise_Institute).

SUPPORT FOR LEGAL FOUNDATIONS

An even more direct way to influence the legal and judicial process is through the support of legal foundations. The models of such legal foundations were provided by the NAACP Legal Defense Fund, which litigated major civil rights cases such as *Brown v. Board of Education* in the 1950s, along with the liberal public interest law movement of the 1960s, started with the strong support of the Ford Foundation. That era saw the creation of the National Women's Law Center and the Center for Law and Social Policy in Washington, D.C. as well as the rise of the Natural Resources Defense Council in New York, and the Environmental Defense Fund. Ralph Nader's Public Citizen Litigation Group, which addressed many consumer issues, was also a precursor to the later conservative legal foundations. Beyond the development of these specialized legal foundations that litigated on behalf of a variety of liberal causes, especially environmental protection, several lobbies and think tanks started their own legal foundations. The Sierra Club, for instance, has its own legal defense fund to litigate environmental issues on its agenda. The National Organization for Women (NOW) also has its own legal defense fund litigating women's issues.

Based on the influence of such legal foundations, the corporate community imitated that movement by launching its own network of conservative legal foundations in the 1970s (Teles, 2008). First among them, and still a prominent actor on the litigation scene, was the Pacific Legal Foundation (PLF), founded in 1973. It has operations in four states, as

well as the nation's capital, and litigates on such issues as civil rights, public lands and takings, endangered species, property rights, natural resources, economic liberties, and freedom of association. Twenty percent of PLF's budget has come from corporate donations, and its earliest supporters included west coast utilities such as Pacific Gas & Electric Company and Southern California Gas & Electric Company.

Similar litigation foundations later formed in other regions of the country. The Mountain States Legal Foundation organized in 1977 and has been heavily involved in natural resource and public lands issues, as well as property rights and gun ownership. Seventy percent of its budget is devoted to litigation, and its litigation committee has legal representatives from every western state. Energy companies are heavily represented on its board of trustees and presumably among its donors as well.

Other conservative legal foundations that emerged in the 1970s include the Center for Individual Rights, the Center for Equal Opportunity, the American Center for Law and Justice (on religious liberty issues), the American Civil Rights Union, the Atlantic Legal Foundation, the Southeastern Legal Foundation, the New England Legal Foundation, and the Washington Legal Foundation. All have litigated cases and represented issues related to liberty and free enterprise.

Depending upon the era, conservative groups and legal foundations were either more or less present in their advocacy before the US Supreme Court. Even after they formed in the mid-1970s, they were not heavily involved in Supreme Court advocacy during the Reagan era. Either as primary litigants or filers of amicus curiae briefs, liberal groups were involved in 37 percent of Supreme Court cases from 1981 to 1987, while conservative groups were involved in only 26 percent (Holyoke, 2014; O'Connor and McFall, 1992). One might argue there was far less need for conservative pressure on the courts during that time period, though, since conservatives would not be litigating against Reagan policies. Further, Reagan's solicitor general was representing key conservative positions before the Court, and Reagan appointees then occupied many positions on the federal bench (Holyoke, 2014). After 2000, however, conservative groups have been involved in a larger percentage of cases than have liberal groups, and the latter lose more often than they win before the Supreme Court (Holyoke, 2014).

AMICUS CURIAE BRIEFS

Beyond litigating cases directly, the legal foundations and public policy groups supported by business are even more active in submitting amicus curiae briefs in leading court cases. It is likely the most important tactic used by business to influence the legal and judicial process, and amicus briefs are 'the most popular form of interest group participation before the Court' (Holyoke, 2014). The entire enterprise of submitting amicus briefs has historical roots and has generated some controversy. The first amicus curiae, or friend-of-the-court briefs, were filed in 1823, but it was not until the Supreme Court formulated rules in 1939 that their use became widespread. 'The rules require any person, interest group, or governmental entity to seek the permission of the parties or of the Court itself to file such briefs, save for the solicitor general or state attorneys general, where no permission is needed' (Solimine, 2013). As implied, the solicitor general will sometimes file an amicus brief and even members of Congress will file such a brief, as did 172 members of the House of Representatives in support of Edith Windsor, in her opposition to the Defense of Marriage Act in *United States v. Windsor* ('Brief … .', 2015). Just as the solicitor general files amicus briefs in Supreme Court cases, so do state attorneys general, especially on commerce clause and states' rights issues. Among the states, Texas

and Virginia have been the most frequent filers. Amicus briefs have also been filed in state Supreme Court cases at increasing and varying rates, with California's Supreme Court having amicus briefs filed in 53 percent of the cases, while the figure in Arizona is 22 percent. Meanwhile, the rate hovers at the ten percent level in federal appellate courts (Anderson, 2015).

The purpose of amicus briefs is to educate the Court on issues or facts not sufficiently addressed by briefs submitted by the contending parties to the case. Some scholars have examined in depth exactly what types of facts should be submitted in amicus briefs (Morrison, 2014). Increasingly, amicus briefs have supplied social science evidence in support of legal claims and analysis. Of cases decided in the 2012–13 term of the Supreme Court, 78 percent had an amicus brief that presented 'medical, historical, or social science' facts (Larsen, 2014). For instance, the effect of violent video games on child brain development was an important issue in *Brown v. Entertainment Merchants Association*. Social science questions in other major cases involve the educational benefits of racial diversity and the medical necessity of partial birth abortions (Larsen, 2014). Supreme Court members ranging from Justice Breyer to Justice Alito have praised the value of amicus briefs in educating the Court, while other experts point to their role in minimizing the search costs for information (Larsen, 2014). In spite of the support for the value of factual information in amicus briefs, one authority questions the accuracy of some of that information (Larsen, 2014).

Presenting factual information to the court through the vehicle of an amicus brief is based on the purpose served in an earlier era by what is called the Brandeis brief. Supreme Court Justice Louis Brandeis often requested information from advocates on social science facts that went beyond the issues of law emphasized in an advocate's brief (Larsen, 2014). The Brandeis brief was based on the school of thought known as sociological jurisprudence, which deemed the factual results or impact of legal decisions as relevant.

The controversy is over whether most briefs really accomplish that purpose or simply voice support for one of the parties to the case. Rather than really being friends of the court, briefs are often friends of one of the parties. One study found that, in 1992, three-fourths of briefs submitted largely repeated and reinforced information found in the briefs submitted by the contending parties (Spriggs and Wahlbeck, 1997). Further, many briefs transmit essentially the same message and information (Caldeira and Wright, 1990). This has led to calls for banning such briefs, although they now seem a fixture in the judicial process. Justice Felix Frankfurter, in opposing the use of amicus briefs, believed that allowing interest groups to lobby the Court would undermine its image (Harper, 2014; Solimine, 2013). When over a 100 briefs are filed in a single case, as occurred in the Affordable Care Act case, *NFIB v. Sebelius,* that may also overburden the Court (Harper, 2014).

Meanwhile, others advocate the extension of the right of international non-governmental organizations and businesses to file amicus briefs before World Trade Organization dispute settlement bodies and appellate panels (Pavel, 2014). Interest groups can already submit amicus briefs to influence North American Free Trade Agreement (NAFTA) arbitrations, and some advocate its use as a means to counter corporate interests (Salazar, 2013). The *United States v. Methanex* tribunal was the first use of amicus briefs in an investor–state arbitration, in 2001. Methanex is a Canadian producer of fuel additives, which were strictly regulated by California, prompting the company to bring an action under Chapter 11 of NAFTA for compensation, viewing the regulation as tantamount to expropriation. In the case, which rejected the claims by Methanex, the tribunal granted petitions to appear as amici curiae in the case by the International Institute for Sustainable Development, Communities for a Better Environment, the Bluewater Network of Earth Island Institute, and the Center for

International Environmental Law, since the public interest was heavily at stake (Mann, 2005). Since in the previous case of *Metalclad Corporation v. US* compensation had been granted to a corporation under a similar claim, providing an amici opportunity to such groups added balance to the deliberation.

One study of the use of amicus briefs in international and foreign courts has found their allowance for purposes of knowledge production, either as experts or activists. Their use in the UK may go back as far as Henry IV in 1403 (Dolidze, 2012).

There are a number of reasons for the proliferation of amicus briefs. Interest groups may believe that such briefs will actually influence the ultimate decision and result in court. At a minimum, the sheer volume of briefs being filed may insure that a petition for certiorari is granted and the Court will actually hear the case. Interest groups will also see an amicus brief as a way to counter the arguments in the briefs filed by the other side in the case. Interest groups that lobby other branches of government, including the legislative and executive branches, may see the amicus brief as another tool in their political arsenal to reinforce their positions with the courts (Solimine, 2013).

The numbers of briefs submitted have proliferated since the Burger Court of the 1980s. One study found that in one sample of cases at least one amicus brief was filed in 62 percent of Supreme Court cases, with two to five briefs filed in 28 percent of the cases. During the Burger Court era, four or more briefs were filed in 32.8 percent of the cases, while during the Roberts Court that number grew to 86 percent of the cases (Epstein et al., 2015). Other numbers reveal the increasing prominence and use of amicus briefs. Between 1945 and 1995, the number of amicus briefs filed in the Supreme Court increased by more than 800%, while the numbers of cases argued have actually declined. Between 1996 and 2003, at least one amicus brief was filed in 95% of all cases (Anderson, 2015; Howard, 2015).

The numbers of amicus briefs filed in the most important cases have increased to impressive levels. The gay rights case *United States v. Windsor* attracted 134 amicus briefs while there were over 140 amicus briefs in the Affordable Care Act case of *NFIB v. Sebelius* (Anderson, 2015). *Hollingsworth v. Perry*, the case involving California's Proposition 8, banning same-sex marriage, attracted 96 amicus briefs (Howard, 2015). In the case of *Citizens United v. FEC*, 25 organizations submitted briefs in support of the appellant Citizens United, while 13 submitted briefs supporting the law and the FEC. In the 2003 landmark affirmative action case of *Grutter v. Bollinger*, involving the program at the University of Michigan Law School, an important amicus brief submitted by 65 corporations supported the affirmative action plan. Companies such as Coca-Cola and Microsoft were leading signatories of the brief. Justice O'Connor, in her concurring opinion in *Grutter v. Bollinger*, 539 US 306 (2003), relied heavily on that brief, and on another amicus brief submitted by the military, in building a leadership rationale for affirmative action and arguing that such plans at elite universities like Michigan provide a filtering device for businesses and law firms recruiting future minority leaders. A counter argument, involving a mismatch theory developed by law professor Richard Sander, appeared in a heavily cited major law review article and amicus brief in the later case of *Fisher v. University of Texas* (Sander, 2014). In *Fisher*,

in addition to an amicus brief from the United States Solicitor General, the University of Texas was supported by briefs from seventeen senators; sixty-six congressmen; fifty-seven of the Fortune 100 American corporations; thirty-seven retired military and defense leaders; fifteen states; and well over one hundred colleges and universities. Most of these briefs generally discussed the importance of preserving racial preferences in education. (Sander, 2014)

Just as the ACLU and NAACP Legal Defense Fund served as models for business-oriented think tanks and legal foundations in the 1970s, so did the practice of the ACLU and NAACP in filing amicus briefs in the 1950s and 1960s serve as models for conservative legal foundations to do the same in later decades. Among the interest groups that file amicus briefs most frequently are the ACLU, the CATO Institute, Chamber of Commerce, and the American Federation of Labor and Congress of Industrial Organizations (Harper, 2014).

Religious groups have also been active in filing amicus briefs on issues of religious values and significance. The Southern Baptist Convention, for example, filed a brief against patenting modified genes in the case of *Association for Molecular Pathology v. Myriad Genetics*, decided by the Supreme Court in 2013. The Court unanimously held that some segments of DNA that constitute human genes are not patentable as products of nature, while other genetic sequences are (Chapman, 2013). Even more prominent as a filer of amicus briefs is the American Center for Law and Justice (ACLJ), which has 70,000 members. It filed two briefs against President Obama's executive order on immigration, on behalf of 68 members of Congress, and in support of 24 states. It also filed a brief on behalf of 21 family business owners and 90,000 supporters, defending freedom of religion in the famous *Hobby Lobby* case. As the ACLJ states:

In today's amicus brief, we argue that if for-profit corporations are not protected in their religious exercise, at least the owners of such corporations should be protected, and in these cases, it is clear that the Mandate forces them to manage their companies in violation of their religious beliefs. In the government's view, when people with religious convictions start and incorporate a business, they must necessarily operate that business as though they had no such convictions; they should leave their religious beliefs at home or at their place of worship. But for many business owners, like those who joined our amicus brief, this is a remarkably narrow view of the role religion plays in both their personal and professional lives. (ACLJ Amicus Brief, 2015)

In the *Sebelius v. Hobby Lobby* case, law professors filed an amicus brief supporting the government's position, which was critiqued by another law professor who supported Hobby Lobby (Bainbridge, 2014). In *Good News Community Church v. Town of Gilbert, AZ*, the ACLJ filed an amicus brief on behalf of the church, arguing against a municipal sign regulation that the ACLJ maintained violated content neutrality and freedom of religion.

As for the overall impact of amicus briefs, a 1988 study (Caldeira and Wright, 1988) found that amicus briefs do not influence the actual substance or outcome of a decision, but their primary influence is on the Supreme Court's decision to grant certiorari on a case. Even then, one authority argues it is not the content or analysis in the briefs that move the Court, but rather the sheer volume of briefs, especially since the Justices or their clerks do not really have time to read all of the briefs (Holyoke, 2014). That has led one political scientist to conclude that the briefs create an 'echo chamber' and are nothing more than 'legal cheerleading' (Holyoke, 2014). One key value of amicus briefs is aiding in organizational maintenance and to please organization constituents and donors (Holyoke, 2014). Meanwhile, another study, using plagiarism detection software, actually found that key phrases used in Supreme Court opinions often reflect those used in amicus briefs, belying the notion that they have no substantive impact on Court opinions. Based on that study, 'the justices systematically incorporate language from amicus briefs into the Court's majority opinions' (Larsen, 2014).

Regarding the overall importance of amicus briefs in advancing any conservative agenda, Daniel Lowenstein of UCLA Law School maintains that:

> To appeal to individual donors in fundraising mailers, the (conservative legal) organizations found it necessary to devote many of their resources to filing amicus briefs that usually had little influence but permitted the firms to claim that they were engaged in numerous cases. Corporate donors favored their short-term goals over basic principles shoring up the market system. (Lowenstein, 2008)

US CHAMBER LITIGATION CENTER

Based on its growing prominence and effectiveness, the newly named US Chamber Litigation Center (formerly National Chamber Litigation Center) deserves separate discussion. The Chamber Litigation Center, founded in 1977, participated in 400 cases during its first 20 years of operation, or 20 per year, while it now participates in over 100 cases a year. In 2014, it moved that number up to 150 cases. Its success rate in having cert petitions granted is also notable. While the ACLU filed only one amicus brief between 2009 and 2012, the Chamber Litigation Center filed 54, with an acceptance rate of 32 percent. Given that the Court accepts only 5 percent of all cert petitions in any term, that is an exceptional acceptance rate (Goldman, 2014).

An analysis of the 'elite litigation unit' concludes:

> the Litigation Center has become a major player. ... (In 2013) its small team, working with top outside litigators, submitted 107 amicus briefs on behalf of the US Chamber to federal agencies and in state and federal courts. ... the chamber was also a plaintiff, petitioner, intervenor, or counsel for an individual litigant in 18 cases, in many instances seeking appellate review of rulings by state and federal regulators. (Goldman, 2014)

LEADING APPELLATE LAW FIRMS

Just as conservative think tanks and legal foundations have become crucial in advancing the law in a direction that favors conservative and often business interests, leading appellate law firms are crucial in influencing the legal and judicial process on grand and large issues. They constitute an elite within the legal community that business can retain when it is facing the most consequential legal challenges and issues. As one experienced corporate counsel puts it, a company would turn to a specialist in a given area of law in the late 1980s to represent its interests at higher court levels, but in 2015, 'Now you want the guy who knows the justices and the justices know. There are 12 lawyers and firms that keep coming up' (Biskupic et al., 2014). In some cases, not only do the elite lawyers know the justices but socialize with them. This stands as strong evidence of the theory of legal realism, that judges and lawyers live not just a life of law but also a life of experience.

Biskupic, Roberts, and Shiffman wrote a special Reuters report nominated for a Pulitzer Prize and winner of the 2015 Hillman Prize for Web Journalism, titled 'The Echo Chamber' (Biskupic et al., 2014). The authors examined 10,000 appeals over nine Supreme Court terms that involved 17,000 lawyers. The series identified 66 lawyers who got an astonishing 43 percent of the cases heard by the Supreme Court. The top firms argued 60 percent of the cases brought on behalf of Big Business, and were successful in getting 18 percent of their petitions for certiorari granted by the Court. One criterion the Court may use in determining whether it will hear a case is which lawyer would likely be arguing the case. The leading law firms included in this elite are Gibson Dunn, Jones Day, and Sidley Austin. To have maximum influence on the Supreme Court in major cases, and to maximize one's chance of winning a major case, it would be prudent for any corporation to select one of the elite law firms to represent its interests.

MAJOR CASES AND JUDICIAL PROCESS ISSUES

As a result of its focus on judicial nominations, on supporting various conservative legal foundations, on filing major amicus briefs, and on retaining elite law firms, business has enjoyed much success before the Roberts Court. Especially when it comes to cases involving the gatekeeper role of the Court, in allowing or restricting access by complaining parties, business has won some notable victories. The US Chamber Litigation Center has been a major player in some of those cases. As one observer summarizes those wins: 'Over the past two decades, the Chamber has embarked on a series of largely successful legislative and litigation-driven campaigns – to frustrate securities class actions, encourage mandatory arbitration agreements, support the preemption of federal over state laws, reduce punitive damage awards, and raise procedural hurdles for standing to sue' (Goldman, 2014).

On class action cases, business won a major victory in the case of *Wal-Mart Stores, Inc. v. Dukes*, 131 S. Ct. 2541 (2011), a precedent which will be a major barrier to other plaintiffs bringing class action lawsuits in the future. In that case, the Court ruled against class certification in a suit on behalf of 1.5 million Wal-Mart female employees, saying there was insufficient commonality of interests among the class members to warrant certification. On the issue of arbitration, the Supreme Court similarly ruled in the interests of business in the case of *AT&T Mobility v. Concepcion*, 131 S. Ct. 1740 (2011). The plaintiffs in that case argued that an arbitration clause that also barred class actions was unconscionable, to which the Court answered that the federal arbitration act pre-empted any lawsuits on that basis and distinctly favored arbitration as a remedy, even though there was no real bargaining over inclusion of the clause.

In other cases, the Supreme Court has expanded the ability of business to defend itself against lawsuits by erecting other barriers against plaintiffs. In the case of *Stoneridge Investment Partners v. Scientific-Atlanta, Inc.*, 552 US 148 (2008), for instance, the Court denied the plaintiffs the right to sue Scientific-Atlanta for aiding and abetting the fraud of Charter Communications, by finding that the plaintiffs had failed to show any reliance on the conduct of Scientific-Atlanta. The Court also expanded the ability of business to rebut claims of reliance in the later case of *Halliburton Co. v. Erica P. John Fund, Inc.*, 134 S. Ct. 2398 (2014).

Business has also enjoyed support from both the Supreme Court and the DC Court of Appeals in its challenges to various federal regulations. The Business Roundtable and the Chamber Litigation Center challenged the rule under the Dodd–Frank Law that allowed shareholder nomination of corporate directors in the case of *Business Roundtable v. SEC*, 647 F.3d 1144 (DC Cir. 2011). The Court held the rule did not meet the cost–benefit test mandated by the Administrative Procedure Act (Mongone, 2012). The Court also occasionally strikes down regulations if they exceed an agency's statutory authority, as it did in overruling the Environmental Protection Agency's (EPA) limits on stationary sources of greenhouse gases in *Utility Air Regulatory Group v. Environmental Protection Agency*, 134 S. Ct. 2427 (2014). In a blow to net neutrality, the DC Court of Appeals also ruled that the FCC lacks the authority to regulate the speed at which content is delivered by internet service providers in *Comcast Corporation v. Federal Communications Commission (FCC)*, 600 F.3d 642 (DC Cir. 2010).

Business and other economic interests have also won cases that have expanded their constitutional rights. For example, in *Citizens United v. Federal Election Commission*, 558 US 310 (2010), the US Supreme Court struck down part of the Bipartisan Campaign Reform Act of 2002 that restricted what any person, including corporations, could spend on candidate-related issue advertising, and reversed two precedents in so doing. The Court also upheld the religious freedom of business owners to resist compliance with a provision of the Affordable Care Act that forced them to provide contraception coverage for their employees, in the case of *Burwell v. Hobby Lobby Stores, Inc.*, 134 S. Ct. 2751 (2014).

CONCLUSION

Interest groups can influence the legal and judicial process in several ways. They can influence the selection of judges, either through lobbying the appointment of federal judges, or by contributing to the campaigns of state judicial candidates. The latter is more problematic and may face ethical and legal barriers, but the former is now a standard tactic of interest groups of various stripes, including business. Business can also educate federal judges through supporting the Law and Economics Center, and can facilitate the advancement and careers of other potential conservative judicial candidates through support of the Federalist Society.

Meanwhile, business also supports the various conservative and free-market think tanks and legal foundations that formed in the 1970s. Filing amicus curiae briefs is a common tactic used by interest groups of various persuasions to influence judicial decisions, and those briefs have their supporters and detractors. They are nonetheless popular vehicles to influence the judiciary, and evidence exists that they are useful and have had a real impact. Among business organizations that are involved in filing amicus briefs and bringing cases directly to court, the US Chamber Litigation Center is most prominent and has grown in impact over recent years.

Finally, business more than other interest groups connects with elite law firms that represent its interests in major Supreme Court cases. Business has, through all its tools of influence, won major victories in cases involving judicial process, federal regulations, and constitutional rights.

Note

1   As noted by Tamanaha (2012):

  … the late great political scientist C. Herman Pritchett was far closer to the mark when he wrote that judges 'are influenced by their own biases and philosophies, which to a large degree predetermine the position they will take on a given question. Private attitudes, in other words, become public law'. When one adds up the preceding five senses of politics in judging, it seems sensible to pay close attention to the political views of judicial appointees. First, judges are a part of the political apparatus of government. Second, judges make public policy in the course of developing the common law and when interpreting statutes and the Constitution. Third, the background ideological views of judges influence how they perceive the facts, interpret the law, apply standards, fill in gaps and resolve contradictions, choose an answer from among equally plausible decisions, pick a theory of interpretation, think about justice, and decide policy questions. Fourth, judges sometimes render decisions that affect the shape and outcome of major political issues of the day. Fifth, screening judges for their political views almost necessarily follows from the above.

REFERENCES

Abramovsky, A. (2012) 'Justice for Sale: Contemplations on the 'Impartial' Judge in a Citizens United World', *Michigan State Law Review*, 2012: 713–733.

ACLJ Amicus Brief (2015) http://aclj.org/obamacare/aclj-files-hhs-mandate-amicus-brief-with-supreme-court, accessed on October 15.

Anderson, H.A. (2015) 'Frenemies of the Court: The Many Faces of Amicus Curiae', *University of Richmond Law Review*, 49: 361–416.

Bainbridge, S.M. (2014) 'A Critique of the Corporate Law Professors' Amicus Brief in Hobby Lobby and Conestoga Wood', *Virginia Law Review Online*, 100: 1.

Banks, C.P. and O'Brien, D.M. (2016) *The Judicial Process: Law, Courts, and Judicial Politics*, Washington, DC: CQ Press.

Biskupic, J., Roberts, J., and Shiffman, J. (2014) *The Echo Chamber, a Reuters Special Report.*

Bonneau, C.W. and Hall, M.G. (2009) *In Defense of Judicial Elections*, New York: Routledge.

Brandenburg, B. and Schotland, R.A. (2008) 'Justice in Peril: The Endangered Balance Between Impartial Courts and Judicial Election Campaigns', *Georgetown Journal of Legal Ethics*, 21: 1229.

'Brief of 172 Members of the U.S. House of Representatives and 40 U.S. Senators as Amici Curiae in Support of Respondent Edith Schlain Windsor, Urging Affirmance on the Merits' (2015) *Columbia Journal of Gender and Law*, 29: 177–228.

Caldeira, G.A., Hojnacki M., and Wright, J.R. (2000) 'The Lobbying Activities of Organized Interests in Federal Judicial Nominations', *Journal of Politics*, 62: 51–69.

Caldeira, G.A. and Wright, J.R. (1988) 'Organized Interests and Agenda Setting in the U.S. Supreme Court', *American Political Science Review*, 82: 1109–1127.

Caldeira, G.A. and Wright, J.R. (1990) 'Amici Curiae before the Supreme Court: Who Participates, When, and How Much?' *American Journal of Political Science*, 42: 499–523.

Carrington, P.D. (1998) 'Judicial Independence and Democratic Accountability in Highest State Courts', *Law and Contemporary Problems*, 61: 79.

Chapman, A.R. (2013) 'Religious Contributions to the Debate on the Patenting of Human Genes', *University of St. Thomas Law Journal*, 10: 650–682.

Chemerinsky, E., Hasen, R., and Sample, J. (2012) 'Citizens United Impact on Judicial Elections', *Drake Law Review*, 60: 685–701.

Ciocchetti, C. (2013) 'The Constitution, the Roberts Court, and Business: The Significant Business Impact of the 2011–2012 Supreme Court Term', *William & Mary Business Law Review*, 4: 385–473.

Coyle, M. (2013) *The Roberts Court: The Struggle for the Constitution*, New York: Simon & Schuster.

CPA (2014) *The 2014 CPA-Zicklin Index of Corporate Political Disclosure and Accountability*, Philadelphia: Center for Political Accountability, Zicklin Center for Business Ethics Research, University of Pennsylvania.

Danelski, D. (1990) 'Ideology as a Ground for the Rejection of the Bork Nomination', *Northwestern University Law Review*, 1990: 900–920.

DeGregorio, C. and Rossotti, J. (1995) 'Campaigning for the Court: Interest Group Participation in the Bork and Thomas Confirmation Processes', in A.J. Cigler and B.A.

Loomis, eds. *Interest Group Politics,* 4th ed. Washington, DC: Congressional Quarterly Press.

Dinan, J. (2013) 'Book Review – The People's Choice: Pursuing Judicial Independence in America', *Texas Law Review,* 91:633–649.

Dolidze, A. (2012) 'Making International Property Law: The Role of Amici Curiae in International Decision-Making', *Syracuse Journal of International Law & Commerce,* 40: 119–153.

Edmonds, J. (2014) 'Scandal: The Growing Need for a Code of Conduct in Attorney General Elections', *Georgetown Journal of Legal Ethics,* 27: 505–519.

Epstein, L., Landes, W.M., and Posner, R.A. (2013) 'How Business Fares in Supreme Court', *Minnesota Law Review,* 97: 1431–1462.

Epstein, L., Landes, W.M., and Posner, R.A. (2015) 'The Best for Last: The Timing of U.S. Supreme Court Decisions', *Duke Law Journal,* 64: 991–1022.

Freedman, M.H. (2013) 'The Unconstitutionality of Electing State Judges', *Georgetown Journal of Legal Ethics,* 26: 217–223.

Gaylord, S.W. (2012) 'Judicial Independence Revisited: Judicial Elections and Missouri Plan Challenges', *North Carolina Law Review Addendum,* 90: 61A–83A.

Geyh, C.G. (2012) 'Judicial Selection Reconsidered: A Plea for a Radical Moderation', *Harvard Journal of Law & Public Policy,* 35: 623–642.

Gibson, J.L. and Caldeira, G.A. (2012) 'Campaign Support, Conflicts of Interest, and Judicial Impartiality: Can the Legitimacy of Courts Be Rescued by Recusals?', *Journal of Politics* 74(1): 18.

Gibson, J.L. and Caldeira, G.A. (2013) 'Judicial Impartiality, Campaign Contributions, and Recusals: Results from a National Survey', *Journal of Empirical Legal Studies,* 10: 76–92.

Gibson, J.L., Gottfried J.A., DelliCarpini, M.X., and Jamieson, K.H. (2011) 'The Effects of Judicial Campaign Activity on the Legitimacy of Courts: A Survey-Based Experiment', *Political Research Quarterly,* 64(3): 545.

Goldman, T.R. (2014) 'Inside the Chamber', *California Lawyer,* July, https://www.callawyer.com/clstory.cfm?eid=935765&wteid=935765_Inside_the_Chamber.

Goodman, S.J. (2012) 'The Danger Inherent in the Public Perception that Justice Is for Sale', *Drake Law Review,* 60: 8–7-825.

Greenhouse, L. (2015) 'The Illusion of a Liberal Supreme Court', *The New York Times,* July 9.

Harper, B.D. (2014) 'The Effectiveness of State-Filed Amicus Briefs at the United States Supreme Court', *University of Pennsylvania Journal of Constitutional Law,* 16: 1503–1529.

Holyoke, T.T. (2014) *Interest Groups and Lobbying: Pursuing Political Interests in America.* Boulder, CO: Westview Press.

Houck, O. (1984) 'With Charity for All', *Yale Law Journal,* 93: 1415.

Howard, A.E. (2015) 'The Changing Face of the Supreme Court', *Virginia Law Review,* 101: 231–316.

Howell, L. (2012) 'Once Upon a Time in the West: Citizens United, Caperton, and the War of the Copper Kings', *Montana Law Review,* 73: 25–58.

Katz, A. (2015) *The Influence Machine: The U.S. Chamber of Commerce and the Corporate Capture of American Life,* New York: Spiegel & Grau.

Larsen, A.O. (2014) 'The Trouble with Amicus Facts', *Virginia Law Review,* 100: 1757–1818.

Liptak, A. (2015) 'Right Divided, a Disciplined Left Steered the Supreme Court', *The New York Times,* June 30.

Lipton, E. (2014a) 'Lobbyists, Bearing Gifts, Pursue Attorneys General', *The New York Times,* October 28, http://www.nytimes.com/2014/10/29/us/lobbyists-bearing-gifts-pursue-attorneys-general.html.

Lipton, E. (2014b) 'Lawyers Create Big Paydays by Coaxing Attorneys General to Sue', *The New York Times,* December 18, http://www.nytimes.com/2014/12/19/us/politics/lawyers-create-big-paydays-by-coaxing-attorneys-general-to-sue-.html.

Lowenstein, D.H. (2008) 'Review of The Rise of the Conservative Legal Movement', *Engage,* 9(3): 116–118.

Mann, H. (2005) *The Final Decision in Methanex v. United States: Some New Wine in Some New Bottles,* New York: International Institute for Sustainable Development.

Mongone, A.W. (2012) 'Business Roundtable: A New Level of Judicial Scrutiny and Its

Implications in a Post Dodd-Frank World', *Columbia Business Law Review*, 2012: 746–797.

Morrison, A.B. (2014) 'The Brandeis Brief and 21st Century Constitutional Litigation', *Lewis & Clark Law Review*, 18: 715–750.

Nyhan, B. (2015) 'Supreme Court: Liberal Drift v. Conservative Overreach', *The New York Times*, June 25.

O'Connor, K. and McFall, B. (1992) 'Conservative Interest Group Litigation in the Reagan Era and Beyond', in M.P. Petracca, ed. *The Politics of Interests: Interest Groups Transformed*. Boulder, CO: Westview Press.

Parlapiano, A., Liptak, A., and Bowers, J. (2015) 'The Roberts Court's Surprising Move Leftward', *The New York Times*, June 23.

Pavel, C. (2014) 'Making a Faustian Bargain Work: What Special Interests Can Tell Us about Representation In the WTO', *Georgetown Journal of Law & Public Policy*, 12: 471–491.

Pierson, J. (2015) *Shattered Consensus*, New York: Encounter Books.

Rowland, C.K. and Carp, R.A. (1996) *Politics and Judgment in Federal District Courts*, Lawrence, KS: University Press of Kansas.

Salazar, A.R. (2013) 'Defragmenting International Investment Law to Protect Citizen-Consumers: The Role of Amici Curiae and Public Interest Groups', *Law and Business Review of the Americas*, 19: 183–199.

Sander, R. (2014) 'Diversity in Legal Education and the Legal Profession: Mismatch and the Empirical Scholars Brief', *Valparaiso University Law Review*, 48: 555–584.

Savage, D. (1992) *Turning Right: The Making of the Rehnquist Supreme Court*, New York: John Wiley & Sons, Inc.

Savelieff, L. (2012) 'Hyper-Partisanship on the Supreme Court Nomination and Confirmation Process', *Georgetown Journal of Law & Public Policy*, 10: 563–588.

Segal, J.A. and Spaeth, H.J. (1993) *The Supreme Court and the Attitudinal Model*, New York: Cambridge University Press.

Segal, J.A. and Spaeth, J.J. (2002) *The Supreme Court and Attitudinal Model Reconsidered*, New York: Cambridge University Press.

Shugerman, J.H. (2012) *The People's Courts: Pursuing Judicial Independence in America*, Cambridge, MA: Harvard University Press.

Solimine, M.E. (2013) 'The Solicitor General Unbound: Amicus Curiae Activism and Deference in the Supreme Court', *Arizona State Law Journal*, 45: 1183–1225.

Spriggs, J.F. and Wahlbeck, P.J. (1997) 'Amicus Curiae and the Role of Information at the Supreme Court', *Political Research Quarterly*, 50: 365–386.

Stefancic, J. and Delgado, R. (1996) *No Mercy: How Conservative Think Tanks and Foundations Changed America's Social Agenda*, Philadelphia, PA: Temple University Press.

Tamanaha, B.Z. (2012) 'The Several Meanings of "Politics" in Judicial Politics Studies: Why "Ideological Influence" Is Not "Partisanship"', *Emory Law Journal*, 61: 759–778.

Tarr, G.A. (2012) *Without Fear or Favor: Judicial Independence and Judicial Accountability in the States*, Stanford, CA: Stanford University Press.

Teles, S.M. (2008) *The Rise of the Conservative Legal Movement: The Battle for Control of the Law*, Princeton, NJ: Princeton University Press.

Wallison, P.J. (2015) *Hidden in Plain Sight: What Really Caused the World's Worst Financial Crisis and Why It Could Happen Again*, New York: Encounter Books.

Watson, G. and Stookey, J. (1988) 'The Bork Hearings: Rocks and Roles', *Judicature*, 71: 194–196.

29

Corporate Issues Management

John Mahon

Corporate issues management is the internal process by which a firm attempts to assess potential and future threats from unfolding situations, social predicaments and other events that arise from either organizational actions and past history, or from external events in what I term the marketplace of ideas (Mahon, 1993; Mahon, 2006; Mahon and Waddock, 1992). Most executives have been trained, and are extremely comfortable dealing in the marketplace. Making products, delivering services, marketing those products and services, financing the operations, and investing in facilities are all skills that managers are educated in and experience as they mature and advance in the modern corporation.

However, there is a parallel marketplace of ideas to the marketplace of goods and services. It is where ideas are formulated, developed, and implemented that often take executives completely by surprise. It may be the imposition of an advertising ban by a regulatory agency (as happened to the tobacco industry), federal legislation to tax an industry to clean up its abandoned wastes (as occurred with the US chemical industry), or the development of new demands on all industries world-wide to meet the challenge of climate change. These actions were not driven by the give and take of competition in the marketplace or by the desires of the customers for different and/or better products and services. They were driven by the advancement of an idea (or, more broadly, an issue) by key stakeholders searching for a specific arena within this marketplace of ideas – it could be in a legislative, regulatory, or judicial arena or in the social network and public media arena – in which to advance the issue and achieve some resolution.

Anticipating, managing, and dealing with issues in this marketplace is a skill set of increasing value to organizations of all types, but is one that is frequently not clearly understood by line managers (and which lead to the subsequent creation of the Issue Management Council). Sadly, the consequences of a poor or not existent issues management capability is felt by all in the organization or across entire industries (Cobb and Elder, 1972; Eyestone, 1978; Heath and Nelson, 1986; Keim and Baysinger, 1988; Kingdon, 1984; Mahon, 1983; Olson, 1965).

Managers have two simple options to select in dealing with issues and social predicaments. The first is to identify all key organizations and groups that are influenced by the organization's decisions or that may affect organizational outcomes with regards to these issues. Sensible managers will recognize that these stakeholders are sometimes parties with whom the organization already has a well-developed, on-going relationship, whereas at other times they are parties that only have relationships with influential actors in the organizational network, but whom can exert indirect influence on the organization through these relationships, and in some situations there are no preexisting relationships of any kind. Once these stakeholders are identified, managers can prioritize them according to their power over the corporation and the urgency and legitimacy of their claims (Mitchell et al., 1997). Realizing that organizational means are always scarce, managers can then use the outcome of this prioritization exercise to accommodate the needs of the most powerful and/or urgent of these stakeholders, provided the organization has carefully identified all the key stakeholders (Freeman, 1984; Mahon and Wartick, 2003).

The second option open to key decision-makers is to focus not so much on these groups *per se*, but rather on the social predicaments facing the organization. Regardless of whether these social predicaments are called strategic, public, or social issues, they all have the potential to interfere with the organization's attempts to realize its strategic intent if they are left unattended. In the traditional issues management process, decision-makers first scan the organizational environment for new predicaments emerging on the horizon. Next, they monitor these issues throughout their life-cycle, in order to interpret their nature and to evaluate their potential consequences. Finally, they come up with an appropriate set of responses, timed to the life-cycle of the issue and to the ability of the organization to influence, shape, or eliminate the issue (Mahon et al., 2004). See Figure 29.1.

Managers will of course realize that separating these two choices is not a practical option in real life. If they focus on their current set of stakeholders only, there is a fair chance that they will miss out on new threats and opportunities emanating in their environments or by stakeholders who champion an issue but have no relationship with the focal organization. If they focus on issues only, they may suffer reputational damage, as they get known as reactive fire-fighters rather than pro-active fire preventers. Yet in the literature (both scholarly and practitioner oriented), Chinese walls seem to separate the bodies of work on issues management and stakeholder theory and practice, to which these options

Figure 29.1 The Simple Model

correspond. This situation is conceptually and practically undesirable, as both perspectives can at best offer only a partial and incomplete understanding of social predicaments (Mahon and Wartick, 2003).

We view such *social predicaments* as controversies (economic, political, social, or any combination) that may have a negative effect on the ability of organizations to realize their strategic intent if left unattended. Social predicaments always have an issue side (in that they involve a disagreement over the distribution of resources and positions) as well as a stakeholder side (in that they affect or address a number of actors, who will then automatically have a stake in whether and how the issue will be resolved). Social predicaments are broader than strategic issues. Strategic issues must of necessity be identified with something – generally an organization in order to be 'strategic'. Social predicaments exist independently of the organization and have a different ontological status. In some ways social predicaments may be analogous to campaigns in the social movement literature. They do have the potential to mature into a social movement if not dealt with in a timely and proper manner (Kingdon, 1984; Mahon et al., 2004).

On the one hand, stakeholders help to frame issues and use symbols to raise the visibility of a particular set of issues in order to build awareness, coalitions, and achieve *their desired solution or preferred outcome(s)* (Cobb and Elder, 1997; Edelman, 1964; Mahon, 1989; Schattschneider, 1960). Alternatively, issues affect a number of parties in any of the arenas in which the issue is played out, and as such they 'hand-pick' certain parties that will become stakeholders, predestinating them into activism because they hurt them in their interests. Although it is important to understand both stakeholders and issues simultaneously and interactively, the focus of this chapter is on issues management. One final caveat – issues management processes emerge, move, die, and are reborn as a consequence of the interactions between the stakeholders involved, the issue itself, the very process of interactions among the players on the issue, and the dynamics of the arena chosen for resolution. A wild card in all of this is the media and how or if the issue captures public attention.

ISSUES MANAGEMENT

From a temporal perspective, we can separate out issues management and stakeholder management. Issues management is the future-oriented long-term assessment by the firm (and others) as to what potential issues (difference in facts, values, or policies) are likely to gain traction in the marketplace of ideas, impact on the organization in what is perceived as negative or limiting ways, or to take advantage of opportunities presented by a specific issue. Stakeholder management is dealing with an issue in the here and now. That is, the issue is no longer a potential 'future' challenge, but one that has emerged and requires an organizational response.

Results in the political system are obtained largely through group pressure (Olson, 1965; Pfeffer and Salancik, 1978; Post, 1978; Ryan et al., 1987; Schattschneider, 1960). Thus, corporations and non-business groups seek to develop coalitions that support their positions (see Chapter 33 in this compendium) and attempt to prevent opposition coalitions from forming. Although these coalitions try to influence action/decisions in the political and social arena, access by coalition members is not guaranteed.

Participation in the formal political system (the legislature, the regulatory bureaucracy, etc.) where alternatives are identified and discussed is highly restricted. The battleground, a 'pressure system', is generally distinguishable by the activities of small groups (Berry, 1984; Olson, 1965; Schattschneider, 1960). Entry to the system is often limited to those 'legitimate' groups who have already gained access to the political arena. This often means that new groups seeking access resort to extralegal behavior or action that is outside the legitimate rules of the game. In recent years, black power groups and pro-abortion and anti-abortion groups have evidenced a willingness to obtain power through illegal actions. The attempts by Iran to influence the availability of *Satanic Verses* is another example of such behavior. The clear lesson is that groups denied access to the system can, and often will, resort to illegal, highly visible means to gain attention for their cause. Much of the Civil Rights movement was oriented towards obtaining for 'outsiders' access to a political system that had denied them entry for years. This extralegal behavior, incidentally, has been reflected in the early history of business (for example, the robber barons) and in the political scandals of the 1960s and 1970s. Business has, from time to time, operated on the fringes of the political decision-making process.

Conflicts in the political system are not always resolved by those organizations or individuals with the most money or, in the case of organizations, the largest membership. Other mechanisms and forces may serve as predictors of success (for example, techniques to increase the visibility of an issue with a broader audience, or the emotional content of an issue like abortion) can lead to a temporary stalemate in which the system's immediate ability to respond to issues and problems is drastically reduced (Pfeffer and Salancik, 1978; Post, 1978; Sethi, 1987). Under such circumstances, the actor who engages a sufficiently broad audience in a timely way and convinces it of his/her position will win, regardless of other strengths of other actors in the contest. Timing is critical: that is, when is the best time to energize the larger audience and how are appeals to that audience made? This requires some understanding of the issues-life-cycle (Bigelow et al., 1993; Mahon, 1993, 2006; Mahon and Waddock, 1992; Mahon and Wartick, 1994).

The issues-life-cycle consists of five stages through which an issue develops. A gestation phase begins when a gap develops between a firm's actual performance and the public's expectation of that performance. In the second stage, as the gap widens over time, more groups and individuals become involved, and the risk increases that the issue will become politicized, and more broadly demand action of some kind. The shift in public sentiment over investment in apartheid-era South Africa is illustrative of stage-1 and stage-2 activities. If the issue remains unresolved (that is, the gap is not narrowed by organizational action), a third phase can occur in which the issue is considered by a specific political or regulatory body. Even if the issue is resolved, a period of litigation often follows during which the interested parties test the scope of the legislative or regulatory solution. Finally, after public policy has prevailed, or the public has exercised its choice through media or community pressure to which the organization acquiesces, there occurs an institutionalization of the matter by the organizations affected. The battles over and the passage of legislation regulating hazardous waste cleanup is illustrative of this life-cycle in its entirety (Mahon, 1983; Mahon and Kelley, 1988).

This issues-life-cycle suggests two clear sets of external strategic action that can be pursued by an organization. The first set of strategies deals with the definition of the issue and associated strategies to keep the issue from achieving broad audience recognition and support, unless, of course, the organization desires to place the issue on an agenda for resolution. In the latter instance, the organization would seek to publicize the issue to an ever-increasing audience. Such actions have the best chance of success when undertaken in the early stages of the issues-life-cycle, specifically in the gestation and widening of the issue states, and the early part of the third stage, as described above. These strategies deal with the management

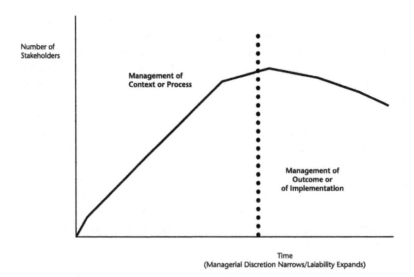

Number of
Stakeholders

Management of
Context or Process

Management of
Outcome or
of Implementation

Time
(Managerial Discretion Narrows/Laiability Expands)

Figure 29.2   Narrowing discretion

of conflict and the building of relationships ('Management of context or process' as shown in Figure 29.2).

The second set of strategies deals with the later phases of the life-cycle. In this situation, the organization is faced with the task of influencing a legislature, a regulatory agency, or a community group after the issue has entered into its realm of action. These strategies are aimed, in general, at shaping the outcomes and processes by which the issue will be resolved. It must be clearly noted that, in dealing with the issue at this stage, the issue can be 're-ignited', that is, the issue can be redefined and altered and as such can result in an entirely new issue emerging.

Here the organization has two sub-strategies from which to choose. The first deals with the content of the proposed action/issue, and the second with the implementation of the regulatory-, legislative-, or community-determined action. The most effective strategy from an organizational standpoint is to prevent issues from expanding onto an agenda or to place issues on an agenda of the organization's choosing. Union Carbide's efforts to have Bhopal claims resolved in Indian

Courts was a notable example of an organization placing the resolution of the issue where the organization desired. The payment of US$426 million was significantly less than the billion-dollar funds required of Robins and Manville in previous cases. Other examples of this type of action include Chrysler's pressing for a federal bailout and Manville's moves to bankruptcy court to preclude the breakup of the firm through enormous liability settlements and the more recent actions by Volkswagen to deal with their emissions problems.

The thrust behind containing the issue and keeping it off the public agenda and away from specific political and regulatory action is to prevent the building of momentum for resolution and to avoid the loss of organizational discretion to act. In the fractionated world noted earlier, organizations need skills to exercise both containment and placement strategies. This requires recognition of the notion of corporate political entrepreneurship; to develop political advantage, the firm must act entrepreneurially in the political and social arena (Keim and Baysinger, 1988; Keim and Zeithaml, 1986; Sethi, 1987; Yoffie and Bergenstein, 1985).

STRATEGIES OF CONTAINMENT: KEEPING ISSUES OFF OF AGENDAS

How can an organization keep an issue off an agenda and out of the limelight, or place an issue on an agenda of its own choosing? First, what is meant by an issue? An issue is '... a conflict between two or more identifiable groups or organizations over procedural or substantive matters relating to the distribution of positions or resources' (Cobb and Elder, 1972: 35). These conflicts are often over scarce resources, and not necessarily scarce '... in any absolute sense but in *light of the expectations of the members of society*' (emphasis added – Cobb and Elder, 1972: 35). Two things are notable here. First, political issues, by definition, are resolved in political situations and in political systems. Second, societal expectations of the issue and of how decisions are made, the content of the issue, and the outcomes of these decisions (expectations and content) need as much managerial attention as the actual resolution of an issue itself.

Of particular relevance are the types of political agendas, and the methods by which an issue is brought to that larger audience noted earlier. It is here that managers find clues and strategies for the prevention of issue expansion. In the formal political system (as opposed to political action by a corporation in dealing with protestors or community groups over a local issue) there are two types of formal political agendas: systemic and institutional (Cobb and Elder, 1972). The systemic agenda comprises all issues that society perceives as requiring public attention; for example, such things as the health, welfare, and safety of society.

This is obviously too broad to be useful. The institutional agenda, on the other hand, is much more restrictive, and is defined as those issues '... explicitly up for the active and serious consideration of authoritative decision makers' (Cobb and Elder, 1972: 87). These are the specific issues being considered by the regulatory agency this year

or quarter, or the issues before Congress or Parliament in this session, or issues that are being actively driven by media coverage. As issues follow the life-cycle, the speed with which they move from the systemic to the institutional agenda will vary greatly. A visible tragedy, however, will move issues along at a rapid pace. The explosion at BP's oil well in the Gulf of Mexico and the accident at Chernobyl quickly raised issues of oil rig safety and nuclear safety to the institutional agenda.

When an organization fails to keep an issue off the agenda, the organization should strive to choose when and on what agenda the issue will appear. This is accomplished through issue containment, of which the most powerful weapon is issue definition. Both business organizations and non-business interest groups argue over the definition of an issue because it is key in attracting other groups and the public's involvement.

DEFINING THE ISSUE

The most powerful technique available for the control of an issue is definition and the symbols and symbolism associated with that definition (Edelman, 1964). For example, in the current US debate over abortion, the two sides have rallied around two very powerful organizing themes – pro-choice and pro-life. Pro-choice conveys to large segments of this society the message that constitutional guarantees of freedom and the right of women to choose how their bodies are to be used is crucial to a free society. Pro-life argues that abortion is murder, forbidden by the laws of this society. Each side has defined the issue in a manner exclusive of the other's position. Therefore, pro-choice advocates, emphasizing the symbolism of freedom of choice, never have to deal with the issue of murder; pro-life advocates, emphasizing the charge of murder, never have to address the choice issue. The problem is emotion-laden: for example, pro-choice advocates are infuriated by the use of the term 'murder' in association with abortion.

We see similar arguments in the ranging debate over climate issues. The original term 'global warming' allowed those unconvinced to point out that places were actually getting colder or that there were more snow storms. More recently, the issue has been redefined to 'climate change' which allows for the uneven, differentiated impact of climate change and eliminates, to a certain extent, the arguments against 'global warming'.

In Procter and Gamble's Rely-tampon problem, the issue was defined as toxic shock, in part because the Centers for Disease Control (CDC), a public agency, was over-zealous. The agency had been suffering from two large public blunders – the swine flu incident and the outbreak of Legionnaires disease. In the swine flu incident, the CDC had predicted a major outbreak, which did not occur, and forced the development of a new vaccine that resulted in several deaths. In the Legionnaires' disease situation, the CDC was perceived as very slow in learning what the problem was and in selecting an appropriate course of action. As a consequence, the CDC was hungry for a public-relations victory to reestablish its image. The problem was that the identification of Rely as the major source of toxic shock obscured the more serious issue, that of toxic shock from any super-absorbent tampon. Continued research into toxic shock supports the contention that the problem was not Rely, but super-absorbent products. Because of the efforts of the Center and because of tremendous infighting in the industry, Procter and Gamble was not able to control the definition of the issue. If the company had been successful in redefining the issue to super-absorbent products, that success would have helped its public image and contributed to the development of sound public policy. In what must strike Procter and Gamble as bittersweet, its early suggestion that warning labels be provided on the

product, which the CDC rejected, was eventually adopted.

There have been several successful attempts to keep longer-term issues off agendas. The American Medical Association (AMA) has long resisted legislation aimed at requiring governmental support of low-cost health care to the poor and elderly by arguing that such programs are 'socialistic'. The use of that symbol has served for years to block efforts at national medical care. In a similar vein, the National Rifle Association (NRA) has repeatedly prevented legislation from being placed on an agenda or being enacted that would place restrictions on individual ownership of guns, despite the numerous examples of mass murders in the US in the last two years. It too has used a powerful symbol – that of Constitutional guarantees to the citizenry of the right to bear arms. Corporations, government officials, interest groups, and community members should exercise care in the choice of a rallying cry and in the symbols they use for their cause. The choice of a symbol with which to associate a movement or issue plays an important role in developing coalitions and attracting a larger audience's interest in the issue.

HOW DOES AN ISSUE GET PLACED ON THE INSTITUTIONAL AGENDA?

Although the control of issue definition is important, it is not always sufficient to keep an issue off an agenda. The tactic of issue definition can, nevertheless, be employed even after an issue appears on an agenda. However, we need to know how word of an issue spreads to broader audiences. The major process by which an issue moves through its life-cycle involves the buildup of interest group and individual attention to the issue. In general, the more people and groups involved, the greater the likelihood that the issue will be placed on a formal agenda for resolution. This process occurs through gradual stages of involvement by the 'public'. Schattschneider noted some time ago that:

> Every fight consists of two parts: (1) a few individuals who are actively engaged at the center, and (2) the audience that is irresistibly attracted to the scene. The latter are an integral part of the overall situation. (1960: 1)

Schattschneider goes on at length to argue for the importance of the involvement of the audience in political issues resolution. This should not play down the role of a committed individual in forcing an organization to respond and actually change corporate policies and action. The Nader attack on General Motors illustrates the impact of one individual. So, too, do the attacks by individuals against certain shows on the Fox Broadcasting Network; they have influenced some advertisers to withdraw their sponsorship of some programs. Other examples include Gordon Anderson, who established Friends of the Earth and forced major legislation for clean air, and William Shurcliff, who singlehandedly toppled the supersonic transport program by constantly challenging the plane, its design, and claims regarding noise and pollution. Individuals do make a difference, but they must know how to use symbols, and gain access to the larger audience. This is generally done through the use of media attention, and the emotionalization of the issue.

The media play a powerful role in shaping societal and corporate views of the world. The choices of which issues to cover and devote time to are crucial to broadening support for an issue. However, the media is a biased observer. Some research has revealed that most major media elite (broadcasters and journalists of the most influential media outlets) have a 'liberal' bias, significantly at variance with the view of the public-at-large (Lichter and Rothman, 1981). The individual and the public should be wary. The media choose to cover stories that will attract readership or listenership. Stories emotional in content or showing the small person being beaten by the large organization are likely to receive attention. Therefore, wherever possible, groups and individuals courting media attention emphasize such characteristics.

A conceptual map for understanding how an issue expands and how various publics get involved is shown in Figure 29.3 (Cobb and Elder, 1972). In essence there are two broad types of publics: (1) specific publics, which include identification and attention groups; and (2) general publics, which include attentive and general publics. The size of these groups and their influence, as shown in Figure 29.3, vary significantly.

The identification group is the first to become involved as the dispute expands beyond the initial participants. Examples of identification groups include such organizations as the local church, the Toastmasters club, and the adult members who coach a Little League team. The tie that binds them is the individual's choice of personal affiliation and connections. In general, such individual groups are relatively powerless, and it is fairly easy for business organizations to cope with them. The major threat is the formation of interlocking networks of individuals and groups that can bring pressure on the organization (Austrom and Lad, 1986; Mahon et al., 2004).

The next group to which an issue will normally expand is an attention group. Attention groups have two key aspects that separate them from other publics. First, they tend to be organized around a small set of issues important to their membership. They are easily mobilized around their issues and become aware of the latter much earlier than the general public. Examples of such groups include the American Civil Liberties Union, the Center for Automotive Safety, Common Cause, and the Gray Panthers. The second key aspect of these groups is that they have resources and access to the media, giving them power to expand the issue beyond their own limited membership. They also have legitimate access to the formal political

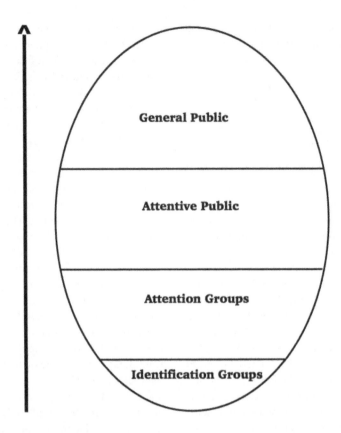

Figure 29.3   How an issue builds support

system, and exercise it frequently. They are more difficult to deal with from an organizational perspective because of their strengths and commitment.

However, if the organization has any desire to contain an issue and prevent it from expanding into more contentious arenas, dealing with this particular set of interest groups early offers the best chance of success. As an example of some success in this regard we can look to the National Coal Policy Project. The project was an attempt by the coal industry to deal with its most knowledgeable and severe critics away from the glare of media attention. A number of breakthroughs occurred in the meetings among the groups, most notable a recognition that neither people in the industry nor in environmental groups were evil personified (Hay and Gray, 1985). Another example is

Clean Sites, which was established in 1984 by the coordinated effort of chemical firms and environmental groups with the support of the Environmental Protection Agency. It is an attempt to speed the cleanup of hazardous waste sites using private monies and is not meant to supplant current federal programs in hazardous waste cleanup and control. Although the organization has met with only moderate success, its impact on the renewal of Superfund in 1984–85 should not be underestimated (Clean Sites, 1985a,b; and personal correspondence between the author and the President of Clean Sites, Inc.). Again, both of these efforts were non-adversarial in approach, and were attempts to gain control of issues and problems before they entered a judicial, legislative, or regulatory arena, where no side (corporate or environmental) has much control over the eventual outcome.

The suggestion here is simple. If an organization wishes to contain an issue, it must deal with the attention groups early. More importantly, there appears to be a critical mass or turning point in the evolution of an issue beyond which containment is not an option. It is argued that this occurs when an issue is named, so that then someone or an industry or an organization is blamed, and afterward claims are made on those blamed to remedy the situation.

In general, firms only recognize this after the fact, through painful failure. Therefore, a clearer understanding of issue expansion (and the use of definition and symbols) helps to narrow the time frame or critical mass of involvement to a smaller window of vulnerability for the corporation. In complex issues, such as biotechnology, this can be done relatively easily. Industry's argument is that regulation and public-policy oversight are much too complicated to be left to the general public, but are better suited to the deliberations and decisions of experts. This argument will probably hold until either an accident occurs, or an attention group changes the definition of the issue and emotionalizes it. Research shows that business has been learning from experience (Boston University Public Affairs Research Group, 1981; and the unpublished results of a 1986 survey by the same group).

The issue, if it expands further, moves into the arena of general publics. The first general public, the 'attentive' public, consists of the well-educated and well-read population. In this group one finds opinion leaders. Finally, an issue expands to the broadest segment of society, the general public itself. An issue reaches this group either because the organization did not contain the issue at the attention-group level and/or because the issue is highly generalizable and symbolic. Often the response of this public is disorganized, neither well-channeled or directed – unless an interest group, organization, or political official/body seizes control of the issue and directs attention to a specific set of actions.

Tylenol's experience with product tampering is an example of an issue reaching the broadest levels of public knowledge. Johnson and Johnson had a clear plan of action – product withdrawal. Volkswagen, as this chapter is written, is engaged in managing the emissions testing issue associated with what appears to be fraudulent performance claims. What then, when an issue emerges, can an organization do to contain it?

TACTICS OF ISSUE CONTAINMENT

In summary, if an organization can keep an issue off an agenda, it stands a greater chance of success, success being defined as the exercise of maximum corporate discretion to deal with the issue, with minimal public and media involvement. Failing that, the second best strategy is to seize the initiative and take control of the issue and its definition, and place it on an agenda of the organization's choosing. A first pass at tactics pursued by organizations in dealing with issues is shown in Figure 29.4. There are two alternatives available to the organization in any political contest – deal with the issue or deal with those who are pressing the issue for resolution.

Obviously an organization can choose to do one or the other, or both simultaneously. If the issue focus is chosen, the organization or public interest group can pursue a direct attack by attempting to defuse the issue. This can often be undertaken by symbolic action that lacks real substance. It is done, however, amid a great deal of publicity, and with appropriate comments as to how the organization will change. The reality is that the organization does not change at all; the situation is not seriously addressed, but everyone feels better. The Grace Commission on Control of Government Expenditures, for example, was announced with great fanfare by President Reagan. It produced an extensive set of recommendations, and died a silent death. The

ORIENTATION

M O D E O F A T T A C K		Issue	Group
	Direct	**Defuse the Issue** e.g. set up a special committee to look into the issue	**Attack the Group** e.g. question the authority, motives and legitimacy of group regarding the issue
	Indirect	**Blur the Issue** e.g. bring in other stake-holders, add issues and refine the current issue	**Undermine the Group** e.g. co-opt the leadership, or bypass the leaders and go directly to membership

Figure 29.4   Attacking the issue or the stakeholder

firing of a chief executive officer in a public manner is often cited as proof of the organization's sincere desire to change – but is it? What happens afterwards is more telling. Does the organization change its behavior and actions? Sadly, not often. Pfeffer and Salancik document several symbolic actions that give the illusion of action but bring little substantive change (Pfeffer and Salancik, 1978).

An indirect attack on the issue could include attempts to redefine the issue, postponement of action to await more study, and discussion of the constraints on organizational behavior that make it impossible to comply or respond to this issue. The Manville and Eastern bankruptcies, shifting and blurring the issue of product liability and union–management disagreements with that of bankruptcy law, is an example of this tactic.

If the organization decides to deal with individuals or groups pressing an issue, it can launch a direct attack, but with great risk to itself. One tactic is to raise questions about the individual's or group's legitimacy in an attempt to discredit them. General

Motors (GM), for instance, tried several years ago to destroy Ralph Nader's credibility, but subsequently apologized before a Congressional committee for its action. GM then lost a court case to Nader and paid him US$500,000. Nader used those funds to establish the Center for Automotive Safety that has been a public and effective critic of the industry since the Center's establishment. Sometimes, however, direct attacks can be successful as it either discourages individuals from pursing an issue or so damages their credibility that their impact on an issue is greatly diminished.

The indirect approach to dealing with groups (or stakeholders) includes co-optation, direct appeals to the membership (bypassing the leadership), and secondary sources of influence. This last technique was used with some success by union organizers. The unions appeal to members of the local community, and to other unionized workers to support efforts in unionization. The President of the United States has used this approach, with little success to date, to appeal to the general public on the issue of gun control and gun violence.

SHAPING STRATEGIES: DEALING WITH ISSUES ON THE AGENDA

Despite an organization's best efforts, issues do get to agendas that are not of the organization's choosing. In this situation, the firm must try to shape the issue, its eventual outcome, and the implementation of that outcome.

In Massachusetts, a controversial bill calling for dramatic changes in health-care costs was proposed in 1982. Several major actors were involved: the state Business Roundtable, the Massachusetts Hospital Association (MHA), Blue Cross, the High-Technology Council, physicians, and the Life Insurance Association of Massachusetts. A principal purpose of the bill was to reduce health-care costs and erode the dominant position that Blue Cross held in the state. It was clear to all that the issue was 'health-care cost containment'. This had great appeal to business, as it would reduce the cost of employee benefits, and to individuals, as it would reduce the costs for health care. The MHA, the physicians, and Blue Cross were less than thrilled by this proposal, but it had great public, business, and political backing and appeal. In assessing the situation, Blue Cross noted that if the legislation passed, then it would force that organization to reduce benefits provided to its 300,000 plus elderly subscribers. It meant that that group would either pay more for benefits, receive less benefits, or both. Blue Cross called all of these subscribers to let them know of this potential impact. Those calls stopped the bill dead. The issue had been shifted to 'erosion of benefits for the elderly', and no group or organization wanted to support that position publicly. The tactic of issue redefinition can still be effective even after issues are on the agenda – and with minimal costs to the organizations involved. In this situation, the only cost to Blue Cross was that of telephone calls. In a similar vein, the Australian government attempted to impose a significant tax increase on mining, feeling that the general public would support such an effort. They were wrong, as the mining industry had spent some time in improving relationships with the public at large and were able to pressure the government, through extensive public involvement, to not implement this new tax.

The gamesmanship surrounding issue definition also occurs at the industry level, as in the 1980 chemical industry response to calls for hazardous waste site cleanup legislation (aka, Superfund). In the early days of the proposed legislation, the industry attempted to define the issue as 'societal'. Since society benefitted from the advances made by chemicals, it should bear the burden of the cleanup of waste sites. When that failed, the industry tried to identify the issue as one of 'orphan sites', that is, that the proposed tax should be used only to clean up sites for which ownership or responsibility could not be determined. Since these sites were not numerous, the proposed tax should be, their reasoning went, very low. Although these attempts failed, it is important to note the persistent attempt to redefine the issue as it was being considered, and the subtle appeal that each redefinition held for different sets of publics interested in the issue.

In the social agenda arena, the Tylenol incident is a successful example of seizing control of an issue once it became widely known. It is not necessary to recount the Tylenol tragedy, but it should be noted that Johnson and Johnson's quick action gained control of the issue early. The company reduced the potential damage to its main product in the first poisoning incident and won time to rethink new product design and packaging. Johnson and Johnson did this by maintaining constant contact with the press and by pushing a public-policy initiative that paid dividends for the company. The initiative advocated an immediate Food and Drug Administration requirement that all products such as Tylenol be placed in tamper-proof containers. Not only did this get good press, as it showed that Johnson and Johnson's first commitment was to people's safety, it also had the effect of increasing overall costs for the industry simultaneously with the increased cost for Tylenol.

STAKEHOLDER AND GROUP POSITIONING AROUND ISSUES ON THE AGENDA

Political and social action should be aimed at identifying those actors likely to become involved in the contest and their relative strengths and weaknesses. The first method of doing this is analysis of the stake of individual actors and groups in the issue at hand (Freeman, 1984; Mitchell et al., 1997). The organization must be concerned with maintaining relationships involving similar stakeholders and groups across the range of issues faced. Today's friend can be tomorrow's enemy and vice versa. This approach also requires simultaneous conflict- and collaboration-management techniques with the same set of stakeholders on a variety of issues and the achievement of favorable outcomes for the organization.

There are five strategies that a firm can pursue, at every stage of the life-cycle, based on its stake in the issue and the degree to which the firm has 'mostly conflicting' or 'mostly common' interests with the opposition or industry critics. These strategies are objectively and directly observable. This framework is useful not only for identifying a particular organization's strategy, but also for assessing the strategy of other groups, individuals, and political officials (see Post, 1978; Thomas, 1976).

Business organizations and non-business interest groups can compete vigorously in an attempt to overwhelm the other side and maintain the status quo (resistance). Management may likewise opt to avoid the problem by ignoring or withdrawing from the situation (avoidance), or by accommodating the opposition. The choice is reflective of the stake of the organization in the issue and

management's desire to act in one manner rather than another. The firm can also work toward mutually satisfactory solutions (collaboration), or the enterprise may seek out an intermediate position which often arises out of a weaker position in terms of outcomes or relationships (shared responsibility). As noted, the positioning and the strategies themselves are a direct function of the organization's stake in the issue and its power relative to other actors in the debate. This analytical process has been used with great success in the infant formula controversy and in the chemical industry's approach to superfund legislation (Mahon, 1983; Post, 1978). This is a simple, but powerful technique for understanding and assessing political strategies and group involvement. Organizations that monitor several issues at a time will find this an effective instrument for cross-issue political impact analysis. An organization that uses this technique to track several issues in the political and social arenas will be able to see how opposing groups trade off political capital and alliances on different issues, and in turn assess their own response to this activity.

It is clear, however, that over the life-cycle of an issue organizations alter their political and social strategies. This suggests that a combination of internal and external forces is at work. In brief, not only is the firm's specific strategy (or, perhaps, tactics) at a given time observable, but so are the broader strategies that an organization follows throughout the issue-life-cycle. These strategies have been characterized as reactive, proactive, and interactive patterns of response (Post, 1978).

A final and more specific set of strategies and tactics is suggested below:

1 **Total resistance** – the organization refuses to change, repulses all challenges, or forces the environment to change or adapt to the organization's goals;
2 **Bargaining** – the organization bargains or compromises so that adjustments on all sides are required;

3 **Capitulation** – the organization ends the bargaining with external actors, seeks a replacement, or changes its environment, all the while seeking the best solution for the organization and exoneration;

4 **Termination** – the organization ends the relationship with the external group, and seeks a replacement; and

5 **Cessation of activity** – the organization, unwilling or unable to adapt or respond to the changes demanded, disbands.

All of these approaches emphasize clear patterns in organizational political strategies that are directly and objectively verifiable. In addition, these techniques provide us with a slightly different frame of reference to view the activity of actors in the political process, and they also provide us with different sets of information about the issue, the actors involved, and their relative strengths and weaknesses. Lastly, organizations that use multiple perspectives to assess political and social action reduce their risk of surprise from unanticipated group involvement or issue redefinition.

CONCLUSION

This chapter has attempted to sketch out how an organization can keep issues off of the agenda (containment) or shape an issue once it has been placed on an agenda for resolution. The tactics described herein are equally appropriate to public-interest-group action and to international political and social action by corporations and other groups.

It should be clear that most political and social action by corporations in dealing with issues is undertaken with specific goals and objectives in mind. At a minimum, the organization does not wish to change the way in which it has been doing business for years. However, if these externally oriented strategies fail, the corporation must take substantive action to change its behavior. As a consequence, the final stage of organizational

adjustment to external pressure, once an issue has been resolved, is what I term 'coping'. Then the strategic action becomes focused internally on managing the required change (for the challenges here see Ackerman, 1975; Ackerman and Bauer, 1976). More importantly, external groups and politicians need to realize that large corporations do not learn quickly, and that they move very slowly. One often needs a crisis to get movement, or the pressure on the corporation must be heavy and sustained. Indeed, the fractionation in political power addressed in this chapter may be tipping the balance in favor of large organizations in their quest not to change and to avoid adapting. It certainly contributes to increased confusion as to who represents the public interest and what that public interest is in a given situation.

What is needed is greater recognition of political and social processes to resolve misunderstandings and difficulties before they enter the formal political, legal, and regulatory arenas. However, the shift of power to the states, growing pressures for resolution of issues on an international scale, and the movement of public interest groups to that level of political action will probably lead to an increase in adversarial confrontations for the near-term future.

The astute management of issues can pay dividends that affect the profitability, cost, and risk associated with large-scale enterprises. First, well-coordinated and thoughtfully implemented issue strategies can contribute to the preservation of profits. Examples include the actions of Johnson and Johnson with Tylenol (which also resulted in good public policy – tamper-proof containers), the bailout of Chrysler, and Procter and Gamble's continued involvement in toxic shock research after the Rely problem.

Second, sound issues strategies can lead to the reduction of risk and costs for the organization. Tylenol is an example of this type of action; so, too, was the successful lobbying aimed at persuading the federal government to provide guarantees to the insurance industry after the riots in inner cities in the late 1960s. The bailout of financial organizations worldwide to avoid even deeper financial problems is yet another example of public policy working on behalf of an industry.

A careful review of these actions, techniques, and approaches – and a host of others in different industries and circumstances – will continue to demonstrate the value of corporate issues management as necessary survival skills for the twenty-first-century organization. As fractionation of political power at the national level continues and globalization of markets grows, more pressure will be placed on organizations to provide solutions and adapt to changing circumstances.

REFERENCES

Ackerman, R. A., 1975. *The Social Challenge to Business.* Cambridge, MA: Harvard University Press.

Ackerman, R. A., and Bauer, R., 1976. *Corporate Responsiveness: The Modern Dilemma.* Reston, VA: Reston.

Austrom, D. R., and Lad. L. 1986. 'Problem Solving Networks: Towards a Synthesis of Innovative Approaches to Social Issues Management', in J. A. Pearce and R. B. Robinson, eds., *Academy of Management Best Paper Proceedings*: 311–315.

Berry, J. M., 1984. *The Interest Group Society.* Boston, MA: Little, Brown and Co.

Bigelow, B., Fahey, L., and Mahon, J. F., 1993. 'A Typology of Issues Evolution', *Business and Society*, 32, (1), Spring: 18–29.

Boston University Public Affairs Research Group, 1981. *Public Affairs Officers and Their Functions: Summary of Survey Responses*, monograph. Boston, MA: Boston University School of Management.

Clean Sites, 1985a. 'Clean Sites Inc., Getting Down to Business', *Chemical and Engineering News*, June 17: 30–31.

Clean Sites, 1985b. 'Clean Sites, Inc., Sweeping Aside Startup Problems and Getting on with the Job', *Chemical Week*, June 5, 1985: 28–31.

Cobb, R. W., and Elder, C. D., 1972. *Participation in American Politics: The Dynamics of Agenda Building.* Boston, MA: Allyn and Bacon. Reissued in 1983, Baltimore, MD: Johns Hopkins Press.

Cobb, R. W., and Ross, M. H., 1997. *Cultural Strategies of Agenda Denial: Avoidance, Attack, and Redefinition.* Lawrence, KS: University Press of Kansas.

Edelman, M., 1964. *The Symbolic Uses of Politics.* Chicago, IL: University of Illinois Press.

Eyestone, R., 1978. *From Social Issues to Public Policy.* New York: Wiley.

Freeman, R. E., 1984. *Strategic Management: A Stakeholder Approach.* Marshfield, MA: Pitman.

Hay, T. M., and Gray, B., 1985. 'The National Coal Policy Project: An Interactive Approach to Corporate Social Responsiveness', in Lee E. Preston, ed., *Research in Corporate Social Performance and Policy*, vol. 7. Greenwich, CT: JAI Press: 191–212.

Heath, R. L., and Nelson, R. A., 1986. *Issues Management.* Beverly Hills, CA: Sage.

Keim, G. D., and Baysinger, B., 1988. 'The Efficacy of Business Political Activity: Competitive Considerations in a Principal-Agent Context', *Journal of Management*, 14, (2): 165.

Keim, G. D., and Zeithaml, C., 1986. 'Corporate Political Strategy and Legislative Decision Making: A Review and Contingency Approach', *Academy of Management Review*, 11, (4): 828–843.

Kingdon, J. W., 1984. *Agendas, Alternatives, and Public Policies.* Boston, MA: Little, Brown and Co.

Lichter, S. R., and Rothman, S., 1981. 'Media and Business Elites', *Public Opinion*, 4, (5): 42–46.

Mahon, J. F., 1983. 'Corporate Political Strategies: An Empirical Study of Chemical Firm Response to Superfund Legislation', in Lee E. Preston, ed., *Research in Corporate Social Performance and Policy*, vol. 5. Greenwich, CT: JAI Press: 143–182.

Mahon, J. F. 1989. 'Corporate Political Strategy', *Business in the Contemporary World*, II, I, Autumn: 50–63.

Mahon, J. F. 1993. 'Shaping Issues/Manufacturing Agents: Corporate Political Sculpting', in Barry Mitnick, ed., *Corporate*

Political Agency: The Construction of Competition in Public Affairs. Newbury Park, CA: Sage: 187–212.

Mahon, J. F., 2006. 'Issuing the Challenge – Naming and Framing Issues in Civil Societies', *Corporate Public Affairs*, 15, (2): 3–5.

Mahon, J. F., Heugens, P. M. A. R., and Lamertz, K., 2004. 'Social Networks and Nonmarket Strategy', *International Journal of Public Affairs*, 4, (2): 170–189.

Mahon, J. F., and Kelley, P. C., 1988. 'The Politics of Toxic Wastes: Multinational Corporations as Facilitators of Transnational Public Policy', in Lee E. Preston, ed., *Research in Corporate Social Performance and Policy*, vol. 10. Greenwich, CT: JAI Press: 59–86.

Mahon, J. F., and Waddock, S. A., 1992. 'Strategic Issues Management: An Integration of Issue Life Cycle Perspectives', *Business & Society*, 31, (1): 19–32.

Mahon, J. F., and Wartick, S. L., 1994. Toward a Substantive Definition of the Corporate Issue Construct: A Review and Synthesis of the Literature', *Business & Society*, 33, (3): 293–311.

Mahon, J. F., and Wartick, S. L., 2003. 'Dealing with Stakeholders: How Reputation, Credibility and Framing Influence the Game', *Corporate Reputation Review*, 6, (1), Spring: 19–35.

Mitchell, R. K., Agle, B. R., and Wood, D. J., 1997. 'Toward A Theory of Stakeholder Identification and Salience: Defining the Principle of Who and What Really Counts', *Academy of Management Review*, 22, (4): 853–886.

Olson, M., 1965. *The Logic of Collective Action: Public Goods and the Theory of Groups.* Cambridge, MA: Harvard University Press.

Pfeffer, J., and Salancik, G., 1978. *The External Control of Organizations.* New York: Harper and Row.

Post, J. E., 1978. *Corporate Behavior and Social Change.* Reston, VA: Reston.

Ryan, M. H., Swanson, C. L., and Buchholz, R. A., 1987. *Corporate Strategy, Public Policy, and the Fortune 500.* Oxford: Basil Blackwell: especially pp. 100–105.

Schattschneider, E. F., 1960. *The Semi-Sovereign People.* New York: Holt.

Sethi, S. P., 1987. 'Corporate Political Activism', in S. Prakash Sethi and Cecilia M. Falbe, eds., *Business and Society – Dimensions of Conflict and Cooperation.* Lexington, MA: Lexington Books: 529–544.

Thomas, K., 1976. 'Conflict and Conflict Management', in M. Dunnette, ed., *Handbook of Industrial and Organizational Psychology.* Chicago, IL: Rand-McNally: 889–935.

Yoffie, D. B., and Bergenstein, S., 1985. 'Creating Political Advantage: The Rise of the Corporate Political Entrepreneur', *California Management Review*, 28, (1), Fall: 124–139.

30

Corporate Social Responsibility, Public Affairs and Corporate Community Involvement: Torn between Instrumentalism and Deliberation

Irina Lock and Peter Seele

The more successful and important corporate social responsibility (CSR) becomes in the business world, the more divided it becomes as a concept. Most companies follow a strategic and instrumental approach in identifying additional value creation. Non-governmental organizations (NGOs) and stakeholders instead emphasize the transformative power of the concept in reducing harm and negative impacts. This divide analogously takes place in the scholarly discussion on CSR, as this article shows. The arena in which these divergent approaches are dealt with is the political arena, where CSR, in at least some countries, has become increasingly more of a compliance exercise. In this process, communities play an increasing role in facilitating institutional change.

Given the effects that CSR as a compliance exercise can have on the bottom line, the political and corporate spheres are growing closer and closer. On the one hand, corporations have become ever more active in the political arena through public affairs (PA) activities because legislation often determines success, failure, or even the license to operate for corporations. On the other hand, researchers have observed a 'new political role of corporations' contributing to solving global public issues as part of their CSR, a recent theoretical stream known as 'political CSR'. In this chapter, we address this interplay focusing on community involvement as an example.

In a nutshell, the goal of corporate political activities is to 'produce public policy outcomes that are favorable to the firm's continued economic survival and success' (Keim & Baysinger, 1988, p. 171). In contrast, political CSR addresses issues such as 'public health, education, social security, and protection of human rights' (among others) that previously belonged to the domain of nation-states (Scherer & Palazzo, 2007, p. 1109; 2011, p. 899) and corporations are called to 'go beyond instrumental (that is, profit-focused) arguments for CSR' (Scherer &

Palazzo, 2007, p. 1113; Whelan, 2012, p. 712).

Thus, on the one hand, we observe a normative approach to CSR which builds on participation, dialogue, and transparency and advocates for corporations to engage more politically. On the other hand, more instrumentally focused activities of PA aim to build relationships with political decision makers to favor the companies' interests. Often, these activities are carried out with the help of communities and their civil engagement.

PA responds to the notion of participation and 'government relation functions' (Baysinger & Woodman, 1982) in that it refers not only to legislators (Grunig & Hunt, 1984) and politicians (Harrison, 2000), as some authors have claimed with regard to lobbying, but expands further to reach other constituents such as communities, any other stakeholder, and regulators, and hence all groups influencing the policy process. PA includes activities such as grassroots lobbying, one of the most effective tools of public affairs (Nownes, 2006), where lobbyists do not approach public policy makers directly, but detour via the constituents of a certain community or issue to reach the policy makers indirectly (Thompson & John, 2007). According to Hillman and Hitt (1999), unlike 'classical' lobbying which is part of an information-seeking strategy, PA falls under the umbrella of constituency-building strategies. In practice, lobbyists may approach citizens via diverse channels to inform them about an issue and make them take action (for example, approach their local politician). Elected politicians are also more eager to respond to such grassroots support from communities because 'classical' lobbying or lobbying techniques based on financial incentives, such as paid travel and honoraria for speeches, are not always as attractive to them (Hillman & Hitt, 1999).

In this chapter, we present the case of Coca-Cola, a sponsor of the Olympic Games in London, and the debate about sugar and obesity in the UK. We also examine how the doctors' associations act as communities and got involved. The London Assembly, a community board controlling the mayor of the city of London, also engaged in the debate. What makes the case more compelling conceptually is that Coca-Cola's CSR strategy was in opposition to what the company planned as sponsor and how it was perceived by the public regarding their health. We conclude this chapter by building on recent literature on CSR and public affairs, and propose strategic alignment between the two, particularly to safeguard the authentic and credible role of communities in the process of deliberation.

CSR, HOW IT ALL STARTED

The modern era of corporate social responsibility began in the 1950s in the US with Bowen and Johnson's book '*The social responsibilities of the businessman*' (1953), in which they recognize the impact of business's actions on society. However, scholars agree that socially responsible actions were already observable in North America in the 1920s with entrepreneurs like Henry Ford, Andrew Carnegie, and John D. Rockefeller (Post, Lawrence, & Weber, 2002, p. 60f). In Europe, socially responsible entrepreneurs were active even earlier in the nineteenth century with Werner von Siemens and Friedrich Krupp, whose companies have grown into multinational corporations (Hiss, 2009). Their activities ranged from donations to charitable foundations to workers rights, housing, and health insurance.

Opposition to these alleged social responsibilities of business emerged in the early 1960s, with Milton Friedman being the most popular adversary voice (Friedman, 1962). Nevertheless, conceptual advancements of CSR were put forward in the years to come (Preston & James, 1975; Zenisek, 1979), broadening the scope of the concept. Carroll (1979) defined CSR as a four-dimensional construct, consisting of economic, legal, ethical, and discretionary responsibilities, which he later recreated in the form of a pyramid (Carroll, 1991). Eilbert and Parket (1973, p. 7) framed CSR as 'good neighborliness', a term that carries the idea that business is and should behave as a good 'neighbor' to its close constituents, a notion that was taken up in the 1980s with the idea of corporate citizenship (Matten & Crane, 2005). Sethi (1975) for the first time put forward the idea of corporate social performance (CSP), marking a shift from abstract responsibility to behavior. This notion was popular until the 1990s (Wood, 1991), but in the new millennium it lost track due to the new concept of instrumental CSR.

Empirical works on CSR took off in the 1980s, along with conceptual alternatives to the already then contested and ill-defined CSR concept. Stakeholder theory (Freeman, 1984) and the emergence of business ethics as a new discipline in the US are examples tracing the idea of performance rather than responsibility. It was also the decade of the emergence of instrumental CSR, where social problems are turned into economic opportunities for firms (Drucker, 1984). Until today, this line proliferates in academia and practice.

Although the 1990s did not see many novel conceptual approaches to CSR (Carroll, 1999), more empirical studies and further alternative concepts emerged, such as corporate citizenship (Matten & Crane, 2005), the pyramid of CSR (Carroll, 1991), and sustainability (Elkington, 1998). Most crucially, CSR found entrance and proliferated in the business world. This set the foundation for the success of instrumental CSR research. However, with globalization, powerful multinational corporations, economic crises, and corporate scandals, a counter stream of CSR research emerged global corporate citizenship (Matten & Crane, 2005) that further develops ideas of the 1970s and political CSR theory that applies critical political philosophy to business's responsibilities (Scherer & Palazzo, 2007). An overview of the two

broad lines in CSR research, instrumental and deliberative, follows.

CSR TODAY: OVERVIEW ON CURRENT THEORIES AND CONCEPTS

Scholars have attempted to classify the existing theoretical approaches taken on CSR: Garriga and Melé (2004) delineate instrumental from political, integrative, and ethical CSR; Lee (2008) and Carroll (1999) describe the evolution of the concept historically; others (Dahlsrud, 2008; Van Marrewijk, 2003) review existing definitions for a classification; most recently, Schultz et al. (2013) have delineated instrumental, political-normative, and communicative approaches.

Following the approach taken by Schultz et al., the following reviews instrumental and political-normative (called here deliberative) approaches to CSR. Instrumental CSR focuses on the business case and the relationship between social and financial performance, a link that has not yet been shown to exist consistently (Wood, 2010). Political-normative theories include the concept of political CSR. This so-called communicative approach to CSR includes attempts to describe CSR as a dynamic process where multiple, uncontrolled forms of dialogue take place with a variety of audiences. Furthermore, it regards CSR as communicatively constructed (Castelló et al., 2013), for instance, in the form of aspirational talk (Christensen et al., 2013) or as a sense making process (Guthey & Morsing, 2014), thereby challenging the consensus view of political CSR. In this review, however, the focus is on instrumental and deliberative CSR because deliberative CSR has communication at its very core (Seele & Lock, 2015). Furthermore, given that the focus of this contribution is to analyze the political activities of companies, the political approach to CSR is taken as a reference as well as for comparison.

INSTRUMENTAL CSR

The twenty-first century brought a shift to the concept of CSR. An increasing number of scholars conceptualized it as a risk or reputation management tool (for example, Francis & Armstrong, 2003) and a strategic management lens was applied to CSR. Developed by marketing researchers such as Kotler & Lee, 2005; Porter & Kramer, 2006), social responsibility concepts were broadened and focused on the business case for the firm. This instrumental viewpoint of CSR is still prevalent in academia and practice, describing a 'shift from obligation to strategy' (Kotler & Lee, 2005, p. 7). Hence, the link between CSR and financial performance, for instance with the study of CSR's effects on customer loyalty and advocacy (Du et al., 2007) or CSR and corporate reputation (Van Riel & Fombrun, 2007), are included within this line of inquiry. Furthermore, from a value chain perspective, researchers have analyzed the extent to which CSR can contribute to establishing new products and markets and help to develop communities at corporate production sites. Most recent notions include the idea of creating shared value (Porter & Kramer, 2011) that takes up Drucker's idea of turning social problems into business opportunities and that has caught on with major corporations such as Nestlé.

Given this proliferation of competing frameworks, the concept of CSR has become more ambiguous than ever before. Not only have competing concepts such as citizenship, sustainability, and creating shared value entered the academic (and popular) literature, but also even more theories, frameworks, and viewpoints have emerged to influence CSR's meaning.

DELIBERATIVE CSR

The instrumental business case perspective on CSR, however, has been criticized for lacking clear research goals and explanatory power, not accounting for individual-level factors of CSR, and being based on the erroneous equation that what is good for society is also good for corporations (Lee, 2008). Van Oosterhout (2010) argued that the narrow 'economizing' perspective on CSR is based on rational choice theory and lacks theoretical foundations, especially regarding legitimacy theory. Furthermore, it disregards current global trends, where the public and private spheres are blurred and globalized business results in ever more responsibilities for corporations, along with increasing power. At the same time, the state is losing power and multinational firms operate outside the spheres of national influence. The Copenhagen Conference on Climate Change, for instance, reflects this lack of state power and nations' inability to solve global problems. On the other hand, companies capitalize on this inability of the (former) nation-state power and operate in ill-defined global governances. That way, companies can hide behind 'organized irresponsibility' and conduct business profitably (Wettstein, 2010).

With the idea of 'global corporate citizenship', Crane et al. (2008) take up the idea of the company being a 'neighbor' (Eilbert & Parket, 1973) or citizen in society. Firms are politically responsible actors that set and implement norms and values in global society by their actions. At the same time, the power of multinational private actors is increasing. Corporations influence public policy to shape global rules, with CSR being a means to influence governments (Wettstein, 2010). Thereby, businesses also assume political responsibilities. Companies, however, are profit-driven, not altruistic actors and thus interested in making profits. That is why these positive political responsibilities have to be completed collectively, including a variety of stakeholder groups in multi-stakeholder initiatives to create self-regulations where hard law legislation is missing due to governance gaps. This new approach is called 'political CSR' (Scherer &

Palazzo, 2007, 2011). The concept refers to an extended model of global public policy in which firms contribute to global regulation and the provision of public goods (Scherer & Palazzo, 2011, p. 901). Practical examples of this idea are the UN Global Compact or the Global Reporting Initiative standards, where firms deliberately join a regulatory framework although they are not forced to do so by any superior authority. Corporations thus become 'politicized' in two ways: they have to conduct business in a broadened definition of responsibility and they have to help solve public issues by cooperating with other societal actors (Scherer & Palazzo, 2011, p. 917).

Political CSR is distinct from instrumental CSR theories because it 'goes beyond' (Scherer & Palazzo, 2011, p. 900) the notion that CSR is merely complying with stakeholder expectations. It employs a broader definition of responsibility that accounts for globalization's effects on business. At its heart stands deliberative democracy theory (Habermas, 1996), which provides a solid theoretical foundation for this approach.

With this political turn, new questions of (democratic) legitimacy (Scherer et al., 2013a) enter the debate. In political CSR, 'moral' legitimacy is proposed. As opposed to the pragmatic and cognitive forms of legitimacy (Suchman, 1995) that are prevalent in instrumental CSR approaches, moral legitimacy 'is based on moral judgments and an exchange of arguments on whether an individual, an institution, or an action can be considered socially acceptable' (Scherer & Palazzo, 2011, p. 915).

Public relations scholars hold that moral legitimacy is an outcome and objective of issues management (Heath & Palenchar, 2008), while organizational scholars hold that it can be achieved by storytelling (Golant & Sillince, 2007). In political CSR, moral legitimacy is reached through discourse oriented toward consensus between the company and society (Habermas, 1996); thus, it is established in a communication process. Contrary to cognitive and pragmatic legitimacy, moral

legitimacy is not attributed, but constructed through communication: 'Moral legitimacy consists of a mutual exchange between "organizational practice" and "societal expectations"' (Scherer et al., 2013a, p. 263). This marks a shift in the source of legitimacy, which ultimately affects the companies' license to operate (Donaldson & Dunfee, 1999) and results in an emphasis of the role of communication in CSR theory. Hence, communication is central to the exercise of political CSR.

CSR AND PUBLIC AFFAIRS: JOINT FORCES OR ANTAGONISTS (IN GENERAL)

As one of the many functions of the public relations realm, PA is a communication exercise. By communicating with an array of different stakeholders, organizations – whether corporations, NGOs, or governments themselves – aim at '[m]anaging relationships between organisations and stakeholders/issues in the public policy (i.e., non-market or socio-political) environment' (Fleisher, 1994). Positive relations with stakeholders contribute to organizational effectiveness, loyalty, advocacy, and crisis resolution (Huang, 2001). In addition to classical lobbying, PA includes political activities such as community relations, donations, grassroots activities, and devious astroturf lobbying (Showalter & Fleisher, 2005; Thomson & John, 2007); 'public affairs extends beyond the function of government relations alone' (Harris & Moss, 2001, p. 104).

PA operates at the crossing of business and public policy. While in management studies scholars hold that the economic and the political spheres are separate (Baron, 1995) and therefore 'corporate political activities' need to bridge these two worlds, political CSR views both spheres as conflated. Thus, a collective approach to problem solution is needed, bringing a multitude of societal actors together to reach consensus discursively (Scherer & Palazzo, 2011). This can take the form of community issues being tackled in local councils or global multi-stakeholder initiatives addressing sustainable forestry, such as the Forest Stewardship Council (FSC).

Thus, CSR and PA activities take place in the same market space. Therefore, their organizational strategies should not be contradictory, but aligned to avoid negative effects on reputation and accusations of greenwashing (Seele & Gatti, 2015) and corporate hypocrisy (Den Hond et al., 2014). In the tobacco industry, for example, companies deliberately have not aligned their CSR and PA efforts, claiming that they would do anything in their CSR strategy to prevent youths from smoking while at the same time lobbying against further regulation (Fooks et al., 2013). While this opportunistic strategy has led to further mistrust on the side of regulators, aligning CSR and PA activities can result in positive outcomes for the firm and society (Lock & Seele, 2016). In fact, CSR can add value to PA activities (Richter, 2011) because it fosters organizational reputation and builds trustful relationships with stakeholders through moral legitimacy (Heath et al., 2013). Furthermore, firms can use their CSR resources to access public policy and to support their PA strategy (Den Hond et al., 2014).

Whether CSR and PA join forces or contradict each other, however, depends on the tactics and strategies organizations use. This becomes especially evident in the realm of corporate community relations (CCR), a sphere of influence for CSR and PA alike.

Tactics of CSR and Public Affairs: the Exemplar of Corporate Community Relations

CSR and PA operate at the intersection of business, society, and public policy. By providing jobs, paying taxes, and having a physical presence that can affect local infrastructure, companies have a big and largely positive impact on the communities in which they operate, rendering them important stakeholders. That is why companies are interested in obtaining and maintaining trustful relationships with the communities in which they operate. Corporate community relations:

> help to build a sense of rapport and understanding of local citizens' concerns and needs, which in turn may assist organisations when seeking planning permission, change of use of a site, or the closure or development of a plant – all of which are likely to be made easier when there is a thorough understanding by the organisation or community of how each other works and its interests. (Harris & Moss, 2001, p. 107)

This can be pursued by establishing contacts with local institutions and politicians, which is part of the PA strategy. Alternatively, companies approach local citizens, often through voluntary activities such as donations, employee voluntarism, and in-kind contributions (Waddock & Boyle, 1995). These activities show overlaps with discretionary CSR actions (Carroll, 1991) and corporate citizenship activities (Matten & Crane, 2005). Recently, the relationship between geographic proximity and local CSR engagement has been analyzed (Husted et al., 2015); the findings show that CSR engagement also depends on high levels of local CSR density. Thus, CSR, PA, and CCR are interlinked: all three build on the idea of stakeholder theory and view local communities as important stakeholders, all three have communication at their core, and all three share common tactics. In fact, rather than viewing the three as distinct corporate strategies, it is more accurate to describe CSR and PA as strategies that come to fruition in CCR. Thus, from a theoretical stance, it appears inevitable for companies to link their CSR and PA strategies, especially when it comes to CCR. Linking CSR, PA, and CCR activities strategically and with regard to resources and communication tactics is efficient for all three strategies (Showalter & Fleisher, 2005).

This link becomes even more evident when looking at the concept of political CSR. Political CSR is built on the idea of political deliberation (Habermas, 1996), where all affected parties of an issue are invited 'to a roundtable' to collectively find a solution to the problem at hand through discourse (Young, 2004). Furthermore, given that political CSR regards corporations as bearing 'new political responsibilities' (Scherer & Palazzo, 2011) that were previously ascribed to the nation-state, companies are called upon to solve public issues. Thus, the distinction between PA and CSR activities is blurred.

With regard to transnationally operating companies as described in political CSR theory, the notion of local communities may not be adequate. As Harris and Moss (2001, p. 107f) suggest, '[with] larger international or multinational corporations, community relations initiatives may take on an international dimension, perhaps embracing issues that transcend national boundaries but which manifest themselves in similar ways in the different communities where an organisation has a presence'. Thus, in line with political CSR, the authors suggest that more global problems such as poverty and obesity may be in the corporations' and communities' spheres of interest and responsibility, thus understanding local communities not primarily as where the companies have their home bases, but enlarging the concept to global society, incorporating the idea of 'glocal' business (Svensson, 2001).

In addition, the PA field has seen conceptual changes. PA, as the recent term for activities that were formerly covered by 'lobbying', responds more to the notion of participation in that it refers not only to legislators (Grunig & Hunt, 1984) or politicians (Harrison, 2000), but also to other constituents such as civil society, stakeholders such as local communities, and, increasingly, regulators. Besides classical lobbying, it includes tactics such as donations to political parties, funding of think tanks, local grassroots campaigns, astroturf lobbying (Thomson &

John, 2007), and corporate political advocacy (Wettstein & Baur, 2012). In fact, some authors already see a 'golden age of grassroots lobbying' (Lerbinger, 2006, p. 252), a tactic that is probably most evident when it comes to CCR. Unlike classic lobbying that belongs to information-seeking strategies, grassroots lobbying is a constituency-building strategy. In a grassroots campaign, professionals try to 'influence public policy by gaining support of individual voters and citizens, who, in turn, express their policy preferences to political decision makers' (Hillman & Hitt, 1999, p. 834). Thus, grassroots activism is 'organized efforts by organizations to inform, recruit and deploy political power from constituents' (Hawkinson, 2005, p. 84f) and 24 percent of this activism is carried out in the firm's local communities. However, communities become 'glocal' and with the rise of the internet as the primary communication medium, grassroots campaigns go increasingly viral and therewith global. Thus, companies are not only politically responsible to their local communities, but also must attend to the expectations of global communities instantly due to modern communication technologies.

WHEN PA AND CSR STRATEGIES DO NOT AGREE: THE EXAMPLE OF COCA-COLA'S FIGHT AGAINST FOOD TRAFFIC LIGHT LABELING

Aligning corporate PA and CSR strategies, hence, seems to be beneficial from both a theoretical and practical point of view (Anastasiadis, 2014; Dahan et al., 2013; Den Hond et al., 2014; Lock & Seele, 2016), especially when it comes to corporate community relations. However, often PA and CSR strategies do not agree; they may even contradict each other. Such misalignments result from opposing strategies that are pursued by different departments within the same firm (Den Hond et al., 2014). This has detrimental effects with regard to legitimacy. Not only does such corporate behavior challenge stakeholders' trust, it also violates the expectation of consistent corporate strategies (Basu & Palazzo, 2008) and thus damages firms' reputation (Anastasiadis, 2014). This harms corporate (moral) legitimacy in the long run. Coca-Cola's lobbying efforts against a traffic light food labeling system at a European level, the headwind the company faced as a sponsor of the Olympics 2012 from the city of London, and its contemporary CSR program with a focus on obesity provide an example of such a misalignment.

To mandate nutritional information on food packages in a traffic light illustration, making it easily 'readable' for consumers, was the legislative proposal for food packaging brought to the European Parliament in 2010. The quantities of salt, sugar, and fat per 100 grams were supposed to be displayed in the form of a traffic light on the front of every packaged food and beverage product. This transparency was intended to make consumers' choice of healthy food easier.

The food industry lobbied massively against this proposal and spent US$1 billion on its PA efforts countering the traffic light. Major players were the industry association CIAA (confederation of the food and drink industries of the European Union (EU)) and the sector-affiliated research institute, the European Food Information Council (EUFIC). As a counter initiative, the food sector proposed a voluntary system called the guideline daily amount (GDA) showing the amount of calories per (individually determined) portion of food. The GDA, however, was criticized as being misleading given the freely determinable 'daily amount' and ineffective due to its voluntary nature. Often, such self-regulation is said to be employed instrumentally to divert policy makers' attention from hard law regulation (Fooks et al., 2013; Moodie et al., 2013).

During the consulting phase of the Parliament, the food lobby approached the Members of the European Parliament (MEPs) aggressively. Food lobbying groups distributed 50 emails within one hour to MEP Liotard, immediately after she was appointed as shadow rapporteur (MEP monitoring a dossier for political groups; EC, 2013). Another shadow rapporteur stated about the consultation discussions: 'In the earlier discussions people were much more open-minded [...] But they have been exposed to so much industry pressure that it shifted focus' (Corporate Europe Observatory, 2010a, p. 6). Several sector associations targeted MEPs with voting recommendations via email shortly before the vote was cast. The meat processing industry, for instance, wrote: '[C]onsumers have the right of not being misled or confused and therefore that a correct enforcement of the existing labeling legislation throughout the EU – rather than new burdensome rules – is urgently needed' (Corporate Europe Observatory, 2010b, p. 16). The International Butchers' Association stated: 'The basic principle for the new regulation must be: a minimum of mandatory labeling elements, to avoid that the consumer will be overstrained with a flood of information or even misled and to avoid that SMEs will have to cope with heavy administrative burdens' (Corporate Europe Observatory, 2010b, pp. 6, 25). At the same time, studies in favor of GDA labeling were published by the industry-sponsored EUFIC, which officially stated its intent 'to enhance the public's understanding of credible, science-based information on the nutritional quality and safety of foods' (EUFIC, 2012, p. 1). One chapter from a peer-reviewed journal indicated that the author was affiliated with EUFIC, but did not mention that EUFIC's research money stems from the food industry. This and following studies, moreover, did not compare the traffic light system and the GDA, but only focused on the latter's advantages. A comparative study, however, was available simultaneously reporting that the traffic light system is easier to understand than the GDA (Corporate Europe Observatory, 2010a).

The food industry's efforts were successful, the proposal was not adopted. Coca-Cola's PA strategy against traffic light food labeling becomes more interesting when compared to the CSR strategy the company pursued at the same time and in the years until 2014.

In its 2010/2011 sustainability report, Coca-Cola recognizes obesity as a global issue, which it addresses by 'by partnering with government, academia, health societies and other responsible members of civil society' (Coca-Cola, 2011, p. 55). Coca-Cola tackles the problem by offering low-calorie beverages that give consumers a choice of what to consume. Moreover, the company claims to support and use science, to market responsibly, and to be 'committed to transparency about the nutritional content of our products' (Coca-Cola, 2011, p. 56). For 2011, the company aimed to provide front-package information on calories on all its products, which it fulfilled by introducing the GDA.

Hence, in 2010, Coca-Cola pursued a double-edged corporate strategy: on the one hand, the company publicly stated that providing nutritional information is important; on the other, it spent large amounts of money to lobby at the EU level against a transparent and understandable system of food labeling (Corporate Europe Observatory, 2010a). Around the same time in the US, Coca-Cola also faced a class action suit attacking its fraudulent claims regarding its newly introduced vitamin water as being a healthy choice (Basso, 2014).

In the year following 2010, Coca-Cola made obesity a central component of its CSR strategy: 'Since 1980, global obesity rates have doubled. In addition to our product innovation of diet and light beverages, we have also increased our support of exercise and nutrition programs' (Coca-Cola, 2013, p. 10). This move probably was made to anticipate ongoing criticism of the company being responsible for increasing obesity rates, especially among children; approximately one-third of children were classified as obese

at the time in the UK (Gallagher, 2012). More headwind from local communities hit Coca-Cola in the wake of the London Olympics 2012. Coca-Cola has been sponsoring the Olympic Games since 1928 (Gallagher, 2012). Some months before the Games started, the British association of doctors criticized the sponsorship of the Olympics in London by Coca-Cola and McDonald's as 'sending the wrong message' to consumers and particularly children (Gallagher, 2012). The association's spokesperson further warned that to change behavior, anti-fast food and soft drink advertising will be needed, just as in the move against smoking: 'It's much more likely, as in smoking, that the solution will lie in changing the environments, changing the way people are exposed to marketing, advertising and pressures to buy these kinds of foods' (Gallagher, 2012).

This parallel between the food and beverage industry's impact on society and smoking was already made visible when Moodie et al. (2013) claimed that the processing food industry used the same lobbying tactics as tobacco companies did when they were high up on the public policy agenda. Also, shortly before the Olympic Games in London in 2012, the London Assembly, a community board controlling the mayor, called for a ban of Coca-Cola and McDonald's as sponsors of the Olympics stating:

> London won the right to host the 2012 Games with the promise to deliver a legacy of more active, healthier children across the world. Yet the same International Olympic Committee that awarded the games to London persists in maintaining sponsorship deals with the purveyors of high calorie junk that contributes to the threat of an obesity epidemic. (Phillips, 2012)

Thus, apparently the enforced sustainability program and 'fight against obesity' that Coca-Cola propagated since 2011 could not outbalance its negative image as a company responsible for obesity due to its products and most likely its fierce lobbying against food labeling. As the opposition by the London Assembly shows, Coca-Cola's claim of 'partnering with government, academia, health societies and other responsible members of civil society' did not work out on a community level. This can be due to its differing strategies for PA and CSR and the resulting loss of trust on the side of communities and public policy bodies.

The International Olympic Committee considered the claim of the city's assembly, but did not ban the sponsors. As top sponsor, Coca-Cola likely pays US$100 million to cover the Olympics, and triples or even quadruples that amount for accompanying marketing campaigns (Gallagher, 2012).

After the ineffective move of the city of London and the resulting press echo, Coca-Cola in the UK intensified its obesity-focused CSR program from 2012 afterward. The company launched the 'Coming together' campaign calling 'Help us fight obesity'. With US$13 million in the first period, Coca-Cola financed fitness classes and nutritional education for children. The program's website featured advice for healthy living under slogans such as 'Hate Exercise? This Will Change Your Thinking'. However, the proven link between sugared beverages and obesity is concealed, shifting the attention toward sports and education (Harvard School of Public Health, 2012). Coca-Cola advertises in its CSR strategy that it 'offer[s] more than 3,500 products, including more than 800 low- and no calorie beverages that add up to a full range of hydration options' (Coca-Cola, 2013, p. 8). In fact, this statement means that 23 percent of Coca-Cola's beverages are with reduced calories, compared to 77 percent of sugared drinks. This strategy also conceals the detrimental side effects of artificial sweeteners like aspartame and sodium cyclamate that are used in diet, light, and 'zero' products (Carroll, 2009).

The contradictions between Coca-Cola's CSR and PA strategies and the reactions of a local community body on a basically positive sponsoring effort show that inconsistencies in corporate strategies are not easily explained to the communities in which corporations operate. The reaction of the London Assembly to Coca-Cola's sponsoring efforts in the Olympic Games in London is exemplary. This may be why Coca-Cola changed its PA strategy and opposition toward the food traffic light in the UK in 2014.

The UK government recommended traffic light food labeling officially in 2013, with many big food producers joining the voluntary initiative (Triggle, 2013). As a result, supermarket chains in the UK and some food producers introduced traffic light labeling voluntarily. Together with Cadbury, Coca-Cola was the only major company that did not join this initiative, unlike its biggest competitor PepsiCo (Hall, 2013). It took until 2014 for Coca-Cola to agree to this labeling system on the products it sells in the UK, not worldwide (Campbell, 2014). The class action against misleading advertisement of vitamin water in the US was settled in 2014, forcing Coca-Cola to delete the health claims regarding vitamin water and to make nutritional information visible on this product in the US (although not in a traffic light fashion).

OUTLOOK: ACHIEVING ALIGNMENT IS KEY

Political CSR theory suggests that transnational corporations are powerful players in globalized business and influence public policy with their vast resources (Schuler, 2008). Thus, companies should take on an active role in public policy to address and help solve public issues. They include issues such as 'public health, education, social security, and protection of human rights' (Scherer & Palazzo, 2007, p. 1109). Obesity belongs to this set of pressing public issues, as in most developed countries it is described as an epidemic. Particularly when it comes to obese children, researchers and health organizations warn about the long-term effects of obesity and the resulting negative impacts on entire societies (Harvard School of Public Health, 2012; Moodie et al., 2013).

As the example of Coca-Cola's fight against the traffic light food labeling shows, corporate lobbies have considerable influence on policy processes, which can be undermined at local, regional, national, and supranational levels. Such PA strategies are often contradictory of other strategies in the firm, especially when it comes to CSR. Thus, the 'new political responsibilities' (Scherer & Palazzo, 2011) of corporations such as Coca-Cola are often not met in a consistent manner. In the case of Coca-Cola, the firm lobbied against the introduction of transparent food labeling, while at the same time claiming in its CSR strategy that transparent information is crucial when fighting obesity. Such a 'disconnect between companies' thinking on lobbying and CSR [...] is dangerous for those firms' ongoing legitimacy' (Anastasiadis, 2014, p. 261). In a study on the tobacco industry, Fooks et al. (2013) find that deliberate misalignment of both strategies can lead to the misuse of CSR for PA strategy. This results in what they call (without addressing Scherer and Palazzo's theory) 'political CSR'. This different 'political CSR' can limit governmental actions and undermine public policy processes. Regarding the effect on the firm, misalignments of PA and CSR threaten the legitimacy and the reputation (Lock & Seele, 2016) of corporations in society. This has long-lasting consequences, as a loss of trust from stakeholders might backfire on companies eventually. The London Assembly's call for a ban of Coca-Cola as a sponsor of the Olympic Games can be seen as such a move.

As Den Hond et al. (2014) argue, aligning CSR and PA provokes synergies for companies. Alignment gives organizations the opportunity to participate in public policy, provide expertise, and thus help solve issues such as obesity. Organizations that communicate one message are perceived more positively than those that speak with differing voices. Mutually trustful relationships with stakeholders are seen as the basis for maintaining legitimacy for companies (Heath et al., 2013). Also, the case of the car industry (Anastasiadis, 2014) shows how inconsistent strategies of CSR and PA challenge companies' legitimacy. CSR and PA are 'both political' (Anastasiadis, 2014, p. 289); hence, they should be aligned to protect a company's reputation, its trustful relationships with stakeholders, and its legitimacy. As the example of Coca-Cola illustrates, there is (on purpose or not) apparently not much coordination between the CSR and PA departments and strategies. Alignment certainly also entails coordination among the departments. Joint goals would have to be formulated and strategies lined up together as the concept of 'deliberative lobbying' suggests (Lock & Seele, 2016). For instance, despite opposing a traffic light food labeling system, Coca-Cola could have opened up a dialogue with public policy bodies and provided expert information on the issue of food labeling and obesity prevention.

Contradictions between CSR and PA strategies should not occur because they can ultimately result in the exclusion of corporations from public policy processes. Moodie et al. (2013, p. 671) call for 'a substantially scaled up response from governments, public health organisations, and civil society to regulate the harmful activities of these industries'. However, the exclusion of companies from public policy processes is not in the interest of corporations. Corporations play a vital role in contributing to solve public issues through PA as they are important political players with vast resources and specific expertise. If they better align CSR and PA, pressing issues such as obesity can be addressed more successfully by multiple societal players together, including corporations. Communities can play a major role here as their authenticity and credibility to politicians as potential voters and to companies as potential consumers is a necessary precondition for the processes of deliberation and discourse on which open democracies depend.

REFERENCES

Anastasiadis, S. (2014). Toward a view of citizenship and lobbying corporate engagement in the political process. *Business & Society*, *53*(2), 260–299.

Baron, D. P. (1995). Integrated strategy; market and nonmarket components. *California Management Review*, *37*, 47–65.

Basso, K. (2014, October 6). Vitaminwater deceptive marketing class action settlement. *Top Class Actions*. Retrieved from http://topclassactions.com/lawsuit-settlements/closed-settlements/41542- vitaminwater-deceptive-marketing-class-action-settlement/.

Basu, K., & Palazzo, G. (2008). Corporate social responsibility: a process model of sensemaking. *Academy of Management Review*, *33*, 122–136.

Baysinger, B. D., & Woodman, R. W. (1982). Dimensions of the public affairs/government relations function in major American corporations. *Strategic Management Journal*, *3*(1), 27–41.

Bowen, H. R., & Johnson, F. E. (1953). *Social responsibility of the businessman*. New York: Harper.

Campbell, D. (2014, September 5). Coca-Cola agrees to traffic-light labelling on drinks sold in UK. *The Guardian*. Retrieved from http://www.theguardian.com/business/2014/sep/05/coca-cola-traffic-light-labelling-drinks-uk-salt-sugar-fat.

Carroll, A. B. (1979). A three-dimensional conceptual model of corporate performance. *Academy of Management Review*, *4*(4), 497–505.

Carroll, A. B. (1991). The pyramid of corporate social responsibility: toward the moral management of organizational stakeholders. *Business Horizons*, *34*(4), 39–48.

Carroll, A. B. (1999). Corporate social responsibility evolution of a definitional construct. *Business & Society*, *38*(3), 268–295.

Carroll, R. (2009, June 11). Chávez bans sale of Coke Zero in Venezuela. *The Guardian*.

Castelló, I., Morsing, M., & Schultz, F. (2013). Communicative dynamics and the polyphony of corporate social responsibility in the network society. *Journal of Business Ethics*, *118*(4), 683–694.

Christensen, L. T., Morsing, M., & Thyssen, O. (2013). CSR as aspirational talk. *Organization*, *20*(3), 372–393.

Coca-Cola (2011). *2010/2011 Sustainability Report*. Retrieved from http://www.coca-colacompany.com/sustainabilityreport/.

Coca-Cola (2013). *Sustainability at Coca-Cola*. Atlanta, GA: The Coca-Cola Company.

Corporate Europe Observatory (2010a, June). *A red light for consumer information: the food industry's €1-billion campaign to block health warnings on food*. Brussels, Belgium: Corporate Europe Observatory.

Corporate Europe Observatory (2010b). *Hardcore lobbying: a sample of 'voting recommendations' sent by lobbyists to MEPs on the new EU food labelling regulation*. Brussels, Belgium: Corporate Europe Observatory.

Crane, A., McWilliams, A., Matten, D., Moon, J., & Siegel, D. S. (Eds.). (2008). *The Oxford handbook of corporate social responsibility*. Oxford: Oxford University Press.

Dahan, N. M., Hadani, M., & Schuler, D. A. (2013). The governance challenges of corporate political activity. *Business & Society*, DOI: 10.1177/0007650313491470.

Dahlsrud, A. (2008). How corporate social responsibility is defined: an analysis of 37 definitions. *Corporate Social Responsibility and Environmental Management*, *15*(1), 1.

Den Hond, F., Rehbein, K. A., Bakker, F. G., & Lankveld, H. K. V. (2014). Playing on two chessboards: reputation effects between corporate social responsibility (CSR) and corporate political activity (CPA). *Journal of Management Studies*, *51*(5), 790–813.

Donaldson, T., & Dunfee, T. W. (1999). *Ties that bind*. Cambridge, MA: Harvard Business School Press.

Drucker, P. F. (1984). Converting social problems into business opportunities: the new meaning of corporate social responsibility. *California Management Review*, *26*, 53.

Du, S., Bhattacharya, C. B., & Sen, S. (2007). Convergence of interests-cultivating consumer trust through corporate social initiatives. *Advances in Consumer Research*, *34*, 687.

Eilbert, H., & Parket, I. R. (1973). The current status of corporate social responsibility. *Business Horizons*, *16*, 5–14.

Elkington, J. (1998). *Cannibals with forks: the triple bottom line of sustainability*. Gabriola Island: New Society Publishers.

European Commission (EC) (2013). *Glossary*. Retrieved from http://ec.europa.eu/codecision/stepbystep/glossary_en.htm.

European Food Information Council (EUFIC) (2012). *Annual Report 2011*. Brussels, Belgium: EUFIC.

Fleisher, C. (1994). Leading-edge measurement and evaluation ideas for managing public affairs. In P. Shafer (Ed.), *Adding value to the public affairs function* (pp. 123–132). Washington, DC: Public Affairs Council.

Fooks, G., Gilmore, A., Collin, J., Holden, C., & Lee, K. (2013). The limits of corporate social responsibility: techniques of neutralization, stakeholder management and political CSR. *Journal of Business Ethics, 112*(2), 283–299.

Francis, R., & Armstrong, A. (2003). Ethics as a risk management strategy: the Australian experience. *Journal of Business Ethics, 45*(4), 375–385.

Freeman, R. E. (1984). *Strategic management: a stakeholder approach*. Marshall, MA: Harpercollins College Div.

Friedman, M. (1962). *Capitalism and freedom*. Chicago, IL: University of Chicago Press.

Gallagher, J. (2012, April 16). Doctors unite to combat obesity. *BBC News*. Retrieved from http://www.bbc.com/news/health-17705228.

Garriga, E., & Mélé, D. (2004). Corporate social responsibility theories: mapping the territory. *Journal of Business Ethics, 53*(1), 51–71.

Golant, B. D., & Sillince, J. A. (2007). The constitution of organizational legitimacy: a narrative perspective. *Organization Studies, 28*(8), 1149–1167.

Grunig, J. E., & Hunt, T. (1984). *Managing public relations* (Vol. 343). New York: Holt, Rinehart and Winston.

Guthey, E., & Morsing, M. (2014). CSR and the mediated emergence of strategic ambiguity. *Journal of Business Ethics, 120*(4), 555–569.

Habermas, J. (1996). *Between facts and norms: contributions to a discourse theory of law and democracy*. Cambridge, MA: MIT Press.

Hall, J. (2013, June 19). Plans for new food labelling to combat UK obesity are dealt blow as Cadbury and Coca-Cola reject 'traffic light' system. *The Independent*.

Harris, P., & Moss, D. (2001). Editorial: In search of public affairs: a function in search of an identity. *Journal of Public Affairs, 1*(2), 102–110.

Harrison, S. (2000). Shouts and whispers: the lobbying campaigns for and against resale price maintenance. *European Journal of Marketing, 34*(1/2), 207–222.

Harvard School of Public Health (2012, June). *Factsheet: sugary drink supersizing and the obesity epidemic*. Boston, MA: Harvard School of Public Health.

Hawkinson, B. 2005. The internal environment of public affairs: organization, process and systems. *The Handbook of Public Affairs* (pp. 76–85). Thousand Oaks, CA: Sage.

Heath, R. L., & Palenchar, M. J. (Eds.). (2008). *Strategic issues management: organizations and public policy challenges*. Thousand Oaks, CA: Sage.

Heath, R.L., Waymer, D., & Palenchar, M.J. (2013). Is the universe of democracy, rhetoric, and public relations whole cloth or three separate galaxies? *Public Relations Review, 39*, 271–279.

Hillman, A. J., & Hitt, M. A. (1999). Corporate political strategy formulation: a model of approach, participation, and strategy decisions. *Academy of Management Review, 24*, 825–842.

Hiss, S. (2009). From implicit to explicit corporate social responsibility: institutional change as a fight for myths. *Business Ethics Quarterly, 19*(03), 433–451.

Huang, Y. H. (2001). OPRA: a cross-cultural, multiple-item scale for measuring organization-public relationships. *Journal of Public Relations Research, 13*(1), 61–90.

Husted, B. W., Jamali, D., & Saffar, W. (2015). Near and Dear? The role of location in CSR engagement. *Strategic Management Journal*, DOI: 10.1002/smj.2437.

Keim, G., & Baysinger, B. (1988). The efficacy of business political activity: competitive considerations in a principal-agent context. *Journal of Management, 14*(2), 163–180.

Kotler, P., & Lee, N. (2005). Corporate social responsibility. *Doing the most good for your company and your cause*. Hoboken: John Wiley & Sons.

Lee, M. D. P. (2008). A review of the theories of corporate social responsibility: its evolutionary path and the road ahead. *International Journal of Management Reviews, 10*(1), 53–73.

Lerbinger, O. (2006). *Corporate public affairs: interacting with interest groups, media, and government*. London: Routledge.

Lock, I., & Seele, P. (2016). Deliberative lobbying: toward a non-contradiction of corporate political activities and corporate social responsibility. *Journal of Management Inquiry, 25*(4), 415–430.

Matten, D., & Crane, A. (2005). Corporate citizenship: toward an extended theoretical conceptualization. *Academy of Management Review, 30*(1), 166–179.

Moodie, R., Stuckler, D., Monteiro, C., Sheron, N., Neal, B., Thamarangsi, T., Lincoln, P., & Casswell, S. (2013). Profits and pandemics: prevention of harmful effects of tobacco, alcohol, and ultra-processed food and drink industries. *The Lancet, 381*, 670–679.

Nownes, A. J. (2006). *Total lobbying: what lobbyists want (and how they try to get it)*. Cambridge: Cambridge University Press.

Phillips, J. (2012, July 5). The movement to ban McDonald's, Coca-Cola from the London Olympics. *The Time*. Retrieved from http://business.time.com/2012/07/05/olympics-2012-the-move-to-ban-mcdonalds-coca-cola-from-the-london-games/.

Porter, M. E., & Kramer, M. R. (2006). The link between competitive advantage and corporate social responsibility. *Harvard Business Review, 84*(12), 78–92.

Porter, M. E., & Kramer, M. R. (2011). Creating shared value. *Harvard Business Review, 89*(1/2), 62–77.

Post, J. E., Frederick, W. C., Lawrence, A. T., & Weber, J. (2002). *Business and society: corporate strategy, public policy, ethics*. Boston, MA: McGraw-Hill.

Preston, L. E., & James, E. (1975). *Post, private management and public policy*. New York: Prentice Hall.

Richter, B. K. (2011). 'Good' and 'evil': The relationship between corporate social responsibility and corporate political activity. Available at *SSRN 1750368*.

Scherer, A. G., Palazzo, G., & Seidl, D. (2013a). Managing legitimacy in complex and heterogeneous environments: sustainable development in a globalized world. *Journal of Management Studies, 50*(2), 259–284.

Scherer, A. G., & Palazzo, G. (2007). Toward a political conception of corporate responsibility: business and society seen from a Habermasian perspective. *Academy of Management Review, 32*(4), 1096–1120.

Scherer, A. G., & Palazzo, G. (2011). The new political role of business in a globalized world: a review of a new perspective on CSR and its implications for the firm, governance, and democracy. *Journal of Management Studies, 48*(4), 899–931.

Scherer, A. G., Baumann-Pauly, D., & Schneider, A. (2013b). Democratizing corporate governance compensating for the democratic deficit of corporate political activity and corporate citizenship. *Business & Society, 52*(3), 473–514.

Schuler, D. A. (2008). Peering in from corporate political activity. *Journal of Management Inquiry, 17*, 162–167.

Schultz, F., Castelló, I., & Morsing, M. (2013). The construction of corporate social responsibility in network societies: A communication view. *Journal of Business Ethics, 115*(4), 681–692.

Seele, P., & Gatti, L. (2015). Greenwashing revisited: in search for a typology and accusation-based definition incorporating legitimacy strategies. *Business Strategy and the Environment*. DOI: 10.1002/bse.1912.

Seele, P., & Lock, I. (2015). Deliberative and/or instrumental? A typology of CSR communication. *Journal of Business Ethics, 131*(2): 401–414.

Sethi, S. P. (1975). Dimensions of corporate social performance: an analytical framework. *California Management Review, 17*, 58.

Showalter, A., & Fleisher, C. S. (2005). The tools and techniques of PA. In P. Harris, & C. S. Fleisher (Eds.), *Handbook of public affairs* (pp. 109–122). Thousand Oaks, CA: Sage.

Suchman, M. C. (1995). Managing legitimacy: Strategic and institutional approaches. *Academy of Management Review, 20*(3), 571–610.

Svensson, G. (2001). 'Glocalization' of business activities: a 'glocal strategy' approach. *Management Decision, 39*(1), 6–18.

Thomson, S., & John, S. (2007). *Public affairs in practice: a practical guide to lobbying (PR in practice)*. London, England: Kogan Page.

Triggle, N. (2013, June 19). Food labelling: consistent system to be rolled out. *BBC News*. Retrieved from http://www.bbc.com/news/health-22959239.

Van Marrewijk, M. (2003). Concepts and definitions of CSR and corporate sustainability: between agency and communion. *Journal of Business Ethics*, *44*(2–3), 95–105.

Van Oosterhout, J. H. (2010). The role of corporations in shaping the global rules of the game: in search of new foundations. *Business Ethics Quarterly*, *20*(02), 253–264.

Van Riel, C. B., & Fombrun, C. J. (2007). *Essentials of corporate communication: Implementing practices for effective reputation management*. London: Routledge.

Waddock, S. A., & Boyle, M. E. (1995). The dynamics of change in corporate community relations. *California Management Review*, *37*(4), 125.

Wettstein, F. (2010). For better or for worse. *Business Ethics Quarterly*, *20*(2), 275–283.

Wettstein, F., & Baur, D. (2012). Why should we care about marriage equality?: Political advocacy as a part of corporate responsibility. *Journal of Business Ethics*, DOI:10.1007/s10551-015-2631-3.

Whelan, G. (2012). The political perspective of corporate social responsibility: A critical research agenda. *Business Ethics Quarterly*, *22*(04), 709–737.

Wood, D. J. (1991). Corporate social performance revisited. *Academy of Management Review*, *16*(4), 691–718.

Wood, D. J. (2010). Measuring corporate social performance: a review. *International Journal of Management Reviews*, *12*(1), 50–84.

Young, I. M. (2004). Responsibility and global labor justice. *Journal of Political Philosophy*, *12*, 365–388.

Zenisek, T. J. (1979). Corporate social responsibility: a conceptualization based on organizational literature. *Academy of Management Review*, 4(3), 359–368.

Making and Managing Lobbying Coalitions

Arco Timmermans

THE COALITION IMPERATIVE IN PUBLIC AFFAIRS

One of the paradoxes of public affairs is that as this organizational function becomes ever more important for success and survival, it also becomes increasingly difficult for single organizations and groups to perform this function well by working alone. Organizations or groups with stakes in political decisions face harsh competition for these stakes to be considered by policymakers, and the accelerating speed of mobilization of critical publics requires them to constantly monitor and invest in their image and reputation. Scarce resources, incomplete information and the need to demonstrate to policymakers a broad enough support basis all induce organizations and groups with interests to work together.

In the same way as individuals, organizations build and maintain ties with friends and all those considered like-minded. It is a selection process that helps people and organizations give and receive trust and create a sense of identity and togetherness. But when facing competition from others, organizations must broaden their basis and may even need to reach out to opponents in the politics of interest representation in order to avoid veto, stalemate, and campaigns of naming and shaming. Thus, there is an imperative for organizations to build coalitions as a tactic in public affairs in order to achieve their goals and minimize threats to their continuity. A survey among lobbyists in the US shows that two thirds of professional lobbyists are active in coalition building more than once per week and work in several coalitions, including other types of organization and other industries (Lobbyists.info, n.d.).

Given these increasing incentives for broadening support and reaching out to opponents, are interest organizations and groups and all the public-affairs professionals representing them successful team players? Do they move well in coalition land as their natural habitat, or do they behave as if on a terrain far outside their organizational comfort zone? After all, coalitions may entail costs as well as benefits. Being a coalition member usually means a readiness to compromise; it may involve risk of identity loss, and it requires a fair level of accountability towards the partners. How often, then, and in what ways are lobbying coalitions formed, how are they managed and what are the effects of such public affairs performed in alliance, compared with cases where organizations lobby alone? What does it take to be an appreciated coalition entrepreneur in a network of actors and issues that may constantly change in composition and in its sense of urgency about matters that some want to raise to prominence but others would rather keep suppressed?

This chapter deals with these important questions about the emergence, management, and effects of alliances made between organizations and groups in public affairs. We may call these alliances lobbying coalitions, and they can vary in coherence and organizational form, more or less tied together, institutionalized and speaking with one voice. Lobbying coalitions may not only seek access and influence in policymaking arenas but also, as in the broader understanding of public affairs, act in the public sphere in order to profile positively in image and reputation.

Lobbying coalitions can be defined as a level of collective action between interest organizations and groups that exchange and pool their resources in order to achieve a common agenda. This agenda may contain just one issue on which coalition members' interests and preferences converge, or it may be composed of more issues or even an entire program (Kingdon, 1984). Lobbying coalitions may be formal or informal, and they can be homogeneous in types of member or instead contain a mix of 'strange bedfellows' – organizations or groups that usually do not ally and may even be antagonistic towards each other. Coalitions may have a logo and an office with staff, or they may be ad hoc,

temporary, and kept together by a rather thin thread as long as this is considered convenient. If coalitions are informal, this may mean that the terms of understanding and agreement, the common-issue agenda, the exchange of resources, and the level of commitment are not spelled out. While opportunistic behavior may occur in any type of alliance – including the most heavily formalized – the risk of it may be most endemic in informal coalitions that refrain from investing in mechanisms of steering and control to keep the partners on track (see, for example, Mitnick, 1993). Thus, in this view, lobbying coalitions are more than the sum of actors that have, at a certain point in time, similar convictions and preferences about issues. There must be additional binding factors to make them act together.

All this variation in properties suggests that the number of possible lobbying coalitions that may emerge in public affairs across the world is practically endless. As we will see below, the multidimensionality of lobbying coalitions in the real world has important implications for theorizing about them.

Thus far, a look across the globe for research on the topic must lead to the conclusion that we know still relatively little about lobbying coalitions. Many talk about them and engage in them, but few actually study them. Writings from within the professional community may be based on experiential learning and a good dose of anecdotes and impressions with intuitive appeal, but how systematic is what we know about coalitions and their effects in practice?

The knowledge that has accumulated is not only limited but is also concentrated in a few regions in the world, mainly the US, where lobbying coalitions started to be considered more systematically in the 1970s and 1980s (Berry, 1977; Loomis, 1986; Salisbury et al., 1987). For a long time, most work done on coalitions in interest representation was qualitative, single-issue and case-study-based; but, later, quantitative studies were also developed (for an overview of this development, see Hojnacki et al., 2012).

Scholarly attention in Europe and other parts of the world followed, but the level has remained low. Bunea and Baumgartner (2014: 1426) report that thus far, only 4 percent of the journal articles on lobbying in the EU was devoted to lobbying coalitions. There are no such figures or even an impression of research done for individual countries, so it is safe to say that the systematic investigation of this phenomenon has just begun. This also is true for international and global coalitions in public affairs (see, for example, on the WTO: Hanegraaff, 2015; Hanegraaff et al., 2015; on climate change: Betzold, 2013; Hadden, 2015). Since the previous edition of the *Handbook of Public Affairs* (Harris and Fleisher, 2005) in which Showalter and Fleisher (2005) started to address coalitions as a tool in public affairs, important steps forward have been taken in the empirical analysis of lobbying coalitions, but much work remains to be done. While, since its launch in 2001, the *Journal of Public Affairs* has highlighted particular themes – for example, issues management (volume 1/2, 2002) – this has not yet been the case for coalitions, and individual contributions dealing with lobbying coalitions are also underrepresented. Most instances where such coalitions enter the analysis are single-case analyses in which they are addressed indirectly and thus remain somewhat hidden.

Even though our research-based picture of lobbying coalitions is still sketchy, with a limited systematic knowledge of where they occur, how participants manage them and harvest payoffs from joint investments, or experience disillusion and obstruction, we can bring together a number of theoretically informed and empirically grounded insights into the politics of lobbying coalitions. The following sections present the emergence of coalitions in public affairs, followed by a discussion of relevant theory and patterns of coalition formation, management, and success. The chapter concludes with an outlook on coalitions in public affairs in the near future.

THE EMERGENCE OF LOBBYING COALITIONS

Lobbying coalitions are work relationships between interest organizations or groups established to pursue a common agenda and pool resources to stand stronger than they would alone. More than from formal and legal routes, they are formed from a network of actors in which ideological or functional work relationships drive their joint pathways in lobbying. These pathways may cross when it happens to be convenient, or they may flow together over a longer period of time and for a broader set of issues. But in all instances, the network context provides the linkages and, from the perspective of individual organizations, the context in which estimates are made about who is near and who is distant – whose work provides added value and who is marginal – and about who is familiar and trusted and who must be treated with extreme caution. Thus old or new coalition players may be closely related in a network, but such network connections also may be loose and fluid (Heaney and Leifeld, 2015).

Issues as Orientation Points

Issues – that is, more or less controversial matters with stakes for organizations – are key orientation points for interest organizations and groups. Coalitions around issues are formed when actors share their views about the required level of attention to these issues, their problem definition, and the best solutions to be promoted to policymakers. Thus, naturally, coalitions are intimately related to issues in politics and society, and they form around them. It may be true that coalitions of interest organizations and groups emerge for reasons other than attempts to jointly influence policy and reputation. Branch organizations, occupational groups, peak and umbrella organizations: these are mostly a formal and permanent type of coalition of members, not only – or not even primarily – seeking to influence their image and policy decisions but to provide internal services to their members. But even if member associations are less central players in lobbying coalitions, the formation and management of such coalitions happens around substantive stakes in policy and public image. In other words: issues management is not only a key organizational task in public affairs, it also requires the coordinated attention of coalitions. Coalitions make issues, and issues make coalitions.

Another basic element in understanding lobbying-coalition dynamics is that, when dealing with issues, coalitions may stretch their activities throughout the policy cycle. That is, while lobbying often is considered to be oriented towards the legislative process (the formal stages of bills or other types of regulation in the policy-making pipeline), it starts earlier – as smart lobby organizations and groups know all too well – in setting the agenda (Baumgartner et al., 2009), and it may also continue – as alert actors in public affairs know too – during the implementation and even the evaluation of policy decisions and programs (Heaney and Lorenz, 2013).

Frequency, Type and Composition of Coalitions

Though large-scale empirical research on issue lobbying and coalition formation is just emerging, analysis done on lobbying and policy change in the US suggests that on most issues only limited numbers of actors are involved, while few issues attract multiple stakeholders (Baumgartner et al., 2009). It is important to realize, however, that this kind of distribution of lobbying actors and issues refers to the larger set of issues that may be lobbied, but not always *are* lobbied.

Most of the data about lobbying coalitions are based on interviews and survey research done in the US and, more recently, the EU. Analysis of coalitions within countries that go beyond single case studies still are scarce. One reason for this is that large-N studies (the N representing issues) of interest groups are resource-intensive. In the previous edition of the *Handbook of Public Affairs*, Hawkinson (2005: 81–2) reported the types of coalition partner approached successfully by business corporations at federal and state level in the US. Typically, at both levels of governance, similar kinds of corporation, association, and company outrank advocacy groups, customers, and suppliers. Sectoral industry actors do particularly well, but while this indicates choice of partners, it does not tell us how often corporations make such choices for coalitions rather than for acting alone. Figure 31.1 shows some findings from research on emerging lobbying coalitions. Generally, most is known about the US. In the extensive work on EU interest groups done by Klüver (2013), lobbying coalitions

Figure 31.1: Empirical findings on the occurrence of coalitions

How frequent?

70 percent of interest groups in US (Scholzman and Tierney, 1986; Kerwin, 2003)
80 percent in US legislative process (Hula, 1999)
40 percent in a sample of issues in US (Baumgartner et al., 2009)
57 percent in US, 15 percent in EU (Mahoney, 2008)
60 to 82 percent in US, varying between issues (Hojnacki, 1997)
60 percent in EU (Bruycker and Beyers, 2015)

What type and composition?
When corporations go in coalitions, 90 percent do this together with other corporations (Hawkinson, 2005)
80 percent of coalitions in EU are homogenous, with similar types of coalition member (Bruycker and Beyers, 2015)
Occupational groups are least coalition-oriented in US (Hojnacki, 1997; 1998)
Mostly homogenous coalitions both in US and EU (Mahoney, 2008)

are analyzed, but they are treated as a given and not taken as a proportion of all cases of lobbying. Van Schendelen (2013) also deals with coalitions in the EU, but he provides no systematic evidence of frequency and type.

Lacking more systematic data on lobbying-coalition formation, and given the hard task of comparing the existing empirical work as approaches differ, it is hard to draw overall conclusions. When summarizing the evidence available thus far, the result is that such coalitions emerge mostly for at least half the number of issues and cases in which interest organizations and groups actively lobby. Much other work in countries across the world may indicate that such coalition lobbying is also a substantive part of public affairs, but the meaning of this information is first of all that much more empirical work remains to be done. The variation in percentages mentioned above reflects not only differences in measurement but also suggests that national institutional context, issue characteristics, and other factors play a part. These conditions for coalition building are discussed later in this chapter.

Compared to executive or legislative coalitions in politics, lobbying coalitions show much more diversity in composition, status, and dynamics. This is so even within a single country, where such lobbying coalitions occur at all levels of governance, in the whole range of policy domains from monetary issues to human rights and from transport to health care. Networks of actors may be more or less densely populated, their ties may be close or distant, and issues may trigger activity of groups and grass roots barely involved in lobbying before, and they may also give rise to group formation, specifically for one lobbying and advocacy cause, what Levi and Murphy (2006) call an 'event coalition'. Lobbying coalitions not only vary in shape, status, and subject matter, they also constantly face the situation or at least the possibility that one or more other coalitions are competing in the same public and political arenas. In fact, this competitive situation

may also be a strong motivation for lobbying coalitions to form and stick together.

Given the limited quantitative empirical basis of lobbying-coalition formation across the world, to some extent the types of coalition can be discussed only with reference to systematic research and thus must be more qualitative. As with coalitions in general, definition of concepts and operationalization in measurement can produce wide variation in findings. Occupational groups seem less prone to lobby together than expressive groups and corporations. They may and often appear to be more sensitive to identity loss and are oriented strongly to internal services for members.

Permanent coalitions with a formal status seem to be less profiled in lobbying compared than informal ad hoc coalitions that are event- or single-issue-driven. If coalitions have a single-issue basis and not a deeper fundamental, shared belief or other sense of ideological affiliation, they are unlikely to last and may even collapse. Coalition 'partners' may then become opponents on another issue. Beer-brewing companies and environmental movements may agree in their view on the risks of shale-gas drilling, as we have witnessed in European countries where shale gas became a political issue, but they may disagree over other issues. Likewise, Jewish and Islamic organizations may stand together in the debate on regulating ritual slaughtering, but otherwise their lobbying goes in widely different directions.

If coalitions require a degree of steering in order to stand and act together, then a next question is what happens with their environment? The message of lobbying coalitions must land there, and democratic legitimacy must be secured in order to convince policymakers that their claims deserve positive decisions. As Schattschneider (1960) noted: 'If a fight starts, watch the crowd'. The politics of attention is also a crucial element of lobbying-coalition behavior (Jones and Baumgartner, 2005; Baumgartner et al., 2009). While on any given issue some interest organizations or groups will try to keep attention low-key and deal with matters in what Cobb and Elder (1983) call a system of limited participation, the threshold for expanding the scope of debate is becoming less a matter of control, as, for example, Coombs (2002) argues in his study of issue 'contamination' – the rapid spread of an issue within a widening circle of participants in the game of making and breaking images of the issue.

This is the process of bandwagons, in which adherence to a case of advocacy happens in a process of positive feedback (Jones and Baumgartner, 2005) and thus cascades and reaches high critical mass and visibility in a short period of time (Baumgartner and Leech, 2001; Halpin, 2011). This is a process similar to media hypes, which can be one venue in which bandwagon effects occur and add to the drama of a lobbying campaign. Social-media use reinforces this process (Coombs, 2002). A given lobbying coalition may benefit from such a strong tailwind, but at the same time it may lose its control of direction of the issue and the debate over it. Coalitions that involve bandwagons become almost unmanageable even for strong coalition leaders.

This brings us at the final point of this section about types and forms of lobbying coalition: they can follow different routes in their lobbying activities, searching widely varying venues of access for attention. Coalitions may be oriented entirely to internal access to formal policymaking institutions, but they also can reach stages of large public visibility and even seek a bandwagon effect, as some types of organization such as advocacy groups are oriented to such outside lobbying (Kollman, 1998; Halpin, 2011; Betzold, 2013). In actual public affairs, coalition behavior will consist of mixes, and such mixed activity becomes more likely as coalitions themselves become more heterogeneous in composition. The base line in this, of course, is to what extent such mixed repertoires of activities still entail a united strategy and avoid the insufficient coordination that leads to a neutralization

or even an undermining of the joint results. If such degenerative effects occur, they are likely to evoke the end of the coalition life cycle.

THEORIZING ABOUT LOBBYING COALITIONS

Thus far, we have considered the occurrence of lobbying coalitions and drawn some headlines of type and composition as they have appeared in the scholarly literature. Most of this literature takes some theoretical point of departure. Elsewhere in this new edition of the SAGE *Handbook of International Corporate and Public Affairs,* the theoretical state of the art of public affairs is one of diversity, speaking to the multidisciplinary perspective that applies in this domain of research and practice. For lobbying coalitions, the plurality of relevant theories and perspectives may be more limited, but it would be a misrepresentation to say that there is one prevailing, one-size-fits-all theory that explains the formation and management of alliances of interest organizations and groups.

Long ago, theorizing about coalitions seemed simple. In William Riker's *The Theory of Political Coalitions* (1962), developed in the US but applied to Western European political systems, it was the so-called *size principle* that was seen to guide actors in their allying behavior. Riker postulated that rational parties construct government coalitions large enough to form a majority but small enough to reap as many benefits of being in office and control as possible. Thus he predicted minimal coalition size for maximum utility of the participant parties; in concrete terms this meant that actors would try to stay as close as possible to the 50 percent plus 1 seat winning threshold. But critics argued that Riker's theory misjudged the required majority for policy proposals, often larger than the minimal size, and also that he had a blind eye for policy considerations. This critique was justified, as empirical tests showed that most political coalitions could *not* be explained by this theory. Subsequent theoretical work took such policy considerations – ideology, preferences, policy production, legacy, etc. – into account, and the explanatory power was enhanced (Laver and Schofield, 1990).

For coalitions of stakeholders, policy considerations and beliefs are crucial (Sabatier, 1988; Haas, 1992; Fischer, 2003), but it is also necessary to revisit the size principle: what does it take to move beyond the winning threshold? How large must a coalition be to have success? Compared to executive coalitions, the tremendous variation in type, composition, formal or informal status, mission statement, etc. of alliances that are all formed in widely different public-affairs contexts means that there is no simple and single arithmetic to winning. Nor is the formation of lobbying coalitions likely to be just a matter of rational calculation. After all: what should we count? In public affairs, we must deal with the sensitivity of policymakers to constituencies, with resources that are much more varied and rarely owned exclusively by single stakeholders, and we must take into account that the arenas of lobbying and advocacy can be much more exposed than a political-coalition laboratory.

What in rational-choice political-economy theory is called the 'bargaining system' (Schofield, 1993) is, in a more comprehensive sense, the network context for the formation of lobbying coalitions. There has been theoretically and empirically sophisticated and relevant work done on networks of actors and issues and the way they provide strong or weak ties where trust and reputation are constructed and opportunity structures in which interest organizations and groups may decide to act in concert or go solo (Granovetter, 1973; Laumann and Knoke, 1987; Heaney, 2006). They also are a context for stakeholder analysis and management (Caroll, 2005). When analyzed by organizations

themselves, networks can provide a cognitive map for coalition building. Demarcations of the sphere of friendly and the sphere of less friendly or antagonistic actors in networks may need to be nuanced in order to build coalitions that can demonstrate a large enough constituency and lead to lobbying success. This may require temporary or even more permanent crossing of such boundaries and brokerage in coalition building.

As a lobbying-coalition context, networks entail constructions of distance and proximity between actors, but this macro context is best understood when relating it to population-ecology theory, which has attracted growing attention from interest-group scholars. In the ecology of interest-group populations, density and the presence of niches are mostly used as concepts and measures for understanding organizational performance and survival, but these policy-domain properties also set the stage for coalition building (Gray and Lowery, 1998; Halpin et al., 2015). As Gray and Lowery (1998) say in population ecology terms: interest organizations may 'lobby alone or in a flock'. Variations in policy domains can be analyzed in terms of the type of actor network (Grossmann, 2013) to see how joint hunting behavior in the pursuit of interests may vary across policy domains.

The actor and issue network and the type of interest-group population it contains is a context that structures the space of maneuver for individual organizations and groups. This space of behavior is not only the sum of actors and their positions on issues but is also structured by institutional arrangements that create opportunities and constraints (Levi and Murphy, 2006). Consider the different political-system types, from open and pluralistic to more closed corporatist, and from majority and adversarial in nature to consensus-oriented (Lijphart, 2012). But as Nelson and Yackee (2012: 351) say, often the aggregate-level analysis of lobby processes and their results are difficult to explain because of a lack of micro-level theorizing. A network may provide opportunity structures and the position in a network space may make actors more or less 'coalitionable'. But what makes an individual organization or group decide to initiate or join a coalition?

Here, theories about information processing, resource exchange, and transaction costs are relevant. Estimates and decisions about other actors' resources, positions, and the costs and benefits of coalition transactions are always bounded by rationality. As Jones and Baumgartner say in their path-breaking work on political attention and priority setting, organizations and the individuals within them display sticky behavior with no changes interrupted by sudden shifts in attention (Jones, 2001; Jones and Baumgartner, 2005, Baumgartner and Jones, 2014). During such shifts, views about the transaction costs of going into a coalition also change (Timmermans, 2006), and so are expectations about success in lobbying in coalition (Levi and Murphy, 2006; Leifeld and Schneider, 2012). Likewise, within a framework of bounded rationality of information processing, interest organizations and groups include in their estimations also the benefits and costs of resource exchanges (Pfeffer and Salancik, 2003; Berkhout, 2013; Braun, 2015).

The next sections of this chapter will employ these theoretical views in discussing the three key elements of lobbying coalitions: their formation, their management, and their effects.

COALITION FORMATION

In this section we consider the relevance of the institutional context for forming or not forming coalitions, the characteristics of issues around which coalitions are formed, and the resources and transaction costs of exchange and deals that individual organizations assess when making decisions about coalition participation. Given that the stakes of actors come into play during the entire policy cycle, from agenda setting to

implementation and on to evaluating policies, coalition building also occurs at each of these stages. Thus coalitions can add critical mass to strategies of agenda denial as much as organizations can push together for extensive government attention to an issue (Cobb and Ross, 1997). Coalitions contribute to shaping the lobby agenda (Kimball et al., 2012).

Institutional Mechanisms Inducing Coalition Formation

If an important incentive for coalition formation is to demonstrate a broad enough support basis to policymakers, then a question is how sensitive such policymakers are to constituencies and what 'broad enough' means. As we saw, coalition size is not a straightforward concept in public affairs: its calculation may include many different factors. A basic factor relevant to any lobbying coalition constructed in a political system is the institutional arrangement for democratic accountability of policymakers. Do policymakers face direct electoral risk when engaging with lobbying coalitions or any other type of single or collective actor with claims that may appear sympathetic or rather undeserving in the eyes of the voting public? This mechanism of democratic accountability is itself nested in macro political structures, in which countries vary, as is well known from the literature. They may be pluralist or corporatist, have a majoritarian and adversarial decision-making regime, or rather one oriented to consensus (Hollingsworth et al., 1994; Lijphart, 2012).

In her comparison of the US and the EU, Mahoney (2008) explains part of the difference between the frequency of lobbying coalitions and their size by the strength of the institutional mechanism for democratic accountability, which is more present in the US. She also finds that groups operating in public affairs in the US are smaller compared to the prominence of larger associations and groups in the EU, and this induces them to ally more and more informally in the US. Since the EU is typically a system of multi-level governance, with its member states and subnational governments, Mahoney argues that in the EU such informal coalitions are more likely to emerge at the member-state level. In the EU, the coalitions in action are often relatively permanent coalitions: associations, umbrella, or representing a branch. We have no systematic data for all the 28 member states, but there is little doubt that the sum of lobbying-coalition activity in all of them is beyond what happens in Brussels. This also may be the case in the US federal system, but the types of coalition are likely to be more similar, as suggested by the patterns of businesses in alliance found by Hawkinson (2005).

Thus, signaling public-affairs messages to policymakers is less of a binding element in coalition building than resource sharing where the chains of democratic delegation and electoral accountability are weak, as in the EU. It must be realized, however, that the EU is a polity in development, with policy-making institutions evolving towards more 'normal' representative and bureaucratic organizations, alike to those in other political systems (Wille, 2013). This also speaks to the findings of Bruycker and Beyers (2015: 9), who conclude that coalitions in the EU are on the rise, and that these emerging coalitions are increasingly heterogeneous, containing diverse organizations from business, nongovernmental organizations (NGOs), and citizen groups. Pijnenburg (1998: 315) found that in the EU ad hoc coalitions of business actors occur when internal divisions exist within the larger associations of which they are members.

Issue Characteristics as Coalition Drivers

Informal and ad hoc coalitions are often a *marriage de raison* – a functional and conditional togetherness – and this acting together may happen more as the scope and definition of issues widens and the level of conflict over it rises. Another factor that may drive otherwise diverse interest organizations together is the existence of strong opposition on the issue – a common enemy helps unity. These factors are found to be highly relevant by Gray and Lowery (1996) in their work on lobbying in states in the US, by Hojnacki (1997), and by Baumgartner and Leech (2001: 1206–7). Similar conclusions were drawn for the EU by Klüver (2013), Bruycker and Beyers (2015), and Beyers and Braun (2014). However, since the EU does not have a real public arena in the way countries have, the salience and media exposure of policy proposals arguably plays less of a part in driving coalitions. This means that while the scope of debate and the level of conflict are relevant, the level of exposure is limited and may play a more relevant part in member states.

Resource Interdependencies and Exchange to Cement Coalitions

Institutions and issues are contextual to coalition building. Another key category of condition in this process is the properties of interest organizations and groups themselves – in particular, their resources and the way they may engage in exchanging them when estimations are made about the costs and benefits of sharing (Pfeffer and Salancik, 2003; Berkhout, 2013). The resource conditions are not an alternative explanation to the previous factors: they must be seen in combination. Thus when Hula (1999) finds that resource-rich organizations are less likely to join coalitions, this does not render them systematic solo players in public affairs. In analyzing information exchange, a type of resource that can entail technical expertise as well as experiential knowledge about the best possible access points for influence, Carpenter et al. (2004) find that in the US, like-minded actors – the 'friendly' potential allies – are the main targets for interest organizations and groups in coalition building. Comparing three EU countries, Binderkrantz and Rasmussen (2015) found that group resources generally are more important in setting up joint lobbying activities at the EU level, while institutional embedding appeared more important at the national level, as we also saw above in the paragraph on institutional mechanisms.

If money generally is found to be a resource that matters but does not determine who wins or loses in lobbying for or against policy change (Baumgartner et al., 2009), it plays mostly a part in those cases of coalition formation where other actors dispose of other resources, such as generic information, technical expertise, and public or political legitimacy. Inside information access is found to provide added value for business corporations to join coalitions in the EU (Pijnenburg, 1998). He found, however, that this incentive does not produce long-lasting coalitions, or broad ones, but rather short-lived, functional coalitions that easily dissolve again. Enlarging the organization or group's own strategic knowledge and intelligence was also found to be a coalition making-factor by Heaney (2006) and Holyoke (2011) in analyzing patterns in the US.

If political legitimacy and support depends in large part on the image of the coalition towards the public, it also bears relevance at the closer circle of actual coalition members. In analyzing lobbying tactics towards the European Parliament, Marshall (2013) found that lobby-group strategies involve seeking the support of political parties that are not only natural ideological allies but also cut across the 'friendly' and 'unfriendly' ties. The patterns he found are distinct from those observed in the US, where alignments between political parties and interest groups are much more between the usual suspects in the separate camps of Democrats and Republicans, albeit with quite different coalition dynamics between the two (Grossmann and Dominguez, 2009).

To Invite or be Invited for Coalitions

This extended look on who gets in and who remains out of lobbying coalitions leads us to a final point to consider for coalition formation: who invites whom? If an actor is invited, this may lead that actor to estimate that those inviting are too weak to put pressure on a lobbied issue themselves, so the aforementioned points about resource exchange and added value of the coalition for reasons of broadening support and legitimacy will play their part.

Heaney and Lorenz (2013) present the concept of the *coalition portfolio*. They show how the position of an interest group in a network determines its degree of effort for leadership within a coalition, and how coalition leadership supports the collective action capacity of the entire coalition. Organizations or groups thus build a portfolio of diverse coalitions in which they participate or lead. Such central or pivotal positions in the coalition-building space vary in stability, however: in only a few instances of an interest organization network can one organization reproduce its centrality over longer periods of time.

While some actors in interest representation may not appear strong players when inviting others to join a coalition, and in such cases will face intense and explicit resource competition, other actors may be empowered to become an ally. Strolovich (2007) found citizen groups to be in such a position, in which they often dispose of limited affairs resources but are supported by state organizations to enter an alliance. Leifeld and Schneider (2012: 741) refer to Van Waarden (1992), who speaks of *sponsored pluralism*. Also, the EU appears to support civil-society organizations, which in this way are induced to 'follow the money' (Mahoney and Beckstrand, 2011).

As the inviting or 'to be invited' dividing line is often thin and may change over time, experience and coalition reputation are the social capital that make organizations and groups welcome guests or players to avoid in public-affairs collaboration. As mentioned, such coalition-participation legacy is not only relevant to the invitation and coalition-enlargement game, it also plays a part in the motivations of organizations to sacrifice a degree of visibility and identity when engaging in joint lobbying activity. Such tradeoffs are particularly relevant to organizations that have important internal functions, such as branch organizations and sectoral business associations, as well as NGOs that need to mobilize public support for their outspoken cases of advocacy. The costs of coalition can be considerable if a member organization or group gets drowned in it and loses its profile towards its own constituency.

COALITION MANAGEMENT AND SUCCESS

Next to the 'coalitionability' of individual organizations and groups, the management of coalitions is crucial to their success. Success factors are in part endogenous – they relate to the properties of actors, to resources, positions within networks, and how some balance between these points is established in the coalition. But success factors may also be external, relating to the way in which issues flow and travel in a political system and cross territorial boundaries. If event coalitions are made, then events may also break them.

Collective Action and Risks of Opportunism

Broad and diversely composed coalitions may enjoy appreciation and goodwill from policymakers, but as Olson (1965) noted, the growing size and heterogeneity of actor constellations also may increase the problem of collective action. Heinz et al. speak of ties held together 'not by magnetism of a dense core but by surface tension' (1993: 302). For this reason, Heaney and Leifeld (2015) argue that interest organizations or groups need to take on coalition leadership to facilitate such concerted action and avert the risk that the coalition will explode or implode. Coalition leadership can help resolve the collective-action problem, but it is in the nature of lobbying coalitions that are ad hoc, informal, temporary, and in other ways highly conditional instances of collaboration that the steering hand of a coalition leader can stretch only so far. Certainly, when bandwagons evolve in a rapid issue-attention wave, then hierarchical coalition control becomes an illusion. This does not derail such coalitions from success, as bandwagon effects can be powerful in the policy process, but it means that the possibility of centrally steering a coalition disappears.

Lobbying coalitions that emerge because actors see the advantages of joint effort in the pursuit of interests in an issue always are vulnerable to opportunistic behavior, in the same ways as multiparty governments or legislative coalitions involve continued trade-offs of costs and benefits by partners when making and enforcing deals (Timmermans, 2006; Martin and Vanberg, 2011). How lobbying coalitions 'police their bargain' is thus a matter of constant internal assessment. The point made above about leadership limits is particularly important because lobbying coalitions have no mechanisms of external control for enforcement. The agenda and agreements over issues made within a coalition are always incomplete contracts – they may not even be made explicit to begin with (Timmermans and Breeman, 2014). This is a reason why so many coalitions end prematurely, either silently or with a lot of noise expressing discontent when objectives are considered fully or in part achieved, or when goals are seen as practically unachievable by one or more of the participants in the collective effort. Dealing with risks of opportunistic behavior, free riding, and shirking require coalitions to design informal but credible arrangements for keeping the coalition on track for as long as it is meant to be lobbying (Levi and Murphy, 2006). Such arrangements for togetherness include incentives, sanctions, and future perspectives for partnership.

The Diffuse Parameters of Success

What, then, about the success of lobbying coalitions? The parameters of success may vary with the size and diversity of composition, the scope of the agenda, and the fluidity of resource exchanges. As mentioned, it is hard to establish a straightforward criterion for winning and success. Of course, it will be known when a coalition achieves its main goals – the least being that it sees its own goals achieved – but it is harder to say what accounts for it. This is the same puzzle as for measuring lobbying influence and success more generally (Lowery, 2013). For coalition activity, we also face the problem of counterfactuals: how can we know that a coalition's lobbying success would not have been achieved by a single-interest organization alone, or that failure would have been averted if one organization had handled all the public affairs?

But when analyzing or engaging in professional lobbying-coalition activity we do not need such a high threshold for causal evidence of success. It is foremost the success or failure itself and its perception that may matter most. For measurement, interest-group scholars are applying spatial approaches based on content analysis in addition to the survey- and interview-based research designs in use for so long in this field (see, for example, Bernhagen et al., 2014). And when coalitions are formed to lobby together and when they operate in concert, this is likely to bring some or all of the advantages mentioned in this chapter. The odds are not of coalition activity as a hindering factor, but they seem to indicate that, with the intense dynamics of issue attention and the sensitivity of policymakers to broadening their constituencies, coalition partners in lobbying can produce significant added value for a public-affairs strategy, as long as they maintain a unified message (Mahoney, 2008; Nelson and Yackee, 2012).

Policymakers across the world, and certainly in the regions for which we have the most systematic empirical data, are increasingly in need of signaling (hence their need of a clear message at the same time). Lobbying coalitions spread as informal, ad hoc, and temporary vehicles for doing this. Thus the available research findings indicate that larger coalitions make a more positive difference than they used to some decades ago (Heinz et al., 1993; Gray and Lowery, 1996). Nelsen and Yackee (2012) mention the positive effects of extended size and composition, with new members and thus some heterogeneity within the coalition adding strength rather than weakness in achieving results. Likewise, Klüver (2013) in her analysis of EU lobbying, finds that lobbying coalitions are most likely to win when they are wide enough and all partners contribute to the exchange of information, support, and economic resources. She did not find evidence for the special role of coalition leaders paving the way towards joint success, instead observing that coalitions work best in their joint efforts when all partners are involved. Bruyker and Beyers (2015) report that business corporations and NGOs in the EU increasingly consider teaming up with each other to be unavoidable, particularly for high-profile issues. Also, the state-driven empowerment of citizen groups – the aforementioned sponsored pluralism – may be seen not only to contribute to the diversity of coalition formation in public affairs, but also to condition of access to policymakers that speaks to the need for increased constituencies of political decision makers.

THE FUTURE OF COALITIONS IN PUBLIC AFFAIRS

This chapter has shown how the playing field – the context in which interest organizations and groups move around issues – sets the stage for lobbying-coalition formation. Network ties and positions matter, as do previously established (or wasted) reputations as an ally for a cause in public affairs. To manage lobbying coalitions and ensure they reach joint goals, the exchange of resources, a good level of tolerance for diversity in composition, and a good deal of compromising are required. Though coalition leadership may not solely determine outcomes, it may be key for setting coalition formation in motion, for expanding a coalition, and for pulling members over a threshold to deliver for collective action. When coalitions grow or are drawn into a rapidly expanding bandwagon, however, the steering potential rapidly declines. We do not know much about bandwagons in public affairs, but they seem to be more frequent than previously, and when they occur they may not always provide a definitive push for policy change. Bandwagons also can be powerful veto mechanisms.

Heterogeneous coalitions seem to be on the rise, and coalitions are becoming more prone to bandwagon effects as issues 'contaminate' at enormous speed. This sets quite demanding conditions for keeping coalitions on track and for obtaining common goals. It also means that coalition management in public affairs is an important area of further professionalization. Here, it is relevant to consider trends in orientation of types of interest and advocacy organization and group, with business corporations becoming ever more aware of the need to build and maintain a public reputation of trust and monitor public opinion, while NGOs extend their repertoire from activism and outside advocacy to taking a seat at the negotiation table. In this sense, diverse actors show some degree of convergence, and stereotypes about their respective lobbying behavior apply less than they used to, a tendency that speaks to what Alinsky (1971) called *rules for radicals*.

Thus, in the near future, the boundaries between inside and outside lobbying,

between organizations with access to information, resources, and policymakers and those lacking it, and between business, branch, and advocacy groups and mobilizing citizens and public organizations as actors will become less marked than they have been. Crossing these boundaries will be a prominent category of competencies as coalitions become ever more important in the successful management of public affairs.

REFERENCES

Alinsky, S.D. (1971). *Rules for Radicals. A Pragmatic Primer for Realistic Radicals*. New York, Random House.

Baumgartner, F.R. and B.R. Jones (2014). *The Politics of Information*. Chicago, University of Chicago Press.

Baumgartner, F.R. and B.L. Leech (2001). 'Issue niches and policy bandwagons: Patterns of interest group involvement in national politics', *Journal of Politics* 63: 1191–1213.

Baumgartner, F.R., J.M. Berry, M. Hojnacki, D.C. Kimball and B.L. Leech (2009). *Lobbying and Policy Change. Who Wins, Who Loses, and Why*. Chicago, University of Chicago Press.

Berkhout, J. (2013). 'Why interest organizations do what they do: Assessing the explanatory potential of 'exchange' approaches', *Interest Groups & Advocacy* 2(2): 227–50.

Bernhagen, P., A. Dür and D. Marshall (2014). 'Measuring lobbying success spatially', *Interest Groups & Advocacy* 3(2): 202–18.

Berry, J. (1977). *Lobbying for the People. The Political Behavior of Public Interest Groups*. New Jersey, Princeton University Press.

Betzold, C. (2013). 'Business insiders and environmental outsiders? Advocacy strategies in international climate change negotiations', *Interest Groups & Advocacy* 2(3): 302–22.

Beyers, J. and C. Braun (2014). 'Ties that count. Explaining interest group access to policymakers', *Journal of Public Policy* 34(1): 93–121.

Binderkrantz, A. and A. Rasmussen (2015). 'Comparing the domestic and the EU lobbying context: Perceived agenda-setting influence in the multi-level system of the

European Union', *Journal of European Public Policy* 22(4): 552–69.

Braun, C. (2015). 'Lobbying as a leverage act: On resource dependencies and lobby presence', in D. Halpin, D. Lowery and V. Gray (eds). *The Organization Ecology of Interest Communities: An Assessment and An Agenda*. Houndsmills, PalgraveMacmillan.

Bruycker, I. de and J. Beyers (2015). 'When politics makes strange bedfellows: Why business interests and NGOs coalesce', paper presented at the 14th EUSA Conference, Boston, March 2015.

Bunea, A. and F.R. Baumgartner (2014). 'The state of the discipline: authorship, research designs and citation patterns in studies of EU interest groups and lobbying', *Journal of European Public Policy* 21(10): 1412–1434.

Carpenter, D., K. Esterling and D. Lazer (2004). 'Friends, brokers and transitivity: who informs whom in Washington politics?', *Journal of Politics* 66(1): 224–46.

Caroll, A.B. (2005). 'Stakeholder management', in P.H. Harris and C.S. Fleisher (eds.). *The Handbook of Public Affairs*. Thousand Oaks, Sage.

Cobb, R.W. and C.D. Elder (1983). *Participation in American Politics: The Dynamics of Agenda-Building*. Second edition. Baltimore, Johns Hopkins University Press.

Cobb, R.W. and M.H. Ross (eds.) (1997). *Cultural Strategies of Agenda Denial: Avoidance, Attack, and Redefinition*. Lawrence, University Press of Kansas.

Coombs, W.T. (2002). 'Assessing online issue threats: Issues contagions and their effect on issue prioritisation', *Journal of Public Affairs* 2(4): 215–29.

Fischer, F. (2003). *Reframing Public Policy*. Oxford, Oxford University Press.

Granovetter, M.S. (1973). 'The strength of weak ties', *American Journal of Sociology* 78(6): 1360–1380.

Gray, V. and D. Lowery (1998). 'To lobby alone or in a flock: Foraging behavior among organized interests', *American Politics Quarterly* 26(1): 5–34.

Grossmann, M. (2013). 'The variable party politics of the policy process', *Journal of Politics* 75(1): 65–79.

Grossmann, M. and C.B.K. Dominguez (2009). 'Party coalitions and interest group networks', *American Politics Research* 37(5): 767–800.

Haas, P.M. (1992). 'Introduction: Epistemic communities and international policy coordination', *International Organization* 46(1): 1–35.

Hadden, J. (2015). *Networks in Contention: The Divisive Politics of Climate Change*. Cambridge, Cambridge University Press.

Halpin, D. (2011). 'Explaining policy bandwagons: Organized interest mobilization and cascades of attention'. *Governance* 24(2): 205–30.

Halpin, D., D. Lowery and V. Gray (eds.) (2015). *The Organization Ecology of Interest Communities*. Houndsmills, PalgraveMacmillan.

Hanegraaff, M.C. (2015). 'Interest groups at transnational conferences: goals, strategies, interactions and influence', *Global Governance: A Review of Multilateralism and International Organizations* 21(4): 599–620.

Hanegraaff, M.C., C. Braun, D. De Bièvre and J. Beyers (2015). 'The domestic and global origins of transnational advocacy: explaining lobbying presence during WTO ministerial conferences', *Comparative Political Studies*, online first publication, 21 July 2015.

Harris, P.H. and C.S. Fleisher (eds.) (2005). *The Handbook of Public Affairs*. Thousand Oaks, Sage.

Hawkinson, B. (2005). 'The internal environment of public affairs', in P.H. Harris and C.S. Fleisher (eds.). *The Handbook of Public Affairs*. Thousand Oaks, Sage.

Heaney, M.T. (2006). 'Brokering health policy: coalitions, parties, and interest group influence', *Journal of Health Politics, Policy and Law*, 31(5): 887–944.

Heaney, M.T. and P. Leifeld (2015). 'Collective action and leadership inside lobbying coalitions', paper presented at the Comparative Political Networks Conference, Madrid, 29–30 June 2015.

Heaney, M.T. and G.M. Lorenz (2013). 'Coalition portfolios and interest group influence over the policy process', *Interest Groups and Advocacy* 2(3): 251–77.

Heinz, J.P., E.O. Laumann, R.L. Nelson and R.H. Salisbury (1993). *The Hollow Core: Private Interests in National Policy Making*. Cambridge, Harvard University Press.

Hojnacki, M. (1997). 'Interest groups' decisions to join alliances or work alone', *American Journal of Political Science*' 41(1): 61–87.

Hojnacki, M. (1998). 'Organized interests' advocacy behavior in alliances', *Political Research Quarterly* 51(2): 437–59.

Hojnacki, M., D.C. Kimball, F.R. Baumgartner, J.M. Berry and B.L. Leech (2012). 'Studying organizational advocacy and influence: Re-examining interest group research'. *Annual Review of Political Science* 15(9): 1–21.

Hollingsworth, J.R., P.C. Schmitter and W. Streeck (1994). *Governing Capitalist Economies: Performance and Control of Economic Sectors*. Oxford, Oxford University Press.

Holyoke, T.T. (2011). *Competitive Interests*. Washington DC, Georgetown University Press.

Hula, K.W. (1999). *Lobbying Together. Interest Group Coalitions in Legislative Politics*. Washington DC, Georgetown University Press.

Jones, B.D. (2001). *Politics and the Architecture of Choice. Bounded Rationality and Governance*. Chicago, University of Chicago Press.

Jones, B.D. and Baumgartner, F.R. (2005). *The Politics of Attention. How Government Prioritizes Problems*. Chicago, University of Chicago Press.

Kerwin, C.M. (2003). *Rulemaking: How Government Agencies Write Law and Make Policy*. 3rd edition, Washington D.C., CQ Press.

Kimball, D.C., F.R. Baumgartner, J.M. Berry, M. Hojnacki, B.L. Leech and B. Summary (2012). 'Who cares about the lobbying agenda?', *Interest Groups & Advocacy* 1(1): 5–25.

Kingdon, J.W. (1984). *Agendas, Alternatives, and Public Policy*. New York, Longman.

Klüver, H. (2013). *Lobbying in the European Union: Interest Groups, Lobbying Coalitions, and Policy Change*. Oxford, Oxford University Press.

Kollman, K. (1998). *Outside Lobbying: Public Opinion and Interest Group Strategies*. Princeton, Princeton University Press.

Laver, M. and N. Schofield (1990). *Multiparty Government. The Politics of Coalition in Europe*. Oxford, Oxford University Press.

Laumann, E.O. and D. Knoke (1987). *The Organizational State*. Madison, University of Wisconsin Press.

Leifeld, P. and V. Schneider (2012). 'Information exchange in policy networks', *American Journal of Political Science* 56(3): 731–44.

Levi, M. and G. Murphy (2006). 'Coalitions of contention: The case of the WTO protests in Seattle', *Political Studies* 54(4): 651–70.

Lijphart, A. (2012). *Patterns of Democracy. Government Forms and Performance in Thirty-Six Countries*. New Haven, Yale University Press.

Lobbyists.info (n.d.). Lobbyist Involvement in Coalition Building. Retrieved from http://www.lobbyists.info/Lobbyist_Involvement_in_Coalition_Building-11-WhitePaper (accessed 29 August, 2016).

Loomis, B.A. (1986). 'Coalitions of interests: building bridges in the Balkanized state', in C.A. Cigler and B.A. Loomis (eds.). *Interest Group Politics*, second edition. Washington DC, Congressional Quarterly Press.

Lowery, D. (2013). 'Lobbying influence: Meaning, measurement and missing', *Interest Groups & Advocacy* 2(1): 1–26.

Mahoney, C. (2008). *Brussels versus the Beltway. Advocacy in the United States and the European Union*. Washington DC, Georgetown University Press.

Mahoney, C. and M.J. Beckstrand (2011). 'Following the money: EU funding of civil society organizations', *Journal of Common Market Studies* 49(6): 1339–1361.

Marshall, D. (2013). 'Explaining interest group interactions with party group members in the European Parliament: Dominant party groups and coalition formation', *Journal of Common Market Studies* 53(3): 311–29.

Martin, L.W. and G. Vanberg (2011). *Parliaments and Coalitions. The Role of Legislative Institutions in Multiparty Governance*. Oxford, Oxford University Press.

Mitnick, B.M. (ed.) (1993). *Corporate Political Agency: The Construction of Competition in Public Affairs*. Thousand Oaks, Sage.

Nelson, D. and S.W. Yackee (2012). 'Lobbying coalitions and government policy change', *Journal of Politics* 74(2): 339–53.

Olson, M. (1965). *The Logic of Collective Action. Public Goods and the Theory of Groups*. Cambridge, Mass., Harvard University Press.

Pfeffer, J. and G.R. Salancik (2003). *The External Control of Organizations. A Resource*

Dependence Perspective. Stanford, Stanford University Press.

Pijnenburg, B. (1998). 'EU lobbying by ad hoc coalitions: an exploratory case study', *Journal of Europen Public Policy* 5(2): 303–21.

Riker, W.H. (1962). *The Theory of Political Coalitions*. New Haven, Yale University Press.

Sabatier, P.A. (1988). 'An advocacy coalition framework of policy change and the role of policy-oriented learning therein', *Policy Sciences* 21: 129–68.

Salisbury, R.H., J.P. Heinz, E.O. Laumann and R.L. Nelson. (1987). 'Who works with whom? Interest group alliances and opposition', *American Political Science Review* 81(4): 1217–234.

Schattschneider, E.E. (1960). *The Semisovereign People*. New York, Holt, Rinehart and Winston.

Schlozman, K. L. and J.T. Tierney (1986). *Organized Interests and American Democracy*. New York, Harper and Row.

Schofield, N. (1993). 'Political competition and multiparty coalition governments', *European Journal of Political Research* 23(1): 1–33.

Strolovich, D. (2007). *Affirmative Advocacy. Race, Class and Gender in Interest Group Politics*. Chicago, University of Chicago Press.

Timmermans, A. (2006). 'Standing apart and sitting together. Enforcing coalition agreements in multiparty systems', *European Journal of Political Research* 45(2): 263–83.

Timmermans, A. and Breeman, G. (2014). The policy agenda in multiparty government: Coalition agreements and legislative activity in the Netherlands. In: C. Green-Pedersen and S. Walgrave (eds.). *Agenda Setting, Policies, and Political Systems: A Comparative Approach*. Chicago: University of Chicago Press.

Van Schendelen, M.P.C.M. (2013). *The Art of Lobbying the EU. More Machiavelli in Brussels*. Amsterdam, Amsterdam University Press.

Van Waarden, F. (1992). 'Dimensions and types of policy networks', *European Journal of Political Research* 21(1–2): 29–52.

Wille, A. (2013). *The Normalization of the European Commission. Politics and Bureaucracy in the EU Executive*. Oxford, Oxford University Press.

PART VI

Case Studies in Public Affairs

Danny Moss

The decade since the first edition of the Handbook of Public Affairs (2005) was published has been marked by profound socio-economic and political change, brought about by a series of seismic upheavals affecting many of the world's economies, social structures and the political landscape across Europe and other parts of the world. Such profound changes have created new challenges for public affairs professionals in understanding and interpreting external change for their organisations, set against a backdrop of increasingly complex and fast-changing environmental pressures, which are often exacerbated by multi-stakeholder expectations and demands. One recurring theme over the past decade has been the increasing *pace* of change and the consequent pressure on organisations and every function within an organisation to try to remain 'agile' and responsive to those forces shaping its operating environment. But, of course, environments are not in themselves tangible; it is through the actions and behaviours of various stakeholders or stakeholder activist groups that environmental pressures are often made manifest. It is in monitoring and anticipating such stakeholder behaviour, and counselling senior management about how best to respond, that public affairs arguably can make its most important and ongoing contribution to organisational success. This role of effective stakeholder intelligence gathering and communication was captured in what Post et al. (1982) termed as functioning as the 'window out and window in' for organisations. This 'two-way' public affairs function has also become more multi-faceted with the 'explosion' in the widespread use of social and digital media over the past decade. Indeed such has been the growth of social media use worldwide that simply keeping track of all the 'chatter' circulating at any time within social media channels has become a major challenge in itself for communications/public affairs professionals, who normally assume this responsibility. On a cautionary note, such has been the rapid proliferation of social media in recent years that some commentators and communication professionals appear to focus on social media almost to the exclusion of all other channels of communication.

While to ignore what is being said about an organisation or issues within social media channels would be irresponsible, it is equally important to keep social media communication in perspective, weighing its potential influence alongside that of other, more traditional communication channels. Moreover, from a public affairs perspective in particular, media coverage in any channel can only go so far in facilitating the types of behavioural outcome critical to the success of most public affairs campaigns. Often public affairs success depends on the deployment of more subtle and 'behind the scenes' exchanges that take place within the so-called 'corridors of power', which public affairs professionals may have access to or can facilitate access to for key figures from their organisation.

Another feature of public affairs work over the past decade has been its increasing internationalisation, which has mirrored the pattern of expansion in international trade, which, according to the World Trade Organization (WTO), has grown on average by 7 percent per annum over the past two decades, reaching $18.8 trillion in 2013. While the majority of business entities remain relatively small and operate largely in domestic markets, for an increasing number of medium-sized and larger enterprises, international trading often represents a significant and important part of their business. In this international business arena, it is not unusual to find that the public affairs function may be asked to assume a broad range of responsibilities across a business's sphere of operations that goes beyond the more conventional political advocacy and influencing role and may embrace working as a 'cultural and political interpreter' or, in some cases, functioning as

a corporate and business communications expert. Here, anecdotal evidence suggests it is often more a case of pragmatism and lack of specialised expertise, particularly in some of the more remote parts of the world, that forces organisations to adopt a more broad-ranging interpretation of the role and scope of public affairs in an international business context. Thus while in some circumstances, notably in highly regulated markets/countries, public affairs may play a more conventional political lobbying and influencing role, in other circumstances it may work as a cultural and political interpreter, helping organisations avoid any potential 'banana skins' in terms of local regulations, customs and practices that may have a profound impact on an organisation's ability to build a position in specific international markets. In short, conventional disciplinary boundaries may count for very little when an organisation is faced with the immediate reality of operating in international markets, where a shortage of local public affairs expertise and a greater demand for broader communications support for business strategies is always likely to result in the hiring of generalist over specialist public affairs professionals.

Earlier chapters of this book have explored in more detail how public affairs is understood, what role it plays in organisations today and how the management of public affairs may vary across different regional, national, industrial and organisational settings. This section of the book comprises a number of case study chapters that serve to illustrate something of this rich tapestry of understanding of public affairs in different geopolitical and industrial contexts, ranging from Japan to the African continent and Europe and spanning the work of public affairs in the corporate, not-for-profit and NGO contexts. The broad scope and focus of the cases included in this section are summarised below.

Chapter 32, which has been researched and authored by Clive Thomas and Kristina Klimovich (University of Alaska Southeast Juneau), actually comprises three shorter case studies, which examine the challenges facing three international not-for-profit organisations working in Latin America. The chapter provides a valuable insight into how public affairs may be understood in the Latin American region, along with an overview of the varied and troubled history of how the distribution of political power has unfolded across the region, and how foreign governments and business have sought to intervene in Latin American affairs over the years. Against this backdrop, the chapter explores the experience of three NGOs working respectively in Bolivia, Brazil and Haiti. The chapter examines the reasons behind Bolivia's first expulsion of an international NGO – a Danish NGO, IBIS, which promoted local education and democratic participation among local communities. Focusing on Brazil, the chapter examines the campaigning work of the World Wildlife Fund (WWF) to influence the Brazilian government's policy to protect the Amazon rainforest. Finally, the chapter explores the work of a number of the major relief agencies that sought to help Haitian communities after the devastating earthquake that hit the country in 2010.

In Chapter 33 David Irwin (independent social entrepreneur and consultant in enterprise and economic development) and Kariuki Waweru (Business Advocacy Fund, Nairobi) offer a detailed examination of the work of the Kenya Chamber of Mines (KCM), an association which was formed to represent the interests of miners, exploration companies and mineral traders in Kenya. The authors examine the effectiveness of the KCM in seeking to influence and shape the final outcome of a new Mining Act in 2014 as it passed through government processes prior to final assent by Kenya's President. In examining this specific case the authors also draw more general conclusions about the role of business associations in influencing public policy, particularly in an African context.

Chapter 34 returns to Western Europe and more specifically to the UK and Ireland, where Conor McGrath (independent scholar and lecturer at the University of Ulster) offers a considered comparison of the recent review and reform of lobbying practices in the UK and Irish political environment, setting this analysis against the background of each country's political history. The author analyses the potential effectiveness of the legislative reforms in each country with respect to the registration of lobbyists and the ability to exercise a degree of control over the influence lobbyists might have on government decisions and policy.

Chapter 35 turns the lens on to Asia and more specifically Japan, where the authors, Koji Haraguchi (International College of Liberal Arts, Yamanashi Gakkuin University) and Ronald Hrebenar (University of Utah), offer a relatively rare and fascinating insight into public affairs and lobbying practice in Japan, highlighting and explaining how and why they are very different to public affairs and lobbying in other developed nations. Here, in essence, they trace these differences to deep-seated cultural and social traditions that continue to affect how public affairs and lobbying impact government policy-making in the Japanese context. The chapter concludes by examining a specific case – the dispute about the US military base on Okinawa – which illustrates many of the principles examined earlier about how public affairs and lobbying take place in a Japanese context.

Chapter 36 takes us back to Africa, this time to Tanzania, where Goodluck Charles (University of Dar es Salaam Business School) analyses the lessons to be learned from reviewing the Tanzanian government's attempts develop a more effective dialogue with the private business sector and encourage greater business advocacy/engagement in policy reforms designed to improve the country's economic performance. The chapter explores the reasons for the limited success of this initiative despite the establishment of a number of regional, sub-national and national consultative working groups and representative bodies designed to engage with the business community.

Finally, in Chapter 37, Gianluca Vinicio Aguggini (Condé Nast International, London) recounts the remarkable rise to political power of the Italian comedian Beppe Grillo and his Movimento 5 Stelle party in the Italian elections of 2013. Essentially, Aguggini argues that the totally unexpected success of Grillo's campaign can be attributed in large part to a highly effective digital- and social-media-led campaign allied to Grillo's personal appearances and engaging campaigning across Italy. What is notable in Grillo's campaign is just how important a part social media, and particularly Grillo's daily blog, appears to have played in mobilizing support for this new political party and its leader, not just among a younger 'cyber-savvy' audience but increasingly among a broader swathe of the Italian population. However, while acknowledging the importance of social- and digital-media campaign tactics to Grillo's success, the chapter also recognises that the resonance of the carefully crafted messages distributed through these channels and the engaging personality of the party leader were equally critical in capturing electoral support for Grillo and his party.

REFERENCES

Post, J.E., Murray, E.A, Dickie, R.B., and Mahon, J.F. (1982). The public affairs function in American corporations: Development and relations with corporate planning. *Long Range Planning*,15(2), 12–21.

Three Case Studies from Latin America: A Living Museum of Government Affairs

Clive S. Thomas and Kristina Klimovich

INTRODUCTION: A LIVING MUSEUM OF PUBLIC AFFAIRS

The term *public affairs* generally has a broad meaning across Latin America and does not only include the relations of business or other interests in their activities in the public sphere and their dealings with government. That is, it does not only include lobbying. In the Latin American case public affairs includes public relations and even organizing conferences and other public events. Dealings with government in the region are usually referred to as *governmental affairs*, *government affairs* or *government relations*. So these are the terms we use in this chapter.

Furthermore, we do not confine our use of government affairs to include only the relations of business and other corporate entities with government. In this chapter we take a broad view of governmental-affairs activity to include all groups and organizations whether formally organized or not that attempt to influence governmental actions by some form of lobbying. This is because, in Latin America as elsewhere, while lobbying by business has probably been and likely remains the most significant aspect of any segment of civil society working to influence government, over the past hundred years many other groups and organizations have become involved in lobbying. Thus to understand the form and extent of government relations in the region it is necessary to view the broad spectrum of groups and techniques now embraced under lobbying in Latin America.

The pattern of political flux and of external influence that have long characterized Latin America has shaped the development of its interest-group systems and the characteristics of government affairs. In turn, both the group systems and the activity of government relations have affected the nature of the region's political systems. In this chapter, three case studies provide a perspective on the 'living museum' (Anderson 1967: 104–5) of Latin American government affairs and interest-group activity, where practices from the past operate alongside modern methods of access and influence.[1]

For most of its history since European settlement, Latin America has been dominated by political, economic, military and religious elites and been on a rollercoaster from authoritarianism to various forms of participatory politics (limited democracy) and populism. This dominant aspect of the region's political development spawned the power group – an influential, often politically dominant, individual or clique – as the major force in the region's governmental affairs and which persists today. With particular reference to business and agribusiness, the role of power groups is the subject of the first case study. The second case illustrates how the vicissitudes and level of political development affects the conduct of public affairs. The example chosen is the labour movement. This embraces what would be termed blue-collar and white-collar unions in Europe and North America, from unskilled labourers to electricians to teachers and nurses, but excludes some professional organizations such as lawyers and physicians. This is because the latter are usually less confrontational with democratic and particularly authoritarian governments. The third case study illustrates the continuing influence of outside forces in the region. In this case it is that of international non-governmental organizations (NGOs) in three countries at different levels of economic and political development. These are, Brazil, Bolivia and Haiti – and the NGOs' varying roles and approach to government affairs, and government reactions to the political role of these NGOs.[2]

POWER GROUPS: A PERENNIAL ASPECT OF GOVERNMENTAL AFFAIRS

The development of the power group has similarities in all political systems. From the earliest days of civilization, people have naturally banded into groups. Group identity based on location, race, tribe, religion, class, economic status and, later, profession and values (such as pro- or anti-slavery) was a major aspect of the dynamics of all societies. As a consequence societies were structured by various groups and interests. Certain groups, such as the noblemen in Europe in the Middle Ages, became major political forces by influencing or, in many cases, controlling government and excluding other groups and interests. This was sometimes to promote their view of life (such as the Catholic Church) or in other cases to secure economic benefits (like import tariffs to protect their products from foreign competition).

In these ways power groups emerged in all societies. These informal political entities, in the form of a group (such as large landowners), a prominent family, a major group of businesses and sometimes a powerful individual, have been the dominant entity engaging in government relations throughout history. They influenced and in some cases continue to influence government policy by a variety of methods, including: like-mindedness and ideological affinity with those in government; close personal, sometimes family, ties with those in power; because they had, and in many cases still have, a service or industry that government could not do without for revenue or other purposes; and the use of bribery and corrupt practices. Most of the activities of power groups take place far from public view and are often subtle in their operation, such as an implicit understanding between the members of the power group and the government.

Power groups continue to be the major vehicle of government relations in authoritarian systems, like North Korea, many African countries and Cuba. Moreover, they continue to exist in democracies of all types, as personal contacts are the essence of any governmental-relations activity no matter what the form of government. In sharp contrast to authoritarian systems, however, one of the major developments in countries that transition from authoritarian to some form of pluralist democratic rule is that more and more interests became formalized interest groups, such as trade unions, business associations and so on, and power groups decline in number relative to formalized interest groups and are pushed into a secondary place as a vehicle of governmental relations. Furthermore, the development of democracy, with its regular elections, increased political participation, activities of a plethora of interest groups and a free media, also involved the major development of the transparency of government actions. This includes many forms of public disclosure of election spending and campaign contributions and in some cases the regulation of lobbying and disclosure of interest-group activities. Consequently, the more advanced the democracy, the more formalized its interest-group system and the more diminished the role of power groups.

To be sure, a plethora of formalized interest groups operate across Latin America today and in some cases have for over 150 years. But because of the region's rollercoaster of political development and the stunted growth of pluralist democracy, power groups are still an important aspect of governmental relations. Other factors contributing to this prominence of power groups in Latin America include: the persistence of political, social and economic elites; the lack of public transparency of government in most countries; the persistence of corruption across the region; extensive poverty that stymies the growth of a middle class in most countries that would increase broader participation in interest groups and act as a counter balance to elite political activities; and, partly as a result of the first four, a deep-rooted scepticism of government among Latin Americans, resulting in a high degree of political apathy. The situation varies, of course, from consolidated democracies, like Costa Rica, Uruguay, Chile and Brazil, to those less developed, like Haiti and Nicaragua, to those with an authoritarian bent, like Bolivia and Venezuela.

Examples of Power Groups Across Latin America Past and Present

To illustrate the long-standing role of power groups in Latin American governmental affairs, we use three categories of power group from the past, and the same three categories operate in the region today. The three categories are: cliques of elites, both domestic and foreign; prominent families; and influential individuals.

The past: from colonial times to the return of democracy in the 1980s

Until after the Second World War the franchise across Latin America was extremely restricted, though it was expanded earlier in some countries, like Uruguay and Costa Rica. When widespread extreme poverty and the lack of literacy of tens of millions across the region are added to the limited franchise, it is easy to see why access to government was extremely restricted. So the overwhelming modus operandi of government affairs was very informal actions by a narrow range of elites. Certainly, many formal interest groups were established across the region in the late nineteenth and early twentieth centuries, such as Chile's National Agricultural Association (SNA), founded in 1838 (Rodríguez and Thomas 2014: 315) and in Brazil, the dominant centre of economic activity, the state of São Paulo, established its major industrial association, Central Industrial Association of the State of São Paulo (CIESP) in 1928 (Schneider 2004: 98). But even these formal organizations usually used informal methods to deal with and influence government.

Across Latin America in the past and to some extent today, there were five cliques of elite that tended to have the most influence on government and public policy. These were landowners, prominent businessmen, the military, the Catholic Church and foreign governments and businesses. These elites, particularly landowners and businessmen, filled the ranks of government officials at various times and thus had access to policy-makers, while excluding the mass of society. Of particular significance were foreign governments and businesses that often influenced the government, because these foreign entities and the domestic government elites had a common interest. Britain, Spain and to a lesser extent France were most influential in the region down to the end of the nineteenth century, but they were all superseded by the dominant influence of the US from the 1880s onward. Foreign businesses included companies constructing railways in Argentina, mining companies in Bolivia, Chile and Peru and companies growing bananas and tropical fruits in Central America.

As government was an important political force in the region, either because of corporatist policies (as with the Getúlio Vargas administrations in Brazil from 1930–45 and again from 1951–4) or in response to populist demands (such as in Argentina under Juan Perón after the Second World War), power groups in government were also an important force. A good example of this type of power group was Venezuela's government oil agency, Petroleos de Venezuela (PDVSA), after the oil industry was nationalized in 1976.

Venezuela stands out in the region as the only country that permitted foreign-owned oil companies ('big oil') to operate its oil industry, decades after Mexico's dramatic nationalization of oil in 1938. Even after nationalization PDVSA was, 'never fully controlled by any of the governments that technically owned it' (Parenti 2006: 8). This was partly because these governments left the former executives of the big oil companies in charge of PDVSA. This choice effectively displaced the Energy Ministry in setting Venezuela's oil policy (López-Maya and Lander 2011: 22).

As a result, the nation's oil policy after nationalization was set by the cadre of Venezuelan engineers and managers within PDVSA who were cultivated by the big oil companies as part of their broader project to legitimize a foreign-owned oil industry

(Tinker Salas 2009). These executives shared big oil's view that 'what was good for the oil industry was good for Venezuela' (Tinker Salas 2009: 5).

The family in Latin America has always been a dominant societal unit, more so than in northern Europe and on a par with southern Europe. Family-owned businesses and their patriarchs often had a major influence on public policy either because of the family's major connections with the government elite (often they were the same people) or because the government needed the industry for revenue and to maintain some semblance of economic stability. Bolivia and Central America provide excellent examples of families and their individuals as power groups.

The first power-group elite in Bolivia was the silver-mining oligarchy centred in Potosi and Sucre. It controlled the Conservative Party, dominated by civilians. A short civil war in 1899 ended the rule of the silver aristocracy. It was replaced by the tin barons centred in La Paz. The major world demand for tin from 1900–27 made Bolivia's three major tin magnates, Carlos Aramayo, Mauricio Hochschild and Simon Patiño, very rich. During these years the government was very dependent on the big three. They earned foreign exchange, provided considerable employment and government revenues and 'owned' most politicians. Into the mid 1930s the government was very much beholden to 'the state that tin made' (Morales 2012: 573) and the big three had a virtual monopoly on what government did or did not do. This entrenched political-economic control of the tin oligarchy and associated establishment was known at *la Rosca* (literally, a screw or screw thread but intended to denote applying pressure – as in tightening a screw – to the government).

Another example of a politically powerful individual from the past is a US immigrant, Samuel Zemurray (1877–1961, 'Sam the Banana Man'), who ran the United Fruit Company (UFC) for a quarter of a century. Operating largely from the US, through his direct contacts in the State Department Zemurray exercised considerable control over Central American governments, particularly Honduras and Nicaragua.

Contemporary Latin America: power groups in the age of democracy

As a society transitions from authoritarianism to democracy with groups and other entities free to organize and lobby, a process of institutionalization occurs. In this process many hitherto informal groups, some of which are power groups, become formalized by officially organizing and are then recognized as members of the interest-group system. Consequently, one of the characteristics of this gradual democratization is that power groups become relatively fewer in number in the political system as more and more formalized groups are established. Nevertheless, power groups persist as part of the democratic system and certainly in Latin America (where power groups in Brazil, Chile and Uruguay, for example, re-established themselves, having been considerably constrained during authoritarian rule). This is for three major reasons.

First, power groups exist in all political systems, including the most advanced democracies. This is because, as government relations is essentially a human-interaction activity, like-minded individuals in and out of government who have a common interest in a policy area will always seek out each other in informal settings. This is the case even where there are extensive public-disclosure laws. Often, though, power groups – including individuals – are also part of a more formal organization. The second reason is that old habits die hard, particularly in a region like Latin America, where power groups have long been the major form of political organisation involved in government relations. This is just the normal way of doing business for most groups and organizations, even if they have a formal organization. And third, as in the past, Latin American countries are still subject to much foreign influence. This was particularly true following the debt crises from the early 1980s into the 1990s, when many Latin American countries needed international loans.

Numerous examples could be used but six will suffice, three general to the region and three specific to particular countries. Across the region, the Catholic Church still operates as a significant power group to influence public policies. This is particularly true on doctrinal matters, especially on issues like abortion and birth control. Latin America is the region in the world with the most countries that ban abortion outright (Elgar 2014). While in most countries the military has left the halls of government and returned to the barracks, they still wield considerable influence across the region from Mexico to Columbia even to Chile, one of the most advanced of Latin America's democracies. Numerous foreign entities also continue to act as power groups, not least the US, through policies like drug eradication (a largely failed policy) and aid to several countries, particularly in Central America and in the Caribbean. In addition, loan organizations like the International Monetary Fund (IMF) and the World Bank are always in the wings because of recurring Latin American debt problems.

As for individual countries, we use examples from Haiti, Brazil and Mexico. In Haiti, power groups include the *mulatto* business class (also represented to some extent in formal organizations), the black government elite and the military. Another power group – more precisely, groups – is that of drug trafficking as part of the underground economy. It is estimated that about one third of all illicit drugs shipped from Latin America to the US and Europe pass through Haiti. In Brazil, a foundation of the military's long-term influence is the Superior War College (ESG), established in 1949, that has not only trained many future politicians but has always had a major role in policy-making. Its significant number of military and civilian alumni forms a loose power group in itself (Wiarda 2014: 116).

Mexico provides a good example of an individual who is, by himself, a powerful force in policy-making. Carlos Helú Slim is now one of the world's richest people. As part of the group close to President Carlos Salinas (1988–94), Slim benefited tremendously from the privatisation of telecommunications in the early 1990s. His Grupo Carso purchased a controlling interest in TELMEX, Mexico's major telecommunications company that operates throughout Latin America (Gentleman 2014: 317). Slim has enormous power and has been able to stop further decentralization and competition that would be disadvantageous to his business interests, though. At the time of writing of this chapter, there was some indication that President Enrique Peña Nieto (2012–) might pursue further privatization that might affect Slim's empire.

LABOUR INTERESTS AND GOVERNMENT RELATIONS

Over the years, the entrenched power of political, economic and military elites, and the periods of authoritarianism in Latin America, have profoundly impacted the nature of labour's relations with government. Indeed, these circumstances have affected the extent to which labour has existed as a formal organizational and political entity and the way that it engages in political relations with government. Four factors are fundamental to understanding the development of and current government relations with labour.

First, while labour unions are almost completely accepted as part of a pluralist society in all advanced democracies, like the US, the Scandinavian countries and Australia, there is still a small minority of the Latin American elite who do not see them as legitimate. So while all Latin American countries have labour unions of various types and have had for over 100 years. In most cases, unions often face barriers to organizing and operating, particularly in the political sphere.

Second, traditionally, labour unions have been the major opposition to various forms of government in Latin America, particularly authoritarian dictatorships – and so together with the media and certain other interest groups they are often the first to be outlawed or otherwise repressed during authoritarian regimes. This, of course, seriously retards their growth as organizations and their ability to develop sophisticated advocacy techniques in dealing with government.

Third, many authoritarian regimes have co-opted labour to join their corporatist-type political arrangements, blunting labour's political effectiveness and stymieing the development of the labour movement as an independent civil-society entity and its ability to become a sophisticated lobbying force. Two prominent examples of this are the Brazilian labour movement under President Getúlio Vargas from the early 1930s to the early 1950s and labour in Mexico under the party corporatism of the Institutional Revolutionary Party (Partido Revolucionario Institucional (PRI)) from the 1940s to the late 1990s (Rosenberg 2001; Oliveira and Thomas 2014: 220–1).

The fourth factor relates to the power relationship between labour and government. This relationship can be contrasted with that of government and business (particularly big business, including agribusiness and large landowners). Authoritarian governments and democratic governments alike needed and continue to need business's cooperation for economic stability and the well-being of their populations. Democratic systems also need unions, particularly left-wing parties and governments, but not to the same extent they need business. Authoritarian governments, on the other hand, see unions in a very negative light, not only because they often are the core of opposition to their regimes, but also because many of those in power in such regimes see unions as illegitimate and want to crush them organizationally and politically. Or, as mentioned above, the regime co-opts the unions and undermines their potential influence. All this boils down to the fact that authoritarian regimes do not need unions like they need business and thus unions are often powerless in such circumstances.

In combination, these four factors have meant that labour's ability to develop a sophisticated set of tools for government relations, both informal and formal, have been seriously undermined in many Latin American countries. This is particularly evident today when labour's government relations are compared with those of business in the region. Again, however, circumstances vary widely across the region.

Variations across Contemporary Latin America

The extent of the operation of labour in government affairs and the techniques it uses can be represented by the particulars of four categories: the relatively advanced pluralist systems; at the other end of the spectrum, the underdeveloped systems; a category of countries in the process of transitioning to a consolidated form of pluralist democracy; and systems based on what, in effect, is an authoritarian populist ideology.

The relatively pluralist systems, like those in Chile, Costa Rica, Uruguay and, to some extent, Brazil and Colombia, have the most developed labour movements in Latin America. In the case of the first three their common political denominator was relatively early development of a free civil society which included the early organization of various interest groups including labour. In Brazil's case there was a major boost in the organized labour movement during the time of the Presidency of Getúlio Vargas, though these were strictly controlled under his corporatist-type system. Despite over half a century of dealing with guerilla groups, Columbia has had a fairly open system of access to government and this has benefited labour. Costa Rica had a well-established labour movement by the time of the short revolution of 1948. Since then, the country has enjoyed almost seven

decades of democratic rule. And even though Brazil, Chile and Uruguay fell under military dictatorships for varying periods from the mid 1960s to the late 1980s, their labour movements were well-established before the onset of the dictatorships and formed major forces of resistance during these dictatorships. Being long-established, they were able to rebound fairly quickly and effectively on the return to democracy.

Today, unions in Brazil, Chile Costa Rica, Colombia and Uruguay use a broad range of governmental-relations techniques, similar to unions in any advanced pluralist democracy. In Uruguay, for example, interviews with group and think-tank leaders and journalists as well as secondary and popular sources attest to the use of a combining of direct and indirect methods of lobbying (Butler 2009; Linn 2009; McDonald and Weinstein 2014; Munyo and Díaz 2009; Pérez 2009; Piacenza and Benavente 2009). In the case of all five countries this includes some form of association with left-wing parties as a means of access when these parties are in power. Nevertheless, the banning or curtailment of unions during the dictatorships deprived the union movement of a generation of leaders who would be more adept at governmental affairs than they are today.

At the other end of the spectrum are several countries that are both economically and politically underdeveloped, where trade unions have never been major players in policy-making and thus remain unsophisticated in their use of governmental-affairs techniques. These countries include Guatemala and Honduras in Central America, Paraguay in South America and, again, Haiti in the Caribbean. These are generally countries that have had a long history of elitist rule, long periods of dictatorships and exclusion of the mass of society from politics, including the suppression of trade unions together with other forces with the potential to oppose the regimes. In Haiti, urban unions have never recovered from the suppression of the dictatorship of Papa Doc Devalier and his son Baby Doc Devalier, from the late 1950s to the mid 1980s. Even today, an insignificant industrial and service industry base, widespread poverty and low levels of education make it difficult for trade unions to build a political power base in Haiti. In Paraguay, Alfredo Stroessner, the country's dictator from 1954–89, discouraged industrialization because of the likelihood of it encouraging the rise of trade unions that might pose a threat to his rule.

These countries exhibit what has been termed a bifurcated interest-group system: one with a small elite of power groups and some formal organizations, but with the rest of society either excluded from relations with government or forced to use outsider tactics, such as demonstrations, protests and sit-ins, to gain the attention of policy-makers (Klimovich and Thomas 2014: 184–6). In these countries, many of the elite still see unions as illegitimate. So while rural and some urban unions exist, in contrast to those in countries like Costa Rica and Uruguay they are far less advanced in their governmental-affairs techniques.

A third category includes those political systems transitioning to some form of pluralist democracy, where trade unions are slowly re-establishing themselves or organizing for the first time and are using more and more direct governmental-affairs techniques. This category includes Mexico, Peru, Columbia, Panama and the Dominican Republic. However, all are suffering from the consequences of prohibition on their freedom to pursue normal lobbying during their dictatorships.

The fourth category is that of authoritarian or semi-authoritarian political systems. These include Venezuela, Bolivia and, to a certain extent, Ecuador. All are left-wing regimes that have a strong populist leader who has imposed populist-type rule with the ideological goal of moving to some form of socialism or egalitarianism. These systems exhibit a very limited pluralist environment for the conduct of governmental affairs by any group, including unions, that is not supportive of the state.

In the case of Venezuela, the late Hugo Chávez, who came to power in 1998, moved to replace the interest-group system that had existed under the previous, largely democratic system with a new system based upon his idea of a Bolivarian state (essentially one where he was the supreme power). During the short-lived coup attempt against Chávez in April 2002, the two-month general strike was led by the leading traditional labour peak association, the Confederation of Venezuelan Workers or CTV, and business's leading association, FEDECAMARAS (Ellner 2008: 143). So in April 2003, Chávez's government allies promoted the formation of a new labour federation, the National Workers Union or UNT (Ellner 2008: 155).

Bolivia under Evo Morales is less exclusionary, but, like President Raphael Correa's Ecuador, gives preferential treatment in the form of political access to unions that support their governments. So even though some of the older unions may have political know-how and experience with sophisticated techniques of governmental affairs, this may be of little use to the political environment in which they operate.

Clearly, then, looking across the region, we find a wide range of political environments in which unions operate that are fundamental to the type and level of their sophistication (or lack thereof) in working with government. So here is another living museum of government affairs, ranging from Uruguay through Haiti and various other countries to the exclusionary regime of Venezuela.[3]

THREE INTERNATIONAL NGOs AND GOVERNMENT AFFAIRS: MODERN ADVOCACY, AUTHORITARIAN ACTION AND SURROGATE GOVERNMENTS

There are several good reasons to include case studies of the activities of international nongovernmental organizations (NGOs) in considering governmental affairs in Latin America. Three are particularly significant.

First, over the years, foreign influence has shaped the political environment in the region in a major way. Much of this stems from Latin America's long period of colonial status as well as relative underdevelopment, placing many of its countries in the developing world until recently, with the developed world providing aid and other assistance. The major influence has been and remains foreign businesses and business organizations but also some governments, particularly the US. However, in contemporary Latin America NGOs have an increasing influence both as advocacy organizations and as service providers. Consequently, NGOs have become an integral part of the public-policy process in all the region's countries. Second, and a corollary of the first point, the various types of relations NGOs have with Latin American governments – how they lobby governments, work with them or avoid them to achieve their goals – offers an insight into one aspect of the development of government relations and the broader category of public affairs in the region. And third, the various levels of political development in the region and the types of political regimes and how they view the political role and the approach to governmental affairs by NGOs, offer another illustration of the living museum of various forms of government affairs existing today between interests and governments.

The UN defines an NGO as 'any nonprofit, voluntary citizens' group which is organized on a local, national or international level' (United Nations 2015). And international NGOs, according to Princen and Finger (1994: 1), are organizations that work across state lines (that is, national borders) to 'link biophysical conditions to the political realm'. While international NGOs have existed for well over 100 years, they rose to prominence during the 1980s and 1990s. In fact, from the beginning of the twentieth century until 1988, the number of international NGOs grew from 37 to 309, while tracked domestic

NGOs grew from 176 to 4,518 (Princen and Finger 1994: 1). It is not possible to determine precise numbers of international NGOs today, however, because there is no centralized organization that keeps global statistics.

Domestic and international NGOs vary greatly by size, sophistication, revenue, and how long they have been in operation. There are well-established organizations, such as Amnesty International, Doctors Without Borders (MSF), Greenpeace, and the World Wildlife Fund (WWF), which have multi-million-dollar budgets and constituencies all over the world, as well as small, privately funded operations with limited resources.

A broad distinction can be made between a service and an advocacy NGO. While the lines between these categories are often blurred in many situations, advocacy organizations elevate and promote issues to place them on the government's agenda. Service organizations provide direct services to civil society and the government, often under a contractual agreement, as consultants or as volunteers. NGOs, however, are not looking to replace or become a government themselves. This means that NGOs are essentially a third sector (in addition to the public and private sectors): that is, entities inhabiting the space between government and civil society.

Whether they are primarily advocacy- or service-oriented, or a combination of the two, there are broadly two views of the role and value of international NGOs. On the one hand, they are seen as improving the lives of individuals and communities by providing information or direct services with a goal to building a sustainable pluralist society. In this regard, international NGOs are seen as providing 'a public good' that is not available from state institutions. On the other hand, critics of foreign-funded NGOs question whether their agendas are determined by their powerful donors rather than their constituencies on the ground, and whether the organizations respect local self-determination and the autonomous development of civil societies. NGOs based in a Western, developed country and doing work in the developing world are often criticized for being extensions of former colonial powers. None of these arguments are new. In fact, they are as old as the NGO sector itself.

The three short case studies presented here illustrate both the two types of international NGO – advocacy and service – and the pro and con view of their role and motives. Consideration of their primary function and how they are viewed provides a perspective on the range of political environments across Latin America in which governmental affairs take place, not only for NGOs but other interest groups and advocacy organizations.

Brazil and the World Wildlife Fund

The major expansion internationally of the World Wildlife Fund (WWF) occurred during the general proliferation of international NGOs during the last decades of the twentieth century. The organization was conceived in New York and formally founded in Switzerland in 1961. During fiscal year 2010, the revenues of the WWF-International were reportedly 525 million euros, with more than half of all contributions coming from individuals. The organization employed more than 5,000 staff and boasted five million supporters worldwide (WWF 2010). Today, the WWF has offices in over 100 countries, including Argentina, Brazil, Chile, Colombia, Costa Rica, Ecuador, Paraguay, Peru and Venezuela (WWF 2015a). The office in Brasília was opened in 1996; in addition, there are four regional offices. WWF-Brazil's mission is to 'contribute to a Brazilian society that conserves its natural environment, harmonizing human activity with the preservation of biodiversity and the sustainable use of natural resources, to the benefit of the citizens of today and of future generations' (WWF 2015b).

Since its establishment in Brazil, WWF has lobbied the federal and state governments on numerous occasions, both through direct lobbying and indirectly, by working to use public opinion, the media and other influences to bring pressure to bear on policy-makers. One such occasion was in 2011, when the Brazilian Congress was considering, and subsequently adopted, a new Forest Code that WWF viewed as putting the rainforest at risk by softening environmental regulations to allow more land to be cleared for farming (Bevins 2012).

The law was hotly debated in both chambers of Congress and heavily reported in the Western media. Once the bill passed in both chambers, President Dilma Rousseff came under pressure from both sides: the powerful agribusiness community and environmental organizations. The agribusiness lobby has worked to weaken the law since the 1990s to allow for more land to be used for cattle and crops. President Rousseff vetoed 12 out of 32 changes to the Forest Code. The new Code provided some protections but significantly relaxed regulations for farming around river banks, potentially increasing the possibility of river pollution.

The WWF employed a wide range of direct and indirect tactics during and after the policy-making process that were very similar to government-relations tactics used in the most advanced democracies. These ranged from activist informal advocacy with public officials to formal lobbying of the federal government. The organization appealed to global civil society by partnering with several high-profile international environmental organizations, such as Avaaz and Greenpeace, to deliver a digital petition to President Rousseff. This was signed by more than two million people worldwide demanding that she veto the newly proposed Forest Code (Avaaz.com 2011).[4]

In terms of media engagement, the WWF's staff was quoted repeatedly in the Western media (including *The Economist*, *The Telegraph* and the BBC) taking a stand against the legislation. For instance, the head of the Brazilian WWF office stated:

The project approved in Congress is the fruit of a torturous legislative process, made to serve the interests of a small part of society that wants to increase the possibility of deforestation and give amnesty to those who have already cut it down illegally. (Bevins 2012)

The organization issued a fact-sheet and developed a webpage that detailed the changes in the Forest Code and how these changes may affect forest management (WWF 2012). The WWF drew on its stature worldwide as well as other sophisticated government-relations techniques to put pressure on the Brazilian president to veto the bill and to publicly 'shame' the administration for relaxing the environmental regulations leading up to the United Nations Conference on Sustainable Development that Brazil volunteered to host in 2012.

In the end, WWF got something but not its ideal policy. The story is not over, however. Brazil's public defender, an office charged with protecting the rights of citizens under the national constitution, sued the government over a number of provisions in the Forest Code. The results of this legal challenge are not clear yet (Haley 2014), but this is just one government-relations effort that WWF has conducted in Brazil over the years. The organization consistently lobbied the Brazilian government to protect the Amazon forest. Past initiatives include lobbying the federal government to sustain the 80-percent legal Forest Reserve and both federal and local governments to adopt appropriate legislation and zoning practices to promote sustainable forest management (AIDEnvironment 2007).

Over the years of working in Brazil, WWF has adapted to the shifting political climate and changed its political goals and government-relations strategies. Whereas before 2007, it was focused on establishing protected land areas and curbing illegal logging, nowadays the organization strives to increase the costs of deforestation and make it more profitable to implement sustainable practices (AIDEnvironment 2007). The latter strategy is focused on incentives and involves a more collaborative relationship with the federal and state governments. This strategy also fits well within the service-organization definition, since the WWF acts as an advisor and capacity builder.

Bolivia and the Expulsion of IBIS

The climate of governmental affairs in which WWF operates in Brazil is similar to those in most advanced pluralist democracies. In particular, WWF is able to strongly oppose federal and state governments without reprisal. This is not the case for many interest groups, including some NGOs in Bolivia with its semi-authoritarian system run by Evo Morales (the first indigenous president) and, in effect, by one political party, the Movement Towards Socialism, commonly known as MAS.

The example we use is IBIS, a Danish NGO operating globally.[5] It is primarily a service NGO, largely supported by the Danish International Development Agency. IBIS sees its goals as working for 'a just world in which all people have equal access to education, influence and resources' (IBIS 2013). It works in Latin America (Bolivia, Guatemala and Nicaragua) and Africa (Ghana, Liberia, Mozambique, Sierra Leone and South Sudan) (IBIS 2015). In fiscal year 2013, the organization had total revenue of over 40 million US dollars (IBIS 2014a). IBIS has worked in Bolivia for 30 years fostering education and the democratic influence of indigenous communities (IBIS 2014b).

In 2013, the Bolivian government accused IBIS of 'meddling in local political affairs' (*Global Post* 2013). The expulsion, according to the government spokesperson, was motivated by the fact that 'they are doing political work against the government'. He added: 'We are tired of tolerating IBIS's promotion of internal conflict among the indigenous organizations themselves' (*MSN News* 2013). The reaction in Denmark was muted and diplomatic. IBIS, in a press release posted on its website, did not denounce or accuse the Bolivian government but simply stated that the organization had not received any complaints from the Ministry of Foreign Affairs and had followed the rules applicable to foreign NGOs on Bolivian soil (IBIS 2013).

Fernando Vargas, one of Bolivia's prominent indigenous leaders, said: 'The NGOs took Evo Morales into power … now he's throwing them out … because he does not want anyone to aid us technically, to orient us, so that [now] we thus have to subordinate ourselves to the Government' (NACLA 2013). IBIS worked with indigenous groups directly by providing them with information, training and resources in order to empower individuals to become advocates for themselves.

Why is IBIS's expulsion significant in terms of throwing light on government affairs in Bolivia in particular and Latin America in general? First, since IBIS facilitated the development of an independent civil society and encourages political participation, the Bolivian government infringed the rights of the indigenous communities served by IBIS. Second, 'meddling in local political affairs' is a dangerous, slippery-slope argument that could be applied to any organization that is viewed as opposing government – in IBIS's case, working with groups that were not supportive of the government (though IBIS was also working with groups that were supportive of the Morales regime). Furthermore, as a service NGO, there is no evidence of IBIS engaging directly with the government, in contrast to WWF's work in Brazil. The comparison of the Brazilian and Bolivian examples shows the clear existence of a living museum in regard to government affairs across Latin America.

The American Red Cross and Relief Efforts in Haiti

As the poorest country in the Americas and one of the poorest in the world, and with extensive corruption and a government long teetering on the edge of being a failed state, Haiti offers a very different perspective on governmental affairs from those in most Latin American countries and those in advanced democracies. As noted earlier, government affairs are most often conducted through power groups, with some protests and demonstrations by dispossessed groups that sometimes have impact. The extreme poverty and service needs of the Haitian population has meant that international NGOs have been a fixture in the country for decades. NGOs often fill the service void that the Haitian government cannot fill due to minimal governmental capacity or will not fill out of choice. Consequently, NGOs often play a unique role in government relations in the country, as both service provider and political advocate. Often, their engagement in political advocacy is out of necessity and not choice; although the widespread corruption and weakness of the Haitian state means that many NGOs circumvent dealing with the state and, in effect, become surrogate or quasi-governments. The case of the American Red Cross provides a good example of an NGO's relationship with the Haitian government where the service and political functions of an NGO merge, and the organization becomes a sort of parallel government.

Before the devastating earthquake of January 2010, aid flows to Haiti were administered through more than 300 foreign nonprofits (Schuller 2007: 104). After the 2010 earthquake, Haiti saw an influx of foreign organizations – governance interests as well as international charities. In 2010, the international community pledged 2.5 million US dollars for the reconstruction of the country. However, the real costs are expected to be at least five times higher (Bilham 2010). The American Red Cross raised nearly half a billion dollars to support its efforts in Haiti after the earthquake, which is more than any other single organization (Elliott 2015).

The relationship between the Red Cross and Rene Preval, Haitian President at the time of the earthquake, got off to a rocky start shortly after the disaster. President Preval, while recognizing the limits of the Haitian government to deal with the disaster, called for relief focused on boosting the agricultural sector rather than direct food aid that would only breed dependency on the donors (LaFranchi 2010). But Red Cross officials declared that the organization would have the power to overrule the Haitian government and provide relief to communities in need (Sheldon 2010).

It is difficult, if not impossible, to imagine an international NGO overruling the government in Germany or France, for instance. This indirect confrontation exhibits lack of formal engagement channels with the Haitian government and a certain level of defiance and distrust on the part of the Red Cross. In a later interview for the US public-radio network, NPR (National Public Radio), President Preval noted that the state does not have sufficient means to undertake the reconstruction efforts, while the NGOs receive significant resources. He went on to say that there was a lack of coordination and NGOs preferred to work on their own without the state (PBS *Newshour* 2010). The Red Cross mentioned in its brochures that the reconstruction efforts involved collaboration with local authorities (American Red Cross 2015). However, it is difficult to envision a productive collaboration with local authorities without a centralized strategy of working with the Haitian government at the highest level.

The Red Cross promised its donors that it would defy the Haitian government to provide 'permanent homes to tens of thousands of people and build brand-new communities. After five years, however, the organization has built just six homes' (Sullivan 2015a). The organization ended up not being able to account for 500 million US dollars, which prompted an investigation by the US Senate (Sullivan 2015b). The Red Cross claimed that local circumstances had prevented it from reaching its goal but also asserted that, since the earthquake, it had 'helped more than 4.5 million Haitians to get back on their feet' (American Red Cross 2015).

Regardless of the claims and counter claims, the presence of international NGOs, like the Red Cross in Haiti, has both broad and narrow implications for the development of governmental affairs in weak states.

Foreign-funded non-profits in Haiti have little need to lobby the state because in many areas non-profits perform the roles that a state is presumed to undertake. As a result, foreign-funded non-profits arguably undermine the government's capacity by dominating various human-services areas and hiring the majority of skilled locals. Moreover, NGOs undermine the state because they are large recipients of foreign funding at the expense of the state, which was reliant on that funding (Schuller 2007). In short, NGOs as surrogate governments inhibit the development of state apparatus that would lay the groundwork for the emergence of an interest-group and government-affairs system necessary for a country to develop a viable pluralist democracy.

CONCLUSION: A PERSISTING LIVING MUSEUM OF GOVERNMENT AFFAIRS ACTIVITY

These case studies illustrate several points about the status of government affairs in Latin America. The most obvious point but, nevertheless, a seminal one is how the level of political development shapes the form and type of government relations. For much of its history government relations was of the informal power-group type. Because of varying levels of political development in contemporary Latin America, the range of government affairs runs the gamut from a level comparable with many long-established democracies, such as in Costa Rica and Uruguay, to underdeveloped systems resulting in large part from histories of authoritarianism, extensive poverty and low levels of political efficacy, such as in Haiti and Paraguay.

So, in sharp contrast to a region like Western Europe, where there are more or less highly developed and sophisticated levels of government relations, Latin America is a living museum of lobbying techniques and attitudes toward civil-society groups dealing with government. Moreover, the wide range of levels of economic and political development means that types of government relation not evident in advanced democracies can be found in Latin America. These include the role of NGOs and the various ways that they relate to government and even the acceptance of certain groups lobbying government, such as certain power groups, that would likely be less acceptable in many advanced democracies.

Clearly, the activity of government relations is a developing area in Latin America. This offers the researcher a museum of a variety of types of relations and the opportunity to study different paths to the development of government relations and the varying attitudes to them.

Notes

1   It was Charles Anderson (1967: 104–5) who observed the fact that across Latin American countries several levels of political and economic development could be observed at any one time. Thus, the region represented 'a living museum' as all the countries continued to develop.
2   For more background on the Latin American political experience and the development of its interest group and government affairs system, see Chapter 22 in this volume, 'Public Affairs in Latin America: The Gradual and Uneven Formalization of a Long-Time Informal Activity'.
3   For the contrasting role of labour organizations and their government relations in a developed versus an underdeveloped interest-groups system, see Alexander (2005).
4   Avaaz is a global civic organization founded in 2007 that promotes activism on issues such as climate change, human rights, animal rights, corruption, poverty, and the reconciliation of conflicts.
5   Information on the IBIS case study draws in part on Biggemann et al. (2014: 275).

REFERENCES

AIDEnvironment. 2007. 'Towards effective conservation strategies: the application of strategic principles to increase the impact and sustainability of WWF conservation efforts,' http://www.panda.org/standards/2_1_wwf_nl_strategic_principles [viewed August 8, 2015].
Alexander, R.J. 2005. *A History of Organized Labor in Uruguay and Paraguay*. Westport, CT: Praeger Publishers.
American Red Cross. 2015. 'Haiti assistance program fact sheet,' http://www.redcross.org/images/MEDIA_CustomProductCatalog/m42240141_Haiti_Assistance_Program_Overview_Factsheet.pdf [viewed August 4, 2015].
Anderson, Charles. 1967. *Politics and Economic Change in Latin America*. New York: Van Norstrand.
Avaaz.com. 2011. 'World to Dilma: save the Amazon,' June 16, http://www.avaaz.org/en/save_the_amazon/ [viewed August 8, 2015].
Bevins, V. 2012. 'Amazon in dire threat as Brazil finalizes forest bill shaped by lobbyists for agricultural industry,' DSR News Service, May 30.
Biggemann, S., K. Klimovich and C.S. Thomas. 2014. 'Interest group dynamics in a weak and transitional state: the case of Bolivia,' *Journal of Public Affairs*, Special Double Issue, 'Interest Groups and Lobbying in Latin America – A New Era or More of the Same,' 14: 3–4, September–November, 254–82.
Bilham, R. 2010. 'Lessons from the Haiti earthquake,' *Nature* 463, 878–9.
Butler, Alejandro. 2009. Director, Improfit Casa de Comunicación [political consulting firm], interview by Clive Thomas, June 11.
Elgar, Richard 2014. 'Women's rights in transition: the collision of women's interest groups, religion and NGOs in Latin America,' *Journal of Public Affairs*, Special Double Issue, 'Interest Groups and Lobbying in Latin America – A New Era or More of the Same,' 14: 3–4, September–November 2014, 359–68.
Elliott, J. 2015. 'Confidential documents: Red Cross itself may not know how millions donated for Haiti were spent,' ProPublica,

21 July, https://www.propublica.org/article/confidential-documents-red-cross-millions-donated-haiti [viewed August 8, 2015].

Ellner, Steve. 2008. *Rethinking Venezuelan Politics: Class, Conflict, and the Chávez Phenomenon*. Boulder, CO: Lynne Rienner.

Gentleman, Judith A. 2014. 'Mexico: Democratization, Development and Internal War.' In *Latin America Politics and Development*, eighth edition, edited by Howard J. Wiarda and Harvey F. Kline. Boulder, CO: Westview Press, pp. 307–33.

Global Post. 2013. 'Bolivia expels Danish NGO for meddling,' http://www.globalpost.com/dispatch/news/afp/131220/bolivia-expels-danish-ngo-meddling-1 [viewed May 24, 2014].

Gozetto, A.C.O., and C.S. Thomas. 2014. 'Interest groups in Brazil: a new era and its challenges,' *Journal of Public Affairs*, Special Double Issue, 'Interest Groups and Lobbying in Latin America – A New Era or More of the Same,' 14: 3–4, September–November, 212–39, 220–1.

Haley, I. 2014. 'Decoding the Amazon: Brazil's controversial new Forest Code,' *Joule: Duquesne Energy & Environmental Journal*, March 7, 2014, http://www.duqlawblogs.org/joule/decoding-the-amazon-brazils-controversial-new-forest-code/ [viewed August 2015].

IBIS. 2013. 'IBIS asked to leave Bolivia,' http://ibis-global.org/press-release/ibis-asked-leave-bolivia/ [viewed May 24, 2014].

IBIS. 2014a. 'Annual report 2013–2014,' http://ibis-global.org/about-ibis/annual-report/ [viewed August 8, 2015].

IBIS. 2014b. 'IBIS Global,' http://ibis-global.org/aboutibisglobal/ [viewed May 24, 2014].

IBIS. 2015. 'Where we work,' http://ibis-global.org/countriesweworkinglobal/ [viewed August 8, 2015].

Klimovich, K. and C.S. Thomas. 2014. 'Power groups, interests and interest groups in consolidated and transitional democracies: comparing Uruguay and Costa Rica with Paraguay and Haiti,' *Journal of Public Affairs*, Special Double Issue, 'Interest Groups and Lobbying in Latin America – A New Era or More of the Same,' 14: 3–4, September–November 2014, 183–211.

LaFranchi, H. 2010. 'Aid after Haiti earthquake: President René Préval sees need for shift,' *Christian Science Monitor*, March 10, 2010, http://www.csmonitor.com/USA/Foreign-Policy/2010/0310/Aid-after-Haiti-earthquake-President-Rene-Preval-sees-need-for-shift [viewed August 4, 2015].

Linn, Tomás. 2009. Freelance political journalist, interview by Clive Thomas, June 4.

López Maya, Margarita and Luis E. Lander. 2011. 'Participatory Democracy in Venezuela: Origins, Ideas, and Implementation.' In *Venezuela's Bolivarian Democracy: Participation, Politics, and Culture under Chávez*, edited by D. Smilde and D. Hellinger. Durham, NC and London: Duke University Press, pp. 58–79.

McDonald, R. and M. Weinstein. 2014. 'Uruguay: Balancing Growth and Democracy.' In *Latin American Politics and Development*, eighth edition, edited by Howard J. Wiarda and Harvey F. Kline. Boulder, CO: Westview Press, pp. 237–54.

Morales, W.Q. 2012. Bolivia. In Vanden, HE and Prevost G, *Politics of Latin America: The Power Game*. Oxford University Press: New York, NY. 4th ed., pp. 557–88.

Munyo, Ignacion [senior economist] and Carlos Díaz [researcher/economist]. 2009. Center for the Study of Economic and Social Reality – CERES [think tank dealing with macroeconomic information], interview by Clive Thomas, June 11.

MSN News. 2013. 'Bolivia expels Danish NGO for "meddling",' http://news.msn.co.nz/worldnews/8774709/bolivia-expels-danish-ngo-for-meddling [viewed March 12, 2014].

NACLA [North American Congress on Latin America]. 2013. 'Close the NGOs: asserting sovereignty or eroding democracy?' https://nacla.org/blog/2013/12/31/close-ngos-asserting-sovereignty-or-eroding-democracy [viewed May 24, 2014].

Parenti, Christian. 2006. 'Venezuela's revolution and the oil company inside,' *NACLA* (North American Congress on Latin America), 39: 8–13.

PBS Newshour. 2010. 'Preval assesses Haiti's quake recovery,' July 13, 2010, http://www.pbs.org/newshour/bb/latin_america-july-dec10-haiti_07–13/ [viewed August 3, 2015].

Pérez, Gustavo. 2009. President of the Central Council, Uruguayan Bank Employees Association (AEBU), interview by Clive Thomas, June 11.

Piacenza, Claudio [assistant manager] and María Dolores Benavente [international affairs manager]. 2009. Uruguayan National Chamber of Commerce and Services, interview by Clive Thomas, June 11.

Princen, T. and M. Finger. 1994. *Environmental NGOs in World Politics: Linking the Local and the Global.* London and New York: Routledge.

Rodríguez, F.H. and C.S. Thomas. 2014. 'The Chilean big business lobby: a long-standing and major influence on public policy,' *Journal of Public Affairs*, Special Double Issue, 'Interest Groups and Lobbying in Latin America – A New Era or More of the Same,' 14: 3–4, September–November 2014, 310–30.

Rosenberg, Jonathan. 2001. 'Mexico: The End of Party Corporatism?' In *Political Parties and Interest Groups: Shaping Democratic Governance*, edited by C. S. Thomas. Boulder, CO: Lynne Rienner, pp. 247–65.

Schneider, B.R. 2004. *Business Politics and the State in Twentieth Century Latin America.* Cambridge: Cambridge University Press.

Schuller, M. 2007. 'Invasion or infusion? Understanding the role of NGOs in Contemporary Haiti,' *Journal of Haitian Studies*, 13: 2, Fall, 96–109.

Sheldon, D. 2010. 'Price says Red Cross will defy Haitian president if necessary,' *Daily Observer* [Antigua, West Indies], March 11, 2010, http://antiguaobserver.com/price-says-red-cross-will-defy-haitian-president-if-necessary/ [viewed August 8, 2015].

Sullivan, L. 2015a. 'Senator Grassley gives Red Cross deadline to explain Haiti spending,' NPR, July 9, http://www.npr.org/sections/thetwoway/2015/07/09/421501644/sen-grassley-gives-red-cross-deadline-to-explain-haiti-spending [viewed August 5, 2015].

Sullivan, L. 2015b. 'In search of the Red Cross' $500 million in Haiti,' NPR, June 3, http://www.npr.org/2015/06/03/411524156/in-search-of-the-red-cross-500-million-in-haiti-relief [viewed August 1, 2015].

Tinker Salas, Miguel. 2009. *The Enduring Legacy: Oil, Culture, and Society in Venezuela.* Durham, NC: Duke University Press.

UN. 2015. 'NGO relations,' http://outreach.un.org/ngorelations/about-us/ [viewed August 5, 2015].

Wiarda, I.S. 2014. 'Brazil: A Unique Country.' In *Latin American Politics and Development*, eighth edition, edited by Howard J. Wiarda and Harvey F. Kline. Boulder, CO: Westview Press, pp. 97–126.

WWF. 2010. 'World Wildlife Fund annual review,' http://assets.panda.org/downloads/int_ar_2010.pdf [viewed August 5, 2015].

WWF. 2012. 'Factsheet: the new Brazilian Forest Code as a harmful subsidy,' http://assets.wwf.org.uk/downloads/forest_code_factsheet.pdf [viewed August 8, 2015].

WWF. 2015a. 'WWF offices and associates around the world,' http://wwf.panda.org/who_we_are/wwf_offices/ [viewed August 1, 2015].

WWF. 2015b. 'WWF's work in Brazil,' http://wwf.panda.org/who_we_are/wwf_offices/brazil/our_work/ [viewed August 8, 2015].

The Kenya Chamber of Mines: A Case Study in Public Sector Advocacy

David Irwin and Kariuki Waweru

INTRODUCTION

It is generally acknowledged that governments create the political and economic environment in which their private sector operates, usually described as the 'enabling environment' or 'investment climate'. In response, business associations seek to influence public policy to make it easier for their members to 'do business'. Whilst many associations have access, this is not the same as influence (Eising 2007), leading Helboe Pedersen to lament the lack of knowledge of 'which groups are influential and to what extent' (2013: 28), while Lowery raises concerns that 'we look for [influence], but rarely find evidence of it' (2013: 1).

There is, therefore, considerable debate about whether, and if so how, business associations gain attention within political circles, whether politicians or public officials are interested in their views and whether they are ultimately successful in influencing policy.

Much of the literature is based on studies of issues, after the event, and the actors who sought to influence those issues. Most of those studies are in the US or EU. And most issues have several, sometimes competing, actors, all vying for attention. Few, if any, studies, follow an issue in real time. This chapter aims to address that gap by following the activities of the Kenya Chamber of Mines (KCM) in its efforts to influence the final shape of a new Mining Act in Kenya in 2014 and early 2015 and to assess the extent of their influence.

In recounting the progress of this legislation through the Kenyan Parliament, we first describe the political context and then introduce KCM and record its efforts to amend the proposed legislation. It reflects on KCM's approach and concludes that whilst KCM did not achieve all its objectives, it did achieve most. Furthermore, it concludes that many of the amendments to the legislation are due solely or largely to the lobbying activities of

KCM. The chapter ends by drawing lessons from KCM's approach that could be helpful to other business associations.

POLITICAL CONTEXT

Politically, Kenya is relatively stable. It achieved independence in 1963, with a bicameral legislature and a federal government. There were two major political parties, which reflected ethnic divides: KANU (the larger party, representing the Kikuyu and Luo) and KADU (Booth et al. 2014). The first president was Jomo Kenyatta. The federal system and the upper chamber were abolished in 1966 and opposition parties were banned in 1969 (Booth et al. 2014). Since independence, there has been considerable involvement of politicians in business and business people in politics. But while a number of individual business people were able to influence politicians, there was little scope for independent business associations directly to influence policy and little public-sector advocacy. Kenyatta was succeeded as president in 1978 by Daniel Arap Moi. Opposition parties were allowed once again in 1991 and the first multi-party election in Kenya held in 1992.

In 2002, Mwai Kibaki of the National Rainbow Coalition (NARC) was elected as the third president of Kenya in an election deemed to be reasonably fair. In 2003, Kibaki invited the private sector to participate in formulating economic policy, based on a recognition that it was the private sector that created jobs, not the government, and established a Presidential Private Sector Working Forum. One of its outputs, the Economic Recovery Strategy for Wealth & Employment Creation (ERS), was published later in 2003. Economic growth followed, and Vision 2030, Kenya's development plan for 2008–30, emerged from ERS. The private sector thus claimed to have conceived Vision 2030, and Fourie (2014) reports that this has

been confirmed by public officials. During this period, there was *de facto* encouragement for ministers and ministries to consult with the private sector. But the position was undoubtedly complicated by the relationships between politicians and business elites.

Booth et al. assert that Kibaki's 'failure to develop an inclusive political agenda [...] widened divisions and laid the foundations for the violent conflict' (2014: 18) that followed the disputed election contest of 2007. Following a conflict in which more than 1,500 people died, in 2008, a government of national unity was formed with Kibaki (leader of the Party of National Unity) as president and, a prime minister, Raila Odinga (leader of the Orange Democratic Movement) – and a commitment to introduce a new constitution. There is some evidence that business associations were becoming more active and indeed were achieving some success in influencing public policy during this period (Irwin & Githinji, 2015). The Kenya Private Sector Alliance (KEPSA) was able, to some extent, to institutionalise dialogue by working with the government to set up ministerial stakeholder fora. Not surprisingly, business associations found it hard to lobby government whilst it was discussing the new constitution and then during the election campaign.

A new constitution was approved by referendum in 2010. This introduced a system much more closely modelled on the US bicameral system than on the UK system: a National Assembly (NA) and a Senate to represent the counties, collectively known as Parliament. Unlike the US, however, the NA has precedence. Members of the NA are still described by everyone as MPs. The NA has a total of 349 members. After the March 2013 general election, the Jubilee Alliance secured 167 seats, so allied with the Amani Coalition, with 24 seats, to give it a total of 191 seats. The opposition Coalition for Reforms and Democracy (CORD), led by Raila Odinga, has 141 seats. There are 17 other members of the NA, who represent unaffiliated smaller parties or stood as independent candidates.

The Senate has 67 members, comprising one senator for each of the 47 counties, together with 16 women members nominated by their political parties, two representing youth and two representing people with disabilities. The new constitution removed the office of prime minister, saw ministries headed up by people known as cabinet secretaries who no longer sit in Parliament and created 47 autonomous counties, each with a directly elected governor.

The counties became effective, once office holders were elected, following the 2013 election, which saw the election of a new president, Uhuru Kenyatta, leader of the Jubilee Alliance. He immediately reduced the number of ministries in line with the new constitution to 18 and largely appointed technocrats with no political experience as cabinet secretaries. The media gained more freedom during the Kibaki years and was further liberated by the new constitution, although this became more constrained with the passing of the Kenya Information and Communications Amendment Act 2013. Kenyatta has tried to cast the government as being business-friendly and is keen to do more to improve the investment climate (Booth et al. 2014). There is talk of pro-market reform, including privatisation, better regulation and trade liberalisation to improve the business environment and, it is hoped, to boost economic growth and employment. Booth et al. (2014) suggest that the government is relatively independent of business – and the reverse is probably also true. They observed that whilst there was a lack of institutionalised political parties, the NA and Senate exert pressure on other parts of government (2014: 27).

At the time of writing, the country was showing signs of settling down into the new arrangements, and it was becoming easier for business associations at least to lobby, though not necessarily easier to influence policy. Not surprisingly, there is a growing need to lobby Parliament as well as the Executive. The constitution requires that all new legislation is rooted in a formal policy document and

the need to create many new policies gives more opportunities to business associations keen to explain and promote the policy most appropriate to their sector. And the new constitution requires much old legislation to be updated, so there is considerable pressure on legislators and ministries. Existing policies and legislation need to be revised to align them to the new governance system, especially where functions have been partially or fully devolved to counties. Priority is currently split between legislation necessary to implement the devolved system of governance and revising other existing legislation.

The county governments also have policy and legislative power, so business associations need to lobby them as well. Counties are expected to prepare and enact legislation to implement and regulate devolved functions while enforcing county-specific revenue-raising measures.

KENYA CHAMBER OF MINES AND THE MINING BILL 2014

Kenya is not a major mining country, though it is believed to have significant and largely unexplored potential. It currently produces soda ash, fluorspar, titanium, rare earth minerals, cement, gemstones, manganese, iron ore, gypsum, carbon dioxide, diatomite, chromites, silica sand, limestone and gold.

Vision 2030 identifies mining as a priority sector. The 2013 government created a stand-alone Ministry of Mining (MoM) in place of a Department of Mines and Geology in the previous Ministry of Environment and Mineral Resources. By 2014, mining contributed around one per cent of GDP though it was expected to grow around 10 per cent in 2014 compared to GDP as a whole, which was expected to grow around four per cent, making it one of the few sectors delivering the Jubilee Coalition's manifesto commitment of a 10 per cent per annum growth rate (Kenyatta et al. 2013). At present, there are fewer than 20 large-scale mining ventures. However, given investment, the sector could grow quickly, potentially contributing three per cent to GDP within four years and 10 per cent by 2030. MoM says government revenue from mining in 2011/12 was just $260,000, rising to $12.5m in 2013/14 and expected to be more than $15m in 2014/15.

Up till 2000, miners were represented by the Kenya African Mining Association though its membership comprised solely of the small-scale miners; large-scale miners were not represented at all. The government was struggling to talk collectively to the miners and so they encouraged the miners to create the Kenya Chamber of Mines. It now represents the interests of Kenya's miners, exploration companies and mineral traders. Initially they had an office within the Office of the Commissioner of Mines in the Ministry, though they quickly moved out.

KCM sees its purpose to be to 'contribute to the creation, maintenance and improvement of a conducive business environment for the successful development and benefit of its members' businesses and of the mineral industry in Kenya as a whole', so its *raison d'être* is influencing public policy. KCM explains on its website that it specifically seeks to associate its interests with national and local community interests and to work with other stakeholders to ensure that its interests do not harm the environment or communities.

KCM has some 213 members (137 corporate and 76 individual members). The corporate members include 12 exploration companies (of which the best known is probably African Barrick Gold); 31 mining companies (including Base Titanium), comprising 15 small-scale miners, nine medium-scale miners and seven large-scale miners; 30 mineral dealers; 30 supplementary-services companies; three academic institutions; and 31 auxiliary-services companies. Members are a mix of foreign investors and small local businesses. Its total income is about $190,000 of which subscriptions account

for around 25 per cent, with the balance coming from additional member donations and contributions for specific projects, Business Advocacy Fund (BAF)[1] and African Development Bank. It does provide some services to members but sees its primary function as advocacy, either for the sector as a whole or occasionally for individual members who have a problem – for example, with licensing. It does help with networking and with linking miners to specific expertise. To some extent, BAF has assisted KCM to build its sustainability. Indeed, it funded the post of policy & research manager, filled by Stephen Mwakesi,[2] whilst KCM built subscription income. Mwakesi is well educated, a lawyer and an excellent communicator.

KCM aims to work with others. Amongst business membership organisations (BMOs), it works with KEPSA, Kenya Association of Manufacturers, Petroleum Institute of East Africa, Geological Society of Kenya and Kenya National Chamber of Commerce & Industry. It works with civil-society organisations, including Kenya National Resources Alliance, CSO Platform for Oil & Gas, Institute for Human Rights & Business and East Africa Tax Justice Network. It would like to cover oil and gas as well, though at present that is covered by a different association. It has a formal dialogue arrangement with MoM, including a regular 'Ministerial Round Table'. Through KEPSA, it participates in Ministerial Round Tables with other ministries. It has been cultivating civil servants. It regarded the Principal Secretary (known as Permanent Secretary before the new Constitution) as a champion, but he moved to the Ministry of Sports, Culture and Arts in August 2014. However, it also had a good relationship with the Commissioner for Mines, and Stephen Mwakesi had a personal relationship with the Personal Adviser to the Cabinet Secretary.

Until the end of 2013, government policy on mining was largely tacit, with the Mining Act dating from 1940. A process of review was initiated in 1992, with United Nations

Development Programme support, and then started again in 2002, with Commonwealth support. In part, issues were addressed by passing additional legislation. With support from BAF, KCM was able in 2009 to secure amendments to the Mining & Minerals Bill as it related to land and mining titles. MoM agreed that the existing legislation was too limited, failing to address emerging issues such as environmental concerns, the importance of communities and equitable sharing of benefits, devolution of decision making, in line with the new constitution, as well as licensing, accountability, efficiency and predictability. And all parties recognised that there was a need for a complete overhaul of the legislation rather than just further tinkering. After some discussion and a number of internal drafts, the government published a Mining Bill in June 2013. KCM was invited to make presentations, both in writing and orally, which they did. (See Figure 33.1 for timeline.)

KCM felt little progress was being made. It met with the Cabinet Secretary in a Ministerial Round Table in February 2014 but felt that he was not sufficiently receptive to its concerns. As a result, it made a formal request to meet with the President. Before that meeting could take place, the government published the Mining Bill 2014 on 17 March. Despite a representative of MoM apparently saying to KCM that it 'had taken care of your interests: you're going to love the Bill', in fact KCM had serious reservations not least because it seemed that little had changed from the previous version. However, the proposed Act is important, giving effect to several articles in the Constitution relating to minerals, prospecting, mining, processing, refining, etc.

With further support from BAF, KCM was already developing policy positions on a number of issues and, by chance, a policy position workshop had been arranged for 24 March, so the timing was propitious. Stephen Mwakesi spent the weekend reading the draft and considering responses. The workshop, in which staff and board members participated, then provided the opportunity to look in detail and debate the potential implications of the Bill. The participants decided to draft an overall critique of the Bill – including detailed recommendations to amend a substantial number of clauses – and to draft four papers, each setting out a policy position to address a specific issue in detail: the need for landowner consent for prospecting, exploration and mining; governance and regulation of the sector by the government; licensing and royalties; and 'state participation' – that is, the state's expectation that it should effectively receive a dividend and even free shares in mining companies in addition to royalties and the usual taxes.

Each of the policy position papers was intended to focus on a single issue that was regarded as being of critical importance, on the basis that each could be argued separately, that different allies might be identified for each issue and, importantly, that combining them might lead to all proposals failing simply because of strong opposition to one. Given an expectation that the Bill could be submitted to Parliament at any time, KCM initially focused all its efforts on the critique – with drafts going backwards and forwards between staff, board, ordinary members and a mentor provided by BAF. In addition, the mentor supported the policy officer to think through and develop a clear advocacy strategy.

The Bill had its first reading in the NA on 22 April and was immediately referred to the Parliamentary Committee on Environment & Natural Resources (ENR). Then, on 29 April, KCM met with the President. He listened carefully to KCM's concerns and instructed that MoM should work with KCM to undertake a joint review and to look for compromises and agreement. Much happened quickly thereafter.

Early in May, KCM organised a three-day 'retreat' with ENR in Mombasa, aimed at setting out and discussing the areas where they felt the Bill needed to be amended. The retreat was well attended, with 52 participants, including 21 members of the

Committee. The Chairman said that 'she was elated' to be able to participate in the retreat and thanked KCM 'for working closely with the committee'(Nyando 2014: 7). However, she reminded participants that 'their principal duty [is] to provide a good law for both Kenya and the investors' (Nyando 2014: 8). She particularly asked KCM to support the legislators with technical information so that they could make informed decisions. The outcome of the meeting was agreement on clauses that needed to be well considered, including, *inter alia*, reducing the powers of the cabinet secretary, removal of hindrances related to the conduct of small-scale mining and setting thresholds for mineral agreements.

Then, on 8 May, KCM met with the Principal Secretary, the Commissioner for Mines and a consultant from Adam Smith International commissioned by MoM to review the Bill and make suggestions for amendment. On 12 May, KCM met with the Cabinet Secretary to review the proposals for amendment, and then the 'technical committee' of MoM and KCM prepared a zero draft of a proposal to go to ENR. On 20 May, KCM met once again with the Cabinet Secretary to agree their final submission. They had agreed that the submission would cover all the areas on which they could agree and that each would separately submit additional proposals on the more contentious issues. The Bill, as originally drafted, had 198 clauses and three schedules. KCM and MoM agreed and proposed 193 amendments to 95 clauses plus one substantial addition (on artisanal mining) and five amendments to all three schedules. There were four proposals made by MoM with which KCM did not agree and four proposals made by KCM that did not secure MoM agreement but were included in the joint submission. Some proposals were very technical or about tightening up loose wording (e.g., '60 days' instead of 'two months'), but some were very detailed (e.g., the new section on artisanal mining). Mwakesi estimates that they secured agreement on perhaps 80 per cent of the issues.

The KCM/MoM (2014) joint submission was sent to ENR on 29 May. KCM followed this with a submission regarding its other issues on 6 June. It continued to work on detailed policy positions, which had grown to seven, and completed these by 26 June:

1 County taxes: there was a concern that counties might seek to impose additional taxes on mining; KCM wanted agreement that nationally imposed royalties would be shared with the counties instead.
2 Free carried interest: the government was seeking a free 'carried interest' of 10 per cent of the share capital of mining companies; effectively they were asking to be given, free, 10 per cent of the shares, but KCM argued that many prospects never deliver and that this would make it harder to raise capital, instead proposing a series of amendments which would allow them to share higher dividends in the event that a mine starts to produce.
3 Local equity participation: the draft legislation called for more local participation and required mining companies to 'offload' 20 per cent of their shares through a local stock exchange within four years of receiving a licence (without defining 'offload' or 'local)'; this could make it harder to raise capital, and mines often take longer than four years to start generating revenue, let alone a profit, and Kenya's own listing rules require firms to be profitable before they list. KCM argued for a watering down of the requirement and that it not be imposed until four years after production starts.
4 Mineral agreements and stability agreements: the mineral agreement is effectively a contract between the mining company and the state; KCM was concerned that the provisions all seemed one way and put too much power in the hands of the cabinet secretary. They proposed that mineral agreements should only apply where there is an investment of more than $250m and that this should be balanced by a stability agreement.
5 Mineral Rights Board: the draft legislation gave the cabinet secretary the power to grant, deny or revoke mineral rights: KCM argued that there should a degree of independence and proposed the establishment of a Mineral Rights Board instead.

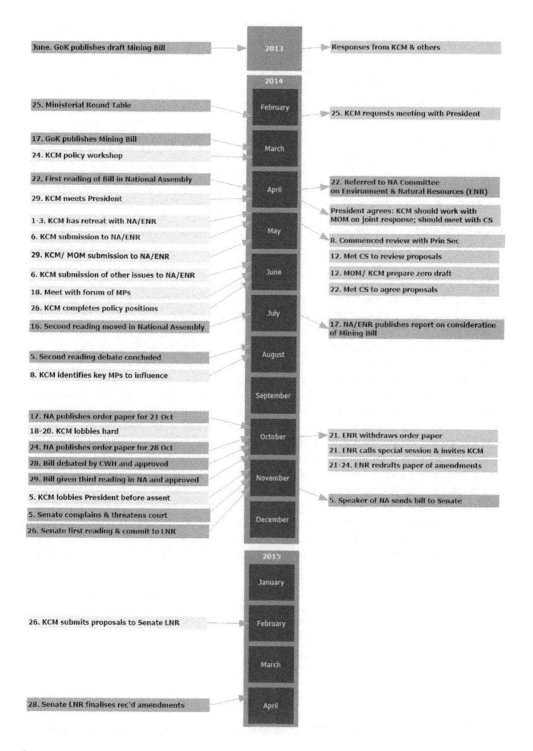

Figure 33.1: Timeline

6 Repeal, savings and transitional provisions: there were already a number of agreements with mining companies; KCM was concerned that these would all be torn up rather than honoured in the transition to the new legislation. They argued that existing arrangements should continue in force until they expire and then be replaced with agreements under the new legislation.

7 Royalties: the draft legislation allowed the cabinet secretary to set royalties, more or less, on a whim; KCM was concerned about the lack of predictability that this would introduce and argued that maximum rates should be enshrined in the legislation and that actual agreed rates should be included in mineral agreements and thus given contractual force.

On 18 June, at Serena Hotel, KCM met with a forum of MPs, which helped them to identify people who they regarded as critical to influence and, in particular, helped them to conclude that the really critical partner was the Parliamentary Committee.

The second reading of the Bill was moved in the NA on 16 July. On 17 July, ENR published its report on its consideration of the Bill. ENR noted in its report that it met with KCM and recorded that 'the Committee listened to the concerns and fears of the investors in the sector', and it further explained that it 'took into consideration these concerns of the investors in a three-day policy retreat'. ENR invited public participation to support its consideration of the Bill and received written and verbal submission. ENR listed the main stakeholders who submitted comments as Commission on Revenue Allocation, Base Titanium Limited (a KCM member), Kenyan African Mining Association, Commission for the Implementation of the Constitution (CIC), Kenya Investment Authority, KCM, African Barrick Gold Ltd (a KCM member) and Farasi Strategy Advisors Ltd (not a member). This report did not include any proposals for amendment – they come later – but KCM perceived that the language captured the spirit of the joint submission and their proposed amendments. Certainly, KCM featured more prominently than any other stakeholder: Figure 33.2 shows the number of times each stakeholder is cited as making a recommendation. It is worth noting that many of the comments from CIC were based on concerns shared bilaterally by KCM with CIC. The language of the report suggests a degree of sympathy for their views.

MoM explained that it was lobbied by other stakeholders, including communities, county governments and MPs from mining areas as well as the treasuries and development partners from countries where some of the mining companies are based, though they did not feature in the ENR review.

On 5 August, the second-reading debate was concluded with a commitment for amendment. During the debate the chair of ENR had voiced the opinion that there should be some amendment, though there was a view that most MPs had not read their report

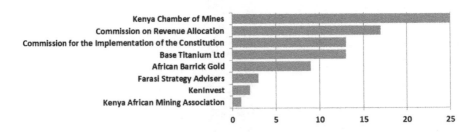

Figure 33.2:   Citations in Report of Departmental Committee on Environment & Natural Resources

Source: Derived from the *Report on the consideration of the mining bill*, Departmental Committee on Environment & Natural Resources, Kenya National Assembly

and that some had not even read the Bill, so the comments in the debate were very general. Some, however, were well briefed and made more pointed contributions. Most of the more informed MPs were part of KCM's target audience and had been well briefed by KCM. The Chair of ENR was a champion on the Bill (balancing KCM and government interests).

The next step was the committee stage, which was considered sufficiently important to constitute a 'committee of the whole house'. Any MP can propose amendments at the committee stage, though the usual approach is for detailed amendments to be made by the Parliamentary committee. Generally, however, the agreement of the committee is needed for amendments to be considered. At this stage, ENR had not concluded its proposals, so KCM continued to make proposals for amendments and also sought to lobby individual MPs. During Parliament's summer break, KCM lobbied MPs who they anticipated would also submit amendments. KCM recognised that it needed to make some effort to bring on side associations and MPs who saw themselves as representing small scale-miners, because they perceived them as thinking that the Bill would do nothing for them and so oppose making it easier for large-scale miners. About this time, KCM saw a preliminary draft of ENR's proposals and concluded that much had been lifted word for word from their submission to ENR, which they saw as positive.

On 17 October, the NA published their 'order of business', listing all the amendments proposed by ENR, for 21 October. The order paper showed ENR making proposals for amendments to 76 clauses and to one schedule; they also proposed 29 additional clauses. An MP, not on the committee, proposed amendments to four clauses. This was the first time that KCM had seen the amendments that were actually being proposed, as opposed to drafts. KCM's analysis (2014) showed that ENR had adopted many of their proposals, in some cases word for word.

However, they also quickly realised that a number of proposed amendments were likely to be detrimental to the industry (including, for example, new permit requirements and additional revenue-sharing requirements). As a result, KCM spent all weekend lobbying key MPs. On the morning of 21 October, the chairman of ENR retracted the list of amendments to allow further consultation and called a special session of the committee, to which KCM was invited. Following a detailed discussion, ENR agreed that KCM should sit with their legal drafter to redraft some of the amendments.

Out of nine drafting changes presented to ENR, six were adopted and incorporated into the committee's revised proposals. Despite many of KCM's original amendments being accepted by the committee, a few critical issues were still outstanding, and KCM resorted to further lobbying. These included (i) the exclusion of prospecting rights from the requirement of consent before granting of rights upon application; (ii) the need to review a clause that would render redundant the force and purpose of mineral agreements; (iii) the need to institute a stabilisation clause; and (iv) criminalising possession of minerals where any person found in possession of minerals is deemed guilty of having committed an offence and is penalised without being accorded an opportunity to prove their innocence. Intensive lobbying over the next days resulted in further amendments, the most significant one being on mineral agreements.

Whilst KCM was not entirely happy with all the revised amendments, it felt that the Bill was much improved. The new order for business for 28 October for the committee of the whole house was published on 23 October. Prior to the committee meeting, KCM lobbied some MPs and texted more specifically about mineral agreements. One MP, Joyce Lay, from a mining area, but also an opposition MP (well known to and well briefed by KCM), made a number of amendments regarded by KCM as progressive.

In total, 110 amendments were proposed, 84 of which originated from ENR and thus mostly from KCM. Most of the ENR amendments were adopted as proposed, while other proposals – perceived by KCM as detrimental – were either defeated on the floor of the house or withdrawn by their proponents. After more than five hours of deliberations, the Mining Bill was agreed by the committee of the whole house and sent to the NA for its third reading on 29 October, which it passed. There seems to be some debate about what happened next. It seems that the NA may have sent the Bill to the President for his assent. However, the Senate then intervened, saying that it should have a chance to debate the Bill. KCM noted that the Executive and the NA often appeared to ignore the Senate, but that the Bill was rather emotive and the Senate felt that some elements were important to the counties. Indeed, the Senate threatened to go to court if it did not get a chance to debate the Bill. It was supported in this by the Commission for the Implementation of the Constitution – so, on 19 November, the Speaker of the NA sent the Bill to the Speaker of the Senate so that they could review the provisions affecting counties, specifically clauses on revenue sharing and consent from county government. Expecting the Bill to go to the President for assent, KCM wrote to the President on 5 November asking for his intervention to amend clauses relating to consents, mineral rights and mineral agreements.

The Senate Standing Committee on Land and Natural Resources started its own hearing – with public submissions – at the end of February 2015 (2015). Whilst the Senate is supposed only to look at impacts on the counties, this provided a further opportunity for KCM to lobby for amendment, and it proposed nine further amendments, not solely focused on counties: it included its proposals for amendment that were not adopted by the NA. According to the Senate report (2015), some 18 submissions were received altogether. The committee made a number of recommendations, including one of the proposals from KCM.

At the time of writing, the Bill is still in the Senate, though it was expected to pass largely as amended. It will then need to come back to the NA. KCM sees this as providing yet a further opportunity to amend some of the clauses with which they are still unhappy. After brief consideration and approval in the NA, it will be sent to the President for assent. It is then possible for the President to send the Bill back to the NA with 'recommendations' for further amendments. KCM does not foresee major amendments being proposed by the President. However, it has prepared a memorandum drawing attention to the clauses that it still feels are problematic. This memorandum has to be presented to and considered by the President within 14 days of receiving the Bill from the NA, after which the law must be promulgated or a communication sent to Parliament proposing further changes. Otherwise the Bill automatically becomes law as it stands.

If the outstanding issues are not resolved at this stage, KCM could simply wait for six months after the Mining Act becomes effective then start to lobby for changes. Positively, however, KCM thinks that it has achieved 80 per cent of its proposed changes. It does not regard what it has done as 'winning' and says that there will be some adverse impact; but it does think that the mining sector can live with what is currently proposed and suggests that it will not decimate the industry (as the Bill as originally drafted would have done).

THE MINISTRY VIEW

MoM explained that it was expected to engage in a process of public participation to provide all stakeholders with a chance to have their say. It organised many workshops. It stated that the Mining Bill had had more public participation than any Bill other than the Land Bills. MoM wanted, through the consultation, to understand all stakeholders' viewpoints, to hear proposals for solutions and to seek convergence. MoM was particularly keen to gather evidence to inform the final wording of the legislation and sought to gather it from experience in mining areas and from reference to international best practice. It invited stakeholders to provide evidence, though it reported that most simply listed issues without offering evidence. It observed that mining companies tended to share evidence that supported its arguments – for example, from Botswana and Tanzania rather than from, say, the US, EU and Australia, where mining legislation is stricter. However, it also commented that KCM members were helpful in sharing evidence on conserving the environment based on best practice in other countries where they mine. MoM said that the process helped it to realise that mining investors are very sensitive to laws and keen to study the legislation closely before they invest.

MoM recognised that there is no perfect law but tried to ensure that the Bill responded to the legitimate concerns of key stakeholders: large miners, small-scale miners and local communities. It perceived that each party felt that they made major compromises. MoM believe that the resulting Act will encourage investment, because it ensures security of tenure of mineral rights and introduces transparency and predictability.

MoM had mixed views on KCM. It described KCM as 'aggressive, confrontational and non-compromising', not always objective and appearing 'elitist' and said that the process may have been smoother and 'less bumpy' without it. However, it did acknowledge that some changes and areas that KCM highlighted may have been overlooked and could not have been changed later. It said that KCM took the lead on behalf of the private sector, ensuring that there was a single message. MoM described KCM's chairman as 'a good mobiliser and organiser', who 'was always a step ahead of the process'. For example, he would meet with MoM one

day and the next be in Parliament talking to MPs before MoM could manage to do so, and often this would make the difference in what the MPs believed. It is noteworthy that MoM described MPs as 'activists', reflecting the assessment of Booth et al. (2014). It said the KCM chairman 'was a strategist', providing intellectual stimulation that forced the government to think further about some of its proposals: 'KCM's involvement brought some balance to the process'. MoM perceived that KCM was often suspicious of and objected to its contributions. 'However, they would come around and agree', though, based on the way in which the wording was changed, in most cases it looks like a suitable compromise was agreed.

THE PARLIAMENTARY VIEW

The Chairman of ENR said that she avoided interacting with KCM until she had learnt about the mining sector, but that it was a good partner with which to work and she enjoyed working with its staff. She was broadly complementary about KCM and its work, noting that the CEO at the start of the lobbying process (Monica Gichuhi) was 'broad and fair', though she felt that KCM's chairman had been prone to 'spread[ing] misinformation'. However, she says that generally 'KCM was professional, especially when giving general information about the sector; KCM input on the broad issues in the mining sector was very helpful'. She notes that working with KCM made 'our work easy in terms of public participation' and 'reduced the number of stakeholders with which we had to engage'. She observed a problem in that KCM did not represent many artisan miners, so the committee aimed to engage with them separately. The committee, however, validated issues with other stakeholders and through a mission to learn about how the mining sector is regulated in Australia. It seemed that whenever the committee felt that KCM was basing arguments on 'misinformation', when it lacked evidential rigour or when it appeared only to be self-serving, then the arguments were rejected out of hand; but when it had good evidence to support its arguments, it appeared 'professional and trustworthy' and its proposals were more acceptable. Overall, the chairman says, 'The Committee incorporated over 95 per cent of KCM's amendments on the broad issues. KCM's proposals helped a great deal in developing a good Mining Bill'.

REFLECTION AND CONCLUSION

Our approach in this single case study, given the chance to follow it from the publication of the Bill in March 2014, has been one of process tracing. It is often not possible in researching business associations easily to observe causes of success, particularly when objectives and actions are assessed after a project has concluded. Clearly, a single case study is not representative, but it is purposive: case studies focus on answering how and why (Yin 2009; Easton 2010) need to catch complexity (Stake 1995: xi) 'to tease out and disentangle [...] relationships' (Easton 2010: 119), including relationships between actor and context (Christie et al. 2000). They provide opportunities for inductively identifying complex interactions, causal mechanisms and results (George & Bennett 2005: 212). They provide a basis on which to draw inferences about causal outcomes that follow from mechanisms acting in contexts (Pawson & Tilley 1997: 58), which is particularly important in contested issues.

The 'why' is relatively easy to identify: mining was and remains an important and growing sector in Kenya and has the potential to contribute considerable tax revenue and to create many jobs. Indeed, ENR makes the point that 'the review of the Mining Sector Policy and legislative reform is driven by the government's recognition of the importance of the mineral sector in national development in line with vision 2030'. The challenge, of course, is that too many arms of government – ministries, agencies and now counties – all want to 'dip their hand' in the revenue stream. The mining companies recognise that they are extracting resources and that once they're gone, that is it, so there needs to be an equitable share with the state. They recognise that the local communities also want a stake in mineral resources. Their objective, however, is to ensure that they can still make a return on the very large investments required. Indeed, one company, African Queen Mines, has already disinvested, citing an environment not sufficiently conducive to business.

Interest groups engaging in public-policy advocacy tend to choose between working 'inside' government – seeking directly to influence officials and politicians – or 'outside' government – essentially through mobilising public opinion (Walker 1991: 103). Business leaders may get privileged access (Walker 1991: 124), though this begs the question of whether they get their privilege by virtue of being seen as leaders, by running businesses that make an important contribution to the economy or by demonstrating credibility and competence. The purpose of business association advocacy is to ensure that government understands how its actions impact on the private sector and to encourage government to act in a way that improves the enabling environment. However, Walker (1983) also suggests that the public sector needs appropriate organisations with which it can consult. As noted, mining is expected to make a much bigger contribution to GDP, and KCM was established at the behest of government, so perhaps it is not surprising that it has good access at all levels from the President down.

At the time, KCM's strategy was predominantly one of working with the Ministry and lobbying the ENR Committee and selected MPs. However, it was also talking with a number of other ministries and departments, though in a minimal manner, including the Office of the President, the Treasury, State Law Office, Ministry of Trade and Commerce and Ministry of Industrialisation. It recognises that it needs to spend more time lobbying the Ministries of Energy, Transport and Labour as well. KCM has sought some media coverage, not to pursue its lobbying of government, but rather to promote the industry and to promote Kenya as a destination for investment. KCM was targeting a wider audience and has had coverage, *inter alia*, on CNBC. KCM is effectively, at the moment, just Stephen Mwakesi and his board. At one stage, meetings were happening so quickly that he simply did not have time to complete the policy position papers. They were completed eventually, however, and focus closely on proposals to amend the legislation and the arguments that support those proposals. They are commendably short and high on evidence, including international comparisons to make the case for change, though they could, arguably, have covered jurisdictions that did not have regulatory regimes that supported KCM's arguments and which would have painted a broader picture. Despite having large mining companies as members, KCM is under-resourced. KCM would have liked the resources to undertake more economic analysis of the key provisions and this would undoubtedly have strengthened the arguments further – and may have ensured that all its proposals were rigorously evidenced. Despite advice from BAF on having their position papers available when speaking to stakeholders, this did not always happen, and Mwakesi now stresses the need, when you are called to public hearings by a Parliamentary committee, to go with a written summary.

Mwakesi was clear that he needed to keep track of what Parliament and ENR were doing. As a result, he spent many hours as an observer in Parliament, watching debates, listening to arguments and trying to understand how MPs think and how they make proposals. He was surprised that more BMOs do not do this in order to gather intelligence.

Having listened to many of the debates, Mwakesi explained his concern that too many Parliamentarians are expected to take decisions on industries about which they know little or nothing, and this perhaps puts the onus on organisations like KCM to ensure that MPs are properly briefed. However, MPs claim to be short of time, so KCM found it difficult to gain enough attention to raise awareness and to brief them. As a result, they used short policy papers and other means such as text messaging. During the lobbying process, KCM members followed the Parliament sessions closely and made contributions to the proposed amendments and devised the advocacy strategy. Their approach was to ensure they undertook sustained engagement where they aimed to educate MPs about the industry and the potential effects of the proposed legislation on the sector.

At every stage in the process, KCM worked hard to understand what precisely was being proposed and was clear about its objectives. Where it was able to reach agreement on specific clauses, it did so, requiring some compromise. But it did not compromise on the whole Bill; instead it has reserved its position on the clauses that it does not like and has continued to lobby on those separately, recognising that other stakeholders would also continue to lobby on those aspects, probably taking a contrary position to KCM. It worked entirely by itself and not in partnership with other BMOs or civil-society organisations, though some of its members lobbied alongside them. Mwakesi suggested that the members, through an active board, are very important to KCM's success. He noted that his international members have a much greater eye for detail and a consideration of the possible implications. He says that this is almost certainly due to a difference in culture but says that local members 'are beginning to take attention to detail more seriously', though he laments that many local companies did not participate closely enough. He also notes that international members are much stricter in relation to being ethical.

There is a belief amongst scholars of a resource-exchange relationship between the public sector, whose officials are short of time and resources (Jones & Baumgartner 2005), and the interest groups that seek to interact with it (Bouwen 2002; Poppelaars 2007; Eising 2007; Beyers & Braun 2014). It is generally the case that interest groups gain access to policy makers and may be able to influence policy in exchange, *inter alia*, for technical expertise and expert knowledge, information, legitimacy, consent or cooperation in introducing the policy – so the better able the interest group is to deliver the needs of the public sector (objective research, carefully argued policy positions, etc.), the more likely it is to secure access and influence (Bouwen 2002; Beyers & Braun 2014). Again, there is little doubt that KCM's well researched positions, well argued proposals and holistic approach to influencing the ENR and MoM simultaneously made a significant difference to what it was able to achieve.

Mwakesi knew the government's proposals intimately, as least as well as the government's own advisers. His view was that associations cannot rely on external consultants because they do not have enough focus. He also notes that consultants sometimes have conflicts of interest. He cites, for example, the same consultant supporting the Ministry, the ENR and the Commission for the Implementation of the Constitution, each of which may have different objectives. KCM has made use of research and evidence but, as he notes, much of their argument to Parliamentarians is based on 'emotion and rationality': he says that you 'cannot bury Parliament with information'.

Empirical evidence suggests that many associations take the building of relationships much further and seek to cultivate and encourage champions, either officials or MPs who may act on their behalf. Baumgartner et al. (2009) commonly found government officials who, far from being neutral, were acting as advocates, often collaborating with others regarded as sharing similar views and actively

lobbying others to adopt a particular position. It does seem that champions – from both the public and private sectors, who invest in the process and drive it forward – can make a real difference (Public Private Dialogue 2015).

KCM has been clear all along that it has lobbied solely on the strength of its arguments and has not offered any bribes, though it also notes that some organisations are alleged to have offered bribes whilst trying to influence the government. KCM explains that its lobbying will be subject to external scrutiny and the way in which it achieved influence will be important. So, on this occasion, at least, KCM did not work through champions, since it was worried that too much contact with one or two individuals might raise suspicions amongst their colleagues. Nevertheless, KCM made an effort, and was able, to engage across government: with the President, with the Cabinet Secretary, with MoM, with the Parliamentary committee and with MPs in general. This was helped by building relationships over many years. After a shaky start, the engagement with MoM has been positive and the Cabinet Secretary engaged KCM in the review process to allow a collaborative view to be presented to the NA.

The literature suggests that, to be effective, business associations need to be competent in their approach, with objective research and evidence that will inform policy makers and with compelling policy positions that will persuade politicians and officials. They need to develop and sustain relationships with ministries, departments and agencies, so that they can adopt an insider approach. It is clear that KCM was very professional in its approach, gathering intelligence, understanding the motives of the MPs, working through MoM and ENR and giving them the ammunition to support amendments once agreed.

Success, for a business association aiming to influence public policy, could be regarded as achieving all of the objectives of a specified advocacy project. Neither access (Eising 2007) nor success (Mahoney 2007) proves that a business association has influence.

A trade association may see a change in public policy that accords with its wishes but which they did not bring about. Total success is rare. Compromise is often necessary (Chapman & Wameyo 2001; Coates & David 2002). Whilst KCM did not achieve all its objectives, it is clear that it had excellent access and it seems that it was influential. Whilst the complexity of issues often makes it difficult to determine cause and effect (Chapman & Wameyo 2001), there seems little doubt in this case that KCM was the driving force behind many of the amendments – persuading MoM or ENR or both of the merits of its case and thus ensuring that ENR adopted its proposals so that it then pushed them through the NA.

There is evidence to suggest that involving the private sector in the process of formulating public policy builds legitimacy, improves legislation and regulation and secures private sector buy-in (Bettcher 2011: 1) as well as leading to economic growth (Qureshi & te Velde 2007: 4). MoM certainly believes that this legislation will pave the way for more investment in mining, and that more mining will lead to considerable growth. It also believes, despite its misgivings, that KCM made a positive contribution to improving the legislation as originally drafted. This view is shared by ENR.

Ultimately, much of KCM's success is due to Stephen Mwakesi. His educational background and legal training helped him to understand the legal language and parliamentary process. His ability to communicate and articulate a message in a well spoken manner has been a great plus. A key lesson for other BMOs is the importance of updating members on progress and regularly seeking their input. Constant updates made KCM members feel part of the process and helped them to understand where and when to contribute.

The legislation will be largely enabling, with technical matters covered in subsequent regulations to be drafted by the Ministry, though they will eventually also need NA approval, so KCM cannot afford to drop its guard. It needs to monitor other developments as well.

For example, the National Environmental Management Agency (NEMA) is currently proposing amendments to the Environmental Management Act which might have a detrimental effect on mining.

The biggest challenge for KCM has been struggling with gathering enough research and preparing documents. It has been somewhat overwhelmed by the process but has come through it, and Stephen Mwakesi is still smiling. He has developed enormously throughout this process; he has outgrown his mentor and indeed, if only time would allow, would probably now make a good mentor for another BMO.

Notes

1 Funded by Danish International Development Assistance (DANIDA) to support business membership organisations (BMO) in Kenya to influence public policy.
2 Stephen Mwakesi was appointed as acting CEO in September 2014.

ACKNOWLEDGEMENTS

A big thank you is due to all the people whom we interviewed in the preparation of this case study, but we are especially grateful to Stephen Mwakesi for his unstinting support and co-operation.

POST SCRIPT

Since writing the case study, a number of developments have taken place, which support the impression that KCM has been able to be influential, at least in relation to this legislation, and has been able to develop and maintain a god relationship with MoM.

The Senate Standing Committee on Land and Natural Resources completed its report in May 2015. It was due to be discussed by the Senate on 31 July but the lack of a quorum meant that the Senate was unable to take its final vote. The vote finally took place on 16 September approving some 29 amendments to the Bill. It was sent back to the NA on 29 September.

On 22 October, the NA ENR rejected 11 of the Senate's amendments and so the Bill was sent to be considered by a mediation committee. They produced their report, and proposed final version of the Bill, in March 2016. This then had to be sent back to both Houses for approval.

Whilst the stakeholders were engaging in debating the draft legislation, the MoM had, in January 2014, initiated a process to prepare a mining policy, which was expected to some extent to guide the regulatory reform required in the sector and provide clear guidance for sustainable mineral resources development. The draft policy was published on the Ministry's website on 23 January and KCM was invited by the Ministry for a consultative forum with the CS on sector issues with the draft policy being central to the discussion. By 30 January, KCM had responded with comments accompanied by a formal letter which requested closer collaboration between them and the Ministry to develop a comprehensive policy framework. The CS responded on 20 February acknowledging KCM's input and expressing the Ministry's willingness to partner with KCM in developing the framework.

BAF supported KCM to engage in dialogue on the policy and legal framework. After several meetings, however, the Ministry seemed more interested in developing the legal framework first and so the policy took a back seat, though the draft Bill was largely aligned to the spirit of the draft policy.

As the Mining Bill approached finalisation, the Ministry sought also to finalise the Mining and Minerals Policy which was approved by the Cabinet on 1 April 2016. The Mining Bill was also, finally, approved by both Houses and sent to the President for assent. It was gazetted on 20 May and came into effect a few days later. Perhaps because of the Government's ambition for the sector ultimately to contribute as much as 10 per cent of GDP (about $3 billion), the President made a formal presentation of the Mining Act to the CS on 13 June.

KCM still has some issues with the new Act, though it is much better than it might have been if they had not lobbied so hard and so vigilantly. However, the legislation will now need to be followed by more detailed regulations and there was a hope within KCM that those regulations might alleviate some of their concerns. Once the Act has been operational for six months, they will be allowed to start lobbying for amendments should they still consider those necessary. There is also considerable jockeying for positions on new organisations such as the Mineral Rights Board (the creation of which was one of their proposals), the National Mining Corporation and the Minerals and Metals Commodities Exchange, with investors pushing hard to be represented.

On 28 July 2016, the Ministry published 14 draft Mining Regulations and Guidelines on its official website and on the same day wrote to KCM. The letter invited comments before 2 September. KCM sees this as another opportunity for the mining and mineral industry to ensure an environment that is consistent with accepted mining practice elsewhere in the world. It does appear that MoM is now much more willing to invite KCM to comment at all stages of development of the regulations.

A new CS for Mining, Dan Kazungu, and a new PS, Dr. Ibrahim M. Mohamed, were appointed on 18 Dec 2015, so KCM has had to work hard to build new relationships. It is particularly interesting however to note the game of musical chairs that has taken place since KCM started its lobbying. In Feb 2016, Monica Gichuhi, KCM's former CEO was appointed to be a Policy, Strategy and Institutional Advisor at the MoM. In April 2016, Moses Njiru, a former Commissioner of Mines at MOM was appointed as KCM's new CEO. And in May 2016, Stephen Mwakesi moved from KCM to take up a position as Private Secretary to the Cabinet Secretary, where he sees his role as being to promote a fairness, objectivity and balance in order to achieve a 'win-win' for both public and private sectors.

Njiru has described the new CS as 'warm and receptive' and reports that he has expressed a readiness to listen to the industry players and address their concerns. KCM has done well in its advocacy and will be working hard to build on those foundations. There seems to be a commitment to dialogue and KCM has demonstrated that it can provide detailed evidence and make compelling arguments. The appointments of KCM staff into government and MoM staff to KCM should make it much easier for KCM to develop and maintain relationships and to be able to continue influencing MoM and the government in relation of mining policy.

REFERENCES

Baumgartner, F.R., Berry, J.M., Hojnacki, M. et al. (2009), *Lobbying and policy change: who wins, who loses and why*, Chicago: University of Chicago Press.

Bettcher, K.E. (2011), *Making the most of public private dialogue: an advocacy approach*, Washington DC: CIPE.

Beyers, J. & Braun, C. (2014), Ties that count: explaining interest group access to policy-makers, *Journal of Public Policy*, vol. 34, no. 1, pp. 93–121.

Booth, D., Cooksey, B., Golooba-mutebi, F. & Kanyinga, K. (2014), *East African prospects: an update on the political economy of Kenya, Rwanda, Tanzania and Uganda*, London: ODI.

Bouwen, P. (2002), Corporate lobbying in the European Union: the logic of access, *Journal of European Public Policy*, vol. 9, no. 3, pp. 365–90.

Chapman, J. & Wameyo, A. (2001), *Monitoring and evaluating advocacy: a scoping study*, London: Action Aid.

Christie, M., Rowe, P., Perry, C. & Chamard, J. (2000), *Implementation of realism in case study research methodology*, International Council for Small Business, Annual Conference, Brisbane.

Coates, B. & David, R. (2002), Learning for change: the art of assessing the impact of advocacy work, *Development in Practice*, vol. 12, no. 3–4, pp. 530–41.

Easton, G. (2010), Critical realism in case study research, *Industrial Marketing Management*, vol. 39, pp. 118–28.

Eising, R. (2007), Institutional contexts, organisational resources and strategic choices, exploring interest group access in the European Union, *European Union Politics*, vol. 8, no. 3, pp. 329–62.

Fourie, E. (2014), Model students: policy emulation, modernisation and Kenya's Vision 2030, *African Affairs*, vol. 113, no. 453, pp. 540–62.

George, A.L. & Bennett, A. (2005), *Case studies and theory development in the social sciences*, Cambridge, MA: MIT Press.

Pederson, H.H. (2013), Is measuring interest group influence a mission impossible? The case of interest group influence in the Danish parliament, *Interest Groups & Advocacy*, vol. 2, no. 1, pp. 27–47.

Irwin, D. & Githinji, M. (2016), Business associations in Kenya: the success factors, *Journal of Public Affairs*, vol. 16, no. 2, pp. 162–80.

Jones, B.D. & Baumgartner, F.R. (2005), *The politics of attention: how government prioritises problems*, Chicago: University of Chicago Press.

Kenya Chamber of Mines (2014), *Analysis of committee on Environment & Natural Resources proposals on the Mining Bill 2014*, Nairobi: Kenya Chamber of Mines.

Kenya Chamber of Mines and Ministry of Mining (2014), *Joint submission on the Mining Bill 2014*, Nairobi: Kenya Chamber of Mines.

Kenyatta, U., Ruto, W., Ngilu, C. & Balala, N. (2013), *Transforming Kenya. Securing Kenya's prosperity 2013–2017: the shared manifesto of the Coalition between the National Alliance (TNA), the United Republican Party (URP), the National Rainbow Coalition (NARC) and the Republican Congress Party (RC)*, Nairobi: http://presidency.go.ke/images/

jubilee-coalition-manifesto.pdf, accessed 20 April 15.

Lowery, D. (2013), Lobbying influence: meaning, measurement and missing, *Interest Groups & Advocacy*, vol. 2, no. 1, pp.1–27.

Mahoney, C. (2007), Networking vs allying: the decision of interest groups to join coalitions in the US and the EU, *Journal of European Public Policy*, vol. 14, no. 3, pp. 366–83.

National Assembly Departmental Committee on Environment & Natural Resources (2014), *Report on the consideration of the Mining Bill 2014*, Nairobi: Kenya National Assembly.

Nyando, L (2014), *The Mining Bill 2014 retreat with Departmental Committee on Environment and Natural Resources*, Nairobi: Kenya Chamber of Mines.

Pawson, R. & Tilley, N. (1997), *Realistic Evaluation*, London: Sage.

Poppelaars, C. (2007), Resource exchange in urban governance: on the means that matter, *Urban Affairs Review*, vol. 43, no. 1, pp. 3–27.

Public Private Dialogue (2015), *Charter of good practice in using Public Private Dialogue for private sector development*. Retrieved from http://www.publicprivatedialogue.org/charter/New%202015%20PPD%20Charter%20of%20Good%20Practice.pdf (accessed 6 September, 2016).

Qureshi, M. & te Velde, D.W. (2007), *State-business relations, investment climate reform and firm productivity in sub-Saharan Africa*, Manchester: IPPG Programme, University of Manchester.

Senate Standing Committee on Land & Natural Resources (2015), *Report on the Mining Bill, 2014*, Nairobi: The Senate.

Stake, R.E. (1995), *The art of case study research*, Thousand Oaks, CA: Sage.

Walker, J.L. (1983), The origins and maintenance of interest groups in America, *American Political Science Review*, vol. 77, no. 2, pp.390–406.

Walker, J.L. (1991), *Mobilizing interest groups in America*, Ann Arbor, MI: University of Michigan Press.

Yin, R.K. (2009), *Case study research: designs and methods*, 4th ed, Thousand Oaks, CA: Sage.

INTERVIEWS

KCM policy position workshop, 24 March 2014

Monica Gichuhi (CEO, Kenya Chamber of Mines), 24 March 2014

Stephen Mwakesi (Acting CEO, Kenya Chamber of Mines), 24 March, 27 March, 10 September, 9 December 2014, 18 February 2015

Shadrack Kimomo (Chief Geologist & Acting Commissioner of Mines), 30 January 2015

Raymond Mutiso (Director of Mines), 30 January 2015

Hon. Amina Abdalla (Chairman, NA Departmental Committee on Environment and Natural Resources), 1 April 2015

34

Lessons in Lobbying Regulation from the UK and Ireland

Conor McGrath

INTRODUCTION

In the period 2012–15, both the UK and Irish governments prepared measures aimed at making the lobbying industry more transparent – ultimately enacted as the Transparency of Lobbying, Non-Party Campaigning and Trade Union Administration Act 2014 and the Regulation of Lobbying Act 2015 respectively. The two governments undertook very different consultation processes and produced quite different pieces of legislation – but both laws are ultimately flawed in key respects.

An unregulated lobbying industry presents three critical difficulties: (1) only a relatively small proportion of the industry will be members of professional associations and thus subject to even minimal self-regulation; (2) the whole of the industry will be insufficiently transparent, thus undermining public confidence in the policymaking process; and (3) no uniform set of enforceable standards

of ethical behavior will have been imposed on the entire industry. Statutory *registration* of lobbyists has the potential to do much to address the first two of these concerns, but the third requires *regulation* as it is only by setting rules that lobbyists' conduct can be controlled. A mandatory system of both registration and regulation, to which all lobbyists must adhere and which requires of them significant disclosure, would enable policymakers and citizens to answer fundamental questions: *Who is attempting to influence whom, on whose behalf, over which public policy issue? What resources are being invested in that effort? Are the tactics employed by lobbyists in that effort legitimate and appropriate?* A regulatory framework which provides the information needed to answer these questions would be a model for other nations to follow, by making lobbying more transparent and policymakers more accountable. Such a regulatory mechanism would benefit all stakeholders (Cohen-Eliya and Hammer, 2011; Holman and Luneburg, 2012):

- *Policymakers* can more easily determine which groups have lobbied on a particular issue and are thus in a better position to assess whether an equitable range of views have been taken into consideration during the policy formulation process.
- *Lobbyists* currently spend much time simply trying to discover which of their competitors have been active on an issue, and would more easily be able to determine whether it was necessary to attempt to counteract such lobbying.
- *The public* could be better reassured that policy-making was conducted in an open and legitimate manner.

In most nations, lobbying remains secretive and closed to external scrutiny, even as it exerts significant influence over the formulation and implementation of public policy. This inevitably raises existential questions which go to the heart of the industry. Is access to the policymaking process available on an equitable basis? Are relationships between government and outside interests conducted appropriately? How can we be confident that influence does not become *undue* influence? The public are largely excluded from the lobbying world and thus find it difficult to assess its scale, effectiveness, and probity. By contrast, the regulatory system which operates at the federal level in the US 'enables interested parties to discern trends and patterns of interest representation' and provides 'a relevant and reliable tool that enables proper scrutiny of the role of lobbying and thus helps to improve the quality of democratic decision-making' (PASC, 2009b, Spinwatch evidence: 223). This chapter argues that in designing any system of lobbying registration a number of fundamental questions must be addressed:

- *Is registration necessary and proportionate?* Any notion that lobbying, and its impact on the policymaking process, is currently sufficiently transparent can frankly no longer be credible. Moreover, the experience of the US, Canada, and Australia demonstrates that even relatively

detailed registration need not be unduly problematic for lobbyists to comply with.
- *Should registration be voluntary or statutory?* There is no evidence from any nation in which self-regulation operates that it has delivered meaningful disclosure or enforceable standards of ethical conduct.
- *Should registration be partial or comprehensive?* The overwhelming virtue of the statutory approach is that no other framework can provide for a uniform system across the whole industry – consultants, in-house staff, companies, charities, trade unions, and so on.
- *How should 'lobbying' and 'lobbyist' be defined?* It is most important here to devise a clear definition of what activities constitute 'lobbying'; thereafter, all those who engage in those activities for remuneration are 'lobbyists'. In addition, since lobbying is essentially an exercise in communication, and given that what may or may not represent an attempt to influence policy is subjective, I would suggest that lobbying activities are defined concretely in terms of communication with a policymaker.
- *What information should be registered?* A simple list of the names of lobbyists and their employers/clients is of relatively little value. As one UK academic says, 'Registration is likely to serve little purpose unless it requires the provision of specified information, most importantly the beneficiaries of lobbying, a list of clients, and the issue of subject-matter' (Rush, 1994: 634). Meaningful registration should enable the citizen to discover more precisely who is being lobbied by whom on specific policy issues, as well as what lobbying techniques and financial resources are being applied to that activity.
- *Is registration adequate or is regulation necessary?* If a new system is to have any impact on public confidence in the integrity of the policymaking process, all lobbying contacts must be registered, and registered lobbyists must operate according to a uniform and rigorous set of ethical standards. Only this dual approach of registration and regulation can provide both transparency and accountability.

Judged against these basic criteria, the newly introduced frameworks in the UK and Ireland are less than ideal, in varying ways. The perfect lobbying regulation does not exist anywhere, but a well crafted framework which provides for meaningful disclosure by all lobbyists is the least that a transparent democracy demands. This chapter introduces some contextual background to lobbying reform in the UK and Ireland, examines the content of each nation's legislation, and draws lessons which can be taken forward by other nations when introducing their own systems.

PRE-LEGISLATIVE DEBATE IN THE UK AND IRELAND

UK

Following a number of high-profile lobbying scandals in the UK during the 1980s and early 1990s, five lobbying firms set up the Association of Professional Political Consultants (APPC) in 1994; as of May 2015 it had grown to 82 member companies, which collectively account for more than 80 per cent of the lobbying consultancy sector in the UK by turnover. APPC members adhere to a code of conduct and publicly register their public affairs staff and clients; both the register and code are available on its website (www.appc.org.uk).

Established in 1969, the Public Relations Consultants Association (PRCA) represents about 350 public relations consultancies in the UK. The 80 or so member firms involved in public affairs and lobbying are required to comply with a Public Affairs Code of Conduct and to make publicly available a register of their public affairs staff and clients (available on the PRCA website at www.prca.org.uk/Public_Affairs_Group).

The third key body involved in the self-regulation of lobbying in the UK is the Chartered Institute of Public Relations (CIPR), which represents individual members of the public relations industry. The CIPR has been in operation since 1948 and has over 10,000 members (see www.cipr.co.uk). It has a network of sectoral groups, one of which is the Public Affairs Group,

with around 700 members. Like the other two organizations, the CIPR Public Affairs Group has adopted a code of conduct for its members, although it is much less detailed and prescriptive than the others. A fuller overview of the UK lobbying landscape can be found in McGrath (forthcoming).

A survey of 163 MPs, in November 2005, found that 62 per cent would support a compulsory register for lobbyists, while 15 per cent opposed a register (ComRes, 2005). Two years later, another survey of 138 MPs showed that 80 per cent would be quite or very supportive of 'Parliament creating and maintaining a "Register of Lobbyists" that would disclose the name and organization of every professional lobbyist who engaged in lobbying activities with parliamentarians', while only nine per cent would be not supportive or not very supportive of such a move. Of the 111 MPs who supported a register, 83 per cent favored a mandatory register, with 15 per cent preferring a voluntary register (Dods, 2007).

The House of Commons Public Administration Select Committee (PASC) held an inquiry into lobbying in the UK, which reported in early 2009 (PASC, 2009a and 2009b). A comprehensive analysis of the inquiry can be found in McGrath (2009a). The committee concluded that: 'In the current climate of public mistrust, voluntary self-regulation of lobbying activity risks being little better than the Emperor's new clothes' (PASC, 2009a: 38). The PASC report recommended the introduction of a mandatory register of lobbying activity, which would encompass the entire industry. In an innovative move, it went on to suggest that the register should also include information provided by policymakers, such as 'diary records and minutes of meetings', so that the public can 'see what contacts are taking place, and to reach a reasonably informed judgement as to whether decision makers are receiving a balanced perspective from those they are meeting' (PASC, 2009a: 54).

In response, the three main industry associations – APPC, CIPR, and PRCA – came together to establish in March 2010 the UK Public Affairs Council (UKPAC). UKPAC's (whose website is at www.publicaffairscouncil.org.uk) key functions are to maintain a register of lobbyists, to adopt a set of guiding principles and assess how they might be translated into a common code of conduct agreeable to each member association, and to promote high ethical standards in lobbying. The compilation of a register should have been a fairly straightforward task: given that the APPC and PRCA already held registers of their member firms and could simply copy that information over to a UKPAC register, the only new material to be included was the registration of individual CIPR members who worked as lobbyists. Despite this, UKPAC struggled with IT platforms for about 18 months before it was able to produce a relatively comprehensive register – and even that only covered members of the three associations. At best, UKPAC registered perhaps 40 per cent of the industry. What appeared to be the final nail in the coffin of lobbying self-regulation in the UK came in December 2011, when the PRCA – one of the three founding members – decided to withdraw from UKPAC, citing disillusionment with UKPAC's inability to publish an accurate and credible register.

In January 2012, the Cabinet Office published a paper setting out the government's intention to introduce legislation. As a consultation exercise, the whole process was quite unsatisfactory. Rather than making all of the submissions available, the Cabinet Office published only 'a summary of consultation responses' (Cabinet Office, 2012a: 3) – and less than two weeks after the consultation paper was published, one of the Cabinet Office civil servants responsible for lobbying reform was suspended for posting a message on Twitter saying that she hoped one of the good-governance groups campaigning for rigorous regulation 'would die' (Wright, 2012).

David Cameron had asserted in February 2010 that the lobbying industry would produce a future scandal in UK politics

(a concern quickly overtaken by the jailing of five former MPs in an unprecedented exposure of parliamentary expenses fraud), but, in the event, his government's initial proposals were weak in the extreme. The consultation paper suggested that a statutory register would be established but would only apply to those who lobby on behalf of a third-party client. In other words, it would be a register solely of lobbying agencies rather than of the entire industry. The information to be registered quarterly was minimal: the names of the lobbying firm, lobbyists, and clients. No detailed financial information about lobbying income or expenditure would be disclosed and nor would details of meetings between lobbyists or clients and policymakers (Cabinet Office, 2012a: 14). Crucially, the government viewed a register simply as a list of names and did not intend that it should be linked to a mandatory code of conduct.

The consultation paper stated that a register would provide information 'about who is lobbying and for whom' (Cabinet Office, 2012a: 9). However, the accompanying Impact Assessment rendered this aim as the provision of information 'about who is lobbying and on what issues' (Cabinet Office, 2012b: 1). These formulations have significant consequences in practice. The purpose of a lobbying register should not simply be to make the lobbying industry more transparent but to better enable the government to be held to account. To take an example: if we know that Tesco lobbied the Treasury, that tells us a little; if we know that Tesco's external consultant lobbied a particular official at the Treasury about environmental issues, that reveals something more; if we know that Tesco's corporate affairs director lobbied the Chancellor of the Exchequer about tax credits for recycling, that tells us even more. The consultation paper talked of regulation as 'an obstacle ... and undue burden' and as 'costly and unnecessary' (Cabinet Office, 2012a: 9, 10) – utterly ignoring the fact that lobbyists in other jurisdictions apparently are able to register without undue difficulty.

In other words, the government was explicitly interested only in registration of lobbying consultancies, not in registration and regulation of the whole industry. It was encouraged to go further by a report from the House of Commons Political and Constitutional Reform Committee, which held an inquiry into the consultation paper (PCRC, 2012a, 2012b), but ultimately the government chose not to impose more rigorous regulation.

Ireland

Beginning in 1999, the Labour Party (then in opposition) began introducing a series of unsuccessful Bills to regulate Irish lobbying (McGrath, 2010). While none became law, they did have the effect of forcing the issue onto the agenda of the Public Relations Institute of Ireland (PRII). In 2003, the PRII introduced a Code of Professional Practice for Public Affairs and Lobbying, which although very basic in its obligations was the first time Irish lobbyists were regulated in any way. However, public distrust of the financial relationship between some politicians and some lobbyists intensified during the 2000s, culminating with the imprisonment of a high-profile lobbyist, Frank Dunlop, on bribery and corruption charges (McGrath, 2009b). Throughout that decade, most Irish lobbyists opposed any form of regulation – many asserted privately that the Dublin political community is so close-knit that 'everyone knows who is lobbying'. In fact, if Ireland were a US state, it would be the 25th most populous – in other words, there are 26 US states which are smaller than Ireland but which all benefit from some form of lobbying regulation despite their own political communities being relatively intimate. Following the 2011 general election, the Labour Party entered into a coalition government with the Fine Gael Party, and the Programme for Government they negotiated together included a commitment to legislate for a lobbying register (McGrath, 2011).

The pre-legislative consultation process undertaken by the Department of Public Expenditure and Reform (DPER) was exemplary. At each stage, all submissions received were published in full; meetings were held with a range of respondents and notes of these meetings were published (http://www.per.gov.ie/regulation-of-lobbying/). Disappointingly, the PRII's response was short-sighted and unpersuasive – even going so far as to insist that 'Ireland does not have a lobbying industry' (PRII, 2012: 3). Its consistent hostility to substantial reform in this area was underlined by its suggestion (PRII, 2012: 15) that a new system should be introduced for up to five years before being placed on a statutory basis.

At the end of April 2013, the DPER produced a draft outline (known as the General Scheme) of a Bill to regulate lobbying (DPER, 2013). It focused on regulating 'lobbying' rather than regulating 'lobbyists', and on 'lobbying communications' rather than the more nebulous phrase used in some nations' legislation regarding 'attempts to influence'. Head 4 of the General Scheme stated straightforwardly that lobbying is 'all communication … on specific policy, legislative matters or prospective decisions' (DPER, 2013: 9), directed at Ministers, parliamentarians, special advisers, senior civil servants, and elected members of local authorities. The system would explicitly encompass the entire spectrum of lobbying organizations – companies, industry and professional associations, representative groups, voluntary bodies, trade unions, chambers of commerce, charities, and non-profit bodies. Interestingly, the General Scheme covered not just direct lobbying but also 'grass-roots communication', which is in itself progressive, as most nations which regulate direct lobbying neglect to cover this sort of indirect lobbying. This was defined as 'appeals to members of the public or members of a particular organization through the mass media or by direct communication that seek to persuade members of the public to communicate directly with [policymakers] in an attempt to influence the [policymakers] to endorse a particular opinion' (DPER, 2013: 6).

The General Scheme set out (DPER, 2013: 17) the categories of information which would be captured on the register. Most were straightforward and appropriate (although it was notable that no financial information was required). In this regard, the Irish government's proposals certainly met the test suggested by the UK House of Commons Public Administration Select Committee that 'If sensibly framed, regulation would simply require those involved in the process of lobbying to provide information which should already be in their hands' (PASC, 2009a: 41). Most lobbying organizations presumably already hold the records of their lobbying activities in the normal course of their internal operation and accounting. It is likely that the time involved in preparing this information for a lobbying register would not be onerous – and certainly the benefits to wider accountability and transparency disproportionately outweigh the costs to each lobbying organization. According to Head 9 of the General Scheme, registration would include 'summary information to determine the type, nature and extent of lobbying activity/communication techniques undertaken'.

There were some significant exemptions contained in the General Scheme. In particular, it suggested that there is no need to register details of discussions held with policymakers regarding 'implementation matters of a purely technical nature' within an already established policy framework (DPER, 2013: 7). To my mind, lobbyists seek legitimately to influence the ways in which policy is implemented, but they cannot reasonably argue that such activity does not constitute lobbying. How policy is implemented matters significantly; often as much is at stake for an organization in the implementation of policy as it is in the formulation of policy. And this exemption raised the possibility of a loophole which could be exploited by lobbyists if they were authorized to determine for themselves

whether any communication was of 'a purely technical nature'.

Head 22 of the General Scheme was one of the most crucial elements of the whole system, dealing with the duty of the registrar to promote both public awareness and compliance with the regime by lobbyists through communication, education and guidance programs. A large element of the registrar's job – certainly in the first two years and less intensively after that – would revolve around meeting lobbyists individually and in groups, providing training and workshops on the new system, issuing guidance notes on how lobbyists can comply with the system, and ensuring that all professionals know when and what they must register. Under the General Scheme (DPER, 2013: 35), the registrar would be empowered to establish a code of conduct which would be binding on all lobbyists on the register. This raised the possibility that the Irish system could go beyond simple registration to include at least basic regulation of behavior. Finally, to address the revolving door, some senior policymakers would be subject to restrictions on future lobbying employment for 12 months after leaving public service.

LOBBYING LEGISLATION IN THE UK AND IRELAND

UK

The legislation ultimately produced by the coalition government – the Transparency of Lobbying, Non-Party Campaigning and Trade Union Administration Bill – was widely criticized on a number of fronts. The conflation of lobbying reform alongside more overtly partisan measures to do with electoral campaigning by groups other than political parties and with the administration of trade unions' membership lists created an impression that the whole Bill was overly politicized. The timing of the Bill's progress through the House of Commons was also unsatisfactory – it was first introduced the day before Parliament began its summer recess, received its second reading on the third day back after recess and its committee stage the following week. This meant that it was impracticable for parliamentary committees to subject the Bill to any form of pre-legislative scrutiny.

So far as its actual content is concerned, the law's requirements regarding lobbying are certainly weak by international standards. The government consistently ignored the advice of virtually all stakeholders – including the lobbying industry itself, other political parties, transparency campaigners, and academics – to strengthen its initial proposals. The Transparency of Lobbying, Non-Party Campaigning and Trade Union Administration Act (2014) which was passed by Parliament and granted Royal Assent on January 30, 2014 provides that:

- It is illegal to work as a consultant lobbyist without having registered as such (section 1);
- The conditions which define 'consultant lobbyist' are: that the person communicates 'in the course of a business' with a UK government minister or permanent secretary (the most senior civil servant in each department) about legislation, government policy, or the awarding of contracts and licenses; and that the person does so on another's behalf in return for payment (section 2);
- However, there are significant exceptions to this definition. In particular, in-house lobbyists and their employers are not required to register – thus the Act is aimed solely at contract or commercial consultants. Nor is registration necessary if the person's business 'consists mainly of non-lobbying activities' and any lobbying communication they make is merely 'incidental' to those non-lobbying activities (Schedule 1);
- Sole practitioners must register individually, but in the case of lobbying agencies only the agency must register and not its individual employees (section 2);
- A post of Registrar of Consultant Lobbyists is established to operate the register, but the Registrar cannot hire subordinate staff, instead he or she may request the secondment of existing civil servants (section 3);

- Each individual or company must provide details on the register of their business name and address, the names of any directors, a statement as to whether or not they subscribe to any relevant voluntary code of conduct, and a list of lobbying clients in that quarter. The register is to be available on a website (sections 4–7);
- The Registrar is required to monitor compliance by lobbyists, and is empowered to seek certain information necessary for such monitoring. A range of criminal and civil penalties are set out to punish those guilty of the offences of operating as an unregistered consultant lobbyist or of failing to provide the Registrar with information (sections 8–20); and
- The Registrar is authorized to issue guidance to lobbyists on how to ensure compliance with the law, and to charge registration fees at a level designed to cover the costs of maintaining the register (sections 21–22).

Since its introduction, this legislation has been criticized by the lobbying industry itself for not being sufficiently rigorous. The APPC pointed out that most lobbyists are in-house employees and that most lobbyists communicate primarily with ordinary MPs and junior civil servants – but that none of that activity would trigger registration. Indeed, analyzing records of ministers' meetings with external organizations, the APPC concluded that just 1 per cent of such meetings were with consultant lobbyists and asserted that 'It would be difficult to produce a worse Bill' (APPC, 2013). The Act does not establish a statutory code of conduct to which all registered lobbyists must adhere; it does not require lobbyists to identify which policymakers they met on behalf of which clients; and it does not include on the register any information about the policy issue which was the subject of lobbying activity.

Alison White was named (on a part-time basis) as the Registrar of Consultant Lobbyists in September 2014; she held the post alongside five other public body appointments. She had no previous experience of the lobbying industry, having trained as an accountant and worked at the Royal

Mail. The register was launched in March 2015 (its website is available at https://www.gov.uk/government/organisations/office-of-the-registrar-of-consultant-lobbyists). By the end of May 2015, one sole practitioner and 69 lobbying firms had registered, a substantial majority of which were already providing significantly more detailed information as registrants to either or both of the APPC and UKPAC registers. Indeed, given that those registers also include many individuals and organizations not signed up to the statutory register (presumably because of the narrow way in which the legislation defines consultant lobbyists), the perverse possibility exists that if the various trade associations withdrew their own voluntary registers, the government's register would provide us with much less transparency than was the case before it was established.

Ireland

Although the pre-legislative consultation process had been both extensive and transparent, and despite the fact that the General Scheme produced in 2013 had been relatively rigorous, when the Irish government published its actual legislation in June 2014 it proved to be significantly less robust in key respects. The legislation passed through the parliamentary process and was enacted on March 11, 2015 as the Regulation of Lobbying Act 2015.

Most strikingly, when the legislation was first introduced, it was as the 'Registration of Lobbying Bill' rather than as the more comprehensive 'Regulation of Lobbying Bill', although this change was reversed by a parliamentary amendment. It did, though, indicate that the purpose of the Bill had been substantially weakened. Similarly, the long title of the Act – which offers a summary of its key measures – did not include important functions which had been set out in the General Scheme, such as making 'information available to the public' and 'providing a framework for holding those engaged in lobbying

accountable for the manner in which they conduct the activity' (DPER, 2013: 4).

As ultimately passed, the Regulation of Lobbying Act (2015) provides that:

- Professional lobbyists are defined as including in-house staff, representative organizations, 'advocacy' bodies ('which exist primarily to take up particular issues'), and lobbying agencies or consultancies (section 5);
- Lobbying communications are oral and written communication between a registered lobbyist and a designated public official 'in relation to a relevant issue' (section 5). The final Act makes no reference to grassroots lobbying, which was previously explicitly defined in the General Scheme – thus squandering an opportunity for Irish legislation to develop a genuinely innovative lobbying regulation;
- Designated public officials include Ministers, parliamentarians, Irish MEPs, special advisers, elected members of local authorities, and senior civil servants (section 6). However, they no longer include the personal staff employed by parliamentarians (who had previously been covered in the General Scheme);
- The 'relevant matters' on which lobbying activity is deemed to occur include 'the initiation, development or modification of any public policy or of any public programme', the 'preparation or amendment' of legislation, and the 'award of any grant, loan or other financial support, contract or other agreement, or of any licence or other authorization involving public funds'. However, three particular exemptions are specified in the Act, so that communications made by a lobbyist need not be registered if they relate 'only to the implementation of any such policy, programme, enactment or award'; or if they provide 'factual information in response to a request for the information'; or if they are merely 'of a technical nature' (section 5);
- The Act establishes a register of lobbyists whose communication with officials relate to such relevant matters. Lobbyists are to update their entries each September, January and May in respect of their activities over the preceding 4 months (section 7);
- The Register of Lobbying is to be maintained by the Standards in Public Office Commission (section 7) and is to be made freely available on the Internet (section 10);

- In each 4-monthly return, the lobbying organization is required to record: which public body and which designated public officials were communicated with; the 'type and extent of the lobbying activities carried on'; the name of the person 'who had primary responsibility for carrying on the lobbying activities'; and the name of any employee or consultant engaged in lobbying activities for the organization who had formerly been a designated public official (section 12). It is worth noting that while the General Scheme proposed that lobbyists would record the 'subject-matter and purpose of the communications in relation to the specific policy or legislative issues or areas of public administration of interest to the lobbyist, including the name of the Bill or other identifier of the legislation, on which lobbying has taken place' (DPER, 2013: 17), the Act now asks for only 'the subject matter of those communications and the results they were intended to secure' (section 12). This will allow lobbyists to submit much less precise information;

- The Standards in Public Office Commission 'may' produce a Code of Conduct 'with a view to promoting high professional standards and good practice'. If it chooses to do so, registered lobbyists 'shall have regard' to the code (section 16). Again, this is a substantial regression from the intent of the General Scheme which referred to 'a statutory code of conduct', and would have required lobbyists to 'comply with the code' (DPER, 2013: 35);

- Similarly, the Commission 'may issue guidance about the operation of this Act' and 'may make available information with a view to promoting awareness and understanding of this Act' (section 17). Very troublingly, the Bill places significantly less emphasis on the importance of education and advice than was originally set out in the General Scheme, which stated that the registrar 'shall' (DPER, 2013: 36) undertake information programs to assist public understanding of the system;

- Several offences are created by the Act, including failing to register as a lobbyist; failing to make a complete return in time, providing any information to the Commission which is 'known to be inaccurate or misleading', and obstructing an investigation undertaken by the Commission (section 18);

- Those who have formerly worked in the public service as a designated public official require the permission of the Commission if they wish to undertake lobbying activities or advise lobbyists for a period of 12 months (section 22); and

- The Commission must publish an annual report on the operation of the Act (section 25). In addition, the Minister of Public Expenditure and Reform is to review the operation of the Act after the first year and thereafter every three years (section 2).

The Register of Lobbying was launched on May 1, 2015 (available at www.lobbying.ie), with the Act coming into force on September 1, 2015, and the first returns being submitted by January 21, 2016. In April 2015, Sherry Perreault was appointed as Head of Lobbying Regulation at the Standards in Public Office Commission, having previously served as director of policy, research, and communications at the Office of the Conflict of Interest and Ethics Commissioner in Canada.

DRAWING LESSONS FROM UK AND IRISH LOBBYING REFORM

It is important to note that in comparative perspective both the UK and Ireland are relatively progressive since, unlike most nations, they now have some form of lobbying register. To that extent, they deserve some credit. However, once we probe a little beyond that basic fact, it becomes apparent that their respective models are not terribly rigorous. They each offer a number of fundamental areas from which other countries considering lobbying reform in the future can learn crucial lessons.

Is Registration Necessary and Proportionate?

Frankly, this is such a fundamental question that it ought always to be answered affirmatively. There is no nation in which public confidence in politics would not be improved by having a lobbying register. No state's policymaking process, institutional framework, or political culture are immune to the benefits which greater lobbying transparency can confer. It is generally the case that abuses come to light through investigative journalism rather than through publicly available information. This adds to the sense that lobbying is a secretive, almost furtive, activity. The UK government has recognized that this lack of transparency in itself presents a problem which registration could address: 'where lobbying is opaque, this creates a market failure caused by imperfect information that can undermine public confidence in the decision making process and its results' (Cabinet Office, 2012b: 1). The integrity – and the perceived integrity – of the policymaking process is such an existential component of the democratic system that lobbying registration should by now be regarded as essential.

Moreover, simple registration of lobbying activity is absolutely proportionate. The basic information which registration makes publicly available is not onerous for interest organizations to provide. They presumably already hold the records of their lobbying activities and expenditure in the normal course of their internal operation and accounting. This point was highlighted to the PASC inquiry in the UK by Owen Espley of Friends of the Earth: 'If I am about to employ a public affairs consultancy, they are going to send me a bill every now and then and I hope they will tell me what issues they have been working on and what work they have been doing for me. They have that information available' (PASC, 2009b: 111). The same is true of all companies, charities, trade unions, and so on, which already internally monitor their own lobbying efforts.

Should Registration be Voluntary or Statutory?

This too is a question which should scarcely need to be asked any longer. In the UK, the PASC thoroughly dismissed the idea of a voluntary register on the grounds that

anything short of full coverage would result in 'uneven and partial information of no real benefit to those wishing to assess the scale and nature of lobbying activity' (PASC, 2009a: 52). Those associations which represent lobbyists can certainly play an active and useful role in defending and explaining the industry's societal utility. But developing voluntary systems of self-regulation is not a productive element of that agenda – even though the principles which tend to underpin self-regulation (that no financial relationship exists between the lobbyist and the lobbied, that lobbying is done transparently, and that lobbyists are accurate and honest) are in themselves good.

The simple truth is that the only way to compel all lobbyists to meet appropriate standards of openness and behavior is to give statutory force to a registration system. Pross asserts (2007: 33) that the effectiveness of any lobbying register depends

> on a level of enforcement that can only be achieved at the governmental level. Only government has the authority to require lobbyists to divulge information. Only government can require officials to report the failure of lobbyists to comply with the rules. Only government can investigate such failures and prosecute breaches of the rules. Only government can impose sanctions such as the denial of access.

I know of no empirical evidence which indicates that the voluntary self-regulation of lobbyists in any country has proved a success. Indeed, it is difficult to imagine what positive evidence is possible if judged against the standards of universal coverage of all lobbyists, of the enforcement of ethical conduct, or of transparency about which policymakers are being lobbied by which organizations in respect of which policy decisions. Self-regulation is inevitably problematic – it applies only to those practitioners who adopt it, it is essentially toothless, and it creates little new information accessible by the public. Human nature being what it is, the reality remains that those lobbyists most likely to choose to adopt a self-regulatory framework are those least likely to transgress.

Should Registration be Partial or Comprehensive?

It is at this point that the UK and Irish reforms begin to diverge. If the experience of lobbying regulation in other nations has any lessons, the first of these is surely that all lobbyists must be subject to the same registration requirements. In the US, the 1946 Regulation of Lobbying Act established that those whose 'principal purpose' was to influence legislation were required to register. The obvious weakness here was that most lobbyists simply decided that lobbying was not their principal purpose but merely secondary to whatever other services they provided, and as a result only perhaps one quarter of all lobbyists chose to register.

It is vital, in my view, that any registration scheme covers all 'paid lobbyists' rather than merely 'paid consultants'. The UK's Transparency of Lobbying, Non-Party Campaigning and Trade Union Administration Act (2014) is fundamentally flawed by the government's arbitrary belief that some lobbying (by commercial consultants) is 'bad' and requires registration, while other lobbying (by firms and civil-society groups) is 'good' and need not be at all transparent. Lobbying is a significant component of the UK politics industry, although its exact size can only be estimated. In February 2015, the 80 firms that were APPC members employed 1,444 registered consultants between them. It is generally believed that the APPC accounts for around 80 per cent of all lobbyists-for-hire, which suggests a total of something like 1,800 consultant lobbyists. Most observers further accept that the ratio of consultants to in-house lobbyists (working in companies, charities, trade unions, trade associations, law firms, and so on) is about 1:4, so that there are likely to be in the region of 7,200 professional lobbyists in the UK. Most of these will not appear on the UK's register of lobbyists. By contrast, the Irish Regulation of Lobbying Act (2015) covers all sectors of the lobbying industry.

How Should 'Lobbying' and 'Lobbyist' be Defined?

What particular activities should be regarded as constituting 'lobbying' and thus subject to registration? There is scope for a legitimate and honest debate around this point, and as Greenwood and Thomas (1998: 489) note: 'Many legislative attempts to regulate lobbying have foundered on definitional terms'. Analyzing a range of definitions used in various jurisdictions, Pross (2007: 15) notes that definitions are the foundation of a regulatory regime, and must be 'clear and unambiguous ... and robust enough to support legal challenges'. One clear lesson to be learned from the experience of the original European Transparency Initiative (ETI) derives from the evident mismatch between an academic analysis on the one hand showing that system almost at the bottom of a 'league table' of worldwide regulatory regimes in terms of its severity or rigor (Chari et al., 2010) and on the other hand the experiences of many Brussels lobbyists who genuinely struggled to know how best to register. Both perspectives are correct: ETI was relatively lax given that it was voluntary and associated with only weak incentives to register, but the fact that the European Commission chose to leave it up to practitioners to decide what information to register meant that lobbyists in Brussels had to arrive at their own methodologies for determining what to count and not count. Notably, the revised European Transparency Register included more detailed guidance for registrants on how to calculate the financial information on their filings. Perhaps, even if it is counter-intuitive, the more tightly defined a registration regime is, the easier in practice it is for lobbyists to comply with.

Most lobbyists work in-house rather than in consultancies; most do not have the word 'lobbyist' in their job title; many will have other functions in addition to lobbying. Many people will spend only a small fraction of their time on lobbying activities, yet their interventions could be crucial to the outcome of a policy decision. In my view, the most crucial issue is to arrive at an explicit statement of what constitutes 'lobbying' – once that is established, then all those who undertake 'lobbying' on a professional basis can be regarded as 'lobbyists'.

Some jurisdictions have found it problematic when they base lobbying regulation on the concept of 'attempting to influence policy'. Such a formulation is too vague to capture in legislation, and thus it is preferable to base a statutory definition instead on the concept of 'communicating in respect of policy'. Both the UK and Irish legislation adopted this approach. Perhaps the most useful and stimulating work yet written on lobbying, in my view, was Lester Milbrath's 1963 study of Washington lobbyists. In that book Milbrath offered the first systematic interpretation of lobbying as a form of political communication: 'lobbying is the stimulation and transmission of a communication, by someone other than a citizen acting on his own behalf, directed to a governmental decision-maker, with the hope of influencing his decision' (Milbrath, 1963: 8). He went on to argue that:

> all officials arrive at decisions on the basis of what they perceive and not on the basis of what is objectively true or not. The only way to influence a decision, then, is to influence the perceptions of official decision-makers. Communication is the only means of influencing or changing a perception; the lobbying process, therefore, is totally a communication process. (Milbrath, 1963: 184–5)

However, 'lobbying' can, and should, be defined as encompassing more than just the direct communication between a lobbyist and a policymaker, in two respects: (1) the whole range of preparatory work which all lobbyists undertake prior to actual direct communication; and (2) the management of indirect communication, or grassroots lobbying campaigns.

First, one of the clichés of lobbying – but no less valid for that – is that every hour of direct contact first requires 10 hours of background research. For instance, the APPC's

original Memorandum of Association states that professional political consultancy is 'the provision of consultancy services (meaning *advice, representation, research, monitoring or administrative assistance*) predominantly related to [government institutions] for third parties for commercial gain' [emphasis added]; of the five activities listed here, four go beyond direct representation which seeks to influence policy (APPC, 1994: 1). But the APPC then told the PASC committee that activities such as 'monitoring and providing intelligence about the political process, and advising about messaging and positioning in the media as well as for public affairs audiences' are indeed a part of 'public affairs' but 'may not be regarded as "lobbying" at all' (PASC, 2009b: 139). A relatively straightforward solution to this semantic confusion would be for the statutory definition of lobbying to include not only direct communication but also those background activities which provide the foundation for communication.

Given that most consultant lobbyists rightly regard their role as being to advise clients on how to contact policymakers themselves, any register based upon direct communication between third-party consultants and policymakers (such as the new UK scheme) might conceivably result in many consultants being able to avoid registration by simply foregoing the relatively small proportion of the work which involves direct representation with policymakers. Something similar has already become an issue in the US, against a context in which registered lobbyists are increasingly criticized and restricted in their activities to the extent that many seek to avoid registering. For instance, a new business model has been developed which is described as a 'non-lobbying entity' – K Street Research is a firm which undertakes the research and preparatory work which lobbyists traditionally need to do themselves to inform their lobbying communications. By subcontracting that work to K Street Research, lobbyists can thus ensure that they spend less than 20 per cent of their time on direct lobbying for a client and so are able to avoid registering (Delaney, 2010).

Second, as noted above, the Irish government originally proposed defining lobbying to include the management and direction of grassroots campaigns – that is, using the mass media or direct mailings to target segments of the public, encouraging them to contact policymakers. However, in its final legislation, the government backed away from this approach. This was unfortunate as incorporating grassroots activity within the statutory definition of lobbying would have been innovative and would have extended the transparency achieved by the register. It is certainly true that other jurisdictions have in the past found it difficult to formulate a workable definition of grassroots lobbying – but it is equally the case that grassroots campaigns are becoming both more common and more controversial in many nations. This is an issue which other states could usefully consider as they develop their own registration schemes in the future.

What Information Should be Registered?

Any lobbying register should be framed in such a way as to require only that information which can be provided with relative ease and only that which is 'of genuine potential value to the general public, to others who might wish to lobby government, and to decision makers' (PASC, 2009a: 52). In my view, the information which should certainly be disclosed would include:

- The individual lobbyist's name and address and those of the client or employer on whose behalf lobbying was undertaken.
- The public bodies which were lobbied: the names of all policymakers with whom a lobbyist communicated should be disclosed in the interests of helping to hold the Government to account. On a particularly busy and meeting-heavy day, the typical lobbyist might perhaps have direct contact with a handful of policymakers.

Recording that information daily would be the work of a couple of minutes. Those lobbyists who file an annual return of the activities may indeed find it burdensome, but all could comfortably set aside five minutes each day to keep their returns up-to-date.

- The issue which was lobbied on: lobbyists should record as precisely as possible the specific issue being lobbied on (such as identifying the particular Bill or regulation) rather than simply a broad policy area. Just as consultancies have multiple clients, so many firms, charities, and other organizations have multiple issues on which they lobby. Transparency requires that we know as precisely as possible the subject matter being lobbied on.
- Any public offices previously or currently held by each individual lobbyist.
- Details of any public funding received by the organization being lobbied on behalf of.

Currently, some of the lobbying registers in operation around the world require that lobbyists give financial information; others do not. Neither of the new UK or Irish registers include financial details. My own view is that some indication of fee income or lobbying expenditure would be useful in the interests of transparency. However, an excessive focus on financial issues can encourage a (generally unfounded) public attitude that influence over public policy equates to money. Most informed observers accept that lobbying effectiveness is much more directly related to expertise, contacts, and skills than to budgetary outlay. That said, financial disclosure has on occasion been crucial in identifying wrongdoing. The most infamous modern Washington lobbyist, Jack Abramoff, first came to the attention of congressional committees and prosecutors as a result of media exposure of the client fees he was obliged to register (Schmidt, 2004).

Financial disclosure is an area which obviously needs to be treated with some caution. As noted above, the original European Transparency Initiative in Brussels gave insufficient guidelines on precisely what activities were to be registered, and thus it became very difficult for organizations to know what to count and what not to count. Unless every registrant is able to use a single, clear method of calculation, then the registered information does not enable observers to make safe assumptions about an organization's lobbying activity or to compare the level of activity across a range of organizations. Registration risks becoming meaningless – or worse, misleading – unless it provides a fair representation of who does what and with what resources. On the other hand, it cannot credibly be argued that financial disclosure would hinder the competitive development of the lobbying market – we need only look to the US to see that lobbying organizations are perfectly able to supply financial information without undermining the industry. For a registration scheme to operate with no reference whatever to financial issues ensures that critics will continue to be dissatisfied with the extent of transparency and accountability it provides. Unhelpful, and frankly inaccurate, myths about lobbying can develop when what appears to most people to be relevant information is not available. A total lack of financial disclosure could therefore hinder the industry in the future as it seeks to engage more positively with public opinion and to build a reputation for openness and accountability. It may therefore be appropriate for future lobbying registers to oblige lobbyists to provide good-faith estimates (perhaps to the nearest £20,000 or local equivalent) of either lobbying income or lobbying expenditure – with expenditure defined as direct costs only (such as salaries, expenses, events, materials), not more indirect costs (such as the proportion of an organization's office rent which is attributed to their lobbying staff).

The Irish Regulation of Lobbying Act (2015) includes several exemptions, or circumstances in which lobbyists are not required to register direct communication with policymakers. One in particular is likely to prove controversial. Lobbyists are not required to register direct communication with policymakers if they are 'providing factual information in response to a request

for the information' (section 5). This distinction, in my view, is almost wholly without foundation. Almost all information in the policymaking arena is capable of being used to advocate for a particular policy decision. To take a straightforward example, the number of people who die each year in road accidents is in itself an objective measure of fact. However, the number of lobbying communications which provide that information and *only* that information are relatively few. Most lobbyists in that area would provide the number and draw from it a subjective opinion as to whether the level of fatalities could be attributed to poor design and manufacturing by car companies, speed limits set too high, dangerous road construction, drink driving, excessive speeds by young male drivers, inadequate roadside signage or lighting, inadequate car-safety inspections, or any one of a host of other contributory factors – each of which would, if accepted by policymakers, point towards a different public policy solution. No material provided by a lobbyist can be regarded as wholly or solely factual as it is part of their overriding narrative designed to influence public policy. This is an ambiguity which will inevitably cause difficulties for the Irish regulator in the future. Granting to lobbyists the ability to decide for themselves that any communication is 'strictly factual' creates a loophole which will be gradually and surreptitiously widened over time.

Is Registration Adequate or is Regulation Necessary?

Lobbying registration is always better than non-registration, but can never be a complete and final policy solution in itself. The UK government, in its original consultation paper, asserted that the setting of ethical standards is 'a matter for the industry itself, not for the operator of the register' (Cabinet Office, 2012a: 15). This perspective ignores entirely the reality that while a register can be useful in terms of ensuring that uniform levels of transparency can be applied to all lobbyists across the whole industry (and the new UK system does not even achieve that much), it is in no way a substitute for the enforcement of a uniform set of ethical standards across the industry. That requires a more comprehensive and rigorous system of regulation than can be achieved through a register. I would strongly urge future governments in other nations to consider giving a lobbying registrar additional powers to set fundamental rules and guidelines concerning what lobbyists may legitimately do and what they may not do. Most lobbying registers around the world are supplemented either by legislation of this nature or by a code of conduct. For the UK to establish a register but fail to provide for a regulatory framework at the same time represented a missed opportunity which will inevitably have to be returned to at a later date. As Mark Ramsdale put it in his written evidence to the Political and Constitutional Reform Committee inquiry, a register 'is of little use without a regulatory framework, adherence to codes of practice, and appropriate sanction regime' (PCRC, 2012a: 143).

The new UK registration model does not provide for a mandatory code of conduct, while the Irish system allows for one to be developed in the future (but does not require that this actually happens). Still, the Irish framework at least offers the potential for the system to move towards regulation at some point. It is important that any nation's code of conduct is directed towards the general public as much as it is towards the lobbying industry. For instance, under the APPC's Code of Conduct, lobbyists must disclose to policymakers the identity of their client, but there is no mechanism by which the public is entitled or enabled to learn specifically who is lobbying whom on whose behalf over which policy issues: the Code treats ethical lobbying standards solely as an internal matter for the industry. It is unfortunate that the UK government appears to accept this perspective – the Cabinet Office has detailed

'non-monetised benefits by "main affected groups"' (Cabinet Office, 2012b: 3) but includes in these groups only government institutions and lobbyists, entirely ignoring the possibility that the registration of lobbyists may benefit ordinary citizens. In fact, a rigorous code of conduct is essential both for the creation of a level playing field for lobbyists, and (no less importantly) for public confidence in the policymaking process.

Future lobbying reform in other nations should grant wide-ranging power to the registrar to modify and update the rules concerning the practice of lobbying in as flexible a manner as possible. No regulatory model is perfect, and some lobbyists will certainly seek to identify any possible loopholes. The registrar needs to be able to close these quickly and to learn from the evolving lessons of his or her counterparts in other jurisdictions. What the loopholes in any country's legislation will prove to be is almost impossible to predict, but there will inevitably be loopholes, and the registrar must be in a position to respond to them. For instance, in 2010 lobbyists in Texas began to avoid lengthy queues to enter the state Capitol by applying for firearms permits so that they could then make use of a separate entrance (Ward, 2010). That will not be an issue in most nations, but the underlying point remains that some lobbyists are adept at finding new ways around existing rules.

Fundamentally, lobbying registration can introduce welcome light and transparency to an opaque process, but only regulation can insist upon standards of ethical behavior by lobbyists.

CONCLUSION

The UK and Irish governments have recently chosen to introduce lobbying registers. Although each of these new systems has a range of significant flaws, they will at least introduce some measure of transparency. In Ireland, it is possible that some basic regulation of the industry can be developed through a code of conduct. Most lobbyists in every developed democracy operate entirely appropriately. That, though, is not a compelling argument against external regulation. Only through regulation can society set out the standards of ethical behavior which all lobbyists must adhere to. Indeed, regulation can bring positive benefits to the industry. It allows lobbyists to demonstrate their commitment to the integrity of the policymaking process, to begin to educate the public about the legitimate role of interest articulation, and, by exposing occasional wrongdoing by a few lobbyists, allows the vast majority of the industry to operate in the open. As one academic notes, 'The absence of a comprehensive system of regulation may lead to suspicions that abuses are more frequent than they actually are, discrediting not only consultants, but also the whole political process' (Grant, 1993: 103).

Lobbying regulation has a purpose which goes beyond ensuring that lobbyists behave properly: lobbying is a fundamental activity in any democracy to the point where it is difficult to conceive of how a democracy might be possible in the absence of lobbying. How, though, can we judge if an organization's lobbying activity was appropriate unless we know first of all what contacts it had with policymakers and the content of those contacts? Only by seeing which organizations have access to policymakers can we judge whether government is weighing competing policy preferences equitably. And only by knowing that all lobbyists are subject to a common set of ethical standards can we be satisfied that policy influence does not become undue policy influence.

As governments around the world begin to consider introducing lobbying registers, they should consider the lessons to be learnt from those nations which have already undertaken reform. First among these is that while registration can deliver greater transparency of the lobbying industry, more stringent regulation

is necessary to achieve genuine accountability for public policymaking.

REFERENCES

APPC (1994) *Memorandum of Association*. London: Association of Professional Political Consultants.

APPC (2013) 'Lobbying Transparency Bill – "It Would be Difficult to Produce a Worse Bill"', August 29. London: Association of Professional Political Consultants. Retrieved from http://www.appc.org.uk/lobbying-transparency-bill-it-would-be-difficult-to-produce-a-worse-bill/ (accessed August 25, 2016).

Cabinet Office (2012a) *Introducing a Statutory Register of Lobbyists: Consultation Paper*, Cm 8233. London: The Stationery Office. Retrieved from https://www.gov.uk/government/uploads/system/uploads/attachment_data/file/78896/IntroduIntr_statutory_register_of_lobbyists.pdf (accessed August 25, 2016).

Cabinet Office (2012b) *Proposals to Introduce a Statutory Register of Lobbyists: Impact Assessment*. London: Cabinet Office. Retrieved from https://www.gov.uk/government/uploads/system/uploads/attachment_data/file/78897/SRL_Impact_Assessment.pdf (accessed August 25, 2016).

Chari, R., Hogan, J. and Murphy, G. (2010) *Regulating Lobbying: A Global Comparison*. Manchester: Manchester University Press.

Cohen-Eliya, M. and Hammer, Y. (2011) 'Nontransparent Lobbying as a Democratic Failure', *William & Mary Policy Review*, 2(2): 265–87.

ComRes (2005) 'Parliamentary Panel Survey – November 2005'. Retrieved from http://www.comres.co.uk/wp-content/themes/comres/poll/Attitudes_towards_Loyybists.pdf (accessed August 25, 2016).

Delaney, A. (2010) 'Lobbying's New Frontier: "Not lobbying"', *Huffington Post*, January 6. Retrieved from http://www.huffingtonpost.com/2010/01/06/lobbyings-new-frontier-no_n_411639.html (accessed August 25, 2016).

Dods (2007) 'Dods/ICM Parliamentary Panel Survey – October–November 2007'.

DPER (2013) *General Scheme of the Regulation of Lobbying Bill 2013*. Dublin: Department of Public Expenditure and Reform. Retrieved from http://per.gov.ie/wp-content/uploads/General-Scheme-of-the-Regulation-of-Lobbying-Bill.pdf (accessed August 25, 2016).

Grant, W. (1993) *Business and Politics in Britain*. Second edition. Basingstoke: Macmillan.

Greenwood, J. and Thomas, C.S. (1998) 'Introduction: Regulating Lobbying in the Western World', *Parliamentary Affairs*, 51(4): 487–99.

Holman, C. and Luneburg, W. (2012) 'Lobbying and Transparency: A Comparative Analysis of Regulatory Reform', *Interest Groups & Advocacy*, 1(1): 75–104.

McGrath, C. (forthcoming) 'United Kingdom', in Bitonti, A. and Harris, P. (eds.) *Lobbying in Europe*. London: Palgrave Macmillan.

McGrath, C. (2011) 'Lobbying in Ireland: A Reform Agenda', *Journal of Public Affairs*, 11(2): 127–34.

McGrath, C. (2010) 'Lobbying Regulation: An Irish Solution to a Universal Problem?', in Hogan, J., Donnelly, P.F. and O'Rourke, B.K. (eds.) *Irish Business and Society: Governing, Participating & Transforming in the 21st Century*. Dublin: Gill and Macmillan; pp. 215–34.

McGrath, C. (2009a) 'Access, Influence and Accountability: Regulating Lobbying in the UK', in McGrath, C. (ed.) *Interest Groups and Lobbying in Europe*. Lewiston, NY: Edwin Mellen Press; pp. 53–123.

McGrath, C. (2009b) 'The Lobbyist with "Balls of Iron and a Spine of Steel": Why Ireland Needs Lobbying Reform', *Journal of Public Affairs*, 9(4): 256–71.

Milbrath, L.W. (1963) *The Washington Lobbyists*. Chicago, IL: Rand McNally.

PASC (2009a) *Lobbying: Access and Influence in Whitehall – Volume I Report*, HC 36-I. London: The Stationery Office. Retrieved from http://www.publications.parliament.uk/pa/cm200809/cmselect/cmpubadm/36/36i.pdf (accessed August 25, 2016).

PASC (2009b) *Lobbying: Access and Influence in Whitehall – Volume II Oral and Written Evidence*, HC 36-II. London: The Stationery Office. Retrieved from http://www.publications.parliament.uk/pa/cm200809/cmselect/cmpubadm/36/36ii.pdf (accessed August 25, 2016).

PCRC (2012a) *Introducing a Statutory Register of Lobbyists – Volume I Report*, HC 163-I. London: The Stationery Office. Retrieved from http://www.publications.parliament.uk/pa/cm201213/cmselect/cmpolcon/153/153.pdf (accessed August 25, 2016).

PCRC (2012b) *Introducing a Statutory Register of Lobbyists – Volume II Additional Written Evidence*, HC 163-II. London: The Stationery Office. Retrieved from http://www.publications.parliament.uk/pa/cm201213/cmselect/cmpolcon/153/153vw.pdf (accessed August 25, 2016).

PRII (2012) 'Response to Department of Public Expenditure & Reform's Public Consultation on the Regulation of Lobbyists'. Dublin: Public Relations Institute of Ireland. Retrieved from www.per.gov.ie/wp-content/uploads/Public-Relations-Institute-of-Ireland.pdf (accessed August 25, 2016).

Pross, A.P. (2007) *Lobbying: Models for Regulation*, GOV/PGC/ETH(2007)4. Paris: Organisation for Economic Co-operation and Development. Retrieved from http://www.oecd.org/officialdocuments/publicdisplaydocumentpdf/?cote=GOV/PGC/ETH(2007)4&docLanguage=En (accessed August 25, 2016).

Regulation of Lobbying Act (2015) Dublin: The Stationery Office.

Rush, M. (1994) 'Registering the Lobbyists: Lessons from Canada', *Political Studies*, 42(4): 630–45.

Schmidt, S. (2004) 'A Jackpot from Indian Gaming Tribes', *Washington Post*, February 22. Retrieved from http://www.washingtonpost.com/wp-dyn/content/article/2006/03/06/AR2006030600702.html (accessed August 25, 2016).

Transparency of Lobbying, Non-Party Campaigning and Trade Union Administration Act (2014). London: The Stationery Office. Retrieved from http://www.legislation.gov.uk/ukpga/2014/4/pdfs/ukpga_20140004_en.pdf (accessed August 25, 2016).

Ward, M. (2010) 'Lobbyists Getting Gun Permits to Speed Access to Capitol', *Austin American-Statesman*, June 1. Retrieved from http://www.statesman.com/news/texas-politics/lobbyists-getting-gun-permits-to-speed-access-to-721535.html (accessed August 25, 2016).

Wright, O. (2012) 'Lobbying Official Turned Down Reform Meetings', *The Independent*, January 30. Retrieved from http://www.independent.co.uk/news/uk/politics/lobbying-official-turned-down-reform-meetings-6296562.html? (accessed August 25, 2016).

35

Public Affairs and National Level Lobbying in Japan: Winners and Losers in the Continuing Issue of the American Bases on Okinawa

Koji Haraguchi and Ronald J. Hrebenar

The study of public affairs and lobbying in Japan is nowhere near as widely researched as in the United States or the European Union. Politics in Japan, in general, is often viewed in one of two very different models: the Japan 'just like us' model and the 'revisionist' model. The latter argues that while Japan may look like 'us' in terms of politics, it is really very different and very difficult for non-Japanese to understand. The former notes that in terms of political institutions the Japanese have a parliamentary system that appears to be built on the Westminster model, with a prime minister, cabinet, and a parliament with two chambers (the House of Representatives and the House of Councillors) that is elected by a mix of single-member districts and proportional representation. There are multiple parties representing a relatively wide range of political views and interests, a large and well-educated electorate (with a new minimum voting age of 18), and a relatively high voter-turnout rate in national elections. Japan also has a huge and popular mass media that is largely free from government censorship. Finally, it has learned modern democratic politics in the past 70 years from its long-time tutor, the United States and thus one would expect to find a pattern of professional public affairs and lobbying at the national level similar to that found in other modern democratic Western nations. However, one must understand that interest representation in Japan is very different from that in the West; it truly is a Japanese style of public affairs. To make a comparison, the Japanese have had the American game of baseball for a century, but those Americans who come to Japan to play baseball for a Japanese professional team such as the Yomiuri Giants or the Hiroshima Carp quickly learn that they're playing a Japanese-style game, not an American-style game. The lobbying game is similar (*Business Week* 1991).

Japan is a very interesting case regarding the nature of its public affairs and lobbying systems (Campbell 1989; Campbell and Scheiner 2008). It was the first Asian nation to modernize, beginning in the 1860s. It was one of two Asian nations never to be colonialized (Thailand was the other one). It was the first parliamentary democracy in Asia (1890) and learned American democracy from nearly a decade of American occupation following World War Two.

Japan has the world's third biggest economy and perhaps one of the top five most powerful militaries. It also has the most developed interest-group system in Asia, but its system of public affairs and lobbying is quite different from those found in other Western, developed nations. There are many reasons why Japan's public affairs are different, but many of them are rooted in the deepseated cultural and social traditions of the people of Japan and how these continue to impact the business of lobbying and government policy making.

It has been argued that Japan's interest-group and lobbying system is a form of *corporatism* similar to but also different from those found in European nations such as Austria, Germany, and some of the Scandinavian states. Japan has also often been described as a political system having three legs of power and influence: bureaucracy, political parties, and interest groups, especially 'Big Business' and agriculture. The conventional knowledge of who has public policy power and influence in Japan has focused on the bureaucracy for much of the post-war years. Japan's governmental bureaucracy has been seen as so powerful in the policy game in Tokyo – perhaps it is similar to the role played by the elite bureaucracy in Paris. In the 1990s, the elite national bureaucracy was considered to be the element cementing the ruling Liberal Democratic Party (LDP) and major interest groups (Hrebenar and Nakamura, 1993).

Recently, revisionists have argued that changes in the Japanese political institutional system have made politicians of the ruling party much more important in the political process. When the opposition party, the Democratic Party (DPJ), took control of the national government in December 2009, its prime minister and his successors made a strong point of saying that they would act to sharply reduce the influence of the bureaucracy in Tokyo's policy-making process. A cold war ensued between the DPJ leadership and top bureaucrats in the national government. The three years (2009–12) for which the DPJ held power are now viewed as a time of DPJ failure – partly as a result of its ill thought-out war with the bureaucracy. The bureaucracy won. We will return to this story later in our case study of the US bases on Okinawa.

This chapter will survey the broad patterns of lobbying and public affairs in Japan. Each of the major-interest sectors will be discussed as well as the major institutional public-policy decision makers in the government, in terms of how these institutions interact with various interests. Since Japanese interest-group lobbying is quite different from that found in other Western countries, the common forms of contemporary Japanese lobbying will also be presented.

THE MAJOR INSTITUTIONS OF JAPANESE NATIONAL GOVERNMENT

Japan's contemporary national-level institutions date back to the early post-World War Two era, when the Americans 'helped' Japanese political leaders to write the Constitution of 1948 that significantly revised the autocratic, pre-war constitutional framework. The new institutions democratized Japanese government – giving the vote to male and female Japanese citizens over 20 – and provided for a popularly elected parliament and a prime minister–cabinet structure somewhat similar to the Westminster model. The new Constitution also established an independent judiciary and a long list of rights to be guaranteed. But in one important aspect the old system was continued. The Americans decided to keep the essence of the pre-war Japanese bureaucracy to help them administer Japan during the occupation. Thus, Japan's new national-level government started the post-war era being guided not by Japan's purged politicians but by the highly educated and politically ambitious elite bureaucrats. Japan's business world was dismantled by the Americans and thus at the beginning of the new world of democratic government only the bureaucracy could wield power over policy making while dealing with the American occupiers.

A second reason why the bureaucrats moved into political power lay in the fragile nature of the immediate post-war political party system. In the pre-1955 period, there were many parties competing in Diet elections – many of them with only a single politician. This chaotic pattern severely undermined the competing power of politicians until the two major parties (LDP and JSP) emerged in 1955, with the former backed by corporate Japan and the latter by organized labor. The LDP then began a record of Diet domination that lasted for almost 70 years except for a couple of years in the 1990s and the more recent 2009–12 period. During its domination, the LDP ruled hand-in-hand with the elite bureaucracy.

In reality, the bureaucracy's greatest advantage lies in its expertise and access to information essential for intelligent policy making. The elite bureaucrats are recruited, as are French bureaucrats, from the nation's elite universities, such as Tokyo and Kyoto universities. They are trained from the bottom up and groomed to be policy 'advisors' to their political masters in the Diet. But, in reality, the political cabinet ministers are usually administrative and policy amateurs and stay in their posts for a year or less. In the Diet debate sessions, the ministers usually let senior bureaucrats answer difficult questions from the opposition. Only recently has Japan acquired a set of NGOs and think tanks

capable of generating independent sources of information and opinion. Consequently, one important generalization about policy making in the Japanese Diet is that most, if not almost all, of the laws and regulations are written by the bureaucracy in cooperation with the Political Affairs Committee of the LDP.

We should mention the Japanese judiciary, which can be generalized as a very passive and conservative branch of government. While there is a clause in the Japanese Constitution legitimizing judicial review of laws passed by the Diet or lower-level legislatures, the Supreme Court is extremely reluctant to do so. In fact, in 70 years the Supreme Court has overturned only a handful of laws, and several of those were declared unconstitutional, although no significant action was taken to enforce the decisions. The Supreme Court members are appointed by the prime minister and cabinet and thus the conservative LDP has made sure over the decades that the court defers to political leaders and their agendas. While a lower court may get a little out of hand with a more liberal agenda, the Supreme Court can be relied upon to bring a more conservative perspective to the issue. Therefore, lobbying the courts is not a very fruitful activity for Japanese interest groups.

Japan is a unitary state somewhat similar to France, but Tokyo can exercise even more power over the sub-divisions than Paris. The 47 prefectures rely on Tokyo for almost all their revenue and policy direction. It is a classic case of the 'Golden Rule of Politics': 'He who has the gold, makes the rules'. Once in a while, a local mayor or governor may embark upon a course of action contrary to the policy of the national government that causes the overall political system to seize up and malfunction for a period of time. Recently, local level politicians have played major roles in policy discussions on re-starting the nuclear-power stations on the main Japanese islands and the movement of American bases on Okinawa.

THE THREE SETS OF MAJOR ACTORS IN JAPANESE 'PUBLIC AFFAIRS'

As was noted previously, almost every analysis of Japanese interest groups, lobbying, public affairs, or policy making uses the three-legged stool as a metaphor for the triumvirate of powerful actors in the political process. The three legs are the Liberal Democratic Party, the elite Japanese national-level bureaucracy, and the major actors in the Japanese corporate and business community.

The political party system is composed of one major ruling party (LDP), a second, devastated party that ruled recently (DPJ), and a collection of smaller parties that represent a variety of largely conservative and a couple of leftist groups.

These smaller parties come and go and actually have relatively little significance in the system. They include the old Japanese Communist Party (JCP) and the Socialist Party. The latter was once the 'wannabe' second party in the Diet but has declined almost to extinction. The JCP wins fewer than a dozen seats each election but has become more popular recently as an effective protest vehicle against Prime Minister Abe's LDP rule. The smaller conservative parties rise and fall with the fates of their leaders and are often splinters from the LDP. The other party that has some policy significance is the Buddhist party: the Clean Government Party, or the Komeito. While some think of it as a leftist party advocating for social-welfare programs, it is really a moderate conservative party that has been a coalition cabinet partner of the LDP for much of the past twenty years. Its Diet members have not been crucial for controlling the House of Representatives but have been useful in controlling the upper chamber, the House of Councillors.

The LDP symbol is an elephant, which is very appropriate, given that the LDP is huge in Japanese politics (Ishida 1974). One can say that literally everything in Japanese policy making on the national level flows through the LDP. It currently holds a huge majority in the House of Representatives and has won the last three elections quite easily. As mentioned, it has controlled the Diet since 1955, forming every cabinet except for a couple of years in the 1990s and 2009–12. Many of the LDP's Diet members are former bureaucrats or former local- or prefectural-level officials, and that cements the policy-making process with the bureaucracy and the actual managers of Japanese government. The LDP has five or six major factions, and their leaders and their senior lieutenants seem to rotate as prime ministers, party leaders, and cabinet ministers. Factional politics in the LDP is extremely expensive. While Diet political campaigns are theoretically relatively cheap by law, the reality is that LDP election campaigns are unending and very expensive. Where does the money come from? The simple but true answer is largely corporate interests, with additional funds coming from some special interests such as religious groups, agricultural groups, medical interests, and even from more marginal groups.

Historically, the LDP had a largely rural base and strong support from the huge agricultural-interest groups. But the agricultural sector now represents a much smaller part of the Japanese economy, and much of the rural population has moved to urban and suburban homes. The LDP has adapted well to the interests of urban Japan: in the last election it won almost identical vote percentages in urban, suburban, and rural districts. It has become a truly national political party.

The LDP has a policy committee (PARC) that mirrors the ministries of the national government, and each section has close contacts with the interest groups that make policy demands of the government. It acts as a filter to study these groups' demands and coordinate with the party leaders and the bureaucrats. The sub-groups of the PARC also interact closely with the bureaucrats of the related ministries. The circle of influence flows through the LDP and the bureaucracy.

We should mention the other party to form cabinets in recent decades: the DPJ.

It was founded in the 1990s by former members of the LDP and a collection of opposition-party Diet members and candidates. It surged to power in the 2009 House elections based on a popular surge of dissatisfaction with the LDP's lack of success in bringing Japan out of its two decades of recession. Its leadership and senior members were largely inexperienced but wanted to project an image of strong leadership and independence from the elite bureaucracy in contrast to the strong ties of the LDP. As we will see later in this chapter, the role of the DPJ in the American bases on Okinawa was characterized by a series of poor political strategies and decisions. It acquired a reputation for failure in that and other policy areas and was nearly destroyed in the December 2012 House elections and then badly beaten again in December 2014.

THE JAPANESE ELITE BUREAUCRACY

Japan's national bureaucracy traces its history back to the Meiji Revolution of the 1860s and the subsequent need to create a modern, Western-style national government. The Meiji leaders decided to create a system of training schools to staff the national government, and thus several Imperial universities (the most prominent were Tokyo University and Kyoto University) were established. An examination system was created to identify the best and the brightest students from these universities for a rigorous selection process for fast-track bureaucratic positions. Now, 150 years later, the national examinations for college graduates pass only a handful of students each year, and that group is divided among the various ministries and earmarked for the track to top positions. Many of these share students share 'school ties' with LDP politicians and the top corporate leadership. Decision making in the bureaucracy is not a top-down process as found in many foreign systems. Many policy initiatives come to the bureaucracy from key

interest groups or LDP Diet members. The LDP has a comprehensive set of *zoku*, or tribes, of Diet members who identify with a specific policy sector such as rice production. The three-legged stool operates nearly perfectly here: the interest groups, the bureaucratic specialty department or ministry, and the interested members of the LDP. Each ministry is headed by an administrative vice-minister, who is a top-level bureaucrat, and he (almost always a male) works directly with the cabinet minister and several political vice-ministers. The top bureaucrat will have survived a winnowing process over about four decades, gradually working his way up the pyramid. He holds that position for about a year and then retires, and another seasoned veteran takes his place. So, in most policy discussions, a relatively inexperienced but senior LDP politician (and his young political aides) is interacting with a bureaucrat (and his senior aides) who has spent his entire government life learning about the activities and policies of a ministry. One additional feature of the bureaucracy should be noted: the ministries encourage the loaning out of junior bureaucrats to other ministries to broaden their knowledge and personal contacts. This helps in making bureaucratic alliances and in resisting political initiatives from the LDP that the ministry sees as harmful.

THE THIRD LEG: INTEREST GROUPS AND SOCIAL MOVEMENTS

In the introduction to this chapter, we wrote that most studies of Japanese interest-group influence named corporate Japan (or Big Business) as the other possible dominating force. The idea of Japan, Inc. emerged in the 1960s, as a pattern of cooperation was frequently seen among the participants in Japanese policy making: the bureaucrats, the relevant interests, and key LDP politicians. They all seemed to be working together to enhance Japan, Inc. Chalmers Johnson, a prominent Japan analyst, wrote the book *MITI*, which featured the national-level ministry then called MITI (Ministry of International Trade and Industry). MITI seemed to have as its central charge the protection of the Japanese economy and its major actors and the expansion of Japanese exports around the globe. The Ministry of Agriculture had a similar charge, to protect Japan's high-quality but inefficient and expensive fruit and rice farms. This pattern of cooperation among the bureaucracy, interest groups, and political leaders is the essence of Japan, Inc.

When we talk about corporate Japan or Big Business we usually point to the outsize role played by the peak organizations in the corporate world and especially the *Keidanren*, the Japanese Federation of Economic Organizations. At its peak, it had over 100 industrial associations and over a thousand major corporations (Kobayashi 1997). The chair of the Keidanren was considered to be business's ambassador to the government and the political world. Several other business groups represented second-tier or local-level businesses. In addition, there are the giant, corporate *keiretsu* (the post-war manifestation of the pre-war *zaibatsu*) – giant industrial families with names such as Mitsubishi, Mitsui, and Sumitomo as well as families organized around powerful companies such as Toyota and Sony (Curtis 1975). The over-two-decades-long recession Japan has experienced since 1990 reduced the influence of the corporate world in their battles with the bureaucrats and the professional politicians; and in today's Japan, when we ask, 'Who has power?' the business world should be mentioned in terms of specific, more narrow issues. The real, long-term battles are between the politicians and the bureaucrats.

Frank Langdon, writing in the *American Political Science Review* (1961) noted:

> The political activities of the business community in Japan have not received the scholarly attention they deserve. Because of the paucity of information and the lack of serious studies, the nature of the political power of Japanese business is poorly understood. The popular notion that big business is influential in politics is quite correct, but just how the influence is exercised, or how much influence can be brought to bear in a particular field of policy, or what conditions limit or augment business influence is far from clear. (Langdon 1966, 527)

Langdon noted that in the case study he researched, business was unable to prevail over the central government bureaucrats:

> The power of business, potentially very great, is exercised in conventional and institutionalized ways within the context of competing groups, competing ideas, and competing policies. All of these affect the influence it can exert. In the case of central bank reform, business, especially banking, was fully consulted and able to take an active part in the formation of policy. It was not able to prevail. On monetary policy at least, even with finance, industry, and the central bank in agreement, business and its allies could not overcome the position of a powerful ministry. (Langdon 1966, 527)

As in the Asian game of paper, rock and scissors where the paper defeats the rock, but the rock defeats the scissors, the Japanese bureaucracy usually defeats Big Business or, at the very least in Japan's game of politics, coopts Big Business's ideas and demands as its own.

In the corporatist interest-group world of parts of Europe, the other major interest included in systemic decision making is organized labor. This is not true in Japan. Immediately after the war, the Americans encouraged the formation and growth of labor unions, but, as the Cold War heated up, the unions were perceived to be 'leftist'- and even communist-dominated, and, with the Americans' approval, the unions were broken in the late 1940s and early 1950s. A pattern of company unions (such as Toyota or Sony unions) replaced the industry unions and largely came under company control. As one of the authors of this chapter wrote previously, the Japanese interest-group system is one of 'corporatism without labor' (Pemple and Tsunekawa 1979). In later decades, the unions tried to build political power by working closely with an opposition party, such as the Socialists up to the early 1990s and the DPJ from the 1990s to 2012. But the labor-supported parties crashed and burned. Quite simply, there is no balance to corporate political power. One might think that the DPJ, now in opposition, might represent the agenda of today's labor in Japanese politics. After all, the *Domei* Labor Confederation, Japan's largest, was instrumental in the formation of the DPJ; but in recent elections many, if not most, workers voted for the conservative LDP. Labor plays a very passive role in Japanese policy making.

Agriculture continues to be a powerful voice, not only in domestic policy making but also in foreign policy, and especially regarding the Trans-Pacific Trade Agreement's impact on the nation's rice and fruit farmers. More than 6 million farmers and farm families are organized in the farmer cooperatives, or *nokyos*. These have been bedrock foundations for the LDP since the 1950s. The agricultural lobby has been undergoing fundamental changes in membership in recent decades with the depopulation of Japan's rural areas as young members of farm families have moved to the cities for lifestyle and employment reasons. Recently, about two thirds of the membership has been part-time farmers. When the LDP Diet base was more rural, the farmers had a powerful hold on the party, but now that the party's base in recent elections has spread across all types of urban–rural districts, the significance of farm associations has declined in the national policy-making process (George 1981).

Japanese media also play a relatively minor role in the policy-making process. The nation has four big national newspapers – each with millions of subscribers. Several of these newspapers own television networks as well as magazines. Only one of these national newspapers, the *Asahi Shimbun*, could be considered to be 'leftist', representing a constituency that might challenge the ruling LDP party and its agenda. The biggest and most powerful newspaper, the *Yomiuri Shimbun*, also owns the nation's most popular baseball team, the Yomiuri Giants, and is

profoundly conservative and supportive of the LDP. The fact that Japanese media tend to be highly concentrated and, by and large, quite conservative produces sterile political discussions. Japan has an extensive public radio and television network (NHK), which historically had been an independent and sometimes challenging voice but has lately been reined in by the Abe government, which has restructured NHK's Board of Directors so that it supports the government's policies.

There are also some non-traditional interests that occasionally are active in Japanese policy making. One of the curious aspects of interest-group politics in Japan is the frequent inclusion of Japan's organized-crime syndicates as significant actors in the political system. In the United States, for example, one almost never sees references to the various American mafia families as seekers of portions of government budgets, such as construction projects. Japanese organized-crime groups operate in many cases in legitimate business sectors. After the 2011 Tohoku Earthquake tsunami and ensuing nuclear disaster, the media reported the role that construction companies with ties to the *yakuza* world had played in the reconstruction efforts.

When, in 2012, DPJ Prime Minister Noda appointed a party member named Tanaka Keishu as Justice Minister, one of Japan's weekly magazines subsequently reported that Tanaka 'had strong ties to the *yakuza*'. It was also reported, in 2007, that the DPJ had sought and received an endorsement for the next House election from two of the most powerful *yakuza* groups. It may seem incredible for a Justice Minister to be closely identified with powerful organized-crime groups, but that is Japan (*Foreign Policy* 2012).

The LDP too has a long reputation of working closely with the *yakuza*. Some have noted that LDP governments have not pursued the *yakuza* in significant ways. Robert Whiting, for example, notes how one of the founders of the LDP had very close ties to organized crime and remained influential in party matters for years. In Japan, organized crime can be considered an interest group in a manner unlike that found in most modern states.

Japan's *yakuza* have business offices in exclusive neighborhoods and members who hand out business cards just like those of the nation's top corporations. The *yakuza* group that operates in Tokyo has its offices across the street from the Ritz-Carlton. They are viewed as 'almost normal' participants in the 'public affairs game' in Japan.

There are also a number of huge and conservative religious organizations that lobby for conservative social policies. These groups are Buddhist and Shinto, and the latter lobbies to restore Shinto to the national religion that it was prior to World War Two. As mentioned earlier, one of the so-called 'New Religions' is the Sokka Gakkai, a Buddhist group that formed its own political party, the Clean Government Party, or Komeito, which has been in coalition with the LDP for most of the last two decades. It started out as semi-socialist and has moved to being a moderate-to-conservative ally of the LDP's rightist policy preferences (Hrebenar 1992, 1998 and 2001).

Some of the most influential interest groups exist largely below the public's awareness. *Nippon Kaigi* (Japan Conference) has been described as one of Japan's most powerful lobby groups. It is a largely secret right-wing organization with almost 300 local chapters, 38,000 dues-paying members, and a leadership that is deep into the Japanese national elite. Its previous chairman was a former chief justice of the Supreme Court and it has one third of the national Diet as well as half of the Abe cabinet as members. The *Nippon Kaigi* pushes a revisionist political agenda: rebuilding the armed forces, rewriting Japanese history books about World War Two, and restoring the emperor as a religious and political figure. It can generate petitions with millions of signatures in support of its policy preferences. One of its major projects is to hold a referendum on Article 9 of the Constitution, for which Prime Minister Abe secured approval by the House

of Representatives in July 2015. Clearly, this little known group has had a run of recent success (*The Economist* 2015).

LOBBYING STRATEGIES AND TACTICS

Lobbying in Tokyo is very different from lobbying in Washington, D.C., London, or Brussels. There are no hordes of lobbyists waiting outside committee rooms to buttonhole Diet members to vote for their private legislation. There are relatively few attempts to use mass media to manipulate public opinion. There are relatively few opportunities for interest groups to play crucial roles in elite political campaigns, and the rules regarding political money restrict the 'buying' of the support of individual politicians. There is no 'K St' such as that in Washington, D.C., with thousands of professional lobbyists working for many thousands of clients. Like many other activities in Japan, 'public affairs' is usually done behind closed doors by people often having personal ties spanning decades (Yoshito 1999).

There are almost no professional lobbyists or lobbying firms in Japan. Even in Eastern Europe in places such as Vilnius, Lithuania, after the fall of communism, a few lobbying or 'public affairs' firms emerged to offer services close to those of their Western models. These are almost non-existent in Japan. A search of the internet in 2015 found one firm comprised of non-Japanese public-relations professionals that advertises PR services in Tokyo. That firm is Langley Esquire, and its web page claims it is 'Japan's most trusted name in public affairs' with 'over 30 years of experience in Japan's public affairs', including 'government outreach and crisis management'. Its website contains a list of 'victories or accomplishments', but there are no major lobbying victories on it (instead, it includes helping to organize an American president's visit to Japan). The organization's founder is Timothy Langley, an international lawyer with close contacts with several of Japan's top politicians and a former counsel for Apple Japan and General Motors-Asia Pacific. The LE 'team' listed on the website has members with impressive academic credentials, but not one of them is Japanese. Public-affairs representation in Japan is almost exclusively public relations for corporations and individuals, not the powerful forms of lobbying found in Western political systems (Solis 2013).

Very few international corporations have traditional lobbyists working in Tokyo. When AT&T and Motorola established a lobbying presence in Tokyo in 1990, it was big news that these two interests were pursuing a new strategy in Japan.

> Few United States companies maintain full-time lobbyists in Japan. Corporate leaders remain skeptical that lobbying offices can lead to new business there. International Business Machines Corporation has had a government affairs office for many years, but most high-tech firms are represented by a single person from the American Electronics Association. … With far less business in Japan, US firms have fewer allies to enlist in lobbying for greater market access. Moreover, because of the political logjam caused by special interest groups, aggrieved sections of Japanese society like consumers, who might otherwise be allies to US corporations, have little power to press for change. … AT&T has hired Glen Fukushima as director of public affairs for AT&T-Japan. Last December, Mr. Fukushima left the United States Trade Representative's office after nearly five years as a top trade negotiator with Japan, including on electronics and telecommunications issues. … AT&T has maintained the public affairs post in Tokyo for several years, but the appointment of Fukushima, who was one of the few US government officials fluent in Japanese, represents a significant upgrading of the position. Fukushima will also direct AT&T-Japan's business development efforts. (Addison, 1990)

THE AMERICAN CASES ON OKINAWA DISPUTE: A POLICY-MAKING CASE STUDY

The central themes of this chapter regarding Japanese national government policy making

have been an emphasis on the continued power of the elite bureaucrats, the lesser influence of Big Business and interest groups, and the mixed record of success of professional politicians. We have selected one recent case study to highlight how these various actors interacted to impact a crucial policy issue between the United States and Japan.

Following World War Two, there were hundreds of American military bases located all over the Japanese islands. One by one the bases were closed or returned to the Japanese, with the major exception of those located on the southern island of Okinawa. By the twenty-first century, there were 23 major bases in Japan – most were on Okinawa, which has 1 percent of the Japanese population but almost half of the American servicemen stationed in Japan. The American bases occupy approximately 10 percent of the island. The Americans ran the island until 1972, when administration reverted to the Japanese. But, the Americans kept the bases. Japanese activists demanded the closure of the bases, especially after a number of sex crimes were committed by American military personnel. After 15 years of negotiations, the United States and Japan agreed in 2006 to move the Marine Corps airbase at Futenma to a more rural part of the island. In 2012, the United States announced a plan to move some marines from Okinawa to the American island of Guam. Then, in 2013, the Joint Statement of the US–Japan Security Consultative Committee confirmed that the agreements on the realignment of the US forces in Japan would be implemented as previously decided. Ministers from both countries then reaffirmed the commitment.

After the LDP Abe administration reaffirmed its commitment to the relocation of the base on Okinawa, activist demonstrations continued on Okinawa and throughout Japan. In 2015, over 35,000 people across Japan marched in opposition to the bases. Okinawa prefectural governor Onaga Takashi and the mayor of Nago City continued to lead the fight against the relocation of the Marine base, but they have not been able to overcome the policy decisions of the national bureaucracy and the ruling party.

The LDP's nearly complete domination of national politics ended in December 2009, when it lost control of the House of Representatives to the DPJ. DPJ rule lasted for only three years. The three DPJ prime ministers of the 2009–12 era were Hatoyama Yukio, Kan Naoto, and Noda Yoshihiko. The first two had major political and security crises to deal with, and the latter had to try to survive the wreckage he inherited. The Hatoyama cabinet's main headache was the agreement with the Americans regarding base realignments in Okinawa. The Kan administration tried to deal with the Great Tohoku Earthquake, tsunami and Fukushima nuclear-power catastrophe. Finally, the Noda administration couldn't climb out of the hole dug by the first two DPJ prime ministers, the bottoming out of the party's public support by late 2012, and the LDP–Komeito's obstructionism to the DPJ's rule. In December 2012, the LDP under Abe won a dramatic victory in the House elections and established LDP conservative rule once again.

There were several causes that contributed to the collapse of the DPJ in 2012. These include the party's poor leadership, the lack of experience in administration and policy making of many of its Diet members, its internal instability, its failure to deal effectively with the political, security, and disaster challenges, and its inability to devise a strategy to survive politically, given that the Japanese electorate is so loosely attached to all the national-level political parties.

Since it had dominated nearly all Japanese cabinets since 1955, the LDP had lots of Diet members with ministerial and vice-ministerial experience. The DPJ was woefully short on such experience, and even its top leadership's experience was largely based on leading small opposition parties, not running huge bureaucracies as ministers or vice-ministers. One of the constant problems faced

by the three DPJ leaders was the constant undermining of their authority and legitimacy by Ozawa Ichiro, who led the party's largest faction. Often, the loudest voices of opposition to the DPJ prime ministers were heard from Ozawa or his faction's spokesmen. In 2010, Ozawa challenged Hatoyama directly in the party's presidential elections and lost a rather close and divisive battle. Later, Ozawa constantly challenged Kan and his cabinet's policies after the Tohoku earthquake and tsunami and then bolted the party when Noda became prime minister, threatening to reduce DPJ Diet member numbers in the House of Representatives to the point that a successful vote of no-confidence against the cabinet was nearly possible. How can you run a ruling party when your former party president and largest faction is trying to undermine you at every opportunity?

During its days in opposition, the DPJ developed ideas about how government should make policy. Since the LDP had a 50-year 'partnership' with Japan's national bureaucracy, the DPJ decided to take a position of hostility toward the national bureaucracy and demanded that future policy be determined by the elected Diet members and not the unelected bureaucrats (Tatsumi 2013). So when it achieved power, the DPJ tried to sharply reduce the traditional role played by the bureaucrats in Japan's various ministries. One of the traditions during the LDP-dominated decades was the weekly meetings of senior bureaucrats to coordinate the policies they would recommend to the political ministers. Hatoyama ended those coordination meetings. Due to this and other instances of DPJ hostility toward the bureaucrats, the latter appeared to adopt a policy of passivity toward their political masters and allowed them to make one serious mistake after another in the areas of foreign policy, security policy, disaster response, welfare policy, and tax policy. The bureaucrats seemed to decide to wait out the DPJ cabinets until the next scheduled House of Representatives elections in 2012 and the hoped-for return to power of their old partners in the LDP. Hatoyama even decided to undermine his own internal party policy-making deliberation processes. He wanted to differentiate the DPJ from the LDP and concluded that one way was to change the DPJ's major internal organizations so they no longer mirrored those of the LDP. Hatoyama thus eliminated the Policy Affairs Committee that had as its major tasks the deliberation of future policy and the establishment of links to key interests in Japanese society to advise the party on policy. When Noda tried to rebuild the party by reestablishing the PARC it was a case of 'too little-too late'.

By alienating the professional bureaucracy, eliminating the internal policy-making organizations, and not fostering good relations with major Japanese interest groups, the DPJ followed a course that was fraught with lots of political dangers. The DPJ lost public support for its foreign and defense policy by failing to fulfill promises it had made before the 2009 election and by responding to crises poorly (*Japan Times* 2012; Tatsumi 2013). The most visible discrepancy between the DPJ's promises and policy outcomes can be found in its handling of the US Marine Corps Air Station Futenma.

In its 2009 manifesto (party platform), the DPJ promised to develop 'close and equal relations' with the United States, which included 'proposing the Status of Forces Agreement' and 'possible revisions' of the US military bases in Japan (Minshuto 2009). Although the manifesto was not specific enough, it was obvious that the 'possible revisions' included the Futenma Air Station. The DPJ had started a study group on a wide range of policy issues on Okinawa in 1999 and issued research titled 'Okinawa Vision' in July 2008 (Minshuto 2008, 2009). The research proposed that the Japanese government 'should seek an alternative location (for the Futenma Air Station) outside Okinawa. If the strategic environment should change, a location outside Japan should be an option, too' (Minshuto 2008). And July 19, 2009,

at a political rally in Okinawa, Hatoyama, campaigning, as DPJ president, to be prime minister, announced that he would relocate the Futenma Air Station to 'at least outside Okinawa' – 'at least' meaning maybe even outside Japan.

Soon after Hatoyama became prime minister, he restarted the negotiation on the Futenma Air Station with the Obama administration. But unlike the LDP, the DPJ excluded the bureaucrats of the Defense and Foreign Affairs ministries from the policy-making process (Heginbotham et al. 2011). The key bureaucratic positions dealing with military-base issues in the Obama administrations were occupied by some of those who had agreed on the relocation of the Futenma Air Station under the Clinton administrations in the mid 1990s. For example, Assistant Secretary of State Curt Campbell under the Obama administration had been Deputy Assistant Secretary of Defense under the Clinton administration and was 'the point man for US–Japan security issues', according to Ambassador Walter Mondale. Prime Minister Hatoyama tried to persuade the leading expert of the Futenma issue in the US government without much input from foreign and defense bureaucrats in his own government.

By mid April 2010, when Hatoyama visited Washington, D.C., President Obama seemed to be skeptical about the prime minister's promise to find an alternative location outside Okinawa. Reportedly, when Obama questioned the feasibility of meeting the May negotiation deadline, Hatoyama replied 'trust me'. But after a troubled search for an alternative location for the base, on May 4, 2010 Hatoyama admitted that his plan to relocate Futenma Air Station off Okinawa would be difficult. Around the same time, it was reported that the Hatoyama administration would accept the 2006 plan to build an alternative airbase in Henoko, Nago City, Okinawa. Henoko is a much less populated area than Futenma, and the new airbase would be built on the tip of a peninsula, with major parts of the airfield suspended over the sea. Governor Nakaima of Okinawa Prefecture had not been opposed to the plan when the LDP administration agreed it with the Bush administration.

But after the DPJ had taken power, Governor Nakaima started opposing any plan to relocate Futenma Air Station within Okinawa Prefecture. Because of the heightened expectation for possible relocation of the most dangerous US military bases outside Okinawa, Japanese public opinion also sharply turned against Prime Minister Hatoyama. Based on a Fujisankei poll published in late April, 72 percent of respondents thought that 'Hatoyama's approach to the Futenma issue had worsened the US–Japan relationship' (Sankei 2010). The DPJ's handling of the base issue was not only criticized severely by the LDP, but it also created the first major conflict within the governing coalition between the DPJ and the Social Democratic Party (SDP). In late May, SDP President Mizuho Fukushima was fired from her cabinet post as Special Minister of Consumer Protection and Food Safety after she refused to sign the cabinet resolution on the Futenma issue. Ratner and Samuels explain the confusion surrounding the Futenma issue as a result of 'the new political environment' in which 'a small party. ... could alter the dynamics of an important defense issue'. On May 30, the SDP officially left the governing coalition. In addition to the failure in the Futenma issue, Hatayama's leadership was weakened by financial scandal, which affected Secretary General Ozawa, too. Hatoyama announced his resignation on June 2, and Kan Naoto was elected prime minister (Hrebenar and Nakamura 2015; Lipscy and Scheiner 2012).

By November 2012, about a month before Prime Minister Noda dissolved the House of Representatives to hold an election, 78 percent of the respondents to a *Sankei Shimbun* (2012) opinion poll had lost confidence in the DPJ's foreign and defense policy. As prime ministers changed almost every year under the DPJ rule, it was difficult even to start negotiations on and commitments to any important long-term foreign issues.

After the LDP took back power from the DPJ in a landslide victory in the House of Representatives election in 2012, the Abe administration rolled back the DPJ's policy on Futenma. On the floor of the House of Representatives in January 2013, Prime Minister Abe expressed his determination to implement the relocation plan of the airbase. He noted that the base should not be permanently in Futenma, and that the burden that Okinawa Prefecture had shouldered by hosting US military bases should be reduced. He repeated the same points when he met President Obama in February, and the two agreed on speeding up the process of relocating the base. Okinawa public opinion and citizen groups remained strongly opposed to the US base. On November 16, Takeshi Onaga, former mayor of Naha City, was elected Governor of Okinawa Prefecture. During his campaign, Onaga promised that he would not allow the building of a new Marine airbase in Henoko, the alternative location for Futenma agreed upon by the US and Japanese governments. The battle over the bases continues.

In this public-affairs case, the bureaucracy and the LDP have been able to effectively deal with the demands of popular interest groups and movements. However, in the bigger picture, it was the elite bureaucracy working with its preferred political party that dominated the Okinawa base controversy. The post-war pattern in Japanese policy making continues.

REFERENCES

Addison, Paul. 1990. 'US Lobbyists in Japan strive to get foot in the door,' *Globe and Mail* (Canada) May 22.
Business Week, 1991. 'Lobbying European Style: Japan, Inc. Catches On,' June 2.
Solis, Mireya. 2013. 'Business Advocacy in Asian PTAs: A Model of Selective Corporate Lobbying with Evidence from Japan,'

Brookings Institute web page, March 15 (accessed 8 September, 2016).

Campbell, John Creighton. 1989. 'Democracy and Bureaucracy in Japan,' in Ishida Takeshi and Ellis S. Krauses, eds, *Democracy in Japan*. Pittsburgh: University of Pittsburgh Press, pp. 113–37.

Campbell, John Creighton and Ethan Scheiner. 2008. 'Fragmentation and Power: Re-conceptualizing Policy Making under Japan's 1955 System,' *Japanese Journal of Political Science,* 9 (1), 89–113.

Curtis, Gerald. 1975. 'Big Business and Political Influence,' in Ezra Vogel, ed., *Modern Japanese Organizations and Decision Making*. Berkeley: University of California Press, pp. 34–70.

The Economist. 2015. 'Politics in Japan: Right Side Up,' June 5, 33.

Eric, Heginbotham, Ely Ratner and Richard Samuels. 2011. 'Tokyo's Transformation: How Japan is Changing – And what it means for the United States,' *Foreign Affairs*, 1 September, 90 (5), 136–148.

Foreign Policy. 2012. 'The Yakuza Lobby,' December 12.

George, Aurelia. 1981. 'The Japanese Farm Lobby and Agricultural Policy Making,' *Pacific Affairs*, 54 (3), 409–30.

Hrebenar, Ronald, 1992. *The Japanese Party System*, Second Edition. Boulder, Co: Westview.

Hrebenar, Ronald and Akira Nakamura. 1993. 'Japan: Associational Politics in a Group Oriented Society,' in Clive S. Thomas, ed. *First World Interest Groups: A Comparative Perspective,* London: Greenwood Press, pp. 199–216.

Hrebenar, Ronald. 2001. 'Japan: Strong State, Spectator democracy, and Modified Corporatism,' in Clive S. Thomas, ed., *Political Parties and Interest Groups*, Boulder: Lynne Rienner.

Hrebenar, Ronald and Akira Nakamura, eds. 2015. *Party Politics in Japan: Political Chaos and Stalemate in the 21st Century*. London: Routledge.

Ishida, Takeshi. 1974. 'Interest Groups under a Semi-permanent Government Party: The Case of Japan,' *Annals of American Academy of Political and Social Science*, 413 (May), 1–10.

Japan Times. 2012. 'DPJ's Promise to Change the System Failed,' December 1.

Kobayashi, Yoshiaki. 1997. *Gendai Nihon-no Seiji Katei* (Policy-making Process in Japan). Tokyo: University of Tokyo Press.

Langdon, Frank. 1961. 'Big Business Lobbying in Japan: The Case of Central Bank Reform,' *American Political Science Review*, 55 (3), 527–38.

Lipscy, Phillip and Ethan Scheiner. 2012. 'Japan under the DPJ: The Paradox of Political Change without Policy Change,' *Journal of East Asian Studies*, 12, 311–22.

Minshuto. 2008. "Okinawa Bijon" (Okinawa Vision), retrieved from www.dpj.or.jp/news/files/okinawa(2).pdf (accessed 8 September, 2016).

Minshuto. 2009. 'Manifesto,' http://www.dpj.or.jp/global/downloads/manifesto2009.txt.

Pemple, T.J. and Keiichi Tsunekawa. 1979. 'Corporatism with Labor: The Japanese Anomaly,' in Phillippe C. Schmitter and Gerhard Lehmbruch, eds. *Trends Toward Corporatist Intermediation*. Beverly Hills: Sage, pp. 231–270.

Sankei Shimbun. 2012. 'Yoron Chosa,' (public-opinion polls) Retrieved from http://sankei.jp.msn.com/politics/news/121105/stt12110517300011-n1.htm. (accessed 8 September, 2016).

Tatsumi, Yuki. 2013. 'Japan under DPJ Rule,' http://harvard.edu/mobile-might/japan-under-dpj-rule.

Whiting, Robert. 1999. Tokyo Underworld. Pantheon: New York.

Yoshito, Yoshio. 1999. 'Interest Groups' Lobbying Tactics in Japan and the United States: The Influence of Political Structures and Conflict on Tactical Choices,' *Southeastern Political Review*, 27 (2), 243–64.

36

Public–Private Dialogue and Policy Reforms: Lessons from Tanzania

Goodluck Charles

INTRODUCTION

Creating an enabling environment for private-sector development is essential for sustaining long-term economic growth and job creation. It is now widely agreed that the private sector must be the engine of growth, and that governments must create an environment that allows it to flourish. In both academic and policy-related literature, it is emphasized that policies which create a 'level playing field', in which all firms operate on an equal footing, are crucial for economic development. At all levels, private enterprises require an operating environment conducive for growth and development, including, for example, peace and stability, good governance, the absence of corruption, adequate infrastructure and an educated workforce. Accordingly, since the post-independence period, the majority of African countries have transformed their socialist economic models to more private-sector-oriented economies (Sen,

2013; Charles, 2014). On account of structural adjustment in the early 1980s, these states have withdrawn from core areas of economic activity, and the market economy has taken centre stage. Consequently, the role of government has largely been in creating policies, institutions and other conditions, including infrastructure, that collectively improve the general business setting, where enterprises and business activities can start, develop and thrive (Konig et al., 2013). We now depend on business and the government to address a wide variety of critical issues, ranging from protecting the environment, businesses and society to providing public goods. It is therefore critical that we better understand how the government and private sector interact with one another and the role played by their interactions in policy reform.

Designing effective government policies and regulations depends, among other things, on input from and consultation with the private sector. Regular sharing of information between the state and businesses ensures that private-sector objectives are met with public actions and that local-level issues are fed into the higher-level policy-making process. The private-sector can identify constraints, opportunities and possible policy options for creating incentives, lowering investment risks and reducing the cost of doing business. Therefore, as in many other Sub-Saharan African countries, the Tanzanian government has begun to interact with the private sector. A number of national public–private-dialogue (PPD) platforms, including the government's roadmap for improving the investment climate, Big Results Now (BRN), the Tanzania National Business Council (TNBC) and local dialogue, have been created to promote participation of the private sector in policy change. In these platforms, state organs and the private sector work jointly to devise proposals that are expected to inform policy reforms. Accordingly, private-sector organizations (PSOs), with the support of development partners, are actively advocating for an improved business environment and investment climate. Sections, several policy studies which inform the dialogue process are identified and reviewed in later sections.

Although the government is determined to improve the business environment, and PSOs are making efforts to influence the policy-making process, the global ranking of Tanzania by the World Bank and other international organizations indicates that the investment climate in the country is deteriorating. Tanzania has always been ranked between 123 and 145 out of 183 countries surveyed by the World Bank in terms of ease of doing business. The Global Competitiveness Report, which assesses the investment climate and business environment in national economies based on 12 pillars of competitiveness, ranked Tanzania 121 out of 144 countries in 2014 (WEF, 2014). This indicates that the country is less competitive in attracting investment. In addition, a number of local studies consistently indicate that the business environment

in Tanzania is unfavourable for private-sector growth because it is dominated by lack of finance, bureaucratic institutions, corruption, poor infrastructure and the inefficient provision of public goods (Kessy and Temu, 2010; Kinda and Loening, 2010; Cooksey, 2011). Thus, it is still debatable whether the ongoing reforms in Tanzania are effective in terms of supporting and transforming the private sector as fast as expected. Coupled with limited studies on reforms and business–state relations, there is limited understanding of the role being played by the private sector in the ongoing reforms.

One specific issue that remains unexplored is the extent to which PPD and private sector advocacy shape the policy-making process. PPD is an institutional arrangement that brings together a group of public- and private-sector actors (Bannock, 2005). Objectives of PPD include building trust and bridging gaps to laying the foundation for a joint problem analysis and identification of policies and institutional reforms that contribute to a more conducive environment for private sector development. While the government recognizes the existence of PSOs and interacts with the private sector through business associations, the question is whether the government really listens to the private sector and implements the reforms recommended by the business community. Policy research evidence shows that the government of Tanzania has been hesitant to implement the policy actions recommended by the private sector (e.g. Confederation of Tanzania Industries (CTI), 2011; Tanzania Milk Processors' Association (TAMPA), 2010; Charles, 2014). Contrary to the argument that effective interactions between the state and business matter for wealth creation (Kathuria et al., 2010; Sen and te Velde, 2009), interactions between the business community and the state in Tanzania appear to be collusive and rent-extracting (Charles, 2014). Consequently, there is considerable debate on how to conceptualize the ways in which different types of interaction between the state and the private sector influence the conduct of industrial policy to create wealth. Although institutions such as the World Bank encourage increased PPD and private-sector advocacy in the belief that this will assist in providing an enabling environment, and many governments now stress that they are more interested in producing 'evidence-based policy' (Irwin, 2008), there is limited research focusing on how the ongoing PPDs and advocacy projects contribute to pro-private-sector policies and an improved business environment.

Although it has been argued that formalized dialogue and sustained private-sector advocacy can promote economic performance, e.g. through improved allocative efficiency of government spending and better growth and industrial policies (Taylor, 2012), a systematic analysis of how they work and the outcome in terms of implementing reforms, particularly in a developing-country setting, has not been undertaken. Whether or not the strategies used by the private sector to engage with the state are effective is not well understood. Whether promoting PPDs in a country like Tanzania is worthwhile is still questionable. It remains debatable whether devoting additional resources to influencing public policy makes businesses more powerful. Even though there has been some analysis of the nature of state–business relations in Africa (e.g. Mauritius, South Africa, Zambia and Egypt) (e.g. te Velde, 2006; Taylor, 2012) and suggestions that countries with stronger private-sector participation in the policy process will have stronger investment and growth (Harris, 2006), there is insufficient data in Sub-Saharan Africa to validate this argument. In particular, we know surprisingly little about the nature of PPD and advocacy, how effective it is, how it evolves and whether it matters for economic performance in Sub-Saharan Africa.

In view of the above background, this chapter aims to present the lessons learnt and the experience of dialogue and advocacy practices in Tanzania, with a special focus on the role of PPD and advocacy in policy reforms.

Based on the cases of the PSO advocacy projects and the experiences gathered from the dialogue platforms, the chapter assesses the extent to which the private sector participates in dialogue and influences the policy-making process. It identifies various strategies used by PSOs to participate in PPDs and their outcomes. The chapter makes a noteworthy contribution to this book in many ways. First, it explores the Sub-Saharan context, which from a Western perspective is unique in terms of institutional settings. Second, the chapter focuses on an important area of public affairs that shows how the private and public sector relate to each other. It presents some empirical cases demonstrating the experience of and lessons drawn from a specific context. The chapter expands the scope of the research on public affairs and forms the basis for further inclusion of PPD issues in an emerging-economy context.

The remaining part of the chapter is organized as follows. Section 2 presents an overview of the major reforms of the business environment in Tanzania. For the purpose of showing the efforts made by the government to improve the business environment, the section describes the major reform initiatives that were intended to improve the performance of the public sector. Section 3 presents both the theoretical and practical arguments on the role of the private sector in promoting reforms and effective policies. It shows the essence of private-sector participation in PPD. Section 4 describes the existing PPD platforms in Tanzania, representation of the private sector in those platforms and the extent to which the private sector's voice is considered in public-policy reforms. Section 5 presents various empirical cases of advocacy projects implemented by PSOs in Tanzania, emphasizing the lessons learnt and experience gained from those projects. The main goal of this section is to demonstrate the extent to which the private sector participates in PPD initiatives and the extent to which advocacy projects implemented through PSOs work toward promoting reforms and an improved investment climate. Section 6 presents critical reflections on the lessons learnt from PPD practices in Tanzania. Section 7 draws key conclusions and presents the policy implications of the findings presented in this chapter.

BUSINESS ENVIRONMENT REFORMS IN TANZANIA

At independence in 1961, Tanzania was one of the poorest countries in the world. Its government chose a path of 'African Socialism' and 'self-reliance' to bring about national development, whereby almost all productive and service activities were put under the direct control of the state. During that time there was little tolerance for private enterprise, especially that of the indigenous majority. While the policy of socialism led to improvements in social development, especially in primary-education and health services, economic growth stagnated as state-run enterprises became increasingly inefficient and ineffective. The economic downturn in the early 1980s led the government to attempt to liberalize the economy and to depart from state control to a market-driven economy and market-friendly policies. The first phase of the structural-adjustment programme (1986–9) focused on macroeconomic stabilization and trade liberalization. The second phase (1989–92) concentrated on the inclusion of key social dimensions of adjustment and laying the groundwork for institutional reforms and foreign-exchange and investment deregulation. The third phase (1993 onwards) focused on reforms in institutional governance, notably civil-service and parastatal reform. Subsequently, in 2000, Tanzania adopted the Poverty Reduction Strategy (PRS), succeeded by the National Strategy for Growth and Reduction of Poverty (MKUKUTA), which has become a formal process and overarching policy for driving economic reform.

As part of the economic liberalization and reforms, the government has implemented a set of measures to improve the business environment, including:

- formation of the Tanzania Revenue Authority (TRA) in 1996 to modernize tax administration, promote voluntary tax compliance and strengthen the government's revenue base;
- transformation of the Investment Promotion Centre (IPC) in 1997 into the Tanzania Investment Centre (TIC), with a focus on making it a one-stop shop to overcome bureaucratic hurdles for potential investors, particularly to attract foreign investment;
- establishment of the Business Registration and Licensing Authority (BRELA) in 1999 to handle business registration outside the mainstream of government bureaucracy, with a view to cutting red tape and making it easier to start a business;
- initiation of the Business Environment Strengthening for Tanzania (BEST) programme in 2000 to comprehensively improve the business environment and bring down the cost of doing business;
- formation of the Tanzania National Business Council (TNBC) in 2000 to serve as the forum for dialogue between the government and the private sector and to build a constructive partnership for policy reform and push for faster economic growth;
- creation of the Fair Competition Commission in 2003; and
- enactment of the Business Activities Registration Act (BARA) of 2007 to further simplify the process of starting businesses by separating business licensing from revenue collection.

Other major areas of reforms have included the Public Sector Reform Programme (PSRP) I and II, Local Government Reform Programme (LGRP) I and II, Public Financial Management Reform Programme (PFMRP), Second Generation Financial Sector Reform Programme, National Anti-Corruption Strategy and Action Plan (NACSAP), Agricultural Sector Reform Programme and Legal Sector Reform Programme (LSRP). These reforms aimed to promote good governance, scale down direct government participation in economic ventures, create a business environment that will attract both local and foreign investments, and increase private-sector participation in the economy. In addition, the government formulated the Five-Year Development Plan (FYDP) (2011/12–2015/16), which aims to unleash the growth potential of the economy. The plan charts a growth path for realizing the Development Vision 2025, which is that Tanzania becomes a semi-industrialized country by 2025 that is capable of withstanding competition in domestic, regional and global markets. The FYDP I intends to effectively tap into Tanzania's resource potential in order to create the conditions for broad-based and pro-poor growth (United Republic of Tanzania (URT), 2011).

It is clear that Tanzania has pursued numerous policy reforms that had a number of implications in terms of improving the business environment and investment climate. The government has established within its various strategy documents a clear rationale for regulatory reform as a major part of its overall private-sector-development strategy. Efforts are being made to improve the consultation process, particularly the capacity of PSOs to advocate for policy change and contribute to effective policy discussion. However, the historical background of Tanzania is an important factor to be considered when looking at the effectiveness of the private sector in terms of policy reforms. The prevalence of socialist governance after independence created a partition between the government and the private sector that has often directly contributed to a climate of distrust between the two parties. The socialist legacy and the remnants of authoritarian rule have often served to create a business environment consisting of an overly complex legal and regulatory framework, burdensome business-registration, licensing and tax regimes and limited availability of business development services, etc. Therefore, the poor enabling environment is one obvious area for fruitful dialogue between the government and the private sector.

ROLE OF PRIVATE SECTOR IN PROMOTING REFORMS

Governments in developing countries have the responsibility to ensure that a favourable business environment exists for all private-sector actors. Accordingly, most efforts to address the constraints for sustainable private-sector development originate in governments and public-development institutions. In view of this, governments need to be aware of the key constraints facing different private-sector entities in realizing their potential to contribute to pro-poor economic growth (Organization for Economic Cooperation and Development (OECD), 2006). However, in order to avoid prescriptive policy making and to reach the required level of change, it is essential to engage the private sector in addressing the development challenge. Because private-sector development cannot be achieved by focusing interventions on either the private or the public sector, and the many constraints that the private sector faces can only be resolved in collaboration with the public sector, the private sector should be integrated into the policy-making process and reform initiatives.

The private sector has an important role to play in identifying bottlenecks, opportunities and possible interventions for private-sector development. Through effective PPDs and sustained interactions between the state and the business community, the private sector can play an effective role in creating awareness of the root causes of the identified constraints to pro-poor private-sector development and economic growth at various levels. This suggests that 'governments that listen to the private sector are more likely to design credible and workable reforms, while entrepreneurs who understand what their government is trying to achieve with a programme of reforms are more likely to accept and support them' (Herzberg and Wright, 2005: 3). In such cases, private-sector hosts can be used as think-tanks that bring ideas to the table and also participate in developing, implementing and monitoring

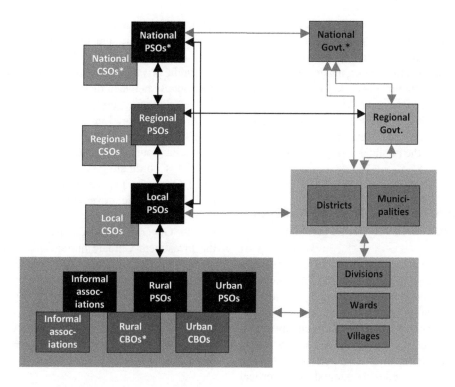

Figure 36.1 Policy dialogue levels in Tanzania

Source: Gerwen, Olomi, van der Poel, 2005

*CSOs – Civil society organizations; *CBOs – Community based organizations, PSOs – Private sector organizations, Govt. – Government

development policies. Consultation with a wide range of PSOs is therefore an important part of the policy-development process. Such consultation needs to be accompanied by mechanisms for regular PPD at the appropriate policy level, combined with bottom-up communication to ensure that local-level issues are fed into the higher-level policy-making process. Making private-sector-development policy more responsive to private-sector needs depends on the way in which PPD is organized, especially with respect to approaches and mechanisms that ensure that the business community can voice its concerns. Private-sector participation speeds up change, ensuring the rapid uptake of new processes and promoting greater efficiency in new administrative regimes. Neglecting private-sector participation during implementation can derail

promising initiatives. Effective participation of the private sector in policy reforms leads to commitment by the government to certain policies that minimize uncertainties concerning future policy actions in the minds of investors. It creates a setting in which the private sector demands high-quality public goods from the state, such as infrastructure, effective public administration and property rights.

From the above observations, it can be argued that governments which engage in PPD and allow effective private-sector advocacy are more likely to promote sensible, workable reforms, while enterprises participating in meaningful PPD are more likely to support these reforms (Herzberg and Wright, 2005). Without more equitable dialogue, governments tend to follow the loudest, most powerful voices, which rarely advocate for broad-based private-sector growth, let alone poverty reduction. Although not the only condition for accelerating pro-poor growth, PPD can be a first important step in an institutional-reform process aimed at improving the business environment for all. It is especially effective where and when there is an explicit commitment and willingness to act on its outcomes by the public and private sector.

PRIVATE-SECTOR PARTICIPATION IN POLICY MAKING IN TANZANIA

Private-sector participation in dialogue and the policy-making process in Tanzania take place through a number of national, sectoral and local government platforms aimed at ensuring consultative decisions and the inclusion of the private sector. According to van der Poel et al. (2005), the PPD framework in Tanzania includes horizontal and vertical linkages among associations and the government from village to national level (Figure 36.1). Parallel to these are civil-society organizations (CSOs), dealing with human rights, inclusion, capacity building, health, democracy and other development issues. Therefore, private-sector institutions (and CSOs) have a hierarchical structure, from the national level (apex organizations) via the regional level to local PSOs active at local government (city, municipal, district) level. At village and ward level, many forms of association exist, and a distinction can be made between informal associations, representing particular informal groups (e.g. fishermen), rural associations such as farmer groups or savings and credit societies, and urban associations such as an association of shop owners in a particular area. At this grassroots level, the distinction between PSOs and CSOs is blurred, as there is often an overlap of similar objectives, such as access to credit, training, etc. The framework shown in Figure 36.1 is inspired by the institutional setting in Tanzania and can be used

for identifying and analysing the different levels of dialogue and decision making on private-sector development, both vertically within the private and public sector as well as horizontally between them.

The dialogue takes place through a range of structured and informal mechanisms. These include The Tanzania National Business Council (TNBC), Regional and District Coordinating Committees (RCCs and DCCs), the local and national government budget cycle, governance structures for business-environment-reform programmes (e.g. the Government Roadmap for Improving the Investment Climate in Tanzania and the recently adopted initiative BRN, sector PPD forums and other stakeholder forums). For illustrative purposes, we present the experience of national dialogue platforms, while the specific cases drawn from sectoral- and local-level dialogue initiatives are presented in the next section.

Tanzania National Business Council

The TNBC was established by a Presidential Circular in 2001 as a forum for facilitating PPD to reach a consensus relating to the efficient management of national resources and the promotion of an enabling environment for economic development. The TNBC is made up of 40 members, 20 from the private sector and 20 from the public sector. All 40 members are appointed by the President of the United Republic of Tanzania, who is also the TNBC's Chairman. Private-sector representatives on the Council are appointed on the basis of recommendations by the Tanzania Private Sector Foundation (TPSF), which is the apex organization for private-sector associations in Tanzania. An Executive Committee of 12 members, six from the private sector and six from the public sector, oversees the functions of the TNBC. The day-to-day functions of the Council are undertaken by a Secretariat headed by the

Executive Secretary. TNBC dialogue is conducted through council meetings, Local and International Investors' Round Tables (LIRTs and IIRTs) and regional and district business councils, which have structures similar to the TNBC. Working Groups, constituting professionals and practitioners from the public and private sector, provide informed opinions and make recommendations on the relevant sectors to the TNBC dialogue process.

The TNBC appears to be one of the key platforms that have the potential to bring both high-level government officials and private-sector representatives and investors to the negotiation table. The level of representation of the public and private sector indicates a good balance required for the dialogue process. However, the TNBC has not been effective enough in achieving its mission for a number of reasons. First, the regional and district business councils, which appear in the structure of the TNBC, are not active in most places. Indeed, although there are several policy issues requiring the attention of local government, most regional and district councils do not meet at all to discuss them. The TNBC has recently initiated a move to revive the regional business councils, but the speed has been slow. The input of national dialogue platforms is therefore limited, partly because of weak business councils at local level. Second, the capacity of the private sector to articulate issues with strong evidence and closely follow them up is still limited. As a result, most TNBC forums are run as talk-show platforms where those from the private and public sector talk without seriously implementing the actions agreed on. Third, the frequency of TNBC meetings at the national level has not been as consistent as expected when it was established. Since 2002, the TNBC has been able to organize seven (53 per cent) national annual meetings rather than the 13 that should have taken place. Some meetings are skipped due to lack of adequate preparation and limited resources to organize them. The last TNBC meeting took place in 2013 and no date has been set for the next meeting. Fourth, most TNBC deliberations produce a list of what should be done without proposing pragmatic action with a specific timeframe. This results in inadequate implementation of the decisions made in the council. In addition, following several initiatives that have emerged over time (e.g. Agriculture First (Kilimo Kwanza) under TNBC, which aims to promote a green revolution by transforming agriculture, and the government roadmap, First FYDP and BRN), there has been a duplication of efforts and lack of focus on more strategic interventions. Although some efforts have been made to link various programmes, over the last ten years the government has been changing its focus, according to which initiative has gained momentum.

The Government Roadmap for Improving the Investment Climate

Initiated by the government in 2010, the doing-business roadmap framework intends to systematically reform Tanzania's business environment and investment climate by addressing the challenges identified in the World Bank Doing Business Report. The roadmap established eight thematic taskforce teams to identify, document and address barriers in the investment climate in nine thematic areas identified by the World Bank Report. Eight Technical Working Groups (TWGs) covering these areas (starting and closing a business, getting credit, trading across borders, employing workers, enforcing contracts, protecting investors, paying taxes and registering property) were established, each under the leadership of a government ministry or agency. A Permanent Secretaries Working Group (PSWG) was also constituted, bringing together Chief Executive Officers of key ministries and government agencies involved in the relevant reforms. Each TWG drew up a comprehensive list of the issues, steps to be taken and government agencies responsible for improving Tanzania's ranking in the Doing Business Report from over 120 to double digits. A comprehensive action plan for 2010/11–2012/13 was developed to implement the recommendations from the roadmap (URT, 2010b). The action plan aims to ensure that Tanzania's business environment becomes globally competitive and vibrant for both domestic- and foreign-owned businesses by: 1) reducing the cost of doing business through reforming or eliminating regulatory procedures and reducing administrative barriers; 2) improving the capacity of the public sector to deliver better services to the private sector; and 3) promoting strategic partnerships between the public and private sector. However, the issues that are being addressed through the roadmap largely focus on trading across borders, getting credit and starting and closing a business (Table 36.1).

To implement the roadmap action plan, all TWGs are supposed to meet quarterly and report progress to the PSWG under the Prime Minister's Office (PMO). The Private-Sector-Driven Working Groups (PSDWGs), which include representatives of the PSOs, were formed by the TSPF to act as a link between the PSWG, private sector and other partners participating in the roadmap process. Their specific functions are: monitoring the implementation of actions agreed on by public sector actors; informing meetings of the

public-sector working groups through regular reports and sending informed representatives to their meetings; providing feedback on the status of implementation as reported by the public sector; advising the public sector on feasible ways of addressing issues in the investment climate and of implementing agreed actions; coordinating and initiating research into issues affecting the private sector to demonstrate the impact of the issues as well as the urgency of implementation; providing information to the private sector on the roadmap process and implementation progress; identifying private-sector actors who may be involved in public-private partnership (PPP) to address some of the identified barriers in the investment climate; advising the TPSF on effective ways of engaging the diverse private-sector actors in the dialogue process; ensuring that the planning of roadmap activities addresses private-sector priorities; establishing an appropriate framework for monitoring roadmap process activities and tracking their operationalization and implementation; and identifying and working on any pertinent emerging issues not already included in the action plan.

However, implementation of the roadmap has been sluggish, with most targeted reforms behind schedule. A study on the status of implementation of the roadmap in 2012 indicated that out of a total of 187 actions or

Table 36.1   Advocacy issues vs roadmap and BRN focus

Issues in order of priority	Roadmap	BRN
1. Levies or fees	None	Taxes, levies and fees
2. Sector regulation	None	Regulations and institutions
3. Taxation	Paying taxes	Taxes, levies and fees
4. Unfair imports	None	Corruption
5. Standards and measures	None	Regulations and institutions
6. Electronic Fiscal Devices (EFDs)	None	None
7. Infrastructure	Trading across borders	Infrastructure, access to land
8. Access to finance	Getting credit	Access to land
9. PPP or Public Private Partnership (PPP)	None	None
10. Business registration and licensing	Starting and closing a business	Regulations and institutions
11. Inclusiveness/Empowerment	None	None
12. Cross border trade	Trading across borders	Infrastructure (port, road)
13. Agriculture subsidies	None	Agriculture

Source: TPSF2015

reforms that were to be implemented only 43 (22.3 per cent) had been implemented, while 93 (about half) had been partially implemented (URT, 2012). About a quarter had not been implemented at all (URT, 2012). As a result, Tanzania's ranking in the annual doing-business surveys deteriorated from 126 in 2009 to 134 in 2013 and 145 in 2014 (World Bank, 2014). The reasons for this were identified as 1) lack of accountability (sanctions) when ministries, departments and agencies (MDAs) do not report to, attend or organize Task Force meetings; 2) the absence of clear terms of reference for the task forces; 3) frequent changes in PSO staff and MDAs, leading to lack of awareness by the government and the private sector; 4) the absence of a clear mechanism for tracking and reporting implementation; and 5) limited financial and human resources in the MDAs' planning units and Attorney General's chambers.

Interviews with PSOs indicate that the TWGs have not been meeting regularly and the private sector has not effectively participated in the roadmap process. As a result, there has been no pressure on the TWGs to meet or work on issues. Some of the achievements recorded at the PSWG level have not been realized, as reported on the ground, and there is no mechanism for giving feedback to the TWGs. PSOs have not been systematically engaged in the roadmap process. Some of them are hardly aware of it, and some may even be developing policy proposals already contained in the Comprehensive Action Plan instead of pushing for their implementation. All these factors indicate that leadership of the roadmap process has been left largely to the public sector, with private-sector representatives being unorganized spectators rather than serious partners in the dialogue process.

Surprisingly, new regulations, fees and levies were introduced without adequate assessment of their impact, thereby reversing the gains made. The roadmap action plan is not monitored systematically at Task Force or Steering Committee level. While the action plan is integrated into MDAs' Medium-Term Expenditure Frameworks (MTEFs) and budgets, its implementation depends on the availability of resources, which are rarely sufficient. Information on MDAs' MTEFs, annual plans, budgets and the availability of funds for implementing actions earmarked in the roadmap is not communicated to the roadmap Task Forces or Steering Committee. It is therefore impossible for them to effectively monitor the implementation of specific actions. Since the government has its own quarterly and annual reporting framework, and given that all actions in the roadmap are implemented by MDAs, it is almost impossible to have a different format for the roadmap.

Big Results Now (BRN)

As one of the efforts to transform the country from a low- to a middle-income economy, Tanzania, with the support of development partners, adopted the Big Results Now initiative in 2013, based on a model of development that has proved successful in Malaysia. This comprehensive system of implementing development, described as a 'fast-track people-centred growth "marathon"'[1], focuses on six priority areas articulated in the Tanzania Development Vision 2025: energy and natural gas, agriculture, water, education, transport and mobilization of resources. It began with an eight-week coaching session (Lab) led by Malaysian policy experts who drew on the experience of Malaysia's Performance Management and Delivery Unit to design and implement a model suited to Tanzania. The lab teams analysed the most important challenges and prioritized areas that would give big results quickly. The TPSF was a key partner both in the preparation of the lab and in the lab itself and, in collaboration with PSOs, made a task force that would participate in both the preparatory committee and the lab to ensure that the private sector was adequately represented.

The labs were expected to introduce a strong and effective system that would oversee, monitor and evaluate the implementation of Tanzania's development plans (particularly the FYDP I) and programmes, prioritizing detailed monitoring tools and performance accountability. The motive was to eliminate the 'culture of business as usual' and needless confidentiality among officials and officers serving the public that has hobbled efforts to move Tanzania forward. BRN is coordinated by the President's Office through the Presidential Delivery Bureau (PDB). This body brings together experts and key stakeholders, who choose and agree on priorities and refine them so that they will be implementable. Through the creation of mechanisms that make sure top government officials address the priorities in concrete ways, deliver results and meet the targets set, each selected Ministry is expected to align its budget to the high-level initiatives of the government as defined in each FYDP, which in turn are targeted at moving the country toward achieving Vision 2025.

As shown in Table 36.1, most issues discussed in the regulatory labs are related to levies, fees and sector regulation, followed by taxation. Business registration and licensing is also an issue but mostly for associations of small enterprises. Some segments in the private sector have been advocating for special treatment (inclusiveness) because existing systems are not working for them. These include graduates (special treatment in start-ups), women (gender-based budgeting) and the disabled (differential treatment in business licensing).

Although this is a recent initiative, some challenges have already been observed. First, the rate of implementation of the reforms identified in BRN is still slow on account of the limited budget made available by the government. Second, the initiative has turned its attention to the BRN agenda, leading to cannibalization of the reforms that were underway through the roadmap. Although the government claims that this initiative is intended to complement other reforms, the focus has largely been on the actions identified in BRN. Third, participation of the private sector in monitoring the implementation of BRN is still limited because it is formal government structures that are accountable. This suggests that without coordination representation of the private sector in public-sector-driven processes may not achieve the intended results.

PARTICIPATION OF BUSINESS ASSOCIATIONS IN DIALOGUE AND POLICY REFORM IN TANZANIA

In the last ten years, a number of PSOs have been entering into dialogue with the state to advocate for a better business environment. For instance, since 2004 the BEST-Dialogue (the programme that promotes private-sector dialogue in Tanzania) has supported over 34 business associations conducting advocacy work (BEST-AC, 2011). In this section, we present the selected business associations

---

Selected Illustrations from PSOs

TANZANIA EXPORTERS ASSOCIATION (TANEXA)

TANEXA was established in 1994 to improve the business environment for exporters. It has 45 members and one employee. TANEXA has been advocating for an improvement in the government's Export Credit Guarantee and SME Credit Guarantee Schemes. Through the research undertaken by the association and the active engagement of the media, members of parliament (MPs) and the Ministry of Industry and Trade (MIT), TANEXA succeeded in influencing the government to introduce the scheme and form the credit-guarantee management committee in 2003. However, the scheme has been ineffective, partly because most entrepreneurs are unaware of how it works. In 2012, TANEXA initiated a project, which is ongoing, advocating for the removal of export permits for exporting food products to Southern African Development Community (SADC) and East African Community (EAC) countries. However, access to credit for exporters is still a challenge as most credit-guarantee schemes have not worked effectively and regulations for accessing credit guarantees mean that they are beyond the reach of the majority of SMEs.

AGRICULTURAL COUNCIL OF TANZANIA (ACT)

This is an apex organization with some direct members. It was formed in 1999 and currently has 84 members and 11 staff. It has been active advocating for an improved crop cess system, a review of the 1999 Land Act, VAT exemption on agricultural equipment, improved distribution of quality agricultural inputs, a reduction in land rent, etc. For example, in terms of improving the crop cess system, ACT undertook a study in 2010, developed a solid policy proposal and created awareness at the local government level. It formed a coalition with government agencies and other PSOs and engaged the media to highlight the issue. Although the level of awareness has increased, most district councils hesitate to reduce the crop cess for financial reasons. In terms of reviewing the Land Act, the government has delayed the process despite the efforts being made to formalize dialogue and work actively with champions. As a result of the lack of clear ownership of land, land conflicts are increasing. However, the association achieved success in the form of VAT concessions in 2010–11 after it lobbied the government to attract agricultural investment. The challenge is that due to the high cost of investing in agriculture, ACT is yet to see positive results in terms of attracting commercial investors.

CONFEDERATION OF TANZANIA INDUSTRIES (CTI)

CTI was launched in 1991 to advocate for an improved business environment and provide services to manufacturing industries. It has 400 active members and 15 staff, three in the policy department. CTI represents its members in a policy forum to ensure that their views are considered in the policy-making process. Over the last ten years, it has advocated for improving the regulatory system, addressing the challenge of supplying power to manufacturers, reducing the number of counterfeit products and improving the tax system. Various techniques are used to advocate for change, such as researching and presenting evidenced-based position papers to MDAs, participating in the tax-reform committee, using the media, entering into a coalition with other PSOs and lobbying parliamentarians. In this way, CTI has succeeded in partnering with the government in BRN and the roadmap and has participated in various working groups. It has influenced the government in improving the tax system and stabilized the cost of electricity. However, CTI has witnessed the introduction of more taxes, a number of legal cases on the emergency power plans and the slow implementation of regulatory reforms.

TANZANIA MILK PROCESSORS ASSOCIATION (TAMPA)

Established in 2001, currently with 130 members and two staff, TAMPA seeks to promote the business interests of milk processors. Over the last ten years, the TAMPA has been in active dialogue with the government on rationalizing the regulations affecting the dairy sub-sector, introducing zero-rated VAT for milk processors, improving milk-collection centres and promoting a milk-drinking culture. In 2007–8, for instance, TAMPA commissioned a study on the impact of regulations in the dairy sub-sector and prepared a position paper on harmonizing the functions of 17 regulators governing the sector. It succeeded in forming a coalition with the Tanzania Dairy Board (TDB) to explore the regulatory overlaps, and it proposed a strategy for harmonizing the regulatory framework. Surprisingly, despite sustained efforts to create awareness and engage with MPs, MDAs and dialogue platforms, the government has not taken serious measures to address the issue. TAMPA succeeded in getting the government to introduce zero-rated VAT on milk and milk products in 2012, but to TAMPA's surprise the government waived the zero-rating privilege in 2014, and the Association has initiated a dialogue as there are more issues emerging in the sector.

TANZANIA CONFEDERATION OF TOURISM (TCT)

TCT is an apex organization formed in 2000, currently with nine association members and four staff. TCT has carried out several advocacy and dialogue initiatives focusing on improving the tourism value chain, tourism marketing and the general business environment in the tourist industry and reducing hunting fees. In 2007, for instance, TCT engaged MPs and decision makers in the Ministry of Tourism and Natural Resources (MTNR) in a dialogue on a reduction in the proposed 500 percent increase in fees for hunting and photographic safaris in the middle of the tourist season. The hunting project was successful in persuading the government to increase the fees by 'only' 200 percent as well as delaying the introduction until the next season. Through the sustained dialogue, in 2009 TCT worked with the government to develop the first comprehensive tourism marketing strategy for Tanzania, which is owned by both the private and public sector. In June 2010, TCT signed a five-year memorandum of understanding with MTNR to partner in dialoguing the industry's issues. Although the resources for implementing the strategy are limited, TCT considers this a success. However, the hunting fees are still considered high and TCT is advocating for a further reduction.

that have been actively advocating for an improved business environment, the issues addressed, the techniques used, the success achieved and the challenges encountered. An analysis of the dialogue practices of the five business associations indicates that the private sector can take initiatives in dialogue by adopting an advocacy approach. It is apparent that in many instances, PPDs arise between a particular industry, cluster or value chain in the private sector and those in government responsible for regulating that area of the economy. In our case, at least five sectors and sub-sectors (trade, manufacturing, tourism, agriculture and dairy) were covered by the associations studied.

REFLECTION OF PPD PRACTICES

Before embarking on dialogue initiatives, most PSOs identify various issues requiring the attention of policy makers. To a large extent, the private sector has been addressing problems associated with the regulatory framework and inadequate provision of public services (Table 36.2). As demonstrated in the cases of TAMPA and CTI, PSOs have been actively advocating for an improvement in the regulatory system to reduce compliance costs and administrative hurdles. Some PSOs have addressed the issues of improving the tax system (e.g. TCT and ACT), improving the power supply (CTI), introducing special exemptions for certain sectors and products (dairy industry and agricultural equipment) and enhancing access to credit (TANEXA). In terms of proposed changes, the majority of PSOs have been advocating for a change in public policy and amendments of laws. A few PSOs (e.g. TAMPA) have attempted to persuade the government to improve the interpretation of existing laws and/or change the administrative arrangements for enforcing the legislation (e.g. ACT). Besides the issues presented by PSOs, a study of 106 PSOs by the TPSF

(2015) (Annex 1) indicates that the private sector has dealt with a wide variety of issues, ranging from multiple regulations, access to resources and compliance with product and service standards to improving national policies. However, the overall assessment by TPSF shows that only 28 per cent of implemented advocacy projects focus on improving the business environment, with the rest relating to human rights, health, access to services and membership services.

With respect to dialogue techniques, the majority of PSOs apply a combination of techniques, including: 1) engaging the media to create awareness of the issues; 2) engaging politicians, particularly MPs; 3) presenting position papers and fact sheets to MDAs; 4) creating a policy coalition with other PSOs and, on a few occasions, with public agencies (e.g. TCT and the Tanzania Tourist Board, ACT and the Ministry of Agriculture, TAMPA and TDB); 5) identifying and cultivating 'champions' within key ministries (e.g. TCT); 6) formalizing dialogue arrangements (e.g. TCT and tourism associations and the Ministry of Natural Resources and Tourism (MNRT); and 7) training members to take an active and consistent approach to advocacy (ACT) and participating in government committees.

In terms of outcomes, there is growing appreciation of the value of the private sector in the policy-making process. The experience of PSOs indicates that in some cases the government has taken on board actions proposed by the private sector (see for example, the proposals made by TANEXA, TAMPA, TCT and CTI). Some of the issues identified at the sectoral level have been moved to the national PPD platforms and become important policy-agenda items. For instance, the issue of multiple regulations is now an important agenda item of BRN and the roadmap for improving the investment climate. In line with previous assessments (e.g. BEST-AC, (2011)), it seems that the government is becoming positive about PSOs' involvement in both policy development and policy implementation, and it is fairly positive about their approach to consultation. From

Table 36.2   Advocacy projects implemented by members of the TPSF (2005-20–15)

Issue	No	Issue	No	Issue	No
Electronic Fiscal Devices (EFDs)	8	Land titling	1	Amendments to the mineral policy	1
Skills Development Levy (SDL)	6	Mineral policy	1	Multiple levies for tourism businesses	1
Sugar importation	6	Management of the Surface and Marine Transport Regulatory Authority (SUMATRA)	1	Obtaining government guarantee	1
Multiple taxation	5	Meat quality	1	Physical security at banks	1
Value Added Tax (VAT)	3	New driving license requirements	1	Produce Cess and industrial service levy	1
Fire levy	2	PPP in health	1	Stable custom in ports	1
Business license fees	2	PPD: Seven agenda tourism pillars	1	Subsidy on farm inputs	1
Unfair weights and measures	2	Public-expenditure tracking system	1	Tobacco regulation	1
Access to finance	1	Public–private Partnership	1	Withdrawal of business licences	1
Access to markets	1	Receipts adjustment	1	VAT zero rating for some products	1
Airport construction	1	Multiple fees and charges	1	Arbitration rules	1
Alcohol Policy	1	Regulating cultural tourism sub-sector	1	Cashew-nut-processing policy	1
Allocating special areas for SMEs	1	Excise duty on money transfer	1	Cross-border trade	1
Sugar imports	1	Solar-energy installation in schools	1	Occupational Safety and Health Act (OSHA)	1
Work premises	1	Special Window facility	1	Hotel-grading system	1
Gender-sensitive budgeting	1	Taxation for Zanzibar traders	1	Food Quality	1
Cashew business management by ACT	1	Teachers' recognition	1	Limited input fund	1
Motor insurance rates	1	Standard mark of quality	1	Information and communication technology (ICT) application in rural areas	1
Common market for agricultural products	1	Fees of Weights and Measures Agency	1	Inclusion of horticulture in government policies/plans	1
Crop cess	1	Tourism Act	1	Livestock keepers grazing in farms	1
Marine Park fees	1	Business registration	1	Payment of debts by the government	1
Edible Oil Imports	1	Border-trade restrictions	1	Road fund	1
Fire and Rescue Policy	1	Conflict at market places	1	Service fee	1
Business licensing for the disabled	1	Dynamite fishing	1	Service levy	1
Improving the warehouse receipt policies	1	Improving agricultural conditions	1	Tree-selling regulations	1
Incentives for start-ups	1	Improving labour-law regulations	1	Introduction of seed subsidy to farmers in Tanzania instead of fertilizers only	1
Fake pharmaceuticals	1				

Source: TPSF 2015

the experience of the cases analysed, it is clear that business associations play a significant role in facilitating the formulation, implementation and monitoring of economic policies and providing feedback to the government (Hisahiro,

2005). This suggests that promoting business associations is likely to increase the consultative approach to policy making.

Despite the recorded achievements, a number of challenges are still observed in the

PPD processes. First, while the government might agree to implement the proposed policy change, actual implementation has been slow and sometimes does not happen at all. In some cases, the government has reinstated some taxes (e.g. the abolition of zero-rated VAT in the dairy sector) after realizing the revenue lost as a result of implementing the policy change. Second, most dialogue interventions have taken place at the national level, driven by national PSOs and CSOs, leaving out PPDs at local government level. The main gap is that national PSOs do not have an in-depth understanding of key sectoral issues and a limited grasp of local concerns. As highlighted earlier, the district business councils are still weak, and other platforms such as district stakeholders' meetings, local budget sessions and business roundtables are dominated by the government. Indeed, observations made in our cases are similar to those elsewhere, i.e. that most PPDs take place at the central level while sub-sector PPDs and processes at the district or municipal level are limited (Bannock, 2005; Herzberg and Wright, 2005). This is contrary to good practice, which shows that PPD is most effective at the lowest level at which entrepreneurs and government services interact (van der Poel et al., 2005). Interactions between local governments or the lowest interface with line ministries for certain sub-sector issues are the most relevant.

Third, coalitions among business associations are still weak, resulting in the duplication of efforts and weak engagement with the state. As a result, private-sector participation in the policy-making process is considerably limited. Fourth, our interaction with business associations indicates that most of them are weak in terms of advocacy capacity and institutional competence. This is in line with BEST's assessment in 2005, which found that most PSOs had a weak institutional foundation, with a small or no secretariat, and funding being a major concern. Therefore, the quality of PPD may suffer from the inability of participants to contribute effectively to an analysis of the root causes and to finding evidence to support requests for policy reform. Such PPDs tend to produce a laundry list of symptoms. Since approaches and tools that facilitate the participatory analysis of problems and the identification of opportunities by local actors exist and can be adapted to local level PPDs, it is important for the actors to emphasize local PPDs. This suggests that the way in which a PPD is designed has to be context-specific and adjusted to prevailing institutional arrangements. Fourth, although most PSOs were able to craft issues and agendas for dialogue with the government, most of them suffer from a lack of resources and inadequate planning to complete the process. This is risky, since good planning is vital, such as the preparation in advance of clear and concise agendas, timeframes that show milestones for each specific outcome, good chairing of meetings (ensuring that all present can participate), agreement on minutes and the accountability of the secretariat to the participants (Bannock, 2005).

CONCLUSION AND POLICY IMPLICATIONS

The main focus of this chapter has been on dialogue practices and policy reforms in the context of a developing economy. The experience of PPD processes in Tanzania shows that there are formal policy-dialogue frameworks ranging from national to local government level. The increased number of interactions between businesses and government is part of the economic transformation occurring in Tanzania and other African countries. Overall, existing frameworks are instrumental in the private sector's interactions with the state and provide inputs into the policy-making process. There seems to be a growing appreciation by the government of the value of the private sector in providing an understanding of what the policy looks like on the ground and as a source of pressure that can transcend departmental boundaries and hierarchies. Thus, structured and inclusive dialogue between the public and private sector can encourage the private sector to participate in the policy-making process. By working jointly with the public sector, business associations can act as a think-tank for the state by informing the government of opportunities and challenges in the business environment. The experience of PSOs and various dialogue platforms shows that most PSOs identify the issues affecting the private sector, undertake studies and prepare position papers/fact sheets before they embark on the policy dialogue. While this seems to be a systematic process, the main challenge is that most agreed policy actions are not implemented, and the government sometimes reverses its decisions. This clearly shows that reforming institutions and policies can be a difficult and time-consuming process and requires a careful mix of contestation and negotiation to overcome resistance to change.

Although it is documented that the presence of well-organized and capable PSOs at various levels makes PPDs more relevant (e.g. Hisahiro, 2005; Taylor, 2012), it appears that most PSOs become active only when there is an urgent issue. Most business associations are inclined to do ad hoc advocacy work, but they often lack the resources to become a serious dialogue partner. Therefore, building and supporting business associations can be helpful in making sure that the concerns of the private sector are heard. In addition, it is observed that many grassroots-level PSOs are not linked to apex organizations which potentially could have taken care of their interests in national-level dialogue processes. So, for the purpose of promoting effective PPDs, there is a need to enhance the capacity of both private and public representative organizations and raise awareness at different levels (national, sub-national and local) of the real, practical and underlying issues that constrain pro-poor private-sector development. This requires building the capacity of both national and local PSOs to engage in sustainable dialogue and develop coalitions that will enable them to become stronger.

The presence of several dialogue frameworks which are not coordinated is likely to encourage duplication of efforts in the dialogue process. For example, the issue of the regulatory framework is one of the agenda items in BRN, the TNBC and the roadmap for improving the investment climate. The risk here is that in all platforms different actions target the same implementers (MDAs), while the resources available for policy implementation are insufficient. As a result, monitoring and following up policy change becomes a challenge for both the private and public sector. Certainly, this requires further documentation and mapping of ongoing policy-reform issues addressed through PPDs, including the action plans developed to monitor progress. Strengthening the capacity of the private sector to monitor the implementation process and inform the government about the duplication of efforts would definitely be useful.

In view of the above, there are a number of policy implications. First, there is a need to build the capacity of business associations, especially at the local level, to conduct more sustainable advocacy and dialogue with the government. Second, more policy studies are needed which feed into the policy-making process by analysing issues, proposing policy changes and providing knowledge on how best to engage with the government. Third, governments in developing countries and in Africa in particular need to speed up implementation of the policy actions agreed on in PPDs and improve the feedback mechanism. Fourth, the private sector must improve its follow-up strategies to ensure that the actions agreed on in the dialogue process are implemented. The problem with any PPD is when the government agrees to take action without devising an adequate follow-up mechanism. The private sector therefore has to be keen to ensure that feedback mechanisms are designed and follow-up strategies developed.

Notes

1 Quoted from the Tanzania Big Results Now (BRN) concept downloaded on http://www.africa-platform.org/resources/tanzanias-big-results-now-initiative in July 2015.

REFERENCES

Bannock Consulting (2005). 'Reforming the business enabling environment, mechanisms and processes for private–public sector dialogue', retrieved from http://www.public-privatedialogue.org/papers/Reforming_the_Business_Enabling_Environment.pdf (accessed 14 September, 2016).

BEST-AC (2005). 'Baseline survey: Advocacy capacity and competency of private sector organisations and business development service providers, final report for external circulation' Dar es Salaam.

BEST-AC (2011). 'Longitudinal Impact Assessment (LIA) Report' by Coffey International Development, Dar es Salaam.

Charles, G. (2014). 'The effect of the regulatory framework on the competitiveness of the dairy sector in Tanzania', *International Journal of Public Sector Management*, 27(4): 296–305.

Confederation of Tanzania Industries (CTI). (2011). Simplifying compliance of multiple regulatory authorities to enhance the ease of doing business: Policy brief published by CTI, Dar es Salaam.

Cooksey, B. (2011). 'Public goods, rents and business in Tanzania. Background paper no. 1'. London: African Power and Politics Retrieved from http://www.institutions-africa.org/publications/author/cooksey/1.html (accessed 17 October, 2016).

Harris, J. (2006). 'Institutions and state–business relations, IPPG briefing note 2', retrieved from http://www.ippg.org.uk/publications.html=br2 (accessed 14 September, 2016).

Herzberg, B. and A. Wright (2005), Competitiveness Partnerships: Building and Maintaining Public-Private Dialogue to Improve the Investment Climate. A resource drawn from 40 countries in OECD (2006), Washington DC: World Bank http://www.publicprivatedialogue.org/papers/competitiveness_partnerships.pdf

Hisahiro, K. (2005). 'Comparative analysis of governance: Relationship between bureaucracy and policy coordination capacity with particular reference to Bangladesh', Japan International Cooperative Agency, retrieved from http://www.jica.go.jp/english/publications/reports/study/topical/index.html (accessed 14 September, 2016).

Irwin, D. (2008). 'Can the private sector successfully advocate change in public policy in Africa?' presented at the Annual Conference of the Institute for Small Business and Entrepreneurship, Belfast, available at: http://irwingrayson.com/dloads/isbe08psaAfrica.pdf (accessed February 2015).

Kathuria, V., Rajesh Raj, S.N. and Sen, K. (2010). 'State–business relations and manufacturing productivity growth in India', *Munich Personal RePEc Archive*, paper 20314.

Kessy, S. and Temu, S. (2010). 'The impact of training on performance of micro and small enterprises served by microfinance institutions in Tanzania', *Research Journal of Business Management,* 4(2): 103–11.

Kinda, T. and Loening, J.L. (2010). 'Small enterprise growth and the rural investment climate: Evidence from Tanzania', *African Development Review*, 22(1): 173–207.

Konig, G., Da Silva, C.A. and Mhlanga, N. (2013). 'Enabling for agri-business and agro-industries development'. Food and Agriculture Organization of the United Nations: Rome.

Organization for Economic Co-Operation and Development (OECD) (2006). 'Promoting pro-poor growth: Private sector development': report extracted from *Policy Guidance for Donors*, retrieved from https://www.oecd.org/dac/povertyreduction/36427804.pdf (accessed 14 September, 2016).

Sen, K. (2013). *State–Business Relations and Economic Development in Africa and India.* Abingdon: Routledge.

Sen, K. and te Velde, D.W. (2009). 'State–business relations and economic growth in Sub-Saharan Africa', *Journal of Development Studies*, 45: 1–17.

Tanzania Milk Processors' Association (TAMPA) (2010). 'Improving competitiveness of the dairy sector: a policy research paper', presented to the Dairy Industry Stakeholders Workshop: Dar es Salaam, 25 March.

Tanzania Private Sector Foundation (TPSF) (2015). 'Mapping of private sector organizations in Tanzania: A consultancy report submitted by the Institute of Management and Entrepreneurship'. Dar es Salaam.

Taylor, S.D. (2012). 'Influence without organizations: State–business relations and their impact on business environments in contemporary Africa', *Business and Politics*, 14 (1): 1–35.

Te Velde, D.W. (2006). 'Effective state-business relations, industrial policy and economic growth', IPPG-ODI briefing: London.

United Republic of Tanzania (URT) (2010b). 'A comprehensive action plan for implementing the road-map for improving investment climate in Tanzania (2010/11–2012/13)'. Dar es Salaam: Prime Minister's Office.

United Republic of Tanzania (URT) (2011). 'The Tanzania Five-Year Development Plan 2011/12–2015/16'. Dar es Salaam: President's Office – Planning Commission.

United Republic of Tanzania (URT) (2012). 'Consultancy report on the status of the road map implementation in Tanzania'. Dar es Salaam: Prime Minister's Office.

van der Poel, N., F. van Gerwen and D. Olomi (2005), Reforming Institutions aimed at Improving the Enabling Environment for Pro-Poor Private Sector Development, Tanzania case study; a paper presented at the conference on designing donor supported reform programs, in Cairo, Egypt, 1st December, 2005

WEF (2014). Global Competitiveness Report (2014-2015), Full Data Edition, World Economic Forum. Retrieved from https://www.weforum.org/reports/global-competitiveness-report-2014-2015/ (accessed 17 October, 2016).

World Bank (2014). 'Understanding regulations for small and medium-size enterprises'. World Bank. A copublication of The World Bank and the International Finance Corporation, Washington DC, World Bank.

37

Beppe Grillo: A Man, A Plan, A Van: The Tsunami campaign and the national elections, February 2013

Gianluca Vinicio Aguggini

Western Europe has been going through a process of irreversible and inescapable political transformation in the last decade; however, traditional parties seem not to realize it (Bigi, 2013). In the meantime, new actors are emerging in the political landscape of many European countries, like the Pirate Party in Germany and Movimento 5 Stelle (5-Star Movement) in Italy, the core subject of this chapter. There are two main reasons that paved the way for the rise of these political movements: one, the increasing level of public distrust in parties and the awful results of recent government attempts to fight the economic crisis that exploded in 2007; and, two, the rise of new digital opportunities to communicate with audiences (and so with electors) and online campaign planning have completely upset the way politics is conceived and made (Kahne and Middaugh, 2012).

The use of the internet as the major source of information and communication between a political party and its audience has been neglected, because of the reliance on traditional media, like television and newspapers. Nevertheless, the almost infinite options for interaction that blogs, social networks and other online platforms make available to the public have revolutionized communication in the social sphere and, as a result, significantly affected the political one. This is what O'Shaughnessy (2004) defined as the embeddedness of politics: politics is not a separate entity but is tightly knit with the cultural and social sphere. Those politicians who appreciated all these considerations managed to keep up with the evolution of the society and its members, using the internet to plan their political campaigns (Hartleb, 2013b).

This is exactly how Beppe Grillo and his Movimento 5 Stelle succeeded in becoming the first single party in Italy (as for polling number), in the political elections in 2013, following only Berlusconi's Popolo delle Libertà and Bersani's Partito Democratico coalitions.

The echo of his victory reverberates even more loudly when we consider how the entire political movement Grillo created started from his personal blog (Bigi, 2013). Thanks to the engagement and interest he aroused around his blog, along with public speeches and shows in squares, Grillo attracted supporters little by little from all over the country and, thereby, set up the first Italian anti-elitist cyber-party, turning upside-down the entire Italian political scenario (Biorcio and Natale, 2013). This chapter illustrates Grillo's triumphal steps towards parliament, analyzing the strategies and tactics he used in his electoral campaign *Tsunami Tour 2013* to conquer seats in the Chamber of Deputies and in the Senate of the Republic.

BACKGROUND OF THE TSUNAMI CAMPAIGN: BEPPE GRILLO AND THE FOUNDATION OF MOVIMENTO 5 STELLE

Beppe Grillo was not born a politician and, according to the way he describes himself, he hasn't become one. He appeared on the public stage in the 1970s as a comedian and a showman with a pronounced propensity for political satire. Despite his popularity, the sharp and straightforward powerful argumentation he used in his prime-time *RAI* shows, mixed with his explosive and unpredictable spirit, triggered RAI's mounting hostility, leading to his eventual dismissal in 1986 and to his consequent ban from every public broadcasting television (Biorcio and Natale, 2013). From that moment on, Grillo decided to opt out of traditional media exposure and kick-started his one-man shows in theatres and public squares, achieving a resounding success all over the country, although far from television screens.

His shows and speeches were built around a wide variety of topics that met with the general public's consent: the fight against corruption, elitism, the inefficiency of government in tackling the economic crisis and the collusion of some of its members with financial institutions (Natale and Ballatore, 2014). He also raised environmental and ecological issues, including clean-energy concerns, which would become cornerstones of the future political campaign of Movimento 5 Stelle. Therefore, the comedian and satirist, gradually and subliminally, turned to a political activist, embodying both the spokesperson and the booster of popular dissatisfaction and distrust (Bigi, 2013).

The turning point of his personal and political trajectory was a meeting with Gianroberto Casaleggio, a leading expert in the field of online marketing strategies and entrepreneur in the field of IT. Grillo understood, unlike his opponents, the potential of the web and of new media technology as vehicles which could spread his political message by reaching out to an unimaginable number of people (Hartleb, 2013a). With Casaleggio's expertise, he launched his personal blog beppegrillo.it on 26 January 2005. This became a historic day, symbolizing how the political revolution Grillo was dreaming of would arrive via a media revolution (Natale and Ballatore, 2014). The blog became the gathering point of every fan and follower of the comedian, who, benefitting from the incomparable advantages of the web, began to have a strong and evident influence not only over public opinion in Italy but also worldwide. *The Guardian* called it one of the most influential blogs in the world (Danna, 2013).

Thanks to the success achieved through daily blogging and massive use of social-media platforms, like Facebook and Twitter, Grillo began to organize offline events: the *vaffa days,* where *vaffa* stood for 'f*** off'. During these events (the first was organized in 2007), Grillo collected signatures to put forward new laws meant to properly clean up government, proposals that regularly ended up rejected by the Parliament (Hartleb, 2013b). Nevertheless, the pairing of an active online presence and offline events represented a winning strategy that led Grillo first to present civic lists in local elections in 2008 and afterwards to arrange these lists in a real political movement, aiming at national elections: Movimento 5 Stelle, was born on 4 October 2009.

The Movement was born in total opposition to the traditional system of parties: as a matter of fact, Grillo contended that neither was it a party, nor was it meant to become one (beppegrillo.it, 2013). It was rather defined as a free association of citizens, founded on a non-statute, where it was stated that the Movement represented the main vehicle to spread and discuss information. The Movement is headquartered online, on Grillo's personal blog; no site exists offline, nor was a real organizational structure defined at a national level (Biorcio and Natale, 2013). However, the online interaction of its members and their participation and commitment, which Grillo succeeded in galvanizing on his blog, were the key factors that allowed Movimento 5 Stelle to participate in the regional elections in 2010 and to win the local elections in Parma in May 2012. For the first time ever, a candidate of Movimento 5 Stelle was elected mayor of a county seat (Ridet, 2014). This was the proof that the Movement was growing significantly stronger; the time was ripe to debate nationally. Once he realized the huge possibilities of digital campaigning, Grillo started to plan the political campaign for the national elections of 2013, baptized as the Tsunami Tour (Hartleb, 2013a).

THE GOAL OF THE CAMPAIGN AND THE TARGET AUDIENCE

The concrete aim of the Tsunami Tour, run between January and February 2013, was to lead Movimento 5 Stelle to win the majority premium in the Chamber of Deputies and in the Senate of the Republic against its top rivals: Berlusconi's Popolo delle Libertà (right-wing) and Bersani's Partito Democratico (left-wing). The ideal was to bring Italian citizens back to the heart of politics, by supporting a parliamentary delegation that represented the socio-demographic and cultural aspects of Italian society (Natale and Ballatore, 2014). Grillo advocated the participation of real citizens in Parliament to make political institutions transparent and to cut back on the costs of politics, starting with the total clean up of the so-called *Casta* (The Clique) of politicians who benefit from unjustified privileges and keep their positions despite being involved in scandals or trials (Biorcio and Natale, 2013).

In order to achieve this, Grillo intended to touch the two sorest points in Italian society: political disenchantment and alienation. The Tsunami Tour fought both: to mobilize enthusiasm for politics, Grillo organized one-man shows and speeches in squares all across Italy, going on tour in a van; and to make people feel part of Italy's political project again, he created discussion groups on his blog and gathered users in thematic meet-ups (Santoro, 2014). In other words, Grillo's ultimate goal was to turn his audience into his electorate and his online followers into hardened political allies. The goal could be effectively summarized with the Latin expression '*fidem facere et animo impellere*, convince rationally and persuade emotionally' (Bigi, 2013, p. 215).

In order to accomplish his plan, Grillo needed to acquire a thorough knowledge of that slice of his audience that could turn into his electorate: it was a matter of understanding and forecasting the voting behaviors and attitudes of his target audience (O'Shaughnessy, 2004). Grillo therefore planned the Tsunami campaign, presenting Movimento 5 Stelle as an anti-elitist cyber-party. He included two big groups in his target audience, aiming to merge them into a big cohesive political force: on the one hand, voters alienated and disenchanted by the traditional two-party system; on the other, the web population that visited his blogs and actively took part in the meet-ups (*The Economist*, 2013b).

The blog gave Grillo the chance not only to reach out to a huge number of potential voters but also to tailor messages to them, without the filters of traditional media. This ensured he achieved a greater intimacy with his audience, from the perspective of political-relationship marketing. He solicited support for the campaign, enabled chat discussions, recruited volunteers, published press releases, and elected members of civic lists. Grillo tried to attract voters by converting those belonging to the dominant parties of the left (mainly Partito Democratico) and right wings (mainly Popolo delle Libertà and Lega). He bet on their sense of abandonment by their parties, with which they could not identify anymore, and offered them a new direction. Likewise, he offered long-standing abstainers a new way of participating again in the political life of their country and offered political neophytes, mainly young people, a way to have a say in political matters. Grillo stated that the electoral audience of his campaign was composed in general of all the people that for years had been counted out of Italian political life, especially young people, women, the worker class and the unemployed (Biorcio and Natale, 2013; *The Economist*, 2013a).

MESSAGE STRATEGY AND PERSUASIVE TECHNIQUES

MYTH: 'a Comedian will Bury you all'

There is no doubt that Movimento 5 Stelle has an undisputed leader: Beppe Grillo conceived the Movement and kick-started the Tsunami campaign. Gianroberto Casaleggio acted more as his digital mentor, devising the online platform and dealing with the implementation of the campaign (Hartleb, 2013a). However, Grillo never defined himself as a political leader, rather stating that 'the only leader is the Movement' and that he was only the

communication director, the spokesperson for the community, or, using a metaphor, 'the megaphone of truth' (Biorcio and Natale, 2013, chapter 7). In general, newspapers, television, and traditional media do not speak that truth, either because they take the side of the corrupted political class or, as the property of private companies, they reflect vested interests.

Grillo's Tsunami campaign stressed that it was 'Us versus Them', reflecting the biblical clash between Good and Evil. The former is represented by his Movement and its members, in the attempt to re-establish real democracy, while the latter is composed of the corrupted political class, mass media, bankers, and, to a large extent, the EU and its institutions (Natale and Ballatore, 2013). It cannot be denied that Grillo has been cultivating populist appeal and promoting the cult of his personality, like other political leaders have done across history, from Mussolini, Mao, Stalin, and Hitler to more contemporary actors, like Berlusconi (Dominijanni, 2014). Grillo embodies the essence of Movimento 5 Stelle: his presence is essential for the unity of the Movement. Moreover, his comedian background and expulsion from the institutional circles of television positioned him at the same level as the people he wants to talk to. He has been increasingly considered a popular hero, who seeks his revenge and asks the masses to fight a common enemy: the political *Casta*. The success of his personality is down to the trust he succeeded in building over the years with his public and the credibility he developed as a savior of real democracy and scourge of corrupted politicians.

The tactics he used to build his personal myth and to support real democracy date back to the era when democracy itself was invented: Ancient Greece. Grillo used the public spaces – squares, mainly – just like Greek orators, philosophers, and politicians used agoras to deliver public speeches (Hartleb, 2013b; Ortoleva, 2009). These one-man shows, held during the tour, scored astounding results in involving potential voters in his political plan and in gathering

sympathizers around his Movement. A reason could be found in the link between his
performances and Carnival celebrations,
or, in general, the ritual of temporary moral
overthrowing, when masses could freely vent
repressed anger and frustrations (Biorcio and
Natale, 2013). As O'Shaughnessy (2004)
highlighted, masses want to be told stories
and need myths, as a cultural point of reference: Grillo built his personal myth through
public speeches and by restaging heroic acts,
like swimming across the Strait of Messina,
between Sicily and Calabria. This act had
an astounding effect on the building of his
personal myth as a popular 'normal hero',
who accomplishes extraordinary feats. The
crossing of the Strait boosted enormously
the appeal among his voters-to-be audience,
because it epitomized the titanic fight against
a seemingly invincible enemy (the *Casta*),
reinforcing social cohesion, instilling iconic
values, and promoting a shared identification in myth among Movement members
(O'Shaughnessy, 2004).

SYMBOLISM: 'Tsunami is Coming, Board the Lifeboats'

The success or failure of political campaigns
in history has always been determined by
their success or failure in creating and controlling symbols, and in how effectively their
leaders conveyed symbolic meanings to the
masses. Symbols, which are essentially con-
densed meanings, are required to unite members of a political association and provide
them with a shared perspective about the
future (O'Shaughnessy, 2004). Grillo's
success lay in his sensitivity to these needs
and in the masterful conception and creation
of the symbols used in the Tsunami campaign. The whole Tsunami campaign started
from the image of the Movement and the
essential and minimalist design of its logo:
two words and a graphic element only.

The word *movimento* in the center of
the circle refers to the verb 'move', that

translated into Grillo's rhetoric, becomes
'take action, make progress, go forth'. The
other writing cites the place of birth of the
whole Movement: Grillo's blog beppegrillo.
it, without which the Movement would not
have existed. The letter *V* is graphically
emphasized, because it recalls one of the most
resounding events organized by the comedian: *V-Day*, September 8 2007, when Grillo
gathered his fans in squares all across Italy
to collect signatures for a popular petition,
to be presented directly to Parliament. This
petition, called *Parlamento Pulito* (Cleaning
Parliament Up), was based on the proposal
to modify laws and procedures about the eli-
gibility of parliamentary candidates, along
with their term of office and the contingent
removal or loss of position (Natale and
Ballatore, 2014). This event was imbued with
symbolism, marking the transition of mass
mobilization from the web to the square and
from the square to Parliament, demonstrating that symbols are not only images but also
events that change the destiny of a political
campaign (O'Shaughnessy, 2004).

The letter *V* has a double metaphorical
meaning: on the one hand, it stands for the
Italian swear word *vaffanculo* (*f*** off*), dedicated to the actual political class. On the other,
it is an homage to the US film *V-for-Vendetta*,
based on the UK graphic novel, in which V,
the protagonist, is a masked avenger who
fights a totalitarian regime, encouraging citizens to rise up against tyranny and oppres-
sion. The message that Grillo intended to
convey to his audience was almost the same,
although the rebellion fomented by the comedian was peaceful, encompassing petitions,
pleas, legal proposals of citizens' initiatives,
and the presentation of civic lists at polling
places. Nevertheless, the mask used in the
movie became a symbol of Grillo's political activists. Meanwhile, the name *V-Day* is
also a clear citation of D-Day, in 1943, when
the Allies landed in Normandy, Grillo imply-
ing that nothing has really changed since.
Yesterday, King Emmanuele III's getaway
– today, the political class locked in its

buildings, while the Nation outside is adrift (Biorcio and Natale, 2013).

Finally, the five stars in the logo illustrate the concept of excellence and superiority – in the hotel sector they stand for superior service and incomparable quality – and mark the five objectives towards which Grillo directs the effort and the energy of the Movement: public water, environmental safeguards, sustainable energy, social services, and free connectivity (beppegrillo.it, 2013). Posters, billboards, and fliers promoting his campaign for the national elections of February 2013 showed Beppe Grillo wearing a helmet with five stars and dominating the waves. What he wanted to express was that he was rowing against the political tide, presenting his Movement, an anti-party, as the solution to restore popular sovereignty: 'I won't stop. Tsunami is coming, politicians, board the lifeboats' (beppegrillo.it, 2014; Pasquino, 2014).

Generally speaking, symbols used in a political campaign can have significant consequences in the long run, even after the end of the single campaign. Grillo had been using the same symbols in local and regional campaigns as in the national one, because he recognized the potential of political-relationship marketing. Symbols foster a sense of political ownership, energize and motivate actions, and create emotional bonds among members of a movement or party far beyond the success of a single campaign (O'Shaughnessy, 2004). This is how he created a loyal electorate and devoted public: brick by brick, in little more than ten years.

(CYBER-)RHETORIC: 'Politicians have to go Home'

Although gradually becoming an entrepreneur and leader of a political movement, Grillo preserved his heritage as a comedian and never repudiated his inclination to satire. On the contrary, the Tsunami campaign owed a lot of its success to his satirical language

and parodic impersonations, with which he mocked politicians of both left- and right-wing parties, stigmatizing their weaknesses and bad habits (Biorcio and Natale, 2013). As O'Shaughnessy (2004) emphasized, rhetoric is essentially emotional persuasion, through which political leaders try to propagate their ideas and brand themselves in distinction to other party leaders.

Grillo, while visiting Italian squares and arenas, spiced the presentation of his political project with metaphors, analogies, and comparisons, openly addressing the politicians he intended to mock. He coined nicknames for most of his political rivals: Matteo Renzi, assistant leader of *Partito Democratico*, now prime minister, was nicknamed *Ebetino* (little, gullible man), whereas Pierluigi Bersani, leader of *Partito Democratico*, was dubbed Gargamella, for his apparent resemblance to the villain of the Smurfs. Mario Monti, ex prime minister, became *Rigor Montis*, for his deathly quality; Silvio Berlusconi was nicknamed *psiconano* (psycho-dwarf); and Giorgio Napolitano, ex president of the republic, was defined as *un morto che cammina* (dead man walking), the first person of the political clique to be removed from his position as soon as Movimento 5 Stelle conquered Parliament. Similarly, newspapers, television, and traditional media were defined as *mummie* (mummies), about to die out and be replaced by new digital media as the main form of interaction between parties and their members (Bigi, 2013).

These tropes, with which he seasoned his public speeches, proved to be crucial in persuading a huge number of people: by using the same way of speaking as his target audience, he first won their approval, then he became familiar to them, and, finally, he won their trust, which in most cases was turned into votes. Tropes and metaphors trigger emotional responses and, to a great extent, they can influence perspectives (O'Shaughnessy, 2004). Moreover, a study conducted by Cavazza and Guidetti (2014) unearthed how curse words can intensify political discourse and increase the believability of a leader's statements. Curse words are the cultural heritage of the masses and can easily penetrate into the common language: that is the reason why Grillo opted for a vernacular, biting, and nasty language. He aimed at identifying with his public, conveying an aura of informality and, thus, enhancing his personal brand image: that is why he directly, though brilliantly, insulted the representatives of the political *Casta* (Ruggiero, 2012; Cavazza and Guidetti, 2014).

Furthermore, Grillo's use of his blog and the wider internet to communicate and conduct his digital campaign gave him an edge over the competition: no other party leader embraced online campaigning so keenly, as no other party leader clearly understood the concrete potential of cyber-rhetoric in chasing the electorate. Actually, it could be stated that all the references to citizens' sovereignty, the fight against political *Casta*, the Movement as the embodiment of every positive value – everything depicts Grillo's rhetoric as markedly populist. Although he never openly denied it, it can be contended that the secret of the Tsunami campaign was his dialectics: simple, straightforward, highly emotionally loaded, and purposely provocative. His comic and apparently unengaged façade, indeed, gave him free range to attack and insult all his political opponent to-be, as a comedian is not usually taken seriously (Urbinati, 1998). Who would have ever guessed that a comedian could really get into Parliament?

STRATEGY AND MEDIA IMPLEMENTATION: BLOG, SOCIAL NETWORKS AND ONE-MAN SHOWS

Grillo's PR skills mixed with Casaleggio's IT expertise were the two secret ingredients in the development of the Tsunami campaign: the union of the aforementioned triune structure (myth, symbolism, and rhetoric) with the boundless opportunities of digital

tools allowed Movimento 5 Stelle to rocket in the preferences of the Italian voting public. The strategy Grillo adopted was to merge the offline one-man shows in city squares with digital interaction, keeping information transparent and keeping in permanent contact with the public being its essential cornerstones (Biorcio and Natale, 2013; Hartleb, 2013a). Grillo has been stating from the very beginning of the campaign that the web was the most democratic arena of political discussion: on the internet parties disappear, along with hierarchies and intermediaries. What remains is citizens who speak with their own voice and can interact through the varied touchpoints that Movimento 5 Stelle made available to realize the e-democracy Grillo conceived (Bigi, 2013).

As Berlusconi exploited Mediaset, his own private television company, for the political campaign in the 1980s, Grillo used his blog beppegrillo.it to create and promote Movimento 5 Stelle (Santoro, 2014). He used it to plan the campaign, publishing the dates of his van tour and asking his public to join him in his political fight. At the top right of the page he provided users with the option to look for the local closest meet-up, subscribe to the Movement, and take an active part in the law proposals. The meet-up network was the backbone of the whole Movement: activists and followers could communicate through it and participate in the political issues of the association, with a particular focus on local matters. The discussion groups proliferated during the two-month campaign: there are now more than 500, present in 381 cities and in 11 countries all over the world (Bigi, 2013).

The blog is also the place where the political project is disclosed in detail, following the schema of the aforementioned 5 stars: public water, other environmental safeguards (optimizing public transport use rather than private cars), sustainable energy (reducing CO_2 emissions and promoting renewable resources), social services (funding the education system and the public health sector) and free connectivity (extending broadband connectivity and reducing phone rates) (beppegrillo.it, 2013; *The Economist*, 2013a). By selecting a blog as the main source of political engagement with his electorate, Grillo completely overthrew the idea that political campaigns had to be run through traditional media in the way Popolo delle Libertà and Partito Democratico, the main opponents, have been doing for as long as anybody can remember.

The blog also links to social networks, like Facebook and Twitter, to engage a younger audience with the campaign. Grillo has built a considerable social-media following over the years: nearly 2 million people have joined his Facebook and Twitter pages. The main reason for this remarkable online success is the communication techniques he applied in the Tsunami campaign. He created slogans and soundbites, which spread virally as they were shared and tweeted by his followers: *ignorateci adesso* (ignore us now) and *li mandiamo tutti a casa* (we kiss off them all). These slogans became anthems for *grillini*, the nickname the media stuck to Grillo's supporters, and strengthened their union. Further, the repetition of slogans during shows and by online word-of-mouth created a free, reverberating echo. Bigi (2013), in fact, has stated that political messages should not be over-articulated but easy to remember and emotionally loaded. Grillo proved to be a mastermind at this. Analyzing his communication techniques on his blog, on social networks, and in his public shows from the Elaboration Likelihood Model perspective, it is quite clear how Grillo favored a peripheral-route, persuasive approach (Petty and Cacioppo, 1986). Surfing the wave of disgust and frustration of the bulk of Italian electorate, Grillo patterned his language to evoke their gut feelings and instinctive reactions.

In his 40 days aboard a camper van Grillo promoted his Movement in 77 Italian squares, starting in Livorno on January 14 and ending, symbolically, in Rome on February 22. He built a team of close assistants, that he always called by their first names: Walter, the van driver; Pietro, the social-network specialist,

and Salvatore, the live-streaming operator and manager of the web channel, who dedicated 12 hours a day to recording the main events of the campaign (Biorcio and Natale, 2013). The public performances emphasized the contact between Grillo and his public and were the moments of maximum expression of his rhetorical power and his ability to create union and cohesion around him.

According to the model proposed by Henneberg's (2006) analysis, Grillo's posture in the Tsunami campaign can be described as halfway between the tactical populist and the relationship builder. Taking cues from the former posture, Grillo strategically planned every action and word in order to be tuned to his audience's mood and need; from the latter, it is evident how the comedian set his objectives beyond national elections in February 2013. The promises he made to his public need to be considered against a wider horizon, oriented to the establishment of a solid relationship not only with voters, but also with his fans and supporters (Collins and Butler, 2003).

In order to strengthen his personal brand image and that of the Movement even further, Grillo involved in the tour two among the most influential Italian personalities in the cultural landscape: the singer–actor Adriano Celentano and the Nobel Prize winner for literature Dario Fo (Hartleb, 2013a). These celebrities are not only deeply rooted in Italian popular imagery for their charisma and the admiration they have generated in their career, but they are also well-known in foreign countries. Therefore, they perfectly fitted the requirements of attractiveness and credibility that Grillo sought in order to endorse the candidacy of Movimento 5 Stelle for a seat in Parliament (Keel and Nataraajan, 2013).

EVALUATION AND CRITIQUE OF THE CAMPAIGN

The election results were unprecedented in the history of the Italian two-party system: no coalition achieved a crushing victory against the other. As a matter of fact, Tables 37.1 and 37.2 show that three parties almost scored a draw in the Chamber of Deputies, with Partito Democratico and Popolo delle Libertà still slightly ahead, 29.6 per cent and 29.2 per cent respectively, but Movimento 5 Stelle just behind, breathing down their necks with an astonishing 25.6 per cent. There were similar results for the Senate of the Republic: 31.6 per cent for Bersani, 30.7 per cent for Berlusconi, and 23.8 per cent for Grillo (Electionresources.org, 2013). The astonishment was provoked by consideration of the

Table 37.1 February 24–25, Chamber of Deputies Election Results

Registered Electors	46,905,154	
Voters	35,270,926	75,2%
Blank or Invalid Ballots	1,265,171	3,6%
Valid Votes	34,005,755	96,5%

LIST	VOTES	%	SEATS
Pier Luigi Bersani	10,049,393	29,6	340
Partito Democratico	8,646,034	25,4	292
Sinistra Ecologia Liberta'	1,089,231	3,2	37
Centro Democratico	167,328	0,5	6
Sudtiroler Volkspartei (SVP)	146,800	0,4	5
Silvio Berlusconi	9,923,600	29,2	124
Il Popolo delle Liberta'	7,332,134	21,6	97
Lega Nord	1,390,534	4,1	18
Fratelli d'Italia	666,765	2,0	9
La Destra	219,585	0,6	0
Grande Sud - MPA	148,248	0,4	0
MIR - Moderati in Rivoluzione	82,557	0,2	0
Partito Pensionati	54,418	0,2	0
Others (Silvio Berlusconi)	29,359	0,1	0
Movimento 5 Stelle - beppegrillo.it	8,691,406	25,6	108
Mario Monti	3,591,541	10,6	45
Scelta Civica - Con Monti per l'Italia	2,823,842	8,3	37
Unione di Centro	608,321	1,8	8
Futuro e Liberta'	159,378	0,5	0
Rivoluzione Civile	765,189	2,3	0
Fare per Fermare il Declino	380,044	1,1	0
Others	604,582	1,8	0

Table 37.2   February 24–25, Senate Election Results

Registered Electors	42,270,824	
Voters	31,751,350	75,1%
Blank or Invalid Ballots	1,133,449	3,6%
Valid Votes	30,617,901	96,4%

LIST	VOTES	%	SEATS
Silvio Berlusconi	**9,405,652**	**30,7**	**116**
Il Popolo delle Liberta'	6,828,994	22,3	98
Lega Nord	1,328,534	4,3	17
Grande Sud	122,262	0,4	1
Fratelli d'Italia	590,645	1,9	0
La Destra	221,368	0,7	0
Partito Pensionati	123,327	0,4	0
MIR - Moderati in Rivoluzione	69,838	0,2	0
MPA - Partito dei Siciliani	48,539	0,2	0
Others (Silvio Berlusconi)	72,235	0,2	0
Pier Luigi Bersani	**9,685,437**	**31,6**	**113**
Partito Democratico	8,400,851	27,4	105
Sinistra Ecologia Liberta'	911,486	3,0	7
Il Megafono - Lista Crocetta	138,564	0,5	1
Centro Democratico	162,418	0,5	0
Partito Socialista Italiano	57,606	0,2	0
Others (Pier Luigi Bersani)	14,512	0,0	0
Movimento 5 Stelle - beppegrillo.it	**7,286,550**	**23,8**	**54**
Con Monti per l'Italia	2,797,734	9,1	18
Rivoluzione Civile	551,064	1,8	0
Fare per Fermare il Declino	278,47	0,9	0
Others	612,994	2,0	0

entire path that Grillo and his *grillini* traveled to achieve this result, from 2005, when beppegrillo.it was founded, to the Tsunami campaign 2013, the capstone of the political journey. No other party has scored better results for the first participation in national elections, and this success is owed to Grillo's political campaign aboard the van and on the web (*The Economist*, 2013c; *The Telegraph*, 2013).

At this point, some might legitimately argue that Grillo did not win the elections, drawing the conclusion that he may have won the political-campaign battle against Bersani and Berlusconi but, on balance, did not win the war, since he was still behind them in the percentages. Several reasons might be advanced to explain the fact that he could not go beyond 25.6 per cent and 23.8 per cent, the main being the fear that behind the populist slogans and attacks on the political class there was no clear political project. How could a leader, who rejects politics as a profession, actually rule a country? Moreover, the candidates elected through the blog were deemed not to have the skills and the knowledge to enter Parliament, since they were not politicians.

In addition, some newspapers argued that Grillo was not as democratic as he wanted to appear, reporting cases of members (like Federica Salsi) who were removed from the Movement because they violated the code of conduct during the campaign (for example, talking to the press or participating in television shows) (Biorcio and Natale, 2013). Likewise, they argued that compliance with this code was ensured through the strict stances adopted by Grillo, who turned out to look more like a dictator, preaching real democracy while actually applying a strictly centralized management of the Movement, where dissenters were hushed up and decisions came from one person only. But another issue raised was the lack of control over the blog and social networks (a typical byproduct of digital communication), the broadened participation in discussions degenerating in some cases into heated debates and off-topic speeches (Natale and Ballatore, 2014).

It is reasonable, then, to raise some doubts about the realization of Grillo's project in Italian politics: despite some victories in local elections, more defined structures and a clear offline organization, beyond the blog and meet-ups, seem mandatory requirements at a national level (Bigi, 2013). This criticism is accepted, though it should not overshadow the success of the Tsunami campaign from a political-marketing perspective, which remains proof of how a political leader can still excite the masses by talking about politics – excitement that, in television talk shows and primetime political broadcasting, seemed

to have been irremediably lost, especially in the younger generations.

Grillo declared during his campaign: 'an actual war is going on between an old, analogue, unfair, polluting world and a digital ecological web-centric and just world' (Natale and Ballatore, 2014, p. 115). He alluded to the genetic mutation that the world of politics is going through now because of the new avenues that digital technologies have opened for political parties to create, shape, and preserve relationships with their public: that is, their voters. Leaders who do not understand the compelling necessity of moving in this direction, towards which their public has already moved, are bound to lose contact with them (Kahne and Middaugh, 2012).

The Movimento 5 Stelle case study demonstrated how the liquid e-democracy, which Grillo exalted in the Tsunami campaign, can provide members with the chance to be engaged and committed in a wide variety of ways (Bigi, 2013). This can be a valid starting point for the actualization of the concept of permanent campaigning – the means to engage and involve the audience, not only asking for their support in a political campaign but also beyond it (Nimmo, 1999).

In a post-political scenario where the distrust-turned-to-apathy towards politics has spread like a virus, especially in the younger generations, Grillo with the Tsunami campaign brought back into focus the urgent need for politics to re-engage in meaningful long-term interactions with people (*The Economist*, 2013c). Maybe Movimento 5 Stelle would not be able to rule the country by itself, but Grillo has definitely provided evidence of how online campaigning can lead to important results in elections.

REFERENCES

beppegrillo.it (2013). Tsunami tour. [online] Available at: http://www.beppegrillo.it/2013/

01/tsunami_tour.html [accessed 2 Apr. 2015].

Bigi, A. (2013). Viral political communication and readability: an analysis of an Italian political blog. *Journal of Public Affairs*, 13(2), pp. 209–17.

Biorcio, R. and Natale, P. (2013). *5 Stars Politics*. Milano: G. Feltrinelli.

Cavazza, N. and Guidetti, M. (2014). Swearing in political discourse: why vulgarity works. *Journal of Language and Social Psychology*, 33(5), pp. 537–47.

Collins, N. and Butler, P. (2003). When marketing models clash with democracy. *Journal of Public Affairs*, 3(1), pp. 52–62.

Danna, S. (2013). Why Beppe Grillo won in Italy: it wasn't because of social media. [online] Available at: http://www.theguardian.com/commentisfree/2013/mar/08/beppe-grillo-success-italy [accessed 6 Apr. 2015].

Dominijanni, I. (2014). The cricket's leap: post-oedipal populism and neoliberal democracy in contemporary Italy. *Cultural Critique*, 87, pp. 167–82.

The Economist (2013a). A dangerous mess. [online] Available at: http://www.economist.com/blogs/charlemagne/2013/02/italian-politics-2 [accessed 13 Apr. 2015].

The Economist (2013b). Five-star menu. [online] Available at: http://www.economist.com/newsbriefing/21571886-comedian-and-populist-whose-result-may-be-underestimated-five-star-menu [accessed 12 Apr. 2015].

The Economist (2013c). Rising star? [online] Available at: http://www.economist.com/blogs/charlemagne/2013/02/beppe-grillo [accessed 13 Apr. 2015].

The Economist (2013d). The crickets come out. [online] Available at: http://www.economist.com/news/europe/21572797-movement-some-   strange-policiesbut-also-some-sensible-ones-crickets-come-out [accessed 2 Apr. 2015].

Electionresources.org (2013). Election resources on the internet: elections to the Italian Parliament – Chamber of Deputies results lookup. [online] Available at: http://electionresources.org/it/chamber.php?election=2013 [accessed 8 Apr. 2015].

Electionresources.org (2013). Election resources on the internet: elections to the Italian Parliament – Senate results lookup. [online] Available at: http://electionresources.org/it/senate.php?election=2013 [accessed 13 Apr. 2015].

Hartleb, F. (2013a). Anti-elitist cyber parties? *Journal of Public Affairs*, 13(4), pp. 355–69. Retrieved from http://onlinelibrary.wiley.com/doi/10.1002/pa.1480/full (accessed 30 Aug. 2016).

Hartleb, F. (2013b). Digital campaigning and the growing anti-elitism: the Pirates and Beppe Grillo. European View, 12(1), pp. 135–42. Retrieved from http://link.springer.com/article/10.1007/s12290-013-0252-8 (accessed 30 Aug. 2016).

Henneberg, S. (2006). Leading or following? *Journal of Political Marketing*, 5(3), pp. 29–46.

Kahne, J. and Middaugh, E. (2012). Digital media shapes youth participation in politics. *Phi Delta Kappan*, 94(3), pp. 52–6.

Keel, A. and Nataraajan, R. (2012). Celebrity endorsements and beyond: new avenues for celebrity branding. *Psychology & Marketing*, 29(9), pp. 690–703.

Natale, S. and Ballatore, A. (2014). The web will kill them all: new media, digital utopia, and political struggle in the Italian 5-Star Movement. Media, Culture & Society, 36(1), pp. 105–21.

Nimmo, D. (1999). The permanent campaign: marketing as a governing tool, in B. Newman (ed.), *Handbook of Political Marketing*. Thousand Oaks: Sage, pp. 73–88.

Ortoleva, P. (2009). Modern mythologies, the media and the social presence of technology. *Observatorio Journal*, 8, pp.1–12.

O'Shaughnessy, N. (2004). *Politics of Propaganda*. Manchester: Manchester University Press.

Pasquino, G. (2014). Italy: the triumph of personalist parties. *Politics & Policy*, 42(4), pp. 548–66.

Petty, R. and Cacioppo, J. (1986). The elaboration likelihood model of persuasion. *Advances in Experimental Social Psychology*, 19, pp. 197–216.

Ridet, P. (2014). Debt reduction and recycling keep Parma's Five Star mayor occupied. [online] Available at: http://www.theguardian.com/world/2014/jul/15/parma-italy-mayor-pizzarotti-five-star [accessed 4 Apr. 2015].

Ruggiero, C. (2012). Forecasting in the politics of spectacle, from Berlusconi to Grillo: the narrative of impolite politics. *Bulletin of Italian Politics*, 4(2), pp. 305–22.

Santoro, G. (2014). Italy from Berlusconi to Grillo. *Cultural Critique*, 87, pp. 193–202.

The Telegraph (2013). Italy elections: results breakdown of lower and upper chambers. [online] Available at: http://www.telegraph. co.uk/news/worldnews/europe/ italy/9894625/Italy-elections-results-break- down-of-lower-and-upper-chambers.html [accessed 3 Apr. 2015].

Urbinati, N. (1998). Democracy and populism. Constellations, 5(1), pp. 110–24. Retrieved from http://onlinelibrary.wiley.com/doi/ 10.1111/1467-8675.00080/full (accessed 31 Aug. 2016).

Index

Page references to Figures or Tables will be in *italics*, followed by the letters 'f' and 't', as appropriate. References to Notes will be followed by the letter 'n' and note number